EIGHTY THIRD E

SINCE 1912

WHO'S WHO IN BASEBALL 1998

Official Lifetime Records
Of Major League Players

Editor
Norman MacLean

Associate Editor
Bill Shannon

Cover Design
James Allocca

Editorial Assistants
Lynn Hudson
Pete Palmer
Alex MacLean

WHO'S WHO IN BASEBALL is published annually by Who's Who in Baseball Magazine Co., Inc., 1115 Broadway, New York, New York 10010. Single copy price: $6.95. Submissions of manuscripts, illlustrations and/or photographs must be accompanied by a stamped, self-addressed envelope. The publisher assumes no responsibility for unsolicited material. Copyright © 1998 by Who's Who in Baseball Magazine Co., Inc. All rights reserved under International and Pan American Copyright Conventions. Reproduction in whole or in part without written permission of the publisher is strictly prohibited. Printed in U.S.A.

BATTERS

ABBOTT, JEFFREY WILLIAM
Born, Atlanta, Georgia, August 17, 1972.
Bats Right. Throws Left. Height, 6 feet, 2 inches. Weight 190 pounds.

Year Club	Lea	Pos	G	AB	R	H	2B	3B	HR	RBI	SB	Avg
1994 White Sox	Gulf Coast	OF	4	15	4	7	1	0	1	3	2	.467
1994 Hickory	So. Atl.	OF	63	224	47	88	16	6	6	48	2	.393
1995 Pr William	Carolina	OF	70	264	41	92	16	0	4	47	7	.348
1995 Birmingham	Southern	OF	55	197	25	63	11	1	3	28	1	.320
1996 Nashville	A.A.	OF	113	440	64	143	27	1	14	60	12	.325
1997 Nashville	A.A.	OF	118	465	88	152	35	3	11	63	12	.327
1997 Chicago	A.L.	OF	19	38	8	10	1	0	1	2	0	.263

ABBOTT, KURT THOMAS
Born, Zanesville, Ohio, June 2, 1968.
Bats Right. Throws Right. Height, 6 feet. Weight, 170 pounds.

Year Club	Lea	Pos	G	AB	R	H	2B	3B	HR	RBI	SB	Avg
1989 So. Oregon	Northwest	SS	5	10	2	1	0	0	0	1	1	.100
1989 Scottsdale Athletics	Ariz.	SS-2B-3B	36	155	27	42	5	3	0	25	0	.271
1990 Madison	Midwest	SS-2B-3B	104	362	38	84	18	0	0	28	21	.232
1991 Modesto	California	SS	58	216	36	55	8	2	3	25	6	.255
1991 Huntsville	Southern	SS	53	182	18	46	6	1	0	11	6	.253
1992 Tacoma	P.C.	SS	11	39	2	6	1	0	0	1	1	.154
1992 Huntsville	Southern	SS	124	452	64	115	14	5	9	52	16	.254
1993 Tacoma	P.C.	SS	133	480	75	153	36	11	12	79	19	.319
1993 Oakland a	A.L.	OF-SS-2B	20	61	11	15	1	0	3	9	2	.246
1994 Florida	N.L.	SS	101	345	41	86	17	3	9	33	3	.249
1995 Charlotte	Int.	SS	5	18	3	5	0	0	1	3	1	.278
1995 Florida b	N.L.	SS	120	420	60	107	18	7	17	60	4	.255
1996 Charlotte	Int.	SS-2B-3B	18	69	20	26	10	1	5	11	2	.377
1996 Florida c	N.L.	SS-3B-2B	109	320	37	81	18	7	8	33	3	.253
1997 Florida	N.L.	2B-OF-SS-3B	94	252	35	69	18	2	6	30	3	.274
Major League Totals	5 Yrs.		444	1398	184	358	72	19	43	165	15	.256
Division Series												
1997 Florida	N.L.	2B	3	8	0	2	0	0	0	0	0	.250
Championship Series												
1997 Florida	N.L.	2B	2	8	0	3	1	0	0	0	0	.375
World Series Record												
1997 Florida	N.L.	DH	3	3	0	0	0	0	0	0	0	.000

a Traded to Florida Marlins for outfielder Kerwin Moore, December 20, 1993.
b On disabled list from April 25 to May 6, 1995.
c On disabled list from May 6 to June 13, 1996.
d Traded to Oakland A's for P Eric Ludwich December 21, 1997.

ABREU, BOB KELLY
Born, Aragua, Venezuela, March 11, 1974.
Bats Left. Throws Right. Height, 6 feet. Weight 160 pounds.

Year Club	Lea	Pos	G	AB	R	H	2B	3B	HR	RBI	SB	Avg
1991 Astros	Gulf Coast	OF-SS	56	183	21	55	7	3	0	20	10	.301
1992 Asheville	So. Atl.	OF	135	480	81	140	21	4	8	48	15	.292
1993 Osceola	Fla. St.	OF	129	474	62	134	21	17	5	55	10	.283
1994 Jackson	Texas	OF	118	400	61	121	25	9	16	73	12	.303
1995 Tucson	P.C.	OF-2B	114	415	72	126	24	17	10	75	16	.304
1996 Tucson	P.C.	OF	132	484	86	138	14	16	13	68	24	.285
1996 Houston	N.L.	OF	15	22	1	5	1	0	0	1	0	.227
1997 Jackson	Texas	OF	3	12	2	2	1	0	0	0	0	.167
1997 New Orleans	A.A.	OF	47	194	25	52	9	4	2	22	7	.268
1997 Houston a-b-c	N.L.	OF	59	188	22	47	10	2	3	26	7	.250
Major League Totals	2 Yrs.		74	210	23	52	11	2	3	27	7	.248
Division Series												
1997 Houston	N.L.	PH	3	3	0	1	0	0	0	0	1	.333

a On disabled list from May 25 to July 1, 1997.
b Selected in expansion draft by Tampa Bay Devil Rays, November 18, 1997.
c Traded to Philadelphia Phillies for infielder Kevin Stocker, November 19, 1997.

ALEXANDER, MANUEL DEJESUS (MANNY)
Born, San Pedro de Marcoris, Dominican Republic, March 20, 1971.
Bats Right. Throws Right. Height, 5 feet, 10 inches. Weight, 165 pounds.

Year	Club	Lea	Pos	G	AB	R	H	2B	3B	HR	RBI	SB	Avg
1988				Played in Dominican Summer League									
1989 Bluefield		Appal.	SS	65	*274	49	*85	13	2	2	34	19	.310
1990 Wausau a		Midwest	SS	44	152	16	27	3	1	0	11	8	.178
1991 Frederick		Carolina	SS	134	548	*81	*143	17	3	3	42	47	.261
1991 Hagerstown		Eastern	SS	3	9	3	3	1	0	0	2	0	.333
1992 Hagerstown		Eastern	SS	127	499	70	129	22	8	2	41	43	.259
1992 Rochester		Int.	SS	6	24	3	7	1	0	0	3	2	.292
1992 Baltimore		A.L.	SS	4	5	1	1	0	0	0	0	0	.200
1993 Rochester		Int.	SS	120	471	55	115	23	8	6	51	19	.244
1993 Baltimore		A.L.	PR	3	0	1	0	0	0	0	0	0	.000
1994 Rochester b		Int.	SS-2B	111	426	63	106	23	6	6	39	30	.249
1995 Baltimore		A.L.	2B-SS-3B	94	242	35	57	9	1	3	23	11	.236
1996 Baltimore		A.L.	SS-2B-3B-OF	54	68	6	7	0	0	0	4	3	.103
1997 St. Lucie c-d		Fla. St.	SS	1	4	0	1	0	0	0	0	0	.250
1997 New York-Chicago e		N.L.	SS-2B-3B	87	248	37	66	12	4	3	22	13	.266
Major League Totals			5 Yrs.	242	563	80	131	21	5	6	49	27	.233
Division Series													
1996 Baltimore		A.L.	DH	3	0	2	0	0	0	0	0	0	.000

a On disabled list from April 26 to July 23, 1990.
b On disabled list from March 25 to May 2, 1994.
c Traded to New York Mets with infielder Scott McClain for pitcher Hector Ramirez, March 22, 1997.
d On disabled list from June 11 to July 10 and July 25 to August 11, 1997.
e Sent to Chicago Cubs as player to be named later for pitcher Mel Rojas, pitcher Turk Wendell and outfielder Brian McRae, August 14, 1997.

ALFONZO, EDGARDO ANTONIO
Born, Santa Teresa, Venezuela, August 11, 1973.
Bats Right. Throws Right. Height, 5 feet, 11 inches. Weight, 185 pounds.

Year	Club	Lea	Pos	G	AB	R	H	2B	3B	HR	RBI	SB	Avg
1991 Mets		Gulf Coast	2B-SS-3B	54	175	29	58	8	4	0	27	6	.331
1992 St. Lucie		Fla. St.	2B-SS	4	5	0	0	0	0	0	0	0	.000
1992 Pittsfield		N.Y.-Penn.	SS	74	298	41	106	13	5	1	44	7	.356
1993 St. Lucie		Fla. St.	SS	128	494	75	145	18	3	11	86	26	.294
1994 Binghamton		Eastern	SS-2B-1B	127	498	89	146	34	2	15	75	14	.293
1995 New York a		N.L.	3B-2B-SS	101	335	26	93	13	5	4	41	1	.278
1996 New York		N.L.	3B-2B	123	368	36	96	15	2	4	40	2	.261
1997 New York		N.L.	3B-SS-2B	151	518	84	163	27	2	10	72	11	.315
Major League Totals			3 Yrs.	375	1221	146	352	55	9	18	153	14	.288

a On disabled list from August 11 to September 1, 1995.

ALICEA, LUIS RENE
Born, Santurce, Puerto Rico, July 29, 1965.
Bats Both. Throws Right. Height, 5 feet, 9 inches. Weight, 177 pounds.

Year	Club	Lea	Pos	G	AB	R	H	2B	3B	HR	RBI	SB	Avg
1986 Erie		N.Y.-Penn.	2B	47	163	40	46	6	1	3	18	27	.282
1986 Arkansas		Texas	2B	25	68	8	16	3	0	0	3	0	.235
1987 Arkansas		Texas	2B	101	337	57	91	14	3	4	47	13	.270
1987 Louisville		A.A.	2B	29	105	18	32	10	2	2	20	4	.305
1988 Louisville		A.A.	2B-SS	49	191	21	53	11	6	1	21	8	.277
1988 St. Louis		N.L.	2B	93	297	20	63	10	4	1	24	1	.212
1989 Louisville		A.A.	2B	124	412	53	102	20	3	8	48	13	.248
1990 St. Petersburg a		Fla. St.	2B-3B	29	95	14	22	1	4	0	12	9	.232
1990 Arkansas		Texas	2B-3B	14	49	11	14	3	1	0	4	2	.286
1990 Louisville		A.A.	2B-3B	25	92	10	32	6	3	0	10	0	.348
1991 Louisville		A.A.	2B	31	112	26	44	6	3	4	16	5	.393
1991 St. Louis b		N.L.	2B-3B-SS	56	68	5	13	3	0	0	0	0	.191
1992 Louisville		A.A.	2B	20	71	11	20	8	0	0	6	0	.282
1992 St. Louis c		N.L.	2B-SS	85	265	26	65	9	11	2	32	2	.245
1993 St. Louis		N.L.	2B-OF-3B	115	362	50	101	19	3	3	46	11	.279
1994 St. Louis d-e		N.L.	2B-OF	88	205	32	57	12	5	5	29	4	.278
1995 Boston f		A.L.	2B	132	419	64	113	20	3	6	44	13	.270
1996 St. Louis g-h-i-j		N.L.	2B	129	380	54	98	26	3	5	42	11	.258
1997 Anaheim k-l		A.L.	2B-3B	128	388	59	98	16	7	5	37	22	.253
Major League Totals			8 Yrs.	826	2384	310	608	115	36	27	254	64	.255

Year	Club	Lea	Pos	G	AB	R	H	2B	3B	HR	RBI	SB	Avg
	Division Series												
1995 Boston	..............A.L.		2B	3	10	1	6	1	0	1	1	1	.600
1996 St. Louis	.............,......N.L.		2B	3	11	1	2	2	0	0	0	0	.182
Division Series Totals	....			6	21	2	8	3	0	1	1	1	.381
	Championship Series												
1996 St. Louis	..............N.L.		2B	5	8	0	0	0	0	0	0	0	.000

a On disabled list from April 6 to June 4, 1990.
b On disabled list from April 25 to May 25, 1991.
c On disabled list from June 1 to July 6, 1992.
d Traded to Boston Red Sox for pitcher Nate Minchey and outfielder Jeff McNeely, December 7, 1994.
e Became restricted free agent under Major League Baseball implemented labor proposal, December 23, 1994.
f Signed with Boston Red Sox, April 7, 1995.
g Waived by Boston Red Sox, March 12, 1996.
h Signed with St. Louis Cardinals, March 17, 1996.
i Filed for free agency, October 31, 1996.
j Signed with Anaheim Angels organization, January 20, 1997.
k Filed for free agency, October 30, 1997.
l Signed with Texas Rangers, December 11, 1997.

ALLENSWORTH, JERMAINE LAMONT
Born, Anderson, Indiana, January 11, 1972.
Bats Right. Throws Right. Height, 6 feet. Weight 189 pounds.

Year	Club	Lea	Pos	G	AB	R	H	2B	3B	HR	RBI	SB	Avg
1993 Welland	........N.Y.-Penn.		OF	67	263	44	81	16	4	1	32	18	.308
1994 Carolina	.........Southern		OF	118	452	63	109	26	8	1	34	16	.241
1995 Carolina	.........Southern		OF	56	219	37	59	14	2	1	14	13	.269
1995 Calgary	..............P.C.		OF	51	190	46	60	13	4	3	11	13	.316
1996 Calgary	..............P.C.		OF	95	352	77	116	23	6	8	43	25	.330
1996 Pittsburgh	.............N.L.		OF	61	229	32	60	9	3	4	31	11	.262
1997 Calgary	...........P.C.		OF	5	20	5	8	3	1	0	1	1	.400
1997 Pittsburgh a	..........N.L.		OF	108	369	55	94	18	2	3	43	14	.255
Major League Totals	....	2 Yrs.	169	598	87	154	27	5	7	74	25	.258

a On disabled list from May 16 to June 23, 1997.

ALOMAR (VELAZQUEZ), ROBERTO
Born, Salinas, Puerto Rico, February 5, 1968.
Bats Both. Throws Right. Height, 6 feet. Weight, 185 pounds.

Year	Club	Lea	Pos	G	AB	R	H	2B	3B	HR	RBI	SB	Avg
1985 Charleston	.........So. Atl.		2B-SS	*137	*546	89	160	14	3	0	54	36	.293
1986 Reno	..............Calif.		2B	90	356	53	123	16	4	4	49	14	*.346
1987 Wichita	..............Texas		SS-2B	130	536	88	171	41	4	12	68	43	.319
1988 Las Vegas	..............P.C.		2B	9	37	5	10	1	0	2	14	3	.270
1988 San Diego	............N.L.		2B	143	545	84	145	24	6	9	41	24	.266
1989 San Diego	............N.L.		2B	158	623	82	184	27	1	7	56	42	.295
1990 San Diego a	............N.L.		2B-SS	147	586	80	168	27	5	6	60	24	.287
1991 Toronto	..............A.L.		2B	161	637	88	188	41	11	9	69	53	.295
1992 Toronto	..............A.L.		2B	152	571	105	177	27	8	8	76	49	.310
1993 Toronto	..............A.L.		2B	153	589	109	192	35	6	17	93	55	.326
1994 Toronto	..............A.L.		2B	107	392	78	120	25	4	8	38	19	.306
1995 Toronto b	..............A.L.		2B	130	517	71	155	24	7	13	66	30	.300
1996 Baltimore	..............A.L.		2B	153	588	132	193	43	4	22	94	17	.328
1997 Baltimore c	..........A.L.		2B	112	412	64	137	23	2	14	60	9	.333
Major League Totals	....	10 Yrs.	1416	5460	893	1659	296	54	113	653	322	.304
	Division Series												
1996 Baltimore	..............A.L.		2B	4	17	2	5	0	0	1	4	0	.294
1997 Baltimore	.............A.L.		2B	4	10	1	3	2	0	0	2	0	.300
Divisional Series Totals	....			8	27	3	8	2	0	1	6	0	.296
	Championship Series												
1991 Toronto	..............A.L.		2B	5	19	3	9	0	0	0	4	2	.474
1992 Toronto	..............A.L.		2B	6	26	4	11	1	0	2	4	5	.423
1993 Toronto	..............A.L.		2B	6	24	3	7	1	0	0	4	4	.292
1996 Baltimore	..............A.L.		2B	5	23	2	5	2	0	0	1	0	.217
1997 Baltimore	..............A.L.		2B	6	22	2	4	0	0	1	2	0	.182
Championship Series Totals	....			28	114	14	36	4	0	3	15	11	.316

4

Year	Club	Lea	Pos	G	AB	R	H	2B	3B	HR	RBI	SB	Avg
	World Series Record												
1992 Toronto .............A.L.			2B	6	24	3	5	1	0	0	0	2	.208
1993 Toronto .............A.L.			2B	6	25	5	12	2	1	0	6	4	.480
World Series Totals				12	49	8	17	3	1	0	6	6	.347

a Traded to Toronto Blue Jays with outfielder Joe Carter for shortstop Tony Fernandez and first baseman Fred McGriff, December 5, 1990.
b Filed for free agency, October 30, 1995. Signed with Baltimore Orioles, December 21, 1995.
c On disabled list from July 30 to August 26, 1997.

ALOMAR (VELAZQUEZ), SANTOS JR. (SANDY)
Born, Salinas, Puerto Rico, June 18, 1966.
Bats Right. Throws Right. Height, 6 feet, 5 inches. Weight, 215 pounds.

Year	Club	Lea	Pos	G	AB	R	H	2B	3B	HR	RBI	SB	Avg
1984 Spokane a ......Northwest			C-1B	59	219	13	47	5	0	0	21	3	.215
1985 Charleston ......So. Atl.			C-OF	100	352	38	73	7	0	3	43	3	.207
1986 Beaumont ....Texas			C	100	346	37	83	15	1	4	27	2	.240
1987 Wichita ....Texas			C	103	375	50	115	19	1	8	65	1	.307
1988 Las Vegas b .........P.C.			C-OF	93	337	59	100	9	5	16	71	1	.297
1988 San Diego .............N.L.			PH	1	1	0	0	0	0	0	0	0	.000
1989 Las Vegas ...........P.C.			C-OF	131	*523	88	160	33	8	13	101	3	.306
1989 San Diego c ...........N.L.			C	7	19	1	4	1	0	1	6	0	.211
1990 Cleveland d ..........A.L.			C	132	445	60	129	26	2	9	66	4	.290
1991 Colorado Springs ....P.C.			C	12	35	5	14	2	0	1	10	0	.400
1991 Cleveland e ..........A.L.			C	51	184	10	40	9	0	0	7	0	.217
1992 Cleveland f-g ........A.L.			C	89	299	22	75	16	0	2	26	3	.251
1993 Charlotte ....Int.			C	12	44	8	16	5	0	1	8	0	.364
1993 Cleveland h ..........A.L.			C	64	215	24	58	7	1	6	32	3	.270
1994 Cleveland i ..........A.L.			C	80	292	44	84	15	1	14	43	8	.288
1995 Canton-Akron ......Eastern			C	6	15	3	6	1	0	0	1	0	.400
1995 Cleveland j ..........A.L.			C	66	203	32	61	6	0	10	35	3	.300
1996 Cleveland ...........A.L.			C-1B	127	418	53	110	23	0	11	50	1	.263
1997 Cleveland ...........A.L.			C	125	451	63	146	37	0	21	83	0	.324
Major League Totals		10 Yrs.		742	2527	309	707	140	4	74	348	22	.280
	Division Series												
1995 Cleveland ...........A.L.			C	3	11	1	2	1	0	0	1	0	.182
1996 Cleveland ...........A.L.			C	4	16	0	2	0	0	0	3	0	.125
1997 Cleveland ...........A.L.			C	5	19	4	6	1	0	2	5	0	.316
Division Series Totals				12	46	5	10	2	0	2	9	0	.217
	Championship Series												
1995 Cleveland ...........A.L.			C	5	15	0	4	1	1	0	1	0	.267
1997 Cleveland ...........A.L.			C	6	24	3	3	0	0	1	4	0	.125
Championship Series Totals				11	39	3	7	1	1	1	5	0	.179
	World Series Record												
1995 Cleveland ...........A.L.			C	5	15	0	3	2	0	0	1	0	.200
1997 Cleveland ...........A.L.			C	7	30	5	11	1	0	2	10	0	.367
World Series Totals				12	45	5	14	3	0	2	11	0	.311

a Batted left and right from 1984 through 1986 season.
b On disabled list from August 14 to September 16, 1988.
c Traded to Cleveland Indians with infielder Carlos Baerga and outfielder Chris James for outfielder Joe Carter, December 7, 1989.
d Selected Rookie of the Year in American League for 1990.
e On disabled list from May 15 to June 17 and July 29 to end of 1991 season.
f On disabled list from May 1 to May 18, 1992.
g Suspended three games by American League for June 8 mound charging from July 29 to August 2, 1992.
h On disabled list May 1 to August 7, 1993.
i On disabled list from April 24 to May 11, 1994.
j On disabled list from April 25 to June 29, 1995.

ALOU, MOISES ROJAS
Born, Atlanta, Georgia, July 3, 1966.
Bats Right. Throws Right. Height, 6 feet, 3 inches. Weight, 190 pounds.

Year	Club	Lea	Pos	G	AB	R	H	2B	3B	HR	RBI	SB	Avg
1986 Watertown ......N.Y.-Penn.			OF	69	254	30	60	9	*8	6	35	14	.236
1987 Macon a ....So. Atl.			OF	4	8	1	1	0	0	0	0	0	.125
1987 Watertown ......N.Y.-Penn.			OF	39	117	20	25	6	2	4	18	6	.214
1988 Augusta ....So. Atl.			OF	105	358	58	112	23	5	7	62	24	.313

Year Club	Lea	Pos	G	AB	R	H	2B	3B	HR	RBI	SB	Avg
1989 Salem . . . . .Carolina	OF	86	321	50	97	29	2	14	53	12	.302
1989 Harrisburg . . . . .Eastern	OF	54	205	36	60	5	2	3	19	8	.293
1990 Buff.-Indianap. . . . . . . .A.A.	OF	90	326	44	86	5	6	5	37	13	.264
1990 Harrisburg . . . . . .Eastern	OF	36	132	19	39	12	2	3	22	7	.295
1990 Pitts.-Montreal b . . . . . .N.L.	OF	16	20	4	4	0	1	0	0	0	.200
1991 Montreal c . . . . .N.L.		INJURED—Did Not Play									
1992 Montreal d . . . . .N.L.	OF	115	341	53	96	28	2	9	56	16	.282
1993 Montreal e . . . . .N.L.	OF	136	482	70	138	29	6	18	85	17	.286
1994 Montreal . . . . .N.L.	OF	107	422	81	143	31	5	22	78	7	.339
1995 Montreal f . . . . .N.L.	OF	93	344	48	94	22	0	14	58	4	.273
1996 Montreal g-h . . . . .N.L.	OF	143	540	87	152	28	2	21	96	9	.281
1997 Florida i . . . . .N.L.	OF	150	538	88	157	29	5	23	115	9	.292
Major League Totals	7 Yrs.	760	2687	431	784	167	21	107	488	62	.292
Division Series											
1997 Florida . . . . .N.L.	OF	3	14	1	3	1	0	0	1	0	.214
Championship Series											
1997 Florida . . . . .N.L.	OF	5	15	0	1	1	0	0	5	0	.067
World Series Record											
1997 Florida . . . . .N.L.	OF	7	28	6	9	2	0	3	9	1	.321

a On disabled list from March 31 to April 18, 1987.
b Traded to Montreal Expos organization to complete August 8 trade in which Pittsburgh Pirates acquired pitcher Zane Smith for pitcher Scott Ruskin, shortstop Willie Greene and player to be named, August 16, 1990.
c On disabled list from March 19 to end of 1991 season.
d On disabled list from July 7 to July 27, 1992.
e On disabled list from September 18 to end of 1993 season.
f On disabled list from August 19 to September 5 and September 11 to October 2, 1995.
g On disabled list from July 8 to July 23, 1996.
h Signed as free agent with Florida Marlins, December 12, 1996.
i Traded to Houston Astros for pitcher Oscar Henriquez, pitcher Manuel Barrios and player to be named later, November 11, 1997.

AMARAL, RICHARD LOUIS

Born, Visalia, California, April 1, 1962.
Bats Right. Throws Right. Height, 6 feet. Weight, 175 pounds.

Year Club	Lea	Pos	G	AB	R	H	2B	3B	HR	RBI	SB	Avg
1983 Geneva . .N.Y.-Penn.	2B-3B	67	269	63	68	17	3	1	24	22	.253
1984 Quad City .Midwest	2B	34	119	21	25	1	0	0	7	12	.210
1985 Win.-Salem . .Carol.	2B	124	428	62	116	15	5	3	36	26	.271
1986 Pittsfield . . .Eastern	2B	114	355	43	89	12	0	0	24	25	.251
1987 Pittsfield . . .Eastern	2B	104	315	45	80	8	5	0	28	28	.254
1988 Pittsfield a . .Eastern	2B-SS	122	422	66	117	15	4	4	47	54	.277
1989 Birmingham .South.	2B-SS	122	432	*90	123	15	6	4	48	57	.285
1990 Vancouver b . . .P.C.	SS-2B-3B-OF	130	462	87	139	*39	5	4	56	20	.301
1991 Calgary . . . . . . .P.C.	SS-2B	86	347	79	120	26	2	3	36	30	*.346
1991 Seattle c . . . . . .A.L.	2B-SS-3B-1B	14	16	2	1	0	0	0	0	0	.063
1992 Calgary . . . . . . .P.C.	SS-2B-OF	106	403	79	128	21	8	0	21	*53	.318
1992 Seattle . . . . . .A.L.	3B-SS-OF-1B-2B	35	100	9	24	3	0	1	7	4	.240
1993 Seattle d . . . . . .A.L.	2B-3B-SS-1B	110	373	53	108	24	1	1	44	19	.290
1994 Calgary . . . . . . .P.C.	2B-OF	13	56	13	18	7	0	0	12	2	.321
1994 Seattle . . . . . . .A.L.	2B-OF-SS-1B	77	228	37	60	10	2	4	18	5	.263
1995 Seattle . . . . . .A.L.	OF	90	238	45	67	14	2	2	19	21	.282
1996 Seattle . . . . . .A.L.	OF-2B-1B-3B	118	312	69	91	11	3	1	29	25	.292
1997 Seattle . . . . . .A.L.	OF-1B-2B-3B	89	190	34	54	5	0	1	21	12	.284
Major League Totals	7 Yrs.	533	1457	249	405	67	8	10	138	86	.278
Division Series											
1997 Seattle . . . . . .A.L.	1B	2	4	2	2	0	0	0	0	0	.500
Championship Series											
1995 Seattle . . . . . .A.L.	PH	2	2	0	0	0	0	0	0	0	.000

a Drafted by Chicago White Sox from Chicago Cubs organization in minor league draft, December 5, 1988.
b Became free agent, October 15; signed with Seattle Mariners organization, November 25, 1990.
c On disabled list from May 29 to July 17, 1991.
d On disabled list from August 1 to August 16, 1993.

ANDERSON, BRADY KEVIN

Born, Silver Spring, Maryland, January 18, 1964.
Bats Left. Throws Left. Height, 6 feet, 1 inch. Weight, 195 pounds.

Year Club	Lea	Pos	G	AB	R	H	2B	3B	HR	RBI	SB	Avg
1985 Elmira . . . . .N.Y.-Penn.	OF	71	215	36	55	7	*6	5	21	13	.256
1986 Winter Haven . . . . . . .Fla. St.	OF	126	417	86	133	19	11	12	87	44	.319
1987 New Britain a . . . . . . .Eastern	OF	52	170	30	50	4	3	6	35	7	.294

Year	Club	Lea	Pos	G	AB	R	H	2B	3B	HR	RBI	SB	Avg
1987 Pawtucket	....	Int.	OF	23	79	18	30	4	0	2	8	2	.380
1988 Pawtucket	....	Int.	OF	49	167	27	48	6	1	4	19	8	.287
1988 Boston-Balt. b	....	A.L.	OF	94	325	31	69	13	4	1	21	10	.212
1989 Rochester	....	Int.	DH	21	70	14	14	1	2	1	8	2	.200
1989 Baltimore	....	A.L.	OF	94	266	44	55	12	2	4	16	16	.207
1990 Hagerstown	....	Eastern	DH	9	34	8	13	0	2	1	5	2	.382
1990 Baltimore c	....	A.L.	OF	89	234	24	54	5	2	3	24	15	.231
1991 Rochester	....	Int.	OF	7	26	5	10	3	0	0	2	4	.385
1991 Baltimore d	....	A.L.	OF	113	256	40	59	12	3	2	27	12	.230
1992 Baltimore	....	A.L.	OF	159	623	100	169	28	10	21	80	53	.271
1993 Baltimore e	....	A.L.	OF	142	560	87	147	36	8	13	66	24	.262
1994 Baltimore	....	A.L.	OF	111	453	78	119	25	5	12	48	31	.263
1995 Baltimore	....	A.L.	OF	143	554	108	145	33	10	16	64	26	.262
1996 Baltimore	....	A.L.	OF	149	579	117	172	37	5	50	110	21	.297
1997 Baltimore f-g	....	A.L.	OF	151	590	97	170	39	7	18	73	18	.288
Major League Totals	....	10 Yrs.		1245	4440	726	1159	240	56	140	529	226	.261
Division Series													
1996 Baltimore	....	A.L.	OF	4	17	3	5	0	0	2	4	0	.294
1997 Baltimore	....	A.L.	OF	4	17	3	6	1	0	1	4	1	.353
Divisional Series Totals	....			8	34	6	11	1	0	3	8	1	.324
Championship Series													
1996 Baltimore	....	A.L.	OF	5	21	5	4	1	0	1	1	0	.190
1997 Baltimore	....	A.L.	OF	6	25	5	9	2	0	2	3	2	.360
Championship Series Totals	....			11	46	10	13	3	0	3	4	2	.283

a On disabled list from June 5 to July 20, 1987.
b Traded to Baltimore Orioles with pitcher Curt Schilling for pitcher Mike Boddicker, July 29, 1988.
c On disabled list from June 8 to July 20, 1990.
d On disabled list from May 28 to June 14, 1991.
e On disabled list from June 23 to July 8, 1993.
f Filed for free agency, October 27, 1997.
g Re-signed with Baltimore Orioles, December 5, 1997.

ANDERSON, GARRET JOSEPH

Born, Los Angeles, California, June 30, 1972.
Bats Left. Throws Left. Height, 6 feet, 3 inches. Weight, 190 pounds.

Year	Club	Lea	Pos	G	AB	R	H	2B	3B	HR	RBI	SB	Avg
1990 Mesa Angels	......	Arizona	OF	32	127	5	27	2	0	0	14	3	.213
1990 Boise	....	Northwest	OF	25	83	11	21	3	1	1	8	0	.253
1991 Quad City	....	Midwest	OF	105	392	40	102	22	2	2	42	5	.260
1992 Palm Springs	....	California	OF	81	322	46	104	15	2	1	62	1	.323
1992 Midland	....	Texas	OF	39	146	16	40	5	0	2	19	2	.274
1993 Vancouver	....	P.C.	OF-1B	124	467	57	137	34	4	4	71	3	.293
1994 Vancouver	....	P.C.	OF-1B	123	505	75	162	42	6	12	102	3	.321
1994 California	....	A.L.	OF	5	13	0	5	0	0	0	1	0	.385
1995 Vancouver	....	P.C.	OF	14	61	9	19	7	0	0	12	0	.311
1995 California	....	A.L.	OF	106	374	50	120	19	1	16	69	6	.321
1996 California	....	A.L.	OF	150	607	79	173	33	2	12	72	7	.285
1997 Anaheim	....	A.L.	OF	154	624	76	189	36	3	8	92	10	.303
Major League Totals	....	4 Yrs.		415	1618	205	487	88	6	36	234	23	.301

ANDREWS, DARRELL SHANE (SHANE)

Born, Dallas, Texas, August 28, 1971.
Bats Right. Throws Right. Height, 6 feet, 1 inch. Weight, 215 pounds.

Year	Club	Lea	Pos	G	AB	R	H	2B	3B	HR	RBI	SB	Avg
1990 Expos	....	Gulf Coast	3B	56	190	31	46	7	1	3	24	11	.242
1991 Sumter	....	So. Atl.	3B	105	356	46	74	16	7	11	49	5	.208
1992 Albany	....	So. Atl.	3B-1B	136	453	76	104	18	1	25	87	8	.230
1993 Harrisburg	....	Eastern	3B-SS	124	442	77	115	29	2	18	70	10	.260
1994 Ottawa	....	Int.	3B-OF	137	460	79	117	25	2	16	85	6	.254
1995 Montreal	....	N.L.	3B-1B	84	220	27	47	10	1	8	31	1	.214
1996 Montreal	....	N.L.	3B	127	375	43	85	15	2	19	64	3	.227
1997 Montreal a	....	N.L.	3B	18	64	10	13	3	0	4	9	0	.203
1997 Ottawa	....	Int.	3B	3	12	3	3	0	0	1	1	0	.250
1997 West Plm Bch	....	Fla. St.	DH-3B	5	17	2	3	2	0	1	5	0	.176
Major League Totals	....	3 Yrs.		229	659	80	145	28	3	31	104	4	.220

a On disabled list from May 1 to September 29, 1997.

ARIAS, ALEJANDRO (ALEX)
Born, New York, New York, November 20, 1967.
Bats Right. Throws Right. Height, 6 feet, 3 inches. Weight, 185 pounds.

Year	Club	Lea	Pos	G	AB	R	H	2B	3B	HR	RBI	SB	Avg
1987 Wytheville	......	Appal.	SS-3B	61	233	41	69	7	0	0	24	16	.296
1988 Charleston, WV		.So. Atl.	SS-3B-2B	127	472	57	122	12	1	0	33	41	.258
1989 Peoria	....	Midwest	SS	*136	506	74	140	10	*11	2	64	31	.277
1990 Charlotte	.....	Southern	SS	119	419	55	103	16	3	4	38	12	.246
1991 Charlotte	.....	Southern	SS	134	488	69	134	26	0	4	47	23	.275
1992 Iowa	....	A.A.	SS-2B	106	409	52	114	23	3	5	40	14	.279
1992 Chicago a	....	N.L.	SS	32	99	14	29	6	0	0	7	0	.293
1993 Florida	....	N.L.	2B-3B-SS	96	249	27	67	5	1	2	20	1	.269
1994 Florida	....	N.L.	SS-3B	59	113	4	27	5	0	0	15	0	.239
1995 Florida	....	N.L.	SS-3B-2B	94	216	22	58	9	2	3	26	1	.269
1996 Florida	....	N.L.	3B-SS-1B-2B	100	224	27	62	11	2	3	26	2	.277
1997 Florida b-c-d		.N.L.	3B-SS	74	93	13	23	2	0	1	11	0	.247
Major League Totals	....		6 Yrs.	455	994	107	266	38	5	9	105	4	.268
Division Series													
1997 Florida	....	.N.L.	PH	1	1	1	1	0	0	0	1	0	1.000
Championship Series													
1997 Florida	....	.N.L.	3B	3	1	0	1	0	0	0	0	0	1.000
World Series Record													
1997 Florida	....	.N.L.	3B-DH	2	1	1	0	0	0	0	0	0	.000

a Traded to Florida Marlins with third baseman Gary Scott for pitcher Greg Hibbard, November 17, 1992.
b On disabled list from June 14 to July 2, 1997.
c Designated for assignment by Florida Marlins, December 8, 1997.
d Signed with Philadelphia Phillies, December 27, 1997.

ARIAS, GEORGE ALBERTO
Born, Tucson, Arizona, March 12, 1972.
Bats Right. Throws Right. Height, 5 feet, 11 inches. Weight 190 pounds.

Year	Club	Lea	Pos	G	AB	R	H	2B	3B	HR	RBI	SB	Avg
1993 Cedar Rapds	......	Midwest	3B-SS	74	253	31	55	13	3	9	41	6	.217
1994 Lake Elsnor	......	California	3B	134	514	89	144	28	3	23	80	6	.280
1995 Midland	....	Texas	3B-SS	134	520	91	145	19	10	30	104	3	.279
1996 Vancouver	....	P.C.	3B	59	243	49	82	24	0	9	55	2	.337
1996 California	....	A.L.	3B	84	252	19	60	8	1	6	28	2	.238
1997 Vancouver	....	P.C.	3B-SS	105	401	71	112	28	3	11	60	3	.279
1997 Las Vegas	....	P.C.	3B	10	30	4	10	4	1	1	5	0	.333
1997 Anaheim	....	A.L.	3B	3	6	1	2	0	0	0	1	0	.333
1997 San Diego a	....	N.L.	3B	11	22	2	5	1	0	0	2	0	.227
Major League Totals	....		2 Yrs.	98	280	22	67	9	1	6	31	2	.239

a Sent to San Diego Padres as player to be named later for outfielder Rickey Henderson, August 19, 1997.

ASHLEY, BILLY MANUAL
Born, Taylor, Michigan, July 11, 1970.
Bats Right. Throws Right. Height, 6 feet, 7 inches. Weight, 227 pounds.

Year	Club	Lea	Pos	G	AB	R	H	2B	3B	HR	RBI	SB	Avg
1988 Sarasota Dodgers	....	Gulf C.	OF	9	26	3	4	0	0	0	0	1	.154
1989 Kissimmee Dodgers	..	Gulf C.	OF	48	160	23	38	6	2	1	19	16	.238
1990 Bakersfield	......	California	OF	99	331	48	72	13	1	9	40	17	.218
1991 Vero Beach	....	Fla. St.	OF	61	206	18	52	11	2	7	42	9	.252
1992 San Antonio	....	Texas	OF	101	380	60	106	23	1	24	66	13	.279
1992 Albuquerque	....	.P.C.	OF	25	95	11	20	7	0	2	10	1	.211
1992 Los Angeles	....	.N.L.	OF	29	95	6	21	5	0	2	6	0	.221
1993 Albuquerque	....	.P.C.	OF	125	482	88	143	31	4	26	100	6	.297
1993 Los Angeles	....	.N.L.	OF	14	37	0	9	0	0	0	0	0	.243
1994 Albuquerque	....	.P.C.	OF	107	388	93	134	19	4	*37	105	6	.345
1994 Los Angeles	....	.N.L.	OF	2	6	0	2	1	0	0	0	0	.333
1995 Los Angeles	....	.N.L.	OF	81	215	17	51	5	0	8	27	0	.237
1996 Albuquerque	....	.P.C.	OF	7	23	6	8	1	0	1	9	2	.348
1996 Los Angeles a	....	.N.L.	OF	71	110	18	22	2	1	9	25	0	.200
1997 Los Angeles	....	.N.L.	OF	71	131	12	32	7	0	6	19	0	.244
Major League Totals	....		6 Yrs.	268	594	53	137	20	1	25	77	0	.231
Division Series													
1995 Los Angeles	....	.N.L.	PH	1	0	0	0	0	0	0	0	0	.000
1996 Los Angeles	....	.N.L.	PH	2	2	0	0	0	0	0	0	0	.000
Division Series Totals	....			3	2	0	0	0	0	0	0	0	.000

a On disabled list from April 21 to May 13, 1996.

AURILIA, RICHARD SANTO (RICH)
Born, Brooklyn, New York, September 2, 1971.
Bats Right. Throws Right. Height, 6 feet. Weight, 170 pounds.

Year	Club	Lea	Pos	G	AB	R	H	2B	3B	HR	RBI	SB	Avg
1992 Butte	. . . .	.Pioneer	SS	59	202	37	68	11	3	3	30	13	.337
1993 Charlotte	. . . .	.Fla. St.	SS	122	440	80	136	16	5	5	56	15	.309
1994 Tulsa	. . . .	.Texas	SS	129	458	67	107	18	6	12	57	10	.234
1995 Shreveport	. . . .	.Texas	SS	64	226	29	74	17	1	4	42	10	.327
1995 Phoenix	. . . .	.P.C.	SS	71	258	42	72	12	0	5	34	2	.279
1995 San Francisco	. . . .	.N.L.	SS	9	19	4	9	3	0	2	4	1	.474
1996 Phoenix	. . . .	.P.C.	SS-2B	7	30	9	13	7	0	0	4	1	.433
1996 San Francisco a	. . . .	.N.L.	SS-2B	105	318	27	76	7	1	3	26	4	.239
1997 Phoenix	. . . .	.P.C.	SS	8	34	9	10	2	0	1	5	2	.294
1997 San Francisco	. . . .	.N.L.	SS	46	102	16	28	8	0	5	19	1	.275
Major League Totals	. . . .		3 Yrs.	160	439	47	113	18	1	10	49	6	.257

a On disabled list from September 24 to September 30, 1996.

AUSMUS, BRADLEY DAVID (BRAD)
Born, New Haven, Connecticut, April 14, 1969.
Bats Right. Throws Right. Height, 5 feet, 11 inches. Weight, 190 pounds.

Year	Club	Lea	Pos	G	AB	R	H	2B	3B	HR	RBI	SB	Avg
1988 Oneonta	. . . .	.N.Y.-Penn.	C	2	4	0	1	0	0	0	0	0	.250
1988 Sarasota Yankees	. . . .	.Gulf C.	C	43	133	22	34	2	0	0	15	5	.256
1989 Oneonta	. . . .	.N.Y.-Penn.	C-3B	52	165	29	43	6	0	1	18	6	.261
1990 Prince William	. . . .	.Carolina	C	107	364	46	86	12	2	0	27	2	.236
1991 Prince William	. . . .	.Carolina	C	63	230	28	70	14	3	2	30	17	.304
1991 Albany	. . . .	.Eastern	C	67	229	36	61	9	2	1	29	14	.266
1992 Albany	. . . .	.Eastern	C	5	18	0	3	0	1	0	1	2	.167
1992 Columbus a	. . . .	.Int.	C-OF	111	364	48	88	14	3	2	35	19	.242
1993 Colorado Springs b	. . . .	.P.C.	C-OF	76	241	31	65	10	4	2	33	10	.270
1993 San Diego	. . . .	.N.L.	C	49	160	18	41	8	1	5	12	2	.256
1994 San Diego	. . . .	.N.L.	C-1B	101	327	45	82	12	1	7	24	5	.251
1995 San Diego	. . . .	.N.L.	C-1B	103	328	44	96	16	4	5	34	16	.293
1996 San Diego c	. . . .	.N.L.	C	50	149	16	27	4	0	1	13	1	.181
1996 Detroit d	. . . .	.A.L.	C	75	226	30	56	12	0	4	22	3	.248
1997 Houston	. . . .	.N.L.	C	130	425	45	113	25	1	4	44	14	.266
Major League Totals	. . . .		5 Yrs.	508	1615	198	415	77	7	26	149	41	.257
Division Series													
1997 Houston	. . . .	.N.L.	C	2	5	1	2	1	0	0	2	0	.400

a Selected by Colorado Rockies from New York Yankees organization in expansion draft, November 17, 1992.
b Traded by Colorado Rockies to San Diego Padres with pitcher Doug Bochtler and player to be named for pitchers Greg W. Harris and Bruce Hurst, July 26; San Diego Padres acquired pitcher Andy Ashby to complete trade, July 28, 1993.
c Traded to Detroit Tigers with infielder Andujar Cedeno for catcher John Flaherty and infielder Chris Gomez, June 18, 1996.
d Traded to Houston Astros with pitcher C.J. Nitkowski, pitcher Jose Lima, pitcher Trever Miller and infielder Daryle Ward for outfielder Brian Hunter, infielder Orlando Miller, pitcher Todd Jones and pitcher Doug Brocail, December 10, 1996.

BAERGA (ORTIZ), CARLOS OBED
Born, San Juan Puerto Rico, November 4, 1968.
Bats Both. Throws Right. Height, 5 feet, 11 inches. Weight, 200 pounds.

Year	Club	Lea	Pos	G	AB	R	H	2B	3B	HR	RBI	SB	Avg
1986 Charleston	. . . .	.So. Atl.	2B-SS	111	378	57	102	14	4	7	41	6	.270
1987 Charleston	. . . .	.So. Atl.	2B-SS	134	515	83	157	23	*9	7	50	26	.305
1988 Wichita	. . . .	.Texas	SS-2B	122	444	67	121	28	1	12	65	4	.273
1989 Las Vegas a	. . . .	.P.C.	3B	132	520	63	143	28	2	10	74	6	.275
1990 Colorado Springs	. . . . .	.P.C.	3B	12	50	11	19	2	1	1	11	1	.380
1990 Cleveland	. . . .	.A.L.	3B-SS-2B	108	312	46	81	17	2	7	47	0	.260
1991 Cleveland	. . . .	.A.L.	3B-2B-SS	158	593	80	171	28	2	11	69	3	.288
1992 Cleveland	. . . .	.A.L.	2B	161	657	92	205	32	1	20	105	10	.312
1993 Cleveland	. . . .	.A.L.	2B	154	624	105	200	28	6	21	114	15	.321
1994 Cleveland	. . . .	.A.L.	2B	103	442	81	139	32	2	19	80	8	.314
1995 Cleveland b	. . . .	.A.L.	2B	135	557	87	175	28	2	15	90	11	.314
1996 Cleveland b	. . . .	.A.L.	2B	100	424	54	113	25	0	10	55	1	.267
1996 New York	. . . .	.N.L.	1B-3B-2B	26	83	5	16	3	0	2	11	0	.193
1997 New York	. . . .	.N.L.	2B	133	467	53	131	25	1	9	52	2	.281
Major League Totals	. . . .		8 Yrs.	1078	4159	603	1231	218	16	114	623	50	.296

9

Year	Club	Lea	Pos	G	AB	R	H	2B	3B	HR	RBI	SB	Avg
	Division Series												
1995	Cleveland ...........A.L.		2B	3	14	2	4	1	0	0	1	0	.286
	Championship Series												
1995	Cleveland ...........A.L.		2B	6	25	3	10	0	0	1	4	0	.400
	World Series Record												
1995	Cleveland ...........A.L.		2B	6	26	1	5	2	0	0	4	0	.192

a Traded by San Diego Padres to Cleveland Indians organization with catcher Sandy Alomar Jr. and outfielder Chris James for outfielder Joe Carter, December 7, 1989.
b Traded to New York Mets with infielder Alvaro Espinoza for infielder Jose Vizcaino and infielder Jeff Kent, July 29, 1996.

BAGWELL, JEFFREY ROBERT

Born, Boston, Massachusetts, May 27, 1968.
Bats Right. Throws Right. Height, 6 feet. Weight, 195 pounds.

Year	Club	Lea	Pos	G	AB	R	H	2B	3B	HR	RBI	SB	Avg
1989	Sarasota Red Sox ....Gulf C.		3B	5	19	3	6	1	0	0	3	0	.316
1989	Winter Haven ....Fla. St.		3B	64	210	27	65	13	2	2	19	1	.310
1990	New Britain a ......Eastern		3B	136	481	63	*160	*34	7	4	61	5	.333
1991	Houston b ...........N.L.		1B	156	554	79	163	26	4	15	82	7	.294
1992	Houston .............N.L.		1B	*162	586	87	160	34	6	18	96	10	.273
1993	Houston .............N.L.		1B	142	535	76	171	37	4	20	88	13	.320
1994	Houston c ...........N.L.		1B-OF	110	400	*104	147	32	2	39	*116	15	.368
1995	Jackson ....Texas		1B	4	12	0	2	0	0	0	0	0	.167
1995	Houston d ...........N.L.		1B	114	448	88	130	29	0	21	87	12	.290
1996	Houston .............N.L.		1B	*162	568	111	179	*48	2	31	120	21	.315
1997	Houston .............N.L.		1B	*162	566	109	162	40	2	43	135	31	.286
Major League Totals			7 Yrs.	1008	3657	654	1112	246	20	187	724	109	.304
	Division Series												
1997	Houston .............N.L.		1B	3	12	0	1	0	0	0	0	0	.083

a Traded by Boston Red Sox to Houston Astros for pitcher Larry Andersen, August 31, 1990.
b Selected Rookie of the Year in National League for 1991.
c Selected Most Valuable Player in National League for 1994.
d On disabled list from July 31 to September 1, 1995.

BAINES, HAROLD DOUGLASS

Born, Easton, Maryland, March 15, 1959.
Bats Left. Throws Left. Height, 6 feet, 2 inches. Weight, 195 pounds.

Year	Club	Lea	Pos	G	AB	R	H	2B	3B	HR	RBI	SB	Avg
1977	Appleton ....Midwest		OF	69	222	37	58	11	2	5	29	2	.261
1978	Knoxville ....Southern		OF-1B	137	502	70	138	16	6	13	72	3	.275
1979	Iowa ................A.A.		OF	125	466	87	139	25	8	22	87	5	.298
1980	Chicago .............A.L.		OF	141	491	55	125	23	6	13	49	2	.255
1981	Chicago .............A.L.		OF	82	280	42	80	11	7	10	41	6	.286
1982	Chicago .............A.L.		OF	161	608	89	165	29	8	25	105	10	.271
1983	Chicago .............A.L.		OF	156	596	76	167	33	2	20	99	7	.280
1984	Chicago .............A.L.		OF	147	569	72	173	28	10	29	94	1	.304
1985	Chicago .............A.L.		OF	160	640	86	198	29	3	22	113	1	.309
1986	Chicago .............A.L.		OF	145	570	72	169	29	2	21	88	2	.296
1987	Chicago a ...........A.L.		OF	132	505	59	148	26	4	20	93	0	.293
1988	Chicago .............A.L.		OF	158	599	55	166	39	1	13	81	0	.277
1989	Chicago-Texas b .....A.L.		OF	146	505	73	156	29	1	16	72	0	.309
1990	Texas-Oakland c .....A.L.		OF	135	415	52	118	15	1	16	65	0	.284
1991	Oakland .............A.L.		DH-OF	141	488	76	144	25	1	20	90	0	.295
1992	Oakland d-e .........A.L.		DH-OF	140	478	58	121	18	0	16	76	1	.253
1993	Bowie ....Eastern		DH	2	6	0	0	0	0	0	0	0	.000
1993	Baltimore f-g .......A.L.		DH	118	416	64	130	22	0	20	78	0	.313
1994	Baltimore h .........A.L.		DH	94	326	44	96	12	1	16	54	0	.294
1995	Baltimore i .........A.L.		DH	127	385	60	115	19	1	24	63	0	.299
1996	Chicago j-k .........A.L.		DH	143	495	80	154	29	0	22	95	3	.311
1997	Chicago-Balt. l-m-n ...A.L.		DH-OF	137	452	55	136	23	0	16	67	0	.301
Major League Totals			18 Yrs.	2463	8818	1168	2561	439	48	339	1423	33	.290
	Division Series												
1997	Baltimore ...........A.L.		DH	2	5	2	2	0	0	1	1	0	.400
	Championship Series												
1983	Chicago .............A.L.		OF	4	16	0	2	0	0	0	0	0	.125
1990	Oakland .............A.L.		DH	4	14	2	5	1	0	0	3	1	.357

Year	Club	Lea	Pos	G	AB	R	H	2B	3B	HR	RBI	SB	Avg
1992 Oakland .............A.L.			DH	6	25	6	11	2	0	1	4	0	.440
1997 Baltimore ...........A.L.			DH	6	17	1	6	0	0	1	2	0	.353
Championship Series Totals				20	72	9	24	3	0	2	9	1	.333
World Series Record													
1990 Oakland .............A.L.			DH	3	7	1	1	0	0	1	2	0	.143

a On disabled list from April 7 to May 8, 1987.
b Traded to Texas Rangers with infielder Fred Manrique for infielder Scott Fletcher, outfielder Sam Sosa and pitcher Wilson Alvarez, July 29, 1989.
c Traded to Oakland Athletics for two players to be named, August 29; Texas Rangers acquired pitchers Joe Bitker and Scott Chiamparino to complete trade, September 4, 1990.
d Filed for free agency, October 27, 1992; re-signed with Oakland Athletics, December 18, 1992.
e Traded to Baltimore Orioles for pitchers Bobby Chouinard and Allen Plaster, January 14, 1993.
f On disabled list from May 5 to May 27, 1993.
g Filed for free agency, November 1; re-signed with Baltimore Orioles, December 2, 1993.
h Filed for free agency, October 14; re-signed with Baltimore Orioles, December 23, 1994.
i Filed for free agency, November 12, 1995.
j Filed for free agency, November 18, 1996.
k Signed with Chicago White Sox, January 10, 1997.
l Traded to Baltimore Orioles for player to be named later, July 29, 1997. Chicago White Sox received infielder Juan Bautista to complete trade, August 18, 1997.
m Filed for free agency, October 29, 1997.
n Re-signed by Baltimore Orioles, December 20, 1997.

BATES, JASON CHARLES

Born, Downey, California, January 5, 1971.
Bats Both. Throws Right. Height, 5 feet, 11 inches. Weight, 170 pounds.

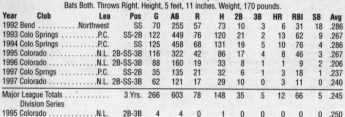

Year	Club	Lea	Pos	G	AB	R	H	2B	3B	HR	RBI	SB	Avg
1992 Bend ....Northwest			SS	70	255	57	73	10	3	6	31	18	.286
1993 Colo Springs ........P.C.			SS-2B	122	449	76	120	21	2	13	62	9	.267
1994 Colo Springs .........P.C.			SS	125	458	68	131	19	5	10	76	4	.286
1995 Colorado .............N.L.			2B-SS-3B	116	322	42	86	17	4	8	46	3	.267
1996 Colorado .............N.L.			2B-SS-3B	88	160	19	33	8	1	1	9	2	.206
1997 Colo Sprngs ..........P.C.			SS-2B	35	135	21	32	6	1	3	18	1	.237
1997 Colorado .............N.L.			2B-SS-3B	62	121	17	29	10	0	3	11	0	.240
Major League Totals			3 Yrs.	266	603	78	148	35	5	12	66	5	.245
Division Series													
1995 Colorado .............N.L.			2B-3B	4	4	0	1	0	0	0	0	0	.250

BATISTA, LEOCADIO FRANCISCO (TONY)

Born, Puerto Plata, Dominican Republic, December 9, 1973.
Bats Right. Throws Right. Height, 6 feet. Weight 180 pounds.

Year	Club	Lea	Pos	G	AB	R	H	2B	3B	HR	RBI	SB	Avg
1992 Athletics ....Arizona			2B-2B-SS-OF	45	167	32	41	6	2	0	22	1	.246
1993 Athletics ....Arizona			3B-2B-SS	24	104	21	34	6	2	2	17	6	.327
1993 Tacoma .............P.C.			SS	4	12	1	2	1	0	0	1	0	.167
1994 Modesto ....California			SS-2B	119	466	91	131	26	3	17	68	7	.281
1995 Huntsville ....Southern			SS-2B	120	419	55	107	23	1	16	61	7	.255
1996 Edmonton ...........P.C.			SS	57	205	33	66	17	4	8	40	2	.322
1996 Oakland .............A.L.			2B-3B-SS	74	238	38	71	10	2	6	25	7	.298
1997 Edmonton ...........P.C.			SS	33	124	25	39	10	1	3	21	2	.315
1997 Oakland a-b ..........A.L.			SS-3B-2B	68	188	22	38	10	1	4	18	2	.202
Major League Totals			2 Yrs.	142	426	60	109	20	3	10	43	9	.256

a On disabled list from August 27 to September 12, 1997.
b Selected in expansion draft by Arizona Diamondbacks, November 18, 1997.

BECKER, RICHARD GODHARD

Born, Aurora, Illinois, February 1, 1972.
Bats Both. Throws Right. Height, 5 feet, 10 inches. Weight, 180 pounds.

Year	Club	Lea	Pos	G	AB	R	H	2B	3B	HR	RBI	SB	Avg
1990 Elizabethton ....Appal.			OF	56	194	54	56	5	1	6	24	18	.289
1991 Kenosha ....Midwest			OF	130	494	100	132	38	3	13	53	19	.267
1992 Visalia ....California			OF	136	506	*118	160	37	2	15	82	29	.316
1993 Nashville ....Southern			OF	138	516	93	148	25	7	15	66	29	.287
1993 Minnesota a .........A.L.			OF	3	7	3	2	2	0	0	0	1	.286
1994 Salt Lake City .........P.C.			OF	71	282	64	89	21	3	2	38	7	.316

Year	Club	Lea	Pos	G	AB	R	H	2B	3B	HR	RBI	SB	Avg
1994 Minnesota b	.........A.L.		OF	28	98	12	26	3	0	1	8	6	.265
1995 Salt Lake	............P.C.		OF	36	123	26	38	7	0	6	28	6	.309
1995 Minnesota	...........A.L.		OF	106	392	45	93	15	1	2	33	8	.237
1996 Minnesota	...........A.L.		OF	148	525	92	153	31	4	12	71	19	.291
1997 Minnesota c	..........A.L.		OF	132	443	61	117	22	3	10	45	17	.264
Major League Totals	....		5 Yrs.	417	1465	213	391	73	8	25	157	51	.267

a On disabled list from September 13 to end of 1993 season.
b On disabled list from April 29 to May 17, 1994.
c Traded to New York Mets for outfielder Alex Ochoa, December 14, 1997.

BELL, DEREK NATHANIEL
Born, Tampa, Florida, December 11, 1968.
Bats Right. Throws Right. Height, 6 feet, 2 inches. Weight, 215 pounds.

Year	Club	Lea	Pos	G	AB	R	H	2B	3B	HR	RBI	SB	Avg
1987 St. Catharines	. . . .N.Y.-Penn.		OF	74	273	46	72	11	3	10	42	12	.264
1988 Myrtle Beach	.........So. Atl.		OF	91	352	55	121	29	5	12	60	18	*.344
1988 Knoxville a	......Southern		OF	14	52	5	13	3	1	0	4	2	.250
1989 Knoxville	.........Southern		OF	136	513	72	124	22	6	16	75	15	.242
1990 Syracuse b	............Int.		OF	109	402	57	105	13	5	7	56	21	.261
1991 Syracuse	..............Int.		OF	119	457	*89	*158	22	*12	13	*93	27	*.346
1991 Toronto	.............A.L.		OF	18	28	5	4	0	0	0	1	3	.143
1992 Dunedin	............Fla. St.		OF	7	25	7	6	2	0	0	4	3	.240
1992 Toronto c-d	..........A.L.		OF	61	161	23	39	6	3	2	15	7	.242
1993 San Diego	..........N.L.		OF-3B	150	542	73	142	19	1	21	72	26	.262
1994 San Diego e-f	.........N.L.		OF	108	434	54	135	20	0	14	54	24	.311
1995 Houston	..........N.L.		OF	112	452	63	151	21	2	8	86	27	.334
1996 Houston	..........N.L.		OF	158	627	84	165	40	3	17	113	29	.263
1997 New Orleans	..........A.A.		OF	5	13	0	2	0	0	0	1	1	.154
1997 Houston g	..........N.L.		OF	129	493	67	136	29	3	15	71	15	.276
Major League Totals	....		7 Yrs.	736	2737	369	772	135	12	77	412	131	.282
Divisional Series													
1997 Houston	..........N.L.		OF	3	13	0	0	0	0	0	0	0	.000

a On disabled list from July 30 to September 1, 1988.
b On disabled list from June 13 to June 21 and July 2 to July 12, 1990.
c On disabled list from April 9 to May 8, 1992.
d Traded to San Diego Padres with outfielder Stoney Briggs for outfielder Darrin Jackson, March 30, 1993.
e Suspended five games by National League for April 30 mound charging from July 14 to July 18, 1994.
f Traded to Houston Astros with outfielder Phil Plantier, shortstop Ricky Gutierrez, pitchers Pedro Martinez and Doug Brocail and infielder Craig Shipley for third baseman Ken Caminiti, shortstop Andujar Cedeño, outfielder Steve Finley, pitcher Brian Williams, first baseman Roberto Petagine and player to be named, December 28, 1994.
g On disabled list from May 14 to June 13, 1997.

BELL, JAY STUART
Born, Eglin Air Force Base, Florida, December 11, 1965.
Bats Right. Throws Right. Height, 6 feet, 1 inch. Weight, 185 pounds.

Year	Club	Lea	Pos	G	AB	R	H	2B	3B	HR	RBI	SB	Avg
1984 Elizabethton	........Appal.		SS	66	245	43	54	12	1	6	30	4	.220
1985 Visalia a	.........California		SS	106	376	56	106	16	6	9	59	10	.282
1985 Waterbury	........Eastern		SS	29	114	13	34	11	2	1	14	3	.298
1986 Waterbury	.........Eastern		SS	138	494	*88	137	28	4	7	74	10	.277
1986 Cleveland	.............A.L.		2B	5	14	3	5	2	0	1	4	0	.357
1987 Buffalo	.............A.A.		SS-2B	110	362	71	94	15	4	17	60	6	.260
1987 Cleveland	.............A.L.		SS	38	125	14	27	9	1	2	13	2	.216
1988 Colorado Springs	......P.C.		SS	49	181	35	50	12	2	7	24	3	.276
1988 Cleveland b	.........A.L.		SS	73	211	23	46	5	1	2	21	4	.218
1989 Buffalo	.............A.A.		SS-3B	86	298	49	85	15	3	10	54	12	.285
1989 Pittsburgh	..............N.L.		SS	78	271	33	70	13	3	2	27	5	.258
1990 Pittsburgh	..............N.L.		SS	159	583	93	148	28	7	7	52	10	.254
1991 Pittsburgh	..............N.L.		SS	157	608	96	164	32	8	16	67	10	.270
1992 Pittsburgh	..............N.L.		SS	159	632	87	167	36	6	9	55	7	.264
1993 Pittsburgh	..............N.L.		SS	154	604	102	187	32	9	9	51	16	.310
1994 Pittsburgh	..............N.L.		SS	110	424	68	117	35	4	9	45	2	.276
1995 Pittsburgh	..............N.L.		SS-3B	138	530	79	139	28	4	13	55	2	.262
1996 Pittsburgh c	...........N.L.		SS	151	527	65	132	29	3	13	71	6	.250
1997 Kansas City d-e	........A.L.		SS-3B	153	573	89	167	28	3	21	92	10	.291
Major League Totals	....		12 Yrs.	1375	5102	752	1369	277	49	104	553	74	.268

Year	Club	Lea	Pos	G	AB	R	H	2B	3B	HR	RBI	SB	Avg
	Championship Series												
1990 Pittsburgh		N.L.	SS	6	20	3	5	1	0	1	1	0	.250
1991 Pittsburgh		N.L.	SS	7	29	2	12	2	0	1	1	0	.414
1992 Pittsburgh		N.L.	SS	7	29	3	5	2	0	1	4	0	.172
Championship Series Totals				20	78	8	22	5	0	3	6	0	.282

a Traded by Minnesota Twins to Cleveland Indians organization with pitchers Curt Wardle and Rich Yett, and outfielder Jim Weaver for pitcher Bert Blyleven, August 1, 1985.
b Traded to Pittsburgh Pirates organization for shortstop Felix Fermin, March 25, 1989.
c Traded with infielder Jeff King to Kansas City Royals for pitchers Jeff Granger, Jeff Martin, Jeff Wallace and third baseman Joe Randa, December 14, 1996.
d Filed for free agency, November 3, 1997.
e Signed with Arizona Diamondbacks, November 17, 1997.

BELLE, ALBERT JOJUAN

Born, Shreveport, Louisiana, August 25, 1966.
Bats Right. Throws Right. Height, 6 feet, 2 inches. Weight, 200 pounds.

Year	Club	Lea	Pos	G	AB	R	H	2B	3B	HR	RBI	SB	Avg
1987 Kinston		Carolina	OF	10	37	5	12	2	0	3	9	0	.324
1988 Waterloo		Midwest	OF	9	28	2	7	1	0	1	2	0	.250
1988 Kinston		Carolina	OF	41	153	21	46	16	0	8	39	2	.301
1989 Canton		Eastern	OF	89	312	48	88	20	0	20	69	8	.282
1989 Cleveland		A.L.	OF	62	218	22	49	8	4	7	37	2	.225
1990 Cleveland		A.L.	OF	9	23	1	4	0	0	1	3	0	.174
1990 Colorado Spgs. a-b		P.C.	OF	24	96	16	33	3	1	5	19	4	.344
1990 Canton		Eastern	OF	9	32	4	8	1	0	0	3	0	.250
1991 Colorado Springs		P.C.	OF	16	61	9	20	3	2	2	16	1	.328
1991 Cleveland c		A.L.	OF	123	461	60	130	31	2	28	95	3	.282
1992 Cleveland d		A.L.	DH-OF	153	585	81	152	23	1	34	112	8	.260
1993 Cleveland e		A.L.	OF	159	594	93	172	36	3	38	*129	23	.290
1994 Cleveland f		A.L.	OF	106	412	90	147	35	2	36	101	9	.357
1995 Cleveland		A.L.	OF	143	546	121	173	52	1	50	126	5	.317
1996 Cleveland g-h		A.L.	OF	158	602	124	187	38	3	48	*148	11	.311
1997 Chicago		A.L.	OF	161	634	90	174	45	1	30	116	4	.274
Major League Totals		9 Yrs.		1074	4075	682	1188	268	17	272	867	65	.292
	Division Series												
1995 Cleveland		A.L.	OF	3	11	3	3	1	0	1	3	0	.273
1996 Cleveland		A.L.	OF	4	15	2	3	0	0	2	6	1	.200
Division Series Totals				7	26	5	6	1	0	3	9	1	.231
	Championship Series												
1995 Cleveland		A.L.	OF	5	18	1	4	1	0	1	1	0	.222
	World Series Record												
1995 Cleveland		A.L.	OF	6	17	4	4	0	0	2	4	0	.235

a Suspended five games by team from June 2 to June 7, 1990.
b On disabled list from June 7 to August 23, 1990.
c Suspended six games by American League for May 1 throwing ball at fan from July 12 to July 17, 1991.
d Suspended three games by American League for May 4 mound charging from August 4 to August 7, 1992.
e Suspended three games by American League for May 13 mound charging from June 4 to June 6, 1993.
f Suspended seven games by American League for July 17 suspected corked bat from August 1 to August 7, 1994.
g Filed for free agency, October 28, 1996.
h Signed with Chicago White Sox, November 19, 1996.

BENARD, MARVIN LARRY

Born, Bluefields, Nicaragua, January 20, 1970.
Bats Left. Throws Left. Height, 5 feet, 9 inches. Weight, 183 pounds.

Year	Club	Lea	Pos	G	AB	R	H	2B	3B	HR	RBI	SB	Avg
1992 Everett		Northwest	OF	64	161	31	38	10	2	1	17	17	.236
1993 Clinton		Midwest	OF	112	349	84	105	14	2	5	50	42	.301
1994 Shreveport		Texas	OF	125	454	66	143	32	3	4	48	24	.315
1995 Phoenix		P.C.	OF	111	378	70	115	14	6	6	32	10	.304
1995 San Francisco		N.L.	OF	13	34	5	13	2	0	1	4	1	.382
1996 Phoenix		P.C.	OF	4	19	2	7	0	0	0	4	1	.368
1996 San Francisco		N.L.	OF	135	488	89	121	17	4	5	27	25	.248
1997 Phoenix		P.C.	OF	17	60	14	20	5	0	0	5	4	.333
1997 San Francisco		N.L.	OF	84	114	13	26	4	0	1	13	3	.228
Major League Totals		3 Yrs.		232	636	107	160	23	4	7	44	29	.252
	Division Series												
1997 San Francisco		N.L.	PH	2	2	0	0	0	0	0	0	0	.000

BENITEZ, YAMIL ANTONIO
Born, San Juan, Puerto Rico, May 10, 1972.
Bats Right. Throws Right. Height, 6 feet, 2 inches. Weight, 195 pounds.

Year	Club	Lea	Pos	G	AB	R	H	2B	3B	HR	RBI	SB	Avg
1990 Expos	.........Gulf Coast		OF	22	83	6	19	1	0	1	5	0	.229
1991 Expos	.........Gulf Coast		OF	54	197	20	47	9	5	5	38	10	.239
1992 Albany	...........So. Atl.		OF	23	79	6	13	3	2	1	6	0	.165
1992 Jamestown	......N.Y.-Penn.		OF	44	162	24	44	6	6	3	23	19	.272
1993 Burlington	.......Midwest		OF	111	411	70	112	21	5	15	61	18	.273
1994 Harrisburg	........Eastern		OF	126	475	58	123	18	4	17	91	18	.259
1995 Ottawa	..............Int.		OF	127	474	66	123	24	6	18	69	14	.259
1995 Montreal	..............N.L.		OF	14	39	8	15	2	1	2	7	0	.385
1996 Ottawa	..............Int.		OF	114	439	56	122	20	2	23	81	11	.278
1996 Montreal	.............N.L.		OF	11	12	0	2	0	0	0	2	0	.167
1997 Omaha a	...........A.A.		OF	92	329	61	97	14	1	21	71	12	.295
1997 Kansas City b	........A.L.		OF	53	191	22	51	7	1	8	21	2	.267
Major League Totals	....	3 Yrs.	78	242	30	68	9	2	10	30	2	.281	

a Traded to Kansas City Royals for pitcher Melvin Bunch, January 28, 1997.
b Selected in expansion draft by Arizona Diamondbacks, November 18, 1997.

BENJAMIN, MICHAEL PAUL
Born, Euclid, Ohio, November 22, 1965.
Bats Right. Throws Right. Height, 6 feet. Weight, 169 pounds.

Year	Club	Lea	Pos	G	AB	R	H	2B	3B	HR	RBI	SB	Avg
1987 Fresno	......California		SS	64	212	25	51	6	4	6	24	6	.241
1988 Shreveport	......Texas		SS	89	309	48	73	19	5	6	37	14	.236
1988 Phoenix	.........P.C.		SS	37	106	13	18	4	1	0	6	2	.170
1989 Phoenix	.........P.C.		SS-2B	113	363	44	94	17	6	3	36	10	.259
1989 San Francisco	.....N.L.		SS	14	6	6	1	0	0	0	0	0	.167
1990 Phoenix	.........P.C.		SS	118	415	61	104	21	7	5	39	13	.251
1990 San Francisco	.....N.L.		SS	22	56	7	12	3	1	2	3	1	.214
1991 Phoenix	.........P.C.		SS	64	226	34	46	13	2	6	31	3	.204
1991 San Francisco	.....N.L.		SS-3B	54	106	12	13	3	0	2	8	3	.123
1992 Phoenix	.........P.C.		SS-2B	31	108	15	33	9	2	0	17	3	.306
1992 San Francisco	.....N.L.		SS-3B	40	75	4	13	2	1	1	3	1	.173
1993 San Jose	.....California		2B-SS	2	8	1	0	0	0	0	0	0	.000
1993 San Francisco b	....N.L.		2B-SS-3B	63	146	22	29	7	0	4	16	0	.199
1994 San Francisco	....N.L.		SS-2B-3B	38	62	9	16	5	1	1	9	5	.258
1995 San Francisco c	....N.L.		3B-SS-2B	68	186	19	41	6	0	3	12	11	.220
1996 Clearwater d	.....Fla.St.		SS	8	23	3	4	1	0	0	0	1	.174
1996 Scranton-WB	......Int.		SS	4	13	2	5	2	0	0	4	0	.385
1996 Philadelphia e-f	....N.L.		SS-2B	35	103	13	23	5	1	4	13	3	.223
1997 Pawtucket	.........Int.		SS-3B-2B	33	105	12	26	4	1	4	12	4	.248
1997 Boston g-h	.........A.L.		3B-SS-2B-1B	49	116	12	27	9	1	0	7	2	.233
Major League Totals	....	9 Yrs.	383	856	104	175	40	5	17	71	26	.204	

a On disabled list from March 31 to June 5, 1992.
b On disabled list from July 8 to August 6, 1993.
c Traded to Philadelphia for pitcher Jeff Juden, October 6, 1995.
d On disabled list from April 1 to April 26 and July 20 to September 30, 1996.
e Filed for free agency, October 8, 1996.
f Signed with Boston Red Sox organization, February 1, 1997.
g Filed for free agency, October 27, 1997.
h Re-signed with Boston Red Sox, November 21, 1997.

BERROA, GERONIMO EMILIANO
Born, Santo Domingo, Dominican Republic, March 18, 1965.
Bats Right. Throws Right. Height, 6 feet. Weight, 195 pounds.

Year	Club	Lea	Pos	G	AB	R	H	2B	3B	HR	RBI	SB	Avg
1984 Bradenton Blue Jays	..Gulf C.		OF	62	235	31	59	16	1	3	34	2	.251
1985 Kinston	..........Carolina		OF	19	43	4	8	0	0	1	4	0	.186
1985 Medicine Hat	.......Pioneer		OF	54	201	39	69	22	2	6	45	7	.343
1985 Florence	............So. Atl.		OF	19	66	7	21	2	0	3	20	0	.318
1986 Ventura	.........California		OF	128	459	76	137	22	5	21	73	12	.298
1986 Knoxville	........Southern		OF	1	4	0	0	0	0	0	0	0	.000
1987 Knoxville	........Southern		OF	134	523	87	150	33	3	36	108	2	.287
1988 Syracuse a	............Int.		OF	131	470	55	122	29	1	8	64	7	.260
1989 Atlanta	..............N.L.		OF	81	136	7	36	4	0	2	9	0	.265
1990 Richmond	............Int.		OF	135	499	56	134	17	2	12	80	4	.269

14

Year	Club	Lea	Pos	G	AB	R	H	2B	3B	HR	RBI	SB	Avg
1990 Atlanta b-c	N.L.	OF	7	4	0	0	0	0	0	0	0	.000
1991 Colorado Springs d	P.C.	OF	125	478	81	154	31	7	18	91	2	.322
1992 Nashville	A.A.	OF	112	461	73	151	33	2	22	88	8	.328
1992 Cincinnati e	N.L.	OF	13	15	2	4	1	0	0	0	0	.267
1993 Florida	N.L.	OF	14	34	3	4	1	0	0	0	0	.118
1993 Edmonton f	P.C.	OF-1B	90	327	64	107	33	4	16	68	1	.327
1994 Oakland g	A.L.	DH-OF-1B	96	340	55	104	18	2	13	65	7	.306
1995 Oakland	A.L.	DH-OF	141	546	87	152	22	3	22	88	7	.278
1996 Oakland	A.L.	DH-OF	153	586	101	170	32	1	36	106	0	.290
1997 Oakland-Baltimore h-i-j-k	A.L.	OF-DH	156	561	88	159	25	0	26	90	4	.283
Major League Totals			8 Yrs.	661	2222	343	629	103	6	99	358	18	.283
Division Series													
1997 Baltimore	A.L.	DH-OF	4	13	4	5	1	0	2	2	0	.385
Championship Series													
1997 Baltimore	A.L.	OF-DH	6	21	1	6	2	0	0	3	0	.286

a Drafted by Atlanta Braves from Toronto Blue Jays organization, December 5, 1988.
b Released, February 4; signed with Seattle Mariners organization, February 13, 1991.
c Sold by Seattle Mariners to Cleveland Indians organization, March 28, 1991.
d Became free agent, October 15; signed with Cincinnati Reds organization, October 31, 1991.
e Released, November 20; signed with Florida Marlins organization, December 8, 1992.
f Released by Florida Marlins, October 4, 1993; signed with Oakland Athletics, January 20, 1994.
g On disabled list from August 3 to end of 1994 season.
h Traded to Baltimore Orioles for pitcher Jimmy Haynes and player to be named later, June 27, 1997.
i Oakland Athletics received pitcher Mark Seaver to complete trade, September 2, 1997.
j Not offered contract by Baltimore Orioles December 8, 1997
k Signed with Cleveland Indians organization, January 28, 1998.

BERRY, SEAN ROBERT

Born, Santa Monica, California, March 22, 1966.
Bats Right. Throws Right. Height, 5 feet, 11 inches. Weight, 200 pounds.

Year	Club	Lea	Pos	G	AB	R	H	2B	3B	HR	RBI	SB	Avg
1986 Eugene	Northwest	3B	63	238	53	76	20	2	5	44	10	.319
1987 Fort Myers a	Fla. St.	3B	67	206	28	52	7	2	2	30	5	.252
1988 Baseball City	Fla. St.	3B	94	304	34	71	6	4	4	30	24	.234
1989 Baseball City	Fla. St.	3B-OF	116	399	67	106	19	7	4	44	37	.266
1990 Memphis	Southern	3B	135	487	73	142	25	4	14	77	18	.292
1990 Kansas City	A.L.	3B	8	23	2	5	1	1	0	4	0	.217
1991 Omaha	A.A.	3B-SS-2B	103	368	62	97	21	9	11	54	8	.264
1991 Kansas City	A.L.	3B	31	60	5	8	3	0	0	1	0	.133
1992 Omaha b	A.A.	3B	122	439	61	126	22	2	21	77	6	.287
1992 Montreal	N.L.	3B	24	57	5	19	1	0	1	4	2	.333
1993 Montreal	N.L.	3B	122	299	50	78	15	2	14	49	12	.261
1994 Montreal	N.L.	3B	103	320	43	89	19	2	11	41	14	.278
1995 Montreal c	N.L.	3B-1B	103	314	38	100	22	1	14	55	3	.318
1996 Houston	N.L.	3B	132	431	55	121	38	1	17	95	12	.281
1997 New Orleans	A.A.	3B	3	9	1	3	0	0	0	0	0	.333
1997 Houston d-e-f	N.L.	3B	96	301	37	77	24	1	8	43	1	.256
Major League Totals			8 Yrs.	619	1805	235	497	123	8	65	292	44	.275
Division Series													
1997 Houston	N.L.	PH	1	1	0	0	0	0	0	0	0	.000

a On disabled list from April 16 to June 3, 1987.
b Traded by Kansas City Royals to Montreal Expos with pitcher Archie Corbin for pitcher Chris Haney and Bill Sampen, August 29, 1992.
c Traded from Montreal Expos to Houston Astros for pitcher Dave Veres and catcher Raul Chavez, December 20, 1995.
d On disabled list from April 7 to April 22 and August 23 to September 7, 1997.
e Not offered contract by Houston Astros, December 8, 1997.
f Re-signed with Houston Astros, December 18, 1997

BERRYHILL, DAMON SCOTT

Born, South Laguna, California, December 3, 1963.
Bats Both. Throws Right. Height, 6 feet. Weight, 205 pounds.

Year	Club	Lea	Pos	G	AB	R	H	2B	3B	HR	RBI	SB	Avg
1984 Quad City a	Midwest	C	62	217	30	60	14	0	0	31	4	.276
1985 Winston-Salem	Carolina	C	117	386	31	90	25	1	9	50	4	.233
1986 Pittsfield	Eastern	C	112	345	33	71	13	1	6	35	2	.206
1987 Iowa	A.A.	C	121	429	54	123	22	1	18	67	5	.287
1987 Chicago	N.L.	C	12	28	2	5	1	0	0	1	0	.179

Year	Club	Lea	Pos	G	AB	R	H	2B	3B	HR	RBI	SB	Avg
1988 Iowa		A.A.	C	21	73	11	16	5	1	2	11	0	.219
1988 Chicago b		N.L.	C	95	309	19	80	19	1	7	38	1	.259
1989 Iowa		A.A.	C	7	30	4	6	1	0	2	4	0	.200
1989 Chicago c		N.L.	C	91	334	37	86	13	0	5	41	1	.257
1990 Peoria		Midwest	C	7	26	10	10	2	0	3	8	0	.385
1990 Iowa		A.A.	C	22	79	8	17	1	0	3	6	0	.215
1990 Chicago d		N.L.	C	17	53	6	10	4	0	1	9	0	.189
1991 Iowa		A.A.	C	26	97	20	32	4	1	8	24	0	.330
1991 Chicago-Atlanta e		N.L.	C	63	160	13	30	7	0	5	14	1	.188
1992 Atlanta		N.L.	C	101	307	21	70	16	1	10	43	0	.228
1993 Atlanta f		N.L.	C	115	335	24	82	18	2	8	43	0	.245
1994 Boston g		A.L.	C	82	255	30	67	17	2	6	34	0	.263
1995 Cincinnati h-i		N.L.	C-1B	34	82	6	15	3	0	2	11	0	.183
1996 Cincinnati i		N.L.	(Did Not Play)										
1997 Phoenix		P.C.	C	4	13	0	5	0	0	0	1	0	.385
1997 San Francisco j-k-l		N.L.	C-1B	73	167	17	43	8	0	3	23	0	.257
Major League Totals		10 Yrs.		683	2030	175	488	106	6	47	257	3	.240
Division Series													
1997 San Francisco		N.L.	PH	1	1	0	0	0	0	0	0	0	.000
Championship Series													
1992 Atlanta		N.L.	C	7	24	1	4	1	0	0	1	0	.167
1993 Atlanta		N.L.	C	6	19	2	4	0	0	1	3	0	.211
Championship Series Totals				13	43	3	8	1	0	1	4	0	.186
World Series Record													
1992 Atlanta		N.L.	C	6	22	1	2	0	0	1	3	0	.091

a Batted righthanded only during 1984 season.
b On disabled list from June 30 to July 15, 1988.
c On disabled list from March 29 to May 1 and August 19 to end of 1989 season.
d On disabled list from April 8 to September 1, 1990.
e Traded to Atlanta Braves with pitcher Mike Bielecki for pitchers Yorkis Perez and Turk Wendell, September 29, 1991.
f Not offered 1994 contract, December 20, 1993; signed with Boston Red Sox organization, February 1, 1994.
g Filed for free agency, October 29; signed with Cincinnati Reds organization, November 4, 1994.
h On disabled list from July 24 to September 1, 1995.
i Signed with San Francisco Giants organization, January 6, 1997.
j On disabled list from May 18 to June 10 and August 18 to September 2, 1997.
k Filed for free agency, October 27, 1997.
l Signed with Oakland Athletics, December 22, 1997.

BICHETTE, ALPHONSE DANTE

Born, West Palm Beach, Florida, November 18, 1963.
Bats Right. Throws Right. Height, 6 feet, 3 inches. Weight, 225 pounds.

Year	Club	Lea	Pos	G	AB	R	H	2B	3B	HR	RBI	SB	Avg
1984 Salem		Northwest	1B-OF-3B	64	250	27	58	9	2	4	30	6	.232
1985 Quad City		Midwest	OF-1B	137	547	58	145	28	4	11	78	25	.265
1986 Palm Springs		Calif.	OF-3B	68	290	39	79	15	0	10	73	2	.272
1986 Midland		Texas	OF-3B	62	243	43	69	16	2	12	36	3	.284
1987 Edmonton a		P.C.	OF	92	360	54	108	20	3	13	50	3	.300
1988 Edmonton		P.C.	OF	132	509	64	136	29	*10	14	81	7	.267
1988 California		A.L.	OF	21	46	1	12	2	0	0	8	0	.261
1989 Edmonton		P.C.	OF	61	226	39	55	11	2	11	40	4	.243
1989 California		A.L.	OF	48	138	13	29	7	0	3	15	3	.210
1990 California b		A.L.	OF	109	349	40	89	15	1	15	53	5	.255
1991 Milwaukee		A.L.	OF-3B	134	445	53	106	18	3	15	59	14	.238
1992 Milwaukee c		A.L.	OF	112	387	37	111	27	2	5	41	18	.287
1993 Colorado		N.L.	OF	141	538	93	167	43	5	21	89	14	.310
1994 Colorado d		N.L.	OF	*116	*484	74	147	33	2	27	95	21	.304
1995 Colorado e		N.L.	OF	139	579	102	197	38	2	40	128	13	.340
1996 Colorado f		N.L.	OF	159	633	114	198	39	3	31	141	31	.313
1997 Colorado		N.L.	OF	151	561	81	173	31	2	26	118	6	.308
Major League Totals		10 Yrs.		1130	4160	608	1229	253	20	183	747	125	.295
Division Series													
1995 Colorado		N.L.	OF	4	17	6	10	3	0	1	3	0	.588

a On disabled list from May 6 to June 23, 1987.
b Traded to Milwaukee Brewers for designated hitter Dave Parker, March 14, 1991.
c Traded to Colorado Rockies for outfielder Kevin Reimer, November 17, 1992.
d Declared restricted free agent under Major League Baseball implemented labor proposal, December 23, 1994.
e Re-signed with Colorado Rockies, April 6, 1995.
f Had reconstructive knee surgery, October, 1996.

BIGGIO, CRAIG ALAN

Born, Smithtown, New York, December 14, 1965.
Bats Right. Throws Right. Height, 5 feet, 11 inches. Weight, 180 pounds.

Year	Club	Lea	Pos	G	AB	R	H	2B	3B	HR	RBI	SB	Avg
1987	Asheville	So. Atl.	C	64	216	59	81	17	2	9	49	31	.375
1988	Tucson	P.C.	C	77	281	60	90	21	4	3	39	19	.320
1988	Houston	N.L.	C	50	123	14	26	6	1	3	5	6	.211
1989	Houston	N.L.	C-OF	134	443	64	114	21	2	13	60	21	.257
1990	Houston	N.L.	C-OF	150	555	53	153	24	2	4	42	25	.276
1991	Houston	N.L.	C-2B-OF	149	546	79	161	23	4	4	46	19	.295
1992	Houston	N.L.	2B	*162	613	96	170	32	3	6	39	38	.277
1993	Houston	N.L.	2B	155	610	98	175	41	5	21	64	15	.287
1994	Houston	N.L.	2B	114	437	88	139	*44	5	6	56	*39	.318
1995	Houston a-b	N.L.	2B	141	553	123	167	30	2	22	77	33	.302
1996	Houston	N.L.	2B	*162	605	113	174	24	4	15	75	25	.288
1997	Houston	N.L.	2B	*162	619	*146	191	37	8	22	81	47	.309
Major League Totals			10 Yrs.	1379	5104	874	1470	282	36	116	545	268	.288
Division Series													
1997	Houston	N.L.	2B	3	12	0	1	0	0	0	0	0	.083

a Filed for free agency, November 12, 1995.
b Re-signed with Houston Astros, December 14, 1995.

BLAUSER, JEFFREY MICHAEL

Born, Los Gatos, California, November 8, 1965.
Bats Rights. Throws Right. Height, 6 feet. Weight, 170 pounds.

Year	Club	Lea	Pos	G	AB	R	H	2B	3B	HR	RBI	SB	Avg
1984	Pulaski	Appal.	SS	62	217	41	54	6	1	3	24	14	.249
1985	Sumter	So. Atl.	SS	125	422	74	99	19	0	5	49	36	.235
1986	Durham	Carolina	SS	123	447	94	128	27	3	13	52	12	.286
1987	Greenville	Southern	SS	72	265	35	66	13	3	4	32	5	.249
1987	Richmond	Int.	SS	33	113	11	20	1	0	1	12	3	.177
1987	Atlanta	N.L.	SS	51	165	11	40	6	3	2	15	7	.242
1988	Richmond	Int.	SS	69	271	40	77	19	1	5	23	6	.284
1988	Atlanta	N.L.	2B-SS	18	67	7	16	3	1	2	7	0	.239
1989	Atlanta	N.L.	3B-2B-SS-OF	142	456	63	123	24	2	12	46	5	.270
1990	Atlanta a	N.L.	SS-2B-3B-OF	115	386	46	104	24	3	8	39	3	.269
1991	Atlanta	N.L.	SS-2B-3B	129	352	49	91	14	3	11	54	5	.259
1992	Atlanta	N.L.	SS-2B-3B	123	343	61	90	19	3	14	46	5	.262
1993	Atlanta	N.L.	SS	161	597	110	182	29	2	15	73	16	.305
1994	Atlanta b-c	N.L.	SS	96	380	56	98	21	4	6	45	1	.258
1995	Atlanta d	N.L.	SS	115	431	60	91	16	2	12	31	8	.211
1996	Atlanta e	N.L.	SS	83	265	48	65	14	1	10	35	6	.245
1997	Atlanta f	N.L.	SS	151	519	90	160	31	4	17	70	5	.308
Major League Totals			11 Yrs.	1184	3961	601	1060	201	28	109	461	61	.268
Division Series													
1995	Atlanta	N.L.	SS	3	6	0	0	0	0	0	0	0	.000
1996	Atlanta	N.L.	SS	3	9	0	1	0	0	0	0	0	.111
1997	Atlanta	N.L.	SS	3	10	2	3	0	0	1	4	0	.300
Division Series Totals				9	25	2	4	0	0	1	4	0	.160
Championship Series													
1991	Atlanta	N.L.	SS	2	2	0	0	0	0	0	0	0	.000
1992	Atlanta	N.L.	SS	7	24	3	5	0	1	1	4	0	.208
1993	Atlanta	N.L.	SS	6	25	5	7	1	0	2	4	0	.280
1995	Atlanta	N.L.	SS	1	4	0	0	0	0	0	0	0	.000
1996	Atlanta	N.L.	SS	7	17	5	3	0	1	0	2	0	.176
1997	Atlanta	N.L.	SS	6	20	5	6	0	0	1	1	0	.300
Championship Series Totals				29	92	18	21	1	2	4	11	0	.228
World Series Record													
1991	Atlanta	N.L.	SS	5	6	0	1	0	0	0	0	0	.167
1992	Atlanta	N.L.	SS	6	24	2	6	0	0	0	0	2	.250
1996	Atlanta	N.L.	SS	6	18	2	3	1	0	0	1	0	.167
World Series Totals				17	48	4	10	1	0	0	1	2	.208

a On disabled list from May 14 to May 30, 1990.
b On disabled list from May 2 to May 20, 1994.
c Filed for free agency, October 18, 1994.
d Re-signed with Atlantic Braves, April 12, 1995.
e On disabled list from April 14 to May 4 and July 16 to September 1, 1996.
f Filed for free agency, November 3, 1997.
g Signed with Chicago Cubs Dec. 9, 1997.

BLOWERS, MICHAEL ROY

Born, Wurzburg, West Germany, April 24, 1965.
Bats Right. Throws Right. Height, 6 feet, 2 inches. Weight, 210 pounds.

Year	Club	Lea	Pos	G	AB	R	H	2B	3B	HR	RBI	SB	Avg
1986 Jamestown	.N.Y.-Penn.		SS	32	95	13	24	9	2	1	6	3	.253
1986 Brad. Expos	.....Gulf C.		SS	31	115	14	25	3	1	2	17	2	.217
1987 West Palm Bch.	.Fla. St.		3B	136	491	68	124	30	3	16	71	4	.253
1988 Jacksonville	...Southern		3B	137	460	58	115	20	6	15	60	6	.250
1989 Indianapolis a	.....A.A.		3B	131	461	49	123	29	6	14	56	3	.267
1989 New York	........A.L.		3B	13	38	2	10	0	0	0	3	0	.263
1990 Columbus	........Int.		3B	62	230	30	78	20	6	6	50	3	.339
1990 New York	........A.L.		3B	48	144	16	27	4	0	5	21	1	.188
1991 New York b	........A.L.		3B	15	35	3	7	0	0	1	1	0	.200
1991 Calgary	..........P.C.		3B-1B-SS	90	329	56	95	20	2	9	59	3	.289
1992 Calgary	..........P.C.		3B-1B-OF	83	300	56	95	28	2	9	67	2	.317
1992 Seattle	...........A.L.		3B-1B	31	73	7	14	3	0	1	2	0	.192
1993 Seattle	...........A.L.		3B-OF-C-1B	127	379	55	106	23	3	15	57	1	.280
1994 Seattle	...........A.L.		3B-1B-OF	85	270	37	78	13	0	9	49	2	.289
1995 Seattle c	..........A.L.		3B-1B-OF	134	439	59	113	24	1	23	96	2	.257
1996 Los Angeles d-e	...N.L.		3B-1B-SS	92	317	31	84	19	2	6	38	0	.265
1997 Seattle f-g	..........A.L.		1B-3B-OF	68	150	22	44	5	0	5	20	0	.293
Major League Totals	....		9 Yrs.	613	1845	232	483	91	6	65	287	6	.262
Division Series													
1995 Seattle	...............A.L.		3B-1B	5	18	0	3	0	0	0	1	0	.167
1997 Seattle	..........A.L.		3B	3	5	0	1	0	0	0	0	0	.200
Divisional Series Totals	....			8	23	0	4	0	0	0	1	0	.174
Championship Series													
1995 Seattle	...............A.L.	—	3B	6	18	1	4	0	0	1	2	0	.222

a Traded by Montreal Expos to New York Yankees to complete August 29 trade in which Montreal acquired pitcher John Candelaria, August 31, 1989.
b Traded to Seattle Mariners organization for player to be named, May 17; New York Yankees acquired pitcher Jim Blueberg to complete trade, June 23, 1991.
c Traded to Los Angeles Dodgers for infielder Miguel Cairo and infielder Willis Otanez, November 29, 1995.
d On disabled list from July 18 to September 30, 1996.
e Filed for free agency, October 15, 1996.
f Filed for free agency, October 28, 1997.
g Signed with Oakland Athletics, December 16, 1997

BOGAR, TIMOTHY PAUL

Born, Indianapolis, Indiana, October 28, 1966.
Bats Right. Throws Right. Height, 6 feet, 2 inches. Weight, 198 pounds.

Year	Club	Lea	Pos	G	AB	R	H	2B	3B	HR	RBI	SB	Avg
1987 Little Falls	.N.Y.-Penn.		SS-2B	58	205	31	48	9	0	0	23	2	.234
1988 Columbia	... .So. Atl.		2B-SS	45	142	19	40	4	2	3	21	5	.282
1988 St. Lucie	.....Fla. St.		2B-SS-3B	76	236	34	65	7	1	2	30	9	.275
1989 Jackson	......Texas		SS	112	406	44	108	13	5	4	45	8	.266
1990 Tidewater a	......Int.		SS	33	117	10	19	2	0	0	4	1	.162
1991 Williamsport	.Eastern		3B-2B-1B-SS	63	243	33	61	12	2	2	25	13	.251
1991 Tidewater	......Int.		SS-2B-3B-1B-OF-C	65	218	23	56	11	0	1	23	1	.257
1992 Tidewater b	......Int.		2B-SS-3B-1B	129	481	54	134	32	1	5	38	7	.279
1993 New York c	.....N.L.		SS-3B-2B	78	205	19	50	13	0	3	25	0	.244
1994 Norfolk	.........Int.		3B-2B	5	19	0	2	0	0	0	1	0	.105
1994 New York d	.....N.L.		3B-1B-SS-2B	50	52	5	8	0	0	2	5	1	.154
1995 New York	......N.L.		3B-1B-SS-2B	78	145	17	42	7	0	1	21	1	.290
1996 New York	......N.L.		1B-3B-SS-2B	91	89	17	19	4	0	0	6	1	.213
1997 Houston e-f	.....N.L.		SS-3B-1B	97	241	30	60	14	4	4	30	4	.249
Major League Totals	......		5 Yrs.	394	732	88	179	38	4	10	87	7	.245

a On disabled list from May 18 to May 29 and June 14 to end of 1990 season.
b Record of 0-0 in one game as pitcher.
c On disabled list from August 15 to September 1, 1993.
d On disabled list from May 6 to June 9, 1994.
e Traded to Houston Astros for infielder Luis Lopez, March 31, 1997.
f On disabled list from September 5 to September 29, 1997.

BOGGS, WADE ANTHONY

Born, Omaha, Nebraska, June 15, 1958.
Bats Left. Throws Right. Height, 6 feet, 2 inches. Weight, 197 pounds.

Year	Club	Lea	Pos	G	AB	R	H	2B	3B	HR	RBI	SB	Avg
1976 Elmira	......N.Y.-Penn.		3B	57	179	29	47	6	0	0	15	2	.263
1977 Wnstn-Salem	....Carol.		3B-SS	117	422	67	140	13	1	2	55	8	.332
1978 Bristol	........Eastern		3B-SS-2B-OF	109	354	63	110	14	2	1	32	1	.311

18

Year	Club	Lea	Pos	G	AB	R	H	2B	3B	HR	RBI	SB	Avg
1979 Bristol a	Eastern		3B-SS-2B	113	406	56	132	17	2	0	41	11	.325
1980 Pawtucket	Int.		3B-1B	129	418	51	128	21	0	1	45	3	.306
1981 Pawtucket	Int.		3B-1B	137	498	67	*167	*41	3	5	60	4	*.335
1982 Boston	A.L.		1B-3B-OF	104	338	51	118	14	1	5	44	1	.349
1983 Boston	A.L.		3B	153	582	100	210	44	7	5	74	3	*.361
1984 Boston	A.L.		3B	158	625	109	203	31	4	6	55	3	.325
1985 Boston	A.L.		3B	161	653	107	*240	42	3	8	78	2	*.368
1986 Boston	A.L.		3B	149	580	107	207	47	2	8	71	0	*.357
1987 Boston	A.L.		3B-1B	147	551	108	200	40	6	24	89	1	*.363
1988 Boston	A.L.		3B	155	584	*128	214	*45	6	5	58	2	*.366
1989 Boston	A.L.		3B	156	621	*113	205	*51	7	3	54	2	.330
1990 Boston	A.L.		3B	155	619	89	187	44	5	6	63	0	.302
1991 Boston	A.L.		3B	144	546	93	181	42	2	8	51	1	.332
1992 Boston b	A.L.		3B	143	514	62	133	22	4	7	50	1	.259
1993 New York	A.L.		3B	143	560	83	169	26	1	2	59	0	.302
1994 New York	A.L.		3B-1B	97	366	61	125	19	1	11	55	2	.342
1995 New York c-d	A.L.		3B-1B	126	460	76	149	22	4	5	63	1	.324
1996 New York	A.L.		3B	132	501	80	156	29	2	2	41	1	.311
1997 New York e-f	A.L.		3B-P	104	353	55	103	23	1	4	28	0	.292
Major League Totals			16 Yrs.	2227	8453	1422	2800	541	56	109	933	20	.331
Division Series													
1995 New York	A.L.		3B	5	19	4	5	2	0	1	3	0	.263
1996 New York	A.L.		3B	3	12	0	1	1	0	0	0	0	.083
1997 New York	A.L.		3B	3	7	1	3	0	0	0	2	0	.429
Division Series Totals				11	38	5	9	3	0	1	5	0	.237
Championship Series													
1986 Boston	A.L.		3B	7	30	3	7	1	1	0	2	0	.233
1988 Boston	A.L.		3B	4	13	2	5	0	0	0	3	0	.385
1990 Boston	A.L.		3B	4	16	1	7	1	0	1	1	0	.438
1996 New York	A.L.		3B	3	15	1	2	0	0	0	0	0	.133
Championship Series Totals				18	74	7	21	2	1	1	6	0	.284
World Series Record													
1986 Boston	A.L.		3B	7	31	3	9	3	0	0	3	0	.290
1996 New York	A.L.		3B	4	11	0	3	1	0	0	2	0	.273
World Series Totals				11	42	3	12	4	0	0	5	0	.286

a On disabled list from April 20 to May 2, 1979.
b Filed for free agency, October 26; signed with New York Yankees, December 15, 1992.
c Filed for free agency, November 12, 1995.
d Re-signed with New York Yankees, December 5, 1995.
e Filed for free agency, November 3, 1997.
f Signed as free agent by Tampa Bay Devil Rays, December 9, 1997.

BONDS, BARRY LAMAR

Born, Riverside, California, July 24, 1964.
Bats Left. Throws Left. Height, 6 feet, 1 inch. Weight, 185 pounds.

Year	Club	Lea	Pos	G	AB	R	H	2B	3B	HR	RBI	SB	Avg
1985 Prince William	Carolina		OF	71	254	49	76	16	4	13	37	15	.299
1986 Pittsburgh	N.L.		OF	113	413	72	92	26	3	16	48	36	.223
1986 Hawaii	P.C.		OF	44	148	30	46	7	2	7	37	16	.311
1987 Pittsburgh	N.L.		OF	150	551	99	144	34	9	25	59	32	.261
1988 Pittsburgh	N.L.		OF	144	538	97	152	30	5	24	58	17	.283
1989 Pittsburgh	N.L.		OF	159	580	96	144	34	6	19	58	32	.248
1990 Pittsburgh a	N.L.		OF	151	519	104	156	32	3	33	114	52	.301
1991 Pittsburgh	N.L.		OF	153	510	95	149	28	5	25	116	43	.292
1992 Pittsburgh b-c-d	N.L.		OF	140	473	*109	147	36	5	34	103	39	.311
1993 San Francisco e	N.L.		OF	159	539	129	181	38	4	*46	*123	29	.336
1994 San Francisco	N.L.		OF	112	391	89	122	18	1	37	81	29	.312
1995 San Francisco	N.L.		OF	144	506	109	149	30	7	33	104	31	.294
1996 San Francisco	N.L.		OF	158	517	122	159	27	3	42	129	40	.308
1997 San Francisco	N.L.		OF	159	532	123	155	26	5	40	101	37	.291
Major League Totals			12 Yrs.	1742	6069	1244	1750	359	56	374	1094	417	.288
Division Series													
1997 San Francisco	N.L.		OF	3	12	0	3	2	0	0	2	1	.250
Championship Series													
1990 Pittsburgh	N.L.		OF	6	18	4	3	0	0	0	1	2	.167
1991 Pittsburgh	N.L.		OF	7	27	1	4	1	0	0	0	3	.148
1992 Pittsburgh	N.L.		OF	7	23	5	6	1	0	1	2	1	.261
Championship Series Totals				420	68	10	13	2	0	1	3	6	.191

a Selected Most Valuable Player in National League for 1990.
b On disabled list from June 15 to July 3, 1992.
c Selected Most Valuable Player in National League for 1992.
d Filed for free agency, October 26; signed with San Francisco Giants, December 6, 1992.
e Selected Most Valuable Player in National League for 1993.

BONILLA, ROBERTO MARTIN ANTONIO
Born, New York, New York, February 23, 1963.
Bats Both. Throws Right. Height, 6 feet, 3 inches. Weight, 240 pounds.

Year	Club	Lea	Pos	G	AB	R	H	2B	3B	HR	RBI	SB	Avg
1981	Brad. Pirates	Gulf C.	1B-C-3B	22	69	6	15	5	0	0	7	2	.217
1982	Brad. Pirates	Gulf C.	1B	47	167	20	38	3	0	5	26	2	.228
1983	Alexandria	Carolina	OF-1B	*136	504	88	129	19	7	11	59	28	.256
1984	Nashua	Eastern	OF-1B	136	484	74	128	19	5	11	71	15	.264
1985	Prince Wm. a-b	Carol.	1B-3B	39	130	15	34	4	1	3	11	1	.262
1986	Chicago c	A.L.	OF-1B	75	234	27	63	10	2	2	26	4	.269
1986	Pittsburgh	N.L.	OF-1B-3B	63	192	28	46	6	2	1	17	4	.240
1987	Pittsburgh	N.L.	3B-OF-1B	141	466	58	140	33	3	15	77	3	.300
1988	Pittsburgh	N.L.	3B	159	584	87	160	32	7	24	100	3	.274
1989	Pittsburgh	N.L.	3B-1B-OF	*163	616	96	173	37	10	24	86	8	.281
1990	Pittsburgh	N.L.	OF-3B-1B	160	625	112	175	39	7	32	120	4	.280
1991	Pittsburgh d	N.L.	OF-3B-1B	157	577	102	174	*44	6	18	100	2	.302
1992	New York e-f	N.L.	OF-1B	128	438	62	109	23	0	19	70	4	.249
1993	New York	N.L.	OF-3B-1B	139	502	81	133	21	3	34	87	3	.265
1994	New York	N.L.	3B	108	403	60	117	24	1	20	67	1	.290
1995	New York	N.L.	3B-OF-1B	80	317	49	103	25	4	18	53	0	.325
1995	Baltimore g	A.L.	OF-3B	61	237	47	79	12	4	10	46	0	.333
1996	Baltimore h-i	A.L.	OF-1B-3B	159	595	107	171	27	5	28	116	1	.287
1997	Florida	N.L.	3B-1B	153	562	77	167	39	3	17	96	6	.297
Major League Totals			12 Yrs.	1746	6348	993	1810	372	57	262	1061	43	.285
Division Series													
1996 Baltimore		A.L.	OF	4	15	4	3	0	0	2	5	0	.200
1997 Florida		N.L.	3B	3	12	1	4	0	0	1	3	0	.333
Division Series Totals				7	27	5	7	0	0	3	8	0	.259
Championship Series													
1990 Pittsburgh		N.L.	OF-3B	6	21	0	4	1	0	0	1	0	.190
1991 Pittsburgh		N.L.	OF	7	23	2	7	2	0	0	1	0	.304
1996 Baltimore		A.L.	OF	5	20	1	1	0	0	1	2	0	.050
1997 Florida		N.L.	3B	6	23	3	6	1	0	0	4	0	.261
Championship Series Totals				24	87	6	18	4	0	1	8	0	.207
World Series Record													
1997 Florida		N.L.	3B	7	29	5	6	1	0	1	3	0	.207

a On disabled list from March 25 to July 19, 1985.
b Drafted by Chicago White Sox from Pittsburgh Pirates organization, December 10, 1985.
c Traded to Pittsburgh Pirates for pitcher Jose DeLeon, July 23, 1986.
d Filed for free agency, October 28; signed with New York Mets, December 2, 1991.
e Suspended two games by National League for June 24 contact with umpire from July 27 to July 28, 1992.
f On disabled list from August 2 to August 19, 1992.
g Traded to Baltimore Orioles with player to be named later for outfielder Alex Ochoa and outfielder Damon Buford, July 28, 1995. Baltimore Orioles received pitcher Jimmy Williams to complete trade, August 16, 1995.
h Filed for free agency, November 18, 1996.
i Signed with Florida Marlins, November 22, 1996.

BOONE, AARON JOHN
Born, LaMesa, California, March 9, 1973.
Bats Right. Throws Right. Height, 6 feet, 2 inches. Weight 190 pounds.

Year	Club	Lea	Pos	G	AB	R	H	2B	3B	HR	RBI	SB	Avg
1994	Billings	Pioneer	3B-1B-SS	67	256	48	70	15	5	7	55	6	.273
1995	Chattanooga	Southern	3B	23	66	6	15	3	0	0	3	2	.227
1995	Winston-Sal	Carolina	3B	108	395	61	103	19	1	14	50	11	.261
1996	Chattanooga	Southern	3B-SS	136	548	86	158	44	7	17	95	21	.288
1997	Indianapols	A.A.	3B-SS-2B	131	476	79	138	30	4	22	75	12	.290
1997	Cincinnati	N.L.	3B-2B	16	49	5	12	1	0	0	5	1	.245

BOONE, BRET ROBERT
Born, El Cajon, California, April 6, 1969.
Bats Right. Throws Right. Height, 5 feet, 10 inches. Weight, 180 pounds.

Year	Club	Lea	Pos	G	AB	R	H	2B	3B	HR	RBI	SB	Avg
1990 Peninsula	Carolina		2B	74	255	42	68	13	2	8	38	5	.267
1991 Jacksonville	Southern		2B	*139	475	64	121	10	1	19	75	9	.255
1992 Calgary	P.C.		2B	118	439	73	138	26	5	13	73	17	.314
1992 Seattle	A.L.		2B-3B	33	129	15	25	4	0	4	15	1	.194
1993 Calgary	P.C.		2B	71	274	48	91	18	3	8	56	3	.332
1993 Seattle a	A.L.		2B	76	271	31	68	12	2	12	38	2	.251
1994 Cincinnati	N.L.		2B-3B	108	381	59	122	25	2	12	68	3	.320
1995 Cincinnati	N.L.		2B	138	513	63	137	34	2	15	68	5	.267
1996 Cincinnati b	N.L.		2B	142	520	56	121	21	3	12	69	3	.233
1997 Indianapols	A.A.		2B	3	7	1	2	1	0	0	1	1	.286
1997 Cincinnati	N.L.		2B	139	443	40	99	25	1	7	46	5	.223
Major League Totals		6 Yrs.		636	2257	264	572	121	10	62	304	19	.253
Division Series													
1995 Cincinnati	N.L.		2B	3	10	4	3	1	0	1	1	1	.300
Championship Series													
1995 Cincinnati	N.L.		2B	4	14	1	3	0	0	0	0	0	.214

a Traded to Cincinnati Reds with pitcher Erik Hanson for pitcher Bobby Ayala and catcher Dan Wilson, November 2, 1993.

b On disabled list from April 1 to April 16, 1996.

BOOTY, JOSHUA GIBSON
Born, Starkville, Mississippi, April 29, 1975.
Bats Right. Throws Right. Height, 6 feet, 3 inches. Weight 210 pounds.

Year	Club	Lea	Pos	G	AB	R	H	2B	3B	HR	RBI	SB	Avg
1994 Marlins	Gulf Coast		SS	10	36	5	8	0	0	1	2	1	.222
1994 Elmira	N.Y.-Penn.		SS	4	16	1	4	1	0	0	1	0	.250
1995 Kane County	Midwest		3B	31	109	6	11	2	0	1	6	1	.101
1995 Elmira	N.Y.-Penn.		3B	74	287	33	63	18	1	6	37	4	.220
1996 Kane County	Midwest		3B	128	475	62	98	25	1	21	87	2	.206
1996 Florida	N.L.		3B	2	2	1	1	0	0	0	0	0	.500
1997 Portland	Eastern		3B	122	448	42	94	19	2	20	69	2	.210
1997 Florida	N.L.		3B	4	5	2	3	0	0	0	1	0	.600
Major League Totals		2 Yrs.		6	7	3	4	0	0	0	1	0	.571

BORDERS, PATRICK LANCE
Born, Lake Wales, Florida, May 14, 1963.
Bats Right. Throws Right. Height, 6 feet, 2 inches. Weight, 200 pounds.

Year	Club	Lea	Pos	G	AB	R	H	2B	3B	HR	RBI	SB	Avg
1982 Medicine Hat	Pioneer		3B	61	217	30	66	12	2	5	33	1	.304
1983 Florence	So. Atl.		3B	131	457	62	125	31	4	5	54	4	.274
1984 Florence	So. Atl.		1B-3B	131	467	69	129	32	5	12	*85	3	.276
1985 Kinston	Carolina		1B	127	460	43	120	16	1	10	60	6	.261
1986 Florence	So. Atl.		C-OF	16	40	8	15	7	0	3	9	0	.375
1986 Kinston	Carolina		C-1B	49	174	24	57	10	0	6	26	0	.328
1986 Knoxville	Southern		C-1B	12	34	3	12	1	0	2	5	0	.353
1987 Dunedin	Fla. St.		1B	3	11	0	4	0	0	0	1	0	.364
1987 Knoxville	Southern		C	94	349	44	102	14	1	11	51	2	.292
1988 Syracuse	Int.		C	35	120	11	29	8	0	3	14	0	.242
1988 Toronto a	A.L.		C-2B	56	154	15	42	6	3	5	21	0	.273
1989 Toronto	A.L.		C	94	241	22	62	11	1	3	29	2	.257
1990 Toronto	A.L.		C	125	346	36	99	24	2	15	49	0	.286
1991 Toronto	A.L.		C	105	291	22	71	17	0	5	36	0	.244
1992 Toronto	A.L.		C	138	480	47	116	26	2	13	53	1	.242
1993 Toronto	A.L.		C	138	488	38	124	30	0	9	55	2	.254
1994 Toronto b	A.L.		C	85	295	24	73	13	1	3	26	1	.247
1995 Kansas City c-d	A.L.		C	52	143	14	33	8	1	4	13	0	.231
1995 Houston e-f	N.L.		C	11	35	1	4	0	0	0	0	0	.114
1996 St. Louis	N.L.		C	26	69	3	22	3	0	0	4	0	.319
1996 Calif.-Chicago g-h-i	A.L.		C-1B	50	151	12	39	4	0	5	14	0	.258
1997 Cleveland j-k	A.L.		C	55	159	17	47	7	1	4	15	0	.296
Major League Totals		10 Yrs.		935	2852	251	732	149	11	66	315	6	.257
Championship Series													
1989 Toronto	A.L.		C	1	1	0	1	0	0	0	1	0	1.000
1991 Toronto	A.L.		C	5	19	0	5	1	0	0	2	0	.263

Year	Club	Lea	Pos	G	AB	R	H	2B	3B	HR	RBI	SB	Avg
1992 Toronto	A.L.	C	6	22	3	7	0	0	1	3	0	.318
1993 Toronto	A.L.	C	6	24	1	6	1	0	0	3	1	.250
Championship Series Totals			18	66	4	19	2	0	1	9	1	.288
World Series Record												
1992 Toronto	A.L.	C	6	20	2	9	3	0	1	3	0	.450
1993 Toronto	A.L.	C	6	23	2	7	0	0	0	1	0	.304
World Series Totals			12	43	4	16	3	0	1	4	0	.372

a On disabled list from July 5 to August 19, 1988.
b Filed for free agency, October 14, 1994.
c Signed with Kansas City Royals, April 7, 1995.
d Traded to Houston Astros for player to be named later, August 11, 1995.
e Kansas City Royals received pitcher Rick Huisman to complete trade, August 17, 1995.
f Filed for free agency, November 12, 1995. Signed with St. Louis Cardinals, January 12, 1996.
g Traded to Chicago White Sox for pitcher Robert Ellis, July 27, 1996.
h Filed for free agency, November 8, 1996.
i Signed with Cleveland Indians, December 13, 1996.
j Filed for free agency, November 7, 1997.
k Re-signed with Cleveland Indians organization, December 17, 1997.

BORDICK, MICHAEL TODD

Born, Marquette, Michigan, July 21, 1965.
Bats Right. Throws Right. Height, 5 feet, 11 inches. Weight, 175 pounds.

Year	Club	Lea	Pos	G	AB	R	H	2B	3B	HR	RBI	SB	Avg
1986 Medford	Northwest	SS	46	187	30	48	3	1	0	19	6	.257
1987 Modesto	California	SS	133	497	73	133	17	0	3	75	8	.268
1988 Huntsville	Southern	2B-SS-3B	*132	481	48	130	13	2	0	38	7	.270
1989 Tacoma	P.C.	2B-SS	136	487	55	117	17	1	1	43	4	.240
1990 Tacoma	P.C.	SS	111	348	49	79	16	1	2	30	3	.227
1990 Oakland	A.L.	3B-SS-2B	25	14	0	1	0	0	0	0	0	.071
1991 Tacoma	P.C.	SS	26	81	15	22	4	1	2	14	0	.272
1991 Oakland	A.L.	SS-2B-3B	90	235	21	56	5	1	0	21	3	.238
1992 Oakland	A.L.	2B-SS	154	504	62	151	19	4	3	48	12	.300
1993 Oakland	A.L.	SS-2B	159	546	60	136	21	2	3	48	10	.249
1994 Oakland	A.L.	SS-2B	114	391	38	99	18	4	2	37	7	.253
1995 Modesto	California	SS	1	2	0	0	0	0	0	0	0	.000
1995 Oakland a	A.L.	SS	126	428	46	113	13	0	8	44	11	.264
1996 Oakland b-c	A.L.	SS	155	525	46	126	18	4	5	54	5	.240
1997 Baltimore	A.L.	SS	153	509	55	120	19	1	7	46	0	.236
Major League Totals	8 Yrs.		976	3152	328	802	113	16	28	298	48	.254
Division Series												
1997 Baltimore	A.L.	SS	4	10	4	4	1	0	0	4	0	.400
Championship Series												
1992 Oakland	A.L.	SS-2B	6	19	1	1	0	0	0	0	1	.053
1997 Baltimore	A.L.	SS	6	19	0	3	1	0	0	2	0	.158
Championship Series Totals			12	38	1	4	1	0	0	2	1	.105
World Series Record												
1990 Oakland	A.L.	SS	3	0	0	0	0	0	0	0	0	.000

a On disabled list from May 8 to May 27, 1995.
b Filed for free agency, October 28, 1996.
c Signed with Baltimore Orioles, December 12, 1996.

BOURNIGAL, RAFAEL ANTONIO

Born, Azusa, Dominican Republic, May 12, 1966.
Bats Right. Throws Right. Height, 5 feet, 11 inches. Weight, 165 pounds.

Year	Club	Lea	Pos	G	AB	R	H	2B	3B	HR	RBI	SB	Avg
1987 Great Falls	Pioneer	2B-SS	30	82	5	12	4	0	0	4	0	.146
1988 Salem	Northwest	SS-2B-3B	70	275	54	86	10	1	0	25	11	.313
1989 Vero Beach	Fla. St.	2B-SS	132	484	74	128	11	1	1	37	18	.264
1990 San Antonio	Texas	SS-2B-3B	69	194	20	41	4	2	0	14	2	.211
1991 Vero Beach	Fla. St.	SS-3B	20	66	6	16	2	0	0	3	2	.242
1991 San Antonio	Texas	3B-SS-2B	16	65	6	21	2	0	0	9	2	.323
1991 Albuquerque	P.C.	SS-2B-3B	66	215	34	63	5	5	0	29	4	.293
1992 Albuquerque	P.C.	SS	122	395	47	128	18	1	0	34	5	.324
1992 Los Angeles	N.L.	SS	10	20	1	3	1	0	0	0	0	.150
1993 Albuquerque	P.C.	SS	134	465	75	129	25	0	4	55	3	.277
1993 Los Angeles	N.L.	2B-SS	8	18	0	9	1	0	0	3	0	.500
1994 Albuquerque	P.C.	SS	61	208	29	69	8	0	1	22	2	.332

Year	Club	Lea	Pos	G	AB	R	H	2B	3B	HR	RBI	SB	Avg
1994 Los Angeles	N.L.	SS	40	116	2	26	3	1	0	11	0	.224
1995 Albuquerque a	P.C.	SS	15	31	2	4	1	0	0	1	0	.129
1995 Ottawa b	Int.	SS	19	54	2	11	4	0	0	6	0	.204
1996 Oakland	A.L.	2B-SS	88	252	33	61	14	2	0	18	4	.242
1997 Modesto	California	SS	7	21	0	5	1	0	0	2	0	.238
1997 Oakland c	A.L.	SS-2B	79	222	29	62	9	0	1	20	2	.279
Major League Totals	5 Yrs.		225	628	65	161	28	3	1	52	6	.256

a Traded to Montreal Expos for pitcher Kris Foster, June 10, 1995.
b Signed with Oakland Athletics organization, January 15, 1996.
c On disabled list from July 1 to July 31, 1997.

BRAGG, DARREN WILLIAM

Born, Waterbury, Connecticut, September 7, 1969.
Bats Left. Throws Right. Height, 5 feet, 9 inches. Weight, 180 pounds.

Year	Club	Lea	Pos	G	AB	R	H	2B	3B	HR	RBI	SB	Avg
1991 Peninsula	Carolina	OF-2B	69	237	42	53	14	0	3	29	21	.224
1992 Peninsula a	Carolina	OF-2B	135	428	83	117	25	5	9	58	44	.273
1993 Jacksonville b	Southern	OF	131	451	74	119	26	3	11	46	19	.264
1994 Calgary	P.C.	OF	126	500	112	175	33	6	17	85	28	.350
1994 Seattle.............	A.L.	OF	8	19	4	3	1	0	0	2	0	.158
1995 Tacoma	P.C.	OF	53	212	24	65	13	3	4	31	10	.307
1995 Seattle	A.L.	OF	52	145	20	34	5	1	3	12	9	.234
1996 Tacoma	P.C.	OF	20	71	17	20	8	0	3	8	1	.282
1996 Seattle-Boston c	A.L.	OF	127	417	74	109	26	2	10	47	14	.261
1997 Boston	A.L.	OF-3B	153	513	65	132	35	2	9	57	10	.257
Major League Totals	4 Yrs.		340	1094	163	278	67	5	22	118	33	.254

a Record of 0-0 in one game as pitcher.
b Record of 0-0 in one game as pitcher.
c Traded to Boston Red Sox for pitcher Jamie Moyer, July 30, 1996.

BRANSON, JEFFREY GLENN

Born, Waynesboro, Mississippi, January 26, 1967.
Bats Left. Throws Right. Height, 6 feet. Weight, 175 pounds.

Year	Club	Lea	Pos	G	AB	R	H	2B	3B	HR	RBI	SB	Avg
1989 Cedar Rapids ..	Midwest	SS	127	469	70	132	28	1	10	68	5	.281
1990 Chattanooga ..	Southern	2B-SS	63	233	19	49	9	1	2	29	3	.210
1990 Cedar Rapids ..	Midwest	SS	62	239	37	60	13	4	6	24	11	.251
1991 Chattanooga ..	Southern	SS-2B	88	304	35	80	13	3	2	28	3	.263
1991 Nashville	A.A.	SS-2B	43	145	10	35	4	1	0	11	5	.241
1992 Nashville	A.A.	SS-3B-2B-OF	36	123	18	40	6	3	4	12	0	.325
1992 Cincinnati	N.L.	2B-3B-SS	72	115	12	34	7	1	0	15	0	.296
1993 Cincinnati	N.L.	SS-2B-3B-1B	125	381	40	92	15	1	3	22	4	.241
1994 Cincinnati	N.L.	2B-3B-SS-1B	58	109	18	31	4	1	6	16	0	.284
1995 Cincinnati	N.L.	3B-SS-2B-1B	122	331	43	86	18	2	12	45	2	.260
1996 Cincinnati	N.L.	3B-SS-2B	129	311	34	76	16	4	9	37	2	.244
1997 Indianapolis	A.A.	SS-3B	15	57	7	12	3	0	1	4	0	.211
1997 Cincinnati a	N.L.	3B-2B-SS	65	98	9	15	3	1	1	5	1	.153
1997 Cleveland	A.L.	2B-3B-SS	29	72	5	19	4	0	2	7	0	.264
Major League Totals	6 Yrs.		600	1417	161	353	67	10	33	147	9	.249
Division Series												
1995 Cincinnati	N.L.	3B	3	7	0	2	1	0	0	2	0	.286
Championship Series												
1995 Cincinnati	N.L.	3B	4	9	2	1	1	0	0	0	1	.111
1997 Cleveland	A.L.	DH	1	2	0	0	0	0	0	0	0	.000
Championship Series Totals			5	11	2	1	1	0	0	0	1	.091
World Series Record												
1997 Cleveland	A.L.	PH	1	1	0	0	0	0	0	0	0	.000

a Traded to Cleveland Indians with pitcher John Smiley for pitcher Danny Graves, pitcher Jim Crowell, pitcher Scott Winchester and infielder Damian Jackson, July 31, 1997.

BREDE, BRENT DAVID

Born, New Baden, Illinois, September 13, 1971.
Bats Left. Throws Left. Height, 6 feet, 4 inches. Weight, 208 pounds.

Year	Club	Lea	Pos	G	AB	R	H	2B	3B	HR	RBI	SB	Avg
1990 Elizabethtn	Appal.	OF	46	143	39	35	5	0	0	14	14	.245
1991 Kenosha	Midwest	OF	53	156	12	30	3	2	0	10	4	.192
1991 Elizabethtn	Appal.	OF-1B	68	253	24	61	13	0	3	36	13	.241

Year Club	Lea	Pos	G	AB	R	H	2B	3B	HR	RBI	SB	Avg
1992 Kenosha ....Midwest		OF-1B-3B	110	363	44	88	15	0	0	29	10	.242
1993 Ft. Myers ....Fla. St.		OF-1B	53	182	27	60	10	1	0	27	8	.330
1994 Ft. Myers ....Fla. St.		OF-1B	116	419	49	110	21	4	2	45	18	.263
1995 New Britain ....Eastern		OF-1B	134	449	71	123	28	2	3	39	14	.274
1996 Salt Lake .............P.C.		OF-1B	132	483	102	168	38	8	11	86	14	.348
1996 Minnesota ...........A.L.		OF	10	20	2	6	0	1	0	2	0	.300
1997 Salt Lake .............P.C.		OF-1B	84	328	82	116	27	4	9	76	4	.354
1997 Minnesota ...........A.L.		OF-1B	61	190	25	52	11	1	3	21	7	.274
Major League Totals	2 Yrs.		71	210	27	58	11	2	3	23	7	.276

BROGNA, RICO JOSEPH
Born, Turners Falls, Massachusetts, April 18, 1970.
Bats Left. Throws Left. Height, 6 feet, 2 inches. Weight, 202 pounds.

Year Club	Lea	Pos	G	AB	R	H	2B	3B	HR	RBI	SB	Avg
1988 Bristol ....Appal.		1B-OF	60	209	37	53	11	2	7	33	3	.254
1989 Lakeland ....Fla. St.		1B	128	459	47	108	20	7	5	51	2	.235
1990 London ....Eastern		1B	137	488	70	128	21	3	*21	*77	1	.262
1991 London ....Eastern		1B-OF	77	293	40	80	13	1	13	51	0	.273
1991 Toledo ....Int.		1B	41	132	13	29	6	1	2	13	2	.220
1992 Toledo ....Int.		1B	121	387	45	101	19	4	10	58	1	.261
1992 Detroit ...............A.L.		1B	9	26	3	5	1	0	1	3	0	.192
1993 Toledo a ....Int.		1B	129	483	55	132	30	3	11	59	7	.273
1994 Norfolk ....Int.		1B	67	258	33	63	14	5	12	37	1	.244
1994 New York ............N.L.		1B	39	131	16	46	11	2	7	20	1	.351
1995 New York ............N.L.		1B	134	495	72	143	27	2	22	76	0	.289
1996 New York b-c ........N.L.		1B	55	188	18	48	10	1	7	30	0	.255
1997 Philadelphia ..........N.L.		1B	148	543	68	137	36	1	20	81	12	.252
Major League Totals	5 Yrs.		385	1383	177	379	85	6	57	210	13	.274

a Traded by Detroit Tigers to New York Mets organization for first baseman Alan Zinter, March 31, 1994.
b On disabled list from June 20 to September 30, 1996.
c Traded to Philadelphia Phillies for pitcher Ricardo Jordan and pitcher Toby Borland, November 27, 1996.

BROSIUS, SCOTT DAVID
Born, Hillsboro, Oregon, August 15, 1966.
Bats Right. Throws Right. Height, 6 feet, 1 inch. Weight, 185 pounds.

Year Club	Lea	Pos	G	AB	R	H	2B	3B	HR	RBI	SB	Avg
1987 Medford .Northwest		SS-3B-2B	65	255	34	73	18	1	3	49	5	.286
1988 Madison ..Midwest		SS-3B-OF-1B	132	504	82	153	28	2	9	58	13	.304
1989 Huntsville .Southern		2B-3B-SS-1B	128	461	68	125	22	2	7	60	4	.271
1990 Huntsville .Southern		SS-2B-3B	*142	547	94	*162	*39	2	23	88	12	.296
1990 Tacoma .......P.C.		2B	3	7	2	1	0	1	0	0	0	.143
1991 Tacoma .......P.C.		3B-SS-2B	65	245	28	70	16	3	8	31	4	.286
1991 Oakland .....A.L.		2B-OF-3B	36	68	9	16	5	0	2	4	3	.235
1992 Tacoma .......P.C.		3B	63	236	29	56	13	0	9	31	8	.237
1992 Oakland a .....A.L.		OF-3B-1B-SS	38	87	13	19	2	0	4	13	3	.218
1993 Tacoma .......P.C.		3B-OF-2B-1B-SS	56	209	38	62	13	2	8	41	8	.297
1993 Oakland .....A.L.		OF-1B-3B-SS	70	213	26	53	10	1	6	25	6	.249
1994 Oakland b .....A.L.		3B-OF-1B	96	324	31	77	14	1	14	49	2	.238
1995 Oakland .....A.L.		3B-OF-1B-2B	123	388	69	102	19	2	17	46	4	.263
1996 Edmonton ......P.C.		3B	3	8	5	5	1	0	0	0	0	.625
1996 Oakland c .....A.L.		3B-1B-OF	114	428	73	130	25	0	22	71	7	.304
1997 Modesto .California		3B	2	3	1	1	0	0	0	1	0	.333
1997 Oakland d-e .A.L.		3B-SS-OF	129	479	59	97	20	1	11	41	9	.203
Major League Totals	7 Yrs.		606	1988	280	494	95	5	76	249	34	.248

a On disabled list from April 18 to May 10 and July 17 to August 3, 1992.
b On disabled list from June 8 to June 26, 1994.
c On disabled list from May 5 to June 25, 1996.
d On disabled list from August 7 to August 29, 1997.
e Sent to New York Yankees as player to be named later for pitcher Kenny Rogers, November 18, 1997.

BUHNER, JAY CAMPBELL
Born, Louisville, Kentucky, August 13, 1964.
Bats Right. Throws Right. Height, 6 feet, 3 inches. Weight, 210 pounds.

Year Club	Lea	Pos	G	AB	R	H	2B	3B	HR	RBI	SB	Avg
1984 Watertown a .....N.Y.-Penn.		OF	65	229	43	74	16	3	9	*58	3	.323
1985 Ft. Lauderdale ....Fla. St.		OF	117	409	65	121	18	10	11	76	6	.296
1986 Ft. Lauderdale b .....Fla. St.		OF	36	139	24	42	9	1	7	31	1	.302

Year Club	Lea	Pos	G	AB	R	H	2B	3B	HR	RBI	SB	Avg
1987 Columbus ....Int.		OF	134	502	83	140	23	1	*31	85	4	.279
1987 New York ...........A.L.		OF	7	22	0	5	2	0	0	1	0	.227
1988 Columbus ....Int.		OF	38	129	26	33	5	0	8	18	1	.256
1988 New York-Seattle c ....A.L.		OF	85	261	36	56	13	1	13	38	1	.215
1989 Calgary .............P.C.		OF	56	196	43	61	12	1	11	45	4	.311
1989 Seattle d ...........A.L.		OF	58	204	27	56	15	1	9	33	1	.275
1990 Calgary .............P.C.		OF	13	34	6	7	1	0	2	5	0	.206
1990 Seattle e ...........A.L.		OF	51	163	16	45	12	0	7	33	2	.276
1991 Seattle ............A.L.		OF	137	406	64	99	14	4	27	77	0	.244
1992 Seattle ............A.L.		OF	152	543	69	132	16	3	25	79	0	.243
1993 Seattle ............A.L.		OF	158	563	91	153	28	3	27	98	2	.272
1994 Seattle f ...........A.L.		OF	101	358	74	100	23	4	21	68	0	.279
1995 Seattle g ...........A.L.		OF	126	470	86	123	23	0	40	121	0	.262
1996 Seattle ............A.L.		OF	150	564	107	153	29	0	44	138	0	.271
1997 Seattle ............A.L.		OF	157	540	104	131	18	2	40	109	0	.243
Major League Totals	11 Yrs.	1025	4094	674	1053	193	18	253	795	6	.257	
Division Series												
1995 Seattle ............A.L.		OF	5	24	2	11	1	0	1	3	0	.458
1997 Seattle ............A.L.		OF	4	13	2	3	0	0	2	2	0	.231
Division Series Totals		9	37	4	14	1	0	3	5	0	.378	
Championship Series												
1995 Seattle ............A.L.		OF	6	23	5	7	2	0	3	5	0	.304

a Traded by Pittsburgh Pirates to New York Yankees organization with infielder Dale Berra and pitcher Alfonso Pulido for outfielder Steve Kemp, infielder Tim Foli and cash, December 20, 1984.
b On disabled list from April 11 to July 27, 1986.
c Traded to Seattle Mariners with pitcher Rick Balabon and player to be named for first baseman Ken Phelps, July 21; Seattle acquired pitcher Troy Evers to complete deal, October 12, 1988.
d On disabled list from June 29 to August 19, 1989.
e On disabled list from March 31 to June 1 and June 17 to August 23, 1990.
f Filed for free agency, October 14; re-signed with Seattle Mariners, December 21, 1994.
g On disabled list from June 6 to June 22, 1995.

BURKS, ELLIS RENA
Born, Vicksburg, Mississippi, September 11, 1964.
Bats Right. Throws Right. Height, 6 feet, 2 inches. Weight, 205 pounds.

Year Club	Lea	Pos	G	AB	R	H	2B	3B	HR	RBI	SB	Avg
1983 Elmira .........N.Y.-Penn.		OF	53	174	30	42	9	0	2	23	9	.241
1984 Winter Haven ....Fla. St.		OF	112	375	52	96	15	4	6	43	29	.256
1985 New Britain ....Eastern		OF	133	476	66	121	25	7	10	61	17	.254
1986 New Britain ....Eastern		OF	124	462	70	126	20	3	14	55	31	.273
1987 Pawtucket ....Int.		OF	11	40	11	9	3	1	3	6	1	.225
1987 Boston .............A.L.		OF	133	558	94	152	30	2	20	59	27	.272
1988 Boston a ...........A.L.		OF	144	540	93	159	37	5	18	92	25	.294
1989 Pawtucket ....Int.		OF	5	21	4	3	1	0	0	0	0	.143
1989 Boston b ...........A.L.		OF	97	399	73	121	19	6	12	61	21	.303
1990 Boston .............A.L.		OF	152	588	89	174	33	8	21	89	9	.296
1991 Boston .............A.L.		OF	130	474	56	119	33	3	14	56	6	.251
1992 Boston c-d ...........A.L.		OF	66	235	35	60	8	3	8	30	5	.255
1993 Chicago e ...........A.L.		OF	146	499	75	137	24	4	17	74	6	.275
1994 Colorado Springs ......P.C.		OF	2	8	4	4	1	0	1	2	0	.500
1994 Colorado f ...........N.L.		OF	42	149	33	48	8	3	13	24	3	.322
1995 Colorado Springs ......P.C.		OF	8	29	9	9	2	1	2	6	0	.310
1995 Colorado g ...........N.L.		OF	103	278	41	74	10	6	14	49	7	.266
1996 Colorado ...........N.L.		OF	156	613	*142	211	45	8	40	128	32	.344
1997 Colorado h ...........N.L.		OF	119	424	91	123	19	2	32	82	7	.290
Major League Totals	11 Yrs.	1288	4757	822	1378	266	50	209	744	148	.290	
Division Series												
1995 Colorado ...........N.L.		OF	2	6	1	2	1	0	0	2	0	.333
Championship Series												
1988 Boston .............A.L.		OF	4	17	2	4	1	0	0	1	0	.235
1990 Boston .............A.L.		OF	4	15	1	4	2	0	0	0	1	.267
1993 Chicago .............A.L.		OF	6	23	4	7	1	0	1	3	0	.304
Championship Series Totals		14	55	7	15	4	0	1	4	1	.273	

a On disabled list from March 27 to April 12, 1988.
b On disabled list from June 16 to August 1, 1989.
c On disabled list from June 25 to end of 1992 season.
d Not offered 1993 contract, December 18, 1992; signed with Chicago White Sox, January 4, 1993.
e Filed for free agency, October 27; signed with Colorado Rockies, November 30, 1993.
f On disabled list from May 18 to July 31, 1994.
g On disabled list from April 25 to May 5, 1995.
h On disabled list from June 28 to July 29, 1997.

BURNITZ, JEROMY NEAL
Born, Westminster, California, April 15, 1969.
Bats Left. Throws Right. Height, 6 feet. Weight, 190 pounds.

Year	Club	Lea	Pos	G	AB	R	H	2B	3B	HR	RBI	SB	Avg
1990 Pittsfield	.......N.Y.-Penn.	OF	51	173	37	52	6	5	6	22	12	.301
1990 St. Lucie	...........Fla. St.	OF	11	32	6	5	1	0	0	3	1	.156
1991 Williamsport	.......Eastern	OF	135	457	80	103	16	10	31	85	31	.225
1992 Tidewater	.............Int.	OF	121	445	56	108	21	3	8	40	30	.243
1993 Norfolk	.............Int.	OF	65	255	33	58	15	3	8	44	10	.227
1993 New York	...........N.L.	OF	86	263	49	64	10	6	13	38	3	.243
1994 New York	...........N.L.	OF	45	143	26	34	4	0	3	15	1	.238
1994 Norfolk a	.............Int.	OF	85	314	58	75	15	5	14	49	18	.239
1995 Buffalo	..............A.A.	OF	128	443	72	126	26	7	19	85	13	.284
1995 Cleveland	...........A.L.	OF	9	7	4	4	1	0	0	0	0	.571
1996 Cleveland-Milwaukee b	.A.L.	OF	94	200	38	53	14	0	9	40	4	.265
1997 Milwaukee	...........A.L.	OF	153	494	85	139	37	8	27	85	20	.281
Major League Totals	....	5 Yrs.	387	1107	202	294	66	14	52	178	28	.266

a Traded by New York Mets to Cleveland Indians with pitcher Joe Roa for pitchers Jerry DiPoto and Paul Byrd and player to be named, November 18; New York Mets acquired second baseman Jesus Azuaje to complete trade, December 6, 1994.

b Traded to Milwaukee Brewers for infielder Kevin Seitzer, August 31, 1996.

BUSH, HOMER GILES
Born, East St. Louis, Illinois, November 12, 1972.
Bats Right. Throws Right. Height, 5 feet, 11 inches. Weight 180 pounds.

Year	Club	Lea	Pos	G	AB	R	H	2B	3B	HR	RBI	SB	Avg
1991 Padres	...........Arizona	3B	32	127	16	41	3	2	0	16	11	.323
1992 Chston-Sc	.........So. Atl.	2B	108	367	37	86	10	5	0	18	14	.234
1993 Waterloo	.........Midwest	2B	130	472	63	152	19	3	5	51	39	.322
1994 Rancho Cuca	....California	2B	39	161	37	54	10	3	0	16	9	.335
1994 Wichita	.............Texas	2B	59	245	35	73	11	4	3	14	20	.298
1995 Memphis	.......Southern	2B	108	432	53	121	12	5	5	37	34	.280
1996 Las Vegas	.............P.C.	2B	32	116	24	42	11	1	2	3	3	.362
1997 Las Vegas	.............P.C.	2B	38	155	25	43	10	1	3	14	5	.277
1997 Columbus a	...........Int.	2B	74	275	36	68	10	3	2	26	12	.247
1997 New York	..............A.L.	2B	10	11	2	4	0	0	0	3	0	.364

a Traded to New York Yankees with pitcher Hideki Irabu and player to be named later for outfielder Ruben Rivera, pitcher Rafael Medina and cash, May 30, 1997. New York Yankees received outfielder Vernon Maxwell to complete trade, June 9, 1997.

BUTLER, RICHARD DWIGHT
Born, Toronto, Ontario, Canada, May 1, 1973.
Bats Left. Throws Right. Height, 6 feet, 1 inch. Weight 180 pounds.

Year	Club	Lea	Pos	G	AB	R	H	2B	3B	HR	RBI	SB	Avg
1991 Blue Jays	.......Gulf Coast	OF	59	213	30	56	6	7	0	13	10	.263
1992 Myrtle Bch	.........So. Atl.	OF	130	441	43	100	14	1	2	43	11	.227
1993 Dunedin	.........Fla. St.	OF	110	444	68	136	19	8	11	65	11	.306
1993 Knoxville	........Southern	OF	6	21	3	2	0	1	0	0	0	.095
1994 Knoxville	........Southern	OF	53	192	29	56	7	4	3	22	7	.292
1994 Syracuse	.............Int.	OF	94	302	34	73	6	2	3	27	8	.242
1995 Syracuse	.............Int.	OF	69	199	24	32	4	2	2	14	2	.161
1995 Knoxville	........Southern	OF	58	217	27	58	12	3	4	33	11	.267
1996 Dunedin	.........Fla. St.	DH	10	28	1	2	0	0	0	0	4	.071
1997 Syracuse	.............Int.	OF-3B	137	537	93	161	30	9	24	87	20	.300
1997 Toronto a	............A.L.	OF	7	14	3	4	1	0	0	2	0	.286

a Selected in expansion draft by Tampa Bay Devil Rays, November 18, 1997.

CABRERA, ORLANDO LUIS
Born, Cartagena, Colombia, November 2, 1974.
Bats Right. Throws Right. Height, 5 feet, 11 inches. Weight 165 pounds.

Year	Club	Lea	Pos	G	AB	R	H	2B	3B	HR	RBI	SB	Avg
1994 Expos	.........Gulf Coast	2B-SS-OF	22	73	13	23	4	1	0	11	6	.315
1995 Wst Plm Bch	.....Fla. St.	SS	3	5	0	1	0	0	0	0	0	.200
1995 Vermont	.....N.Y.-Penn.	2B-SS	65	248	37	70	12	5	3	33	15	.282
1996 Delmarva	.........So. Atl.	SS-2B	134	512	86	129	28	4	14	65	51	.252
1997 Wst Plm Bch	.....Fla. St.	SS-2B	69	279	56	77	19	2	5	26	32	.276

Year Club	Lea	Pos	G	AB	R	H	2B	3B	HR	RBI	SB	Avg
1997 Harrisburg ....Eastern		SS-2B	35	133	34	41	13	2	5	20	7	.308
1997 Ottawa ....Int.		SS-2B	31	122	17	32	5	2	2	14	8	.262
1997 Montreal ............N.L.		SS-2B	16	18	4	4	0	0	0	2	1	.222

CAIRO, MIGUEL JESUS
Born, Anaco, Venezuela, May 4, 1974.
Bats Right. Throws Right. Height, 6 feet. Weight 160 pounds.

Year Club	Lea	Pos	G	AB	R	H	2B	3B	HR	RBI	SB	Avg
1992 Dodgers ....Gulf Coast		SS-3B	21	76	10	23	5	2	0	9	1	.303
1992 Vero Beach ....Fla. St.		2B-SS	36	125	7	28	0	0	0	7	5	.224
1993 Vero Beach ....Fla. St.		2B-SS-3B	90	346	50	109	10	1	1	23	23	.315
1994 Bakersfield ......California		2B-SS	133	533	76	155	23	4	2	48	44	.291
1995 San Antonio a-b ......Texas		2B-SS	107	435	53	121	20	1	1	41	33	.278
1996 Syracuse ....Int.		2B-3B-SS	120	465	71	129	14	4	3	48	27	.277
1996 Toronto c ............A.L.		2B	9	27	5	6	2	0	0	1	0	.222
1997 Iowa ................A.A.		2B-SS	135	569	82	159	35	4	5	46	40	.279
1997 Chicago d ...........N.L.		2B-SS	16	29	7	7	1	0	0	1	0	.241
Major League Totals	2 Yrs.		25	56	12	13	3	0	0	2	0	.232

a Traded to Seattle Mariners with infielder Willie Otanez for third baseman Mike Blowers, November 29, 1995.
b Traded to Toronto Blue Jays for pitcher Bill Risley for pitchers Edwin Hurtado and Paul Menhart, December 18, 1995.
c On disabled list, May 27 to June 5, 1996.
d Selected in expansion draft by Tampa Bay Devil Rays, November 18, 1997.

CAMERON, MICHAEL TERRANCE
Born, La Grange, Georgia, January 8, 1973.
Bats Right. Throws Right. Height, 6 feet, 2 inches. Weight, 190 pounds.

Year Club	Lea	Pos	G	AB	R	H	2B	3B	HR	RBI	SB	Avg
1991 White Sox ....Gulf Coast		OF	44	136	20	30	3	0	0	11	13	.221
1992 Utica ...........N.Y.-Penn.		OF	28	87	15	24	1	4	2	12	3	.276
1992 South Bend ....Midwest		OF	35	114	19	26	8	1	1	9	2	.228
1993 South Bend ....Midwest		OF	122	411	52	98	14	5	0	30	19	.238
1994 Pr William ....Carolina		OF	131	468	86	116	15	17	6	48	22	.248
1995 Birmingham ......Southern		OF	107	350	64	87	20	5	11	60	21	.249
1995 Chicago .............A.L.		OF	28	38	4	7	2	0	1	2	0	.184
1996 Birmingham ......Southern		OF	123	473	120	142	34	12	28	77	39	.300
1996 Chicago .............A.L.		OF	11	11	1	1	0	0	0	0	0	.091
1997 Nashville .............A.A.		OF	30	120	21	33	7	3	6	17	4	.275
1997 Chicago .............A.L.		OF	116	379	63	98	18	3	14	55	23	.259
Major League Totals	3 Yrs.		155	428	68	106	20	3	15	57	23	.248

CAMINITI, KENNETH GENE
Born, Hanford, California, April 21, 1963.
Bats Both. Throws Right. Height, 6 feet. Weight, 200 pounds.

Year Club	Lea	Pos	G	AB	R	H	2B	3B	HR	RBI	SB	Avg
1985 Osceola ....Fla.St.		3B	126	468	83	133	26	9	4	73	14	.284
1986 Columbus ....Southern		3B	137	513	82	154	29	3	12	82	5	.300
1987 Columbus ....Southern		3B	95	375	66	122	25	2	15	69	11	.325
1987 Houston .............N.L.		3B	63	203	10	50	7	1	3	23	0	.246
1988 Tucson ..............P.C.		3B	109	416	54	113	24	7	5	66	13	.272
1988 Houston .............N.L.		3B	30	83	5	15	2	0	1	7	0	.181
1989 Houston .............N.L.		3B	161	585	71	149	31	3	10	72	4	.255
1990 Houston .............N.L.		3B	153	541	52	131	20	2	4	51	9	.242
1991 Houston .............N.L.		3B	152	574	65	145	30	3	13	80	4	.253
1992 Houston a ...........N.L.		3B	135	506	68	149	31	2	13	62	10	.294
1993 Houston .............N.L.		3B	143	543	75	142	31	0	13	75	8	.262
1994 Houston b ...........N.L.		3B	111	406	63	115	28	2	18	75	4	.283
1995 San Diego ...........N.L.		3B	143	526	74	159	33	0	26	94	12	.302
1996 San Diego c-d .......N.L.		3B	146	546	109	178	37	2	40	130	11	.326
1997 San Diego e .........N.L.		3B	137	486	92	141	28	0	26	90	11	.290
Major League Totals	11 Yrs.		1374	4999	684	1374	278	15	167	759	73	.275
Division Series												
1996 San Diego ...........N.L.		3B	4	10	3	3	0	0	3	3	0	.300

a On disabled list from April 19 to May 11, 1992.
b Traded to San Diego Padres with outfielder Steve Finley, shortstop Andujar Cedeño, pitcher Brian Williams, first baseman Roberto Petagine and player to be named for outfielders Derek Bell and Phil Plantier, shortstop Ricky Gutierrez, pitchers Pedro Martinez and Doug Brocail and infielder Craig Shipley, December 28, 1994.
c Selected Most Valuable Player in National League for 1996.
d Underwent rotator cuff surgery right arm, November 1996.
e On disabled list from May 12 to May 27, 1997.

CANGELOSI, JOHN ANTHONY
Born, Brooklyn, New York, March 10, 1963.
Bats Both. Throws Left. Height, 5 feet, 8 inches. Weight, 150 pounds.

Year	Club	Lea	Pos	G	AB	R	H	2B	3B	HR	RBI	SB	Avg
1982	Niagara Falls	N.Y.-Penn.	OF	76	277	60	80	15	4	5	38	45	.289
1983	Appleton	Midwest	OF	128	439	87	124	12	4	1	48	87	.282
1984	Glens Falls	Eastern	OF	138	464	91	133	17	1	1	38	65	.287
1985	Mexico City Reds a	..Mex.	OF	61	201	46	71	9	4	1	30	17	.353
1985	Chicago	A.L.	OF	5	2	2	0	0	0	0	0	0	.000
1985	Buffalo	A.A.	OF	78	244	34	58	8	5	1	21	14	.238
1986	Chicago b	A.L.	OF	137	438	65	103	16	3	2	32	50	.235
1987	Pittsburgh	N.L.	OF	104	182	44	50	8	3	4	18	21	.275
1988	Buffalo	A.A.	OF	37	145	23	48	6	0	0	10	14	.331
1988	Pittsburgh c-d	N.L.	OF-P	75	118	18	30	4	1	0	8	9	.254
1989	Pittsburgh	N.L.	OF	112	160	18	35	4	2	0	9	11	.219
1990	Buffalo	A.A.	OF	24	89	17	31	2	2	0	7	15	.348
1990	Pittsburgh e	N.L.	OF	58	76	13	15	2	0	0	1	7	.197
1991	Vancouver f	P.C.	OF	30	102	15	25	1	0	0	10	9	.245
1991	Denver g	A.A.	OF-P-1B	83	303	69	89	8	3	3	25	26	.294
1992	Texas h	A.L.	OF	73	85	12	16	2	0	1	6	6	.188
1992	Toledo	Int.	OF	27	74	9	20	3	0	0	6	11	.270
1993	Toledo i	Int.	OF-P	113	439	73	128	23	4	6	42	39	.292
1994	New York	N.L.	OF	62	111	14	28	4	0	0	4	5	.252
1995	Tucson	P.C.	OF	30	106	18	39	4	1	0	9	11	.368
1995	Houston j-k-l	N.L.	OF-P	90	201	46	64	5	2	2	18	21	.318
1996	Houston m-n	N.L.	OF	108	262	49	69	11	4	1	16	17	.263
1997	Florida	N.L.	OF-P	103	192	28	47	8	0	1	12	5	.245
Major League Totals	....		11 Yrs.	927	1827	309	457	64	15	11	124	152	.250
	Division Series												
1997	Florida	.... N.L.	PH	1	1	0	0	0	0	0	0	0	.000
	Championship Series												
1997	Florida	.... N.L.	OF	3	5	0	1	0	0	0	0	0	.200
	World Series Record												
1997	Florida	.... N.L.	PH	3	3	0	1	0	0	0	0	0	.333

a Loaned to Mexico City Reds with infielder Manny Salinas, March 4, as part of deal in which Chicago White Sox acquired infielder Nelson Barrera; returned to Chicago organization, June 1, 1985.
b Traded to Pittsburgh Pirates for pitcher Jim Winn, March 30, 1987.
c On disabled list from June 6 to June 27, 1988.
d Record of 0-0 in one game as pitcher.
e Not offered 1991 contract, December 20, 1990; signed with Chicago White Sox organization, February 11, 1991.
f Traded by Chicago White Sox to Milwaukee Brewers organization for shortstop Estaban Beltre, May 23, 1991.
g Became free agent, October 15; signed with Texas Rangers organization, November 7, 1991.
h Released, July 19; signed with Detroit Tigers organization, November 20, 1992.
i Became free agent, October 15; signed with New York Mets organization, November 17, 1993.
j Signed with Houston Astros organization, February 1, 1995.
k Filed for free agency, November 12, 1995.
l Signed with Houston Astros organization, December 7, 1995.
m Filed for free agency, November 18, 1996.
n Signed with Florida Marlins, November 26, 1996.

CANSECO (CAPAS), JOSE
Born, Havana, Cuba, July 2, 1964.
Bats Right. Throws Right. Height, 6 feet, 4 inches. Weight, 240 pounds.

Year	Club	Lea	Pos	G	AB	R	H	2B	3B	HR	RBI	SB	Avg
1982	Miami	Fla. St.	OF	6	9	0	1	0	0	0	0	0	.111
1982	Idaho Falls	Pioneer	OF-3B	28	57	13	15	3	0	2	7	3	.263
1983	Madison	Midwest	OF	34	88	8	14	4	0	3	10	2	.159
1983	Medford	Northwest	OF	59	197	34	53	15	2	11	40	6	.269
1984	Modesto	Calif.	OF	116	410	61	113	21	2	15	73	10	.276
1985	Huntsville a	Southern	OF	58	211	47	67	10	2	25	80	6	.318
1985	Tacoma	P.C.	OF	60	233	41	81	16	1	11	47	5	.348
1985	Oakland	A.L.	OF	29	96	16	29	3	0	5	13	1	.302
1986	Oakland b	A.L.	OF	157	600	85	144	29	1	33	117	15	.240
1987	Oakland	A.L.	OF	159	630	81	162	35	3	31	113	15	.257

Year	Club	Lea	Pos	G	AB	R	H	2B	3B	HR	RBI	SB	Avg
1988 Oakland c	A.L.	OF	158	610	120	187	34	0	*42	*124	40	.307
1989 Huntsville	Southern	OF	9	29	2	6	0	0	0	3	1	.207
1989 Oakland d	A.L.	OF	65	227	40	61	9	1	17	57	6	.269
1990 Oakland e	A.L.	OF	131	481	83	132	14	2	37	101	19	.274
1991 Oakland	A.L.	OF	154	572	115	152	32	1	*44	122	26	.266
1992 Oakland-Texas f-g	A.L.	OF	119	439	74	107	15	0	26	87	6	.244
1993 Texas h-i	A.L.	OF	60	231	30	59	14	1	10	46	6	.255
1994 Texas j	A.L.	DH	111	429	88	121	19	2	31	90	15	.282
1995 Pawtucket	Int.	DH	2	6	1	1	0	0	0	1	0	.167
1995 Boston k-l-m	A.L.	DH-OF	102	396	64	121	25	1	24	81	4	.306
1996 Pawtucket n	Int.	DH	2	5	0	1	0	0	0	0	0	.200
1996 Boston o	A.L.	DH-OF	96	360	68	104	22	1	28	82	3	.289
1997 Oakland p-q-r	A.L.	DH-OF	108	388	56	91	19	0	23	74	8	.235
Major League Totals	13 Yrs.		1449	5459	920	1470	270	13	351	1107	164	.269
Division Series												
1995 Boston	A.L.	DH-OF	3	13	0	0	0	0	0	0	0	.000
Championship Series												
1988 Oakland	A.L.	OF	4	16	4	5	1	0	3	4	1	.313
1989 Oakland	A.L.	OF	5	17	1	5	0	0	1	3	0	.294
1990 Oakland	A.L.	OF	4	11	3	2	0	0	0	1	2	.182
Championship Series Totals			13	44	8	12	1	0	4	8	3	.273
World Series Record												
1988 Oakland	A.L.	OF	5	19	1	1	0	0	1	5	1	.053
1989 Oakland	A.L.	OF	4	14	5	5	0	0	1	3	1	.357
1990 Oakland	A.L.	OF	4	12	1	1	0	0	1	2	0	.083
World Series Totals			13	45	7	7	0	0	3	10	2	.156

a On disabled list from May 14 to June 3, 1985.
b Selected Rookie of the Year in American League for 1986.
c Selected Most Valuable Player in American League for 1988.
d On disabled list from March 23 to July 13, 1989.
e On disabled list from June 8 to June 23, 1990.
f On disabled list from July 1 to July 16, 1992.
g Traded to Texas Rangers for outfielder Ruben Sierra, pitchers Jeff Russell and Bobby Witt, and cash, August 31, 1992.
h Record of 0-0 in one game as pitcher.
i On disabled list from June 25 to end of 1993 season.
j Traded to Boston Red Sox for outfielder Otis Nixon and third baseman Luis Ortiz, December 9, 1994.
k On disabled list from May 15 to June 20, 1995.
l Filed for free agency, October 30, 1995.
m Re-signed with Boston Red Sox December 8, 1995.
n On disabled list from April 24 to May 9 and July 26 to September 17, 1996.
o Traded to Oakland for pitcher John Wasdin, January 27, 1997.
p On disabled list from August 1 to August 20 and August 27 to September 29, 1997.
q Filed for free agency, October 31, 1997.
r Signed as free agent with Cleveland Indians, February 4, 1998.

CARR, CHARLES LEE GLENN (CHUCK)

Born, San Bernardino, California, August 10, 1967.
Bats Both. Throws Right. Height, 5 feet, 10 inches. Weight, 165 pounds.

Year	Club	Lea	Pos	G	AB	R	H	2B	3B	HR	RBI	SB	Avg
1986 Sarasota Reds a	Gulf C.	2B-SS	44	123	13	21	5	0	0	10	9	.171
1987 Bellingham	Northwest	SS-OF-2B-3B	44	165	31	40	1	1	1	11	20	.242
1988 Wausau	Midwest	OF-SS	82	304	58	91	14	2	6	30	41	.299
1988 Vermont b	Eastern	OF	41	159	26	39	4	2	1	13	21	.245
1989 Jackson	Texas	OF	116	444	45	107	13	1	0	22	47	.241
1990 Jackson	Texas	OF	93	361	60	93	19	9	3	24	48	.258
1990 New York	N.L.	OF	4	2	0	0	0	0	0	0	1	.000
1990 Tidewater	Int.	OF	20	81	13	21	5	1	0	8	6	.259
1991 Tidewater	Int.	OF	64	246	34	48	6	1	1	11	27	.195
1991 New York c-d	N.L.	OF	12	11	1	2	0	0	0	1	1	.182
1992 Arkansas	Texas	OF	28	111	17	29	5	1	1	6	8	.261
1992 Louisville	A.A.	OF	96	377	68	116	11	9	3	28	*53	.308
1992 St. Louis e	N.L.	OF	22	64	8	14	3	0	0	3	10	.219
1993 Kissimmee Marlins	Gulf C.	OF	3	12	4	5	1	0	1	3	3	.417
1993 Florida f	N.L.	OF	142	551	75	147	19	2	4	41	*58	.267
1994 Florida	N.L.	OF	106	433	61	114	19	2	2	30	32	.263
1995 Charlotte	Int.	OF	7	23	5	5	8	0	1	1	2	.217
1995 Florida g-h	N.L.	OF	105	308	54	70	20	0	2	20	25	.227
1996 New Orleans i	A.A.	OF	4	13	2	5	1	0	0	1	2	.385
1996 Milwaukee	A.L.	OF	27	106	18	29	6	1	0	11	5	.274
1997 New Orleans	A.A.	OF	19	65	8	16	1	0	0	3	5	.246

Year	Club	Lea	Pos	G	AB	R	H	2B	3B	HR	RBI	SB	Avg
1997 Milwaukee j		.A.L.	OF	26	46	3	6	3	0	0	0	1	.130
1997 Houston k		.N.L.	OF	63	192	34	53	11	2	4	17	11	.276
Major League Totals				8 Yrs.	507	1713	254	435	81	7	13	123	144	.254
Division Series													
1997 Houston		.N.L.	OF	2	4	1	1	0	0	1	1	0	.250

a Released by Cincinnati Reds, March 30; signed with Seattle Mariners organization, June 15, 1987.
b Traded by Seattle Mariners to New York Mets organization for pitcher Reggie Dobie, November 18, 1988.
c On disabled list from July 14 to August 9 and August 28 to September 13, 1991.
d Traded to St. Louis Cardinals organization for pitcher Clyde Keller, December 13, 1991.
e Selected by Florida Marlins in expansion draft, November 17, 1992.
f On disabled list from July 1 to July 18, 1993.
g On disabled list from May 15 to June 11, 1995.
h Traded to Milwaukee Brewers for pitcher Juan Gonzalez, December 4, 1995.
i On disabled list from April 22 to May 11 and May 31 to September 30, 1996.
j Released by Milwaukee Brewers, May 20, 1997.
k Signed with Houston Astros organization, June 1, 1997.
i Not offered contract by Houston Astros, December 8, 1997.

CARTER, JOSEPH CHRIS
Born, Oklahoma City, Oklahoma, March 7, 1960.
Bats Right. Throws Right. Height, 6 feet, 3 inches. Weight, 225 pounds.

Year	Club	Lea	Pos	G	AB	R	H	2B	3B	HR	RBI	SB	Avg
1981 Midland		.Texas	OF	67	249	42	67	15	3	5	35	12	.269
1982 Midland a		.Texas	OF	110	427	84	136	22	8	25	98	15	.319
1983 Iowa		.A.A.	OF	124	*522	82	160	27	6	22	83	40	.307
1983 Chicago		.N.L.	OF	23	51	6	9	1	1	0	1	1	.176
1984 Cleveland b-c		.A.L.	OF-1B	66	244	32	67	6	1	13	41	2	.275
1984 Iowa		.A.A.	OF	61	248	45	77	12	7	14	67	11	.310
1985 Cleveland		.A.L.	OF-1B-3B-2B	143	489	64	128	27	0	15	59	24	.262
1986 Cleveland		.A.L.	OF-1B	162	663	108	200	36	9	29	*121	29	.302
1987 Cleveland		.A.L.	OF-1B	149	588	83	155	27	2	32	106	31	.264
1988 Cleveland		.A.L.	OF	157	621	85	168	36	6	27	98	27	.271
1989 Cleveland d		.A.L.	OF-1B	*162	*651	84	158	32	4	35	105	13	.243
1990 San Diego e		.N.L.	OF-1B	*162	*634	79	147	27	1	24	115	22	.232
1991 Toronto		.A.L.	OF	*162	638	89	174	42	3	33	108	20	.273
1992 Toronto f		.A.L.	OF-1B	158	622	97	164	30	7	34	119	12	.264
1993 Toronto		.A.L.	OF	155	603	92	153	33	5	33	121	8	.254
1994 Toronto		.A.L.	OF	111	435	70	118	25	2	27	103	11	.271
1995 Toronto		.A.L.	OF-1B	139	558	70	141	23	0	25	76	12	.253
1996 Toronto		.A.L.	OF-1B	157	625	84	158	35	7	30	107	7	.253
1997 Toronto g-h		.A.L.	DH-OF-1B	157	612	76	143	30	4	21	102	8	.234
Major League Totals				15 Yrs.	2063	8034	1119	2083	410	52	378	1382	227	.259
Championship Series													
1991 Toronto		.A.L.	OF	5	19	3	5	2	0	1	4	0	.263
1992 Toronto		.A.L.	OF-1B	6	26	2	5	0	0	1	3	2	.192
1993 Toronto		.A.L.	OF	6	27	2	7	0	0	0	2	0	.259
Championship Series Totals				17	72	7	17	2	0	2	9	2	.236
World Series Record													
1992 Toronto		.A.L.	OF-1B	6	22	2	6	2	0	2	3	1	.273
1993 Toronto		.A.L.	OF	6	25	6	7	1	0	2	8	0	.280
World Series Totals				12	47	8	13	3	0	4	11	1	.277

a On disabled list from April 9 to April 19, 1982.
b Traded by Chicago Cubs to Cleveland Indians with outfielder Mel Hall and pitchers Don Schulze and Darryl Banks for pitchers George Frazier and Rick Sutcliffe and catcher Ron Hassey, June 14, 1984.
c On disabled list from July 2 to July 17, 1984.
d Traded to San Diego Padres for catcher Sandy Alomar Jr., infielder Carlos Baerga and outfielder Chris James, December 7, 1989.
e Traded to Toronto Blue Jays with second baseman Roberto Alomar for shortstop Tony Fernandez and first baseman Fred McGriff, December 5, 1990.
f Filed for free agency, October 30; re-signed with Toronto Blue Jays, December 7, 1992.
g Filed for free agency, October 28, 1997.
h Signed as free agent by Baltimore Orioles, December 12, 1997.

CASANOVA, RAUL
Born, Humacao, Puerto Rico, August 23, 1972.
Bats Both. Throws Right. Height, 6 feet. Weight 192 pounds.

Year	Club	Lea	Pos	G	AB	R	H	2B	3B	HR	RBI	SB	Avg
1990 Mets		.Gulf Coast	C	23	65	4	5	0	0	0	1	0	.077
1991 Mets		.Gulf Coast	C	32	111	19	27	4	2	0	9	3	.243
1991 Kingsport		.Appal.	C	5	18	0	1	0	0	0	0	0	.056

Year	Club	Lea	Pos	G	AB	R	H	2B	3B	HR	RBI	SB	Avg
1992	Columbia	So.Atl.	C	5	18	2	3	0	0	0	1	0	.167
1992	Kingsport	Appal.	C	42	137	25	37	9	1	4	27	3	.270
1993	Waterloo	Midwest	C-3B	76	227	32	58	12	0	6	30	0	.256
1994	Rancho Cuca	California	C	123	471	83	160	27	2	23	120	1	.340
1995	Memphis	Southern	C	89	306	42	83	18	0	12	44	4	.271
1996	Jacksnville	Southern	C	8	30	5	10	2	0	4	9	0	.333
1996	Toledo	Int.	C	49	161	23	44	11	0	8	28	0	.273
1996	Detroit a	A.L.	C	25	85	6	16	1	0	4	9	0	.188
1997	Toledo	Int.	C	12	41	1	8	0	0	1	3	0	.195
1997	Detroit	A.L.	C	101	304	27	74	10	1	5	24	1	.243
Major League Totals			2 Yrs.	126	389	33	90	11	1	9	33	1	.231

a On disabled list from June 19 to August 13, 1996.

CASTILLA (SORIA), VINICIO
Born, Oaxaca, Mexico, July 4, 1967.
Bats Right. Throws Right. Height, 6 feet, 1 inch. Weight, 180 pounds.

Year	Club	Lea	Pos	G	AB	R	H	2B	3B	HR	RBI	SB	Avg
1987	Saltillo	Mexican	3B	13	27	0	5	2	0	0	1	0	.185
1988	Saltillo-Monclova	Mex.	SS-3B	50	124	22	30	2	2	5	18	1	.242
1989	Saltillo a	Mexican	SS	128	462	70	142	25	13	10	58	11	.307
1990	Sumter	So. Atl.	SS	93	339	47	91	15	2	9	53	2	.268
1990	Greenville	Southern	SS	46	170	20	40	5	1	4	16	4	.235
1991	Greenville	Southern	SS	66	259	34	70	17	3	7	44	0	.270
1991	Richmond	Int.	SS	67	240	25	54	7	4	7	36	1	.225
1991	Atlanta	N.L.	SS	12	5	1	1	0	0	0	0	0	.200
1992	Richmond	Int.	SS	127	449	49	113	29	1	7	44	1	.252
1992	Atlanta b	N.L.	3B-SS	9	16	1	4	1	0	0	1	0	.250
1993	Colorado c	N.L.	SS	105	337	36	86	9	7	9	30	2	.255
1994	Colorado Springs	P.C.	3B-2B-SS	22	78	13	19	6	1	1	11	0	.244
1994	Colorado	N.L.	SS-2B-3B-1B	52	130	16	43	11	1	3	18	2	.331
1995	Colorado	N.L.	3B-SS	139	527	82	163	34	2	32	90	2	.309
1996	Colorado	N.L.	3B	160	629	97	191	34	0	40	113	7	.304
1997	Colorado	N.L.	3B	159	612	94	186	25	2	40	113	2	.304
Major League Totals			7 Yrs.	636	2256	327	674	114	12	124	365	15	.299
Division Series													
1995	Colorado	N.L.	3B	4	15	3	7	1	0	3	6	0	.467

a Sold by Saltillo Sarape Makers of Mexican League to Atlanta Braves organization, March 19, 1990.
b Selected by Colorado Rockies in expansion draft, November 17, 1992.
c On disabled list from May 22 to June 4, 1993.

CASTILLO, ALBERTO TERRERO
Born, San Juan De La Maguana, Dominican Republic, February 10, 1970.
Bats Right. Throws Right. Height, 6 feet. Weight, 185 pounds.

Year	Club	Lea	Pos	G	AB	R	H	2B	3B	HR	RBI	SB	Avg
1987	Kingsport	Appal.	C-P	7	9	1	1	0	0	0	0	1	.111
1988	Mets	Gulf Coast	C	22	68	7	18	4	0	0	10	2	.265
1988	Kingsport	Appal.	C	24	75	7	22	3	0	1	14	0	.293
1989	Kingsport	Appal.	C-1B	27	74	15	19	4	0	3	12	2	.257
1989	Pittsfield	N.Y.-Penn.	C	34	123	13	29	8	0	1	13	2	.236
1990	Columbia	So. Atl.	C	30	103	8	24	4	3	1	14	1	.233
1990	Pittsfield	N.Y.-Penn.	C-OF-1B	58	187	19	41	8	1	4	24	3	.219
1990	St. Lucie	Fla. St.	C	3	11	4	4	0	0	1	3	0	.364
1991	Columbia	So. Atl.	C	90	267	35	74	20	3	3	47	6	.277
1992	St. Lucie	Fla. St.	C	60	162	11	33	6	0	3	17	0	.204
1993	St. Lucie	Fla. St.	C	105	333	37	86	21	0	5	42	0	.258
1994	Binghamton	Eastern	C-1B	90	315	33	78	14	0	7	42	1	.248
1995	Norfolk	Int.	C	69	217	23	58	13	1	4	31	2	.267
1995	New York	N.L.	C	13	29	2	3	0	0	0	0	1	.103
1996	Norfolk	Int.	C	113	341	34	71	12	1	11	39	2	.208
1996	New York	N.L.	C	6	11	1	4	0	0	0	0	0	.364
1997	Norfolk	Int.	C-OF	34	83	4	18	1	0	1	8	1	.217
1997	New York a	N.L.	C	35	59	3	12	1	0	0	7	0	.203
Major League Totals			3 Yrs.	54	99	6	19	1	0	0	7	1	.192

a Traded to New York Yankees with outfielder Chris Singleton for infielder Charlie Hayes, November 11, 1997.

CASTILLO, LUIS ANTONIO

Born, San Pedro De Macoris, Dominican Republic, September 12, 1975.
Bats Both. Throws Right. Height, 5 feet, 11 inches. Weight 145 pounds.

Year Club	Lea	Pos	G	AB	R	H	2B	3B	HR	RBI	SB	Avg
1994 Marlins	Gulf Coast	2B-SS	57	216	49	57	8	0	0	16	31	.264
1995 Kane County	Midwest	2B	89	340	71	111	4	4	0	23	41	.326
1996 Portland	Eastern	2B	109	420	83	133	15	7	1	35	51	.317
1996 Florida	N.L.	2B	41	164	26	43	2	1	1	8	17	.262
1997 Florida a	N.L.	2B	75	263	27	63	8	0	0	8	16	.240
1997 Charlotte	Int.	2B	37	130	25	46	5	0	0	5	8	.354
Major League Totals		2 Yrs.	116	427	53	106	10	1	1	16	33	.248

a On disabled list from May 7 to May 22, 1997.

CASTRO, JUAN GABRIEL

Born, Los Mochis, Mexico, June 20, 1972.
Bats Right. Throws Right. Height, 5 feet, 10 inches. Weight, 165 pounds.

Year Club	Lea	Pos	G	AB	R	H	2B	3B	HR	RBI	SB	Avg
1991 Great Falls	Pioneer	SS-2B	60	217	36	60	4	2	1	27	7	.276
1992 Bakersfield	California	SS	113	446	56	116	15	4	4	42	14	.260
1993 San Antonio	Texas	SS-2B	118	424	55	117	23	8	7	41	12	.276
1994 San Antonio	Texas	SS	123	445	55	128	25	4	4	44	4	.288
1995 Albuquerque	P.C.	SS-2B	104	341	51	91	18	4	3	42	4	.267
1995 Los Angeles	N.L.	3B-SS	11	4	0	1	0	0	0	0	0	.250
1996 Albuquerque	P.C.	3B-SS-2B	17	56	12	21	4	2	1	8	1	.375
1996 Los Angeles	N.L.	SS-3B-2B-OF	70	132	16	26	5	3	0	5	1	.197
1997 Albuquerque	P.C.	SS-2B	27	101	11	31	5	2	2	11	1	.307
1997 Los Angeles a	N.L.	SS-2B-3B	40	75	3	11	3	1	0	4	0	.147
Major League Totals		3 Yrs.	121	211	19	38	8	4	0	9	1	.180
Division Series												
1996 Los Angeles	N.L.	2B	2	5	0	1	1	0	0	1	0	.200

a On disabled list from June 5 to August 2, 1997.

CATALANOTTO, FRANK JOHN

Born, Smithtown, New York, April 27, 1974.
Bats Left. Throws Right. Height, 6 feet. Weight 170 pounds.

Year Club	Lea	Pos	G	AB	R	H	2B	3B	HR	RBI	SB	Avg
1992 Bristol	Appal.	2B-1B	21	50	6	10	2	0	0	4	0	.200
1993 Bristol	Appal.	2B	55	199	37	61	9	5	3	22	3	.307
1994 Fayetteville	So. Atl.	2B	119	458	72	149	24	8	3	56	4	.325
1995 Jacksonville	Southern	2B	134	491	66	111	19	5	8	48	13	.226
1996 Jacksonville	Southern	2B	132	497	105	148	34	6	17	67	15	.298
1997 Toledo	Int.	2B-3B-OF	134	500	75	150	32	3	16	68	12	.300
1997 Detroit	A.L.	2B	13	26	2	8	2	0	0	3	0	.308

CEDENO, DOMINGO ANTONIO

Born, La Romana, Dominican Republic, November 4, 1968.
Bats Both. Throws Right. Height, 6 feet. Weight, 170 pounds.

Year Club	Lea	Pos	G	AB	R	H	2B	3B	HR	RBI	SB	Avg
1988		Played in Dominican Summer League										
1989 Myrtle Beach	So. Atl.	SS	9	35	4	7	0	0	0	2	1	.200
1989 Dunedin	Fla. St.	SS	9	28	3	6	0	1	0	1	0	.214
1989 Medicine Hat	Pioneer	SS	53	194	28	45	6	4	1	20	6	.232
1990 Dunedin	Fla. St.	SS	124	493	64	109	12	10	7	61	10	.221
1991 Knoxville	Southern	SS	100	336	39	75	7	6	1	26	11	.223
1992 Knoxville	Southern	2B-SS	106	337	31	76	7	7	2	21	8	.226
1992 Syracuse	Int.	2B-SS	18	57	4	11	4	0	0	5	0	.193
1993 Syracuse	Int.	SS-2B	103	382	58	104	16	10	2	28	15	.272
1993 Toronto	A.L.	SS-2B	15	46	5	8	0	0	0	7	1	.174
1994 Syracuse	Int.	2B-OF-SS	22	80	11	23	5	1	1	9	3	.287
1994 Toronto	A.L.	2B-SS-3B-OF	47	97	14	19	2	3	0	10	1	.196
1995 Toronto	A.L.	SS-2B-3B	51	161	18	38	6	1	4	14	0	.236
1996 Toronto-Chicago b-c-d	A.L.	2B-SS-3B	89	301	46	82	12	2	2	20	6	.272
1997 Tulsa	Texas	SS	2	9	0	4	0	1	0	0	0	.444
1997 Okla City	A.A.	2B-SS	6	28	0	10	2	0	0	2	0	.357
1997 Texas e	A.L.	2B-SS-3B	113	365	49	103	19	6	4	36	3	.282
Major League Totals		5 Yrs.	315	970	132	250	39	12	10	87	11	.258

a On disabled list from April 22 to May 28, 1991.
b Traded to Chicago White Sox with pitcher Tony Castillo for pitcher Luis Andujar and pitcher Allen Halley, August 22, 1996.
c Designated for assignment by Chicago White Sox December 12, 1996.
d Signed with Texas Rangers organization, January 15, 1997.
e On disabled list from April 8 to May 15, 1997.

CEDENO, ROGER LEANDRO
Born, Valencia, Venezuela, August 16, 1974.
Bats Both. Throws Right. Height, 6 feet, 1 inch. Weight, 165 pounds.

Year	Club	Lea	Pos	G	AB	R	H	2B	3B	HR	RBI	SB	Avg
1992 Great Falls	Pioneer	OF	69	256	60	81	6	5	2	27	40	.316
1993 San Antonio	Texas	OF	122	465	70	134	12	8	4	30	28	.288
1993 Albuquerque	P.C.	OF	6	18	1	4	1	1	0	4	0	.222
1994 Albuquerque	P.C.	OF	104	383	84	123	18	5	4	49	30	.321
1995 Albuquerque	P.C.	OF	99	367	67	112	19	9	2	44	23	.305
1995 Los Angeles	N.L.	OF	40	42	4	10	2	0	0	3	1	.238
1996 Albuquerque	P.C.	OF	33	125	16	28	2	3	1	10	6	.224
1996 Los Angeles	N.L.	OF	86	211	26	52	11	4	2	18	5	.246
1997 Albuquerque	P.C.	OF	29	113	21	40	4	4	2	9	5	.354
1997 Los Angeles a	N.L.	OF	80	194	31	53	10	2	3	17	9	.273
Major League Totals		3 Yrs.	206	447	61	115	23	3	5	38	15	.257

a On disabled list from April 1 to April 21 and August 26 to September 29, 1997.

CHAVEZ, RAUL ALEXANDER
Born, Valencia, Venezuela, March 18, 1973.
Bats Right. Throws Right. Height, 5 feet, 11 inches. Weight 175 pounds.

Year	Club	Lea	Pos	G	AB	R	H	2B	3B	HR	RBI	SB	Avg
1990 Astros	Gulf Coast	SS-2B-3B	48	155	23	50	8	1	0	23	5	.323
1991 Burlington	Midwest	SS-3B	114	420	54	108	17	0	3	41	1	.257
1992 Asheville	So. Atl.	C	95	348	37	99	22	1	2	40	1	.284
1993 Osceola	Fla. St.	C	58	197	13	45	5	1	0	16	1	.228
1994 Jackson	Texas	C	89	251	17	55	7	0	1	22	1	.219
1995 Jackson	Texas	C-3B	58	188	16	54	8	0	4	25	0	.287
1995 Tucson	P.C.	C	32	103	14	27	5	0	0	10	0	.262
1996 Ottawa a	Int.	C	60	198	15	49	10	0	2	24	0	.247
1996 Montreal	N.L.	C	4	5	1	1	0	0	0	0	1	.200
1997 Ottawa	Int.	C	92	310	31	76	17	0	4	46	1	.245
1997 Montreal	N.L.	C	13	26	0	7	0	0	0	2	1	.269
Major League Totals		2 Yrs.	17	31	1	8	0	0	0	2	2	.258

a Traded to Montreal Expos with pitcher Dave Veres for third baseman Sean Berry, December 20, 1995.

CIANFROCCO, ANGELO DOMINIC (ARCHI)
Born, Rome, New York, October 6, 1966.
Bats Right. Throws Right. Height, 6 feet, 5 inches. Weight, 215 pounds.

Year	Club	Lea	Pos	G	AB	R	H	2B	3B	HR	RBI	SB	Avg
1987 Jamestown	N.Y.-Penn.	2B-SS	70	251	28	62	8	4	2	27	2	.247
1988 Rockford	Midwest	3B	126	455	54	115	34	0	15	65	6	.253
1989 Jacksonville	Southern	3B	132	429	46	105	22	7	7	50	3	.245
1990 Jacksonville	Southern	1B-3B-2B	62	196	18	43	10	0	5	29	0	.219
1991 Harrisburg	Eastern	1B	124	456	71	144	21	10	9	77	11	.316
1992 Montreal	N.L.	1B-3B-OF	86	232	25	56	5	2	6	30	2	.241
1992 Indianapolis	A.A.	1B-3B-SS	15	59	12	18	3	0	4	16	1	.305
1993 Ottawa	Int.	OF-1B-3B	50	188	21	56	14	2	4	27	4	.298
1993 Mont.-San Diego a	N.L.	3B-1B	96	296	30	72	11	2	12	48	2	.243
1994 Las Vegas	P.C.	OF-3B	32	112	11	34	11	1	1	21	0	.304
1994 San Diego b	N.L.	3B-1B-SS	59	146	9	32	8	0	4	13	2	.219
1995 Las Vegas	P.C.	1B-3B-OF	89	322	51	100	20	2	10	58	5	.311
1995 San Diego	N.L.	1B-SS-OF-2B	51	118	22	31	7	0	5	31	0	.263
1996 San Diego c	N.L.	1B-3B-SS-OF	79	192	21	54	13	3	2	32	1	.281
1997 San Diego	N.L.	1B-3B-2B-SS	89	220	25	54	12	0	4	26	7	.245
Major League Totals		6 Yrs.	460	1204	132	299	56	7	33	180	15	.248
Division Series													
1996 San Diego	N.L.	1B	1	3	1	1	0	0	0	0	0	.333

a Traded to San Diego Padres for pitcher Tim Scott, June 23, 1993.
b Released, November 28; re-signed with San Diego Padres organization, December 1, 1994.
c On disabled list from May 6 to May 21 and July 7 to July 23, 1996.

CIRILLO, JEFFREY HOWARD
Born, Pasadena, California, September 23, 1969.
Bats Right. Throws Right. Height, 6 feet, 2 inches. Weight, 190 pounds.

Year	Club	Lea	Pos	G	AB	R	H	2B	3B	HR	RBI	SB	Avg
1991	Helena	Pioneer	3B-OF	*70	286	60	100	16	2	10	51	3	.350
1992	Stockton	California	3B	7	27	2	6	1	0	0	5	0	.222
1992	Beloit	Midwest	3B-2B	126	444	65	135	27	3	9	71	21	.304
1993	El Paso	Texas	2B-3B	67	249	53	85	16	2	9	41	2	.341
1993	New Orleans	A.A.	3B-2B-SS	58	215	31	63	13	2	3	32	2	.293
1994	New Orleans	A.A.	3B-2B-SS	61	236	45	73	18	2	10	46	4	.309
1994	Milwaukee	A.L.	3B-2B	39	126	17	30	9	0	3	12	0	.238
1995	Milwaukee	A.L.	3B-2B-1B-SS	125	328	57	91	19	4	9	39	7	.277
1996	Milwaukee	A.L.	3B-1B-2B	158	566	101	184	46	5	15	83	4	.325
1997	Milwaukee	A.L.	3B	154	580	74	167	46	2	10	82	4	.288
Major League Totals			4 Yrs.	476	1600	249	472	120	11	37	216	15	.295

CLARK, ANTHONY CHRISTOPHER (TONY)
Born, Newton, Kansas, June 15, 1972.
Bats Both. Throws Right. Height, 6 feet, 7 inches. Weight, 240 pounds.

Year	Club	Lea	Pos	G	AB	R	H	2B	3B	HR	RBI	SB	Avg
1990	Bristol	Appal.	OF	25	73	2	12	2	0	1	8	0	.164
1991	Niagara Falls a ..	N.Y.-Penn.					INJURED—Did Not Play						
1992	Niagara Falls b ..	N.Y.-Penn.	OF	27	85	12	26	9	0	5	17	1	.306
1993	Lakeland c	Fla. St.	OF	36	117	14	31	4	14	1	22	0	.265
1994	Trenton	Eastern	1B	107	394	50	110	25	0	21	86	0	.279
1994	Toledo	Int.	1B	25	92	10	24	4	0	2	13	2	.261
1995	Toledo	Int.	1B	110	405	50	98	17	2	14	63	0	.242
1995	Detroit	A.L.	1B	27	101	10	24	5	1	3	11	0	.238
1996	Toledo	Int.	1B	55	194	42	58	7	1	14	36	1	.299
1996	Detroit	A.L.	1B	100	376	56	94	14	0	27	72	0	.250
1997	Detroit	A.L.	1B	159	580	105	160	28	3	32	117	1	.276
Major League Totals			3 Yrs.	286	1057	171	278	47	4	62	200	1	.263

a On disabled list from May 30 to June 17; transferred to temporary inactive list from June 17 to end of 1991 season.
b On temporary inactive list from August 17 to end of 1992 season.
c On disabled list from August 24 to end of 1993 season.

CLARK, DAVID EARL
Born, Tupelo, Mississippi, September 3, 1962.
Bats Left. Throws Right. Height, 6 feet, 2 inches. Weight, 209 pounds.

Year	Club	Lea	Pos	G	AB	R	H	2B	3B	HR	RBI	SB	Avg
1983	Waterloo	Midwest	OF	58	159	20	44	8	1	4	20	2	.277
1984	Waterloo	Midwest	OF	110	363	74	112	16	3	15	63	20	.309
1984	Buffalo	Eastern	OF	17	56	12	10	1	0	3	10	1	.179
1985	Waterbury	Eastern	OF	132	463	75	140	24	7	12	64	27	.302
1986	Maine	Int.	OF	106	355	56	99	17	2	19	58	6	.279
1986	Cleveland	A.L.	OF	18	58	10	16	1	0	3	9	1	.276
1987	Buffalo	A.A.	OF	108	420	83	143	22	3	30	80	14	.340
1987	Cleveland	A.L.	OF	29	87	11	18	5	0	3	12	1	.207
1988	Cleveland	A.L.	OF	63	156	11	41	4	1	3	18	0	.263
1988	Colorado Springs	P.C.	OF	47	165	27	49	10	2	4	31	4	.297
1989	Cleveland a	A.L.	OF	102	253	21	60	12	0	8	29	0	.237
1990	Chicago b	N.L.	OF	84	171	22	47	4	2	5	20	7	.275
1991	Omaha	A.A.	OF-1B	104	359	45	108	24	3	13	64	6	.301
1991	Kansas City c	A.L.	OF	11	10	1	2	0	0	0	1	0	.200
1992	Buffalo	A.A.	OF-1B	78	253	43	77	17	6	11	55	6	.304
1992	Pittsburgh d	N.L.	OF	23	33	3	7	0	0	2	7	0	.212
1993	Pittsburgh	N.L.	OF	110	277	43	75	11	2	11	46	1	.271
1994	Pittsburgh	N.L.	OF	86	223	37	66	11	1	10	46	2	.296
1995	Pittsburgh e	N.L.	OF	77	196	30	55	6	0	4	24	3	.281
1996	Pitts.-Los Angeles f-g-h ..	N.L.	OF	107	226	28	61	12	2	8	36	2	.270
1997	Chicago i-j	N.L.	OF	102	143	19	43	8	0	5	32	1	.301
Major League Totals			12 Yrs.	812	1833	236	491	74	8	62	280	18	.268
Division Series													
1996	Los Angeles	N.L.	PH	2	2	0	0	0	0	0	0	0	.000

a Traded to Chicago Cubs for outfielder Mitch Webster, November 20, 1989.
b Released, March 31; signed with Kansas City Royals organization, April 29, 1991.
c Released, January 2; signed with Pittsburgh Pirates organization, January 24, 1992.

d Became free agent, October 15; re-signed with Pittsburgh Pirates organization, November 20, 1992.
e On disabled list from July 26 to September 11, 1995.
f Traded to Los Angeles Dodgers for pitcher Carl South, August 31, 1996.
g Filed for free agency, October 28, 1996.
h Signed with Chicago Cubs organization January 29, 1997.
i Filed for free agency, October 27, 1997.
j Signed with Houston Astros, November 24, 1997.

CLARK, WILLIAM NUSCHLER, JR.

Born, New Orleans, Louisiana, March 13, 1964.
Bats Left. Throws Left. Height, 6 feet, 1 inch. Weight 196 pounds.

Year	Club	Lea	Pos	G	AB	R	H	2B	3B	HR	RBI	SB	Avg
1985 Fresno	California		1B-OF	65	217	41	67	14	0	10	48	11	.309
1986 San Francisco a	N.L.		1B	111	408	66	117	27	2	11	41	4	.287
1986 Phoenix	P.C.		DH	6	20	3	5	0	0	0	1	1	.250
1987 San Francisco	N.L.		1B	150	529	89	163	29	5	35	91	5	.308
1988 San Francisco	N.L.		1B	*162	575	102	162	31	6	29	*109	9	.282
1989 San Francisco	N.L.		1B	159	588	*104	196	38	9	23	111	8	.333
1990 San Francisco	N.L.		1B	154	600	91	177	25	5	19	95	8	.295
1991 San Francisco	N.L.		1B	148	565	84	170	32	7	29	116	4	.301
1992 San Francisco	N.L.		1B	144	513	69	154	40	1	16	73	12	.300
1993 San Francisco b-c	N.L.		1B	132	491	82	139	27	2	14	73	2	.283
1994 Texas	A.L.		1B	110	389	73	128	24	2	13	80	5	.329
1995 Texas	A.L.		1B	123	454	85	137	27	3	16	92	0	.302
1996 Tulsa	Texas		1B	3	9	3	2	0	0	0	0	0	.222
1996 Texas d	A.L.		1B	117	436	69	124	25	1	13	72	2	.284
1997 Texas	A.L.		1B	110	393	56	128	29	1	12	51	0	.326
Major League Totals	12 Yrs.			1620	5941	970	1795	354	44	230	1004	59	.302
Division Series													
1996 Texas	A.L.		1B	4	16	1	2	0	0	0	0	0	.125
Championship Series													
1987 San Francisco	N.L.		1B	7	25	3	9	2	0	1	3	1	.360
1989 San Francisco	N.L.		1B	5	20	8	13	3	1	2	8	0	.650
Championship Series Totals				12	45	11	22	5	1	3	11	1	.489
World Series Record													
1989 San Francisco	N.L.		1B	4	16	2	4	1	0	0	0	0	.250

a On disabled list from June 4 to July 24, 1986.
b On disabled list from August 26 to September 10, 1993.
c Filed for free agency, October 25; signed with Texas Rangers, November 22, 1993.
d On disabled list from June 8 to June 23 and June 30 to July 16 and July 17 to August 4, 1996.
e On disabled list from April 1 to April 18 and August 25 to September 29, 1997.

CLAYTON, ROYCE SPENCER

Born, Burbank, California, January 2, 1970.
Bats Right. Throws Right. Height, 6 feet. Weight, 183 pounds.

Year	Club	Lea	Pos	G	AB	R	H	2B	3B	HR	RBI	SB	Avg
1988 Everett	Northwest		SS	60	212	35	55	4	0	3	29	10	.259
1989 Clinton	Midwest		SS	104	385	39	91	13	3	0	24	28	.236
1989 San Jose	California		SS	28	92	5	11	2	0	0	4	10	.120
1990 San Jose	California		SS	123	460	80	123	15	10	7	71	33	.267
1991 Shreveport	Texas		SS	126	485	84	136	22	8	5	68	36	.280
1991 San Francisco	N.L.		SS	9	26	0	3	1	0	0	2	0	.115
1992 Phoenix	P.C.		SS	48	192	30	46	6	2	3	18	15	.240
1992 San Francisco	N.L.		SS-3B	98	321	31	72	7	4	4	24	8	.224
1993 San Francisco	N.L.		SS	153	549	54	155	21	5	6	70	11	.282
1994 San Francisco	N.L.		SS	108	385	38	91	14	6	3	30	23	.236
1995 San Francisco a	N.L.		SS	138	509	56	124	29	3	5	58	24	.244
1996 St. Louis	N.L.		SS	129	491	64	136	20	4	6	35	33	.277
1997 St. Louis	N.L.		SS	154	576	75	153	39	5	9	61	30	.266
Major League Totals	7 Yrs.			789	2857	318	734	131	27	33	280	129	.257
Division Series													
1996 St. Louis	N.L.		SS	2	6	1	2	0	0	0	0	0	.333
Championship Series													
1996 St. Louis	N.L.		SS	5	20	4	7	0	0	0	1	1	.350

a Traded from San Francisco Giants to St. Louis Cardinals for pitchers Allen Watson, Rich DeLucia, and Doug Creek, December 14, 1995.

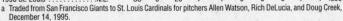

COLBRUNN, GREGORY JOSEPH
Born Fontana, California, July 26, 1969.
Bats Right. Throws Right. Height, 6 feet. Weight, 200 pounds.

Year	Club	Lea	Pos	G	AB	R	H	2B	3B	HR	RBI	SB	Avg
1988 Rockford	Midwest		C	115	417	55	111	18	2	7	46	5	.266
1989 West Palm Beach	Fla. St.		C	59	228	20	54	8	0	0	25	3	.237
1989 Jacksonville	Southern		C	55	178	21	49	11	1	3	18	0	.275
1990 Jacksonville	Southern		C	125	458	57	138	29	1	13	76	1	.301
1991 Indianapolis a	A.A.						INJURED—Did Not Play						
1992 Indianapolis	A.A.		1B	57	216	32	66	19	1	11	48	1	.306
1992 Montreal b	N.L.		1B	52	168	12	45	8	0	2	18	3	.268
1993 West Palm Beach	Fla. St.		1B	8	31	6	12	2	1	1	5	0	.387
1993 Ottawa	Int.		1B	6	22	4	6	1	0	0	8	1	.273
1993 Montreal c-d	N.L.		1B	70	153	15	39	9	0	4	23	4	.255
1994 Edmonton	P.C.		1B	7	17	2	4	0	0	1	2	0	.235
1994 Brevard City	Fla. St.		1B	7	11	3	6	2	0	1	2	0	.545
1994 Florida e	N.L.		1B	47	155	17	47	10	0	6	31	1	.303
1995 Florida	N.L.		1B	138	528	70	146	22	1	23	89	11	.277
1996 Florida f-g	N.L.		1B	141	511	60	146	26	2	16	69	4	.286
1997 Minnesota h	A.L.		1B	70	217	24	61	14	0	5	26	1	.281
1997 Atlanta i-j	N.L.		1B	28	54	3	15	3	0	2	9	0	.278
Major League Totals			6 Yrs.	546	1786	201	499	92	3	58	265	24	.279
Division Series													
1997 Atlanta	N.L.		PH	1	1	0	1	0	0	0	2	0	1.000
Championship Series													
1997 Atlanta	N.L.		PH	3	3	0	2	0	0	0	0	0	.667

a On disabled list from March 28 to end of 1991 season.
b On disabled list from August 2 to August 18, 1992.
c On disabled list from April 4 to April 23 and July 19 to end of 1993 season.
d Claimed on waivers by Florida Marlins, October 7, 1993.
e On disabled list from April 9 to May 27 and July 15 to July 30, 1994.
f On disabled list from July 24 to August 8, 1996.
g Florida declined to offer a 1997 contract, December 20, 1996.
h Traded to Atlanta Braves for player to be named later, August 14, 1997.
i Minnesota Twins received outfielder Marc Lewis to complete trade, October 1, 1997.
j Filed for free agency, October 23, 1997.
k Signed with Colorado Rockies organization, December 23, 1997.

CONINE, JEFFREY GUY
Born, Tacoma, Washington, June 27, 1966.
Bats Right. Throws Right. Height, 6 feet, 1 inch. Weight, 220 pounds.

Year	Club	Lea	Pos	G	AB	R	H	2B	3B	HR	RBI	SB	Avg
1988 Baseball City	Fla. St.		1B-3B	118	415	63	112	23	9	10	59	26	.272
1989 Baseball City	Fla. St.		1B	113	425	89	116	12	7	14	60	32	.273
1990 Memphis	Southern		1B-3B	137	487	89	156	37	8	15	95	21	.320
1990 Kansas City	A.L.		1B	9	20	3	5	2	0	0	2	0	.250
1991 Omaha a	A.A.		1B-OF	51	171	23	44	9	1	3	15	0	.257
1992 Omaha	A.A.		1B-OF	110	397	69	120	24	5	20	72	4	.302
1992 Kansas City b	A.L.		OF-1B	28	91	10	23	5	2	0	9	0	.253
1993 Florida	N.L.		OF-1B	*162	595	75	174	24	3	12	79	2	.292
1994 Florida	N.L.		OF-1B	115	451	60	144	27	6	18	82	1	.319
1995 Florida	N.L.		OF-1B	133	483	72	146	26	2	25	105	2	.302
1996 Florida	N.L.		OF-1B	157	597	84	175	32	2	26	95	1	.293
1997 Florida c	N.L.		1B-OF	151	405	46	98	13	1	17	61	2	.242
Major League Totals			7 Yrs.	755	2642	350	765	129	16	98	433	8	.290
Division Series													
1997 Florida	N.L.		1B	3	11	3	4	1	0	0	0	0	.364
Championship Series													
1997 Florida	N.L.		1B	6	18	1	2	0	0	0	1	0	.111
World Series Record													
1997 Florida	N.L.		1B	6	13	1	3	0	0	0	2	0	.231

a On disabled list from June 28 to end of 1991 season.
b Selected by Florida Marlins in expansion draft, November 17, 1992.
c Traded to Kansas City Royals for pitcher Blaine Mull, November 21, 1997.

COOMER, RONALD BRYAN (RON)
Born, Crest Hill, Illinois, November 18, 1966.
Bats Right. Throws Right. Height, 5 feet, 11 inches. Weight, 195 pounds.

Year	Club	Lea	Pos	G	AB	R	H	2B	3B	HR	RBI	SB	Avg
1987 Medford	Northwest		3B-1B-P	45	168	23	58	10	2	1	26	1	.345
1988 Modesto	California		DH-3B-1B	131	495	67	138	23	2	17	85	2	.279
1989 Madison	Midwest		3B-1B	61	216	28	69	15	0	4	28	0	.319

36

Year	Club	Lea	Pos	G	AB	R	H	2B	3B	HR	RBI	SB	Avg
1990 Huntsville	Southern		2B-1B-3B	66	194	22	43	7	0	3	27	3	.222
1991 Birmingham	Southern		3B-1B-2B	137	505	81	129	27	5	13	76	0	.255
1992 Vancouver		P.C.	3B	86	262	29	62	10	0	9	40	3	.237
1993 Birmingham	Southern		3B-1B	69	262	44	85	18	0	13	50	1	.324
1993 Nashville		A.A.	3B	59	211	34	66	19	0	13	51	1	.313
1994 Albuquerque		P.C.	3B-2B	127	535	89	181	34	6	22	123	4	.338
1995 Albuquerque		P.C.	3B-1B	85	323	54	104	23	2	16	76	5	.322
1995 Minnesota a		A.L.	1B-3B-OF	37	101	15	26	3	1	5	19	0	.257
1996 Minnesota		A.L.	1B-OF-3B	95	233	34	69	12	1	12	41	3	.296
1997 Minnesota		A.L.	3B-1B-OF	140	523	63	156	30	2	13	85	4	.298
Major League Totals			3 Yrs.	272	857	112	251	45	4	30	145	7	.293

a Traded to Minnesota Twins with pitcher Jose Parra and pitcher Greg Hansell for pitcher Kevin Tapani and pitcher Mark Guthrie, July 31, 1995. Minnesota received outfielder Chris Latham to complete trade, October 30, 1995.

CORA, JOSE MANUEL

Born, Caguas, Puerto Rico, May 14, 1965.
Bats Both. Throws Right. Height, 5 feet, 8 inches. Weight, 155 pounds.

Year	Club	Lea	Pos	G	AB	R	H	2B	3B	HR	RBI	SB	Avg
1985 Spokane	Northwest		2B	43	170	48	55	11	2	3	26	13	.324
1986 Beaumont		Texas	2B-SS	81	315	54	96	5	5	3	41	24	.305
1987 Las Vegas		P.C.	2B	81	293	50	81	9	1	1	24	12	.276
1987 San Diego		N.L.	2B-SS	77	241	23	57	7	2	0	13	15	.237
1988 Las Vegas		P.C.	2B	127	460	73	136	15	3	3	55	31	.296
1989 Las Vegas a		P.C.	2B	119	507	79	157	25	4	0	37	40	.310
1989 San Diego		N.L.	SS-3B-2B	12	19	5	6	1	0	0	1	1	.316
1990 Las Vegas		P.C.	SS-2B	51	211	41	74	13	9	0	24	15	.351
1990 San Diego b		N.L.	SS-2B-C	51	100	12	27	3	0	0	2	8	.270
1991 South Bend		Midwest	2B	1	5	1	1	0	0	0	0	1	.200
1991 Chicago c		A.L.	2B-SS	100	228	37	55	2	3	0	18	11	.241
1992 Chicago		A.L.	2B-SS-3B	68	122	27	30	7	1	0	9	10	.246
1993 Chicago		A.L.	2B-3B	153	579	95	155	15	13	2	51	20	.268
1994 South Bend		Midwest	2B	3	11	3	5	1	0	0	1	1	.455
1994 Chicago d-e		A.L.	2B	90	312	55	86	13	4	2	30	8	.276
1995 Seattle f		A.L.	2B-SS	120	427	64	127	19	2	3	39	18	.297
1996 Seattle		A.L.	2B-3B	144	530	90	154	37	6	6	45	5	.291
1997 Seattle g-h		A.L.	2B	149	574	105	172	40	4	11	54	6	.300
Major League Totals			10 Yrs.	964	3132	513	869	144	35	24	262	102	.277
Division Series													
1995 Seattle		A.L.	2B	5	19	7	6	1	0	1	1	1	.316
1997 Seattle		A.L.	2B	4	17	1	3	0	0	0	0	0	.176
Division Series Totals				9	36	8	9	1	0	1	1	1	.250
Championship Series													
1993 Chicago		A.L.	2B	6	22	1	3	0	0	0	1	0	.136
1995 Seattle		A.L.	2B	6	23	2	4	1	0	0	0	2	.174
Championship Series Totals				12	45	3	7	1	0	0	1	2	.156

a On disabled list from May 15 to May 31, 1989.
b Traded to Chicago White Sox with infielder Kevin Garner and outfielder Warren Newson for pitchers Adam Peterson and Steve Rosenberg, March 31, 1991.
c On disabled list from June 22 to July 11, 1991.
d On disabled list from June 30 to July 14, 1994.
e Not offered 1995 contract, December 23, 1994.
f Signed with Seattle Mariners, April 6, 1995.
g Filed for free agency, November 6, 1997.
h Re-signed with Seattle Mariners, November 18, 1997.

CORDERO, WILFRED NIEVA

Born, Mayaguez, Puerto Rico, October 3, 1971.
Bats Right. Throws Right. Height, 6 feet, 2 inches. Weight, 190 pounds.

Year	Club	Lea	Pos	G	AB	R	H	2B	3B	HR	RBI	SB	Avg
1988 Jamestown	N.Y.-Penn.		SS	52	190	18	49	3	0	2	22	3	.258
1989 West Palm Beach	Fla. St.		SS	78	289	37	80	12	2	6	29	2	.277
1989 Jacksonville	Southern		SS	39	121	9	26	6	1	3	17	1	.215
1990 Jacksonville	Southern		SS	131	444	63	104	18	4	7	40	9	.234
1991 Indianapolis a	A.A.		SS	98	360	48	94	16	4	11	52	9	.261
1992 Indianapolis b	A.A.		SS	52	204	32	64	11	1	6	27	6	.314
1992 Montreal	N.L.		SS-2B	45	126	17	38	4	1	2	8	0	.302

Year Club	Lea	Pos	G	AB	R	H	2B	3B	HR	RBI	SB	Avg
1993 Montreal .............N.L.		SS-3B	138	475	56	118	32	2	10	58	12	.248
1994 Montreal .............N.L.		SS	110	415	65	122	30	3	15	63	16	.294
1995 Montreal c ...........N.L.		SS-OF	131	514	64	147	35	2	10	49	9	.286
1996 Red Sox ....Gulf Coast		DH-2B	3	10	1	3	0	0	1	3	0	.300
1996 Pawtucket ....Int.		2B	4	10	2	3	1	0	1	2	0	.300
1996 Boston d ............A.L.		2B-1B	59	198	29	57	14	0	3	37	2	.288
1997 Boston e ............A.L.		OF-2B	140	570	82	160	26	3	18	72	1	.281
Major League Totals	6 Yrs.		623	2298	313	642	141	11	58	287	40	.279

a On disabled list from July 31 to end of 1991 season.
b On disabled list from May 12 to June 11 and July 7 to July 20, 1992.
c Traded to the Boston Red Sox with pitcher Bryan Eversgerd for pitcher Rheal Cormier, first baseman Ryan McGuire and pitcher Shane Bennett, January 10, 1996.
d On disabled list from May 21 to August 12, 1996.
e Released by Boston Red Sox, September 28, 1997.

CORDOVA, MARTIN KEEVIN (MARTY)

Born, Las Vegas, Nevada, July 10, 1969.
Bats Right. Throws Right. Height, 6 feet. Weight, 200 pounds.

Year Club	Lea	Pos	G	AB	R	H	2B	3B	HR	RBI	SB	Avg
1989 Elizabethtn ......Appal.		DH-3B-OF-2B	38	148	32	42	2	3	8	29	2	.284
1990 Kenosha ......Midwest		OF	81	269	35	58	7	5	7	25	6	.216
1991 Visalia ....California		OF	71	189	31	40	6	1	7	19	2	.212
1992 Visalia ....California		OF	134	513	103	175	31	6	28	131	13	.341
1993 Nashville .....Southern		OF	138	508	83	127	30	5	19	77	10	.250
1994 Salt Lake .........P.C.		OF	103	385	69	138	25	4	19	66	17	.358
1995 Minnesota a .....A.L.		OF	137	512	81	142	27	4	24	84	20	.277
1996 Minnesota .......A.L.		OF	145	569	97	176	46	1	16	111	11	.309
1997 Salt Lake .........P.C.		DH-OF	6	24	5	9	4	0	1	4	1	.375
1997 Minnesota b .......A.L.		OF	103	378	44	93	18	4	15	51	5	.246
Major League Totals	3 Yrs.		385	1459	222	411	91	9	55	246	36	.282

a Selected Rookie of the Year in American League for 1995.
b On disabled list from April 10 to May 26, 1997.

COUNSELL, CRAIG JOHN

Born, South Bend, Indiana, August 21, 1970.
Bats Left. Throws Right. Height, 6 feet. Weight, 170 pounds.

Year Club	Lea	Pos	G	AB	R	H	2B	3B	HR	RBI	SB	Avg
1992 Bend ....Northwest		2B-SS	18	61	11	15	6	1	0	8	1	.246
1993 Central Val ......California		SS	131	471	79	132	26	3	5	59	14	.280
1994 New Haven ....Eastern		SS-2B	83	300	47	84	20	1	5	37	4	.280
1995 Colo Sprngs ..........P.C.		SS	118	399	60	112	22	6	5	53	10	.281
1995 Colorado ............N.L.		SS	3	1	0	0	0	0	0	0	0	.000
1996 Colo Sprngs ..........P.C.		2B-3B-SS	25	75	17	18	3	0	2	10	4	.240
1997 Colo Sprngs ..........P.C.		2B-SS	96	376	77	126	31	6	5	63	12	.335
1997 Colorado-Florida a ....N.L.		2B	52	164	20	49	9	2	1	16	1	.299
Major League Totals	2 Yrs.		55	165	20	49	9	2	1	16	1	.297
Division Series												
1997 Florida .............N.L.		2B	3	5	0	2	1	0	0	1	0	.400
Championship Series												
1997 Florida .............N.L.		2B	5	14	0	6	0	0	0	2	0	.429
World Series Record												
1997 Florida .............N.L.		2B	7	22	4	4	1	0	0	2	1	.182

a Traded to Florida Marlins for pitcher Mark Hutton, July 27, 1997.

CRUZ, DEIVI

Born, Bani, Dominican Republic, November 6, 1975.
Bats Right. Throws Right. Height, 5 feet, 11 inches. Weight 160 pounds.

Year Club	Lea	Pos	G	AB	R	H	2B	3B	HR	RBI	SB	Avg
1993 Giants ....Arizona		3B-SS-1B	29	82	8	28	3	0	0	15	3	.341
1994 Giants ....Arizona		SS-3B	18	53	10	16	8	0	0	5	0	.302
1995 Burlington ....Midwest		2B-3B-SS	16	58	2	8	1	0	1	9	1	.138
1995 Bellingham ......Northwest		3B-2B	62	223	32	66	17	0	3	28	6	.296
1996 Burlington ....Midwest		SS-3B	127	517	72	152	27	2	9	64	12	.294
1997 Detroit...............A.L.		SS	147	436	35	105	26	0	2	40	3	.241

38

CRUZ, JOSE L.
Born, Arroyo, Puerto Rico, April 19, 1974.
Bats Both. Throws Right. Height, 6 feet. Weight 190 pounds.

Year	Club	Lea	Pos	G	AB	R	H	2B	3B	HR	RBI	SB	Avg
1995 Everett	....	Northwest	OF	3	11	6	5	0	0	0	2	1	.455
1995 Riverside	....	California	OF	35	144	34	37	7	1	7	29	3	.257
1996 Lancaster	....	California	OF	53	203	38	66	17	1	6	43	7	.325
1996 Port City	....	Southern	OF	47	181	39	51	10	2	3	31	5	.282
1996 Tacoma	....	P.C.	OF	22	76	15	18	1	2	6	15	1	.237
1997 Tacoma	....	P.C.	OF	50	190	33	51	16	2	6	30	3	.268
1997 Seattle-Toronto a	.....	A.L.	OF	104	395	59	98	19	1	26	68	7	.248

a Traded to Toronto Blue Jays for pitchers Mike Timlin and Paul Spoljaric, July 31, 1997.

CRUZ, LUIS IVAN
Born, Fajardo, Puerto Rico, May 3, 1968.
Bats Left. Throws Left. Height, 6 feet, 3 inches. Weight 210 pounds.

Year	Club	Lea	Pos	G	AB	R	H	2B	3B	HR	RBI	SB	Avg
1989 Niagara Fls	....	N.Y.-Penn.	1B	64	226	43	62	11	2	7	40	2	.274
1990 Lakeland	....	Fla. St.	1B	118	414	61	118	23	2	11	73	8	.285
1991 Toledo	....	Int.	1B	8	29	2	4	0	0	1	4	0	.138
1991 London	....	Eastern	1B	121	443	46	110	21	0	9	47	3	.248
1992 London	....	Eastern	1B	134	524	71	143	25	1	14	104	1	.273
1993 Toledo	....	Int.	DH-1B	115	402	44	91	18	4	13	50	1	.226
1994 Toledo	....	Int.	1B	97	303	36	75	11	2	15	43	1	.248
1995 Toledo	....	Int.	1B	11	36	5	7	2	0	0	3	0	.194
1995 Jacksnville a-b	....	Southern	1B	108	397	65	112	17	1	31	93	0	.282
1996 Columbus	....	Int.	1B	130	446	84	115	26	0	28	96	2	.258
1997 Columbus	....	Int.	1B	116	417	69	125	35	1	24	95	4	.300
1997 New York	....	A.L.	1B-OF	11	20	0	5	1	0	0	3	0	.250

a Released by Detroit Tigers organization, October 17, 1995.
b Signed by New York Yankees organization, November 27, 1995.

CUMMINGS, MIDRE ALMERIC
Born, St. Croix, U.S. Virgin Islands, October 14, 1971.
Bats Left. Throws Right. Height, 6 feet. Weight, 195 pounds.

Year	Club	Lea	Pos	G	AB	R	H	2B	3B	HR	RBI	SB	Avg
1990 Twins	....	Gulf Coast	OF	47	177	28	56	3	4	5	28	14	.316
1991 Kenosha	....	Midwest	OF	106	382	59	123	20	4	4	54	28	.322
1992 Salem a	....	Carolina	OF	113	420	55	128	20	5	14	75	23	.305
1993 Carolina	....	Southern	OF	63	237	33	70	17	2	6	26	5	.295
1993 Buffalo	....	A.A.	OF	60	232	36	64	12	1	9	21	5	.276
1993 Pittsburgh	....	N.L.	OF	13	36	5	4	1	0	0	3	0	.111
1994 Buffalo	....	A.A.	OF	49	183	23	57	12	4	2	22	5	.311
1994 Pittsburgh	....	N.L.	OF	24	86	11	21	4	0	1	12	0	.244
1995 Calgary	....	P.C.	OF	45	159	19	44	9	1	1	16	1	.277
1995 Pittsburgh	....	N.L.	OF	59	152	13	37	7	1	2	15	1	.243
1996 Pittsburgh	....	N.L.	OF	24	85	11	19	3	1	3	7	0	.224
1996 Calgary	....	P.C.	OF	97	368	60	112	24	3	8	55	6	.304
1997 Pitt.-Phila. b	....	N.L.	OF	115	314	35	83	22	6	4	31	2	.264
Major League Totals	....		5 Yrs.	235	673	75	164	37	8	10	68	3	.244

a Traded by Minnesota Twins to Pittsburgh with pitcher Denny Neagle for pitcher John Smiley, March 17, 1992.
b Claimed on waivers by Philadelphia Phillies, July 8, 1997.

CURTIS, CHAD DAVID
Born, Marion, Indiana, November 6, 1968.
Bats Right. Throws Right. Height, 5 feet, 10 inches. Weight, 175 pounds.

Year	Club	Lea	Pos	G	AB	R	H	2B	3B	HR	RBI	SB	Avg
1989 Mesa Angels	....	Arizona	2B-OF	32	122	30	37	4	4	3	20	17	.303
1989 Quad City	....	Midwest	OF	23	78	7	19	3	0	2	11	7	.244
1990 Quad City	....	Midwest	2B-OF	*135	*492	87	*151	28	1	14	65	64	.307
1991 Edmonton	....	P.C.	3B-OF-2B	115	431	81	136	28	7	9	61	46	.316
1992 California	....	A.L.	OF	139	441	59	114	16	2	10	46	43	.259
1993 California	....	A.L.	OF-2B	152	583	94	166	25	3	6	59	48	.285
1994 California	....	A.L.	OF	114	453	67	116	23	4	11	50	25	.256
1995 Detroit a	....	A.L.	OF	144	586	96	157	29	3	21	67	27	.268

Year	Club	Lea	Pos	G	AB	R	H	2B	3B	HR	RBI	SB	Avg
1996 Detroit b	............A.L.		OF	104	400	65	105	20	1	10	37	16	.262
1996 Los Angeles c-d	.......N.L.		OF	43	104	20	22	5	0	2	9	2	.212
1997 Akron e	..........Eastern		OF	4	18	5	7	1	0	3	6	0	.389
1997 Cleveland-New York f	...A.L.		OF	115	349	59	99	22	1	15	55	12	.284
Major League Totals	....		6 Yrs.	811	2916	460	779	140	14	75	323	173	.267
Division Series													
1996 Los Angeles	............N.L.		OF	1	2	0	0	0	0	0	0	0	.000
1997 New York	............A.L.		OF	4	6	0	1	0	0	0	0	0	.167
Divisional Series Totals	....			5	8	0	1	0	0	0	0	0	.125

a Traded to Detroit Tigers for outfielder Tony Phillips, April 13, 1995.
b Traded to Los Angeles Dodgers for pitcher Joey Eischen and pitcher John Cummings, July 31, 1996.
c Filed for free agency, October 15, 1996.
d Signed with Cleveland Indians December 18, 1996.
e Traded to New York Yankees for pitcher Dave Weathers, June 9, 1997.
f On disabled list from May 14 to June 9, 1997.

DAMON, JOHNNY DAVID
Born, Fort Riley, Kansas, November 5, 1973.
Bats Left. Throws Left. Height, 6 feet. Weight, 175 pounds.

Year	Club	Lea	Pos	G	AB	R	H	2B	3B	HR	RBI	SB	Avg
1992 Royals	.........Gulf Coast		OF	50	192	58	67	12	9	4	24	23	.349
1992 Baseball City	........Fla. St.		OF	1	1	0	0	0	0	0	0	0	.000
1993 Rockford	.........Midwest		OF	127	511	82	148	25	13	5	50	59	.290
1994 Wilmington	.......Carolina		OF	119	472	96	149	25	13	6	75	44	.316
1995 Wichita	.............Texas		OF	111	423	83	145	15	9	16	54	26	.343
1995 Kansas City	...........A.L.		OF	47	188	32	53	11	5	3	23	7	.282
1996 Kansas City	...........A.L.		OF	145	517	61	140	22	5	6	50	25	.271
1997 Kansas City	...........A.L.		OF	146	472	70	130	12	8	8	48	16	.275
Major League Totals	....		3 Yrs.	338	1177	163	323	45	18	17	121	48	.274

DAVIS, CHARLES THEODORE (CHILI)
Born, Kingston, Jamaica, January 17, 1960.
Bats Both. Throws Right. Height, 6 feet, 3 inches. Weight, 217 pounds.

Year	Club	Lea	Pos	G	AB	R	H	2B	3B	HR	RBI	SB	Avg
1978 Cedar Rapids	......Midwest		C-OF	124	424	63	119	18	5	16	73	15	.281
1979 Fresno	.........California		OF-C	134	490	91	132	24	5	21	95	30	.269
1980 Shreveport	.........Texas		OF-C	129	442	50	130	30	4	12	67	19	.294
1981 Phoenix a	.............P.C.		OF	88	334	76	117	16	6	19	75	40	.350
1981 San Francisco	...........N.L.		OF	8	15	1	2	0	0	0	0	2	.133
1982 San Francisco	...........N.L.		OF	154	641	86	167	27	6	19	76	24	.261
1983 San Francisco	...........N.L.		OF	137	486	54	113	21	2	11	59	10	.233
1983 Phoenix	.............P.C.		OF	10	44	12	13	2	0	2	9	5	.295
1984 San Francisco	...........N.L.		OF	137	499	87	157	21	6	21	81	12	.315
1985 San Francisco	...........N.L.		OF	136	481	53	130	25	2	13	56	15	.270
1986 San Francisco	...........N.L.		OF	153	526	71	146	28	3	13	70	16	.278
1987 San Francisco b	.......N.L.		OF	149	500	80	125	22	1	24	76	16	.250
1988 California	.............A.L.		OF	158	600	81	161	29	3	21	93	9	.268
1989 California	.............A.L.		OF	154	560	81	152	24	1	22	90	3	.271
1990 California c-d	.........A.L.		OF	113	412	58	109	17	1	12	58	1	.265
1991 Minnesota	............A.L.		DH-OF	153	534	84	148	34	1	29	93	5	.277
1992 Minnesota e			A.L. DH-OF-1B	138	444	63	128	27	2	12	66	4	.288
1993 California f	............A.L.		DH	153	573	74	139	32	0	27	112	4	.243
1994 California	............A.L.		DH-OF	108	392	72	122	18	1	26	84	3	.311
1995 California g-h	.........A.L.		DH	119	424	81	135	23	0	20	86	3	.318
1996 California i	............A.L.		DH	145	530	73	155	24	0	28	95	5	.292
1997 Kansas City j-k-l	....A.L.		DH	140	477	71	133	20	0	30	90	6	.279
Major League Totals	....		17 Yrs.	2255	8094	1170	2222	392	29	328	1285	138	.275
Championship Series													
1987 San Francisco	.........N.L.		OF	6	20	2	3	1	0	0	0	0	.150
1991 Minnesota	...........A.L.		DH	5	17	3	5	2	0	0	2	1	.294
Championship Series Totals	......			11	37	5	8	3	0	0	2	1	.216
World Series Record													
1991 Minnesota	............A.L.		DH-OF	6	18	4	4	0	0	2	4	0	.222

a On disabled list from August 19 to August 28, 1981.
b Filed for free agency, October 28; signed with California Angels, December 1, 1987.
c On disabled list from July 17 to August 9, 1990.

40

d Granted special free agency by arbitrator, December 7, 1990; signed with Minnesota Twins, January 29, 1991.
e Filed for free agency, November 3; signed with California Angels, December 11, 1992.
f Record of 0-0 in one game as pitcher.
g Re-signed with California Angels, May 4, 1995.
h On disabled list from June 20 to July 18, 1995.
i Traded to Kansas City Royals for pitcher Mark Gubicza and pitcher Mike Bovee, October 28, 1996.
j On disabled list from April 1 to April 14, 1997.
k Filed for free agency, October 29, 1997.
l Signed as free agent with New York Yankees, December 10, 1997.

DAVIS, ERIC KEITH
Born, Los Angeles, California, May 29, 1962.
Bats Right. Throws Right. Height, 6 feet, 3 inches. Weight, 185 pounds.

Year	Club	Lea	Pos	G	AB	R	H	2B	3B	HR	RBI	SB	Avg
1980	Eugene	Northwest	SS-2B	33	73	12	16	1	0	1	11	0	.219
1981	Eugene	Northwest	OF	62	214	*67	69	10	4	11	39	*40	.322
1982	Cedar Rapids	Midwest	OF	111	434	80	120	20	5	15	56	53	.276
1983	Waterbury	Eastern	OF	89	293	56	85	13	1	15	43	39	.290
1983	Indianapolis	A.A.	OF	19	77	18	23	4	0	7	19	9	.299
1984	Wichita	A.A.	OF	52	194	42	61	9	5	14	34	27	.314
1984	Cincinnati a	N.L.	OF	57	174	33	39	10	1	10	30	10	.224
1985	Cincinnati	N.L.	OF	56	122	26	30	3	3	8	18	16	.246
1985	Denver	A.A.	OF	64	206	48	57	10	2	15	38	35	.277
1986	Cincinnatti	N.L.	OF	132	415	97	115	15	3	27	71	80	.277
1987	Cincinnati	N.L.	OF	129	474	120	139	23	4	37	100	50	.293
1988	Cincinnatti	N.L.	OF	135	472	81	129	18	3	26	93	35	.273
1989	Cincinnatti b	N.L.	OF	131	462	74	130	14	2	34	101	21	.281
1990	Cincinnatti c	N.L.	OF	127	453	84	118	25	2	24	86	21	.260
1991	Cincinnati d-e	N.L.	OF	89	285	39	67	10	0	11	33	14	.235
1992	Los Angeles f-g	N.L.	OF	76	267	21	61	8	1	5	32	19	.228
1993	Los Angeles h	N.L.	OF	108	376	57	88	17	0	14	53	33	.234
1993	Detroit	A.L.	OF	23	75	14	19	1	1	6	15	2	.253
1994	Detroit i-j	A.L.	OF	37	120	19	22	4	0	3	13	5	.183
1995 k						DID NOT PLAY							
1996	Cincinnati l-m-n	N.L.	OF-1B	129	415	81	119	20	0	26	83	23	.287
1997	Baltimore o	A.L.	OF	42	158	29	48	11	0	8	25	6	.304
Major League Totals			13 Yrs.	1271	4268	775	1124	180	20	239	753	335	.263
Division Series													
1997	Baltimore	A.L.	OF	3	9	0	2	0	0	0	2	0	.222
Championship Series													
1990	Cincinnatti	N.L.	OF	6	23	2	4	1	0	0	2	0	.174
1997	Baltimore	A.L.	OF-DH	6	13	1	2	0	0	1	1	0	.154
Championship Series Totals				12	36	3	6	1	0	1	3	0	.167
World Series Record													
1990	Cincinnatti	N.L.	OF	4	14	3	4	0	0	1	5	0	.286

a On disabled list from August 16 to September 1, 1984.
b On disabled list from May 3 to May 18, 1989.
c On disabled list from April 25 to May 19, 1990.
d On disabled list from June 12 to June 27 and July 31 to August 26, 1991.
e Traded to Los Angeles Dodgers with pitcher Kip Gross for pitchers Tim Belcher and John Wetteland, November 27, 1991.
f On disabled list from May 23 to June 19 and August 5 to August 25, 1992.
g Filed for free agency, November 3; re-signed with Los Angeles Dodgers, December 1, 1992.
h Traded to Detroit Tigers for player to be named, August 31; Los Angeles Dodgers acquired pitcher John DeSilva to complete trade, September 7, 1993.
i On disabled list from May 23 to July 19 and July 27 to end of 1994 season.
j Filed for free agency, October 17, 1994.
k Signed with Cincinnati Reds organization, January 2, 1996.
l On disabled list from May 26 to June 10, 1996.
m Filed for free agency, October 28, 1996.
n Signed with Baltimore Orioles, December 19, 1996.
o On disabled list from May 26 to September 15, 1997.

DAVIS, RUSSELL STUART
Born, Birmingham, Alabama, September 13, 1969.
Bats Right. Throws Right. Height, 6 feet. Weight, 170 pounds.

Year	Club	Lea	Pos	G	AB	R	H	2B	3B	HR	RBI	SB	Avg
1988	Sarasota Yankees	Gulf C.	3B	58	213	33	49	11	3	2	30	6	.230
1989	Fort Lauderdale	Fla. St.	3B	48	147	8	27	5	1	2	22	3	.184
1989	Oneonta	N.Y.-Penn.	3B	65	236	33	68	7	5	7	42	3	.288

Year	Club	Lea	Pos	G	AB	R	H	2B	3B	HR	RBI	SB	Avg
1990 Prince William .....Carolina			3B	137	510	55	127	*37	3	16	71	3	.249
1991 Albany ....Eastern			3B	135	473	57	103	23	3	8	58	3	.218
1992 Albany ....Eastern			3B	132	491	77	140	23	4	22	71	3	.285
1993 Columbus ....Int.			3B	113	424	63	108	24	1	26	83	1	.255
1994 Columbus ....Int.			3B-1B	117	416	76	115	30	2	25	69	3	.276
1994 New York ...........A.L.			3B	4	14	0	2	0	0	0	1	0	.143
1995 Columbus ....Int.			3B-1B	20	76	12	19	4	1	2	15	0	.250
1995 New York a ...........A.L.			3B-1B	40	98	14	27	5	2	2	12	0	.276
1996 Seattle b ...........A.L.			3B	51	167	24	39	9	0	5	18	2	.234
1997 Seattle c ...........A.L.			3B	119	420	57	114	29	1	20	63	6	.271
Major League Totals			4 Yrs.	214	699	95	182	43	3	27	94	8	.260
Division Series													
1995 New York ...........A.L.			3B	2	5	0	1	0	0	0	0	0	.200

a Traded to Seattle Mariners with pitcher Sterling Hitchcock for first baseman Tino Martinez, pitcher Jeff Nelson and pitcher Jim Mecir, December 7, 1995.
b On disabled list from June 8 to September 30, 1996.
c On disabled list from August 25 to September 26, 1997.

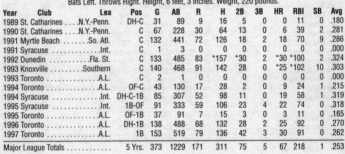

DELGADO (HERNANDEZ), CARLOS JUAN

Born, Aguadilla, Puerto Rico, June 25, 1972.
Bats Left. Throws Right. Height, 6 feet, 3 inches. Weight, 220 pounds.

Year	Club	Lea	Pos	G	AB	R	H	2B	3B	HR	RBI	SB	Avg
1989 St. Catharines ....N.Y.-Penn.			DH-C	31	89	9	16	5	0	0	11	0	.180
1990 St. Catharines ....N.Y.-Penn.			C	67	228	30	64	13	0	6	39	2	.281
1991 Myrtle Beach ....So. Atl.			C	132	441	72	126	18	2	18	70	9	.286
1991 Syracuse ....Int.			C	1	3	0	0	0	0	0	0	0	.000
1992 Dunedin ....Fla. St.			C	133	485	83	*157	*30	2	*30	*100	2	.324
1993 Knoxville ....Southern			C	140	468	91	142	28	0	*25	*102	10	.303
1993 Toronto .............A.L.			C	2	1	0	0	0	0	0	0	0	.000
1994 Toronto .............A.L.			OF-C	43	130	17	28	2	0	9	24	1	.215
1994 Syracuse ....Int.			DH-C-1B	85	307	52	98	11	0	19	58	1	.319
1995 Syracuse ....Int.			1B-OF	91	333	59	106	23	4	22	74	0	.318
1995 Toronto .............A.L.			OF-1B	37	91	7	15	3	0	3	11	0	.165
1996 Toronto .............A.L.			DH-1B	138	488	68	132	28	2	25	92	0	.270
1997 Toronto .............A.L.			1B	153	519	79	136	42	3	30	91	0	.262
Major League Totals			5 Yrs.	373	1229	171	311	75	5	67	218	1	.253

DESHIELDS, DELINO LAMONT

Born, Seaford, Delaware, January 15, 1969.
Bats Left. Throws Right. Height, 6 feet, 1 inch. Weight, 175 pounds.

Year	Club	Lea	Pos	G	AB	R	H	2B	3B	HR	RBI	SB	Avg
1987 Bradenton Expos ....Gulf C.			SS	31	111	17	24	5	2	1	4	16	.216
1987 Jamestown ......N.Y.-Penn.			SS	34	96	16	21	1	2	1	5	14	.219
1988 Rockford ....Midwest			SS	129	460	97	116	26	6	12	46	59	.252
1989 Jacksonville .....Southern			SS	93	307	55	83	10	6	3	35	37	.270
1989 Indianapolis ..........A.A.			SS	47	181	29	47	8	4	2	14	16	.260
1990 Montreal a .........N.L.			2B	129	499	69	144	28	6	4	45	42	.289
1991 Montreal ...........N.L.			2B	151	563	83	134	15	4	10	51	56	.238
1992 Montreal ...........N.L.			2B	135	530	82	155	19	8	7	56	46	.292
1993 Montreal b-c .........N.L.			2B	123	481	75	142	17	7	2	29	43	.295
1994 Los Angeles d .........N.L.			2B-SS	89	320	51	80	11	3	2	33	27	.250
1995 Los Angeles .........N.L.			2B	127	425	66	109	18	3	8	37	39	.256
1996 Los Angeles e-f .........N.L.			2B	154	581	75	130	12	8	5	41	48	.224
1997 St. Louis ...........N.L.			2B	150	572	92	169	26	*14	11	58	55	.295
Major League Totals			8 Yrs.	1058	3971	593	1063	146	53	49	350	356	.268
Division Series													
1995 Los Angeles .........N.L.			2B	3	12	1	3	0	0	0	0	0	.250
1996 Los Angeles .........N.L.			2B	2	4	0	0	0	0	0	0	0	.000
Division Series Totals				5	16	1	3	0	0	0	0	0	.188

a On disabled list from June 16 to July 12, 1990.
b On disabled list from August 12 to September 11, 1993.
c Traded to Los Angeles Dodgers for pitcher Pedro Martinez, November 19, 1993.
d On disabled list from May 26 to June 19, 1994.
e Filed for free agency, October 29, 1996.
f Signed with St. Louis Cardinals, November 20, 1996.

DIAZ, ALEXIS

Born, Brooklyn, New York, October 5, 1968.
Bats Both. Throws Right. Height, 5 feet, 11 inches. Weight, 180 pounds.

Year	Club	Lea	Pos	G	AB	R	H	2B	3B	HR	RBI	SB	Avg
1987 Kingsport	....	Appal.	SS	54	212	29	56	9	1	0	13	*34	.264
1987 Little Falls	...	N.Y.-Penn.	SS	12	47	7	16	4	1	0	8	2	.340
1988 Columbia	......	So. Atl.	SS	123	481	82	126	14	*11	0	37	28	.262
1988 St. Lucie	....	Fla. St.	SS	3	6	2	0	0	0	0	1	0	.000
1989 St. Lucie	....	Fla. St.	SS-OF	102	416	54	106	11	10	1	33	43	.255
1989 Jackson	....	Texas	2B-OF-SS	23	95	11	26	5	1	2	9	3	.274
1990 Tidewater a	....	Int.	OF-2B-SS	124	437	55	112	15	2	1	36	23	.256
1991 Indianapolis b	.....	A.A.	OF-SS-3B-2B	108	370	48	90	14	4	1	21	17	.243
1992 Denver	....	A.A.	OF-2B-SS	106	455	67	122	17	4	1	41	42	.268
1992 Milwaukee	....	A.L.	OF	22	9	5	1	0	0	0	1	3	.111
1993 New Orleans	......	A.A.	OF	16	55	8	16	2	0	0	5	7	.291
1993 Milwaukee c-d	.....	A.L.	OF	32	69	9	22	2	0	0	1	5	.319
1994 Milwaukee e-f	.....	A.L.	OF-2B	79	187	17	47	5	7	1	17	5	.251
1995 Tacoma	....	P.C.	OF	10	40	3	10	1	0	0	4	1	.250
1995 Seattle	....	A.L.	OF	103	270	44	67	14	0	3	27	18	.248
1996 Tacoma g	....	P.C.	OF-3B	44	176	19	43	5	0	0	7	5	.244
1996 Seattle h-i	....	A.L.	OF	38	79	11	19	2	0	1	5	6	.241
1997 Norfolk	....	Int.	OF	7	26	0	2	1	0	0	1	0	.077
1997 Oklahoma City j	....	A.A.	OF-2B-SS	104	423	64	122	25	2	12	49	25	.288
1997 Texas	....	A.L.	OF-1B-2B	28	90	8	20	4	0	2	12	1	.222
Major League Totals	....		6 Yrs.	302	704	94	176	27	7	7	63	38	.250
Division Series													
1995 Seattle	....	A.L.	OF	2	3	0	1	0	0	0	0	0	.333
Championship Series													
1995 Seattle	....	A.L.	OF	4	7	0	3	1	0	0	0	0	.429

a Traded by New York Mets to Montreal Expos organization with outfielder Darren Reed for outfielder Terrel Hansen and pitcher David Sommer, April 2, 1991.
b Traded by Montreal Expos to Milwaukee Brewers organization for first baseman George Canale, October 16, 1991.
c On disabled list from May 2 to August 29, 1993.
d Not offered 1994 contract, December 20; re-signed with Milwaukee Brewers, December 21, 1993.
e On disabled list from August 2 to end of 1994 season.
f Claimed on waivers by Seattle Mariners, October 14, 1994.
g On disabled list from June 5 to August 4 and August 12 to September 2, 1996.
h Filed for free agency, October 8, 1996.
i Signed with New York Mets organization, November 21, 1996.
j Signed with Texas Rangers orgainzation, May 1, 1997.

DISARCINA, GARY THOMAS

Born, Malden, Massachusetts, November 19, 1967.
Bats Right. Throws Right. Height, 6 feet, 1 inch. Weight, 178 pounds.

Year	Club	Lea	Pos	G	AB	R	H	2B	3B	HR	RBI	SB	Avg
1988 Bend	....	Northwest	SS	71	295	40	90	11	*5	2	39	7	.305
1989 Midland	....	Texas	SS	126	441	65	126	18	7	4	54	11	.286
1989 California	....	A.L.	SS	2	0	0	0	0	0	0	0	0	.000
1990 Edmonton	....	P.C.	SS	97	330	46	70	12	2	4	37	5	.212
1990 California	....	A.L.	SS-2B	18	57	8	8	1	1	0	0	1	.140
1991 Edmonton	....	P.C.	SS-2B	119	390	61	121	21	4	4	58	16	.310
1991 California	....	A.L.	SS-2B-3B	18	57	5	12	2	0	0	3	0	.211
1992 California	....	A.L.	SS	157	518	48	128	19	0	3	42	9	.247
1993 California a	....	A.L.	SS	126	416	44	99	20	1	3	45	5	.238
1994 California	....	A.L.	SS	112	389	53	101	14	2	3	33	3	.260
1995 California b	....	A.L.	SS	99	362	61	111	28	6	5	41	7	.307
1996 California	....	A.L.	SS	150	536	62	137	26	4	5	48	2	.256
1997 Anaheim	....	A.L.	SS	154	549	52	135	28	2	4	47	7	.246
Major League Totals	....		9 Yrs.	836	2884	333	731	138	16	23	259	34	.253

a On disabled list from August 27 to end of 1993 season.
b On disabled list from August 4 to September 17, 1995.

DUCEY, ROBERT THOMAS

Born, Toronto, Ontario, May 24, 1965.
Bats Left. Throws Right. Height, 6 feet, 2 inches. Weight, 185 pounds.

Year	Club	Lea	Pos	G	AB	R	H	2B	3B	HR	RBI	SB	Avg
1984 Medicine Hat	....	Pioneer	OF-1B	63	235	49	71	10	3	12	49	13	.302
1985 Florence	....	So. Atl.	OF-1B	134	529	78	133	22	2	13	86	12	.251
1986 Ventura	....	California	OF-1B	47	178	36	60	11	3	12	38	17	.337

Year Club	Lea	Pos	G	AB	R	H	2B	3B	HR	RBI	SB	Avg
1986 Knoxville . . . . .Southern	OF	88	344	49	106	22	3	11	58	7	.308	
1987 Syracuse . . . . .Int.	OF	100	359	62	102	14	10	10	60	7	.284	
1987 Toronto . . . . .A.L.	OF	34	48	12	9	1	0	1	6	2	.188	
1988 Syracuse . . . . .Int.	OF	90	317	40	81	14	4	7	42	7	.256	
1988 Toronto . . . . .A.L.	OF	27	54	15	17	4	1	0	6	1	.315	
1989 Syracuse . . . . .Int.	OF	10	29	0	3	0	1	0	3	0	.103	
1989 Toronto a . . . . .A.L.	OF	41	76	5	16	4	0	0	7	2	.211	
1990 Syracuse . . . . .Int.	OF	127	438	53	117	32	7	7	47	14	.267	
1990 Toronto . . . . .A.L.	OF	19	53	7	16	5	0	0	7	1	.302	
1991 Syracuse . . . . .Int.	OF	72	266	53	78	10	3	8	40	5	.293	
1991 Toronto . . . . .A.L.	OF	39	68	8	16	2	2	1	4	2	.235	
1992 Toronto-Calif. b-c . . . . .A.L.	OF	54	80	7	15	4	0	0	2	2	.188	
1993 Okla City . . . . .A.A.	OF	105	389	68	118	17	10	17	56	17	.303	
1993 Texas . . . . .A.L.	OF	27	85	15	24	6	3	2	9	2	.282	
1994 Texas . . . . .A.L.	OF	11	29	1	5	1	0	0	1	0	.172	
1994 Okla City d-e . . . . .A.A.	OF	115	403	69	108	27	9	17	65	9	.268	
1995 Nippon . . . . .Japan Pac.	OF	117	425	61	106	19	4	25	61	7	.249	
1996 Nippon . . . . .Japan Pac.	OF	120	427	68	105	17	5	26	59	3	.246	
1997 Tacoma f . . . . .P.C.	OF	23	74	8	24	8	0	0	11	0	.324	
1997 Seattle g-h . . . . .A.L.	OF	76	143	25	41	15	2	5	10	3	.287	
Major League Totals	9 Yrs.	328	636	95	159	42	8	9	52	15	.250	
Division Series												
1997 Seattle . . . . .A.L.	OF	2	4	0	2	0	0	0	1	0	.500	

a On disabled list from June 9 to September 2, 1989.
b Traded to California Angels with catcher Greg Myers for pitcher Mark Eichhorn, July 30, 1992.
c Refused assignment to minor leagues and became free agent, November 9; signed with Texas Rangers org December 18, 1992.
d Released by Texas Rangers, October 14, 1994.
e Signed with Nippon Ham Fighters (Japan), February 18, 1995.
f Signed with Seattle Mariners organization, January 22, 1997.
g On disabled list from August 3 to August 21, 1997.
h Re-signed with Seattle Mariners, December 11, 1997.

DUNSTON, SHAWON DONNELL

Born, Brooklyn, New York, March 21, 1963.
Bats Right. Throws Right. Height, 6 feet, 1 inch. Weight, 180 pounds.

Year Club	Lea	Pos	G	AB	R	H	2B	3B	HR	RBI	SB	Avg
1982 Sarasota Cubs . . .Gulf Coast	SS-3B	53	190	27	61	11	0	2	28	32	.321	
1983 Quad Cities a . . . . . .Midwest	SS	117	455	65	141	17	8	4	62	58	.310	
1984 Midland . . . . .Texas	SS	73	298	44	98	13	3	3	34	11	.329	
1984 Iowa . . . . .A.A.	SS	61	210	25	49	11	1	7	27	9	.233	
1985 Chicago . . . . .N.L.	SS	74	250	40	65	12	4	4	18	11	.260	
1985 Iowa . . . . .A.A.	SS	73	272	24	73	9	6	2	28	17	.268	
1986 Chicago . . . . .N.L.	SS	150	581	66	145	37	3	17	68	13	.250	
1987 Iowa . . . . .A.A.	SS	5	19	1	8	1	0	0	2	1	.421	
1987 Chicago b . . . . .N.L.	SS	95	346	40	85	18	3	5	22	12	.246	
1988 Chicago . . . . .N.L.	SS	155	575	69	143	23	6	9	56	30	.249	
1989 Chicago . . . . .N.L.	SS	138	471	52	131	20	6	9	60	19	.278	
1990 Chicago . . . . .N.L.	SS	146	545	73	143	22	8	17	66	25	.262	
1991 Chicago . . . . .N.L.	SS	142	492	59	128	22	7	12	50	21	.260	
1992 Chicago c . . . . .N.L.	SS	18	73	8	23	3	1	0	2	2	.315	
1993 Chicago d . . . . .N.L.	SS	7	10	3	4	2	0	0	2	0	.400	
1994 Chicago . . . . .N.L.	SS	88	331	38	92	19	0	11	35	3	.278	
1995 Chicago e . . . . .N.L.	SS	127	477	58	141	30	6	14	69	10	.296	
1996 San Francisco f-g-h . . .N.L.	SS	82	287	27	86	12	2	5	25	8	.300	
1997 Chicago-Pitt i-j-k . . . . . .N.L.	SS-OF	132	490	71	147	22	5	14	57	32	.300	
Major League Totals	13 Yrs.	1354	4928	604	1333	242	51	117	530	186	.270	
Championship Series												
1989 Chicago . . . . .N.L.	SS	5	19	2	6	0	0	0	0	1	.316	

a On disabled list from May 31 to June 10, 1983.
b On disabled list from June 16 to August 21, 1987.
c On disabled list from May 5 to end of 1992 season.
d On disabled list from March 29 to September 1, 1993.
e Filed for free agency, November 12, 1995. Signed with San Francisco Giants, January 8, 1996.
f On disabled list from April 24 to May 13 and August 5 to September 30, 1996.
g Filed for free agency, November 18, 1996.
h Signed with Chicago Cubs, December 2, 1996.
i On disabled list from June 9 to June 24, 1997.
j Traded to Pittsburgh Pirates for player to be named later, August 31, 1997.
k Filed for free agency, October 28, 1997.

DUNWOODY, TODD FRANKLIN
Born, Lafayette, Indiana, April 11, 1975.
Bats Left. Throws Left. Height, 6 feet, 1 inch. Weight 190 pounds.

Year Club	Lea	Pos	G	AB	R	H	2B	3B	HR	RBI	SB	Avg
1993 Marlins ....Gulf Coast	OF	31	109	13	21	2	2	0	7	5	.193
1994 Kane County ......Midwest	OF	15	45	7	5	0	0	1	1	1	.111
1994 Marlins ....Gulf Coast	OF	46	169	32	44	6	6	1	25	11	.260
1995 Kane County .....Midwest	OF	132	494	89	140	20	8	14	89	39	.283
1996 Portland ....Eastern	OF	138	552	88	153	30	6	24	93	24	.277
1997 Florida .............N.L.	OF	19	50	7	13	2	2	2	7	2	.260
1997 Charlotte ....Int.	OF	107	401	74	105	16	7	23	62	25	.262

DURHAM, RAY
Born, Charlotte, North Carolina, November 30, 1971.
Bats Both. Throws Right. Height, 5 feet, 8 inches. Weight, 170 pounds.

Year Club	Lea	Pos	G	AB	R	H	2B	3B	HR	RBI	SB	Avg
1990 Sarasota White Sox ..Gulf C.	2B	35	116	18	32	3	3	0	13	23	.276
1991 Sarasota White Sox ..Gulf C.	2B	6	23	3	7	1	0	0	4	5	.304
1991 Utica ..........N.Y.-Penn.	2B	39	142	29	36	2	7	0	17	12	.254
1992 Sarasota White Sox ..Gulf C.	DH	5	13	3	7	2	0	0	2	1	.538
1992 Sarasota a ....Fla. St.	2B	57	202	37	55	6	3	0	7	28	.272
1993 Birmingham .....Southern	2B	137	528	83	143	22	10	3	37	39	.271
1994 Nashville ..............A.A.	2B	133	527	89	156	33	*12	16	66	34	.296
1995 Chicago ..............A.L.	2B	125	471	68	121	27	6	7	51	18	.257
1996 Chicago ..............A.L.	2B	156	557	79	153	33	5	10	65	30	.275
1997 Chicago ..............A.L.	2B	155	634	106	172	27	5	11	53	33	.271
Major League Totals	3 Yrs.	436	1662	253	446	87	16	28	169	81	.268

a On disabled list from June 16 to July 9, 1992.

DYE, JERMAINE TERRELL
Born, Oakland, California, January 28, 1974.
Bats Right. Throws Right. Height, 6 feet, 4 inches. Weight 210 pounds.

Year Club	Lea	Pos	G	AB	R	H	2B	3B	HR	RBI	SB	Avg
1993 Braves ....Gulf Coast	OF-3B	31	124	17	43	14	0	0	27	5	.347
1993 Danville ....Appal.	OF	25	94	6	26	6	1	2	12	4	.277
1994 Macon ....So.Atl.	OF	135	506	73	151	41	1	15	98	19	.298
1995 Greenville ....Southern	OF	104	403	50	115	26	4	15	71	4	.285
1996 Richmond ....Int.	OF	36	142	25	33	7	1	6	19	3	.232
1996 Atlanta ..............N.L.	OF	98	292	32	82	16	0	12	37	1	.281
1997 Omaha ..............A.A.	OF	39	144	21	44	6	0	10	25	0	.306
1997 Kansas City a-b .......A.L.	OF	75	263	26	62	14	0	7	22	2	.236
Major League Totals	2 Yrs.	173	555	58	144	30	0	19	59	3	.259
Division Series											
1996 Atlanta ..............N.L.	OF	3	11	1	2	0	0	1	1	1	.182
Championship Series											
1996 Atlanta ..............N.L.	OF	7	28	2	6	1	0	0	4	0	.214
World Series Record											
1996 Atlanta ..............N.L.	OF	5	17	0	2	0	0	0	1	0	.118

a Traded to Kansas City Royals with pitcher Jamie Walker for infielder Keith Lockhart and outfielder Michael Tucker, March 27, 1997.

b On disabled list from April 17 to May 3 and July 3 to August 13, 1997.

DYKSTRA, LEONARD KYLE
Born, Santa Ana, California, February 10, 1963.
Bats Left. Throws Left. Height, 5 feet, 10 inches. Weight, 195 pounds.

Year Club	Lea	Pos	G	AB	R	H	2B	3B	HR	RBI	SB	Avg
1981 Shelby ....So. Atl.	OF-SS	48	157	34	41	7	2	0	18	15	.261
1982 Shelby ....So. Atl.	OF	120	413	95	120	13	7	3	38	77	.291
1983 Lynchburg ....Carolina	OF-	*136	*525	*132	*188	24	*14	8	81	*105	*.358
1984 Jackson ....Texas	OF	131	501	*100	138	25	7	6	52	53	.275
1985 Tidewater ....Int.	OF	58	229	44	71	8	6	1	25	26	.310
1985 New York ............N.L.	OF	83	236	40	60	9	3	1	19	15	.254
1986 New York ............N.L.	OF	147	431	77	127	27	7	8	45	31	.295
1987 New York ............N.L.	OF	132	431	86	123	37	3	10	43	27	.285
1988 New York ............N.L.	OF	126	429	57	116	19	3	8	33	30	.270

45

Year	Club	Lea	Pos	G	AB	R	H	2B	3B	HR	RBI	SB	Avg
1989 N.Y.-Philadelphia a	.....N.L.	OF	146	511	66	121	32	4	7	32	30	.237
1990 Philadelphia	..........N.L.	OF	149	590	106	*192	35	3	9	60	33	.325
1991 Philadelphia b	..........N.L.	OF	63	246	48	73	13	5	3	12	24	.297
1992 Philadelphia c	........N.L.	OF	85	345	53	104	18	0	6	39	30	.301
1993 Philadelphia	..........N.L.	OF	161	*637	*143	*194	44	6	19	66	37	.305
1994 Scranton	......Int.	OF	3	7	1	2	1	1	0	1	0	.286
1994 Philadelphia d	........N.L.	OF	84	315	68	86	26	5	5	24	15	.273
1995 Philadelphia e	......N.L.	OF	62	254	37	67	15	1	2	18	10	.264
1996 Philadelphia f	........N.L.	OF	40	134	21	35	6	3	3	13	3	.261
1997 Philadelphia g	N.L.	INJURED—Did Not Play										
Major League Totals	....	12 Yrs.	1278	4559	802	1298	281	43	81	404	285	.285
Championship Series												
1986 New York	............N.L.	OF	6	23	3	7	1	1	1	3	1	.304
1988 New York	............N.L.	OF	7	14	6	6	3	0	1	3	0	.429
1993 Philadelphia	..........N.L.	OF	6	25	5	7	1	0	2	2	0	.280
Championship Series Totals	....	19	62	14	20	5	1	4	8	1	.323
World Series Record												
1986 New York	............N.L.	OF	7	27	4	8	0	0	2	3	0	.296
1993 Philadelphia	..........N.L.	OF	6	23	9	8	1	0	4	8	4	.348
World Series Totals	....	13	50	13	16	1	0	6	11	4	.320

a Traded to Philadelphia Phillies with pitcher Roger McDowell and player to be named for outfielder Juan Samuel, June 18; Philadelphia acquired pitcher Tom Edens to complete trade, July 28, 1989.
b On disabled list from May 6 to July 15 and August 27 to end of 1991 season.
c On disabled list from April 4 to April 24, June 29 to July 16 and August 16 to end of 1992 season.
d On disabled list from June 18 to July 23, 1994.
e On disabled list from June 4 to June 24 and July 28 to October 2, 1995.
f On disabled list from May 19 to September 30, 1996.
g On disabled list entire 1997 season.

EASLEY, JACINTO DAMION

Born, New York, New York, November 11, 1969.
Bats Right. Throws Right. Height, 5 feet, 11 inches. Weight, 185 pounds.

Year	Club	Lea	Pos	G	AB	R	H	2B	3B	HR	RBI	SB	Avg
1989 Bend	.......Northwest	SS	36	131	34	39	5	1	4	21	9	.298
1990 Quad City	.....Midwest	SS-3B	103	365	59	100	19	3	10	56	25	.274
1991 Midland	.........Texas	SS	127	452	73	115	24	4	6	57	23	.254
1992 Edmonton	..........P.C.	SS-3B	108	429	61	124	18	3	3	44	26	.289
1992 California	........A.L.	3B-SS	47	151	14	39	5	0	1	12	9	.258
1993 California a	......A.L.	2B-3B	73	230	33	72	13	2	2	22	6	.313
1994 California b	........A.L.	3B-2B	88	316	41	68	16	1	6	30	4	.215
1995 California	........A.L.	2B-SS	114	357	35	77	14	2	4	35	5	.216
1996 Midland	.........Texas	3B-SS	4	14	1	6	2	0	0	2	1	.429
1996 Vancouver c	.......P.C.	SS-2B-3B	12	48	13	15	2	1	2	8	4	.313
1996 California-Detroit d	.A.L.	SS-2B-3B-OF	49	112	14	30	2	0	4	17	3	.268
1997 Detroit	...........A.L.	2B-SS	151	527	97	139	37	3	22	72	28	.264
Major League Totals	....	6 Yrs.	522	1693	234	425	87	8	39	188	55	.251

a On disabled list from June 19 to July 4 and July 28 to end of 1993 season.
b On disabled list from May 30 to June 17, 1994.
c On disabled list from April 1 to May 10, 1996.
d Traded to Detroit Tigers for pitcher Greg Gohr, July 31, 1996.

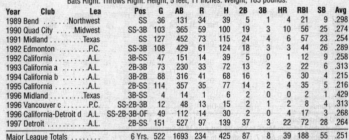

EDMONDS, JAMES PATRICK

Born, Fullerton, California, June 27, 1970.
Bats Left. Throws Left. Height, 6 feet, 1 inch. Weight, 190 pounds.

Year	Club	Lea	Pos	G	AB	R	H	2B	3B	HR	RBI	SB	Avg
1988 Bend	...........Northwest	OF	35	122	23	27	4	0	0	13	4	.221
1989 Quad City a	.......Midwest	OF	31	92	11	24	4	0	1	4	1	.261
1990 Palm Springs	........California	OF	91	314	36	92	18	6	3	56	5	.293
1991 Palm Springs b-c	..California	OF-1B	60	187	28	55	15	1	2	27	2	.294
1992 Midland	.............Texas	OF	70	246	42	77	15	2	8	32	3	.313
1992 Edmonton	..........P.C.	OF	50	194	37	58	15	2	6	36	3	.299
1993 Vancouver d	.........P.C.	OF	95	356	59	112	28	4	9	74	6	.315
1993 California	............A.L.	OF	18	61	5	15	4	1	0	4	0	.246
1994 California	............A.L.	OF-1B	94	289	35	79	13	1	5	37	4	.273
1995 California	...........A.L.	OF	141	558	120	162	30	4	33	107	1	.290
1996 Lk Elsinore e	.....California	OF	5	15	4	6	2	0	1	4	0	.400

Year	Club	Lea	Pos	G	AB	R	H	2B	3B	HR	RBI	SB	Avg
1996 California	A.L.		OF	114	431	73	131	28	3	27	66	4	.304
1997 Anaheim f	A.L.		OF-1B	133	502	82	146	27	0	26	80	5	.291
Major League Totals		5 Yrs.	500	1841	315	533	102	9	91	294	14	.290

a On disabled list from June 19 to end of 1989 season.
b Record of 0-0 in one game as pitcher.
c On disabled list from April 10 to May 7 and July 23 to end of 1991 season.
d On disabled list from June 29 to July 19, 1993.
e On disabled list from May 26 to June 10 and June 12 to July 18, 1996.
f On disabled list from July 31 to August 16, 1997.

EISENREICH, JAMES MICHAEL
Born, St. Cloud, Minnesota, April 18, 1959.
Bats Left. Throws Left. Height, 5 feet, 11 inches. Weight, 200 pounds.

Year	Club	Lea	Pos	G	AB	R	H	2B	3B	HR	RBI	SB	Avg
1980 Elizabethon ...	.Appalachian	OF	67	258	47	77	12	*4	3	41	12	.298
1980 Wis. Rapids	.Midwest	DH	5	16	4	7	0	0	0	5	1	.438
1981 Wis. Rapids	.Midwest	OF	*134	489	101	*152	*27	0	23	99	9	.311
1982 Minnesota a	.A.L.	OF	34	99	10	30	6	0	2	9	0	.303
1983 Minnesota b	.A.L.	OF	2	7	1	2	1	0	0	0	0	.286
1984 Minnesota c	.A.L.	OF	12	32	1	7	1	0	0	3	2	.219
1985–1986						Out of Organized Baseball						
1987 Memphis d	.Southern	DH	70	275	60	105	36	*10	11	57	13	.382
1987 Kansas City e	.A.L.	DH	44	105	10	25	8	2	4	21	1	.238
1988 Omaha	.A.A.	OF	36	142	28	41	8	3	4	14	9	.289
1988 Kansas City	.A.L.	OF	82	202	26	44	8	1	1	19	9	.218
1989 Kansas City f	.A.L.	OF	134	475	64	139	33	7	9	59	27	.293
1990 Kansas City	.A.L.	OF	142	496	61	139	29	7	5	51	12	.280
1991 Kansas City g	.A.L.	OF-1B	135	375	47	113	22	3	2	47	5	.301
1992 Kansas City h-i	.A.L.	OF	113	353	31	95	13	3	2	28	11	.269
1993 Philadelphia j	.N.L.	OF-1B	153	362	51	115	17	4	7	54	5	.318
1994 Philadelphia	.N.L.	OF	104	290	42	87	15	4	4	43	6	.300
1995 Philadelphia k	.N.L.	OF	129	377	46	119	22	2	10	55	10	.316
1996 Philadelphia l-m	.N.L.	OF	113	338	45	122	24	3	3	41	11	.361
1997 Florida	.N.L.	OF-1B	120	293	36	82	19	1	2	34	0	.280
Major League Totals		14 Yrs.	1317	3804	471	1119	218	37	51	464	99	.294
Division Series												
1997 Florida	.N.L.	PH	2	0	0	0	0	0	0	0	0	.000
Championship Series												
1993 Philadelphia	.N.L.	OF	6	15	0	2	1	0	0	1	0	.133
1997 Florida	.N.L.	OF	1	3	0	0	0	0	0	0	0	.000
Championship Series Totals			7	18	0	2	1	0	0	1	0	.111
World Series Record												
1993 Philadelphia	.N.L.	OF	6	26	3	6	0	0	1	7	0	.231
1997 Florida	.N.L.	1B-DH	5	8	1	4	0	0	1	3	0	.500
World Series Totals			11	34	4	10	0	0	2	10	0	.294

a On disabled list from May 6 to May 28 and June 18 to September 1, 1982.
b On disabled list from April 7; transferred to voluntarily retired list, May 27 to end of 1983 season.
c On disabled list from April 26 to May 18, 1984; on voluntarily retired list from June 4, 1984 to September 29, 1986.
d Claimed on waivers by Kansas City Royals, October 2, 1986.
e On disabled list from August 25 to September 9, 1987.
f On disabled list from July 22 to August 6, 1989.
g Filed for free agency, November 11; re-signed with Kansas City Royals, December 19, 1991.
h On disabled list from August 12 to September 7, 1992.
i Filed for free agency, October 30, 1992; signed with Philadelphia Phillies, January 19, 1993.
j Filed for free agency, October 28; re-signed with Philadelphia Phillies, November 24, 1993.
k Filed for free agency, November 12, 1995, re-signed with Philadelphia Phillies, December 7, 1995.
l Filed for free agency, November 18, 1996.
m Signed with Florida Marlins, December 3, 1996.

ELSTER, KEVIN DANIEL C.
Born, San Pedro, California, August 3, 1964.
Bats Right. Throws Right. Height, 6 feet, 2 inches. Weight, 200 pounds.

Year	Club	Lea	Pos	G	AB	R	H	2B	3B	HR	RBI	SB	Avg
1984 Little Falls	.N.Y.-Penn.	SS	71	257	35	66	7	3	3	35	13	.257
1985 Lynchburg	.Carolina	SS	59	224	41	66	9	0	7	26	8	.295
1985 Jackson a	.Texas	SS	59	214	30	55	13	0	2	22	2	.257

47

Year Club	Lea	Pos	G	AB	R	H	2B	3B	HR	RBI	SB	Avg
1986 Jackson ....Texas	Texas	SS	127	435	69	117	19	3	2	52	7	.269
1986 New York ...........N.L.	N.L.	SS	19	30	3	5	1	0	0	0	0	.167
1987 Tidewater ....Int.	Int.	SS	134	*549	83	*170	33	7	8	74	7	.310
1987 New York ...........N.L.	N.L.	SS	5	10	1	4	2	0	0	1	0	.400
1988 New York ...........N.L.	N.L.	SS	149	406	41	87	11	1	9	37	2	.214
1989 New York ...........N.L.	N.L.	SS	151	458	52	106	25	2	10	55	4	.231
1990 New York b .........N.L.	N.L.	SS	92	314	36	65	20	1	9	45	2	.207
1991 New York c .........N.L.	N.L.	SS	115	348	33	84	16	2	6	36	2	.241
1992 New York d-e .......N.L.	N.L.	SS	6	18	0	4	0	0	0	0	0	.222
1993 San Antonio f-g ......Texas	Texas	SS	10	39	5	11	2	1	0	7	0	.282
1994 Tampa ....Fla. St.	Fla. St.	2B-3B	3	11	2	2	1	0	0	2	0	.182
1994 Albany ....Eastern	Eastern	SS-3B-2B	41	135	19	33	7	0	2	21	2	.244
1994 New York h ..........A.L.	A.L.	SS	7	20	0	0	0	0	0	0	0	.000
1995 New York ...........A.L.	A.L.	SS-2B	10	17	1	2	1	0	0	0	0	.118
1995 Omaha ............A.A.	A.A.	SS	11	42	5	10	4	0	0	6	0	.238
1995 Scranton-WB ....Int.	Int.	SS	5	17	2	5	3	0	0	2	0	.294
1995 Philadelphia .........N.L.	N.L.	SS-1B-3B	26	53	10	11	4	1	1	9	0	.208
1996 Texas i-j-k .........A.L.	A.L.	SS	157	515	79	130	32	2	24	99	4	.252
1997 Pittsburgh l-m-n .......N.L.	N.L.	SS	39	138	14	31	6	2	7	25	0	.225
Major League Totals		11 Yrs.	776	2327	270	529	118	11	66	307	14	.227
Division Series												
1996 Texas ..............A.L.	A.L.	SS	4	12	2	4	2	0	0	0	1	.333
Championship Series												
1986 New York ...........N.L.	N.L.	SS	4	3	0	0	0	0	0	0	0	.000
1988 New York ...........N.L.	N.L.	SS	5	8	1	2	1	0	0	1	0	.250
Championship Series Totals			9	11	1	2	1	0	0	1	0	.182
World Series Record												
1986 New York ...........N.L.	N.L.	SS	1	1	0	0	0	0	0	0	0	.000

a On disabled list from August 11 to end of 1985 season.
b On disabled list from August 4 to end of 1990 season.
c On disabled list from May 6 to May 21, 1991.
d On disabled list from April 13 to end of 1992 season.
e Not offered 1993 contract, December 18, 1992, signed with Los Angeles Dodgers organization, January 12, 1993.
f Became free agent, October 15, 1993, signed with San Diego Padres organization, January 5, 1994.
g Released by San Diego Padres, March 27, signed with New York Yankees organization, April 2, 1994.
h On disabled list from July 7 to end of 1994 season.
i Signed with Texas Rangers organization, January 16, 1996.
j Filed for free agency, October 31, 1996.
k Signed with Pittsburgh Pirates, December 19, 1996.
l On disabled list from May 17 to September 29, 1997.
m Filed for free agency, October 28, 1997.
n Signed with Texas Rangers, December 8, 1997.

ENCARNACION, ANGELO BENJAMIN

Born, Santo Domingo, Dominican Republic, April 18, 1973.
Bats Right. Throws Right. Height, 5 feet, 8 inches. Weight, 180 pounds.

Year Club	Lea	Pos	G	AB	R	H	2B	3B	HR	RBI	SB	Avg
1991 Welland ........N.Y.-Penn.	N.Y.-Penn.	C	50	181	21	46	3	2	0	15	4	.254
1992 Augusta ....So. Atl.	So. Atl.	C	94	314	39	80	14	3	1	29	2	.255
1993 Salem ....Carolina	Carolina	C-OF	70	238	20	61	12	1	3	24	1	.256
1993 Buffalo ..............A.A.	A.A.	C	3	9	1	3	0	0	0	2	0	.333
1994 Carolina ....Southern	Southern	C	67	227	26	66	17	0	3	32	2	.291
1995 Calgary .............P.C.	P.C.	C	21	80	8	20	3	0	1	6	1	.250
1995 Pittsburgh ...........N.L.	N.L.	C	58	159	18	36	7	2	2	10	1	.226
1996 Calgary .............P.C.	P.C.	C	75	263	38	84	18	0	4	31	6	.319
1996 Pittsburgh ...........N.L.	N.L.	C	7	22	3	7	2	0	0	1	0	.318
1997 Las Vegas ...........P.C.	P.C.	C-OF	79	253	27	62	12	1	3	23	1	.245
1997 Anaheim a ............A.L.	A.L.	C	11	17	2	7	1	0	1	4	2	.412
Major League Totals		3 Yrs.	76	198	23	50	10	2	3	15	3	.253

a Traded to San Diego Padres with outfielder Trey Beamon for outfielder Mark Smith and pitcher Hal Garrett, March 29, 1997.

ENCARNACION, JUAN DE DIOS

Born, Las Matas De Faran, Dominican Republic, March 8, 1976.
Bats Right. Throws Right. Height, 6 feet, 2 inches. Weight 160 pounds.

Year Club	Lea	Pos	G	AB	R	H	2B	3B	HR	RBI	SB	Avg
1994 Fayetteville ....So. Atl.	So. Atl.	OF	24	83	6	16	1	1	1	4	1	.193
1994 Bristol ....Appal.	Appal.	OF	54	197	16	49	7	1	4	31	9	.249
1994 Lakeland ....Fla. St.	Fla. St.	OF	3	6	1	2	0	0	0	0	0	.333

Year	Club	Lea	Pos	G	AB	R	H	2B	3B	HR	RBI	SB	Avg
1995 Fayettevlle	So. Atl.	OF	124	457	62	129	31	7	16	72	5	.282
1996 Lakeland	Fla. St.	OF	131	499	54	120	31	2	15	58	11	.240
1997 Jacksnville	Southern	OF	131	493	91	159	31	4	26	90	17	.323
1997 Detroit	A.L.	OF	11	33	3	7	1	1	1	5	3	.212

ERSTAD, DARIN CHARLES
Born, Jamestown, North Dakota, June 4, 1974.
Bats Left. Throws Left. Height, 6 feet, 2 inches. Weight, 195 pounds.

Year	Club	Lea	Pos	G	AB	R	H	2B	3B	HR	RBI	SB	Avg
1995 Angels	Arizona	OF	4	18	2	10	1	0	0	1	1	.556
1995 Lk Elsinore	California	OF	25	113	24	41	7	3	5	24	3	.363
1996 Vancouver	P.C.	OF-1B	85	351	63	107	22	5	6	41	11	.305
1996 California	A.L.	OF	57	208	34	59	5	1	4	20	3	.284
1997 Anaheim	A.L.	1B-OF	139	539	99	161	34	4	16	77	23	.299
Major League Totals			2 Yrs.	196	747	133	220	39	5	20	97	26	.295

ESTALELLA, ROBERT M. (BOBBY)
Born, Hialeah, Fla., August 23, 1974.
Bats Right. Throws Right. Height, 6 feet, 1 inch. Weight, 195 pounds.

Year	Club	Lea	Pos	G	AB	R	H	2B	3B	HR	RBI	SB	Avg
1993 Martinsvlle	Appal.	C	35	122	14	36	11	0	3	19	0	.295
1993 Clearwater	Fla.St.	C	11	35	4	8	0	0	0	4	0	.229
1994 Spartanburg	So.Atl.	C	86	299	34	65	19	1	9	41	0	.217
1994 Clearwater	Fla.St.	C	13	46	3	12	1	0	2	9	0	.261
1995 Clearwater	Fla.St.	C	117	404	61	105	24	1	15	58	0	.260
1995 Reading	Eastern	C	10	34	5	8	1	0	2	9	0	.235
1996 Reading	Eastern	C	111	365	48	89	14	2	23	72	2	.244
1996 Scranton-WB	Int.	C	11	36	7	9	3	0	3	8	0	.250
1996 Philadelphia	N.L.	C	7	17	5	6	0	0	2	4	1	.353
1997 Scranton-W.B.	Int.	C	123	433	63	101	32	0	16	65	3	.233
1997 Philadelphia	N.L.	C	13	29	9	10	1	0	4	9	0	.345
Major League Totals			2 Yrs.	20	46	14	16	1	0	6	13	1	.348

EUSEBIO, RAUL ANTONIO BARE
Born, San Jose de Los Llamos, Dominican Republic, April 27, 1967.
Bats Right. Throws Right. Height, 6 feet, 2 inches. Weight, 180 pounds.

Year	Club	Lea	Pos	G	AB	R	H	2B	3B	HR	RBI	SB	Avg
1985 Sarasota Astros	Gulf C.	C	1	1	0	0	0	0	0	0	0	.000
1986	....		Played in Dominican Summer League										
1987 Sarasota Astros	Gulf C.	C-1B	42	125	26	26	1	2	1	15	8	.208
1988 Osceola	Fla. St.	C-OF	118	392	45	96	6	3	0	40	20	.245
1989 Columbus	Southern	C	65	203	20	38	6	1	0	18	7	.187
1989 Osceola	Fla. St.	C	52	175	22	50	6	3	0	30	5	.286
1990 Columbus a	Southern	C	92	318	36	90	18	0	4	37	6	.283
1991 Tucson	P.C.	C	5	20	5	8	1	0	0	2	1	.400
1991 Jackson	Texas	C	66	222	27	58	8	3	2	31	3	.261
1991 Houston	N.L.	C	10	19	4	2	1	0	0	0	0	.105
1992 Jackson	Texas	C	94	339	33	104	9	3	5	44	1	.307
1993 Tucson b	P.C.	C	78	281	39	91	20	1	1	43	1	.324
1994 Houston	N.L.	C	55	159	18	47	9	1	5	30	0	.296
1995 Houston	N.L.	C	113	368	46	110	21	1	6	58	0	.299
1996 Tucson c	P.C.	C	15	53	8	22	4	0	0	14	0	.415
1996 Houston	N.L.	C	58	152	15	41	7	2	1	19	0	.270
1997 Houston	N.L.	C	60	164	12	45	2	0	1	18	0	.274
Major League Totals			5 Yrs.	296	862	95	245	40	4	13	125	0	.284
Division Series													
1997 Houston	N.L.	C	1	3	1	2	0	0	0	0	1	.667

a On disabled list from August 5 to end of 1990 season.
b On disabled list from August 24 to end of 1993 season.
c On disabled list from May 8 to June 17 and June 22 to August 7, 1996.

EVERETT, CARL EDWARD

Born, Tampa, Florida, June 3, 1970.
Bats Both. Throws Right. Height, 6 feet. Weight, 190 pounds.

Year Club	Lea	Pos	G	AB	R	H	2B	3B	HR	RBI	SB	Avg
1990 Tampa Yankees	Gulf C.	OF	48	185	28	48	8	5	1	14	15	.259
1991 Greensboro	So. Atl.	OF	123	468	96	127	18	0	4	40	28	.271
1992 Fort Lauderdale	Fla. St.	OF	46	183	30	42	8	2	2	9	11	.230
1992 Prince William a	Carolina	OF	6	22	7	7	0	0	4	9	1	.318
1993 High Desert	California	OF	59	253	48	73	12	6	10	52	24	.289
1993 Florida	N.L.	OF	11	19	0	2	0	0	0	0	1	.105
1993 Edmonton	P.C.	OF	35	136	28	42	13	4	6	16	12	.309
1994 Edmonton	P.C.	OF	78	321	63	108	17	2	11	47	16	.336
1994 Florida b-c	N.L.	OF	16	51	7	11	1	0	2	6	4	.216
1995 Norfolk	Int.	OF-SS	67	260	52	78	16	4	6	35	12	.300
1995 New York d	N.Y.	OF	79	289	48	75	13	1	12	54	2	.260
1996 New York d	N.L.	OF	101	192	29	46	8	1	1	16	6	.240
1997 New York e	N.L.	OF	142	443	58	110	28	3	14	57	17	.248
Major League Totals		5 Yrs.	349	994	142	244	50	5	29	133	30	.245

a Selected by Florida Marlins from New York Yankees organization in expansion draft, November 17, 1992.
b On disabled list from July 23 to August 10, 1994.
c Traded to New York Mets for second baseman Quilvio Veras, November 29, 1994.
d On disabled list from April 12 to April 27, 1996.
e Traded to Houston Astros for pitcher John Hudek, December 22, 1997.

FABREGAS, JORGE

Born, Miami, Florida, March 13, 1970.
Bats Left. Throws Right. Height, 6 feet, 3 inches. Weight, 205 pounds.

Year Club	Lea	Pos	G	AB	R	H	2B	3B	HR	RBI	SB	Avg
1992 Palm Springs	California	C	70	258	35	73	13	0	0	40	0	.283
1993 Midland	Texas	C	113	409	63	118	26	3	6	56	1	.289
1993 Vancouver	P.C.	C	4	13	1	3	1	0	0	1	0	.231
1994 Vancouver	P.C.	C	66	211	17	47	6	1	1	24	1	.223
1994 California	A.L.	C	43	127	12	36	3	0	0	16	2	.283
1995 Vancouver	P.C.	C	21	73	9	18	3	0	4	10	0	.247
1995 California	A.L.	C	73	227	24	56	10	0	1	22	0	.247
1996 Vancouver	P.C.	DH-C-1B	10	37	4	11	3	0	0	5	0	.297
1996 California	A.L.	C	90	254	18	73	6	0	2	26	0	.287
1997 Anaheim-Chicago a-b	A.L.	C-1B	121	360	33	93	11	1	7	51	1	.258
Major League Totals		4 Yrs.	327	968	87	258	30	1	10	115	3	.267

a Traded to Chicago White Sox with pitcher Chuck McElroy for outfielder Tony Phillips and catcher Chad Kreuter, May 18, 1997.
b Selected in expansion draft by Arizona Diamondbacks, November 18, 1997.

FERNANDEZ, OCTAVIO ANTONIO (TONY)

Born, San Pedro de Macoris, Dominican Republic, June 30, 1962.
Bats Both. Throws Right. Height, 6 feet, 2 inch. Weight, 175 pounds.

Year Club	Lea	Pos	G	AB	R	H	2B	3B	HR	RBI	SB	Avg
1980 Kinston	Carolina	SS	62	187	28	52	6	2	0	12	7	.278
1981 Kinston	Carolina	SS	75	280	57	89	10	6	1	13	15	.318
1981 Syracuse a	Int.	SS	31	115	13	32	6	2	1	9	9	.278
1982 Syracuse	Int.	SS	134	523	78	158	21	6	4	56	22	.302
1983 Syracuse	Int.	SS	117	437	65	131	18	6	5	38	35	.300
1983 Toronto	A.L.	SS	15	34	5	9	1	1	0	2	0	.265
1984 Toronto	A.L.	SS-3B	88	233	29	63	5	3	3	19	5	.270
1984 Syracuse	Int.	SS	26	94	12	24	1	0	0	6	1	.255
1985 Toronto	A.L.	SS	161	564	71	163	31	10	2	51	13	.289
1986 Toronto	A.L.	SS	*163	*687	91	213	33	9	10	65	25	.310
1987 Toronto	A.L.	SS	146	578	90	186	29	8	5	67	32	.322
1988 Toronto	A.L.	SS	154	648	76	186	41	4	5	70	15	.287
1989 Toronto b	A.L.	SS	140	573	64	147	25	9	11	64	22	.257
1990 Toronto c	A.L.	SS	161	635	84	175	27	*17	4	66	26	.276
1991 San Diego	N.L.	SS	145	558	81	152	27	5	4	38	23	.272
1992 San Diego d	N.L.	SS	155	622	84	171	32	4	4	37	20	.275
1993 New York e	N.L.	SS	48	173	20	39	5	2	1	14	6	.225
1993 Toronto f	A.L.	SS	94	353	45	108	18	9	4	50	15	.306
1994 Cincinnati g	N.L.	3B-SS-2B	104	366	50	102	18	6	8	50	12	.279
1995 New York h-i-j	A.L.	SS-2B	108	384	57	94	20	2	5	45	6	.245
1997 Cleveland k	A.L.	2B-SS	120	409	55	117	21	1	11	44	6	.286
Major League Totals		14 Yrs.	1802	6817	902	1925	333	90	77	682	226	.282

Year	Club	Lea	Pos	G	AB	R	H	2B	3B	HR	RBI	SB	Avg
Division Series													
1995 New York	A.L.	SS	5	21	0	5	2	0	0	0	0	.238
1997 Cleveland	A.L.	2B	4	11	0	2	1	0	0	4	0	.182
Division Series Totals			9	32	0	7	3	0	0	4	0	.219
Championship Series													
1985 Toronto	A.L.	SS	7	24	2	8	2	0	0	2	0	.333
1989 Toronto	A.L.	SS	5	20	6	7	3	0	0	1	5	.350
1993 Toronto	A.L.	SS	6	22	1	7	0	0	0	1	0	.318
1997 Cleveland	A.L.	2B	5	14	1	5	1	0	1	2	0	.357
Championship Series Totals			23	80	10	27	6	0	1	6	5	.338
World Series Record													
1993 Toronto	A.L.	SS	6	21	2	7	1	0	0	9	0	.333
1997 Cleveland	A.L.	2B	5	17	1	8	1	0	0	4	0	.481
World Series Totals			11	38	3	15	2	0	0	13	0	.395

a On disabled list from August 10 to August 27, 1981.
b On disabled list from April 8 to May 2, 1989.
c Traded to San Diego Padres with first baseman Fred McGriff for outfielder Joe Carter and second baseman Roberto Alomar, December 5, 1990.
d Traded to New York Mets for pitcher Wally Whitehurst, outfielder D. J. Dozier and player to be named, October 26; San Diego Padres acquired catcher Raul Casanova to complete trade, December 7, 1992.
e Traded to Toronto Blue Jays for outfielder Darrin Jackson, June 11, 1993.
f Filed for free agency, November 3, 1993; signed with Cincinnati Reds, March 8, 1994.
g Refused assignment to minor leagues and became free agent, October 20; signed with New York Yankees, December 15, 1994.
h On disabled list from May 21 to June 8, 1995.
i On disabled list entire 1996 season, released by New York Yankees.
j Signed with Cleveland Indians, December 26, 1996.
k Filed for free agency, October 30, 1997.
l Signed with Toronto Blue Jays, December 8, 1997.

FIELDER, CECIL GRANT

Born, Los Angeles, California, September 21, 1963.
Bats Right. Throws Right. Height, 6 feet, 3 inches. Weight, 250 pounds.

Year	Club	Lea	Pos	G	AB	R	H	2B	3B	HR	RBI	SB	Avg
1982 Butte a	Pioneer	1B	69	273	73	88	*28	0	*20	68	3	.322
1983 Florence	So. Atl.	1B	140	500	81	156	28	2	16	94	2	.312
1983 Kingston	Carolina	1B	61	222	42	63	12	1	19	49	2	.284
1984 Knoxville	Southern	1B	64	236	33	60	12	2	9	44	0	.254
1985 Knoxville	Southern	1B	96	361	52	106	26	2	18	81	0	.294
1985 Toronto	A.L.	1B	30	74	6	23	4	0	4	16	0	.311
1986 Toronto	A.L.	1B-3B-OF	34	83	7	13	2	0	4	13	0	.157
1986 Syracuse	Int.	OF-1B	88	325	47	91	13	3	18	68	0	.280
1987 Toronto	A.L.	1B-3B	82	175	30	47	7	1	14	32	0	.269
1988 Toronto	A.L.	1B	74	174	24	40	6	1	9	23	0	.230
1989 Hanshin Tigers c	Jpn. Cent.	1B	106	384	60	116	11	0	38	81	0	.302
1990 Detroit	A.L.	1B	159	573	104	159	25	1	*51	*132	0	.277
1991 Detroit	A.L.	1B	*162	624	102	163	25	0	*44	*133	0	.261
1992 Detroit	A.L.	1B	155	594	80	145	22	0	35	*124	0	.244
1993 Detroit	A.L.	1B	154	573	80	153	23	0	30	117	0	.267
1994 Detroit	A.L.	1B	109	425	67	110	16	2	28	90	0	.259
1995 Detroit	A.L.	1B	136	494	70	120	18	1	31	82	0	.243
1996 Detroit-New York d	A.L.	1B-DH	160	591	85	149	20	0	39	117	2	.252
1997 New York e-f-g	A.L.	DH-1B	98	361	40	94	15	0	13	61	0	.260
Major League Totals		12 Yrs.	1353	4741	695	1216	183	6	302	940	2	.256
Division Series													
1996 New York	A.L.	DH	3	11	2	4	0	0	1	4	0	.364
1997 New York	A.L.	DH	2	8	0	1	0	0	0	1	0	.125
Division Series Totals			5	19	2	5	0	0	1	5	0	.263
Championship Series													
1996 New York	A.L.	DH	5	18	3	3	0	0	2	8	0	.167
World Series													
1996 New York	A.L.	1B-DH	6	23	1	9	2	0	0	2	0	.391

a Traded by Kansas City Royals to Toronto Blue Jays organization for outfielder Leon Roberts, February 4, 1983.
b Sold to Hanshin Tigers of Japanese Central League, December 22, 1988.
c Signed with Detroit Tigers, January 16, 1990.
d Traded to New York Yankees for outfielder Ruben Sierra and pitcher Matt Drews, July 31, 1996.
e On disabled list from July 16 to September 16, 1997.
f Filed for free agency, October 27, 1997.
g Signed as free agent by Anaheim Angels, December 20, 1997.

51

FINLEY, STEVEN ALLEN
Born, Union City, Tennessee, May 12, 1965.
Bats Left. Throws Left. Height, 6 feet, 2 inches. Weight, 180 pounds.

Year	Club	Lea	Pos	G	AB	R	H	2B	3B	HR	RBI	SB	Avg
1987 Newark	N.Y.-Penn.	OF	54	222	40	65	13	2	3	33	26	.293
1987 Hagerstown	Carolina	OF	15	65	9	22	3	2	1	5	7	.338
1988 Hagerstown	Carolina	OF	8	28	2	6	2	0	0	3	4	.214
1988 Charlotte	Southern	OF	10	40	7	12	4	2	1	6	2	.300
1988 Rochester	Int.	OF	120	456	61	*143	19	7	5	54	20	*.314
1989 Hagerstown	Southern	OF	11	48	11	20	3	1	0	7	4	.417
1989 Rochester	Int.	OF	7	25	2	4	0	0	0	2	3	.160
1989 Baltimore a	A.L.	OF	81	217	35	54	5	2	2	25	17	.249
1990 Baltimore b	A.L.	OF	142	464	46	119	16	4	3	37	22	.256
1991 Houston	N.L.	OF	159	596	84	170	28	10	8	54	34	.285
1992 Houston	N.L.	OF	*162	607	84	177	29	13	5	55	44	.292
1993 Houston c	N.L.	OF	142	545	69	145	15	*13	8	44	19	.266
1994 Jackson	Texas	OF	5	13	3	4	0	0	0	0	1	.308
1994 Houston d-e	N.L.	OF	94	373	64	103	16	5	11	33	13	.276
1995 San Diego	N.L.	OF	139	562	104	167	23	8	10	44	36	.297
1996 San Diego	N.L.	OF	161	655	126	195	45	9	30	95	22	.298
1997 Mobile	Southern	DH	1	4	1	2	0	0	1	2	0	.500
1997 Rancho Cuca	California	DH-OF	4	14	3	4	0	0	2	3	1	.286
1997 San Diego f	N.L.	OF	143	560	101	146	26	5	28	92	15	.261
Major League Totals			9 Yrs.	1223	4579	713	1276	203	69	105	479	222	.279
Division Series													
1996 San Diego	N.L.	OF	3	12	0	1	0	0	0	1	1	.083

a On disabled list from April 4 to April 21 and July 30 to September 1, 1989.
b Traded to Houston Astros with pitchers Pete Harnisch and Curt Schilling for first baseman Glenn Davis, January 10, 1991.
c On disabled list from April 25 to May 14, 1993.
d On disabled list from June 13 to July 3, 1994.
e Traded to San Diego Padres with third baseman Ken Caminiti, shortstop Andujar Cedeño, pitcher Brian Williams, first baseman Roberto Petagine and player to be named for outfielders Derek Bell and Phil Plantier, pitchers Doug Brocail and Pedro Martinez, shortstop Ricky Gutierrez and infielder Craig Shipley, December 28, 1994.
f On disabled list from April 20 to May 6, 1997.

FLAHERTY, JOHN TIMOTHY
Born, New York, New York, October 21, 1967.
Bats Right. Throws Right. Height, 6 feet, 1 inch. Weight, 195 pounds.

Year	Club	Lea	Pos	G	AB	R	H	2B	3B	HR	RBI	SB	Avg
1988 Elmira	N.Y.-Penn.	C	46	162	17	38	3	0	3	16	2	.235
1989 Winter Haven	Fla. St.	C-1B	95	334	31	87	14	2	4	28	1	.260
1990 Pawtucket	Int.	C-3B	99	317	35	72	18	0	4	32	1	.227
1990 Lynchburg	Carolina	C	1	4	0	0	0	0	0	1	0	.000
1991 New Britain	Eastern	C	67	225	27	65	9	0	3	18	0	.289
1991 Pawtucket	Int.	C	45	156	18	29	7	0	3	13	0	.186
1992 Pawtucket	Int.	C	31	104	11	26	3	0	0	7	0	.250
1992 Boston	A.L.	C	35	66	3	13	2	0	0	2	0	.197
1993 Pawtucket	Int.	C	105	365	29	99	22	0	6	35	0	.271
1993 Boston a	A.L.	C	13	25	3	3	2	0	0	2	0	.120
1994 Toledo	Int.	C	44	151	20	39	10	2	7	17	3	.258
1994 Detroit	A.L.	C	34	40	2	6	1	0	0	4	0	.150
1995 Detroit	A.L.	C	112	354	39	86	22	1	11	40	0	.243
1996 Detroit	A.L.	C	47	152	18	38	12	0	4	23	1	.250
1996 San Diego b	N.L.	C	72	264	22	80	12	0	9	41	2	.303
1997 San Diego c	N.L.	C	129	439	38	120	21	1	9	46	4	.273
Major League Totals			6 Yrs.	442	1340	125	346	72	2	33	158	7	.258

a Traded to Detroit Tigers for catcher Rich Rowland, April 1, 1994.
b Traded to San Diego Padres with infielder Chris Gomez for catcher Brad Ausmus and infielder Andujar Cedeno, June 18, 1996.
c Traded to Tampa Bay Devil Rays for pitcher Brian Boehringer and infielder Andy Sheets, November 19, 1997

FLETCHER, DARRIN GLEN
Born, Elmhurst, Illinois, October 3, 1966.
Bats Left. Throws Right. Height, 6 feet, 1 inch. Weight, 198 pounds.

Year	Club	Lea	Pos	G	AB	R	H	2B	3B	HR	RBI	SB	Avg
1987 Vero Beach	Fla. St.	C	43	124	13	33	7	0	0	15	0	.266
1988 San Antonio	Texas	C	89	279	19	58	8	0	1	20	2	.208
1989 Albuquerque	P.C.	C	100	315	34	86	16	1	5	44	1	.273

Year	Club	Lea	Pos	G	AB	R	H	2B	3B	HR	RBI	SB	Avg
1989 Los Angeles	N.L.	C	5	8	1	4	0	0	1	2	0	.500
1990 Albuquerque	P.C.	C	105	350	58	102	23	1	13	65	1	.291
1990 Los Angeles-Phil. a	N.L.	C	11	23	3	3	1	0	0	1	0	.130
1991 Scranton	Int.	C-1B	90	306	39	87	13	1	8	50	1	.284
1991 Philadelphia b	N.L.	C	46	136	5	31	8	0	1	12	0	.228
1992 Indianapolis	A.A.	C	13	51	2	13	2	0	1	9	0	.255
1992 Montreal c	N.L.	C	83	222	13	54	10	2	2	26	0	.243
1993 Montreal	N.L.	C	133	396	33	101	20	1	9	60	0	.255
1994 Montreal	N.L.	C	94	285	28	74	18	1	10	57	0	.260
1995 Montreal	N.L.	C	110	350	42	100	21	1	11	45	0	.286
1996 Montreal	N.L.	C	127	394	41	105	22	0	12	57	0	.266
1997 Montreal d-e-f	N.L.	C	96	310	39	86	20	1	17	55	1	.277
Major League Totals		9 Yrs.	705	2124	205	558	120	6	63	315	1	.263

a Traded to Philadelphia Phillies for pitcher Dennis Cook, September 13, 1990.
b Traded to Montreal Expos with cash for pitcher Barry Jones, December 9, 1991.
c On disabled list from May 12 to June 15, 1992.
d On disabled list from June 18 to July 3, 1997.
e Filed for free agency, October 27, 1997.
f Signed with Toronto Blue Jays, November 26, 1997.

FLOYD, CORNELIUS CLIFFORD

Born, Chicago, Illinois, December 5, 1972.
Bats Left. Throws Right. Height, 6 feet 4 inches. Weight, 220 pounds.

Year	Club	Lea	Pos	G	AB	R	H	2B	3B	HR	RBI	SB	Avg
1991 Bradenton Expos	Gulf C.	1B	56	214	35	56	9	3	6	30	13	.262
1992 Albany	So. Atl.	OF-1B	134	516	83	157	24	*16	16	*97	32	.304
1992 West Palm Beach	Fla. St.	OF	1	4	0	0	0	0	0	1	0	.000
1993 Harrisburg	Eastern	1B-OF	101	380	82	125	17	4	*26	*101	31	.329
1993 Ottawa	Int.	1B	32	125	12	30	2	2	2	18	2	.240
1993 Montreal	N.L.	1B	10	31	3	7	0	0	1	2	0	.226
1994 Montreal	N.L.	1B-OF	100	334	43	94	19	4	4	41	10	.281
1995 Montreal a	N.L.	1B-OF	29	69	6	9	1	0	1	8	3	.130
1996 Ottawa	Int.	OF-3B	20	76	7	23	3	1	1	8	2	.303
1996 Montreal	N.L.	OF-1B	117	227	29	55	15	4	6	26	7	.242
1997 Charlotte	Int.	OF-1B	39	131	27	48	10	0	9	33	7	.366
1997 Florida b-c	N.L.	OF-1B	61	137	23	32	9	1	6	19	6	.234
Major League Totals		5 Yrs.	317	798	104	197	44	9	18	96	26	.247
World Series Record												
1997 Florida	N.L.	DH	4	2	1	0	0	0	0	0	0	.000

a On disabled list from May 16 to September 11, 1995.
b Traded to Florida Marlins for pitcher Dustin Hermanson and outfielder Joe Orsulak, March 26, 1997.
c On disabled list from May 9 to May 24 and June 21 to September 1, 1997.

FONVILLE, CHAD EVERETT

Born, Jacksonville, North Carolina, March 5, 1971.
Bats Both. Throws Right. Height, 5 feet, 6 inches. Weight, 155 pounds.

Year	Club	Lea	Pos	G	AB	R	H	2B	3B	HR	RBI	SB	Avg
1992 Everett	Northwest	2B-SS	63	260	56	71	9	1	1	33	36	.273
1993 Clinton	Midwest	SS-2B-3B	120	447	80	137	16	10	1	44	52	.306
1994 San Jose	California	SS-2B-OF	68	283	58	87	9	6	0	26	22	.307
1995 Montreal-Los Angeles a .	N.L.	SS-2B-OF	102	320	43	89	6	1	0	16	20	.278
1996 Albuquerque	P.C.	SS-2B-OF	25	96	17	23	1	0	0	5	7	.240
1996 Los Angeles	N.L.	OF-2B-SS-3B	103	201	34	41	4	1	0	13	7	.204
1997 Albuquerque	P.C.	OF-2B-SS	102	371	49	81	5	2	0	22	23	.218
1997 Los Angeles b	N.L.	2B	9	14	1	2	0	0	0	1	0	.143
1997 Chicago c	A.L.	OF-2B-SS	9	9	1	1	0	0	0	1	2	.111
Major League Totals		3 Yrs.	223	544	79	133	10	2	0	31	29	.244
Division Series												
1995 Los Angeles	N.L.	SS	3	12	1	6	0	0	0	0	0	.500

a Claimed on waivers by Los Angeles Dodgers, May 31, 1995.
b Sent to Chicago White Sox as player to be named later for outfielder Darren Lewis, September 2, 1997.
c Claimed on waivers by Cleveland Indians, November 25, 1997.

FOX, ANDREW JUNIPERO (ANDY)
Born, Sacramento, California, January 12, 1971.
Bats Left. Throws Right. Height, 6 feet, 4 inches. Weight, 205 pounds.

Year Club	Lea	Pos	G	AB	R	H	2B	3B	HR	RBI	SB	Avg
1989 Yankees	Gulf Coast	3B	40	141	26	35	9	2	3	25	6	.248
1990 Greensboro	So.Atl.	3B	134	455	68	99	19	4	9	55	26	.218
1991 Pr William	Carolina	3B	126	417	60	96	22	2	10	46	15	.230
1992 Pr William	Carolina	3B-SS	125	473	75	113	18	3	7	42	28	.239
1993 Albany	Eastern	3B	65	236	44	65	16	1	3	24	12	.275
1994 Albany	Eastern	3B-SS-2B	121	472	75	105	20	3	11	43	22	.222
1995 Norwich	Eastern	SS	44	175	23	36	3	5	5	17	8	.206
1995 Columbus	Int.	3B-SS-OF-2B	82	302	61	105	16	6	9	37	22	.348
1996 New York	A.L.	2B-3B-SS-OF	113	189	26	37	4	0	3	13	11	.196
1997 Columbus	Int.	3B-2B-SS-OF	95	318	66	87	11	4	6	33	28	.274
1997 New York	A.L.	3B-2B-SS-OF	22	31	13	7	1	0	0	1	2	.226
Major League Totals		2 Yrs.	135	220	39	44	5	0	3	14	13	.200
Division Series												
1996 New York	A.L.	DH-PR	2	0	0	0	0	0	0	0	0	.000
1997 New York	A.L.	2B	2	0	0	0	0	0	0	0	0	.000
Division Series Totals			4	0	0	0	0	0	0	0	0	.000
Championship Series												
1996 New York	A.L.	PR	2	0	0	0	0	0	0	0	0	.000
World Series												
1996 New York	A.L.	2B-3B	4	0	1	0	0	0	0	0	0	.000

FRANCO, JULIO CESAR
Born, San Pedro de Macoris, Dominican Republic, August 23, 1961.
Bats Right. Throws Right. Height, 6 feet, 1 inch. Weight, 190 pounds.

Year Club	Lea	Pos	G	AB	R	H	2B	3B	HR	RBI	SB	Avg
1978 Butte	Pioneer	SS	47	141	34	43	5	2	3	28	4	.305
1979 Bend	Northwest	SS	*71	299	57	*98	15	5	*10	45	22	.328
1980 Peninsula	Carolina	SS	*140	*555	105	178	25	6	11	*99	44	.321
1981 Reading	Eastern	SS	*139	*532	70	160	17	3	8	74	27	.301
1982 Oklahoma City	A.A.	SS-3B	120	463	80	139	19	5	21	66	33	.300
1982 Philadelphia a	N.L.	SS-3B	16	29	3	8	1	0	0	3	0	.276
1983 Cleveland	A.L.	SS	149	560	68	153	24	8	8	80	32	.273
1984 Cleveland	A.L.	SS	160	*658	82	188	22	5	3	79	19	.286
1985 Cleveland	A.L.	SS-2B	160	636	97	183	33	4	6	90	13	.288
1986 Cleveland	A.L.	SS-2B	149	599	80	183	30	5	10	74	10	.306
1987 Cleveland b	A.L.	SS	128	495	86	158	24	3	8	52	32	.319
1988 Cleveland c	A.L.	2B	152	613	88	186	23	6	10	54	25	.303
1989 Texas	A.L.	2B	150	548	80	173	31	5	13	92	21	.316
1990 Texas	A.L.	2B	157	582	96	172	27	1	11	69	31	.296
1991 Texas	A.L.	2B	146	589	108	201	27	3	15	78	36	*.341
1992 Texas d	A.L.	DH-2B-OF	35	107	19	25	7	0	2	8	1	.234
1993 Texas e	A.L.	DH	144	532	85	154	31	3	14	84	9	.289
1994 Chicago f	A.L.	DH-1B	112	433	72	138	19	2	20	98	8	.319
1995 Chiba Lotte g	Japan Pac.	1B	126	474	60	145	25	3	10	58	11	.306
1996 Cleveland h	A.L.	1B	112	432	72	139	20	1	14	76	8	.322
1997 Cleveland-Milwaukee i-j-k	A.L.	DH-2B-1B	120	430	68	116	16	1	7	44	15	.270
Major League Totals		15 Yrs.	1890	7243	1104	2177	335	47	141	981	260	.301

a Traded to Cleveland Indians with second baseman Manny Trillo, outfielder George Vukovich, catcher Gerald Willard and pitcher Jay Baller for outfielder Von Hayes, December 9, 1982.
b On disabled list from July 13 to August 8, 1987.
c Traded to Texas Rangers for first baseman Pete O'Brien, outfielder Oddibe McDowell and second baseman Jerry Browne, December 6, 1988.
d On disabled list from April 3 to April 19, May 4 to June 1 and July 9 to end of 1992 season.
e Filed for free agency, October 27; signed with Chicago White Sox, December 15, 1993.
f Filed for free agency, October 14; signed with Chiba Lotte Marines of Japan Pacific League, December 21, 1994.
g Signed with Cleveland Indians December 5, 1995.
h On disabled list from July 7 to July 25 and August 4 to August 30, 1996.
i Released by Cleveland Indians, August 8, 1997.
j Signed with Milwaukee Brewers, August 14, 1997.
k Filed for free agency, October 28, 1997.

FRANCO, MATTHEW NEIL
Born, Santa Monica, California, August 19, 1969.
Bats Left. Throws Right. Height, 6 feet, 2 inches. Weight, 210 pounds.

Year Club	Lea	Pos	G	AB	R	H	2B	3B	HR	RBI	SB	Avg
1987 Wytheville	Appal.	3B-1B-2B	62	202	25	50	10	1	1	21	4	.248
1988 Wytheville	Appal.	3B-1B-OF	20	79	14	31	9	1	0	16	0	.392

Year	Club	Lea	Pos	G	AB	R	H	2B	3B	HR	RBI	SB	Avg
1988	Geneva	N.Y.-Penn.	3B-1B	44	164	19	42	2	0	3	21	2	.256
1989	Chston-Wv	So. Atl.	3B-1B-OF	109	377	42	102	16	1	5	48	2	.271
1989	Peoria	Midwest	3B	16	58	4	13	4	0	0	9	0	.224
1990	Peoria	Midwest	1B-3B	123	443	52	125	33	2	6	65	4	.282
1991	Winston-Sal	Carolina	1B-3B-SS	104	307	47	66	12	1	4	41	4	.215
1992	Charlotte	Southern	3B-1B-OF	108	343	35	97	18	3	2	31	3	.283
1993	Orlando	Southern	1B-3B	68	237	31	75	20	1	7	37	3	.316
1993	Iowa	A.A.	1B-OF-2B	62	199	24	58	17	4	5	29	4	.291
1994	Iowa	A.A.	1B-3B-OF	128	437	63	121	32	4	11	71	3	.277
1995	Iowa	A.A.	3B-1B-C	121	455	51	128	28	5	6	58	1	.281
1995	Chicago	N.L.	2B-1B-3B	16	17	3	5	1	0	0	1	0	.294
1996	Norfolk a	Int.	3B-1B	133	508	74	164	40	2	7	81	5	.323
1996	New York	N.L.	3B-1B	14	31	3	6	1	0	1	2	0	.194
1997	Norfolk	Int.	OF-1B-3B	7	26	5	7	2	0	0	0	0	.269
1997	New York	N.L.	3B-1B-OF	112	163	21	45	5	0	5	21	1	.276
Major League Totals			3 Yrs.	142	211	27	56	7	0	6	24	1	.265

a   Traded by Chicago Cubs to New York Mets for a player-to-be-named later, April 8, 1996. Chicago received pitcher Chris DeWitt, June 11, 1996.

FRIAS, HANLEY
Born, Villa Altagracia, Dominican Republic, December 5, 1973.
Bats Both. Throws Right. Height, 6 feet. Weight 160 pounds.

Year	Club	Lea	Pos	G	AB	R	H	2B	3B	HR	RBI	SB	Avg
1992	Rangers	Gulf Coast	2B-SS	58	205	37	50	9	2	0	28	28	.244
1993	Chston-Sc	So. Atl.	2B-OF-SS	132	473	61	109	20	4	4	37	27	.230
1994	High Desert	California	SS	124	452	70	115	17	6	3	59	37	.254
1995	Charlotte	Fla. St.	SS	33	120	23	40	6	3	0	14	8	.333
1995	Tulsa	Texas	SS	93	360	44	101	18	4	0	27	14	.281
1996	Tulsa	Texas	SS	134	505	73	145	24	12	2	41	9	.287
1997	Okla City	A.A.	SS-2B	132	484	64	128	17	4	5	46	35	.264
1997	Texas a	A.L.	SS-2B	14	26	4	5	1	0	0	1	0	.192

a   Selected in expansion draft by Arizona Diamondbacks, November 18, 1997.

FRYE, JEFFREY DUSTIN
Born, Oakland, California, August 31, 1966.
Bats Right. Throws Right. Height, 5 feet, 9 inches. Weight, 165 pounds.

Year	Club	Lea	Pos	G	AB	R	H	2B	3B	HR	RBI	SB	Avg
1988	Butte	Pioneer	2B	55	185	47	53	7	1	0	14	16	.286
1989	Gastonia	So. Atl.	2B	125	464	85	145	26	3	1	40	33	*.313
1990	Charlotte	Fla. St.	2B	131	503	77	137	16	7	0	50	29	.272
1991	Tulsa	Texas	2B	131	503	92	152	32	11	4	41	15	.302
1992	Oklahoma City ...	A.A.	2B-3B	87	337	64	101	26	2	2	28	11	.300
1992	Texas	A.L.	2B	67	199	24	51	9	1	1	12	1	.256
1993	Texas a	A.L.		INJURED—Did Not Play									
1994	Oklahoma City ...	A.A.	2B	17	68	7	19	3	0	1	5	2	.279
1994	Texas b	A.L.	2B-3B	57	205	37	67	20	3	0	18	6	.327
1995	Texas c-d	A.L.	2B	90	313	38	87	15	2	4	29	3	.278
1996	Okla City	A.A.	2B-SS-OF-3B	49	181	25	43	10	0	1	18	10	.238
1996	Boston e-f-g	A.L.	2B-OF-SS	105	419	74	120	27	2	4	41	18	.286
1997	Boston	A.L.	2B-3B-OF	127	404	56	126	36	2	3	51	19	.312
Major League Totals			5 Yrs.	446	1540	229	451	107	10	12	151	47	.293

a   On disabled list from March 27 to end of 1993 season.
b   On disabled list from June 9 to June 24, 1994.
c   On disabled list from June 21 to July 6 and June 3 to June 18, 1995.
d   Not offered contract by Texas Rangers, October 20, 1995.
e   Signed with Texas Rangers organization, March 25, 1996.
f   Released by Texas Rangers, June 5, 1996.
g   Signed with Boston Red Sox, June 6, 1996.

FRYMAN, DAVID TRAVIS
Born, Lexington, Kentucky, April 25, 1969.
Bats Right. Throws Right. Height, 6 feet, 1 inch. Weight, 194 pounds.

Year	Club	Lea	Pos	G	AB	R	H	2B	3B	HR	RBI	SB	Avg
1987	Bristol	Appal.	SS	67	248	25	58	9	0	2	20	6	.234
1988	Fayetteville	So. Atl.	SS	123	411	44	96	17	4	0	47	18	.234
1989	London	Eastern	SS	118	426	52	113	*30	1	9	56	5	.265

Year	Club	Lea	Pos	G	AB	R	H	2B	3B	HR	RBI	SB	Avg
1990 Toledo	....	Int.	SS	87	327	38	84	22	2	10	53	4	.257
1990 Detroit	....	A.L.	3B-SS	66	232	32	69	11	1	9	27	3	.297
1991 Detroit	....	A.L.	3B-SS	149	557	65	144	36	3	21	91	12	.259
1992 Detroit	....	A.L.	SS-3B	161	*659	87	175	31	4	20	96	8	.266
1993 Detroit	....	A.L.	SS-3B	151	607	98	182	37	5	22	97	9	.300
1994 Detroit	....	A.L.	3B	114	*464	66	122	34	5	18	85	2	.263
1995 Detroit	....	A.L.	3B	144	567	79	156	21	5	15	81	4	.275
1996 Detroit	....	A.L.	3B-SS	157	616	90	165	32	3	22	100	4	.268
1997 Detroit a-b	....	A.L.	3B	154	595	90	163	27	3	22	102	16	.274
Major League Totals	....		8 Yrs.	1096	4297	607	1176	229	29	149	679	58	.274

a Traded to Arizona Diamondbacks for third baseman Joe Randa, infielder Gabe Alvarez and pitcher Matt Drews, November 19, 1997.

b Traded to Cleveland Indians with pitcher Tom Martin for infielder Matt Williams, December 1, 1997.

FULLMER, BRADLEY RYAN (BRAD)
Born, Chatsworth, California, January 17, 1975.
Bats Left. Throws Right. Height, 6 feet, 1 inch. Weight 185 pounds.

Year	Club	Lea	Pos	G	AB	R	H	2B	3B	HR	RBI	SB	Avg
1995 Albany	....	So. Atl.	DH-3B-1B	123	468	69	151	38	4	8	67	10	.323
1996 Wst Plm Bch	....	Fla. St.	OF-1B	102	380	52	115	29	1	5	63	4	.303
1996 Harrisburg	....	Eastern	OF-1B	24	98	11	27	4	1	4	14	0	.276
1997 Harrisburg	....	Eastern	1B-OF-3B	94	357	60	111	24	2	19	62	6	.311
1997 Ottawa	....	Int.	1B-OF	24	91	13	27	7	0	3	17	1	.297
1997 Montreal	....	N.L.	1B-OF	19	40	4	12	2	0	3	8	0	.300

GAETTI, GARY JOSEPH
Born, Centralia, Illinois, August 19, 1958.
Bats Right. Throws Right. Height, 6 feet. Weight, 200 pounds.

Year	Club	Lea	Pos	G	AB	R	H	2B	3B	HR	RBI	SB	Avg
1979 Elizabethton	....	Appal.	3B-SS	66	230	50	59	15	2	14	42	6	.257
1980 Wis. Rapids	...	Midwest	3B	138	503	77	134	27	3	*22	82	24	.266
1981 Orlando	.....	Southern	3B-1B	137	495	92	137	19	2	30	93	15	.277
1981 Minnesota	......	A.L.	3B	9	26	4	5	0	0	2	3	0	.192
1982 Minnesota	......	A.L.	3B-SS	145	508	59	117	25	4	25	84	0	.230
1983 Minnesota	......	A.L.	3B-SS	157	584	81	143	30	3	21	78	7	.245
1984 Minnesota	....	A.L.	3B-OF-SS	*162	588	55	154	29	4	5	65	11	.262
1985 Minnesota	......	A.L.	3B-OF	160	560	71	138	31	0	20	63	13	.246
1986 Minnesota	......	A.L.	3B-SS-OF-2B	157	596	91	171	34	1	34	108	14	.287
1987 Minnesota a	......	A.L.	3B	154	584	95	150	36	2	31	109	10	.257
1988 Minnesota b	......	A.L.	3B-SS	133	468	66	141	29	2	28	88	7	.301
1989 Minnesota c	......	A.L.	3B-1B	130	498	63	125	11	4	19	75	6	.251
1990 Minnesota d	......	A.L.	3B-1B-SS	154	577	61	132	27	5	16	85	6	.229
1991 California	....	A.L.	3B	152	586	58	144	22	1	18	66	5	.246
1992 California	....	A.L.	3B-1B	130	456	41	103	13	2	12	48	3	.226
1993 Cal.-Kansas City e-f	A.L.		3B-1B	102	331	40	81	20	1	14	50	1	.245
1994 Kansas City g-h	...	A.L.	3B-1B	90	327	53	94	15	3	12	57	0	.287
1995 Kansas City i-j	....	A.L.	3B-1B	137	514	76	134	27	0	35	96	3	.261
1996 St. Louis k	....	N.L.	3B-1B	141	522	71	143	27	4	23	80	2	.274
1997 St. Louis l	....	N.L.	3B-1B-P	148	502	63	126	24	1	17	69	7	.251
Major League Totals	....		17 Yrs.	2261	8227	1048	2101	400	37	332	1224	95	.255
Division Series													
1996 St. Louis	....	N.L.	3B	3	11	1	1	1	0	0	1	3	0	.091
Championship Series													
1987 Minnesota	......	A.L.	3B	5	20	5	6	1	0	2	5	0	.300
1996 St. Louis	....	N.L.	3B	7	24	1	7	0	0	1	4	0	.292
Championship Series Totals	....		3B	12	44	6	13	1	0	3	9	0	.295
World Series Record													
1987 Minnesota	......	A.L.	3B	7	27	4	7	2	1	1	4	2	.259

a Filed for free agency, October 30, 1987; re-signed with Minnesota Twins, January 7, 1988.

b On disabled list from August 21 to September 6, 1988.

c On disabled list from August 26 to September 13, 1989.

d Granted special free agency by arbitrator, December 7, 1990; signed with California Angels, January 24, 1991.

e Released, June 3; signed with Kansas City Royals, June 19, 1993.

f Filed for free agency, October 25; re-signed with Kansas City Royals, December 16, 1993.

g On disabled list from July 5 to July 20, 1994.

h Filed for free agency, October 26; re-signed with Kansas City Royals, December 13, 1994.

i Filed for free agency, November 12, 1995.

j Signed with St. Louis Cardinals, December 18, 1995.
k On disabled list from April 28 to May 14, 1996.
l Filed for free agency, October 27, 1997.

GAGNE, GREGORY CARPENTER

Born, Fall River, Massachusetts, November 12, 1961.
Bats Right. Throws Right. Height, 5 feet, 11 inches. Weight, 180 pounds.

Year	Club	Lea	Pos	G	AB	R	H	2B	3B	HR	RBI	SB	Avg
1979 Paintsville	Appal.		SS	41	106	10	19	2	3	0	7	13	.179
1980 Greensboro	So. Atl.		SS-2B-3B	98	337	39	91	20	5	3	32	8	.270
1981 Greensboro	So. Atl.		2B-SS-3B	104	364	71	108	21	3	9	48	14	.297
1982 Fort Laud. a	Fla. St.		SS	1	3	0	1	0	0	0	0	0	.333
1982 Orlando	Southern		SS-2B	136	504	73	117	23	5	11	57	8	.232
1983 Toledo	Int.		SS	119	392	61	100	22	4	17	66	6	.255
1983 Minnesota	A.L.		SS	10	27	2	3	1	0	0	3	0	.111
1984 Toledo b	Int.		3B-SS-2B	70	236	31	66	7	2	9	27	2	.280
1984 Minnesota	A.L.		PH-PR	2	1	0	0	0	0	0	0	0	.000
1985 Minnesota c	A.L.		SS	114	293	37	66	15	3	2	23	10	.225
1986 Minnesota	A.L.		SS-2B	156	472	63	118	22	6	12	54	12	.250
1987 Minnesota	A.L.		SS-OF-2B	137	437	68	116	28	7	10	40	6	.265
1988 Minnesota	A.L.		SS-3B	149	461	70	109	20	6	14	48	15	.236
1989 Minnesota	A.L.		SS-OF	149	460	69	125	29	7	9	48	11	.272
1990 Minnesota	A.L.		SS-OF	138	388	38	91	22	3	7	38	8	.235
1991 Minnesota	A.L.		SS	139	408	52	108	23	3	8	42	11	.265
1992 Minnesota d	A.L.		SS	146	439	53	108	23	0	7	39	6	.246
1993 Kansas City	A.L.		SS	159	540	66	151	32	3	10	57	10	.280
1994 Kansas City	A.L.		SS	107	375	39	97	23	3	7	51	6	.259
1995 Kansas City e-f-g	A.L.		SS	120	430	58	110	25	4	6	49	3	.256
1996 Albuquerque h	P.C.		SS	4	11	1	3	1	0	0	1	0	.273
1996 Los Angeles	N.L.		SS	128	428	48	109	13	2	10	55	4	.255
1997 Los Angeles i	N.L.		SS	144	514	49	129	20	3	9	57	2	.251
Major League Totals		15 Yrs.		1798	5673	712	1440	296	50	111	604	108	.254
Division Series													
1996 Los Angeles	N.L.		SS	3	11	2	3	1	0	0	0	0	.273
Championship Series													
1987 Minnesota	A.L.		SS	5	18	5	5	3	0	2	3	0	.278
1991 Minnesota	A.L.		SS	5	17	1	4	0	0	0	1	0	.235
Championship Series Totals				10	35	6	9	3	0	2	4	0	.257
World Series Record													
1987 Minnesota	A.L.		SS	7	30	5	6	1	0	1	3	0	.200
1991 Minnesota	A.L.		SS	7	24	1	4	1	0	1	3	0	.167
World Series Totals				14	54	6	10	2	0	2	6	0	.185

a Traded by New York Yankees to Minnesota Twins organization with pitchers Paul Boris and Ron Davis and cash
   for pitcher Gary Serum and shortstop Roy Smalley, April 10, 1982.
b On disabled list from June 13 to July 18, 1984.
c On disabled list from August 10 to September 1, 1985.
d Filed for free agency, October 27; signed with Kansas City Royals, December 8, 1992.
e On disabled list from June 22 to July 13, 1995.
f Filed for free agency, November 12, 1995.
g Signed with Los Angeles Dodgers, November 30, 1995.
h On disabled list from May 18 to June 20, 1996.
i Filed for free agency, October 8, 1997.

GALARRAGA, ANDRES JOSE

Born, Caracas, Venezuela, June 18, 1961.
Bats Right. Throws Right. Height, 6 feet, 3 inches. Weight, 235 pounds.

Year	Club	Lea	Pos	G	AB	R	H	2B	3B	HR	RBI	SB	Avg
1979 W. Palm Beach	Fla. St.		1B	7	23	3	3	0	0	0	1	0	.130
1979 Calgary	Pioneer		1B-3B-C	42	112	14	24	3	1	4	16	1	.214
1980 Calgary	Pioneer		1B-3B-C-OF	759	190	27	50	11	4	4	22	3	.263
1981 Jamestown	N.Y.-Penn.		C-OF-3B	47	154	24	40	5	4	6	26	0	.260
1982 W. Palm Beach	Fla. St.		1B-OF	105	338	39	95	20	2	14	51	2	.281
1983 W. Palm Beach	Fla. St.		1B	104	401	55	116	18	3	10	66	7	.289
1984 Jacksonville	Southern		1B	143	533	81	154	28	4	27	87	2	.289
1985 Indianapolis	Int.		1B-OF	121	439	*75	118	15	8	25	87	3	.269
1985 Montreal	N.L.		1B	24	75	9	14	1	0	2	4	1	.187
1986 Montreal a	N.L.		1B	105	321	39	87	13	0	10	42	6	.271
1987 Montreal	N.L.		1B	147	551	72	168	40	3	13	90	7	.305

Year	Club	Lea	Pos	G	AB	R	H	2B	3B	HR	RBI	SB	Avg
1988 Montreal	N.L.	1B	157	609	99	*184	*42	8	29	92	13	.302
1989 Montreal	N.L.	1B	152	572	76	147	30	1	23	85	12	.257
1990 Montreal	N.L.	1B	155	579	65	148	29	0	20	87	10	.256
1991 Montreal b-c	N.L.	1B	107	375	34	82	13	2	9	33	5	.219
1992 Louisville	A.A.	1B	11	34	3	6	0	1	2	3	1	.176
1992 St. Louis d-e	N.L.	1B	95	325	38	79	14	2	10	39	5	.243
1993 Colorado f-g	N.L.	1B	120	470	71	174	35	4	22	98	2	*.370
1994 Colorado h	N.L.	1B	103	417	77	133	21	0	31	85	8	.319
1995 Colorado	N.L.	1B	143	554	89	155	29	3	31	106	12	.280
1996 Colorado	N.L.	1B-3B	159	626	119	190	39	3	*47	*150	15	.304
1997 Colorado i-j	N.L.	1B	154	600	120	191	31	3	41	*140	15	.318
Major League Totals			13 Yrs.	1621	6074	908	1752	337	29	288	1051	114	.288
Division Series													
1995 Colorado	N.L.	1B	4	18	1	5	1	0	0	2	0	.278

a On disabled list from July 10 to September 4, 1986.
b On disabled list from May 26 to July 4, 1991.
c Traded to St. Louis Cardinals for pitcher Ken Hill, November 25, 1991.
d On disabled list from April 8 to May 22, 1992.
e Filed for free agency, October 27; signed with Colorado Rockies, November 17, 1992.
f On disabled list from May 10 to May 28 and July 25 to August 19, 1993.
g Filed for free agency, October 25; re-signed with Colorado Rockies, December 6, 1993.
h On disabled list from July 26 to end of 1994 season.
i Filed for free agency, October 27, 1997.
j Signed by Atlanta Braves, November 20, 1997.

GALLEGO, MICHAEL ANTHONY

Born, Whittier, California, October 31, 1960.
Bats Right. Throws Right. Height, 5 feet, 8 inches. Weight, 175 pounds.

Year	Club	Lea	Pos	G	AB	R	H	2B	3B	HR	RBI	SB	Avg
1981 Modesto	Calif.	2B	60	202	38	55	9	3	0	23	9	.272
1982 West Haven	Eastern	2B-SS	54	139	17	25	1	0	0	5	3	.180
1982 Tacoma	P.C.	2B-3B-SS	44	136	12	30	3	1	0	11	4	.221
1983 Tacoma a	P.C.	2B	2	2	0	0	0	0	0	0	0	.000
1983 Albany	Eastern	2B-SS-3B	90	274	31	61	6	0	0	18	3	.223
1984 Tacoma	P.C.	2B-SS-3B	101	288	29	70	8	1	0	18	7	.243
1985 Modesto	Calif.	2B-3B	6	25	1	5	1	0	0	2	1	.200
1985 Oakland	A.L.	2B-SS-3B	76	77	13	16	5	1	1	9	1	.208
1986 Tacoma	P.C.	SS-3B-2B	132	443	58	122	16	5	4	46	3	.275
1986 Oakland	A.L.	2B-3B-SS	20	37	2	10	2	0	0	4	0	.270
1987 Tacoma	P.C.	2B	10	41	6	11	0	2	0	6	1	.268
1987 Oakland b	A.L.	2B-3B-SS	72	124	18	31	6	0	2	14	0	.250
1988 Oakland	A.L.	2B-SS-3B	129	277	38	58	8	0	2	20	2	.209
1989 Oakland	A.L.	SS-2B-3B	133	357	45	90	14	2	3	30	7	.252
1990 Oakland	A.L.	2B-SS-3B-OF	140	389	36	80	13	2	3	34	5	.206
1991 Oakland c	A.L.	2B-SS	159	482	67	119	15	4	12	49	6	.247
1992 Ft. Lauderdale ...	Fla. St.	SS	3	10	0	2	1	0	0	2	1	.200
1992 New York d	A.L.	2B-SS	53	173	24	44	7	1	3	14	0	.254
1993 New York e	A.L.	SS-2B-3B	119	403	63	114	20	1	10	54	3	.283
1994 New York f-g	A.L.	SS-2B	89	306	39	73	17	1	6	41	0	.239
1995 Edmonton	P.C.	2B-3B-SS	6	18	1	5	1	0	0	1	0	.278
1995 Oakland h-i-j-k	A.L.	2B-3B-SS	43	120	11	28	0	0	0	8	0	.233
1996 St. Petersburg l ..	Fla.St.	2B-3B-SS	14	51	7	15	0	0	0	5	0	.294
1996 St. Louis m	N.L.	2B-3B-SS	51	143	12	30	2	0	0	4	0	.210
1997 Louisville	A.A.	SS	6	18	0	5	1	0	0	1	1	.278
1997 St. Louis n	N.L.	2B-SS-3B	27	43	6	7	2	0	0	1	0	.163
Major League Totals			13 Yrs.	1111	2931	374	700	111	12	42	282	24	.239
Division Series													
1996 St. Louis	N.L.	2B	2	1	0	0	0	0	0	0	0	.000
Championship Series													
1988 Oakland	A.L.	2B	4	12	1	1	0	0	0	0	0	.083
1989 Oakland	A.L.	2B-SS	4	11	3	3	1	0	0	1	0	.273
1990 Oakland	A.L.	SS-2B	4	10	1	4	1	0	0	2	0	.400
1996 St. Louis	N.L.	2B-3B	7	14	1	2	0	0	0	0	0	.143
Championship Series Totals			19	47	6	10	2	0	0	3	0	.213
World Series Record													
1988 Oakland	A.L.	2B	1	0	0	0	0	0	0	0	0	.000
1989 Oakland	A.L.	2B-3B	2	1	0	0	0	0	0	0	0	.000
1990 Oakland	A.L.	SS	4	11	0	1	0	0	0	0	1	.091
World Series Totals			47	12	0	1	0	0	0	0	1	.083

a On temporary inactive list from April 10 to May 20, 1983.
b On disabled list from June 13 to July 29, 1987.
c Filed for free agency, November 6, 1991; signed with New York Yankees, January 7, 1992.
d On disabled list from March 28 to May 17 and July 8 to September 18, 1992.
e On disabled list from June 11 to June 26, 1993.
f On disabled list from June 29 to July 19, 1994.
g Filed for free agency, October 22, 1994.
h Signed with Oakland Athletics organization, April 12, 1995.
i On disabled list from May 18 to August 10, 1995.
j Filed for free agency, November 12, 1995.
k Signed with St. Louis Cardinals, January 9, 1996.
l On disabled list from April 1 to July 12, 1996.
m Filed for free agency, October 29, 1996.
n Waived by St. Louis Cardinals, July 29, 1997.

GANT, RONALD EDWIN

Born, Victoria, Texas, March 2, 1965.
Bats Right. Throws Right. Height, 6 feet. Weight, 172 pounds.

Year	Club	Lea	Pos	G	AB	R	H	2B	3B	HR	RBI	SB	Avg
1983	Bradenton Braves	Gulf C.	SS	56	193	32	45	2	2	1	14	4	.233
1984	Anderson	So. Atl.	2B	105	359	44	85	14	6	3	38	13	.237
1985	Sumter	So. Atl.	2B-SS	102	305	46	78	14	4	7	37	19	.256
1986	Durham	Carolina	2B	137	512	108	142	31	10	*26	102	35	.277
1987	Greenville	Southern	2B	140	527	78	130	27	3	14	82	24	.247
1987	Atlanta	N.L.	2B	21	83	9	22	4	0	2	9	4	.265
1988	Richmond	Int.	2B	12	45	3	14	2	2	0	4	1	.311
1988	Atlanta	N.L.	2B-3B	146	563	85	146	28	8	19	60	19	.259
1989	Atlanta	N.L.	3B-OF	75	260	26	46	8	3	9	25	9	.177
1989	Sumter	So. Atl.	OF	12	39	13	15	4	1	1	5	4	.385
1989	Richmond	Int.	OF-3B	63	225	42	59	13	2	11	27	6	.262
1990	Atlanta	N.L.	OF	152	575	107	174	34	3	32	84	33	.303
1991	Atlanta a	N.L.	OF	154	561	101	141	35	3	32	105	34	.251
1992	Atlanta	N.L.	OF	153	544	74	141	22	6	17	80	32	.259
1993	Atlanta b	N.L.	OF	157	606	113	166	27	4	36	117	26	.274
1994	Cincinnati c	N.L.				INJURED—Did Not Play								
1995	Cincinnati d-e	N.L.	OF	119	410	79	113	19	4	29	88	23	.276
1996	St. Louis f	N.L.	OF	122	419	74	103	14	2	30	82	13	.246
1997	St. Louis	N.L.	OF	139	502	68	115	21	4	17	62	14	.229
Major League Totals		10 Yrs.	1238	4523	736	1167	212	37	223	712	207	.258
Division Series													
1995	Cincinnati	N.L.	OF	3	13	3	3	0	0	1	2	0	.231
1996	St. Louis	N.L.	OF	3	10	3	4	1	0	1	4	2	.400
Division Series Totals			6	23	6	7	1	0	2	6	2	.304
Championship Series													
1991	Atlanta	N.L.	OF	7	27	4	7	1	0	1	3	7	.259
1992	Atlanta	N.L.	OF	7	22	5	4	0	0	2	6	1	.182
1993	Atlanta	N.L.	OF	6	27	4	5	3	0	0	3	0	.185
1995	Cincinnati	N.L.	OF	4	16	1	3	0	0	0	1	0	.188
1996	St. Louis	N.L.	OF	7	25	3	6	1	0	2	4	0	.240
Championship Series Totals			31	117	17	25	5	0	5	17	8	.214
World Series Record													
1991	Atlanta	N.L.	OF	7	30	3	8	0	1	0	4	1	.267
1992	Atlanta	N.L.	OF	4	8	2	1	1	0	0	0	2	.125
World Series Totals			411	38	5	9	1	1	0	4	3	.237

a Suspended one game by National League for July 4 umpire bumping, July 31, 1991.
b Released, March 15; signed with Cincinnati Reds, June 21, 1994.
c On disabled list from June 21 to end of 1994 season.
d Filed for free agency, November 12, 1995.
e Signed with St. Louis Cardinals, December 25, 1995.
f On disabled list from May 11 to June 14, 1996.

GARCIA (GUERRERO), CARLOS JESUS

Born, Tachira, Venezuela, October 15, 1967.
Bats Right. Throws Right. Height, 6 feet, 1 inch. Weight, 193 pounds.

Year	Club	Lea	Pos	G	AB	R	H	2B	3B	HR	RBI	SB	Avg
1987	Macon	So. Atl.	SS	110	373	44	95	14	5	3	38	20	.255
1988	Augusta	So. Atl.	SS	73	269	32	78	13	2	1	45	11	.290
1988	Salem	Carolina	SS	62	236	21	65	9	3	1	28	8	.275
1989	Salem	Carolina	SS	81	304	45	86	12	4	7	49	19	.283

Year Club	Lea	Pos	G	AB	R	H	2B	3B	HR	RBI	SB	Avg
1989 Harrisburg ....Eastern	SS	54	188	28	53	5	5	3	25	6	.282
1990 Harrisburg ....Eastern	SS	65	242	36	67	11	2	5	25	12	.277
1990 Buffalo ............A.A.	SS	63	197	23	52	10	0	5	18	7	.264
1990 Pittsburgh ..........N.L.	SS	4	4	1	2	0	0	0	0	0	.500
1991 Buffalo ............A.A.	SS	127	463	62	123	21	6	7	60	30	.266
1991 Pittsburgh ..........N.L.	SS-3B-2B	12	24	2	6	0	2	0	1	0	.250
1992 Buffalo ............A.A.	SS-2B	113	426	73	129	28	9	13	70	21	.303
1992 Pittsburgh ..........N.L.	2B-SS	22	39	4	8	1	0	0	4	0	.205
1993 Pittsburgh ..........N.L.	2B-SS	141	546	77	147	25	5	12	47	18	.269
1994 Pittsburgh ..........N.L.	2B	98	412	49	114	15	2	6	28	18	.277
1995 Pittsburgh a ........N.L.	2B-SS	104	367	41	108	24	2	6	50	8	.294
1996 Calgary b-c ........P.C.	2B-SS	2	6	0	2	0	1	0	0	0	.333
1996 Pittsburgh d ........N.L.	2B-SS-3B	101	390	66	111	18	4	6	44	16	.285
1997 Toronto ............A.L.	2B-SS-3B	103	350	29	77	18	2	3	23	11	.220
Major League Totals .... 8 Yrs.		585	2132	269	573	101	17	33	197	71	.269
Championship Series											
1992 Pittsburgh ..........N.L.	2B	1	1	0	0	0	0	0	0	0	.000

a On disabled list from July 28 to August 14, 1995.
b On disabled list from May 2 to May 17 and July 22 to August 27, 1996.
c Traded to Toronto Blue Jays with outfielder Orlando Merced and pitcher Dan Plesac for pitcher Jose Silva, pitcher Jose Pett, infielder Brandon Cromer, player to be named later and infielder Abra, November 14, 1996.
d Pittsburgh Pirates received pitcher Mike Halperin, infielder Abraham Nunez and catcher Craig Wilson to complete trade, December 11, 1996.
e Toronto declined to offer a 1998 contract, December 22, 1997

GARCIA, GUSTAVO KARIM
Born, Ciudad Obregon, Mexico, October 29, 1975.
Bats Left. Throws Left. Height, 6 feet. Weight 200 pounds.

Year Club	Lea	Pos	G	AB	R	H	2B	3B	HR	RBI	SB	Avg
1993 Bakersfield ....California	OF	123	460	61	111	20	9	19	54	5	.241
1994 Vero Beach ....Fla. St.	OF	121	452	72	120	28	10	21	84	8	.265
1995 Albuquerque ........P.C.	OF	124	474	88	151	26	10	20	91	12	.319
1995 Los Angeles ........N.L.	OF	13	20	1	4	0	0	0	0	0	.200
1996 San Antonio ....Texas	OF	35	129	21	32	6	1	5	22	1	.248
1996 Albuquerque ........P.C.	OF	84	327	54	97	17	10	13	58	6	.297
1996 Los Angeles ........N.L.		1	1	0	0	0	0	0	0	0	.000
1997 Los Angeles a-b .......N.L.	OF	15	39	5	5	0	0	1	8	0	.128
1997 Albuquerque ........P.C.	OF	71	262	53	80	17	6	20	66	11	.305
Major League Totals .... 3 Yrs.		29	60	6	9	0	0	1	8	0	.150

a On disabled list from September 19 to September 29, 1997.
b Selected in expansion draft by Arizona Diamondbacks, November 18, 1997.

GARCIAPARRA, ANTHONY NOMAR (NOMAR)
Born, Whittier, Calif., July 23, 1973.
Bats Right. Throws Right. Height, 6 feet. Weight, 167 pounds.

Year Club	Lea	Pos	G	AB	R	H	2B	3B	HR	RBI	SB	Avg
1994 Sarasota ....Fla.St.	SS	28	105	20	31	8	1	1	16	5	.295
1995 Trenton ....Eastern	SS	125	513	77	137	20	8	8	47	35	.267
1996 Red Sox ....Gulf Coast	SS	5	14	4	4	2	1	0	5	0	.286
1996 Pawtucket ....Int.	SS	43	172	40	59	15	2	16	46	3	.343
1996 Boston ............A.L.	SS-2B	24	87	11	21	2	3	4	16	5	.241
1997 Boston a ............A.L.	SS	153	*684	122	*209	44	*11	30	98	22	.306
Major League Totals .... 2 Yrs.		177	771	133	230	46	14	34	114	27	.298

a Selected Rookie of the Year in American League for 1997.

GATES, BRENT ROBERT
Born, Grand Rapids, Michigan, March 14, 1970.
Bats Both. Throws Right. Height, 6 feet, 1 inch. Weight, 180 pounds.

Year Club	Lea	Pos	G	AB	R	H	2B	3B	HR	RBI	SB	Avg
1991 So. Oregon ..Northwest	SS-2B-3B	58	219	41	63	11	0	3	26	8	.288
1991 Madison .....Midwest	SS-3B	4	12	4	4	2	0	0	1	1	.333
1992 Modesto .....California	2B	133	505	94	162	39	2	10	88	9	.321
1993 Huntsville ....Southern	2B	12	45	7	15	4	0	1	11	0	.333
1993 Tacoma ..........P.C.	2B	12	44	7	15	7	0	1	4	2	.341

Year	Club	Lea	Pos	G	AB	R	H	2B	3B	HR	RBI	SB	Avg
1993 Oakland .........A.L.			2B	139	535	64	155	29	2	7	69	7	.290
1994 Oakland a ........A.L.			2B-1B	64	233	29	66	11	1	2	24	3	.283
1995 Oakland .........A.L.			2B-1B	136	524	60	133	24	4	5	56	3	.254
1996 Oakland b .......A.L.			2B	64	247	26	65	19	2	2	30	1	.263
1997 Tacoma .........P.C.			2B-SS	7	33	7	15	3	0	0	6	0	.455
1997 Seattle c-d-e .....A.L.			3B-2B-SS-1B	65	151	18	36	8	0	3	20	0	.238
Major League Totals			5 Yrs.	468	1690	197	455	91	9	19	199	14	.269
Division Series													
1997 Seattle ..........A.L.			3B	2	4	0	0	0	0	0	0	0	.000

a On disabled list from April 10 to May 5 and July 17 to end of 1994 season.
b On disabled list from June 16 to September 30, 1996.
c Released by Oakland Athletics, March 10, 1997.
d Signed with Seattle Mariners, March 16, 1997.
e Signed as free agent with Minnesota Twins organization, December 23, 1997.

GIAMBI, JASON GILBERT
Born, W. Covina, California, January 8, 1971.
Bats Left. Throws Right. Height, 6 feet, 2 inches. Weight, 200 pounds.

Year	Club	Lea	Pos	G	AB	R	H	2B	3B	HR	RBI	SB	Avg
1992 South Oregon ....Northwest			3B	13	41	9	13	3	0	3	13	1	.317
1993 Modesto ....California			3B	89	313	72	91	16	2	12	60	2	.291
1994 Huntsville ......Southern			3B-1B	56	193	31	43	9	0	6	30	0	.223
1994 Tacoma .............P.C.			3B-1B-SS	52	176	28	56	20	0	4	38	1	.318
1995 Edmonton ...........P.C.			3B-1B	55	190	34	65	26	1	3	41	0	.342
1995 Oakland .............A.L.			3B-1B	54	176	27	45	7	0	6	25	2	.256
1996 Oakland .............A.L.			1B-OF-3B	140	536	84	156	40	1	20	79	0	.291
1997 Oakland .............A.L.			OF-1B	142	519	66	152	41	2	20	81	0	.293
Major League Totals			3 Yrs.	336	1231	177	353	88	3	46	185	2	.287

GIL (AGUILAR), ROMAR BENJAMIN
Born, Tijuana, Mexico, October 6, 1972.
Bats Right. Throws Right. Height, 6 feet, 2 inches. Weight, 182 pounds.

Year	Club	Lea	Pos	G	AB	R	H	2B	3B	HR	RBI	SB	Avg
1991 Butte ....Pioneer			SS	32	129	25	37	4	3	2	15	9	.287
1992 Gastonia ....So. Atl.			SS-OF	132	482	75	132	21	1	9	55	26	.274
1993 Texas .............A.L.			SS	22	57	3	7	0	0	0	2	1	.123
1993 Tulsa ....Texas			SS	101	342	45	94	9	1	17	59	20	.275
1994 Oklahoma City .......A.A.			SS	139	487	62	121	20	6	10	55	14	.248
1995 Texas .............A.L.			SS	130	415	36	91	20	3	9	46	2	.219
1996 Charlotte ....Fla.St.			SS	11	31	2	8	6	0	1	7	0	.258
1996 Okla City ...........A.A.			SS	84	292	32	65	15	1	6	28	4	.223
1996 Texas a ...........A.L.			SS	5	5	0	2	0	0	0	1	0	.400
1997 Texas .............A.L.			SS	110	317	35	71	13	2	5	31	1	.224
Major League Totals			4 Yrs.	267	794	74	171	33	5	14	80	4	.215

a On disabled list from April 1 to May 22, 1996.
b Traded to Chicago White Sox for pitchers Al Levine and Larry Thomas, December 19, 1997.

GILES, BRIAN STEPHEN
Born, El Cajon, California, January 21, 1971.
Bats Left. Throws Left. Height, 5 feet, 11 inches. Weight, 195 pounds.

Year	Club	Lea	Pos	G	AB	R	H	2B	3B	HR	RBI	SB	Avg
1989 Burlington ....Appal.			OF	36	129	18	40	7	0	0	20	6	.310
1990 Watertown ......N.Y.-Penn.			OF	70	246	44	71	15	2	1	23	11	.289
1991 Kinston ....Carolina			OF	125	394	71	122	14	0	4	47	19	.310
1992 Canton-Akrn ......Eastern			OF	23	74	6	16	4	0	0	3	3	.216
1992 Kinston ....Carolina			OF	42	140	28	37	5	1	3	18	3	.264
1993 Canton-Akrn ......Eastern			OF	123	425	64	139	17	6	8	64	18	.327
1994 Charlotte ....Int.			OF	128	434	74	136	18	3	16	58	8	.313
1995 Buffalo .............A.A.			OF	123	413	67	128	18	8	15	67	7	.310
1995 Cleveland ..........A.L.			OF	6	9	6	5	0	0	1	3	0	.556
1996 Buffalo .............A.A.			OF	83	318	65	100	17	6	20	64	1	.314
1996 Cleveland ..........A.L.			DH-OF	51	121	26	43	14	1	5	27	3	.355
1997 Cleveland ..........A.L.			OF	130	377	62	101	15	3	17	61	13	.268
Major League Totals			3 Yrs.	187	507	94	149	29	4	23	91	16	.294

Year	Club	Lea	Pos	G	AB	R	H	2B	3B	HR	RBI	SB	Avg
Division Series													
1996 Cleveland	...........A.L.	PH	1	1	0	0	0	0	0	0	0	0	.000
1997 Cleveland	...........A.L.	OF	3	7	0	1	0	0	0	0	0	.143
Division Series Totals	....		4	8	0	1	0	0	0	0	0	.125
Championship Series													
1997 Cleveland	...........A.L.	OF	6	16	1	3	3	0	0	0	0	.188
World Series Record													
1997 Cleveland	...........A.L.	OF	5	4	1	2	1	0	0	2	0	.400

GILKEY, OTIS BERNARD
Born, St. Louis, Missouri, September 24, 1966.
Bats Right. Throws Right. Height, 6 feet. Weight, 190 pounds.

Year	Club	Lea	Pos	G	AB	R	H	2B	3B	HR	RBI	SB	Avg
1985 Erie	...........N.Y.-Penn.	OF	*77	*294	57	60	9	1	7	27	34	.204
1986 Savannah	.........So. Atl.	OF	105	374	64	88	15	4	6	36	32	.235
1987 Springfield a	......Midwest	OF	46	162	30	37	5	0	0	9	18	.228
1988 Springfield	.......Midwest	OF	125	492	84	120	19	6	6	36	54	.244
1989 Arkansas	...........Texas	OF	131	500	*104	139	25	3	6	57	*53	.278
1990 Louisville	............A.A.	OF	132	499	83	147	26	8	3	46	45	.295
1990 St. Louis	...........N.L.	OF	18	64	11	19	5	2	1	3	6	.297
1991 Louisville	............A.A.	OF	11	41	5	6	2	0	0	2	1	.146
1991 St. Louis b	...........N.L.	OF	81	268	28	58	7	2	5	20	14	.216
1992 St. Louis	...........N.L.	OF	131	384	56	116	19	4	7	43	18	.302
1993 St. Louis c	...........N.L.	OF-1B	137	557	99	170	40	5	16	70	15	.305
1994 St. Louis	...........N.L.	OF	105	380	52	96	22	1	6	45	15	.253
1995 Louisville d	...........A.A.	OF	2	6	3	2	1	0	1	1	0	.333
1995 St. Louis	...........N.L.	OF	121	480	73	143	33	4	17	69	12	.298
1996 New York e	...........N.L.	OF	153	571	108	181	44	3	30	117	17	.317
1997 New York	...........N.L.	OF	145	518	85	129	31	1	18	78	7	.249
Major League Totals	....	8 Yrs.	891	3222	512	912	201	22	100	445	104	.283

a On disabled list from May 29 to end of 1987 season.
b On disabled list from June 14 to July 11, 1991.
c On disabled list from April 29 to May 14, 1993.
d On disabled list from June 28 to July 17, 1995.
e Traded to New York Mets for pitcher Eric Ludwick, pitcher Erik Hiljus and outfielder Yudith Ozorio, January 22, 1996.

GIOVANOLA, EDWARD THOMAS (ED)
Born, Los Gatos, California, March 4, 1969.
Bats Left. Throws Right. Height, 5 feet, 10 inches. Weight, 170 pounds.

Year	Club	Lea	Pos	G	AB	R	H	2B	3B	HR	RBI	SB	Avg
1990 Idaho Falls	.....Pioneer	2B	25	98	25	38	6	0	0	13	6	.388
1990 Sumter	........So.Atl.	2B	35	119	20	29	4	0	0	8	8	.244
1991 Durham	.......Carolina	3B-SS-2B	101	299	50	76	9	0	6	27	18	.254
1992 Greenville	...Southern	3B	75	270	39	72	5	0	5	30	4	.267
1993 Greenville	...Southern	3B-2B	120	384	70	108	21	5	5	43	6	.281
1994 Greenville	...Southern	3B	25	84	13	20	6	1	4	16	2	.238
1994 Richmond	.........Int.	3B-SS-2B	98	344	48	97	16	2	6	30	7	.282
1995 Richmond	.........Int.	SS-3B	99	321	45	103	18	2	4	36	8	.321
1995 Atlanta	...........N.L.	2B-3B-SS	13	14	2	1	0	0	0	0	0	.071
1996 Richmond	.........Int.	SS-2B-3B-OF	62	210	29	62	15	1	3	16	2	.295
1996 Atlanta	...........N.L.	SS-3B-2B	43	82	10	19	2	0	0	7	1	.232
1997 Richmond	.........Int.	3B-SS-OF	116	395	65	115	23	5	2	46	2	.291
1997 Atlanta	...........N.L.	3B-2B-SS	14	8	0	2	0	0	0	0	0	.250
Major League Totals	....	3 Yrs.	70	104	12	22	2	0	0	7	1	.212

GIRARDI, JOSEPH ELLIOTT
Born, Peoria, Illinois, October 14, 1964.
Bats Right. Throws Right. Height, 5 feet, 11 inches. Weight, 195 pounds.

Year	Club	Lea	Pos	G	AB	R	H	2B	3B	HR	RBI	SB	Avg
1986 Peoria a	.........Midwest	C	68	230	36	71	13	1	3	28	6	.309
1987 Winston-Salem	...Carolina	C	99	364	51	102	9	8	8	46	9	.280
1988 Pittsfield b	........Eastern	C-OF	104	357	44	97	14	1	7	41	7	.272
1989 Iowa	...............A.A.	C	32	110	12	27	4	2	2	11	3	.245

Year Club	Lea	Pos	G	AB	R	H	2B	3B	HR	RBI	SB	Avg
1989 Chicago ...............N.L.		C	59	157	15	39	10	0	1	14	2	.248
1990 Chicago ...............N.L.		C	133	419	36	113	24	2	1	38	8	.270
1991 Iowa ................A.A.		C	12	36	3	8	1	0	0	4	2	.222
1991 Chicago c ............N.L.		C	21	47	3	9	2	0	0	6	0	.191
1992 Chicago d .............N.L.		C	91	270	19	73	3	1	1	12	0	.270
1993 Colorado Springs ......P.C.		C	8	31	6	15	1	1	1	6	1	.484
1993 Colorado e ............N.L.		C	86	310	35	90	14	5	3	31	6	.290
1994 Colorado f ............N.L.		C	93	330	47	91	9	4	4	34	3	.276
1995 Colorado g ............N.L.		C	125	462	63	121	17	2	8	55	3	.262
1996 New York h-i .........A.L.		C	124	422	55	124	22	3	2	45	13	.294
1997 New York .............A.L.		C	112	398	38	105	23	1	1	50	2	.264
Major League Totals	9 Yrs.		844	2815	311	765	124	18	21	285	37	.272
Division Series												
1995 Colorado ..............N.L.		C	4	16	0	2	0	0	0	0	0	.125
1996 New York .............A.L.		C	4	9	1	2	0	0	0	0	0	.222
1997 New York .............A.L.		C	5	15	2	2	0	0	0	0	0	.133
Division Series Totals			13	40	3	6	0	0	0	0	0	.150
Championship Series												
1989 Chicago ..............N.L.		C	4	10	1	1	0	0	0	0	0	.100
1996 New York ............A.L.		C	4	12	1	3	0	1	0	0	0	.250
Championship Series Totals			8	22	2	4	0	1	0	0	0	.182
World Series												
1996 New York ............A.L.		C	4	10	1	2	0	1	0	1	0	.200

a On disabled list from August 27 to end of 1986 season.
b On disabled list from August 8 to end of 1988 season.
c On disabled list from April 17 to August 5, 1991.
d Selected by Colorado Rockies in expansion draft, November 17, 1992.
e On disabled list from June 5 to August 11, 1993.
f On disabled list from July 11 to July 26, 1994.
g Traded to New York Yankees for pitcher Mike DeJean and player to be named, November 20, 1995.
h Filed for free agency, November 4, 1996.
i Re-signed with New York Yankees, December 3, 1996.

GLANVILLE, DOUGLAS METUNWA

Born, Hackensack, New Jersey, August 25, 1970.
Bats Right. Throws Right. Height, 6 feet, 2 inches. Weight, 175 pounds.

Year Club	Lea	Pos	G	AB	R	H	2B	3B	HR	RBI	SB	Avg
1991 Geneva ........N.Y.-Penn.		OF	36	152	29	46	8	0	2	12	17	.303
1992 Winston-Sal ....Carolina		OF	120	485	72	125	18	4	4	36	32	.258
1993 Daytona ....Fla. St.		OF	61	239	47	70	10	1	2	21	18	.293
1993 Orlando ....Southern		OF	73	296	42	78	14	4	9	40	15	.264
1994 Orlando ....Southern		OF	130	483	53	127	22	2	5	52	26	.263
1995 Iowa ................A.A.		OF	112	419	48	113	16	2	4	37	13	.270
1996 Iowa ................A.A.		OF	90	373	53	115	23	3	3	34	15	.308
1996 Chicago ..............N.L.		OF	49	83	10	20	5	1	1	10	2	.241
1997 Chicago a .............N.L.		OF	146	474	79	142	22	5	4	35	19	.300
Major League Totals	2 Yrs.		195	557	89	162	27	6	5	45	21	.291

a Traded to Philadelphia Phillies for second baseman Mickey Morandini, December 23, 1997.

GOMEZ, CHRISTOPHER CORY

Born, Los Angeles, California, June 16, 1971.
Bats Right. Throws Right. Height, 6 feet, 1 inch. Weight, 183 pounds.

Year Club	Lea	Pos	G	AB	R	H	2B	3B	HR	RBI	SB	Avg
1992 London ....Eastern		SS-3B	64	220	20	59	13	2	1	19	1	.268
1993 Toledo ....Int.		SS	87	277	29	68	12	2	0	20	6	.245
1993 Detroit ..............A.L.		SS-2B	46	128	11	32	7	1	0	11	2	.250
1994 Detroit ..............A.L.		SS-2B	84	296	32	76	19	0	8	53	5	.257
1995 Detroit ..............A.L.		SS-2B	123	431	49	96	20	2	11	50	4	.223
1996 Detroit ..............A.L.		SS	48	128	21	31	5	0	1	16	1	.242
1996 San Diego a ..........N.L.		SS	89	328	32	86	16	1	3	29	2	.262
1997 San Diego ...........N.L.		SS	150	522	62	132	19	2	5	54	5	.253
Major League Totals	5 Yrs.		540	1833	207	453	86	6	28	213	19	.247
Division Series												
1996 San Diego ............N.L.		SS	3	1	2	0	2	0	0	1	0	.167

a Traded to San Diego Padres with catcher John Flaherty for catcher Brad Ausmus and infielder Andujar Cedeno, June 18, 1996.

GONZALEZ, ALEXANDER SCOTT
Born, Miami, Florida, April 8, 1973.
Bats Right. Throws Right. Height, 6 feet. Weight, 182 pounds.

Year	Club	Lea	Pos	G	AB	R	H	2B	3B	HR	RBI	SB	Avg
1991	Charlotte Blue Jays	Gulf C.	SS	53	191	29	40	5	4	0	10	7	.209
1992	Myrtle Beach	So. Atl.	SS	134	535	82	145	22	9	10	62	26	.271
1993	Knoxville	Southern	SS	142	561	*93	162	29	7	16	69	38	.289
1994	Toronto a	A.L.	SS	15	53	7	8	3	1	0	1	3	.151
1994	Syracuse	Int.	SS	110	437	69	124	22	4	12	57	23	.284
1995	Toronto	A.L.	SS-3B	111	367	51	89	19	4	10	42	4	.243
1996	Toronto	A.L.	SS	147	527	64	124	30	5	14	64	16	.235
1997	Toronto b	A.L.	SS	126	426	46	102	23	2	12	35	15	.239
Major League Totals		4 Yrs.		399	1373	168	323	75	12	36	142	38	.235

a On disabled list from April 29 to May 27, 1994.
b On disabled list from August 14 to September 14, 1997.

GONZALEZ (VAZQUEZ), JUAN ALBERTO
Born, Vega Baja, Puerto Rico, October 16, 1969.
Bats Right. Throws Right. Height, 6 feet, 3 inches. Weight, 215 pounds.

Year	Club	Lea	Pos	G	AB	R	H	2B	3B	HR	RBI	SB	Avg
1986	Sarasota Rangers	Gulf C.	OF	60	*233	24	56	4	1	0	36	7	.240
1987	Gastonia	So. Atl.	OF	127	509	69	135	21	2	14	74	9	.265
1988	Charlotte a	Fla. St.	OF	77	277	25	71	14	3	8	43	5	.256
1989	Texas	A.L.	OF	24	60	6	9	3	0	1	7	0	.150
1990	Oklahoma City	A.A.	OF	128	496	78	128	29	4	*29	*101	2	.258
1990	Texas	A.L.	OF	25	90	11	26	7	1	4	12	0	.289
1991	Texas b	A.L.	OF	142	545	78	144	34	1	27	102	4	.264
1992	Texas	A.L.	OF	155	584	77	152	24	2	*43	109	0	.260
1993	Texas	A.L.	OF	140	536	105	166	33	1	*46	118	4	.310
1994	Texas	A.L.	OF	107	422	57	116	18	4	19	85	6	.275
1995	Texas c	A.L.	DH-OF	90	352	57	104	20	2	27	82	0	.295
1996	Texas d-e	A.L.	OF	134	541	89	170	33	2	47	144	2	.314
1997	Texas f	A.L.	DH-OF	133	533	87	158	24	3	42	131	0	.296
Major League Totals		9 Yrs.		950	3663	567	1045	196	16	256	790	16	.285
Division Series													
1996	Texas	A.L.	OF	4	16	5	7	0	0	5	9	0	.438

a On disabled list from April 27 to June 17, 1988.
b On disabled list from March 30 to April 26, 1991.
c On disabled list from April 25 to June 1 and July 27 to August 16, 1995.
d Selected Most Valuable Player in American League for 1996.
e On disabled list from May 8 to June 1, 1996.
f On disabled list from April 1 to May 2, 1997.

GONZALEZ, LUIS EMILIO
Born, Tampa, Florida, September 3, 1967.
Bats Left. Throws Right. Height, 6 feet, 2 inches. Weight, 180 pounds.

Year	Club	Lea	Pos	G	AB	R	H	2B	3B	HR	RBI	SB	Avg
1988	Asheville	So. Atl.	3B	31	115	13	29	7	1	2	14	2	.252
1988	Auburn	N.Y.-Penn.	3B	39	157	32	49	10	3	5	27	2	.312
1989	Osceola a	Fla. St.	DH	86	287	46	82	16	7	6	38	2	.286
1990	Columbus	Southern	1B-3B	138	495	86	131	30	6	*24	89	27	.265
1990	Houston	N.L.	3B-1B	12	21	1	4	2	0	0	0	0	.190
1991	Houston b	N.L.	OF	137	473	51	120	28	9	13	69	10	.254
1992	Tucson	P.C.	OF	13	44	11	19	4	2	1	9	4	.432
1992	Houston c	N.L.	OF	122	387	40	94	19	3	10	55	7	.243
1993	Houston	N.L.	OF	154	540	82	162	34	3	15	72	20	.300
1994	Houston	N.L.	OF	112	392	57	107	29	4	8	67	15	.273
1995	Houston-Chicago d-e	N.L.	OF	133	471	69	130	29	8	13	69	6	.276
1996	Chicago f-g	N.L.	OF-1B	146	483	70	131	30	4	15	79	9	.271
1997	Houston h-i	N.L.	OF-1B	152	550	78	142	31	2	10	68	10	.258
Major League Totals		8 Yrs.		968	3317	448	890	202	33	84	479	77	.268
Division Series													
1997	Houston	N.L.	OF	3	12	0	4	0	0	0	0	0	.333

a On disabled list from May 26 to July 5, 1989.
b On disabled list from August 29 to September 13, 1991.
c On disabled list from July 21 to August 5, 1992.
d Traded to Chicago Cubs with catcher Scott Servais for catcher Rick Wilkins, June 28, 1995.
e Was not offered contract by Chicago Cubs, December 20, 1995.

f Filed for free agency, October 28, 1996.
g Signed with Houston Astros, December 19, 1996.
h Filed for free agency, October 28, 1997.
i Signed with Detroit Tigers, December 9, 1997.

GOODWIN, CURTIS LA MAR

Born, Oakland, California, September 30, 1972.
Bats Left. Throws Left. Height, 5 feet, 11 inches. Weight, 180 pounds.

Year	Club	Lea	Pos	G	AB	R	H	2B	3B	HR	RBI	SB	Avg
1991 Orioles	Gulf Coast	OF	48	151	32	39	5	0	0	9	26	.258
1992 Kane County	Midwest	OF	134	542	85	153	7	5	1	42	52	.282
1993 Frederick	Carolina	OF	138	555	98	156	15	10	2	42	61	.281
1994 Bowie	Eastern	OF	142	597	105	171	18	8	2	37	59	.286
1995 Rochester	Int.	OF	36	140	24	37	3	3	0	7	17	.264
1995 Baltimore a-b	A.L.	OF	87	289	40	76	11	3	1	24	22	.263
1996 Indianapolis	A.A.	OF	91	337	57	88	19	4	2	30	40	.261
1996 Cincinnati	N.L.	OF	49	136	20	31	3	0	0	5	15	.228
1997 Cincinnati	N.L.	OF	85	265	27	67	11	0	1	12	22	.253
1997 Indianapols	A.A.	OF	30	116	14	32	4	1	1	7	11	.276
Major League Totals			3 Yrs.	221	690	87	174	25	3	2	41	59	.252

a On disabled list from August 20 to September 4, 1995.
b Traded to Cincinnati Reds with outfielder Trovin Valdez for pitcher David Wells, December 26, 1995.

GOODWIN, THOMAS JONES

Born, Fresno, California, July 27, 1968.
Bats Left. Throws Right. Height, 6 feet, 1 inch. Weight, 170 pounds.

Year	Club	Lea	Pos	G	AB	R	H	2B	3B	HR	RBI	SB	Avg
1989 Great Falls	Pioneer	OF	63	240	55	74	12	3	2	33	*60	.308
1990 Bakersfield	California	OF	32	134	24	39	6	2	0	13	22	.291
1990 San Antonio	Texas	OF	102	428	76	119	14	4	0	28	*60	.278
1991 Albuquerque	P.C.	OF	132	509	84	139	19	4	1	45	48	.273
1991 Los Angeles	N.L.	OF	16	7	3	1	0	0	0	0	1	.143
1992 Albuquerque	P.C.	OF	82	319	48	96	10	4	2	28	27	.301
1992 Los Angeles	N.L.	OF	57	73	15	17	1	1	0	3	7	.233
1993 Albuquerque	P.C.	OF	85	289	48	75	5	5	1	28	21	.260
1993 Los Angeles a	N.L.	OF	30	17	6	5	1	0	0	1	1	.294
1994 Kansas City	A.L.	OF	2	2	0	0	0	0	0	0	0	.000
1994 Omaha	A.A.	OF	113	429	67	132	17	7	2	34	*50	.308
1995 Kansas City	A.L.	OF	133	480	72	138	16	3	4	28	50	.287
1996 Kansas City	A.L.	OF	143	524	80	148	14	4	1	35	66	.282
1997 Kansas City-Texas b	A.L.	OF	150	574	90	149	26	6	2	39	50	.260
Major League Totals			7 Yrs.	531	1677	266	458	58	14	7	106	175	.273

a Claimed on waivers by Kansas City Royals, January 6, 1994.
b Traded to Texas Rangers for infielder Dean Palmer, July 26, 1997.

GRACE, MARK EUGENE

Born, Winston-Salem, North Carolina, June 28, 1964.
Bats Left. Throws Left. Height, 6 feet, 2 inches. Weight, 190 pounds.

Year	Club	Lea	Pos	G	AB	R	H	2B	3B	HR	RBI	SB	Avg
1986 Peoria	Midwest	1B	126	465	81	*159	30	4	15	95	6	*.342
1987 Pittsfield	Eastern	1B	123	453	81	151	29	8	17	*101	5	.333
1988 Iowa	A.A.	1B	21	67	11	17	4	0	0	14	1	.254
1988 Chicago	N.L.	1B	134	486	65	144	23	4	7	57	3	.296
1989 Chicago a	N.L.	1B	142	510	74	160	28	3	13	79	14	.314
1990 Chicago	N.L.	1B	157	589	72	182	32	1	9	82	15	.309
1991 Chicago	N.L.	1B	160	*619	87	169	28	5	8	58	3	.273
1992 Chicago	N.L.	1B	158	603	72	185	37	5	9	79	6	.307
1993 Chicago b	N.L.	1B	155	594	86	193	39	4	14	98	8	.325
1994 Chicago b	N.L.	1B	106	403	55	120	23	3	6	44	0	.298
1995 Chicago c-d-e	N.L.	1B	143	552	97	180	51	3	16	92	6	.326
1996 Chicago f	N.L.	1B	142	547	88	181	39	1	9	75	2	.331
1997 Chicago g	N.L.	1B	151	555	87	177	32	5	13	78	2	.319
Major League Totals			10 Yrs.	1448	5458	783	1691	332	34	104	742	59	.310
Championship Series													
1989 Chicago	N.L.	1B	5	17	3	11	3	1	1	8	1	.647

a On disabled list from June 5 to June 23, 1989.
b Filed for free agency, October 17, 1994.
c Re-signed with Chicago Cubs, April 7, 1995.
d Filed for free agency, November 12, 1995.
e Re-signed with Chicago Cubs, December 19, 1995.
f On disabled list from June 11 to June 28, 1996.
g On disabled list from April 4 to April 19, 1997.

GRAFFANINO, ANTHONY JOSEPH
Born, Amityville, New York, June 6, 1972.
Bats Right. Throws Right. Height, 6 feet, 1 inch. Weight, 175 pounds.

Year	Club	Lea	Pos	G	AB	R	H	2B	3B	HR	RBI	SB	Avg
1990 Pulaski	. . . .	.Appal.	SS	42	131	23	27	5	1	0	11	6	.206
1991 Idaho Falls	. . . .	.Pioneer	SS	66	274	53	95	16	4	4	56	19	.347
1992 Macon	. . . . . .	.So. Atl.	2B	112	400	50	96	15	5	10	31	9	.240
1993 Durham	. . . . . .	.Carolina	2B-SS	123	459	78	126	30	5	15	69	24	.275
1994 Greenville	. . . .	.Southern	2B	124	440	66	132	28	3	7	52	29	.300
1995 Richmond	. . . .	.Int.	2B	50	179	20	34	6	0	4	17	2	.190
1996 Richmond	. . . .	.Int.	2B	96	353	57	100	29	2	7	33	11	.283
1996 Atlanta	. . . .	.N.L.	2B	22	46	7	8	1	1	0	2	0	.174
1997 Atlanta	. . . .	.N.L.	2B-3B-SS-1B	104	186	33	48	9	1	8	20	6	.258
Major League Totals	. . . .		2 Yrs.	126	232	40	56	10	2	8	22	6	.241
Division Series													
1997 Atlanta	. . . .	.N.L.	2B	3	3	0	0	0	0	0	0	0	.000
Championship Series													
1997 Atlanta	. . . .	.N.L.	2B	3	8	1	2	1	0	0	0	0	.250

GREBECK, CRAIG ALLEN
Born, Johnstown, Pennsylvania, December 29, 1964.
Bats Right. Throws Right. Height, 5 feet, 7 inches. Weight, 148 pounds.

Year	Club	Lea	Pos	G	AB	R	H	2B	3B	HR	RBI	SB	Avg
1987 Peninsula	. . . .	.Carolina	SS	104	378	63	106	22	3	15	67	3	.280
1988 Birmingham	. .	.Southern	SS	133	450	57	126	21	1	9	53	5	.280
1989 Birmingham	. .	.Southern	SS-3B-2B	*143	*533	85	*153	25	4	5	80	14	.287
1990 Chicago	. . . .	.A.L.	3B-SS-2B	59	119	7	20	3	1	1	9	0	.168
1990 Vancouver	. . . .	.P.C.	SS-3B	12	41	8	8	0	0	1	3	1	.195
1991 Chicago	. . . .	.A.L.	3B-2B-SS	107	224	37	63	16	3	6	31	1	.281
1992 Chicago a	. . . .	.A.L.	SS-3B-OF	88	287	24	77	21	2	3	35	0	.268
1993 Chicago	. . . .	.A.L.	SS-2B-3B	72	190	25	43	5	0	1	12	1	.226
1994 Nashville	. . . .	.A.A.	SS	5	15	3	6	2	0	0	4	0	.400
1994 Chicago b	. . . .	.A.L.	2B-SS-3B	35	97	17	30	5	0	0	5	0	.309
1995 Chicago c	. . . . . .	.A.L.	SS-3B-2B	53	154	19	40	12	0	1	18	0	.260
1996 Florida d-e-f	. . . . . .	.N.L.	2B-SS-3B	50	95	8	20	1	0	1	9	0	.211
1997 Anaheim g-h	. .	.A.L.	2B-SS-3B-OF	63	126	12	34	9	0	1	6	0	.270
Major League Totals	. . . .		8 Yrs.	527	1292	149	327	72	6	14	125	2	.253
Championship Series													
1993 Chicago	. . . .	.A.L.		38	1	1	1	0	0	0	0	0	1.000

a On disabled list from August 10 to end of 1992 season.
b On disabled list from May 21 to June 30, 1994.
c Signed with Florida Marlins organization, December 22, 1995.
d On disabled list from July 4 to August 13, 1996.
e Filed for free agency, October 31, 1996.
f Signed with California Angels, December 6, 1996.
g Filed for free agency, October 9, 1997.
h Signed with Toronto Blue Jays organization, November 26, 1997.

GREEN, SHAWN DAVID
Born, Des Plaines, Illinois, November 10, 1972.
Bats Left. Throws Left. Height, 6 feet, 4 inches. Weight, 190 pounds.

Year	Club	Lea	Pos	G	AB	R	H	2B	3B	HR	RBI	SB	Avg
1992 Dunedin	. . . .	.Fla. St.	OF	114	417	44	114	21	3	1	49	22	.273
1993 Knoxville	. . . .	.Southern	OF	99	360	40	102	14	2	4	34	4	.283
1993 Toronto	. . . .	.A.L.	OF	3	6	0	0	0	0	0	0	0	.000
1994 Syracuse	. . . .	.Int.	OF	109	433	82	149	27	3	13	61	19	*.344
1994 Toronto	. . . .	.A.L.	OF	14	33	1	3	1	0	0	1	1	.091
1995 Toronto	. . . .	.A.L.	OF	121	379	52	109	31	4	15	54	1	.288

Year Club	Lea	Pos	G	AB	R	H	2B	3B	HR	RBI	SB	Avg
1996 Toronto .............A.L.		OF	132	422	52	118	32	3	11	45	5	.280
1997 Toronto .............A.L.		OF	135	429	57	123	22	4	16	53	14	.287
Major League Totals			5 Yrs.	405	1269	162	353	86	11	42	153	21	.278

GREENE, TODD ANTHONY
Born, Augusta, Georgia, May 8, 1971.
Bats Right. Throws Right. Height, 5 feet, 10 inches. Weight, 200 pounds.

Year Club	Lea	Pos	G	AB	R	H	2B	3B	HR	RBI	SB	Avg
1993 Boise ....Northwest		OF-3B	76	305	55	82	15	3	15	71	4	.269
1994 Lake Elsnor ......California		C-OF-1B	133	524	98	158	39	2	35	124	10	.302
1995 Midland ....Texas		C-1B	82	318	59	104	19	1	26	57	3	.327
1995 Vancouver .............P.C.		C	43	168	28	42	3	1	14	35	1	.250
1996 Vancouver .............P.C.		C	60	223	28	68	18	0	5	33	0	.305
1996 California .............A.L.		C	29	79	9	15	1	0	2	9	2	.190
1997 Vancouver .............P.C.		C-1B-OF	64	260	51	92	22	0	25	75	5	.354
1997 Anaheim a ............A.L.		C	34	124	24	36	6	0	9	24	2	.290
Major League Totals			2 Yrs.	63	203	33	51	7	0	11	33	4	.251

a On disabled list from August 21 to September 29, 1997.

GREENE, WILLIE LOUIS
Born, Milledgeville, Georgia, September 23, 1971.
Bats Left. Throws Right. Height, 5 feet, 11 inches. Weight, 184 pounds.

Year Club	Lea	Pos	G	AB	R	H	2B	3B	HR	RBI	SB	Avg
1989 Bradenton Pirates .Gulf C.		SS	23	86	17	24	3	3	5	11	4	.279
1989 Princeton ....Appal.		SS	39	136	22	44	6	4	2	24	4	.324
1990 Augusta ....So. Atl.		SS	86	291	59	75	12	4	11	47	7	.258
1990 Salem a ....Carolina		SS	17	60	9	11	1	1	3	9	0	.183
1990 Rockford .....Midwest		SS	11	35	4	14	3	0	0	2	2	.400
1991 W. Palm Beach b .Fla. St.		3B	99	322	46	70	9	3	12	43	9	.217
1992 Cedar Rapids ..Midwest		3B	34	120	26	34	8	2	12	40	3	.283
1992 Chattanooga ..Southern		3B	96	349	47	97	19	2	15	66	9	.278
1992 Cincinnati .........N.L.		3B	29	93	10	25	5	2	2	13	0	.269
1993 Indianapolis .......A.A.		3B-SS	98	341	62	91	19	0	22	58	2	.267
1993 Cincinnati c ........N.L.		SS-3B	15	50	7	8	1	1	2	5	0	.160
1994 Indianapolis .......A.A.		3B-SS	114	435	77	124	24	1	23	80	8	.285
1994 Cincinnati ........N.L.		3B-OF	16	37	5	8	2	0	0	3	0	.216
1995 Indianapolis .......A.A.		3B-SS-OF	91	325	57	79	12	2	19	45	3	.243
1995 Cincinnati .........N.L.		3B	8	19	1	2	0	0	0	0	0	.105
1996 Cincinnati d .......N.L.		3B-OF-1B-2B	115	287	46	70	5	5	19	63	0	.244
1997 Cincinnati ........N.L.		3B-OF-1B-SS	151	495	62	125	22	1	26	91	6	.253
Major League Totals			6 Yrs.	334	981	133	238	35	9	49	175	6	.243

a Traded by Pittsburgh Pirates to Montreal Expos organization with pitcher Scott Ruskin and player to be named
   for pitcher Zane Smith, August 8; Montreal acquired outfielder Moises Alou to complete trade, August 16, 1990.
b Traded by Montreal Expos to Cincinnati Reds organization with outfielder Dave Martinez and pitcher Scott Ruskin
   for pitchers John Wetteland and Bill Risley, December 11, 1991.
c On disabled list from August 21 to end of 1993 season.
d On disabled list from June 27 to July 12, 1996.

GREER, THURMAN CLYDE (RUSTY)
Born, Fort Rucker, Alabama, January 21, 1969.
Bats Left. Throws Left. Height, 6 feet. Weight, 190 pounds.

Year Club	Lea	Pos	G	AB	R	H	2B	3B	HR	RBI	SB	Avg
1990 Butte ....Pioneer		OF	62	226	48	78	12	6	10	50	9	.345
1991 Charlotte ....Fla. St.		OF-1B	111	388	52	114	25	1	5	48	12	.294
1991 Tulsa ....Texas		OF	20	64	12	19	3	2	3	12	2	.297
1992 Tulsa ....Texas		1B-OF	106	359	47	96	22	4	5	37	2	.267
1993 Tulsa ....Texas		1B	129	474	70	138	25	6	15	59	10	.291
1993 Oklahoma City ......A.A.		OF	8	27	6	6	2	0	1	4	0	.222
1994 Oklahoma City ......A.A.		OF-1B	31	111	18	35	12	1	3	13	1	.315
1994 Texas .............A.L.		OF-1B	80	277	36	87	16	1	10	46	0	.314
1995 Texas .............A.L.		1B-OF	131	417	58	113	21	2	13	61	3	.271
1996 Texas .............A.L.		OF-1B	139	542	96	180	41	6	18	100	9	.332
1997 Texas .............A.L.		OF	157	601	112	193	42	3	26	87	9	.321
Major League Totals			4 Yrs.	507	1837	302	573	120	12	67	294	21	.312

Year	Club	Lea	Pos	G	AB	R	H	2B	3B	HR	RBI	SB	Avg
	Division Series												
1996 Texas	A.L.		OF	4	16	2	2	0	0	0	0	0	.125

GRIEVE, BENJAMIN
Born, Arlington, Texas, May 4, 1976.
Bats Left. Throws Right. Height, 6 feet, 4 inches. Weight, 220 pounds.

Year	Club	Lea	Pos	G	AB	R	H	2B	3B	HR	RBI	SB	Avg
1994 Sou Oregon	Northwest	OF	72	252	44	83	13	0	7	50	2	.329
1995 W. Michigan	Midwest	OF	102	371	53	97	16	1	4	62	11	.261
1995 Modesto	California	OF	28	107	17	28	5	0	2	14	2	.262
1996 Modesto	California	OF	72	281	61	100	20	1	11	51	8	.356
1996 Huntsville	Southern	OF	63	232	34	55	8	1	8	32	0	.237
1997 Huntsville	Southern	OF	100	372	100	122	29	2	24	108	5	.328
1997 Edmonton	P.C.	OF	27	108	27	46	11	1	7	28	0	.426
1997 Oakland	A.L.	OF	24	93	12	29	6	0	3	24	0	.312

GRIFFEY, GEORGE KENNETH, JR. (JUNIOR)
Born, Donora, Pennsylvania, November 21, 1969.
Bats Left. Throws Left. Height, 6 feet, 3 inches. Weight, 205 pounds.

Year	Club	Lea	Pos	G	AB	R	H	2B	3B	HR	RBI	SB	Avg
1987 Bellingham	Northwest	OF	54	182	43	57	9	1	14	40	13	.313
1988 San Bernardino a ..	California	OF	58	219	50	74	13	3	11	42	32	.338
1988 Vermont	Eastern	OF	17	61	10	17	5	1	2	10	4	.279
1989 Seattle b	A.L.	OF	127	455	61	120	23	0	16	61	16	.264
1990 Seattle	A.L.	OF	155	597	91	179	28	7	22	80	16	.300
1991 Seattle	A.L.	OF	154	548	76	179	42	1	22	100	18	.327
1992 Seattle c	A.L.	OF	142	565	83	174	39	4	27	103	10	.308
1993 Seattle	A.L.	OF-1B	156	582	113	180	38	3	45	109	17	.309
1994 Seattle	A.L.	OF	111	433	94	140	24	4	*40	90	11	.323
1995 Tacoma	P.C.	DH	1	3	0	0	0	0	0	0	0	.000
1995 Seattle d	A.L.	OF	72	260	52	67	7	0	17	42	4	.258
1996 Seattle e	A.L.	OF	140	545	125	165	26	2	49	140	16	.303
1997 Seattle f	A.L.	OF	157	608	*125	185	34	3	*56	*147	15	.304
Major League Totals		9 Yrs.	1214	4593	820	1389	261	24	294	872	123	.302
	Division Series												
1995 Seattle	A.L.	OF	5	23	9	9	0	0	5	7	1	.391
1997 Seattle	A.L.	OF	4	15	0	2	0	0	0	2	2	.133
Division Series Totals			9	38	9	11	0	0	5	9	3	.289
	Championship Series												
1995 Seattle	A.L.	OF	6	21	2	7	2	0	1	2	2	.333

a On disabled list from June 9 to August 15, 1988.
b On disabled list from July 24 to August 20, 1989.
c On disabled list from June 9 to June 25, 1992.
d On disabled list from May 27 to August 15, 1995.
e On disabled list from June 20 to July 13, 1996.1
f Selected Most Valuable Player in American League for 1997.

GRISSOM, MARQUIS DEON
Born, Atlanta, Georgia, April 17, 1967.
Bats Right. Throws Right. Height, 5 feet, 11 inches. Weight, 190 pounds.

Year	Club	Lea	Pos	G	AB	R	H	2B	3B	HR	RBI	SB	Avg
1988 Jamestown	N.Y.-Penn.	OF	74	291	*69	94	14	7	8	39	23	.323
1989 Jacksonville	Southern	OF	78	278	43	83	15	4	3	31	24	.299
1989 Indianapolis	A.A.	OF	49	187	28	52	10	4	2	21	16	.278
1989 Montreal	N.L.	OF	26	74	16	19	2	0	1	2	1	.257
1990 Indianapolis	A.A.	OF	5	22	3	4	0	0	2	3	1	.182
1990 Montreal a	N.L.	OF	98	288	42	74	14	2	3	29	22	.257
1991 Montreal	N.L.	OF	148	558	73	149	23	9	6	39	*76	.267
1992 Montreal	N.L.	OF	159	*653	99	180	39	6	14	66	*78	.276
1993 Montreal	N.L.	OF	157	630	104	188	27	2	19	95	53	.298
1994 Montreal b	N.L.	OF	110	475	96	137	25	4	11	45	36	.288
1995 Atlanta c-d	N.L.	OF	139	551	80	142	23	3	12	42	29	.258
1996 Atlanta	N.L.	OF	158	671	106	207	32	10	23	74	28	.308
1997 Cleveland e-f-g ...	A.L.	OF	144	558	74	146	27	6	12	66	22	.262
Major League Totals		9 Yrs.	1139	4458	690	1242	212	42	101	458	345	.279

68

Year	Club	Lea	Pos	G	AB	R	H	2B	3B	HR	RBI	SB	Avg
	Division Series												
1995 Atlanta	...............N.L.		OF	4	21	5	11	2	0	3	4	2	.524
1996 Atlanta	...............N.L.		OF	3	12	2	1	0	0	0	0	1	.083
1997 Cleveland	............A.L.		OF	5	17	3	4	0	1	0	0	0	.235
Division Series Totals	....			12	50	10	16	2	1	3	4	3	.320
	Championship Series												
1995 Atlanta	...............N.L.		OF	4	19	2	5	0	1	0	0	0	.263
1996 Atlanta	...............N.L.		OF	7	35	7	10	1	0	1	3	2	.286
1997 Cleveland	............A.L.		OF	6	23	2	6	0	0	1	4	3	.261
Championship Series Totals	....			17	77	11	21	1	1	2	7	5	.273
	World Series Record												
1995 Atlanta	...............N.L.		OF	6	25	3	9	1	0	0	1	3	.360
1996 Atlanta	...............N.L.		OF	6	27	4	12	2	1	0	5	1	.444
1997 Cleveland	............A.L.		OF	7	25	5	9	1	0	0	2	0	.360
World Series Totals	....			19	77	12	30	4	1	0	8	4	.390

a On disabled list from May 29 to June 30, 1990.
b Declared restricted free agent under Major League Baseball implemented labor proposal, December 23, 1994.
c Traded to Atlanta Braves for outfielder Roberto Kelly, outfielder Tony Tarasco and pitcher Esteban Yan, April 6, 1995.
d Signed with Atlanta Braves, April 25, 1995.
e Traded to Cleveland Indians with outfielder David Justice for outfielder Kenny Lofton and pitcher Alan Embree, March 25, 1997.
f On disabled list from April 20 to May 5, 1997.
g Traded to Milwaukee Brewers with pitcher Jeff Jodar for pitchers Ben McDonald, Mike Fetters and Ron Villone, December 8, 1997.

GRUDZIELANEK, MARK JAMES

Born, Milwaukee, Wisconsin, June 30, 1970.
Bats Right. Throws Right. Height, 6 feet, 1 inch. Weight, 185 pounds.

Year	Club	Lea	Pos	G	AB	R	H	2B	3B	HR	RBI	SB	Avg
1991 Jamestown	......N.Y.-Penn.	SS	72	275	44	72	9	3	2	32	14	.262
1992 Rockford	.........Midwest	SS	128	496	64	122	12	5	5	54	25	.246
1993 West Palm Beach	...Fla. St.	2B-SS-3B	86	300	41	80	11	6	1	34	17	.267
1994 Harrisburg	........Eastern	SS-3B	122	488	92	157	37	3	11	66	32	.322
1995 Ottawa	...............Int.	SS	49	181	26	54	9	1	1	22	12	.298
1995 Montreal	....N.L.	SS-3B-2B	78	269	27	66	12	2	1	20	8	.245
1996 Montreal	.............N.L.	SS	153	657	99	201	34	4	6	49	33	.306
1997 Montreal	.............N.L.	SS	156	*649	76	177	*54	3	4	51	25	.273
Major League Totals	....	3 Yrs.	387	1575	202	444	100	9	11	120	66	.282

GUERRERO, VLADIMIR

Born, Nizao Bani, Dominican Republic, February 9, 1976.
Bats Right. Throws Right. Height, 6 feet, 2 inches. Weight, 195 pounds.

Year	Club	Lea	Pos	G	AB	R	H	2B	3B	HR	RBI	SB	Avg
1994 Montreal	.............DSL		25	92	34	39	11	0	12	35	5	.424
1994 Expos	..........Gulf Coast	OF	37	137	24	43	13	3	5	25	0	.314
1995 Albany	..........So.Atl.	OF	110	421	77	140	21	10	16	63	12	.333
1996 Wst Plm Bch	........Fla.St.	OF	20	80	16	29	8	0	5	18	2	.363
1996 Harrisburg	........Eastern	OF	118	417	84	150	32	8	19	78	17	.360
1996 Montreal	.............N.L.	OF	9	27	2	5	0	0	1	1	0	.185
1997 Wst. Plm. Bch	......Fla. St.	OF	3	10	0	4	2	0	0	2	1	.400
1997 Montreal a	...........N.L.	OF	90	325	44	98	22	2	11	40	3	.302
Major League Totals	....	2 Yrs.	99	352	46	103	22	2	12	41	3	.293

On disabled list from April 1 to May 2 and June 6 to June 21 and July 12 to July 27, 1997.

GUERRERO, WILTON

Born, Don Gregorio, Dominican Republic, October 24, 1974.
Bats Right. Throws Right. Height, 5 feet, 11 inches. Weight, 145 pounds.

Year	Club	Lea	Pos	G	AB	R	H	2B	3B	HR	RBI	SB	Avg
1993 Great Falls	........Pioneer	SS	66	256	44	76	5	1	0	21	20	.297
1994 Vero Beach	........Fla. St.	SS	110	402	55	118	11	4	1	32	23	.294
1995 San Antonio	........Texas	SS	95	382	53	133	13	6	0	26	21	.348
1995 Albuquerque	...........P.C.	SS-OF	14	49	10	16	1	1	0	2	2	.327
1996 Albuquerque	..........P.C.	2B-SS	98	425	79	146	17	12	0	38	26	.344
1996 Los Angeles	..........N.L.		5	2	1	0	0	0	0	0	0	.000

Year	Club	Lea	Pos	G	AB	R	H	2B	3B	HR	RBI	SB	Avg
1997 Albuquerque .........P.C.			SS-2B	10	45	9	18	0	1	0	5	3	.400
1997 Los Angeles .........N.L.			2B-SS	111	357	39	104	10	9	4	32	6	.291
Major League Totals			2 Yrs.	116	359	40	104	10	9	4	32	6	.290

GUILLEN, JOSE MANUEL

Born, San Cristobal, Dominican Republic, May 17, 1976.
Bats Right. Throws Right. Height, 5 feet, 11 inches. Weight 165 pounds.

Year	Club	Lea	Pos	G	AB	R	H	2B	3B	HR	RBI	SB	Avg
1994 Pirates ....Gulf Coast			OF	30	110	17	29	4	1	4	11	2	.264
1995 Erie ............N.Y.-Penn.			OF	66	258	41	81	17	1	12	46	1	.314
1995 Augusta ....So. Atl.			OF	10	34	6	8	1	1	2	6	0	.235
1996 Lynchburg ....Carolina			OF	136	528	78	170	30	0	21	94	24	.322
1997 Pittsburgh ............N.L.			OF	143	498	58	133	20	5	14	70	1	.267

GUILLEN (BARRIOS), OSWALDO JOSE

Born, Oculare del Tuy, Venezuela, January 20, 1964.
Bats Left. Throws Right. Height, 5 feet, 11 inches. Weight, 164 pounds.

Year	Club	Lea	Pos	G	AB	R	H	2B	3B	HR	RBI	SB	Avg
1981 Bradenton ....Gulf Coast			SS-2B	55	189	26	49	4	1	0	16	8	.259
1982 Reno ....California			SS	130	528	*103	*183	33	1	2	54	25	.347
1983 Beaumont ....Texas			SS	114	427	62	126	20	4	2	48	7	.295
1984 Las Vegas a ..........P.C.			SS-2B	122	463	81	137	26	6	5	53	9	.296
1985 Chicago b ...........A.L.			SS	150	491	71	134	21	9	1	33	7	.273
1986 Chicago ............A.L.			SS	159	547	58	137	19	4	2	47	8	.250
1987 Chicago ............A.L.			SS	149	560	64	156	22	7	2	51	25	.279
1988 Chicago ............A.L.			SS	156	566	58	148	16	7	0	39	25	.261
1989 Chicago ............A.L.			SS	155	597	63	151	20	8	1	54	36	.253
1990 Chicago ............A.L.			SS	160	516	61	144	21	4	1	58	13	.279
1991 Chicago ............A.L.			SS	154	524	52	143	20	3	3	49	21	.273
1992 Chicago c ...........A.L.			SS	12	40	5	8	4	0	0	7	1	.200
1993 Chicago ............A.L.			SS	134	457	44	128	23	4	4	50	5	.280
1994 Chicago ............A.L.			SS	100	365	46	105	9	5	1	39	5	.288
1995 Chicago ............A.L.			SS	122	415	50	103	20	3	1	41	6	.248
1996 Chicago ............A.L.			SS-OF	150	499	62	131	24	8	4	45	6	.263
1997 Chicago d-e .........A.L.			SS	142	490	59	120	21	6	4	52	5	.245
Major League Totals			13 Yrs.	1743	6067	693	1608	240	68	24	565	163	.265
Championship Series													
1993 Chicago .............A.L.			SS	6	22	4	6	1	0	0	2	1	.273

a Traded by San Diego Padres to Chicago White Sox with pitchers Tim Lollar and Bill Long and infielder Luis Salazar for pitchers LaMarr Hoyt, Todd Simmons and Kevin Kristan, December 6, 1984.
b Selected Rookie of the Year in American League for 1985.
c On disabled list from April 21 to end of 1992 season.
d Filed for free agency, November 3, 1997.
e Signed with Baltimore Orioles organization, January 29, 1998.

GUTIERREZ, RICARDO

Born, Miami, Florida, May 23, 1970.
Bats Right. Throws Right. Height, 6 feet, 1 inch. Weight, 175 pounds.

Year	Club	Lea	Pos	G	AB	R	H	2B	3B	HR	RBI	SB	Avg
1988 Bluefield ....Appal.			SS	62	208	35	51	8	2	2	19	5	.245
1989 Frederick .....Carolina			SS	127	456	48	106	16	2	3	41	15	.232
1990 Hagerstown ...Eastern			SS	20	64	4	15	0	1	0	6	2	.234
1990 Frederick .....Carolina			SS	112	425	54	117	16	4	1	46	12	.275
1991 Hagerstown ...Eastern			SS	84	292	47	69	6	4	0	30	11	.236
1991 Rochester ....Int.			SS-3B	49	157	23	48	5	3	0	15	4	.306
1992 Rochester a ......Int.			2B-SS	125	431	54	109	9	3	0	41	14	.253
1992 Las Vegas .......P.C.			2B-SS	3	6	0	1	0	0	0	1	0	.167
1993 Las Vegas .......P.C.			2B-SS	5	24	4	10	4	0	0	4	4	.417
1993 San Diego ........N.L.			SS-2B-OF-3B	133	438	76	110	10	5	5	26	4	.251
1994 San Diego b .......N.L.			SS-2B	90	275	27	66	11	2	1	28	2	.240
1995 Tucson ...........P.C.			SS	64	236	46	71	12	4	1	26	9	.301
1995 Houston .........N.L.			SS-3B	52	156	22	43	6	0	0	12	5	.276
1996 Houston .........N.L.			SS-3B-2B	89	218	28	62	8	1	1	15	6	.284

Year	Club	Lea	Pos	G	AB	R	H	2B	3B	HR	RBI	SB	Avg
1997 New Orleans ......A.A.			SS	7	27	2	5	1	0	0	4	0	.185
1997 Houston c ...........N.L.			SS-3B-2B	102	303	33	79	14	4	3	34	5	.261
Major League Totals				5 Yrs.	466	1390	186	360	49	12	10	115	22	.259
Division Series													
1997 Houston .........N.L.			SS	3	8	0	1	0	0	0	0	0	.125

a Traded by Baltimore Orioles to San Diego Padres organization to complete August 31 trade in which Baltimore acquired pitcher Craig Lefferts for pitcher Erik Schullstrom, September 4, 1992.

b Traded to Houston Astros with outfielders Derek Bell and Phil Plantier, pitchers Doug Brocail and Pedro Martinez and infielder Craig Shipley for third baseman Ken Caminiti, shortstop Andujar Cedeño, outfielder Steve Finley, pitcher Brian Williams, first baseman Roberto Petagine and player to be named, December 28, 1994.

c On disabled list from April 1 to May 6, 1997.

GWYNN, ANTHONY KEITH (TONY)

Born, Los Angeles, California, May 9, 1960.
Bats Left. Throws Left. Height, 5 feet, 11 inches. Weight, 215 pounds.

Year	Club	Lea	Pos	G	AB	R	H	2B	3B	HR	RBI	SB	Avg
1981 Walla Walla .....Northwest			OF	42	178	46	59	12	1	2	37	17	*.331
1981 Amarillo ....Texas			OF	23	91	22	42	8	2	4	19	5	.462
1982 Hawaii ................P.C.			OF	93	366	65	120	23	2	5	46	14	.328
1982 San Diego a .........N.L.			OF	54	190	33	55	12	2	1	17	8	.289
1983 Las Vegas b ..........P.C.			OF	17	73	15	25	6	0	0	7	3	.342
1983 San Diego ...........N.L.			OF	86	304	34	94	12	2	1	37	7	.309
1984 San Diego ...........N.L.			OF	158	606	88	*213	21	10	5	71	33	*.351
1985 San Diego ...........N.L.			OF	154	622	90	197	29	5	6	46	14	.317
1986 San Diego ...........N.L.			OF	160	*642	*107	*211	33	7	14	59	37	.329
1987 San Diego ...........N.L.			OF	157	589	119	*218	36	13	7	54	56	*.370
1988 San Diego c .........N.L.			OF	133	521	64	163	22	5	7	70	26	*.313
1989 San Diego ...........N.L.			OF	158	604	82	*203	27	7	4	62	40	*.336
1990 San Diego ...........N.L.			OF	141	573	79	177	29	10	4	72	17	.309
1991 San Diego ...........N.L.			OF	134	530	69	168	27	11	4	62	8	.317
1992 San Diego ...........N.L.			OF	128	520	77	165	27	3	6	41	3	.317
1993 San Diego ...........N.L.			OF	122	489	70	175	41	3	7	59	14	.358
1994 San Diego ...........N.L.			OF	110	419	79	*165	35	1	12	64	5	*.394
1995 San Diego ...........N.L.			OF	135	535	82	197	33	1	9	90	17	*.368
1996 San Diego d .........N.L.			OF	116	451	67	159	27	2	3	50	11	*.353
1997 San Diego ...........N.L.			OF	149	592	97	*220	49	2	17	119	12	*.372
Major League Totals				16 Yrs.	2095	8187	1237	2780	460	84	107	973	308	.340
Division Series													
1996 San Diego ...........N.L.			OF	3	13	0	4	1	0	0	1	1	.308
Championship Series													
1984 San Diego ...........N.L.			OF	5	19	6	7	3	0	0	3	0	.368
World Series Record													
1984 San Diego ...........N.L.			OF	5	19	1	5	0	0	0	0	1	.263

a On disabled list from August 25 to September 10, 1982.

b On disabled list from March 26 to June 21, 1983.

c On disabled list from May 8 to May 28, 1988.

d On disabled list from July 2 to August 6, 1996.

HALE, WALTER WILLIAM (CHIP)

Born, Santa Clara, California, December 2, 1964.
Bats Left. Throws Right. Height, 5 feet, 11 inches. Weight, 191 pounds.

Year	Club	Lea	Pos	G	AB	R	H	2B	3B	HR	RBI	SB	Avg
1987 Kenosha .....Midwest			2B	87	339	65	117	12	7	7	65	3	*.345
1988 Orlando ......Southern			2B	133	482	62	126	20	1	11	65	8	.261
1989 Portland ..........P.C.			2B-3B	108	411	49	112	16	9	2	34	3	.273
1989 Minnesota ........A.L.			2B-3B	28	67	6	14	3	0	0	4	0	.209
1990 Portland ..........P.C.			2B-3B-SS	130	479	71	134	24	2	3	40	6	.280
1990 Minnesota ........A.L.			2B	1	2	0	0	0	0	0	2	0	.280
1991 Portland ..........P.C.			2B	110	352	45	85	16	3	1	37	3	.241
1992 Portland a .......P.C.			2B-OF	132	474	77	135	25	8	1	53	3	.285
1993 Portland ..........P.C.			2B-3B-SS	55	211	37	59	15	3	1	24	2	.280
1993 Minnesota ........A.L.			2B-3B-1B	69	186	25	62	6	1	3	27	2	.333
1994 Minnesota ........A.L.			3B-1B-2B	67	118	13	31	9	0	1	11	0	.263
1995 Salt Lake ........P.C.			3B-2B-1B	16	49	5	14	4	0	0	2	0	.286
1995 Minnesota ........A.L.			DH-2B-3B-1B	69	103	10	27	4	0	2	18	0	.262
1996 Minnesota b-c .....A.L.			2B-1B-3B	85	87	8	24	5	0	1	16	0	.276

Year	Club	Lea	Pos	G	AB	R	H	2B	3B	HR	RBI	SB	Avg
1997 Los Angeles	N.L.		3B	14	12	0	1	0	0	0	0	0	.083
1997 Albuquerque d-e	...P.C.	1B-2B-3B-OF		88	247	43	66	16	0	2	30	3	.267
Major League Totals			7 Yrs.	333	575	62	159	27	1	7	78	2	.277

a Record of 0-0 in one game as pitcher.
b Filed for free agency, October 4, 1996.
c Signed with Los Angeles Dodgers, October 30, 1996.
d Released by Los Angeles Dodgers, September 3, 1997.
e Signed by Anaheim Angels organization, December 22, 1997.

HALTER, SHANE DAVID
Born, LaPlata, Maryland, November 8, 1969.
Bats Right. Throws Right. Height, 5 feet, 10 inches. Weight, 160 pounds.

Year	Club	Lea	Pos	G	AB	R	H	2B	3B	HR	RBI	SB	Avg
1991 Eugene	.....Northwest		SS	64	236	41	55	9	1	1	18	12	.233
1992 Appleton	......Midwest		SS	80	313	50	83	22	3	3	33	21	.265
1992 Baseball Cy	....Fla. St.		SS	44	117	11	28	1	0	1	14	5	.239
1993 Wilmington	....Carolina		SS	54	211	44	63	8	5	5	32	5	.299
1993 Memphis	.....Southern		SS	81	306	50	79	7	0	4	20	4	.258
1994 Memphis	.....Southern		SS	129	494	61	111	23	1	6	35	10	.225
1995 Omaha	.........A.A.		SS-2B	124	392	42	90	19	3	8	39	2	.230
1996 Charlotte	..........Int.		OF-2B-3B	16	41	3	12	1	0	0	4	0	.293
1996 Omaha	............A.A.		OF-3B-SS-2B	93	299	43	77	24	0	3	33	7	.258
1997 Omaha	..........A.A.		3B-OF-2B-SS	14	49	10	13	1	1	2	9	0	.265
1997 Kansas City	.......A.L.		OF-2B-3B-SS	74	123	16	34	5	1	2	10	4	.276

HAMELIN, ROBERT JAMES
Born, Elizabeth, New Jersey, November 29, 1967.
Bats Left. Throws Left. Height, 6 feet. Weight, 235 pounds.

Year	Club	Lea	Pos	G	AB	R	H	2B	3B	HR	RBI	SB	Avg
1988 Eugene	........Northwest		1B	70	235	42	70	19	1	*17	61	9	.298
1989 Memphis a	........Southern		1B	68	211	45	65	12	5	16	47	3	.308
1990 Omaha b	.............A.A.		1B	90	271	31	63	11	2	8	30	2	.232
1991 Omaha c	.............A.A.		DH-1B	37	127	13	24	3	1	4	19	0	.189
1992 Baseball City d	.....Fla. St.		DH-1B	11	44	7	12	0	1	1	6	0	.273
1992 Memphis	........Southern		1B	35	120	23	40	8	0	6	22	0	.333
1992 Omaha	.............A.A.		1B	27	95	9	19	3	1	5	15	0	.200
1993 Omaha	.............A.A.		1B	137	479	77	124	19	3	29	84	8	.259
1993 Kansas City	............A.L.		1B	16	49	2	11	3	0	2	5	0	.224
1994 Kansas City e	.........A.L.		DH-1B	101	312	64	88	25	1	24	65	4	.282
1995 Omaha	.............A.A.		1B	36	119	25	35	12	0	10	32	2	.294
1995 Kansas City	.........A.L.		DH-1B-C	72	208	20	35	7	1	7	25	0	.168
1996 Omaha	.............A.A.		1B	4	16	4	5	1	0	1	0	1	.313
1996 Kansas City f	.........A.L.		DH-1B	89	239	31	61	14	1	9	40	5	.255
1997 Toledo	.............Int.		1B	27	91	14	22	7	0	6	24	0	.242
1997 Detroit g-h-i	..........A.L.		DH-1B	110	318	47	86	15	0	18	52	2	.270
Major League Totals			5 Yrs.	388	1126	164	281	64	3	60	187	11	.250

a On disabled list from June 25 to July 2 and August 3 to end of 1989 season.
b On disabled list from August 8 to end of 1990 season.
c On disabled list from May 27 to end of 1991 season.
d On disabled list from April 9 to June 10, 1992.
e Selected Rookie of the Year in American League for 1994.
f On disabled list from June 17 to July 15, 1996.
g Outrighted by Kansas City Royals, March 25, 1997.
h Signed with Detroit Tigers organization, April 8, 1997.
i Released by Detroit Tigers, December 12, 1997.

HAMILTON, DARRYL QUINN
Born, Baton Rouge, Louisiana, December 3, 1964.
Bats Left. Throws Right. Height, 6 feet, 1 inch. Weight, 180 pounds.

Year	Club	Lea	Pos	G	AB	R	H	2B	3B	HR	RBI	SB	Avg
1986 Helena	............Pioneer		OF	65	248	*72	*97	12	*6	0	35	34	*.391
1987 Stockton	.............Calif.		OF	125	494	102	162	17	6	8	61	43	.328
1988 Denver	..............A.A.		OF	72	277	55	90	11	4	0	32	23	.325
1988 Milwaukee	............A.L.		OF	44	103	14	19	4	0	1	11	7	.184
1989 Denver	..............A.A.		OF	129	497	72	142	24	4	2	40	20	.286

Year	Club	Lea	Pos	G	AB	R	H	2B	3B	HR	RBI	SB	Avg
1990 Milwaukee	A.L.	OF	89	156	27	46	5	0	1	18	10	.295
1991 Milwaukee a	A.L.	OF	122	405	64	126	15	6	1	57	16	.311
1992 Milwaukee b	A.L.	OF	128	470	67	140	19	7	5	62	41	.298
1993 Milwaukee c	A.L.	OF	135	520	74	161	21	1	9	48	21	.310
1994 Milwaukee d	A.L.	OF	36	141	23	37	10	1	1	13	3	.262
1995 Milwaukee e	A.L.	OF	112	398	54	108	20	6	5	44	11	.271
1996 Texas f	A.L.	OF	148	627	94	184	29	4	6	51	15	.293
1997 Phoenix	P.C.	OF	3	14	1	4	1	0	1	2	0	.286
1997 San Francisco h	N.L.	OF	125	460	78	124	23	3	5	43	15	.270
Major League Totals		9 Yrs.	939	3280	495	945	146	28	34	347	139	.288
Division Series												
1997 San Francisco	N.L.	OF	2	5	1	0	0	0	0	0	0	.000
Division Series Totals			6	24	1	3	0	0	0	0	0	.125

a On disabled list from May 22 to June 15, 1991.
b On disabled list from May 6 to May 24, 1992.
c On disabled list from May 2 to May 16, 1993.
d On disabled list from May 11 to May 26 and June 10 to end of 1994 season.
e Filed for free agency, November 12, 1995; signed with Texas Rangers, December 14, 1995.
f Filed for free agency, November 18, 1996.
g Signed with San Francisco Giants, January 10, 1997.
h On disabled list from April 17 to May 9, 1997.

HAMMONDS, JEFFREY BRYAN

Born, Plainfield, New Jersey, March 5, 1971.
Bats Right. Throws Right. Height, 6 feet. Weight, 195 pounds.

Year	Club	Lea	Pos	G	AB	R	H	2B	3B	HR	RBI	SB	Avg
1993 Rochester	Int.	OF	36	151	25	47	9	1	5	23	6	.311
1993 Bowie	Eastern	OF	24	92	13	26	3	0	3	10	4	.283
1993 Baltimore a	A.L.	OF	33	105	10	32	8	0	3	19	4	.305
1994 Baltimore b	A.L.	OF	68	250	45	74	18	2	8	31	5	.296
1995 Bowie	Eastern	OF	9	31	7	12	3	1	1	11	3	.387
1995 Baltimore c	A.L.	OF	57	178	18	43	9	1	4	23	4	.242
1996 Rochester d	Int.	OF	34	125	24	34	4	2	3	19	3	.272
1996 Baltimore	A.L.	OF	71	248	38	56	10	1	9	27	3	.226
1997 Baltimore	A.L.	OF	118	397	71	105	19	3	21	55	15	.264
Major League Totals		5 Yrs.	347	1178	182	310	66	7	45	155	31	.263
Division Series												
1997 Baltimore	A.L.	OF	4	10	3	1	1	0	0	2	1	.100
Championship Series												
1997 Baltimore	A.L.	OF	5	3	0	0	0	0	0	0	1	.000

a On disabled list from August 8 to September 1 and September 28 to end of 1993 season.
b On disabled list from May 4 to June 16, 1994.
c On disabled list from July 18 to September 3, 1995.
d On disabled list from August 16 to September 22, 1996.

HANSEN, DAVID ANDREW

Born Long Beach, California, November 24, 1968.
Bats Left. Throws Right. Height, 6 feet. Weight, 195 pounds.

Year	Club	Lea	Pos	G	AB	R	H	2B	3B	HR	RBI	SB	Avg
1986 Great Falls	Pioneer	OF-3B	61	204	39	61	7	3	1	36	9	.229
1987 Bakersfield	California	3B-OF	132	432	68	113	22	1	3	38	4	.262
1988 Vero Beach	Fla. St.	3B	135	512	68	*149	*28	6	7	*81	2	.291
1989 San Antonio	Texas	3B	121	464	72	138	21	4	6	52	3	.297
1989 Albuquerque	P.C.	3B	6	30	6	8	1	0	2	10	0	.267
1990 Albuquerque	P.C.	3B-SS-OF	135	487	90	154	20	3	11	92	9	.316
1990 Los Angeles	N.L.	3B	5	7	0	1	0	0	0	1	0	.143
1991 Albuquerque	P.C.	3B	68	254	42	77	11	1	5	40	4	.303
1991 Los Angeles	N.L.	3B-SS	53	56	3	15	4	0	1	5	1	.268
1992 Los Angeles	N.L.	3B	132	341	30	73	11	0	6	22	0	.214
1993 Los Angeles	N.L.	3B	84	105	13	38	3	0	4	30	0	.362
1994 Los Angeles a	N.L.	3B	40	44	3	15	3	0	0	5	0	.341
1995 Los Angeles b	N.L.	3B	100	181	19	52	10	0	1	14	0	.287
1996 Los Angeles c	N.L.	3B-1B	80	104	7	23	1	0	0	6	0	.221
1997 Chicago e	N.L.	3B-1B-2B	90	151	19	47	8	2	3	21	1	.311
Major League Totals		8 Yrs.	584	989	94	264	40	2	15	104	2	.267
Division Series												
1995 Los Angeles	N.L.	PH	3	3	0	2	0	0	0	0	0	.667

73

a On disabled list from May 9 to May 28, 1994.
b Re-signed with Los Angeles Dodgers, December 14, 1995.
c Filed for free agency, November 27, 1996.
d Signed with Chicago Cubs organization, January 22, 1997.
e Filed for free agency, October 27, 1997.

HANSEN, JED RAMON

Born, Tacoma, Washington, August 19, 1972.
Bats Right. Throws Right. Height, 6 feet, 1 inch. Weight 195 pounds.

Year Club	Lea	Pos	G	AB	R	H	2B	3B	HR	RBI	SB	Avg
1994 Eugene ....Northwest		2B	66	235	26	57	8	2	3	17	6	.243
1995 Springfield ....Midwest		2B	122	414	86	107	27	7	9	50	44	.258
1996 Wichita ....Texas		2B-OF	99	405	60	116	27	4	12	50	14	.286
1996 Omaha .............A.A.		2B	29	99	14	23	4	0	3	9	2	.232
1997 Omaha ...........A.A.		2B-SS-3B	114	380	43	102	20	2	11	44	8	.268
1997 Kansas City ..........A.L.		2B	34	94	11	29	6	1	1	14	3	.309

HARDTKE, JASON ROBERT

Born, Milwaukee, Wisconsin, September 15, 1971.
Bats Both. Throws Right. Height, 5 feet, 10 inches. Weight 175 pounds.

Year Club	Lea	Pos	G	AB	R	H	2B	3B	HR	RBI	SB	Avg
1990 Burlington ....Appal.		SS-2B	39	142	18	38	7	0	4	16	11	.268
1991 Columbus ....So. Atl.		SS-2B	139	534	104	155	26	8	12	81	23	.290
1992 Kinston a ....Carolina		SS-2B	6	19	3	4	0	0	0	1	0	.211
1992 Waterloo ....Midwest		2B	110	411	75	125	27	4	8	47	9	.304
1992 High Desert ......California		DH	10	41	9	11	1	0	2	8	1	.268
1993 Rancho Cuca ....California		2B-3B-1B	130	523	98	167	38	7	11	85	7	.319
1994 Wichita ....Texas		3B-2B	75	255	26	60	15	1	5	29	1	.235
1994 Rancho Cuca b ....California		2B-3B	4	13	2	4	0	0	0	0	0	.308
1995 Norfolk ....Int.		2B	4	7	1	2	1	0	0	0	1	.286
1995 Binghamton ....Eastern		2B-3B	121	455	65	130	42	4	4	52	6	.286
1996 Binghamton ....Eastern		2B	35	137	23	36	11	0	3	16	0	.263
1996 Norfolk ....Int.		2B	71	257	49	77	17	2	9	35	4	.300
1996 New York c .........N.L.		2B	19	57	3	11	5	0	0	6	0	.193
1997 Norfolk ....Int.		2B	97	388	46	107	23	3	11	45	3	.276
1997 Binghamton ....Eastern		2B	6	26	3	10	2	0	1	4	0	.385
1997 New York d .........N.L.		2B-3B	30	56	9	15	2	0	2	8	1	.268
Major League Totals		2 Yrs.	49	113	12	26	7	0	2	14	1	.230

a Traded by Cleveland Indians to San Diego Padres for outfielder Thomas Howard, April 14, 1992.
b Selected by New York Mets in Rule V draft, December 5, 1994.
c Re-signed by New York Mets as a free agent, November 14, 1996.
d Claimed on waivers by Chicago Cubs, October 15, 1997.

HARRIS, LEONARD ANTHONY

Born, Miami, Florida, October 28, 1964.
Bats Left. Throws Right. Height, 5 feet, 10 inches. Weight, 220 pounds.

Year Club	Lea	Pos	G	AB	R	H	2B	3B	HR	RBI	SB	Avg
1983 Billings ....Pioneer		3B	56	224	37	63	8	1	1	26	7	.281
1984 Cedar Rapids ..Midwest		3B	132	468	52	115	15	3	6	53	31	.246
1985 Tampa ....Fla. St.		3B	132	499	66	129	11	8	3	51	15	.259
1986 Vermont ....Eastern		3B	119	450	68	114	17	2	10	52	36	.253
1987 Nashville a .......A.A.		SS-3B	120	403	45	100	12	3	2	31	30	.248
1988 Glens Falls .....Eastern		2B	17	65	9	22	5	1	1	7	6	.338
1988 Nashville .........A.A.		2B	107	422	46	117	20	2	0	35	*45	.277
1988 Cincinnati .......N.L.		3B-2B	16	43	7	16	1	0	0	8	4	.372
1989 Nashville .........A.A.		2B	8	34	6	9	2	0	3	6	0	.265
1989 Cincin.-L.A. b .....N.L.		2B-3B-OF-SS	115	335	36	79	10	1	3	26	14	.236
1990 Los Angeles .....N.L.		3B-2B-OF-SS	137	431	61	131	16	4	2	29	15	.304
1991 Los Angeles .....N.L.		3B-2B-SS-OF	145	429	59	123	16	1	3	38	12	.287
1992 Los Angeles .....N.L.		2B-3B-OF-SS	135	347	28	94	11	0	0	30	19	.271
1993 Los Angeles c .....N.L.		2B-3B-SS-OF	107	160	20	38	6	1	2	11	3	.237
1994 Cincinnati .......N.L.		3B-1B-OF-2B	66	100	13	31	3	1	0	14	7	.310
1995 Cincinnati .......N.L.		3B-1B-OF-2B	101	197	32	41	8	3	2	16	10	.208
1996 Cincinnati d-e .....N.L.		OF-3B-1B-2B	125	302	33	86	17	2	5	32	14	.285
1997 Cincinnati ........N.L.		OF-2B-3B-1B	120	238	32	65	13	1	3	28	4	.273
Major League Totals		10 Yrs.	1067	2582	321	704	101	14	20	232	102	.273

Year	Club	Lea	Pos	G	AB	R	H	2B	3B	HR	RBI	SB	Avg
	Championship Series												
1995 Cincinnati	N.L.		PH	3	2	0	2	0	0	0	1	1	1.000

a Loaned by Cincinnati Reds to Detroit Tigers organization for 1987 season.
b Traded to Los Angeles Dodgers with outfielder Kal Daniels for pitcher Tim Leary and infielder Mariano Duncan, July 18, 1989.
c Released, October 8; signed with Cincinnati Reds, November 24, 1993.
d Filed for free agency, October 31, 1996.
e Re-signed with Cincinnati Reds, November 18, 1996.

HASELMAN, WILLIAM JOSEPH

Born, Long Branch, New Jersey, May 25, 1966.
Bats Right. Throws Right. Height, 6 feet, 3 inches. Weight, 220 pounds.

Year	Club	Lea	Pos	G	AB	R	H	2B	3B	HR	RBI	SB	Avg
1987 Gastonia	So. Atl.		C	61	235	35	72	13	1	8	33	11	.306
1988 Charlotte	Fla. St.		C	122	453	56	111	17	2	10	54	8	.245
1989 Tulsa	Texas		C	107	352	38	95	17	2	7	36	5	.270
1990 Tulsa	Texas		C	120	430	68	137	39	2	18	80	3	.319
1990 Texas	A.L.		C	7	13	0	2	0	0	0	3	0	.154
1991 Oklahoma City	A.A.		C	126	442	57	113	22	2	9	60	10	.256
1992 Oklahoma City a-b	A.A.		OF-C	17	58	8	14	5	0	1	9	1	.241
1992 Calgary	P.C.		C-OF-1B	88	302	49	77	14	2	19	53	3	.255
1992 Seattle	A.L.		C-OF	8	19	1	5	0	0	0	0	0	.263
1993 Seattle c	A.L.		C-OF	58	137	21	35	8	0	5	16	2	.255
1994 Calgary	P.C.		C-1B	44	163	44	54	10	0	15	46	1	.331
1994 Seattle d	A.L.		C-OF	38	83	11	16	7	1	1	8	1	.193
1995 Boston e	A.L.		C-1B-3B	64	152	22	37	6	1	5	23	0	.243
1996 Boston	A.L.		C-1B	77	237	33	65	13	1	8	34	4	.274
1997 Red Sox	Gulf Coast		DH	4	16	2	2	0	0	0	1	1	.125
1997 Trenton	Eastern		C	7	26	3	6	1	0	2	3	0	.231
1997 Boston f	A.L.		C	67	212	22	50	15	0	6	26	0	.236
Major League Totals		7 Yrs.		319	853	110	210	49	3	25	110	7	.246
	Division Series												
1995 Boston	A.L.		C	1	2	0	0	0	0	0	0	0	.000

a On disabled list from March 28 to May 4, 1992.
b Claimed on waivers by Seattle Mariners organization from Texas Rangers, May 29, 1992.
c Suspended three games by American League for June 6 mound charging from July 22 to July 24, 1993.
d Refused assignment to minor leagues and became free agent, October 14; signed with Boston Red Sox organization, November 7, 1994.
e Signed with Boston Red Sox organization, December 19, 1995.
f On disabled list from June 30 to August 8, 1997.

HATTEBERG, SCOTT ALLEN

Born, Salem, Oregon, December 14, 1969.
Bats Left. Throws Right. Height, 6 feet, 1 inch. Weight, 195 pounds.

Year	Club	Lea	Pos	G	AB	R	H	2B	3B	HR	RBI	SB	Avg
1991 Winter Havn	Fla. St.		C	56	191	21	53	7	3	1	25	1	.277
1991 Lynchburg	Carolina		C	8	25	4	5	1	0	0	2	0	.200
1992 New Britain	Eastern		C-1B	103	297	28	69	13	2	1	30	1	.232
1993 New Britain	Eastern		C	68	227	35	63	10	2	7	28	1	.278
1993 Pawtucket	Int.		C	18	53	6	10	0	0	1	2	0	.189
1994 New Britain	Eastern		C	20	68	6	18	4	1	1	9	0	.265
1994 Pawtucket	Int.		C	78	238	26	56	14	0	7	19	2	.235
1995 Pawtucket	Int.		C	85	251	36	68	15	1	7	27	2	.271
1995 Boston	A.L.		C	2	2	1	1	0	0	0	0	0	.500
1996 Pawtucket	Int.		C	90	287	52	77	16	0	12	49	0	.268
1996 Boston	A.L.		C	10	11	3	2	1	0	0	0	0	.182
1997 Boston	A.L.		C	114	350	46	97	23	1	10	44	0	.277
Major League Totals		3 Yrs.		126	363	50	100	24	1	10	44	0	.275

HAYES, CHARLES DEWAYNE

Born, Hattiesburg, Mississippi, May 29, 1965.
Bats Right. Throws Right. Height, 6 feet. Weight, 215 pounds.

Year	Club	Lea	Pos	G	AB	R	H	2B	3B	HR	RBI	SB	Avg
1983 Great Falls a	Pioneer		3B	34	111	9	29	4	2	0	9	1	.261
1984 Clinton	Midwest		3B	116	392	41	96	17	2	2	51	4	.245
1985 Fresno	California		3B	131	467	73	132	17	2	4	68	7	.283

Year	Club	Lea	Pos	G	AB	R	H	2B	3B	HR	RBI	SB	Avg
1986 Shreveport	Texas	3B	121	434	52	107	23	2	5	45	1	.247
1987 Shreveport	Texas	3B	128	487	66	148	33	3	14	75	5	.304
1988 Phoenix	P.C.	OF-3B	131	492	71	151	26	4	7	71	4	.307
1988 San Francisco	N.L.	OF	7	11	0	1	0	0	0	0	0	.091
1989 Phoenix b	P.C.	3B-OF	61	229	25	65	15	1	7	27	0	.284
1989 Scranton	Int.	3B	7	27	4	11	3	1	1	3	0	.407
1989 S.F.-Philadelphia	N.L.	3B	87	304	26	78	15	1	8	43	3	.257
1990 Philadelphia	N.L.	3B-1B-2B	152	561	56	145	20	0	10	57	4	.258
1991 Philadelphia c	N.L.	3B-SS	142	460	34	106	23	1	12	53	3	.230
1992 New York d	A.L.	3B-1B	142	509	52	131	19	2	18	66	3	.257
1993 Colorado e	N.L.	3B-SS	157	573	89	175	*45	2	25	98	11	.305
1994 Colorado f	N.L.	3B	113	423	46	122	23	4	10	50	3	.288
1995 Philadelphia g-h-i	N.L.	3B	141	529	58	146	30	3	11	85	5	.276
1996 Pittsburgh	N.L.	3B	128	459	51	114	21	2	10	62	6	.248
1996 New York j	A.L.	3B	20	67	7	19	3	0	2	13	0	.284
1997 New York k	A.L.	3B-2B	100	353	39	91	16	0	11	53	3	.258
Major League Totals	10 Yrs.		1189	4249	458	1128	215	15	117	580	41	.265
Division Series												
1996 New York	A.L.	3B	3	5	0	1	0	0	0	1	0	.200
1997 New York	A.L.	3B-2B	5	15	0	5	0	0	0	1	0	.333
Division Series Totals			8	20	0	6	0	0	0	2	0	.300
Championship Series												
1996 New York	A.L.	3B	4	7	0	1	0	0	0	0	0	.143
World Series												
1996 New York	A.L.	3B-1B	5	16	2	3	0	0	0	1	0	.188

a On disabled list from July 20 to end of 1983 season.
b Traded by San Francisco Giants to Philadelphia Phillies with pitchers Dennis Cook and Terry Mulholland for pitcher Steve Bedrosian and player to be named, June 18; San Francisco acquired infielder Rick Parker to complete trade, August 6, 1989.
c Traded to New York Yankees for pitcher Darrin Chapin, January 8, 1992.
d Selected by Colorado Rockies in expansion draft, November 17, 1992.
e Suspended three games by National League for June 15 fight from August 10 to August 12, 1993.
f Not offered 1995 contract, December 23, 1994.
g Signed with Philadelphia Phillies, April 6, 1995.
h Filed for free agency, November 12, 1995.
i Signed with Pittsburgh Pirates, December 28, 1995.
j Traded to New York Yankees for player to be named later, August 30, 1996.
k Traded to San Francisco Giants for outfielder Chris Singleton and pitcher Alberto Castillo, November 11, 1997.

HELTON, TODD LYNN

Born, Knoxville, Tennessee, August 20, 1973.
Bats Left. Throws Left. Height, 6 feet, 2 inches. Weight, 195 pounds.

Year	Club	Lea	Pos	G	AB	R	H	2B	3B	HR	RBI	SB	Avg
1995 Asheville	So. Atl.	1B	54	201	24	51	11	1	1	15	1	.254
1996 New Haven	Eastern	1B	93	319	46	106	24	2	7	51	2	.332
1996 Colo Sprngs	P.C.	1B-OF	21	71	13	25	4	1	2	13	0	.352
1997 Colo Sprngs	P.C.	1B-OF	99	392	87	138	31	2	16	88	3	.352
1997 Colorado	N.L.	OF-1B	35	93	13	26	2	1	5	11	0	.280

HENDERSON, RICKEY HENLEY

Born, Chicago, Illinois, December 25, 1958.
Bats Right. Throws Left. Height, 5 feet, 10 inches. Weight, 190 pounds.

Year	Club	Lea	Pos	G	AB	R	H	2B	3B	HR	RBI	SB	Avg
1976 Boise	Northwest	OF	46	140	34	47	13	2	3	23	29	.336
1977 Modesto	California	OF	134	481	120	166	18	4	11	69	*95	.345
1978 Jersey City	Eastern	OF	133	455	81	141	14	4	0	34	*81	.310
1979 Ogden	P.C.	OF	71	259	66	80	11	8	3	26	44	.309
1979 Oakland	A.L.	OF	89	351	49	96	13	3	1	26	33	.274
1980 Oakland	A.L.	OF	158	591	111	179	22	4	9	53	*100	.303
1981 Oakland	A.L.	OF	108	423	*89	*135	18	7	6	35	*56	.319
1982 Oakland	A.L.	OF	149	536	119	143	24	4	10	51	*130	.267
1983 Oakland	A.L.	OF	145	513	105	150	25	7	9	49	*108	.292
1984 Oakland a	A.L.	OF	142	502	113	147	27	4	16	58	*66	.293
1985 Ft. Lauderdale	Fla. St.	OF	3	6	5	1	0	1	0	3	1	.167
1985 New York b	A.L.	OF	143	547	*146	172	28	5	24	72	*80	.314
1986 New York	A.L.	OF	153	608	*130	160	31	5	28	74	*87	.263
1987 New York c	A.L.	OF	95	358	78	104	17	3	17	37	41	.291

Year	Club	Lea	Pos	G	AB	R	H	2B	3B	HR	RBI	SB	Avg
1988 New York ..........A.L.			OF	140	554	118	169	30	2	6	50	*93	.305
1989 N.Y.-Oakland d-e ......A.L.			OF	150	541	*113	148	26	3	12	57	*77	.274
1990 Oakland f ..........A.L.			OF	136	489	*119	159	33	3	28	61	*65	.325
1991 Oakland g ..........A.L.			OF	134	470	105	126	17	1	18	57	*58	.268
1992 Oakland h ..........A.L.			OF	117	396	77	112	18	3	15	46	48	.283
1993 Oakland-Toronto i-j .....A.L.			OF	134	481	114	139	22	2	21	59	53	.289
1994 Oakland k ..........A.L.			OF	87	296	66	77	13	0	6	20	22	.260
1995 Oakland l-m ..........A.L.			OF	112	407	67	122	31	1	9	54	32	.300
1996 San Diego ..........N.L.			OF	148	465	110	112	17	2	9	29	37	.241
1997 San Diego n-o .........N.L.			OF	88	288	63	79	11	0	6	27	29	.274
1997 Anaheim p-q ..........A.L.			DH-OF	32	115	21	21	3	0	2	7	16	.183
Major League Totals	19 Yrs.			2460	8931	1913	2550	426	59	252	921	1231	.286
Division Series													
1981 Oakland ............A.L.			OF	3	11	3	2	0	0	0	0	2	.182
1996 San Diego ..........N.L.			OF	3	12	2	4	0	0	0	1	0	.333
Division Series Totals				6	23	5	6	0	0	0	1	2	.261
Championship Series													
1981 Oakland ............A.L.			OF	3	11	0	4	2	1	0	1	2	.364
1989 Oakland ............A.L.			OF	5	15	8	6	1	1	2	5	8	.400
1990 Oakland ............A.L.			OF	4	17	1	5	0	0	0	3	2	.294
1992 Oakland ............A.L.			OF	6	23	5	6	0	0	0	1	2	.261
1993 Toronto ............A.L.			OF	6	25	4	3	2	0	0	0	2	.120
Championship Series Totals				24	91	18	24	5	2	2	10	16	.264
World Series Record													
1989 Oakland ............A.L.			OF	4	19	4	9	1	2	1	3	3	.474
1990 Oakland ............A.L.			OF	4	15	2	5	2	0	1	1	3	.333
1993 Toronto ............A.L.			OF	6	22	6	5	2	0	0	2	1	.227
World Series Totals				14	56	12	19	5	2	2	6	7	.339

a Traded to New York Yankees with pitcher Bert Bradley and cash for pitchers Jay Howell, Jose Rijo, Eric Plunk and Tim Birtsas and outfielder Stan Javier, December 5, 1984.
b On disabled list from March 30 to April 22, 1985.
c On disabled list from June 5 to June 29 and July 26 to September 1, 1987.
d Traded to Oakland Athletics for pitchers Eric Plunk and Greg Cadaret and outfielder Luis Polonia, June 21, 1989.
e Filed for free agency, November 2; re-signed with Oakland Athletics, November 28, 1989.
f Selected Most Valuable Player in American League for 1990.
g On disabled list from April 12 to April 27, 1991.
h On disabled list from May 28 to June 17 and June 30 to July 16, 1992.
i Traded to Toronto Blue Jays for pitcher Steve Karsay and player to be named, July 31; Oakland Athletics acquired outfielder Jose Herrera to complete trade, August 6, 1993.
j Filed for free agency, October 27; signed with Oakland Athletics, December 17, 1993.
k On disabled list from May 10 to May 27, 1994.
l Filed for free agency, October 30, 1995.
m Signed with San Diego Padres organization, December 29, 1995.
n On disabled list from May 9 to May 24, 1997.
o Traded to Anaheim Angels for pitcher Ryan Hancock, pitcher Steven Agosto and player to be named later, August 13, 1997. San Diego Padres received infielder George Arias to complete trade, August 19, 1997.
p Filed for free agency, October 27, 1997.
q Signed with Oakland Athletics, January 22, 1998.

HERNANDEZ (ALMEIDA), CARLOS ALBERTO

Born, San Felix, Venezuela, May 24, 1967.
Bats Right. Throws Right. Height, 5 feet, 11 inches. Weight, 218 pounds.

Year	Club	Lea	Pos	G	AB	R	H	2B	3B	HR	RBI	SB	Avg
1985 Bradenton Dodgers ..Gulf C.			3B-1B	22	49	3	12	1	0	0	6	0	.245
1986 Sarasota Dodgers ....Gulf C.			C	57	205	19	64	7	0	1	31	1	.312
1987 Bakersfield ......California			C	48	462	22	37	6	1	3	22	8	.228
1988 Bakersfield ......California			C	92	333	37	103	15	2	5	52	3	.309
1988 Albuquerque ..........P.C.			C	3	8	0	1	0	0	0	1	0	.125
1989 San Antonio ....Texas			C	99	370	37	111	16	3	8	41	2	.300
1989 Albuquerque ..........P.C.			C	4	14	1	3	0	0	0	1	0	.214
1990 Albuquerque ..........P.C.			C	52	143	11	45	8	1	0	16	2	.315
1990 Los Angeles ..........N.L.			C	10	20	2	4	1	0	0	1	0	.200
1991 Albuquerque ..........P.C.			C	95	345	60	119	24	2	8	44	5	.345
1991 Los Angeles ..........N.L.			C-3B	15	14	1	3	1	0	0	1	1	.214
1992 Los Angeles ..........N.L.			C	69	173	11	45	4	0	3	17	0	.260
1993 Los Angeles ..........N.L.			C	50	99	6	25	5	0	2	7	0	.253
1994 Los Angeles a .........N.L.			C	32	64	6	14	2	0	2	6	0	.219
1995 Los Angeles ..........N.L.			C	45	94	3	14	1	0	2	8	0	.149
1996 Albuquerque ..........P.C.			C-1B-3B	66	233	19	56	11	0	5	30	5	.240
1996 Los Angeles b-c .......N.L.			C	13	14	1	4	0	0	0	0	0	.286

77

Year Club	Lea	Pos	G	AB	R	H	2B	3B	HR	RBI	SB	Avg
1997 Rancho Cuca .....California		C	1	4	0	1	0	0	0	0	0	.250
1997 Las Vegas ............P.C.		C	3	10	1	4	0	0	1	5	0	.400
1997 San Diego d-e-f .......N.L.		C-1B	50	134	15	42	7	1	3	14	0	.313
Major League Totals	8 Yrs.		284	612	45	151	21	1	12	54	1	.247

a On disabled list from April 8 to April 22, 1994.
b On disabled list from May 17 to June 14, 1996.
c Signed with San Diego Padres organization, December 2, 1996.
d On disabled list from July 13 to August 15, 1997.
e Filed for free agency, October 31, 1997.
f Re-signed with San Diego Padres, November 12, 1997.

HERNANDEZ, JOSE ANTONIO

Born, Vega Alta, Puerto Rico, July 14, 1969.
Bats Right. Throws Right. Height, 6 feet. Weight, 180 pounds.

Year Club	Lea	Pos	G	AB	R	H	2B	3B	HR	RBI	SB	Avg
1987 Sarasota Rangers .Gulf C.		SS	24	52	5	9	1	1	0	2	2	.173
1988 Sarasota Rangers .Gulf C.		3B-2B-SS-1B	55	162	19	26	7	1	1	13	4	.160
1989 Gastonia ....So. Atl.		3B-SS-2B-OF	91	215	35	47	7	6	1	16	9	.219
1990 Charlotte ....Fla. St.		SS-OF	121	388	43	99	14	7	1	44	11	.255
1991 Oklahoma City ....A.A.		SS	14	46	6	14	1	1	1	3	0	.304
1991 Tulsa ....Texas		SS	91	301	36	72	17	4	1	20	4	.239
1991 Texas a .........A.L.		SS-3B	45	98	8	18	2	1	0	4	0	.184
1992 Canton ....Eastern		SS	130	404	56	103	16	4	3	46	7	.255
1992 Cleveland .........A.L.		SS	3	4	0	0	0	0	0	0	0	.000
1993 Canton b ......Eastern		SS-3B	45	150	19	30	6	0	2	17	9	.200
1993 Orlando .....Southern		SS	71	263	42	80	8	3	8	33	8	.304
1993 Iowa ...........A.A.		SS	6	24	3	6	1	0	0	3	0	.250
1994 Chicago ..........N.L.		3B-2B-SS-2B-OF	56	132	18	32	2	3	1	9	2	.242
1995 Chicago ..........N.L.		SS-2B-3B	93	245	37	60	11	4	13	40	1	.245
1996 Chicago ..........N.L.		SS-3B-2B-OF	131	331	52	80	14	1	10	41	4	.242
1997 Chicago ..........N.L.		3B-SS-2B-OF	121	183	33	50	8	5	7	26	2	.273
Major League Totals	6 Yrs.		449	993	148	240	37	14	31	120	9	.242

a Claimed on waivers by Cleveland Indians from Texas Rangers, April 3, 1992.
b Traded by Cleveland Indians to Chicago Cubs organization for pitcher Heathcliff Slocumb, June 1, 1993.

HIDALGO, RICHARD JOSE

Born, Caracas, Venezuela, July 2, 1975.
Bats Right. Throws Right. Height, 6 feet, 3 inches. Weight, 190 pounds.

Year Club	Lea	Pos	G	AB	R	H	2B	3B	HR	RBI	SB	Avg
1992 Astros ....Gulf Coast		OF	51	184	20	57	7	3	1	27	14	.310
1993 Asheville ....So. Atl.		OF	111	403	49	109	23	3	10	55	21	.270
1994 Quad City ....Midwest		OF	124	476	68	139	47	6	12	76	12	.292
1995 Jackson ....Texas		OF	133	489	59	130	28	6	14	59	8	.266
1996 Jackson ....Texas		OF	130	513	66	151	34	2	14	78	11	.294
1997 New Orleans ..........A.A.		OF	134	526	74	147	37	5	11	78	6	.279
1997 Houston .............N.L.		OF	19	62	8	19	5	0	2	6	1	.306
Division Series												
1997 Houston .............N.L.		OF	2	5	1	0	0	0	0	0	0	.000

HIGGINSON, ROBERT LEIGH (BOBBY)

Born, Philadelphia, Pennsylvania, August 18, 1970.
Bats Left. Throws Right. Height, 5 feet, 11 inches. Weight, 180 pounds.

Year Club	Lea	Pos	G	AB	R	H	2B	3B	HR	RBI	SB	Avg
1992 Niagara Falls .....N.Y.-Penn.		OF	70	232	35	68	17	4	2	37	12	.293
1993 Lakeland ....Fla. St.		OF	61	223	42	67	11	7	3	25	8	.300
1993 London ....Eastern		OF	63	224	25	69	15	4	4	35	3	.308
1994 Toledo ....Int.		OF	137	476	81	131	28	3	23	67	16	.275
1995 Detroit .............A.L.		OF	131	410	61	92	17	5	14	43	6	.224
1996 Toledo a ....Int.		OF	3	13	4	4	0	1	0	1	0	.308
1996 Detroit .............A.L.		OF	130	440	75	141	35	0	26	81	6	.320
1997 Detroit b ............A.L.		OF	146	546	94	163	30	5	27	101	12	.299
Major League Totals	3 Yrs.		407	1396	230	396	82	10	67	225	24	.284

a On disabled list from May 11 to June 7, 1996.
b On disabled list from June 11 to June 26, 1997.

HILL, GLENALLEN

Born, Santa Cruz, California, March 22, 1965.
Bats Right. Throws Right. Height, 6 feet, 2 inches. Weight, 220 pounds.

Year	Club	Lea	Pos	G	AB	R	H	2B	3B	HR	RBI	SB	Avg
1983 Medicine Hat	Pioneer	OF	46	133	26	34	3	4	6	27	4	.256
1984 Florence	So. Atl.	OF	129	440	75	105	19	5	16	64	30	.239
1985 Kinston	Carolina	OF	131	466	57	98	13	0	20	56	42	.210
1986 Knoxville	Southern	OF	141	*570	87	158	23	6	*31	97	18	.277
1987 Syracuse	Int.	OF	137	536	65	126	25	6	16	77	22	.235
1988 Syracuse	Int.	OF	51	172	21	40	7	0	4	19	7	.233
1988 Knoxville	Southern	OF	79	269	37	71	13	2	12	38	10	.264
1989 Syracuse	Int.	OF	125	483	86	155	31	15	21	72	21	.321
1989 Toronto	A.L.	OF	19	52	4	15	0	0	1	7	2	.288
1990 Toronto a	A.L.	OF	84	260	47	60	11	3	12	32	8	.231
1991 Tor.-Cleveland b	A.L.	OF	72	221	29	57	8	2	8	25	6	.258
1992 Canton	Eastern	OF	3	9	1	1	1	0	0	1	0	.111
1992 Cleveland c	A.L.	OF	102	369	38	89	16	1	18	49	9	.241
1993 Cleveland d	A.L.	OF	66	174	19	39	7	2	5	25	7	.224
1993 Chicago	N.L.	OF	31	87	14	30	7	0	10	22	1	.345
1994 Chicago e	N.L.	OF	89	269	48	80	12	1	10	38	19	.297
1995 San Francisco f-g	N.L.	OF	132	497	71	131	29	4	24	86	25	.264
1996 Phoenix h	P.C.	OF	5	17	4	6	1	0	2	2	1	.353
1996 San Francisco	N.L.	OF	98	379	56	106	26	0	19	67	6	.280
1997 San Francisco i	N.L.	OF	128	398	47	104	28	4	11	64	7	.261
Major League Totals		9 Yrs.	821	2706	373	711	144	17	118	415	90	.263
Division Series												
1997 San Francisco	N.L.	OF	3	7	0	0	0	0	0	0	0	.000

a On disabled list from July 6 to July 21, 1990.
b Traded to Cleveland Indians with outfielder Mark Whiten, pitcher Denis Boucher and player to be named for pitcher Tom Candiotti and outfielder Turner Ward, June 27; trade settled for cash, October 22, 1991.
c On disabled list from April 23 to May 22, 1992.
d Traded to Chicago Cubs for outfielder Candy Maldonado, August 19, 1993.
e Declared restricted free agent under Major League Baseball implemented labor proposal, December 23, 1994.
f Designated for assignment by Chicago Cubs, April 7, 1995.
g Signed with San Francisco Giants, April 9, 1995.
h On disabled list from May 27 to August 5, 1996.
i Filed for free agency, October 29, 1997.

HOCKING, DENNIS LEE

Born, Torrance, California, April 2, 1970.
Bats Both. Throws Right. Height, 5 feet, 10 inches. Weight, 180 pounds.

Year	Club	Lea	Pos	G	AB	R	H	2B	3B	HR	RBI	SB	Avg
1990 Elizabethton	Appal.	SS-2B-3B	54	201	45	59	6	2	6	30	14	.294
1991 Kenosha	Midwest	SS	125	432	72	110	17	8	2	36	22	.255
1992 Visalia	California	SS	135	550	117	*182	34	9	7	81	38	.331
1993 Nashville	Southern	SS	107	409	54	109	9	4	8	50	15	.267
1993 Minnesota	A.L.	SS-2B	15	36	7	5	1	0	0	0	1	.139
1994 Salt Lake City	P.C.	SS	112	394	61	110	14	6	5	57	13	.279
1994 Minnesota	A.L.	SS	11	31	3	10	3	0	0	2	2	.323
1995 Salt Lake	P.C.	SS-2B	117	397	51	112	24	2	8	75	12	.282
1995 Minnesota	A.L.	SS	9	25	4	5	0	2	0	3	1	.200
1996 Salt Lake a	P.C.	SS-OF-1B	37	130	18	36	6	2	3	22	2	.277
1996 Minnesota	A.L.	OF-SS-2B-1B	49	127	16	25	6	0	1	10	3	.197
1997 Minnesota	A.L.	SS-3B-OF-2B	115	253	28	65	12	4	2	25	3	.257
Major League Totals		5 Yrs.	199	472	58	110	22	6	3	40	10	.233

a On disabled list from April 1 to April 30 and May 30 to June 29 and July 31 to September 8, 1996.

HOILES, CHRISTOPHER ALLEN

Born, Bowling Green, Ohio, March 20, 1965.
Bats Right. Throws Right. Height, 6 feet. Weight, 213 pounds.

Year	Club	Lea	Pos	G	AB	R	H	2B	3B	HR	RBI	SB	Avg
1986 Bristol	Appal.	1B-C	*68	253	42	81	*19	2	13	*57	10	.320
1987 Glens Falls	Eastern	C	108	380	47	105	12	0	13	53	1	.276
1988 Toledo	Int.	C	22	69	4	11	1	0	2	6	1	.159
1988 Glens Falls a	Eastern	C	103	360	67	102	21	3	*17	73	4	.283
1989 Rochester	Int.	C	96	322	41	79	19	1	10	51	1	.245
1989 Baltimore	A.L.	C	6	9	0	1	1	0	0	1	0	.111
1990 Rochester	Int.	C	74	247	52	86	20	1	18	56	4	.348

79

Year Club	Lea	Pos	G	AB	R	H	2B	3B	HR	RBI	SB	Avg
1990 Baltimore	A.L.	C-1B	23	63	7	12	3	0	1	6	0	.190
1991 Baltimore	A.L.	C-1B	107	341	36	83	15	0	11	31	0	.243
1992 Hagerstown	Eastern	C	7	24	7	11	1	0	1	5	0	.458
1992 Baltimore b	A.L.	C	96	310	49	85	10	1	20	40	0	.274
1993 Baltimore c	A.L.	C	126	419	80	130	28	0	29	82	1	.310
1994 Baltimore d	A.L.	C	99	332	45	82	10	0	19	53	2	.247
1995 Baltimore e	A.L.	C	114	352	53	88	15	1	19	58	1	.250
1996 Baltimore	A.L.	C-1B	127	407	64	105	13	0	25	73	0	.258
1997 Bowie	Eastern	C	3	7	1	1	1	0	0	2	0	.143
1997 Baltimore f	A.L.	C-1B-3B	99	320	45	83	15	0	12	49	1	.259
Major League Totals		9 Yrs.	797	2553	379	669	110	2	136	393	5	.262
Division Series												
1996 Baltimore	A.L.	C	4	7	1	1	0	0	0	0	0	.143
1997 Baltimore	A.L.	C	3	7	1	1	0	0	1	1	0	.143
Division Series Totals			7	14	2	2	0	0	1	1	0	.143
Championship Series												
1996 Baltimore	A.L.	C	4	12	1	2	0	0	1	2	0	.167
1997 Baltimore	A.L.	C	4	14	1	2	0	0	0	0	0	.143
Championship Series Totals			8	26	2	4	0	0	1	2	0	.154

a Traded by Detroit Tigers to Baltimore Orioles organization with pitchers Robinson Garces and Cesar Mejia to complete August 31 trade in which Detroit acquired outfielder Fred Lynn, September 12, 1988.
b On disabled list from June 22 to August 18, 1992.
c On disabled list from August 3 to August 24, 1993.
d Declared restricted free agent under Major League Baseball implemented labor proposal, December 23, 1994.
e On disabled list from July 16 to July 31, 1995.
f On disabled list from June 17 to July 18, 1997.

HOLLANDSWORTH, TODD MATHEW
Born, Dayton, Ohio, April 20, 1973.
Bats Left. Throws Left. Height, 6 feet, 2 inches. Weight, 195 pounds.

Year Club	Lea	Pos	G	AB	R	H	2B	3B	HR	RBI	SB	Avg
1991 Dodgers	Gulf Coast	OF	6	16	1	5	0	0	0	0	0	.313
1991 Yakima	Northwest	OF	56	203	34	48	5	1	8	33	11	.236
1992 Bakersfield	California	OF	119	430	70	111	23	5	13	58	27	.258
1993 San Antonio	Texas	OF	126	474	57	119	24	9	17	63	24	.251
1994 Albuquerque	P.C.	OF	132	505	80	144	31	5	19	91	15	.285
1995 San Bernardino	California	OF	1	2	0	1	0	0	0	0	0	.500
1995 Albuquerque	P.C.	OF	10	38	9	9	2	0	2	4	1	.237
1995 Los Angeles a	N.L.	OF	41	103	16	24	2	0	5	13	2	.233
1996 Los Angeles b	N.L.	OF	149	478	64	139	26	4	12	59	21	.291
1997 Albuquerque	P.C.	OF	13	56	13	24	4	3	1	14	2	.429
1997 San Berndno	California	OF	2	8	1	2	0	1	0	2	0	.250
1997 Los Angeles c	N.L.	OF	106	296	39	73	20	2	4	31	5	.247
Major League Totals		3 Yrs.	296	877	119	236	48	6	21	103	28	.269
Division Series												
1995 Los Angeles	N.L.	OF	2	2	0	0	0	0	0	0	0	.000
1996 Los Angeles	N.L.	OF	3	12	1	4	3	0	0	1	0	.333
Division Series Totals			5	14	1	4	3	0	0	1	0	.286

a On disabled list from May 3 to July 7 and August 9 to September 12, 1995.
b Selected Rookie of the Year in National League for 1996.
c On disabled list from August 1 to August 16 and August 17 to September 6, 1997.

HOLLINS, DAVID MICHAEL
Born, Buffalo, New York, May 25, 1966.
Bats Both. Throws Right. Height, 6 feet, 1 inch. Weight, 215 pounds.

Year Club	Lea	Pos	G	AB	R	H	2B	3B	HR	RBI	SB	Avg
1987 Spokane	Northwest	3B	75	278	52	86	14	4	2	44	20	.309
1988 Riverside	California	3B	139	516	90	157	32	1	9	92	13	.304
1989 Wichita a	Texas	3B	131	459	69	126	29	4	9	79	8	.275
1990 Philadelphia	N.L.	3B-1B	72	114	14	21	0	0	5	15	0	.184
1991 Scranton	Int.	3B-1B	72	229	37	61	11	6	8	35	4	.266
1991 Philadelphia b	N.L.	3B-1B	56	151	18	45	10	2	6	21	1	.298
1992 Philadelphia	N.L.	3B-1B	156	586	104	158	28	4	27	93	9	.270
1993 Philadelphia c	N.L.	3B	143	543	104	148	30	4	18	93	2	.273
1994 Scranton	Int.	OF	6	19	6	4	0	0	1	3	0	.211
1994 Philadelphia d	N.L.	3B-OF	44	162	28	36	7	1	4	26	1	.222

80

Year	Club	Lea	Pos	G	AB	R	H	2B	3B	HR	RBI	SB	Avg
1995 Philadelphia	.N.L.	1B	65	205	46	47	12	2	7	25	1	.229	
1995 Boston e-f-g	.A.L.	OF	5	13	2	2	0	0	0	1	0	.154	
1996 Minnesota-Seattle h-i-j	.A.L.	3B-1B-SS	149	516	88	135	29	0	16	78	6	.262	
1997 Anaheim	.A.L.	3B-1B	149	572	101	165	29	2	16	85	16	.288	
Major League Totals		8 Yrs.	839	2862	505	757	145	15	99	437	36	.265	
Championship Series													
1993 Philadelphia	.N.L.	3B	6	20	2	4	1	0	2	4	1	.200	
World Series Record													
1993 Philadelphia	.N.L.	3B	6	23	5	6	1	0	0	2	0	.261	

a Drafted by Philadelphia Phillies from San Diego Padres organization, December 4, 1989.
b On disabled list from August 16 to September 6, 1991.
c On disabled list from June 11 to June 28, 1993.
d On disabled list from May 23 to July 23 and July 24 to end of 1994 season.
e Traded to Boston Red Sox for outfielder Mark Whiten, July 24, 1995.
f On disabled list from August 9 to October 2 and June 12 to June 27, 1995.
g Was not offered contract by Boston, December 21, 1995; signed with Minnesota Twins organization, December 25, 1995.
h Traded to Seattle Mariners for player to be named later, August 29, 1996.
i Filed for free agency, October 31, 1996.
j Signed with California Angels, November 20, 1996.

HOUSTON, TYLER SAM

Born, Las Vegas, Nevada, January 17, 1971.
Bats Left. Throws Right. Height, 6 feet, 2 inches. Weight, 212 pounds.

Year	Club	Lea	Pos	G	AB	R	H	2B	3B	HR	RBI	SB	Avg
1989 Idaho Falls	Pioneer	DH-C	50	176	30	43	11	0	4	24	4	.244	
1990 Sumter	So.Atl.	C	117	442	58	93	14	3	13	56	6	.210	
1991 Macon	So.Atl.	C	107	351	41	81	16	3	8	47	10	.231	
1992 Durham	Carolina	C-3B-1B	117	402	39	91	17	1	7	38	5	.226	
1993 Greenville	Southern	C-OF	84	262	27	73	14	1	5	33	5	.279	
1993 Richmond	Int.	C	13	36	4	5	1	1	1	3	0	.139	
1994 Richmond	Int.	1B-C-OF	97	312	33	76	15	2	4	33	3	.244	
1995 Richmond	Int.	1B-C-OF-3B	103	349	41	89	10	3	12	42	3	.255	
1996 Atlanta-Chicago a	.N.L.	C-1B-3B-2B	79	142	21	45	9	1	3	27	3	.317	
1997 Iowa	.A.A.	3B-C	6	23	0	5	2	0	0	4	0	.217	
1997 Rockford	Midwest	3B-C	2	6	1	3	1	0	0	1	0	.500	
1997 Chicago b	.N.L.	C-3B-1B-2B	72	196	15	51	10	0	2	28	1	.260	
Major League Totals		2 Yrs.	151	338	36	96	19	1	5	55	4	.284	

a Traded to Chicago Cubs for pitcher Ishmael Villegas, June 26, 1996.
b On disabled list from May 3 to May 19 and June 11 to July 11, 1997.

HOWARD, DAVID WAYNE

Born, Sarasota, Florida, February 26, 1967.
Bats Both. Throws Right. Height, 6 feet. Weight, 175 pounds.

Year	Club	Lea	Pos	G	AB	R	H	2B	3B	HR	RBI	SB	Avg
1987 Fort Myers	Fla. St.	SS	89	289	26	56	9	4	1	19	11	.194	
1988 Appleton	Midwest	SS	110	368	48	82	9	4	1	22	10	.223	
1989 Baseball City a	Fla. St.	SS-OF	83	267	36	63	7	3	3	30	12	.236	
1990 Memphis	Southern	SS-2B	116	384	41	96	10	4	5	44	15	.250	
1991 Omaha	.A.A.	SS-2B	14	41	2	5	0	0	0	2	1	.122	
1991 Kansas City b	.A.L.	SS-2B-3B-OF	94	236	20	51	7	0	1	17	3	.216	
1992 Kansas City b	.A.L.	SS-OF	74	219	19	49	6	2	1	18	3	.224	
1992 Baseball City	Fla. St.	SS	3	9	3	4	1	0	0	0	0	.444	
1992 Omaha	.A.A.	SS	19	68	5	8	1	0	0	5	1	.118	
1993 Omaha	.A.A.	SS	47	157	15	40	8	2	0	18	3	.255	
1993 Kansas City c-d	.A.L.	2B-SS-3B-OF	15	24	5	8	0	1	0	2	1	.333	
1994 Kansas City e	.A.L.	3B-SS-2B-OF	46	83	9	19	4	0	1	13	3	.229	
1995 Kansas City f	.A.L.	2B-SS-OF-1B	95	255	23	62	13	4	0	19	6	.243	
1996 Kansas City	.A.L.	SS-2B-1B-OF	143	420	51	92	14	5	4	48	5	.219	
1997 Kansas City g-h	.A.L.	2B-OF-SS-3B	80	162	24	39	8	1	1	13	2	.241	
Major League Totals		7 Yrs.	547	1399	151	320	52	13	8	130	23	.229	

a On disabled list from May 12 to May 31 and July 23 to August 9, 1989.
b On disabled list from April 22 to July 6, 1992.
c On disabled list from April 20 to May 17 and June 7 to August 11, 1993.
d Not offered 1994 contract, December 20, 1993; re-signed with Kansas City Royals, January 18, 1994.
e Record of 0-0 in one game as pitcher.
f On disabled list from May 27 to June 17, 1995.
g On disabled list from August 14 to September 1, 1997.
h Filed for free agency, October 28, 1997.

HOWARD, THOMAS SYLVESTER
Born, Middletown, Ohio, December 11, 1964.
Bats Both. Throws Right. Height 6 feet, 2 inches. Weight, 208 pounds.

Year	Club	Lea	Pos	G	AB	R	H	2B	3B	HR	RBI	SB	Avg
1986	Spokane	Northwest	OF	13	55	16	23	3	3	2	17	2	.418
1986	Reno	California	OF	61	223	35	57	7	3	10	39	10	.256
1987	Wichita	Texas	OF	113	401	72	133	27	4	14	60	26	.332
1988	Las Vegas	P.C.	OF	44	167	29	42	9	1	0	15	3	.251
1988	Wichita	Texas	OF	29	103	15	31	9	2	0	16	6	.301
1989	Las Vegas a	P.C.	OF	80	303	45	91	18	3	3	31	22	.300
1990	Las Vegas	P.C.	OF	89	341	58	112	26	8	5	51	27	.328
1990	San Diego	N.L.	OF	20	44	4	12	2	0	0	0	0	.273
1991	Las Vegas	P.C.	OF	25	94	22	29	3	1	2	16	11	.309
1991	San Diego	N.L.	OF	106	281	30	70	12	3	4	22	10	.249
1992	San Diego b	N.L.	PH-PR	5	3	1	1	0	0	0	0	0	.333
1992	Cleveland	A.L.	OF	117	358	36	99	15	2	2	32	15	.277
1993	Cleveland c	A.L.	OF	74	178	26	42	7	0	3	23	5	.236
1993	Cincinnati	N.L.	OF	38	141	22	39	8	3	4	13	5	.277
1994	Cincinnati	A.L.	OF	83	178	24	47	11	0	5	24	4	.264
1995	Cincinnati	N.L.	OF	113	281	42	85	15	2	3	26	17	.302
1996	Chattanooga d	Southern	OF	8	30	4	10	1	0	1	2	1	.333
1996	Indianapolis e	A.A.	OF	1	5	2	2	0	0	1	2	0	.400
1996	Cincinnati f	N.L.	OF	121	360	50	98	19	10	6	42	6	.272
1997	Houston g	N.L.	OF	107	255	24	63	16	1	3	22	1	.247
Major League Totals		8 Yrs.		784	2079	259	556	105	21	30	204	63	.267
Division Series													
1995	Cincinnati	N.L.	OF	3	10	0	1	1	0	0	0	0	.100
1997	Houston	N.L.	PH	2	1	0	0	0	0	0	0	0	.000
Divisional Series Totals				5	11	0	1	1	0	0	0	0	.091
Championship Series													
1995	Cincinnati	N.L.	OF	4	8	0	2	1	0	0	1	0	.250

a   On disabled list from June 5 to July 19, 1989.
b   Traded to Cleveland Indians for shortstop Jason Hardtke and player to be named, April 14; San Diego Padres
    acquired pitcher Chris Maffett to complete trade, July 10, 1992.
c   Traded to Cincinnati Reds to complete August 17 trade in which Cleveland Indians acquired first baseman Randy
    Milligan for player to be named, August 20, 1993.
d   On disabled list from April 1 to April 20, 1996.
e   Released by Cincinnati Reds, November 16, 1996.
f   Signed with Houston Astros, December 4, 1996.
g   Filed for free agency, October 28, 1997.

HOWELL, JACK ROBERT
Born, Tucson, Arizona, August 18, 1961.
Bats Left. Throws Right. Height, 6 feet. Weight, 190 pounds.

Year	Club	Lea	Pos	G	AB	R	H	2B	3B	HR	RBI	SB	Avg
1984	Redwood	California	3B-1B	135	451	62	111	21	5	5	64	12	.246
1985	Edmonton	P.C.	3B-SS	79	284	55	106	22	3	13	48	3	.373
1985	California	A.L.	3B	43	137	19	27	4	0	5	18	1	.197
1986	Edmonton	P.C.	3B	44	156	39	56	17	3	3	28	1	.359
1986	California	A.L.	3B-OF	63	151	26	41	14	2	4	21	2	.272
1987	California	A.L.	OF-3B-2B	138	449	64	110	18	5	23	64	4	.245
1988	California	A.L.	3B-OF	154	500	59	127	32	2	16	63	2	.254
1989	California	A.L.	3B-OF	144	474	56	108	19	4	20	52	0	.228
1990	Edmonton	P.C.	3B-1B	20	75	14	25	7	1	2	15	3	.333
1990	California a	A.L.	3B-1B-SS	105	316	35	72	19	1	8	33	3	.228
1991	California b	A.L.	2B-3B-OF-1B	32	81	11	17	2	0	2	7	1	.210
1991	San Diego c	A.L.	3B	58	160	24	33	3	1	6	16	0	.206
1992	Yakult d	Japan Cent.	3B	113	387	67	128	21	1	38	87	3	.331
1993	Yakult	Japan Cent.	3B	121	396	72	117	15	1	28	88	3	.295
1994	Yakult e	Japan Cent.	3B	105	363	54	91	14	0	20	56	4	.251
1995	Yomiuri f-g	Japan Cent.	3B	66	219	35	61	10	0	14	41	1	.279
1996	Lk Elsinore h	California	3B	4	12	2	2	1	0	1	3	0	.167
1996	California i-j	A.L.	3B-1B-2B	66	126	20	34	4	1	8	21	0	.270
1997	Anaheim k-l	A.L.	3B-1B	77	174	25	45	7	0	14	34	1	.259
Major League Totals		9 Yrs.		880	2568	339	614	122	16	106	329	14	.239

a   On disabled list from May 23 to June 9.
b   Traded to San Diego Padres for outfielder Shawn Abner, July 30, 1991.
c   Filed for free agency, October 28, 1991.
d   Signed with Yakult Swallows, December 8, 1991.
e   Released by Yakult Swallows, October 31, 1994.
f   Signed with Yomiuri Giants, December 7, 1994.

g Announced retirement to return to United States, July 25, 1995.
h Signed by California Angels organization, December 5, 1995.
i Filed for free agency, November 18, 1996.
j On disabled list from June 16 to July 19, 1996.
k Filed for free agency, October 30, 1997.
l Signed with Houston Astros, December 10, 1997.

HUDLER, REX ALLEN

Born, Tempe, Arizona, September 2, 1960.
Bats Right. Throws Right. Height, 6 feet. Weight, 195 pounds.

Year	Club	Lea	Pos	G	AB	R	H	2B	3B	HR	RBI	SB	Avg
1978	Oneonta	NY-Penn.	2B	58	221	33	62	5	5	0	24	16	.281
1979	Ft. Lauderdale	Fla. St.	2B	116	414	37	104	14	1	1	25	23	.251
1980	Ft. Lauderdale	Fla. St.	2B	37	125	14	26	4	0	0	6	2	.208
1980	Greensboro	So. Atl.	2B	20	75	7	17	3	1	2	9	1	.227
1981	Ft. Lauderdale	Fla. St.	2B	79	259	35	77	11	1	2	26	6	.297
1982	Nashville	Southern	2B	89	299	27	71	14	1	0	24	9	.237
1982	Ft. Lauderdale	Fla. St.	2B	9	32	2	8	1	0	1	6	0	.250
1983	Ft. Lauderdale	Fla. St.	2B	91	345	55	93	15	2	2	50	30	.270
1983	Columbus	Int.	2B	40	118	17	36	5	0	1	11	1	.305
1984	Columbus	Int.	2B	114	394	49	115	26	1	1	35	11	.292
1984	New York	A.L.	2B	9	7	2	1	1	0	0	0	0	.143
1985	Columbus	Int.	2B-SS	106	380	62	95	13	4	3	18	29	.250
1985	New York a	N.L.	2B-SS-1B	20	51	4	8	0	1	0	1	0	.157
1986	Rochester	Int.	2B-3B-OF-SS	77	219	29	57	12	3	2	13	12	.260
1986	Baltimore	A.L.	2B-3B	14	1	1	0	0	0	0	0	1	.000
1987	Rochester b	Int.	OF-2B	31	106	22	27	5	1	5	10	9	.255
1988	Indianapolis	A.A.	2B	67	234	36	71	11	3	7	25	14	.303
1988	Montreal	N.L.	2B-SS-OF	77	216	38	59	14	2	4	14	29	.273
1989	Montreal	N.L.	2B-OF-SS	92	155	21	38	7	0	6	13	15	.245
1990	Mont.-St. Louis c	N.L.	OF-2B-3B-1B	93	220	31	62	11	2	7	22	18	.282
1991	St. Louis	N.L.	OF-1B-2B	101	207	21	47	10	2	1	15	12	.227
1992	St. Louis d-e	N.L.	2B-OF-1B	61	98	17	24	4	0	3	5	2	.245
1993	Yakult Swal. f-g	Jpn. Cen.	2B	120	410	48	123	26	3	14	64	1	.300
1994	California h-i	A.L.	2B-OF-3B-1B	56	124	17	37	8	0	8	20	2	.298
1995	California	A.L.	2B-OF-1B	84	223	30	59	16	0	6	27	12	.265
1996	California j-k	A.L.	2B-OF-1B	92	302	60	94	20	3	16	40	14	.311
1997	Reading	Eastern	OF-2B	6	23	5	8	2	0	1	5	0	.348
1997	Clearwater	Fla. St.	DH-OF-2B	9	34	8	11	2	1	3	6	1	.324
1997	Scranton-WB	Int.	DH-2B	3	9	0	3	0	0	0	0	0	.333
1997	Philadelphia l	N.L.	OF-2B	50	122	17	27	4	0	5	10	1	.221
Major League Totals			12 Yrs.	749	1726	259	456	95	10	56	167	107	.264

a Traded to Baltimore Orioles organization with pitcher Rich Bordi for outfielder Gary Roenicke and third baseman Leo Hernandez, December 11, 1985.
b Became free agent, October 15; signed with Montreal Expos organization, December 8, 1987.
c Traded to St. Louis Cardinals for pitcher John Costello, April 23, 1990.
d On disabled list from May 17 to June 29, 1992.
e Released to sign with Yakult Swallows of Japan Central League, December 8, 1992.
f Signed with San Francisco Giants organization, December 21, 1993.
g Released by San Francisco Giants, March 22; signed with California Angels, March 28, 1994.
h On disabled list from May 28 to June 14, 1994.
i Filed for free agency, October 27; re-signed with California Angels, December 5, 1994.
j Filed for free agency, October 28, 1996.
k Signed with Philadelphia Phillies, November 21, 1996.
l On disabled list from April 12 to May 7 and June 9 to August 7, 1997.

HUNDLEY, TODD RANDOLPH

Born, Martinsville, Virginia, May 27, 1969.
Bats Both. Throws Right. Height, 5 feet, 11 inches. Weight, 185 pounds.

Year	Club	Lea	Pos	G	AB	R	H	2B	3B	HR	RBI	SB	Avg
1987	Little Falls	N.Y.-Penn.	C	34	103	12	15	4	0	1	10	0	.146
1988	Little Falls	N.Y.-Penn.	C	52	176	23	33	8	0	2	18	1	.188
1988	St. Lucie	Fla. St.	C	1	1	0	0	0	0	0	0	0	.000
1989	Columbia	So. Atl.	C-OF	125	439	67	118	23	4	11	66	6	.269
1990	Jackson	Texas	C-3B	81	279	27	74	12	2	1	35	5	.265
1990	New York	N.L.	C	36	67	8	14	6	0	0	2	0	.209
1991	Tidewater a	Int.	C	125	454	62	124	24	4	14	66	1	.273
1991	New York	N.L.	C	21	60	5	8	0	1	1	7	0	.133
1992	New York	N.L.	C	123	358	32	75	17	0	7	32	3	.209
1993	New York	N.L.	C	130	417	40	95	17	2	11	53	1	.228

Year	Club	Lea	Pos	G	AB	R	H	2B	3B	HR	RBI	SB	Avg
1994 New York	............N.L.		C	91	291	45	69	10	1	16	42	2	.237
1995 New York b-c	...N.L.		C	90	275	39	77	11	0	15	51	1	.280
1996 New York	............N.L.		C	153	540	85	140	32	1	41	112	1	.259
1997 New York	............N.L.		C	132	417	78	114	21	2	30	86	2	.273
Major League Totals		8 Yrs.		776	2425	332	592	114	7	121	385	10	.244

a On disabled list from June 29 to July 6, 1991.
b Signed with New York Mets, April 28, 1995.
c On disabled list from July 23 to October 2, 1995.

HUNTER, BRIAN LEE
Born, Portland, Oregon, March 5, 1971.
Bats Right. Throws Right. Height, 6 feet, 4 inches. Weight, 180 pounds.

Year	Club	Lea	Pos	G	AB	R	H	2B	3B	HR	RBI	SB	Avg
1989 Kissimmee Astros	...Gulf C.		OF	51	206	15	35	2	0	0	13	12	.170
1990 Asheville	.......So. Atl.		OF	127	444	84	111	14	6	0	16	45	.250
1991 Osceola	..........Fla. St.		OF	118	392	51	94	15	3	1	30	32	.240
1992 Osceola	..........Fla. St.		OF	131	489	62	146	18	9	1	62	39	.299
1993 Jackson	............Texas		OF	133	523	84	154	22	5	10	52	*35	.294
1994 Tucson	...............P.C.		OF	128	513	*113	*191	28	9	10	51	*49	*.372
1994 Houston	..............N.L.		OF	6	24	2	6	1	0	0	0	2	.250
1995 Tucson	...............P.C.		OF	38	155	28	51	5	1	1	16	11	.329
1995 Jackson	............Texas		OF	2	6	1	3	0	0	0	0	0	.500
1995 Houston	..............N.L.		OF	78	321	52	97	14	5	2	28	24	.302
1996 Tucson a	...............P.C.		OF	3	14	3	5	0	1	0	1	3	.357
1996 Houston b	...........N.L.		OF	132	526	74	145	27	2	5	35	35	.276
1997 Detroit	...............A.L.		OF	162	658	112	177	29	7	4	45	*74	.269
Major League Totals		4 Yrs.		378	1529	240	425	71	14	11	108	135	.278

a On disabled list from June 29 to July 27, 1996.
b Traded to Detroit Tigers with infielder Orlando Miller, pitcher Todd Jones and pitcher Doug Brocail for catcher Brad Ausmus, pitcher C.J. Nitkowski, pitcher Jose Lima, pitcher Trever Miller and infielder Daryle Ward, December 10, 1996.

HUSKEY, ROBERT LEON (BUTCH)
Born, Anadarko, Oklahoma, November 10, 1971.
Bats Right. Throws Right. Height, 6 feet, 3 inches. Weight, 244 pounds.

Year	Club	Lea	Pos	G	AB	R	H	2B	3B	HR	RBI	SB	Avg
1989 Mets	..........Gulf Coast		3B-1B	54	190	27	50	14	2	6	34	4	.263
1990 Kingsport	..........Appal.		3B	72	279	39	75	13	0	14	53	7	.269
1991 Columbia	.........So. Atl.		3B	134	492	88	141	27	5	26	99	22	.287
1992 St. Lucie	..........Fla. St.		3B	134	493	65	125	17	1	18	75	7	.254
1993 Binghamton	........Eastern		3B-SS	139	526	72	132	23	1	25	98	11	.251
1993 New York	..............N.L.		3B	13	41	2	6	1	0	0	3	0	.146
1994 Norfolk	................Int.		3B	127	474	59	108	23	3	10	57	16	.228
1995 Norfolk	...............Int.		3B-OF-1B	109	394	66	112	18	1	28	87	8	.284
1995 New York	..............N.L.		3B-OF	28	90	8	17	1	0	3	11	1	.189
1996 New York a	...........N.L.		1B-OF-3B	118	414	43	115	16	2	15	60	1	.278
1997 New York	..............N.L.		OF-1B-3B	142	471	61	135	26	2	24	81	8	.287
Major League Totals		4 Yrs.		301	1016	114	273	44	4	42	155	10	.269

a On disabled list from August 6 to September 1, 1996.

JACKSON, DARRIN JAY
Born, Los Angeles, California, August 22, 1963.
Bats Right. Throws Right. Height, 6 feet. Weight, 185 pounds.

Year	Club	Lea	Pos	G	AB	R	H	2B	3B	HR	RBI	SB	Avg
1981 Sara Cubs	......Gulf Coast		OF	62	210	29	39	5	0	1	15	18	.186
1982 Quad City	.........Midwest		OF	132	529	86	146	23	5	5	48	58	.276
1983 Salinas	.........California		OF	129	509	70	126	18	5	6	54	36	.248
1984 Midland	.............Texas		OF	132	496	63	134	18	2	15	54	13	.270
1985 Iowa	................A.A.		OF	10	40	0	7	2	1	0	1	1	.175
1985 Chicago	..............N.L.		OF	5	11	0	1	0	0	0	0	0	.091
1985 Pittsfield	.........Eastern		OF	91	325	38	82	10	1	3	30	8	.252
1986 Pittsfield	.........Eastern		OF	137	520	82	139	28	2	15	64	42	.267
1987 Iowa	................A.A.		OF	132	474	81	130	32	5	23	81	13	.274
1987 Chicago	..............N.L.		OF	7	5	2	4	1	0	0	0	0	.800

Year	Club	Lea	Pos	G	AB	R	H	2B	3B	HR	RBI	SB	Avg
1988 Chicago	....	N.L.	OF	100	188	29	50	11	3	6	20	4	.266
1989 Iowa	....	A.A.	OF	30	120	18	31	4	1	7	17	4	.258
1989 Chicago-San Diego a		N.L.	OF	70	170	17	37	7	0	4	20	1	.218
1990 Las Vegas	....	P.C.	OF	29	98	14	27	4	0	5	15	3	.276
1990 San Diego	....	N.L.	OF	58	113	10	29	3	0	3	9	3	.257
1991 San Diego b	....	N.L.	OF-P	122	359	51	94	12	1	21	49	5	.262
1992 San Diego c		N.L.	OF	155	587	72	146	23	5	17	70	14	.249
1993 Toronto	....	A.L.	OF	46	176	15	38	8	0	5	19	0	.216
1993 New York e-f	....	N.L.	OF	31	87	4	17	1	0	1	7	0	.195
1994 Chicago g-h		A.L.	OF	104	369	43	115	17	3	10	51	7	.312
1997 Salt Lake i-j	....	P.C.	OF	19	80	14	24	3	3	1	12	3	.300
1997 Minnesota-Milwaukee k-l		A.L.	OF	75	211	26	55	9	1	5	36	4	.261
Major League Totals	....		10 Yrs.	773	2276	269	586	92	13	72	281	38	.257

a Traded to San Diego Padres with pitcher Calvin Schiraldi and player to be named for infielder/outfielder Luis Salazar and outfielder Marvell Wynne, August 30; San Diego acquired outfielder/first baseman Phil Stephenson to complete trade September 5, 1989.
b Record of 0-0 in one game as pitcher.
c Traded to Toronto Blue Jays for outfielder Derek Bell and Stoney Briggs, March 30, 1993.
d Traded to New York Mets for shortstop Tony Fernandez, June 11, 1993.
e On disabled list from July 19 to September 1, 1993.
f Not offered 1994 contract, December 20; signed with Chicago White Sox, December 28, 1993.
g Filed for free agency, October 25, 1994.
h Played in Japan.
i Signed with Minnesota Twins, April 24, 1997.
j Traded to Milwaukee Brewers for player to be named later, August 30, 1997.
k Filed for free agency, October 27, 1997.
l Signed with Milwaukee Brewers organization, November 19, 1997.

JAHA, JOHN EMIL

Born, Portland, Oregon, May 27, 1966.
Bats Right. Throws Right. Height, 6 feet, 1 inch. Weight, 205 pounds.

Year	Club	Lea	Pos	G	AB	R	H	2B	3B	HR	RBI	SB	Avg
1985 Helena	....	Pioneer	3B	24	68	13	18	3	0	2	14	4	.265
1986 Tri-Cities a	......	Northwest	1B-3B	73	258	65	82	13	2	*15	67	9	.318
1987 Beloit	....	Midwest	3B-1B	122	377	68	101	22	0	7	47	10	.268
1988 Stockton	....	California	1B	99	302	58	77	14	6	8	54	10	.255
1989 Stockton	....	California	1B-3B	140	479	83	140	26	5	25	91	8	.292
1990 Stockton b		California	DH	26	84	12	22	5	0	4	19	0	.262
1991 El Paso	....	Texas	1B	130	486	*121	167	38	3	*30	*134	12	.344
1992 Denver	....	A.A.	1B-OF	79	274	61	88	18	2	18	69	6	.321
1992 Milwaukee	....	A.L.	1B-OF	47	133	17	30	3	1	2	10	0	.226
1993 Milwaukee	....	A.L.	1B-2B-3B	153	515	78	136	21	0	19	70	13	.264
1994 New Orleans		A.A.	1B	18	62	8	25	7	1	2	16	2	.403
1994 Milwaukee	....	A.L.	1B	84	291	45	70	14	0	12	39	3	.241
1995 Beloit	....	Midwest	DH	1	4	1	0	0	0	0	0	0	.000
1995 New Orleans		A.A.	DH-1B	3	10	2	4	1	0	1	3	0	.400
1995 Milwaukee c		A.L.	1B	88	316	59	99	20	2	20	65	2	.313
1996 Milwaukee	....	A.L.	1B	148	543	108	163	28	1	34	118	3	.300
1997 Milwaukee d		A.L.	1B	46	162	25	40	7	0	11	26	1	.247
Major League Totals	....		6 Yrs.	566	1960	332	538	93	4	98	328	32	.274

a Loaned by Milwaukee Brewers to cooperative Tri-Cities Triplets of Northwest League from June 5 to end of 1986 season.
b On disabled list from March 28 to July 10, 1990.
c On disabled list from May 21 to June 6 and June 24 to July 27, 1995.
d On disabled list from June 1 to September 29, 1997.

JAVIER, STANLEY JULIAN

Born, San Francisco Macoris, Dominican Republic, September 1, 1965.
Bats Both. Throws Right. Height, 6 feet. Weight, 185 pounds.

Year	Club	Lea	Pos	G	AB	R	H	2B	3B	HR	RBI	SB	Avg
1981 Johnson City	....	Appal.	OF	53	144	30	36	5	4	3	19	2	.250
1982 Johnson City	....	Appal.	OF	57	185	45	51	3	*4	8	36	11	.276
1983 Greensboro	......	So. Atl.	OF	129	489	109	152	*34	6	12	77	33	.311
1984 New York	....	A.L.	OF	7	7	1	1	0	0	0	0	0	.143
1984 Nashville a	......	Southern	OF	76	262	40	76	17	4	7	38	17	.290
1984 Columbus b	....	Int.	OF	32	99	12	22	3	1	0	7	1	.222
1985 Huntsville	....	Southern	OF	140	486	105	138	22	8	9	64	61	.284
1986 Tacoma	....	P.C.	OF-1B	69	248	50	81	16	2	4	51	18	.327

Year Club	Lea	Pos	G	AB	R	H	2B	3B	HR	RBI	SB	Avg
1986 Oakland .............A.L.		OF	59	114	13	23	8	0	0	8	8	.202
1987 Tacoma .............P.C.		OF	15	51	6	11	2	0	0	2	3	.216
1987 Oakland c ...........A.L.		OF	81	151	22	28	3	1	2	9	3	.185
1988 Oakland d ...........A.L.		OF	125	397	49	102	13	3	2	35	20	.257
1989 Oakland e ..........A.L.	OF-1B-2B		112	310	42	77	12	3	1	28	12	.248
1990 Oakland f ...........A.L.		OF	19	33	4	8	0	2	0	3	0	.242
1990 Los Angeles .........N.L.		OF	104	276	56	84	9	4	3	24	15	.304
1991 Los Angeles .........N.L.		OF-1B	121	176	21	36	5	3	1	11	7	.205
1992 L.A.-Philadelphia g-h ...N.L.		OF	130	334	42	83	17	1	1	29	18	.249
1993 California i ...........A.L.	OF-1B-2B		92	237	33	69	10	4	3	28	12	.291
1994 Oakland .............A.L.	OF-1B-3B		109	419	75	114	23	0	10	44	24	.272
1995 Oakland j ...........A.L.	OF-3B		130	442	81	123	20	2	8	56	36	.278
1996 San Jose ....California		OF	3	5	1	2	0	0	0	1	0	.400
1996 San Francisco k ......N.L.		OF	71	274	44	74	25	0	2	22	14	.270
1997 San Francisco l-m .....N.L.		OF-1B	142	440	69	126	16	4	8	50	25	.286
Major League Totals		13 Yrs.	1302	3610	552	948	161	27	41	347	194	.263
Division Series												
1997 San Francisco .........N.L.		OF	3	12	2	5	1	0	0	1	1	.417
Championship Series												
1988 Oakland .............A.L.		OF	2	4	0	2	0	0	0	1	0	.500
1989 Oakland .............A.L.		OF	1	2	0	0	0	0	0	0	0	.000
Championship Series Totals			3	6	0	2	0	0	0	1	0	.333
World Series Record												
1988 Oakland .............A.L.		OF	3	4	0	2	0	0	0	2	0	.500
1989 Oakland .............A.L.		OF	1	0	0	0	0	0	0	0	0	.000
World Series Totals			44	4	0	2	0	0	0	2	0	.500

a Traded by St. Louis Cardinals to New York Yankees with shortstop Bobby Meacham for outfielder Bob Helsom and pitchers Marty Mason and Steve Fincher, December 14, 1982.

b Traded by New York Yankees to Oakland A's with pitchers Jay Howell, Jose Rijo, Eric Plunk and Tim Birtsas for outfielder Rickey Henderson and pitcher Bert Bradley, December 5, 1984.

c On disabled list from August 3 to September 1, 1987.

d On disabled list from August 18 to September 5, 1988.

e On disabled list from July 9 to July 24, 1989.

f Traded to Los Angeles Dodgers for second baseman Willie Randolph, May 11, 1990.

g Traded to Philadelphia Phillies for pitcher Steve Searcy and player to be named, July 2; Los Angeles Dodgers acquired outfielder Julio Peguero to complete trade, July 28, 1992.

h Filed for free agency, October 27, 1992; signed with California Angels organization, January 15, 1993.

i Filed for free agency, October 28; signed with Oakland Athletics, December 7, 1993.

j Filed for free agency, November 12, 1995; signed by San Francisco Giants, December 8, 1995.

k On disabled list from April 13 to April 29 and July 17 to September 30, 1996.

l Filed for free agency, October 28, 1997.

m Re-signed with Oakland Athletics, November 26, 1997.

JEFFERIES, GREGORY SCOTT
Born, Burlingame, California, August 1, 1967.
Bats Both. Throws Right. Height, 5 feet, 10 inches. Weight, 185 pounds.

Year Club	Lea	Pos	G	AB	R	H	2B	3B	HR	RBI	SB	Avg
1985 Kingsport ......Appalachian		SS	47	166	27	57	18	2	3	29	21	.343
1985 Columbia ....So. Atl.		SS	20	64	7	18	2	2	1	12	7	.281
1986 Columbia ....So. Atl.		SS	25	112	29	38	6	1	5	24	13	.339
1986 Lynchburg ....Carolina		SS	95	390	66	138	25	9	11	80	43	.354
1986 Jackson ....Texas		SS	5	19	1	8	1	1	0	7	1	.421
1987 Jackson ....Texas		SS-3B	134	510	81	187	48	5	20	101	26	.367
1987 New York ...........N.L.		PH	6	6	0	3	1	0	0	2	0	.500
1988 Tidewater ....Int.		3B-SS-2B	132	504	62	142	28	4	7	61	32	.282
1988 New York ...........N.L.		3B-2B	29	109	19	35	8	2	6	17	5	.321
1989 New York ...........N.L.		2B-3B	141	508	72	131	28	2	12	56	21	.258
1990 New York ...........N.L.		2B-3B	153	604	96	171	*40	3	15	68	11	.283
1991 New York a-b .......N.L.		2B-3B	136	486	59	132	19	2	9	62	26	.272
1992 Kansas City c ........A.L.		3B-2B	152	604	66	172	36	3	10	75	19	.285
1993 St. Louis ...........N.L.		1B-2B	142	544	89	186	24	3	16	83	46	.342
1994 St. Louis d ..........N.L.		1B	103	397	52	129	27	1	12	55	12	.325
1995 Philadelphia e .......N.L.		1B-OF	114	480	69	147	31	2	11	56	9	.306
1996 Scranton-WB f ....Int.		1B	4	17	1	2	0	1	0	0	0	.118
1996 Philadelphia .........N.L.		1B-OF	104	404	59	118	17	3	7	51	20	.292
1997 Philadelphia g .......N.L.		OF	130	476	68	122	25	3	11	48	12	.256
Major League Totals		11 Yrs.	1210	4618	649	1346	256	24	109	573	181	.291
Championship Series												
1988 New York ...........N.L.		3B	7	27	2	9	2	0	0	1	0	.333

a On disabled list from April 27 to May 13, 1991.
b Traded to Kansas City Royals with outfielder Kevin McReynolds and infielder/outfielder Keith Miller for pitcher Bret Saberhagen and infielder Bill Pecota, December 11, 1991.
c Traded to St. Louis Cardinals with outfielder Ed Gerald for outfielder Felix Jose and infielder Craig Wilson, February 13, 1993.
d Filed for free agency, October 17; signed with Philadelphia Phillies, December 14, 1994.
e On disabled list from June 17 to July 2, 1995.
f On disabled list from April 5 to June 4, 1996.
g On disabled list from August 18 to September 2, 1997.

JEFFERSON, REGINALD JIROD

Born, Tallahassee, Florida, September 25, 1968.
Bats Both. Throws Left. Height, 6 feet, 4 inches. Weight, 215 pounds.

Year	Club	Lea	Pos	G	AB	R	H	2B	3B	HR	RBI	SB	Avg
1986 Sarasota Reds	......	Gulf C.	1B	59	208	28	54	4	*5	3	33	10	.260
1987 Cedar Rapids a-b	...	Midwest	1B	15	54	9	12	5	0	3	11	1	.222
1987 Billings	....	Pioneer	1B	8	22	10	8	1	0	1	0	1	.364
1988 Cedar Rapids	......	Midwest	1B	135	517	76	149	26	2	18	*90	2	.288
1989 Chattanooga	......	Southern	1B	135	487	66	140	19	3	17	80	2	.287
1990 Nashville c	....	A.A.	1B	37	126	24	34	11	2	5	23	1	.270
1991 Nashville	....	A.A.	1B	28	103	15	33	3	1	3	20	3	.320
1991 Cincinnati d	....	N.L.	1B	5	7	1	1	0	0	1	1	0	.143
1991 Canton e	....	Eastern	1B	6	25	2	7	1	0	0	4	0	.280
1991 Colorado Springs	......	P.C.	1B	39	136	29	42	11	0	3	21	0	.309
1991 Cleveland	....	A.L.	1B	26	101	10	20	3	0	2	12	0	.198
1992 Colorado Springs	......	P.C.	1B	57	218	49	68	11	4	11	44	1	.312
1992 Cleveland f	....	A.L.	1B	24	89	8	30	6	2	1	6	0	.337
1993 Cleveland g	....	A.L.	DH-1B	113	366	35	91	11	2	10	34	1	.249
1994 Seattle h	....	A.L.	DH-1B-OF	63	162	24	53	11	0	8	32	0	.327
1995 Boston i-j	....	A.L.	DH-1B-OF	46	121	21	35	8	0	5	26	0	.289
1996 Boston	....	A.L.	DH-OF-1B	122	386	67	134	30	4	19	74	0	.347
1997 Boston	....	A.L.	DH-1B	136	489	74	156	33	1	13	67	1	.319
Major League Totals	....		7 Yrs.	535	1721	240	520	102	9	59	252	2	.302
Division Series													
1995 Boston	....	A.L.	DH	1	4	1	1	0	0	0	0	0	.250

a Batted lefthanded only from 1987 through 1988 season.
b On disabled list from May 14 to June 12 and July 8 to end of 1987 season.
c On disabled list from May 25 to end of 1990 season.
d Traded to Cleveland Indians organization for infielder Tim Costo, June 14, 1991.
e On disabled list from June 14 to June 30, 1991.
f On disabled list from March 28 to July 3, 1992.
g Traded to Seattle Mariners with shortstop Felix Fermin for shortstop Omar Vizquel, December 20, 1993.
h On disabled list from May 21 to June 10, 1994.
i Signed with Boston Red Sox, April 9, 1995.
j On disabled list from July 10 to September 19, 1995.

JETER, DEREK SANDERSON

Born, Pequannock, New Jersey, June 26, 1974.
Bats Right. Throws Right. Height, 6 feet, 3 inches. Weight, 175 pounds.

Year	Club	Lea	Pos	G	AB	R	H	2B	3B	HR	RBI	SB	Avg
1992 Tampa Yankees	......	Gulf C.	SS	47	173	19	35	10	0	3	25	2	.202
1992 Greensboro	....	So. Atl.	SS	11	37	4	9	0	0	1	4	0	.243
1993 Greensboro	....	So. Atl.	SS	128	515	85	152	14	11	5	71	18	.295
1994 Tampa	....	Fla. St.	SS	69	292	61	96	13	8	0	39	28	.329
1994 Albany	....	Eastern	SS	34	122	17	46	7	2	2	13	12	.377
1994 Columbus	....	Int.	SS	35	126	25	44	7	1	3	16	10	.349
1995 Columbus	....	Int.	SS	123	486	96	154	27	9	2	45	20	.317
1995 New York	....	A.L.	SS	15	48	5	12	4	1	0	7	0	.250
1996 New York a	....	A.L.	SS	157	582	104	183	25	6	10	78	14	.314
1997 New York	....	A.L.	SS	159	654	116	190	31	7	10	70	23	.291
Major League Totals	....		3 Yrs.	331	1284	225	385	60	14	20	155	37	.300
Division Series													
1996 New York	....	A.L.	SS	4	17	2	7	1	0	0	1	0	.412
1997 New York	....	A.L.	SS	5	21	6	7	1	0	2	2	1	.333
Division Series Totals	....			9	38	8	14	2	0	2	3	1	.368
Championship Series													
1996 New York	....	A.L.	SS	5	24	5	10	2	0	1	1	2	.417
World Series													
1996 New York	....	A.L.	SS	6	20	5	5	0	0	0	1	1	.250

a Selected Rookie of the Year in American League for 1996.

JOHNSON, BRIAN DAVID

Born, Oakland, California, January 8, 1968.
Bats Right. Throws Right. Height, 6 feet, 2 inches. Weight, 210 pounds.

Year	Club	Lea	Pos	G	AB	R	H	2B	3B	HR	RBI	SB	Avg
1989	Sarasota Yankees	Gulf C.	C	17	61	7	22	1	1	0	8	0	.361
1990	Greensboro	So. Atl.	C-3B-1B	137	496	58	118	15	0	7	51	4	.238
1991	Fort Lauderdale	Fla. St.	C-1B-3B	113	394	35	94	19	0	1	44	4	.239
1991	Albany a	Eastern	C-1B	2	8	0	0	0	0	0	0	0	.000
1992	Wichita	Texas	C-3B	75	245	30	71	20	0	3	26	3	.290
1993	Las Vegas	P.C.	C-3B-OF	115	416	58	141	35	6	10	71	0	.339
1994	Las Vegas	P.C.	C	15	51	6	11	1	0	2	9	0	.216
1994	San Diego	N.L.	C-1B	36	93	7	23	4	1	3	16	0	.247
1995	San Diego	N.L.	C-1B	68	207	20	52	9	0	3	29	0	.251
1996	San Diego	N.L.	C-1B-3B	82	243	18	66	13	1	8	35	0	.272
1997	Toledo	Int.	C	7	21	0	3	2	0	0	1	0	.143
1997	Detroit b	A.L.	C	45	139	13	33	6	1	2	18	1	.237
1997	San Francisco	N.L.	C-1B	56	179	19	50	7	2	11	27	0	.279
Major League Totals			4 Yrs.	287	861	77	224	39	5	27	125	1	.260
Division Series													
1996	San Diego	N.L.	C	2	8	2	3	1	0	0	0	0	.286
1997	San Francisco	N.L.	C	3	10	2	1	0	0	1	1	0	.100
Division Series Totals				5	18	4	4	1	0	1	1	0	.222

a Drafted by San Diego Padres from New York Yankees organization in minor league draft, December 9, 1991.
b Traded to San Francisco Giants for catcher Marcus Jensen, July 16, 1997.

JOHNSON, CHARLES EDWARD

Born, Fort Pierce, Florida, July 20, 1971.
Bats Right. Throws Right. Height, 6 feet, 2 inches. Weight, 215 pounds.

Year	Club	Lea	Pos	G	AB	R	H	2B	3B	HR	RBI	SB	Avg
1993	Kane County	Midwest	C	135	488	74	134	29	5	19	94	9	.275
1994	Portland	Eastern	C	132	443	64	117	29	1	*28	80	4	.264
1994	Florida	N.L.	C	4	11	5	5	1	0	1	4	0	.455
1995	Portland	Eastern	C	2	7	0	0	0	0	0	0	0	.000
1995	Florida a	N.L.	C	97	315	40	79	15	1	11	39	0	.251
1996	Florida b	N.L.	C	120	386	34	84	13	1	13	37	1	.218
1997	Florida	N.L.	C	124	416	43	104	26	1	19	63	0	.250
Major League Totals			4 Yrs.	345	1128	122	272	55	3	44	143	1	.241
Division Series													
1997	Florida	N.L.	C	3	8	5	2	1	0	1	2	0	.250
Championship Series													
1997	Florida	N.L.	C	6	17	1	2	2	0	0	5	0	.118
World Series Record													
1997	Florida	N.L.	C	7	28	4	10	0	0	1	3	0	.357

a On disabled list from August 9 to September 1, 1995.
b On disabled list from July 28 to September 1, 1996.

JOHNSON, KENNETH LANCE

Born, Cincinnati, Ohio, July 7, 1963.
Bats Left. Throws Left. Height, 5 feet, 11 inches. Weight, 160 pounds.

Year	Club	Lea	Pos	G	AB	R	H	2B	3B	HR	RBI	SB	Avg
1984	Erie	N.Y.-Penn.	OF	71	283	*63	*96	7	5	1	28	29	.339
1985	St. Petersburg	Fla. St.	OF	129	497	68	134	17	10	2	55	33	.270
1986	Arkansas	Texas	OF	127	445	82	128	24	6	2	33	*49	.288
1987	Louisville	A.A.	OF	116	477	89	159	21	11	5	50	42	.333
1987	St. Louis a	N.L.	OF	33	59	4	13	2	1	0	7	6	.220
1988	Vancouver	P.C.	OF	100	411	71	126	12	6	2	36	49	.307
1988	Chicago	A.L.	OF	33	124	11	23	4	1	0	6	6	.185
1989	Vancouver	P.C.	OF	106	408	69	124	11	7	0	28	33	.304
1989	Chicago	A.L.	OF	50	180	28	54	8	2	0	16	16	.300
1990	Chicago	A.L.	OF	151	541	76	154	18	9	1	51	36	.285
1991	Chicago	A.L.	OF	159	588	72	161	14	*13	0	49	26	.274
1992	Chicago	A.L.	OF	157	567	67	158	15	*12	3	47	41	.279
1993	Chicago	A.L.	OF	147	540	75	168	18	*14	0	47	35	.311
1994	Chicago	A.L.	OF	106	412	56	114	11	*14	3	54	26	.277
1995	Chicago b	A.L.	OF	142	607	98	186	18	12	10	57	40	.306
1996	New York	N.L.	OF	160	*682	117	*227	31	*21	9	69	50	.333
1997	New York-Chicago c-d	N.L.	OF	111	410	60	126	16	8	5	39	20	.307
Major League Totals			11 Yrs.	1249	4710	664	1384	155	107	31	442	302	.294

Year	Club	Lea	Pos	G	AB	R	H	2B	3B	HR	RBI	SB	Avg
	Championship Series												
1987	St. Louis .............N.L.		PR	1	0	1	0	0	0	0	0	1	.000
1993	Chicago ....,....A.L.		OF	6	23	2	5	1	1	1	6	1	.217
Championship Series Totals				7	23	3	5	1	1	1	6	2	.217
	World Series Record												
1987	St. Louis .............N.L.		PR	1	0	0	0	0	0	0	0	1	.000

a Traded to Chicago White Sox with pitcher Ricky Horton for pitcher Jose DeLeon, February 9, 1988.
b Filed for free agency, November 12, 1995; signed with New York Mets, December 14, 1995.
c On disabled list from May 2 to June 16, 1997.
d Traded to Chicago Cubs with pitcher Mark Clark and player to be named later for pitcher Mel Rojas, pitcher Turk Wendell and outfielder Brian McRae, August 8, 1997. Chicago Cubs received infielder Manny Alexander to complete trade, August 14, 1997.

JOHNSON, WILLIAM RUSSELL
Born, Baton Rouge, Louisiana, February 22, 1973.
Bats Right. Throws Right. Height, 5 feet, 10 inches. Weight, 185 pounds.

Year	Club	Lea	Pos	G	AB	R	H	2B	3B	HR	RBI	SB	Avg
1995	Jackson ....Texas		SS	132	475	65	118	16	2	9	53	10	.248
1996	Jackson ....Texas		SS	132	496	86	154	24	5	15	74	9	.310
1997	New Orleans .........A.A.		3B-SS	122	445	72	123	16	6	4	49	7	.276
1997	Houston ..............N.L.		3B-2B	21	60	7	18	1	0	2	9	1	.300
	Division Series												
1997	Houston ..............N.L.		PH	1	1	0	0	0	0	0	0	0	.000

JONES, ANDRUW RUDOLF
Born, Curacao, Neth. Antilles, April 23, 1977.
Bats Right. Throws Right. Height, 6 feet, 1 inch. Weight, 185 pounds.

Year	Club	Lea	Pos	G	AB	R	H	2B	3B	HR	RBI	SB	Avg
1994	Braves ....Gulf Coast		OF	27	95	22	21	5	1	2	10	5	.221
1994	Danville ....Appal.		OF	36	143	20	48	9	2	1	16	16	.336
1995	Macon ....So.Atl.		OF	139	537	104	149	41	5	25	100	56	.277
1996	Durham ....Carolina		OF	66	243	65	76	14	3	17	43	16	.313
1996	Greenville ....Southern		OF	38	157	39	58	10	1	12	37	12	.369
1996	Richmond ....Int.		OF	12	45	11	17	3	1	5	12	2	.378
1996	Atlanta ..............N.L.		OF	31	106	11	23	7	1	5	13	3	.217
1997	Atlanta ..............N.L.		OF	153	399	60	92	18	1	18	70	20	.231
Major League Totals		2 Yrs.	184	505	71	115	25	2	23	83	23	.228
	Division Series												
1996	Atlanta ..............N.L.		OF	3	0	0	0	0	0	0	0	0	.000
1997	Atlanta ..............N.L.		OF	3	5	1	0	0	0	0	1	0	.000
Division Series Totals				6	5	1	0	0	0	0	1	0	.000
	Championship Series												
1996	Atlanta ..............N.L.		OF	5	9	3	2	0	0	1	3	0	.222
1997	Atlanta ..............N.L.		OF	5	9	0	4	0	0	0	1	0	.444
Championship Series Totals				10	18	3	6	0	0	1	4	0	.333
	World Series												
1996	Atlanta ..............N.L.		OF	6	20	4	8	1	0	2	6	1	.400

JONES, CHRISTOPHER CARLOS
Born, Utica, New York, December 16, 1965.
Bats Right. Throws Right. Height, 6 feet, 2 inches. Weight, 205 pounds.

Year	Club	Lea	Pos	G	AB	R	H	2B	3B	HR	RBI	SB	Avg
1984	Billings ....Pioneer		3B	21	73	8	11	2	0	2	13	4	.151
1985	Billings ....Pioneer		OF	63	240	43	62	12	5	4	33	13	.258
1986	Cedar Rapids ......Midwest		OF	128	473	65	117	13	9	20	78	23	.247
1987	Vermont ....Eastern		OF	113	383	50	88	11	4	10	39	13	.230
1988	Chattanooga ......Southern		OF	116	410	50	111	20	7	4	61	11	.271
1989	Nashville .............A.A.		OF	21	49	8	8	1	0	2	5	2	.163
1989	Chattanooga ......Southern		OF	103	378	47	95	18	2	10	54	10	.251
1990	Nashville .............A.A.		OF	134	436	53	114	23	3	10	52	12	.261
1991	Nashville .............A.A.		OF	73	267	29	65	5	4	9	33	10	.243
1991	Cincinnati a ...........N.L.		OF	52	89	14	26	1	2	2	6	2	.292
1992	Tucson ..............P.C.		OF	45	170	25	55	9	8	3	28	7	.324

89

Year Club	Lea	Pos	G	AB	R	H	2B	3B	HR	RBI	SB	Avg
1992 Houston b	N.L.	OF	54	63	7	12	2	1	1	4	3	.190
1993 Colorado Springs	P.C.	OF	46	168	41	47	5	5	12	40	8	.280
1993 Colorado	N.L.	OF	86	209	29	57	11	4	6	31	9	.273
1994 Colorado Springs	P.C.	OF	98	386	77	124	22	4	20	75	12	.321
1994 Colorado c	N.L.	OF	21	40	6	12	2	1	0	2	0	.300
1995 Norfolk	Int.	OF	33	114	20	38	12	1	3	19	5	.333
1995 New York	N.L.	OF-1B	79	182	33	51	6	2	8	31	2	.280
1996 New York d-e	N.L.	OF-1B	89	149	22	36	7	0	4	18	1	.242
1997 San Diego f-g-h	N.L.	OF	92	152	24	37	9	0	7	25	7	.243
Major League Totals	7 Yrs.	473	884	135	231	38	10	28	117	24	.261	

a Released, December 12, 1991; signed with Houston Astros organization, January 2, 1992.
b Refused assignment to minor leagues and became free agent, October 21; signed with Colorado Rockies, October 26, 1992.
c Became free agent, October 15; signed with New York Mets organization, December 7, 1994.
d Outrighted by New York Mets, October 7, 1996.
e Signed with San Diego Padres organization, November 4, 1996.
f On disabled list from May 22 to June 10, 1997.
g Filed for free agency, October 7, 1997.
h Signed with Arizona Diamondbacks, November 21, 1997.

JONES, LARRY WAYNE (CHIPPER)
Born, Deland, Florida, April 24, 1972.
Bats Both. Throws Right. Height, 6 feet, 3 inches. Weight, 185 pounds.

Year Club	Lea	Pos	G	AB	R	H	2B	3B	HR	RBI	SB	Avg
1990 Bradenton Braves	Gulf C.	SS	44	140	20	32	1	1	1	18	5	.229
1991 Macon	So. Atl.	SS	136	473	*104	154	24	11	15	98	40	.326
1992 Durham	Carolina	SS	70	264	43	73	22	1	4	31	10	.277
1992 Greenville	Southern	SS	67	266	43	92	17	11	9	42	14	.346
1993 Richmond	Int.	SS	139	536	97	174	31	12	13	89	23	.325
1993 Atlanta	N.L.	SS	8	3	2	2	1	0	0	0	0	.667
1994 Atlanta a	N.L.	INJURED—Did Not Play										
1995 Atlanta	N.L.	3B-OF	140	524	87	139	22	3	23	86	8	.265
1996 Atlanta b	N.L.	3B-SS-OF	157	598	114	185	32	5	30	110	14	.309
1997 Atlanta	N.L.	3B-OF	157	597	100	176	41	3	21	111	20	.295
Major League Totals	4 Yrs.	462	1722	303	502	96	11	74	307	42	.292	
Division Series												
1995 Atlanta	N.L.	3B	4	18	4	7	2	0	2	4	0	.389
1996 Atlanta	N.L.	3B	3	9	2	2	0	0	1	2	1	.222
1997 Atlanta	N.L.	3B	3	8	3	4	0	0	1	2	1	.500
Division Series Totals		10	35	9	13	2	0	4	8	2	.371	
Championship Series												
1995 Atlanta	N.L.	3B	4	16	3	7	0	0	1	3	1	.438
1996 Atlanta	N.L.	3B	7	25	6	11	2	0	0	4	1	.440
1997 Atlanta	N.L.	3B	6	24	5	7	1	0	2	4	0	.292
Championship Series Totals		17	65	14	25	3	0	3	11	2	.385	
World Series Record												
1995 Atlanta	N.L.	3B	6	21	3	6	3	0	0	1	0	.286
1996 Atlanta	N.L.	3B-SS	6	21	3	6	3	0	0	3	1	.286
World Series Totals		12	42	6	12	3	0	0	4	0	.286	

a On disabled list from March 20 to end of 1994 season.
b On disabled list from April 1 to April 6, 1996.

JORDAN, BRIAN O'NEAL
Born, Baltimore, Maryland, March 29, 1967.
Bats Right. Throws Right. Height, 6 feet, 1 inch. Weight, 205 pounds.

Year Club	Lea	Pos	G	AB	R	H	2B	3B	HR	RBI	SB	Avg
1988 Hamilton a	N.Y.-Penn.	OF	19	71	12	22	3	1	4	12	3	.310
1989 St. Petersburg	Fla. St.	OF	11	43	7	15	4	1	2	11	0	.349
1990 Arkansas b	Texas	OF	16	50	4	8	1	0	0	0	0	.160
1990 St. Petersburg	Fla. St.	OF	9	30	3	5	0	1	0	1	0	.167
1991 Louisville	A.A.	OF	61	212	35	56	11	4	4	24	0	.264
1992 St. Louis c	N.L.	OF	55	193	17	40	9	4	5	22	7	.207
1992 Louisville	Int.	OF	43	155	23	45	3	1	4	16	13	.290
1993 Louisville	A.A.	OF	38	144	24	54	13	2	5	35	9	.375
1993 St. Louis	N.L.	OF	67	223	33	69	10	6	10	44	6	.309
1994 St. Louis d	N.L.	OF-1B	53	178	14	46	8	2	5	15	4	.258

Year	Club	Lea	Pos	G	AB	R	H	2B	3B	HR	RBI	SB	Avg
1995 St. Louis	....	N.L.	OF	131	490	83	145	20	4	22	81	24	.296
1996 St. Louis e	....	N.L.	OF-1B	140	513	82	159	36	1	17	104	22	.310
1997 Louisville	....	A.A.	OF	6	20	1	3	0	0	0	2	0	.150
1997 St. Louis f	....	N.L.	OF	47	145	17	34	5	0	0	10	6	.234
Major League Totals	....		6 Yrs.	493	1742	246	493	88	17	59	276	69	.283
Division Series													
1996 St. Louis	....	N.L.	OF	3	12	4	4	0	0	1	3	1	.333
Championship Series													
1996 St. Louis	....	N.L.	OF	7	25	3	6	1	1	1	2	0	.240

a Batted left and right during 1988 season.
b On disabled list from May 6 to May 17 and June 8 to end of 1990 season.
c On disabled list from May 25 to June 22, 1992.
d On disabled list from July 11 to end of 1994 season.
e On disabled list from April 1 to April 15, 1996.
f On disabled list from May 6 to June 13 and June 27 to August 10 and August 25 to September 29, 1997.

JORDAN, KEVIN WAYNE
Born, San Francisco, California, October 9, 1969.
Bats Right. Throws Right. Height, 6 feet, 1 inch. Weight, 206 pounds.

Year	Club	Lea	Pos	G	AB	R	H	2B	3B	HR	RBI	SB	Avg
1990 Oneonta	....	N.Y.-Penn.	2B	73	276	47	92	13	7	4	54	19	.333
1991 Ft. Laurdrle	....	Fla. St.	2B-1B	121	448	61	122	25	5	4	53	14	.272
1992 Pr William	....	Carolina	2B-3B	112	438	67	136	29	8	8	63	6	.311
1993 Albany a	....	Eastern	2B	135	513	87	145	33	4	16	87	8	.283
1994 Scranton-WB	....	Int.	2B-3B	81	314	44	91	22	1	12	57	0	.290
1995 Scranton-WB	....	Int.	2B	106	410	61	127	29	4	5	60	3	.310
1995 Philadelphia	....	N.L.	2B-3B	24	54	6	10	1	0	2	6	0	.185
1996 Philadelphia b	....	N.L.	1B-2B-3B	43	131	15	37	10	0	3	12	2	.282
1997 Scranton-WB	....	Int.	3B-2B-1B	7	30	5	9	2	2	0	2	2	.300
1997 Philadelphia	....	N.L.	1B-3B-2B	84	177	19	47	8	0	6	30	0	.266
Major League Totals	....		3 Yrs.	151	362	40	94	19	0	11	48	2	.260

a Traded by New York Yankees to Philadelphia Phillies with pitchers Bobby Munoz and Ryan Karp for pitchers Terry Mulholland and Jeff Patterson, February 9, 1994.
b On disabled list from June 17 to end of 1996 season.

JOYNER, WALLACE KEITH
Born, Atlanta, Georgia, June 16, 1962.
Bats Left. Throws Left. Height, 6 feet, 2 inches. Weight, 200 pounds.

Year	Club	Lea	Pos	G	AB	R	H	2B	3B	HR	RBI	SB	Avg
1983 Peoria	....	Midwest	1B	54	192	25	63	16	2	3	33	1	.328
1984 Waterbury	....	Eastern	1B-OF	134	467	81	148	24	7	12	72	0	.317
1985 Edmonton	....	P.C.	1B	126	477	68	135	29	5	12	73	2	.283
1986 California	....	A.L.	1B	154	593	82	172	27	3	22	100	5	.290
1987 California	....	A.L.	1B	149	564	100	161	33	1	34	117	8	.285
1988 California	....	A.L.	1B	158	597	81	176	31	2	13	85	8	.295
1989 California	....	A.L.	1B	159	593	78	167	30	2	16	79	3	.282
1990 California a	....	A.L.	1B	83	310	35	83	15	0	8	41	2	.268
1991 California b	....	A.L.	1B	143	551	79	166	34	3	21	96	2	.301
1992 Kansas City	....	A.L.	1B	149	572	66	154	36	2	9	66	11	.269
1993 Kansas City	....	A.L.	1B	141	497	83	145	36	3	15	65	5	.292
1994 Kansas City c	....	A.L.	1B	97	363	52	113	20	3	8	57	3	.311
1995 Kansas City d	....	A.L.	1B	131	465	69	144	28	0	12	83	3	.310
1996 Rancho Cuca	.....	California	1B	3	10	1	3	1	0	0	2	0	.300
1996 San Diego e	....	N.L.	1B	121	433	59	120	29	1	8	65	5	.277
1997 Las Vegas	....	P.C.	1B	3	8	1	2	0	0	0	1	0	.250
1997 San Diego f	....	N.L.	1B	135	455	59	149	29	2	13	83	3	.327
Major League Totals	....		12 Yrs.	1620	5993	843	1750	348	22	179	937	58	.292
Championship Series													
1986 California	....	A.L.	1B	3	11	3	5	2	0	1	2	0	.455

a On disabled list from July 12 to end of 1990 season.
b Filed for free agency, October 28; signed with Kansas City Royals, December 9, 1991.
c On disabled list from June 26 to July 14, 1994.
d Traded to San Diego Padres with pitcher Aaron Dorlarque for infielder/outfielder Bip Roberts and pitcher Bryan Wolff, December 21, 1995.
e On disabled list from June 2 to July 11, 1996.
f On disabled list from April 28 to May 13, 1997.

JUSTICE, DAVID CHRISTOPHER

Born, Cincinnati, Ohio, April 14, 1966.
Bats Left. Throws Left. Height, 6 feet, 3 inches. Weight, 200 pounds.

Year Club	Lea	Pos	G	AB	R	H	2B	3B	HR	RBI	SB	Avg
1985 Pulaski	Appal.	OF	66	204	39	50	8	0	*10	46	0	.245
1986 Sumter	So. Atl.	OF	61	220	48	66	16	0	10	61	10	.300
1986 Durham	Carolina	OF	67	229	47	64	9	1	12	44	2	.279
1987 Greenville	Southern	OF	93	348	38	79	12	4	6	40	3	.227
1988 Richmond	Int.	OF	70	227	27	46	9	1	8	28	4	.203
1988 Greenville	Southern	OF	58	198	34	55	13	1	9	37	6	.278
1989 Richmond	Int.	1B	115	391	47	102	24	3	12	58	12	.261
1989 Atlanta	N.L.	OF	16	51	7	12	3	0	1	3	2	.235
1990 Richmond	Int.	OF-1B	12	45	7	16	5	1	2	7	0	.356
1990 Atlanta a	N.L.	1B-OF	127	439	76	124	23	2	28	78	11	.282
1991 Macon	So. Atl.	OF	3	10	2	2	0	0	2	5	0	.200
1991 Atlanta b	N.L.	OF	109	396	67	109	25	1	21	87	8	.275
1992 Atlanta c	N.L.	OF	144	484	78	124	19	5	21	72	2	.256
1993 Atlanta	N.L.	OF	157	585	90	158	15	4	40	120	3	.270
1994 Atlanta	N.L.	OF	104	352	61	110	16	2	19	59	2	.313
1995 Atlanta d	N.L.	OF	120	411	73	104	17	2	24	78	4	.253
1996 Atlanta	N.L.	OF	40	140	23	45	9	0	6	25	1	.321
1997 Cleveland g-h	A.L.	OF	139	495	84	163	31	1	33	101	3	.329
Major League Totals		9 Yrs.	956	3353	559	949	158	17	193	623	36	.283
Division Series												
1995 Atlanta	N.L.	OF	4	13	2	3	0	0	0	0	0	.231
1997 Cleveland	A.L.	DH	5	19	3	5	2	0	1	2	0	.263
Division Series Totals			9	32	5	8	2	0	1	2	0	.250
Championship Series												
1991 Atlanta	N.L.	OF	7	25	4	5	1	0	1	2	0	.200
1992 Atlanta	N.L.	OF	7	25	5	7	1	0	2	6	0	.280
1993 Atlanta	N.L.	OF	6	21	2	3	1	0	0	4	0	.143
1995 Atlanta	N.L.	OF	3	11	1	3	0	0	0	1	0	.274
1997 Cleveland	A.L.	DH	6	21	3	7	1	0	0	0	0	.333
Championship Series Totals			29	103	15	25	4	0	3	13	0	.243
World Series Record												
1991 Atlanta	N.L.	OF	7	27	5	7	0	0	2	6	2	.259
1992 Atlanta	N.L.	OF	6	19	4	3	0	0	1	3	1	.158
1995 Atlanta	N.L.	OF	6	20	3	5	1	0	1	5	0	.250
1997 Cleveland	A.L.	OF-DH	7	27	4	5	0	0	0	4	0	.185
World Series Totals			26	93	16	20	1	0	4	18	3	.215

a Selected Rookie of the Year in National League for 1990.
b On disabled list from June 27 to August 20, 1991.
c On disabled list from April 12 to April 27, 1992.
d On disabled list from June 2 to June 17, 1995.
e On disabled list from May 16 to September 30, 1996.
f Traded to Chicago Cubs, January 22, 1997.
g Traded to Cleveland Indians with outfielder Marquis Grissom for outfielder Kenny Lofton and pitcher Alan Embree, March 25, 1997.
h On disabled list from June 23 to July 10, 1997.

KARKOVICE, RONALD JOSEPH

Born, Union, New Jersey, August 8, 1963.
Bats Right. Throws Right. Height, 6 feet, 1 inch. Weight, 219 pounds.

Year Club	Lea	Pos	G	AB	R	H	2B	3B	HR	RBI	SB	Avg
1982 Sarasota White Sox	Gulf C.	C	60	214	34	56	6	0	7	32	5	.262
1983 Appleton	Midwest	C	97	326	54	78	17	3	13	48	10	.239
1984 Glens Falls	Eastern	C	88	260	37	56	9	1	13	39	3	.215
1984 Denver	A.A.	C	31	86	7	19	1	0	2	10	1	.221
1985 Glens Falls	Eastern	C	99	324	37	70	9	3	11	37	6	.216
1986 Birmingham	Southern	C	97	319	62	90	13	1	20	53	2	.282
1986 Chicago	A.L.	C	37	97	13	24	7	0	4	13	1	.247
1987 Chicago	A.L.	C	39	85	7	6	0	0	2	7	3	.071
1987 Hawaii	P.C.	C	34	104	15	19	3	0	4	11	3	.183
1988 Vancouver	P.C.	C	39	116	12	29	10	0	2	13	2	.250
1988 Chicago	A.L.	C	46	115	10	20	4	0	3	9	4	.174
1989 Chicago	A.L.	C	71	182	21	48	9	2	3	24	0	.264
1990 Chicago	A.L.	C	68	183	30	45	10	0	6	20	2	.246
1991 Chicago a	A.L.	C-OF	75	167	25	41	13	0	5	22	0	.246
1992 Chicago	A.L.	C-OF	123	342	39	81	12	1	13	50	10	.237
1993 Chicago b	A.L.	C	128	403	60	92	17	1	20	54	2	.228

Year	Club	Lea	Pos	G	AB	R	H	2B	3B	HR	RBI	SB	Avg
1994 Chicago c	......	.A.L.	C	77	207	33	44	9	1	11	29	0	.213
1995 Chicago d-e	......	.A.L.	C	113	323	44	70	14	1	13	51	2	.217
1996 Chicago	......	.A.L.	C	111	355	44	78	22	0	10	38	0	.220
1997 Chicago f	......	.A.L.	C	51	138	10	25	3	0	6	18	0	.181
Major League Totals			12 Yrs.	939	2597	336	574	120	6	96	335	24	.221
Championship Series													
1993 Chicago	......	.A.L.	C	6	15	0	0	0	0	0	0	0	.000

a On disabled list from May 20 to July 4, 1991.
b On disabled list from June 20 to July 6, 1993.
c On disabled list from July 18 to end of 1994 season.
d Not offered 1996 contract, November 9, 1995.
e Re-signed with Chicago White Sox, November 10, 1995.
f Filed for free agency, November 3, 1997.

KARROS, ERIC PETER
Born, Hackensack, New Jersey, November 4, 1967.
Bats Right. Throws Right. Height, 6 feet, 4 inches. Weight, 216 pounds.

Year	Club	Lea	Pos	G	AB	R	H	2B	3B	HR	RBI	SB	Avg
1988 Great Falls	Pioneer		1B-3B	66	268	68	98	12	1	12	55	8	.366
1989 Bakersfield	California		1B-3B	*142	545	86	*165	*40	1	15	86	18	.303
1990 San Antonio	Texas		1B	*131	509	91	*179	*45	2	18	78	8	*352
1991 Albuquerque	.P.C.		1B	132	488	88	154	33	8	22	101	3	.316
1991 Los Angeles	.N.L.		1B	14	14	0	1	1	0	0	1	0	.071
1992 Los Angeles a	.N.L.		1B	149	545	63	140	30	1	20	88	2	.257
1993 Los Angeles	.N.L.		1B	158	619	74	153	27	2	23	80	0	.247
1994 Los Angeles	.N.L.		1B	111	406	51	108	21	1	14	46	2	.266
1995 Los Angeles	.N.L.		1B	143	551	83	164	29	3	32	105	4	.298
1996 Los Angeles	.N.L.		1B	154	608	84	158	29	1	34	111	8	.260
1997 Los Angeles	.N.L.		1B	162	628	86	167	28	0	31	104	15	.266
Major League Totals			7 Yrs.	891	3371	441	891	165	8	154	535	31	.264
Division Series													
1995 Los Angeles	.N.L.		1B	3	12	3	6	1	0	2	4	0	.500
1996 Los Angeles	.N.L.		1B	3	9	0	0	0	0	0	0	0	.000
Division Series Totals				6	21	3	6	1	0	2	4	0	.286

a Selected Rookie of the Year in National League for 1992.

KELLY, MICHAEL RAYMOND
Born, Los Angeles, California, June 2, 1970.
Bats Right. Throws Right. Height, 6 feet, 4 inches. Weight, 195 pounds.

Year	Club	Lea	Pos	G	AB	R	H	2B	3B	HR	RBI	SB	Avg
1991 Durham	Carolina		DH-OF	35	124	29	31	6	1	6	17	6	.250
1992 Greenville	Southern		OF	133	471	83	108	18	4	25	71	22	.229
1993 Richmond	.Int.		OF	123	424	63	103	13	1	19	58	11	.243
1994 Atlanta	.N.L.		OF	30	77	14	21	10	1	2	9	0	.273
1994 Richmond	.Int.		OF	81	313	46	82	14	4	15	45	9	.262
1995 Richmond	.Int.		OF	15	45	5	13	1	0	2	8	0	.289
1995 Atlanta a	.N.L.		OF	97	137	26	26	6	1	3	17	7	.190
1996 Cincinnati	.N.L.		OF	19	49	5	9	4	0	1	7	4	.184
1996 Indianapolis	.A.A.		OF	88	292	43	61	10	1	8	30	13	.209
1997 Chattanooga	Southern		OF	15	60	14	21	7	0	3	12	3	.350
1997 Indianapolis	.A.A.		OF	27	92	28	32	8	0	7	18	7	.348
1997 Cincinnati b	.N.L.		OF	73	140	27	41	13	2	6	19	6	.293
Major League Totals			4 Yrs.	219	403	72	97	33	4	12	52	17	.241

a Traded to Cincinnati Reds for pitcher Chad Fox and a player to be named, January 9, 1996.
b Traded to Tampa Bay Devil Rays for player to be named later, November 11, 1997. Cincinnati Reds received infielder
   Dmitri Young to complete trade, November 18, 1997.

KELLY, PATRICK FRANKLIN
Born, Philadelphia, Pennsylvania, October 14, 1967.
Bats Right. Throws Right. Height, 6 feet. Weight, 182 pounds.

Year	Club	Lea	Pos	G	AB	R	H	2B	3B	HR	RBI	SB	Avg
1988 Oneonta	N.Y.-Penn.		2B-SS	71	281	49	92	11	6	2	34	25	.327
1989 Prince William	Carolina		2B	124	436	61	116	21	*7	3	45	31	.266
1990 Albany	Eastern		2B	126	418	67	113	19	6	8	44	31	.270

Year	Club	Lea	Pos	G	AB	R	H	2B	3B	HR	RBI	SB	Avg
1991 Columbus ....Int.			2B	31	116	27	39	9	2	3	19	8	.336
1991 New York ............A.L.			3B-2B	96	298	35	72	12	4	3	23	12	.242
1992 Albany ....Eastern			2B	2	6	1	0	0	0	0	0	0	.000
1992 New York a ..........A.L.			2B	106	318	38	72	22	2	7	27	8	.226
1993 New York ............A.L.			2B	127	406	49	111	24	1	7	51	14	.273
1994 Albany ....Eastern			2B	1	4	1	1	0	0	0	0	1	.250
1994 New York b ..........A.L.			2B	93	286	35	80	21	2	3	41	6	.280
1995 Yankees ....Gulf Coast			2B	1	2	2	0	0	0	0	1	0	.000
1995 Tampa ....Fla. St.			2B	3	17	0	4	1	0	0	2	0	.235
1995 New York c ..........A.L.			2B	89	270	32	64	12	1	4	29	8	.237
1996 Yankees ....Gulf Coast			2B	5	17	7	6	2	0	1	1	3	.353
1996 Tampa ....Fla.St.			2B	6	22	6	6	0	0	1	2	0	.273
1996 Columbus ....Int.			2B	8	37	6	14	1	1	2	7	3	.378
1996 Norwich d ....Eastern			2B	4	17	3	5	2	1	0	0	1	.294
1996 New York ............A.L.			2B	13	21	4	3	0	0	0	2	0	.143
1997 Columbus ....Int.			2B	11	44	8	15	4	0	2	6	1	.341
1997 New York e-f-g .......A.L.			2B	67	120	25	29	6	1	2	10	8	.242
Major League Totals			7 Yrs.	591	1719	218	431	97	11	26	183	56	.251
Division Series													
1995 New York ............A.L.			2B	4	3	3	0	0	0	0	1	0	.000

a On disabled list from April 21 to May 7, 1992.
b On disabled list from June 22 to July 7, 1994.
c On disabled list from May 27 to July 7, 1995.
d On disabled list from April 1 to July 26 and July 27 to August 12 and August 23 to September 7, 1996.
e On disabled list from May 10 to June 3 and August 17 to September 1, 1997.
f Filed for free agency, November 7, 1997.
g Signed with Toronto Blue Jays organization, November 26, 1997.

KELLY, ROBERTO CONRADO

Born, Panama City, Panama, October 1, 1964.
Bats Right. Throws Right. Height, 6 feet, 2 inches. Weight, 202 pounds.

Year	Club	Lea	Pos	G	AB	R	H	2B	3B	HR	RBI	SB	Avg
1982 Bradenton Yankees ...Gulf C.			OF	31	86	13	17	1	1	1	18	3	.198
1983 Greensboro ....So. Atl.			OF	20	49	6	13	0	0	0	3	3	.265
1983 Oneonta .......N.Y.-Penn.			OF	48	167	17	36	1	2	2	17	12	.216
1984 Greensboro ....So. Atl.			OF	111	361	68	86	13	2	1	26	42	.238
1985 Ft. Lauderdale ....Fla. St.			OF	114	417	86	103	4	*13	3	38	49	.247
1986 Albany a ....Eastern			OF	86	299	42	87	11	4	2	43	10	.291
1987 Columbus ....Int.			OF	118	471	77	131	19	8	13	62	51	.278
1987 New York ............A.L.			OF	23	52	12	14	3	0	1	7	9	.269
1988 Columbus ....Int.			OF	30	120	25	40	8	1	3	16	11	.333
1988 New York b ..........A.L.			OF	38	77	9	19	4	1	1	7	5	.247
1989 New York c ..........A.L.			OF	137	441	65	133	18	3	9	48	35	.302
1990 New York ............A.L.			OF	*162	641	85	183	32	4	15	61	42	.285
1991 New York d ..........A.L.			OF	126	486	68	130	22	2	20	69	32	.267
1992 New York e ..........A.L.			OF	152	580	81	158	31	2	10	66	28	.272
1993 Cincinnati f ..........N.L.			OF	78	320	44	102	17	3	9	35	21	.319
1994 Cincinnati-Atlanta g ....N.L.			OF	110	434	73	127	23	3	9	45	19	.293
1995 Montreal-Los Ange. h-j ..N.L.			OF	136	504	58	140	23	2	7	57	19	.278
1996 Minnesota k-l ..........A.L.			OF	98	322	41	104	17	4	6	47	10	.323
1997 Ft. Myers m-n ....Fla. St.			OF	4	11	2	4	0	0	1	3	0	.364
1997 Minnesota-Seattle o-p ..A.L.			OF	105	368	58	107	26	2	12	59	9	.291
Major League Totals			11 Yrs.	1165	4225	594	1217	216	26	99	501	229	.288
Division Series													
1995 Los Angeles ..........N.L.			OF	3	11	0	4	0	0	0	0	0	.364
1997 Seattle ............A.L.			OF	4	13	1	4	3	0	0	1	0	.308
Divisional Series Totals			7	24	1	8	3	0	0	1	0	.333		

a On disabled list from July 10 to August 22, 1986.
b On disabled list from June 29 to September 2, 1988.
c On disabled list from May 26 to June 11, 1989.
d On disabled list from July 6 to August 13, 1991.
e Traded to Cincinnati Reds for outfielder Paul O'Neill and first baseman Joe DeBerry, November 3, 1992.
f On disabled list from July 14 to end of 1993 season.
g Traded to Atlanta Braves with pitcher Roger Etheridge for outfielder Deion Sanders, May 29, 1994.
h Traded to Montreal Expos with outfielder Tony Tarasco and pitcher Esteban Yan for outfielder Marquis Grissom, April 6, 1995.
i Traded to Los Angeles Dodgers with pitcher Joey Eischen for outfielder Henry Rodriguez and infielder Jeff Treadway, May 24, 1995.
j Filed for free agency, November 12, 1995.
k Signed with Minnesota Twins organization, January 29, 1996.

l On disabled list from June 27 to July 12, 1996.
m On disabled list from April 1 to April 16, 1997.
n Traded to Seattle Mariners for player to be named later and pitcher Jeromy Palki), August 20, 1997. Minnesota Twins received pitcher Joe Mays and pitcher Jeromy Palki to complete trade, October 9, 1997.
o Filed for free agency, October 31, 1997.
p Signed as free agent with Texas Rangers, December 9, 1997.

KENDALL, JASON DANIEL

Born, San Diego, California, June 26, 1974.
Bats Right. Throws Right. Height, 6 feet. Weight, 181 pounds.

Year	Club	Lea	Pos	G	AB	R	H	2B	3B	HR	RBI	SB	Avg
1992 Pirates	Gulf Coast	C	33	111	7	29	2	0	0	10	2	.261
1993 Augusta	So.Atl.	C	102	366	43	101	17	4	1	40	8	.276
1994 Salem	Carolina	C	101	371	68	118	19	2	7	66	14	.318
1994 Carolina	Southern	C	13	47	6	11	2	0	0	6	0	.234
1995 Carolina	Southern	C	117	429	87	140	26	1	8	71	10	.326
1996 Pittsburgh	N.L.	C	130	414	54	124	23	5	3	42	5	.300
1997 Pittsburgh	N.L.	C	144	486	71	143	36	4	8	49	18	.294
Major League Totals		2 Yrs.	274	900	125	267	59	9	11	91	23	.297

KENT, JEFFREY FRANKLIN

Born, Bellflower, California, March 7, 1968.
Bats Right. Throws Right. Height, 6 feet, 1 inch. Weight, 185 pounds.

Year	Club	Lea	Pos	G	AB	R	H	2B	3B	HR	RBI	SB	Avg
1989 St. Catharines	N.Y.-Penn.	3B-SS	73	268	34	60	14	1	*13	37	5	.224
1990 Dunedin	Fla. St.	2B	132	447	72	124	32	2	16	60	17	.277
1991 Knoxville	Southern	2B	139	445	68	114	34	1	12	61	25	.256
1992 Toronto a	A.L.	3B-2B	65	192	36	46	13	1	8	35	2	.240
1992 New York	N.L.	2B-3B-SS	37	113	16	27	8	1	3	15	0	.239
1993 New York	N.L.	2B-3B-SS	140	496	65	134	24	0	21	80	4	.270
1994 New York	N.L.	2B	107	415	53	121	24	5	14	68	1	.292
1995 New York b	N.L.	2B	125	472	65	131	22	3	20	65	3	.278
1996 New York c	N.L.	3B	89	335	45	97	20	1	9	39	4	.290
1996 Cleveland d	A.L.	1B-2B-3B	39	102	16	27	7	0	3	16	2	.265
1997 San Francisco	N.L.	2B-1B	155	580	90	145	38	2	29	121	11	.250
Major League Totals		6 Yrs.	757	2705	386	728	156	13	107	439	27	.269
Division Series													
1996 Cleveland	A.L.	2B-1B-3B	4	8	2	1	1	0	0	0	0	.125
1997 San Francisco	N.L.	2B-1B	3	10	2	3	0	0	2	2	0	.300
Division Series Totals			7	18	4	4	1	0	2	2	0	.222

a Traded to New York Mets with player to be named for pitcher David Cone, August 27; New York acquired outfielder Ryan Thompson to complete trade, September 1, 1992.
b On disabled list from July 6 to July 21, 1995.
c Traded to Cleveland Indians with infielder Jose Vizcaino for infielder Carlos Baerga and infielder Alvaro Espinoza, July 29, 1996.
d Traded to San Francisco Giants with pitcher Julian Taverez, infielder Jose Vizcaino and player to be named later for infielder Matt Williams and player to be named later, November 13, 1996.

KING, JEFFREY WAYNE

Born, Marion, Indiana, December 26, 1964.
Bats Right. Throws Right. Height, 6 feet, 1 inch. Weight, 183 pounds.

Year	Club	Lea	Pos	G	AB	R	H	2B	3B	HR	RBI	SB	Avg
1986 Prince William	Carolina	3B	37	132	18	31	4	1	6	20	1	.235
1987 Salem	Carolina	1B-3B	90	310	68	86	9	1	26	71	6	.277
1987 Harrisburg	Eastern	1B	26	100	12	24	7	0	2	25	0	.240
1988 Harrisburg	Eastern	3B-SS	117	411	49	105	21	1	14	66	5	.255
1989 Buffalo	A.A.	1B-3B	51	169	26	43	5	2	6	29	7	.254
1989 Pittsburgh	N.L.	1B-3B-2B-SS	75	215	31	42	13	3	5	19	4	.195
1990 Pittsburgh	N.L.	3B-1B	127	371	46	91	17	1	14	53	3	.245
1991 Buffalo	A.A.	3B	9	18	3	4	1	1	0	2	1	.222
1991 Pittsburgh a	N.L.	3B	33	109	16	26	1	1	4	18	3	.239
1992 Pittsburgh	3B-1B-2B-SS-OF	130	480	56	111	21	2	14	65	4	.231
1992 Buffalo	A.A.	3B	7	29	6	10	2	0	2	5	1	.345
1993 Pittsburgh	N.L.	3B-2B-SS	158	611	82	180	35	3	9	98	8	.295
1994 Pittsburgh b	N.L.	3B-2B	94	339	36	89	23	0	5	42	3	.263
1995 Pittsburgh c	N.L.	3B-1B-2B-SS	122	445	61	118	27	2	18	87	7	.265

95

Year Club	Lea	Pos	G	AB	R	H	2B	3B	HR	RBI	SB	Avg
1996 Pittsburgh d . . .N.L.		1B-2B-3B	155	591	91	160	36	4	30	111	15	.271
1997 Kansas City . . .A.L.		1B	155	543	84	129	30	1	28	112	16	.238
Major League Totals	9 Yrs.		1049	3704	503	946	203	17	127	605	63	.255
Championship Series												
1990 Pittsburgh . . . .N.L.		3B	5	10	0	1	0	0	0	0	0	.100
1992 Pittsburgh . . . .N.L.		3B	7	29	4	7	4	0	0	2	0	.241
Championship Series Totals			412	39	4	8	4	0	0	2	0	.205

a On disabled list from May 5 to May 31 and June 13 to end of 1991 season.
b On disabled list from May 25 to June 9, 1994.
c On disabled list from June 16 to July 1, 1995.
d Traded with shortstop Jay Bell to Kansas City Royals for pitchers Jeff Wallace, Jeff Martin, Jeff Granger and third baseman Joe Randa, December 14, 1996.

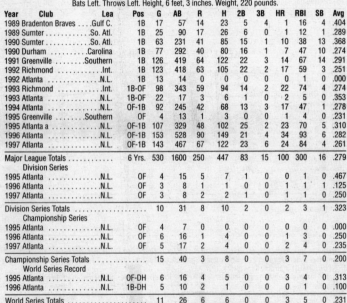

KLESKO, RYAN ANTHONY
Born, Westminster, California, June 12, 1971.
Bats Left. Throws Left. Height, 6 feet, 3 inches. Weight, 220 pounds.

Year Club	Lea	Pos	G	AB	R	H	2B	3B	HR	RBI	SB	Avg
1989 Bradenton Braves . . . .Gulf C.		1B	17	57	14	23	5	4	1	16	4	.404
1989 Sumter . . . . .So. Atl.		1B	25	90	17	26	6	0	1	12	1	.289
1990 Sumter . . . . .So. Atl.		1B	63	231	41	85	15	1	10	38	13	.368
1990 Durham . . . . .Carolina		1B	77	292	40	80	16	1	7	47	10	.274
1991 Greenville . . . . . .Southern		1B	126	419	64	122	22	3	14	67	14	.291
1992 Richmond . . . . .Int.		1B	123	418	63	105	22	2	17	59	3	.251
1992 Atlanta . . . . .N.L.		1B	13	14	0	0	0	0	0	1	0	.000
1993 Richmond . . . . .Int.		1B-OF	98	343	59	94	14	2	22	74	4	.274
1993 Atlanta . . . . .N.L.		1B-OF	22	17	3	6	1	0	2	5	0	.353
1994 Atlanta . . . . .N.L.		OF-1B	92	245	42	68	13	3	17	47	1	.278
1995 Greenville . . . . . . .Southern		OF	4	13	1	3	0	0	1	4	0	.231
1995 Atlanta a . . . . .N.L.		OF-1B	107	329	48	102	25	2	23	70	5	.310
1996 Atlanta . . . . .N.L.		OF-1B	153	528	90	149	21	4	34	93	6	.282
1997 Atlanta . . . . .N.L.		OF-1B	143	467	67	122	23	6	24	84	4	.261
Major League Totals	6 Yrs.		530	1600	250	447	83	15	100	300	16	.279
Division Series												
1995 Atlanta . . . . .N.L.		OF	4	15	5	7	1	0	0	1	0	.467
1996 Atlanta . . . . .N.L.		OF	3	8	1	1	0	0	1	1	1	.125
1997 Atlanta . . . . .N.L.		OF	3	8	2	2	1	0	1	1	0	.250
Division Series Totals			10	31	8	10	2	0	2	3	1	.323
Championship Series												
1995 Atlanta . . . . .N.L.		OF	4	7	0	0	0	0	0	0	0	.000
1996 Atlanta . . . . .N.L.		OF	6	16	1	4	0	0	1	3	0	.250
1997 Atlanta . . . . .N.L.		OF	5	17	2	4	0	0	2	4	0	.235
Championship Series Totals			15	40	3	8	0	0	3	7	0	.200
World Series Record												
1995 Atlanta . . . . .N.L.		OF-DH	6	16	4	5	0	0	3	4	0	.313
1996 Atlanta . . . . .N.L.		1B-DH	5	10	2	1	0	0	0	1	0	.100
World Series Totals			11	26	6	6	0	0	3	5	0	.231

a On disabled list from May 3 to May 18, 1995.

KNOBLAUCH, EDWARD CHARLES (CHUCK)
Born, Houston, Texas, July 7, 1968.
Bats Right. Throws Right. Height, 5 feet, 9 inches. Weight, 181 pounds.

Year Club	Lea	Pos	G	AB	R	H	2B	3B	HR	RBI	SB	Avg
1989 Kenosha . . . . .Midwest		SS	51	196	29	56	13	1	2	19	9	.286
1989 Visalia . . . . .California		SS	18	77	20	28	10	0	0	21	4	.364
1990 Orlando . . . . .Southern		2B	118	432	74	125	23	6	2	53	23	.289
1991 Minnesota a . . . . .A.L.		2B-SS	151	565	78	159	24	6	1	50	25	.281
1992 Minnesota . . . . .A.L.		2B-SS	155	600	104	178	19	6	2	56	34	.297
1993 Minnesota . . . . .A.L.	2B-SS-OF		153	602	82	167	27	4	2	41	29	.277
1994 Minnesota . . . . .A.L.		2B-SS	109	445	85	139	*45	3	5	51	35	.312
1995 Minnesota . . . . .A.L.		2B-SS	136	538	107	179	34	8	11	63	46	.333
1996 Minnesota . . . . .A.L.		2B	153	578	140	197	35	*14	13	72	45	.341
1997 Minnesota b-c . . . . .A.L.		2B-SS	156	611	117	178	26	10	9	58	62	.291
Major League Totals	7 Yrs.		1013	3939	713	1197	210	51	43	391	276	.304
Championship Series												
1991 Minnesota . . . . .A.L.		2B	5	20	5	7	2	0	0	3	2	.350

Year	Club	Lea	Pos	G	AB	R	H	2B	3B	HR	RBI	SB	Avg
	World Series Record												
1991 Minnesota	...........A.L.		2B	7	26	3	8	1	0	0	2	4	.308

a Selected Rookie of the Year in American League for 1991.
b Filed for free agency, October 28, 1997.
c Traded to New York Yankees for pitchers Eric Milton and Danny Mota, outfielder Brian Buchanan and infielder Cristian Guzman and reported $3 million, February 6, 1998.

KNORR, RANDY DUANE
Born, San Gabriel, California, November 12, 1968.
Bats Right. Throws Right. Height, 6 feet, 2 inches. Weight, 215 pounds.

Year	Club	Lea	Pos	G	AB	R	H	2B	3B	HR	RBI	SB	Avg
1986 Medicne Hat	....Pioneer		1B	55	215	21	58	13	0	4	32	0	.270
1987 Medicne Hat	....Pioneer		DH-C	26	106	21	31	7	0	10	24	0	.292
1987 Myrtle Bch	......So.Atl.		DH-C-1B-2B	46	129	17	34	4	0	6	21	0	.264
1988 Myrtle Bch	....So.Atl.		C	117	364	43	85	13	0	9	42	0	.234
1989 Dunedin	........Fla.St.		C	33	122	13	32	6	0	6	23	0	.262
1990 Knoxville	.....Southern		C	116	392	51	108	12	1	13	64	0	.276
1991 Knoxville	.....Southern		C-1B	24	74	7	13	4	0	0	4	2	.176
1991 Syracuse	..........Int.		C	91	342	29	89	20	1	5	44	1	.260
1991 Toronto	..........A.L.		C	3	1	0	0	0	0	0	0	0	.000
1992 Syracuse	..........Int.		C	61	228	27	62	13	1	11	27	1	.272
1992 Toronto	..........A.L.		C	8	19	1	5	0	0	1	2	0	.263
1993 Toronto	..........A.L.		C	39	101	11	25	3	2	4	20	0	.248
1994 Toronto	..........A.L.		C	40	124	20	30	2	0	7	19	0	.242
1995 Syracuse	..........Int.		C	18	67	6	18	5	1	1	6	0	.269
1995 Toronto	..........A.L.		C	45	132	18	28	8	0	3	16	0	.212
1996 Syracuse	..........Int.		C	12	36	1	10	5	0	0	5	0	.278
1996 Houston a-b	......N.L.		C	37	87	7	17	5	0	1	7	0	.195
1997 New Orleans	.....A.A.		C	72	244	22	58	10	0	5	27	0	.238
1997 Houston c-d-e	.....N.L.		C-1B	4	8	1	3	0	0	1	1	0	.375
Major League Totals	....	7 Yrs.		176	472	58	108	18	2	17	65	0	.229

a Sold to Houston Astros, May 17, 1996.
b Houston Astros declined to offer contract, December 20, 1996.
c On disabled list from August 28 to September 12, 1997.
d Filed for free agency, October 14, 1997.
e Signed with Florida Marlins, December 22, 1997.

KONERKO, PAUL HENRY
Born, Providence, Rhode Island, March 5, 1976.
Bats Right. Throws Right. Height, 6 feet, 3 inches. Weight, 205 pounds.

Year	Club	Lea	Pos	G	AB	R	H	2B	3B	HR	RBI	SB	Avg
1994 Yakima	........Northwest		C	67	257	25	74	15	2	6	58	1	.288
1995 San Berndno	.....California		C	118	448	77	124	21	1	19	77	3	.277
1996 San Antonio	........Texas		1B	133	470	78	141	23	2	29	86	1	.300
1996 Albuquerque	..........P.C.		1B	4	14	2	6	0	0	1	2	0	.429
1997 Albuquerque	..........P.C.	3B-1B-2B		130	483	97	156	31	1	37	127	2	.323
1997 Los Angeles	..........N.L.		1B-3B	6	7	0	1	0	0	0	0	0	.143

KOTSAY, MARK STEVEN
Born, Woodier, California, December 2, 1975.
Bats Left. Throws Left. Height, 6 feet. Weight, 180 pounds.

Year	Club	Lea	Pos	G	AB	R	H	2B	3B	HR	RBI	SB	Avg
1996 Kane County	......Midwest		OF	17	60	16	17	5	0	2	8	3	.283
1997 Florida	..........N.L.		OF	14	52	5	10	1	1	0	4	3	.192
1997 Portland	..........Eastern		OF	114	438	103	134	27	2	20	77	17	.306

KREUTER, CHAD MICHAEL
Born, Marin County, California, August 16, 1964.
Bats Both. Throws Right. Height, 6 feet, 2 inches. Weight, 195 pounds.

Year	Club	Lea	Pos	G	AB	R	H	2B	3B	HR	RBI	SB	Avg
1985 Burlington a	.......Midwest		C	69	199	25	53	10	0	4	26	3	.266
1986 Salem	...........Carolina		C	125	387	55	85	21	2	6	49	5	.220
1987 Charlotte	...........Fla. St.		C	85	281	36	61	18	1	9	40	1	.217
1988 Tulsa	...............Texas		C	108	358	46	95	24	6	3	51	2	.265
1988 Texas	...............A.L.		C	16	51	3	14	2	1	1	5	0	.275

97

Year	Club	Lea	Pos	G	AB	R	H	2B	3B	HR	RBI	SB	Avg
1989 Oklahoma City .......A.A.			C	26	87	10	22	3	0	0	6	1	.253
1989 Texas .............A.L.			C	87	158	16	24	3	0	5	9	0	.152
1990 Oklahoma City b ......A.A.			C	92	291	41	65	17	1	7	35	0	.223
1990 Texas .............A.L.			C	22	22	2	1	1	0	0	2	0	.045
1991 Oklahoma City .......A.A.			C	24	70	14	19	6	0	1	12	2	.271
1991 Texas .............A.L.			C	3	4	0	0	0	0	0	0	0	.000
1991 Tulsa c ....Texas			C	42	128	23	30	5	1	2	10	1	.234
1992 Detroit ............A.L.			C	67	190	22	48	9	0	2	16	0	.253
1993 Detroit ............A.L.			C-1B	119	374	59	107	23	3	15	51	2	.286
1994 Detroit d ...........A.L.			C-1B-OF	65	170	17	38	8	0	1	19	0	.224
1995 Tacoma ............P.C.			C	15	48	6	14	5	0	1	11	0	.292
1995 Seattle e-f-g ........A.L.			C	26	75	12	17	5	0	1	8	0	.227
1996 Chicago h-i .........A.L.			C-1B	46	114	14	25	8	0	3	18	0	.219
1997 Chicago-Anaheim j-k-l ..A.L.			C-1B	89	255	25	59	9	2	5	21	0	.231
Major League Totals			10 Yrs.	540	1413	170	333	68	6	33	149	2	.236

a Batted righthanded only from 1985 through 1987 season.
b Batted righthanded only during 1990 season.
c Became free agent, October 15; signed with Detroit Tigers organization, December 17, 1991.
d Not offered 1995 contract, December 23, 1994.
e Signed with Seattle Mariners, April 8, 1995.
f On disabled list from June 19 to July 6, 1995.
g Became free agent, October 15, 1995; signed with Chicago White Sox organization, December 11, 1995.
h On disabled list from July 20 to September 30, 1996.
i Filed for free agency, October 14, 1996. Resigned with Chicago White Sox.
j Traded to Anaheim Angels with outfielder Tony Phillips for pitcher Chuck McElroy and catcher Jorge Fabregas, May 18, 1997.
k Filed for free agency, November 3, 1997.
l Signed with Florida Marlins organization, December 22, 1997.

LAMPKIN, THOMAS MICHAEL
Born, Cincinnati, Ohio, March 4, 1964.
Bats Left. Throws Right. Height, 5 feet, 11 inches. Weight, 190 pounds.

Year	Club	Lea	Pos	G	AB	R	H	2B	3B	HR	RBI	SB	Avg
1986 Batavia .........N.Y.-Penn.			C	63	190	24	49	5	1	1	20	4	.258
1987 Waterloo ....Midwest			C	118	397	49	106	19	2	7	55	5	.267
1988 Williamsport ....Eastern			C	80	263	38	71	10	0	3	23	1	.270
1988 Colorado Springs ......P.C.			C	34	107	14	30	5	0	0	7	0	.280
1988 Cleveland ...........A.L.			C	4	0	0	0	0	0	0	0	0	.000
1989 Colorado Springs a .....P.C.			C	63	209	26	67	10	3	4	32	4	.321
1990 Colo. Spr.-Las Vegas b ..P.C.			C	70	201	32	45	7	5	1	18	7	.224
1990 San Diego ...........N.L.			C	26	63	4	14	0	1	1	4	0	.222
1991 Las Vegas .........P.C.			C-1B-OF	45	164	25	52	11	1	2	29	2	.317
1991 San Diego ...........N.L.			C	38	58	4	11	3	1	0	3	0	.190
1992 Las Vegas .........P.C.			C	108	340	45	104	17	4	3	48	15	.306
1992 San Diego c ..........N.L.			C-OF	9	17	3	4	0	0	0	0	2	.235
1993 New Orleans .........A.A.			C-OF	25	80	18	26	5	0	2	10	5	.325
1993 Milwaukee d ..........A.L.			C-OF	73	162	22	32	8	0	4	25	7	.198
1994 Phoenix .............P.C.			C-OF	118	453	76	136	32	8	8	70	8	.300
1995 San Francisco ........N.L.			C-OF	65	76	8	21	2	0	1	9	2	.276
1996 San Jose e ......California			C	2	7	2	2	0	1	0	2	0	.286
1996 San Francisco f ........N.L.			C	66	177	26	41	8	0	6	29	1	.232
1997 St. Louis ...........N.L.			C	108	229	28	56	8	1	7	22	2	.245
Major League Totals			8 Yrs.	389	786	95	179	29	3	19	92	14	.228

a On disabled list from July 6 to end of 1989 season.
b Traded by Cleveland Indians to San Diego Padres organization for outfielder Alex Cole, July 11, 1990.
c Traded to Milwaukee Brewers for future considerations, March 25, 1993.
d Not offered 1994 contract, December 20, 1993; signed with San Francisco Giants organization, January 5, 1994.
e On disabled list from April 1 to April 24 and August 26 to September 30, 1996.
f Traded to St. Louis Cardinals for player to be named or cash, December 19, 1996, with pitcher René Arocha sent to San Francisco to complete deal, February 12, 1997.

LANKFORD, RAYMOND LEWIS
Born, Modesto, California, June 5, 1967.
Bats Left. Throws Left. Height, 5 feet, 11 inches. Weight, 198 pounds.

Year	Club	Lea	Pos	G	AB	R	H	2B	3B	HR	RBI	SB	Avg
1987 Johnson City ....Appal.			OF	66	253	45	78	17	4	3	32	14	.308
1988 Springfield ....Midwest			OF	135	532	90	151	26	*16	11	66	33	.284
1989 Arkansas ....Texas			OF	*134	498	98	*158	28	*12	11	98	38	.317

Year Club	Lea	Pos	G	AB	R	H	2B	3B	HR	RBI	SB	Avg
1990 Louisville ..........A.A.		OF	132	473	61	123	25	8	10	72	29	.260
1990 St. Louis ............N.L.		OF	39	126	12	36	10	1	3	12	8	.286
1991 St. Louis ............N.L.		OF	151	566	83	142	23	*15	9	69	44	.251
1992 St. Louis ............N.L.		OF	153	598	87	175	40	6	20	86	42	.293
1993 St. Louis a ..........N.L.		OF	127	407	64	97	17	3	7	45	14	.238
1994 St. Louis b ..........N.L.		OF	109	416	89	111	25	5	19	57	11	.267
1995 St. Louis c ..........N.L.		OF	132	483	81	134	35	2	25	82	24	.277
1996 St. Louis ............N.L.		OF	149	545	100	150	36	8	21	86	35	.275
1997 Pr William ....Carolina		OF	4	13	3	4	1	0	0	4	1	.308
1997 St. Louis ............N.L.		OF	133	465	94	137	36	3	31	98	21	.295
Major League Totals	8 Yrs.		993	3606	610	982	222	43	135	535	199	.272
Division Series												
1996 St. Louis ............N.L.		OF	1	2	1	1	0	0	0	0	0	.500

a On disabled list from June 24 to July 9, 1993.
b Declared restricted free agent under Major League Baseball implemented labor proposal, December 23, 1994.
c Re-signed with St. Louis Cardinals, May 18, 1995.
d On disabled list from April 1 to April 22, 1997.

LANSING, MICHAEL THOMAS

Born, Rawlins, Wyoming, April 3, 1968.
Bats Right. Throws Right. Height, 6 feet. Weight, 180 pounds.

Year Club	Lea	Pos	G	AB	R	H	2B	3B	HR	RBI	SB	Avg
1990 Miami ....Fla. St.		SS	61	207	20	50	5	2	2	11	15	.242
1991 Miami a ....Fla. St.		SS-2B	104	384	54	110	20	7	6	55	29	.286
1992 Harrisburg ....Eastern		SS	128	483	66	135	20	6	6	54	46	.280
1993 Montreal ............N.L.		3B-SS-2B	141	491	64	141	29	1	3	45	23	.287
1994 Montreal ............N.L.		2B-3B-SS	106	394	44	105	21	2	5	35	12	.266
1995 Montreal b ..........N.L.		2B-SS	127	467	47	119	30	2	10	62	27	.255
1996 Montreal ............N.L.		2B-SS	159	641	99	183	40	2	11	53	23	.285
1997 Montreal c ..........N.L.		2B	144	572	86	161	45	2	20	70	11	.281
Major League Totals	5 Yrs.		677	2565	340	709	165	9	49	265	96	.276

a Purchased by Montreal Expos from independent Miami Miracle, September 18, 1991.
b On disabled list from May 31 to June 15, 1995.
c Traded to Colorado Rockies for pitcher Jake Westbrook, pitcher John Nicholson and outfielder Mike Hamlin, November 18, 1997.

LARKIN, BARRY LOUIS

Born, Cincinnati, Ohio, April 28, 1964.
Bats Right. Throws Right. Height, 6 feet. Weight, 196 pounds.

Year Club	Lea	Pos	G	AB	R	H	2B	3B	HR	RBI	SB	Avg
1985 Vermont ....Eastern		SS	72	255	42	68	13	2	1	31	0	.267
1986 Denver ..............A.A.		SS-2B	103	413	67	136	31	10	10	51	19	.329
1986 Cincinnati ..........N.L.		SS-2B	41	159	27	45	4	3	3	19	8	.283
1987 Cincinnati a .........N.L.		SS	125	439	64	107	16	2	12	43	21	.244
1988 Cincinnati ..........N.L.		SS	151	588	91	174	32	5	12	56	40	.296
1989 Nashville ...........A.A.		SS	2	5	2	5	1	0	0	0	0	1.000
1989 Cincinnati b .........N.L.		SS	97	325	47	111	14	4	4	36	10	.342
1990 Cincinnati ..........N.L.		SS	158	614	85	185	25	6	7	67	30	.301
1991 Cincinnati c .........N.L.		SS	123	464	88	140	27	4	20	69	24	.302
1992 Cincinnati d .........N.L.		SS	140	533	76	162	32	6	12	78	15	.304
1993 Cincinnati e .........N.L.		SS	100	384	57	121	20	3	8	51	14	.315
1994 Cincinnati ..........N.L.		SS	110	427	78	119	23	5	9	52	26	.279
1995 Cincinnati f .........N.L.		SS	131	496	98	158	29	6	15	66	51	.319
1996 Cincinnati ..........N.L.		SS	152	517	117	154	32	4	33	89	36	.298
1997 Cincinnati g .........N.L.		SS	73	224	34	71	17	3	4	20	14	.317
Major League Totals	12 Yrs.		1401	5170	862	1547	271	51	139	646	289	.299
Division Series												
1995 Cincinnati ..........N.L.		SS	3	13	2	5	0	0	0	1	4	.385
Championship Series												
1990 Cincinnati ...........N.L.		SS	6	23	5	6	2	0	0	1	3	.261
1995 Cincinnati ...........N.L.		SS	4	18	1	7	2	1	0	0	1	.389
Championship Series Totals			10	41	6	13	4	1	0	1	4	.317
World Series Record												
1990 Cincinnati ...........N.L.		SS	4	17	3	6	1	1	0	1	0	.353

a On disabled list from April 13 to May 2, 1987.
b On disabled list from July 13 to September 1, 1989.

c On disabled list from May 18 to June 4, 1991.
d On disabled list from April 19 to May 8, 1992.
e On disabled list from August 5 to end of 1993 season.
f Selected Most Valuable Player in National League for 1995.
g On disabled list from June 17 to August 2 and September 1 to September 29, 1997.

LAWTON, MATTHEW (MATT)

Born, Gulfport, Mississippi, November 3, 1971.
Bats Left. Throws Right. Height, 5 feet, 9 inches. Weight, 180 pounds.

Year	Club	Lea	Pos	G	AB	R	H	2B	3B	HR	RBI	SB	Avg
1992 Twins	Gulf Coast	2B	53	173	39	45	8	3	2	26	20	.260
1993 Ft. Wayne	Midwest	DH-OF	111	340	50	97	21	3	9	38	23	.285
1994 Ft. Myers	Fla. St.	OF	122	446	79	134	30	1	7	51	42	.300
1995 New Britain	Eastern	OF	114	412	75	111	19	5	13	54	26	.269
1995 Minnesota	A.L.	OF	21	60	11	19	4	1	1	12	1	.317
1996 Salt Lake	P.C.	OF	53	212	40	63	16	1	7	33	2	.297
1996 Minnesota	A.L.	OF	79	252	34	65	7	1	6	42	4	.258
1997 Minnesota	A.L.	OF	142	460	74	114	29	3	14	60	7	.248
Major League Totals		3 Yrs.	242	772	119	198	40	5	21	114	12	.256

LEDESMA, AARON DAVID

Born, Union City, California, June 3, 1971.
Bats Right. Throws Right. Height, 6 feet, 2 inches. Weight, 205 pounds.

Year	Club	Lea	Pos	G	AB	R	H	2B	3B	HR	RBI	SB	Avg
1990 Kingsport	Appal.	SS	66	243	50	81	11	1	5	38	27	.333
1991 Columbia a	So. Atl.	SS	33	115	19	39	8	0	1	14	3	.339
1992 St. Lucie	Fla. St.	SS	134	456	51	120	17	2	2	50	20	.263
1993 Binghamton	Eastern	DH-SS	66	206	23	55	12	0	5	22	2	.267
1994 Norfolk	Int.	SS	119	431	49	118	20	1	3	56	18	.274
1995 New York	N.L.	3B-1B-SS	21	33	4	8	0	0	0	3	0	.242
1995 Norfolk b	Int.	3B-1B-SS	56	201	26	60	12	1	0	28	6	.299
1996 Vancouver c	P.C.	SS-3B	109	440	60	134	27	4	1	51	2	.305
1997 Rochester	Int.	SS-1B	85	326	40	106	26	1	3	43	12	.325
1997 Baltimore d	A.L.	2B-3B-1B-SS	43	88	24	31	5	1	2	11	1	.352
Major League Totals		2 Yrs.	64	121	28	39	5	1	2	14	1	.322

a On disabled list April 1 to May 24 and June 26 to end of 1991 season.
b Traded by New York Mets to California Angels for outfielder Kevin Flora, January 18, 1996.
c Released by California Angels organization; signed by Baltimore Orioles, January 3, 1997.
d Selected in expansion draft by Tampa Bay Devil Rays, November 18, 1997.

LEE, DERREK LEON

Born, Sacramento, California, September 6, 1975.
Bats Right. Throws Right. Height, 6 feet, 5 inches. Weight 205 pounds.

Year	Club	Lea	Pos	G	AB	R	H	2B	3B	HR	RBI	SB	Avg
1993 Padres	Arizona	1B	15	52	11	17	1	1	2	5	4	.327
1993 Rancho Cuca	California	1B	20	73	13	20	5	1	1	10	0	.274
1994 Rancho Cuca	California	3B-1B	126	442	66	118	19	2	8	53	18	.267
1995 Rancho Cuca	California	1B	128	502	82	151	25	2	23	95	14	.301
1995 Memphis	Southern	1B	2	9	0	1	0	0	0	1	0	.111
1996 Memphis	Southern	1B-3B	134	500	98	140	39	2	34	104	13	.280
1997 Las Vegas	P.C.	1B	124	468	85	152	29	2	13	64	17	.325
1997 San Diego	N.L.	1B	22	54	9	14	3	0	1	4	0	.259

LEMKE, MARK ALAN

Born, Utica, New York, August 13, 1965.
Bats Both. Throws Right. Height, 5 feet, 9 inches. Weight, 167 pounds.

Year	Club	Lea	Pos	G	AB	R	H	2B	3B	HR	RBI	SB	Avg
1983 Bradenton Braves	Gulf C.	2B	53	209	37	55	6	0	0	19	10	.263
1984 Anderson	So. Atl.	2B	42	121	18	18	2	0	0	5	3	.149
1984 Bradenton Braves	Gulf C.	2B	*63	*243	41	67	11	0	3	32	2	.276
1985 Sumter	So. Atl.	2B	90	231	25	50	6	0	0	20	2	.216
1986 Sumter	So. Atl.	3B-2B	126	448	99	122	24	2	18	66	11	.272
1987 Durham	Carolina	2B	127	489	76	143	28	3	20	68	10	.292

Year Club	Lea	Pos	G	AB	R	H	2B	3B	HR	RBI	SB	Avg
1987 Greenville ....Southern		3B	6	26	0	6	0	0	0	4	0	.231
1988 Greenville ....Southern		2B	143	567	81	*153	29	4	16	80	18	.270
1988 Atlanta .............N.L.		2B	16	58	8	13	4	0	0	2	0	.224
1989 Richmond ....Int.		2B	146	518	69	143	22	7	5	61	4	.276
1989 Atlanta .............N.L.		2B	14	55	4	10	2	1	2	10	0	.182
1990 Bradenton Braves ....Gulf C.		2B-3B	4	11	2	4	0	0	1	5	0	.364
1990 Atlanta a ...........N.L.	3B-2B-SS		102	239	22	54	13	0	0	21	0	.226
1991 Atlanta .............N.L.		2B-3B	136	269	36	63	11	2	2	23	1	.234
1992 Atlanta .............N.L.		2B-3B	155	427	38	97	7	4	6	26	0	.227
1993 Atlanta .............N.L.		2B	151	493	52	124	19	2	7	49	1	.252
1994 Atlanta b ...........N.L.		2B	104	350	40	103	15	0	3	31	0	.294
1995 Atlanta .............N.L.		2B	116	399	42	101	16	5	5	38	2	.253
1996 Atlanta e-f-g .......N.L.		2B	135	498	64	127	17	0	5	37	5	.255
1997 Atlanta h-i .........N.L.		2B	109	351	33	86	17	1	2	26	2	.245
Major League Totals		10 Yrs.	1038	3139	339	778	121	15	32	263	11	.248
Division Series												
1995 Atlanta .............N.L.		2B	4	19	3	4	1	0	0	1	0	.211
1996 Atlanta .............N.L.		2B	3	12	1	2	1	0	0	2	0	.167
Division Series Totals			7	31	4	6	2	0	0	3	0	.194
Championship Series												
1991 Atlanta .............N.L.		2B	7	20	1	4	1	0	0	1	0	.200
1992 Atlanta .............N.L.		2B-3B	7	21	2	7	1	0	0	2	0	.333
1993 Atlanta .............N.L.		2B	6	24	2	5	2	0	0	4	0	.208
1995 Atlanta .............N.L.		2B	4	18	2	3	0	0	0	1	0	.167
1996 Atlanta .............N.L.		2B	7	27	4	12	2	0	1	5	0	.444
Championship Series Totals			31	110	11	31	6	0	1	13	0	.282
World Series Record												
1991 Atlanta .............N.L.		2B	6	24	4	10	1	3	0	4	0	.417
1992 Atlanta .............N.L.		2B	6	19	0	4	0	0	0	2	0	.211
1995 Atlanta .............N.L.		2B	6	22	1	6	0	0	0	0	0	.273
1996 Atlanta .............N.L.		2B	6	26	2	6	1	0	0	2	0	.231
World Series Totals			24	91	7	26	2	3	0	8	0	.286

a On disabled list from May 28 to July 17, 1990.
b Declared restricted free agent under Major League Baseball implemented labor proposal, December 23, 1994.
c Re-signed with Atlanta Braves, April 7, 1995.
d On disabled list from June 25 to July 18, 1995.
e On disabled list from May 27 to June 13, 1996.
f Filed for free agency, October 30, 1996.
g Re-signed with Atlanta Braves, December 22, 1996.
h On disabled list from August 21 to September 29, 1997.
i Filed for free agency, November 4, 1997.

LESHER, BRIAN HERBERT

Born, Antwerp, Belgium, March 5, 1971.
Bats Right. Throws Right. Height, 6 feet, 5 inches. Weight, 205 pounds.

Year Club	Lea	Pos	G	AB	R	H	2B	3B	HR	RBI	SB	Avg
1992 Sou Oregon .....Northwest		OF-1B	46	136	21	26	7	1	3	18	3	.191
1993 Madison ....Midwest		OF-P	119	394	63	108	13	5	5	47	20	.274
1994 Modesto ....California		OF-1B	117	393	76	114	21	0	14	68	11	.290
1995 Huntsville ....Southern		OF-1B	127	471	78	123	23	2	19	71	7	.261
1996 Edmonton ............P.C.		1B-OF	109	414	57	119	29	2	18	75	6	.287
1996 Oakland ..............A.L.		OF-1B	26	82	11	19	3	0	5	16	0	.232
1997 Edmonton ............P.C.		OF-1B	110	415	85	134	27	5	21	78	14	.323
1997 Oakland ..............A.L.		OF-1B	46	131	17	30	4	1	4	16	4	.229
Major League Totals		2 Yrs.	72	213	28	49	7	1	9	32	4	.230

LEVIS, JESSE

Born, Philadelphia, Pennsylvania, April 14, 1968.
Bats Left. Throws Right. Height 5 feet, 9 inches. Weight, 180 pounds.

Year Club	Lea	Pos	G	AB	R	H	2B	3B	HR	RBI	SB	Avg
1989 Colo Sprngs ..........P.C.			1	1	0	0	0	0	0	0	0	.000
1989 Burlington ....Appal.		C	27	93	11	32	4	0	4	16	1	.344
1989 Kinston ....Carolina		DH-C	27	87	11	26	6	0	2	11	1	.299
1990 Kinston ....Carolina		C	107	382	63	113	18	3	7	64	4	.296
1991 Canton-Akrn ....Eastern		C	115	382	31	101	17	3	6	45	2	.264
1992 Colo Sprngs ..........P.C.		C	87	253	39	92	20	1	6	44	1	.364

Year	Club	Lea	Pos	G	AB	R	H	2B	3B	HR	RBI	SB	Avg
1992 Cleveland	A.L.	C	28	43	2	12	4	0	1	3	0	.279
1993 Cleveland	A.L.	C	31	63	7	11	2	0	0	4	0	.175
1993 Charlotte	Int.	C	47	129	10	32	6	1	2	20	0	.248
1994 Cleveland			1	1	0	1	0	0	0	0	0	1.000
1994 Charlotte	Int.	C	111	375	55	107	20	0	10	59	2	.285
1995 Buffalo	A.A.	C	66	196	26	61	16	0	4	20	0	.311
1995 Cleveland	A.L.	C	12	18	1	6	2	0	0	3	0	.333
1996 Milwaukee a	A.L.	C	104	233	27	55	6	1	1	21	0	.236
1997 Milwaukee	A.L.	C	99	200	19	57	7	0	1	19	1	.285
Major League Totals			6 Yrs.	275	558	56	142	21	1	3	50	1	.254

a Traded to Milwaukee Brewers for pitcher Scott Nate and player to be named later, April 4, 1996. Cleveland Indians received pitcher Jared Camp to complete trade, June 7, 1996.

LEWIS, DARREN JOEL
Born, Berkeley, California, August 28, 1967.
Bats Right. Throws Right. Height, 6 feet. Weight, 189 pounds.

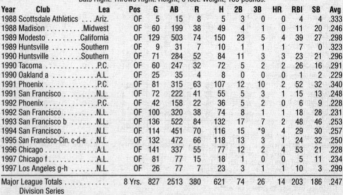

Year	Club	Lea	Pos	G	AB	R	H	2B	3B	HR	RBI	SB	Avg
1988 Scottsdale Athletics	Ariz.	OF	5	15	8	5	3	0	0	4	4	.333
1988 Madison	Midwest	OF	60	199	38	49	4	1	0	11	20	.246
1989 Modesto	California	OF	129	503	74	150	23	5	4	39	27	.298
1989 Huntsville	Southern	OF	9	31	7	10	1	1	1	7	0	.323
1990 Huntsville	Southern	OF	71	284	52	84	11	3	3	23	21	.296
1990 Tacoma	P.C.	OF	60	247	32	72	5	2	2	26	16	.291
1990 Oakland a	A.L.	OF	25	35	4	8	0	0	0	1	2	.229
1991 Phoenix	P.C.	OF	81	315	63	107	12	10	2	52	32	.340
1991 San Francisco	N.L.	OF	72	222	41	55	5	3	1	15	13	.248
1992 Phoenix	P.C.	OF	42	158	22	36	5	2	0	6	9	.228
1992 San Francisco	N.L.	OF	100	320	38	74	8	1	1	18	28	.231
1993 San Francisco b	N.L.	OF	136	522	84	132	17	7	2	48	46	.253
1994 San Francisco	N.L.	OF	114	451	70	116	15	*9	4	29	30	.257
1995 San Francisco-Cin. c-d-e	N.L.	OF	132	472	66	118	13	3	1	24	32	.250
1996 Chicago	A.L.	OF	141	337	55	77	12	2	4	53	21	.228
1997 Chicago f	A.L.	OF	81	77	15	18	1	0	0	5	11	.234
1997 Los Angeles g-h	N.L.	OF	26	77	7	23	3	1	1	10	3	.299
Major League Totals			8 Yrs.	827	2513	380	621	74	26	14	203	186	.247

Division Series

Year	Club	Lea	Pos	G	AB	R	H	2B	3B	HR	RBI	SB	Avg
1995 Cincinnati	N.L.	OF	3	3	0	0	0	0	0	0	0	.000

a Traded to San Francisco Giants with player to be named for infielder Ernest Riles, December 4; San Francisco acquired pitcher Pedro Pena to complete trade, December 17, 1990.

b On disabled list from August 21 to September 4, 1993.

c Traded to Cincinnati Reds with pitcher Mark Portugal and pitcher Dave Burba for outfielder Deion Sanders, pitcher John Roper, pitcher Ricky Pickett, pitcher Scott Service and infielder David McCarty, July 21, 1995.

d Waived by Cincinnati Reds, December 1, 1995; claimed on waivers by Texas Rangers, December 6, 1995.

e Waiver claim rejected, became unrestricted free agent, December 11, 1995; signed with Chicago White Sox, December 12, 1995.

f Traded to Los Angeles Dodgers for player to be named later, August 27, 1997. Chicago White Sox received infielder Chad Fonville to complete trade, September 2, 1997.

g Filed for free agency, October 27, 1997.

h Signed as free agent with Boston Red Sox, December 23, 1997.

LEWIS, MARK DAVID
Born, Hamilton, Ohio, November 30, 1969.
Bats Right. Throws Right. Height, 6 feet, 1 inch. Weight, 190 pounds.

Year	Club	Lea	Pos	G	AB	R	H	2B	3B	HR	RBI	SB	Avg
1988 Burlington	Appal.	SS	61	227	39	60	13	1	7	43	14	.264
1989 Kinston a	Carolina	SS	93	349	50	94	16	3	1	32	17	.269
1989 Canton	Eastern	SS	7	25	4	5	1	0	0	1	0	.200
1990 Canton	Eastern	SS	102	390	55	106	19	3	10	60	8	.272
1990 Colorado Springs	P.C.	SS	34	124	17	38	8	1	1	21	2	.306
1991 Colorado Springs	P.C.	SS-2B	46	179	29	50	10	3	2	31	3	.279
1991 Cleveland	A.L.	2B-SS	84	314	29	83	15	1	0	30	2	.264
1992 Cleveland	A.L.	SS-3B	122	413	44	109	21	0	5	30	4	.264
1993 Charlotte	Int.	SS	126	507	93	144	30	4	17	67	9	.284
1993 Cleveland	A.L.	SS	14	52	6	13	2	0	1	5	3	.250
1994 Charlotte	Int.	SS-2B-3B	86	328	56	85	16	1	8	34	2	.259
1994 Cleveland b	A.L.	SS-3B-2B	20	73	6	15	5	0	1	8	1	.205
1995 Cincinnati	N.L.	3B-2B-SS	81	171	25	58	13	1	3	30	0	.339

Year Club	Lea	Pos	G	AB	R	H	2B	3B	HR	RBI	SB	Avg
1996 Detroit c .............A.L.		2B	145	545	69	147	30	3	11	55	6	.270
1997 San Francisco d-e-f ....N.L.		3B-2B	118	341	50	91	14	6	10	42	3	.267
Major League Totals	7 Yrs.		584	1909	229	516	100	11	31	200	19	.270
Division Series												
1995 Cincinnati ...........N.L.		3B	2	2	2	1	0	0	1	5	0	.500
1997 San Francisco .........N.L.		2B	1	5	0	3	0	0	0	1	0	.600
Division Series Totals			3	7	2	4	0	0	1	6	0	.571
Championship Series												
1995 Cincinnati ...........N.L.		3B	2	4	0	1	0	0	0	0	0	.250

a On disabled list from May 29 to June 20, 1989.
b Traded to Cincinnati Reds for infielder/outfielder Tim Costo, December 14, 1994.
c Traded to San Francisco Giants for 1B Jesus Ibarra, December 16, 1996.
d On disabled list from April 1 to April 13, 1997.
e San Francisco declined to offer contract, December 20, 1997.
f Signed with Philadelphia Phillies, December 23, 1997

LEYRITZ, JAMES JOSEPH

Born, Lakewood, Ohio, December 27, 1963.
Bats Right. Throws Right. Height, 6 feet. Weight, 195 pounds.

Year Club	Lea	Pos	G	AB	R	H	2B	3B	HR	RBI	SB	Avg
1986 Oneonta a .N.Y.-Penn.		C	23	91	12	33	3	1	4	15	1	.363
1986 Ft. Lauderdale .Fla. St.		C	12	34	3	10	1	1	0	1	0	.294
1987 Ft. Lauderdale .Fla. St.		C	102	374	48	115	22	0	6	51	2	.307
1988 Albany ....Eastern		C-3B	112	382	40	92	18	3	5	50	3	.241
1989 Albany ....Eastern		C-OF	114	375	53	118	18	2	10	66	2	.315
1990 Columbus .....Int.		3B	59	204	36	59	11	1	8	32	4	.289
1990 New York .....A.L.		3B-OF-C	92	303	28	78	13	1	5	25	2	.257
1991 Columbus b ....Int.		C-3B-2B-SS	79	270	50	72	24	1	11	48	1	.267
1991 New York .....A.L.		3B-C-1B	32	77	8	14	3	0	0	4	0	.182
1992 New York .....A.L.		C-1B-3B-OF-2B	63	144	17	37	6	0	7	26	0	.257
1993 New York .....A.L.		1B-OF-C	95	259	43	80	14	0	14	53	0	.309
1994 New York .....A.L.		C-1B	75	249	47	66	12	0	17	58	0	.265
1995 New York .....A.L.		C-1B	77	264	37	71	12	0	7	37	1	.269
1996 New York c .....A.L.		C-3B-1B	88	265	23	70	10	0	7	40	2	.264
1997 Ana.-Tex. d-e .A.L.		C-1B	121	379	58	105	11	0	11	64	2	.277
Major League Totals	8 Yrs.		643	1940	261	521	81	1	68	307	7	.269
Division Series												
1995 New York .....A.L.		C	2	7	1	1	0	0	1	2	0	.143
1996 New York .....A.L.		C	2	3	0	0	0	0	0	0	0	.000
Division Series Totals			4	10	1	1	0	0	1	2	0	.100
Championship Series												
1996 New York .....A.L.		C-OF	3	8	1	2	0	0	1	2	0	.250
World Series												
1996 New York .....A.L.		C	4	8	1	3	0	0	1	3	1	.375

a Batted left and right from 1986 through 1987 season.
b Suspended by New York Yankees organization from August 11 to August 15, 1991.
c Traded to California Angels for players to be named later, December 5, 1996.
d Traded to Texas Rangers with player to be named later for pitcher Ken Hill, July 29, 1997. Texas Rangers received infielder Rob Sasser to complete trade, October 31, 1997.
e Traded to Boston Red Sox with outfielder Damon Buford for pitchers Aaron Sele and Mark Brandenburg, November 6, 1997.

LIEBERTHAL, MICHAEL SCOTT (MIKE)

Born, Glendale, California, January 18, 1972.
Bats Right. Throws Right. Height, 6 feet. Weight, 179 pounds.

Year Club	Lea	Pos	G	AB	R	H	2B	3B	HR	RBI	SB	Avg
1990 Martinsville ....Appal.		C	49	184	26	42	9	0	4	22	2	.228
1991 Spartanburg ..So. Atl.		C	72	243	34	74	17	0	0	31	1	.305
1991 Clearwater ....Fla. St.		C	16	52	7	15	2	0	0	7	0	.288
1992 Reading ....Eastern		C	86	309	30	88	16	1	2	37	4	.285
1992 Scranton a ....Int.		C	16	45	4	9	1	0	0	4	0	.200
1993 Scranton ....Int.		C	112	382	35	100	17	0	7	40	2	.262
1994 Scranton ....Int.		C	84	296	23	69	16	0	1	32	1	.233
1994 Philadelphia .........N.L.		C	24	79	6	21	3	1	1	5	0	.266
1995 Scranton-WB ....Int.		C-3B	85	278	44	78	20	2	6	42	1	.281
1995 Philadelphia .........N.L.		C	16	47	1	12	2	0	0	4	0	.255

Year	Club	Lea	Pos	G	AB	R	H	2B	3B	HR	RBI	SB	Avg
1996 Philadelphia b	.......N.L.		C	50	166	21	42	8	0	7	23	0	.253
1997 Philadelphia	.........N.L.		C	134	455	59	112	27	1	20	77	3	.246
Major League Totals			4 Yrs.	224	747	87	187	40	2	28	109	3	.250

a On disabled list from August 31 to end of 1992 season.
b On disabled list from August 22 to September 30, 1996.

LIRIANO, NELSON ARTURO

Born, Puerto Plata, Dominican Republic, June 3, 1964.
Bats Both. Throws Right. Height, 5 feet, 10 inches. Weight, 165 pounds.

Year	Club	Lea	Pos	G	AB	R	H	2B	3B	HR	RBI	SB	Avg
1983 Florence	.......So. Atl.		2B	129	478	87	124	24	5	6	57	27	.259
1984 Kinston	......Carolina		2B	132	512	68	125	22	4	5	50	10	.246
1985 Kinston	......Carolina		2B	134	451	68	130	23	1	6	36	25	.288
1986 Knoxville	....Southern		2B-3B-SS	135	557	88	159	25	15	7	59	35	.285
1987 Syracuse	.........Int.		2B	130	531	72	133	19	*10	10	55	36	.250
1987 Toronto	.........A.L.		2B	37	158	29	38	6	2	2	10	13	.241
1988 Syracuse	.........Int.		2B	8	31	2	6	1	1	0	1	2	.194
1988 Toronto	.........A.L.		2B	99	276	36	73	6	2	3	23	12	.264
1989 Toronto	.........A.L.		2B	132	418	51	110	26	3	5	53	16	.263
1990 Tor.-Minnesota a-b	A.L.		2B	103	355	46	83	12	9	1	28	8	.234
1991 Omaha	..........A.A.		2B-SS	86	292	50	80	16	9	2	36	6	.274
1991 Kansas City c	.....A.L.		2B	10	22	5	9	0	0	0	1	0	.409
1992 Colorado Springs d	.P.C.		2B-3B-SS	106	362	73	110	19	9	5	51	20	.304
1993 Central Valley	.California		3B-SS-2B	6	22	3	8	0	2	0	4	0	.364
1993 Colorado Springs	..P.C.		2B-SS-3B	79	293	48	105	23	6	6	46	9	.358
1993 Colorado	.........N.L.		SS-2B-3B	48	151	28	46	6	3	2	15	6	.305
1994 Colorado e	.......N.L.		2B-SS-3B	87	255	39	65	17	5	3	31	0	.255
1995 Pittsburgh f	.....N.L.		2B-3B-SS	107	259	29	74	12	1	5	38	2	.286
1996 Pittsburgh g	.....N.L.		2B-3B-SS	112	217	23	58	14	2	3	30	2	.267
1997 Los Angeles h-i-j	...N.L.		2B-1B-3B-SS	76	88	10	20	6	0	1	11	0	.227
Major League Totals	.... Championship Series		10 Yrs.	811	2199	296	576	105	27	25	240	59	.262
1989 Toronto	.............A.L.		2B	3	7	1	3	0	0	0	1	3	.429

a Traded to Minnesota Twins with outfielder Pedro Munoz for pitcher John Candelaria, July 27, 1990.
b Released, April 2; signed with Kansas City Royals organization, May 1, 1991.
c Became free agent, October 15, 1991; signed with Cleveland Indians organization, January 31, 1992.
d Became free agent, October 15; signed with Colorado Rockies, October 26, 1992.
e Claimed on waivers by Pittsburgh Pirates, October 14, 1994.
f Re-signed with Pittsburgh Pirates, November 29, 1995.
g Claimed on waivers by Los Angeles Dodgers, November 20, 1996.
h On disabled list from April 1 to April 12, 1997.
i Filed for free agency, October 3, 1997.
j Signed with Colorado Rockies organization, December 21, 1997.

LIVINGSTONE, SCOTT LOUIS

Born, Dallas, Texas, July 15, 1965.
Bats Left. Throws Right. Height, 6 feet. Weight, 198 pounds.

Year	Club	Lea	Pos	G	AB	R	H	2B	3B	HR	RBI	SB	Avg
1988 Lakeland	......Fla. St.		3B	53	180	28	51	8	1	2	25	1	.283
1989 London	......Eastern		3B-SS	124	452	46	98	18	1	14	71	1	.217
1990 Toledo	...........Int.		3B	103	345	44	94	19	0	6	36	1	.272
1991 Toledo	...........Int.		3B	92	331	48	100	13	3	3	62	2	.302
1991 Detroit	..........A.L.		3B	44	127	19	37	5	0	2	11	2	.291
1992 Detroit	..........A.L.		3B	117	354	43	100	21	0	4	46	1	.282
1993 Detroit	..........A.L.		3B	98	304	39	89	10	2	2	39	1	.293
1994 Detroit a	..........A.L.		1B-3B	15	23	0	5	1	0	0	1	0	.217
1994 San Diego	.......N.L.		3B	57	180	11	49	12	1	2	10	2	.272
1995 San Diego b	.......N.L.		1B-3B-2B	99	196	26	66	15	0	5	32	2	.337
1996 San Diego c	......N.L.		1B-3B	102	172	20	51	4	1	2	20	0	.297
1997 Rancho Cuca	..California		DH	3	8	2	2	0	0	0	0	0	.250
1997 Louisville d-e	.....A.A.		1B	9	25	4	9	1	0	0	2	0	.360
1997 San Diego-St. Louis f	........N.L.		3B-1B-2B-OF	65	67	4	11	2	0	0	6	1	.164
Major League Totals	....		7 Yrs.	597	1423	162	408	70	4	17	165	9	.287

a Traded to San Diego Padres for pitcher Gene Harris, May 11, 1994.
b Re-signed with San Diego Padres, December 8, 1995.
c On disabled list from June 3 to June 23, 1996.

d Traded to St. Louis Cardinals with outfielder Phil Plantier and pitcher Fernando Valenzuela for pitcher Danny Jackson, pitcher Rich Batchelor and outfielder Mark Sweeney, June 14, 1997.
e On disabled list from April 29 to May 26 and August 11 to September 1, 1997.
f Filed for free agency, November 7, 1997.

LOCKHART, KEITH VIRGIL

Born, Whittier, California, November 10, 1964.
Bats Left. Throws Right. Height, 5 feet, 10 inches. Weight, 170 pounds.

Year Club	Lea	Pos	G	AB	R	H	2B	3B	HR	RBI	SB	Avg
1986 Billings	Pioneer	2B-3B	53	202	51	70	11	3	7	31	4	.347
1986 Cedar Rapids	Midwest	2B-3B	13	42	4	8	2	0	0	1	1	.190
1987 Cedar Rapids	Midwest	3B-2B	140	511	101	160	37	5	23	84	20	.313
1988 Chattanooga	Southern	3B-2B	139	515	74	137	27	3	12	67	7	.266
1989 Nashville	A.A.	2B	131	479	77	128	21	6	14	58	4	.267
1990 Nashville	A.A.	2B-3B-OF	126	431	48	112	25	4	9	63	8	.260
1991 Nashville	A.A.	3B-2B-OF	116	411	53	107	25	3	8	36	3	.260
1992 Tacoma	P.C.	2B-3B-SS	107	363	44	101	25	3	5	37	5	.278
1993 Louisville	A.A.	3B-2B-OF	132	467	66	140	24	3	13	68	3	.300
1994 San Diego	N.L.	3B-2B-SS-OF	27	43	4	9	0	0	2	6	1	.209
1994 Las Vegas a	P.C.	OF-SS-2B-3B	89	331	61	106	15	5	7	43	3	.320
1995 Omaha	A.A.	3B	44	148	24	56	7	1	5	19	1	.378
1995 Kansas City	A.L.	2B-3B	94	274	41	88	19	3	6	33	8	.321
1996 Kansas City	A.L.	2B-3B	138	433	49	118	33	3	7	55	11	.273
1997 Atlanta b-c	N.L.	2B-3B	96	147	25	41	5	3	6	32	0	.279
Major League Totals		4 Yrs.	355	897	119	256	57	9	21	126	20	.285
Division Series												
1997 Atlanta	N.L.	2B	2	6	0	0	0	0	0	0	0	.000
Championship Series												
1997 Atlanta	N.L.	2B	5	16	4	8	1	1	0	3	0	.500

a Signed with Kansas City Royals, November 14, 1994.
b Traded to Atlanta Braves with outfielder Michael Tucker for outfielder Jermaine Dye and pitcher Jamie Walker, March 27, 1997.
c On disabled list from August 6 to August 22, 1997.

LOFTON, KENNETH

Born, East Chicago, Indiana, May 31, 1967.
Bats Left. Throws Left. Height, 6 feet. Weight, 180 pounds.

Year Club	Lea	Pos	G	AB	R	H	2B	3B	HR	RBI	SB	Avg
1988 Auburn	N.Y.-Penn.	OF	48	187	23	40	6	1	1	14	26	.214
1989 Auburn	N.Y.-Penn.	OF	34	110	21	29	3	1	0	8	26	.264
1989 Asheville	So. Atl.	OF	22	82	14	27	2	0	1	9	14	.329
1990 Osceola	Fla. St.	OF	124	481	98	*159	15	5	2	35	62	.331
1991 Tucson	P.C.	OF	130	545	93	*168	19	*17	2	50	40	.308
1991 Houston a	N.L.	OF	20	74	9	15	1	0	0	2	2	.203
1992 Cleveland	A.L.	OF	148	576	96	164	15	8	5	42	*66	.285
1993 Cleveland	A.L.	OF	148	569	116	185	28	8	1	42	*70	.325
1994 Cleveland	A.L.	OF	112	459	105	*160	32	9	12	57	*60	.349
1995 Cleveland b	A.L.	OF	118	481	93	149	22	13	7	53	54	.310
1996 Cleveland	A.L.	OF	154	*662	132	210	35	4	14	67	75	.317
1997 Atlanta c-d-e-f	N.L.	OF	122	493	90	164	20	6	5	48	27	.333
Major League Totals		7 Yrs.	822	3314	641	1047	153	48	44	309	354	.316
Division Series												
1995 Cleveland	A.L.	OF	3	13	1	2	0	0	0	0	0	.154
1996 Cleveland	A.L.	OF	4	18	3	3	0	0	0	1	5	.167
1997 Atlanta	N.L.	OF	3	13	2	2	1	0	0	0	0	.154
Division Series Totals			10	44	6	7	1	0	0	1	5	.159
Championship Series												
1995 Cleveland	A.L.	OF	6	24	4	11	0	2	0	3	5	.458
1997 Atlanta	N.L.	OF	6	27	3	5	0	1	0	1	1	.185
Championship Series Totals			12	51	7	16	0	3	0	4	6	.314
World Series Record												
1995 Cleveland	A.L.	OF	6	25	6	5	1	0	0	0	6	.200

a Traded to Cleveland Indians with infielder Dave Rohde for pitcher Willie Blair and catcher Ed Taubensee, December 10, 1991.
b On disabled list from July 17 to August 1, 1995.
c Traded to Atlanta Braves with pitcher Alan Embree for outfielder Marquis Grissom and outfielder David Justice, March 25, 1997.

d On disabled list from June 18 to July 5 and July 6 to July 28, 1997.
e Filed for free agency, October 28, 1997.
f Signed as free agent with Cleveland Indians, December 8, 1997.

LOPEZ, JAVIER TORRES
Born, Ponce, Puerto Rico, November 5, 1970.
Bats Right. Throws Right. Height, 6 feet, 3 inches. Weight, 185 pounds.

Year	Club	Lea	Pos	G	AB	R	H	2B	3B	HR	RBI	SB	Avg
1988 Bradenton Braves	Gulf C.	C	31	94	8	18	4	0	1	9	1	.191
1989 Pulaski	Appal.	C	51	153	27	40	8	1	3	27	3	.261
1990 Burlington	Midwest	C	116	422	48	112	17	3	11	55	0	.265
1991 Durham	Carolina	C	113	384	43	94	14	2	11	51	10	.245
1992 Greenville	Southern	C	115	442	64	142	28	3	16	60	7	.321
1992 Atlanta	N.L.	C	9	16	3	6	2	0	0	2	0	.375
1993 Richmond	Int.	C	100	380	56	116	23	2	17	74	1	.305
1993 Atlanta	N.L.	C	8	16	1	6	1	1	1	2	0	.375
1994 Atlanta	N.L.	C	80	277	27	68	9	0	13	35	0	.245
1995 Atlanta	N.L.	C	100	333	37	105	11	4	14	51	0	.315
1996 Atlanta	N.L.	C	138	489	56	138	19	1	23	69	1	.282
1997 Atlanta a	N.L.	C	123	414	52	122	28	1	23	68	1	.295
Major League Totals		6 Yrs.	458	1545	176	445	70	7	74	227	2	.288
Division Series													
1995 Atlanta	N.L.	C	3	9	0	4	0	0	0	3	0	.444
1996 Atlanta	N.L.	C	2	7	1	2	0	0	1	1	1	.286
1997 Atlanta	N.L.	C	2	7	3	2	2	0	0	1	0	.286
Division Series Totals			7	23	4	8	2	0	1	5	1	.348
Championship Series													
1992 Atlanta	N.L.	C	1	1	0	0	0	0	0	0	0	.000
1995 Atlanta	N.L.	C	3	14	2	5	1	0	1	3	0	.357
1996 Atlanta	N.L.	C	7	24	8	13	5	0	2	6	1	.542
1997 Atlanta	N.L.	C	5	17	0	1	1	0	0	2	0	.059
Championship Series Totals			16	56	10	19	7	0	3	11	1	.339
World Series Record													
1995 Atlanta	N.L.	C	6	17	1	3	2	0	1	3	0	.176
1996 Atlanta	N.L.	C	6	21	3	4	0	0	0	1	0	.190
World Series Totals			12	38	4	7	2	0	1	4	0	.184

a On disabled list from July 6 to July 22, 1997.

LOPEZ, LUIS MANUEL
Cidra, Puerto Rico, September 4, 1970.
Bats Both. Throws Right. Height, 5 feet, 11 inches. Weight, 175 pounds.

Year	Club	Lea	Pos	G	AB	R	H	2B	3B	HR	RBI	SB	Avg
1988 Spokane	Northwest	SS	70	312	50	95	13	1	0	35	14	.304
1989 Chston-Sc	So.Atl.	SS	127	460	50	102	15	1	1	29	12	.222
1990 Riverside	California	SS	14	46	5	17	3	1	1	4	4	.370
1991 Wichita	Texas	2B-SS	125	452	43	121	17	1	1	41	6	.268
1992 Las Vegas	P.C.	SS-OF	120	395	44	92	8	8	1	31	6	.233
1993 Las Vegas	P.C.	SS-2B	131	491	52	150	36	6	6	58	8	.305
1993 San Diego	N.L.	2B	17	43	1	5	1	0	0	1	0	.116
1994 Las Vegas	P.C.	2B	12	49	2	10	2	2	0	6	0	.204
1994 San Diego	N.L.	SS-2B-3B	77	235	29	65	16	1	2	20	3	.277
1996 Las Vegas a	P.C.	2B-SS	18	68	4	14	3	0	1	12	0	.206
1996 San Diego	N.L.	SS-2B-3B	63	139	10	25	3	0	2	11	0	.180
1997 Norfolk b-c	Int.	SS-2B	48	203	32	67	12	1	4	19	2	.330
1997 New York	N.L.	SS-2B-3B	78	178	19	48	12	1	1	19	2	.270
Major League Totals		4 Yrs.	235	595	59	143	32	2	5	51	5	.240
Division Series													
1996 San Diego		PR	1	0	0	0	0	0	0	0	0	.000

a On disabled list from April 1 to April 18 and July 31 to September 1, 1996.
b Traded to Houston Astros for pitcher Sean Runyan, March 16, 1997.
c Traded to New York Mets for infielder Tim Bogar, March 31, 1997.

LORETTA, MARK DAVID
Born, Santa Monica, California, August 14, 1971.
Bats Right. Throws Right. Height, 6 feet. Weight, 175 pounds.

Year	Club	Lea	Pos	G	AB	R	H	2B	3B	HR	RBI	SB	Avg
1993 Helena	Pioneer	SS	6	28	5	9	1	0	1	8	0	.321
1993 Stockton	California	SS-3B	53	201	36	73	4	1	4	31	8	.363

Year	Club	Lea	Pos	G	AB	R	H	2B	3B	HR	RBI	SB	Avg
1994 El Paso	Texas	SS-P		77	302	50	95	13	6	0	38	8	.315
1994 New Orleans	A.A.	SS-2B		43	138	16	29	7	0	1	14	2	.210
1995 New Orleans	A.A.	SS-3B-2B		127	479	48	137	22	5	7	79	8	.286
1995 Milwaukee	A.L.	SS-2B		19	50	13	13	3	0	1	3	1	.260
1996 New Orleans	A.A.	SS		19	71	10	18	5	1	0	11	1	.254
1996 Milwaukee	A.L.	2B-3B-SS		73	154	20	43	3	0	1	13	2	.279
1997 Milwaukee	A.L.	2B-SS-1B-3B		132	418	56	120	17	5	5	47	5	.287
Major League Totals		3 Yrs.		224	622	89	176	23	5	7	63	8	.283

MABRY, JOHN STEVEN

Born, Wilmington, Delaware, October 17, 1970.
Bats Left. Throws Right. Height, 6 feet, 4 inches. Weight, 195 pounds.

Year	Club	Lea	Pos	G	AB	R	H	2B	3B	HR	RBI	SB	Avg
1991 Hamilton	N.Y.-Penn.	OF	49	187	25	58	11	0	1	31	9	.310
1991 Savannah	So. Atl.	OF	22	86	10	20	6	1	0	8	1	.233
1992 Springfield	Midwest	OF	115	438	63	115	13	6	11	57	2	.263
1993 Arkansas	Texas	OF	136	528	68	153	32	2	16	72	7	.290
1993 Louisville	A.A.	OF	4	7	0	1	0	0	0	1	0	.143
1994 Louisville	A.A.	OF	122	477	76	125	30	1	15	68	2	.262
1994 St. Louis	N.L.	OF	6	23	2	7	3	0	0	3	0	.304
1995 Louisville	A.A.	OF	4	12	0	1	0	0	0	0	0	.083
1995 St. Louis	N.L.	1B-OF	129	388	35	119	21	1	5	41	0	.307
1996 St. Louis	N.L.	1B-OF	151	543	63	161	30	2	13	74	3	.297
1997 St. Louis a	N.L.	OF-1B-3B	116	388	40	110	19	0	5	36	0	.284
Major League Totals		4 Yrs.	402	1342	140	397	73	3	23	154	3	.296
Division Series												
1996 St. Louis	N.L.	1B	3	10	1	3	0	1	0	1	0	.300
Championship Series												
1996 St. Louis	N.L.	1B-OF	7	23	1	6	0	0	0	0	0	.261

a On disabled list from August 20 to September 24, 1997.

MACFARLANE, MICHAEL ANDREW

Born, Stockton, California, April 12, 1964.
Bats Right. Throws Right. Height, 6 feet, 1 inch. Weight, 205 pounds.

Year	Club	Lea	Pos	G	AB	R	H	2B	3B	HR	RBI	SB	Avg
1985 Memphis	Southern	C	65	223	29	60	15	4	8	39	0	.269
1986 Memphis	Southern	DH	40	141	26	34	7	2	12	29	0	.241
1987 Omaha :..........	A.A.	C	87	302	53	79	25	1	13	50	0	.262
1987 Kansas City	A.L.	C	8	19	0	4	1	0	0	3	0	.211
1988 Omaha	A.A.	C	21	76	8	18	7	2	2	8	0	.237
1988 Kansas City a	A.L.	C	70	211	25	56	15	0	4	26	0	.265
1989 Kansas City	A.L.	C	69	157	13	35	6	0	2	19	0	.223
1990 Kansas City	A.L.	C	124	400	37	102	24	4	6	58	1	.255
1991 Kansas City b	A.L.	C	84	267	34	74	18	2	13	41	1	.277
1992 Kansas City	A.L.	C	129	402	51	94	28	3	17	48	1	.234
1993 Kansas City	A.L.	C	117	388	55	106	27	0	20	67	2	.273
1994 Kansas City c	A.L.	C	92	314	53	80	17	3	14	47	1	.255
1995 Boston d-e-f-g	A.L.	C	115	364	45	82	18	1	15	51	2	.225
1996 Kansas City	A.L.	C	112	379	58	104	24	2	19	54	3	.274
1997 Kansas City h-i-j	A.L.	C	82	257	34	61	14	2	8	35	0	.237
Major League Totals		11 Yrs.	1002	3158	405	798	192	17	118	449	11	.253
Division Series												
1995 Boston	A.L.	C	3	9	0	3	0	0	0	1	0	.333

a On disabled list from August 15 to end of 1988 season.
b On disabled list from July 16 to September 14, 1991.
c Filed for free agency, October 21, 1994.
d Signed with Boston Red Sox, April 8, 1995.
e Not offered 1996 contract, October 30, 1995.
f Filed for free agency, November 12, 1995.
g Signed with Kansas City Royals, December 17, 1995.
h On disabled list from April 1 to April 13 and May 2 to May 23, 1997.
i Filed for free agency, October 28, 1997.
j Re-signed with Kansas City Royals, November 25, 1997.

MACK, SHANE LEE

Born, Los Angeles, California, December 7, 1963.
Bats Right. Throws Right. Height, 6 feet. Weight, 190 pounds.

Year	Club	Lea	Pos	G	AB	R	H	2B	3B	HR	RBI	SB	Avg
1985 Beaumont	.........Texas	OF-3B	125	430	59	112	23	3	6	55	12	.260
1986 Beaumont	.........Texas	OF	115	452	61	127	26	3	15	68	14	.281
1986 Las Vegas	.........P.C.	OF	19	69	13	25	1	6	0	6	3	.362
1987 Las Vegas	.........P.C.	OF	39	152	38	51	11	1	5	26	13	.336
1987 San Diego	.........N.L.	OF	105	238	28	57	11	3	4	25	4	.239
1988 Las Vegas	.........P.C.	OF	55	196	43	68	7	1	10	40	7	.347
1988 San Diego	.........N.L.	OF	56	119	13	29	3	0	0	12	5	.244
1989 Las Vegas a-b	.........P.C.	OF	24	80	10	18	3	1	1	8	4	.225
1990 Minnesota	.........A.L.	OF	125	313	50	102	10	4	8	44	13	.326
1991 Minnesota	.........A.L.	OF	143	442	79	137	27	8	18	74	13	.310
1992 Minnesota	.........A.L.	OF	156	600	101	189	31	6	16	75	26	.315
1993 Minnesota c	.........A.L.	OF	128	503	66	139	30	4	10	61	15	.276
1994 Minnesota d-e	.........A.L.	OF	81	303	55	101	21	2	15	61	4	.333
1995 Yomiuri	.......Japan Cent.	OF	128	477	79	131	18	0	20	52	12	.275
1996 Yomiuri f	.......Japan Cent.	OF	121	484	71	142	28	0	22	75	12	.293
1997 Boston g-h-i	.........A.L.	OF	60	130	13	41	7	0	3	17	2	.315
Major League Totals	....	8 Yrs.	854	2648	405	795	140	27	74	369	82	.300
Championship Series													
1991 Minnesota	.........A.L.	OF	5	18	4	6	1	1	0	3	2	.333
World Series Record													
1991 Minnesota	.........A.L.	OF	6	23	0	3	1	0	0	1	0	.130

a   On disabled list from March 25 to May 4 and June 9 to end of 1989 season.
b   Drafted by Minnesota Twins from San Diego Padres organization, December 4, 1989.
c   On disabled list from May 16 to May 30, 1993.
d   On disabled list from March 29 to May 3, 1994.
e   Filed for free agency, October 14, 1994; signed with Yomiuri Giants of Japan Central League, January 5, 1995.
f   Signed with Boston Red Sox, December 13, 1996.
g   On disabled list from August 7 to September 1, 1997.
h   Filed for free agency, October 28, 1997.
i   Signed as free agent with Oakland Athletics, December 22, 1997.

MAGADAN, DAVID JOSEPH

Born, Tampa, Florida, September 30, 1962.
Bats Left. Throws Right. Height, 6 feet, 3 inches. Weight, 205 pounds.

Year	Club	Lea	Pos	G	AB	R	H	2B	3B	HR	RBI	SB	Avg
1983 Columbia	.......S. Atlantic	1B	64	220	41	74	13	1	3	32	2	.336
1984 Lynchburg a	.......Carolina	1B	112	371	78	130	22	4	0	62	2	*.350
1985 Jackson	...........Texas	3B-1B	134	466	84	144	22	0	0	76	0	.309
1986 Tidewater	..........Int.	3B-1B	133	473	68	147	33	6	1	64	2	.311
1986 New York	.........N.L.	1B	10	18	3	8	0	0	0	3	0	.444
1987 New York b	.........N.L.	3B-1B	85	192	21	61	13	1	3	24	0	.318
1988 New York c	.........N.L.	1B-3B	112	314	39	87	15	0	1	35	0	.277
1989 New York	.........N.L.	1B-3B	127	374	47	107	22	3	4	41	1	.286
1990 New York	.........N.L.	1B-3B	144	451	74	148	28	6	6	72	2	.328
1991 New York	.........N.L.	1B	124	418	58	108	23	0	4	51	1	.258
1992 New York d-e	.........N.L.	3B-1B	99	321	33	91	9	1	3	28	1	.283
1993 Florida f	.........N.L.	3B-1B	66	227	22	65	12	0	4	29	0	.286
1993 Seattle g	.........A.L.	1B-3B	71	228	27	59	11	0	1	21	2	.259
1994 Florida h-i	.........N.L.	3B-1B	74	211	30	58	7	0	1	17	0	.275
1995 Houston j-k	.........N.L.	3B-1B	127	348	44	109	24	0	2	51	2	.313
1996 Daytona	.........Fla. St.	3B	7	20	5	6	1	0	0	3	0	.300
1996 Iowa l	.........A.A.	3B	3	9	0	2	1	0	0	1	0	.222
1996 Chicago m-n	.........N.L.	3B-1B	78	169	23	43	10	0	3	17	0	.254
1997 Oakland o-p	.........A.L.	3B-1B	128	271	38	82	10	1	4	30	1	.303
Major League Totals	....	12 Yrs.	1245	3542	459	1026	184	12	36	419	10	.290
Championship Series													
1988 New York	.........N.L.	PH	3	3	0	0	0	0	0	0	0	.000

a   On disabled list from August 7 to September 10, 1984.
b   On disabled list from March 29 to April 17, 1987.
c   On disabled list from May 5 to May 20, 1988.
d   On disabled list from August 9 to end of 1992 season.
e   Filed for free agency, October 27; signed with Florida Marlins organization, December 8, 1992.
f   Traded to Seattle Mariners for outfielder Henry Cotto and pitcher Jeff Darwin, June 27, 1993.
g   Traded to Florida Marlins with cash for pitcher Jeff Darwin, November 9, 1993.
h   On disabled list from March 29 to April 13 and July 21 to end of 1994 season.
i   Filed for free agency, October 17, 1994.
j   Signed with Houston Astros, April 13, 1995.

k Filed for free agency, October 30, 1995.
l On disabled list from April 1 to April 15 and April 15 to June 1, 1996.
m Filed for free agency, November 18, 1996.
n Signed with Oakland A's organization, January 23, 1997.
o Filed for free agency, October 27, 1997.
p Re-signed with Oakland Athletics, November 12, 1997.

MANTO, JEFFREY PAUL (JEFF)

Born, Bristol, Pennsylvania, August 23, 1964.
Bats Right. Throws Right. Height, 6 feet, 3 inches. Weight, 210 pounds.

Year	Club	Lea	Pos	G	AB	R	H	2B	3B	HR	RBI	SB	Avg
1985	Quad City	Midwest	OF-3B	74	233	34	46	5	2	11	34	3	.197
1986	Quad City	Midwest	3B	73	239	31	59	13	0	8	49	2	.247
1987	Palm Springs	California	3B-1B	112	375	61	96	21	4	7	63	8	.256
1988	Midland	Texas	3B-1B-2B	120	408	88	123	23	3	24	101	7	.301
1989	Edmonton	P.C.	3B-1B	127	408	89	113	25	3	23	67	4	.277
1990	Colorado Springs	P.C.	3B-1B	96	316	73	94	27	1	18	82	10	.297
1990	Cleveland	A.L.	1B-3B	30	760	12	17	5	1	2	14	0	.224
1991	Colorado Springs	P.C.	3B-1B-C-SS	43	153	36	49	16	0	6	36	1	.320
1991	Cleveland	A.L.	3B-1B-C-OF	47	128	15	27	7	0	2	13	2	.211
1992	Richmond	Int.	3B-2B-1B	127	450	65	131	24	1	13	68	1	.291
1993	Scranton-WB	Int.	3B-1B-C	106	388	62	112	30	1	17	88	4	.289
1993	Philadelphia	N.L.	3B-SS	8	18	0	1	0	0	0	0	0	.056
1994	Norfolk	Int.	3B-1B-2B	37	115	20	30	6	0	4	17	1	.261
1994	Rochester	Int.	3B-1B	94	329	61	102	25	2	27	83	2	.310
1995	Bowie	Eastern	DH	1	4	1	1	0	0	0	0	0	.250
1995	Frederick	Carolina	3B	2	8	1	3	0	0	1	3	0	.375
1995	Baltimore a	A.L.	3B-1B	89	254	31	65	9	0	17	38	0	.256
1996	Pawtucket	Int.	3B-2B	12	45	6	11	5	0	2	6	1	.244
1996	Trenton	Eastern	3B-2B-SS	6	21	3	6	0	0	0	5	0	.286
1996	Boston-Seattle-Boston b-c-d-e-f-g	A.L.	3B-2B-SS-1B	43	102	15	20	6	1	3	10	0	.196
1997	Syracuse	Int.	DH-3B-OF-1B	40	132	18	27	5	1	3	11	1	.205
1997	Buffalo	A.A.	3B-1B-OF	54	187	37	60	11	0	20	54	0	.321
1997	Cleveland h-i-j	A.L.	3B-1B-OF	16	30	3	8	3	0	2	7	0	.267
Major League Totals			6 Yrs.	233	608	76	138	30	2	26	82	2	.227

a On disabled list from June 26 to July 13, 1995.
b Sold to Yomiuri Giants, January 25, 1996.
c Signed with Boston Red Sox organization, May 8, 1996.
d On disabled list from May 26 to June 27, 1996.
e Traded to Seattle Mariners for infielder Arquimedez Pozo, July 23, 1996.
f Claimed on waivers by Boston Red Sox, August 29, 1996.
g Filed for free agency, October 8, 1996.
h Traded to Cleveland Indians for outfielder Ryan Thompson, June 6, 1997.
i Filed for free agency, November 17, 1997.
j Re-signed with Cleveland Indians organization, December 17, 1997

MANWARING, KIRT DEAN

Born, Elmira, New York, July 15, 1965.
Bats Right. Throws Right. Height, 5 feet, 11 inches. Weight, 203 pounds.

Year	Club	Lea	Pos	G	AB	R	H	2B	3B	HR	RBI	SB	Avg
1986	Clinton	Midwest	C	49	147	18	36	7	1	2	16	1	.245
1987	Shreveport	Texas	C	98	307	27	82	13	2	2	22	1	.267
1987	San Francisco	N.L.	C	6	7	0	1	0	0	0	0	0	.143
1988	Phoenix	P.C.	C	81	273	29	77	12	2	2	35	3	.282
1988	San Francisco	N.L.	C	40	116	12	29	7	0	1	15	0	.250
1989	San Francisco a	N.L.	C	85	200	14	42	4	2	0	18	2	.210
1990	Phoenix	P.C.	C	74	247	20	58	10	2	3	14	0	.235
1990	San Francisco	N.L.	C	8	13	0	2	0	1	0	1	0	.154
1991	San Francisco b	N.L.	C	67	178	16	40	9	0	0	13	1	.225
1991	Phoenix	P.C.	C	24	81	8	18	0	0	4	14	0	.222
1991	San Jose	California	C	1	3	1	0	0	0	0	0	0	.000
1992	San Francisco c	N.L.	C	109	349	24	85	10	5	4	26	2	.244
1993	San Francisco	N.L.	C	130	432	48	119	15	1	5	49	1	.275
1994	San Francisco	N.L.	C	97	316	30	79	17	1	1	29	1	.250
1995	San Francisco	N.L.	C	118	379	21	95	15	2	4	36	1	.251
1996	Phoenix	P.C.	C	4	11	1	2	0	0	0	1	0	.182
1996	San Francisco-Houston d-e-f-g	N.L.	C	86	227	14	52	9	0	1	18	0	.229
1997	Colorado	N.L.	C	104	337	22	76	6	4	1	27	1	.226
Major League Totals			11 Yrs.	850	2554	201	620	92	16	17	238	9	.243

Year	Club	Lea	Pos	G	AB	R	H	2B	3B	HR	RBI	SB	Avg
	Championship Series												
1989 San Francisco .........N.L.			C	3	2	0	0	0	0	0	0	0	.000
	World Series Record												
1989 San Francisco .........N.L.			C	1	1	1	1	1	0	0	0	0	1.000

a On disabled list from August 31 to September 15, 1989.
b On disabled list from May 21 to July 11, 1991.
c On disabled list from July 22 to August 6, 1992.
d On disabled list from April 10 to May 23, 1996.
e Traded to Houston Astros for catcher Rick Wilkins, July 26, 1996.
f Filed for free agency, October 28, 1996.
g Signed with Colorado Rockies, December 9, 1996.

MARRERO, ELIESER
Born, Havana, Cuba, November 17, 1973.
Bats Right. Throws Right. Height, 6 feet, 1 inch. Weight 180 pounds.

Year	Club	Lea	Pos	G	AB	R	H	2B	3B	HR	RBI	SB	Avg
1993 Johnson Cty ....Appal.			C	18	61	10	22	8	0	2	14	2	.361
1994 Savannah ....So. Atl.			C	116	421	71	110	16	3	21	79	5	.261
1995 St. Petersburg ......Fla. St.			C	107	383	43	81	16	1	10	55	9	.211
1996 Arkansas ....Texas			C	116	374	65	101	17	3	19	65	9	.270
1997 Louisville ............A.A.			C	112	395	60	108	21	7	20	68	4	.273
1997 St. Louis ............N.L.			C	17	45	4	11	2	0	2	7	4	.244

MARTIN, ALBERT LEE
Born, West Covina, California, November 24, 1967.
Bats Left. Throws Left. Height, 6 feet, 2 inches. Weight, 210 pounds.

Year	Club	Lea	Pos	G	AB	R	H	2B	3B	HR	RBI	SB	Avg
1985 Bradenton Braves ....Gulf C.			1B-OF	40	138	16	32	3	0	0	9	1	.232
1986 Idaho Falls ....Pioneer			OF-1B	63	242	39	80	17	*6	4	44	11	.331
1986 Sumter ....So. Atl.			1B	44	156	23	38	5	0	1	24	6	.244
1987 Sumter ....So. Atl.			OF-1B	117	375	59	95	18	5	12	64	27	.253
1988 Burlington ....Midwest			OF	123	480	69	134	21	3	7	42	40	.279
1989 Durham ....Carolina			OF	128	457	*84	124	26	3	9	48	27	.271
1990 Greenville ....Southern			OF	133	455	64	110	17	5	10	50	20	.242
1991 Greenville ....Southern			OF	86	301	38	73	13	3	7	38	19	.243
1991 Richmond a ....Int.			OF	44	151	20	42	11	1	5	18	11	.278
1992 Buffalo ..............A.A.			OF	125	420	85	128	16	*15	20	59	20	.305
1992 Pittsburgh ...........N.L.			OF	12	12	1	2	0	1	0	2	0	.167
1993 Pittsburgh ...........N.L.			OF	143	480	85	135	26	8	18	64	16	.281
1994 Pittsburgh b .........N.L.			OF	82	276	48	79	12	4	9	33	15	.286
1995 Pittsburgh ...........N.L.			OF	124	439	70	124	25	3	13	41	20	.282
1996 Pittsburgh ...........N.L.			OF	155	630	101	189	40	1	18	72	38	.300
1997 Carolina ....Southern			OF	3	9	0	1	0	0	0	0	0	.111
1997 Pittsburgh c .........N.L.			OF	113	423	64	123	24	7	13	59	23	.291
Major League Totals			6 Yrs.	629	2260	369	652	127	24	71	271	112	.288

a Became free agent, October 15; signed with Pittsburgh Pirates organization, November 11, 1991.
b On disabled list from July 11 to end of 1994 season.
c On disabled list from May 22 to June 24, 1997.

MARTIN, NORBERTO EDONA
Born, Santo Domingo, Dominican Republic, December 10, 1966.
Bats Right. Throws Right. Height, 5 feet, 10 inches. Weight, 164 pounds.

Year	Club	Lea	Pos	G	AB	R	H	2B	3B	HR	RBI	SB	Avg
1984 Sarasota White Sox Gulf C.			SS-OF	56	205	36	56	8	2	1	30	18	.273
1985 Appleton ......Midwest			SS	30	96	15	19	2	0	0	5	2	.198
1985 Niagara Falls .N.Y.-Penn.			SS	60	217	22	55	9	0	1	13	6	.253
1986 Sarasota White Sox Gulf C.			PR	0	0	0	0	0	0	0	0	0	.000
1986 Appleton a ....Midwest			SS	9	33	4	10	2	0	0	2	1	.303
1987 Charleston, WV .So. Atl.			SS-OF-2B	68	250	44	78	14	1	5	35	14	.312
1987 Peninsula ....Carolina			2B	41	162	21	42	6	1	1	18	11	.259
1988 Tampa ....Fla. St.			2B	101	360	44	93	10	4	2	33	24	.258
1989 Birmingham b .Southern			INJURED—Did Not Play										
1990 Vancouver .......P.C.			2B	130	508	77	135	20	4	3	45	10	.266
1991 Vancouver c .......P.C.			2B-SS	93	338	39	94	9	0	0	20	11	.278
1992 Vancouver .......P.C.			2B	135	497	72	143	12	7	0	29	29	.288

Year	Club	Lea	Pos	G	AB	R	H	2B	3B	HR	RBI	SB	Avg
1993 Nashville	....	A.A.	2B-SS	137	580	87	179	21	6	9	74	31	.309
1993 Chicago	....	A.L.	2B	8	14	3	5	0	0	0	2	0	.357
1994 Nashville	....	A.A.	SS-3B-2B	43	172	26	44	8	0	2	12	4	.256
1994 Chicago	....	A.L.	2B-SS-3B-OF	45	131	19	36	7	1	1	16	4	.275
1995 Chicago	....	A.L.	2B-OF-3B	72	160	17	43	7	4	2	17	5	.269
1996 Nashville	....	A.A.	2B-SS-3B	17	68	9	14	3	0	2	8	1	.206
1996 Chicago d	....	A.L.	SS-3B-3B	70	140	30	49	7	0	1	14	10	.350
1997 Chicago e	....	A.L.	SS-3B-2B	71	213	24	64	7	1	2	27	1	.300
Major League Totals	....		5 Yrs.	266	658	93	197	28	6	6	76	20	.299

a On disabled list from April 10 to May 5 and May 14 to end of 1986 season.
b On disabled list from April 7 to end of 1989 season.
c On disabled list from May 5 to June 9, 1991.
d On disabled list from April 6 to June 5, 1996.
d Designated for assignment by Chicago White Sox December 21, 1997
e On disabled list from June 15 to July 3 and July 22 to August 9, 1997.

MARTINEZ, CONSTANTINO (TINO)
Born, Tampa, Florida, December 7, 1967.
Bats Left. Throws Right. Height, 6 feet, 2 inches. Weight, 210 pounds.

Year	Club	Lea	Pos	G	AB	R	H	2B	3B	HR	RBI	SB	Avg
1989 Williamsport	....	Eastern	1B	*137	*509	51	131	29	2	13	64	7	.257
1990 Calgary	....	P.C.	1B	128	453	83	145	28	1	17	93	8	.320
1990 Seattle		A.L.	1B	24	68	4	15	4	0	0	5	0	.221
1991 Calgary	....	P.C.	1B-3B	122	442	94	144	34	5	18	86	3	.326
1991 Seattle	....	A.L.	1B	36	112	11	23	2	0	4	9	0	.205
1992 Seattle	....	A.L.	1B	136	460	53	118	19	2	16	66	2	.257
1993 Seattle a	....	A.L.	1B	109	408	48	108	25	1	17	60	0	.265
1994 Seattle	....	A.L.	1B	97	329	42	86	21	0	20	61	1	.261
1995 Seattle b	....	A.L.	1B	141	519	92	152	35	3	31	111	0	.293
1996 New York	....	A.L.	1B	155	595	82	174	28	0	25	117	2	.292
1997 New York	....	A.L.	1B	158	594	96	176	31	2	44	141	3	.296
Major League Totals	....		8 Yrs.	856	3085	428	852	165	8	157	570	8	.276
Division Series													
1995 Seattle	....	A.L.	1B	5	22	4	9	1	0	1	5	0	.409
1996 New York	....	A.L.	1B	4	15	3	4	2	0	0	0	0	.267
1997 New York	....	A.L.	1B	5	18	1	4	1	0	1	4	0	.222
Division Series Totals	....			14	55	8	17	4	0	2	9	0	.309
Championship Series													
1995 Seattle	....	A.L.	1B	6	22	0	3	0	0	0	0	0	.136
1996 New York	....	A.L.	1B	5	22	3	4	1	0	0	0	0	.182
Championship Series Totals	....			11	44	3	7	0	0	0	0	0	.159
World Series													
1996 New York	....	A.L.	1B	6	11	0	1	0	0	0	0	0	.091

a On disabled list from August 13 to end of 1993 season.
b Traded to New York Yankees with pitchers Jeff Nelson and Jim Mecir for infielder Russ Davis and pitcher Sterling Hitchcock, November 7, 1995.

MARTINEZ, DAVID
Born, New York, New York, September 26, 1964.
Bats Left. Throws Left. Height, 5 feet, 10 inches. Weight, 175 pounds.

Year	Club	Lea	Pos	G	AB	R	H	2B	3B	HR	RBI	SB	Avg
1983 Quad Cities	......	Midwest	OF	44	119	17	29	6	2	0	10	10	.244
1983 Geneva	....	N.Y.-Penn.	OF	64	241	35	63	15	2	5	33	16	.261
1984 Quad Cities a	....	Midwest	OF	12	41	6	9	2	2	0	5	3	.220
1985 Winston-Salem	....	Carolina	OF	115	386	52	132	14	4	5	54	38	*.342
1986 Iowa	....	A.A.	OF	83	318	52	92	11	5	5	32	42	.289
1986 Chicago	....	N.L.	OF	53	108	13	15	1	1	1	7	4	.139
1987 Chicago	....	N.L.	OF	142	459	70	134	18	8	8	36	16	.292
1988 Chicago-Montreal b	....	N.L.	OF	138	447	51	114	13	6	6	46	23	.255
1989 Montreal	....	N.L.	OF	126	361	41	99	16	7	3	27	23	.274
1990 Montreal c	....	N.L.	OF	118	391	60	109	13	5	11	39	13	.279
1991 Montreal d	....	N.L.	OF	124	396	47	117	18	5	7	42	16	.295
1992 Cincinnati e	....	N.L.	OF-1B	135	393	47	100	20	5	3	31	12	.254
1993 Phoenix	....	P.C.	OF	3	15	4	7	0	0	0	2	1	.467
1993 San Francisco f	....	N.L.	OF	91	241	28	58	12	1	5	27	6	.241
1994 San Francisco g	....	N.L.	OF-1B	97	235	23	58	9	3	4	27	3	.247

Year	Club	Lea	Pos	G	AB	R	H	2B	3B	HR	RBI	SB	Avg
1995 Chicago h-i-j	A.L.	OF-1B-P	119	303	49	93	16	4	5	37	8	.307
1996 Chicago	A.L.	OF-1B	146	440	85	140	20	8	10	53	15	.318
1997 Chicago k	A.L.	OF-1B	145	504	78	144	16	6	12	55	12	.286
Major League Totals		12 Yrs.	1434	4278	592	1181	172	59	75	427	151	.276

a On disabled list from April 27 to end of 1984 season.
b Traded to Montreal Expos for outfielder Mitch Webster, July 14, 1988.
c Record of 0-0 in game as pitcher.
d Traded to Cincinnati Reds with pitcher Scott Ruskin and shortstop Willie Greene for pitchers John Wetteland and Bill Risley, December 11, 1991.
e Filed for free agency, October 27; signed with San Francisco Giants, December 9, 1992.
f On disabled list from April 30 to June 4, 1993.
g Refused assignment to minor leagues and became free agent, October 14, 1994.
h Signed with Chicago White Sox, April 4, 1995.
i Filed for free agency, November 12, 1995.
j Re-signed with Chicago White Sox, November 14, 1995.
k Filed for free agency, October 27, 1997.

MARTINEZ, EDGAR

Born, New York, New York, January 2, 1963.
Bats Right. Throws Right. Height, 5 feet, 11 inches. Weight, 190 pounds.

Year	Club	Lea	Pos	G	AB	R	H	2B	3B	HR	RBI	SB	Avg
1983 Bellingham	Northwest	3B	32	104	14	18	1	1	0	5	1	.173
1984 Wausau	Midwest	3B	126	433	72	131	32	2	15	66	11	.303
1985 Chattanooga	Southern	3B	111	357	43	92	15	5	3	47	1	.258
1985 Calgary	P.C.	3B	20	68	8	24	7	1	0	14	1	.353
1986 Chattanooga	Southern	3B	132	451	71	119	29	5	6	74	2	.264
1987 Calgary	P.C.	3B	129	438	75	144	31	1	10	66	3	.329
1987 Seattle	A.L.	3B	13	43	6	16	5	2	0	5	0	.372
1988 Calgary	P.C.	3B	95	331	63	120	19	4	8	64	9	*.363
1988 Seattle	A.L.	3B	14	32	0	9	4	0	0	5	0	.281
1989 Calgary	P.C.	3B-2B	32	113	30	39	11	0	3	23	2	.345
1989 Seattle	A.L.	3B	65	171	20	41	5	0	2	20	2	.240
1990 Seattle	A.L.	3B	144	487	71	147	27	2	11	49	1	.302
1991 Seattle	A.L.	3B	150	544	98	167	35	1	14	52	0	.307
1992 Seattle	A.L.	3B-1B	135	528	100	181	*46	3	18	73	14	*.343
1993 Jacksonville	Southern	DH	4	14	2	5	0	0	1	3	0	.357
1993 Seattle a	A.L.	DH-3B	42	135	20	32	7	0	4	13	0	.237
1994 Seattle b	A.L.	3B	89	326	47	93	23	1	13	51	6	.285
1995 Seattle	A.L.	DH-3B-1B	145	511	121	182	52	0	29	113	4	.356
1996 Seattle c	A.L.	DH-1B-3B	139	499	121	163	52	2	26	103	3	.327
1997 Seattle	A.L.	DH-1B-3B	155	542	104	179	35	1	28	108	2	.330
Major League Totals		11 Yrs.	1091	3818	708	1210	291	12	145	592	32	.317
Division Series													
1995 Seattle	A.L.	DH	5	21	6	12	3	0	2	10	0	.571
1997 Seattle	A.L.	DH	4	16	2	3	0	0	2	3	0	.188
Division Series Totals			9	37	8	15	3	0	4	13	0	.405
Championship Series													
1995 Seattle	A.L.	DH	6	23	0	2	0	0	0	0	1	.087

a On disabled list from April 3 to May 17, June 15 to July 21, and August 17 to end of 1993 season.
b On disabled list from April 16 to May 6, 1994.
c On disabled list from July 21 to August 12, 1996.

MARTINEZ, FELIX

Born, Nagua, Dominican Republic, May 18, 1974.
Bats Both. Throws Right. Height, 6 feet. Weight, 168 pounds.

Year	Club	Lea	Pos	G	AB	R	H	2B	3B	HR	RBI	SB	Avg
1993 Royals	Gulf Coast	SS-2B-3B	57	165	23	42	5	1	0	12	22	.255
1994 Wilmington	Carolina	SS	117	400	65	107	16	4	2	43	19	.268
1995 Wichita	Texas	SS	127	426	53	112	15	3	3	30	44	.263
1996 Omaha	A.A.	SS	118	395	54	93	13	3	5	35	18	.235
1997 Omaha	A.A.	SS	112	410	55	104	19	4	2	36	21	.254
1997 Kansas City	A.L.	SS	16	31	3	7	1	1	0	3	0	.226

MARZANO, JOHN ROBERT

Born, Philadelphia, Pennsylvania, February 14, 1963.
Bats Right. Throws Right. Height, 5 feet, 11 inches. Weight, 200 pounds.

Year	Club	Lea	Pos	G	AB	R	H	2B	3B	HR	RBI	SB	Avg
1985 New Britain	....	Eastern	C	103	350	36	86	14	6	4	51	4	.246
1986 New Britain	....	Eastern	C-3B	118	445	55	126	28	2	10	62	2	.283
1987 Pawtucket	....	Int.	C	70	255	46	72	22	0	10	35	2	.282
1987 Boston	....	A.L.	C	52	168	20	41	11	0	5	24	0	.244
1988 Pawtucket	....	Int.	C	33	111	7	22	2	1	0	5	1	.198
1988 New Britain	....	Eastern	C	35	112	11	23	6	1	0	5	1	.205
1988 Boston	....	A.L.	C	10	29	3	4	1	0	0	1	0	.138
1989 Pawtucket	....	Int.	C	106	322	27	68	11	0	8	36	1	.211
1989 Boston	....	A.L.	C	7	18	5	8	3	0	1	3	0	.444
1990 Pawtucket	....	Int.	C-3B	26	75	16	24	4	1	2	8	6	.320
1990 Boston	....	A.L.	C	32	83	8	20	4	0	0	6	0	.241
1991 Boston	....	A.L.	C	49	114	10	30	8	0	0	9	0	.263
1992 Pawtucket	....	Int.	C	18	62	5	18	1	0	2	12	0	.290
1992 Boston a	....	A.L.	C	19	50	4	4	2	1	0	1	0	.080
1993 Charlotte b-c-d	...	Int.	C	3	9	0	1	0	0	0	0	0	.111
1994 Scranton-WB e-f	......	Int.	C-OF	88	280	25	59	19	2	1	19	2	.211
1995 Okla City g	....	A.A.	C	120	427	55	132	41	3	9	56	0	.309
1995 Texas	....	A.L.	C	2	6	1	2	0	0	0	0	0	.333
1996 Seattle h	....	A.L.	C	41	106	8	26	6	0	0	6	0	.245
1997 Seattle i-j	....	A.L.	C	39	87	7	25	3	0	1	10	0	.287
Major League Totals	....		9 Yrs.	251	661	66	160	38	1	7	60	0	.242

a On disabled list April 6 to July 26, 1992.
b Released by Boston Red Sox, March 24, 1993.
c Signed by Cleveland Indians, May 5, 1993.
d On disabled list May 8 through end of 1993 season.
e Signed as free agent with Philadelphia Phillies, December 14, 1993.
f Filed for free agency, October 17, 1994.
g Signed as free agent with Texas Rangers, April 2, 1995.
h Signed as free agent with Seattle Mariners, December 14, 1995.
i Filed for free agency, October 29, 1997.
j Signed with Seattle Mariners December 8, 1997

MASHORE, DAMON WAYNE

Born, Ponce, Puerto Rico, October 31, 1969.
Bats Right. Throws Right. Height, 5 feet, 11 inches. Weight, 195 pounds.

Year	Club	Lea	Pos	G	AB	R	H	2B	3B	HR	RBI	SB	Avg
1991 Sou Oregon	......	Northwest	OF	73	264	48	72	17	6	6	31	15	.273
1992 Modesto	....	California	OF	124	471	91	133	22	3	18	64	29	.282
1993 Huntsville	....	Southern	OF	70	253	35	59	7	2	3	20	18	.233
1994 Athletics	....	Arizona	OF	11	34	6	14	2	0	0	6	1	.412
1994 Huntsville	....	Southern	OF	59	210	24	47	11	2	3	21	6	.224
1995 Edmonton	....	P.C.	OF	117	337	50	101	19	5	1	37	17	.300
1996 Edmonton	....	P.C.	OF	50	183	32	49	9	1	8	29	6	.268
1996 Oakland a	....	A.L.	OF	50	105	20	28	7	1	3	12	4	.267
1997 Oakland b-c	....	A.L.	OF	92	279	55	69	10	2	3	18	5	.247
Major League Totals	....		2 Yrs.	142	384	75	97	17	3	6	30	9	.253

a On disabled list from August 13 to September 30, 1996.
b On disabled list from July 27 to September 29, 1997.
c Outrighted by Oakland Athletics, October 13, 1997.

MATHENY, MICHAEL SCOTT

Born, Columbus, Ohio, September 22, 1970.
Bats Right. Throws Right. Height, 6 feet, 3 inches. Weight, 205 pounds.

Year	Club	Lea	Pos	G	AB	R	H	2B	3B	HR	RBI	SB	Avg
1991 Helena	....	Pioneer	C	64	253	35	72	14	0	2	34	2	.285
1992 Stockton	....	California	C	106	333	42	73	13	2	6	46	2	.219
1993 El Paso	....	Texas	C	107	339	39	86	21	2	2	28	1	.254
1994 New Orleans	....	A.A.	C-1B	57	177	20	39	10	1	4	21	1	.220
1994 Milwaukee	....	A.L.	C	28	53	3	12	3	0	1	2	0	.226
1995 New Orleans	....	A.A.	C	6	17	3	6	2	0	3	4	0	.353
1995 Milwaukee	....	A.L.	C	80	166	13	41	9	1	0	21	2	.247
1996 New Orleans	....	A.A.	C	20	66	3	15	4	0	1	6	1	.227

Year	Club	Lea	Pos	G	AB	R	H	2B	3B	HR	RBI	SB	Avg
1996 Milwaukee	A.L.	C	106	313	31	64	15	2	8	46	3	.204
1997 Milwaukee a	A.L.	C-1B	123	320	29	78	16	1	4	32	0	.244
Major League Totals		4 Yrs.	337	852	76	195	43	4	13	101	5	.229

a Re-signed as free agent with Milwaukee Brewers, December 12, 1997.

MAYNE, BRENT DANEM
Born, Loma Linda, California, April 19, 1968.
Bats Left. Throws Right. Height, 6 feet, 1 inch. Weight, 190 pounds.

Year	Club	Lea	Pos	G	AB	R	H	2B	3B	HR	RBI	SB	Avg
1989 Baseball City a	Fla. St.	C	7	24	5	13	3	1	0	8	0	.542
1990 Memphis	Southern	C	115	412	48	110	16	3	2	61	5	.267
1990 Kansas City	A.L.	C	5	13	2	3	0	0	0	1	0	.231
1991 Kansas City	A.L.	C	85	231	22	58	8	0	3	31	2	.251
1992 Kansas City	A.L.	C-3B	82	213	16	48	10	0	0	18	0	.225
1993 Kansas City	A.L.	C	71	205	22	52	9	1	2	22	3	.254
1994 Kansas City	A.L.	C	46	144	19	37	5	1	2	20	1	.257
1995 Kansas City b	A.L.	C	110	307	23	77	18	1	1	27	0	.251
1996 New York c	N.L.	C	70	99	9	26	6	0	1	6	0	.263
1997 Edmonton	P.C.	C	2	3	0	0	0	0	0	0	0	.000
1997 Oakland d-e	A.L.	C	85	256	29	74	12	0	6	22	1	.289
Major League Totals		8 Yrs.	554	1468	142	375	68	3	15	147	7	.255

a On disabled list from July 24 to end of 1989 season.
b Traded to New York Mets for outfielder, Al Shirley, December 14, 1995.
c Signed with Seattle Mariners organization, January 11, 1997.
d Filed for free agency, October 30, 1997.
e Signed with San Francisco Giants, November 21, 1997.

McCRACKEN, QUINTON ANTOINE
Born, Wilmington, North Carolina, March 16, 1970.
Bats Both. Throws Right. Height, 5 feet, 8 inches. Weight, 170 pounds.

Year	Club	Lea	Pos	G	AB	R	H	2B	3B	HR	RBI	SB	Avg
1992 Bend	Northwest	2B-OF	67	232	37	65	13	2	0	27	18	.280
1993 Central Valley	California	OF-2B	127	483	94	141	17	7	2	58	60	.292
1994 New Haven	Eastern	OF	136	544	94	151	27	4	5	39	36	.278
1995 New Haven	Eastern	OF	55	221	33	79	11	4	1	26	26	.357
1995 Colorado Springs	P.C.	OF	61	244	55	88	14	6	3	28	17	.361
1995 Colorado	N.L.	OF	3	1	0	0	0	0	0	0	0	.000
1996 Colorado	N.L.	OF	124	283	50	82	13	6	3	40	17	.290
1997 Colorado a	N.L.	OF	147	325	69	95	11	1	3	36	28	.292
Major League Totals		3 Yrs.	274	609	119	177	24	7	6	76	45	.291

a Selected in expansion draft by Tampa Bay Devil Rays, November 18, 1997.

MCDONALD, JASON ADAM
Born, Modesto, California, March 20, 1972.
Bats Both. Throws Right. Height, 5 feet, 8 inches. Weight, 175 pounds.

Year	Club	Lea	Pos	G	AB	R	H	2B	3B	HR	RBI	SB	Avg
1993 Sou Oregon	Northwest	2B	35	112	26	33	5	2	0	8	22	.295
1994 W Michigan	Midwest	2B-OF-SS-P	116	404	67	96	11	9	2	31	52	.238
1995 Modesto	California	SS-OF-2B	133	493	109	129	25	7	6	50	70	.262
1996 Edmonton	P.C.	2B-OF	137	479	71	114	7	5	8	46	33	.238
1997 Edmonton	P.C.	OF	79	276	74	73	14	6	4	30	31	.264
1997 Oakland	A.L.	OF	78	236	47	62	11	4	4	14	13	.263

McGEE, WILLIE DEAN
Born, San Francisco, California, November 2, 1958.
Bats Both. Throws Right. Height, 6 feet, 1 inch. Weight, 185 pounds.

Year	Club	Lea	Pos	G	AB	R	H	2B	3B	HR	RBI	SB	Avg
1977 Oneonta	N.Y.-Penn.	OF	65	225	31	53	4	3	2	22	13	.236
1978 Ft. Lauderdale	Fla. St.	OF	124	423	62	106	6	6	0	37	25	.251
1979 West Haven	Eastern	OF	49	115	21	28	3	1	1	8	7	.243
1979 Ft. Lauderdale	Fla. St.	OF	46	176	25	56	8	3	1	18	16	.318
1980 Nashville a	Southern	OF	78	223	35	63	4	5	1	22	7	.283
1981 Nashville b-c	Southern	OF	100	388	7	125	20	5	7	63	24	.322

Year	Club	Lea	Pos	G	AB	R	H	2B	3B	HR	RBI	SB	Avg
1982 Louisville d	.A.A.	OF	13	55	11	16	2	2	1	3	5	.291
1982 St. Louis	.N.L.	OF	123	422	43	125	12	8	4	56	24	.296
1983 St. Louis e	.N.L.	OF	147	601	75	172	22	8	5	75	39	.286
1983 Arkansas	.Texas	OF	7	29	5	8	1	1	0	2	0	.276
1984 St. Louis f	.N.L.	OF	145	571	82	166	19	11	6	50	43	.291
1985 St. Louis g	.N.L.	OF	152	612	114	*216	26	*18	10	82	56	*.353
1986 St. Louis h	.N.L.	OF	124	497	65	127	22	7	7	48	19	.256
1987 St. Louis	.N.L.	OF	153	620	76	177	37	11	11	105	16	.285
1988 St. Louis	.N.L.	OF	137	562	73	164	24	6	3	50	41	.292
1989 Louisville	.A.A.	OF	8	27	5	11	4	0	0	4	3	.407
1989 St. Louis i	.N.L.	OF	58	199	23	47	10	2	3	17	8	.236
1990 St. Louis j	.N.L.	OF	125	501	76	168	32	5	3	62	28	*.335
1990 Oakland k	.A.L.	OF	29	113	23	31	3	2	0	15	3	.274
1991 Phoenix	.P.C.	OF	4	10	4	5	1	0	0	1	2	.500
1991 San Francisco l	.N.L.	OF	131	497	67	155	30	3	4	43	17	.312
1992 San Francisco	.N.L.	OF	138	474	56	141	20	2	1	36	13	.297
1993 San Francisco m	.N.L.	OF	130	475	53	143	28	1	4	46	10	.301
1994 San Francisco n-o	.N.L.	OF	45	156	19	44	3	0	5	23	3	.282
1995 Pawtucket	.Int.	OF	5	21	9	10	0	0	0	2	2	.476
1995 Boston p-q	.A.L.	OF	67	200	32	57	11	3	2	15	5	.285
1996 St. Louis r-s	.N.L.	OF-1B	123	309	52	95	15	2	5	41	5	.307
1997 St. Louis t-u	.N.L.	OF	122	300	29	90	19	4	3	38	8	.300
Major League Totals	16 Yrs.	1949	7109	958	2118	333	93	76	802	338	.298		
Division Series													
1995 Boston	.A.L.	OF	2	4	0	1	0	0	0	1	0	.250
1996 St. Louis	.N.L.	OF	3	10	1	1	0	0	0	1	0	.100
Division Series Totals			5	14	1	2	0	0	0	2	0	.143	
Championship Series													
1982 St. Louis	.N.L.	OF	3	13	4	4	0	2	1	5	0	.308
1985 St. Louis	.N.L.	OF	6	26	6	7	1	0	0	3	2	.269
1987 St. Louis	.N.L.	OF	7	26	2	8	1	1	0	2	0	.308
1990 Oakland	.A.L.	OF	3	9	3	2	1	0	0	0	2	.222
1996 St. Louis	.N.L.	OF	6	15	0	5	0	0	0	0	0	.333
Championship Series Totals			25	89	15	26	3	3	1	10	4	.292	
World Series Record													
1982 St. Louis	.N.L.	OF	6	25	6	6	0	0	2	5	2	.240
1985 St. Louis	.N.L.	OF	7	27	2	7	2	0	1	2	1	.259
1987 St. Louis	.N.L.	OF	7	27	2	10	2	0	0	4	0	.370
1990 Oakland	.A.L.	OF	4	10	1	2	1	0	0	0	1	.214
World Series Totals			24	89	11	25	5	0	3	11	4	.281	

a On disabled list from May 22 to June 7 and July 14 to August 7, 1980.
b On disabled list from April 24 to June 4, 1981.
c Traded by New York Yankees to St. Louis Cardinals organization for pitcher Bob Sykes, October 21, 1981.
d On disabled list from April 13 to April 23, 1982.
e On disabled list from April 2 to April 29, 1983.
f On disabled list from July 12 to July 27, 1984.
g Selected Most Valuable Player in National League for 1985.
h On disabled list from August 3 to August 27, 1986.
i On disabled list from June 7 to July 18 and July 25 to August 14, 1989.
j Traded to Oakland Athletics for outfielder Felix Jose, third baseman Stan Royer and pitcher Daryl Greene, August 29, 1990.
k Filed for free agency, October 26; signed with San Francisco Giants, December 3, 1990.
l On disabled list from July 12 to August 1, 1991.
m On disabled list from July 11 to July 30, 1993.
n On disabled list from June 8 to end of 1994 season.
o Released, October 6, 1994.
p Signed with Boston Red Sox organization, June 6, 1995.
q Filed for free agency, November 12, 1995.
r Filed for free agency, November 13, 1996.
s Re-signed with St. Louis Cardinals, December 4, 1996.
t On disabled list from July 12 to July 29, 1997.
u Filed for free agency, October 29, 1997.

McGRIFF, FREDERICK STANLEY (FRED)
Born, Tampa, Florida, October 31, 1963.
Bats Left. Throws Left. Height, 6 feet, 3 inches. Weight, 215 pounds.

Year	Club	Lea	Pos	G	AB	R	H	2B	3B	HR	RBI	SB	Avg
1981 Bradenton Yankees	...Gulf C.	1B	29	81	6	12	2	0	0	9	0	.148
1982 Bradenton Yankees a	.Gulf C.	1B	62	217	38	59	11	1	*9	*41	6	.272
1983 Florence	.So. Atl.	1B	33	119	26	37	3	1	7	26	3	.311

115

Year	Club	Lea	Pos	G	AB	R	H	2B	3B	HR	RBI	SB	Avg
1983 Kinston ....Carolina			1B	94	350	53	85	14	1	21	57	3	.243
1984 Knoxville ....Southern			1B	56	189	29	47	13	2	9	25	0	.249
1984 Syracuse ....Int.			1B	70	238	28	56	10	1	13	28	0	.235
1985 Syracuse b ....Int.			1B	51	176	19	40	8	2	5	20	0	.227
1986 Syracuse ....Int.			1B-OF	133	468	69	121	23	4	19	74	0	.259
1986 Toronto .............A.L.			1B	3	5	1	1	0	0	0	0	0	.200
1987 Toronto .............A.L.			1B	107	295	58	73	16	0	20	43	3	.247
1988 Toronto .............A.L.			1B	154	536	100	151	35	4	34	82	6	.282
1989 Toronto .............A.L.			1B	161	551	98	148	27	3	*36	92	7	.269
1990 Toronto c ............A.L.			1B	153	557	91	167	21	1	35	88	5	.300
1991 San Diego ...........N.L.			1B	153	528	84	147	19	1	31	106	4	.278
1992 San Diego d .........N.L.			1B	152	531	79	152	30	4	*35	104	8	.286
1993 San Diego-Atlanta e .N.L.			1B	151	557	111	162	29	2	37	101	5	.291
1994 Atlanta ..............N.L.			1B	113	424	81	135	25	1	34	94	7	.318
1995 Atlanta f-g ...........N.L.			1B	144	528	85	148	27	1	27	93	3	.280
1996 Atlanta ..............N.L.			1B	159	617	81	182	37	1	28	107	7	.295
1997 Atlanta h .............N.L.			1B	152	564	77	156	25	1	22	97	5	.277
Major League Totals		12 Yrs.		1602	5693	946	1622	291	19	339	1007	60	.285
Division Series													
1995 Atlanta ..............N.L.			1B	4	18	4	6	0	0	2	6	0	.333
1996 Atlanta ..............N.L.			1B	3	9	1	3	1	0	1	3	0	.333
1997 Atlanta ..............N.L.			1B	3	9	4	2	0	0	0	1	0	.222
Division Series Totals				10	36	9	11	1	0	3	10	0	.306
Championship Series													
1989 Toronto .............A.L.			1B	5	21	1	3	0	0	0	3	0	.143
1993 Atlanta ..............N.L.			1B	6	23	6	10	2	0	1	4	0	.435
1995 Atlanta ..............N.L.			1B	4	16	5	7	4	0	0	0	0	.438
1996 Atlanta ..............N.L.			1B	7	28	6	7	0	1	2	7	0	.250
1997 Atlanta ..............N.L.			1B	6	21	0	7	1	0	0	4	0	.333
Championship Series Totals				28	109	18	34	7	1	3	18	0	.312
World Series Record													
1995 Atlanta ..............N.L.			1B	6	23	5	6	2	0	2	3	1	.261
1996 Atlanta ..............N.L.			1B	6	20	4	6	0	0	2	6	0	.300
World Series Totals				12	43	9	12	2	0	4	9	1	.279

a Traded by New York Yankees to Toronto Blue Jays organization with outfielder Dave Collins and pitcher Mike Morgan for catcher-outfielder Tom Dodd and pitcher Dale Murray, December 9, 1982.
b On disabled list from June 5 to August 14, 1985.
c Traded to San Diego Padres with shortstop Tony Fernandez for outfielder Joe Carter and second baseman Roberto Alomar, December 5, 1990.
d Suspended four games by National League for June 18 mound charging and fighting, June 23 to June 26, 1992.
e Traded to Atlanta Braves for outfielders Melvin Nieves and Vince Moore and pitcher Donnie Elliott, July 18, 1993.
f Filed for free agency, November 12, 1995.
g Re-signed with Atlanta Braves, December 2, 1995.
h Traded to Tampa Bay Devil Rays for player to be named later, November 18, 1997.

MCGUIRE, RYAN BYRON

Born, Wilson, North Carolina, November 23, 1971.
Bats Left. Throws Left. Height, 6 feet, 2 inches. Weight 210 pounds.

Year	Club	Lea	Pos	G	AB	R	H	2B	3B	HR	RBI	SB	Avg
1993 Ft. Laudrdle ....Fla. St.			1B	58	213	23	69	12	2	4	38	2	.324
1994 Lynchburg ....Carolina			1B	137	489	70	133	29	0	10	73	10	.272
1995 Trenton ....Eastern			1B-OF	109	414	59	138	29	1	7	59	11	.333
1996 Ottawa ....Int.			1B-OF	134	451	62	116	21	2	12	60	11	.257
1997 Ottawa ....Int.			1B	50	184	37	55	11	1	3	15	5	.299
1997 Montreal .............N.L.			OF-1B	84	199	22	51	15	2	3	17	1	.256

McGWIRE, MARK DAVID

Born, Claremont, California, October 1, 1963.
Bats Right. Throws Right. Height, 6 feet, 5 inches. Weight, 225 pounds.

Year	Club	Lea	Pos	G	AB	R	H	2B	3B	HR	RBI	SB	Avg
1984 Modesto ....California			1B	16	55	7	11	3	0	1	1	0	.200
1985 Modesto ....California			3B-1B	138	489	95	134	23	3	*24	*106	1	.274
1986 Tacoma .............P.C.			3B	78	280	42	89	21	5	13	59	1	.318
1986 Huntsville ....Southern			3B	55	195	40	59	15	0	10	53	3	.303
1986 Oakland .............A.L.			3B	18	53	10	10	1	0	3	9	0	.189
1987 Oakland a ...........A.L.			1B-3B-OF	151	557	97	161	28	4	*49	118	1	.289

Year	Club	Lea	Pos	G	AB	R	H	2B	3B	HR	RBI	SB	Avg
1988 Oakland		A.L.	1B-OF	155	550	87	143	22	1	32	99	0	.260
1989 Oakland b		A.L.	1B	143	490	74	113	17	0	33	95	1	.231
1990 Oakland		A.L.	1B	156	523	87	123	16	0	39	108	2	.235
1991 Oakland		A.L.	1B	154	483	62	97	22	0	22	75	2	.201
1992 Oakland c-d		A.L.	1B	139	467	87	125	22	0	42	104	0	.268
1993 Oakland e		A.L.	1B	27	84	16	28	6	0	9	24	0	.333
1994 Oakland f		A.L.	1B	47	135	26	34	3	0	9	25	0	.252
1995 Oakland g		A.L.	1B	104	317	75	87	13	0	39	90	1	.274
1996 Oakland h		A.L.	1B	130	423	104	132	21	0	*52	113	0	.312
1997 Oakland i		A.L.	1B	105	366	48	104	24	0	34	81	1	.284
1997 St. Louis		N.L.	1B	51	174	38	44	3	0	24	42	2	.253
Major League Totals			12 Yrs.	1380	4622	811	1201	198	5	387	983	10	.260
Championship Series													
1988 Oakland		A.L.	1B	4	15	4	5	0	0	1	3	0	.333
1989 Oakland		A.L.	1B	5	18	3	7	1	0	1	3	0	.389
1990 Oakland		A.L.	1B	4	13	2	2	0	0	0	2	0	.154
1992 Oakland		A.L.	1B	6	20	1	3	0	0	1	3	0	.150
Championship Series Totals				19	66	10	17	1	0	3	11	0	.258
World Series Record													
1988 Oakland		A.L.	1B	5	17	1	1	0	0	1	1	0	.059
1989 Oakland		A.L.	1B	4	17	0	5	1	0	0	1	0	.294
1990 Oakland		A.L.	1B	4	14	1	3	0	0	0	0	0	.214
World Series Totals				13	48	2	9	1	0	1	2	0	.188

a Selected Rookie of the Year in American League for 1987.
b On disabled list from April 10 to April 26, 1989.
c On disabled list from August 22 to September 11, 1992.
d Filed for free agency, October 26; re-signed with Oakland Athletics, December 24, 1992.
e On disabled list from May 14 to end of 1993 season.
f On disabled list from April 30 to June 18 and August 1 to end of 1994 season.
g On disabled list from July 18 to August 2 and August 5 to August 26, 1995.
h On disabled list from April 1 to April 23, 1996.
i Traded to St. Louis Cardinals for pitchers T.J. Mathews, Eric Ludwick and Blake Stein, July 31, 1997.

McLEMORE, MARK TREMMELL
Born, San Diego, California, October 4, 1964.
Bats Both. Throws Right. Height, 5 feet, 11 inches. Weight, 207 pounds.

Year	Club	Lea	Pos	G	AB	R	H	2B	3B	HR	RBI	SB	Avg
1982 Salem		Northwest	2B-SS	55	165	42	49	6	2	0	25	14	.297
1983 Peoria		Midwest	2B-SS	95	329	42	79	7	3	0	18	15	.240
1984 Redwood		California	2B-SS	134	482	102	142	8	3	0	45	59	.295
1985 Midland a		Texas	2B-SS	117	458	80	124	17	6	2	46	31	.271
1986 Midland		Texas	2B	63	237	54	75	9	1	1	29	38	.316
1986 Edmonton		P.C.	2B	73	286	41	79	13	1	0	23	29	.276
1986 California		A.L.	2B	5	4	0	0	0	0	0	0	0	.000
1987 California		A.L.	2B-SS	138	433	61	102	13	3	3	41	25	.236
1988 Palm Springs		California	2B	11	44	9	15	3	1	0	6	3	.341
1988 Edmonton		P.C.	2B	12	45	7	12	3	0	0	6	1	.267
1988 California b		A.L.	2B-3B	77	233	38	56	11	2	2	16	13	.240
1989 Edmonton		P.C.	2B	114	430	60	105	13	2	2	34	26	.244
1989 California		A.L.	2B	32	103	12	25	3	1	0	14	6	.243
1990 Palm Springs		California	2B	6	22	3	6	0	0	0	2	0	.273
1990 Edm.-Colo. Spr.		P.C.	2B-SS-3B	23	93	15	25	4	0	1	10	5	.269
1990 Cal.-Cleveland c-d-e		A.L.	2B-SS	28	60	6	9	2	0	0	2	1	.150
1991 Houston		N.L.	2B	21	61	6	9	1	0	0	2	0	.148
1991 Tucson		P.C.	2B	4	14	2	5	1	0	0	0	0	.357
1991 Jackson f-g		Texas	2B	7	22	6	5	3	0	1	4	1	.227
1991 Rochester		Int.	2B-1B	57	228	32	64	11	4	1	28	12	.281
1992 Baltimore h		A.L.	2B	101	228	40	56	7	2	0	27	11	.246
1993 Baltimore		A.L.	OF-2B-3B	148	581	81	165	27	5	4	72	21	.284
1994 Baltimore i		A.L.	2B-OF	104	343	44	88	11	1	3	29	20	.257
1995 Texas		A.L.	OF-2B	129	467	73	122	20	5	5	41	21	.261
1996 Texas j-k		A.L.	2B-OF	147	517	84	150	23	4	5	46	27	.290
1997 Charlotte		Fla. St.	2B	2	7	1	4	1	0	0	3	1	.571
1997 Okla City		A.A.	2B	3	10	0	1	0	0	0	1	1	.100
1997 Texas l		A.L.	2B-OF	89	349	47	91	17	2	1	25	7	.261
Major League Totals			12 Yrs.	1019	3379	492	873	135	25	23	315	152	.258

a On disabled list from May 15 to May 27, 1985.
b On disabled list from May 24 to August 15, 1988.
c On disabled list from May 17 to August 14, 1990.

d Traded to Cleveland Indians organization to complete September 6, 1989 trade in which California Angels acquired catcher Ron Tingley, August 17, 1990.
e Released, December 13, 1990; signed with Houston Astros organization, January 31, 1991.
f On disabled list from May 9 to June 25, 1991.
g Released by Houston Astros, June 25; signed with Baltimore Orioles organization, July 5, 1991.
h Not offered 1993 contract, December 18, 1992; re-signed with Baltimore Orioles organization, January 8, 1993.
i Filed for free agency, October 17; signed with Texas Rangers, December 13, 1994.
j Filed for free agency, October 28, 1996.
k Re-signed with Texas Rangers, December 11, 1996.
l On disabled list from May 14 to June 12 and August 19 to September 29, 1997.

McMILLON, WILLIAM EDWARD (BILLY)
Born, Otero, New Mexico, November 17, 1971.
Bats Left. Throws Left. Height, 5 feet, 11 inches. Weight, 180 pounds.

Year	Club	Lea	Pos	G	AB	R	H	2B	3B	HR	RBI	SB	Avg
1993 Elmira	N.Y.-Penn.	OF	57	226	38	69	14	2	6	35	5	.305
1994 Kane County	Midwest	OF	137	496	88	125	25	3	17	101	7	.252
1995 Portland	Eastern	OF	141	518	92	162	29	3	14	93	15	.313
1996 Charlotte	Int.	OF	97	347	72	122	32	2	17	70	5	.352
1996 Florida	N.L.	OF	28	51	4	11	0	0	0	4	0	.216
1997 Charlotte	Int.	OF	57	204	34	57	18	0	8	26	8	.279
1997 Scranton-WB a	Int.	OF	26	92	18	27	8	1	4	21	2	.293
1997 Florida-Philadelphia	N.L.	OF	37	90	10	23	5	1	2	14	2	.256
Major League Totals			2 Yrs.	65	141	14	34	5	1	2	18	2	.241

a Traded by Florida Marlins to Philadelphia Phillies for outfielder Darren Daulton, July 21, 1997.

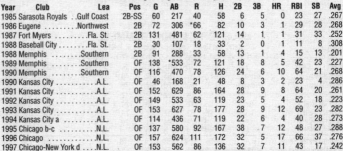

McRAE, BRIAN WESLEY
Born, Bradenton, Florida, August 27, 1967.
Bats Both. Throws Right. Height, 6 feet. Weight, 185 pounds.

Year	Club	Lea	Pos	G	AB	R	H	2B	3B	HR	RBI	SB	Avg
1985 Sarasota Royals	Gulf Coast	2B-SS	60	217	40	58	6	5	0	23	27	.267
1986 Eugene	Northwest	2B	72	306	*66	82	10	3	1	29	28	.268
1987 Fort Myers	Fla. St.	2B	131	481	62	121	14	1	1	31	33	.252
1988 Baseball City	Fla. St.	2B	30	107	18	33	2	0	1	11	8	.308
1988 Memphis	Southern	2B	91	288	33	58	13	1	4	15	13	.201
1989 Memphis	Southern	OF	138	*533	72	121	18	8	5	42	23	.227
1990 Memphis	Southern	OF	116	470	78	126	24	6	10	64	21	.268
1990 Kansas City	A.L.	OF	46	168	21	48	8	3	2	23	4	.286
1991 Kansas City	A.L.	OF	152	629	86	164	28	9	8	64	20	.261
1992 Kansas City	A.L.	OF	149	533	63	119	23	5	4	52	18	.223
1993 Kansas City	A.L.	OF	153	627	78	177	28	9	12	69	23	.282
1994 Kansas City a	A.L.	OF	114	436	71	119	22	6	4	40	28	.273
1995 Chicago b-c	N.L.	OF	137	580	92	167	38	7	12	48	27	.288
1996 Chicago	N.L.	OF	157	624	111	172	32	5	17	66	37	.276
1997 Chicago-New York d	N.L.	OF	153	562	86	136	32	7	11	43	17	.242
Major League Totals			8 Yrs.	1061	4159	608	1102	211	51	70	405	174	.265

a Declared restricted free agent under Major League Baseball implemented labor proposal, December 23, 1994.
b Traded to Chicago Cubs for pitcher Derek Wallace and pitcher Geno Morones, April 5, 1995.
c Re-signed with Chicago Cubs, April 19, 1995.
d Traded to New York Mets with pitchers Mel Rojas and Turk Wendell for outfielder Lance Johnson, pitcher Mark Clark and player to be named later, August 8, 1997. Chicago Cubs received infielder Manny Alexander to complete trade, August 14, 1997.

MEARES, PATRICK JAMES
Born, Salina, Kansas, September 6, 1968.
Bats Right. Throws Right. Height, 6 feet. Weight, 184 pounds.

Year	Club	Lea	Pos	G	AB	R	H	2B	3B	HR	RBI	SB	Avg
1990 Kenosha	Midwest	3B-2B	52	197	26	47	10	2	4	22	2	.239
1991 Visalia	California	2B-3B-OF	89	360	53	109	21	4	6	44	15	.303
1992 Orlando a	Southern	SS	81	300	42	76	19	0	3	23	5	.253
1993 Portland	P.C.	SS	18	54	6	16	5	0	0	3	0	.296
1993 Minnesota	A.L.	SS	111	346	33	87	14	3	0	33	4	.251
1994 Minnesota b	A.L.	SS	80	229	29	61	12	1	2	24	5	.266
1995 Minnesota	A.L.	SS-OF	116	390	57	105	19	4	12	49	10	.269
1996 Minnesota	A.L.	SS-OF	152	517	66	138	26	7	8	67	9	.267
1997 Minnesota c	A.L.	SS	134	439	63	121	23	3	10	60	7	.276
Major League Totals			5 Yrs.	593	1921	248	512	94	18	32	233	35	.267

a On disabled list from July 3 to July 28, 1992.
b On disabled list from June 22 to July 7, 1994.
c On disabled list from August 11 to August 26, 1997.

MENDOZA, CARLOS RAMON

Born, Bolivar, Venezuela, November 4, 1974.
Bats Left. Throws Left. Height, 5 feet, 11 inches. Weight, 160 pounds.

Year Club	Lea	Pos	G	AB	R	H	2B	3B	HR	RBI	SB	Avg
1994 N.Y. Mets . . . . .Dominican		OF	57	197	66	69	11	1	1	25	15	.350
1995 Kingsport . . . . .Appal.		OF	51	192	56	63	9	0	1	24	28	.328
1996 Columbia . . . . .So. Atl.		OF	85	300	61	101	10	2	0	37	31	.337
1997 Binghamton . . . . . . .Eastern		OF	59	228	36	87	12	2	1	13	14	.382
1997 Norfolk . . . . .Int.		OF	10	35	3	5	0	1	0	0	1	.143
1997 New York a . . . . .N.L.		OF	15	12	6	3	0	0	0	1	0	.250

a Selected in expansion draft by Tampa Bay Devil Rays, November 18, 1997.

MERCED (VILLANUEVA), ORLANDO LUIS

Born, Hato Rey, Puerto Rico, November 2, 1966.
Bats Both. Throws Right. Height, 5 feet, 11 inches. Weight, 185 pounds.

Year Club	Lea	Pos	G	AB	R	H	2B	3B	HR	RBI	SB	Avg
1985 Brad. Pirates Gulf C.		SS-3B-1B	40	136	16	31	6	0	1	13	3	.228
1986 Macon . . . . .So. Atl.		OF-3B	65	173	20	34	4	1	2	24	5	.197
1986 Watertown .N.Y.-Pa.		3B-1B-OF	27	89	12	16	0	1	3	9	6	.180
1987 Macon a . . . .So. Atl.		OF	4	4	1	0	0	0	0	0	0	.000
1987 Watertown b .N.Y.-Pa.		2B	4	12	4	5	0	1	0	3	1	.417
1988 Augusta . . . .So. Atl.		2B-3B-SS	37	136	19	36	6	3	1	17	2	.265
1988 Salem . . . .Carolina		3B-2B-OF-1B-SS	80	298	47	87	12	7	7	42	13	.292
1989 Harrisburg .Eastern		1B-OF-3B	95	341	43	82	16	4	6	48	13	.240
1989 Buffalo . . . . .A.A.		1B-OF-3B	35	129	18	44	5	3	1	16	0	.341
1990 Buffalo . . . . . . .A.A.		1B-3B	101	378	52	99	12	6	9	55	14	.262
1990 Pittsburgh . . .N.L.		C-OF	25	24	3	5	1	0	0	0	0	.208
1991 Buffalo . . . . . . .A.A.		OF	3	12	1	2	0	0	0	0	1	.167
1991 Pittsburgh . . .N.L.		1B-OF	120	411	83	113	17	2	10	50	8	.275
1992 Pittsburgh . . .N.L.		1B-OF	134	405	50	100	28	5	6	60	5	.247
1993 Pittsburgh . . .N.L.		OF-1B	137	447	68	140	26	4	8	70	3	.313
1994 Pittsburgh . . .N.L.		OF-1B	108	386	48	105	21	3	9	51	4	.272
1995 Pittsburgh . . .N.L.		OF-1B	132	487	75	146	29	4	15	83	7	.300
1996 Pittsburgh c-d-e .N.L.		OF-1B	120	453	69	130	24	1	17	80	8	.287
1997 Toronto f-g . . .A.L.		OF-1B	98	368	45	98	23	2	9	40	7	.266
Major League Totals		8 Yrs.	874	2981	441	837	169	21	74	434	42	.281
Championship Series												
1991 Pittsburgh . . .N.L.		1B	3	9	1	2	0	0	1	1	0	.222
1992 Pittsburgh . . .N.L.		1B	4	10	0	1	1	0	0	2	0	.100
Championship Series Totals			7	19	1	3	1	0	1	3	0	.158

a On disabled list from April 18 to April 28, 1987.
b On disabled list from June 23 to end of 1987 season.
c On disabled list from May 1 to May 18 and August 1 to August 16 and August 22 to September 6, 1996.
d Traded to Toronto Blue Jays with infielder Carlos Garcia and pitcher Dan Plesac for pitcher Jose Silva, pitcher Jose Pett, infielder Brandon Cromer, player to be named later and infielder Abra, November 14, 1996.
e Pittsburgh Pirates received pitcher Mike Halperin, infielder Abraham Nunez and catcher Craig Wilson to complete trade, December 11, 1996.
f On disabled list from July 30 to September 29, 1997.
g Released by Toronto Blue Jays, December 8, 1997.

MIESKE, MATTHEW TODD

Born, Midland, Michigan, February 13, 1968.
Bats Right. Throws Right. Height, 6 feet. Weight, 185 pounds.

Year Club	Lea	Pos	G	AB	R	H	2B	3B	HR	RBI	SB	Avg
1990 Spokane . . . . . . .Northwest		OF	*76	*291	*59	99	20	0	*12	*63	26	.340
1991 High Desert a . . . . .California		OF	133	492	108	*168	*36	6	15	119	39	*.341
1992 Denver . . . . .A.A.		OF	134	*524	80	140	29	11	19	77	13	.267
1993 New Orleans . . . . .A.A.		OF	60	219	36	57	14	2	8	22	6	.260
1993 Milwaukee . . . . .A.L.		OF	23	58	9	14	0	0	3	7	0	.241
1994 New Orleans . . . . .A.A.		OF	2	8	2	2	0	0	1	3	1	.250
1994 Milwaukee . . . . .A.L.		OF	84	259	39	67	13	1	10	38	3	.259
1995 Milwaukee . . . . .A.L.		OF	117	267	42	67	13	1	12	48	2	.251

Year	Club	Lea	Pos	G	AB	R	H	2B	3B	HR	RBI	SB	Avg
1996 Milwaukee	A.L.	OF	127	374	46	104	24	3	14	64	1	.278
1997 Milwaukee b-c-d	A.L.	OF	84	253	39	63	15	3	5	21	1	.249
Major League Totals		5 Yrs.	435	1211	175	315	65	8	44	178	7	.260

a Traded by San Diego Padres to Milwaukee Brewers organization with pitcher Ricky Bones and infielder Jose Valentin for infielder Gary Sheffield and pitcher Geoff Kellogg, March 27, 1992.
b On disabled list from August 8 to September 2, 1997.
c Released by Milwaukee Brewers, December 22, 1997.
d Signed as free agent with Chicago Cubs, December 29, 1997

MILLER, DAMIAN DONALD
Born, LaCrosse, Wisconsin, October 13, 1969.
Bats Right. Throws Right. Height, 6 feet, 3 inches. Weight 202 pounds.

Year	Club	Lea	Pos	G	AB	R	H	2B	3B	HR	RBI	SB	Avg
1990 Elizabethtn	Appal.	C	14	45	7	10	1	0	1	6	1	.222
1991 Kenosha	Midwest	C-1B-OF	80	267	28	62	11	1	3	34	3	.232
1992 Kenosha	Midwest	C	115	377	53	110	27	2	5	56	6	.292
1993 Ft. Myers	Fla. St.	C	87	325	31	69	12	1	1	26	6	.212
1993 Nashville	Southern	C	4	13	0	3	0	0	0	0	0	.231
1994 Nashville	Southern	C	103	328	36	88	10	0	8	35	4	.268
1995 Salt Lake	P.C.	C-OF	83	295	39	84	23	1	3	41	2	.285
1996 Salt Lake	P.C.	C-1B	104	385	54	110	27	1	7	55	1	.286
1997 Salt Lake	P.C.	C	85	314	48	106	19	3	11	82	6	.338
1997 Minnesota a	A.L.	C	25	66	5	18	1	0	2	13	0	.273

a Selected in expansion draft by Arizona Diamondbacks, November 18, 1997.

MILLER, ORLANDO SALMON
Born, Changuinola, Panama, January 13, 1969.
Bats Right. Throws Right. Height, 6 feet, 1 inch. Weight, 180 pounds.

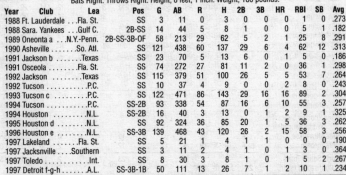

Year	Club	Lea	Pos	G	AB	R	H	2B	3B	HR	RBI	SB	Avg
1988 Ft. Lauderdale ...	Fla. St.	SS	3	11	0	3	0	0	0	1	0	.273
1988 Sara. Yankees ...	Gulf C.	2B-SS	14	44	5	8	1	0	0	5	1	.182
1989 Oneonta a ...	N.Y.-Penn.	2B-SS-3B-OF	58	213	29	62	5	2	1	25	8	.291
1990 Asheville	So. Atl.	SS	121	438	60	137	29	6	4	62	12	.313
1991 Jackson b	Texas	SS	23	70	5	13	6	0	1	5	0	.186
1991 Osceola	Fla. St.	SS	74	272	27	81	11	2	0	36	1	.298
1992 Jackson	Texas	SS	115	379	51	100	26	5	5	53	7	.264
1992 Tucson	P.C.	SS	10	37	4	9	0	0	2	8	0	.243
1993 Tucson c	P.C.	SS	122	471	86	143	29	16	16	89	2	.304
1994 Tucson	P.C.	SS-2B	93	338	54	87	16	6	10	55	3	.257
1994 Houston	N.L.	SS-2B	16	40	3	13	0	1	2	9	1	.325
1995 Houston d	N.L.	SS	92	324	36	85	20	1	5	36	3	.262
1996 Houston e	N.L.	SS-3B	139	468	43	120	26	2	15	58	3	.256
1997 Lakeland	Fla. St.	SS	5	21	1	4	1	0	0	0	0	.190
1997 Jacksnville ...	Southern	SS	3	11	2	4	1	0	1	3	0	.364
1997 Toledo	Int.	SS	30	3	8	1	0	1	5	2		.267
1997 Detroit f-g-h	A.L.	SS-3B-1B	50	111	13	26	7	1	2	10	1	.234
Major League Totals		4 Yrs.	297	943	95	244	53	5	24	113	8	.259

a Traded by New York Yankees to Houston Astros organization for shortstop Dave Silvestri, March 13, 1990.
b On disabled list from May 10 to May 20, 1991.
c On disabled list from April 8 to April 15 and April 17 to April 24, 1993.
d On disabled list from August 26 to September 10, 1995.
e Traded to Detroit Tigers with outfielder Brian Hunter, pitcher Todd Jones and pitcher Doug Brocail for catcher Brad Ausmus, pitcher C.J. Nitkowski, pitcher Jose Lima, pitcher Trever Miller and infielder Daryle Ward, December 10, 1996.
f On disabled list from April 1 to June 10, 1997.
g Claimed on waivers by Kansas City Royals, December 1, 1997.
h Released by Kansas City Royals, December 8, 1997.

MILLIARD, RALPH GREGORY
Born, Willemstad, Curacao, December 30, 1973.
Bats Right. Throws Right. Height, 5 feet, 11 inches. Weight, 170 pounds.

Year	Club	Lea	Pos	G	AB	R	H	2B	3B	HR	RBI	SB	Avg
1993 Marlins	Gulf Coast	2B-3B	53	192	35	45	15	0	0	25	11	.234
1994 Kane County	Midwest	2B	133	515	97	153	34	2	8	67	10	.297
1995 Portland	Eastern	2B	128	464	104	124	22	3	11	40	22	.267

Year	Club	Lea	Pos	G	AB	R	H	2B	3B	HR	RBI	SB	Avg
1996 Charlotte	.Int.	2B	69	250	47	69	15	2	6	26	8	.276
1996 Portland	.Eastern	2B	6	20	2	4	0	1	0	2	1	.200
1996 Florida	.N.L.	2B	24	62	7	10	2	0	0	1	2	.161
1997 Florida	.N.L.	2B	8	30	2	6	0	0	0	2	1	.200
1997 Charlotte	.Int.	2B	33	132	19	35	5	1	4	18	5	.265
1997 Portland a	.Eastern	2B	19	69	13	19	1	2	0	5	3	.275
Major League Totals		2 Yrs.	32	92	9	16	2	0	0	3	3	.174

a   Traded to New York Mets with pitcher Al Leiter for pitchers Jesus Sanchez and A. J. Burnett and outfielder Robert
    Stratton, February 6, 1998.

MOLITOR, PAUL LEO

Born, St. Paul, Minnesota, August 22, 1956.
Bats Right. Throws Right. Height, 6 feet. Weight, 180 pounds.

Year	Club	Lea	Pos	G	AB	R	H	2B	3B	HR	RBI	SB	Avg
1977 Burlington	.Midwest	SS	64	228,	52	79	12	0	8	50	14	.346
1978 Milwaukee	.A.L.	SS-2B-3B	125	521	73	142	26	4	6	45	30	.273
1979 Milwaukee	.A.L.	2B-SS	140	584	88	188	27	16	9	62	33	.322
1980 Milwaukee a	.A.L.	2B-SS-3B	111	450	81	137	29	2	9	37	34	.304
1981 Milwaukee b	.A.L.	OF	64	251	45	67	11	0	2	19	10	.267
1982 Milwaukee	.A.L.	3B-SS	160	*666	*136	201	26	8	19	71	41	.302
1983 Milwaukee	.A.L.	3B	152	608	95	164	28	6	15	47	41	.270
1984 Milwaukee c	.A.L.	3B	13	46	3	10	1	1	0	6	1	.217
1985 Milwaukee d	.A.L.	3B	140	576	93	171	28	3	10	48	21	.297
1986 Milwaukee e	.A.L.	3B-OF	105	437	62	123	24	6	9	55	20	.281
1987 Milwaukee f-g	.A.L.	3B-2B	118	465	*114	164	*41	5	16	75	45	.353
1988 Milwaukee	.A.L.	3B-2B	154	609	115	190	34	6	13	60	41	.312
1989 Milwaukee h	.A.L.	3B-2B	155	615	84	194	35	4	11	56	27	.315
1990 Beloit	.Midwest	DH	1	4	1	2	0	0	1	1	0	.500
1990 Milwaukee i	.A.L.	2B-1B-3B	103	418	64	119	27	6	12	45	18	.285
1991 Milwaukee	.A.L.	1B	158	*665	*133	*216	32	*13	17	75	19	.325
1992 Milwaukee j	.A.L.	DH-1B	158	609	89	195	36	7	12	89	31	.320
1993 Toronto	.A.L.	DH-1B	160	636	121	*211	37	5	22	111	22	.332
1994 Toronto	.A.L.	DH-1B	*115	454	86	155	30	4	14	75	20	.341
1995 Toronto k	.A.L.	DH	130	525	63	142	31	2	15	60	12	.270
1996 Minnesota	.A.L.	DH-1B	161	660	99	*225	41	8	9	113	18	.341
1997 Minnesota l-m-n	.A.L.	DH-1B	135	538	63	164	32	4	10	89	11	.305
Major League Totals		20 Yrs.	2557	10333	1707	3178	576	109	230	1238	495	.308
Division Series												
1981 Milwaukee	.A.L.	OF	5	20	2	5	0	0	1	1	0	.250
Championship Series												
1982 Milwaukee	.A.L.	3B	5	19	4	6	1	0	2	5	1	.316
1993 Toronto	.A.L.	DH	6	23	7	9	2	1	1	5	0	.391
Championship Series Totals			11	42	11	15	3	1	3	10	1	.357
World Series Record												
1982 Milwaukee	.A.L.	3B	7	31	5	11	0	0	0	2	1	.355
1993 Toronto	.A.L.	DH-3B-1B	6	24	10	12	2	2	2	8	1	.500
World Series Totals			13	55	15	23	2	2	2	11	2	.418

a   On disabled list from June 24 to July 18, 1980.
b   On disabled list from May 4 to August 12, 1981.
c   On disabled list from May 3 to end of 1984 season.
d   On disabled list from August 13 to August 29, 1985.
e   On disabled list from May 10 to May 30, June 2 to June 17, and June 19 to July 8, 1986.
f   On disabled list from April 30 to May 26 and June 27 to July 16, 1987.
g   Filed for free agency, November 5, 1987; re-signed with Milwaukee Brewers, January 5, 1988.
h   On disabled list from March 30 to April 14, 1989.
i   On disabled list from April 2 to April 27 and June 17 to July 31, 1990.
j   Filed for free agency, October 30; signed with Toronto Blue Jays, December 7, 1992.
k   Waived by Toronto Blue Jays, November 1, 1995; signed by Minnesota Twins, December 8, 1995.
l   On disabled list from April 14 to May 2, 1997.
m Filed for free agency, October 28, 1997.
n Re-signed with Minnesota Twins, December 7, 1997.

MONDESI, RAUL RAMON

Born, San Cristobal, Dominican Republic, March 12, 1971.
Bats Right. Throws Right. Height, 5 feet 11 inches. Weight, 202 pounds.

Year	Club	Lea	Pos	G	AB	R	H	2B	3B	HR	RBI	SB	Avg
1988-89				Played in Dominican Summer League									
1990 Great Falls	.Pioneer	OF	44	175	35	53	10	4	8	31	30	.303
1991 Bakersfield a	.California	OF	28	106	23	30	7	2	3	13	9	.283

Year	Club	Lea	Pos	G	AB	R	H	2B	3B	HR	RBI	SB	Avg
1991 San Antonio ....Texas			OF	53	213	32	58	11	5	5	26	8	.272
1991 Albuquerque ..........P.C.			OF	2	9	3	3	0	1	0	0	1	.333
1992 Albuquerque ..........P.C.			OF	35	138	23	43	4	7	4	15	2	.312
1992 San Antonio b ....Texas			OF	18	68	8	18	2	2	2	14	3	.265
1993 Albuquerque ..........P.C.			OF	110	425	65	119	22	7	12	65	13	.280
1993 Los Angeles .........N.L.			OF	42	86	13	25	3	1	4	10	4	.291
1994 Los Angeles c ....N.L.			OF	112	434	63	133	27	8	16	56	11	.306
1995 Los Angeles .........N.L.			OF	139	536	91	153	23	6	26	88	27	.285
1996 Los Angeles .........N.L.			OF	157	634	98	188	40	7	24	88	14	.297
1997 Los Angeles .........N.L.			OF	159	616	95	191	42	5	30	87	32	.310
Major League Totals			5 Yrs.	609	2306	360	690	135	27	100	329	88	.299
Division Series													
1995 Los Angeles ..........N.L.			OF	3	9	0	2	0	0	0	1	0	.222
1996 Los Angeles ..........N.L.			OF	3	11	0	2	2	0	0	1	0	.182
Division Series Totals				6	20	0	4	2	0	0	2	0	.200

a On disabled list from May 8 to July 5, 1991.
b On disabled list from May 8 to May 16, June 2 to June 16, June 24 to August 10, and August 24 to end of 1992 season.
c Selected Rookie of the Year in National League for 1994.

MORANDINI, MICHAEL ROBERT
Born, Kittanning, Pennsylvania, April 22, 1966.
Bats Left. Throws Right. Height, 5 feet, 11 inches. Weight, 180 pounds.

Year	Club	Lea	Pos	G	AB	R	H	2B	3B	HR	RBI	SB	Avg
1989 Spartanburg ....So. Atl.			SS	63	231	43	78	19	1	1	30	9	.338
1989 Clearwater ....Fla. St.			SS	17	63	14	19	4	1	0	4	1	.302
1989 Reading ....Eastern			SS	48	188	39	66	12	1	5	29	5	.351
1990 Scranton ....Int.			2B	138	502	77	131	24	*10	1	31	16	.261
1990 Philadelphia .........N.L.			2B	25	79	9	19	4	0	1	3	3	.241
1991 Scranton ....Int.			2B	12	46	7	12	4	0	1	9	2	.261
1991 Philadelphia .........N.L.			2B	98	325	38	81	11	4	1	20	13	.249
1992 Philadelphia .........N.L.			2B-SS	127	422	47	112	8	8	3	30	8	.265
1993 Philadelphia .........N.L.			2B	120	425	57	105	19	9	3	33	13	.247
1994 Philadelphia .........N.L.			2B	87	274	40	80	16	5	2	26	10	.292
1995 Philadelphia .........N.L.			2B	127	494	65	140	34	7	6	49	9	.283
1996 Philadelphia a .......N.L.			2B	140	539	64	135	24	6	3	32	26	.250
1997 Philadelphia b .......N.L.			2B-SS	150	553	83	163	40	2	1	39	16	.295
Major League Totals			8 Yrs.	874	3111	403	835	156	41	20	232	98	.268
Championship Series													
1993 Philadelphia ..........N.L.			2B	4	16	1	4	0	1	0	2	1	.250
World Series Record													
1993 Philadelphia ..........N.L.			2B	3	5	1	1	0	0	0	0	0	.200

a On disabled list from June 15 to June 30, 1996.
b Traded to Chicago Cubs for outfielder Doug Glanville, December 23, 1997.

MORDECAI, MICHAEL HOWARD
Born, Birmingham, Alabama, December 13, 1967.
Bats Both. Throws Right. Height, 5 feet, 11 inches. Weight, 175 pounds.

Year	Club	Lea	Pos	G	AB	R	H	2B	3B	HR	RBI	SB	Avg
1989 Burlington ....Midwest			SS-3B-2B	65	241	39	61	11	1	1	22	12	.253
1989 Greenville ....Southern			3B-2B	4	8	0	3	0	0	0	1	0	.375
1990 Durham ......Carolina			SS	72	271	42	76	11	7	3	36	10	.280
1991 Durham ......Carolina			SS	109	397	52	104	15	2	4	42	30	.262
1992 Greenville ....Southern			SS	65	222	31	58	13	1	4	31	9	.261
1992 Richmond ....Int.			SS-2B-3B-OF	36	118	12	29	3	0	1	6	0	.246
1993 Richmond ....Int.			2B-SS-3B-OF	72	205	29	55	8	1	2	14	10	.268
1994 Richmond ....Int.			SS-1B-2B-3B	99	382	67	107	25	1	14	57	14	.280
1994 Atlanta ...........N.L.			SS	4	4	1	1	0	0	1	3	0	.250
1995 Atlanta ..........N.L.			2B-1B-3B-SS	69	75	10	21	6	0	3	11	0	.280
1996 Richmond ....Int.			SS	3	11	2	2	0	0	1	2	0	.182
1996 Atlanta a .......N.L.			2B-3B-SS-1B	66	108	12	26	5	0	2	8	1	.241
1997 Richmond ....Int.			2B-3B-SS	31	122	23	38	10	0	3	15	0	.311
1997 Atlanta b .......N.L.			3B-2B-SS-1B	61	81	8	14	2	1	0	3	0	.173
Major League Totals			4 Yrs.	200	268	31	62	13	1	6	25	1	.231
Division Series													
1995 Atlanta ..........N.L.			SS	2	3	1	2	1	0	0	2	0	.667

Year	Club	Lea	Pos	G	AB	R	H	2B	3B	HR	RBI	SB	Avg
	Championship Series												
1995	Atlanta ..........N.L.		SS	2	2	0	0	0	0	0	0	0	.000
1996	Atlanta ..........N.L.		3B	4	4	1	1	0	0	0	0	0	.250
Championship Series Totals				6	6	1	1	0	0	0	0	0	.167
	World Series												
1995	Atlanta ..........N.L.		SS-DH	3	3	0	.1	0	0	0	0	0	.333
1996	Atlanta ..........N.L.		PH	1	1	0	0	0	0	0	0	0	.000
World Series Totals				4	4	0	1	0	0	0	0	0	.250

a On disabled list from April 19 to May 11, 1996.
b Released by Atlanta Braves, December 22, 1997.

MORRIS, WILLIAM HAROLD (HAL)

Born, Fort Rucker, Alabama, April 9, 1965.
Bats Left. Throws Left. Height, 6 feet, 4 inches. Weight, 210 pounds.

Year	Club	Lea	Pos	G	AB	R	H	2B	3B	HR	RBI	SB	Avg
1986	Oneonta ........N.Y.-Penn.		1B	36	127	26	48	9	2	3	30	1	.378
1986	Albany ....Eastern		1B	25	79	7	17	5	0	0	4	0	.215
1987	Albany ....Eastern		1B	135	*530	65	*173	31	4	5	73	7	.326
1988	Columbus ....Int.		OF-1B	121	452	41	134	19	4	3	38	8	.296
1988	New York ...........A.L.		OF	15	20	1	2	0	0	0	0	0	.100
1989	Columbus ....Int.		1B-OF	111	417	70	136	24	1	17	66	5	*.326
1989	New York a ........A.L.		OF-1B	15	18	2	5	0	0	0	4	0	.278
1990	Nashville ...........A.A.		OF	16	64	8	22	5	0	1	10	4	.344
1990	Cincinnati ...........N.L.		1B-OF	107	309	50	105	22	3	7	36	9	.340
1991	Cincinnati ...........N.L.		1B-OF	136	478	72	152	33	1	14	59	10	.318
1992	Nashville ...........A.A.		1B	2	6	1	1	1	0	0	0	0	.167
1992	Cincinnati ...........N.L.		1B	115	395	41	107	21	3	6	53	6	.271
1993	Indianapolis .........A.A.		1B	3	13	4	6	0	1	1	5	0	.462
1993	Cincinnati c-d ......N.L.		1B	101	379	48	120	18	0	7	49	2	.317
1994	Cincinnati ...........N.L.		1B	112	436	60	146	30	4	10	78	6	.335
1995	Indianapolis .........A.A.		1B	2	5	2	2	0	0	0	1	0	.400
1995	Cincinnati e-f .......N.L.		1B	101	359	53	100	25	2	11	51	1	.279
1996	Indianapolis g .......A.A.		1B	1	4	1	2	1	0	1	1	0	.500
1996	Cincinnati ...........N.L.		1B	142	528	82	165	32	4	16	80	7	.313
1997	Cincinnati h-i-j ........N.L.		1B	96	333	42	92	20	1	1	33	3	.276
Major League Totals		10 Yrs.		940	3255	451	994	201	18	72	443	44	.305
	Division Series												
1995	Cincinnati ...........N.L.		1B	3	10	5	5	1	0	0	2	1	.500
	Championship Series												
1990	Cincinnati ...........N.L.		1B	5	12	3	5	1	0	0	1	0	.417
1995	Cincinnati ...........N.L.		1B	4	12	0	2	1	0	0	1	1	.167
Championship Series Totals				9	24	3	7	2	0	0	2	1	.292
	World Series Record												
1990	Cincinnati ...........N.L.		1B	4	14	0	1	0	0	0	2	0	.071

a Traded to Cincinnati Reds with pitcher Rodney Imes for pitcher Tim Leary and outfielder Van Snider, December 12, 1989.
b On disabled list from April 16 to May 17 and August 5 to August 21, 1992.
c On disabled list from March 31 to June 7, 1993.
d Suspended one game and fined by National League for March 30 brawl, August 10, 1993.
e On disabled list from June 18 to July 13, 1995.
f Filed for free agency November 12, 1995; re-signed with Cincinnati Reds, December 6, 1995.
g On disabled list from July 2 to July 17, 1996.
h On disabled list from August 2 to September 10 and September 24 to September 29, 1997.
i Filed for free agency, October 29, 1997.
j Signed with Kansas City Royals, December 22, 1997.

MOUTON, JAMES RALEIGH

Born, Denver, Colorado, December 29, 1968.
Bats Right. Throws Right. Height, 5 feet, 9 inches. Weight, 175 pounds.

Year	Club	Lea	Pos	G	AB	R	H	2B	3B	HR	RBI	SB	Avg
1991	Auburn ..........N.Y.-Penn.		2B	76	288	71	76	15	*10	2	40	*60	.264
1992	Osceola ....Fla. St.		2B	133	507	*110	143	*30	6	11	62	*51	.282
1993	Tucson .............P.C.		2B	134	546	*126	*172	42	12	16	92	40	.315
1994	Tucson .............P.C.		OF	4	17	2	7	1	0	1	1	1	.412
1994	Houston ...........N.L.		OF	99	310	43	76	11	0	2	16	24	.245
1995	Tuscon .............P.C.		OF	3	11	1	5	0	0	1	1	0	.455
1995	Houston a .........N.L.		OF	104	298	42	78	18	2	4	27	25	.262

Year	Club	Lea	Pos	G	AB	R	H	2B	3B	HR	RBI	SB	Avg
1996 Tucson	....	P.C.	OF	1	4	1	1	0	0	0	0	0	.250
1996 Houston	....	N.L.	OF	122	300	40	79	15	1	3	34	21	.263
1997 Houston	....	N.L.	OF	86	180	24	38	9	1	3	23	9	.211
Major League Totals			4 Yrs.	411	1088	149	271	53	4	12	100	79	.249

a On disabled list from June 12 to June 30, 1995.

MOUTON, LYLE JOSEPH
Born, Lafayette, Louisiana, May 13, 1969.
Bats Right. Throws Right. Height, 6 feet, 4 inches. Weight, 240 pounds.

Year	Club	Lea	Pos	G	AB	R	H	2B	3B	HR	RBI	SB	Avg
1991 Oneonta	....	N.Y.-Penn.	OF	70	272	53	84	11	2	7	41	15	.309
1992 Prince William	.....	Carolina	OF	50	189	28	50	14	1	6	34	4	.265
1992 Albany	....	Eastern	OF	64	214	25	46	12	2	2	27	1	.215
1993 Albany	....	Eastern	OF	135	491	74	125	22	3	16	76	18	.255
1994 Albany	....	Eastern	OF-3B	74	274	42	84	23	1	12	42	7	.307
1994 Columbus	....	Int.	OF	59	204	26	64	14	5	4	32	5	.314
1995 Nashville	....	A.A.	OF	71	267	40	79	17	0	8	41	10	.296
1995 Chicago a	....	A.L.	OF	58	179	23	54	16	0	5	27	1	.302
1996 Chicago	....	A.L.	OF	87	214	25	63	8	1	7	39	3	.294
Major League Totals			2 Yrs.	145	393	48	117	24	1	12	66	4	.298

a Signed with Chicago White Sox, April 22, 1995.

MUELLER, WILLIAM RICHARD (BILL)
Born, Maryland Heights, Missouri, March 17, 1971.
Bats Both. Throws Right. Height, 5 feet, 11 inches. Weight, 175 pounds.

Year	Club	Lea	Pos	G	AB	R	H	2B	3B	HR	RBI	SB	Avg
1993 Everett	....	Northwest	2B-SS	58	200	31	60	8	2	1	24	13	.300
1994 San Jose	....	California	3B-2B-SS	120	431	79	130	20	9	5	72	4	.302
1995 Shreveport	....	Texas	3B-2B	88	330	56	102	16	2	1	39	6	.309
1995 Phoenix	....	P.C.	3B-2B	41	172	23	51	13	6	2	19	0	.297
1996 Phoenix	....	P.C.	3B-SS-2B	106	440	73	133	14	6	4	36	2	.302
1996 San Francisco	....	N.L.	3B-2B	55	200	31	66	15	1	0	19	0	.330
1997 San Francisco a	......	N.L.	3B	128	390	51	114	26	3	7	44	4	.292
Major League Totals			2 Yrs.	183	590	82	180	41	4	7	63	4	.305
Division Series													
1997 San Francisco	....	N.L.	3B	3	12	1	3	0	0	1	1	0	.250

a On disabled list from June 30 to July 17, 1997.

MYERS, GREGORY RICHARD
Born, Riverside, California, April 14, 1966.
Bats Left. Throws Right. Height, 6 feet, 2 inches. Weight, 215 pounds.

Year	Club	Lea	Pos	G	AB	R	H	2B	3B	HR	RBI	SB	Avg
1984 Medicine Hat	....	Pioneer	C	38	133	20	42	9	0	2	20	0	.316
1985 Florence	....	So. Atl.	C	134	489	52	109	19	2	5	62	0	.223
1986 Ventura	....	California	C	124	451	65	133	23	4	20	79	9	.295
1987 Syracuse	....	Int.	C	107	342	35	84	19	1	10	47	3	.246
1987 Toronto	....	A.L.	C	7	9	1	1	0	0	0	0	0	.111
1988 Syracuse a	....	Int.	C	34	120	18	34	7	1	7	21	1	.283
1989 Knoxville b	....	Southern	C	29	90	11	30	10	0	5	19	1	.333
1989 Syracuse	....	Int.	C	24	89	8	24	6	0	1	11	0	.270
1989 Toronto	....	A.L.	C	17	44	0	5	2	0	0	1	0	.114
1990 Syracuse	....	Int.	C	3	11	0	2	1	0	0	2	0	.182
1990 Toronto c	....	A.L.	C	87	250	33	59	7	1	5	22	0	.236
1991 Toronto	....	A.L.	C	107	309	25	81	22	0	8	36	0	.262
1992 Toronto-California d-e	...	A.L.	C	30	78	4	18	7	0	1	13	0	.231
1993 California	....	A.L.	C	108	290	27	74	10	0	7	40	3	.255
1994 Lake Elsinore	.....	California	C	10	32	4	8	2	0	0	5	0	.250
1995 California f	....	A.L.	C	45	126	10	31	6	0	2	8	0	.246
1995 California g-h	....	A.L.	C	85	273	35	71	12	2	9	38	0	.260
1996 Minnesota i	....	A.L.	C	97	329	37	94	22	3	6	47	0	.286
1997 Minnesota	....	A.L.	C	62	165	24	44	11	1	5	28	0	.267
1997 Atlanta j-k-l-m	....	N.L.	C	9	9	0	1	0	0	0	1	0	.111
Major League Totals			10 Yrs.	654	1882	196	479	99	7	43	234	3	.255

a On disabled list from June 17 to September 2, 1988.
b On disabled list from March 26 to June 5, 1989.
c On disabled list from May 5 to May 25, 1990.
d Traded to California Angels with outfielder Rob Ducey for pitcher Mark Eichhorn, July 30, 1992.
e On disabled list from August 27 to end of 1992 season.
f On disabled list from April 24 to June 20, 1994.
g On disabled list from April 21 to May 6 and June 1 to June 21 and September 30 to October 3, 1995.
h Filed for free agency, November 12, 1995; signed with Minnesota Twins, December 8, 1995.
i On disabled list from July 14 to August 2, 1996.
j On disabled list from August 9 to August 24, 1997.
k Traded to Atlanta Braves for player to be named later, September 5, 1997.
l Filed for free agency, October 28, 1997.
m Signed with San Diego Padres, November 25, 1997.

MYERS, RODERICK DEMOND

Born, Conroe, Texas, January 14, 1973.
Bats Left. Throws Left. Height, 6 feet, 1 inch. Weight, 190 pounds.

Year	Club	Lea	Pos	G	AB	R	H	2B	3B	HR	RBI	SB	Avg
1991 Royals	Gulf Coast	OF	44	133	14	37	2	3	1	18	12	.278
1991 Baseball Cy	Fla. St.	OF	4	11	1	2	0	0	0	0	1	.182
1992 Appleton	Midwest	OF	71	218	31	48	10	2	4	30	25	.220
1993 Rockford	Midwest	OF	129	474	69	123	24	5	9	68	49	.259
1994 Wilmington	Carolina	OF	126	457	76	120	20	4	12	65	31	.263
1995 Wichita	Texas	OF-1B	131	499	71	153	22	6	7	62	29	.307
1996 Omaha	A.A.	OF	112	411	68	120	27	1	16	54	37	.292
1996 Kansas City	A.L.	OF	22	63	9	18	7	0	1	11	3	.286
1997 Wichita	Texas	OF	4	16	3	5	2	0	0	3	0	.313
1997 Omaha	A.A.	OF	38	143	21	36	10	0	2	10	6	.252
1997 Kansas City a	A.L.	OF	31	101	14	26	7	0	2	9	4	.257
Major League Totals		2 Yrs.	53	164	23	44	14	0	3	20	7	.268

a On disabled list from April 1 to July 10, 1997.

NAEHRING, TIMOTHY JAMES

Born, Cincinnati, Ohio, February 1, 1967.
Bats Right. Throws Right. Height, 6 feet, 2 inches. Weight, 205 pounds.

Year	Club	Lea	Pos	G	AB	R	H	2B	3B	HR	RBI	SB	Avg
1988 Elmira	N.Y.-Penn.	SS	19	59	6	18	3	0	1	13	0	.305
1988 Winter Haven	Fla. St.	SS	42	141	17	32	7	0	0	10	1	.227
1989 Lynchburg	Carolina	SS	56	209	24	63	7	1	4	37	2	.301
1989 Pawtucket	Int.	SS-3B	79	273	32	75	16	1	3	31	2	.275
1990 Pawtucket	Int.	SS-3B	82	290	45	78	16	1	15	47	0	.269
1990 Boston a	A.L.	SS-3B-2B	24	85	10	23	6	0	2	12	0	.271
1991 Boston b	A.L.	SS-3B-2B	20	55	1	6	1	0	0	3	0	.109
1992 Pawtucket	Int.	2B	11	34	7	10	0	0	2	5	1	.294
1992 Boston c	A.L.	SS-2B-3B-OF	72	186	12	43	8	0	3	14	0	.231
1993 Pawtucket	Int.	3B-SS-2B	55	202	38	62	9	1	7	36	0	.307
1993 Boston d-e	A.L.	2B-3B-SS	39	127	14	42	10	0	1	17	1	.331
1994 Pawtucket	Int.	2B-3B	4	15	2	2	2	0	0	3	0	.133
1994 Boston f-g	A.L.	2B-3B-1B-SS	80	297	41	82	18	1	7	42	1	.276
1995 Boston h	A.L.	3B	126	433	61	133	27	2	10	57	0	.307
1996 Trenton i	Eastern	3B	3	9	2	2	1	0	1	2	0	.222
1996 Boston	A.L.	3B-2B	116	430	77	124	16	0	17	65	2	.288
1997 Boston j	A.L.	3B	70	259	38	74	18	1	9	40	1	.286
Major League Totals		8 Yrs.	547	1872	254	527	104	4	49	250	5	.282
Division Series													
1995 Boston	A.L.	3B	3	13	2	4	0	0	1	1	0	.308

a On disabled list from August 16 to end of 1990 season.
b On disabled list from May 18 to end of 1991 season.
c On disabled list from July 25 to September 3, 1992.
d On disabled list from April 1 to July 3, 1993.
e Not offered 1994 contract, December 20, 1993; re-signed with Boston Red Sox organization, January 18, 1994.
f On disabled list from June 2 to July 6, 1994.
g Declared restricted free agent under Major League Baseball implemented labor proposal, December 23, 1994.
h Re-signed with Boston Red Sox, April 5, 1995.
i On disabled list from April 15 to May 3, 1996.
j On disabled list from June 24 to September 29, 1997.

NATAL, ROBERT MARCILINO
Born, Long Beach, California, November 13, 1965.
Bats Right. Throws Right. Height, 5 feet, 11 inches. Weight, 190 pounds.

Year	Club	Lea	Pos	G	AB	R	H	2B	3B	HR	RBI	SB	Avg
1987	Jamestown	N.Y.-Penn.	C	57	180	26	58	8	4	7	32	6	.322
1988	West Palm Beach	Fla. St.	C	113	387	57	93	17	0	6	51	3	.240
1989	Jacksonville	Southern	C	46	141	12	29	8	1	0	11	2	.206
1989	West Palm Beach	Fla. St.	C	15	48	5	6	0	0	1	2	1	.125
1990	Jacksonville	Southern	C	62	171	23	42	7	1	7	25	0	.246
1991	Harrisburg	Eastern	C	100	336	47	86	16	3	13	53	1	.256
1991	Indianapolis	A.A.	C	16	41	2	13	4	0	0	9	1	.317
1992	Indianapolis	A.A.	C	92	344	50	104	19	3	12	50	3	.302
1992	Montreal a	N.L.	C	5	6	0	0	0	0	0	0	0	.000
1993	Edmonton	P.C.	C	17	66	16	21	6	1	3	16	0	.318
1993	Florida b	N.L.	C	41	117	3	25	4	1	1	6	1	.214
1994	Edmonton	P.C.	C	37	115	12	32	5	2	3	19	1	.278
1994	Florida	N.L.	C	10	29	2	8	2	0	0	2	1	.276
1995	Charlotte	Int.	C-3B-1B	53	191	23	60	14	0	3	24	0	.314
1995	Florida	N.L.	C	16	43	2	10	2	1	2	6	0	.233
1996	Florida	N.L.	C	44	90	4	12	1	1	0	2	0	.133
1997	Charlotte	Int.	C-OF	78	251	34	67	17	2	11	49	2	.267
1997	Florida	N.L.	C	4	4	2	2	1	0	1	3	0	.500
Major League Totals			6 Yrs.	120	289	13	57	10	3	4	19	2	.197

a Selected by Florida Marlins in expansion draft, November 17, 1992.
b On disabled list from June 2 to June 23, 1993.

NEVIN, PHILLIP
Born, Fullerton, California, January 19, 1971.
Bats Right. Throws Right. Height, 6 feet, 2 inches. Weight, 185 pounds.

Year	Club	Lea	Pos	G	AB	R	H	2B	3B	HR	RBI	SB	Avg
1993	Tucson	P.C.	3B-OF	123	448	67	128	21	3	10	93	8	.286
1994	Tucson	P.C.	3B-OF	118	445	67	117	20	1	12	79	3	.263
1995	Tucson	P.C.	3B	62	223	31	65	16	0	7	41	2	.291
1995	Toledo	Int.	OF	7	23	3	7	2	0	1	3	0	.304
1995	Houston	N.L.	3B	18	60	4	7	1	0	0	1	1	.117
1995	Detroit a	A.L.	OF	29	96	9	21	3	1	2	12	0	.219
1996	Jacksonville	Southern	C-3B-OF	98	344	77	101	18	1	24	69	6	.294
1996	Detroit	A.L.	3B-OF-C	38	120	15	35	5	0	8	19	1	.292
1997	Lakeland	Fla. St.	1B-3B	3	9	3	5	1	0	1	4	0	.556
1997	Toledo	Int.	1B-3B	5	19	1	3	0	0	1	3	0	.158
1997	Detroit b-c	A.L.	OF-3B-1B	93	251	32	59	16	1	9	35	0	.235
Major League Totals			3 Yrs.	178	527	60	122	25	2	19	67	2	.231

a Mike Henneman was traded to Houston Astros for player to be named later, August 10, 1995. Detroit Tigers received infielder Phil Nevin to complete trade, August 15, 1995.
b On disabled list from April 1 to April 16, 1997.
c Traded to Anaheim Angels with player to be named later for pitcher Nick Skuse, November 21, 1997.

NEWFIELD, MARC ALEXANDER
Born, Sacramento, California, October 19, 1972.
Bats Right. Throws Right. Height, 6 feet, 4 inches. Weight, 205 pounds.

Year	Club	Lea	Pos	G	AB	R	H	2B	3B	HR	RBI	SB	Avg
1990	Tempe Mariners	Arizona	1B-OF	51	192	34	60	13	2	6	38	4	.313
1991	San Bernardino	California	OF-1B	125	440	64	132	22	3	11	68	12	.300
1991	Jacksonville	Southern	OF-1B	6	26	4	6	3	0	0	2	0	.231
1992	Jacksonville a	Southern	DH-OF	45	162	15	40	12	0	4	19	1	.247
1993	Jacksonville	Southern	1B-OF	91	336	48	103	18	0	19	51	1	.307
1993	Seattle	A.L.	DH-OF	22	66	5	15	3	0	1	7	0	.227
1994	Calgary	P.C.	OF	107	430	89	150	*44	2	19	83	0	.349
1994	Seattle	A.L.	OF	12	38	3	7	1	0	1	4	0	.184
1995	Tacoma	P.C.	OF	53	198	30	55	11	0	5	30	1	.278
1995	Las Vegas	P.C.	OF-1B	20	70	10	24	5	1	3	12	2	.343
1995	Seattle	A.L.	OF	24	85	7	16	3	0	3	14	0	.188
1995	San Diego b	N.L.	OF	21	55	6	17	5	1	1	7	0	.309
1996	San Diego c-d	N.L.	OF-1B	84	191	27	48	11	0	5	26	1	.251
1996	Milwaukee	A.L.	OF	49	179	21	55	15	0	7	31	0	.307
1997	Tucson	P.C.	DH	8	31	4	10	1	0	1	3	0	.323
1997	Milwaukee e	A.L.	OF	50	157	14	36	8	0	1	18	0	.229
Major League Totals			5 Yrs.	262	771	83	194	46	1	19	107	1	.252

a On disabled list from June 3 to end of 1992 season.
b Traded to San Diego Padres with pitcher Ron Villone for pitcher Andy Benes and player to be named later, July 31, 1995. Seattle Mariners received pitcher Greg Keagle to complete trade, September 16, 1995.
c Traded to Milwaukee Brewers with pitcher Bryce Florie and pitcher Ron Villone for outfielder Greg Vaughan and player to be named later, July 31, 1996.
d San Diego Padres received outfielder Gerald Parent to complete trade, September 16, 1996.
e On disabled list from May 29 to July 5 and July 23 to September 29, 1997.

NEWSON, WARREN DALE

Born, Newnan, Georgia, July 3, 1964.
Bats Left. Throws Left. Height, 5 feet, 7 inches. Weight, 202 pounds.

Year Club	Lea	Pos	G	AB	R	H	2B	3B	HR	RBI	SB	Avg
1986 Spokane . . . . Northwest		OF	56	159	29	37	8	1	2	31	3	.233
1987 Charleston, SC . . . . .So. Atl.		OF	58	191	50	66	12	2	7	32	13	.346
1987 Reno . . . . .California		OF	51	165	44	51	7	2	6	28	2	.309
1988 Riverside . . . . .California		OF	130	438	98	130	23	*7	*22	91	36	.297
1989 Wichita . . . . .Texas		OF	128	427	94	130	20	6	18	70	20	.304
1990 Las Vegas a . . . . .P.C.		OF	123	404	80	123	20	3	13	58	13	.304
1991 Vancouver . . . . .P.C.		OF	33	111	19	41	12	1	2	19	5	.369
1991 Chicago . . . . .A.L.		OF	71	132	20	39	5	0	4	25	2	.295
1992 Vancouver . . . . .P.C.		OF	19	59	7	15	0	0	0	9	3	.254
1992 Chicago . . . . .A.L.		OF	63	136	19	30	3	0	1	11	3	.221
1993 Nashville . . . . .A.A.		OF	61	176	40	60	8	2	4	21	5	.341
1993 Chicago . . . . .A.L.		DH-OF	26	40	9	12	0	0	2	6	0	.300
1994 Chicago . . . . .A.L.		OF	63	102	16	26	5	0	2	7	1	.255
1995 Chicago-Seattle b-c-d-e .A.L.		OF	84	157	34	41	2	2	5	15	2	.261
1996 Texas . . . . .A.L.		OF	91	235	34	60	14	1	10	31	3	.255
1997 Tulsa . . . . .Texas		DH	2	7	1	1	0	0	1	2	0	.143
1997 Texas f-g . . . . .A.L.		OF	81	169	23	36	10	1	10	23	3	.213
Major League Totals	7 Yrs.		479	971	155	244	39	4	34	118	14	.251
Division Series												
1995 Seattle . . . . .A.L.		PH	1	1	0	0	0	0	0	0	0	.000
1996 Texas . . . . .A.L.		PH	3	1	0	0	0	0	0	0	0	.000
Division Series Totals			4	2	0	0	0	0	0	0	0	.000
Championship Series												
1993 Chicago . . . . .A.L.		DH	2	5	1	1	0	0	1	1	0	.200

a Traded by San Diego Padres to Chicago White Sox organization with infielders Joey Cora and Kevin Garner for pitchers Adam Peterson and Steve Rosenberg, March 31, 1991.
b Traded to Seattle Mariners for player to be named later, July 18, 1995.
c Chicago White Sox received pitcher Jeff Darwin to Majors October 16, to complete trade, October 9, 1995.
d Waived by Seattle Mariners, November 16, 1995.
e Signed with Texas Rangers, December 6, 1995.
f On disabled list from April 5 to April 20 and August 25 to September 29, 1997.
g Filed for free agency, October 2, 1997.

NIEVES, MELVIN RAMOS

Born, San Juan, Puerto Rico, December 28, 1971.
Bats Both. Throws Right. Height, 6 feet, 2 inches. Weight, 210 pounds.

Year Club	Lea	Pos	G	AB	R	H	2B	3B	HR	RBI	SB	Avg
1988 Bradenton Braves . . . .Gulf C.		OF	56	176	16	30	6	0	1	12	5	.170
1989 Pulaski . . . . .Appal.		OF	64	231	43	64	16	3	9	46	6	.277
1990 Sumter . . . . .So. Atl.		OF	126	459	60	130	24	7	9	59	10	.283
1991 Durham a . . . . .Carolina		OF	64	201	31	53	11	0	9	25	3	.264
1992 Durham . . . . .Carolina		OF	31	106	18	32	9	1	8	32	4	.302
1992 Greenville . . . . . . .Southern		OF	100	350	61	99	23	5	18	76	6	.283
1992 Atlanta . . . . .N.L.		OF	12	19	0	4	1	0	0	1	0	.211
1993 Richmond b . . . . .Int.		OF	78	273	38	76	10	3	10	36	4	.278
1993 Las Vegas . . . . .P.C.		OF	43	159	31	49	10	1	7	24	2	.308
1993 San Diego . . . . .N.L.		OF	19	47	4	9	0	0	2	3	0	.191
1994 Las Vegas . . . . .P.C.		OF-1B	111	406	81	125	17	6	25	90	1	.308
1994 San Diego . . . . .N.L.		OF	10	19	2	5	1	0	1	4	0	.263
1995 San Diego . . . . .N.L.		OF-1B	98	234	32	48	6	1	14	38	2	.205
1996 Detroit c-d . . . . .A.L.		OF	120	431	71	106	23	4	24	60	1	.246
1997 Detroit e-f . . . . .A.L.		OF	116	359	46	82	18	1	20	64	1	.228
Major League Totals	6 Yrs.		375	1109	155	254	49	6	61	170	4	.229

a On disabled list from April 11 to June 13, 1991.
b Traded by Atlanta Braves to San Diego Padres organization with outfielder Vince Moore and pitcher Donnie Elliott for first baseman Fred McGriff, July 18, 1993.

c Traded to Detroit Tigers with catcher Raul Casanove and pitcher Richie Lewis for pitcher Sean Bergman, pitcher Cade Gaspar and outfielder Todd Steverson, March 22, 1996.
d On disabled list from June 5 to June 20 and August 2 to August 19, 1996.
e On disabled list from August 4 to August 19, 1997.
f Traded to Cincinnati Reds for pitcher Donne Wall and catcher Paul Bako, November 11, 1997.

NILSSON, DAVID WAYNE

Born, Brisbane, Queensland, Australia, December 14, 1969.
Bats Both. Throws Right. Height, 6 feet, 3 inches. Weight, 215 pounds.

Year	Club	Lea	Pos	G	AB	R	H	2B	3B	HR	RBI	SB	Avg
1987	Helena a	Pioneer	C	20	59	6	20	5	1	0	11	0	.339
1988	Beloit	Midwest	C	95	332	28	74	15	2	4	41	1	.223
1989	Stockton	California	C-3B	125	472	59	115	16	6	5	56	2	.244
1990	Stockton b	California	C	107	359	70	104	22	3	7	47	6	.290
1991	El Paso	Texas	C	65	249	52	104	24	3	5	57	4	.418
1991	Denver	A.A.	C-1B	28	95	10	22	8	0	1	14	1	.232
1992	Denver	A.A.	C-1B-3B	66	240	38	76	16	7	3	39	10	.317
1992	Milwaukee c	A.L.	C-1B	51	164	15	38	8	0	4	25	2	.232
1993	El Paso	Texas	C	5	17	5	8	1	0	1	7	1	.471
1993	New Orleans	A.A.	C	17	61	9	21	6	0	1	9	0	.344
1993	Milwaukee d	A.L.	C-1B	100	296	35	76	10	2	7	40	3	.257
1994	Milwaukee	A.L.	C-1B	109	397	51	109	28	3	12	69	1	.275
1995	Beloit	Midwest	DH	3	11	2	6	3	0	1	7	0	.545
1995	El Paso	Texas	OF	5	15	1	7	1	0	1	4	1	.467
1995	New Orleans	A.A.	DH-OF	3	9	1	4	0	0	1	4	0	.444
1995	Milwaukee e	A.L.	OF-1B-C	81	263	41	73	12	1	12	53	2	.278
1996	New Orleans f	A.A.	DH-1B	7	26	3	7	1	0	1	2	0	.269
1996	Milwaukee	A.L.	OF-1B-C	123	453	81	150	33	2	17	84	2	.331
1997	Milwaukee	A.L.	1B-OF	156	554	71	154	33	0	20	81	2	.278
Major League Totals			6 Yrs.	620	2127	294	600	124	8	72	352	12	.282

a Batted lefthanded only from 1987 through end of 1990 season.
b On disabled list from April 30 to May 25, 1990.
c On disabled list from July 6 to July 26, 1992.
d On disabled list from March 29 to April 14 and May 18 to June 21, 1993.
e On disabled list from April 25 to June 24, 1995.
f On disabled list from April 4 to May 8, 1996.

NIXON, OTIS JUNIOR

Born, Evergreen, North Carolina, January 9, 1959.
Bats Both. Throws Right. Height, 6 feet, 2 inches. Weight, 180 pounds.

Year	Club	Lea	Pos	G	AB	R	H	2B	3B	HR	RBI	SB	Avg
1979	Paintsville	Appal.	OF	63	203	58	58	10	3	1	25	5	.286
1980	Greensboro	So. Atl.	OF	136	493	*124	137	12	5	3	48	*67	.278
1981	Nashville	Southern	OF	127	407	89	102	9	2	0	20	71	.251
1982	Nashville	Southern	OF	72	283	47	80	3	2	0	20	61	.283
1982	Columbus	Int.	OF	59	207	43	58	4	0	0	14	46	.280
1983	Columbus	Int.	OF	138	*557	*129	*162	11	6	0	41	*94	.291
1983	New York a	A.L.	OF	13	14	2	2	0	0	0	0	2	.143
1984	Cleveland	A.L.	OF	49	91	16	14	0	0	0	1	12	.154
1984	Maine	Int.	OF	72	253	42	70	5	1	0	22	39	.277
1985	Cleveland	A.L.	OF	104	162	34	38	4	0	3	9	20	.235
1986	Cleveland	A.L.	OF	105	95	33	25	4	1	0	8	23	.263
1987	Buffalo	A.A.	OF	59	249	51	71	13	4	2	23	36	.285
1987	Cleveland b	A.L.	OF	19	17	2	1	0	0	0	1	2	.059
1988	Indianapolis	A.A.	OF	67	235	52	67	6	3	0	19	40	.285
1988	Montreal	N.L.	OF	90	271	47	66	8	2	0	15	46	.244
1989	Montreal	N.L.	OF	126	258	41	56	7	2	0	21	37	.217
1990	Montreal c	N.L.	OF-SS	119	231	46	58	6	2	1	20	50	.251
1991	Atlanta d-e-f	N.L.	OF	124	401	81	119	10	1	0	26	72	.297
1992	Atlanta	N.L.	OF	120	456	79	134	14	2	2	22	41	.294
1993	Atlanta g	N.L.	OF	134	461	77	124	12	3	1	24	47	.269
1994	Boston h	A.L.	OF	103	398	60	109	15	1	0	25	42	.274
1995	Texas i	A.L.	OF	139	589	87	174	21	2	0	45	50	.295
1996	Toronto j	A.L.	OF	125	496	87	142	15	1	1	29	54	.286
1997	Toronto k	A.L.	OF	103	401	54	105	12	1	1	26	47	.262
1997	Los Angeles l-m	N.L.	OF	42	175	30	48	6	2	1	18	12	.274
Major League Totals			15 Yrs.	1515	4516	776	1215	134	20	10	290	557	.269

Year	Club	Lea	Pos	G	AB	R	H	2B	3B	HR	RBI	SB	Avg
Championship Series													
1992 Atlanta	N.L.		OF	7	28	5	8	2	0	0	2	3	.286
1993 Atlanta	N.L.		OF	6	23	3	8	2	0	0	4	0	.348
Championship Series Totals				13	51	8	16	4	0	0	6	3	.314
World Series Record													
1992 Atlanta	N.L.		OF	6	27	3	8	1	0	0	1	5	.296

a Traded to Cleveland Indians with pitchers George Frazier and Gary Elston for third baseman Toby Harrah and pitcher Rick Browne, February 5, 1984.
b Became free agent, October 15, 1987; signed with Montreal Expos organization, March 5, 1988.
c Traded to Atlanta Braves with infielder Boi Rodriguez for catcher Jimmy Kremers and player to be named, April 1; Montreal Expos acquired pitcher Keith Morrison to complete trade, June 2, 1991.
d Suspended four games by National League for June 4 fight, August 13 to August 16, 1991.
e Suspended 60 playing days by Commissioner's Office for violating substance abuse after-care program, September 16, 1991 to April 24, 1992.
f Filed for free agency, November 11, re-signed with Atlanta Braves, December 12, 1991.
g Filed for free agency, October 25; signed with Boston Red Sox, December 7, 1993.
h Traded to Texas Rangers with third baseman Luis Ortiz for outfielder Jose Canseco, December 9, 1994.
i Filed for free agency, November 12, 1995; signed with Toronto Blue Jays, December 7, 1995.
j On disabled list from June 11 to June 26, 1996.
k Traded to Los Angeles Dodgers for catcher Bobby Cripps, August 12, 1997.
l Filed for free agency, October 27, 1997.
m Signed with Minnesota Twins, December 11, 1997.

NUNEZ, ABRAHAM ORLANDO
Born, Santo Domingo, Dominican Republic, March 16, 1976.
Bats Both. Throws Right. Height, 5 feet, 11 inches. Weight 160 pounds.

Year	Club	Lea	Pos	G	AB	R	H	2B	3B	HR	RBI	SB	Avg
1994 Toronto #2	Dominican		2B	59	188	31	47	5	0	0	15	22	.250
1995 Toronto	Dominican			54	186	49	56	10	3	4	25	24	.301
1996 St. Cathrnes	N.Y.-Penn.		SS-2B	75	297	43	83	6	4	3	26	37	.279
1997 Lynchburg	Carolina		SS	78	304	45	79	9	4	3	32	29	.260
1997 Carolina	Southern		SS	47	198	31	65	6	1	1	14	10	.328
1997 Pittsburgh	N.L.		SS-2B	19	40	3	9	2	2	0	6	1	.225

NUNNALLY, JONATHAN KEITH
Born, Pelham, North Carolina, November 9, 1971.
Bats Left. Throws Right. Height, 5 feet, 10 inches. Weight, 195 pounds.

Year	Club	Lea	Pos	G	AB	R	H	2B	3B	HR	RBI	SB	Avg
1992 Watertown	N.Y.-Penn.		OF	69	246	39	59	10	4	5	43	12	.240
1993 Columbus	So. Atl.		2B-OF	125	438	81	110	15	2	15	56	17	.251
1994 Kinston	Carolina		OF	132	483	70	129	29	2	22	74	23	.267
1995 Kansas City a	A.L.		OF	119	303	51	74	15	6	14	42	6	.244
1996 Omaha	A.A.		OF	103	345	76	97	21	4	25	77	10	.281
1996 Kansas City	A.L.		OF	35	90	16	19	5	1	5	17	0	.211
1997 Omaha	A.A.		OF	68	230	35	64	11	1	15	33	8	.278
1997 Kansas City b	A.L.		OF	13	29	8	7	0	1	1	4	0	.241
1997 Cincinnati	N.L.		OF	65	201	38	64	12	3	13	35	7	.318
Major League Totals			3 Yrs.	232	623	113	164	32	11	33	98	13	.263

a Selected by Kansas City Royals from Cleveland Indians organization in Rule V draft, December 5, 1994.
b Traded to Cincinnati Reds with outfielder Chris Stynes for pitcher Hector Carrasco and pitcher Scott Service, July 15, 1997.

OBANDO, SHERMAN OMAR
Born, Changuinola, Panama, January 23, 1970.
Bats Right. Throws Right. Height, 6 feet, 4 inches. Weight, 215 pounds.

Year	Club	Lea	Pos	G	AB	R	H	2B	3B	HR	RBI	SB	Avg
1988 Sarasota Yankees	Gulf Coast		OF	49	172	26	44	10	2	4	27	8	.256
1989 Oneonta	N.Y.-Penn.		OF	70	276	50	86	23	3	6	45	8	.312
1990 Prince William	Carolina		OF	121	439	67	117	24	6	10	67	5	.267
1991 Yankees	Gulf Coast		DH	4	17	3	5	2	0	0	1	0	.294
1991 Prince William a	Carolina		DH-OF	42	140	25	37	11	1	7	31	0	.264

Year	Club	Lea	Pos	G	AB	R	H	2B	3B	HR	RBI	SB	Avg
1992	Albany b-c ....Eastern		DH-1B	109	381	71	107	19	3	17	56	3	.281
1993	Bowie ....Eastern		OF-1B	19	58	8	14	2	0	3	12	1	.241
1993	Baltimore d ..........A.L.		DH-OF	31	92	8	25	2	0	3	15	0	.272
1994	Rochester ....Int.		OF	109	403	67	133	36	7	20	69	1	.330
1995	Baltimore ...........A.L.		OF	16	38	0	10	1	0	0	3	1	.263
1995	Rochester ....Int.		DH-OF-1B	85	324	42	96	26	6	9	53	1	.296
1996	Montreal e-f .........N.L.		OF	89	178	30	44	9	0	8	22	2	.247
1997	Ottawa ....Int.		DH-OF	7	21	5	5	0	0	3	8	0	.238
1997	Montreal g-h .........N.L.		OF	41	47	3	6	1	0	2	9	0	.128
Major League Totals			4 Yrs.	177	355	41	85	13	0	13	49	3	.239

a On disabled list from May 3 to July 25, 1991.
b On disabled list from April 9 to May 11, 1992.
c Drafted by Balitmore Orioles from New York Yankees organization, December 7, 1992.
d On disabled list from May 25 to June 24 and June 27 to July 10, 1993.
e Traded to Montreal Expos for outfielder Tony Tarasco, March 13, 1996.
f On disabled list from July 21 to August 9, 1996.
g On disabled list from July 27 to September 29, 1997.
h Filed for free agency, October 8, 1997.

O'BRIEN, CHARLES HUGH
Born, Tulsa, Oklahoma, May 1, 1961.
Bats Right. Throws Right. Height, 6 feet, 2 inches. Weight, 205 pounds.

Year	Club	Lea	Pos	G	AB	R	H	2B	3B	HR	RBI	SB	Avg
1982	Medford ....Northwest		C	17	60	11	17	3	0	3	14	0	.283
1982	Modesto ....Calif.		C	41	140	23	42	6	0	3	32	7	.300
1983	Albany a ....Eastern		C-1B	92	285	50	83	12	1	14	56	3	.291
1984	Modesto b ....Calif.		C	9	32	8	9	2	0	1	5	1	.281
1984	Tacoma ..............P.C.		C-OF	69	195	33	44	11	0	9	22	0	.226
1985	Huntsville ....Southern		C	33	115	20	24	5	0	7	16	0	.209
1985	Oakland ............A.L.		C	16	11	3	3	1	0	0	1	0	.273
1985	Modesto ....Calif.		C	9	27	5	8	4	1	1	2	0	.296
1985	Tacoma c ............P.C.		C	18	57	5	9	4	0	0	7	0	.158
1986	Vancouver ...........P.C.		C	6	17	1	2	0	0	0	1	0	.118
1986	El Paso ....Texas		C-OF-1B	92	336	72	109	20	3	15	75	0	.324
1987	Denver ..............A.A.		C	80	266	37	75	12	1	8	35	5	.282
1987	Milwaukee ..........A.L.		C	10	35	2	7	3	1	0	0	0	.200
1988	Denver ..............A.A.		C	48	153	16	43	5	0	4	25	1	.281
1988	Milwaukee ..........A.L.		C	40	118	12	26	6	0	2	9	0	.220
1989	Milwaukee ..........A.L.		C	62	188	22	44	10	0	6	35	0	.234
1990	Milwaukee d .........A.L.		C	46	145	11	27	7	2	0	11	0	.186
1990	New York ...........N.L.		C	28	68	6	11	3	0	0	9	0	.162
1991	New York ...........N.L.		C	69	168	16	31	6	0	2	14	0	.185
1992	New York ...........N.L.		C	68	156	15	33	12	0	2	13	0	.212
1993	New York e .........N.L.		C	67	188	15	48	11	0	4	23	1	.255
1994	Atlanta .............N.L.		C	51	152	24	37	11	0	8	28	0	.243
1995	Atlanta f-g .........N.L.		C	67	198	18	45	7	0	9	23	0	.227
1996	Toronto .............A.L.		C	109	324	33	77	17	0	13	44	0	.238
1997	Toronto h-i .........A.L.		C	69	225	22	49	15	1	4	27	0	.218
Major League Totals			12 Yrs.	702	1976	199	438	109	4	50	237	1	.222
Division Series													
1995	Atlanta .............N.L.		C	2	5	0	1	0	0	0	0	0	.200
Championship Series													
1995	Atlanta .............N.L.		C	2	5	1	2	0	0	1	3	0	.400
World Series Record													
1995	Atlanta .............N.L.		C	2	3	0	0	0	0	0	0	0	.000

a On disabled list from July 31 to end of 1983 season.
b On disabled list from April 13 to May 15, 1984.
c Traded by Oakland Athletics to Milwaukee Brewers with infielder Steve Kiefer and pitchers Mike Fulmer and Pete Kendrick for pitcher Moose Haas, March 30, 1986.
d Traded to New York Mets with player to be named for two players to be named, August 31; Milwaukee Brewers acquired pitchers Kevin Brown and Julio Machado, September 7, and New York acquired pitcher Kevin Carmody to complete trade, September 11, 1990.
e Filed for free agency, October 25; signed with Atlanta Braves, November 27, 1993.
f Filed for free agency, October 30, 1995.
g Signed with Toronto Blue Jays, December 15, 1995.
h Filed for free agency, October 27, 1997.
i Signed with Chicago White Sox, December 10, 1997.

OCHOA, ALEX

Born, Miami Lakes, Florida, March 29, 1972.
Bats Right. Throws Right. Height, 6 feet. Weight, 185 pounds.

Year	Club	Lea	Pos	G	AB	R	H	2B	3B	HR	RBI	SB	Avg
1991 Orioles	Gulf Coast		OF	53	179	26	55	8	3	1	30	11	.307
1992 Kane County	Midwest		OF	133	499	65	147	22	7	1	59	31	.295
1993 Frederick	Carolina		OF	137	532	84	147	29	5	13	90	34	.276
1994 Bowie	Eastern		OF	134	519	77	156	25	2	14	82	28	.301
1995 Rochester	Int.		OF	91	336	41	92	18	2	8	46	17	.274
1995 Norfolk	Int.		OF	34	123	17	38	6	2	2	15	7	.309
1995 New York a	N.L.		OF	11	37	7	11	1	0	0	1	0	.297
1996 Norfolk	Int.		OF	67	233	45	79	12	4	8	39	5	.339
1996 New York	N.L.		OF	82	282	37	83	19	3	4	33	4	.294
1997 New York b	N.L.		OF	113	238	31	58	14	1	3	22	3	.244
Major League Totals		3 Yrs.	206	557	75	152	34	4	7	55	8	.273

a Traded to New York Mets with outfielder Damon Buford for infielder Bobby Bonilla and player to be named later,
  July 28, 1995. Baltimore Orioles received pitcher Jimmy Williams to complete trade, August 16, 1995.
b Traded to Minnesota Twins for outfielder Rich Becker, December 14, 1997.

OFFERMAN (DONO), JOSE ANTONIO

Born, San Pedro de Macoris, Dominican Republic, November 8, 1968.
Bats Both. Throws Right. Height, 6 feet. Weight, 165 pounds.

Year	Club	Lea	Pos	G	AB	R	H	2B	3B	HR	RBI	SB	Avg
1988 Great Falls	Pioneer		SS	60	251	75	83	11	5	2	28	*57	.331
1989 Bakersfield	California		SS	62	245	53	75	9	4	2	22	37	.306
1989 San Antonio	Texas		SS	68	278	47	80	6	3	2	22	32	.288
1990 Albuquerque	P.C.		SS	117	454	104	148	16	11	0	56	*60	.326
1990 Los Angeles	N.L.		SS	29	58	7	9	0	0	1	7	1	.155
1991 Albuquerque	P.C.		SS	76	289	58	86	8	4	0	29	32	.298
1991 Los Angeles	N.L.		SS	52	113	10	22	2	0	0	3	3	.195
1992 Los Angeles	N.L.		SS	149	534	67	139	20	8	1	30	23	.260
1993 Los Angeles	N.L.		SS	158	590	77	159	21	6	1	62	30	.269
1994 Los Angeles	N.L.		SS	72	243	27	51	8	4	1	25	2	.210
1994 Albuquerque	P.C.		SS	56	224	43	74	7	5	1	31	9	.330
1995 Los Angeles a	N.L.		SS	119	429	69	123	14	6	4	33	2	.287
1996 Kansas City	A.L.	1B-2B-SS-OF	151	561	85	170	33	8	5	47	24	.303
1997 Kansas City b	A.L.		2B	106	424	59	126	23	6	2	39	9	.297
Major League Totals		8 Yrs.	836	2952	401	799	121	38	15	246	94	.271
Divisional Series													
1995 Los Angeles	N.L.		PR	1	0	0	0	0	0	0	0	0	.000

a Traded to Kansas City Royals for pitcher Billy Brewer, December 17, 1995.
b On disabled list from April 6 to April 29 and July 7 to July 22 and August 14 to September 6, 1997.

O'LEARY, TROY FRANKLIN

Born, Compton, California, August 4, 1969.
Bats Left. Throws Left. Height, 6 feet. Weight, 190 pounds.

Year	Club	Lea	Pos	G	AB	R	H	2B	3B	HR	RBI	SB	Avg
1987 Helena	Pioneer		OF	3	5	0	2	0	0	0	1	0	.400
1988 Helena	Pioneer		OF	67	203	40	70	11	1	0	27	10	.345
1989 Beloit	Midwest		OF	42	115	7	21	4	0	0	8	1	.183
1989 Helena	Pioneer		OF	68	263	54	89	16	3	11	56	9	.338
1990 Beloit	Midwest		OF	118	436	73	130	29	1	6	62	12	.298
1990 Stockton	California		OF	2	6	1	3	1	0	0	0	0	.500
1991 Stockton	California		OF	126	418	63	110	20	4	5	46	4	.263
1992 El Paso	Texas		OF	135	506	92	169	27	8	5	79	28	.334
1993 New Orleans	A.A.		OF-1B	111	388	65	106	32	1	7	59	6	.273
1993 Milwaukee	A.L.		OF	19	41	3	12	2	0	0	3	0	.293
1994 New Orleans	A.A.		OF-1B	63	225	44	74	18	5	8	43	10	.329
1994 Milwaukee	A.L.		OF	27	66	9	18	1	1	2	7	1	.273
1995 Boston a	A.L.		OF	112	399	60	123	31	6	10	49	5	.308
1996 Boston	A.L.		OF	149	497	68	129	28	5	15	81	3	.260
1997 Boston	A.L.		OF	146	499	65	154	32	4	15	80	0	.309
Major League Totals		5 Yrs.	453	1502	205	436	95	16	42	.220	9	.290

a Claimed on waivers by Boston Red Sox, April 14, 1995.

OLERUD, JOHN GARRETT

Born, Bellevue, Washington, August 5, 1968.
Bats Left. Throws Left. Height, 6 feet, 5 inches. Weight, 218 pounds.

Year	Club	Lea	Pos	G	AB	R	H	2B	3B	HR	RBI	SB	Avg
1989 Toronto		A.L.	1B	6	8	2	3	0	0	0	0	0	.375
1990 Toronto		A.L.	1B	111	358	43	95	15	1	14	48	0	.265
1991 Toronto		A.L.	1B	139	454	64	116	30	1	17	68	0	.256
1992 Toronto		A.L.	1B	138	458	68	130	28	0	16	66	1	.284
1993 Toronto		A.L.	1B	158	551	109	200	*54	2	24	107	0	*.363
1994 Toronto		A.L.	1B	108	384	47	114	29	2	12	67	1	.297
1995 Toronto		A.L.	1B	135	492	72	143	32	0	8	54	0	.291
1996 Toronto a		A.L.	1B	125	398	59	109	25	0	18	61	1	.274
1997 New York b-c		N.L.	1B	154	524	90	154	34	1	22	102	0	.294
Major League Totals		9 Yrs.	1074	3627	554	1064	247	7	131	573	3	.293
Championship Series													
1991 Toronto		A.L.	1B	5	19	1	3	0	0	0	3	0	.158
1992 Toronto		A.L.	1B	6	23	4	8	2	0	1	4	0	.348
1993 Toronto		A.L.	1B	6	23	5	8	1	0	0	3	0	.348
Championship Series Totals			17	65	10	19	3	0	1	10	0	.292
World Series Record													
1992 Toronto		A.L.	1B	4	13	2	4	0	0	0	0	0	.308
1993 Toronto		A.L.	1B	5	17	5	4	1	0	1	2	0	.235
World Series Totals			9	30	7	8	1	0	1	2	0	.267

a Traded to New York Mets for RHP Robert Person December 21, 1996.
b Filed for free agency, October 27, 1997.
c Re-signed with New York Mets, November 24, 1997.

OLIVER, JOSEPH MELTON

Born, Memphis, Tennessee, July 24, 1965.
Bats Right. Throws Right. Height, 6 feet, 3 inches. Weight, 220 pounds.

Year	Club	Lea	Pos	G	AB	R	H	2B	3B	HR	RBI	SB	Avg
1983 Billings		Pioneer	C	56	186	21	40	4	0	4	28	1	.215
1984 Cedar Rapids		Midwest	C	102	335	34	73	11	0	3	29	2	.218
1985 Tampa		Fla. St.	C	112	386	38	104	23	2	7	62	1	.269
1986 Vermont a		Eastern	C	84	282	32	78	18	1	6	41	2	.277
1987 Vermont b		Eastern	C	66	236	31	72	13	2	10	60	0	.305
1988 Chattanooga		Southern	C	28	105	9	26	6	0	3	12	0	.248
1988 Nashville		A.A.	C	73	220	19	45	7	2	4	24	0	.205
1989 Nashville		A.A.	C	71	233	22	68	13	0	6	31	0	.292
1989 Cincinnati		N.L.	C	49	151	13	41	8	0	3	23	0	.272
1990 Cincinnati		N.L.	C	121	364	34	84	23	0	8	52	1	.231
1991 Cincinnati		N.L.	C	94	269	21	58	11	0	11	41	0	.216
1992 Cincinnati		N.L.	C-1B	143	485	42	131	25	1	10	57	2	.270
1993 Cincinnati		N.L.	C-1B-OF	139	482	40	115	28	0	14	75	0	.239
1994 Cincinnati c-d		N.L.	C	6	19	1	4	0	0	1	5	0	.211
1995 New Orleans		A.A.	C	4	13	0	1	1	0	0	0	0	.077
1995 Milwaukee e-f-g		A.L.	C-1B	97	337	43	92	20	0	12	51	2	.273
1996 Cincinnati h-i		N.L.	C-1B-OF	106	289	31	70	12	1	11	46	2	.242
1997 Indianapols		A.A.	C	2	9	1	3	0	0	1	1	0	.333
1997 Cincinnati j-k		N.L.	C-1B	111	349	28	90	13	0	14	43	1	.258
Major League Totals		9 Yrs.	866	2745	253	685	140	2	84	393	8	.250
Championship Series													
1990 New York		N.L.	C	5	14	1	2	0	0	0	0	0	.143
World Series Record													
1990 Cincinnati		N.L.	C	4	18	2	6	3	0	0	2	0	.333

a On disabled list from April 23 to May 6, 1986.
b On disabled list from July 6 to end of 1987 season.
c On disabled list from April 12 to end of 1994 season.
d Released, November 3, 1994.
e Signed with Milwaukee Brewers organization, March 22, 1995.
f On disabled list from July 14 to August 15, 1995.
g Filed for free agency, November 12, 1995.
h Filed for free agency, November 18, 1996.
i Signed with Cincinnati Reds organization, February 7, 1997.
j Filed for free agency, October 30, 1997.
k Signed with Detroit Tigers organization December 22, 1997

O'NEILL, PAUL ANDREW

Born, Columbus, Ohio, February 25, 1963.
Bats Left. Throws Left. Height, 6 feet, 4 inches. Weight, 215 pounds.

Year	Club	Lea	Pos	G	AB	R	H	2B	3B	HR	RBI	SB	Avg
1981 Billings	Pioneer	OF	66	241	37	76	7	2	3	29	6	.315
1982 Cedar Rapids	Midwest	OF	116	386	50	105	19	2	8	71	12	.272
1983 Tampa	Fla. St.	OF-1B	121	413	62	115	23	7	8	51	20	.278
1983 Waterbury	Eastern	OF	14	43	6	12	0	0	0	6	2	.279
1984 Vermont	Eastern	OF	134	475	70	126	31	5	16	76	29	.265
1985 Denver	A.A.	OF-1B	*137	*509	63	*155	*32	3	7	74	5	.305
1985 Cincinnati	N.L.	OF	5	12	1	4	1	0	0	1	0	.333
1986 Denver	A.A.	OF	55	193	20	49	9	2	5	27	1	.254
1986 Cincinnati	N.L.	PH	3	2	0	0	0	0	0	0	0	.000
1987 Nashville	A.A.	OF	11	37	12	11	0	0	3	6	1	.297
1987 Cincinnati	N.L.	OF	84	160	24	41	14	1	7	28	2	.256
1988 Cincinnati	N.L.	OF-1B	145	485	58	122	25	3	16	73	8	.252
1989 Nashville	A.A.	OF	4	12	1	4	0	0	0	0	1	.333
1989 Cincinnati a	N.L.	OF	117	428	49	118	24	2	15	74	20	.276
1990 Cincinnati	N.L.	OF	145	503	59	136	28	0	16	78	13	.270
1991 Cincinnati	N.L.	OF	152	532	71	136	36	0	28	91	12	.256
1992 Cincinnati b	N.L.	OF	148	496	59	122	19	1	14	66	6	.246
1993 New York	A.L.	OF	141	498	71	155	34	1	20	75	2	.311
1994 New York	A.L.	OF	103	368	68	132	25	1	21	83	5	*.359
1995 New York c	A.L.	OF	127	460	82	138	30	4	22	96	1	.300
1996 New York	A.L.	OF-1B	150	546	89	165	35	1	19	91	0	.302
1997 New York	A.L.	OF-1B	149	553	89	179	42	0	21	117	10	.324
Major League Totals		13 Yrs.	1469	5043	720	1448	313	14	199	873	79	.287
Division Series												
1995 New York	A.L.	OF	5	18	5	6	0	0	3	6	0	.333
1996 New York	A.L.	OF	4	15	0	2	0	0	0	0	0	.133
1997 New York	A.L.	OF	5	19	5	8	2	0	2	7	0	.421
Division Series Totals			14	52	10	16	2	0	5	13	0	.308
Championship Series												
1990 Cincinnati	N.L.	OF	5	17	1	8	3	0	1	4	1	.471
1996 New York	A.L.	OF	4	11	1	3	0	0	1	2	0	.273
Championship Series Totals			9	28	2	11	3	0	2	6	1	.393
World Series Record												
1990 Cincinnati	N.L.	OF	4	12	2	1	0	0	0	1	1	.108
1996 New York	A.L.	OF	5	12	1	2	2	0	0	0	0	.167
World Series Totals			9	24	2	3	2	0	0	1	1	.125

a On disabled list from July 21 to September 1, 1989.
b Traded to New York Yankees with first baseman Joe DeBerry for outfielder Roberto Kelly, November 3, 1992.
c On disabled list from May 7 to May 23, 1995.

ORDONEZ, MAGGLIO

Born, Caracas, Venezuela, January 28, 1974.
Bats Right. Throws Right. Height, 5 feet, 11 inches. Weight, 170 pounds.

Year	Club	Lea	Pos	G	AB	R	H	2B	3B	HR	RBI	SB	Avg
1993 Hickory	So. Atl.	OF	84	273	32	59	14	4	3	20	5	.216
1994 Hickory	So. Atl.	OF	132	490	86	144	24	5	11	69	16	.294
1995 Pr William	Carolina	OF	131	487	61	116	24	2	12	65	11	.238
1996 Birmingham	Southern	OF	130	479	66	126	41	0	18	67	9	.263
1997 Nashville	A.A.	OF	135	523	65	172	29	3	14	90	14	.329
1997 Chicago	A.L.	OF	21	69	12	22	6	0	4	11	1	.319

ORDONEZ, REYNALDO (REY)

Born, Havana, Cuba, November 11, 1972.
Bats Right. Throws Right. Height, 5 feet, 9 inches. Weight, 159 pounds.

Year	Club	Lea	Pos	G	AB	R	H	2B	3B	HR	RBI	SB	Avg
1993 St. Paul	Northern	SS-2B	15	60	10	17	4	0	0	7	3	.283
1994 St. Lucie	Fla. St.	SS	79	314	47	97	21	2	2	40	11	.309
1994 Binghamton	Eastern	SS	48	191	22	50	10	2	1	20	4	.262
1995 Norfolk	Int.	SS	125	439	49	94	21	4	2	50	11	.214
1996 New York	N.L.	SS	151	502	51	129	12	4	1	30	1	.257
1997 New York a	N.L.	SS	120	356	35	77	5	3	1	33	11	.216
Major League Totals		2 Yrs.	271	858	86	206	17	7	2	63	12	.240

a On disabled list from June 2 to July 11, 1997.

ORIE, KEVIN LEONARD
Born, West Chester, Pennsylvania, September 1, 1972.
Bats Right. Throws Right. Height, 6 feet, 4 inches. Weight, 210 pounds.

Year	Club	Lea	Pos	G	AB	R	H	2B	3B	HR	RBI	SB	Avg
1993 Peoria	..........Midwest		SS-OF	65	238	28	64	17	1	7	45	3	.269
1994 Daytona	...........Fla. St.		DH	6	17	4	7	3	1	1	5	0	.412
1995 Daytona	...........Fla. St.		3B	119	409	54	100	17	4	9	51	5	.244
1996 Orlando	.........Southern		3B	82	296	42	93	25	0	8	58	2	.314
1996 Iowa	.................A.A.		3B	14	48	5	10	1	0	2	6	0	.208
1997 Orlando	.........Southern		DH	3	13	3	5	2	0	2	6	0	.385
1997 Iowa	.................A.A.		3B	9	32	7	12	4	0	1	8	0	.375
1997 Chicago a	............N.L.		3B-SS	114	364	40	100	23	5	8	44	2	.275

a On disabled list from April 30 to May 30, 1997.

ORSULAK, JOSEPH MICHAEL
Born, Glen Ridge, New Jersey, May 31, 1962.
Bats Left. Throws Left. Height, 6 feet, 1 inch. Weight, 205 pounds.

Year	Club	Lea	Pos	G	AB	R	H	2B	3B	HR	RBI	SB	Avg
1981 Greenwood a	.......So. Atl.		OF	118	460	80	145	18	8	6	70	18	.315
1982 Alexandria	........Carolina		OF	129	463	92	134	18	4	14	65	28	.289
1983 Hawaii	...............P.C.		OF	139	538	87	154	12	*13	10	58	38	.286
1983 Pittsburgh	.............N.L.		OF	7	11	0	2	0	0	0	1	0	.182
1984 Pittsburgh	.............N.L.		OF	32	67	12	17	1	2	0	3	3	.254
1984 Hawaii	...............P.C.		OF	98	388	51	110	19	12	3	53	14	.284
1985 Pittsburgh b	...........N.L.		OF	121	397	54	119	14	6	0	21	24	.300
1986 Pittsburgh	.............N.L.		OF	138	401	60	100	19	6	2	19	24	.249
1987 Vancouver c-d	.........P.C.		OF	39	143	20	33	6	1	1	12	2	.231
1988 Baltimore	.............A.L.		OF	125	379	48	109	21	3	8	27	9	.288
1989 Baltimore	.............A.L.		OF	123	390	59	111	22	5	7	55	5	.285
1990 Baltimore	.............A.L.		OF	124	413	49	111	14	3	11	57	6	.269
1991 Baltimore	.............A.L.		OF	143	486	57	135	22	1	5	43	6	.278
1992 Baltimore e-f	.........A.L.		OF	117	391	45	113	18	3	4	39	5	.289
1993 New York	...........N.L.		OF-1B	134	409	59	116	15	4	8	35	5	.284
1994 New York	...........N.L.		OF-1B	96	292	39	76	3	0	8	42	4	.260
1995 New York g	.........N.L.		OF-1B	108	290	41	82	19	2	1	37	1	.283
1996 Florida	...............N.L.		OF-1B	120	217	23	48	6	1	2	19	1	.221
1997 Montreal h	............N.L.		OF-1B	106	150	13	34	12	1	1	7	0	.227

Major League Totals .... 14 Yrs. 1494 4293 559 1173 186 37 57 405 93 .273

a On temporarily inactive list from July 10 to July 27, 1981.
b On disabled list, May 25 through June 9, 1985.
c On disabled list from March 31 to May 22, 1987.
d Traded by Pittsburgh Pirates to Baltimore Orioles for infielders Rico Rossy and Terry Crowley Jr., November 10, 1987.
e On disabled list from August 16 to September 1, 1992.
f Filed for free agency, October 28; signed with New York Mets, December 18, 1992.
g Filed for free agency, November 12, 1995; signed with Florida Marlins, December 5, 1995.
h Traded to Montreal Expos with pitcher Dustin Hermanson for infielder Cliff Floyd, March 26, 1997.

ORTIZ, DAVID AMERICO
Born, Santo Domingo, Dominican Republic, November 18, 1975.
Bats Left. Throws Left. Height, 6 feet, 4 inches. Weight 230 pounds.

Year	Club	Lea	Pos	G	AB	R	H	2B	3B	HR	RBI	SB	Avg
1994 Mariners	.........Arizona		1B	53	167	14	41	10	1	2	20	1	.246
1995 Mariners	.........Arizona		1B	48	184	30	61	18	4	4	37	2	.332
1996 Wisconsin	........Midwest		1B	129	485	89	156	34	2	18	93	3	.322
1997 Ft. Myers	.........Fla. St.		1B	61	239	45	79	15	0	13	58	2	.331
1997 New Britain	........Eastern		DH-1B	69	258	40	83	22	2	14	56	2	.322
1997 Salt Lake	...........P.C.		1B	10	42	5	9	1	0	4	10	0	.214
1997 Minnesota	.............A.L.		1B	15	49	10	16	3	0	1	6	0	.327

OSIK, KEITH RICHARD
Born, Port Jefferson, N.Y., October 22, 1968.
Bats Right. Throws Right. Height, 6 feet. Weight, 185 pounds.

Year	Club	Lea	Pos	G	AB	R	H	2B	3B	HR	RBI	SB	Avg
1990 Welland	........N.Y.-Penn.		3B-C-1B	29	97	13	27	4	0	1	20	2	.278
1991 Carolina	.........Southern		C-3B	17	43	9	13	3	1	0	5	0	.302

Year	Club	Lea	Pos	G	AB	R	H	2B	3B	HR	RBI	SB	Avg
1991 Salem ....Carolina			C-3B-2B	87	300	31	81	12	1	6	35	2	.270
1992 Carolina .....Southern			3B-C-2B-P	129	425	41	110	17	1	5	45	2	.259
1993 Carolina .....Southern			C-3B	103	371	47	104	21	2	10	47	0	.280
1994 Buffalo ..........A.A.			C-OF-1B	83	260	27	55	16	0	5	33	0	.212
1995 Calgary ..........P.C.			C-1B-OF-P	90	301	40	101	25	1	10	59	2	.336
1996 Erie ........N.Y.-Penn.			C	3	10	1	3	1	0	0	2	0	.300
1996 Pittsburgh a ......N.L.			C-3B-OF	48	140	18	41	14	1	1	14	1	.293
1997 Pittsburgh ......N.L.			C-2B-1B-3B	49	105	10	27	9	1	0	7	0	.257
Major League Totals			2 Yrs.	97	245	28	68	23	2	1	21	1	.278

a On disabled list from July 16 to August 13, 1996.

OTERO, RICHARD (RICKY)
Born, Vega Baja, Puerto Rico, April 15, 1972.
Bats Both. Throws Right. Height, 5 feet, 7 inches. Weight, 150 pounds.

Year	Club	Lea	Pos	G	AB	R	H	2B	3B	HR	RBI	SB	Avg
1991 Kingsport ....Appal.			OF	66	236	47	81	16	3	7	52	12	.343
1991 Pittsfield ........N.Y.-Penn.			OF	6	24	4	7	0	0	0	2	4	.292
1992 Columbia ....So. Atl.			OF	96	353	57	106	24	4	8	60	39	.300
1992 St. Lucie ....Fla. St.			OF	40	151	20	48	8	4	0	19	10	.318
1993 Binghamton ....Eastern			OF	124	503	63	133	21	10	2	54	29	.264
1994 Binghamton ....Eastern			OF	128	531	96	156	31	9	7	57	33	.294
1995 Norfolk ....Int.			OF	72	295	37	79	8	6	1	23	16	.268
1995 New York a-b ........N.L.			OF	35	51	5	7	2	0	0	1	2	.137
1996 Scranton-WB ....Int.			OF	46	177	38	53	9	8	1	9	15	.299
1996 Philadelphia .........N.L.			OF	104	411	54	112	11	7	2	32	16	.273
1997 Philadelphia c .........N.L.			OF	50	151	20	38	6	2	0	3	0	.252
1997 Scranton-WB ....Int.			OF	38	160	24	53	10	5	1	15	5	.331
Major League Totals			3 Yrs.	189	613	79	157	19	9	2	36	18	.256

a Outrighted by New York Mets, November 20, 1995.
b Traded by New York Mets to Philadelphia Phillies organization for outfielder Phil Geisler, December 14, 1995.
c Filed for free agency, October 3, 1997.

OWENS, ERIC BLAKE
Born, Danville, Virginia, February 3, 1971.
Bats Right. Throws Right. Height, 6 feet, 1 inch. Weight, 185 pounds.

Year	Club	Lea	Pos	G	AB	R	H	2B	3B	HR	RBI	SB	Avg
1992 Billings ....Pioneer			SS-3B	67	239	41	72	10	3	3	26	15	.301
1993 Winston-Salem .Carolina			SS	122	487	74	132	25	4	10	63	21	.271
1994 Chattanooga ..Southern			3B-2B	134	523	73	133	17	3	3	36	38	.254
1995 Indianapolis .......A.A.			2B	108	427	86	134	24	8	12	63	33	.314
1995 Cincinnati a .......N.L.			3B	2	2	0	2	0	0	0	1	0	.000
1996 Indianapolis ......A.A.			SS-3B-2B-OF	33	128	24	41	8	2	4	14	6	.320
1996 Cincinnati .......N.L.			OF-2B-3B	88	205	26	41	6	0	0	9	16	.200
1997 Cincinnati .......N.L.			OF-2B	27	57	8	15	0	0	0	3	3	.263
1997 Indianapols ......A.A.			2B-SS-OF-3B	104	391	56	112	15	4	11	44	23	.286
Major League Totals			3 Yrs.	117	264	34	58	6	0	0	13	19	.220

a On disabled list from October 1 to October 2, 1995.

PAGNOZZI, THOMAS ALAN
Born, Tucson, Arizona, July 30, 1962.
Bats Right. Throws Right. Height, 6 feet, 1 inch. Weight, 190 pounds.

Year	Club	Lea	Pos	G	AB	R	H	2B	3B	HR	RBI	SB	Avg
1983 Erie ....NY-Penn.			C	45	168	28	52	9	1	6	22	3	.310
1983 Macon ....So. Atl.			C	18	57	7	14	2	1	0	6	0	.246
1984 Springfield ....Midwest			C	114	396	57	112	20	4	10	68	3	.283
1985 Arkansas ....Texas			C-1B	41	139	15	43	7	1	5	29	0	.309
1985 Louisville ..........A.A.			C	76	268	29	72	13	2	5	40	0	.269
1986 Louisville a ..........A.A.			C	30	106	12	31	4	0	1	18	0	.292
1987 Louisville ..........A.A.			C	84	320	53	100	20	2	14	71	0	.313
1987 St. Louis ...........N.L.			C-1B	27	48	8	9	1	0	2	9	1	.188
1988 St. Louis ...........N.L.			1B-C-3B	81	195	17	55	9	0	0	15	0	.282
1989 St. Louis ...........N.L.			C-1B-3B	52	80	3	12	2	0	0	3	0	.150
1990 St. Louis ...........N.L.			C-1B	69	220	20	61	15	0	2	23	1	.277
1991 St. Louis ...........N.L.			C-1B	140	459	38	121	24	5	2	57	9	.264

Year	Club	Lea	Pos	G	AB	R	H	2B	3B	HR	RBI	SB	Avg
1992 St. Louis	N.L.	C	139	485	33	121	26	3	7	44	2	.249
1993 Louisville	A.A.	C	12	43	5	12	3	0	1	1	0	.279
1993 St. Louis b	N.L.	C	92	330	31	85	15	1	7	41	1	.258
1994 Louisville	A.A.	C	10	25	4	6	3	0	0	3	0	.240
1994 St. Louis c	N.L.	C-1B	70	243	21	66	12	1	7	40	0	.272
1995 Louisville	A.A.	C	5	16	4	8	2	0	1	3	0	.500
1995 St. Louis d	N.L.	C	62	219	17	47	14	1	2	15	0	.215
1996 Louisville e	A.A.	C	8	26	5	4	0	0	2	3	0	.154
1996 St. Louis f-g	N.L.	C-1B	119	407	48	110	23	0	13	55	4	.270
1997 Louisville	A.A.	C	3	5	0	0	0	0	0	0	0	.000
1997 Arkansas	Texas	C	21	63	8	20	0	0	5	17	0	.317
1997 St. Louis h	N.L.	C-1B-3B	25	50	4	11	3	0	1	8	0	.220
Major League Totals			11 Yrs.	876	2736	240	698	144	11	43	310	18	.255
Division Series													
1996 St. Louis	N.L.	C	3	11	0	3	0	0	0	2	0	.273
Championship Series													
1987 St. Louis	N.L.	PH	1	1	0	0	0	0	0	0	0	.000
1996 St. Louis	N.L.	C	7	19	1	3	1	0	0	1	0	.158
Championship Series Totals			9	23	1	4	1	0	0	1	0	.174
World Series Record													
1987 St. Louis	N.L.	DH	2	4	0	1	0	0	0	0	0	.250

a On disabled list from May 23 to end of 1986 season.
b On disabled list from May 10 to June 16, 1993.
c On disabled list from March 26 to May 5, 1994.
d On disabled list from July 18 to August 26, 1995.
e On disabled list from April 1 to April 15, 1996.
f Filed for free agency, October 31, 1996.
g Re-signed with St. Louis Cardinals, December 6, 1996.
h On disabled list from April 1 to April 25 and April 30 to August 12, 1997.

PALMEIRO, ORLANDO

Born, Hoboken, New Jersey, January 19, 1969.
Bats Left. Throws Right. Height, 5 feet, 11 inches. Weight, 155 pounds.

Year	Club	Lea	Pos	G	AB	R	H	2B	3B	HR	RBI	SB	Avg
1995 Vancouver	P.C.	OF	107	398	66	122	21	4	0	47	16	.307
1995 California	A.L.	OF	15	20	3	7	0	0	0	1	0	.350
1996 Vancouver	P.C.	OF	62	245	40	75	13	4	0	33	7	.306
1996 California	A.L.	OF	50	87	6	25	6	1	0	6	0	.287
1997 Anaheim a	A.L.	OF	74	134	19	29	2	2	0	8	2	.216
Major League Totals			3 Yrs.	139	241	28	61	8	3	0	15	2	.253

a On disabled list from August 23 to September 7, 1997.

PALMEIRO, RAFAEL CORRALES

Born, Havana, Cuba, September 24, 1964.
Bats Left. Throws Left. Height 6 feet. Weight, 188 pounds.

Year	Club	Lea	Pos	G	AB	R	H	2B	3B	HR	RBI	SB	Avg
1985 Peoria	Midwest	OF	73	279	34	83	22	4	5	51	9	.297
1986 Pittsfield	Eastern	OF	*140	509	66	*156	29	2	12	*95	15	.306
1986 Chicago	N.L.	OF	22	73	9	18	4	0	3	12	1	.247
1987 Iowa	A.A.	OF	57	214	36	64	14	3	11	41	4	.299
1987 Chicago	N.L.	OF-1B	84	221	32	61	15	1	14	30	2	.276
1988 Chicago a	N.L.	OF-1B	152	580	75	178	41	5	8	53	12	.307
1989 Texas	A.L.	1B	156	559	76	154	23	4	8	64	4	.275
1990 Texas	A.L.	1B	154	598	72	*191	35	6	14	89	3	.319
1991 Texas	A.L.	1B	159	631	115	203	*49	3	26	88	4	.322
1992 Texas	A.L.	1B	159	608	84	163	27	4	22	85	2	.268
1993 Texas b	A.L.	1B	160	597	*124	176	40	2	37	105	22	.295
1994 Baltimore	A.L.	1B	111	436	82	139	32	0	23	76	7	.319
1995 Baltimore	A.L.	1B	143	554	89	172	30	2	39	104	3	.310
1996 Baltimore	A.L.	1B	162	626	110	181	40	2	39	142	8	.289
1997 Baltimore	A.L.	1B	158	614	95	156	24	2	38	110	5	.254
Major League Totals			12 Yrs.	1620	6097	963	1792	360	31	271	958	73	.294
Division Series													
1996 Baltimore	A.L.	1B	4	17	4	3	1	0	1	2	0	.176
1997 Baltimore	A.L.	1B	4	12	2	3	2	0	0	0	0	.250
Division Series Totals			8	29	6	6	3	0	1	2	0	.207

Year	Club	Lea	Pos	G	AB	R	H	2B	3B	HR	RBI	SB	Avg
	Championship Series												
1996 Baltimore ...........A.L.			1B	5	17	4	4	0	0	2	4	0	.235
1997 Baltimore ...........A.L.			1B	6	25	3	7	2	0	1	2	0	.280
Championship Series Totals				11	42	7	11	2	0	3	6	0	.262

a Traded to Texas Rangers with pitchers Jamie Moyer and Drew Hall for infielders Curtis Wilkerson and Luis Benetiz, outfielder Pablo Delgado, and pitchers Mitch Williams, Paul Kilgus and Steve Wilson, December 5, 1988.
b Filed for free agency, October 25; signed with Baltimore Orioles, December 13, 1993.

PALMER, DEAN WILLIAM

Born, Tallahassee, Florida, December 27, 1968.
Bats Right. Throws Right. Height, 6 feet, 2 inches. Weight, 195 pounds.

Year	Club	Lea	Pos	G	AB	R	H	2B	3B	HR	RBI	SB	Avg
1986 Sara. Rangers	Gulf C.		3B	50	163	19	34	7	1	0	12	6	.209
1987 Gastonia	So. Atl.		3B	128	484	51	104	16	0	9	54	5	.215
1988 Charlotte a	Fla. St.		3B	74	305	38	81	12	1	4	35	0	.266
1989 Tulsa	Texas		3B	133	498	82	125	31	5	*25	90	15	.251
1989 Texas	A.L.	3B-SS-OF	16	19	0	2	0	0	0	1	0	.105
1990 Tulsa	Texas		3B	7	24	4	7	0	1	3	9	0	.292
1990 Oklahoma City b	A.A.	3B-1B	88	316	33	69	17	4	12	39	1	.218
1991 Oklahoma City	A.A.	3B	60	234	45	70	11	2	22	59	4	.299
1991 Texas	A.L.	3B-OF	81	268	38	50	9	2	15	37	0	.187
1992 Texas	A.L.	3B	152	541	74	124	25	0	26	72	10	.229
1993 Texas	A.L.	3B-SS	148	519	88	127	31	2	33	96	11	.245
1994 Texas c	A.L.	3B	93	342	50	84	14	2	19	59	3	.246
1995 Texas d-e	A.L.	3B	36	119	30	40	6	0	9	24	1	.336
1996 Texas	A.L.	3B	154	582	98	163	26	2	38	107	2	.289
1997 Texas-Kansas City f-g-h	A.L.	3B	143	542	70	139	31	1	23	86	2	.256
Major League Totals		8 Yrs.		823	2932	448	729	144	9	163	482	29	.249
	Division Series												
1996 Texas	A.L.	3B	4	19	3	4	1	0	1	2	0	.211

a On disabled list from July 4 to end of 1988 season.
b On disabled list from July 27 to August 5, 1990.
c On disabled list from April 30 to May 14, 1994.
d Signed with Texas Rangers, May 15, 1995.
e On disabled list from June 4 to September 22, 1995.
f Traded to Kansas City Royals for outfielder Tom Goodwin, July 26, 1997.
g Filed for free agency, October 27, 1997.
h Re-signed with Kansas City Royals December 15, 1997.

PAQUETTE, CRAIG HOWARD

Born, Long Beach, California, March 28, 1969.
Bats Right. Throws Right. Height, 6 feet. Weight, 190 pounds.

Year	Club	Lea	Pos	G	AB	R	H	2B	3B	HR	RBI	SB	Avg
1989 Southern Oregon	Northwest	3B	71	277	53	93	*22	3	14	56	9	.336
1990 Modesto	California	3B	130	495	65	118	23	4	15	59	8	.238
1991 Huntsville a ...	Southern	3B	102	378	50	99	18	1	8	60	0	.262
1992 Huntsville	Southern	3B	115	450	59	116	25	4	17	71	13	.258
1992 Tacoma	P.C.	3B	17	66	10	18	7	0	2	11	3	.273
1993 Tacoma	P.C.	3B-2B-SS	50	183	29	49	8	0	8	29	3	.268
1993 Oakland	A.L.	3B-OF	105	393	35	86	20	4	12	46	4	.219
1994 Tacoma	P.C.	3B	65	245	39	70	12	3	17	48	3	.286
1994 Oakland	A.L.	3B	14	49	0	7	2	0	0	0	1	.143
1995 Oakland	A.L.	3B-OF-SS-1B	105	283	42	64	13	1	13	49	5	.226
1996 Omaha	A.A.	DH-3B-1B-OF	18	63	9	21	3	0	4	13	1	.333
1996 Kansas City b	A.L.	3B-OF-1B-SS	118	429	61	111	15	1	22	67	5	.259
1997 Kansas City c-d ..	A.L.	3B-OF	77	252	26	58	15	1	8	33	2	.230
1997 Omaha	A.A.	3B	23	91	9	28	6	0	3	20	0	.308
Major League Totals		5 Yrs.		419	1406	164	326	65	7	55	195	17	.232

a On disabled list from April 1 to May 5 and June 1 to June 11, 1991.
b Signed with Kansas City Royals organization, April 3, 1996.
c Released by Kansas City Royals, August 7, 1997.
d Signed as free agent with New York Mets organization, December 23, 1997.

PARENT, MARK ALAN
Born, Ashland, Oregon, September 16, 1961.
Bats Right. Throws Right. Height, 6 feet, 5 inches. Weight, 225 pounds.

Year	Club	Lea	Pos	G	AB	R	H	2B	3B	HR	RBI	SB	Avg
1979	Walla Walla	Northwest	C-OF	40	126	8	24	4	0	1	11	8	.190
1980	Reno	California	C	30	99	8	20	3	0	0	12	0	.202
1980	Grays Harbor	Northwest	C-1B	66	239	29	55	11	2	7	32	1	.230
1981	Salem	Carolina	C	123	438	44	103	16	3	6	47	10	.235
1982	Amarillo	Texas	C	26	89	12	17	3	1	1	13	2	.191
1982	Salem	Carolina	C-1B	99	360	39	81	15	2	6	41	2	.225
1983	Beaumont	Texas	C	81	282	38	71	22	1	7	33	1	.252
1984	Beaumont	Texas	C-1B	111	380	52	109	24	3	7	60	1	.287
1985	Las Vegas	P.C.	C-1B	105	361	36	87	23	3	7	45	1	.241
1986	Las Vegas	P.C.	C-1B	86	267	29	77	10	4	5	40	0	.288
1986	San Diego	N.L.	C	8	14	1	2	0	0	0	0	0	.143
1987	Las Vegas	P.C.	C	105	387	50	113	23	2	4	42	2	.292
1987	San Diego	N.L.	C	12	25	0	2	0	0	0	2	0	.080
1988	San Diego	N.L.	C	41	118	9	23	3	0	6	15	0	.195
1989	San Diego	N.L.	C-1B	52	141	12	27	4	0	7	21	1	.191
1990	San Diego a	N.L.	C	65	189	13	42	11	0	3	16	1	.222
1991	Oklahoma City	A.A.	C	5	8	0	2	0	0	0	1	0	.250
1991	Texas b-c	A.L.	C	3	1	0	0	0	0	0	0	0	.000
1992	Rochester	Int.	C	101	356	52	102	24	0	17	69	4	.287
1992	Baltimore	A.L.	C	17	34	4	8	1	0	2	4	0	.235
1993	Rochester	Int.	C	92	332	47	82	15	0	14	56	0	.247
1993	Baltimore d	A.L.	C	22	54	7	14	2	0	4	12	0	.259
1994	Chicago e	N.L.	C	44	99	8	26	4	0	3	16	0	.263
1995	Pittsburgh-Chicago f-g	N.L.	C	81	265	30	62	11	0	18	38	0	.234
1996	Detroit-Baltimore h-i	A.L.	C-1B	56	137	17	31	7	0	9	23	0	.226
1997	Philadelphia	N.L.	C	39	113	4	17	3	0	0	8	0	.150
Major League Totals			12 Yrs.	440	1190	105	254	46	0	52	155	2	.213
Division Series													
1996	Baltimore	A.L.	C	4	5	0	1	0	0	0	0	0	.200
Championship Series													
1996	Baltimore	A.L.	C	2	6	0	1	0	0	0	0	0	.167

a Traded to Texas Rangers for third baseman Scott Coolbaugh, December 12, 1990.
b On disabled list from March 9 to September 6, 1991.
c Refused assignment to minor leagues and became free agent, October 15, 1991; signed with Baltimore Orioles organization, February 5, 1992.
d Refused assignment to minor leagues and became free agent, October 20; signed with Chicago Cubs organization, December 14, 1993.
e Claimed on waivers by Pittsburgh Pirates, October 11, 1994.
f Traded to Chicago Cubs for player to be named, August 31, 1995.
g Filed for free agency, November 12, 1995; signed with Detroit Tigers, December 13, 1995.
h Filed for free agency, November 18, 1996.
i Signed with Philadelphia Phillies, December 11, 1996.

PENA (PADILLA), ANTONIO FRANCISCO (TONY)
Born, Monte Cristi, Dominican Republic, June 4, 1957.
Bats Right. Throws Right. Height, 6 feet. Weight, 185 pounds.

Year	Club	Lea	Pos	G	AB	R	H	2B	3B	HR	RBI	SB	Avg
1976	Brad. Pirates	Gulf C.	OF-1B-C-3B	33	110	10	23	2	2	1	11	5	.209
1976	Charleston	W. Carol.	C	14	49	4	11	2	0	1	8	0	.224
1977	Charleston	W. Carol.	C	29	101	10	24	4	0	3	16	2	.238
1977	Salem	Carolina	C	84	319	36	88	15	3	7	46	3	.276
1978	Shreveport	Texas	C	104	348	34	80	14	0	8	42	3	.230
1979	Buffalo	Eastern	C	134	515	89	161	16	4	34	97	5	.313
1980	Portland	P.C.	C	124	452	57	148	24	13	9	77	5	.327
1980	Pittsburgh	N.L.	C	8	21	1	9	1	1	0	1	0	.429
1981	Pittsburgh	N.L.	C	66	210	16	63	9	1	2	17	1	.300
1982	Pittsburgh	N.L.	C	138	497	53	147	28	4	11	63	2	.296
1983	Pittsburgh	N.L.	C	151	542	51	163	22	3	15	70	6	.301
1984	Pittsburgh	N.L.	C	147	546	77	156	27	2	15	78	12	.286
1985	Pittsburgh	N.L.	C-1B	147	546	53	136	27	2	10	59	12	.249
1986	Pittsburgh a	N.L.	C-1B	144	510	56	147	26	2	10	52	9	.288
1987	Louisville	A.A.	C	2	8	0	3	0	0	0	0	0	.375
1987	St. Louis b	N.L.	C-1B	116	384	40	82	13	4	5	44	6	.214
1988	St. Louis	N.L.	C-1B	149	505	55	133	23	1	10	51	6	.263
1989	St. Louis c	N.L.	C-OF	141	424	36	110	17	2	4	37	5	.259
1990	Boston	A.L.	C-1B	143	491	62	129	19	1	7	56	8	.263
1991	Boston	A.L.	C	141	464	45	107	23	2	5	48	8	.231

Year Club	Lea	Pos	G	AB	R	H	2B	3B	HR	RBI	SB	Avg
1992 Boston	A.L.	C	133	410	39	99	21	1	1	38	3	.241
1993 Boston d	A.L.	C	126	304	20	55	11	0	4	19	1	.181
1994 Cleveland e	A.L.	C	40	112	18	33	8	1	2	10	0	.295
1995 Cleveland f	A.L.	C	91	263	25	69	15	0	5	28	1	.262
1996 Cleveland g-h	A.L.	C	67	174	14	34	4	0	1	27	0	.195
1997 Chicago i-j	A.L.	C-3B	31	67	4	11	1	0	0	8	0	.164
1997 Houston k	N.L.	C	9	19	2	4	3	0	0	2	0	.211
Major League Totals		18 Yrs.	1988	6489	667	1687	298	27	107	708	80	.260
Division Series												
1995 Cleveland	A.L.	C	2	2	1	1	0	0	1	1	0	.500
1996 Cleveland	A.L.	C	1	0	0	0	0	0	0	0	0	.000
1997 Houston	N.L.	C	2	0	0	0	0	0	0	0	0	.000
Division Series Totals			5	2	1	1	0	0	1	1	0	.500
Championship Series												
1987 St. Louis	N.L.	C	7	21	5	8	0	1	0	0	1	.381
1990 Boston	A.L.	C	4	14	0	3	0	0	0	0	0	.214
1995 Cleveland	A.L.	C	4	6	1	2	1	0	0	0	0	.333
Championship Series Totals			15	41	6	13	1	1	0	0	1	.317
World Series Record												
1987 St. Louis	N.L.	C	7	22	2	9	1	0	0	4	1	.409
1995 Cleveland	A.L.	C	2	6	0	1	0	0	0	0	0	.167
World Series Totals			9	28	2	10	1	0	0	4	1	.357

a Traded to St. Louis Cardinals for catcher Mike LaValliere, pitcher Mike Dunne and outfielder Andy Van Slyke, April 1, 1987.
b On disabled list from April 11 to May 22, 1987.
c Filed for free agency, October 30; signed with Boston Red Sox, November 27, 1989.
d Filed for free agency, October 26, 1993; signed with Cleveland Indians organization February 8, 1994.
e Filed for free agency, October 21; re-signed with Cleveland Indians organization, December 13, 1994.
f Filed for free agency, November 12, 1995; re-signed with Cleveland Indians, December 6, 1995.
g Filed for free agency, November 18, 1996.
h Signed with Chicago White Sox organization, January 11, 1997.
i On disabled list from June 3 to June 20, 1997.
j Traded to Houston Astros for pitcher Julien Tucker, August 14, 1997.
k Filed for free agency, October 30, 1997.

PENDLETON, TERRY LEE

Born, Los Angeles, California, July 16, 1960.
Bats Both. Throws Right. Height, 5 feet, 9 inches. Weight, 195 pounds.

Year Club	Lea	Pos	G	AB	R	H	2B	3B	HR	RBI	SB	Avg
1982 Johnson City	Appal.	3B	43	181	38	58	14	4	4	27	13	.320
1982 St. Petersburg	Fla. St.	3B	20	69	4	18	2	1	1	7	1	.261
1983 Arkansas a	Texas	3B	48	185	29	51	10	3	4	20	7	.276
1984 Louisville	A.A.	3B-2B	91	330	52	98	23	5	4	44	6	.297
1984 St. Louis	N.L.	3B	67	262	37	85	16	3	1	33	20	.324
1985 St. Louis b	N.L.	3B	149	559	56	134	16	3	5	69	17	.240
1986 St. Louis	N.L.	3B-OF	159	578	56	138	26	5	1	59	24	.239
1987 St. Louis	N.L.	3B	159	583	82	167	29	4	12	96	19	.286
1988 St. Louis c	N.L.	3B	110	391	44	99	20	2	6	53	3	.253
1989 St. Louis	N.L.	3B	162	613	83	162	28	5	13	74	9	.264
1990 St. Louis d-e	N.L.	3B	121	447	46	103	20	2	6	58	7	.230
1991 Atlanta f	N.L.	3B	153	586	94	*187	34	8	22	86	10	*.319
1992 Atlanta	N.L.	3B	160	640	98	*199	39	1	21	105	5	.311
1993 Atlanta	N.L.	3B	161	633	81	172	33	1	17	84	5	.272
1994 Greenville	Southern	3B	2	6	0	3	1	0	0	2	0	.500
1994 Atlanta g-h	N.L.	3B	77	309	25	78	18	3	7	30	2	.252
1995 Florida i	N.L.	3B	133	513	70	149	32	1	14	78	1	.290
1996 Florida-Atlanta j-k-l	N.L.	3B	153	568	51	135	26	1	11	75	2	.238
1997 Indianapols	A.A.	3B	4	12	2	2	0	0	0	2	0	.167
1997 Cincinnati m-n	N.L.	3B	50	113	11	28	9	0	1	17	2	.248
Major League Totals		14 Yrs.	1814	6795	834	1836	346	39	137	917	126	.270
Division Series												
1996 Atlanta	N.L.	3B	1	1	0	0	0	0	0	0	0	.000
Championship Series												
1985 St. Louis	N.L.	3B	6	24	2	5	1	0	0	4	0	.208
1987 St. Louis	N.L.	3B	6	19	3	4	0	1	0	1	0	.211
1991 Atlanta	N.L.	3B	7	30	1	5	1	1	0	1	0	.167
1992 Atlanta	N.L.	3B	7	30	2	7	2	0	0	3	0	.233

Year	Club	Lea	Pos	G	AB	R	H	2B	3B	HR	RBI	SB	Avg
1993 Atlanta	..............N.L.		3B	6	26	4	9	1	0	1	5	0	.346
1996 Atlanta	..............N.L.		PH	6	6	0	0	0	0	0	0	0	.000
Championship Series Totals	....			38	135	12	30	5	2	1	14	0	.222
World Series Record													
1985 St. Louis	.............N.L.		3B	7	23	3	6	1	1	0	3	0	.261
1987 St. Louis	.............N.L.		DH	3	7	2	3	0	0	0	1	2	.429
1991 Atlanta	.............N.L.		3B	7	30	6	11	3	0	2	3	0	.367
1992 Atlanta	.............N.L.		3B	6	25	2	6	2	0	0	2	0	.240
1996 Atlanta	......:.......N.L.		DH-3B	4	9	1	2	1	0	0	0	0	.222
World Series Totals	......:........			27	94	14	28	7	1	2	9	2	.298

a On disabled list from April 8 to May 23 and July 16 to September 5, 1983.
b On disabled list from June 15 to June 30, 1985.
c On disabled list from May 28 to June 24, 1988.
d On disabled list from April 23 to May 9, 1990.
e Filed for free agency, October 23; signed with Atlanta Braves, December 3, 1990.
f Selected Most Valuable Player in National League for 1991.
g On disabled list from June 22 to July 25, 1994.
h Filed for free agency, October 26, 1994.
i Signed with Florida Marlins, April 7, 1995.
j Traded to Atlanta Braves for outfielder Roosevelt Brown, August 13, 1996.
k Filed for free agency, October 29, 1996.
l Signed with Cincinnati Reds organization January 27, 1997.
m Released by Cincinnati Reds, July 23, 1997.
n On disabled list from April 1 to April 29 and July 7 to July 23, 1997.

PEREZ, EDUARDO (EDDIE)
Born, Ponce, Puerto Rico, May 4, 1968.
Bats Right. Throws Right. Height, 6 feet, 1 inch. Weight, 175 pounds.

Year	Club	Lea	Pos	G	AB	R	H	2B	3B	HR	RBI	SB	Avg
1987 Braves	.........Gulf Coast		C	31	89	8	18	1	0	1	5	0	.202
1988 Burlington	.......Midwest		C-1B	64	186	14	43	8	0	4	19	1	.231
1989 Sumter	...........So. Atl.		C-1B	114	401	39	93	21	0	5	44	2	.232
1990 Sumter	...........So. Atl.		C-1B	41	123	11	22	7	1	3	17	0	.179
1990 Durham	.........Carolina		C-1B	31	93	9	22	1	0	3	10	0	.237
1991 Durham	.........Carolina		C-1B	92	277	38	75	10	1	9	41	0	.271
1991 Greenville	........Southern		1B	1	4	0	1	0	0	0	0	0	.250
1992 Greenville	........Southern		C-1B	91	275	28	63	16	0	6	41	3	.229
1993 Greenville	........Southern		1B-C	28	84	15	28	6	0	6	17	1	.333
1994 Richmond	............Int.		C-1B	113	338	37	101	16	2	9	49	1	.260
1995 Richmond	............Int.		C-1B	92	324	31	86	19	0	5	40	1	.265
1995 Atlanta	.............N.L.		C-1B	7	13	1	4	1	0	1	4	0	.308
1996 Atlanta a	.............N.L.		C-1B	68	156	19	40	9	1	4	17	0	.256
1997 Atlanta	.............N.L.		C-1B	73	191	20	41	5	0	6	18	0	.215
Major League Totals	....		3 Yrs.	148	360	40	85	15	1	11	39	0	.236
Division Series													
1996 Atlanta	.............N.L.		C	1	3	0	1	0	0	0	0	0	.333
1997 Atlanta	.............N.L.		C	1	3	0	0	0	0	0	0	0	.000
Division Series Totals	....			2	6	0	1	0	0	0	0	0	.167
Championship Series													
1996 Atlanta	.............N.L.		C-1B	4	1	0	0	0	0	0	0	0	.000
1997 Atlanta	.............N.L.		C	2	3	0	0	0	0	0	0	0	.000
Championship Series Totals	....			6	4	0	0	0	0	0	0	0	.000
World Series													
1996 Atlanta	.............N.L.		C	2	1	0	0	0	0	0	0	0	.000

a On disabled list from August 30 to September 14, 1996.

PEREZ, EDUARDO ATANASIO
Born, Cincinnati, Ohio, September 11, 1969.
Bats Right. Throws Right. Height, 6 feet, 4 inches. Weight, 215 pounds.

Year	Club	Lea	Pos	G	AB	R	H	2B	3B	HR	RBI	SB	Avg
1991 Boise	..........Northwest		OF-1B	46	160	35	46	13	0	1	22	12	.287
1992 Palm Springs	....California		3B-SS-OF	54	204	37	64	8	4	3	35	14	.314
1992 Midland	........Texas		3B-OF-1B	62	.235	27	54	8	1	3	23	19	.230
1993 Vancouver	...........P.C.		3B-1B-OF	96	363	66	111	23	6	12	70	21	.306
1993 California	...........A.L.		3B	52	180	16	45	6	2	4	30	5	.250
1994 California	...........A.L.		1B	38	129	10	27	7	0	5	16	3	.209

Year	Club	Lea	Pos	G	AB	R	H	2B	3B	HR	RBI	SB	Avg
1994 Vancouver	P.C.	3B	61	219	37	65	14	3	7	38	9	.297
1995 Vancouver	P.C.	3B-1B	69	246	39	80	12	7	6	37	6	.325
1995 California	A.L.	3B	29	71	9	12	4	1	1	7	0	.169
1996 Indianapolis	A.A.	3B-1B	122	451	84	132	29	5	21	84	11	.293
1996 Cincinnati a	N.L.	1B-3B	18	36	8	8	0	0	3	5	0	.222
1997 Cincinnati	N.L.	1B-OF-3B	106	297	44	75	18	0	16	52	5	.253
Major League Totals			5 Yrs.	243	713	87	167	35	3	29	110	13	.234

a Traded to Cincinnati Reds for outfielder Will Pennyfeather, April 5, 1996.

PEREZ, NEIFI NEFTALI
Born, Villa Mella, Dominican Republic, February 2, 1975.
Bats Both. Throws Right. Height, 6 feet. Weight, 176 pounds.

Year	Club	Lea	Pos	G	AB	R	H	2B	3B	HR	RBI	SB	Avg
1993 Bend	Northwest	SS-2B	75	296	35	77	11	4	3	32	19	.260
1994 Central Val	California	SS	134	506	64	121	16	7	1	35	9	.239
1995 Colo Sprngs	P.C.	SS	11	36	4	10	4	0	0	2	1	.278
1995 New Haven	Eastern	SS	116	427	59	108	28	3	5	43	5	.253
1996 Colo Sprngs	P.C.	SS	133	570	77	180	28	12	7	72	16	.316
1996 Colorado	N.L.	SS-2B	17	45	4	7	2	0	0	3	2	.156
1997 Colo Sprngs	P.C.	SS	68	303	68	110	24	3	8	46	8	.363
1997 Colorado	N.L.	SS-2B-3B	83	313	46	91	13	10	5	31	4	.291
Major League Totals			2 Yrs.	100	358	50	98	15	10	5	34	6	.274

PEREZ, ROBERT ALEXANDER
Born, Bolivar, Venezuela, June 4, 1969.
Bats Right. Throws Right. Height, 6 feet, 3 inches. Weight, 205 pounds.

Year	Club	Lea	Pos	G	AB	R	H	2B	3B	HR	RBI	SB	Avg
1990 St. Catharines	N.Y.-Penn.	OF	52	207	21	54	10	2	5	25	7	.261
1990 Myrtle Beach	So. Atl.	OF	21	72	8	21	2	0	1	10	2	.292
1991 Dunedin	Fla. St.	OF	127	480	50	145	28	6	4	50	8	.302
1991 Syracuse	Int.	OF	4	20	2	4	1	0	0	1	0	.200
1992 Knoxville	Southern	OF	139	526	59	137	25	5	9	59	11	.260
1993 Syracuse	Int.	OF	138	524	72	154	26	10	12	64	13	.294
1994 Syracuse	Int.	OF	128	510	63	155	28	3	10	65	4	.304
1994 Toronto	A.L.	OF	4	8	0	1	0	0	0	0	0	.125
1995 Syracuse	Int.	OF	122	502	70	172	38	6	9	66	7	.343
1995 Toronto	A.L.	OF	17	48	2	9	2	0	1	3	0	.188
1996 Toronto	A.L.	OF	86	202	30	66	10	0	2	21	3	.327
1997 Toronto	A.L.	OF	37	78	4	15	4	1	2	6	0	.192
Major League Totals			4 Yrs.	144	336	36	91	16	1	5	30	3	.271

PEREZ, TOMAS ORLANDO
Born, Barquismeto, Venezuela, December 29, 1973.
Bats Right. Throws Right. Height, 5 feet, 11 inches. Weight, 165 pounds.

Year	Club	Lea	Pos	G	AB	R	H	2B	3B	HR	RBI	SB	Avg
1993 Expos	Gulf Coast	SS	52	189	27	46	3	1	2	21	8	.243
1994 Burlington	Midwest	SS-2B	119	465	76	122	22	1	8	47	8	.262
1995 Toronto	A.L.	SS-2B-3B	41	98	12	24	3	1	1	8	0	.245
1996 Syracuse	Int.	SS-2B	40	123	15	34	10	1	1	13	8	.276
1996 Toronto	A.L.	2B-3B-SS	91	295	24	74	13	4	1	19	1	.251
1997 Syracuse	Int.	SS	89	303	32	68	13	0	1	20	3	.224
1997 Toronto a	A.L.	SS-2B	40	123	9	24	3	2	0	9	1	.195
Major League Totals			3 Yrs.	172	516	45	122	19	7	2	36	2	.236

a On disabled list from June 26 to July 24, 1997.

PHILLIPS, KEITH ANTHONY (TONY)
Born, Atlanta, Georgia, April 25, 1959.
Bats Both. Throws Right. Height, 5 feet, 10 inches. Weight, 175 pounds.

Year	Club	Lea	Pos	G	AB	R	H	2B	3B	HR	RBI	SB	Avg
1978 W. Palm Bch a	Fla. St.	SS-2B	32	54	8	9	0	0	0	3	2	.167
1978 Jamestown	N.Y.-Penn.	SS-2B-3B	52	152	24	29	5	2	1	17	3	.191

Year Club	Lea	Pos	G	AB	R	H	2B	3B	HR	RBI	SB	Avg
1979 W. Palm Bch. .Fla. St.		2B-SS	60	203	30	47	5	1	0	18	7	.232
1979 Memphis .Southern		SS-2B	52	156	31	44	4	2	3	11	3	.282
1980 Memphis b Southern		SS-2B	136	502	100	125	18	4	5	41	50	.249
1981 West Haven Eastern		SS-2B	131	461	79	114	25	3	9	64	40	.247
1981 Tacoma c .....P.C.		2B-SS	4	11	1	4	1	0	0	2	0	.364
1982 Tacoma .......P.C.		SS-2B	86	300	76	89	18	5	4	47	29	.297
1982 Oakland ......A.L.		SS	40	81	11	17	2	2	0	8	2	.210
1983 Oakland ......A.L.		SS-3B	148	412	54	102	12	3	4	35	16	.248
1984 Oakland ......A.L.		SS-2B-OF	154	451	62	120	24	3	4	37	10	.266
1985 Tacoma .......P.C.		3B-2B	20	69	9	9	1	0	0	5	3	.130
1985 Oakland d ....A.L.		2B	42	161	23	45	12	2	4	17	3	.280
1986 Oakland e .....A.L.		2B-3B-SS-OF	118	441	76	113	14	5	5	52	15	.256
1987 Tacoma .......P.C.		2B	7	26	5	9	2	1	1	6	1	.346
1987 Oakland f-g ..A.L.		2B-3B-SS-OF	111	379	48	91	20	0	10	46	7	.240
1988 Tacoma .......P.C.		2B-SS-OF	16	59	10	16	0	0	2	8	0	.271
1988 Oakland h ....A.L.		3B-2B-OF-SS	79	212	32	43	8	4	2	17	0	.203
1989 Oakland i .....A.L.		2B-3B-SS-OF-1B	143	451	48	118	15	6	4	47	3	.262
1990 Detroit ......A.L.		3B-2B-SS-OF	152	573	97	144	23	5	8	55	19	.251
1991 Detroit .......A.L.		OF-3B-2B-SS	146	564	87	160	28	4	17	72	10	.284
1992 Detroit .......A.L.		OF-2B-3B-SS	159	606	*114	167	32	3	10	64	12	.276
1993 Detroit .......A.L.		OF-2B-3B	151	566	113	177	27	0	7	57	16	.313
1994 Detroit .......A.L.		OF-2B	114	438	91	123	19	3	19	61	13	.281
1995 California j-k ..A.L.		3B-OF	139	525	119	137	21	1	27	61	13	.261
1996 Chicago l .....A.L.		OF-2B-1B	153	581	119	161	29	3	12	63	13	.277
1997 Chi.-Ana. m-n-o A.L.		OF-2B-DH-3B	141	534	96	147	34	2	8	57	13	.275
Major League Totals	16 Yrs.		1990	6975	1190	1865	320	46	141	749	165	.267
Championship Series												
1988 Oakland .........A.L.		OF-2B	2	7	0	2	1	0	0	0	0	.286
1989 Oakland .........A.L.		2B-3B	5	18	1	3	1	0	0	1	2	.167
Championship Series Totals			7	25	1	5	2	0	0	1	2	.200
World Series Record												
1988 Oakland .....A.L.		OF-2B	2	4	1	1	0	0	0	0	0	.250
1989 Oakland .....A.L.		2B-3B-OF	4	17	2	4	1	0	1	3	0	.235
World Series Totals			6	21	3	5	1	0	1	3	0	.238

a On temporarily inactive list from April 11 to May 4, 1978.
b Traded by Montreal Expos to San Diego Padres organization for first baseman Willie Montanez, August 31, 1980.
c Traded by San Diego Padres to Oakland Athletics organization with pitcher Eric Mustad and infielder Kevin Bell for pitchers Bob Lacey and Roy Moretti, March 27, 1981.
d On disabled list from March 24 to August 22, 1985.
e On disabled list from August 19 to end of 1986 season.
f On disabled list from July 12 to August 28, 1987.
g Not offered 1988 contract, December 18, 1987; re-signed with Oakland Athletics, March 9, 1988.
h On disabled list from May 18 to July 10, 1988.
i Filed for free agency, October 31; signed with Detroit Tigers, December 5, 1989.
j Traded to California Angels for outfielder Chad Curtis, April 13, 1995.
k Filed for free agency, November 12, 1995.
l Signed with Chicago White Sox, January 20, 1996.
n Traded to Anaheim Angels with catcher Chad Kreuter for pitcher Chuck McElroy and catcher Jorge Fabregas, May 18, 1997.
o Released by Anaheim Angels, December 22, 1997.

PIAZZA, MICHAEL JOSEPH
Born, Norristown, Pennsylvania, September 4, 1968.
Bats Right. Throws Right. Height, 6 feet, 3 inches. Weight, 197 pounds.

Year Club	Lea	Pos	G	AB	R	H	2B	3B	HR	RBI	SB	Avg
1989 Salem ....Northwest		C	57	198	22	53	11	0	8	25	0	.268
1990 Vero Beach ....Fla. St.		C-1B	88	272	27	68	20	0	6	45	0	.250
1991 Bakersfield ....California		C-1B	117	448	71	124	27	2	29	80	0	.277
1992 San Antonio ....Texas		C	31	114	18	43	11	0	7	20	0	.377
1992 Albuquerque ..........P.C.		C-1B	94	358	54	122	22	5	16	69	1	.341
1992 Los Angeles ..........N.L.		C	21	69	5	16	3	0	1	7	0	.232
1993 Los Angeles a .........N.L.		C-1B	149	547	81	174	24	2	35	112	3	.318
1994 Los Angeles ..........N.L.		C	107	405	64	129	18	0	24	92	1	.319
1995 Los Angeles b .........N.L.		C	112	434	82	150	17	0	32	93	1	.346
1996 Los Angeles ..........N.L.		C	148	547	87	184	16	0	36	105	0	.336
1997 Los Angeles ..........N.L.		C	152	556	104	201	32	1	40	124	5	.362
Major League Totals	6 Yrs.		689	2558	423	854	110	3	168	533	10	.334

Year	Club	Lea	Pos	G	AB	R	H	2B	3B	HR	RBI	SB	Avg
	Division Series												
1995 Los Angeles	..........N.L.		C	3	14	1	3	1	0	1	1	0	.214
1996 Los Angeles	..........L.A.		C	3	10	1	3	0	0	0	2	0	.300
Division Series Totals	....			6	24	2	6	1	0	1	3	0	.250

a Selected Rookie of the Year in National League for 1993.
b On disabled list from May 11 to June 4, 1995.

PLANTIER, PHILIP ALAN

Born, Manchester, New Hampshire, January 27, 1969.
Bats Left. Throws Right. Height, 5 feet, 11 inches. Weight, 195 pounds.

Year	Club	Lea	Pos	G	AB	R	H	2B	3B	HR	RBI	SB	Avg
1987 Elmira	..........N.Y.-Penn.		3B	28	80	7	14	2	0	2	9	0	.175
1988 Winter Haven	.......Fla. St.	OF-3B-2B		111	337	29	81	13	1	4	32	0	.240
1989 Lynchburg	........Carolina		OF	131	443	73	133	26	1	*27	*105	4	.300
1990 Pawtucket	............Int.		OF	123	430	83	109	22	3	*33	79	1	.253
1990 Boston	..............A.L.		OF	14	15	1	2	1	0	0	3	0	.133
1991 Pawtucket	............Int.		OF	84	298	69	91	19	4	16	61	6	.305
1991 Boston	..............A.L.		OF	53	148	27	49	7	1	11	35	1	.331
1992 Pawtucket	............Int.		OF	12	40	7	17	0	0	5	14	0	.425
1992 Boston a	.............A.L.		OF	108	349	46	86	19	0	7	30	2	.246
1993 San Diego b	.........N.L.		OF	138	462	67	111	20	1	34	100	4	.240
1994 San Diego c	.........N.L.		OF	96	341	44	75	21	0	18	41	3	.220
1995 Tucscon	.............P.C.		OF	10	24	6	6	2	0	1	4	0	.250
1995 Houston-San Diego d-e-f-g	.N.L.		OF	76	216	33	55	6	0	9	34	1	.255
1996 Edmonton	.............P.C.		OF	34	122	25	43	7	1	9	45	1	.352
1996 Oakland h-i-j-k	.......A.L.		OF	73	231	29	49	8	1	7	31	2	.212
1997 Las Vegas	.............P.C.		OF	15	56	13	24	6	0	5	9	1	.429
1997 Rancho Cuca	.....California		OF	4	17	1	4	1	1	0	3	1	.235
1997 Louisville l-m	.........A.A.		OF	9	31	6	8	3	0	1	10	0	.258
1997 San Diego-St. Louis n	. .N.L.		OF	52	121	13	30	8	0	5	18	0	.248
Major League Totals	....	8 Yrs.		610	1883	260	457	90	3	91	292	13	.243

a Traded to San Diego Padres for pitcher Jose Melendez, December 9, 1992.
b On disabled list from April 26 to May 11, 1993.
c Traded to Houston Astros with outfielder Derek Bell, shortstop Ricky Gutierrez, infielder Craig Shipley and pitchers Doug Brocail and Pedro Martinez for third baseman Ken Caminiti, shortstop Andujar Cedeño, first baseman Roberto Petagine, pitcher Brian Williams and player to be named, December 28, 1994.
d On disabled list from May 17 to July 7, 1995.
e Traded to San Diego Padres for pitcher Jeff Tabaka and pitcher Rich Loiselle, July 19, 1995.
f Released by San Diego Padres, November 20, 1995.
g Signed by Detroit Tigers, December 7, 1995.
h Traded to Oakland Athletics for infielder Fausto Cruz and pitcher Ramon Fermin, March 22, 1996.
i Designated for assignment by Oakland Athletics, June 24, 1996.
j Outrighted by Oakland Athletics, August 30, 1996.
k Signed with San Diego Padres organization, January 17, 1997,
l Traded to St. Louis Cardinals with infielder Scott Livingstone and pitcher Fernando Valenzuela for pitcher Danny Jackson, pitcher Rich Batchelor and outfielder Mark Sweeney, June 14, 1997.
m On disabled list from May 8 to July 13 and August 4 to August 25, 1997.
n Filed for free agency, October 28, 1997.

POLCOVICH, KEVIN MICHAEL

Born, Auburn, New York, June 28, 1970.
Bats Right. Throws Right. Height, 5 feet, 9 inches. Weight, 170 pounds.

Year	Club	Lea	Pos	G	AB	R	H	2B	3B	HR	RBI	SB	Avg
1992 Carolina	.....Southern		SS	13	35	1	6	0	0	0	1	0	.171
1992 Augusta	.......So. Atl.		SS-2B-3B	46	153	24	40	6	2	0	10	7	.261
1993 Augusta	.......So. Atl.		SS-2B	14	48	9	13	2	0	0	4	2	.271
1993 Carolina	.....Southern		2B-SS	4	11	1	3	0	0	0	1	0	.273
1993 Salem	.......Carolina	SS-2B-3B-OF		94	282	44	72	10	3	1	25	13	.255
1994 Carolina	.....Southern		SS	125	406	46	95	14	2	2	33	9	.234
1995 Carolina	.....Southern		SS	64	221	27	70	8	0	3	18	10	.317
1995 Calgary	.........P.C.		SS	62	213	31	60	8	1	3	27	5	.282
1996 Calgary	.........P.C.		SS-2B	104	336	53	92	21	3	1	46	7	.274
1997 Carolina	.....Southern		3B-2B-SS	17	50	13	16	5	0	3	7	4	.320
1997 Calgary	.........P.C.		SS	17	62	7	19	4	0	1	9	0	.306
1997 Pittsburgh a	.......N.L.		SS-2B-3B	84	245	37	67	16	1	4	21	2	.273

a On disabled list from August 30 to September 15, 1997.

POLONIA (ALMONTE), LUIS ANDREW

Born, Santiago City, Dominican Republic, October 12, 1964.
Bats Left. Throws Left. Height, 5 feet, 8 inches. Weight, 150 pounds.

Year	Club	Lea	Pos	G	AB	R	H	2B	3B	HR	RBI	SB	Avg
1984 Madison	Midwest		OF	135	*528	103	*162	21	10	8	64	55	.307
1985 Huntsville	Southern		OF	130	515	82	149	15	*18	2	36	39	.289
1986 Tacoma	P.C.		OF	134	*549	98	*165	20	4	3	63	56	.301
1987 Tacoma	P.C.		OF	14	56	18	18	1	2	0	8	4	.321
1987 Oakland	A.L.		OF	125	435	78	125	16	10	4	49	29	.287
1988 Tacoma	P.C.		OF	65	254	58	85	13	5	2	27	31	.335
1988 Oakland	A.L.		OF	84	288	51	84	11	4	2	27	24	.292
1989 Oakland-New York a	A.L.		OF	125	433	70	130	17	6	3	46	22	.300
1990 New York-California b	A.L.		OF	120	403	52	135	7	9	2	35	21	.335
1991 California	A.L.		OF	150	604	92	179	28	8	2	50	48	.296
1992 California	A.L.		OF	149	577	83	165	17	4	0	35	51	.286
1993 California c	A.L.		OF	152	576	75	156	17	6	1	32	55	.271
1994 New York	A.L.		OF	95	350	62	109	21	6	1	36	20	.311
1995 New York	A.L.		OF	67	238	37	62	9	3	2	15	10	.261
1995 Atlanta d-e-f	N.L.		OF	28	53	6	14	7	0	0	2	3	.264
1996 Rochester g-h	Int.		OF	13	50	9	12	2	0	0	3	5	.240
1996 Baltimore i-j	A.L.		OF	58	175	25	42	4	1	2	14	8	.240
1996 Atlanta k-l	N.L.		OF	22	31	3	13	0	0	0	2	1	.419
1997 Mexico City Tigers m	Mex.		OF	105	408	105	154	29	5	7	59	48	.377
Major League Totals			10 Yrs.	1175	4163	634	1214	154	57	19	343	292	.292
Division Series													
1995 Atlanta	N.L.		PH	3	3	0	1	0	0	0	2	1	.333
1996 Atlanta	N.L.		PH	2	2	0	0	0	0	0	0	0	.000
Division Series Totals				5	5	0	1	0	0	0	2	1	.200
Championship Series													
1988 Oakland	A.L.		OF	3	5	0	2	0	0	0	0	0	.400
1995 Atlanta	N.L.		OF	3	2	0	1	0	0	0	1	0	.500
1996 Atlanta	N.L.		PH	3	3	0	0	0	0	0	0	0	.000
Championship Series Totals				9	10	0	3	0	0	0	1	0	.300
World Series Record													
1988 Oakland	A.L.		OF	3	9	1	1	0	0	0	0	0	.111
1995 Atlanta	N.L.		OF	6	14	3	4	1	0	1	4	1	.286
1996 Atlanta	N.L.		PH	6	5	0	0	0	0	0	0	0	.000
World Series Totals				15	28	4	5	1	0	1	4	1	.179

a Traded to New York Yankees with pitchers Eric Plunk and Greg Cadaret for outfielder Rickey Henderson, June 21, 1989.
b Traded to California Angels for outfielder Claudell Washington and pitcher Rich Monteleone, April 29, 1990.
c Filed for free agency, November 2; signed with New York Yankees, December 20, 1993.
d Designated for assignment by New York Yankees, August 4, 1995.
e Traded to Atlanta Braves for outfielder Troy Hughes, August 11, 1995.
f Filed for free agency, November 12, 1995.
g Signed with Seattle Mariners organization, February 1, 1996.
h Released by Seattle Mariners, March 26, 1996.
i Signed with Baltimore Orioles organization, April 19, 1996.
j Designated for assignment by Baltimore Orioles, August 2, 1996.
k Signed with Atlanta Braves, August 16, 1996.
l Filed for free agency, November 18, 1996.
m Signed with Tampa Bay Devil Rays, February 1, 1997.

POSADA, JORGE RAFAEL

Year	Club	Lea	Pos	G	AB	R	H	2B	3B	HR	RBI	SB	Avg
1991 Oneonta	N.Y.-Penn		2B-C	71	217	34	51	5	5	4	33	6	.235
1992 Greensboro	So. Atl.		DH-C-3B	101	339	60	94	22	4	12	58	11	.277
1993 Pr William	Carolina		C-3B	118	410	71	106	27	2	17	61	17	.259
1993 Albany	Eastern		C	7	25	3	7	0	0	0	0	0	.280
1994 Columbus	Int.		C-OF	92	313	46	75	13	3	11	48	5	.240
1995 Columbus	Int.		C	108	368	60	94	32	5	8	51	4	.255
1995 New York	A.L.		C	1	0	0	0	0	0	0	0	0	.000
1996 Columbus	Int.		C-OF	106	354	76	96	22	6	11	62	3	.271
1996 New York	A.L.		C	8	14	1	1	0	0	0	0	0	.071
1997 New York	A.L.		C	60	188	29	47	12	0	6	25	1	.250
Major League Totals			3 Yrs.	69	202	30	48	12	0	6	25	1	.238
Division Series													
1995 New York	A.L.		C	1	0	1	0	0	0	0	0	0	.000
1997 New York	A.L.		C	2	2	0	0	0	0	0	0	0	.000
Division Series Totals				3	2	1	0	0	0	0	0	0	.000

POWELL, LE JON DANTE
Born, Long Beach, California, August 25, 1973.
Bats Right. Throws Right. Height, 6 feet, 2 inches. Weight, 185 pounds.

Year	Club	Lea	Pos	G	AB	R	H	2B	3B	HR	RBI	SB	Avg
1994 Everett	....	Northwest	OF	41	165	31	51	15	1	5	25	27	.309
1994 San Jose		California	OF	1	4	0	2	0	1	0	0	0	.500
1995 San Jose	....	California	OF	135	505	74	125	23	8	10	70	43	.248
1996 Shreveport	....	Texas	OF	135	508	92	142	27	2	21	78	43	.280
1996 Phoenix	....	P.C.	OF	2	8	0	2	0	1	0	0	0	.250
1997 Phoenix	....	P.C.	OF	108	452	91	109	24	4	11	42	34	.241
1997 San Francisco	....	N.L.	OF	27	39	8	12	1	0	1	3	1	.308
Division Series													
1997 San Francisco	....	N.L.	OF	1	0	0	0	0	0	0	0	0	.000

POZO, ARQUIMEDEZ
Born, Santo Domingo, Dominican Republic, August 24, 1973.
Bats Right. Throws Right. Height, 5 feet, 10 inches. Weight, 160 pounds.

Year	Club	Lea	Pos	G	AB	R	H	2B	3B	HR	RBI	SB	Avg
1992 San Bernardino	...	California	2B	54	199	33	52	8	4	3	19	13	.261
1992 Bellingham	......	Northwest	2B	39	149	37	48	12	0	7	21	9	.322
1993 Riverside	....	California	2B	127	515	98	176	44	6	13	83	10	.342
1994 Jacksonville	......	Southern	2B	119	447	70	129	31	4	14	54	11	.289
1995 Tacoma	....	P.C.	2B-3B	122	450	57	135	19	6	10	62	3	.300
1995 Seattle	....	A.L.	2B	1	1	0	0	0	0	0	0	0	.000
1996 Tacoma	....	P.C.	3B-2B	95	365	55	102	12	5	15	64	3	.279
1996 Pawtucket	....	Int.	3B	11	37	6	9	1	0	1	3	0	.243
1996 Boston a	....	A.L.	2B-3B	21	58	4	10	3	1	1	11	1	.172
1997 Pawtucket	....	Int.	3B-2B	101	377	61	107	18	1	22	70	4	.284
1997 Boston	....	A.L.	3B	4	15	0	4	1	0	0	3	0	.267
Major League Totals	....	3 Yrs.		26	74	4	14	4	1	1	14	1	.189

a Traded to Boston Red Sox for infielder Jeff Manto, July 23, 1996.

PRATT, TODD ALAN
Born, Bellevue, Nebraska, February 9, 1967.
Bats Right. Throw Right. Height, 6 feet, 3 inches. Weight, 228 pounds.

Year	Club	Lea	Pos	G	AB	R	H	2B	3B	HR	RBI	SB	Avg
1985 Elmira	....	N.Y.-Penn.	C	39	119	7	16	1	1	0	5	0	.134
1986 Greensboro	....	So. Atl.	C-1B	107	348	63	84	16	0	12	56	0	.241
1987 Winter Haven	....	Fla. St.	C-1B-OF	118	407	57	105	22	0	12	65	0	.258
1988 New Britain	....	Eastern	C-1B	124	395	41	89	15	2	8	49	1	.225
1989 New Britain	....	Eastern	C-1B	109	338	30	77	17	1	2	35	1	.228
1990 New Britain	....	Eastern	DH-C-1B	70	195	15	45	14	1	2	22	0	.231
1991 Pawtucket a-b	....	Int.	C-1B	68	219	27	64	16	0	11	41	0	.292
1992 Reading	....	Eastern	DH-C-1B	41	132	20	44	6	1	6	26	2	.333
1992 Scranton-WB	....	Int.	C-1B	41	125	20	40	9	1	7	28	1	.320
1992 Philadelphia	....	N.L.	C	16	46	6	13	1	0	2	10	0	.283
1993 Scranton-WB	....	Int.	C	3	9	1	2	1	0	0	1	0	.222
1993 Philadelphia	....	N.L.	C	33	87	8	25	6	0	5	13	0	.287
1994 Philadelphia	....	N.L.	C	28	102	10	20	6	1	2	9	0	.196
1995 Chicago c	....	N.L.	C	25	60	3	8	2	0	0	4	0	.133
1995 Iowa	....	A.A.	C-1B	23	58	3	19	1	0	0	5	0	.328
1996 Seattle d-e-f		A.L.			(Did Not Play in Organized Baseball)									
1997 Norfolk	....	Int.	C	59	206	42	62	8	3	9	34	1	.301
1997 New York	....	N.L.	C	39	106	12	30	6	0	2	19	0	.283
Major League Totals	....	5 Yrs.		141	401	39	96	21	1	11	55	0	.239

a On disabled list from July 30 to end of 1991 season.
b Selected by Philadelphia Phillies from Boston Red Sox organization in Rule V draft, December 9, 1991.
c Signed with Chicago Cubs as a free agent, April 8, 1995.
d Signed with Seattle Mariners as a free agent, January 24, 1996.
e Released by Seattle Mariners, March 26, 1996.
f Signed by New York Mets as a free agent, December 23, 1996.

PRIDE, CURTIS JOHN
Born, Washington, D.C., December 17, 1968.
Bats Left. Throws Right. Height, 6 feet. Weight, 200 pounds.

Year	Club	Lea	Pos	G	AB	R	H	2B	3B	HR	RBI	SB	Avg
1986 Kingsport	....	Appal.	OF	27	46	5	5	0	0	1	4	5	.109
1987 Kingsport	....	Appal.	OF	31	104	22	25	4	0	1	9	14	.240
1988 Kingsport	....	Appal.	OF	70	268	59	76	13	1	8	27	23	.284

Year Club	Lea	Pos	G	AB	R	H	2B	3B	HR	RBI	SB	Avg
1989 Pittsfield ........N.Y.-Penn		OF	55	212	35	55	7	3	6	23	9	.259
1990 Columbia ....So. Atl.		OF	53	191	38	51	4	4	6	25	11	.267
1991 St. Lucie ....Fla. St.		OF	116	392	57	102	21	7	9	37	24	.260
1992 Binghamton ....Eastern		OF	118	388	54	88	15	3	10	42	14	.227
1993 Harrisburg ....Eastern		OF	50	180	51	64	6	3	15	39	21	.356
1993 Ottawa ....Int.		OF	69	262	55	79	11	4	6	22	29	.302
1993 Montreal ............N.L.		OF	10	9	3	4	1	1	1	5	1	.444
1994 West Palm Beach ....Fla. St.		OF	3	8	5	6	1	0	1	3	2	.750
1994 Ottawa ....Int.		OF	82	300	56	77	16	4	9	32	22	.257
1995 Ottawa ....Int.		OF	42	154	25	43	8	3	4	24	8	.279
1995 Montreal a ..........N.L.		OF	48	63	10	11	1	0	_ 0	2	3	.175
1996 Toledo b ....Int.		DH-OF	9	26	4	6	1	0	1	2	4	.231
1996 Detroit ..............A.L.		OF	95	267	52	80	17	5	10	31	11	.300
1997 Pawtucket ....Int.		OF	1	3	0	0	0	0	0	0	0	.000
1997 Detroit-Boston c-d-e ....A.L.		OF-DH	81	164	22	35	4	4	3	20	6	.213
Major League Totals	4 Yrs.		234	503	87	130	23	10	14	58	21	.258

a Outrighted by Montreal Expos, October 13, 1995.
b On disabled list from April 13 to May 10, 1996.
c Released by Detroit Tigers, August 21, 1997.
d Signed with Boston Red Sox organization, August 30, 1997.
e Outrighted by Boston Red Sox, October 15, 1997.

PRINCE, THOMAS ALBERT
Born, Kankakee, Illinois, August 13, 1964.
Bats Right. Throws Right. Height, 5 feet, 11 inches. Weight, 185 pounds.

Year Club	Lea	Pos	G	AB	R	H	2B	3B	HR	RBI	SB	Avg
1984 Watertown .......N.Y.-Penn		C	23	69	6	14	3	0	2	13	0	.203
1984 Bradenton Pirates ....Gulf C.		C	18	48	4	11	0	0	1	6	1	.229
1985 Macon ....So. Atl.		C	124	360	60	75	20	1	10	42	13	.208
1986 Prince William .....Carolina		C	121	395	59	100	34	1	10	47	4	.253
1987 Harrisburg ....Eastern		C	113	365	41	112	23	2	6	54	6	.307
1987 Pittsburgh ............N.L.		C	4	9	1	2	1	0	1	2	0	.222
1988 Buffalo .............A.A.		C	86	304	35	79	16	0	14	42	3	.260
1988 Pittsburgh ...........N.L.		C	29	74	3	13	2	0	0	6	0	.176
1989 Buffalo .............A.A.		C	65	183	21	37	8	1	6	33	2	.202
1989 Pittsburgh ...........N.L.		C	21	52	1	7	4	0	0	5	1	.135
1990 Buffalo .............A.A.		C	94	284	38	64	13	0	7	37	4	.225
1990 Pittsburgh ...........N.L.		C	4	10	1	1	0	0	0	0	0	.000
1991 Buffalo .............A.A.		C	80	221	29	46	8	3	6	32	3	.208
1991 Pittsburgh a ..........N.L.		C-1B	26	34	4	9	3	0	1	2	0	.265
1992 Buffalo .............A.A.		C-3B-OF	75	244	34	64	17	0	9	35	3	.262
1992 Pittsburgh ...........N.L.		C-3B	27	44	1	4	2	0	0	5	1	.091
1993 Pittsburgh b ..........N.L.		C	66	179	14	35	14	0	2	24	1	.196
1994 Albuquerque .........P.C.		C	103	330	61	94	31	2	20	54	2	.285
1994 Los Angeles .........N.L.		C	3	6	2	2	0	0	0	1	0	.333
1995 Albuquerque .........P.C.		C	61	192	30	61	15	0	7	36	0	.318
1995 Los Angeles c-d-e ......N.L.		C	18	40	3	8	2	1	1	4	0	.200
1996 Albuquerque .........P.C.		C-3B-OF	32	95	24	39	5	1	7	22	0	.411
1996 Los Angeles ..........N.L.		C	40	64	6	19	6	0	1	11	0	.297
1997 Los Angeles ..........N.L.		C	47	100	17	22	5	0	3	14	0	.220
Major League Totals	11 Yrs.		285	612	53	122	39	1	9	74	3	.199

a On disabled list from August 12 to September 1, 1991.
b Refused assignment to minor leagues and became free agent, November 1; signed with Los Angeles Dodgers organization, November 8, 1993.
c Released, December 5, 1994; re-signed with Los Angeles Dodgers organization, January 5, 1995.
d On disabled list from June 4 to July 10, 1995.
e Filed for free agency, October 17, 1995.

PULLIAM, HARVEY JEROME, JR.
Born, San Francisco, California, October 20, 1967.
Bats Right. Throws Right. Height, 6 feet. Weight, 218 pounds.

Year Club	Lea	Pos	G	AB	R	H	2B	3B	HR	RBI	SB	Avg
1986 Royals ....Gulf Coast		OF	48	168	14	35	3	0	4	23	3	.208
1987 Appleton ....Midwest		OF	110	395	54	109	20	1	9	55	21	.276
1988 Baseball Cy ....Fla. St.		OF	132	457	56	111	19	4	4	42	21	.243
1989 Omaha ..............A.A.		OF	7	22	3	4	2	0	0	2	0	.182
1989 Memphis ....Southern		OF	116	417	67	121	28	8	10	67	5	.290

Year	Club	Lea	Pos	G	AB	R	H	2B	3B	HR	RBI	SB	Avg
1990 Omaha	.............A.A.		OF	123	436	72	117	18	5	16	72	9	.268
1991 Omaha	.............A.A.		OF	104	346	35	89	18	2	6	39	2	.257
1991 Kansas City	..........A.L.		OF	18	33	4	9	1	0	3	4	0	.273
1992 Kansas City	..........A.L.		OF	4	5	2	1	1	0	0	0	0	.200
1992 Kansas City	..........A.A.		OF	100	359	55	97	12	2	16	60	4	.270
1993 Kansas City	..........A.L.		OF	27	62	7	16	5	0	1	6	0	.258
1993 Omaha	.............A.A.		OF	54	208	28	55	10	0	5	26	1	.264
1994 Las Vegas a	.........P.C.		OF	95	314	48	72	10	0	20	53	0	.229
1995 Colo Sprngs b	........P.C.		OF	115	407	90	133	30	6	25	91	6	.327
1995 Colorado	.............N.L.		OF	5	5	1	2	1	0	1	3	0	.400
1996 Colorado	.............N.L.		OF	10	15	2	2	0	0	0	0	0	.133
1996 Colo Sprngs	..........P.C.		OF	79	283	46	78	13	1	10	58	2	.276
1997 Colo Sprngs	..........P.C.		OF	40	137	44	55	10	2	12	43	1	.401
1997 Colorado c	...........N.L.		OF	59	67	15	19	3	0	3	9	0	.284
Major League Totals	....	6 Yrs.		123	187	31	49	11	0	8	22	0	.262

a Signed as free agent with San Diego Padres, February 3, 1994.
b Signed as free agent with Colorado Rockies, January 31, 1995.
c Traded to Arizona Diamondbacks for pitcher Chuck McElroy, November 19, 1997.

RAINES, TIMOTHY (TIM)

Born, Sanford, Florida, September 16, 1959.
Bats Both. Throws Right. Height, 5 feet, 8 inches. Weight, 186 pounds.

Year	Club	Lea	Pos	G	AB	R	H	2B	3B	HR	RBI	SB	Avg
1977 Sarasota Expos	......Gulf C.		2B-3B-OF	49	161	28	45	6	2	0	21	29	.280
1978 W. Palm Beach a	....Fla. St.		2B-SS	100	359	67	103	10	0	0	23	57	.287
1979 Memphis	.........Southern		2B	*145	552	*104	160	25	10	5	50	59	.290
1979 Montreal	.............N.L.		PR	6	0	3	0	0	0	0	0	2	.000
1980 Montreal	.............N.L.		2B-OF	15	20	5	1	0	0	0	0	5	.050
1980 Denver	.............A.A.		2B	108	429	105	152	23	*11	6	64	77	*.354
1981 Montreal	.............N.L.		OF-2B	88	313	61	95	13	7	5	37	*71	.304
1982 Montreal	.............N.L.		OF-2B	156	647	90	179	32	8	4	43	*78	.277
1983 Montreal	.............N.L.		OF-2B	156	615	*133	183	32	8	11	71	*90	.298
1984 Montreal	.............N.L.		OF-2B	160	622	106	192	*38	9	8	60	75	.309
1985 Montreal	.............N.L.		OF	150	575	115	184	30	13	11	41	70	.320
1986 Montreal b	.............N.L.		OF	151	580	91	194	35	10	9	62	70	*.334
1987 Montreal	.............N.L.		OF	139	530	*123	175	34	8	18	68	50	.330
1988 Montreal c	.............N.L.		OF	109	429	66	116	19	7	12	48	33	.270
1989 Montreal	.............N.L.		OF	145	517	76	148	29	6	9	60	41	.286
1990 Montreal d-e	.............N.L.		OF	130	457	65	131	11	5	9	62	49	.287
1991 Chicago	.............A.L.		OF	155	609	102	163	20	6	5	50	51	.268
1992 Chicago	.............A.L.		OF	144	551	102	162	22	9	7	54	45	.294
1993 Nashville	.............A.A.		OF	3	11	3	5	1	0	0	2	2	.455
1993 Chicago f-g	.............A.L.		OF	115	415	75	127	16	4	16	54	21	.306
1994 Chicago	.............A.L.		OF	101	384	80	102	15	5	10	52	13	.266
1995 Chicago h	.............A.L.		OF	133	502	81	143	25	4	12	67	13	.285
1996 Yankees	.......Gulf Coast		DH	1	5	2	3	2	0	0	3	0	.600
1996 Columbus	...........Int.		OF	4	12	3	3	1	0	0	0	1	.250
1996 Tampa	............Fla. St.		OF	9	36	9	13	2	0	2	11	0	.361
1996 Norwich	.......Eastern		OF	8	27	8	5	1	0	1	1	2	.185
1996 New York i	.............A.L.		OF	59	201	45	57	10	0	9	33	10	.284
1997 Yankees	.......Gulf Coast		OF	1	4	0	1	0	0	0	2	0	.250
1997 Norwich	..........Eastern		OF	2	7	0	2	1	0	0	2	0	.286
1997 Tampa	............Fla. St.		OF	11	35	8	12	0	0	2	5	1	.343
1997 Columbus	.............Int.		OF	4	13	1	2	0	0	0	0	0	.154
1997 New York j-k-l	.........A.L.		OF	74	271	56	87	20	2	4	38	8	.321
Major League Totals	....	19 Yrs.		2186	8238	1475	2439	401	111	159	900	795	.296
Division Series													
1996 New York	.............A.L.		OF	4	16	3	4	0	0	0	0	0	.250
1997 New York	...........A.L.		OF-DH	5	19	4	4	0	0	1	3	2	.211
Division Series Totals	....			9	35	7	8	0	0	1	3	2	.229
Championship Series													
1981 Montreal	.............N.L.		OF	5	21	1	5	2	0	0	1	0	.238
1993 Chicago	.............A.L.		OF	6	27	5	12	3	0	0	1	1	.444
1996 New York	.............A.L.		OF	5	15	2	4	1	0	0	0	0	.267
Championship Series Totals	....			16	63	8	21	6	0	0	2	1	.333
World Series													
1996 New York	.............A.L.		OF	4	14	2	3	0	0	0	0	0	.214

a On disabled list from May 23 to June 5, 1978.
b Granted free agency, January 8; re-signed with Montreal Expos, May 1, 1987.

c On disabled list from June 24 to July 9, 1988.
d On disabled list from June 25 to July 10, 1990.
e Traded to Chicago White Sox with pitcher Jeff Carter and player to be named for outfielder Ivan Calderon and pitcher Barry Jones, December 23, 1990; Chicago acquired pitcher Mario Brito to complete trade, February 15, 1991.
f On disabled list from April 9 to May 22, 1993.
g Filed for free agency, November 1; re-signed with Chicago White Sox, December 22, 1993.
h Traded to New York Yankees for future considerations, December 28, 1995.
i On disabled list from April 1 to April 16 and May 22 to August 11, 1996.
j On disabled list from April 1 to April 11 and June 2 to August 12, 1997.
k Filed for free agency, October 29, 1997.
l Re-signed with New York Yankees, December 21, 1997.

RAMIREZ, MANUEL ARISTIDES
Born, Brooklyn, New York, May 30, 1972.
Bats Right. Throws Right. Height, 6 feet. Weight, 190 pounds.

Year	Club	Lea	Pos	G	AB	R	H	2B	3B	HR	RBI	SB	Avg
1991 Burlington	Appal.	OF	59	215	44	70	11	4	19	63	7	.326
1992 Kinston a	Carolina	OF	81	291	52	81	18	4	13	63	1	.278
1993 Canton	Eastern	OF	89	344	67	117	32	0	17	79	2	.340
1993 Charlotte	Int.	OF	40	145	38	46	12	0	14	36	1	.317
1993 Cleveland	A.L.	DH-OF	22	53	5	9	1	0	2	5	0	.170
1994 Cleveland	A.L.	OF	91	290	51	78	22	0	17	60	4	.269
1995 Cleveland	A.L.	OF	137	484	85	149	26	1	31	107	6	.308
1996 Cleveland	A.L.	OF	152	550	94	170	45	3	33	112	8	.309
1997 Cleveland	A.L.	OF	150	561	99	184	40	0	26	88	2	.328
Major League Totals		5 Yrs.	552	1938	334	590	134	4	109	372	20	.304
Division Series												
1995 Cleveland	A.L.	OF	3	12	1	0	0	0	0	0	0	.000
1996 Cleveland	A.L.	OF	4	16	4	6	2	0	2	2	0	.375
1997 Cleveland	A.L.	OF	5	21	2	3	1	0	0	3	0	.143
Division Series Totals			12	49	7	9	3	0	2	5	0	.184
Championship Series												
1995 Cleveland	A.L.	OF	6	21	2	6	0	0	2	2	0	.286
1997 Cleveland	A.L.	OF	6	21	3	6	1	0	2	3	0	.286
Championship Series Totals			12	42	5	12	1	0	4	5	0	.286
World Series Record												
1995 Cleveland	A.L.	OF	6	18	2	4	0	0	1	2	1	.222
1997 Cleveland	A.L.	OF	7	26	3	4	0	0	2	6	0	.154
World Series Totals			13	44	5	8	0	0	3	8	1	.182

a On disabled list from July 10 to end of 1992 season.

RANDA, JOSEPH GREGORY (JOE)
Born, Milwaukee, Wisconsin, December 18, 1962.
Bats Right. Throws Right. Height, 5 feet, 11 inches. Weight, 190 pounds.

Year	Club	Lea	Pos	G	AB	R	H	2B	3B	HR	RBI	SB	Avg
1991 Eugene	Northwest	3B	72	275	53	93	20	2	11	59	6	.338
1992 Appleton	Midwest	3B	72	266	55	80	13	0	5	43	6	.301
1992 Baseball City	Fla. St.	3B-SS	51	189	22	52	7	0	1	12	4	.275
1993 Memphis	Southern	3B	131	505	74	149	31	5	11	72	8	.295
1994 Omaha	A.A.	3B	127	455	65	125	27	2	10	51	5	.275
1995 Omaha	A.A.	3B	64	233	33	64	10	2	8	33	2	.275
1995 Kansas City	A.L.	3B-2B	34	70	6	12	2	0	1	5	0	.171
1996 Omaha a	A.A.	3B	3	9	1	1	0	1	0	0	0	.111
1996 Kansas City b	A.L.	3B-2B-1B	110	337	36	102	24	1	6	47	13	.303
1997 Calgary	P.C.	3B	3	11	4	4	1	0	1	4	0	.364
1997 Pittsburgh c-d-e	N.L.	3B-2B	126	443	58	134	27	9	7	60	4	.302
Major League Totals		3 Yrs.	270	850	100	248	53	10	14	112	17	.292

a On disabled list from May 5 to May 27, 1996.
b Traded to Pittsburgh Pirates with pitchers Jeff Granger, Jeff Martin and Jeff Wallace for infielders Jay Bell and Jeff King, December 14, 1996.
c On disabled list from June 28 to July 27, 1997.
d Selected on expansion draft by Arizona Diamondbacks, November 18, 1997.
e Traded to Detroit Tigers with infielder Gabe Alvarez and pitcher Matt Drews for infielder Travis Fryman, November 19, 1997.

REBOULET, JEFFREY ALLEN

Born, Dayton, Ohio, April 30, 1964.
Bats Right. Throws Right. Height, 6 feet. Weight, 169 pounds.

Year	Club	Lea	Pos	G	AB	R	H	2B	3B	HR	RBI	SB	Avg
1986	Visalia	California	SS	72	254	54	73	13	1	0	29	14	.287
1987	Orlando	Southern	SS-2B	129	422	52	108	15	1	1	35	9	.256
1988	Orlando	Southern	SS	125	439	57	112	24	2	4	41	18	.255
1988	Portland	P.C.	2B-SS	4	12	0	1	0	0	0	1	0	.083
1989	Portland	P.C.	SS-2B	26	65	9	16	1	0	0	3	2	.246
1989	Orlando	Southern	SS-2B	81	291	43	63	5	1	0	26	11	.216
1990	Orlando	Southern	2B-SS-3B	97	287	43	66	12	2	2	28	10	.230
1991	Portland	P.C.	SS-2B	134	391	50	97	27	3	3	46	2	.248
1992	Portland	P.C.	SS-3B	48	161	21	46	11	1	2	21	3	.286
1992	Minnesota	A.L.	SS-3B-2B-OF	58	137	15	26	7	1	1	16	3	.190
1993	Minnesota	A.L.	SS-3B-2B-OF	109	240	33	62	8	0	1	15	5	.258
1994	Minnesota	A.L.	SS-2B-1B-3B	74	189	28	49	11	1	3	23	0	.259
1995	Minnesota	A.L.	SS-3B-1B-2B	87	216	39	63	11	0	4	23	1	.292
1996	Minnesota a	A.L.	SS-3B-2B-1B	107	234	20	52	9	0	0	23	4	.222
1997	Baltimore b	A.L.	2B-SS-3B-OF	99	228	26	54	9	0	4	27	3	.237
Major League Totals			6 Yrs.	549	1244	161	306	55	2	13	127	16	.246
Division Series													
1997	Baltimore	A.L.	2B	2	5	1	1	0	0	1	1	0	.200
Championship Series													
1997	Baltimore	A.L.	SS	1	2	1	0	0	0	0	0	0	.000

a Filed for free agency, October 4, 1996.
b Signed with Baltimore Orioles organization, January 30, 1997.

REED, JEFFREY SCOTT

Born, Joliet, Illinois, November 12, 1962.
Bats Left. Throws Right. Height, 6 feet, 2 inches. Weight, 190 pounds.

Year	Club	Lea	Pos	G	AB	R	H	2B	3B	HR	RBI	SB	Avg
1980	Elizabethton	Appal.	C	65	225	39	64	15	1	1	20	2	.284
1981	Wisconsin Rapids	Midwest	C	106	312	63	73	12	1	4	34	4	.234
1981	Orlando	Southern	C	3	4	0	1	0	0	0	0	0	.250
1982	Visalia	California	C	125	395	69	130	19	2	5	54	1	.329
1983	Orlando	Southern	C	118	379	52	100	16	5	6	45	2	.264
1983	Toledo	Int.	C	14	41	5	7	1	1	0	3	4	.171
1984	Minnesota	A.L.	C	18	21	3	3	3	0	0	1	1	.143
1984	Toledo	Int.	C	94	301	30	80	16	3	3	35	1	.266
1985	Toledo	Int.	C	122	404	53	100	15	3	5	36	1	.248
1985	Minnesota	A.L.	C	7	10	2	2	0	0	0	0	0	.200
1986	Minnesota	A.L.	C	68	165	13	39	6	1	2	9	1	.236
1986	Toledo a	Int.	C	25	71	10	22	5	3	1	14	0	.310
1987	Montreal b	N.L.	C	75	207	15	44	11	0	1	21	0	.213
1987	Indianapolis	A.A.	C	5	17	0	3	0	0	0	0	0	.176
1988	Indianapolis	A.A.	C	8	22	1	7	3	0	0	1	0	.318
1988	Montreal-Cincinnati c	N.L.	C	92	265	20	60	9	2	1	16	1	.226
1989	Cincinnati	N.L.	C	102	287	16	64	11	0	3	23	0	.223
1990	Cincinnati	N.L.	C	72	175	12	44	8	1	3	16	0	.251
1991	Cincinnati d	N.L.	C	91	270	20	72	15	2	3	31	0	.267
1992	Nashville	A.A.	C	14	25	1	6	1	0	1	2	0	.240
1992	Cincinnati e-f	N.L.	C	15	25	2	4	0	0	0	2	0	.160
1993	San Jose	California	C	4	10	2	5	1	0	0	2	0	.500
1993	San Francisco g	N.L.	C	66	119	10	31	3	0	6	12	0	.261
1994	San Francisco	N.L.	C	50	103	11	18	3	0	1	7	0	.175
1995	San Francisco h-i	N.L.	C	66	113	12	30	2	0	0	9	0	.265
1996	Colorado	N.L.	C	116	341	34	97	20	1	8	37	2	.284
1997	Colorado j-k	N.L.	C	90	256	43	76	10	0	17	47	2	.297
Major League Totals			14 Yrs.	928	2357	213	584	101	7	45	231	6	.248
Championship Series													
1990	Cincinnati	N.L.	C	4	7	0	0	0	0	0	0	0	.000

a Traded by Minnesota Twins to Montreal Expos with pitchers Yorkis Perez and Al Cardwood for pitcher Jeff Reardon and catcher Tom Nieto, February 3, 1987.
b On disabled list from April 20 to May 25, 1987.
c Traded to Cincinnati Reds with outfielder Herm Winningham and pitcher Randy St. Claire for outfielder Tracy Jones and pitcher Pat Pacillo, July 13, 1988.
d On disabled list from July 1 to July 19, 1991.
e On disabled list from April 26 to September 1, 1992.
f Filed for free agency, October 27, 1992; signed with San Francisco Giants organization, January 18, 1993.
g On disabled list from June 30 to August 3, 1993.
h Filed for free agency, November 12, 1995.

i Signed with Colorado Rockies, December 18, 1995.
j Filed for free agency, October 27, 1997.
k Re-signed with Colorado Rockies, November 18, 1997.

REESE, CALVIN (POKEY)

Born, Columbia, South Carolina, June 10, 1973.
Bats Right. Throws Right. Height, 5 feet, 11 inches. Weight, 180 pounds.

Year	Club	Lea	Pos	G	AB	R	H	2B	3B	HR	RBI	SB	Avg
1991	Princeton	Appal.	SS-OF	62	231	30	55	8	3	3	27	10	.238
1992	Chston-Wv	So. Atl.	SS	106	380	50	102	19	3	6	53	19	.268
1993	Chattanooga	Southern	SS	102	345	35	73	17	4	3	37	8	.212
1994	Chattanooga	Southern	SS	134	484	77	130	23	4	12	49	21	.269
1995	Indianapols	A.A.	SS	89	343	51	82	21	1	10	46	8	.239
1996	Indianapols	A.A.	SS-3B	79	280	26	65	16	0	1	23	5	.232
1997	Indianapols	A.A.	SS-2B	17	72	12	17	7	0	4	11	4	.236
1997	Cincinnati	N.L.	SS-2B-3B	128	397	48	87	15	0	4	26	25	.219

RENTERIA, EDGAR ENRIQUE

Born, Barranquilla, Colombia, August 7, 1975.
Bats Right. Throws Right. Height, 6 feet, 1 inch. Weight, 172 pounds.

Year	Club	Lea	Pos	G	AB	R	H	2B	3B	HR	RBI	SB	Avg
1992	Marlins	Gulf Coast	SS	43	163	25	47	8	1	0	9	10	.288
1993	Kane County	Midwest	SS	116	384	40	78	8	0	1	35	7	.203
1994	Brevard Cty	Fla. St.	SS	128	439	46	111	15	1	0	36	6	.253
1995	Portland	Eastern	SS	135	508	70	147	15	7	7	68	30	.289
1996	Charlotte	Int.	SS	35	132	17	37	8	0	2	16	10	.280
1996	Florida a	N.L.	SS	106	431	68	133	18	3	5	31	16	.309
1997	Florida	N.L.	SS	154	617	90	171	21	3	4	52	32	.277
Major League Totals			2 Yrs.	260	1048	158	304	39	6	9	83	48	.290
Division Series													
1997	Florida	N.L.	SS	3	13	1	2	0	0	0	1	0	.154
Championship Series													
1997	Florida	N.L.	SS	6	22	4	5	1	0	0	0	1	.227
World Series Record													
1997	Florida	N.L.	SS	7	31	3	9	2	0	0	3	0	.290

a On disabled list from June 24 to July 11, 1996

RIPKEN, CALVIN EDWIN JR.

Born, Havre de Grace, Maryland, August 24, 1960.
Bats Right. Throws Right. Height, 6 feet, 4 inches. Weight, 220 pounds.

Year	Club	Lea	Pos	G	AB	R	H	2B	3B	HR	RBI	SB	Avg
1978	Bluefield	Appal.	SS	63	239	27	63	7	1	0	24	1	.264
1979	Miami	Fla. St.	3B-SS-2B	105	393	51	119	*28	1	5	54	4	.303
1979	Charlotte	Southern	3B	17	61	6	11	0	1	3	8	1	.180
1980	Charlotte	Southern	2B-SS	*144	522	91	144	28	5	25	78	4	.276
1981	Rochester	Int.	3B-SS	114	437	74	126	31	4	23	75	0	.288
1981	Baltimore	A.L.	SS-3B	23	39	1	5	0	0	0	0	0	.128
1982	Baltimore a	A.L.	SS-3B	160	598	90	158	32	5	28	93	3	.264
1983	Baltimore b	A.L.	SS	*162	*663	*121	*211	*47	2	27	102	0	.318
1984	Baltimore	A.L.	SS	*162	641	103	195	37	7	27	86	2	.304
1985	Baltimore	A.L.	SS	161	642	116	181	32	5	26	110	2	.282
1986	Baltimore	A.L.	SS	162	627	98	177	35	1	25	81	4	.282
1987	Baltimore	A.L.	SS	*162	624	97	157	28	3	27	98	3	.252
1988	Baltimore	A.L.	SS	161	575	87	152	25	1	23	81	2	.264
1989	Baltimore	A.L.	SS	*162	646	80	166	30	0	21	93	3	.257
1990	Baltimore	A.L.	SS	161	600	78	150	28	4	21	84	3	.250
1991	Baltimore c	A.L.	SS	*162	650	99	210	46	5	34	114	6	.323
1992	Baltimore	A.L.	SS	*162	637	73	160	29	1	14	72	4	.251
1993	Baltimore	A.L.	SS	*162	*641	87	165	26	3	24	90	1	.257
1994	Baltimore	A.L.	SS	112	444	71	140	19	3	13	75	1	.315
1995	Baltimore	A.L.	SS	144	550	71	144	33	2	17	88	0	.262
1996	Baltimore	A.L.	SS-3B	*163	640	94	178	40	1	26	102	1	.278
1997	Baltimore	A.L.	3B-SS	162	615	79	166	30	0	17	84	1	.270
Major League Totals			17 Yrs.	2543	9832	1445	2715	517	43	370	1453	36	.276

150

Year	Club	Lea	Pos	G	AB	R	H	2B	3B	HR	RBI	SB	Avg
	Division Series												
1996 Baltimore	...........A.L.		SS	4	18	2	8	3	0	0	2	0	.444
1997 Baltimore	...........A.L.		3B	4	16	1	7	2	0	0	1	0	.438
Division Series Totals	....			8	34	3	15	5	0	0	3	0	.441
	Championship Series												
1983 Baltimore	...........A.L.		SS	4	15	5	6	2	0	0	1	0	.400
1996 Baltimore	...........A.L.		SS	5	20	1	5	1	0	0	0	0	.250
1997 Baltimore	...........A.L.		3B	6	23	3	8	2	0	1	3	0	.348
Championship Series Totals	....			15	58	9	19	5	0	1	4	0	.328
	World Series Record												
1983 Baltimore	...........A.L.		SS	5	18	2	3	0	0	0	1	0	.167

a Selected Rookie of the Year in American League for 1982.
b Selected Most Valuable Player in American League for 1983.
c Selected Most Valuable Player in American League for 1991.

RIPKEN, WILLIAM OLIVER

Born, Havre de Grace, Maryland, December 16, 1964.
Bats Right. Throws Right. Height, 6 feet, 1 inch. Weight, 187 pounds.

Year	Club	Lea	Pos	G	AB	R	H	2B	3B	HR	RBI	SB	Avg
1982 Bluefield	.......Appal.	SS-3B-2B	27	45	8	11	1	0	0	4	0	.244	
1983 Bluefield	.......Appal.	SS-3B	48	152	24	33	6	0	0	13	7	.217	
1984 Hagerstown a	....Carol.	SS-2B	115	409	48	94	15	3	2	40	3	.230	
1985 Charlotte	....Southern	SS	18	51	2	7	1	0	0	3	0	.137	
1985 Daytona Bch b	..Fla. St.	SS-3B-2B	67	222	23	51	11	0	0	18	7	.230	
1985 Hagerstown	....Carol.	3B-2B	14	47	9	12	0	1	0	0	0	.255	
1986 Charlotte	....Southern	2B	141	530	58	142	20	3	5	62	9	.268	
1987 Rochester	.........Int.	2B	74	238	32	68	15	0	0	11	7	.286	
1987 Baltimore	.........A.L.	2B	58	234	27	72	9	0	2	20	4	.308	
1988 Baltimore	.........A.L.	2B-3B	150	512	52	106	18	1	2	34	8	.207	
1989 Baltimore c	.......A.L.	2B	115	318	31	76	11	2	2	26	1	.239	
1990 Baltimore d	.......A.L.	2B	129	406	48	118	28	1	3	38	5	.291	
1991 Frederick	.....Carolina	2B	1	4	2	1	0	0	0	1	0	.250	
1991 Hagerstown	....Eastern	2B	1	5	1	3	0	0	0	0	1	.600	
1991 Baltimore e	.....A.L.	2B	104	287	24	62	11	1	0	14	0	.216	
1992 Baltimore f	.......A.L.	2B	111	330	35	76	15	0	4	36	2	.230	
1993 Texas g-h	.......A.L.	2B-SS-3B	50	132	12	25	4	0	0	11	0	.189	
1994 Texas i-j	.......A.L.	3B-2B-SS-1B	32	81	9	25	5	0	0	6	2	.309	
1995 Buffalo	..........A.A.	SS-2B	130	448	51	131	34	1	4	56	5	.292	
1995 Cleveland k-l	......A.L.	2B-3B	8	17	4	7	0	0	2	3	0	.412	
1996 Baltimore m-n	.....A.L.	3B-2B-1B	57	135	19	31	8	0	2	12	0	.230	
1997 Texas o-p	.......A.L.	SS-2B-3B-1B	71	203	18	56	9	1	3	24	0	.276	
Major League Totals	....	11 Yrs.	885	2655	279	654	118	6	20	224	22	.246	

a On disabled list from April 20 to May 3, 1984.
b On disabled list from June 23 to July 6, 1985.
c On disabled list from March 28 to April 14 and August 23 to September 7, 1989.
d On disabled list from August 5 to August 20, 1990.
e On disabled list from July 15 to August 15, 1991.
f Released, December 11, 1992; signed with Texas Rangers, February 1, 1993.
g On disabled list from May 12 to May 27 and June 21 to September 1, 1993.
h Refused assignment to minor leagues and became free agent, October 4; re-signed with Texas Rangers organization, December 16, 1993.
i On disabled list from May 10 to May 24 and July 16 to end of 1994 season.
j Refused assignment to minor leagues and became free agent, October 13, 1994.
k Signed with Cleveland Indians organization, March 22, 1995.
l Filed for free agency, November 12, 1995. Signed with Baltimore Orioles organization, December 23, 1995.
m Filed for free agency, October 29, 1996.
n Signed with Texas Rangers, December 10, 1996.
o On disabled list from June 18 to July 6 and July 23 to August 8, 1997.
p Filed for free agency, October 30, 1997.

RIVERA, RUBEN

Born, Chorrera, Panama, November 14, 1973.
Bats Right. Throws Right. Height, 6 feet, 3 inches. Weight, 200 pounds.

Year	Club	Lea	Pos	G	AB	R	H	2B	3B	HR	RBI	SB	Avg
1992 Yankees	........Gulf Coast	OF	53	194	37	53	10	3	1	20	21	.273	
1993 Oneonta	........N.Y.-Penn.	OF	55	199	45	55	7	6	13	47	12	.276	

Year	Club	Lea	Pos	G	AB	R	H	2B	3B	HR	RBI	SB	Avg
1994 Greensboro	So. Atl.	OF	105	400	83	115	24	3	28	81	36	.287
1994 Tampa	Fla. St.	OF	34	134	18	35	4	3	5	20	12	.261
1995 Norwich	Eastern	OF	71	256	49	75	16	8	9	39	16	.293
1995 Columbus	Int.	OF	48	174	37	47	8	2	15	35	8	.270
1995 New York	A.L.	OF	5	1	0	0	0	0	0	0	0	.000
1996 Columbus	Int.	OF	101	362	59	85	20	4	10	46	15	.235
1996 New York	A.L.	OF	46	88	17	25	6	1	2	16	6	.284
1997 Rancho Cuca	California	DH	6	23	6	4	1	0	1	3	1	.174
1997 Las Vegas	P.C.	DH-1B	12	48	6	12	5	1	1	6	1	.250
1997 San Diego a-b	N.L.	OF	17	20	2	5	1	0	0	1	2	.250
Major League Totals			3 Yrs.	68	109	19	30	7	1	2	17	8	.275
Division Series													
1996 New York	A.L.	OF	2	1	0	0	0	0	0	0	0	.000

a Traded to San Diego Padres with pitcher Rafael Medina and cash for pitcher Hideki Irabu, infielder Homer Bush and player to be named later, May 30, 1997. New York Yankees received outfielder Vernon Maxwell to complete trade, June 9, 1997.
b On disabled list from April 1 to August 13, 1997.

ROBERTS, LEON JOSEPH (BIP)
Born, Berkeley, California, October 27, 1963.
Bats Right. Throws Right. Height, 5 feet, 7 inches. Weight, 165 pounds.

Year	Club	Lea	Pos	G	AB	R	H	2B	3B	HR	RBI	SB	Avg
1982 Brad. Pirates	Gulf C.	2B	6	23	4	7	1	0	0	1	4	.304
1982 Greenwood	So. Atl.	2B	33	107	15	23	3	1	0	6	10	.215
1983 Greenwood	So. Atl.	2B	122	438	78	140	20	5	6	63	27	.320
1984 Prince William	Carolina	2B	134	498	81	*150	25	5	8	77	50	.301
1985 Nashua a	Eastern	2B	105	401	64	109	19	5	1	23	*40	.272
1986 San Diego b	N.L.	2B	101	241	34	61	5	2	1	12	14	.253
1987 Las Vegas	P.C.	OF-2B	98	359	66	110	18	10	1	38	27	.306
1988 Las Vegas	P.C.	3B-2B-OF	100	343	73	121	21	8	7	51	29	.353
1988 San Diego	N.L.	2B-3B	5	9	1	3	0	0	0	0	0	.333
1989 San Diego	N.L.	OF-3B-SS-2B	117	329	81	99	15	8	3	25	21	.301
1990 San Diego	N.L.	OF-3B-SS-2B	149	556	104	172	36	3	9	44	46	.309
1991 San Diego c-d	N.L.	2B-OF	117	424	66	119	13	3	3	32	26	.281
1992 Cincinnati	N.L.	OF-2B-OF	147	532	92	172	34	6	4	45	44	.323
1993 Cincinnati e-f	N.L.	2B-OF-3B-SS	83	292	46	70	13	0	1	18	26	.240
1994 San Diego g	N.L.	2B-OF	105	403	52	129	15	5	2	31	21	.320
1995 Las Vegas	P.C.	SS-2B	3	12	1	4	0	0	0	2	1	.333
1995 Rancho Cuca	California	DH	1	3	1	0	0	0	0	0	1	.000
1995 San Diego h-i	N.L.	OF-2B-SS	73	296	40	90	14	0	2	25	20	.304
1996 Kansas City j	A.L.	2B-OF	90	339	39	96	21	2	0	52	12	.283
1997 Kansas City-Cleveland k-l-m-n	A.L.	OF-2B-3B	120	431	63	130	20	2	4	44	18	.302
Major League Totals			11 Yrs.	1107	3852	618	1141	186	31	29	328	248	.296
Division Series													
1997 Cleveland	A.L.	OF-2B	5	19	1	6	0	0	0	1	2	.316
Championship Series													
1997 Cleveland	A.L.	2B-OF	5	20	0	3	1	0	0	0	1	.150
World Series Record													
1997 Cleveland	A.L.	2B-OF	6	22	3	6	4	0	0	4	0	.273

a Drafted by San Diego Padres from Pittsburgh Pirates organization, December 4, 1985.
b On disabled list from May 21 to June 5, 1986.
c On disabled list from August 8 to September 9, 1991.
d Traded to Cincinnati Reds with player to be named for pitcher Randy Myers, December 8; Cincinnati acquired outfielder Craig Pueschner to complete trade, December 9, 1991.
e On disabled list from July 2 to July 17 and August 4 to end of 1993 season.
f Filed for free agency, October 26, 1993; signed with San Diego Padres, January 10, 1994.
g Filed for free agency, October 17; re-signed with San Diego Padres, December 22, 1994.
h On disabled list from June 28 to July 13 and July 14 to August 22, 1995.
i Traded to Kansas City Royals with pitcher Bryan Wolff for first baseman Wally Joyner and pitcher Aaron Dorlarque, December 21, 1995.
j On disabled list from June 10 to July 19 and August 7 to September 1, 1996.
k On disabled list from June 15 to July 10, 1997.
l Traded to Cleveland Indians for pitcher Roland De La Maza, August 31, 1997.
m Filed for free agency, November 3, 1997.
n Signed with Detroit Tigers, December 12, 1997.

RODRIGUEZ, ALEXANDER EMMANUEL

Born, New York, New York, July 27, 1975.
Bats Right. Throws Right. Height, 6 feet, 3 inches. Weight, 190 pounds.

Year	Club	Lea	Pos	G	AB	R	H	2B	3B	HR	RBI	SB	Avg
1994 Appleton	.........Midwest	SS	65	248	49	79	17	6	14	55	16	.319
1994 Jacksonville	......Southern	SS	17	59	7	17	4	1	1	8	2	.288
1994 Seattle	................A.L.	SS	17	54	4	11	0	0	0	2	3	.204
1994 Calgary	.............P.C.	SS	32	119	22	37	7	4	6*	21	2	.311
1995 Tacoma	.............P.C.	SS	54	214	37	77	12	3	15	45	2	.360
1995 Seattle	................A.L.	SS	48	142	15	33	6	2	5	19	4	.232
1996 Tacoma a	...........P.C.	SS	2	5	0	1	0	0	0	0	0	.200
1996 Seattle	................A.L.	SS	146	601	*141	215	*54	1	36	123	15	*.358
1997 Seattle b	...........A.L.	SS	141	587	100	176	40	3	23	84	29	.300
Major League Totals	.... 4 Yrs.		352	1384	260	435	100	6	64	228	51	.314
Division Series												
1995 Seattle	..............A.L.	SS	1	1	1	0	0	0	0	0	0	.000
1997 Seattle	..............A.L.	SS	4	16	1	5	1	0	1	1	0	.313
Divisional Series Totals	....		5	17	2	5	1	0	1	1	0	.294
Championship Series												
1995 Seattle	................A.L.	PH	1	1	0	0	0	0	0	0	0	.000

a On disabled list from April 22 to May 7, 1996.
b On disabled list from June 12 to June 27, 1997.

RODRIGUEZ (LORENZO), HENRY ANDERSON

Born, Santo Domingo, Dominican Republic, November 8, 1967.
Bats Left. Throws Left. Height, 6 feet, 1 inch. Weight, 200 pounds.

Year	Club	Lea	Pos	G	AB	R	H	2B	3B	HR	RBI	SB	Avg
1987 Sarasota Dodgers	....Gulf C.	1B	49	148	23	49	7	3	0	15	3	.331
1988 Santo Domingo	..Dom. Sum.	OF	19	21	9	8	2	0	0	10	4	.381
1988 Salem	.........Northwest	1B	72	291	47	84	14	4	2	38	14	.289
1989 Vero Beach	...‥.....Fla. St.	1B	126	433	53	123	*33	1	10	73	7	.284
1989 Bakersfield	.........California	1B	3	9	2	2	0	0	1	2	0	.222
1990 San Antonio	........Texas	OF	129	495	82	144	21	9	*28	*109	5	.291
1991 Albuquerque	..........P.C.	OF-1B	121	446	61	121	22	5	10	67	4	.271
1992 Albuquerque	.........P.C.	1B-OF	94	365	59	111	21	5	14	72	1	.304
1992 Los Angeles	..........N.L.	OF-1B	53	146	11	32	7	0	3	14	0	.219
1993 Albuquerque	.........P.C.	1B-OF	46	179	26	53	13	5	4	30	1	.296
1993 Los Angeles	..........N.L.	OF-1B	76	176	20	39	10	0	8	23	1	.222
1994 Los Angeles	..........N.L.	OF-1B	104	306	33	82	14	2	8	49	0	.268
1995 Ottawa	..............Int.	DH	4	15	0	3	1	0	0	2	0	.200
1995 Los Angeles-Montreal a-b	.N.L.	OF-1B	45	138	13	33	4	1	2	15	0	.239
1996 Montreal	.............N.L.	OF-1B	145	532	81	147	42	1	36	103	2	.276
1997 Montreal c	..........N.L.	OF-1B	132	476	55	116	28	3	26	83	3	.244
Major League Totals	.... 6 Yrs.		555	1774	213	449	105	7	83	287	6	.253

a Traded to Montreal Expos with infielder Jeff Treadway for outfielder Roberto Kelly and pitcher Joey Eischen, May 24, 1995.
b On disabled list from June 2 to October 2, 1995.
c Traded to Chicago Cubs for pitcher Miquel Batista, December 12, 1997.

RODRIGUEZ (TORRES), IVAN

Born, Vega Baja, Puerto Rico, November 30, 1971.
Bats Right. Throws Right. Height, 5 feet, 9 inches. Weight, 205 pounds.

Year	Club	Lea	Pos	G	AB	R	H	2B	3B	HR	RBI	SB	Avg
1989 Gastonia	..........So. Atl.	C	112	386	38	92	22	1	7	42	2	.238
1990 Charlotte	..........Fla. St.	C	109	408	48	117	17	7	2	55	1	.287
1991 Tulsa	...............Texas	C	50	175	16	48	7	2	3	28	1	.274
1991 Texas	...............A.L.	C	88	280	24	74	16	0	3	27	0	.264
1992 Texas a	.............A.L.	C	123	420	39	109	16	1	8	37	0	.260
1993 Texas	............:.....A.L.	C	137	473	56	129	28	4	10	66	8	.273
1994 Texas	...............A.L.	C	99	363	56	108	19	1	16	57	6	.298
1995 Texas	...............A.L.	C	130	492	56	149	32	2	12	67	0	.303
1996 Texas	...............A.L.	C	153	639	116	192	47	3	19	86	5	.300
1997 Texas	...............A.L.	C	150	597	98	187	34	4	20	77	7	.313
Major League Totals	.... 7 Yrs.		880	3264	445	948	192	15	88	417	26	.290
Division Series												
1996 Texas	...............A.L.	C	4	16	1	6	1	0	0	2	0	.375

a On disabled list from June 6 to June 27, 1992.

ROLEN, SCOTT BRUCE
Born, Evansville, Indiana, April 4, 1975.
Bats Right. Throws Right. Height, 6 feet, 4 inches. Weight, 195 pounds.

Year	Club	Lea	Pos	G	AB	R	H	2B	3B	HR	RBI	SB	Avg
1993 Martinsvlle	Appal.	3B	25	80	8	25	5	0	0	12	3	.313
1994 Spartanburg	So.Atl.	3B	138	513	83	151	34	5	14	72	6	.294
1995 Clearwater	Fla.St.	3B	66	238	45	69	13	2	10	39	4	.290
1995 Reading	Eastern	3B	20	76	16	22	3	0	3	15	1	.289
1996 Reading	Eastern	3B	61	230	44	83	22	2	9	42	8	.361
1996 Scranton-WB	Int.	3B	45	168	23	46	17	0	2	19	4	.274
1996 Philadelphia	N.L.	3B	37	130	10	33	7	0	4	18	0	.254
1997 Philadelphia a	N.L.	3B	156	561	93	159	35	3	21	92	16	.283
Major League Totals			2 Yrs.	193	691	103	192	42	3	25	110	16	.278

a Selected Rookie of the Year in National League for 1997.

ROSE, PETER EDWARD JR.
Born, Cincinnati, Ohio, November 16, 1969.
Bats Left. Throws Right. Height, 6 feet, 1 inch. Weight, 180 pounds.

Year	Club	Lea	Pos	G	AB	R	H	2B	3B	HR	RBI	SB	Avg
1989 Frederick	Carolina	3B	24	67	3	12	3	0	0	7	1	.179
1989 Erie	N.Y.-Penn.	3B	58	228	30	63	13	5	2	26	1	.276
1990 Frederick	Carolina	3B	97	323	32	75	14	2	1	41	0	.232
1991 Sarasota	Fla. St.	3B-2B	99	323	31	70	12	2	0	35	5	.217
1992 Columbus	So. Atl.	3B	131	510	67	129	24	6	9	54	4	.253
1993 Kinston	Carolina	3B	74	284	33	62	10	1	7	30	1	.218
1994 Hickory	So. Atl.	3B	32	114	14	25	4	1	0	12	0	.219
1994 White Sox	Gulf Coast	3B	2	4	1	2	0	0	0	1	0	.500
1994 Pr William	Carolina	3B	45	146	18	41	3	1	4	22	0	.281
1995 Birmingham	Southern	3B	5	13	1	5	1	0	0	2	0	.385
1995 South Bend	Midwest	3B-1B	116	423	56	117	24	6	4	65	2	.277
1996 Birmingham	Southern	3B-1B-2B	108	399	40	97	13	1	3	44	1	.243
1997 Indianapolis	A.A.	3B	12	40	2	9	2	0	0	1	0	.225
1997 Chattanooga	Southern	3B	112	445	75	137	31	0	25	98	0	.308
1997 Cincinnati	N.L.	3B-1B	11	14	2	2	0	0	0	0	0	.143

SALMON, TIMOTHY JAMES
Born, Long Beach, California, August 24, 1968.
Bats Right. Throws Right. Height, 6 feet, 3 inches. Weight, 220 pounds.

Year	Club	Lea	Pos	G	AB	R	H	2B	3B	HR	RBI	SB	Avg
1989 Bend	Northwest	OF	55	196	37	48	6	5	6	31	2	.245
1990 Palm Springs	California	OF	36	118	19	34	6	0	2	21	11	.288
1990 Midland	Texas	OF	27	97	17	26	3	1	3	16	1	.268
1991 Midland	Texas	OF	131	465	100	114	26	4	23	94	12	.245
1992 Edmonton	P.C.	OF	118	409	*101	142	38	4	*29	*105	9	.347
1992 California	A.L.	OF	23	79	8	14	1	0	2	6	1	.177
1993 California a	A.L.	OF	142	515	93	146	35	1	31	95	5	.283
1994 California b	A.L.	OF	100	373	67	107	18	2	23	70	1	.287
1995 California	A.L.	OF	143	537	111	177	34	3	34	105	5	.330
1996 California	A.L.	OF	156	581	90	166	27	4	30	98	4	.286
1997 Anaheim	A.L.	OF	157	582	95	172	28	1	33	129	9	.296
Major League Totals			6 Yrs.	721	2667	464	782	143	11	153	503	25	.293

a Selected Rookie of the Year in American League for 1993.
b On disabled list from July 18 to August 3, 1994.

SAMUEL, JUAN MILTON
Born, San Pedro de Macoris, Dominican Republic, December 9, 1960.
Bats Right. Throws Right. Height, 5 feet, 11 inches. Weight, 170 pounds.

Year	Club	Lea	Pos	G	AB	R	H	2B	3B	HR	RBI	SB	Avg
1980 Cen. Oregon	Northwest	2B	69	*298	66	84	11	2	17	44	26	.282
1981 Spartanburg	So. Atl.	2B	135	512	88	127	22	8	11	74	53	.248
1982 Peninsula	Carolina	2B	135	494	*111	158	29	6	28	94	64	.320
1983 Reading	Eastern	2B	47	184	36	43	10	0	11	39	19	.234
1983 Portland	P.C.	2B	65	261	59	86	14	8	15	52	33	.330
1983 Philadelphia	N.L.	2B	18	65	14	18	1	2	2	5	3	.277
1984 Philadelphia	N.L.	2B	160	*701	105	191	36	*19	15	69	72	.272

Year	Club	Lea	Pos	G	AB	R	H	2B	3B	HR	RBI	SB	Avg
1985 Philadelphia ......N.L.			2B	161	*663	101	175	31	13	19	74	53	.264
1986 Philadelphia a .....N.L.			2B	145	591	90	157	36	12	16	78	42	.266
1987 Philadelphia ......N.L.			2B	160	*655	113	178	37	*15	28	100	35	.272
1988 Philadelphia ......N.L.			2B-OF-3B	157	629	68	153	32	9	12	67	33	.243
1989 Phil.-N. Y. b-c-d ....N.L.			- OF	137	532	69	125	16	2	11	48	42	.235
1990 Los Angeles e .....N.L.			2B-OF	143	492	62	119	24	3	13	52	38	.242
1991 Los Angeles f .....N.L.			2B	153	594	74	161	22	6	12	58	23	.271
1992 Los Angeles g-h ....N.L.			2B-OF	47	122	7	32	3	1	0	15	2	.262
1992 Kansas City i ......A.L.			OF-2B	29	102	15	29	5	3	0	8	6	.284
1993 Cincinnati j ......N.L.			2B-1B-3B-OF	103	261	31	60	10	4	4	26	9	.230
1994 Detroit k ........A.L.			OF-2B-1B	59	136	32	42	9	5	5	21	5	.309
1995 Detroit-K.C. l-m-n-o-p ..A.L.			1B-OF-2B	91	205	31	54	10	1	12	39	6	.263
1996 Toronto q-r-s ......A.L.			OF-1B	69	188	34	48	8	3	8	26	9	.255
1997 Toronto t-u ......A.L.			DH-3B-1B-2B	45	95	13	27	5	4	3	15	5	.284
Major League Totals	15 Yrs.			1677	6031	859	1569	285	102	160	701	383	.260
Championship Series													
1983 Philadelphia ......N.L.			PR	1	0	0	0	0	0	0	0	0	.000
World Series Record													
1983 Philadelphia ......N.L.			PR-PH	3	1	0	0	0	0	0	0	0	.000

a On disabled list from April 13 to May 2, 1986.
b On disabled list from March 18 to April 19, 1989.
c Traded to New York Mets for pitcher Roger McDowell, outfielder Len Dykstra and player to be named, June 18; Philadelphia Phillies acquired pitcher Tom Edens to complete trade, July 28, 1989.
d Traded to Los Angeles Dodgers for outfielder/first baseman Mike Marshall and pitcher Alejandro Pena, December 20, 1989.
e Filed for free agency, October 23; re-signed with Los Angeles Dodgers, December 19, 1990.
f Filed for free agency, October 28; re-signed with Los Angeles Dodgers, December 19, 1991.
g On disabled list from April 28 to June 11, 1992.
h Released, July 30; signed with Kansas City Royals, August 6, 1992.
i Released, October 22; signed with Cincinnati Reds organization, December 11, 1992.
j Filed for free agency, October 25, 1993; signed with Detroit Tigers, February 14, 1994.
k Filed for free agency, October 17, 1994.
l Signed with Detroit Tigers organization, April 7, 1995.
m Traded to Kansas City Royals for player to be named later, September 8, 1995.
n Detroit Tigers received infielder Phil Hiatt to complete trade, September 14, 1995.
o Filed for free agency, November 12, 1995.
p Signed with Toronto Blue Jays organization, January 16, 1996.
q On disabled list from June 26 to July 11, 1996.
r Filed for free agency, November 18, 1996.
s Re-signed with Toronto Blue Jays organization, December 18, 1996.
t Filed for free agency, October 28, 1997.
u Re-signed with Toronto Blue Jays organization, December 8, 1997

SANCHEZ (GUADALUPE), REY FRANCISCO

Born, Rio Piedras, Puerto Rico, October 5, 1967.
Bats Right. Throws Right. Height, 5 feet, 9 inches. Weight, 170 pounds.

Year	Club	Lea	Pos	G	AB	R	H	2B	3B	HR	RBI	SB	Avg
1986 Sarasota Rangers ....Gulf C.			SS	52	169	27	49	3	1	0	23	10	.290
1987 Gastonia ....So. Atl.			SS	50	160	19	35	1	2	1	10	6	.219
1987 Butte ....Pioneer			SS	49	189	36	69	10	6	0	25	22	.365
1988 Charlotte ....Fla. St.			SS	128	418	60	128	6	5	0	38	29	.306
1989 Oklahoma City a .......A.A.			SS	134	464	38	104	10	4	1	39	4	.224
1990 Iowa b .............A.A.			INJURED—Did Not Play										
1991 Iowa ..............A.A.			SS	126	417	60	121	16	5	2	46	13	.290
1991 Chicago ...........N.L.			SS-2B	13	23	1	6	0	0	0	2	0	.261
1992 Iowa ..............A.A.			SS-2B	20	76	12	26	3	0	0	3	6	.342
1992 Chicago c .........N.L.			SS-2B	74	255	24	64	14	3	1	19	2	.251
1993 Chicago ...........N.L.			SS	105	344	35	97	11	2	0	28	1	.282
1994 Chicago ...........A.L.			2B-SS-3B	96	291	26	83	13	1	0	24	2	.285
1995 Chicago d .........N.L.			2B-SS	114	428	57	119	22	2	3	27	6	.278
1996 Iowa e .............A.A.			SS	3	12	2	2	0	0	0	1	2	.167
1996 Chicago ...........N.L.			SS	95	289	28	61	9	0	1	12	7	.211
1997 Chicago f .........N.L.			SS-2B-3B	97	205	14	51	9	0	1	12	4	.249
1997 New York g-h ......A.L.			2B-SS	38	138	21	43	12	0	1	15	0	.312
Major League Totals	7 Yrs.			632	1973	206	524	90	8	7	139	22	.266
Division Series													
1997 New York ...........A.L.			2B	5	15	1	3	1	0	0	1	0	.200

a Traded by Texas Rangers to Chicago Cubs organization for infielder Bryan House, January 3, 1990.
b On disabled list from April 6 to end of 1990 season.
c On disabled list from May 6 to May 21, 1992.
d On disabled list from July 24 to August 9, 1995.

e On disabled list from June 5 to July 20 and August 11 to September 1, 1996.
f Traded to New York Yankees for pitcher Frisco Parotte, August 16, 1997.
g Filed for free agency, November 3, 1997.
h Signed with San Francisco Giants, January 22, 1998.

SANDBERG, RYNE DEE

Born, Spokane, Washington, September 18, 1959.
Bats Right. Throws Right. Height, 6 feet, 2 inches. Weight, 190 pounds.

Year	Club	Lea	Pos	G	AB	R	H	2B	3B	HR	RBI	SB	Avg
1978 Helena	Pioneer		SS	56	190	34	59	6	6	1	23	15	.311
1979 Spartanburg	W.Carol.		SS	*138	*539	83	133	21	7	4	47	21	.247
1980 Reading	Eastern		SS-3B	129	490	95	152	21	12	11	79	32	.310
1981 Okla. City	A.A.		SS	133	519	78	152	17	5	9	62	32	.293
1981 Philadelphia a	N.L.		SS	13	6	2	1	0	0	0	0	0	.167
1982 Chicago	N.L.		3B-2B	156	635	103	172	33	5	7	54	32	.271
1983 Chicago	N.L.		2B-SS	158	633	94	165	25	4	8	48	37	.261
1984 Chicago b	N.L.		2B	156	636	*114	200	36	*19	19	84	32	.314
1985 Chicago	N.L.		2B-SS	153	609	113	186	31	6	26	83	54	.305
1986 Chicago	N.L.		2B	154	627	68	178	28	5	14	76	34	.284
1987 Chicago c	N.L.		2B	132	523	81	154	25	2	16	59	21	.294
1988 Chicago	N.L.		2B	155	618	77	163	23	8	19	69	25	.264
1989 Chicago	N.L.		2B	157	606	*104	176	25	5	30	76	15	.290
1990 Chicago	N.L.		2B	155	615	*116	188	30	3	*40	100	25	.306
1991 Chicago	N.L.		2B	158	585	104	170	32	2	26	100	22	.291
1992 Chicago	N.L.		2B	158	612	100	186	32	8	26	87	17	.304
1993 Daytona	Fla. St.		2B	2	5	2	1	0	0	1	2	0	.200
1993 Orlando	Southern		2B	4	9	0	2	0	0	1	0	0	.222
1993 Chicago d	N.L.		2B	117	456	67	141	20	0	9	45	9	.309
1994 Chicago e-f	N.L.		2B	57	223	36	53	9	5	5	24	2	.238
1995 Chicago	N.L.		(Voluntarily Retired)										
1996 Chicago g-h			2B	150	554	85	135	28	4	25	92	12	.244
1997 Chicago	N.L.		2B	135	447	54	118	26	0	12	64	7	.264
Major League Totals			16 Yrs.	2164	8385	1318	2386	403	76	282	1061	344	.285
Championship Series													
1984 Chicago	N.L.		2B	5	19	3	7	2	0	0	2	3	.368
1989 Chicago	N.L.		2B	5	20	6	8	3	1	1	4	0	.400
Championship Series Totals				10	39	9	15	5	1	1	6	3	.385

a Traded to Chicago Cubs with shortstop Larry Bowa for shortstop Ivan DeJesus, January 27, 1982.
b Selected Most Valuable Player in National League for 1984.
c On disabled list from June 14 to July 11, 1987.
d On disabled list from March 27 to April 30, 1993.
e Announced retirement, June 13, 1994.
f Returned to active roster, December 15, 1995.
g Filed for free agency, November 5, 1996.
h Re-signed with Chicago Cubs, November 27, 1996.

SANDERS, DEION LUWYNN

Born, Fort Myers, Florida, August 9, 1967.
Bats Left. Throws Left. Height, 6 feet, 1 inch. Weight, 195 pounds.

Year	Club	Lea	Pos	G	AB	R	H	2B	3B	HR	RBI	SB	Avg
1988 Sarasota Yankees	Gulf C.		OF	17	75	7	21	4	2	0	6	11	.280
1988 Ft. Lauderdale	Fla. St.		OF	6	21	5	9	2	0	0	2	2	.429
1988 Columbus	Int.		OF	5	20	3	1	0	0	0	0	1	.150
1989 Albany	Eastern		OF	33	119	28	34	2	2	1	6	17	.286
1989 Columbus	Int.		OF	70	259	38	72	12	7	5	30	16	.278
1989 New York	A.L.		OF	14	47	7	11	2	0	2	7	1	.234
1990 New York	A.L.		OF	57	133	24	21	2	2	3	9	8	.158
1990 Columbus a-b	Int.		OF	22	84	21	27	7	1	2	10	9	.321
1991 Richmond	Int.		OF	29	130	20	34	6	3	5	16	12	.262
1991 Atlanta c	N.L.		OF	54	110	16	21	1	2	4	13	11	.191
1992 Atlanta	N.L.		OF	97	303	54	92	6	*14	8	28	26	.304
1993 Atlanta d-e	N.L.		OF	95	272	42	75	18	6	6	28	19	.276
1994 Atl.-Cincinnati f	N.L.		OF	92	375	58	106	17	4	4	28	38	.283
1995 Chattanooga	Southern		OF	2	7	1	4	0	0	1	2	1	.571
1995 Cincinnati-San Fran. g	N.L.		OF	85	343	48	92	11	8	6	28	24	.268
1996			(Did Not Play in Organized Baseball)										
1997 Cincinnati h-i	N.L.		OF	115	465	53	127	13	7	5	23	56	.273
Major League Totals			8 Yrs.	609	2048	302	545	70	43	38	164	183	.266

Year	Club	Lea	Pos	G	AB	R	H	2B	3B	HR	.RBI	SB	Avg
Championship Series													
1992 Atlanta	N.L.	OF	4	5	0	0	0	0	0	0	0	0	.000
1993 Atlanta	N.L.	OF	5	3	0	0	0	0	0	0	0	0	.000
Championship Series Totals			9	8	0	0	0	0	0	0	0	0	.000
World Series Record													
1992 Atlanta	N.L.	OF	4	15	4	8	2	0	0	1	5	.533

a On disqualified list from August 1 to September 22, 1990.
b Waived by New York Yankees, September 22; claimed by Chicago White Sox, September 30; rejected claim and became free agent, October 2, 1990; signed with Atlanta Braves organization, January 30, 1991.
c On ineligible list from August 1 to September 23, 1991.
d On disqualified list from April 27 to May 21, 1993.
e On disabled list from August 22 to September 6, 1993.
f Traded to Cincinnati Reds for outfielder Roberto Kelly and pitcher Roger Etheridge, May 29, 1994.
g Traded to San Francisco Giants with pitcher John Roper, pitcher Ricky Pickett, pitcher Scott Service and infielder David McCarty for pitcher Mark Portugal, pitcher Dave Burba and outfielder Darren Lewis, July 21, 1995.
h Signed with Cincinnati Reds, January 30, 1997.
i Filed for free agency, November 5, 1997.

SANDERS, REGINALD LAVERN

Born, Florence, South Carolina, December 1, 1967.
Bats Right. Throws Right. Height, 6 feet, 1 inch. Weight, 180 pounds.

Year	Club	Lea	Pos	G	AB	R	H	2B	3B	HR	RBI	SB	Avg
1988 Billings	Pioneer	SS	17	64	11	15	1	1	0	3	10	.234
1989 Greensboro a	So. Atl.	SS	81	315	53	91	18	5	9	53	21	.289
1990 Cedar Rapids	Midwest	OF	127	466	89	133	21	4	17	63	40	.285
1991 Chattanooga	Southern	OF	86	302	50	95	15	8	8	49	15	.315
1991 Cincinnati b	N.L.	OF	9	40	6	8	0	0	1	3	1	.200
1992 Cincinnati c	N.L.	OF	116	385	62	104	26	6	12	36	16	.270
1993 Cincinnati	N.L.	OF	138	496	90	136	16	4	20	83	27	.274
1994 Cincinnati d	N.L.	OF	107	400	66	105	20	8	17	62	21	.262
1995 Cincinnati e	N.L.	OF	133	484	91	148	36	6	28	99	36	.306
1996 Indianapolis f	A.A.	OF	4	12	3	5	2	0	0	1	0	.417
1996 Cincinnati	N.L.	OF	81	287	49	72	17	1	14	33	24	.251
1997 Chattanooga	Southern	OF	3	11	3	6	1	1	1	3	0	.545
1997 Indianapolis	A.A.	OF	5	19	1	4	0	0	0	1	0	.211
1997 Cincinnati g	N.L.	OF	86	312	52	79	19	2	19	56	13	.253
Major League Totals		7 Yrs.	670	2404	416	652	134	27	111	372	138	.271
Division Series												
1995 Cincinnati	N.L.	OF	3	13	3	2	1	0	1	2	2	.154
Championship Series												
1995 Cincinnati	N.L.	OF	4	16	0	2	0	0	0	0	0	.125

a On disabled list from July 20 to end of 1989 season.
b On disabled list from August 26 to September 20, 1991.
c On disabled list from May 13 to May 28 and July 17 to August 2, 1992.
d Suspended five games and fined by National League for April 13 charging mound and inciting brawl from June 3 to June 8, 1994.
e On disabled list from June 1 to July 16, 1995.
f On disabled list from April 20 to May 22 and May 31 to June 15 and September 17 to September 30, 1996.
g On disabled list from April 19 to May 6 and May 24 to July 22, 1997.

SANTANGELO, FRANK-PAUL (F.P.)

Born, Livonia, Michigan, October 24, 1967.
Bats Both. Throws Right. Height, 5 feet, 10 inches. Weight, 165 pounds.

Year	Club	Lea	Pos	G	AB	R	H	2B	3B	HR	RBI	SB	Avg
1989 Jamestown . . .	N.Y.-Penn	2B	2	6	0	3	1	0	0	1	.500
1989 West Palm Bch.	Fla. St.	DH-SS-2B-OF	57	173	18	37	4	0	0	14	3	.214
1990 West Palm Bch.	Fla. St.	SS-OF-2B	116	394	63	109	19	2	0	38	22	.277
1991 Harrisburg	Eastern	2B-OF-SS-3B	132	462	78	113	12	7	5	42	21	.245
1992 Indianapolis	A.A.	OF-2B-SS-3B	137	462	83	123	25	0	5	34	12	.266
1993 Ottawa	Int.	OF-SS-3B-2B	131	453	86	124	21	2	4	45	18	.274
1994 Ottawa	Int.	OF-SS-3B	119	413	62	104	28	1	5	41	7	.252
1995 Ottawa	Int.	3B-2B-0F-SS	95	267	37	68	15	3	2	25	7	.255
1995 Montreal a	N.L.	OF-2B	35	98	11	29	5	1	1	9	1	.296
1996 Montreal	N.L.	OF-3B-2B-SS	152	393	54	109	20	5	7	56	5	.277
1997 Montreal	N.L.	OF-3B-2B-SS	130	350	56	87	19	5	5	31	8	.249
Major League Totals		3 Yrs.	317	841	121	225	44	11	13	96	14	.268

a Outrighted by Montreal Expos, October 17, 1995.

SANTIAGO (RIVERA), BENITO

Born, Ponce, Puerto Rico, March 9, 1965.
Bats Right. Throws Right. Height, 6 feet, 1 inch. Weight, 185 pounds.

Year	Club	Lea	Pos	G	AB	R	H	2B	3B	HR	RBI	SB	Avg
1983 Miami	Fla. St.	C	122	429	34	106	25	3	5	56	3	.247
1984 Reno	California	C	114	416	64	116	20	6	16	83	5	.279
1985 Beaumont a	Texas	C-1B-3B	101	372	55	111	16	6	5	52	12	.298
1986 Las Vegas	P.C.	C	117	436	55	125	26	3	17	71	19	.287
1986 San Diego	N.L.	C	17	62	10	18	2	0	3	6	0	.290
1987 San Diego b	N.L.	C	146	546	64	164	33	2	18	79	21	.300
1988 San Diego	N.L.	C	139	492	49	122	22	2	10	46	15	.248
1989 San Diego	N.L.	C	129	462	50	109	16	3	16	62	11	.236
1990 Las Vegas	P.C.	C	6	20	5	6	2	0	1	8	0	.300
1990 San Diego c	N.L.	C	100	344	42	93	8	5	11	53	5	.270
1991 San Diego	N.L.	C-OF	152	580	60	155	22	3	17	87	8	.267
1992 Las Vegas	P.C.	C	4	13	3	4	0	0	1	2	0	.308
1992 San Diego d-e	N.L.	C	106	386	37	97	21	0	10	42	2	.251
1993 Florida	N.L.	C-OF	139	469	49	108	19	6	13	50	10	.230
1994 Florida f	N.L.	C	101	337	35	92	14	2	11	41	1	.273
1995 Cincinnati g-h-i	N.L.	C-1B	81	266	40	76	20	0	11	44	2	.286
1996 Philadelphia j-k-l	N.L.	C-1B	136	481	71	127	21	2	30	85	2	.264
1997 Toronto m	A.L.	C	97	341	31	83	10	0	13	42	1	.243
Major League Totals			12 Yrs.	1343	4766	538	1244	208	25	163	637	78	.261
Division Series													
1995 Cincinnati	N.L.	C	3	9	2	3	0	0	1	3	0	.333
Championship Series													
1995 Cincinnati	N.L.	C	4	13	0	3	0	0	0	0	0	.231

a On disabled list from June 21 to July 2, 1985.
b Selected Rookie of the Year in National League for 1987.
c On disabled list from June 15 to August 10, 1990.
d On disabled list from May 31 to July 11, 1992.
e Filed for free agency, October 26; signed with Florida Marlins, December 16, 1992.
f Filed for free agency, October 14, 1994.
g Signed with Cincinnati Reds, April 17, 1995.
h On disabled list from May 8 to July 4, 1995.
i Filed for free agency, November 12, 1995.
j Signed with Philadelphia Phillies, January 30, 1996.
k Filed for free agency, November 18, 1996.
l Signed with Toronto Blue Jays, December 9, 1996.
m On disabled list from April 14 to April 29, 1997.

SEFCIK, KEVIN JOHN

Born, Oak Lawn, Illinois, February 10, 1971.
Bats Right. Throws Right. Height, 5 feet, 10 inches. Weight, 175 pounds.

Year	Club	Lea	Pos	G	AB	R	H	2B	3B	HR	RBI	SB	Avg
1993 Batavia	N.Y.-Penn.	2B-3B	74	281	49	84	24	4	2	28	20	.299
1994 Clearwater	Fla. St.	3B-2B	130	516	83	147	29	8	2	46	30	.285
1995 Scranton-WB	Int.	2B	7	26	5	9	6	1	0	6	0	.346
1995 Reading	Eastern	SS-3B	128	508	68	138	18	4	4	46	14	.272
1995 Philadelphia	N.L.	3B	5	4	1	0	0	0	0	0	0	.000
1996 Scranton-WB	Int.	SS-2B-3B	45	180	34	60	7	5	0	19	11	.333
1996 Philadelphia	N.L.	SS-3B-2B	44	116	10	33	5	3	0	9	3	.284
1997 Scranton-WB	Int.	2B-3B-OF	29	123	19	41	11	2	1	7	5	.333
1997 Philadelphia	N.L.	2B-SS-3B	61	119	11	32	3	0	2	6	1	.269
Major League Totals			3 Yrs.	110	239	22	65	8	3	2	15	4	.272

SEGUI, DAVID VINCENT

Born, Kansas City, Missouri, July 19, 1966.
Bats Both. Throws Left. Height, 6 feet, 1 inch. Weight, 202 pounds.

Year	Club	Lea	Pos	G	AB	R	H	2B	3B	HR	RBI	SB	Avg
1988 Hagerstown	Carolina	1B-OF	60	190	35	51	12	4	3	31	0	.268
1989 Frederick	Carolina	1B	83	284	43	90	19	0	10	50	2	.317
1989 Hagerstown	Eastern	1B	44	173	22	58	14	1	1	26	0	.324
1990 Rochester	Int.	1B	86	307	55	103	28	0	2	51	5	.336
1990 Baltimore	A.L.	1B	40	123	14	30	7	0	2	15	0	.244
1991 Rochester a	Int.	1B-OF	28	96	9	26	2	0	1	10	1	.271
1991 Baltimore	A.L.	1B-OF	86	212	15	59	7	0	2	22	1	.278
1992 Baltimore	A.L.	1B-OF	115	189	21	44	9	0	1	17	1	.233

Year	Club	Lea	Pos	G	AB	R	H	2B	3B	HR	RBI	SB	Avg
1993 Baltimore b-c	....	A.L.	1B	146	450	54	123	27	0	10	60	2	.273
1994 New York d	....	N.L.	1B-OF	92	336	46	81	17	1	10	43	0	.241
1995 New York-Montreal e	...	N.L.	1B-OF	130	456	68	141	25	4	12	68	2	.309
1996 Montreal f	....	N.L.	1B	115	416	69	119	30	1	11	58	4	.286
1997 Montreal g-h-i	...	N.L.	1B	125	459	75	141	22	3	21	68	1	.307
Major League Totals	....	8 Yrs.		849	2641	362	738	144	9	69	351	11	.279

a On disabled list from April 15 to April 25, 1991.
b Suspended three games by American League for June 6 fight from August 16 to August 19, 1993.
c Traded to New York Mets for shortstop Kevin Daez and pitcher Tom Wegmann, March 27, 1994.
d On disabled list from June 20 to July 4, 1994.
e Traded to Montreal Expos for pitcher Reid Cornelius, June 8, 1995.
f On disabled list from July 4 to August 16, 1996.
g On disabled list from June 4 to June 21, 1997.
h Filed for free agency, October 28, 1997.
i Signed with Seattle Mariners, December 12, 1997.

SEITZER, KEVIN LEE
Born, Springfield, Illinois, March 26, 1962.
Bats Right. Throws Right. Height, 5 feet, 11 inches. Weight, 190 pounds.

Year	Club	Lea	Pos	G	AB	R	H	2B	3B	HR	RBI	SB	Avg
1983 Butte	......	Pioneer	3B-SS	68	238	60	82	14	1	2	45	11	.345
1984 Charleston	..	So. Atl.	3B	*141	489	*96	*145	26	5	8	79	23	.297
1985 Fort Myers	..	Fla. St.	1B-3B	90	290	61	91	10	5	3	46	28	.314
1985 Memphis	.	Southern	3B-1B-OF	52	187	26	65	6	2	1	20	9	.348
1986 Memphis	.	Southern	1B	4	11	4	3	0	0	0	1	2	.273
1986 Omaha	....	A.A.	OF-1B-3B	129	432	86	138	20	11	13	74	20	.319
1986 Kansas City	.	A.L.	1B-OF-3B	28	96	16	31	4	1	2	11	0	.323
1987 Kansas City	.	A.L.	3B-1B-OF	161	641	105	*207	33	8	15	83	12	.323
1988 Kansas City	.	A.L.	3B-OF	149	559	90	170	32	5	5	60	10	.304
1989 Kansas City	.	A.L.	3B-SS-OF-1B	160	597	78	168	17	2	4	48	17	.281
1990 Kansas City	.	A.L.	3B-2B	158	622	91	171	31	5	6	38	7	.275
1991 Kansas City a-b		A.L.	3B	85	234	28	62	11	3	1	25	4	.265
1992 Milwaukee c	..	A.L.	3B-2B-1B	148	540	74	146	35	1	5	71	13	.270
1993 Oak.-Milw. d-e-f		A.L.	3B-1B-OF-2B-SS	120	417	45	112	16	2	11	57	7	.269
1994 Beloit	....	Midwest	3B	3	12	3	4	3	0	0	3	2	.333
1994 Milwaukee g	..	A.L.	3B-1B	80	309	44	97	24	2	5	49	2	.314
1995 Milwaukee h	..	A.L.	3B-1B	132	492	56	153	33	3	5	69	2	.311
1996 Milw.-Cleve. i	.	A.L.	DH-1B-3B	154	573	85	187	35	3	13	78	6	.326
1997 Cleveland j	.	A.L.	DH-1B-3B	64	198	27	53	14	0	2	24	0	.268
Major League Totals	....	12 Yrs.		1439	5278	739	1557	285	35	74	613	80	.295
Division Series													
1996 Cleveland	....	A.L.	1B	4	17	1	5	1	0	0	4	1	.294
1997 Cleveland	....	A.L.	1B	1	4	0	0	0	0	0	0	0	.000
Division Series Totals	....			5	21	1	5	1	0	0	4	1	.238
Championship Series													
1997 Cleveland	....	A.L.	1B	4	4	0	0	0	0	0	0	0	.000
World Series Record													
1997 Cleveland	....	A.L.	PH	1	1	0	0	0	0	0	0	0	.000

a On disabled list from April 27 to May 31, 1991.
b Released, March 27; signed with Milwaukee Brewers, April 5, 1992.
c Filed for free agency, October 27, 1992.
d Record of 0-0 in one game as pitcher.
e Claimed on waivers by Milwaukee Brewers, July 29, 1993.
f Filed for free agency, November 3, 1993; re-signed with Milwaukee Brewers organization, February 11, 1994.
g On disabled list from May 10 to June 14, 1994.
h Filed for free agency, November 12, 1995; re-signed with Milwaukee Brewers, December 10, 1995.
i Traded to Cleveland Indians for outfielder Jeromy Burnitz, August 31, 1996.
j Filed for free agency, October 29, 1997.

SERVAIS, SCOTT DANIEL
Born, LaCrosse, Wisconsin, June 4, 1967.
Bats Right. Throws Right. Height, 6 feet, 2 inches. Weight, 195 pounds.

Year	Club	Lea	Pos	G	AB	R	H	2B	3B	HR	RBI	SB	Avg
1989 Osceola	....	Fla. St.	C	46	153	16	41	9	0	2	23	0	.268
1989 Columbus	....	Southern	C	63	198	20	47	5	0	1	22	0	.237
1990 Tucson	....	P.C.	C	89	303	37	66	11	3	5	37	0	.218
1991 Tucson	....	P.C.	C	60	219	34	71	12	0	2	27	0	.324

Year	Club	Lea	Pos	G	AB	R	H	2B	3B	HR	RBI	SB	Avg
1991 Houston a .........N.L.			C	16	37	0	6	3	0	0	6	0	.162
1992 Houston .............N.L.			C	77	205	12	49	9	0	0	15	0	.239
1993 Houston .............N.L.			C	85	258	24	63	11	0	11	32	0	.244
1994 Houston b .........N.L.			C	78	251	27	49	15	1	9	41	0	.195
1995 Houston-Chicago c-d-e .N.L.			C	80	264	38	70	22	0	13	47	2	.265
1996 Chicago .............N.L.			C-1B	129	445	42	118	20	0	11	63	0	.265
1997 Chicago .............N.L.			C-1B	122	385	36	100	21	0	6	45	0	.260
Major League Totals	7 Yrs.			587	1845	179	455	101	1	50	249	2	.247

a On disabled list from August 4 to September 7, 1991.
b Not offered 1995 contract, December 23, 1994.
c Re-signed with Houston Astros, April 5, 1995.
d Traded to Chicago Cubs with outfielder Luis Gonzalez for catcher Rick Wilkins, June 28, 1995.
e On disabled list from July 10 to August 3, 1995.

SHEAFFER, DANNY TODD

Born, Jacksonville, Florida, August 21, 1961.
Bats Right. Throws Right. Height, 6 feet. Weight, 190 pounds.

Year	Club	Lea	Pos	G	AB	R	H	2B	3B	HR	RBI	SB	Avg
1981 Bristol ....Eastern			OF-C	8	12	0	0	0	0	0	1	0	.000
1981 Elmira ......N.Y.-Penn.			C	62	198	39	57	9	0	8	29	2	.288
1982 Winter Haven ...Fla. St.			C	82	260	20	65	4	0	5	25	2	.250
1983 Wins.-Salem ...Carolina			1B-C	112	380	48	105	14	2	15	63	1	.276
1984 New Britain ....Eastern			C-OF	93	303	33	73	10	0	1	27	2	.241
1985 Pawtucket ....Int.			C	77	243	24	63	9	0	8	33	0	.259
1986 Pawtucket ....Int.			C-OF	79	265	34	90	16	1	2	30	9	.340
1987 Pawtucket ....Int.			C-1B-OF	69	242	32	62	13	2	2	25	6	.256
1987 Boston ...........A.L.			C	25	66	5	8	1	0	1	5	0	.121
1988 Pawtucket a ....Int.			C-1B-3B	98	299	30	82	17	1	1	28	20	.274
1989 Cleveland ........A.L.			3B-OF	7	16	1	1	0	0	0	0	0	.063
1989 Colorado Springs b .P.C.			OF-C-3B	107	401	62	113	26	2	3	47	6	.282
1990 Buffalo c ........A.A.			C-OF-1B	55	144	23	35	7	0	2	19	4	.243
1991 Portland d ........P.C.			C-1B-OF-3B	93	330	46	100	14	2	1	43	2	.303
1992 Portland e .......P.C.			C-OF-1B	116	442	54	122	23	4	5	56	3	.276
1993 Colorado ........N.L.			C-1B-OF-3B	82	216	26	60	9	1	4	32	2	.278
1994 Colorado ........N.L.			C-1B-OF	44	110	11	24	4	0	1	12	0	.218
1995 St. Louis f ......N.L.			C-1B-3B	76	208	24	48	10	1	5	30	0	.231
1996 St. Louis ........N.L.			C-3B-1B-OF	79	198	10	45	9	3	2	20	3	.227
1997 St. Louis ........N.L.			3B-OF-C-2B	76	132	10	33	5	0	0	11	1	.250
Major League Totals	7 Yrs.			389	946	87	219	38	5	13	110	6	.232
Championship Series													
1996 St. Louis ........N.L.			C	2	3	0	0	0	0	0	0	0	.000

a Became free agent, October 15; signed with Cleveland Indians organization, November 15, 1988.
b Became free agent, October 15; signed with Pittsburgh Pirates organization, November 25, 1989.
c Became free agent, October 15; signed with Minnesota Twins organization, December 20, 1990.
d Record of 0-0 in one game as pitcher.
e Became free agent, October 15; signed with Colorado Rockies, October 29, 1992.
f Signed with St. Louis Cardinals, December 19, 1995.

SHEETS, ANDREW MARK (ANDY)

Born, Baton Rouge, Louisiana, November 19, 1971.
Bats Right. Throws Right. Height, 6 feet, 2 inches. Weight, 180 pounds.

Year	Club	Lea	Pos	G	AB	R	H	2B	3B	HR	RBI	SB	Avg
1993 Riverside ....California			SS	52	176	23	34	9	1	1	12	2	.193
1993 Appleton ....Midwest			SS-2B-OF	69	259	32	68	10	4	1	25	7	.263
1994 Riverside ....California			SS	31	100	17	27	5	1	2	10	6	.270
1994 Calgary .............P.C.			SS	26	93	22	32	8	1	2	16	1	.344
1994 Jacksonville ......Southern			SS	70	232	26	51	12	0	0	17	3	.220
1995 Tacoma .............P.C.			SS-3B-2B	132	437	57	128	29	9	2	47	6	.293
1996 Tacoma .............P.C.			SS-2B-3B	62	232	44	83	16	5	5	33	6	.358
1996 Seattle ............A.L.			3B-2B-SS	47	110	18	21	8	0	0	9	2	.191
1997 Tacoma .............P.C.			SS-2B-3B	113	401	57	104	23	0	14	53	7	.259
1997 Seattle a-b .........A.L.			3B-SS-2B	32	89	18	22	3	0	4	9	2	.247
Major League Totals	2 Yrs.			79	199	36	43	11	0	4	18	4	.216
Division Series													
1997 Seattle .............A.L.			3B	2	3	0	1	0	0	0	0	0	.333

a Selected in expansion draft by Tampa Bay Devil Rays, November 18, 1997.
b Traded to San Diego Padres with pitcher Brian Boehringer for catcher John Flaherty, November 19, 1997.

SHEFFIELD, GARY ANTONIAN

Born, Tampa, Florida, November 18, 1968.
Bats Right. Throws Right. Height, 5 feet, 11 inches. Weight, 190 pounds.

Year	Club	Lea	Pos	G	AB	R	H	2B	3B	HR	RBI	SB	Avg
1986 Helena	Pioneer	SS	57	222	53	81	12	2	15	71	14	.365
1987 Stockton	California	SS	129	469	84	130	23	3	17	*103	25	.277
1988 El Paso	Texas	SS	77	296	70	93	19	3	19	65	5	.314
1988 Denver	A.A.	3B-SS	57	212	42	73	9	5	9	54	8	.344
1988 Milwaukee	A.L.	SS	24	80	12	19	1	0	4	12	3	.238
1989 Denver a	A.A.	SS	7	29	3	4	1	1	0	0	0	.138
1989 Milwaukee	A.L.	SS-3B	95	368	34	91	18	0	5	32	10	.247
1990 Milwaukee b	A.L.	3B	125	487	67	143	30	1	10	67	25	.294
1991 Milwaukee c-d	A.L.	3B	50	175	25	34	12	2	2	22	5	.194
1992 San Diego	N.L.	3B	146	557	87	184	34	3	33	100	5	*.330
1993 San Diego-Florida e-f	N.L.	3B	140	494	67	145	20	5	20	73	17	.294
1994 Portland	Eastern	OF	2	7	1	2	1	0	0	0	0	.286
1994 Florida g	N.L.	OF	87	322	61	89	16	1	27	78	12	.276
1995 Florida h	N.L.	OF	63	213	46	69	8	0	16	46	19	.324
1996 Florida	N.L.	OF	161	519	118	163	33	1	42	120	16	.314
1997 Florida i	N.L.	OF	135	444	86	111	22	1	21	71	11	.250
Major League Totals		10 Yrs.	1026	3659	603	1048	194	14	180	621	123	.286
Division Series													
1997 Florida	N.L.	OF	3	9	2	5	1	0	1	1	1	.556
Championship Series													
1997 Florida	N.L.	OF	6	17	6	4	0	0	1	1	0	.235
World Series Record													
1997 Florida	N.L.	OF	7	24	4	7	1	0	1	5	0	.292

a On disabled list from July 14 to September 9, 1989.
b Suspended three games by American League for June 30 fight, August 31 to September 2, 1990.
c On disabled list from June 2 to July 3 and July 25 to end of 1991 season.
d Traded to San Diego Padres with pitcher Geoff Kellogg for pitcher Ricky Bones, infielder Jose Valentin and outfielder Matt Mieske, March 27, 1992.
e Suspended three games by National League for June 10 fight from July 9 to July 11, 1993.
f Traded to Florida Marlins with pitcher Rich Rodriguez for pitchers Trevor Hoffman, Andres Berumen and Jose Martinez, June 25, 1993.
g On disabled list from May 10 to May 25 and May 28 to June 11, 1994.
h On disabled list from June 11 to September 1, 1995.
i On disabled list from May 14 to May 29, 1997.

SHIPLEY, CRAIG BARRY

Born, Parramatta, New South Wales, Australia, January 7, 1963.
Bats Right. Throws Right. Height, 6 feet, 1 inch. Weight, 190 pounds.

Year	Club	Lea	Pos	G	AB	R	H	2B	3B	HR	RBI	SB	Avg
1984 Vero Beach	Fla. St.	SS	85	293	56	82	11	2	0	28	18	.280
1985 Albuquerque a	P.C.	SS	124	414	50	100	9	2	0	30	24	.242
1986 Albuquerque	P.C.	SS	61	203	33	59	8	2	0	16	6	.291
1986 Los Angeles	N.L.	SS-2B-3B	12	27	3	3	1	0	0	4	0	.111
1987 San Antonio	Texas	3B	33	127	14	30	5	3	2	9	2	.236
1987 Albuquerque	P.C.	SS	49	139	17	31	6	1	1	15	6	.223
1987 Los Angeles b	N.L.	SS-3B	26	35	3	9	1	0	0	2	0	.257
1988 Jackson	Texas	SS	89	335	41	88	14	3	6	41	6	.263
1988 Tidewater	Int.	2B-SS	40	151	12	41	5	0	1	13	0	.272
1989 Tidewater c	Int.	SS-3B	44	131	6	27	1	0	2	9	0	.206
1989 New York	N.L.	SS-3B	4	7	3	1	0	0	0	0	0	.143
1990 Tidewater d-e	Int.	PH	4	3	1	0	0	0	0	0	0	.000
1991 Las Vegas	P.C.	SS	65	230	27	69	9	5	5	34	2	.300
1991 San Diego	N.L.	SS-2B	37	91	6	25	3	0	1	6	0	.275
1992 San Diego	N.L.	SS-2B-3B	52	105	7	26	6	0	0	7	1	.248
1993 San Diego f	N.L.	SS-3B-2B-OF	105	230	25	54	9	0	4	22	12	.235
1994 San Diego g-h	N.L.	3B-SS-2B-OF	81	240	32	80	14	4	4	30	6	.333
1995 Houston	N.L.	3B-SS-2B-1B	92	232	23	61	8	1	3	24	6	.263
1996 Las Vegas	P.C.	SS	1	2	1	0	0	0	0	0	0	.000
1996 Padres	Arizona	SS-3B	3	7	4	5	1	0	0	1	0	.714
1996 San Diego i-j	N.L.	2B-SS-3B-OF	33	92	13	29	5	0	1	7	7	.315
1997 Las Vegas	P.C.	SS-2B-3B-OF	6	19	0	6	3	0	0	1	0	.316
1997 San Diego k-l-m	N.L.	SS-2B-1B-3B	63	139	22	38	9	0	5	19	1	.273
Major League Totals		10 Yrs.	505	1198	137	326	56	5	18	121	33	.272

a Batted left and right from 1985 through 1991 season.
b Traded to New York Mets organization for catcher John Gibbons, April 1, 1988.
c On disabled list from April 20 to May 5 and May 11 to July 31, 1989.
d On disabled list from April 11 to May 2, 1990.

e Drafted by San Diego Padres from New York Mets organization in minor league draft, December 3, 1990.
f On disabled list from May 6 to May 22, 1993.
g On disabled list from April 25 to May 20, 1994.
h Traded to Houston Astros with outfielders Derek Bell and Phil Plantier, pitchers Doug Brocail and Pedro Martinez and shortstop Ricky Gutierrez for third baseman Ken Caminiti, shortstop Andujar Cedeño, outfielder Steve Finley, pitcher Brian Williams, first baseman Roberto Petagine and player to be named, December 28, 1994.
i Signed with San Diego Padres, January 5, 1996.
j On disabled list from April 23 to May 8 and May 17 to July 31, 1996.
k On disabled list from April 1 to May 13 and June 8 to July 2, 1997.
l Filed for free agency, November 3, 1997.
m Released by San Diego Padres, December 22, 1997.

SHUMPERT, TERRANCE DARNELL
Born, Paducah, Kentucky, August 16, 1966.
Bats Right. Throws Right. Height, 5 feet, 11 inch. Weight, 190 pounds.

Year	Club	Lea	Pos	G	AB	R	H	2B	3B	HR	RBI	SB	Avg
1987 Eugene	.....Northwest		2B	48	186	38	54	16	1	4	22	16	.290
1988 Appleton	......Midwest		2B-OF	114	422	64	102	*37	2	7	38	36	.242
1989 Omaha	..........A.A.		2B	113	355	54	88	29	2	4	22	23	.248
1990 Omaha	..........A.A.		2B	39	153	24	39	6	4	2	12	18	.255
1990 Kansas a	.........A.L.		2B	32	91	7	25	6	1	0	8	3	.275
1991 Kansas City	.....A.L.		2B	144	369	45	80	16	4	5	34	17	.217
1992 Kansas City	.....A.L.		2B-SS	36	94	6	14	5	1	1	11	2	.149
1992 Omaha b	.........A.A.		2B-SS	56	210	23	42	12	0	1	14	3	.200
1993 Omaha	..........A.A.		2B	111	413	70	124	29	1	14	59	36	.300
1993 Kansas City	.....A.L.		2B	8	10	0	1	0	0	0	0	1	.100
1994 Kansas City c	......A.L.		2B-3B-SS	64	183	28	44	6	2	8	24	18	.240
1995 Pawtucket	.........Int.		3B-2B-OF	37	133	17	36	7	0	2	11	10	.271
1995 Boston d	.........A.L.		2B-3B-SS	21	47	6	11	3	0	0	3	3	.234
1996 Iowa e	.........A.A.		2B-3B-1B-SS	72	246	45	68	13	4	5	32	13	.276
1996 Chicago f	.........N.L.		3B-2B-SS	27	31	5	7	1	0	2	6	0	.226
1997 San Diego	.........N.L.		2B-OF-3B	13	33	4	9	3	0	1	6	0	.273
1997 Las Vegas g	......P.C.		3B-2B-SS	32	109	18	31	8	1	1	16	3	.284
1997 New Haven h	...Eastern		2B	5	17	2	4	0	0	1	1	0	.235
1997 Colo Sprngs	......P.C.		SS-2B-3B-OF	10	37	8	11	3	0	1	2	0	.297
Major League Totals	....	8 Yrs.	345	858	101	191	40	8	17	92	44	.223

a On disabled list from June 3 to September 10, 1990.
b On disabled list from August 7 to September 7, 1992.
c Traded to Boston Red Sox for player to be named, December 13, 1994.
d Designated for assignment by Boston Red Sox, June 27, 1995.
e On disabled list from August 19 to September 3, 1996.
f Signed with San Diego Padres organization, November 4, 1996.
g Released by San Diego Padres, August 5, 1997.
h Signed with Colorado Rockies organization, August 13, 1997.

SIMON, RANDALL CARLITO
Born, Willemstad, Curacao, May 26, 1975.
Bats Left. Throws Left. Height, 6 feet. Weight, 180 pounds.

Year	Club	Lea	Pos	G	AB	R	H	2B	3B	HR	RBI	SB	Avg
1993 Danville	...........Appal.		1B	61	232	28	59	17	1	3	31	1	.254
1994 Macon	.............So. Atl.		1B-OF	106	358	45	105	23	1	10	54	7	.293
1995 Durham	.........Carolina		1B	122	420	56	111	18	1	18	79	6	.264
1996 Greenville	.......Southern		1B-OF	134	498	74	139	26	2	18	77	4	.279
1997 Richmond	.............Int.		1B	133	519	62	160	45	1	14	102	1	.308
1997 Atlanta	.............N.L.		1B	13	14	2	6	1	0	0	1	0	.429

SMITH, MARK EDWARD
Born, Pasadena, California, May 7, 1970.
Bats Right. Throws Right. Height, 6 feet, 3 inches. Weight, 205 pounds.

Year	Club	Lea	Pos	G	AB	R	H	2B	3B	HR	RBI	SB	Avg
1991 Frederick	.........Carolina		OF	38	148	20	37	5	1	4	29	1	.250
1992 Hagerstown	........Eastern		OF	128	472	51	136	32	6	4	62	15	.288
1993 Rochester	.............Int.		OF	129	485	69	136	27	1	12	68	4	.280
1994 Rochester	.............Int.		OF	114	437	69	108	27	1	19	66	4	.247
1994 Baltimore	.............A.L.		OF	3	7	0	1	0	0	0	2	0	.143
1995 Rochester	.............Int.		OF	96	364	55	101	25	3	12	66	7	.277
1995 Baltimore	.............A.L.		OF	37	104	11	24	5	0	3	15	3	.231

Year Club	Lea	Pos	G	AB	R	H	2B	3B	HR	RBI	SB	Avg
1996 Rochester a ....Int.		OF	39	132	24	46	14	1	8	32	10	.348
1996 Baltimore ...........A.L.		OF	27	78	9	19	2	0	4	10	0	.244
1996 Frederick ....Carolina		DH	1	1	0	0	0	0	0	0	0	.000
1996 Bowie b ....Eastern		DH	6	22	1	2	0	0	1	2	0	.091
1997 Calgary .............P.C.		OF	39	137	37	51	14	1	14	42	2	.372
1997 Carolina ....Southern		OF	3	12	5	5	1	0	3	4	0	.417
1997 Pittsburgh c-d .........N.L.		OF-1B	71	193	29	55	13	1	9	35	3	.285
Major League Totals	4 Yrs.		138	382	49	99	20	1	16	62	6	.259

a On disabled list from July 23 to September 30, 1996.
b Traded to San Diego Padres for catcher Leroy McKinnis, January 9, 1997.
c Traded to Pittsburgh Pirates with pitcher Hal Garrett for outfielder Trey Beamon and catcher Angelo Encarnacion, March 29, 1997.
d On disabled list from May 23 to June 15, 1997.

SNOPEK, CHRISTOPHER CHARLES (CHRIS)

Born, Cynthiana, Kentucky, September 20, 1970.
Bats Right. Throws Right. Height, 6 feet, 1 inch. Weight, 185 pounds.

Year Club	Lea	Pos	G	AB	R	H	2B	3B	HR	RBI	SB	Avg
1992 Utica ...........N.Y.-Penn.		3B-SS	73	245	49	69	15	1	2	29	14	.282
1993 South Bend ......Midwest		3B	22	72	20	28	8	1	5	18	1	.389
1993 Sarasota ....Fla. St.		3B-SS	107	371	61	91	21	4	10	50	3	.245
1994 Birmingham ......Southern		3B-SS	106	365	58	96	25	3	6	54	9	.263
1995 Nashville ...........A.A.		3B-SS	113	393	56	127	23	4	12	55	2	.323
1995 Chicago ............A.L.		3B-SS	22	68	12	22	4	0	1	7	1	.324
1996 Nashville ...........A.A.		SS-3B	40	153	18	38	8	0	2	12	2	.248
1996 Chicago ............A.L.		3B-SS	46	104	18	27	6	1	6	18	0	.260
1997 Chicago ............A.L.		3B-SS	86	298	27	65	15	0	5	35	3	.218
1997 Nashville ...........A.A.		SS-3B	20	73	8	17	4	0	3	8	0	.233
Major League Totals	3 Yrs.		154	470	57	114	25	1	12	60	4	.243

SNOW, JACK THOMAS (J.T.)

Born, Long Beach, California, February 26, 1968.
Bats Both. Throws Left. Height, 6 feet, 2 inches. Weight, 202 pounds.

Year Club	Lea	Pos	G	AB	R	H	2B	3B	HR	RBI	SB	Avg
1989 Oneonta ........N.Y.-Penn.		1B	73	274	41	80	18	2	8	51	4	.292
1990 Prince William .....Carolina		1B	*138	520	57	133	25	1	8	72	2	.256
1991 Albany ....Eastern		1B	132	477	78	133	33	3	13	76	5	.279
1992 Columbus ....Int.		1B-OF	135	492	81	154	26	4	15	78	3	*.313
1992 New York a ..........A.L.		1B	7	14	1	2	1	0	0	2	0	.143
1993 Vancouver ...........P.C.		1B	23	94	19	32	9	1	5	24	0	.340
1993 California ...........A.L.		1B	129	419	60	101	18	2	16	57	3	.241
1994 Vancouver ...........P.C.		1B	53	189	35	56	13	2	8	43	1	.296
1994 California ...........A.L.		1B	61	223	22	49	4	0	8	30	0	.220
1995 California ...........A.L.		1B	143	544	80	157	22	1	24	102	2	.289
1996 California b ..........A.L.		1B	155	575	69	148	20	1	17	67	1	.257
1997 San Francisco .........N.L.		1B	157	531	81	149	36	1	28	104	6	.281
Major League Totals	6 Yrs.		652	2306	313	606	101	5	93	362	12	.263
Division Series												
1997 San Francisco .........N.L.		1B	3	6	0	1	0	0	0	0	0	.167

a Traded to California Angels with pitchers Jerry Nielsen and Russ Springer for pitcher Jim Abbott, December 6, 1992.
b Traded to San Francisco Giants for pitcher Allen Watson and pitcher Fausto Macey, November 27, 1996.

SOJO, LUIS BELTRAN

Born, Barquisimeto, Venezuela, January 3, 1966.
Bats Right. Throws Right. Height, 5 feet, 11 inches. Weight, 174 pounds.

Year Club	Lea	Pos	G	AB	R	H	2B	3B	HR	RBI	SB	Avg
1987 Myrtle Beach .So. Atl.		SS-2B	72	223	23	47	5	4	2	15	5	.211
1988 Myrtle Beach .So. Atl.		SS	135	536	83	*155	22	5	5	56	14	.289
1989 Syracuse ......Int.		SS-3B	121	482	54	133	20	5	3	54	9	.276
1990 Syracuse ......Int.		2B-SS	75	297	39	88	12	3	6	25	10	.296
1990 Toronto a .....A.L.		2B-SS-OF-3B	33	80	14	18	3	0	1	9	1	.225
1991 California .....A.L.		2B-SS-3B-OF	113	364	38	94	14	1	3	20	4	.258
1992 Edmonton .....P.C.		3B-2B-SS	37	145	22	43	9	1	1	24	4	.297

Year	Club	Lea	Pos	G	AB	R	H	2B	3B	HR	RBI	SB	Avg
1992 California b	A.L.		2B-3B-SS	106	368	37	100	12	3	7	43	7	.272
1993 Toronto c-d	A.L.		2B-SS-3B	19	47	5	8	2	0	0	6	0	.170
1993 Syracuse	Int.		2B-OF-3B-1B-SS	43	142	17	31	7	2	1	12	2	.218
1994 Calgary	P.C.		SS-2B	24	102	19	33	9	3	1	18	5	.324
1994 Seattle	A.L.		2B-SS-3B	63	213	32	59	9	2	6	22	2	.277
1995 Tacoma	P.C.		2B-SS	4	17	1	3	0	0	1	1	0	.176
1995 Seattle e	A.L.		SS-2B-OF	102	339	50	98	18	2	7	39	4	.289
1996 Seattle-New York f	A.L.		2B-3B-SS	95	287	23	63	10	1	1	21	2	.220
1997 New York g-h-i	A.L.		2B-SS-3B-1B	77	215	27	66	6	1	2	25	3	.307
Major League Totals		8 Yrs.		608	1913	226	506	74	10	27	185	23	.265
Division Series													
1995 Seattle	A.L.		SS	5	20	0	5	0	0	0	3	0	.250
1996 New York	A.L.		2B	2	0	0	0	0	0	0	0	0	.000
Division Series Totals				7	20	0	5	0	0	0	3	0	.250
Championship Series													
1995 Seattle	A.L.		SS	6	20	2	5	2	0	0	1	0	.250
1996 New York	A.L.		2B	3	5	0	1	0	0	0	0	0	.000
Championship Series Totals				9	25	2	6	2	0	0	1	0	.240
World Series													
1996 New York	A.L.		2B	5	5	0	3	1	0	0	1	0	.600

a Traded to California Angels with outfielder Junior Felix and player to be named for outfielder Devon White, pitcher Willie Fraser and player to be named, December 2; Toronto Blue Jays acquired pitcher Marcus Moore and California acquired catcher Ken Rivers to complete trade, December 5, 1990.
b Traded to Toronto Blue Jays for third baseman Kelly Gruber and cash, December 8, 1992.
c On disabled list from May 10 to May 30, 1993.
d Refused assignment to minor leagues and became free agent, October 15, 1993; signed with Seattle Mariners organization, January 10, 1994.
e On disabled list from June 7 to June 23, 1995.
f Claimed on waivers by New York Yankees, August 22, 1996.
g On disabled list from August 15 to September 29, 1997.
h Filed for free agency, October 31, 1997.
i Re-signed with New York Yankees, December 10, 1997.

SORRENTO, PAUL ANTHONY
Born, Somerville, Massachusetts, November 17, 1965.
Bats Left. Throws Right. Height, 6 feet, 2 inches. Weight, 220 pounds.

Year	Club	Lea	Pos	G	AB	R	H	2B	3B	HR	RBI	SB	Avg
1986 Quad Cities	Midwest		OF	53	177	33	63	11	2	6	34	0	.356
1986 Palm Springs	California		OF	16	62	5	15	3	0	1	7	0	.242
1987 Palm Springs	California		OF	114	370	66	83	14	2	8	45	1	.224
1988 Palm Springs a	California		1B-OF	133	465	91	133	30	6	14	99	3	.286
1989 Orlando	Southern		1B	140	509	81	130	*35	2	27	*112	1	.255
1989 Minnesota	A.L.		1B	14	21	2	5	0	0	0	1	0	.238
1990 Portland	P.C.		1B	102	354	59	107	27	1	19	72	3	.302
1990 Minnesota	A.L.		1B	41	121	11	25	4	1	5	13	1	.207
1991 Portland	P.C.		1B-OF	113	409	59	126	30	2	13	79	1	.308
1991 Minnesota b	A.L.		1B	26	47	6	12	2	0	4	13	0	.255
1992 Cleveland	A.L.		1B	140	458	52	123	24	1	18	60	0	.269
1993 Cleveland	A.L.		1B-OF	148	463	75	119	26	1	18	65	3	.257
1994 Cleveland	A.L.		1B	95	322	43	90	14	0	14	62	0	.280
1995 Cleveland c-d	A.L.		1B	104	323	50	76	14	0	25	79	1	.235
1996 Seattle	A.L.		1B	143	471	67	136	32	1	23	93	0	.289
1997 Seattle e-f	A.L.		1B	146	457	68	123	19	0	31	80	0	.269
Major League Totals		9 Yrs.		857	2683	374	709	135	4	138	466	5	.264
Division Series													
1995 Cleveland	A.L.		1B	3	10	2	3	0	0	0	1	0	.300
1997 Seattle	A.L.		1B	4	10	2	3	1	0	1	1	0	.300
Division Series Totals				7	20	4	6	1	0	1	2	0	.300
Championship Series													
1991 Minnesota	A.L.		PH	1	1	0	0	0	0	0	0	0	.000
1995 Cleveland	A.L.		1B	4	13	2	2	1	0	0	0	0	.154
Championship Series Totals				5	14	2	2	1	0	0	0	0	.143
World Series Record													
1991 Minnesota	A.L.		1B	3	2	0	0	0	0	0	0	0	.000
1995 Cleveland	A.L.		1B	5	11	0	2	1	0	0	0	0	.182
World Series Totals				8	13	0	2	1	0	0	0	0	.154

a Traded by California Angels to Minnesota Twins organization with pitchers Mike Cook and Rob Wassenaar for pitchers Bert Blyleven and Kevin Trudeau, November 3, 1988.
b Traded to Cleveland Indians for pitchers Oscar Munoz and Curt Leskanic, March 28, 1992.

c Not offered 1996 contract, November 2, 1995.
d Signed with Seattle Mariners, January 3, 1996.
e Filed for free agency, October 27, 1997.
f Signed with Tampa Bay Devil Rays, December 8, 1997.

SOSA, SAMUEL

Born, San Pedro de Macoris, Dominican Republic, November 12, 1968.
Bats Right. Throws Right. Height, 6 feet. Weight, 185 pounds.

Year	Club	Lea	Pos	G	AB	R	H	2B	3B	HR	RBI	SB	Avg
1986	Sarasota Rangers	Gulf C.	OF	61	229	38	63	*19	1	4	28	11	.275
1987	Gastonia	So. Atl.	OF	129	519	73	145	27	4	11	59	22	.279
1988	Charlotte	Fla. St.	OF	131	507	70	116	13	*12	9	51	42	.229
1989	Tulsa	Texas	OF	66	273	45	81	15	4	7	31	16	.297
1989	Oklahoma City a	A.A.	OF	10	39	2	4	2	0	0	3	4	.103
1989	Vancouver	P.C.	OF	13	49	7	18	3	0	1	5	2	.367
1989	Texas-Chicago	A.L.	OF	58	183	27	47	8	0	4	13	7	.257
1990	Chicago	A.L.	OF	153	532	72	124	26	10	15	70	32	.233
1991	Vancouver	P.C.	OF	32	116	19	31	7	2	3	19	9	.267
1991	Chicago b	A.L.	OF	116	316	39	64	10	1	10	33	13	.203
1992	Chicago c	N.L.	OF	67	262	41	68	7	2	8	25	15	.260
1992	Iowa	A.A.	OF	5	19	3	6	2	0	0	1	5	.316
1993	Chicago	N.L.	OF	159	598	92	156	25	5	33	93	36	.261
1994	Chicago d	N.L.	OF	105	426	59	128	17	6	25	70	22	.300
1995	Chicago e	N.L.	OF	144	564	89	151	17	3	36	119	34	.268
1996	Chicago f	N.L.	OF	124	498	84	136	21	2	40	100	18	.273
1997	Chicago	N.L.	OF	162	642	90	161	31	4	36	119	22	.251
Major League Totals		9 Yrs.		1088	4021	593	1035	162	33	207	642	199	.257

a Traded by Texas Rangers to Chicago White Sox organization with infielder Scott Fletcher and pitcher Wilson Alvarez
   for outfielder/designated hitter Harold Baines and infielder Fred Manrique, July 29, 1989.
b Traded to Chicago Cubs with pitcher Ken Patterson for outfielder George Bell, March 30, 1992.
c On disabled list from June 13 to July 27 and August 7 to September 16, 1992.
d Declared restricted free agent under Major League Baseball implemented labor proposal, December 23, 1994.
e Re-signed with Chicago Cubs, April 23, 1995.
f On disabled list from August 21 to September 30, 1996.

SPIERS, WILLIAM JAMES III

Born, Orangeburg, South Carolina, June 5, 1966.
Bats Left. Throws Right. Height, 6 feet, 2 inches. Weight, 190 pounds.

Year	Club	Lea	Pos	G	AB	R	H	2B	3B	HR	RBI	SB	Avg
1987	Helena	Pioneer	SS	6	22	4	9	1	0	0	3	2	.409
1987	Beloit	Midwest	SS	64	258	43	77	10	1	3	26	11	.298
1988	Stockton	California	SS	84	353	68	95	17	3	5	52	27	.269
1988	El Paso	Texas	SS	47	168	22	47	5	2	3	21	4	.280
1989	Denver	A.A.	SS	14	47	9	17	2	1	2	8	1	.362
1989	Milwaukee	A.L.	SS-3B-2B-1B	114	345	44	88	9	3	4	33	10	.255
1990	Denver	A.A.	SS	11	38	6	12	0	0	1	7	1	.316
1990	Milwaukee a	A.L.	SS	112	363	44	88	15	3	2	36	11	.242
1991	Milwaukee	A.L.	SS-OF	133	414	71	117	13	6	8	54	14	.283
1992	Beloit	Midwest	SS	16	55	9	13	3	0	0	7	4	.236
1992	Milwaukee b	A.L.	SS-2B-3B	12	16	2	5	2	0	0	2	1	.313
1993	Milwaukee c	A.L.	2B-OF-SS	113	340	43	81	8	4	2	36	9	.238
1994	Milwaukee d	A.L.	3B-SS-OF-1B	73	214	27	54	10	1	0	17	7	.252
1995	Norfolk	Int.	2B-3B	12	41	4	9	2	0	0	4	0	.220
1995	New York e-f-g ...	N.L.	3B-2B	63	72	5	15	2	1	0	11	0	.208
1996	Houston h-i	N.L.	3B-2B-1B-SS	122	218	27	55	10	1	6	26	7	.252
1997	Houston j-k	N.L.	3B-SS-1B-2B	132	291	51	93	27	4	4	48	10	.320
Major League Totals		9 Yrs.		874	2273	314	596	96	23	26	263	69	.262
Division Series													
1997	Houston	N.L.	3B	3	11	1	0	0	0	0	0	0	.000

a On disabled list from April 1 to May 15, 1990.
b On disabled list from April 5 to September 2, 1992.
c Not offered 1994 contract, December 20; re-signed with Milwaukee Brewers, December 21, 1993.
d Claimed on waivers by New York Mets, October 25, 1994.
e On disabled list from May 15 to June 5 and June 26 to July 16, 1995.
f Filed for free agency, November 12, 1995.
g Signed with Houston Astros organization, January 9, 1996.
h Filed for free agency, November 14, 1996.
i Re-signed with Houston Astros, December 2, 1996.
j Filed for free agency, November 3, 1997.
k Re-signed with Houston Astros, November 25, 1997.

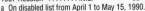

SPIEZIO, SCOTT EDWARD

Born, Joliet, Illinois, September 21, 1972.
Bats Both. Throws Right. Height, 6 feet, 2 inches. Weight, 208 pounds.

Year	Club	Lea	Pos	G	AB	R	H	2B	3B	HR	RBI	SB	Avg
1993 Sou Oregon	Northwest	3B-1B	31	125	32	41	10	2	3	19	0	.328
1993 Modesto	California	3B-1B	32	110	12	28	9	1	1	13	1	.255
1994 Modesto	California	3B-2B-SS	127	453	84	127	32	5	14	68	5	.280
1995 Huntsville	Southern	3B-1B-2B	141	528	78	149	33	8	13	86	10	.282
1996 Edmonton	P.C.	3B-1B	140	523	87	137	30	4	20	91	6	.262
1996 Oakland	A.L.	3B	9	29	6	9	2	0	2	8	0	.310
1997 Sou Oregon	Northwest	2B	2	9	1	5	0	0	0	2	0	.556
1997 Oakland a	A.L.	2B-3B	147	538	58	131	28	4	14	65	9	.243
Major League Totals			2 Yrs.	156	567	64	140	30	4	16	73	9	.247

a On disabled list from June 8 to June 25, 1997.

SPRAGUE, EDWARD NELSON JR.

Born, Castro Valley, California, July 25, 1967.
Bats Right. Throws Right. Height, 6 feet, 2 inches. Weight, 210 pounds.

Year	Club	Lea	Pos	G	AB	R	H	2B	3B	HR	RBI	SB	Avg
1989 Dunedin	Fla. St.	3B	52	192	21	42	9	2	7	23	1	.219
1989 Syracuse	Int.	3B	86	288	23	60	14	1	5	33	0	.208
1990 Syracuse	Int.	3B-1B-C	*142	*519	60	124	23	5	20	75	4	.239
1991 Syracuse	Int.	C-3B	23	88	24	32	8	0	5	25	2	.364
1991 Toronto	A.L.	3B-1B-C	61	160	17	44	7	0	4	20	0	.275
1992 Syracuse	Int.	C-1B-3B	99	369	49	102	18	2	16	50	0	.276
1992 Toronto	A.L.	C-1B-3B	22	47	6	11	2	0	1	7	0	.234
1993 Toronto	A.L.	3B	150	546	50	142	31	1	12	73	1	.260
1994 Toronto	A.L.	3B-1B	109	405	38	97	19	1	11	44	1	.240
1995 Toronto a	A.L.	3B-1B	144	521	77	127	27	2	18	74	0	.244
1996 Toronto	A.L.	3B	159	591	88	146	35	2	36	101	0	.247
1997 Toronto b	A.L.	3B	138	504	63	115	29	4	14	48	0	.228
Major League Totals			7 Yrs.	783	2774	339	682	150	10	96	367	2	.246
Championship Series													
1992 Toronto	A.L.	PH	2	2	0	1	0	0	0	0	0	.500
1993 Toronto	A.L.	3B	6	21	0	6	0	1	0	4	0	.286
Championship Series Totals				8	23	0	7	0	1	0	4	0	.304
World Series Record													
1992 Toronto	A.L.	1B	3	2	1	1	0	0	1	2	0	.500
1993 Toronto	A.L.	3B-1B	5	15	0	1	0	0	0	2	0	.067
World Series Totals				8	17	1	2	0	0	1	4	0	.118

a Signed with Toronto Blue Jays, April 28, 1995.
b On disabled list from September 4 to September 29, 1997.

STAHOVIAK, SCOTT EDMUND

Born, Waukegan, Illinois, March 6, 1970.
Bats Left. Throws Left. Height, 6 feet, 5 inches. Weight, 208 pounds.

Year	Club	Lea	Pos	G	AB	R	H	2B	3B	HR	RBI	SB	Avg
1991 Visalia	California	3B	43	158	29	44	9	1	1	25	9	.278
1992 Visalia	California	3B	110	409	62	126	26	3	5	68	17	.308
1993 Nashville	Southern	3B-1B-SS	93	331	40	90	25	1	12	56	10	.272
1993 Minnesota	A.L.	3B	20	57	1	11	4	0	0	1	0	.193
1994 Salt Lake	P.C.	3B-1B	123	437	96	139	41	6	13	94	6	.318
1995 Salt Lake	P.C.	3B-1B	9	33	6	10	1	0	0	5	2	.303
1995 Minnesota	A.L.	1B-3B	94	263	28	70	19	0	3	23	5	.266
1996 Minnesota a-b	A.L.	1B	130	405	72	115	30	3	13	61	3	.284
1997 Salt Lake	P.C.	1B	8	28	5	6	0	0	2	10	0	.214
1997 Minnesota c	A.L.	1B	91	275	33	63	17	0	10	33	5	.229
Major League Totals			4 Yrs.	335	1000	134	259	70	3	26	118	13	.259

a On disabled list from August 12 to September 1, 1996.
b Outrighted by Montreal Expos, October 16, 1996.
c On disabled list from April 2 to May 16, 1997.

STAIRS, MATTHEW WADE (MATT)

Born, Fredericton, New Brunswick, Canada, February 27, 1969.
Bats Left. Throws Right. Height, 5 feet, 9 inches. Weight, 175 pounds.

Year	Club	Lea	Pos	G	AB	R	H	2B	3B	HR	RBI	SB	Avg
1989 Jamestown	N.Y.Penn.	2B-3B	14	43	8	11	1	0	1	5	1	.256
1989 West Palm Bch.	Fla. St.	3B-SS-2B	36	111	12	21	3	1	1	9	0	.189
1989 Rockford	Midwest	3B	44	141	20	40	9	2	2	14	5	.284
1990 West Palm Bch.	Fla. St.	3B-SS	55	183	30	62	9	3	3	30	15	.339
1990 Jacksonville	Southern	3B-OF-2B	79	280	26	71	17	0	3	34	5	.254
1991 Harrisburg	Eastern	2B-3B-OF	129	505	87	168	30	10	13	78	23	.333
1992 Montreal	N.L.	OF	13	30	2	5	2	0	0	5	0	.167
1992 Indianapolis	A.A.	OF	110	401	57	107	23	4	11	56	11	.267
1993 Ottawa	Int.	OF	34	125	18	35	4	2	3	20	4	.280
1993 Montreal	N.L.	OF	6	8	1	3	1	0	0	2	0	.375
1994 New Britain	Eastern	OF-1B	93	317	44	98	25	2	9	61	10	.309
1995 Pawtucket	Int.	OF	75	271	40	77	17	0	13	56	3	.284
1995 Boston a	A.L.	OF	39	88	8	23	7	1	1	17	0	.261
1996 Edmonton	P.C.	DH-OF-1B	51	180	35	62	16	1	8	41	0	.344
1996 Oakland	A.L.	OF-1B	61	137	21	38	5	1	10	23	1	.277
1997 Oakland	A.L.	OF-1B	133	352	62	105	19	0	27	73	3	.298
Major League Totals		5 Yrs.	252	615	94	174	34	2	38	120	4	.283
Division Series												
1995 Boston	A.L.	PH	1	1	F0	0	0	0	0	0	0	.000

a Signed with Oakland Athletics organization, December 2, 1995.

STANLEY, ROBERT MICHAEL (MIKE)

Born, Fort Lauderdale, Florida, June 25, 1963.
Bats Right. Throws Right. Height, 6 feet. Weight, 192 pounds.

Year	Club	Lea	Pos	G	AB	R	H	2B	3B	HR	RBI	SB	Avg
1985 Salem	Carolina	1B-C	4	9	2	5	0	0	0	3	0	.556
1985 Burlington	Midwest	C-1B-OF	13	42	8	13	2	0	1	6	0	.310
1985 Tulsa	Texas	C-1B-OF-2B	46	165	24	51	10	0	3	17	6	.309
1986 Tulsa	Texas	C-1B-3B	67	235	41	69	16	2	6	35	5	.294
1986 Texas	A.L.	3B-C-OF	15	30	4	10	3	0	1	1	1	.333
1986 Oklahoma City	A.A.	C-3B-1B	56	202	37	74	13	3	5	49	1	.366
1987 Oklahoma City	A.A.	C	46	182	43	61	8	3	13	54	2	.335
1987 Texas	A.L.	C-1B-OF	78	216	34	59	8	1	6	37	3	.273
1988 Texas a	A.L.	C-1B-3B	94	249	21	57	8	0	3	27	0	.229
1989 Texas b	A.L.	C-1B-3B	67	122	9	30	3	1	1	11	1	.246
1990 Texas c	A.L.	C-3B-1B	103	189	21	47	8	1	2	19	1	.249
1991 Texas d	A.L.	C-1B-3B-OF	95	181	25	45	13	1	3	25	0	.249
1992 New York	A.L.	C-1B	68	173	24	43	7	0	8	27	0	.249
1993 New York	A.L.	C	130	423	70	129	17	1	26	84	1	.305
1994 New York e	A.L.	C-1B	82	290	54	87	20	0	17	57	0	.300
1995 New York f	A.L.	C	118	399	63	107	29	1	18	83	1	.268
1996 Boston	A.L.	C	121	397	73	107	20	1	24	69	2	.270
1997 Boston-New York g-h-i	A.L.	DH-1B-C	125	347	61	103	25	0	16	65	0	.297
Major League Totals		12 Yrs.	1096	3016	459	824	161	7	125	505	10	.273
Division Series												
1995 New York	A.L.	C	5	16	2	5	0	0	1	3	0	.313
1997 New York	A.L.	DH	2	4	1	3	1	0	0	1	0	.750
Divisional Series Totals			6	20	3	8	1	0	1	4	0	.400

a On disabled list from July 23 to August 13, 1988.
b On disabled list from August 19 to September 2, 1989.
c Refused assignment to minor leagues and became free agent, October 27, 1990; re-signed with Texas Rangers organization, February 4, 1991.
d Refused assignment to minor leagues and became free agent, October 17, 1991; signed with New York Yankees organization, January 21, 1992.
e On disabled list from May 15 to May 29, 1994.
f Filed for free agency, November 12, 1995; signed with Boston Red Sox, December 14, 1995.
g Traded to New York Yankees with infielder Randy Brown for pitcher Tony Armas and player to be named later, August 13, 1997.
h Boston Red Sox received pitcher Jim Mecir to complete trade, September 29, 1997.
i Filed for free agency, October 27, 1997.
j Signed with Toronto Blue Jays, December 9, 1997

STEINBACH, TERRY LEE
Born, New Ulm, Minnesota, March 2, 1962.
Bats Right. Throws Right. Height, 6 feet, 1 inch. Weight, 195 pounds.

Year Club	Lea	Pos	G	AB	R	H	2B	3B	HR	RBI	SB	Avg
1983 Medford . . . . .Northwest		3B-OF-1B	62	219	42	69	16	0	6	38	8	.315
1984 Madison a . . . . .Midwest		3B-1B	135	474	57	140	24	6	11	79	5	.295
1985 Huntsville b . . . . .South.		C-3B-1B-OF	128	456	64	124	31	3	9	72	4	.272
1986 Huntsville . . . . .Southern		C-1B-3B	138	505	113	164	33	2	24	*132	10	.325
1986 Oakland . . . . .A.L.		C	6	15	3	5	0	0	2	4	0	.333
1987 Oakland . . . . .A.L.		C-3B-1B	122	391	66	111	16	3	16	56	1	.284
1988 Oakland c . . . . .A.L.		C-3B-1B-OF	104	351	42	93	19	1	9	51	3	.265
1989 Oakland . . . . .A.L.		C-OF-1B-3B	130	454	37	124	13	1	7	42	1	.273
1990 Oakland d . . . . .A.L.		C-1B	114	379	32	95	15	2	9	57	0	.251
1991 Oakland . . . . .A.L.		C-1B	129	456	50	125	31	1	6	67	2	.274
1992 Oakland e-f . . . . . .A.L.		C-1B	128	438	48	122	20	1	12	53	2	.279
1993 Oakland g . . . . .A.L.		C-1B	104	389	47	111	19	1	10	43	3	.285
1994 Oakland . . . . .A.L.		C-1B	103	369	51	105	21	2	11	57	2	.285
1995 Oakland h . . . . .A.L.		C-1B	114	406	43	113	26	1	15	65	1	.278
1996 Oakland i-j . . . . . . .A.L.		C-1B	145	514	79	140	25	1	35	100	0	.272
1997 Minnesota . . . . .A.L.		C-1B	122	447	60	111	27	1	12	54	6	.248
Major League Totals		12 Yrs.	1321	4609	558	1255	.232	15	144	649	21	.272
Championship Series												
1988 Oakland . . . . .A.L.		C	2	4	0	1	0	0	0	0	0	.250
1989 Oakland . . . . .A.L.		C	4	15	0	3	0	0	0	1	0	.200
1990 Oakland . . . . .A.L.		C	3	11	2	5	0	0	0	1	0	.455
1992 Oakland . . . . .A.L.		C	6	24	1	7	0	0	1	5	0	.292
Championship Series Totals			15	54	3	16	0	0	1	7	0	.296
World Series Record												
1988 Oakland . . . . .A.L.		C	3	11	0	4	1	0	0	0	0	.364
1989 Oakland . . . . .A.L.		C	4	16	3	4	0	1	1	7	0	.250
1990 Oakland . . . . .A.L.		C	3	8	0	1	0	0	0	0	0	.125
World Series Totals			10	35	3	9	1	1	1	7	0	.257

a Record of 0-0 in two games as pitcher.
b Record of 0-0 in one game as pitcher.
c On disabled list from May 6 to June 1, 1988.
d On disabled list from July 3 to July 27, 1990.
e On disabled list from April 10 to April 25, 1992.
f Filed for free agency, October 26; re-signed with Oakland Athletics, December 14, 1992.
g On disabled list from August 16 to end of 1993 season.
h On disabled list from August 13 to August 29, 1995.
i Filed for free agency, November 17, 1996.
j Signed with Minnesota Twins, December 5, 1996.

STEVENS, DE WAIN LEE
Born, Kansas City, Missouri, July 10, 1967.
Bats Left. Throws Left. Height, 6 feet, 4 inches. Weight, 226 pounds.

Year Club	Lea	Pos	G	AB	R	H	2B	3B	HR	RBI	SB	Avg
1986 Salem . . . . .Northwest		OF-1B	72	267	45	75	18	2	6	47	13	.281
1987 Palm Sprngs . . . . .California		1B-OF	140	532	82	130	29	2	19	97	1	.244
1988 Midland . . . . .Texas		OF-1B	116	414	79	123	26	2	23	76	0	.297
1989 Edmonton . . . . .P.C.		1B-OF	127	446	72	110	29	9	14	74	5	.247
1990 Edmonton . . . . .P.C.		OF-1B	90	338	57	99	31	2	16	66	1	.293
1990 California . . . . .A.L.		1B	67	248	28	53	10	0	7	32	1	.214
1991 Edmonton . . . . .P.C.		OF-1B	123	481	75	151	29	3	19	96	3	.314
1991 California . . . . .A.L.		1B-OF	18	58	8	17	7	0	0	9	1	.293
1992 California . . . . .A.L.		1B	106	312	25	69	19	0	7	37	1	.221
1993 Syracuse a-b-c-d-f . . . . . .Int.		1B-OF	116	401	61	106	30	1	14	66	2	.264
1994 Kintetsu . . . . .Japan Pac.		OF-1B	93	302	44	87	21	0	20	66	0	.288
1995 Kintetsu g . . . . . .Japan Pac.		1B-OF	129	476	54	117	*29	1	23	70	0	.246
1996 Okla City h-i . . . . .A.A.		DH-1B-OF	117	431	84	140	37	2	32	94	3	.325
1996 Texas j . . . . .A.L.		1B-OF	27	78	6	18	2	3	3	12	0	.231
1997 Texas . . . . .A.L.		1B-OF	137	426	58	128	24	2	21	74	1	.300
Major League Totals		5 Yrs.	355	1122	125	285	62	5	38	164	4	.254

a Traded to Montreal Expos for pitcher Jeff Tuss, January 15, 1993.
b Released by Montreal Expos organization, March 30, 1993.
c Signed as free agent with Toronto Blue Jays organization, April 8, 1993.
d Filed for free agency, October 15, 1993.
e Signed with California Angels organization, October 25, 1993.
f Released by California Angels, November 16, 1993.
g Signed free agent with Cincinnati Reds organization, March 8, 1996.

h Released by Cincinnati Reds, March 25, 1996.
i Signed as free agent by Texas Rangers organization, April 4, 1996.
j On disabled list August 4 to September 1, 1996.

STEWART, SHANNON HAROLD

Born, Cincinnati, Ohio, February 25, 1974.
Bats Right. Throws Right. Height, 6 feet, 1 inch. Weight, 194 pounds.

Year	Club	Lea	Pos	G	AB	R	H	2B	3B	HR	RBI	SB	Avg
1992 Blue Jays	Gulf Coast	OF	50	172	44	40	1	0	1	11	32	.233
1993 St. Cathrnes	N.Y.-Penn.	DH-OF	75	301	53	84	15	2	3	29	25	.279
1994 Hagerstown	So. Atl.	OF	56	225	39	73	10	5	4	25	15	.324
1995 Knoxville	Southern	OF	138	498	89	143	24	6	5	55	42	.287
1995 Toronto	A.L.	OF	12	38	2	8	0	0	0	1	2	.211
1996 Syracuse	Int.	OF	112	420	77	125	26	8	6	42	35	.298
1996 Toronto a	A.L.	OF	7	17	2	3	1	0	0	2	1	.176
1997 Syracuse	Int.	OF	58	208	41	72	13	1	5	24	9	.346
1997 Toronto	A.L.	OF	44	168	25	48	13	7	0	22	10	.286
Major League Totals			3 Yrs.	63	223	29	59	14	7	0	25	13	.265

a On disabled list May 13 to May 31, 1996.

STINNETT, KELLY LEE

Born, Lawton, Oklahoma, February 4, 1970.
Bats Right. Throws Right. Height, 5 feet, 11 inches. Weight, 195 pounds.

Year	Club	Lea	Pos	G	AB	R	H	2B	3B	HR	RBI	SB	Avg
1990 Watertown	N.Y.-Penn.	C-1B	60	192	29	46	10	2	2	21	3	.240
1991 Columbus	So. Atl.	C-1B	102	384	49	101	15	1	14	74	4	.263
1992 Canton-Akrn	Eastern	C	91	296	37	84	10	0	6	32	7	.284
1993 Charlotte a	Int.	C	98	288	42	79	10	3	6	33	0	.274
1994 New York	N.L.	C	47	150	20	38	6	2	2	14	2	.253
1995 New York b	N.L.	C	77	196	23	43	8	1	4	18	2	.219
1996 New Orleans	A.A.	C-3B	95	334	63	96	21	1	27	70	3	.287
1996 Milwaukee	A.L.	C	14	26	1	2	0	0	0	0	0	.077
1997 Tucson	P.C.	C-1B	64	209	50	67	15	3	10	43	1	.321
1997 Milwaukee c-d	A.L.	C	30	36	2	9	4	0	0	3	0	.250
Major League Totals			4 Yrs.	168	408	46	92	18	3	6	35	4	.225

a Selected by New York Mets from Cleveland Indians organization in Rule V draft, December 13, 1993.
b Traded to Milwaukee Brewers for pitcher Cory Lidle, January 17, 1996.
c On disabled list from July 25 to August 31, 1997.
d Selected in expansion draft by Arizona Diamondbacks, November 18, 1997.

STOCKER, KEVIN DOUGLAS

Born, Spokane, Washington, February 13, 1970.
Bats Both. Throws Right. Height, 6 feet, 1 inches. Weight, 175 pounds.

Year	Club	Lea	Pos	G	AB	R	H	2B	3B	HR	RBI	SB	Avg
1991 Spartanburg	So. Atl.	SS	70	250	26	55	11	1	0	20	15	.220
1992 Clearwater	Fla. St.	SS	63	244	43	69	13	4	1	33	15	.283
1992 Reading	Eastern	SS	62	240	31	60	9	2	1	13	17	.250
1993 Scranton	Int.	SS	83	313	54	73	14	1	3	17	17	.233
1993 Philadelphia	N.L.	SS	70	259	46	84	12	3	2	31	5	.324
1994 Scranton	Int.	SS	4	13	1	4	1	0	0	2	0	.308
1994 Philadelphia a	N.L.	SS	82	271	38	74	11	2	2	28	2	.273
1995 Philadelphia	N.L.	SS	125	412	42	90	14	3	1	32	6	.218
1996 Scranton-WB	Int.	SS	12	44	5	10	3	0	2	6	1	.227
1996 Philadelphia	N.L.	SS	119	394	46	100	22	6	5	41	6	.254
1997 Philadelphia b	N.L.	SS	149	504	51	134	23	5	4	40	11	.266
Major League Totals			5 Yrs.	545	1840	223	482	82	19	14	172	30	.262
Championship Series													
1993 Philadelphia	N.L.	SS	6	22	0	4	1	0	0	1	0	.182
World Series Record													
1993 Philadelphia	N.L.	SS	6	19	1	4	1	0	0	1	0	.211

a On disabled list from April 28 to June 1, 1994.
b Traded to Tampa Bay Devil Rays for outfielder Bob Abreu, November 19, 1997.

STRANGE, JOSEPH DOUGLAS
Born, Greenville, South Carolina, April 13, 1964.
Bats Both. Throws Right. Height, 6 feet, 2 inches. Weight, 170 pounds.

Year	Club	Lea	Pos	G	AB	R	H	2B	3B	HR	RBI	SB	Avg
1985 Bristol	....	Appal.	OF-2B	65	226	43	69	16	1	6	45	6	.305
1986 Lakeland	....	Fla. St.	3B	126	466	59	119	29	4	2	63	18	.255
1987 Glens Falls	.....	Eastern	3B	115	431	63	130	31	1	13	70	4	.302
1987 Toledo	....	Int.	3B	16	45	7	11	2	0	1	5	3	.244
1988 Toledo	....	Int.	3B	82	278	23	56	8	2	6	19	9	.201
1988 Glens Falls	....	Eastern	3B	57	218	32	61	11	1	1	36	11	.280
1989 Toledo	....	Int.	3B-SS	83	304	38	75	15	2	8	42	38	.247
1989 Detroit a	....	A.L.	3B-2B-SS	64	196	16	42	4	1	1	14	3	.214
1990 Tucson b	....	P.C.	3B	37	98	7	22	3	0	0	7	0	.224
1990 Iowa	....	A.A.	3B	82	269	31	82	17	1	5	35	6	.305
1991 Iowa	....	A.A.	3B-2B-SS	131	509	76	149	35	5	8	56	10	.293
1991 Chicago	....	N.L.	3B	3	9	0	4	1	0	0	1	1	.444
1992 Iowa	....	A.A.	2B-3B-1B	55	212	32	65	16	1	4	26	3	.307
1992 Chicago c	....	N.L.	3B-2B	52	94	7	15	1	0	1	5	1	.160
1993 Texas	....	A.L.	2B-3B-SS	145	484	58	124	29	0	7	60	6	.256
1994 Texas d-e	....	A.L.	2B-3B-OF	73	226	26	48	12	1	5	26	1	.212
1995 Seattle f	....	A.L.	3B-2B-OF	74	155	19	42	9	2	2	21	0	.271
1996 Seattle g-h	....	A.L.	3B-OF-1B	88	183	19	43	7	1	3	23	1	.235
1997 Ottawa	....	Int.	3B	2	7	3	3	1	0	0	0	0	.429
1997 Montreal i-j-k	......	N.L.	3B-2B-OF-1B	118	327	40	84	16	2	12	47	0	.257
Major League Totals	....		8 Yrs.	617	1674	185	402	79	7	31	197	13	.240
Division Series													
1995 Seattle	....	A.L.	3B	2	4	0	0	0	0	0	1	0	.000
Championship Series													
1995 Seattle	....	A.L.	3B	4	4	0	0	0	0	0	0	0	.000

a Traded to Houston Astros organization for infielder/outfielder Lou Frazier, March 30, 1990.
b Released by Houston Astros, May 25; signed with Chicago Cubs organization, June 11, 1990.
c Not offered 1993 contract, December 18, 1992; signed with Texas Rangers, January 11, 1993.
d On disabled list from July 2 to July 17, 1994.
e Not offered 1995 contract, December 23, 1994.
f Signed with Seattle Mariners, March 25, 1995.
g Filed for free agency, October 8, 1996.
h Signed with Montreal Expos organization February 4, 1997.
i On disabled list from June 17 to July 2, 1997.
j Filed for free agency, November 5, 1997.
k Signed with Montreal Expos, December 2, 1997.

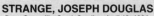

STRAWBERRY, DARRYL EUGENE
Born, Los Angeles, California, March 12, 1962.
Bats Left. Throws Left. Height, 6 feet, 6 inches. Weight, 215 pounds.

Year	Club	Lea	Pos	G	AB	R	H	2B	3B	HR	RBI	SB	Avg
1980 Kingsport	....	Appal.	OF	44	157	27	42	5	2	5	20	5	.268
1981 Lynchburg	....	Carolina	OF	123	420	84	107	22	6	13	78	31	.255
1982 Jackson	....	Texas	OF	129	435	93	123	19	9	*34	97	45	.283
1983 Tidewater	....	Int.	OF	16	57	12	19	4	1	3	13	7	.333
1983 New York a	....	N.L.	OF	122	420	63	108	15	7	26	74	19	.257
1984 New York	....	N.L.	OF	147	522	75	131	27	4	26	97	27	.251
1985 New York b	....	N.L.	OF	111	393	78	109	15	4	29	79	26	.277
1986 New York	....	N.L.	OF	136	475	76	123	27	5	27	93	28	.259
1987 New York	....	N.L.	OF	154	532	108	151	32	5	39	104	36	.284
1988 New York	....	N.L.	OF	153	543	101	146	27	3	*39	101	29	.269
1989 New York	....	N.L.	OF	134	476	69	107	26	1	29	77	11	.225
1990 New York c	....	N.L.	OF	152	542	92	150	18	1	37	108	15	.277
1991 Los Angeles d	....	N.L.	OF	139	505	86	134	22	4	28	99	10	.265
1992 Los Angeles e	....	N.L.	OF	43	156	20	37	8	0	5	25	3	.237
1993 Albuquerque	....	P.C.	OF	5	19	3	6	2	0	1	2	1	.316
1993 Los Angeles f-g-h	......	N.L.	OF	32	100	12	14	2	0	5	12	1	.140
1994 Phoenix	....	P.C.	OF	3	10	3	3	0	0	2	3	0	.300
1994 San Francisco i-j	......	N.L.	OF	29	92	13	22	3	1	4	17	0	.239
1995 Yankees	....	Gulf Coast	OF	7	20	3	5	2	0	0	4	2	.250
1995 Tampa	....	Fla. St.	DH	2	9	1	2	1	0	1	2	0	.222
1995 Columbus	....	Int.	DH-OF	22	83	20	25	3	1	7	29	1	.301
1995 New York k-l	....	A.L.	DH-OF	32	87	15	24	4	1	3	13	0	.276
1996 St. Paul	....	Northern	OF	29	108	31	47	7	0	18	39	4	.435
1996 Columbus	....	Int.	DH	2	8	3	3	0	0	3	5	0	.375
1996 New York m	....	A.L.	OF	63	202	35	53	13	0	11	36	6	.262
1997 Norwich	....	Eastern	OF	1	2	0	0	0	0	0	0	0	.000

Year	Club	Lea	Pos	G	AB	R	H	2B	3B	HR	RBI	SB	Avg
1997 Tampa	............Fla. St.		DH	4	16	2	7	1	0	0	4	0	.438
1997 Columbus	............Int.		DH	11	38	8	11	3	0	6	19	0	.289
1997 New York n-o-p	.......A.L.		OF	11	29	1	3	1	0	0	2	0	.103
Major League Totals		15 Yrs.	1458	5074	844	1312	240	36	308	937	211	.259	
Division Series													
1995 New York	...........A.L.		PH	2	2	0	0	0	0	0	0	0	.000
1996 New York	.............A.L.		DH	2	5	0	0	0	0	0	0	0	.000
Division Series Totals	....			4	7	0	0	0	0	0	0	0	.000
Championship Series													
1986 New York	............N.L.		OF	6	22	4	5	1	0	2	5	1	.227
1988 New York	............N.L.		OF	7	30	5	9	2	0	1	6	0	.300
1996 New York	............A.L.		OF	4	12	4	5	0	0	3	5	0	.417
Championship Series Totals	....			17	64	13	19	3	0	6	16	1	.297
World Series Record													
1986 New York	............N.L.		OF	7	24	4	5	1	0	1	1	3	.208
1996 New York	............A.L.		OF	5	16	0	3	0	0	0	1	0	.188
World Series Totals	....			12	40	4	8	1	0	1	2	3	.200

a Selected Rookie of the Year in National League for 1983.
b On disabled list from May 12 to June 28, 1985.
c Filed for free agency, October 22; signed with Los Angeles Dodgers, November 8, 1990.
d On disabled list from June 18 to July 3, 1991.
e On disabled list from May 14 to July 6 and July 21 to September 1, 1992.
f On disabled list from May 13 to June 5 and June 17 to end of 1993 season.
g On disabled list from April 3 to May 26, 1994.
h Released by Los Angeles Dodgers, May 26; signed with San Francisco Giants, July 3, 1994.
i Suspended 60 days by Major League Baseball for violating drug abuse aftercare program, February 6; suspension to be served from April 2, 1995.
j Released, February 6, 1995.
k Signed with New York Yankees, June 19, 1995.
l Contract option not picked up, November 30, 1995.
m Signed with New York Yankees, July 4, 1996.
n On disabled list from April 7 to August 15, 1997.
o Filed for free agency, October 30, 1997.
p Re-signed with New York Yankees, January 8, 1998.

STYNES, CHRISTOPHER DESMOND (CHRIS)
Born, Queens, New York, January 19, 1973.
Bats Right. Throws Right. Height, 5 feet, 9 inches. Weight, 170 pounds.

Year	Club	Lea	Pos	G	AB	R	H	2B	3B	HR	RBI	SB	Avg
1991 Blue Jays	.......Gulf Coast		3B	57	219	29	67	15	1	4	39	10	.306
1992 Myrtle Beach	.......So. Atl.		3B-2B	127	489	67	139	36	0	7	46	28	.284
1993 Dunedin	...........Fla. St.		3B	123	496	72	151	28	5	7	48	19	.304
1994 Knoxville	........Southern		2B	136	545	79	173	32	4	8	79	28	.317
1995 Omaha	..............A.A.		2B-3B	83	306	51	84	12	5	9	42	4	.275
1995 Kansas City a	.........A.L.		2B	22	35	7	6	1	0	0	2	0	.171
1996 Omaha	..............A.A.		OF-3B-2B	72	284	50	101	22	2	10	40	7	.356
1996 Kansas City	...........A.L.		OF-2B-3B	36	92	8	27	6	0	0	6	5	.293
1997 Omaha	..............A.A.		2B-OF-3B	82	332	53	88	18	1	8	44	3	.265
1997 Indianapolis	...........A.A.		2B	21	86	14	31	8	0	1	17	4	.360
1997 Cincinnati b	...........N.L.		OF-2B-3B	49	198	31	69	7	1	6	28	11	.348
Major League Totals		3 Yrs.	107	325	46	102	14	1	6	36	16	.314	

a Traded to Kansas City Royals with infielder Anthony Medrano and pitcher David Sinnes for pitcher David Cone, April 6, 1995.
b Traded to Cincinnati Reds with outfielder Jon Nunnally for pitcher Hector Carrasco and pitcher Scott Service, July 15, 1997.

SURHOFF, WILLIAM JAMES (B.J.)
Born, Bronx, New York, August 4, 1964.
Bats Left. Throws Right. Height, 6 feet, 1 inch. Weight, 200 pounds.

Year	Club	Lea	Pos	G	AB	R	H	2B	3B	HR	RBI	SB	Avg
1985 Beloit	.....Midwest		C	76	289	39	96	13	4	7	58	10	.332
1986 Vancouver	....P.C.		C	116	458	71	141	19	3	5	59	21	.308
1987 Milwaukee	....A.L.		C-3B-1B	115	395	50	118	22	3	7	68	11	.299
1988 Milwaukee	....A.L.		C-3B-1B-SS-OF	139	493	47	121	21	0	5	38	21	.245
1989 Milwaukee	....A.L.		C-3B	126	436	42	108	17	4	5	55	14	.248
1990 Milwaukee a	...A.L.		C-3B	135	474	55	131	21	4	6	59	18	.276

Year Club	Lea	Pos	G	AB	R	H	2B	3B	HR	RBI	SB	Avg
1991 Milwaukee ....A.L.		C-3B-OF-2B	143	505	57	146	19	4	5	68	5	.289
1992 Milwaukee .......A.L.		C-1B-OF-3B	139	480	63	121	19	1	4	62	14	.252
1993 Milwaukee .......A.L.		3B-OF-1B-C	148	552	66	151	38	3	7	79	12	.274
1994 El Paso ....Texas		OF	3	12	2	3	1	0	0	0	0	.250
1994 New Orleans .....A.A.		3B-1B-OF-C	5	19	3	6	2	0	0	1	0	.316
1994 Milwaukee b-c .....A.L.		3B-C-1B-OF	40	134	20	35	11	2	5	22	0	.261
1995 Milwaukee d-e-f ..A.L.		OF-1B-C	117	415	72	133	26	3	13	73	7	.320
1996 Baltimore .........A.L.		3B-OF-1B	143	537	74	157	27	6	21	82	0	.292
1997 Baltimore ......A.L.		OF-1B-3B	147	528	80	150	30	4	18	88	1	.284
Major League Totals	11 Yrs.		1392	4949	626	1371	251	34	96	694	103	.277
Division Series												
1996 Baltimore .....A.L.		OF	4	13	3	5	0	0	0	3	5	0	.385
1997 Baltimore .....A.L.		OF	3	11	0	3	1	0	0	0	2	0	.273
Division Series Totals			7	24	3	8	1	0	3	7	0	.333
Championship Series												
1996 Baltimore .....A.L.		OF	5	15	0	4	0	0	0	2	0	.267
1997 Baltimore .....A.L.		OF-1B	6	25	1	5	2	0	0	1	0	.200
Championship Series Totals			11	40	1	9	2	0	0	3	0	.225

a Suspended three games by American League for June 30 fight from August 24 to August 26, 1990.
b On disabled list from March 29 to April 16, April 20 to May 23, and July 7 to end of 1994 season.
c Filed for free agency, October 19, 1994.
d Signed with Milwaukee Brewers organization, April 8, 1995.
e Filed for free agency, November 12, 1995.
f Signed with Baltimore Orioles, December 20, 1995.

SUTTON, LARRY JAMES

Born, West Covina, California, May 14, 1970.
Bats Left. Throws Left. Height, 5 feet, 11 inches. Weight, 175 pounds.

Year Club	Lea	Pos	G	AB	R	H	2B	3B	HR	RBI	SB	Avg
1992 Eugene ....Northwest		1B	70	238	45	74	17	3	15	58	3	.311
1992 Appleton ....Midwest		DH	1	2	1	0	0	0	0	0	0	.000
1993 Rockford ....Midwest		1B	113	361	67	97	24	1	7	50	3	.269
1994 Wilmington ....Carolina		1B	129	480	91	147	33	1	26	94	2	.306
1995 Wichita ....Texas		1B	53	197	31	53	11	1	5	32	1	.269
1996 Wichita ....Texas		1B-OF	125	463	84	137	22	2	22	84	4	.296
1997 Omaha .............A.A.		1B	106	380	61	114	27	1	19	72	0	.300
1997 Kansas City ...........A.L.		1B-OF	27	69	9	20	2	0	2	8	0	.290

SVEUM, DALE CURTIS

Born, Richmond, California, November 23, 1963.
Bats Both. Throws Right. Height, 6 feet, 2 inches. Weight, 215 pounds.

Year Club	Lea	Pos	G	AB	R	H	2B	3B	HR	RBI	SB	Avg
1984 El Paso ....Texas		3B-SS	131	523	92	172	41	8	9	84	6	.329
1985 Vancouver .......P.C.		3B-SS	122	415	42	98	17	3	6	48	4	.236
1986 Vancouver ........P.C.		3B	28	105	16	31	3	2	1	23	0	.295
1986 Milwaukee a .......A.L.		3B-2B-SS	91	317	35	78	13	2	7	35	4	.246
1987 Milwaukee .......A.L.		SS-2B	153	535	86	135	27	3	25	95	2	.252
1988 Milwaukee .......A.L.		SS-2B	129	467	41	113	14	4	9	51	1	.242
1989 Beloit b ......Midwest		DH	6	15	0	2	1	0	0	2	0	.133
1989 Stockton .....California		DH	11	43	5	8	0	0	1	5	0	.186
1990 Denver ...........A.A.		3B-SS-1B-2B	57	218	25	63	17	2	2	26	1	.289
1990 Milwaukee .......A.L.		3B-2B-1B-SS	48	117	15	23	7	0	1	12	0	.197
1991 Milwaukee c ......A.L.		SS-3B-2B	90	266	33	64	19	1	4	43	2	.241
1992 Philadelphia d-e ..N.L.		SS-3B-1B	54	135	13	24	4	0	2	16	0	.178
1992 Chicago f .......A.L.		SS-1B-3B	40	114	15	25	9	0	2	12	1	.219
1993 Tacoma .........P.C.		2B-1B-SS	12	43	10	15	1	0	2	6	2	.349
1993 Oakland .........A.L.		1B-3B-2B-SS	30	79	12	14	2	1	2	6	0	.177
1993 Calgary g .......P.C.		DH-3B-1B	33	120	31	36	11	1	6	26	0	.300
1994 Seattle .........A.L.		3B	10	27	3	5	0	0	1	2	0	.185
1994 Calgary h .......P.C.		3B-1B-OF	102	393	71	111	21	3	22	78	1	.282
1995 Calgary .........P.C.		3B-1B-P	118	408	71	116	34	1	12	70	2	.284
1996 Calgary .........P.C.		3B-1B-2B	101	343	62	103	28	2	23	84	2	.300
1996 Pittsburgh .......N.L.		3B	12	34	9	12	5	0	1	5	0	.353
1997 Pittsburgh i-j ......N.L.		3B-SS-1B-2B	126	306	30	80	20	1	12	47	0	.261
Major League Totals	10 Yrs.		783	2397	292	573	120	12	66	324	10	.239

a On disabled list from July 23 to August 9, 1986.
b On disabled list from March 19 to end of 1989 season.

c Traded to Philadelphia Phillies for pitcher Bruce Ruffin, December 11, 1991.
d On disabled list from April 8 to April 24, 1992.
e Traded to Chicago White Sox for pitcher Keith Shepherd, August 10, 1992.
f Filed for free agency, October 26, 1992; signed with Oakland Athletics organization, January 21, 1993.
g Released by Oakland Athletics, June 22; signed with Seattle Mariners organization, June 26, 1993.
h Signed as free agent by Pittsburgh Pirates, November 14, 1994.
i Filed for free agency, October 28, 1997.
j Signed with New York Yankees, November 25, 1997.

SWEENEY, MARK PATRICK

Born, Framingham, Massachusetts, October 26, 1969.
Bats Left. Throws Left. Height, 6 feet, 1 inch. Weight, 195 pounds.

Year Club	Lea	Pos	G	AB	R	H	2B	3B	HR	RBI	SB	Avg
1991 Boise . . . . .Northwest	OF	70	234	45	66	10	3	4	34	9	.282
1992 Quad City . . . . .Midwest	OF	120	424	65	115	20	5	14	76	15	.271
1993 Palm Springs . . . . California	OF-1B	66	245	41	87	18	3	3	47	9	.355
1993 Midland . . . . .Texas	OF	51	188	41	67	13	2	9	32	1	.356
1994 Midland . . . . .Texas	OF	14	50	13	15	3	0	3	18	1	.300
1994 Vancouver . . . . .P.C.	DH-1B-OF	103	344	59	98	12	3	8	49	3	.285
1995 Vancouver . . . . .P.C.	OF-1B	69	226	48	78	14	2	7	59	3	.345
1995 Louisville . . . . .A.A.	1B	22	76	15	28	8	0	2	22	2	.368
1995 St. Louis a . . . . .N.L.	1B-OF	37	77	5	21	2	0	2	13	1	.273
1996 St. Louis . . . . .N.L.	OF-1B	98	170	32	45	9	0	3	22	3	.265
1997 St. Louis-San Diego b . .N.L.	OF-1B	115	164	16	46	7	0	2	23	2	.280
Major League Totals		3 Yrs.	250	411	53	112	18	0	7	58	6	.273

a Traded to St. Louis Cardinals with player to be named later for pitcher John Habyan, July 8, 1995.
b Traded to San Diego Padres with pitcher Danny Jackson and pitcher Rich Batchelor for outfielder Phil Plantier, infielder Scott Livingstone and pitcher Fernando Valenzuela, June 14, 1997.

SWEENEY, MICHAEL JOHN (MIKE)

Born, Orange, California, July 22, 1973.
Bats Right. Throws Right. Height, 6 feet, 1 inch. Weight, 195 pounds.

Year Club	Lea	Pos	G	AB	R	H	2B	3B	HR	RBI	SB	Avg
1991 Royals . . . . .Gulf Coast	C-1B	38	102	8	22	3	0	1	11	1	.216
1992 Eugene . . . . .Northwest	C	59	199	17	44	12	1	4	28	3	.221
1993 Eugene . . . . .Northwest	C	53	175	32	42	10	2	6	29	1	.240
1994 Rockford . . . . .Midwest	C	86	276	47	83	20	3	10	52	0	.301
1995 Wilmington . . . . . . .Carolina	C-3B	99	332	61	103	23	1	18	53	6	.310
1995 Kansas City . . . . .A.L.	C	4	4	1	1	0	0	0	0	0	.250
1996 Wichita . . . . .Texas	DH-C	66	235	45	75	18	1	14	51	3	.319
1996 Omaha . . . . .A.A.	C	25	101	14	26	9	0	3	16	0	.257
1996 Kansas City . . . . .A.L.	C	50	165	23	46	10	0	4	24	1	.279
1997 Omaha . . . . .A.A.	C	40	144	22	34	8	1	10	29	0	.236
1997 Kansas City . . . . .A.L.	C	84	240	30	58	8	0	7	31	3	.242
Major League Totals		3 Yrs.	138	409	54	105	18	0	11	55	4	.257

TARASCO, ANTHONY GIACINTO (TONY)

Born, New York, New York, December 9, 1970.
Bats Left. Throws Right. Height, 6 feet. Weight, 205 pounds.

Year Club	Lea	Pos	G	AB	R	H	2B	3B	HR	RBI	SB	Avg
1988 Idaho Falls · . . . . .Pioneer	OF	7	10	1	0	0	0	0	1	1	.000
1988 Bradenton Braves . . . .Gulf C.	OF	21	64	10	15	6	1	0	4	3	.234
1989 Pulaski a . . . . .Appal.	OF	49	156	22	53	8	2	2	22	7	.340
1990 Sumter b . . . . .So. Atl.	OF	107	355	42	94	13	3	3	37	9	.265
1991 Durham . . . . .Carolina	OF	78	248	31	62	8	2	12	38	11	.250
1992 Greenville . . . . .Southern	OF-2B	133	489	73	140	22	2	15	54	33	.286
1993 Richmond . . . . .Int.	OF	93	370	73	122	15	7	15	53	19	.330
1993 Atlanta . . . . .N.L.	OF	24	35	6	8	2	0	0	2	0	.229
1994 Atlanta . . . . .N.L.	OF	87	132	16	36	6	0	5	19	5	.273
1995 Montreal c . . . . .N.L.	OF	126	438	64	109	18	4	14	40	24	.249
1996 Rochester . . . . .Int.	DH-OF	29	104	18	27	6	0	2	9	4	.260
1996 Orioles . . . . .Gulf Coast	DH	3	8	2	3	1	0	0	3	0	.375
1996 Frederick . . . . .Carolina	DH	9	35	6	8	3	0	1	5	0	.229
1996 Baltimore d-e . . . . .A.L.	OF	31	84	14	20	3	0	1	9	5	.238

Year	Club	Lea	Pos	G	AB	R	H	2B	3B	HR	RBI	SB	Avg
1997 Rochester ....Int.			OF	10	35	4	7	0	0	2	6	0	.200
1997 Baltimore ............A.L.			OF	100	166	26	34	8	1	7	26	2	.205
Major League Totals			5 Yrs.	368	855	126	207	37	5	27	96	36	.242
Championship Series													
1993 Atlanta ..............N.L.			OF	2	1	0	0	0	0	0	0	0	.000
1996 Baltimore ............A.L.			OF	2	1	0	0	0	0	0	0	0	.000
Championship Series Totals				4	2	0	0	0	0	0	0	0	.000

a On disabled list from August 14 to September 1, 1989.
b On disabled list from May 27 to June 6, 1990.
c Traded to Montreal Expos with outfielder Roberto Kelly and pitcher Esteban Yan for outfielder Marquis Grissom, April 6, 1995.
d Traded to Baltimore Orioles for outfielder Sherman Obando, March 13, 1996.
e On disabled list from August 25 to September 13, 1996.

TATIS, FERNANDO

Born, San Pedro De Macoris, Dominican Republic, January 1, 1975.
Bats Right. Throws Right. Height, 6 feet, 1 inch. Weight, 175 pounds.

Year	Club	Lea	Pos	G	AB	R	H	2B	3B	HR	RBI	SB	Avg
1994 Rangers ....Gulf Coast			3B-2B	60	212	34	70	10	2	6	32	21	.330
1995 Chston-Sc ....So. Atl.			3B	131	499	74	151	43	4	15	84	22	.303
1996 Charlotte ....Fla. St.			3B	85	325	46	93	25	0	12	53	9	.286
1996 Okla City .............A.A.			3B	2	4	0	2	1	0	0	0	0	.500
1997 Tulsa ....Texas			3B	102	382	73	120	26	1	24	61	17	.314
1997 Texas ..............A.L.			3B	60	223	29	57	9	0	8	29	3	.256

TAUBENSEE, EDWARD KENNETH (EDDIE)

Born, Beeville, Texas, October 31, 1968.
Bats Left. Throws Right. Height, 6 feet, 4 inches. Weight, 205 pounds.

Year	Club	Lea	Pos	G	AB	R	H	2B	3B	HR	RBI	SB	Avg
1986 Sarasota Reds ...Gulf Coast			C	35	107	8	21	3	0	1	11	0	.196
1987 Billings ....Pioneer			C	55	162	24	43	7	0	5	28	2	.265
1988 Greensboro ....So. Atl.			C	103	330	36	85	16	1	10	41	8	.258
1988 Chattanooga ......Southern			C	5	12	2	2	0	0	1	1	0	.167
1989 Cedar Rapids ......Midwest			C	59	196	25	39	5	0	8	22	4	.199
1989 Chattanooga ......Southern			C	45	127	11	24	2	0	3	13	0	.189
1990 Cedar Rapids ......Midwest			C	122	417	57	108	21	1	16	62	11	.259
1991 Colorado Springs ......P.C.			C	91	287	53	89	23	3	13	39	0	.310
1991 Cleveland c ..........A.L.			C	26	66	5	16	2	1	0	8	0	.242
1992 Tucson ..............P.C.			C	20	74	13	25	8	1	1	10	0	.338
1992 Houston .............N.L.			C	104	297	23	66	15	0	5	28	2	.222
1993 Houston .............N.L.			C	94	288	26	72	11	1	9	42	1	.250
1994 Houston-Cincinnati d ...N.L.			C	66	187	29	53	8	2	8	21	2	.283
1995 Cincinnati ...........N.L.			C-1B	80	218	32	62	14	2	9	44	2	.284
1996 Cincinnati ...........N.L.			C	108	327	46	95	20	0	12	48	3	.291
1997 Cincinnati ...........N.L.			C-OF-1B	108	254	26	68	18	0	10	34	0	.268
Major League Totals			7 Yrs.	586	1637	187	432	88	6	53	225	10	.264
Championship Series													
1995 Cincinnati ...........N.L.			C	2	2	0	1	0	0	0	0	0	.500

a Drafted by Oakland Athletics from Cincinnati Reds organization, December 3, 1990.
b Claimed on waivers by Cleveland Indians from Oakland Athletics, April 4, 1991.
c Traded to Houston Astros with pitcher Willie Blair for outfielder Ken Lofton and infielder Dave Rohde, December 10, 1991.
d Traded to Cincinnati Reds for pitchers Ross Powell and Martin Lister, April 19, 1994.

TEJADA, MIGUEL ODALIS

Born, Bani, Dominican Republic, May 25, 1976.
Bats Right. Throws Right. Height, 5 feet, 10 inches. Weight, 170 pounds.

Year	Club	Lea	Pos	G	AB	R	H	2B	3B	HR	RBI	SB	Avg
1994 Oakland ....Dominican			2B	74	218	51	64	9	1	18	62	13	.294
1995 Sou Oregon ......Northwest			SS	74	269	45	66	15	5	8	44	19	.245
1996 Modesto ....California			SS-3B	114	458	97	128	12	5	20	72	27	.279
1997 Huntsville ....Southern			SS	128	502	85	138	20	3	22	97	15	.275
1997 Oakland .............A.L.			SS	26	99	10	20	3	2	2	10	2	.202

THOMAS, FRANK EDWARD

Born, Columbus, Georgia, May 27, 1968.
Bats Right. Throws Right. Height, 6 feet, 5 inches. Weight, 257 pounds.

Year	Club	Lea	Pos	G	AB	R	H	2B	3B	HR	RBI	SB	Avg
1989 Sarasota White Sox	..Gulf C.		1B	16	48	7	16	5	0	1	11	4	.333
1989 Sarasota	..........Fla. St.		1B	55	188	27	52	9	1	4	30	0	.277
1990 Birmingham	.....Southern		1B	109	353	84	114	27	5	18	71	7	.323
1990 Chicago	.............A.L.		1B	60	191	39	63	11	3	7	31	0	.330
1991 Chicago	.............A.L.		1B	158	559	104	178	31	2	32	109	1	.318
1992 Chicago	.............A.L.		1B	160	573	108	185	*46	2	24	115	6	.323
1993 Chicago a	...........A.L.		1B	153	549	106	174	36	0	41	128	4	.317
1994 Chicago b	...........A.L.		1B	113	399	*106	141	34	1	38	101	2	.353
1995 Chicago	.............A.L.		1B	145	493	102	152	27	0	40	111	3	.308
1996 Chicago c	...........A.L.		1B	141	527	110	184	26	0	40	134	1	.349
1997 Chicago d	...........A.L.		1B	146	530	110	184	35	0	35	125	1	.347
Major League Totals	....		8 Yrs.	1076	3821	785	1261	246	8	257	854	18	.330
Championship Series													
1993 Chicago	.............A.L.		1B	6	17	2	6	0	0	1	3	0	.353

a Selected Most Valuable Player in American League for 1993.
b Selected Most Valuable Player in American League for 1994.
c On disabled list from July 8 to July 30, 1996.
d On disabled list from June 7 to June 22, 1997.

THOME, JAMES HOWARD

Born, Peoria, Illinois, August 27, 1970.
Bats Left. Throws Right. Height, 6 feet, 4 inches. Weight, 220 pounds.

Year	Club	Lea	Pos	G	AB	R	H	2B	3B	HR	RBI	SB	Avg
1989 G.C. Indians	.....Gulf Coast		SS-3B	55	186	22	44	5	3	0	22	6	.237
1990 Burlington	.........Appal.		3B	34	118	31	44	7	1	12	34	6	.373
1990 Kinston	..........Carolina		3B	33	117	19	36	4	1	4	16	4	.308
1991 Canton	..........Eastern		3B	84	294	47	99	20	2	5	45	8	.337
1991 Colorado Springs	......P.C.		3B	41	151	20	43	7	3	2	28	0	.285
1991 Cleveland	...........A.L.		3B	27	98	7	25	4	2	1	9	1	.255
1992 Colorado Springs	......P.C.		3B	12	48	11	15	4	1	2	14	0	.313
1992 Cleveland a	...........A.L.		3B	40	117	8	24	3	1	2	12	2	.205
1993 Charlotte	.............Int.		3B	115	410	85	136	21	4	25	*102	1	*.332
1993 Cleveland	...........A.L.		3B	47	154	28	41	11	0	7	22	2	.266
1994 Cleveland	...........A.L.		3B	98	321	58	86	20	1	20	52	3	.268
1995 Cleveland	...........A.L.		3B	137	452	92	142	29	3	25	73	4	.314
1996 Cleveland	...........A.L.		3B	151	505	122	157	28	5	38	116	2	.311
1997 Cleveland	...........A.L.		1B	147	496	104	142	25	0	40	102	1	.286
Major League Totals	....		7 Yrs.	647	2143	419	617	120	12	133	386	15	.288
Division Series													
1995 Cleveland	...........A.L.		3B	3	13	1	2	0	0	1	3	0	.154
1996 Cleveland	...........A.L.		3B	4	10	1	3	0	0	0	0	0	.300
1997 Cleveland	...........A.L.		1B	5	15	1	3	0	0	0	1	0	.200
Division Series Totals	....			12	38	3	8	0	0	1	4	0	.211
Championship Series													
1995 Cleveland	...........A.L.		3B	5	15	2	4	0	0	2	5	0	.267
1997 Cleveland	...........A.L.		1B	6	14	3	1	0	0	0	0	0	.071
Championship Series Totals	....			11	29	5	5	0	0	2	5	0	.172
World Series Record													
1995 Cleveland	...........A.L.		3B	6	19	1	4	1	0	1	2	0	.211
1997 Cleveland	...........A.L.		1B	7	28	8	8	0	1	2	4	0	.286
World Series Totals	....			13	47	9	12	1	1	3	6	0	.255

a On disabled list from March 28 to May 18 and May 29 to June 15, 1992.

TIMMONS, OSBORNE LLEWELLYN (OZZIE)

Born, Tampa, Florida, September 18, 1970.
Bats Right. Throws Right. Height, 6 feet, 2 inches. Weight, 205 pounds.

Year	Club	Lea	Pos	G	AB	R	H	2B	3B	HR	RBI	SB	Avg
1991 Geneva	.........N.Y.-Penn.		OF	73	294	35	65	10	1	12	47	4	.221
1992 Charlotte	..........Southern		OF	36	122	13	26	7	0	3	13	2	.213
1992 Winston-Salem	....Carolina		OF	86	305	64	86	18	0	18	56	11	.282
1993 Orlando	..........Southern		OF	107	359	65	102	22	2	18	58	5	.284
1994 Iowa	...............A.A.		OF	126	440	63	116	30	2	22	66	0	.264
1995 Chicago	.............N.L.		OF	77	171	30	45	10	1	8	28	3	.263

Year	Club	Lea	Pos	G	AB	R	H	2B	3B	HR	RBI	SB	Avg
1996 Iowa	A.A.	OF	59	213	32	53	7	0	17	40	1	.249
1996 Chicago	N.L.	OF	65	140	18	28	4	0	7	16	1	.200
1997 Cincinnati a	N.L.	OF	6	9	1	3	1	0	0	0	0	.333
1997 Indianapols	A.A.	OF	125	407	46	103	14	1	14	55	1	.253
Major League Totals			3 Yrs.	148	320	49	76	15	1	15	44	4	.237

a Traded to Cincinnati Reds with pitcher Jayson Peterson for pitcher Curt Lyons, March 31, 1997.

TINSLEY, LEE OWEN
Born, Shelbyville, Kentucky, March 4, 1969.
Bats Both. Throws Right. Height, 5 feet, 10 inches. Weight, 185 pounds.

Year	Club	Lea	Pos	G	AB	R	H	2B	3B	HR	RBI	SB	Avg
1987 Medford	Northwest	OF	45	132	22	23	3	2	0	13	9	.174
1988 Southern Oregon	Northwest	OF	72	256	56	64	8	2	3	28	*42	.250
1989 Madison	Midwest	OF	123	397	51	72	10	2	6	31	19	.181
1990 Madison	Midwest	OF	132	482	88	121	14	12	12	59	44	.251
1991 Huntsville a	Southern	OF	92	303	47	68	7	6	2	24	36	.224
1991 Canton	Eastern	OF	38	139	26	41	7	2	3	8	18	.295
1992 Colorado Springs	P.C.	OF	27	81	19	19	2	1	0	4	3	.235
1992 Canton b	Eastern	OF	96	349	65	100	9	8	5	38	18	.287
1993 Seattle	A.L.	OF	11	19	2	3	1	0	1	2	0	.158
1993 Calgary c	P.C.	OF	111	450	94	136	25	*18	10	63	34	.302
1994 Boston	A.L.	OF	78	144	27	32	4	0	2	14	13	.222
1995 Trenton	Eastern	OF	4	18	3	7	1	0	0	3	1	.389
1995 Boston d	A.L.	OF	100	341	61	97	17	1	7	41	18	.284
1996 Clearwater	Fla.St.	OF	4	17	4	5	0	1	0	3	2	.294
1996 Philadelphia	N.L.	OF	31	52	1	7	0	0	0	2	1	.135
1996 Boston e-f-g	A.L.	OF	92	192	28	47	6	1	3	14	6	.245
1997 Tacoma	P.C.	OF	31	105	15	19	2	1	2	7	1	.181
1997 Seattle h	A.L.	OF	49	122	12	24	6	2	0	6	2	.197
Major League Totals			5 Yrs.	361	870	131	210	34	4	13	79	41	.241
Division Series													
1995 Boston	A.L.	OF	1	5	0	0	0	0	0	0	0	.000

a Traded by Oakland Athletics to Cleveland Indians with pitcher Apolinar Garcia for infielder Brook Jacoby, July 26, 1991.
b Claimed on waivers by Seattle Mariners from Cleveland Indians organization, September 18, 1992.
c Traded to Boston Red Sox for player to be named, March 22; Seattle Mariners acquired pitcher Tim Smith to complete trade, September 15, 1994.
d On disabled list from May 19 to June 8 and August 23 to September 8, 1995.
e On disabled list from May 5 to May 22, 1996.
f Traded to Boston Red Sox for pitcher Scott Bakkum, June 9, 1996.
g Traded to Seattle Mariners for player to be named later, November 25, 1996.
h On disabled list from May 3 to August 2 and August 18 to September 3, 1997.

TRAMMELL, THOMAS BUBBA
Born, Knoxville, Tennessee, November 6, 1971.
Bats Right. Throws Right. Height, 6 feet, 3 inches. Weight, 205 pounds.

Year	Club	Lea	Pos	G	AB	R	H	2B	3B	HR	RBI	SB	Avg
1994 Jamestown	N.Y.-Penn.	OF	65	235	37	70	18	6	5	41	9	.298
1995 Lakeland	Fla. St.	OF	122	454	61	129	32	3	16	72	13	.284
1996 Jacksnville	Southern	OF	83	311	63	102	23	2	27	75	3	.328
1996 Toledo	Int.	OF	51	180	32	53	14	1	6	24	5	.294
1997 Toledo	Int.	OF	90	319	56	80	15	1	28	75	2	.251
1997 Detroit a	A.L.	OF	44	123	14	28	5	0	4	13	3	.228

a Selected in expansion draft by Tampa Bay Devil Rays, November 18, 1997.

TUCKER, MICHAEL ANTHONY
Born, S. Boston, Virginia, June 25, 1971.
Bats Left. Throws Right. Height, 6 feet, 2 inches. Weight, 185 pounds.

Year	Club	Lea	Pos	G	AB	R	H	2B	3B	HR	RBI	SB	Avg
1993 Wilmington	Carolina	2B	61	239	42	73	14	2	6	44	12	.305
1993 Memphis	Southern	2B	72	244	38	68	7	4	9	35	12	.279
1994 Omaha	A.A.	OF	132	485	75	134	16	7	21	77	11	.276

Year Club	Lea	Pos	G	AB	R	H	2B	3B	HR	RBI	SB	Avg
1995 Omaha .............A.A.		OF	71	275	37	84	18	4	4	28	11	.305
1995 Kansas City ..........A.L.		OF	62	177	23	46	10	0	4	17	2	.260
1996 Wichita a ....Texas		OF-1B	6	20	4	9	1	3	0	7	0	.450
1996 Kansas City ..........A.L.		OF-1B	108	339	55	88	18	4	12	53	10	.260
1997 Atlanta b .............N.L.		OF	138	499	80	141	25	7	14	56	12	.283
Major League Totals		3 Yrs.	308	1015	158	275	53	11	30	126	24	.271
Division Series												
1997 Atlanta ..............N.L.		OF	2	6	0	1	0	0	0	1	0	.167
Championship Series												
1997 Atlanta ..............N.L.		OF	5	10	1	1	0	0	1	1	0	.100

a On disabled list from June 4 to June 21 and August 28 to September 30, 1996.
b Traded to Atlanta Braves with infielder Keith Lockhart for outfielder Jermaine Dye and pitcher Jamie Walker, March 27, 1997.

TURNER, CHRISTOPHER WAN (CHRIS)
Born, Bowling Green, Kentucky, March 23, 1969.
Bats Right. Throws Right. Height, 6 feet, 2 inches. Weight, 190 pounds.

Year Club	Lea	Pos	G	AB	R	H	2B	3B	HR	RBI	SB	Avg
1991 Boise ....Northwest		C-OF-3B	52	163	26	37	5	0	2	29	10	.227
1992 Quad City ....Midwest		C-1B	109	330	66	83	18	1	9	53	8	.252
1993 Vancouver ............P.C.		C-1B	90	283	50	78	12	1	4	57	6	.276
1993 California .............A.L.		C	25	75	9	21	5	0	1	13	1	.280
1994 Vancouver ............P.C.		DH-C	3	10	1	2	1	0	0	1	0	.200
1994 California .............A.L.		C	58	149	23	36	7	1	1	12	3	.242
1995 Vancouver ............P.C.		C-3B-1B	80	282	44	75	20	2	3	48	3	.266
1995 California .............A.L.		C	5	10	0	1	0	0	0	1	0	.100
1996 Vancouver ............P.C.		C-OF-3B	113	390	51	100	19	1	2	47	1	.256
1996 California .............A.L.		C-OF	4	3	1	1	0	0	0	1	0	.333
1997 Lk Elsinore ....California		C	3	12	0	1	0	1	0	1	0	.083
1997 Vancouver ............P.C.		1B-C-OF	37	135	26	50	10	0	4	22	0	.370
1997 Anaheim a-b ..........A.L.		C-1B-OF	13	23	4	6	1	1	1	2	0	.261
Major League Totals		5 Yrs.	105	260	37	65	13	2	3	29	4	.250

a On disabled list from April 1 to July 10, 1997.
b Filed for free agency, October 10, 1997.

UNROE, TIMOTHY BRIAN (TIM)
Born, Round Lake Beach, Illinois, October 7, 1970.
Bats Right. Throws Right. Height, 6 feet, 3 inches. Weight, 200 pounds.

Year Club	Lea	Pos	G	AB	R	H	2B	3B	HR	RBI	SB	Avg
1992 Helena ....Pioneer		3B-1B-2B	74	266	61	74	13	2	16	58	3	.278
1993 Stockton .....California		3B-OF	108	382	57	96	21	6	12	63	9	.251
1994 El Paso ....Texas		3B-1B-OF	126	474	97	147	36	7	15	103	14	.310
1995 New Orleans ......A.A.		3B-1B-OF	102	371	43	97	21	2	6	45	4	.261
1995 Milwaukee .......A.L.		1B	2	4	0	1	0	0	0	0	0	.250
1996 New Orleans ......A.A.		3B-1B-SS-OF	109	404	72	109	26	4	25	67	8	.270
1996 Milwaukee .......A.L.		1B-3B-OF	14	16	5	3	0	0	0	0	0	.188
1997 Milwaukee .......A.L.		1B-3B-OF-2B	32	16	3	4	1	0	2	5	2	.250
1997 Tucson ...........P.C.		3B-OF-2B	63	234	45	68	17	1	9	46	3	.291
Major League Totals		3 Yrs.	48	36	8	8	1	0	2	5	2	.222

VALDEZ, MARIO A.
Born, Obregon, Mexico, November 19, 1974.
Bats Left. Throws Left. Height, 6 feet, 2 inches. Weight, 190 pounds.

Year Club	Lea	Pos	G	AB	R	H	2B	3B	HR	RBI	SB	Avg
1994 White Sox ....Gulf Coast		1B-OF	53	157	20	37	11	2	2	25	0	.236
1995 Hickory ....So. Atl.		1B	130	441	65	120	30	5	11	56	9	.272
1996 South Bend ......Midwest		1B	61	202	46	76	19	0	10	43	2	.376
1996 Birmingham ......Southern		1B-OF	50	168	22	46	10	2	3	28	0	.274
1997 Nashville ..............A.A.		1B	81	282	44	79	20	1	15	61	1	.280
1997 Chicago ..............A.L.		1B-3B	54	115	11	28	7	0	1	13	1	.243

VALENTIN, JOHN WILLIAM

Born, Mineola, New York, February 18, 1967.
Bats Right. Throws Right. Height, 6 feet. Weight, 180 pounds.

Year	Club	Lea	Pos	G	AB	R	H	2B	3B	HR	RBI	SB	Avg
1988 Elmira	.........N.Y.-Penn.		SS	60	207	18	45	5	1	2	16	5	.217
1989 Winter Haven	.......Fla. St.		SS	55	215	27	58	13	1	3	18	4	.270
1989 Lynchburg	.......Carolina		SS	75	264	47	65	7	2	8	34	5	.246
1990 New Britain	.......Eastern		SS	94	312	20	68	18	1	2	31	1	.218
1991 New Britain	.......Eastern		SS	23	81	8	16	3	0	0	5	1	.198
1991 Pawtucket a	..........Int.		SS	100	329	52	87	22	4	9	49	0	.264
1992 Pawtucket	...........Int.		SS	97	331	47	86	18	1	9	29	1	.260
1992 Boston	..............A.L.		SS	58	185	21	51	13	0	5	25	1	.276
1993 Pawtucket	..........Int.		SS	2	9	3	3	0	0	1	1	0	.333
1993 Boston b	............A.L.		SS	144	468	50	130	40	3	11	66	3	.278
1994 Pawtucket	..........Int.		SS	5	18	2	6	0	0	1	2	0	.333
1994 Boston c	..............A.L.		SS	84	301	53	95	26	2	9	49	3	.316
1995 Boston	..............A.L.		SS	135	520	108	155	37	2	27	102	20	.298
1996 Boston d	..............A.L.		SS-3B	131	527	84	156	29	3	13	59	9	.296
1997 Boston	..............A.L.		2B-3B	143	575	95	176	47	5	18	77	7	.306
Major League Totals	....		6 Yrs.	695	2576	411	763	192	15	83	378	43	.296
Division Series													
1995 Boston	..............A.L.		SS	3	12	1	3	1	0	1	2	0	.250

a On disabled list from August 9 to August 16, 1991.
b On disabled list from April 1 to April 20, 1993.
c On disabled list from May 4 to June 5, 1994.
d On disabled list from August 3 to August 18, 1996.

VALENTIN, JOSE ANTONIO

Born, Manati, Puerto Rico, October 12, 1969.
Bats Both. Throws Right. Height, 5 feet, 10 inches. Weight, 175 pounds.

Year	Club	Lea	Pos	G	AB	R	H	2B	3B	HR	RBI	SB	Avg
1987 Spokane	.......Northwest		SS	70	244	52	61	8	2	2	24	8	.250
1988 Charleston, SC	......So. Atl.		SS	133	444	56	103	20	1	6	44	11	.232
1989 Riverside	........California		SS	114	381	40	74	10	5	10	41	8	.194
1989 Wichita	.............Texas		SS-3B	18	49	8	12	1	0	2	5	1	.245
1990 Wichita a	............Texas		SS	11	36	4	10	2	0	0	2	2	.278
1991 Wichita b	............Texas		SS	129	447	73	112	22	5	17	68	8	.251
1992 Denver	.............A.A.		SS	139	492	78	118	19	11	3	45	9	.240
1992 Milwaukee	...........A.L.		2B-SS	4	3	1	0	0	0	0	1	0	.000
1993 New Orleans	.........A.A.		SS-1B	122	389	56	96	22	5	9	53	9	.247
1993 Milwaukee	...........A.L.		SS	19	53	10	13	1	2	1	7	1	.245
1994 Milwaukee	...........A.L.		SS-2B-3B	97	285	47	68	19	0	11	46	12	.239
1995 Milwaukee	...........A.L.		SS-3B	112	338	62	74	23	3	11	49	16	.219
1996 Milwaukee	...........A.L.		SS	154	552	90	143	33	7	24	95	17	.259
1997 Beloit	...........Midwest		SS	2	6	3	3	1	0	0	1	0	.500
1997 Milwaukee c	...........A.L.		SS	136	494	58	125	23	1	17	58	19	.253
Major League Totals	....		6 Yrs.	522	1725	268	423	99	13	64	256	65	.245

a On disabled list from April 16 to May 1, and May 18 to end of 1990 season.
b Traded by San Diego Padres to Milwaukee Brewers organization with pitcher Ricky Bones and outfielder Matt Mieske for outfielder/infielder Gary Sheffield and pitcher Geoff Kellogg, March 27, 1992.
c On disabled list from April 14 to May 5, 1997.

VANDERWAL, JOHN HENRY

Born, Grand Rapids, Michigan, April 29, 1966.
Bats Left. Throws Left. Height, 6 feet, 2 inches. Weight, 190 pounds.

Year	Club	Lea	Pos	G	AB	R	H	2B	3B	HR	RBI	SB	Avg
1987 Jamestown	......N.Y.-Penn.		OF	18	69	24	33	12	3	3	15	3	.478
1987 West Palm Beach	....Fla. St.		OF	50	189	29	54	11	2	2	22	8	.286
1988 West Palm Beach	....Fla. St.		OF	62	231	50	64	15	2	10	33	11	.277
1988 Jacksonville	......Southern		OF	58	208	22	54	14	0	3	14	3	.260
1989 Jacksonville	......Southern		OF	71	217	30	55	9	2	6	24	2	.253
1990 Jacksonville	......Southern		OF	77	277	45	84	25	3	8	40	6	.303
1990 Indianapolis	.........A.A.		OF	51	135	16	40	6	0	2	14	0	.296
1991 Indianapolis	.........A.A.		OF	133	478	84	140	36	8	15	71	6	.293
1991 Montreal	............N.L.		OF	21	61	4	13	4	1	1	8	0	.213
1992 Montreal	............N.L.		OF-1B	105	213	21	51	8	2	4	20	3	.239
1993 Montreal a	.........N.L.		1B-OF	106	215	34	50	7	4	5	30	6	.233

Year	Club	Lea	Pos	G	AB	R	H	2B	3B	HR	RBI	SB	Avg
1994 Colorado ............N.L.			1B-OF	91	110	12	27	3	1	5	15	2	.245
1995 Colorado ............N.L.			1B-OF	105	101	15	35	8	1	5	21	1	.347
1996 Colorado ............N.L.			OF-1B	104	151	20	38	6	2	5	31	2	.252
1997 Colo Sprngs ........P.C.			1B-OF	25	103	29	42	12	1	3	19	1	.408
1997 Colorado ............N.L.			OF-1B	76	92	7	16	2	0	1	11	1	.174
Major League Totals			7 Yrs.	608	943	113	230	38	11	26	136	15	.244
Division Series													
1995 Colorado ............N.L.			PH	4	4	0	0	0	0	0	0	0	.000

a Traded to Colorado Rockies for player to be named and cash, March 31; Montreal Expos acquired outfielder Ronnie Hall to complete trade, June 11, 1994.

VARITEK, JASON A.
Born, Rochester, Minnesota, April 11, 1972.
Bats Both. Throws Right. Height, 6 feet, 2 inches. Weight, 210 pounds.

Year	Club	Lea	Pos	G	AB	R	H	2B	3B	HR	RBI	SB	Avg
1995 Port City ....Southern			C	104	352	42	79	14	2	10	44	0	.224
1996 Port City ....Southern			C-3B-OF	134	503	63	132	34	1	12	67	7	.262
1997 Tacoma ............P.C.			C	87	307	54	78	13	0	15	48	0	.254
1997 Pawtucket ....Int.			C	20	66	6	13	5	0	1	5	0	.197
1997 Boston a ............A.L.			C	1	1	0	1	0	0	0	0	0	1.000

a Traded to Boston Red Sox with pitcher Derek Lowe for pitcher Heathcliff Slocumb, July 31, 1997.

VAUGHN, GREGORY LAMONT
Born, Sacramento, California, July 3, 1965.
Bats Right. Throws Right. Height, 6 feet. Weight, 205 pounds.

Year	Club	Lea	Pos	G	AB	R	H	2B	3B	HR	RBI	SB	Avg
1986 Helena ....Pioneer			OF	66	258	64	75	13	2	16	54	23	.291
1987 Beloit ....Midwest			OF	139	492	*120	150	31	6	*33	105	36	.305
1988 El Paso ....Texas			OF	131	505	*104	152	*39	4	*28	*105	22	.301
1989 Denver ............A.A.			OF	110	387	74	107	17	5	*26	*92	20	.276
1989 Milwaukee ............A.L.			OF	38	113	18	30	3	0	5	23	4	.265
1990 Milwaukee a ............A.L.			OF	120	382	51	84	26	2	17	61	7	.220
1991 Milwaukee ............A.L.			OF	145	542	81	132	24	5	27	98	2	.244
1992 Milwaukee ............A.L.			OF	141	501	77	114	18	2	23	78	15	.228
1993 Milwaukee ............A.L.			OF	154	569	97	152	28	2	30	97	10	.267
1994 Beloit ....Midwest			DH	2	6	1	1	0	0	0	0	0	.167
1994 Milwaukee b ............A.L.			OF	95	370	59	94	24	1	19	55	9	.254
1995 Milwaukee ............A.L.			DH	108	392	67	88	19	1	17	59	10	.224
1996 Milwaukee ............A.L.			OF	102	375	78	105	16	0	31	95	5	.280
1996 San Diego c-d ........N.L.			OF	43	141	20	29	3	1	10	22	4	.206
1997 San Diego ............N.L.			OF	120	361	60	78	10	0	18	57	7	.216
Major League Totals			9 Yrs.	1066	3746	608	906	171	14	197	645	73	.242
Division Series													
1996 San Diego ............N.L.			OF	3	3	0	0	0	0	0	0	0	.000

a On disabled list from May 27 to June 10, 1990.
b On disabled list from April 8 to April 27, 1994.
c Filed for free agency, October 28, 1996.
d Re-signed with San Diego Padres, December 13, 1996.

VAUGHN, MAURICE SAMUEL
Born, Norwalk, Connecticut, December 15, 1967.
Bats Left. Throws Right. Height, 6 feet, 1 inch. Weight, 225 pounds.

Year	Club	Lea	Pos	G	AB	R	H	2B	3B	HR	RBI	SB	Avg
1989 New Britain ....Eastern			1B	73	245	28	68	15	0	8	38	1	.278
1990 Pawtucket a ....Int.			1B	108	386	62	114	26	1	22	72	3	.295
1991 Pawtucket ....Int.			1B	69	234	35	64	10	0	14	50	2	.274
1991 Boston ............A.L.			1B	74	219	21	57	12	0	4	32	2	.260
1992 Pawtucket ....Int.			1B	39	149	15	42	6	0	6	28	1	.282
1992 Boston ............A.L.			1B	113	355	42	83	16	2	13	57	3	.234
1993 Boston ............A.L.			1B	152	539	86	160	34	1	29	101	4	.297
1994 Boston ............A.L.			1B	111	394	65	122	25	1	26	82	4	.310
1995 Boston b ............A.L.			1B	140	550	98	165	28	3	39	126	11	.300

Year	Club	Lea	Pos	G	AB	R	H	2B	3B	HR	RBI	SB	Avg
1996 Boston	A.L.	1B	161	635	118	207	29	1	44	143	2	.326
1997 Boston c	A.L.	1B	141	527	91	166	24	0	35	96	2	.315
Major League Totals		7 Yrs.	892	3219	521	960	168	8	190	637	28	.298
Division Series												
1995 Boston	A.L.	1B	3	14	0	0	0	0	0	0	0	.000

a On disabled list from May 1 to June 5, 1990.
b Selected Most Valuable Player in American League for 1995.
c On disabled list from June 17 to July 10, 1997.

VELANDIA, JORGE LUIS
Born, Caracas, Venezuela, January 12, 1975.
Bats Right. Throws Right. Height, 5 feet, 9 inches. Weight, 160 pounds.

Year	Club	Lea	Pos	G	AB	R	H	2B	3B	HR	RBI	SB	Avg
1992 Bristol	Appal.	SS-2B	45	119	20	24	6	1	0	9	3	.202
1993 Fayettevlle	So. Atl.	SS-2B-3B	37	106	15	17	4	0	0	11	5	.160
1993 Niagara Fls	N.Y.-Penn.	SS	72	212	30	41	11	0	1	22	22	.193
1994 Lakeland	Fla. St.	SS-2B-3B	22	60	8	14	4	0	0	3	0	.233
1994 Springfield	Midwest	SS-2B	98	290	42	71	14	0	4	36	5	.245
1995 Memphis	Southern	SS	63	186	23	38	10	2	4	17	0	.204
1995 Las Vegas	P.C.	SS	66	206	25	54	12	3	0	25	0	.262
1996 Memphis	Southern	SS	122	392	42	94	19	0	9	48	3	.240
1997 Las Vegas	P.C.	SS	114	405	46	110	15	2	3	35	13	.272
1997 San Diego a	N.L.	SS-2B-3B	14	29	0	3	2	0	0	0	0	.103

a Traded to Oakland Athletics with pitcher Doug Bochtler for pitcher Don Wengert and infielder David Newhan, November 26, 1997.

VELARDE, RANDY LEE
Born, Midland, Texas, November 24, 1962.
Bats Right. Throws Right. Height, 6 feet. Weight, 192 pounds.

Year	Club	Lea	Pos	G	AB	R	H	2B	3B	HR	RBI	SB	Avg
1985 Niagara Fls. ..	N.Y.-Penn.	OF-SS-2B-3B	67	218	28	48	7	3	1	16	8	.220
1986 Appleton	Midwest	SS-3B-OF	124	417	55	105	31	4	11	50	13	.252
1986 Buffalo a	A.A.	SS	9	20	2	4	1	0	0	2	1	.200
1987 Albany	Eastern	SS	71	263	40	83	20	2	7	32	8	.316
1987 Columbus	Int.	SS	49	185	21	59	10	6	5	33	8	.319
1987 New York	A.L.	SS-2B	8	22	1	4	0	0	0	1	0	.182
1988 Columbus	Int.	SS	78	293	39	79	23	4	5	37	7	.270
1988 New York	A.L.	2B-SS-3B	48	115	18	20	6	0	5	12	1	.174
1989 Columbus	Int.	SS-3B	103	387	59	103	26	3	11	53	3	.266
1989 New York b	A.L.	3B-SS	33	100	12	34	4	2	2	11	0	.340
1990 New York	A.L.	3B-SS-OF-2B	95	229	21	48	6	2	5	19	0	.210
1991 New York	A.L.	3B-SS-OF	80	184	19	45	11	1	1	15	3	.245
1992 New York	A.L.	SS-3B-OF-2B	121	412	57	112	24	1	7	46	7	.272
1993 Albany	Eastern	SS-OF	5	17	2	4	0	0	1	2	0	.235
1993 New York c	A.L.	OF-SS-3B	85	226	28	68	13	2	7	24	2	.301
1994 New York d-e	A.L.	SS-3B-OF-2B	77	280	47	78	16	1	9	34	4	.279
1995 New York f-g-h ..	A.L.	2B-SS-OF-3B	111	367	60	102	19	1	7	46	5	.278
1996 California	A.L.	2B-3B-SS	136	530	82	151	27	3	14	54	7	.285
1997 Anaheim i	A.L.		1	0	0	0	0	0	0	0	0	.000
Major League Totals		11 Yrs.	795	2465	345	662	126	13	57	262	29	.269
Division Series												
1995 New York	A.L.	2B-3B-OF	5	17	3	3	0	0	0	1	0	.176

a Traded by Chicago White Sox to New York Yankees organization with pitcher Pete Filson for pitcher Scott Nielson and infielder Mike Soper, January 5, 1987.
b On disabled list from August 9 to August 29, 1989.
c On disabled list from June 6 to July 30, 1993.
d Filed for free agency, October 25, 1994; ruled ineligible by Player Relations Committee due to insufficient service time.
e Not offered 1995 contract, December 20, 1994.
f Re-signed with New York Yankees, April 11, 1995.
g Filed for free agency, November 12, 1995.
h Signed with California Angels, November 22, 1995.
i On disabled list from April 1 to September 1 and September 7 to September 29, 1997.

VENTURA, ROBIN MARK

Born, Santa Maria, California, July 14, 1967.
Bats Left. Throws Right. Height, 6 feet, 1 inch. Weight, 198 pounds.

Year	Club	Lea	Pos	G	AB	R	H	2B	3B	HR	RBI	SB	Avg
1989 Birmingham	Southern		3B	129	454	75	126	25	2	3	67	9	.278
1989 Chicago	A.L.		3B	16	45	5	8	3	0	0	7	0	.178
1990 Chicago	A.L.		3B-1B	150	493	48	123	17	1	5	54	1	.249
1991 Chicago	A.L.		3B-1B	157	606	92	172	25	1	23	100	2	.284
1992 Chicago	A.L.		3B-1B	157	592	85	167	38	1	16	93	2	.282
1993 Chicago	A.L.		3B-1B	157	554	85	145	27	1	22	94	1	.262
1994 Chicago	A.L.	3B-1B-SS		109	401	57	113	15	1	18	78	3	.282
1995 Chicago	A.L.		3B-1B	135	492	79	145	22	0	26	93	4	.295
1996 Chicago	A.L.		3B-1B	158	586	96	168	31	2	34	105	1	.287
1997 Nashville	A.A.		3B	5	15	3	6	1	0	2	5	0	.400
1997 Birmingham	Southern		3B	4	17	3	5	1	0	1	2	0	.294
1997 Chicago a	A.L.		3B	54	183	27	48	10	1	6	26	0	.262
Major League Totals			9 Yrs.	1093	3952	574	1089	188	8	150	650	14	.276
Championship Series													
1993 Chicago	A.L.		3B-1B	6	20	2	4	0	0	1	5	0	.200

a On disabled list from April 1 to July 24, 1997.

VERAS (PEREZ), QUILVIO ALBERTO

Born, Santo Domingo, Dominican Republic, April 3, 1971.
Bats Both. Throws Right. Height, 5 feet, 9 inches. Weight, 166 pounds.

Year	Club	Lea	Pos	G	AB	R	H	2B	3B	HR	RBI	SB	Avg
1990 Sarasota Mets	Gulf C.		2B	30	98	26	29	3	3	1	5	16	.296
1990 Kingsport	Appal.		2B	24	94	21	36	6	0	1	14	14	.383
1991 Kingsport	Appal.		2B	64	226	*54	76	11	4	1	16	*38	.336
1991 Pittsfield	N.Y.-Penn.	2B-SS		5	15	3	4	0	1	0	2	2	.267
1992 Columbia	So. Atl.		2B	117	414	97	132	24	10	2	40	*66	*.319
1993 Binghamton	Eastern		2B	128	444	87	136	19	7	2	51	52	.306
1994 Norfolk a	Int.		2B	123	457	71	114	22	4	0	43	40	.249
1995 Florida	N.L.	2B-OF		124	440	86	115	20	7	5	32	56	.261
1996 Charlotte b	Int.		2B	28	104	22	34	5	-2	2	8	8	.327
1996 Florida c	N.L.		2B	73	253	40	64	8	1	4	14	8	.253
1997 San Diego	N.L.		2B	145	539	74	143	23	1	3	45	33	.265
Major League Totals			3 Yrs.	342	1232	200	322	51	9	12	91	97	.261

a Traded by New York Mets to Florida Marlins for outfielder Carl Everett, November 29, 1994.
b On disabled list from May 10 to June 21, 1996.
c Traded to San Diego Padres for pitcher Dustin Hermanson, November 21, 1996.

VIDRO, JOSE ANGEL

Born, Mayaguez, Puerto Rico, August 27, 1974.
Bats Both. Throws Right. Height, 5 feet, 11 inches. Weight, 175 pounds.

Year	Club	Lea	Pos	G	AB	R	H	2B	3B	HR	RBI	SB	Avg
1992 Expos	Gulf Coast		2B	54	200	29	66	6	2	4	31	10	.330
1993 Burlington	Midwest		2B	76	287	39	69	19	0	2	34	3	.240
1994 Wst Plm Bch	Fla. St.		2B	125	465	57	124	30	2	4	49	8	.267
1995 Harrisburg	Eastern	2B-SS-3B		64	246	33	64	16	2	4	38	3	.260
1995 Wst Plm Bch	Fla. St.	2B-SS-3B		44	163	20	53	15	2	3	24	0	.325
1996 Harrisburg	Eastern	3B-2B-SS		126	452	57	117	25	3	18	82	3	.259
1997 Ottawa	Int.		3B-2B	73	279	40	90	17	0	13	47	2	.323
1997 Montreal	N.L.		3B-2B	67	169	19	42	12	1	2	17	1	.249

VINA, FERNANDO

Born, Sacramento, California, April 16, 1969.
Bats Left. Throws Right. Height, 5 feet, 9 inches. Weight, 170 pounds.

Year	Club	Lea	Pos	G	AB	R	H	2B	3B	HR	RBI	SB	Avg
1990 Kingsport	Appal.			Did Not Play									
1991 Columbia	So. Atl.		2B	129	498	77	135	23	6	6	50	42	.271
1992 St. Lucie	Fla. St.		2B	111	421	61	124	15	5	1	42	36	.295
1992 Tidewater a	Int.		2B	11	30	3	6	0	0	0	0	2	.200
1993 Seattle b	A.L.		2B-SS	24	45	5	10	2	0	0	2	6	.222
1993 Norfolk	Int.		SS-2B-OF	73	287	24	66	6	4	4	27	16	.230
1994 Norfolk	Int.		SS-2B	6	17	2	3	0	0	0	1	1	.176

181

Year	Club	Lea	Pos	G	AB	R	H	2B	3B	HR	RBI	SB	Avg
1994 New York c-d ......N.L.		2B-3B-SS-OF	79	124	20	31	6	0	0	6	3	.250
1995 Milwaukee ........A.L.		2B-SS-3B	113	288	46	74	7	7	3	29	6	.257
1996 Milwaukee ........A.L.		2B	140	554	94	157	19	10	7	46	16	.283
1997 Stockton .....California		2B	3	9	2	4	0	1	0	3	0	.444
1997 Tucson ...........P.C.		2B	6	19	3	9	3	0	1	5	0	.474
1997 Milwaukee e .......A.L.		2B	79	324	37	89	12	2	4	28	8	.275
Major League Totals	5 Yrs.		435	1335	202	361	46	19	14	111	39	.270

a Drafted by Seattle Mariners from New York Mets organization, December 7, 1992.
b Returned to New York Mets organization, June 15, 1993.
c On disabled list from May 22 to June 6, 1994.
d Traded to Milwaukee Brewers to complete November 30 trade in which New York Mets acquired pitcher Doug Henry for two players to be named and Milwaukee acquired catcher Javier Gonzalez on December 6 as partial completion, December 22, 1994.
e On disabled list from April 20 to July 18, 1997.

VITIELLO, JOSEPH DAVID (JOE)

Born, Cambridge, Massachusetts, April 11, 1970.
Bats Right. Throws Right. Height, 6 feet, 2 inches. Weight, 215 pounds.

Year	Club	Lea	Pos	G	AB	R	H	2B	3B	HR	RBI	SB	Avg
1991 Eugene ....Northwest		OF-1B	19	64	16	21	2	0	6	21	1	.328
1991 Memphis ....Southern		OF-1B	36	128	15	28	4	1	0	18	0	.219
1992 Baseball City ......Fla. St.		1B	115	400	52	113	16	1	8	65	0	.283
1993 Memphis ....Southern		1B	117	413	62	119	25	2	15	66	2	.288
1994 Omaha ...........A.A.		1B	98	352	46	121	28	3	10	61	3	.344
1995 Omaha ...........A.A.		1B-OF	59	229	33	64	14	2	12	42	0	.279
1995 Kansas City ..........A.L.		DH-1B	53	130	13	33	4	0	7	21	0	.254
1996 Omaha ...........A.A.		1B	36	132	26	37	7	0	9	31	1	.280
1996 Kansas City ..........A.L.		DH-1B-OF	85	257	29	62	15	1	8	40	2	.241
1997 Omaha ...........A.A.		DH-OF	13	42	5	9	1	0	3	9	0	.214
1997 Kansas City a .........A.L.		OF-1B	51	130	11	31	6	0	5	18	0	.238
Major League Totals	3 Yrs.		189	517	53	126	25	1	20	79	2	.244

a On disabled list from June 16 to July 28 and August 10 to September 29, 1997.

VIZCAINO (PIMENTAL), JOSE LUIS

Born, Palenque de San Cristobal, Dominican Republic, March 26, 1968.
Bats Both. Throws Right. Height, 6 feet, 1 inch. Weight, 180 pounds.

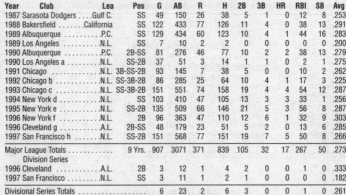

Year	Club	Lea	Pos	G	AB	R	H	2B	3B	HR	RBI	SB	Avg
1987 Sarasota Dodgers ....Gulf C.		SS	49	150	26	38	5	1	0	12	8	.253
1988 Bakersfield ....California		SS	122	433	77	126	11	4	0	38	13	.291
1989 Albuquerque ..........P.C.		SS	129	434	60	123	10	4	1	44	16	.283
1989 Los Angeles .........N.L.		SS	7	10	2	2	0	0	0	0	0	.200
1990 Albuquerque ..........P.C.		2B-SS	81	276	46	77	10	2	2	38	13	.279
1990 Los Angeles a .........N.L.		SS-2B	37	51	3	14	1	1	0	2	1	.275
1991 Chicago ...........N.L.		3B-SS-2B	93	145	7	38	5	0	0	10	2	.262
1992 Chicago b ..........N.L.		SS-3B-2B	86	285	25	64	10	4	1	17	3	.225
1993 Chicago c ..........N.L.		SS-3B-2B	151	551	74	158	19	4	4	54	12	.287
1994 New York d .........N.L.		SS	103	410	47	105	13	3	3	33	1	.256
1995 New York e .........N.L.		SS-2B	135	509	66	146	21	5	3	56	8	.287
1996 New York f .........N.L.		2B	96	363	47	110	12	6	1	32	9	.303
1996 Cleveland g ..........A.L.		2B-SS	48	179	23	51	5	2	0	13	6	.285
1997 San Francisco h .......N.L.		SS-2B	151	568	77	151	19	7	5	50	8	.266
Major League Totals	9 Yrs.		907	3071	371	839	105	32	17	267	50	.273
Division Series												
1996 Cleveland ..........A.L.		2B	3	12	1	4	2	0	0	1	0	.333
1997 San Francisco .........N.L.		SS	3	11	1	2	1	0	0	0	0	.182
Divisional Series Totals			6	23	2	6	3	0	0	1	0	.261

a Traded to Chicago Cubs for infielder Greg Smith, December 14, 1990.
b On disabled list from April 20 to May 6 and August 26 to September 16, 1992.
c Traded to New York Mets for pitchers Anthony Young and Ottis Smith, March 30, 1994.
d Declared restricted free agent under Major League Baseball implemented labor proposal, December 23, 1994.
e Re-signed with New York Mets, April 28, 1995.
f Traded to Cleveland Indians with infielder Jeff Kent for infielder Carlos Baerga and infielder Alvaro Espinoza, July 29, 1996.
g Traded to San Francisco Giants with infielder Jeff Kent, pitcher Julian Taverez and player to be named later for infielder Matt Williams and player to be named later, November 13, 1996.
h Filed for free agency, October 29, 1997.
i Signed with Los Angeles Dodgers December 8, 1997.

VIZQUEL, OMAR ENRIQUE

Born, Caracas, Venezuela, April 24, 1967.
Bats Both. Throws Right. Height, 5 feet, 9 inches. Weight, 165 pounds.

Year	Club	Lea	Pos	G	AB	R	H	2B	3B	HR	RBI	SB	Avg
1984 Butte a	Pioneer	SS-2B	15	45	7	14	2	0	0	4	2	.311
1985 Bellingham	Northwest	SS-2B	50	187	24	42	9	0	5	17	4	.225
1986 Wausau	Midwest	SS-2B	105	352	60	75	13	2	4	28	19	.213
1987 Salinas	California	SS-2B	114	407	61	107	12	8	0	38	25	.263
1988 Vermont	Eastern	SS	103	375	54	95	18	2	2	35	30	.253
1988 Calgary	P.C.	SS	33	107	10	24	2	3	1	12	2	.224
1989 Seattle	A.L.	SS	143	387	45	85	7	3	1	20	1	.220
1989 Calgary	P.C.	SS	7	28	3	6	2	0	0	3	0	.214
1990 San Bernardino	California	SS	6	28	5	7	0	0	0	3	1	.250
1990 Calgary	P.C.	SS	48	150	18	35	6	2	0	8	4	.233
1990 Seattle b	A.L.	SS	81	255	19	63	3	2	2	18	4	.247
1991 Seattle	A.L.	SS-2B	142	426	42	98	16	4	1	41	7	.230
1992 Seattle c	A.L.	SS	136	483	49	142	20	4	0	21	15	.294
1992 Calgary	P.C.	SS	6	22	0	6	1	0	0	2	0	.273
1993 Seattle d	A.L.	SS	158	560	68	143	14	2	2	31	12	.255
1994 Charlotte	Int.	SS	7	26	3	7	1	0	0	1	1	.269
1994 Cleveland e	A.L.	SS	69	286	39	78	10	1	1	33	13	.273
1995 Cleveland f	A.L.	SS	136	542	87	144	28	0	6	56	29	.266
1996 Cleveland	A.L.	SS	151	542	98	161	36	1	9	64	35	.297
1997 Cleveland	A.L.	SS	153	565	89	158	23	6	5	49	43	.280
Major League Totals		9 Yrs.	1169	4046	536	1072	157	23	27	333	159	.265
Division Series												
1995 Cleveland	A.L.	SS	3	12	2	2	1	0	0	4	1	.167
1996 Cleveland	A.L.	SS	4	14	4	6	1	0	0	2	4	.429
1997 Cleveland	A.L.	SS	5	18	3	9	0	0	0	1	4	.500
Division Series Totals			12	44	9	17	2	0	0	7	9	.386
Championship Series												
1995 Cleveland	A.L.	SS	6	23	2	2	1	0	0	2	3	.087
1997 Cleveland	A.L.	SS	6	25	1	1	0	0	0	0	0	.040
Championship Series Totals			12	48	3	3	1	0	0	2	3	.063
World Series Record												
1995 Cleveland	A.L.	SS	6	23	3	4	0	1	0	1	1	.174
1997 Cleveland	A.L.	SS	7	30	5	7	2	0	0	1	5	.233
World Series Totals			13	53	8	11	2	1	0	2	6	.208

a Batted righthanded only from 1984 through 1988 season.
b On disabled list from April 7 to May 14, 1990.
c On disabled list from April 13 to May 11, 1992.
d Traded to Cleveland Indians for shortstop Felix Fermin and first baseman Reggie Jefferson, December 20, 1993.
e On disabled list from April 23 to June 13, 1994.
f Re-signed with Cleveland Indians, December 13, 1995.

WALBECK, MATTHEW LOVICK

Born, Sacramento, California, October 2, 1969.
Bats Both. Throws Right. Height, 5 feet, 11 inches. Weight, 190 pounds.

Year	Club	Lea	Pos	G	AB	R	H	2B	3B	HR	RBI	SB	Avg
1987 Wytheville	Appal.	C	51	169	24	53	9	3	1	28	0	.314
1988 Charleston, WV	So. Atl.	C	104	312	28	68	9	0	2	24	7	.218
1989 Peoria a	Midwest	C	94	341	38	86	19	0	4	47	5	.252
1990 Peoria b	Midwest	C	25	66	2	15	1	0	0	5	1	.227
1991 Winston-Salem	Carolina	C	91	260	25	70	11	0	3	41	3	.269
1992 Charlotte c	Southern	C-1B	105	385	48	116	22	1	7	42	0	.301
1993 Iowa	A.A.	C	87	331	31	93	18	2	6	43	1	.281
1993 Chicago d	N.L.	C	11	30	2	6	2	0	1	6	0	.200
1994 Minnesota	A.L.	C	97	338	31	69	12	0	5	35	1	.204
1995 Minnesota	A.L.	C	115	393	40	101	18	1	1	44	3	.257
1996 Ft. Myers	Fla.St.	C	9	33	4	9	1	1	0	9	0	.273
1996 New Britain e	Eastern	DH-C	7	24	1	5	0	0	0	0	0	.208
1996 Minnesota f	A.L.	C	63	215	25	48	10	0	2	24	3	.223
1997 Lakeland	Fla. St.	C	4	10	4	5	1	0	0	3	0	.500
1997 Toledo	Int.	C	17	59	6	18	2	1	1	8	0	.305
1997 Detroit g-h	A.L.	C	47	137	18	38	3	0	3	10	3	.277
Major League Totals		5 Yrs.	333	1113	116	262	45	1	12	119	10	.235

a On disabled list from July 31 to end of 1989 season.
b On disabled list from April 12 to July 11, 1990.
c On disabled list from September 5 to end of 1992 season.

d Traded by Chicago Cubs to Minnesota Twins with pitcher Dave Stevens for pitcher Willie Banks, November 24, 1993.
e On disabled list from April 1 to June 17, 1996.
f Traded to Minnesota Twins for pitcher Brent Stentz, December 11, 1996.
g On disabled list from April 19 to July 9, 1997.
h Signed with Anaheim Angels, December 8, 1997

WALKER, LARRY KENNETH ROBERT

Born, Maple Ridge, British Columbia, December 1, 1966.
Bats Left. Throws Right. Height, 6 feet, 3 inches. Weight, 215 pounds.

Year	Club	Lea	Pos	G	AB	R	H	2B	3B	HR	RBI	SB	Avg
1985 Utica	N.Y.-Penn.	1B-3B	62	215	24	48	8	2	2	26	12	.223
1986 Burlington	Midwest	OF-3B	95	332	67	96	12	6	29	74	16	.289
1986 West Palm Beach	Fla. St.	OF	38	113	20	32	7	5	4	16	2	.283
1987 Jacksonville	Southern	OF	128	474	91	136	25	7	26	83	24	.287
1988 Montreal a	N.L.		INJURED—Did Not Play									
1989 Indianapolis	A.A.	OF	114	385	68	104	18	2	12	59	36	.270
1989 Montreal	N.L.	OF	20	47	4	8	0	0	0	4	1	.170
1990 Montreal	N.L.	OF	133	419	59	101	18	3	19	51	21	.241
1991 Montreal b	N.L.	OF-1B	137	487	59	141	30	2	16	64	14	.290
1992 Montreal	N.L.	OF	143	528	85	159	31	4	23	93	18	.301
1993 Montreal c	N.L.	OF-1B	138	490	85	130	24	5	22	86	29	.265
1994 Montreal d	N.L.	OF-1B	103	395	76	127	44	2	19	86	15	.322
1995 Colorado e	N.L.	OF	131	494	96	151	31	5	36	101	16	.306
1996 Salem	Carolina	DH	2	8	3	4	3	0	1	1	0	.500
1996 Colo Sprngs	P.C.	OF	3	11	2	4	0	0	2	8	0	.364
1996 Colorado f	N.L.	OF	83	272	58	75	18	4	18	58	18	.276
1997 Colorado g	N.L.	OF-1B	153	568	143	208	46	4	*49	130	33	.366
Major League Totals			9 Yrs.	1041	3700	665	1100	242	29	202	673	165	.297
Division Series													
1995 Colorado	N.L.	OF	4	14	3	3	0	0	1	3	1	.214

a On disabled list from March 28 to end of 1988 season.
b On disabled list from June 28 to July 13, 1991.
c On disabled list from May 30 to June 10, 1993.
d Filed for free agency, October 18, 1994.
e Signed with Colorado Rockies, April 8, 1995.
f On disabled list from June 10 to August 15, 1996.
g Selected Most Valuable Player in National League for 1997.

WALKER, TODD ARTHUR

Born, Bakersfield, California, May 25, 1973.
Bats Left. Throws Right. Height, 6 feet. Weight, 170 pounds.

Year	Club	Lea	Pos	G	AB	R	H	2B	3B	HR	RBI	SB	Avg
1994 Ft. Myers	Fla.St.	2B	46	171	29	52	5	2	10	34	6	.304
1995 New Britain	Eastern	2B-3B	137	513	83	149	27	3	21	85	23	.290
1996 Salt Lake	P.C.	3B-2B	135	551	94	187	41	9	28	111	13	.339
1996 Minnesota	A.L.	3B-2B	25	82	8	21	6	0	0	6	2	.256
1997 Salt Lake	P.C.	3B	83	322	69	111	20	1	11	53	5	.345
1997 Minnesota	A.L.	3B-2B	52	156	15	37	7	1	3	16	7	.237
Major League Totals			2 Yrs.	77	238	23	58	13	1	3	22	9	.244

WALTON, JEROME O'TERRELL

Born, Newnan, Georgia, July 8, 1965.
Bats Right. Throws Right. Height, 6 feet, 1 inch. Weight, 175 pounds.

Year	Club	Lea	Pos	G	AB	R	H	2B	3B	HR	RBI	SB	Avg
1986 Wytheville	Appal.	OF	62	229	48	66	7	4	5	34	21	.288
1987 Peoria	Midwest	OF	128	472	102	158	24	11	6	38	49	.335
1988 Pittsfield	Eastern	OF	120	414	64	137	26	2	3	49	42	*.331
1989 Iowa	A.A.	OF	4	18	4	6	1	0	1	3	2	.333
1989 Chicago a-b	N.L.	OF	116	475	64	139	23	3	5	46	24	.293
1990 Iowa	A.A.	OF	4	16	3	3	0	0	1	1	0	.188
1990 Chicago c	N.L.	OF	101	392	63	103	16	2	2	21	14	.263
1991 Chicago	N.L.	OF	123	270	42	59	13	1	5	17	7	.219
1992 Iowa	A.A.	OF	7	27	8	8	2	1	0	3	1	.296
1992 Chicago d-e	N.L.	OF	30	55	7	7	0	1	0	1	1	.127
1993 Vancouver	P.C.	OF	54	176	34	55	11	1	2	20	5	.313

184

Year	Club	Lea	Pos	G	AB	R	H	2B	3B	HR	RBI	SB	Avg
1993 California f	A.L.	OF	5	2	2	0	0	0	0	0	1	.000
1994 Cincinnati g	N.L.	OF-1B	46	68	10	21	4	0	1	9	1	.309
1995 Cincinnati h	N.L.	OF-1B	102	162	32	47	12	1	8	22	10	.290
1996 Atlanta	N.L.	OF	37	47	9	16	5	0	1	4	0	.340
1996 Greenville i	Southern	OF	3	5	0	1	0	1	0	0	0	.200
1996 Richmond j-k	Int.	OF	6	18	3	8	2	1	1	5	0	.444
1997 Frederick	Carolina	OF-1B	7	19	1	4	0	0	1	2	1	.211
1997 Baltimore l-m	A.L.	OF-1B	26	68	8	20	1	0	3	9	0	.294
Major League Totals			9 Yrs.	586	1539	237	412	74	8	25	129	58	.268
Division Series													
1995 Cincinnati	N.L.	OF	3	3	0	0	0	0	0	0	0	.000
1997 Baltimore	A.L.	1B	2	4	0	0	0	0	0	0	0	.000
Division Series Totals			5	7	0	0	0	0	0	0	0	.000
Championship Series													
1989 Chicago	N.L.	OF	5	22	4	8	0	0	0	2	0	.364
1995 Cincinnati	N.L.	OF	2	7	0	0	0	0	0	0	0	.000
1997 Baltimore	A.L.	OF	1	0	0	0	0	0	0	0	0	.000
Championship Series Totals			8	29	4	8	0	0	0	2	0	.276

a On disabled list from May 11 to June 11, 1989.
b Selected Rookie of the Year in National League for 1989.
c On disabled list from June 18 to August 2, 1990.
d On disabled list from March 28 to April 24, 1992.
e Not offered 1993 contract, December 18, 1992; signed with California Angels organization, January 29, 1993.
f Released, August 19; signed with Cincinnati Reds organization, November 14, 1993.
g On disabled list from July 1 to July 23 and July 27 to end of 1994 season.
h Not offered contract by Cincinnati Reds, December 20, 1995; Signed by Atlanta Braves, January 3, 1996.
i On disabled list from May 30 to September 30, 1996.
j Filed for free agency, October 29, 1996.
k Signed with Baltimore Orioles organization, December 18, 1996.
l On disabled list from April 25 to September 1, 1997.
m Filed for free agency, October 30, 1997.

WARD, TURNER MAX
Born, Orlando, Florida, April 11, 1965.
Bats Both. Throws Right. Height, 6 feet, 2 inches. Weight, 182 pounds.

Year	Club	Lea	Pos	G	AB	R	H	2B	3B	HR	RBI	SB	Avg
1986 Oneonta	N.Y.-Penn.	OF-1B-3B	63	221	42	62	4	1	1	19	6	.281
1987 Ft. Lauderdale	Fla. St.	OF-1B	130	493	83	145	15	2	7	55	25	.294
1988 Columbus a	Int.	OF	134	490	55	123	24	1	7	50	28	.251
1989 Sara. Indians	Gulf Coast	OF	4	15	2	3	0	0	0	1	1	.200
1989 Canton-Akron b	Eastern	OF	30	93	19	28	5	1	0	3	1	.301
1990 Colorado Springs	P.C.	OF	133	495	89	148	24	9	6	65	22	.299
1990 Cleveland	A.L.	OF	14	46	10	16	2	1	1	10	3	.348
1991 Colorado Springs	P.C.	OF	14	51	5	10	1	1	1	3	2	.196
1991 Syracuse	Int.	OF	59	218	40	72	11	3	7	32	9	.330
1991 Cleve.-Toronto c	A.L.	OF	48	113	12	27	7	0	0	7	0	.239
1992 Syracuse	Int.	OF	81	280	41	67	10	2	10	29	7	.239
1992 Toronto	A.L.	OF	18	29	7	10	3	0	1	3	0	.345
1993 Knoxville	Southern	OF	7	23	6	6	2	0	0	2	3	.261
1993 Toronto d-e	A.L.	OF-1B	72	167	20	32	4	2	4	28	3	.192
1994 Milwaukee	A.L.	OF-3B	102	367	55	85	15	2	9	45	6	.232
1995 Beloit	Midwest	OF	2	5	0	0	0	0	0	0	0	.000
1995 New Orleans	A.A.	OF	11	33	3	8	1	1	1	3	0	.242
1995 Milwaukee f	A.L.	OF	44	129	19	34	3	1	4	16	6	.264
1996 New Orleans g	A.A.	DH	9	23	4	8	1	0	1	1	0	.348
1996 Milwaukee h	A.L.	OF	43	67	7	12	2	1	2	10	3	.179
1997 Calgary	P.C.	OF-1B	59	209	44	71	18	3	9	44	7	.340
1997 Pittsburgh i	N.L.	OF	71	167	33	59	16	1	7	33	4	.353
Major League Totals			8 Yrs.	412	1085	163	275	52	8	28	152	25	.253

a Traded by New York Yankees to Cleveland Indians organization with catcher Joel Skinner for outfielder Mel Hall, March 19, 1989.
b On disabled list from April 7 to July 24, 1989.
c Traded to Toronto Blue Jays with pitcher Tom Candiotti for outfielders Glenallen Hill and Mark Whiten, pitcher Denis Boucher and player to be named, June 27; trade settled for cash, October 22, 1991.
d On disabled list from August 2 to September 1, 1993.
e Claimed on waivers by Milwaukee Brewers, November 24, 1993.
f On disabled list from June 7 to June 22 and July 2 to July 19 and July 24 to October 2, 1995.
g On disabled list from May 25 to September 1, 1996.
h Outrighted by Milwaukee Brewers, November 1, 1996.
i Signed with Pittsburgh Pirates organization, April 22, 1997.

WATKINS, WILLIAM PATRICK
Born, Raleigh, North Carolina, September 2, 1972.
Bats Right. Throws Right. Height, 6 feet, 2 inches. Weight, 185 pounds.

Year Club	Lea	Pos	G	AB	R	H	2B	3B	HR	RBI	SB	Avg
1993 Billings	Pioneer	OF	66	235	46	63	10	3	6	30	15	.268
1994 Winston-Sal	Carolina	OF	132	524	107	152	24	5	27	83	31	.290
1995 Winston-Sal	Carolina	OF	27	107	14	22	3	1	4	13	1	.206
1995 Chattanooga	Southern	OF	105	358	57	104	26	2	12	57	5	.291
1996 Chattanooga	Southern	OF	127	492	63	136	31	2	8	59	15	.276
1997 Chattanooga	Southern	OF	46	177	35	62	15	1	7	30	9	.350
1997 Indianapols	A.A.	OF	84	325	46	91	14	7	9	35	13	.280
1997 Cincinnati	N.L.	OF	17	29	2	6	2	0	0	0	1	.207

WEBSTER, LEONARD IRELL (LENNY)
Born, New Orleans, Louisiana, February 10, 1965.
Bats Right. Throws Right. Height, 5 feet, 9 inches. Weight, 195 pounds.

Year Club	Lea	Pos	G	AB	R	H	2B	3B	HR	RBI	SB	Avg
1986 Kenosha	Midwest	C	22	65	2	10	2	0	0	8	0	.154
1986 Elizabethton	Appal.	C	48	152	29	35	4	0	3	14	1	.230
1987 Kenosha	Midwest	C	52	140	17	35	7	0	3	17	2	.250
1988 Kenosha	Midwest	C	129	465	82	134	23	2	11	87	3	.288
1989 Visalia	California	C	63	231	36	62	7	0	5	39	2	.268
1989 Orlando	Southern	C	59	191	29	45	7	0	2	17	2	.236
1989 Minnesota	A.L.	C	14	20	3	6	2	0	0	1	0	.300
1990 Orlando	Southern	C	126	455	69	119	31	0	8	71	0	.262
1990 Minnesota	A.L.	C	2	6	1	2	1	0	0	0	0	.333
1991 Portland	P.C.	C	87	325	43	82	18	0	7	34	1	.252
1991 Minnesota	A.L.	C	18	34	7	10	1	0	3	8	0	.294
1992 Minnesota	A.L.	C	53	118	10	33	10	1	1	13	0	.280
1993 Minnesota a	A.L.	C	49	106	14	21	2	0	1	8	1	.198
1994 Montreal b	N.L.	C	57	143	13	39	10	0	5	23	0	.273
1995 Philadelphia c	N.L.	C	49	150	18	40	9	0	4	14	0	.267
1996 Montreal d	N.L.	C	78	174	18	40	10	0	2	17	0	.230
1997 Baltimore e-f	A.L.	C	98	259	29	66	8	1	7	37	0	.255
Major League Totals		9 Yrs.	418	1010	113	257	53	2	23	121	1	.254
Division Series												
1997 Baltimore	A.L.	C	3	6	1	1	0	0	0	1	0	.167
Championship Series												
1997 Baltimore	A.L.	C	4	9	0	2	0	0	0	0	0	.222

a Traded to Montreal Expos for player to be named, March 14, 1994.
b Not offered 1995 contract, December 23, 1994.
c Signed with Philadelphia Phillies organization, April 4, 1995.
d Filed for free agency, October 16, 1996.
e Filed for free agency, October 30, 1997.
f Re-signed with Baltimore Orioles, November 25, 1997.

WEISS, WALTER WILLIAM (WALT)
Born, Tuxedo, New York, November 28, 1963.
Bats Both. Throws Right. Height, 6 feet. Weight, 175 pounds.

Year Club	Lea	Pos	G	AB	R	H	2B	3B	HR	RBI	SB	Avg
1985 Pocatello	Pioneer	SS	40	158	19	49	9	3	0	21	6	.310
1985 Modesto	California	SS	30	122	17	24	4	1	0	7	3	.197
1986 Huntsville	Southern	SS	46	160	19	40	2	1	0	13	5	.250
1986 Madison	Midwest	SS	84	322	50	97	15	5	2	54	12	.301
1987 Huntsville	Southern	SS	91	337	43	96	16	2	1	32	23	.285
1987 Tacoma	P.C.	SS	46	179	35	47	4	3	0	17	8	.263
1987 Oakland	A.L.	SS	16	26	3	12	4	0	0	1	1	.462
1988 Oakland a	A.L.	SS	147	452	44	113	17	3	3	39	4	.250
1989 Modesto	California	SS	5	8	1	3	0	0	0	1	0	.375
1989 Tacoma	P.C.	SS	2	9	1	1	1	0	0	1	0	.111
1989 Oakland b	A.L.	SS	84	236	30	55	11	0	3	21	6	.233
1990 Oakland c	A.L.	SS	138	445	50	118	17	1	2	35	9	.265
1991 Oakland d	A.L.	SS	40	133	15	30	6	1	0	13	6	.226
1992 Tacoma	P.C.	SS	4	13	2	3	1	0	0	3	0	.231
1992 Oakland e-f	A.L.	SS	103	316	36	67	5	2	0	21	6	.212
1993 Florida g	N.L.	SS	158	500	50	133	14	2	1	39	7	.266
1994 Colorado	N.L.	SS	110	423	58	106	11	4	1	32	12	.251
1995 Colorado h-i	N.L.	SS	137	427	65	111	17	3	1	25	15	.260

Year Club	Lea	Pos	G	AB	R	H	2B	3B	HR	RBI	SB	Avg
1996 Colorado	N.L.	SS	155	517	89	146	20	2	8	48	10	.282
1997 Colorado j-k-l	N.L.	SS	121	393	52	106	23	5	4	38	5	.270
Major League Totals		11 Yrs.	1209	3868	492	997	145	23	23	312	81	.258
Division Series												
1995 Colorado	N.L.	SS	4	12	1	2	0	0	0	0	1	.167
Championship Series												
1988 Oakland	A.L.	SS	4	15	2	5	2	0	0	2	0	.333
1989 Oakland	A.L.	SS	4	9	2	1	1	0	0	0	1	.111
1990 Oakland	A.L.	SS	2	7	2	0	0	0	0	0	0	.000
1992 Oakland	A.L.	SS	3	6	1	1	0	0	0	0	2	.167
Championship Series Totals			13	37	7	7	3	0	0	2	3	.189
World Series Record												
1988 Oakland	A.L.	SS	5	16	1	1	0	0	0	0	1	.063
1989 Oakland	A.L.	SS	4	15	3	2	0	0	1	1	0	.133
World Series Totals			9	31	4	3	0	0	1	1	1	.097

a Selected Rookie of the Year in American League for 1988.
b On disabled list from May 18 to July 31, 1989.
c On disabled list from August 23 to September 7, 1990.
d On disabled list from April 15 to April 30 and June 7 to end of 1991 season.
e On disabled list from March 31 to June 6, 1992.
f Traded to Florida Marlins for catcher Eric Helfand and player to be named, November 17; Oakland Athletics acquired pitcher Scott Baker to complete trade, November 20, 1992.
g Filed for free agency, October 25, 1993; signed with Colorado Rockies, January 7, 1994.
h Filed for free agency, November 12, 1995.
i Re-signed with Colorado Rockies, November 20, 1995.
j On disabled list from July 22 to August 8, 1997.
k Filed for free agency, October 27, 1997.
l Signed with Atlanta Braves, November 17, 1997.

WHITE, DEVON MARKES

Born, Kingston, Jamaica, December 29, 1962.
Bats Both. Throws Right. Height, 6 feet, 2 inches. Weight, 190 pounds.

Year Club	Lea	Pos	G	AB	R	H	2B	3B	HR	RBI	SB	Avg
1981 Idaho Falls	Pioneer	OF-3B-1B	30	106	10	19	2	0	0	10	4	.179
1982 Danville a	Midwest	OF	57	186	21	40	6	1	1	11	11	.215
1983 Nashua	Midwest	OF	17	70	11	18	7	2	0	2	5	.257
1983 Peoria	Eastern	OF	117	430	69	109	17	6	13	66	32	.253
1984 Redwood	California	OF	138	520	101	147	25	5	7	55	36	.283
1985 Midland	Texas	OF	70	260	52	77	10	4	4	35	38	.296
1985 Edmonton	P.C.	OF	66	277	53	70	16	5	4	39	21	.253
1985 California	A.L.	OF	21	7	7	1	0	0	0	0	3	.143
1986 Edmonton b	P.C.	OF	112	461	84	134	25	10	14	60	*42	.291
1986 California	A.L.	OF	29	51	8	12	1	1	1	3	13	.235
1987 California	A.L.	OF	159	639	103	168	33	5	24	87	32	.263
1988 California c	A.L.	OF	122	455	76	118	22	2	11	51	17	.259
1989 California	A.L.	OF	156	636	86	156	18	13	12	56	44	.245
1990 Edmonton	P.C.	OF	14	55	9	20	4	4	0	6	4	.364
1990 California d	A.L.	OF	125	443	57	96	17	3	11	44	21	.217
1991 Toronto	A.L.	OF	156	642	110	181	40	10	17	60	33	.282
1992 Toronto	A.L.	OF	153	641	98	159	26	7	17	60	37	.248
1993 Toronto	A.L.	OF	146	598	116	163	42	6	15	52	34	.273
1994 Toronto	A.L.	OF	100	403	67	109	24	6	13	49	11	.270
1995 Toronto e-f	A.L.	OF	101	427	61	121	23	5	10	53	11	.283
1996 Florida	N.L.	OF	146	552	77	151	37	6	17	84	22	.274
1997 Florida g-h	N.L.	OF	74	265	37	65	13	1	6	34	13	.245
Major League Totals		13 Yrs.	1488	5759	903	1500	296	65	154	633	284	.260
Division Series												
1997 Florida	N.L.	OF	3	11	1	2	0	0	1	4	0	.182
Championship Series												
1986 California	A.L.	OF	4	2	2	1	0	0	0	0	0	.500
1991 Toronto	A.L.	OF	5	22	5	8	1	0	0	0	3	.364
1992 Toronto	A.L.	OF	6	23	2	8	2	0	0	2	0	.348
1993 Toronto	A.L.	OF	6	27	3	12	1	1	1	2	0	.444
1997 Florida	N.L.	OF	6	21	4	4	1	0	0	1	1	.190
Championship Series Totals			27	95	16	33	5	1	1	5	4	.347
World Series Record												
1992 Toronto	A.L.	OF	6	26	2	6	1	0	0	2	1	.231
1993 Toronto	A.L.	OF	6	24	8	7	3	2	1	7	1	.292
1997 Florida	N.L.	OF	7	33	0	8	3	1	0	2	1	.242
World Series Totals			19	83	10	21	7	3	1	11	3	.253

a On suspended list from June 11 to June 12 and July 19 to end of 1982 season.
b On disabled list from May 12 to May 22, 1986.
c On disabled list from May 7 to June 10, 1988.
d Traded to Toronto Blue Jays with pitcher Willie Fraser and player to be named for outfielder Junior Felix, infielder
   Luis Sojo and player to be named, December 2; California Angels acquired catcher Ken Rivers and Toronto acquired
   pitcher Marcus Moore to complete trade, December 5, 1990.
e Filed for free agency, November 12, 1995.
f Signed with Florida Marlins, November 21, 1995.
g On disabled list from April 25 to May 30 and June 8 to July 28, 1997.
h Traded to Arizona Diamondbacks for pitcher Jesus Martinez, November 19, 1997.

WHITE, RONDELL BERNARD
Born, Milledgeville, Georgia, February 23, 1972.
Bats Right. Throws Right. Height, 6 feet, 1 inch. Weight, 205 pounds.

Year Club	Lea	Pos	G	AB	R	H	2B	3B	HR	RBI	SB	Avg
1990 Bradenton Expos	Gulf Coast	OF	57	221	33	66	7	4	5	34	10	.299
1991 Sumter	So. Atl.	OF	123	465	80	122	23	6	13	68	50	.262
1992 West Palm Beach	Fla. St.	OF	111	450	80	142	10	12	4	41	42	.316
1992 Harrisburg	Eastern	OF	21	89	22	27	7	1	2	7	6	.303
1993 Ottawa	Int.	OF	37	150	28	57	8	2	7	32	10	.380
1993 Harrisburg	Eastern	OF-1B	91	373	72	122	16	10	12	52	21	.327
1993 Montreal	N.L.	OF	23	73	9	19	3	1	2	15	1	.260
1994 Ottawa	Int.	OF	42	169	23	46	7	0	7	18	9	.272
1994 Montreal	N.L.	OF	40	97	16	27	10	1	2	13	1	.278
1995 Montreal	N.L.	OF	130	474	87	140	33	4	13	57	25	.295
1996 Wst Plm Bch	Fla.St.	DH-OF	3	10	0	2	1	0	0	2	0	.200
1996 Expos	Gulf Coast	OF	3	12	3	3	0	0	2	4	1	.250
1996 Harrisburg a	Eastern	OF	5	20	5	7	1	0	3	6	1	.350
1996 Montreal	N.L.	OF	88	334	35	98	19	4	6	41	14	.293
1997 Montreal	N.L.	OF	151	592	84	160	29	5	28	82	16	.270
Major League Totals		5 Yrs.	432	1570	231	444	94	15	51	208	57	.283

a On disabled list from April 28 to July 16, 1996.

WIDGER, CHRISTOPHER JON (CHRIS)
Born, Wilmington, Delaware, May 21, 1971.
Bats Right. Throws Right. Height, 6 feet, 3 inches. Weight, 195 pounds.

Year Club	Lea	Pos	G	AB	R	H	2B	3B	HR	RBI	SB	Avg
1992 Bellingham	Northwest	C	51	166	28	43	7	2	5	30	8	.259
1993 Riverside	California	C-OF	97	360	44	95	28	2	9	58	5	.264
1994 Jacksonville	Southern	C-OF-1B	116	388	58	101	15	3	16	59	8	.260
1995 Tacoma	P.C.	C-OF	50	174	29	48	11	1	9	21	0	.276
1995 Seattle	A.L.	C-OF	23	45	2	9	0	0	1	2	0	.200
1996 Tacoma	P.C.	C	97	352	42	107	20	2	13	48	7	.304
1996 Seattle a	A.L.	C	8	11	1	2	0	0	0	0	0	.182
1997 Montreal	N.L.	C	91	278	30	65	20	3	7	37	2	.234
Major League Totals		3 Yrs.	122	334	33	76	20	3	8	39	2	.228
Division Series												
1995 Seattle	A.L.	C	2	3	0	0	0	0	0	0	0	.000
Championship Series												
1995 Seattle	A.L.	C	3	1	0	0	0	0	0	0	0	.000

a Traded to Montreal Expos with pitcher Matt Wagner and pitcher Trey Moore for pitcher Jeff Fassero and pitcher
   Alex Pachecho, October 29, 1996.

WILKINS, RICHARD DAVID
Born, Jacksonville, Florida, July 4, 1967.
Bats Right. Throws Right. Height, 6 feet, 2 inches. Weight, 210 pounds.

Year Club	Lea	Pos	G	AB	R	H	2B	3B	HR	RBI	SB	Avg
1987 Geneva	N.Y.-Penn.	C	75	243	35	61	8	2	8	43	7	.251
1988 Peoria	Midwest	C	137	490	54	119	30	1	8	63	4	.243
1989 Winston-Salem	Carolina	C	132	445	61	111	24	1	12	54	6	.249
1990 Charlotte	Southern	C	127	449	48	102	18	1	17	71	4	.227
1991 Iowa	A.A.	C	38	107	12	29	3	1	5	14	1	.271
1991 Chicago	N.L.	C	86	203	21	45	9	0	6	22	3	.222
1992 Chicago	N.L.	C	83	244	20	66	9	1	8	22	0	.270
1993 Chicago	N.L.	C	136	446	78	135	23	1	30	73	2	.303
1994 Chicago	N.L.	C-1B	100	313	44	71	25	2	7	39	4	.227

Year	Club	Lea	Pos	G	AB	R	H	2B	3B	HR	RBI	SB	Avg
1995 Jackson	Texas		C	4	11	0	0	0	0	0	0	0	.000
1995 Tucson	P.C.		C	4	12	0	4	0	0	0	4	0	.333
1995 Chicago-Houston a-b	N.L.		C-1B	65	202	30	41	3	0	7	19	0	.203
1996 Houston-San Francisco c	N.L.		C-1B	136	411	53	100	18	2	14	59	0	.243
1997 Tacoma	P.C.		C-1B	17	68	16	23	8	0	1	14	0	.338
1997 San Francisco d	N.L.		C	66	190	18	37	5	0	6	23	0	.195
1997 Seattle e-f-g-h	A.L.		C	5	12	2	3	1	0	1	4	0	.250
Major League Totals			7 Yrs.	677	2021	266	498	93	6	79	261	9	.246
Division Series													
1997 Seattle	A.L.		C	1	0	0	0	0	0	0	0	0	.000

a Traded to Houston Astros for outfielder Luis Gonzalez and catcher Scott Servais, June 28, 1995.
b On disabled list from July 2 to September 5, 1995.
c Traded to San Francisco Giants for catcher Kirt Manwaring, July 26, 1996.
d Released by San Francisco Giants, August 1, 1997.
e Signed with Seattle Mariners, August 15, 1997.
f On disabled list from August 15 to September 3, 1997.
g Filed for free agency, November 3, 1997.
h Signed with Seattle Mariners, December 8, 1997

WILLIAMS (FIGUEROA), BERNABE (BERNIE)

Born, San Juan, Puerto Rico, September 13, 1968.
Bats Both. Throws Right. Height, 6 feet, 2 inches. Weight, 200 pounds.

Year	Club	Lea	Pos	G	AB	R	H	2B	3B	HR	RBI	SB	Avg
1986 Sarasota Yankees a	Gulf C.		OF	61	230	*45	62	5	3	2	25	33	.270
1987 Fort Lauderdale b	Fla. St.		OF	25	71	11	11	3	0	0	4	9	.155
1987 Oneonta	N.Y.-Penn.		OF	25	93	13	32	4	0	0	15	9	.344
1988 Prince William c	Carolina		OF	92	337	72	113	16	7	7	45	29	*.335
1989 Albany	Eastern		OF	91	314	63	79	11	8	11	42	26	.252
1989 Columbus	Int.		OF	50	162	21	35	8	1	2	16	11	.216
1990 Albany	Eastern		OF	134	466	*91	131	28	5	8	54	*39	.281
1991 Columbus	Int.		OF	78	306	52	90	14	6	8	37	9	.294
1991 New York	A.L.		OF	85	320	43	76	19	4	3	34	10	.238
1992 Columbus	Int.		OF	95	363	68	111	23	9	8	50	20	.306
1992 New York	A.L.		OF	62	261	39	73	14	2	5	26	7	.280
1993 New York d	A.L.		OF	139	567	67	152	31	4	12	68	9	.268
1994 New York	A.L.		OF	108	408	80	118	29	1	12	57	16	.289
1995 New York	A.L.		OF	144	563	93	173	29	9	18	82	8	.307
1996 New York e	A.L.		OF	143	551	108	168	26	7	29	102	17	.305
1997 New York f	A.L.		OF	129	509	107	167	35	6	21	100	15	.328
Major League Totals			7 Yrs.	810	3179	537	927	183	33	100	469	82	.292
Division Series													
1995 New York	A.L.		OF	5	21	8	9	2	0	2	5	1	.429
1996 New York	A.L.		OF	4	15	5	7	0	0	3	5	1	.467
1997 New York	A.L.		OF	5	17	3	2	1	0	0	1	0	.118
Division Series Totals				14	53	16	18	3	0	5	11	2	.340
Championship Series													
1996 New York	A.L.		OF	5	19	6	9	3	0	2	6	1	.474
World Series													
1996 New York	A.L.		OF	6	24	3	4	0	0	1	4	1	.167

a Batted righthanded only from 1986 through 1988 season.
b On disabled list from May 17 to June 17, 1987.
c On disabled list from July 14 to end of 1988 season.
d On disabled list from May 14 to June 7, 1993.
e On disabled list from May 11 to May 26, 1996.
f On disabled list from June 15 to July 2 and July 14 to August 1, 1997.

WILLIAMS, GEORGE ERIK

Born, LaCrosse, Wisconsin, April 22, 1969.
Bats Both. Throws Right. Height, 5 feet, 10 inches. Weight, 190 pounds.

Year	Club	Lea	Pos	G	AB	R	H	2B	3B	HR	RBI	SB	Avg
1991 South Oregon	Northwest		3B-C-OF	55	174	24	41	10	0	2	24	9	.236
1992 Madison	Midwest		C-3B-OF	115	349	56	106	18	2	5	42	9	.304
1993 Huntsville	Southern		C-OF-3B	124	434	80	128	26	2	14	77	6	.295
1994 W Michigan	Midwest		DH-C	63	221	40	67	20	1	8	48	6	.303
1995 Edmonton	P.C.		C-OF	81	290	53	90	20	0	13	55	0	.310
1995 Oakland	A.L.		C	29	79	13	23	5	1	3	14	0	.291
1996 Edmonton	P.C.		C-OF	14	57	10	23	5	0	5	18	0	.404

Year	Club	Lea	Pos	G	AB	R	H	2B	3B	HR	RBI	SB	Avg
1996 Oakland	....	A.L.	C	56	132	17	20	5	0	3	10	0	.152
1997 Edmonton	....	P.C.	C	3	7	0	0	0	0	0	0	0	.000
1997 Modesto	....	California	C	13	44	8	14	4	0	1	6	0	.318
1997 Oakland a	....	A.L.	C	76	201	30	58	9	1	3	22	0	.289
Major League Totals		3 Yrs.	161	412	60	101	19	2	9	46	0	.245

a On disabled list from April 14 to May 5 and July 20 to August 21, 1997.

WILLIAMS, GERALD FLOYD (ICE)
Born, New Orleans, Louisiana, August 10, 1966.
Bats Right. Throws Right. Height, 6 feet, 2 inches. Weight, 190 pounds.

Year	Club	Lea	Pos	G	AB	R	H	2B	3B	HR	RBI	SB	Avg
1987 Oneonta	....	N.Y.-Penn.	OF	29	115	26	42	6	2	2	29	6	.365
1988 Prince William	....	Carolina	OF	54	159	20	29	3	0	2	18	6	.182
1988 Fort Lauderdale	....	Fla. St.	OF	63	212	21	40	7	2	2	17	4	.189
1989 Prince William	....	Carolina	OF	134	454	63	104	19	6	13	69	15	.229
1990 Fort Lauderdale	....	Fla. St.	OF	50	204	25	59	4	5	7	43	19	.289
1990 Albany	....	Eastern	OF	96	324	54	81	17	2	13	58	18	.250
1991 Albany	....	Eastern	OF	45	175	28	50	15	0	5	32	18	.286
1991 Columbus	....	Int.	OF	61	198	20	51	8	3	2	27	9	.258
1992 Columbus	....	Int.	OF	142	547	92	156	31	6	16	86	14	.285
1992 New York	....	A.L.	OF	15	27	7	8	2	0	3	6	2	.296
1993 Columbus	....	Int.	OF	87	336	53	95	19	6	8	38	29	.283
1993 New York	....	A.L.	OF	42	67	11	10	2	3	0	6	2	.149
1994 New York	....	A.L.	OF	57	86	19	25	8	0	4	13	1	.291
1995 New York	....	A.L.	OF	100	182	33	45	18	2	6	28	4	.247
1996 New York-Milwaukee a	.	A.L.	OF	125	325	43	82	19	4	5	34	10	.252
1997 Milwaukee b	....	A.L.	OF	155	566	73	143	32	2	10	41	23	.253
Major League Totals		6 Yrs.	494	1253	186	313	81	11	28	128	42	.250
Division Series													
1995 New York	....	A.L.	OF	5	5	1	0	0	0	0	0	0	.000

a Traded to Milwaukee Brewers with pitcher Bob Wickman for pitcher Graeme Lloyd, pitcher Ricky Bones and player
   to be named later, August 23, 1996. New York Yankees received infielder Gabby Martinez to complete trade,
   November 5, 1996.

b Traded to Atlanta Braves for pitcher Chad Fox, December 11, 1997.

WILLIAMS, MATTHEW DERRICK
Born, Bishop, California, November 28, 1965.
Bats Right. Throws Right. Height, 6 feet, 2 inches. Weight, 216 pounds.

Year	Club	Lea	Pos	G	AB	R	H	2B	3B	HR	RBI	SB	Avg
1986 Everett	....	Northwest	SS	4	17	3	4	0	1	1	10	0	.235
1986 Clinton	....	Midwest	SS	68	250	32	60	14	3	7	29	3	.240
1987 Phoenix	....	P.C.	3B	56	211	36	61	15	1	6	37	6	.289
1987 San Francisco	....	N.L.	SS-3B	84	245	28	46	9	2	8	21	4	.188
1988 Phoenix	....	P.C.	3B	82	306	45	83	19	1	12	51	6	.271
1988 San Francisco	....	N.L.	3B-SS	52	156	17	32	6	1	8	19	0	.205
1989 Phoenix	....	P.C.	3B-SS	76	284	61	91	20	2	26	61	9	.320
1989 San Francisco	....	N.L.	3B-SS	84	292	31	59	18	1	18	50	1	.202
1990 San Francisco	....	N.L.	3B	159	617	87	171	27	2	33	*122	7	.277
1991 San Francisco	....	N.L.	3B-SS	157	589	72	158	24	5	34	98	5	.268
1992 San Francisco	....	N.L.	3B	146	529	58	120	13	5	20	66	7	.227
1993 San Francisco a	....	N.L.	3B	145	579	105	170	33	4	38	110	1	.294
1994 San Francisco	....	N.L.	3B	112	445	74	119	16	3	*43	96	1	.267
1995 San Jose	....	California	3B	4	11	2	2	0	0	1	2	0	.182
1995 San Francisco b-c	......	N.L.	3B	76	283	53	95	17	1	23	65	2	.336
1996 San Francisco d-e	....	N.L.	3B-1B-SS	105	404	69	122	16	1	22	85	1	.302
1997 Cleveland f	....	A.L.	3B	151	596	86	157	32	3	32	105	12	.263
Major League Totals		11 Yrs.	1271	4735	680	1249	211	28	279	837	41	.264
Division Series													
1997 Cleveland	....	A.L.	3B	5	17	4	4	1	0	1	3	0	.235
Championship Series													
1989 San Francisco	....	N.L.	3B-SS	5	20	2	6	1	0	2	9	0	.300
1997 Cleveland	....	A.L.	3B	6	23	1	5	1	0	0	2	1	.217
Championship Series Totals			11	43	3	11	2	0	2	11	1	.256
World Series Record													
1989 San Francisco	....	N.L.	3B-SS	4	16	1	2	0	0	1	1	0	.125
1997 Cleveland	....	A.L.	3B	7	26	8	10	1	0	1	3	0	.385
World Series Totals			11	42	9	12	1	0	2	4	0	.286

a On disabled list from June 28 to July 14, 1993.
b Traded to Houston Astros for catcher Eddie Tucker, May 15, 1995.
c On disabled list from June 4 to August 19, 1995.
d On disabled list from August 5 to September 30, 1996.
e Traded to Cleveland Indians with player to be named later for infielder Jeff Kent, pitcher Julian Taverez, infielder Jose Vizcaino and player to be named later, November 13, 1996.
f Traded to Arizona Diamondbacks for infielder Travis Fryman and pitcher Tom Martin, December 1, 1997.

WILLIAMSON, ANTHONY JOSEPH

Born, Harbor City, California, July 18, 1973.
Bats Left. Throws Right. Height, 6 feet, 1 inch. Weight, 195 pounds.

Year Club	Lea	Pos	G	AB	R	H	2B	3B	HR	RBI	SB	Avg
1994 Helena ....Pioneer	DH-3B	6	26	5	11	2	1	0	4	0	.423
1994 Stockton ....California	3B	23	85	6	19	4	0	3	13	0	.224
1994 El Paso ....Texas	3B	14	48	8	12	3	0	1	9	0	.250
1995 El Paso ....Texas	3B-1B	104	392	62	121	30	6	7	90	3	.309
1996 New Orleans ..........A.A.	1B-3B	55	199	23	52	10	1	5	23	1	.261
1997 Milwaukee ..........A.L.	1B	24	54	2	11	3	0	0	6	0	.204
1997 Tucson ..............P.C.	1B-3B	83	304	53	87	20	5	5	41	3	.286

WILSON, DANIEL ALLEN (DAN)

Born, Arlington Heights, Illinois, March 25, 1969.
Bats Right. Throws Right. Height, 6 feet, 3 inches. Weight, 190 pounds.

Year Club	Lea	Pos	G	AB	R	H	2B	3B	HR	RBI	SB	Avg
1990 Charleston, WV .....So. Atl.	C	32	113	16	28	9	1	2	17	0	.248
1991 Charleston, WV .....So. Atl.	C	52	197	25	62	11	1	3	29	1	.315
1991 Chattanooga ......Southern	C	81	292	32	75	19	2	2	38	2	.257
1992 Nashville ............A.A.	C	106	366	27	92	16	1	4	34	1	.251
1992 Cincinnati ............N.L.	C	12	25	2	9	1	0	0	3	0	.360
1993 Indianapolis .........A.A.	C	51	191	18	50	11	1	1	17	1	.262
1993 Cincinnati a ..........N.L.	C	36	76	6	17	3	0	0	8	0	.224
1994 Seattle ..............A.L.	C	91	282	24	61	14	2	3	27	1	.216
1995 Seattle ..............A.L.	C	119	399	40	111	22	3	9	51	2	.278
1996 Seattle ..............A.L.	C	138	491	51	140	24	0	18	83	1	.285
1997 Seattle ..............A.L.	C	146	508	66	137	31	1	15	74	7	.270
Major League Totals		6 Yrs.	542	1781	189	475	95	6	45	246	11	.267
Division Series												
1995 Seattle ..............A.L.	C	5	17	0	2	0	0	0	1	0	.118
1997 Seattle ..............A.L.	C	4	13	0	0	0	0	0	0	0	.000
Division Series Totals		9	30	0	2	0	0	0	1	0	.067
Championship Series												
1995 Seattle ..............A.L.	C	6	16	0	0	0	0	0	0	0	.000

a Traded to Seattle Mariners with pitcher Bobby Ayala for pitcher Erik Hanson and second baseman Bret Boone, November 2, 1993.

WOMACK, ANTHONY DARRELL

Born, Chatham, Virginia, September 25, 1969.
Bats Left. Throws Right. Height, 5 feet, 9 inches. Weight, 160 pounds.

Year Club	Lea	Pos	G	AB	R	H	2B	3B	HR	RBI	SB	Avg
1991 Welland ........N.Y.-Penn.	SS-2B	45	166	30	46	3	0	1	8	26	.277
1992 Augusta ....So. Atl.	SS-2B	102	380	62	93	8	3	0	18	50	.245
1993 Salem ....Carolina	SS	72	304	41	91	11	3	2	18	28	.299
1993 Carolina ....Southern	SS	60	247	41	75	7	2	0	23	21	.304
1993 Pittsburgh ............N.L.	SS	15	24	5	2	0	0	0	0	2	.083
1994 Pittsburgh ............N.L.	2B-SS	5	12	4	4	0	0	0	1	0	.333
1994 Buffalo ..............A.A.	SS-2B	106	421	40	93	9	2	0	18	41	.221
1995 Calgary ..............P.C.	2B-SS	30	107	12	30	3	1	0	6	7	.280
1995 Carolina ....Southern	SS-2B	82	332	52	85	9	4	1	19	27	.256
1996 Calgary ............P.C.	SS-2B-OF	131	506	75	152	19	11	1	47	37	.300
1996 Pittsburgh ............N.L.	OF-2B	17	30	11	10	3	1	0	7	2	.333
1997 Pittsburgh ............N.L.	2B-SS	155	641	85	178	26	9	6	50	60	.278
Major League Totals		4 Yrs.	192	707	105	194	29	10	6	58	64	.274

YOUNG, DMITRI DELL

Born, Vicksburg, Mississippi, November 11, 1973.
Bats Both. Throws Right. Height, 6 feet, 2 inches. Weight, 240 pounds.

Year	Club	Lea	Pos	G	AB	R	H	2B	3B	HR	RBI	SB	Avg
1991	Johnson Cty	Appal.	3B	37	129	22	33	10	0	2	22	2	.256
1992	Springfield	Midwest	3B	135	493	74	153	36	6	14	72	14	.310
1993	St. Pete	Fla.St.	3B-1B	69	270	31	85	13	3	5	43	3	.315
1993	Arkansas	Texas	1B-3B	45	166	13	41	11	2	3	21	4	.247
1994	Arkansas	Texas	OF-1B	125	453	53	123	33	2	8	54	0	.272
1995	Arkansas	Texas	OF	97	367	54	107	18	6	10	62	2	.292
1995	Louisville	A.A.	OF	2	7	3	2	0	0	0	0	0	.286
1996	Louisville	A.A.	1B	122	459	90	153	31	8	15	64	16	.333
1996	St. Louis	N.L.	1B	16	29	3	7	0	0	0	2	0	.241
1997	Louisville	A.A.	OF-1B	24	83	10	23	7	0	4	14	1	.277
1997	St. Louis a-b-c-d	N.L.	1B-OF	110	333	38	86	14	3	5	34	6	.258
Major League Totals			2 Yrs.	126	362	41	93	14	3	5	36	6	.257
Championship Series													
1996	St. Louis	N.L.	1B	4	7	1	2	0	1	0	2	0	.286

a On disabled list from May 11 to May 29, 1997.
b Traded to Cincinnati Reds for pitcher Jeff Brantley, November 10, 1997.
c Sent to Cincinnati Reds as player to be named later for outfielder Mike Kelly, November 18, 1997.
d Selected in expansion draft by Tampa Bay Devil Rays, November 18, 1997.

YOUNG, ERIC ORLANDO

Born, Jacksonville, Florida, November 26, 1966.
Bats Right. Throws Right. Height, 5 feet, 9 inches. Weight, 180 pounds.

Year	Club	Lea	Pos	G	AB	R	H	2B	3B	HR	RBI	SB	Avg
1989	Kissimmee Dodgers	Gulf C.	2B-3B-C	56	197	53	65	11	5	2	22	*41	.330
1990	Vero Beach	Fla. St.	2B-OF	127	460	*101	132	23	7	2	50	*76	.287
1991	San Antonio	Texas	2B-OF	127	461	82	129	17	4	3	35	*71	.280
1991	Albuquerque	P.C.	2B	1	5	0	2	0	0	0	0	0	.400
1992	Albuquerque	P.C.	2B-OF	94	350	61	118	16	5	3	49	28	.337
1992	Los Angeles a	N.L.	2B	49	132	9	34	1	0	1	11	6	.258
1993	Colorado	N.L.	2B-OF	144	490	82	132	16	8	3	42	42	.269
1994	Colorado	N.L.	OF-2B	90	228	37	62	13	1	7	30	18	.272
1995	Colorado	N.L.	2B-OF	120	366	68	116	21	9	6	36	35	.317
1996	New Haven	Eastern	2B	3	15	0	1	0	0	0	0	0	.067
1996	Salem	Carolina	2B	3	10	2	3	3	0	0	0	2	.300
1996	Colo Sprngs b	P.C.	2B	7	23	4	6	1	1	0	3	0	.261
1996	Colorado	N.L.	2B	141	568	113	184	23	4	8	74	53	.324
1997	Colorado-Los Angeles c	N.L.	2B	155	622	106	174	33	8	8	61	45	.280
Major League Totals			6 Yrs.	699	2406	415	702	107	30	33	254	199	.292
Division Series													
1995	Colorado	N.L.	2B	4	16	3	7	1	0	1	2	1	.438

a Selected by Colorado Rockies in expansion draft, November 17, 1992.
b On disabled list from April 1 to April 22, 1996.
c Traded to Los Angeles Dodgers for pitcher Pedro Astacio, August 18, 1997.

YOUNG, ERNEST WESLEY (ERNIE)

Born, Chicago, Illinois, July 8, 1969.
Bats Right. Throws Right. Height, 6 feet, 1 inch. Weight, 190 pounds.

Year	Club	Lea	Pos	G	AB	R	H	2B	3B	HR	RBI	SB	Avg
1990	South Oregon	Northwest	OF	50	168	34	47	6	2	6	23	4	.280
1991	Madison	Midwest	OF	114	362	75	92	19	2	15	71	20	.254
1992	Modesto	California	OF	74	253	55	63	12	4	11	33	11	.249
1993	Modesto	California	OF	85	301	83	92	18	6	23	71	23	.306
1993	Huntsville	Southern	OF	45	120	26	25	5	0	5	15	8	.208
1994	Tacoma	P.C.	OF	29	102	19	29	4	0	6	16	0	.284
1994	Oakland	A.L.	OF	11	30	2	2	1	0	0	3	0	.067
1994	Huntsville	Southern	OF	72	257	45	89	19	4	14	55	5	.346
1995	Edmonton	P.C.	OF	95	347	70	96	21	4	15	72	2	.277
1995	Oakland	A.L.	OF	26	50	9	10	3	0	2	5	0	.200
1996	Oakland	A.L.	OF	141	462	72	112	19	4	19	64	7	.242
1997	Edmonton	P.C.	OF	54	195	39	63	10	0	9	45	5	.323
1997	Oakland	A.L.	OF	71	175	22	39	7	0	5	15	1	.223
Major League Totals			4 Yrs.	249	717	105	163	30	4	26	87	8	.227

YOUNG, KEVIN STACEY

Born, Alpena, Michigan, June 16, 1969.
Bats Right. Throws Right. Height, 6 feet, 3 inches. Weight, 221 pounds.

Year	Club	Lea	Pos	G	AB	R	H	2B	3B	HR	RBI	SB	Avg
1990 Welland	N.Y.-Penn.	3B	72	238	46	58	16	2	5	30	10	.244
1991 Salem	Carolina	3B	56	201	38	63	12	4	6	28	3	.313
1991 Carolina	Southern	3B-1B	75	263	36	90	19	6	3	33	9	.342
1991 Buffalo	A.A.	3B-1B	4	9	1	2	1	0	0	2	1	.222
1992 Buffalo	A.A.	3B-SS-1B	137	490	91	154	29	6	8	65	18	.314
1992 Pittsburgh	N.L.	3B-1B	10	7	2	4	0	0	0	4	1	.571
1993 Pittsburgh	N.L.	1B-3B	141	449	38	106	24	3	6	47	2	.236
1994 Pittsburgh	N.L.	1B-3B-OF	59	122	15	25	7	2	1	11	0	.205
1994 Buffalo	A.A.	3B-1B	60	228	26	63	14	5	5	27	6	.276
1995 Calgary	P.C.	3B-1B	45	163	24	58	23	1	8	34	6	.356
1995 Pittsburgh a-b	N.L.	3B	56	181	13	42	9	0	6	22	1	.232
1996 Omaha	A.A.	1B-3B	50	186	29	57	11	1	13	46	3	.306
1996 Kansas City c-d	A.L.	1B-OF-3B	55	132	20	32	6	0	8	23	3	.242
1997 Pittsburgh e	N.L.	1B-3B-OF	97	333	59	100	18	3	18	74	11	.300
Major League Totals		6 Yrs.	418	1224	147	309	64	8	39	181	18	.252

a Released by Pittsburgh Pirates, March 26, 1996.
b Signed as free agent with Kansas City organization, March 29, 1996.
c Released by Kansas City, November 20, 1996.
d Signed as free agent by Pittsburgh Pirates, December 19, 1996.
e On disabled list from August 3 to September 12, 1997.

ZAUN, GREGORY OWEN (GREG)

Born, Glendale, California, April 14, 1971.
Bats Both. Throws Right. Height, 5 feet, 10 inches. Weight, 170 pounds.

Year	Club	Lea	Pos	G	AB	R	H	2B	3B	HR	RBI	SB	Avg
1990 Wausau	Midwest	C	37	100	3	13	0	1	1	7	0	.130
1990 Bluefield	Appal.	C-3B-SS-P	61	184	29	55	5	2	2	21	5	.299
1991 Kane County	Midwest	C	113	409	67	112	17	5	4	51	4	.274
1992 Frederick	Carolina	C-2B	108	383	54	96	18	6	6	52	3	.251
1993 Bowie	Eastern	C-2B-3B	79	258	25	79	10	0	3	38	4	.306
1993 Rochester	Int.	C	21	78	10	20	4	2	1	11	0	.256
1994 Rochester	Int.	C	123	388	61	92	16	4	7	43	4	.237
1995 Rochester	Int.	C	42	140	26	41	13	1	6	18	0	.293
1995 Baltimore	A.L.	C	40	104	18	27	5	0	3	14	1	.260
1996 Rochester	Int.	C	14	47	11	15	2	0	0	4	0	.319
1996 Baltimore a	A.L.	C	50	108	16	25	8	1	1	13	0	.231
1996 Florida	N.L.	C	10	31	4	9	1	0	1	2	1	.290
1997 Florida	N.L.	C-1B	58	143	21	43	10	2	2	20	1	.301
Major League Totals		3 Yrs.	158	386	59	104	24	3	7	49	3	.269
Championship Series													
1997 Florida	N.L.	C	1	0	0	0	0	0	0	0	0	.000
World Series Record													
1997 Florida	N.L.	C	2	2	0	0	0	0	0	0	0	.000

a Traded to Florida Marlins as player to be named to complete the deal of August 21 that sent pitcher Terry Mathews to Baltimore Orioles, August 24, 1996.

ZEILE, TODD EDWARD

Born, Van Nuys, California, September 9, 1965.
Bats Right. Throws Right. Height, 6 feet, 1 inch. Weight, 190 pounds.

Year	Club	Lea	Pos	G	AB	R	H	2B	3B	HR	RBI	SB	Avg
1986 Erie	N.Y.-Penn.	C	70	248	40	64	14	1	14	63	5	.258
1987 Springfield	Midwest	C	130	487	94	142	24	4	25	*106	2	.292
1988 Arkansas	Texas	C	129	430	95	117	33	2	19	75	6	.272
1989 Louisville	A.A.	C	118	453	71	131	26	3	19	85	0	.289
1989 St. Louis	N.L.	C	28	82	7	21	3	1	1	8	0	.256
1990 St. Louis	N.L.	C-3B-1B-OF	144	495	62	121	25	3	15	57	2	.244
1991 St. Louis	N.L.	3B	155	565	76	158	36	3	11	81	17	.280
1992 St. Louis	N.L.	3B	126	439	51	113	18	4	7	48	7	.257
1992 Louisville	A.A.	3B	21	74	11	23	4	1	5	13	0	.311
1993 St. Louis	N.L.	3B	157	571	82	158	36	1	17	103	5	.277
1994 St. Louis a	N.L.	3B	113	415	62	111	25	1	19	75	1	.267
1995 Louisville	A.A.	1B	2	8	0	1	0	0	0	0	0	.125
1995 St.L-Chic. b-c-d-e	N.L.	3B-1B-OF	113	426	50	105	22	0	14	52	1	.246
1996 Philadelphia f	N.L.	3B-1B	134	500	61	134	24	0	20	80	1	.268

193

Year	Club	Lea	Pos	G	AB	R	H	2B	3B	HR	RBI	SB	Avg
1996 Baltimore g-h	.A.L.		3B	29	117	17	28	8	0	5	19	0	.239
1997 Los Angeles	.N.L.		3B	160	575	89	154	17	0	31	90	8	.268
Major League Totals			9 Yrs.	1159	4185	557	1103	214	13	140	613	42	.264
Division Series													
1996 Baltimore	.A.L.		3B	4	19	2	5	1	0	0	0	0	.263
Championship Series													
1996 Baltimore	.A.L.		3B	5	22	3	8	0	0	3	5	0	.364

a Declared restricted free agent under Major League Baseball implemented labor proposal, December 23, 1994.
b Re-signed with St. Louis Cardinals, April 5, 1995.
c On disabled list from April 25 to May 9, 1995.
d Traded to Chicago Cubs for pitcher Mike Morgan, infielder Paul Torres and catcher Francisco Morales, June 16, 1995.
e Filed for free agency, November 12, 1995; signed with Philadelphia Phillies, December 23, 1995.
f Traded to Baltimore Orioles with outfielder Pete Incaviglia for pitcher Kevin Gallagher and infielder Pedro Santana, August 27, 1996.
g Filed for free agency, October 27, 1996.
h Signed with Los Angeles Dodgers, December 8, 1996.

PITCHERS

ACEVEDO, JUAN CARLOS
Born, Juarez, Mexico, May 5, 1970.
Bats Right. Throws Right. Height, 6 feet, 2 inches, Weight, 195 pounds.

Year	Club	Lea	G	IP	W	L	Pct	SO	BB	H	ERA	SAVES
1992 Bend	Northwest	1	2	0	0	.000	3	1	4	13.50	0
1992 Visalia	California	12	64²/₃	3	4	.429	37	33	75	5.43	0
1993 Central Valley	California	27	118²/₃	9	8	.529	107	58	119	4.40	0
1994 New Haven	Eastern	26	174²/₃	17	6	.739	161	38	142	2.37	0
1995 Colorado Springs	P.C.	3	14²/₃	1	1	.500	7	7	18	6.14	0
1995 Norfolk	Int.	2	3	0	0	.000	2	1	0	0.00	0
1995 Colorado a	N.L.	17	65²/₃	4	6	.400	40	20	82	6.44	0
1996 Norfolk	Int.	19	102²/₃	4	8	.333	83	53	116	5.96	0
1997 Norfolk	Int.	18	116²/₃	6	6	.500	99	34	111	3.86	0
1997 New York	N.L.	25	47²/₃	3	1	.750	33	22	52	3.59	0
Major League Totals	2 Yrs.	42	113¹/₃	7	7	.500	73	42	134	5.24	0

a Traded to New York Mets with pitcher Arnold Gooch for pitcher Bret Saberhagen and player to be named later, July 21, 1995.

ADAMS, TERRY WAYNE
Born, Mobile, Alabama, March 6, 1973.
Bats Right. Throws Right. Height, 6 feet, 3 inches, Weight, 205 pounds.

Year	Club	Lea	G	IP	W	L	Pct	SO	BB	H	ERA	SAVES
1991 Huntington	Appal.	14	57²/₃	0	9	.000	52	62	67	5.77	0
1992 Peoria	Midwest	25	157	7	12	.368	96	86	144	4.41	0
1993 Daytona	Fla. St.	13	70²/₃	3	5	.375	35	43	78	4.97	0
1994 Daytona	Fla. St.	39	84¹/₃	9	10	.474	64	46	87	4.38	7
1995 Orlando	Southern	37	37²/₃	2	3	.400	26	16	23	1.43	19
1995 Iowa	A.A.	7	6¹/₃	0	0	.000	10	2	3	0.00	5
1995 Chicago	N.L.	18	18	1	1	.500	15	10	22	6.50	1
1996 Chicago	N.L.	69	101	3	6	.333	78	49	84	2.94	4
1997 Chicago	N.L.	74	74	2	9	.182	64	40	91	4.62	18
Major League Totals	3 Yrs.	161	193	6	16	.273	157	99	197	3.92	23

ADAMS, WILLIAM EDWARD (WILLIE)
Born, Gallup, New Mexico, October 8, 1972.
Bats Right. Throws Right. Height, 6 feet, 7 inches. Weight, 215 pounds.

Year	Club	Lea	G	IP	W	L	Pct	SO	BB	H	ERA	SAVES
1993 Madison	Midwest	5	18²/₃	0	2	.000	22	8	21	3.38	0
1994 Modesto	California	11	45¹/₃	7	1	.875	42	10	41	3.38	2
1994 Huntsville	Southern	10	60²/₃	4	3	.571	33	23	58	4.30	0
1995 Huntsville	Southern	13	80²/₃	6	5	.545	72	17	75	3.01	0
1995 Edmonton	P.C.	11	68	2	5	.286	40	15	73	4.37	0
1996 Edmonton	P.C.	19	112	10	4	.714	80	39	95	3.78	0
1996 Oakland	A.L.	12	76¹/₃	3	4	.429	68	23	76	4.01	0
1997 Oakland	A.L.	13	58¹/₃	3	5	.375	37	32	73	8.18	0
1997 Edmonton	P.C.	13	75¹/₃	5	4	.556	58	19	105	6.45	0
Major League Totals	2 Yrs.	25	134²/₃	6	9	.400	105	55	149	5.81	0

ADAMSON, JOEL LEE
Born, Bellflower, California, July 2, 1971.
Bats Left. Throws Left. Height, 6 feet, 4 inches. Weight, 185 pounds.

Year	Club	Lea	G	IP	W	L	Pct	SO	BB	H	ERA	SAVES
1990 Princeton	Appal.	12	48²/₃	2	5	.286	40	12	56	3.88	1
1991 Spartanburg	So. Atl.	14	81	4	4	.500	84	22	72	2.56	0
1991 Clearwater	Fla. St.	5	29²/₃	2	1	.667	20	7	28	3.03	0
1992 Clearwater	Fla. St.	15	89²/₃	5	6	.455	52	19	90	3.41	0
1992 Reading	Eastern	10	59	3	6	.333	35	13	68	4.27	0
1993 Edmonton a	P.C.	5	26	1	2	.333	7	13	39	6.92	0
1993 High Desert	California	22	129²/₃	5	5	.500	72	30	160	4.58	0

Year Club	Lea	G	IP	W	L	Pct	SO	BB	H	ERA	SAVES
1994 Portland ....Eastern	33	91⅓	5	6	.455	59	32	95	4.34	7
1995 Charlotte b ....Int.	19	115	8	4	.667	80	20	113	3.29	0
1996 Florida ...............N.L.	9	11	0	0	.000	7	7	18	7.36	0
1996 Charlotte c ....Int.	44	97⅔	6	6	.500	84	28	108	3.78	3
1997 Tucson ................P.C.	7	33	2	1	.667	24	8	38	4.36	0
1997 Milwaukee d ..........A.L.	30	76⅓	5	3	.625	56	19	78	3.54	0
Major League Totals ....2 Yrs.	39	87⅓	5	3	.625	63	26	96	4.02	0

a Traded by Philadelphia Phillies organization to Florida Marlins with pitcher Matt Whisenant for pitcher Danny Jackson, November 17, 1992.
b On disabled list from June 8 to July 23, 1995.
c Traded to Milwaukee Brewers for pitcher Eddie Collins, November 25, 1996.
d Selected in expansion draft by Arizona Diamondbacks, November 18, 1997.

AGUILERA, RICHARD WARREN
Born, San Gabriel, California, December 31, 1961.
Bats Right. Throws Right. Height, 6 feet, 5 inches. Weight, 203 pounds.

Year Club	Lea	G	IP	W	L	Pct	SO	BB	H	ERA	SAVES
1983 Little Falls .......N.Y.-Penn.	16	104	5	6	.455	84	26	*109	3.72	0
1984 Lynchburg ....Carolina	13	88⅓	8	3	.727	101	28	72	2.34	0
1984 Jackson a ....Texas	11	67	4	4	.500	71	19	68	4.57	0
1985 New York ...............N.L.	21	122⅓	10	7	.588	74	37	118	3.24	0
1985 Tidewater ....Int.	11	79	6	4	.600	55	17	64	2.51	0
1986 New York .............N.L.	28	141⅔	10	7	.588	104	36	145	3.88	0
1987 Tidewater ....Int.	3	13	1	1	.500	10	1	8	0.69	0
1987 New York b ............N.L.	18	115	11	3	.786	77	33	124	3.60	0
1988 St. Lucie ....Fla. St.	2	7	0	0	.000	5	1	8	1.29	0
1988 Tidewater ....Int.	1	6	0	0	.000	4	1	1	1.50	0
1988 New York c ............N.L.	11	24⅔	0	4	.000	16	10	29	6.93	0
1989 New York d .............N.L.	36	69⅓	6	6	.500	80	21	59	2.34	7
1989 Minnesota ..............A.L.	11	75⅔	3	5	.375	57	17	71	3.21	0
1990 Minnesota ..............A.L.	56	65⅓	5	3	.625	61	19	55	2.76	32
1991 Minnesota ..............A.L.	63	69	4	5	.444	61	30	44	2.35	42
1992 Minnesota ..............A.L.	64	66⅔	2	6	.250	52	17	60	2.84	41
1993 Minnesota ..............A.L.	65	72⅓	4	3	.571	59	14	60	3.11	34
1994 Minnesota ..............A.L.	44	44⅔	1	4	.200	46	10	57	3.63	23
1995 Minnesota-Boston e-f-g ..A.L.	52	55⅓	3	3	.500	52	13	46	2.60	32
1996 Ft. Myers h ....Fla. St.	2	12	2	0	1.000	12	1	13	3.75	0
1996 Minnesota ..............A.L.	19	111⅓	8	6	.571	83	27	124	5.42	0
1997 Minnesota ..............A.L.	61	68⅓	5	4	.556	68	22	65	3.82	26
Major League Totals ....13 Yrs.	549	1101⅔	72	66	.522	890	306	1057	3.50	237
Division Series										
1995 Boston ...............A.L.	1	0⅔	0	0	.000	1	0	3	13.50	0
Championship Series										
1986 New York .............N.L.	2	5	0	0	.000	2	2	2	0.00	0
1988 New York .............N.L.	3	7	0	0	.000	4	2	3	1.29	0
1991 Minnesota ..............A.L.	3	3⅓	0	0	.000	3	0	1	0.00	3
Championship Series Totals 8		15⅓	0	0	.000	9	4	6	0.59	3
World Series Record										
1986 New York .............N.L.	2	3	1	0	1.000	4	1	8	12.00	0
1991 Minnesota ..............A.L.	4	5	1	1	.500	3	1	6	1.80	2
World Series Totals 5		8	2	1	.667	7	2	14	5.63	2

a On disabled list from September 3 to September 14, 1984.
b On disabled list from May 30 to August 24, 1987.
c On disabled list from April 19 to June 19 and July 12 to September 7, 1988.
d Traded to Minnesota Twins with pitchers Dave West, Tim Drummond and Kevin Tapani and player to be named for pitcher Frank Viola, July 31; Minnesota acquired pitcher Jack Savage to complete trade, October 16, 1989.
e Traded to Boston Red Sox for pitcher Frank Rodriguez and player to be named later, July 6, 1995.
f Minnesota Twins received outfielder Jermane Johnson to complete trade, October 11, 1995.
g Filed for free agency, November 12, 1995; signed with Minnesota Twins, December 11, 1995.
h On disabled list from April 1 to April 20 and April 20 to June 11, 1996.

ALDRED, SCOTT PHILLIP
Born, Flint, Michigan, June 12, 1968.
Bats Left. Throws Left. Height, 6 feet, 4 inches. Weight, 228 pounds.

Year Club	Lea	G	IP	W	L	Pct	SO	BB	H	ERA	SAVES
1987 Fayetteville ....So. Atl.	21	111	4	9	.308	91	69	101	3.57	0
1988 Lakeland ....Fla. St.	25	131⅓	8	7	.533	102	72	122	3.56	0

Year Club	Lea	G	IP	W	L	Pct	SO	BB	H	ERA	SAVES
1989 London	Eastern	20	122	10	6	.625	97	59	98	3.84	0
1990 Toledo	Int.	29	158	6	15	.286	133	81	145	4.90	0
1990 Detroit	A.L.	4	14⅓	1	2	.333	7	10	13	3.77	0
1991 Toledo	Int.	22	135⅓	8	8	.500	95	72	127	3.92	1
1991 Detroit	A.L.	11	57⅓	2	4	.333	35	30	58	5.18	0
1992 Toledo	Int.	16	86	4	6	.400	81	47	92	5.13	0
1992 Detroit a	A.L.	16	65	3	8	.273	34	33	80	6.78	0
1993 Colorado b	N.L.	5	6⅔	0	0	.000	5	9	10	10.80	0
1993 Montreal c-d	N.L.	3	5⅓	1	0	1.000	4	1	9	6.75	0
1994 e			(INJURED—Did Not Play)								
1995 Lakeland	Fla. St.	13	67⅔	4	2	.667	64	19	57	3.19	2
1995 Jacksnville	Southern	2	12	1	0	1.000	11	1	9	0.00	0
1996 Detroit	A.L.	11	43⅓	0	4	.000	36	26	60	9.35	0
1996 Minnesota f	A.L.	25	122	6	5	.545	75	42	134	5.09	0
1997 Minnesota	A.L.	-17	77⅓	2	10	.167	33	28	102	7.68	0
1997 Salt Lake g-h-i ..	P.C.	7	39⅔	3	3	.500	23	16	56	7.03	0
Major League Totals ...... 6 Yrs.		92	391⅓	15	33	.313	229	179	466	6.44	0

a Drafted by Colorado Rockies in expansion draft, November 17, 1992.
b Claimed off waivers by Montreal Expos, April 29, 1993.
c On disabled list from May 15 to September 10, 1993.
d Released, September 13, 1993.
e Signed as free agent by Detroit Tigers organization, October 5, 1994.
f Claimed off waivers by Minnesota Twins, May 28, 1996.
g Released by Minnesota Twins, June 22, 1997.
h Filed for free agency, October 8, 1997.
i Signed as free agent by Tampa Bay Devil Rays, December 19, 1997.

ALFONSECA, ANTONIO

Born, LaRomana, Dominican Republic, April 16, 1972.
Bats Right. Throws Right. Height, 6 feet, 5 inches. Weight, 235 pounds.

Year Club	Lea	G	IP	W	L	Pct	SO	BB	H	ERA	SAVES
1991 Expos	Gulf Coast	11	51	3	3	.500	38	25	46	3.88	0
1992 Expos	Gulf Coast	12	66	3	4	.429	62	35	55	3.68	0
1993 Jamestown a	N.Y.-Penn.	15	33⅔	2	2	.500	29	22	31	6.15	1
1994 Kane County	Midwest	32	86⅓	6	5	.545	74	21	78	4.07	0
1995 Portland b	Eastern	19	96⅓	9	3	.750	75	42	81	3.64	0
1996 Charlotte c	Int.	14	71⅔	4	4	.500	51	22	86	5.53	1
1997 Charlotte	Int.	46	58⅓	7	2	.778	45	20	58	4.32	7
1997 Florida	N.L.	17	25⅔	1	3	.250	19	10	36	4.91	0
World Series Record											
1997 Florida	N.L.	3	6⅓	0	0	.000	5	1	6	0.00	0

a Drafted by Florida Marlins from Montreal Expos organization in Rule V draft, December 13, 1993.
b On disabled list May 15 to June 15, 1995.
c On disabled list July 12 to September 3, 1996.

ALVAREZ, WILSON EDUARDO

Born, Maracaibo, Venezuela, March 24, 1970.
Bats Left. Throws Left. Height, 6 feet, 1 inch. Weight, 235 pounds.

Year Club	Lea	G	IP	W	L	Pct	SO	BB	H	ERA	SAVES
1987 Gastonia	So. Atl.	8	32	1	5	.167	19	23	39	6.47	0
1987 G.C. Rangers	Gulf Coast	10	44⅔	2	5	.286	46	21	41	5.24	0
1988 Gastonia	So. Atl.	23	127	4	11	.267	134	50	113	2.98	0
1988 Oklahoma City ...	P.C.	5	16⅔	1	1	.500	9	6	17	3.78	0
1989 Charlotte	Fla. St.	13	81	7	4	.636	46	21	68	2.11	0
1989 Tulsa	Texas	7	48	2	2	.500	29	16	40	2.06	0
1989 Texas a	A.L.	1	0	0	1	.000	0	2	3	x	0
1989 Birmingham	Southern	6	35⅔	2	1	.667	18	16	32	3.03	0
1990 Birmingham	Southern	7	46⅓	5	1	.833	36	25	44	4.27	0
1990 Vancouver	P.C.	17	75	7	7	.500	35	51	91	6.00	0
1991 Birmingham	Southern	23	152⅓	10	6	.625	165	74	109	1.83	0
1991 Chicago b	A.L.	10	56⅓	3	2	.600	32	29	47	3.51	0
1992 Chicago	A.L.	34	100⅓	5	3	.625	66	65	103	5.20	1
1993 Nashville	A.A.	1	6⅓	0	1	.000	8	2	7	2.84	0
1993 Chicago	A.L.	31	207⅔	15	8	.652	155	*122	168	2.95	0
1994 Chicago	A.L.	24	161⅔	12	8	.600	108	62	147	3.45	0
1995 Chicago c	A.L.	29	175	8	11	.421	118	93	171	4.32	0
1996 Chicago	A.L.	35	217⅓	15	10	.600	181	97	216	4.22	0

Year	Club	Lea	G	IP	W	L	Pct	SO	BB	H	ERA	SAVES
1997 Chicago d	A.L.	22	145⅔	9	8	.529	110	55	126	3.03	0
1997 San Francisco e-f	N.L.	11	66⅓	4	3	.571	69	36	54	4.48	0
Major League Totals	8 Yrs.	197	1130⅓	71	54	.568	839	561	1035	3.83	1
Division Series											
1997 San Francisco	N.L.	1	6	0	1	.000	4	4	6	6.00	0
Championship Series											
1993 Chicago	A.L.	1	9	1	0	1.000	6	2	7	1.00	0

a Traded by Texas Rangers to Chicago White Sox with outfielder Sammy Sosa and infielder Scott Fletcher for outfielder/designated hitter Harold Baines and infielder Fred Manrique, July 29, 1989.
b Pitched no-hit, no-run game against Baltimore Orioles, winning 7-0, August 11, 1991.
c Signed with Chicago White Sox, April 28, 1995.
d Traded to San Francisco Giants with pitcher Danny Darwin and pitcher Roberto Hernandez for infielder Mike Caruso, outfielder Brian Manning, pitcher Lorenzo Barcelo, pitcher Keith Foulke, pitcher Bob Howry and pitcher Ken Vining, July 31, 1997.
e Filed for free agency, November 3, 1997.
f Signed with Tampa Bay Devil Rays, December 3, 1997.

ANDERSON, BRIAN JAMES
Born, Portsmouth, Virginia, April 16, 1972.
Bats Left. Throws Left. Height, 6 feet 1 inch. Weight, 190 pounds.

Year	Club	Lea	G	IP	W	L	Pct	SO	BB	H	ERA	SAVES
1993 Midland	Texas	2	10⅔	0	1	.000	9	0	16	3.38	0
1993 Vancouver	P.C.	2	8	0	1	.000	2	6	13	12.38	0
1993 California	A.L.	4	11⅓	0	0	.000	4	2	11	3.97	0
1994 Lake Elsinore	California	2	12	0	1	.000	9	0	6	3.00	0
1994 California a	A.L.	18	101⅔	7	5	.583	47	27	120	5.22	0
1995 Lake Elsinore	California	3	14	1	1	.500	13	1	10	1.93	0
1995 California b	A.L.	18	99⅔	6	8	.429	45	30	110	5.87	0
1996 Buffalo	A.A.	19	128	11	5	.688	85	28	125	3.59	0
1996 Cleveland c	A.L.	10	51⅓	3	1	.750	21	14	58	4.91	0
1997 Buffalo	A.A.	15	85⅔	7	1	.875	60	15	78	3.05	0
1997 Cleveland d-e	A.L.	8	48	4	2	.667	22	11	55	4.69	0
Major League Totals	5 Yrs.	58	312	20	16	.556	139	84	354	5.25	0
Championship Series											
1997 Cleveland	A.L.	3	6⅓	1	0	1.000	7	3	1	1.42	0
World Series Record											
1997 Cleveland	A.L.	3	3⅔	0	0	.000	2	0	2	2.45	1

a On disabled list from May 7 to June 7, 1994.
b On disabled list from May 6 to June 20, 1995.
c Traded to Cleveland Indians for pitcher Jason Grimsley and pitcher Pep Harris, February 15, 1996.
d On disabled list from July 5 to August 12, 1997.
e Selected in expansion draft by Arizona Diamondbacks, November 18, 1997.

ANDUJAR, LUIS
Born, Bani, Dominican Republic, November 22, 1972.
Bats Right. Throws Right. Height, 6 feet, 2 inches, Weight, 175 pounds.

Year	Club	Lea	G	IP	W	L	Pct	SO	BB	H	ERA	SAVES
1991 White Sox	Gulf Coast	10	62⅓	4	4	.500	52	10	60	2.45	0
1992 South Bend	Midwest	32	120⅓	6	5	.545	91	47	109	2.92	3
1993 Sarasota	Fla. St.	18	86	6	6	.500	76	28	67	1.99	1
1993 Birmingham	Southern	6	39⅔	5	0	1.000	48	18	31	1.82	0
1994 White Sox	Gulf Coast	2	6	1	0	1.000	6	1	3	0.00	0
1994 Birmingham	Southern	15	76⅔	3	7	.300	64	25	90	5.05	0
1995 Birmingham	Southern	27	167⅓	14	8	.636	146	44	147	2.85	0
1995 Chicago	A.L.	5	30⅓	2	1	.667	9	14	26	3.26	0
1996 White Sox	Gulf Coast	1	6	1	0	1.000	3	0	3	0.00	0
1996 Nashville	A.A.	8	38	1	4	.200	24	8	50	5.92	0
1996 Syracuse	Int.	2	12	0	0	.000	10	2	17	2.25	0
1996 Chicago-Toronto a	A.L.	8	37⅓	1	3	.250	11	16	46	6.99	0
1997 Syracuse	Int.	13	39	1	6	.143	29	14	37	5.54	1
1997 Toronto b-c-d	A.L.	17	50	0	6	.000	28	21	76	6.48	0
Major League Totals	3 Yrs.	30	117⅔	3	10	.231	48	51	148	5.81	0

a Traded to Toronto Blue Jays with pitcher Allen Halley for pitcher Tony Castillo and infielder Domingo Cedeno, August 22, 1996.
b On disabled list from September 4 to September 29, 1997.
c Filed for free agency, October 5, 1997.
d Signed with Toronto Blue Jays organization, November 11, 1997.

APPIER, ROBERT KEVIN

Born, Lancaster, California, December 6, 1967.
Bats Right. Throws Right. Height, 6 feet, 2 inches. Weight, 195 pounds.

Year Club	Lea	G	IP	W	L	Pct	SO	BB	H	ERA	SAVES
1987 Eugene	Northwest	15	77	5	2	.714	72	29	81	3.04	0
1988 Baseball City	Fla. St.	24	147⅓	10	9	.526	112	39	134	2.75	0
1988 Memphis	Southern	3	19⅔	2	0	1.000	18	7	11	1.83	0
1989 Omaha	A.A.	22	139	8	8	.500	109	42	141	3.95	0
1989 Kansas City	A.L.	6	21⅔	1	4	.200	10	12	34	9.14	0
1990 Omaha	A.A.	3	18	2	0	1.000	17	3	15	1.50	0
1990 Kansas City	A.L.	32	185⅔	12	8	.600	127	54	179	2.76	0
1991 Kansas City	A.L.	34	207⅔	13	10	.565	158	61	205	3.42	0
1992 Kansas City	A.L.	30	208⅓	15	8	.652	150	68	167	2.46	0
1993 Kansas City	A.L.	34	238⅔	18	8	.692	186	81	183	*2.56	0
1994 Kansas City a	A.L.	23	155	7	6	.538	145	63	137	3.83	0
1995 Kansas City b-c	A.L.	31	201⅓	15	10	.600	185	80	163	3.89	0
1996 Kansas City	A.L.	32	211⅓	14	11	.560	207	75	192	3.62	0
1997 Kansas City	A.L.	34	235⅔	9	13	.409	196	74	215	3.40	0
Major League Totals	9 Yrs.	256	1665⅓	104	78	.571	1364	568	1475	3.30	0

a Declared restricted free agent under Major League Baseball implemented labor proposal, December 23, 1994.
b Re-signed with Kansas City Royals, May 23, 1995.
c On disabled list from July 16 to August 12, 1995.

ASHBY, ANDREW JASON

Born, Kansas City, Missouri, July 11, 1967.
Bats Right. Throws Right. Height, 6 feet, 5 inches. Weight, 190 pounds.

Year Club	Lea	G	IP	W	L	Pct	SO	BB	H	ERA	SAVES
1986 Bend	Northwest	16	60	1	2	.333	45	34	56	4.95	2
1987 Spartanburg	So. Atl.	13	64⅓	4	6	.400	52	38	73	5.60	0
1987 Utica	N.Y.-Penn.	13	60	3	7	.300	51	36	56	4.05	0
1988 Batavia a	N.Y.-Penn.	6	44⅔	3	1	.750	32	16	25	1.61	0
1988 Spartanburg	So. Atl.	3	16⅔	1	1	.500	16	7	13	2.70	0
1989 Spartanburg b	So. Atl.	17	106⅔	5	9	.357	100	49	95	2.87	0
1989 Clearwater	Fla. St.	6	43⅔	1	4	.200	44	21	28	1.24	0
1990 Reading	Eastern	23	139⅔	10	7	.588	94	48	134	3.42	0
1991 Scranton	Int.	26	161⅓	11	11	.500	113	60	144	3.46	0
1991 Philadelphia	N.L.	8	42	1	5	.167	26	19	41	6.00	0
1992 Philadelphia c	N.L.	10	37	1	3	.250	24	21	42	7.54	0
1992 Scranton d	Int.	7	33	0	3	.000	18	14	23	3.00	0
1993 Colorado Springs	P.C.	7	41⅔	4	2	.667	35	12	45	4.10	0
1993 Colorado-San Diego e	N.L.	32	123	3	10	.231	77	56	168	6.80	1
1994 San Diego	N.L.	24	164⅓	6	11	.353	121	43	145	3.40	0
1995 San Diego	N.L.	31	192⅔	12	10	.545	150	62	180	2.94	0
1996 San Diego f	N.L.	24	150⅔	9	5	.643	85	34	147	3.23	0
1997 San Diego g	N.L.	30	200⅔	9	11	.450	144	49	207	4.13	0
Major League Totals	7 Yrs.	159	910⅓	41	55	.427	627	284	930	4.18	1
Division Series											
1996 San Diego	N.L.	1	5⅓	0	0	.000	5	1	7	6.75	0

a On disabled list from March 31 to July 10, 1988.
b On disabled list from April 2 to April 26, 1989.
c On disabled list from April 27 to August 10, 1992.
d Selected by Colorado Rockies from Philadelphia Phillies organization in expansion draft, November 17, 1992.
e Traded to San Diego Padres to complete July 26 trade in which Colorado acquired pitchers Greg W. Harris and Bruce Hurst for catcher Brad Ausmus and pitcher Doug Bochtler for player to be named, July 28, 1993.
f On disabled list from June 6 to June 22 and June 29 to July 15 and July 27 to September 1, 1996.
g On disabled list from May 20 to June 15, 1997.

ASSENMACHER, PAUL ANDRE

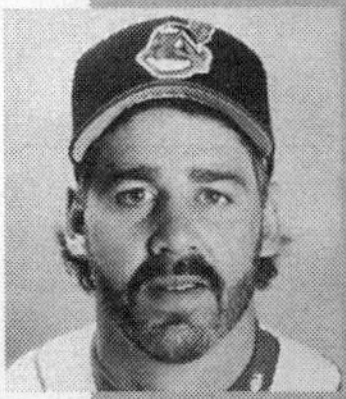

Born, Detroit, Michigan, December 10, 1960.
Bats Left. Throws Left. Height, 6 feet, 3 inches. Weight, 210 pounds.

Year Club	Lea	G	IP	W	L	Pct	SO	BB	H	ERA	SAVES
1983 Bradenton Braves	Gulf C.	10	36⅔	1	0	1.000	44	4	35	2.21	2
1984 Durham	Carolina	26	147⅓	6	11	.353	147	52	153	4.28	0
1985 Durham	Carolina	14	38⅓	3	2	.600	36	13	38	3.29	1
1985 Greenville	W.Carolinas	29	52⅔	6	0	1.000	59	11	47	2.56	4
1986 Atlanta	N.L.	61	68⅓	7	3	.700	56	26	61	2.50	7

Year	Club	Lea	G	IP	W	L	Pct	SO	BB	H	ERA	SAVES
1987 Richmond	Int.	4	24²/₃	1	2	.333	21	8	30	3.65	0
1987 Atlanta a	N.L.	52	54²/₃	1	1	.500	39	24	58	5.10	2
1988 Atlanta b	N.L.	64	79¹/₃	8	7	.533	71	32	72	3.06	5
1989 Atlanta-Chicago c	N.L.	63	76²/₃	3	4	.429	79	28	74	3.99	0
1990 Chicago	N.L.	74	103	7	2	.778	95	36	90	2.80	10
1991 Chicago	N.L.	75	102²/₃	7	8	.467	117	31	85	3.24	15
1992 Chicago d	N.L.	70	68	4	4	.500	67	26	72	4.10	8
1993 Chicago e	N.L.	46	38²/₃	2	1	.667	34	13	44	3.49	0
1993 New York f	A.L.	26	17¹/₃	2	2	.500	11	9	10	3.12	0
1994 Chicago g	N.L.	44	33	1	2	.333	29	13	26	3.55	1
1995 Cleveland h	A.L.	47	38¹/₃	6	2	.750	40	12	32	2.82	0
1996 Cleveland	A.L.	63	46²/₃	4	2	.667	44	14	46	3.09	1
1997 Cleveland i-j	A.L.	75	49	5	0	1.000	53	15	43	2.94	4
Major League Totals	12 Yrs.	760	775²/₃	57	38	.600	735	279	713	3.35	53
Division Series											
1995 Chicago	A.L.	3	1²/₃	0	0	.000	3	0	0	0.00	0
1996 Cleveland	A.L.	3	1²/₃	1	0	1.000	2	1	0	0.00	0
1997 Cleveland	A.L.	4	3¹/₃	0	0	.000	2	2	2	5.40	0
Divisional Series Totals	10	6²/₃	1	0	1.000	7	3	2	2.70	0
Championship Series											
1989 Chicago	N.L.	2	0²/₃	0	0	.000	0	0	3	13.50	0
1995 Chicago	A.L.	3	1¹/₃	0	0	.000	2	1	0	0.00	0
1997 Cleveland	A.L.	5	2	1	0	1.000	3	1	5	9.00	0
Championship Series Totals	10	4	1	0	1.000	5	2	8	6.75	0
World Series Record											
1995 Chicago	A.L.	4	1¹/₃	0	0	.000	3	3	1	6.75	0
1997 Cleveland	A.L.	5	4	0	0	.000	6	0	5	0.00	0
World Series Totals	9	5¹/₃	0	0	.000	9	3	6	1.69	0

a On disabled list from April 24 to May 9, 1987.
b On disabled list from August 10 to August 25, 1988.
c Traded to Chicago Cubs for two players to be named, August 24; Atlanta Braves acquired pitcher Pat Gomez, August 31, and catcher Kelly Mann to complete trade, September 1, 1989.
d On disabled list from May 19 to June 4, 1992.
e Traded to New York Yankees as part of three-team trade in which Chicago Cubs acquired outfielder Karl Rhodes from Kansas City Royals organization and Kansas City acquired pitcher John Habyan from New York, July 30, 1993.
f Traded to Chicago White Sox for pitcher Brian Boehringer, March 21, 1994.
g Filed for free agency, October 17, 1984.
h Signed with Cleveland Indians, April 10, 1995.
i Filed for free agency, November 3, 1997.
j Re-signed with Cleveland Indians, November 12, 1997.

ASTACIO, PEDRO JULIO

Born, Hato Mayor, Dominican Republic, November 28, 1969.
Bats Right. Throws Right. Height, 6 feet, 2 inches. Weight, 190 pounds.

Year	Club	Lea	G	IP	W	L	Pct	SO	BB	H	ERA	SAVES
1988 Santo Domingo	Dom. Sum.	8	47²/₃	4	2	.667	20	18	43	2.08	0
1989 Kissimmee Dodgers	Gulf C.	12	76²/₃	7	3	.700	52	12	77	3.17	0
1990 Vero Beach	Fla. St.	8	47	1	5	.167	41	23	54	6.32	0
1990 Bakersfield	California	10	52	5	2	.714	34	15	46	2.77	0
1991 Vero Beach	Fla. St.	9	59¹/₃	5	3	.625	45	8	44	1.67	0
1991 San Antonio	Texas	19	113	4	11	.267	62	39	142	4.78	0
1992 Albuquerque	P.C.	24	98²/₃	6	6	.500	66	44	115	5.47	0
1992 Los Angeles	N.L.	11	82	5	5	.500	43	20	80	1.98	0
1993 Los Angeles	N.L.	31	186¹/₃	14	9	.609	122	68	165	3.57	0
1994 Los Angeles	N.L.	23	149	6	8	.429	108	47	142	4.29	0
1995 Los Angeles	N.L.	48	104	7	8	.467	80	29	103	4.24	0
1996 Los Angeles	N.L.	35	211²/₃	9	8	.529	130	67	207	3.44	0
1997 Los Angeles-Col. a	N.L.	33	202¹/₃	12	10	.545	166	61	200	4.14	0
Major League Totals	6 Yrs.	181	935¹/₃	53	48	.525	649	292	897	3.71	0
Division Series											
1995 Los Angeles	N.L.	3	3¹/₃	0	0	.000	5	0	1	0.00	0
1996 Los Angeles	N.L.	1	1²/₃	0	0	.000	1	0	0	0.00	0
Division Series Totals	4	5	0	0	.000	6	0	1	0.00	0

a Traded to Colorado Rockies for infielder Eric Young, August 18, 1997.

AVERY, STEVEN THOMAS

Born, Trenton, Michigan, April 14, 1970.
Bats Left. Throws Left. Height, 6 feet, 4 inches. Weight, 190 pounds.

Year	Club	Lea	G	IP	W	L	Pct	SO	BB	H	ERA	SAVES
1988 Pulaski		Appal.	10	66	7	1	.875	80	19	38	1.50	0
1989 Durham		Carolina	13	86⅔	6	4	.600	90	20	59	1.45	0
1989 Greenville		Southern	13	84⅓	6	3	.667	73	34	69	2.77	0
1990 Richmond		Int.	13	82⅓	5	5	.500	69	21	85	3.50	0
1990 Atlanta		N.L.	21	99	3	11	.214	75	45	121	5.64	0
1991 Atlanta a		N.L.	35	210⅓	18	8	.692	137	65	189	3.38	0
1992 Atlanta		N.L.	35	233⅔	11	11	.500	129	71	216	3.20	0
1993 Atlanta		N.L.	35	223⅓	18	6	.750	125	43	216	2.94	0
1994 Atlanta b		N.L.	24	151⅔	8	3	.727	122	55	127	4.04	0
1995 Atlanta c		N.L.	29	173⅓	7	13	.350	141	52	165	4.67	0
1996 Greenville d		Southern	1	0⅔	0	0	.000	0	0	0	0.00	0
1996 Atlanta e-f		N.L.	24	131	7	10	.412	86	40	146	4.47	0
1997 Sarasota		Fla. St.	1	3	0	0	.000	3	1	2	0.00	0
1997 Red Sox		Gulf Coast	1	6	0	0	.000	8	0	5	1.50	0
1997 Pawtucket		Int.	1	5	1	0	1.000	1	3	1	0.00	0
1997 Boston g		A.L.	22	96⅔	6	7	.462	51	49	127	6.42	0
Major League Totals	8 Yrs.		225	1319	78	69	.531	866	420	1307	4.02	0
Division Series												
1995 Atlanta		N.L.	1	0⅔	0	0	.000	1	0	1	13.50	0
Championship Series												
1991 Atlanta		N.L.	2	16⅓	2	0	1.000	17	4	9	0.00	0
1992 Atlanta		N.L.	3	8	1	1	.500	3	2	13	9.00	0
1993 Atlanta		N.L.	2	13	0	0	.000	10	6	9	2.77	0
1995 Atlanta		N.L.	2	6	1	0	1.000	6	4	2	0.00	0
1996 Atlanta		N.L.	2	2	0	0	.000	1	1	2	0.00	0
Championship Series Totals	11			45⅓	4	1	.800	37	17	35	2.38	0
World Series Record												
1991 Atlanta		N.L.	2	13	0	0	.000	8	1	10	3.46	0
1992 Atlanta		N.L.	2	12	0	1	.000	11	3	11	3.75	0
1995 Atlanta		N.L.	1	6	1	0	1.000	3	5	3	1.50	0
1996 Atlanta		N.L.	1	0⅔	0	1	.000	0	3	1	13.50	0
World Series Totals	6			31⅔	1	2	.333	22	12	25	3.41	0

a Appeared in one additional game as pinch runner and one additional game as pinch hitter.
b Declared restricted free agent under Major League Baseball implemented labor proposal, December 23, 1994.
c Re-signed with Atlanta Braves, May 3, 1995.
d On disabled list from July 13 to September 2, 1996.
e Filed for free agency, October 31, 1996.
f Signed with Boston Red Sox, January 10, 1997.
g On disabled list from May 4 to July 5, 1997.

AYALA, ROBERT JOSEPH

Born, Ventura, California, July 8, 1969.
Bats Right. Throws Right. Height, 6 feet, 3 inches. Weight, 200 pounds.

Year	Club	Lea	G	IP	W	L	Pct	SO	BB	H	ERA	SAVES
1988 Sarasota Reds		Gulf Coast	20	33	0	4	.000	24	12	34	3.82	3
1989 Greensboro		So. Atl.	22	105⅓	5	8	.385	70	50	97	4.10	0
1990 Cedar Rapids		Midwest	18	53⅓	3	2	.600	59	18	40	3.38	1
1990 Charleston, WV		So. Atl.	21	74	6	1	.857	73	21	48	2.43	2
1991 Chattanooga		Southern	39	90⅔	3	1	.750	92	58	79	4.67	4
1992 Chattanooga		Southern	27	162⅓	12	6	.667	154	58	152	3.54	0
1992 Cincinnati		N.L.	5	29	2	1	.667	23	13	33	4.34	0
1993 Indianapolis		A.A.	5	27	0	2	.000	19	12	36	5.67	0
1993 Cincinnati a		N.L.	43	98	7	10	.412	65	45	106	5.60	3
1994 Seattle		A.L.	46	56⅔	4	3	.571	76	26	42	2.86	18
1995 Seattle		A.L.	63	71	6	5	.545	77	30	73	4.44	19
1996 Port City		Southern	2	1⅔	0	0	.000	2	1	0	0.00	0
1996 Tacoma b		P.C.	1	1	0	0	.000	1	1	0	0.00	0
1996 Seattle		A.L.	50	67⅓	6	3	.667	61	25	65	5.88	3
1997 Seattle		A.L.	71	96⅔	10	5	.667	92	41	91	3.82	8
Major League Totals	6 Yrs.		278	418⅔	35	27	.565	394	180	410	4.58	51
Division Series												
1995 Seattle		A.L.	2	0⅔	0	0	.000	0	1	6	54.0	0
1997 Seattle		A.L.	1	1⅓	0	0	.000	3	1	4	40.50	0
Divisional Series Totals	3			2	0	0	.000	3	2	10	45.00	0

Year	Club	Lea	G	IP	W	L	Pct	SO	BB	H	ERA	SAVES
	Championship Series											
1995 Seattle		A.L.	2	3⅔	0	0	.000	3	3	3	2.45	0

a Traded to Seattle Mariners with catcher Dan Wilson for pitcher Erik Hanson and second baseman Bret Boone, November 2, 1993.
b On disabled list from April 23 to June 20, 1996.

AYBAR, MANUEL ANTONIO
Born, Bani, Dominican Republic, October 5, 1974.
Bats Right. Throws Right. Height, 6 feet, 1 inch. Weight, 165 pounds.

Year	Club	Lea	G	IP	W	L	Pct	SO	BB	H	ERA	SAVES
1994 Cardinals	Arizona	13	72⅓	6	1	.857	79	9	69	2.12	0	
1995 Savannah	So. Atl.	18	112⅔	3	8	.273	99	36	82	3.04	0	
1995 St. Pete	Fla. St.	9	48⅓	2	5	.286	43	16	42	3.35	0	
1996 Arkansas	Texas	20	121	8	6	.571	83	34	120	3.05	0	
1996 Louisville	A.A.	5	30⅔	2	2	.500	25	7	26	3.23	0	
1997 Louisville	A.A.	22	137	5	8	.385	114	45	131	3.48	0	
1997 St. Louis	N.L.	12	68	2	4	.333	41	29	66	4.24	0	

BAILEY, CHARLES ROGER (ROGER)
Born, Chattachoochee, Florida, October 3, 1970.
Bats Right. Throws Right. Height, 6 feet, 1 inch, Weight, 180 pounds.

Year	Club	Lea	G	IP	W	L	Pct	SO	BB	H	ERA	SAVES
1992 Bend	Northwest	11	65⅓	5	2	.714	81	30	48	2.20	0	
1993 Central Valley	California	22	111⅔	4	7	.364	84	56	139	4.84	0	
1994 New Haven	Eastern	25	159	9	9	.500	112	56	157	3.23	0	
1995 Colorado Springs	P.C.	3	16⅔	0	0	.000	7	8	15	2.70	0	
1995 Colorado	N.L.	39	81⅓	7	6	.538	33	39	88	4.98	0	
1996 Colo Sprngs a	P.C.	9	48⅔	4	4	.500	27	20	60	6.29	0	
1996 Colorado	N.L.	24	83⅔	2	3	.400	45	52	94	6.24	1	
1997 Colorado b	N.L.	29	191	9	10	.474	84	70	210	4.29	0	
Major League Totals	3 Yrs.	92	356	18	19	.486	162	161	392	4.90	1	

a On disabled list from April 8 to May 1, 1996.
b On disabled list from June 30 to July 15, 1997.

BAILEY, PHILLIP CORY
Born, Marion, Illinois, January 24, 1971.
Bats Right. Throws Right. Height, 6 feet, 1 inch. Weight, 210 pounds.

Year	Club	Lea	G	IP	W	L	Pct	SO	BB	H	ERA	SAVES
1991 Winter Haven Red Sox ...	G.C.	1	2	0	0	.000	1	1	2	0.00	1	
1991 Elmira	N.Y.-Penn.	28	39	2	4	.333	54	12	19	1.85	*15	
1992 Lynchburg	Carolina	49	66⅓	5	7	.417	87	30	43	2.44	*23	
1993 Pawtucket	Int.	52	65⅔	4	5	.444	59	31	48	2.88	20	
1993 Boston	A.L.	11	15⅔	0	1	.000	11	12	12	3.45	0	
1994 Pawtucket	Int.	53	61⅓	4	3	.571	52	38	44	3.23	19	
1994 Boston	A.L.	5	4⅓	0	1	.000	4	3	10	12.46	0	
1995 Louisville a	A.A.	55	59⅓	5	3	.625	49	30	51	4.55	25	
1995 St. Louis	N.L.	3	3⅔	0	0	.000	5	2	2	7.36	0	
1996 Louisville	A.A.	22	34	2	4	.333	27	20	29	5.82	1	
1996 St. Louis	N.L.	51	57	5	2	.714	38	30	57	3.00	0	
1997 Okla City b	A.A.	42	50⅓	3	4	.429	38	23	49	3.40	15	
1997 Phoenix	P.C.	13	17⅓	4	0	1.000	14	6	16	1.56	3	
1997 San Francisco	N.L.	7	9⅔	0	1	.000	5	4	15	8.38	0	
Major League Totals	5 Yrs.	77	90⅓	5	5	.500	63	51	96	4.28	0	

a Traded to St. Louis Cardinals with infielder Scott Cooper and player to be named for pitcher Rheal Cormier and outfielder Mark Whiten, April 8, 1995.
b Traded to San Francisco Giants for pitcher Chad Hartvigson, July 29, 1997.

BALDWIN, JAMES JR.

Born, South Pines, North Carolina, July 15, 1971.
Bats Right. Throws Right. Height, 6 feet, 3 inches. Weight, 210 pounds.

Year	Club	Lea	G	IP	W	L	Pct	SO	BB	H	ERA	SAVES
1990 Sarasota White Sox	...Gulf C.		9	37⅓	1	6	.143	32	18	32	4.10	0
1991 Sarasota White Sox	...Gulf C.		6	34	3	1	.750	48	16	16	2.12	0
1991 Utica	...........N.Y.-Penn.		7	37⅓	1	4	.200	23	27	40	5.30	0
1992 South Bend	....Midwest		21	137⅔	9	5	.643	137	45	118	2.42	0
1992 Sarasota	...........Fla. St.		6	37⅔	1	2	.333	39	7	31	2.87	0
1993 Birmingham	......Southern		17	120	8	5	.615	107	43	*94	*2.25	0
1993 Nashville	............A.A.		10	69	5	4	.556	61	36	43	2.61	0
1994 Nashville	............A.A.		26	162	12	6	.667	*156	83	144	3.72	0
1995 Chicago	............A.L.		6	14⅔	0	1	.000	10	9	32	12.89	0
1995 Nashville	............A.A.		18	95⅓	5	9	.357	89	44	120	5.85	0
1996 Nashville	............A.A.		2	14	1	1	.500	15	4	5	0.64	0
1996 Chicago	............A.L.		28	169	11	6	.647	127	57	168	4.42	0
1997 Chicago	............A.L.		32	200	12	15	.444	140	83	205	5.26	0
Major League Totals	........3 Yrs.		66	383⅔	23	22	.511	277	149	405	5.18	0

BANKS, WILLIE ANTHONY

Born, Jersey City, New Jersey, February 27, 1969.
Bats Right. Throws Right. Height, 6 feet, 1 inch. Weight, 216 pounds.

Year	Club	Lea	G	IP	W	L	Pct	SO	BB	H	ERA	SAVES
1987 Elizabethtn	...Appal.		13	65⅔	1	8	.111	71	62	73	6.99	0
1988 Kenosha	.........Midwest		24	125⅔	10	10	.500	113	107	109	3.72	0
1989 Visalia	..........California		27	174	12	9	.571	173	85	122	2.59	0
1989 Orlando	.........Southern		1	7	1	0	1.000	9	0	10	5.14	0
1990 Orlando	.........Southern		28	162⅔	7	9	.438	114	98	161	3.93	0
1991 Portland	.............P.C.		25	146⅓	9	8	.529	63	76	156	4.55	0
1991 Minnesota	.............A.L.		5	17⅓	1	1	.500	16	12	21	5.71	0
1992 Portland	.............P.C.		11	75	6	1	.857	41	34	62	1.92	0
1992 Minnesota	.............A.L.		16	71	4	4	.500	37	37	80	5.70	0
1993 Minnesota a	.............A.L.		31	171⅓	11	12	.478	138	78	186	4.04	0
1994 Chicago	.............N.L.		23	138⅓	8	12	.400	91	56	139	5.40	0
1995 Chicago b	.............N.L.		10	11⅔	0	1	.000	9	12	27	15.43	0
1995 Los Angeles-Florida c-d	.N.L.		15	79	2	5	.286	53	46	79	4.21	0
1996 Phila e-f	...............N.L.				INJURED—Did Not Play							
1997 Columbus	.............Int.		33	154	14	5	.737	130	45	164	4.27	3
1997 New York	.............A.L.		5	14	3	0	1.000	8	6	9	1.93	0
Major League Totals	........6 Yrs.		105	502⅔	29	35	.453	352	247	541	4.94	0

a Traded to Chicago Cubs for catcher Matt Walbeck and pitcher Dave Stevens, November 24, 1993.
b Traded to Los Angeles Dodgers for pitcher Dax Winslett, June 19, 1995.
c Claimed on waivers by Florida Marlins, August 10, 1995.
d Claimed on waivers by Philadelphia Phillies, October 4, 1995.
e Released by Philadelphia Phillies, March 8, 1996.
f Signed by New York Yankees organization, January 3, 1997.

BATCHELOR, RICHARD ANTHONY

Born, Florence, South Carolina, April 8, 1967.
Bats Right. Throws Right. Height, 6 feet, 1 inch. Weight, 195 pounds.

Year	Club	Lea	G	IP	W	L	Pct	SO	BB	H	ERA	SAVES
1990 Greensboro	.........So. Atl.		27	51⅓	2	2	.500	38	14	39	1.58	8
1991 Fort Lauderdale	.....Fla. St.		50	62	4	7	.364	58	22	55	2.76	25
1991 Albany	.......Eastern		1	1	0	0	.000	0	1	5	45.00	0
1992 Albany	...........Eastern		58	70⅔	4	5	.444	45	34	79	4.20	7
1993 Albany	...........Eastern		36	40⅓	1	3	.250	40	12	27	0.89	19
1993 Columbus a	............Int.		15	16⅓	1	1	.500	17	8	14	2.76	6
1993 St. Louis	.............N.L.		9	10	0	0	.000	4	3	14	8.10	0
1994 Louisville	.............A.A.		53	81⅓	1	2	.333	50	32	85	3.54	0
1995 Louisville	.............A.A.		50	85	5	4	.556	61	16	85	3.28	0
1996 Louisville	.............A.A.		51	54⅔	5	2	.714	57	19	59	4.12	28
1996 St. Louis	.............N.L.		11	15	2	0	1.000	11	1	9	1.20	0
1997 Louisville	.............A.A.		12	14	0	2	.000	10	6	18	4.50	5
1997 St. Louis-San Diego b	...N.L.		23	28⅔	3	1	.750	18	14	40	5.97	0
1997 Las Vegas c-d	.........P.C.		15	21	3	0	1.000	19	8	23	6.43	0
Major League Totals	........3 Yrs.		43	53⅔	5	1	.833	33	18	63	5.03	0

a Traded by New York Yankees to St. Louis Cardinals for pitcher Lee Smith, August 31, 1993.

b Traded to San Diego Padres with pitcher Danny Jackson and outfielder Mark Sweeney for outfielder Phil Plantier, infielder Scott Livingstone and pitcher Fernando Valenzuela, June 14, 1997.
c Waived by San Diego Padres, November 25, 1997.
d Signed with Cleveland Indians, December 5, 1997.

BATISTA, MIGUEL JEREZ
Born, Santo Domingo, Dominican Republic, February 19, 1971.
Bats Right. Throws Right. Height, 6 feet. Weight, 160 pounds.

Year	Club	Lea	G	IP	W	L	Pct	SO	BB	H	ERA	SAVES
1990	Expos	Gulf Coast	9	39⅓	4	3	.571	21	17	33	2.06	0
1990	Rockford	Midwest	3	12⅓	0	1	.000	7	5	16	8.76	0
1991	Rockford a	Midwest	23	133⅔	11	5	.688	90	57	126	4.04	0
1992	Pittsburgh b	N.L.	1	2	0	0	.000	1	3	4	9.00	0
1992	Wst Plm Bch	Fla. St.	24	135⅓	7	7	.500	92	54	130	3.79	0
1993	Harrisburg	Eastern	26	141	13	5	.722	91	86	139	4.34	0
1994	Harrisburg c-d-e	Eastern	3	11⅓	0	1	.000	5	9	8	2.38	0
1995	Charlotte	Int.	34	116⅓	6	12	.333	58	60	118	4.80	0
1996	Charlotte	Int.	47	77	4	3	.571	56	39	93	5.38	4
1996	Florida f	N.L.	9	11⅓	0	0	.000	6	7	9	5.56	0
1997	Iowa	A.A.	31	122	9	4	.692	95	38	117	4.20	0
1997	Chicago g	N.L.	11	36⅓	0	5	.000	27	24	36	5.70	0
Major League Totals		3 Yrs.	21	49⅔	0	5	.000	34	34	49	5.80	0

a Drafted from Montreal Expos organization in Rule V draft by Pittsburgh Pirates, December 9, 1991.
b Returned to Montreal Expos by Pittsburgh Pirates, April 23, 1992.
c On disabled list April 14 to 30 and May 7 to September 26, 1994.
d Released by Montreal Expos, November 18, 1994.
e Signed as free agent by Florida Marlins organization, December 9, 1994.
f Claimed on waivers by Chicago Cubs, December 10, 1996.
g Traded to Montreal Expos for outfielder Henry Rodriguez, December 12, 1997.

BECK, RODNEY ROY (ROD)
Born, Burbank, California, August 3, 1968.
Bats Right. Throws Right. Height, 6 feet, 1 inch. Weight, 236 pounds.

Year	Club	Lea	G	IP	W	L	Pct	SO	BB	H	ERA	SAVES
1986	Medford	Northwest	13	32⅔	1	3	.250	21	11	47	5.23	1
1987	Medford a	Northwest	17	92	5	8	.385	69	26	106	5.18	0
1988	Clinton	Midwest	28	177	12	7	.632	123	27	177	3.00	0
1989	San Jose	California	13	97⅓	11	2	*.846	88	26	91	2.40	0
1989	Shreveport	Texas	16	99	7	3	.700	74	16	108	3.55	0
1990	Shreveport	Texas	14	93	10	3	.769	71	17	85	2.23	0
1990	Phoenix	P.C.	12	76⅔	4	7	.364	43	18	100	4.93	0
1991	Phoenix	P.C.	23	71⅓	4	3	.571	35	13	56	2.02	6
1991	San Francisco	N.L.	31	52⅓	1	1	.500	38	13	53	3.78	1
1992	San Francisco	N.L.	65	92	3	3	.500	87	15	62	1.76	17
1993	San Francisco	N.L.	76	79⅓	3	1	.750	86	13	57	2.16	48
1994	San Francisco b	N.L.	48	48⅔	2	4	.333	39	13	49	2.77	28
1995	San Francisco	N.L.	60	58⅔	5	6	.455	42	21	60	4.45	33
1996	San Francisco	N.L.	63	62	0	9	.000	48	10	56	3.34	35
1997	San Francisco c-d	N.L.	73	70	7	4	.636	53	8	67	3.47	37
Major League Totals		7 Yrs.	416	463	21	28	.429	393	93	404	2.97	199
Division Series												
1997	San Francisco	N.L.	1	1⅓	0	0	.000	1	0	1	0.00	0

a Traded by Oakland Athletics to San Francisco Giants organization for pitcher Charlie Korbel, March 23, 1988.
b On disabled list from April 6 to April 30, 1994.
c Filed for free agency, October 27, 1997.
d Signed as free agent with Chicago Cubs, January 15, 1998.

BEECH, LUCAS MATTHEW (MATT)
Born, Oakland, California, January 20, 1972.
Bats Left. Throws Left. Height, 6 feet, 2 inches. Weight, 190 pounds.

Year	Club	Lea	G	IP	W	L	Pct	SO	BB	H	ERA	SAVES
1994	Batavia	N.Y.-Penn.	4	18⅔	2	1	.667	27	12	9	1.93	0
1994	Spartanburg	So.Atl.	10	69⅔	4	4	.500	83	23	51	2.58	0
1995	Clearwater	Fla.St.	15	86	9	4	.692	85	30	87	4.19	0
1995	Reading	Eastern	14	79	2	4	.333	70	33	67	2.96	0
1996	Reading	Eastern	21	133⅓	11	6	.647	132	32	108	3.17	0

Year	Club	Lea	G	IP	W	L	Pct	SO	BB	H	ERA	SAVES
1996 Scranton-WB	.........Int.		2	15	2	0	1.000	14	1	9	2.40	0
1996 Philadelphia	.N.L.		8	41⅓	1	4	.200	33	11	49	6.97	0
1997 Clearwater	.........Fla. St.		1	5⅔	0	0	.000	9	4	1	0.00	0
1997 Scranton-WB	...........Int.		5	30	3	1	.750	38	10	24	5.70	0
1997 Philadelphia a	.........N.L.		24	136⅔	4	9	.308	120	57	147	5.07	0
Major League Totals	........2 Yrs.		32	178	5	13	.278	153	68	196	5.51	0

a On disabled list from May 9 to May 25, 1997.

BELCHER, TIMOTHY WAYNE (TIM)
Born, Mount Gilead, Ohio, October 19, 1961.
Bats Right. Throws Right. Height, 6 feet, 3 inches. Weight, 220 pounds.

Year	Club	Lea	G	IP	W	L	Pct	SO	BB	H	ERA	SAVES
1984 Madison a	.........Midwest		16	98⅓	9	4	.692	111	48	80	3.57	0
1984 Albany	.............Eastern		10	54	3	4	.429	40	41	37	3.33	0
1985 Huntsville	.........Southern		29	149⅔	11	10	.524	90	99	145	4.69	0
1986 Huntsville b	......Southern		9	37	2	5	.286	25	22	50	6.57	0
1987 Tacoma c	.............P.C.		29	163	9	11	.450	136	*133	143	4.42	0
1987 Los Angeles	...........N.L.		6	34	4	2	.667	23	7	30	2.38	0
1988 Los Angeles	...........N.L.		36	179⅔	12	6	.667	152	51	143	2.91	4
1989 Los Angeles	...........N.L.		39	230	15	12	.556	200	80	182	2.82	1
1990 Los Angeles d	.........N.L.		24	153	9	9	.500	102	48	136	4.00	0
1991 Los Angeles e	.........N.L.		33	209⅓	10	9	.526	156	75	189	2.62	0
1992 Cincinnati	...........N.L.		35	227⅔	15	14	.517	149	80	201	3.91	0
1993 Cincinnati f	...........N.L.		22	137	9	6	.600	101	47	134	4.47	0
1993 Chicago g	...........A.L.		12	71⅔	3	5	.375	34	27	64	4.40	0
1994 Detroit h	...........A.L.		25	162	7	*15	.318	76	78	192	5.89	0
1995 Indianapolis i-j	...........A.A.		2	10	0	0	.000	8	1	6	1.80	0
1995 Seattle k	...........A.L.		28	179⅓	10	12	.455	96	88	188	4.52	0
1996 Kansas City l	...........A.L.		35	238⅔	15	11	.577	113	68	262	3.92	0
1997 Kansas City	...........A.L.		32	213⅓	13	12	.520	113	70	242	5.02	0
Major League Totals	.......11 Yrs.		327	2035⅔	122	113	.519	1315	719	1963	3.93	5
Division Series												
1995 Seattle	...............A.L.		2	4⅓	0	1	.000	0	5	4	6.23	0
Championship Series												
1988 Los Angeles	...........N.L.		2	15⅓	2	0	1.000	16	4	12	4.11	0
1993 Chicago	...........A.L.		1	3⅔	1	0	1.000	1	3	3	2.45	0
1995 Seattle	...............A.L.		1	5⅔	0	1	.000	1	2	9	6.35	0
Championship Series Totals	4			24⅔	3	1	.750	18	9	24	4.38	0
World Series Record												
1988 Los Angeles	...........N.L.		2	8⅔	1	0	1.000	10	6	10	6.23	0

a Selected by Oakland Athletics from New York Yankees organization in player pool as compensation for loss of free agent pitcher Tom Underwood, February 8, 1984.
b On disabled list from April 10 to May 4 and May 5 to July 23, 1986.
c Traded by Oakland Athletics to Los Angeles Dodgers to complete August 29 trade in which Oakland acquired pitcher Rick Honeycutt, September 2, 1987.
d On disabled list from August 17 to end of 1990 season.
e Traded to Cincinnati Reds with pitcher John Wetteland for outfielder Eric Davis and pitcher Kip Gross, November 27, 1991.
f Traded to Chicago White Sox for pitchers Johnny Ruffin and Jeff Pierce, July 31, 1993.
g Filed for free agency, October 26, 1993; signed with Detroit Tigers, February 7, 1994.
h Filed for free agency, October 17, 1994.
i Signed with Cincinnati Reds organization, May 3, 1995.
j Traded to Seattle Mariners for pitcher Roger Salkeld, May 15, 1995.
k Filed for free agency, November 12, 1995.
l Signed with Kansas City Royals, February 1, 1996.

BELINDA, STANLEY PETER
Born, Huntington, Pennsylvania, August 6, 1966.
Bats Right. Throws Right. Height, 6 feet, 3 inches. Weight, 215 pounds.

Year	Club	Lea	G	IP	W	L	Pct	SO	BB	H	ERA	SAVES
1986 Bradenton Pirates	....Gulf C.		17	20⅓	3	2	.600	9	8	23	2.66	7
1986 Watertown	.......N.Y.-Penn.		5	8	0	0	.000	5	2	5	3.38	2
1987 Macon	.............So. Atl.		50	82	6	4	.600	75	27	59	2.09	16
1988 Salem	.............Carolina		53	71⅓	6	4	.600	63	32	54	2.76	14
1989 Harrisburg	.........Eastern		32	38⅔	1	4	.200	33	25	32	2.33	13
1989 Buffalo	...............A.A.		19	28⅓	2	2	.500	28	13	13	0.95	9
1989 Pittsburgh	...............N.L.		8	10⅓	0	1	.000	10	2	13	6.10	0

Year	Club	Lea	G	IP	W	L	Pct	SO	BB	H	ERA	SAVES
1990 Buffalo		A.A.	15	23⅔	3	1	.750	25	8	20	1.90	5
1990 Pittsburgh		N.L.	55	58⅓	3	4	.429	55	29	48	3.55	8
1991 Pittsburgh		N.L.	60	78⅓	7	5	.583	71	35	50	3.45	16
1992 Pittsburgh a		N.L.	59	71⅓	6	4	.600	57	29	58	3.15	18
1993 Pittsburgh a		N.L.	40	42⅓	3	1	.750	30	11	35	3.61	19
1993 Kansas City		A.L.	23	27⅓	1	1	.500	25	6	30	4.28	0
1994 Kansas City b		A.L.	37	49	2	2	.500	37	24	47	5.14	1
1995 Sarasota		Fla. St.	1	2	0	0	.000	2	0	2	4.50	0
1995 Boston c-d		A.L.	63	69⅔	8	1	.889	57	28	51	3.10	10
1996 Sarasota		Fla.St.	1	1	0	1	.000	1	1	6	45.00	0
1996 Pawtucket e		Int.	6	7⅔	1	0	1.000	7	2	2	0.00	0
1996 Boston f-g		A.L.	31	28⅔	2	1	.667	18	20	31	6.59	2
1997 Cincinnati		N.L.	84	99⅓	1	5	.167	114	33	84	3.71	1
Major League Totals	9 Yrs.		460	534⅔	33	25	.569	474	217	447	3.85	75
Division Series												
1995 Boston		A.L.	1	0⅓	0	0	.000	0	0	0	0.00	0
Championship Series												
1990 Pittsburgh		N.L.	3	3⅔	0	0	.000	4	0	3	2.45	0
1991 Pittsburgh		N.L.	3	5	1	0	1.000	4	3	0	0.00	0
1992 Pittsburgh		N.L.	2	1⅔	0	0	.000	2	0	2	0.00	0
Championship Series Totals	8		10⅓		1	0	1.000	10	3	5	0.87	0

a Traded to Kansas City Royals for pitchers John Lieber and Dan Miceli, July 31, 1993.
b Not offered 1995 contract, December 23, 1994.
c Signed with Boston Red Sox, April 9, 1995.
d On disabled list from April 21 to May 6, 1995.
e On disabled list from April 1 to April 6 and May 20 to July 26 and August 20 to September 30, 1996.
f Filed for free agency, October 14, 1996.
g Signed with Cincinnati Reds organization, December 20, 1997.

BELTRAN, RIGOBERTO

Born, Tijuana, Mexico, November 13, 1969.
Bats Left. Throws Left. Height, 5 feet, 11 inches. Weight, 185 pounds.

Year	Club	Lea	G	IP	W	L	Pct	SO	BB	H	ERA	SAVES
1991 Hamilton		N.Y.-Penn.	21	48	5	2	.714	69	19	41	2.63	0
1992 Savannah		So. Atl.	13	83	6	1	.857	106	40	38	2.17	0
1992 St. Pete		Fla. St.	2	8	0	0	.000	3	2	6	0.00	0
1993 Arkansas		Texas	18	88⅔	5	5	.500	82	38	74	3.25	0
1994 Arkansas		Texas	4	28	4	0	1.000	21	3	12	0.64	0
1994 Louisville		A.A.	23	138⅓	11	11	.500	87	68	147	5.07	0
1995 Louisville		A.A.	24	129⅔	8	9	.471	92	34	156	5.21	0
1996 Louisville		A.A.	38	130⅓	8	6	.571	132	24	132	4.35	0
1997 Louisville		A.A.	9	54⅓	5	2	.714	46	21	45	2.32	0
1997 St. Louis		N.L.	35	54⅓	1	2	.333	50	17	47	3.48	1

BENES, ALAN PAUL

Born, Evansville, Indiana, January 21, 1972.
Bats Right. Throws Right. Height, 6 feet, 5 inches. Weight, 215 pounds.

Year	Club	Lea	G	IP	W	L	Pct	SO	BB	H	ERA	SAVES
1993 Glens Falls		N.Y.-Penn.	7	37	0	4	.000	29	14	39	3.65	0
1994 Savannah		So. Atl.	4	24⅓	2	0	1.000	24	7	21	1.48	0
1994 St. Petersburg		Fla. St.	11	78⅓	7	1	.875	69	15	55	1.61	0
1994 Arkansas		Texas	13	87⅔	7	2	.778	75	26	58	2.98	0
1994 Louisville		A.A.	2	15⅓	1	0	1.000	16	4	10	2.93	0
1995 Louisville		A.A.	11	56	4	2	.667	54	14	37	2.41	0
1995 St. Louis		N.L.	3	16	1	2	.333	20	4	24	8.44	0
1996 St. Louis		N.L.	34	191	13	10	.565	131	87	192	4.90	0
1997 St. Louis a		N.L.	26	177	10	7	.588	175	61	149	3.10	0
Major League Totals	3 Yrs.		63	384	24	19	.558	326	152	365	4.22	0
Championship Series												
1996 St. Louis		N.L.	2	6⅓	0	1	.000	5	2	3	2.84	0

a On disabled list from July 31 to September 29, 1997.

BENES, ANDREW CHARLES

Born, Evansville, Indiana, August 20, 1967.
Bats Right. Throws Right. Height, 6 feet, 6 inches. Weight, 240 pounds.

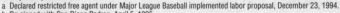

Year Club	Lea	G	IP	W	L	Pct	SO	BB	H	ERA	SAVES
1989 Wichita ....Texas	16	108⅓	8	4	.667	115	39	79	2.16	0
1989 Las Vegas .............P.C.	5	26⅔	2	1	.667	29	12	41	8.10	0
1989 San Diego ............N.L.	10	56⅔	6	3	.667	66	31	51	3.51	0
1990 San Diego ............N.L.	32	192⅓	10	11	.476	140	69	177	3.60	0
1991 San Diego ............N.L.	33	223	15	11	.577	167	59	194	3.03	0
1992 San Diego ............N.L.	34	231⅓	13	14	.481	169	61	*230	3.35	0
1993 San Diego ............N.L.	34	230⅔	15	15	.500	179	86	200	3.78	0
1994 San Diego a .........N.L.	25	172⅓	6	*14	.300	*189	51	155	3.86	0
1995 San Diego ............N.L.	19	118⅓	4	7	.364	126	45	121	4.17	0
1995 Seattle b-c-d-e ........A.L.	12	63	7	2	.778	45	33	72	5.86	0
1996 St. Louis ............N.L.	36	230⅓	18	10	.643	160	77	215	3.83	1
1997 Louisville ...........A.A.	1	5	0	0	.000	5	1	3	1.80	0
1997 Arkansas ....Texas	1	7	1	0	1.000	6	2	2	1.29	0
1997 Pr William ....Carolina	1	5	0	0	.000	9	1	3	0.00	0
1997 St. Louis f-g .........N.L.	23	161⅔	9	9	.500	160	68	128	2.89	0
Major League Totals ....9 Yrs.	258	1690	103	96	.518	1401	580	1543	3.63	1
Division Series										
1995 Seattle ..............A.L.	2	11⅔	0	0	.000	8	9	10	5.40	0
1996 St. Louis ............N.L.	1	7	0	0	.000	9	1	6	5.14	0
Division Series Totals 3	18⅔	0	0	.000	17	10	16	5.30	0
Championship Series										
1995 Seattle ..............A.L.	1	2⅓	0	1	.000	3	2	6	23.14	0
1996 St. Louis ............N.L.	3	15⅓	0	0	.000	9	3	19	5.28	0
Championship Series Totals 4	17⅔	0	1	.000	12	5	25	7.64	0

a Declared restricted free agent under Major League Baseball implemented labor proposal, December 23, 1994.
b Re-signed with San Diego Padres, April 5, 1995.
c Traded to Seattle Mariners with player to be named later for pitcher Ron Villone and outfielder Marc Newfield, July 31, 1995.
d Seattle Mariners received pitcher Greg Keagle to complete trade, September 16, 1995.
e Filed for free agency, November 12, 1995.
f On disabled list from April 1 to April 28, 1997.
g Filed for free agency, November 3, 1997.

BENITEZ, ARMANDO GERMAN

Born, Ramon Santana, Dominican Republic, November 3, 1972.
Bats Right. Throws Right. Height, 6 feet, 4 inches. Weight, 180 pounds.

Year Club	Lea	G	IP	W	L	Pct	SO	BB	H	ERA	SAVES
1991 Sarasota Orioles .....Gulf C.	14	36⅓	3	2	.600	33	11	35	2.72	0
1992 Bluefield ....Appal.	25	31⅓	1	2	.333	37	23	35	4.31	5
1993 Albany ....So. Atl.	40	53⅓	5	1	.833	83	19	31	1.52	14
1993 Frederick ....Carolina	12	13⅔	3	0	1.000	29	4	7	0.66	4
1994 Bowie ....Eastern	53	71⅔	8	4	.667	106	39	41	3.14	16
1994 Baltimore ............A.L.	3	10	0	0	.000	14	4	8	0.90	0
1995 Rochester ....Int.	17	21⅓	2	2	.500	37	7	10	1.25	8
1995 Baltimore ............A.L.	44	47⅔	1	5	.167	56	37	37	5.66	2
1996 Orioles ....Gulf Coast	1	2	1	0	1.000	5	0	1	0.00	0
1996 Bowie ....Eastern	4	6	0	0	.000	8	0	7	4.50	0
1996 Rochester ....Int.	2	4	0	0	.000	5	1	3	2.25	0
1996 Baltimore a ...........A.L.	18	14⅓	1	0	1.000	20	6	7	3.77	4
1997 Baltimore ............A.L.	71	73⅓	4	5	.444	106	43	49	2.45	9
Major League Totals ....4 Yrs.	136	145⅓	6	10	.375	196	90	101	3.53	15
Division Series										
1996 Baltimore ............A.L.	3	4	2	0	1.000	6	2	1	2.25	0
1997 Baltimore ............A.L.	3	3	0	0	.000	4	2	3	3.00	0
Division Series Totals 6	7	2	0	1.000	10	4	4	2.57	0
Championship Series										
1996 Baltimore ............A.L.	3	2⅓	0	0	.000	2	3	3	7.71	1
1997 Baltimore ............A.L.	4	3	0	2	.000	6	4	3	12.00	0
Championship Series Totals 7	5⅓	0	2	.000	8	7	6	10.13	1

a On disabled list from April 20 to August 26, 1996.

BERE, JASON PHILLIP

Born, Cambridge, Massachusetts, May 26, 1971
Bats Right. Throws Right. Height, 6 feet, 3 inches. Weight, 185 pounds.

Year	Club	Lea	G	IP	W	L	Pct	SO	BB	H	ERA	SAVES
1990	Sarasota White Sox	Gulf C.	16	38	0	4	.000	41	19	26	2.37	1
1991	South Bend	Midwest	27	163	9	12	.429	158	100	116	2.87	0
1992	Sarasota	Fla. St.	18	116	7	2	.778	106	34	84	2.41	0
1992	Birmingham	Southern	8	54	4	4	.500	45	20	44	3.00	0
1992	Vancouver	P.C.	1	1	0	0	.000	2	0	2	0.00	0
1993	Nashville	A.A.	8	49⅓	5	1	.833	52	25	36	2.37	0
1993	Chicago	A.L.	24	142⅔	12	5	.706	129	81	109	3.47	0
1994	Chicago	A.L.	24	141⅔	12	2	*.857	127	80	119	3.81	0
1995	Nashville	A.A.	1	5⅓	1	0	1.000	7	2	6	3.38	0
1995	Chicago a	A.L.	27	137⅔	8	15	.348	110	106	151	7.19	0
1996	White Sox	Gulf Coast	1	3	0	1	.000	3	1	3	6.00	0
1996	Hickory	So.Atl.	1	5	1	0	1.000	5	0	3	0.00	0
1996	Birmingham	Southern	1	4⅓	0	0	.000	5	4	4	4.15	0
1996	Nashville	A.A.	3	12⅔	0	0	.000	15	4	9	1.42	0
1996	Chicago b	A.L.	5	16⅔	0	1	.000	19	18	26	10.26	0
1997	White Sox	Gulf Coast	2	5	0	0	.000	5	0	2	0.00	0
1997	Hickory	So. Atl.	1	3	0	0	.000	2	0	4	6.00	0
1997	Birmingham	Southern	2	7	0	1	.000	7	2	8	7.71	0
1997	Nashville	A.A.	4	19⅓	1	1	.500	13	7	23	5.59	0
1997	Chicago c	A.L.	6	28⅔	4	2	.667	21	17	20	4.71	0
Major League Totals	5 Yrs.		86	467⅓	36	25	.590	406	302	425	4.99	0
Championship Series												
1993	Chicago	A.L.	1	2⅓	0	0	.000	3	2	5	11.57	0

a On disabled list from August 5 to August 20, 1995.
b On disabled list from April 22 to September 3 and September 14 to September 30, 1996.
c On disabled list from April 1 to August 19, 1997.

BERGMAN, SEAN FREDERICK

Born, Joliet, Illinois, April 11, 1970.
Bats Right. Throws Right. Height, 6 feet, 4 inches. Weight, 205 pounds.

Year	Club	Lea	G	IP	W	L	Pct	SO	BB	H	ERA	SAVES
1991	Niagara Falls	N.Y.-Penn.	15	84⅔	5	7	.417	77	42	87	4.46	0
1992	Lakeland	Fla. St.	13	83	5	2	.714	67	14	61	2.49	0
1992	London	Eastern	14	88⅓	4	7	.364	59	45	85	4.28	0
1993	Detroit	A.L.	9	39⅔	1	4	.200	19	23	47	5.67	0
1993	Toledo	Int.	19	117	8	9	.471	91	53	124	4.38	0
1994	Toledo	Int.	25	154⅔	11	8	.579	145	53	147	3.72	0
1994	Detroit	A.L.	3	17⅔	2	1	.667	12	7	22	5.60	0
1995	Toledo	Int.	1	3	0	1	.000	4	0	4	6.00	0
1995	Detroit a	A.L.	28	135⅓	7	10	.412	86	67	169	5.12	0
1996	San Diego b	N.L.	41	113⅓	6	8	.429	85	33	119	4.37	0
1997	San Diego	N.L.	44	99	2	4	.333	74	38	126	6.09	0
Major League Totals	5 Yrs.		125	405	18	27	.400	276	168	483	5.22	0

a On disabled list from June 26 to July 17, 1995.
b Traded to San Diego Padres with pitcher Cade Gaspar and outfielder Todd Steverson for outfielder Melvin Nieves, catcher Raul Casanove and pitcher Richie Lewis, March 22, 1996.

BIELECKI, MICHAEL JOSEPH

Born, Baltimore, Maryland, July 31, 1959.
Bats Right. Throws Right. Height, 6 feet, 3 inches. Weight, 200 pounds.

Year	Club	Lea	G	IP	W	L	Pct	SO	BB	H	ERA	SAVES
1979	Bradenton Pirates	Gulf C.	9	51	1	4	.200	35	21	48	2.29	0
1980	Shelby	So. Atl.	29	99	3	5	.375	78	58	106	4.55	3
1981	Greenwood	So. Atl.	28	192	12	11	.522	163	82	172	3.42	0
1982	Buffalo	Eastern	25	157⅓	7	12	.368	135	75	165	4.86	0
1983	Lynn	Eastern	25	163⅔	*15	7	.682	*143	69	126	3.19	0
1984	Hawaii	P.C.	28	187⅔	*19	3	.864	*162	88	162	2.97	0
1984	Pittsburgh	N.L.	4	4⅓	0	0	.000	1	0	4	0.00	0
1985	Hawaii	P.C.	20	129	8	6	.571	111	56	117	3.83	0
1985	Pittsburgh	N.L.	12	45⅔	2	3	.400	22	31	45	4.53	0
1986	Pittsburgh	N.L.	31	148⅔	6	11	.353	83	83	149	4.66	0
1987	Vancouver	P.C.	26	181	12	10	.545	140	78	194	3.78	0
1987	Pittsburgh a	N.L.	8	45⅔	2	3	.400	25	12	43	4.73	0
1988	Iowa	A.A.	23	54⅔	3	2	.600	50	20	34	2.63	5

208

Year	Club	Lea	G	IP	W	L	Pct	SO	BB	H	ERA	SAVES
1988 Chicago	N.L.	19	48⅓	2	2	.500	33	16	55	3.35	0
1989 Chicago	N.L.	33	212⅓	18	7	.720	147	81	187	3.14	0
1990 Chicago	N.L.	36	168	8	11	.421	103	70	188	4.93	1
1991 Chicago-Atlanta b	N.L.	41	173⅔	13	11	.542	75	56	171	4.46	0
1992 Atlanta c-d	N.L.	19	80⅔	2	4	.333	62	27	77	2.57	0
1993 Cleveland e	A.L.	13	68⅓	4	5	.444	38	23	90	5.90	0
1993 Rochester f	Int.	9	48⅓	5	3	.625	31	16	56	5.03	0
1994 Atlanta g	N.L.	19	27	2	0	1.000	18	12	28	4.00	0
1995 Lake Elsinore	California	3	3⅔	0	0	.000	2	2	2	4.91	0
1995 Vancouver	P.C.	3	5	1	0	1.000	4	2	2	0.00	0
1995 California h-i-j	A.L.	22	75⅓	4	6	.400	45	31	80	5.97	0
1996 Atlanta k-l	N.L.	40	75⅓	4	3	.571	71	33	63	2.63	2
1997 Atlanta m-n	N.L.	50	57⅓	3	7	.300	60	21	56	4.08	2
Major League Totals	14 Yrs.	347	1231	70	73	.490	783	496	1236	4.18	5
Division Series											
1996 Atlanta	N.L.	1	0⅔	0	0	.000	1	1	0	0.00	0
Championship Series											
1989 Chicago	N.L.	2	12⅓	0	1	.000	11	6	7	3.65	0
1996 Atlanta	N.L.	3	3	0	0	.000	5	1	0	0.00	0
Championship Series Totals	5	15⅓	0	1	.000	16	7	7	2.93	0
World Series Record											
1996 Atlanta	N.L.	2	3	0	0	.000	6	3	0	0.00	0

a Traded to Chicago Cubs organization for pitcher Mike Curtis, March 31, 1988.
b Traded to Atlanta Braves with catcher Damon Berryhill for pitchers Yorkis Perez and Turk Wendell, September 29, 1991.
c On disabled list from July 29 to end of 1992 season.
d Filed for free agency, October 30; signed with Cleveland Indians organization, December 14, 1992.
e Released, June 18; signed with Baltimore Orioles organization, June 30, 1993.
f Released by Baltimore Orioles, August 15, 1993; signed with Atlanta Braves organization, February 10, 1994.
g Refused assignment to minor leagues and became free agent, October 12, 1994.
h Signed with California Angels organization, April 11, 1995.
i On disabled list from July 17 to October 3, 1995.
j Filed for free agency, November 12, 1995.
k Filed for free agency, October 31, 1996.
l Accepted Sacam arbitration, re-signed with Atlanta, December 19, 1996.
m On disabled list from August 17 to September 29, 1997.
n Filed for free agency, November 7, 1997.

BLAIR, WILLIAM ALLEN (WILLIE)

Born, Paintsville, Kentucky, December 18, 1965.
Bats Right. Throws Right. Height, 6 feet, 1 inch. Weight, 185 pounds.

Year	Club	Lea	G	IP	W	L	Pct	SO	BB	H	ERA	SAVES
1986 St. Catharines	N.Y.-Penn.	21	53⅔	5	0	1.000	55	20	32	1.68	*12
1987 Dunedin	Fla. St.	50	85⅓	2	9	.182	72	29	99	4.43	13
1988 Dunedin a	Fla. St.	4	6⅔	2	0	1.000	5	4	5	2.70	0
1988 Knoxville	Southern	34	102	5	5	.500	76	35	94	3.62	3
1989 Syracuse b	Int.	19	106⅓	5	6	.455	76	38	94	3.97	0
1990 Syracuse	Int.	3	19	0	2	.000	6	8	20	4.74	0
1990 Toronto c	A.L.	27	68⅔	3	5	.375	43	28	66	4.06	0
1991 Colorado Springs	P.C.	26	113⅔	9	6	.600	57	30	130	4.99	4
1991 Cleveland d	A.L.	11	36	2	3	.400	13	10	58	6.75	0
1992 Tucson	P.C.	21	53	4	4	.500	35	12	50	2.39	2
1992 Houston e	N.L.	29	78⅔	5	7	.417	48	25	74	4.00	0
1993 Colorado	N.L.	46	146	6	10	.375	84	42	184	4.75	0
1994 Colorado f	N.L.	47	77⅔	0	5	.000	68	39	98	5.79	3
1995 San Diego g-h	N.L.	40	114	7	5	.583	83	45	112	4.34	0
1996 San Diego	N.L.	60	88	2	6	.250	67	29	80	4.60	1
1997 W Michigan	Midwest	1	5	0	0	.000	7	0	1	0.00	0
1997 Toledo	Int.	1	7	0	0	.000	4	2	1	0.00	0
1997 Detroit i-j-k	A.L.	29	175	16	8	.667	90	46	186	4.17	0
Major League Totals	8 Yrs.	289	784	41	49	.456	496	264	858	4.60	4
Division Series											
1996 San Diego	N.L.	1	2	0	0	.000	3	2	1	0.00	0

a On disabled list from April 8 to May 4, 1988.
b On disabled list from May 20 to June 28, 1989.
c Traded to Cleveland Indians for pitcher Alex Sanchez, November 6, 1990.
d Traded to Houston Astros with catcher Ed Taubensee for outfielder Kenny Lofton and infielder Dave Rohde, December 10, 1991.
e Selected by Colorado Rockies in expansion draft, November 17, 1992.
f Released, December 20, 1994.

g Signed with San Diego Padres organization, April 6, 1995.
h Not offered contract by San Diego Padres, December 20, 1995.
i On disabled list from May 5 to June 3, 1997.
j Filed for free agency, October 27, 1997.
k Signed as free agent with Arizona Diamondbacks, December 8, 1997.

BLAZIER, RONALD PATRICK (RON)
Born, Altoona, Pennsylvania, July 30, 1971.
Bats Right. Throws Right. Height, 6 feet, 6 inches. Weight, 215 pounds.

Year Club	Lea	G	IP	W	L	Pct	SO	BB	H	ERA	SAVES
1990 Princeton	Appal.	14	78⅔	3	5	.375	45	29	77	4.46	0
1991 Batavia	N.Y.-Penn.	24	72⅓	7	5	.583	77	17	81	4.60	2
1992 Spartanburg	So. Atl.	30	159⅔	14	7	.667	149	32	141	2.65	0
1993 Clearwater	Fla. St.	27	155⅓	9	8	.529	86	40	171	3.94	0
1994 Clearwater	Fla. St.	29	173⅓	13	5	.722	120	36	177	3.38	0
1995 Reading	Eastern	56	106⅔	4	5	.444	102	31	93	3.29	1
1996 Scranton-WB	Int.	33	42	4	0	1.000	38	9	33	2.57	12
1996 Philadelphia	N.L.	27	38⅓	3	1	.750	25	10	49	5.87	0
1997 Clearwater	Fla. St.	15	30⅔	2	3	.400	45	8	24	2.93	3
1997 Scranton-WB	Int.	11	14⅔	0	3	.000	10	3	17	3.68	1
1997 Philadelphia	N.L.	36	53⅔	1	1	.500	42	21	62	5.03	0
Major League Totals	2 Yrs.	63	92	4	2	.667	67	31	111	5.38	0

BOCHTLER, DOUGLAS EUGENE (DOUG)
Born, West Palm Beach, Florida, July 5, 1970.
Bats Right. Throws Right. Height, 6 feet, 3 inches. Weight, 205 pounds.

Year Club	Lea	G	IP	W	L	Pct	SO	BB	H	ERA	SAVES
1989 Expos	Gulf Coast	9	47⅔	2	2	.500	45	20	46	3.21	0
1990 Rockford	Midwest	25	139	9	12	.429	109	54	142	3.50	0
1991 West Palm Beach	Fla. St.	26	160⅓	12	9	.571	109	55	148	2.92	0
1992 Harrisburg	Eastern	13	77⅔	6	5	.545	89	36	50	2.32	0
1993 Central Valley	California	8	47⅔	3	1	.750	43	28	40	3.40	0
1993 Colorado Springs	P.C.	12	50⅔	1	4	.200	38	26	71	6.93	0
1993 Las Vegas	P.C.	7	39⅔	0	5	.000	30	11	52	5.22	0
1994 Las Vegas	P.C.	22	100⅓	3	7	.300	86	48	116	5.20	0
1995 Las Vegas	P.C.	18	36	2	3	.400	32	26	31	4.25	1
1995 San Diego	N.L.	34	45⅓	4	4	.500	45	19	38	3.57	1
1996 San Diego	N.L.	63	65⅔	2	4	.333	68	39	45	3.02	3
1997 San Diego a-b	N.L.	54	60⅓	3	6	.333	46	50	51	4.77	2
Major League Totals	3 Yrs.	151	171⅓	9	14	.391	159	108	134	3.78	6
Division Series											
1996 San Diego	N.L.	1	0⅓	0	1	.000	0	2	0	27.00	0

a On disabled list from July 2 to July 17, 1997.
b Traded to Oakland Athletics with infielder Jorge Velandia for pitcher Don Wengert and infielder David Newhan, November 26, 1997.

BOEHRINGER, BRIAN EDWARD
Born, St. Louis, Missouri, January 8, 1970.
Bats Both. Throws Right. Height, 6 feet, 2 inches. Weight, 191 pounds.

Year Club	Lea	G	IP	W	L	Pct	SO	BB	H	ERA	SAVES
1991 Utica	N.Y.-Penn.	4	19	1	1	.500	19	8	14	2.37	0
1992 White Sox	Gulf Coast	2	12	1	1	.500	8	2	9	1.50	0
1992 South Bend	Midwest	15	86⅓	6	7	.462	59	40	87	4.38	0
1993 Sarasota	Fla. St.	18	119	10	4	.714	92	51	103	2.80	0
1993 Birmingham	Southern	7	40⅔	2	1	.667	29	14	41	3.54	0
1994 Albany	Eastern	27	171⅔	10	11	.476	145	57	165	3.62	0
1995 New York	A.L.	7	17⅔	0	3	.000	10	22	24	13.75	0
1995 Columbus	Int.	17	104	8	6	.571	58	31	101	2.77	0
1996 Columbus	Int.	25	153	11	7	.611	132	56	155	4.00	0
1996 New York	A.L.	15	46⅓	2	4	.333	37	21	46	5.44	0
1997 Yankees	Gulf Coast	1	2	0	0	.000	2	0	1	0.00	0
1997 Tampa	Fla. St.	3	9	0	1	.000	8	5	9	5.00	0
1997 New York a-b-c	A.L.	34	48	3	2	.600	53	32	39	2.63	0
Major League Totals	3 Yrs.	56	112	5	9	.357	100	75	109	5.54	0

Year	Club	Lea	G	IP	W	L	Pct	SO	BB	H	ERA	SAVES
Division Series												
1996 New York		A.L.	2	1⅓	1	0	1.000	0	2	3	6.75	0
1997 New York		A.L.	1	1⅔	0	0	.000	2	1	1	0.00	0
Divisional Series Totals		.3	3	1	0	1.000	2	3	4	3.00	0	
World Series Record												
1996 New York		A.L.	2	5	0	0	.000	5	0	5	5.40	0

a On disabled list from May 24 to August 19, 1997.
b Selected on expansion draft by Tampa Bay Devil Rays, November 18, 1997.
c Traded to San Diego Padres with infielder Andy Sheets for catcher John Flaherty, November 19, 1997.

BOHANON, BRIAN EDWARD JR.

Born, Denton, Texas, August 1, 1968.
Bats Left. Throws Left. Height, 6 feet, 2 inches. Weight, 220 pounds.

Year	Club	Lea	G	IP	W	L	Pct	SO	BB	H	ERA	SAVES
1987 G.C. Rangers	Gulf Coast	5	21	0	2	.000	21	5	15	4.71	0	
1988 Charlotte a	Fla. St.	2	6⅔	0	1	.000	9	5	6	5.40	0	
1989 Charlotte b	Fla. St.	11	54⅔	0	3	.000	33	20	40	1.81	1	
1989 Tulsa	Texas	11	73⅔	5	0	1.000	44	27	60	2.20	0	
1990 Texas c	A.L.	11	34	0	3	.000	15	18	40	6.62	0	
1990 Oklahoma City	A.A.	14	32	1	2	.333	22	8	35	3.66	1	
1991 Charlotte	Fla. St.	2	11⅔	1	0	1.000	7	4	6	3.86	0	
1991 Tulsa	Texas	2	11⅔	0	1	.000	6	11	9	2.31	0	
1991 Oklahoma City	A.A.	7	46⅓	0	4	.000	37	15	49	2.91	0	
1991 Texas d	A.L.	11	61⅓	4	3	.571	34	23	66	4.84	0	
1992 Oklahoma City	A.A.	9	56	4	2	.667	24	15	53	2.73	0	
1992 Texas e	A.L.	18	45⅔	1	1	.500	29	25	57	6.31	0	
1992 Tulsa	Texas	6	28⅓	2	1	.667	25	9	25	1.27	0	
1993 Oklahoma City	A.A.	2	7	0	1	.000	7	3	7	6.43	0	
1993 Texas f	A.L.	36	92⅔	4	4	.500	45	46	107	4.76	0	
1994 Oklahoma City	A.A.	15	98⅓	5	10	.333	88	33	106	4.12	0	
1994 Texas g	A.L.	11	37⅓	2	2	.500	26	8	51	7.23	0	
1995 Detroit h-i	A.L.	52	105⅔	1	1	.500	63	41	121	5.54	1	
1996 Toronto j-k	A.L.	20	22	0	1	.000	17	19	27	7.77	1	
1996 Syracuse	Int.	31	58⅓	4	3	.571	38	17	56	3.86	0	
1997 Norfolk	Int.	15	96	9	3	.750	84	32	88	2.63	0	
1997 New York l-m-n	N.L.	19	94⅓	6	4	.600	66	34	95	3.82	0	
Major League Totals	.8 Yrs.	178	493	18	19	.486	295	214	564	5.35	2	

a On disabled list from April 18 to end of 1988 season.
b On disabled list from March 31 to May 2, 1989.
c On disabled list from June 13 to July 19, 1990.
d On disabled list from April 8 to July 3, 1991.
e On disabled list from April 28 to May 12, 1992.
f On disabled list from June 8 to June 29, 1993.
g Not offered 1995 contract, December 23, 1994.
h Signed with Detroit Tigers organization, April 6, 1995.
i Waived by Detroit Tigers, October 16, 1995.
j Outrighted by Toronto Blue Jays, May 31, 1996.
k Filed for free agency, October 3, 1996.
l Signed as free agent with New York Mets, December 18, 1996.
m Outrighted by New York Mets, May 6, 1997.
n Re-signed by New York Mets, December 19, 1997.

BONES, RICARDO (RICKY)

Born, Salinas, Puerto Rico, April 7, 1969.
Bats Right. Throws Right. Height, 6 feet. Weight, 190 pounds.

Year	Club	Lea	G	IP	W	L	Pct	SO	BB	H	ERA	SAVES
1986 Spokane	Northwest	18	58	1	3	.250	46	29	63	5.59	0	
1987 Charleston, SC	So. Atl.	26	170⅓	12	5	.706	130	45	*183	3.65	0	
1988 Riverside	California	25	175⅓	15	6	.714	129	64	162	3.64	0	
1989 Wichita	Texas	24	136⅓	10	9	.526	88	47	162	5.74	0	
1990 Wichita	Texas	21	137	6	4	.600	96	45	138	3.48	0	
1990 Las Vegas	P.C.	5	36⅓	2	1	.667	25	10	45	3.47	0	
1991 Las Vegas	P.C.	23	136⅓	8	6	.571	95	43	155	4.22	0	
1991 San Diego	N.L.	11	54	4	6	.400	31	18	57	4.83	0	
1992 Milwaukee a	A.L.	31	163⅓	9	10	.474	65	48	169	4.57	0	
1993 Milwaukee	A.L.	32	203⅔	11	11	.500	63	63	222	4.86	0	
1994 Milwaukee	A.L.	24	170⅔	10	9	.526	57	45	166	3.43	0	
1995 Milwaukee	A.L.	32	200⅓	10	12	.455	77	83	218	4.63	0	

Year	Club	Lea	G	IP	W	L	Pct	SO	BB	H	ERA	SAVES
1996 Milwaukee-New York b-c-d	.A.L.	36	152	7	14	.333	63	68	184	6.21	0
1997 Tucson	.P.C.	8	42	5	0	1.000	22	8	40	2.79	0
1997 Cincinnati e	.N.L.	9	17²/₃	0	1	.000	8	11	31	10.19	0
1997 Kansas City f-g-h	.A.L.	21	78¹/₃	4	7	.364	36	25	102	5.97	0
Major League Totals	7 Yrs.	196	1040	55	70	.440	400	361	1149	4.91	0

a Traded to Milwaukee Brewers with infielder Jose Valentin and outfielder Matt Mieske for infielder Gary Sheffield and pitcher Geoff Kellogg, March 27, 1992.
b Traded to New York Yankees with pitcher Graeme Lloyd and infielder Pat Listach for outfielder Gerald Williams and pitcher Bob Wickman, August 23, 1996. Listach trade voided due to prior injury New York Yankees received infielder Gabby Martinez to complete deal, November 5, 1996.
c Filed for free agency, October 25, 1996.
d Signed with Cincinnati Reds, December 10, 1996.
e Released by Cincinnati Reds, May 6, 1997.
f Signed as free agent with Kansas City Royals, June 26, 1997.
g Filed for free agency, November 4, 1997.
h Signed with Minnesota Twins organization, January 6, 1998.

BORLAND, TOBY SHAWN

Born, Quitman, Louisiana, May 29, 1969.
Bats Right. Throws Right. Height, 6 feet, 6 inches. Weight, 186 pounds.

Year	Club	Lea	G	IP	W	L	Pct	SO	BB	H	ERA	SAVES
1988 Martinsville	.Appal.	34	49	2	3	.400	43	29	42	4.04	*12
1989 Spartanburg	.So. Atl.	47	66²/₃	4	5	.444	48	35	62	2.97	9
1990 Clearwater	.Fla. St.	44	59²/₃	1	2	.333	44	35	44	2.26	5
1990 Reading	.Eastern	14	25	4	1	.800	26	11	16	1.44	0
1991 Reading	.Eastern	*59	76²/₃	8	3	.727	72	56	68	2.70	*24
1992 Scranton	.Int.	27	27¹/₃	0	1	.000	25	26	25	7.24	1
1992 Reading	.Eastern	32	42	2	4	.333	45	32	39	3.43	5
1993 Scranton	.Int.	26	29²/₃	2	4	.333	26	20	31	5.76	1
1993 Reading	.Eastern	44	53²/₃	2	2	.500	74	20	38	2.52	13
1994 Scranton	.Inc.	27	53²/₃	4	1	.800	61	21	36	1.68	4
1994 Philadelphia	.N.L.	24	34¹/₃	1	0	1.000	26	14	31	2.36	1
1995 Scranton-WB	.Int.	8	11¹/₃	0	0	.000	15	6	5	0.00	1
1995 Philadelphia a	.N.L.	50	74	1	3	.250	59	37	81	3.77	6
1996 Philadelphia b	.N.L.	69	90²/₃	7	3	.700	76	43	83	4.07	0
1997 New York c	.N.L.	13	13¹/₃	0	1	.000	7	14	11	6.07	1
1997 Boston d-e	.A.L.	3	3¹/₃	0	0	.000	1	7	6	13.50	0
1997 Pawtucket	.Int.	28	47¹/₃	2	0	1.000	46	25	50	3.99	2
Major League Totals	4 Yrs.	159	215²/₃	9	7	.563	169	115	212	3.96	8

a On disabled list from June 14 to July 8, 1995.
b Traded to New York Mets with pitcher Ricardo Jordan for infielder Rico Brogna, November 27, 1996.
c Traded to Boston Red Sox for pitcher Ricky Trlicek, May 12, 1997.
d Outrighted by Boston Red Sox, May 27, 1997.
e Signed as free agent with Cincinnati Reds organization, November 27, 1997.

BOSKIE, SHAWN KEALOHA

Born, Hawthorne, Nevada, March 28, 1967.
Bats Right. Throws Right. Height, 6 feet, 3 inches. Weight, 200 pounds.

Year	Club	Lea	G	IP	W	L	Pct	SO	BB	H	ERA	SAVES
1986 Wytheville	.Appal.	14	54	4	4	.500	40	57	42	5.33	0
1987 Peoria	.Midwest	26	149	9	11	.450	100	56	149	4.35	0
1988 Winston-Salem	.Carolina	27	186	12	7	.632	164	89	176	3.39	0
1989 Charlotte	.Southern	28	181	11	8	.579	*164	84	*196	4.38	0
1990 Iowa	.A.A.	8	51	4	2	.667	51	21	46	3.18	0
1990 Chicago a	.N.L.	15	97²/₃	5	6	.455	49	31	99	3.69	0
1991 Iowa	.A.A.	7	45¹/₃	2	2	.500	29	11	43	3.57	0
1991 Chicago b	.N.L.	28	129	4	9	.308	62	52	150	5.23	0
1992 Chicago c	.N.L.	23	91²/₃	5	11	.313	39	36	96	5.01	0
1992 Iowa	.A.A.	2	7¹/₃	0	0	.000	3	3	8	3.68	0
1993 Iowa	.A.A.	11	71²/₃	6	1	.857	35	21	70	4.27	0
1993 Chicago d	.N.L.	39	65²/₃	5	3	.625	39	21	63	3.43	0
1994 Chicago-Phil. e-f-g	.N.L.	20	88	4	6	.400	61	29	88	5.01	0
1994 Seattle h-i	.A.L.	2	2²/₃	0	1	.000	0	1	4	6.75	0
1995 Lake Elsinore	.California	3	11	0	0	.000	8	4	15	4.09	0
1995 Vancouver	.P.C.	1	6	1	0	1.000	1	4	4	3.00	0
1995 California j-k-l	.A.L.	20	111²/₃	7	7	.500	51	25	127	5.64	0
1996 California m	.A.L.	37	189¹/₃	12	11	.522	133	67	226	5.32	0
1997 Baltimore i	.A.L.	28	77	6	6	.500	50	26	95	6.43	1
Major League Totals	8 Yrs.	212	852²/₃	48	60	.444	484	288	948	5.06	1

a On disabled list from August 5 to September 26, 1990.
b Appeared in one additional game as pinch runner and one additional game as pinch hitter.
c On disabled list from July 17 to September 1, 1992.
d Not offered 1994 contract, December 20; re-signed with Chicago Cubs, December 22, 1993.
e Traded to Philadelphia Phillies for pitcher Kevin Foster, April 12, 1994.
f Appeared in one additional game as pinch runner.
g Traded to Seattle Mariners for player to be named, July 21; Philadelphia Phillies acquired first baseman Fred McNair to complete trade, September 6, 1994.
h On disabled list from August 2 to end of 1994 season.
i Released, November 18, 1994.
j Signed with California Angels organization, March 3, 1995.
k On disabled list from July 6 to October 3, 1995.
l Granted free agency by California Angels, December 19, 1995.
m Filed for free agency, October 31, 1996.
h On disabled list from August 16 to September 1, 1997.
i Filed for free agency, October 29, 1997.

BOTTALICO, RICKY PAUL
Born, New Britain, Connecticut, August 26, 1969.
Bats Left. Throws Right. Height, 6 feet, 1 inch. Weight, 200 pounds.

Year	Club	Lea	G	IP	W	L	Pct	SO	BB	H	ERA	SAVES
1991 Martinsville	Appal.	7	33	3	2	.600	38	13	32	4.09	0
1991 Spartanburg	So. Atl.	2	15	2	0	1.000	11	2	4	0.00	0
1992 Spartanburg	So. Atl.	42	119²/₃	5	10	.333	118	56	94	2.41	13
1993 Clearwater	Fla. St.	13	19²/₃	1	0	1.000	19	5	19	2.75	4
1993 Reading	Eastern	49	72	3	3	.500	65	26	63	2.25	20
1994 Scranton	Int.	19	22¹/₃	3	1	.750	22	22	32	8.87	3
1994 Reading	Eastern	38	42²/₃	2	2	.500	51	10	29	2.53	22
1994 Philadelphia	N.L.	3	3	0	0	.000	3	1	3	0.00	0
1995 Philadelphia	N.L.	62	87²/₃	5	3	.625	87	42	50	2.46	1
1996 Philadelphia	N.L.	61	67²/₃	4	5	.444	74	23	47	3.19	34
1997 Philadelphia	N.L.	69	74	2	5	.286	89	42	68	3.65	34
Major League Totals	4 Yrs.	195	232¹/₃	11	13	.458	253	108	168	3.02	69

BOTTENFIELD, KENT DENNIS
Born, Portland, Oregon, November 14, 1968.
Bats Both. Throws Right. Height, 6 feet, 3 inches. Weight, 225 pounds.

Year	Club	Lea	G	IP	W	L	Pct	SO	BB	H	ERA	SAVES
1986 Bradenton Expos	Gulf C.	13	74¹/₃	5	6	.455	41	30	73	3.27	0
1987 Burlington	Midwest	27	161	9	13	.409	103	42	175	4.53	0
1988 West Palm Beach	Fla. St.	27	181	10	8	.556	120	47	165	3.33	0
1989 Jacksonville	Southern	25	138²/₃	3	*17	.150	91	73	137	5.26	0
1990 Jacksonville	Southern	29	169	12	10	.545	·121	67	158	3.41	0
1991 Indianapolis	A.A.	29	166¹/₃	8	15	.348	108	61	155	4.06	0
1992 Indianapolis	A.A.	25	152¹/₃	12	8	.600	111	58	139	3.43	0
1992 Montreal	N.L.	10	32¹/₃	1	2	.333	14	11	26	2.23	1
1993 Mont-Colorado a	N.L.	37	159²/₃	5	10	.333	62	71	179	5.07	0
1994 Colo. Springs-Phoenix	P.C.	13	66	3	3	.500	28	22	65	3.68	0
1994 Colo.-San Fran. b-c-d	N.L.	16	26¹/₃	3	1	.750	15	10	33	6.15	1
1995 Toledo	Int.	27	136²/₃	5	11	.313	68	55	148	4.54	1
1996 Iowa	A.A.	28	24²/₃	1	2	.333	14	8	19	2.19	18
1996 Chicago	N.L.	48	61²/₃	3	5	.375	33	19	59	2.63	1
1997 Chicago h-i	N.L.	64	84	2	3	.400	74	35	82	3.86	2
Major League Totals	5 Yrs.	175	364	14	21	.400	199	146	379	4.20	5

a Traded to Colorado Rockies for pitcher Butch Henry, July 17, 1993.
b On disabled list from March 27 to May 9, 1994.
c Refused assignment to minor leagues and became free agent, June 27; signed with San Francisco Giants, June 30, 1994.
d Released by San Francisco Giants, November 8, 1994.
e Signed as free agent with Detroit Tigers organization, April 3, 1995.
f Opted for free agency, October 16, 1995.
g Signed as free agent with Chicago Cubs organization, March 9, 1996.
h Released by Chicago Cubs, December 19, 1997.
i Signed with St. Louis Cardinals, January 6, 1998.

BOVEE, MICHAEL CRAIG

Born, San Diego, California, August 21, 1973.
Bats Right. Throws Right. Height, 5 feet, 10 inches. Weight, 200 pounds.

Year	Club	Lea	G	IP	W	L	Pct	SO	BB	H	ERA	SAVES
1991	Royals	Gulf Coast	11	61²/₃	3	1	.750	76	12	52	2.04	0
1992	Appleton	Midwest	28	149¹/₃	9	10	.474	120	41	143	3.56	0
1993	Rockford	Midwest	20	109	5	9	.357	111	30	118	4.21	0
1994	Wilmington	Carolina	28	169²/₃	13	4	.765	154	32	149	2.65	0
1995	Wichita	Texas	20	114	8	6	.571	72	43	118	4.18	0
1996	Wichita a	Texas	27	176²/₃	10	11	.476	102	40	223	4.84	0
1997	Midland	Texas	20	102	8	2	.800	61	23	117	4.24	0
1997	Vancouver	P.C.	12	89	4	3	.571	71	25	92	3.44	0
1997	Anaheim	A.L.	3	3¹/₃	0	0	.000	5	1	3	5.40	0

a Traded to California Angels with pitcher Mark Gubicza for outfielder Chili Davis, October 29, 1996.

BRANDENBURG, MARK CLAY

Born, Houston, Texas, July 14, 1970.
Bats Right. Throws Right. Height, 6 feet. Weight, 180 pounds.

Year	Club	Lea	G	IP	W	L	Pct	SO	BB	H	ERA	SAVES
1992	Butte	Pioneer	24	62	7	1	.875	78	14	70	4.06	2
1993	Charleston-Sc.	So. Atl.	44	80	6	3	.667	67	22	62	1.46	4
1994	Charlotte	Fla. St.	25	41¹/₃	0	2	.000	44	15	23	0.87	5
1994	Tulsa	Texas	37	62	5	4	.556	63	12	50	1.74	8
1995	Oklahoma City	A.A.	35	58	0	5	.000	51	15	52	2.02	2
1995	Texas	A.L.	11	27¹/₃	0	1	.000	21	7	36	5.93	0
1996	Texas-Boston	A.L.	55	76	5	5	.500	66	33	76	3.43	0
1997	Sarasota	Fla. St.	1	3	0	0	.000	1	0	3	0.00	0
1997	Pawtucket	Int.	9	18²/₃	2	1	.667	23	3	13	2.41	0
1997	Boston a-b	A.L.	31	41	0	2	.000	34	16	49	5.49	0
Major League Totals		3 Yrs.	97	144¹/₃	5	8	.385	121	56	161	4.49	0

a On disabled list from April 1 to June 2, 1997.
b Traded to Texas Rangers with pitcher Aaron Sele for catcher Jim Leyritz and outfielder Damon Buford, November 6, 1997.

BRANTLEY, JEFFREY HOKE

Born, Florence, Alabama, September 5, 1963.
Bats Right. Throws Right. Height, 5 feet, 10 inches. Weight, 189 pounds.

Year	Club	Lea	G	IP	W	L	Pct	SO	BB	H	ERA	SAVES
1985	Fresno	California	14	94²/₃	8	2	.800	85	37	83	3.33	0
1986	Shreveport	Texas	26	165²/₃	8	10	.444	125	69	139	3.48	0
1987	Shreveport	Texas	2	11²/₃	0	1	.000	7	4	12	3.09	0
1987	Phoenix	P.C.	29	170¹/₃	6	11	.353	111	82	187	4.65	0
1988	Phoenix	P.C.	27	122²/₃	9	5	.643	83	39	130	4.33	0
1988	San Francisco	N.L.	9	20²/₃	0	1	.000	11	6	22	5.66	1
1989	Phoenix	P.C.	7	14¹/₃	1	1	.500	20	2	6	1.26	3
1989	San Francisco	N.L.	59	97¹/₃	7	1	.875	69	37	101	4.07	0
1990	San Francisco	N.L.	55	86²/₃	5	3	.625	61	33	77	1.56	19
1991	San Francisco	A.L.	67	95¹/₃	5	2	.714	81	52	78	2.45	15
1992	San Francisco	N.L.	56	91²/₃	7	7	.500	86	45	67	2.95	7
1993	San Francisco a	N.L.	53	113²/₃	5	6	.455	76	46	112	4.28	0
1994	Cincinnati	N.L.	50	65¹/₃	6	6	.500	63	28	46	2.48	15
1995	Cincinnati b	N.L.	56	70¹/₃	3	2	.600	62	20	53	2.82	28
1996	Cincinnati	N.L.	66	71	1	2	.333	76	28	54	2.41	44
1997	Cincinnati c-d	N.L.	13	11²/₃	1	1	.500	16	7	9	3.86	1
Major League Totals		10 Yrs.	484	723²/₃	40	31	.563	601	302	619	3.06	130
Division Series												
1995	Cincinnati	N.L.	3	3	0	0	.000	2	0	5	6.00	1
Championship Series												
1989	San Francisco	N.L.	3	5	0	0	.000	3	2	1	0.00	0
1995	Cincinnati	N.L.	2	2²/₃	0	0	.000	1	2	0	0.00	0
Championship Series Totals		5	7²/₃		0	0	.000	4	4	1	0.00	0
World Series Record												
1989	San Francisco	N.L.	3	4¹/₃	0	0	.000	1	3	5	4.15	0

a Not offered 1994 contract, December 20, 1993; signed with Cincinnati Reds January 6, 1994.
b On disabled list from April 1 to April 6, 1996.
c On disabled list from April 1 to April 15 and May 20 to September 29, 1997.
d Traded to St. Louis Cardinals for infielder Dmitri Young, November 10, 1997.

BREWER, WILLIAM ROBERT (BILLY)

Born, Fort Worth, Texas, April 15, 1968.
Bats Left. Throws Left. Height, 6 feet, 1 inch. Weight, 175 pounds.

Year Club	Lea	G	IP	W	L	Pct	SO	BB	H	ERA	SAVES
1990 Jamestown	N.Y.-Penn.	11	27⅔	2	2	.500	37	13	23	2.93	1
1991 Rockford	Midwest	29	41	3	3	.500	43	25	32	1.98	5
1992 West Palm Beach	Fla. St.	28	36⅓	2	2	.500	37	14	27	1.73	8
1992 Harrisburg a	Eastern	20	23⅓	2	0	1.000	18	18	25	5.01	0
1993 Kansas City	A.L.	46	39	2	2	.500	28	20	31	3.46	0
1994 Kansas City	A.L.	50	38⅔	4	1	.800	25	16	28	2.56	3
1995 Springfield	Midwest	1	2	0	0	.000	2	1	2	0.00	1
1995 Omaha	A.A.	6	7	0	0	.000	5	7	1	0.00	0
1995 Kansas City b	A.L.	48	45⅓	2	4	.333	31	20	54	5.56	0
1996 Albuquerque	P.C.	31	31⅔	2	2	.500	33	22	28	3.13	2
1996 Columbus	Int.	13	25	0	2	.000	27	19	27	7.20	0
1996 New York c	A.L.	4	5⅔	1	0	1.000	8	8	7	9.53	0
1997 Visalia	California	2	3	0	0	.000	5	4	1	0.00	0
1997 Edmonton	P.C.	7	8	0	0	.000	11	6	8	5.63	1
1997 Scranton-WB	Int.	11	9	2	1	.667	9	5	10	3.00	1
1997 Oakland d	A.L.	3	2	0	0	.000	1	2	4	13.50	0
1997 Philadelphia e-f-g	N.L.	25	22	1	2	.333	16	11	15	3.27	0
Major League Totals	5 Yrs.	176	152⅔	10	9	.526	109	77	139	4.19	3

a Drafted by Kansas City Royals from Montreal Expos organization, December 7, 1992.
b Traded to Los Angeles Dodgers for infielder Jose Offerman, December 17, 1995.
c Traded by Los Angeles organization to New York Yankees for pitcher Mike Judd, June 21, 1996.
d Released by Oakland Athletics, May 22, 1997.
e On disabled list from April 6 to April 28 and August 18 to September 29, 1997.
f Filed for free agency, October 8, 1997.
g Signed as free agent with Philadelphia Phillies organization, December 15, 1997.

BROCAIL, DOUGLAS KEITH (DOUG)

Born, Clearfield, Pennsylvania, May 16, 1967.
Bats Left. Throws Right. Height, 6 feet, 5 inches. Weight, 235 pounds.

Year Club	Lea	G	IP	W	L	Pct	SO	BB	H	ERA	SAVES
1986 Spokane	Northwest	16	85	5	4	.556	77	53	85	3.81	0
1987 Charleston	So. Atl.	19	92⅓	2	6	.250	68	28	94	4.09	0
1988 Charleston	So. Atl.	22	107	8	6	.571	108	25	107	2.69	2
1989 Wichita	Texas	23	134⅔	5	9	.357	95	50	158	5.21	0
1990 Wichita a	Texas	12	52	2	2	.500	27	24	53	4.33	0
1991 Wichita	Texas	34	146⅓	10	7	.588	108	43	147	3.87	6
1992 Las Vegas	P.C.	29	172⅓	10	10	.500	103	63	187	3.97	0
1992 San Diego	N.L.	3	14	0	0	.000	15	5	17	6.43	0
1993 Las Vegas	P.C.	10	51⅓	4	2	.667	32	14	51	3.68	1
1993 San Diego b	N.L.	24	128⅓	4	13	.235	70	42	143	4.56	0
1994 Wichita	Texas	2	4	0	0	.000	2	1	3	0.00	0
1994 Las Vegas	P.C.	7	12⅔	0	0	.000	8	2	21	7.11	0
1994 San Diego c-d-e	N.L.	12	17	0	0	.000	11	5	21	5.82	0
1995 Tucson	P.C.	3	16⅓	1	0	1.000	16	4	18	3.86	0
1995 Houston	N.L.	36	77⅓	6	4	.600	39	22	87	4.19	1
1996 Jackson	Texas	2	4	0	0	.000	5	1	1	0.00	0
1996 Tucson	P.C.	5	7⅓	0	1	.000	4	1	12	7.36	0
1996 Houston f-g	N.L.	23	53	1	5	.167	34	23	58	4.58	0
1997 Detroit	A.L.	61	78	3	4	.429	60	36	74	3.23	2
Major League Totals	6 Yrs.	159	367⅔	14	26	.350	229	133	400	4.33	3

a On disabled list from May 1 to May 11 and June 8 to August 17, 1990.
b Appeared in six additional games as pinch runner.
c On disabled list from April 3 to June 29, 1994.
d Appeared in two additional games as pinch runner.
e Traded to Houston Astros with outfielders Phil Plantier and Derek Bell, shortstop Ricky Gutierrez, infielder Craig Shipley and pitcher Pedro Martinez for third baseman Ken Caminiti, shortstop Andujar Cedeño, outfielder Steve Finley, pitcher Brian Williams, first baseman Roberto Petagine and player to be named, December 28, 1994.
f On disabled list from May 11 to August 15, 1996.
g Traded to Detroit Tigers with outfielder Brian Hunter, infielder Orlando Miller and pitcher Todd Jones for catcher Brad Ausmus, pitcher C.J. Nitkowski, pitcher Jose Lima, pitcher Trever Miller and infielder Daryle Ward, December 10, 1996.

BROWN, JAMES KEVIN

Born, McIntyre, Georgia, March 14, 1965.
Bats Right. Throws Right. Height, 6 feet, 4 inches. Weight, 195 pounds.

Year	Club	Lea	G	IP	W	L	Pct	SO	BB	H	ERA	SAVES
1986	Sarasota Rangers	Gulf C.	3	6	0	0	.000	1	2	7	6.00	0
1986	Tulsa	Texas	3	10	0	0	.000	10	5	9	4.50	0
1986	Texas	A.L.	1	5	1	0	1.000	4	0	6	3.60	0
1987	Tulsa	Texas	8	42	1	4	.200	25	18	53	7.29	0
1987	Oklahoma City	A.A.	5	24⅓	0	5	.000	9	17	32	10.73	0
1987	Charlotte	Fla. St.	6	36⅓	0	2	.000	21	17	33	2.72	0
1988	Tulsa	Texas	26	174⅓	12	10	.545	118	61	174	3.51	0
1988	Texas	A.L.	4	23⅓	1	1	.500	12	8	33	4.24	0
1989	Texas	A.L.	28	191	12	9	.571	104	70	167	3.35	0
1990	Texas a-b	A.L.	26	180	12	10	.545	88	60	175	3.60	0
1991	Texas	A.L.	33	210⅔	9	12	.429	96	90	233	4.40	0
1992	Texas	A.L.	35	*265⅔	*21	11	.656	173	76	*262	3.32	0
1993	Texas c-d	A.L.	34	233	15	12	.556	142	74	228	3.59	0
1994	Texas e	A.L.	26	170	7	9	.438	123	50	*218	4.82	0
1995	Baltimore f-g-h	A.L.	26	172⅓	10	9	.526	117	48	155	3.60	0
1996	Florida i	N.L.	32	233	17	11	.607	159	33	187	1.89	0
1997	Florida j-k	N.L.	33	237⅓	16	8	.667	205	66	214	2.69	0
Major League Totals		11 Yrs.	278	1921⅓	121	92	.568	1223	575	1878	3.42	0
Division Series												
1997	Florida	N.L.	1	7	0	0	.000	5	0	4	1.29	0
Championship Series												
1997	Florida	N.L.	2	15	2	0	1.000	11	5	16	4.20	0
World Series Record												
1997	Florida	N.L.	2	11	0	2	.000	6	5	15	8.18	0

a On disabled list from August 14 to August 29, 1990.
b Appeared in one additional game as pinch hitter.
c On disabled list from March 27 to April 11, 1993.
d Appeared in one additional game as pinch runner.
e Filed for free agency, October 21, 1994.
f Signed with Baltimore Orioles, April 8, 1995.
g Filed for free agency, November 12, 1995.
h Signed with Florida Marlins, December 22, 1995.
i On disabled list from May 13 to May 28, 1996.
j Pitched no-hit, no-run game against San Francisco Giants, winning 3-0, June 10, 1997.
k Traded to San Diego Padres for pitchers Steve Hoff and Rafael Medina and first baseman Derrek Lee, December 15, 1997.

BRUSKE, JAMES SCOTT

Born, East St. Louis, Illinois, October 7, 1964.
Bats Right. Throws Right. Height, 6 feet, 1 inch. Weight, 185 pounds.

Year	Club	Lea	G	IP	W	L	Pct	SO	BB	H	ERA	SAVES
1986	Batavia	N.Y.-Penn.	1	1	0	0	.000	3	3	1	18.00	0
1989	Canton-Akrn	Eastern	2	2	0	0	.000	1	2	3	13.50	0
1990	Canton-Akrn	Eastern	32	118	9	3	.750	62	42	118	3.28	0
1991	Canton-Akrn	Eastern	17	80⅓	5	2	.714	35	27	73	3.47	1
1991	Colo Sprngs	P.C.	7	25⅔	4	0	1.000	13	8	19	2.45	2
1992	Colo Sprngs a	P.C.	7	17⅔	2	0	1.000	8	6	24	4.58	0
1992	Jackson	Texas	13	61⅔	4	3	.571	48	14	54	2.63	0
1993	Jackson	Texas	15	97⅓	9	5	.643	83	22	86	2.31	0
1993	Tucson	P.C.	12	66⅔	4	2	.667	42	18	77	3.78	1
1994	Tucson	P.C.	7	39	3	1	.750	25	8	47	4.15	0
1995	Albuquerque b	P.C.	43	114	7	5	.583	99	41	128	4.11	4
1995	Los Angeles	N.L.	9	10	0	0	.000	5	4	12	4.50	1
1996	Albuquerque	P.C.	36	62	5	2	.714	51	21	63	4.06	4
1996	Los Angeles c	N.L.	11	12⅔	0	0	.000	12	3	17	5.68	0
1997	Las Vegas	P.C.	17	68	5	4	.556	67	22	73	4.90	0
1997	San Diego d-e	N.L.	28	44⅔	4	1	.800	32	25	37	3.63	0
Major League Totals		3 Yrs.	48	67⅓	4	1	.800	49	32	66	4.14	1

a Signed as minor league free agent from Cleveland Indians organization by Houston Astros, June 15, 1992.
b Signed as a minor league free agent by Los Angeles Dodgers, January 18, 1995.
c Signed by San Diego Padres as minor league free agent, December 3, 1996.
d On disabled list from August 6 to August 25, 1997.
e Claimed on waivers by Los Angeles Dodgers, October 6, 1997.

BULLINGER, JAMES ERIC

Born, New Orleans, Louisiana, August 21, 1965.
Bats Right. Throws Right. Height, 6 feet, 2 inches. Weight, 185 pounds.

Year	Club	Lea	G	IP	W	L	Pct	SO	BB	H	ERA	SAVES
1989	Charlotte	Southern	2	3	0	0	.000	5	3	2	0.00	0
1990	Winston-Salem	Carolina	14	90	7	6	.538	85	46	81	3.70	0
1990	Charlotte	Southern	9	44	3	4	.429	33	18	42	5.11	0
1991	Charlotte	Southern	20	142²/₃	9	9	.500	128	61	132	3.53	0
1991	Iowa	A.A.	8	46²/₃	3	4	.429	30	23	47	5.40	0
1992	Iowa	A.A.	20	22	1	2	.333	15	12	17	2.45	14
1992	Chicago	N.L.	39	85	2	8	.200	36	54	72	4.66	7
1993	Iowa	A.A.	49	73²/₃	4	6	.400	74	43	64	3.42	20
1993	Chicago	N.L.	15	16²/₃	1	0	1.000	10	9	18	4.32	1
1994	Chicago	N.L.	33	100	6	2	.750	72	34	87	3.60	2
1995	Orlando	Southern	1	4	0	0	.000	2	1	3	0.00	0
1995	Chicago a	N.L.	24	150	12	8	.600	93	65	152	4.14	0
1996	Chicago b	N.L.	37	129¹/₃	6	10	.375	90	68	144	6.54	1
1997	Montreal c-d	N.L.	36	155¹/₃	7	12	.368	87	74	165	5.56	0
Major League Totals	6 Yrs.		184	636¹/₃	34	40	.459	388	304	638	4.96	11

Record as Position Player

Year	Club	Lea	Pos	G	AB	R	H	2B	3B	HR	RBI	SB	Avg
1986	Geneva	N.Y.-Penn.	SS	*78	248	35	61	*16	1	3	33	7	.246
1987	Winston-Salem	Carolina	SS	129	437	58	112	12	3	9	48	3	.256
1988	Pittsfield	Eastern	SS	88	242	21	41	6	1	3	33	1	.169
1988	Winston-Salem	Carolina	SS	32	104	13	20	4	2	1	11	4	.192
1989	Charlotte	Southern	SS	124	320	34	69	13	1	3	28	3	.216

a On disabled list from May 21 to June 22, 1995.
b Filed for free agency, October 28, 1996. Signed with Montreal Expos, January 16, 1997.
c Filed for free agency, October 6, 1997.
d Signed with Chicago White Sox organization, January 9, 1998.

BURBA, DAVID ALLEN

Born, Dayton, Ohio, July 7, 1966.
Bats Right. Throws Right. Height, 6 feet, 4 inches. Weight, 240 pounds.

Year	Club	Lea	G	IP	W	L	Pct	SO	BB	H	ERA	SAVES
1987	Bellingham	Northwest	5	23¹/₃	3	1	.750	24	3	20	1.93	0
1987	Salinas	California	9	54²/₃	1	6	.143	46	29	53	4.61	0
1988	San Bernardino	California	20	114	5	7	.417	102	54	106	2.68	0
1989	Williamsport	Eastern	25	156²/₃	11	7	.611	89	55	138	3.16	0
1990	Calgary a	P.C.	31	113²/₃	10	6	.625	47	45	124	4.67	2
1990	Seattle	A.L.	6	8	0	0	.000	4	2	8	4.50	0
1991	Calgary	P.C.	23	71¹/₃	6	4	.600	42	27	82	3.53	4
1991	Seattle b	A.L.	22	36²/₃	2	2	.500	16	14	34	3.68	1
1992	San Francisco	N.L.	23	70²/₃	2	7	.222	47	31	80	4.97	0
1992	Phoenix	P.C.	13	74¹/₃	5	5	.500	44	24	86	4.72	0
1993	San Francisco	N.L.	54	95¹/₃	10	3	.769	88	37	95	4.25	0
1994	San Francisco	N.L.	57	74	3	6	.333	84	45	59	4.38	0
1995	San Fran.-Cincinnati c	N.L.	52	106²/₃	10	4	.714	96	51	90	3.96	0
1996	Cincinnati	N.L.	34	195	11	13	.458	148	97	179	3.83	0
1997	Cincinnati d	N.L.	30	160	11	10	.524	131	73	157	4.72	0
Major League Totals	8 Yrs.		278	746¹/₃	49	45	.521	614	350	702	4.26	1
Division Series												
1995	Cincinnati	N.L.	1	1	1	0	1.000	0	1	2	0.00	0
Championship Series												
1995	Cincinnati	N.L.	2	3²/₃	0	0	.000	0	4	3	0.00	0

a On disabled list from May 19 to June 2, 1990.
b Traded to San Francisco Giants with pitchers Bill Swift and Mike Jackson for outfielder Kevin Mitchell and pitcher Mike Remlinger, December 11, 1991.
c Traded to Cincinnati Reds with pitcher Mark Portugal and outfielder Darren Lewis for outfielder Deion Sanders, pitcher John Roper, pitcher Ricky Pickett, pitcher Scott Service and infielder David McCarty, July 21, 1995.
d On disabled list from August 7 to August 27, 1997.

BURKE, JOHN C.

Born, Durango, Colorado, February 9, 1970.
Bats Both. Throws Right. Height, 6 feet, 4 inches. Weight, 215 pounds.

Year	Club	Lea	G	IP	W	L	Pct	SO	BB	H	ERA	SAVES
1992	Bend	Northwest	10	41	2	0	1.000	32	18	38	2.41	0
1993	Central Val	California	20	119	7	8	.467	114	64	104	3.18	0

Year	Club	Lea	G	IP	W	L	Pct	SO	BB	H	ERA	SAVES
1993 Colo Sprngs	.P.C.		8	48⅔	3	2	.600	38	23	44	3.14	0
1994 Colo Sprngs	.P.C.		8	11	0	0	.000	6	22	16	19.64	0
1994 Asheville	.So. Atl.		4	17	0	1	.000	16	5	5	1.06	0
1995 Colo Sprngs	.P.C.		19	87	7	1	.875	65	48	79	4.55	1
1996 Salem	.Carolina		3	12	0	1	.000	12	9	10	6.00	0
1996 Colo Sprngs	.P.C.		24	63⅔	2	4	.333	54	28	75	5.94	1
1996 Colorado	.N.L.		11	15⅓	2	1	.667	19	7	21	7.47	0
1997 Colorado	.N.L.		17	59	2	5	.286	39	26	83	6.56	0
1997 Colo. Sprngs	.P.C.		3	17	1	2	.333	15	14	23	5.82	0
Major League Totals	.2 Yrs.		28	74⅔	4	6	.400	58	33	104	6.75	0

BURKETT, JOHN DAVID

Born, New Brighton, Pennsylvania, November 28, 1964.
Bats Right. Throws Right. Height, 6 feet, 2 inches. Weight, 211 pounds.

Year	Club	Lea	G	IP	W	L	Pct	SO	BB	H	ERA	SAVES
1983 Great Falls	.Pioneer		13	50⅓	2	6	.250	38	30	73	6.26	0
1984 Clinton	.Midwest		20	126⅔	7	6	.538	83	38	120	4.33	0
1985 Fresno	.California		20	109⅔	7	4	.636	72	46	98	2.87	0
1986 Fresno	.California		4	24⅔	0	3	.000	14	8	34	5.47	0
1986 Shreveport	.Texas		22	128⅓	10	6	.625	73	42	99	2.66	0
1987 Shreveport	.Texas		27	*177⅔	*14	8	.636	126	53	181	3.34	0
1987 San Francisco	.N.L.		3	6	0	0	.000	5	3	7	4.50	0
1988 Shreveport	.Texas		7	50⅓	5	1	.833	34	18	33	2.13	0
1988 Phoenix	.P.C.		21	114	5	11	.313	74	49	142	5.21	0
1989 Phoenix	.P.C.		28	167⅔	10	11	.476	105	59	197	5.05	0
1990 Phoenix	.P.C.		3	23	2	1	.667	9	3	18	2.74	0
1990 San Francisco	.N.L.		33	204	14	7	.667	118	61	201	3.79	1
1991 San Francisco	.N.L.		36	206⅔	12	11	.522	131	60	223	4.18	0
1992 San Francisco	.N.L.		32	189⅔	13	9	.591	107	45	194	3.84	0
1993 San Francisco	.N.L.		34	231⅔	*22	7	.759	145	40	224	3.65	0
1994 San Francisco a-b	.N.L.		25	159⅓	6	8	.429	85	36	176	3.62	0
1995 Florida c	.N.L.		30	188⅓	14	14	.500	126	57	208	4.30	0
1996 Florida	.N.L.		24	154	6	10	.375	108	42	154	4.32	0
1996 Texas d	.A.L.		10	68⅔	5	2	.714	47	16	75	4.06	0
1997 Okla City	.A.A.		1	5	1	0	1.000	3	2	6	3.60	0
1997 Texas e	.A.L.		30	189⅓	9	12	.429	139	30	240	4.56	0
Major League Totals	.9 Yrs.		257	1597⅔	101	80	.558	1011	390	1702	4.03	1
Division Series												
1996 Texas	.A.L.		1	9	1	0	1.000	7	1	10	2.00	0

a Traded to Texas Rangers for first baseman/outfielder Desi Wilson and shortstop Rich Aurelia, December 22, 1994.
b Declared restricted free agent under Major League Baseball implemented labor proposal, December 23, 1994.
c Signed with Florida Marlins, April 8, 1995.
d Traded to Texas Rangers for pitcher Ryan Dempster and player to be named later, August 8, 1996.
e On disabled list from August 5 to August 31, 1997.

BYRD, PAUL GREGORY

Born, Louisville, Kentucky, December 3, 1970.
Bats Right. Throws Right. Height, 6 feet, 1 inches. Weight, 185 pounds.

Year	Club	Lea	G	IP	W	L	Pct	SO	BB	H	ERA	SAVES
1991 Kinston	.Carolina		14	62⅔	4	3	.571	62	36	40	3.16	0
1992 Canton-Akron	.Eastern		24	151⅓	14	6	.700	118	75	122	3.01	0
1993 Canton-Akron	.Eastern		2	10	0	0	.000	8	3	7	3.60	0
1993 Charlotte	.Int.		14	81	7	4	.636	54	30	80	3.89	0
1994 Canton-Akron	.Eastern		21	139⅓	5	9	.357	106	52	135	3.81	0
1994 Charlotte	.Int.		9	36⅔	2	2	.500	15	11	33	3.93	1
1995 Norfolk	.Int.		22	87	3	5	.375	61	21	71	2.79	6
1995 New York	.N.L.		17	22	2	0	1.000	26	7	18	2.05	0
1996 Norfolk	.Int.		5	7⅔	2	0	1.000	8	4	4	3.52	1
1996 New York a-b	.N.L.		38	46⅔	1	2	.333	31	21	48	4.24	0
1997 Richmond	.Int.		3	17	2	1	.667	14	1	14	3.18	0
1997 Atlanta	.N.L.		31	53	4	4	.500	37	28	47	5.26	0
Major League Totals	.3 Yrs.		86	121⅔	7	6	.538	94	56	113	4.29	0

a On disabled list from April 1 to June 9, 1996.
b Traded to Atlanta Braves with player to be named later for pitcher Greg McMichael, November 25, 1996.

CABRERA, JOSE ALBERTO

Born, Santiago, Dominican Republic, March 24, 1972.
Bats Right. Throws Right. Height, 6 feet. Weight, 200 pounds.

Year	Club	Lea	G	IP	W	L	Pct	SO	BB	H	ERA	SAVES
1992 Burlington	Appal.	13	92⅓	8	3	.727	79	18	74	1.75	0
1993 Columbus	So. Atl.	26	155⅓	11	6	.647	105	53	122	2.67	0
1994 Kinston	Carolina	24	133⅔	4	13	.235	110	43	134	4.44	0
1995 Canton-Akrn	Eastern	24	85	5	3	.625	61	21	83	3.28	0
1996 Bakersfield	California	7	41⅓	2	2	.500	52	21	40	3.92	0
1996 Kinston	Carolina	4	17⅔	1	1	.500	19	8	7	1.02	0
1996 Canton-Akrn	Eastern	15	62⅓	4	3	.571	40	17	78	5.63	0
1997 Buffalo	A.A.	5	15	3	0	1.000	11	7	8	1.20	0
1997 New Orleans a	A.A.	31	46	2	2	.500	48	13	31	2.54	0
1997 Houston	N.L.	12	15⅓	0	0	.000	18	6	6	1.17	0

a Traded by Cleveland Indians organization to Houston Astros for pitcher Alvin Morman, May 9, 1997.

CANDIOTTI, THOMAS CAESAR

Born, Walnut Creek, California, August 31, 1957.
Bats Right. Throws Right. Height, 6 feet, 2 inches. Weight, 215 pounds.

Year	Club	Lea	G	IP	W	L	Pct	SO	BB	H	ERA	SAVES
1979 Victoria a	Northwest	12	70	5	1	.833	66	16	63	2.44	1
1980 Jacksonville b	Southern	17	117	7	8	.467	93	40	98	2.77	0
1980 Ft. Myers c	Fla. St.	7	44	3	2	.600	31	9	32	2.25	0
1981 El Paso d	Texas	21	119	7	6	.538	68	27	137	2.80	0
1982 Vancouver e	P.C.					INJURED—Did Not Play					
1983 El Paso	Texas	7	24⅔	1	0	1.000	18	7	23	2.92	2
1983 Vancouver	P.C.	15	99⅓	6	4	.600	61	17	87	2.81	0
1983 Milwaukee	A.L.	10	55⅔	4	4	.500	21	16	62	3.23	0
1984 Vancouver f	P.C.	15	96⅔	8	4	.667	53	22	96	2.89	0
1984 Beloit g	Midwest	2	10	0	1	.000	12	5	12	2.70	0
1984 Milwaukee	A.L.	8	32⅓	2	2	.500	23	10	38	5.29	0
1985 Vancouver h	P.C.	24	150⅔	9	13	.409	97	36	178	3.94	0
1985 El Paso	Texas	4	29⅓	1	0	1.000	16	7	29	2.76	0
1986 Cleveland	A.L.	36	252⅓	16	12	.571	167	106	234	3.57	0
1987 Cleveland	A.L.	32	201⅔	7	18	.280	111	93	193	4.78	0
1988 Cleveland i	A.L.	31	216⅔	14	8	.636	137	53	225	3.28	0
1989 Cleveland j	A.L.	31	206	13	10	.565	124	55	188	3.10	0
1990 Cleveland k	A.L.	31	202	15	11	.577	128	55	207	3.65	0
1991 Cleveland-Toronto l-m	A.L.	34	238	13	13	.500	167	73	202	2.65	0
1992 Los Angeles n	N.L.	32	203⅔	11	*15	.423	152	63	177	3.00	0
1993 Los Angeles o	N.L.	33	213⅔	8	10	.444	155	71	192	3.12	0
1994 Los Angeles	N.L.	23	153	7	7	.500	102	54	149	4.12	0
1995 Los Angeles o	N.L.	30	190⅓	7	14	.333	141	58	187	3.50	0
1996 San Berndno	California	2	9	0	1	.000	10	4	11	5.00	0
1996 Los Angeles p	N.L.	28	152⅓	9	11	.450	79	43	172	4.49	0
1997 Los Angeles g-h	N.L.	41	135	10	7	.588	89	40	128	3.60	0
Major League Totals	14 Yrs.	400	2452⅔	136	142	.489	1596	790	2354	3.54	0
Division Series											
1996 Los Angeles	N.L.	1	2	0	0	.000	1	0	0	0.00	0
Championship Series											
1991 Toronto	A.L.	2	7⅔	0	1	.000	5	2	17	8.22	0

a Released by Victoria, January, 4; signed with Kansas City Royals organization, January 5, 1980.
b On disabled list from June 7 to 26, 1980.
c Drafted from Kansas City Royals by Milwaukee Brewers organization, December 9, 1980.
d On disabled list from April 10 to May 12, 1981.
e On disabled list from April 13 to end of 1982 season.
f On disabled list from May 30 to June 15, 1984.
g On disabled list from August 2 to September 1, 1984.
h Became free agent, October 15; signed with Cleveland Indians organization, December 12, 1985.
i On disabled list from August 4 to August 21, 1988.
j On disabled list from July 2 to July 17, 1989.
k On disabled list from May 7 to May 21, 1990.
l Traded to Toronto Blue Jays with outfielder Turner Ward for outfielders Glenallen Hill and Mark Whiten, pitcher Denis Boucher and player to be named, June 27; trade settled for cash, October 22, 1991.
m Filed for free agency, November 1; signed with Los Angeles Dodgers, December 3, 1991.
n On disabled list from August 9 to August 24, 1992.
o Not offered 1996 contract, November 1, 1995.
p On disabled list from July 20 to August 13, 1996.
g Filed for free agency, October 28, 1997.
h Signed with Oakland Athletics, December 9, 1997.

CARLSON, DANIEL STEVEN (DAN)

Born, Portland, Oregon, January 26, 1970.
Bats Right. Throws Right. Height, 6 feet, 1 inch. Weight, 185 pounds.

Year	Club	Lea	G	IP	W	L	Pct	SO	BB	H	ERA	SAVES
1990 Everett	.........Northwest		17	62⅓	2	6	.250	77	33	60	5.34	0
1991 Clinton	...........Midwest		27	181⅓	16	7	.696	164	76	149	3.08	0
1992 Shreveport	...........Texas		27	186	15	9	.625	157	60	166	3.19	0
1993 Phoenix	.............P.C.		13	70	5	6	.455	48	32	79	6.56	0
1993 Shreveport	...........Texas		15	100⅓	7	4	.636	81	26	86	2.24	0
1994 Phoenix	.............P.C.		31	151⅓	13	6	.684	117	55	173	4.64	1
1995 Phoenix	.............P.C.		23	132⅔	9	5	.643	93	66	138	4.27	0
1996 Phoenix	.............P.C.		33	146⅔	13	6	.684	123	46	135	3.44	1
1996 San Francisco	.........N.L.		5	10	1	0	1.000	4	2	13	2.70	0
1997 Bakersfield	...........California		2	6	0	0	.000	7	1	3	0.00	0
1997 San Francisco a-b	......N.L.		6	15⅓	0	0	.000	14	8	20	7.63	0
1997 Phoenix	.............P.C.		29	109	13	3	.813	108	36	102	3.88	3
Major League Totals	........2 Yrs.		11	25⅓	1	0	1.000	18	10	33	5.68	0

a On disabled list from April 1 to April 11, 1997.
b Selected in expansion draft by Tampa Bay Devil Rays, November 18, 1997.

CARPENTER, CHRISTOPHER JOHN (CHRIS)

Born, Exeter, New Hampshire, April 27, 1975.
Bats Right. Throws Right. Height, 6 feet, 6 inches. Weight, 215 pounds.

Year	Club	Lea	G	IP	W	L	Pct	SO	BB	H	ERA	SAVES
1994 Medicne Hat	........Pioneer		15	84⅔	6	3	.667	80	39	76	2.76	0
1995 Dunedin	...........Fla. St.		15	99⅓	3	5	.375	56	50	83	2.17	0
1995 Knoxville	........Southern		12	64⅓	3	7	.300	53	31	71	5.18	0
1996 Knoxville	........Southern		28	171⅓	7	9	.438	150	91	161	3.94	0
1997 Syracuse	.............Int.		19	120	4	9	.308	97	53	113	4.50	0
1997 Toronto	.............A.L.		14	81⅓	3	7	.300	55	37	108	5.09	0

CARRASCO, HECTOR PACHECO PIPO (KING)

Born, San Pedro De Macoris, Dominican Republic, October 22, 1969.
Bats Right. Throws Right. Height, 6 feet, 2 inches. Weight, 175 pounds.

Year	Club	Lea	G	IP	W	L	Pct	SO	BB	H	ERA	SAVES
1988 Sarasota Mets	.......Gulf C.		14	36⅔	0	2	.000	21	13	37	4.17	0
1989 Kingsport	...........Appal.		12	53⅓	1	6	.143	55	34	69	5.74	0
1990 Kingsport	...........Appal.		3	6⅔	0	0	.000	5	1	8	4.05	0
1991 Pittsfield a	.......N.Y.-Penn.		12	23⅓	0	1	.000	20	21	25	5.40	1
1992 Asheville b	.........So. Atl.		49	78⅓	5	5	.500	67	47	66	2.99	8
1993 Kane County c	........Midwest		28	149	6	12	.333	127	76	153	4.11	0
1994 Cincinnati d	...........N.L.		45	56⅓	5	6	.455	41	30	42	2.24	6
1995 Cincinnati	...........N.L.		64	87⅓	2	7	.222	64	46	86	4.12	5
1996 Indianapolis	...........A.A.		13	21	0	1	.000	17	13	18	2.14	0
1996 Cincinnati	...........N.L.		56	74⅓	4	3	.571	59	45	58	3.75	0
1997 Indianapols	...........A.A.		3	4⅓	0	0	.000	4	3	5	6.23	1
1997 Cincinnati e	...........N.L.		38	51⅓	1	2	.333	46	25	51	3.68	0
1997 Kansas City f	..........A.L.		28	34⅔	1	6	.143	30	16	29	5.45	0
Major League Totals	........4 Yrs.		231	304	13	24	.351	240	162	266	3.76	11
Championship Series												
1995 Cincinnati	.............N.L.		1	1⅓	0	0	.000	3	0	1	0.00	0

a Released by New York Mets, January 6; signed with Houston Astros organization, January 21, 1992.
b Traded by Houston Astros to Florida Marlins organization with pitcher Brian Griffiths for pitcher Tom Edens, November 17, 1992.
c Traded by Florida Marlins to Cincinnati Reds to complete March 27 trade in which Florida acquired pitcher Chris Hammond for infielder Gary Scott and player to be named, September 10, 1993.
d On disabled list from May 12 to June 1, 1994.
e Traded to Kansas City Royals with pitcher Scott Service for outfielder Jon Nunnally and outfielder Chris Stynes, July 15, 1997.
f Selected in expansion draft by Arizona Diamondbacks, November 18, 1997.

CASTILLO, ANTONIO JOSE

Born, Lara, Venezuela, March 1, 1963.
Bats Left. Throws Left. Height 5 feet, 10 inches. Weight, 188 pounds.

Year	Club	Lea	G	IP	W	L	Pct	SO	BB	H	ERA	SAVES
1983	Bradenton Jays	Gulf C.	1	3	0	0	.000	4	0	3	3.00	1
1984	Florence	So. Atl.	25	137⅓	11	8	.579	96	50	123	3.41	0
1985	Kinston	Carolina	36	127⅔	11	7	.611	136	48	111	1.90	3
1986	Knoxville a	Southern			INJURED—Did Not Play							
1987	Dunedin	Fla. St.	39	69⅔	6	2	.750	62	19	62	3.36	6
1988	Dunedin	Fla. St.	30	42⅔	4	3	.571	46	10	31	1.48	12
1988	Knoxville	Southern	5	8	1	0	1.000	11	1	2	0.00	2
1988	Toronto	A.L.	14	15	1	0	1.000	14	2	10	3.00	0
1989	Syracuse	Int.	27	41⅓	1	3	.250	37	15	33	2.61	5
1989	Toronto b	A.L.	17	17⅔	1	1	.500	10	10	23	6.11	1
1989	Atlanta	N.L.	12	9⅓	0	1	.000	5	4	8	4.82	0
1990	Richmond	Int.	5	25	3	1	.750	27	6	14	2.52	0
1990	Atlanta	N.L.	52	76⅔	5	1	.833	64	20	93	4.23	1
1991	Richmond	Int.	23	118	5	6	.455	78	32	89	2.90	0
1991	Atlanta-New York c-d	N.L.	17	32⅓	2	1	.667	18	11	40	3.34	0
1992	Toledo e	Int.	12	44⅔	2	3	.400	24	14	48	3.63	2
1993	Syracuse	Int.	1	6	0	0	.000	2	0	4	0.00	0
1993	Toronto	A.L.	51	50⅔	3	2	.600	28	22	44	3.38	0
1994	Toronto	A.L.	41	68	5	2	.714	43	28	66	2.51	1
1995	Toronto	A.L.	55	72⅔	1	5	.167	38	24	64	3.22	13
1996	Toronto-Chicago f	A.L.	55	95	5	4	.556	57	24	95	3.60	2
1997	Chicago g	A.L.	64	62⅓	4	4	.500	42	23	74	4.91	4
Major League Totals		9 Yrs.	378	499⅔	27	21	.563	319	168	517	3.71	22
Championship Series												
1993	Toronto	A.L.	2	2	0	0	.000	1	1	0	0.00	0
World Series Record												
1993	Toronto	A.L.	2	3⅓	1	0	1.000	1	3	6	8.10	0

a On disabled list from April 10 to end of 1986 season.
b Traded to Atlanta Braves with player to be named for pitcher Jim Acker, August 24; Atlanta acquired catcher Francisco Cabrera to complete trade, September 1, 1989.
c Traded to New York Mets with player to be named for pitcher Alejandro Pena, August 28; New York acquired pitcher Joe Roa to complete trade, September 9, 1991.
d Traded to Detroit Tigers with outfielder Mark Carreon for pitchers Paul Gibson and Randy Marshall, January 22, 1992.
e On disabled list from April 5 to August 2, 1992; signed with Toronto Blue Jays organization, January 11, 1993.
f Traded to Chicago White Sox with infielder Domingo Cedeno for pitcher Luis Andujar and pitcher Allen Halley, August 22, 1996.
g On disabled list from May 13 to May 28, 1997.

CASTILLO, CARLOS

Born, Boston, Massachusetts, April 21, 1975.
Bats Right. Throws Right. Height, 6 feet, 2 inches. Weight, 240 pounds.

Year	Club	Lea	G	IP	W	L	Pct	SO	BB	H	ERA	SAVES
1994	White Sox	Gulf Coast	12	59	4	3	.571	57	10	53	2.59	0
1994	Hickory	So. Atl.	3	12	2	0	1.000	17	2	3	0.00	0
1995	Hickory	So. Atl.	14	79⅔	5	6	.455	67	18	85	3.73	1
1996	South Bend	Midwest	20	133⅓	9	9	.500	128	29	131	4.05	0
1996	Pr William	Carolina	6	43⅓	2	4	.333	30	4	45	3.95	0
1997	Chicago	A.L.	37	66⅓	2	1	.667	43	33	68	4.48	1
1997	Nashville	A.A.	4	6	0	0	.000	4	0	4	1.50	3

CASTILLO, FRANK ANTHONY

Born, El Paso, Texas, April 1, 1969.
Bats Right. Throws Right. Height, 6 feet, 1 inch. Weight, 190 pounds.

Year	Club	Lea	G	IP	W	L	Pct	SO	BB	H	ERA	SAVES
1987	Wytheville	Appal.	12	90⅓	*10	1	*.909	83	21	86	2.29	0
1987	Geneva	N.Y.-Penn.	1	6	1	0	1.000	6	1	3	0.00	0
1988	Peoria a	Midwest	9	51	6	1	.857	58	10	25	0.71	0
1989	Winston-Salem	Carolina	18	129⅓	9	6	.600	114	24	118	2.51	0
1989	Charlotte	Southern	10	68	3	4	.429	43	12	73	3.84	0
1990	Charlotte b	Southern	18	111⅓	6	6	.500	112	27	113	3.88	0
1991	Iowa	A.A.	4	25	3	1	.750	20	7	20	2.52	0
1991	Chicago c	N.L.	18	111⅔	6	7	.462	73	33	107	4.35	0
1992	Chicago	N.L.	33	205⅓	10	11	.476	135	63	179	3.46	0

Year Club	Lea	G	IP	W	L	Pct	SO	BB	H	ERA	SAVES
1993 Chicago	N.L.	29	141⅓	5	8	.385	84	39	162	4.84	0
1994 Daytona	Fla. St.	1	4	0	1	.000	1	0	7	4.50	0
1994 Orlando	Southern	1	7	1	0	1.000	2	1	4	1.29	0
1994 Iowa	A.A.	11	66	4	2	.667	64	10	57	3.27	0
1994 Chicago d	N.L.	4	23	2	1	.667	19	5	25	4.30	0
1995 Chicago	N.L.	29	188	11	10	.524	135	52	179	3.21	0
1996 Chicago	N.L.	33	182⅓	7	16	.304	139	46	209	5.28	0
1997 Chicago-Colorado e-f-g	N.L.	34	184⅓	12	12	.500	126	69	220	5.42	0
Major League Totals ....7 Yrs.		180	1036	53	65	.449	711	307	1081	4.39	0

a On disabled list from April 16 to July 11, 1988.
b On disabled list from April 6 to June 15, 1990.
c On disabled list from April 12 to June 6 and August 11 to August 27, 1991.
d On disabled list from March 20 to May 12, 1994.
e Traded to Colorado Rockies for pitcher Matt Pool, July 15, 1997.
f Filed for free agency, October 30, 1997.
g Signed as free agent with Detroit Tigers, December 11, 1997.

CATHER, MICHAEL PETER

Born, San Diego, California, December 17, 1970.
Bats Right. Throws Right. Height, 6 feet, 2 inches. Weight, 195 pounds.

Year Club	Lea	G	IP	W	L	Pct	SO	BB	H	ERA	SAVES
1993 Rangers	Gulf Coast	25	30⅔	1	1	.500	30	9	20	1.76	4
1994 Charlotte	Fla. St.	44	60⅓	8	6	.571	53	40	56	3.88	6
1995 Tulsa a	Texas	18	21⅔	0	2	.000	15	7	20	3.32	0
1995 Winnipeg	Northern	27	31	4	2	.667	35	12	18	1.45	8
1996 Greenville b	Southern	53	87⅔	3	4	.429	61	29	89	3.70	5
1997 Greenville	Southern	22	37⅓	5	2	.714	29	7	37	4.34	1
1997 Richmond	Int.	13	26	0	0	.000	22	9	17	1.73	3
1997 Atlanta	N.L.	35	37⅔	2	4	.333	29	19	23	2.39	0
Division Series											
1997 Atlanta	N.L.	1	2	0	0	.000	2	1	0	0.00	0
Championship Series											
1997 Atlanta	N.L.	4	2⅔	0	0	.000	3	0	3	0.00	0

a Released by Texas Rangers organization, June 9, 1995.
b Signed as free agent by Atlanta Braves organization, February 9, 1996.

CHARLTON, NORMAN WOOD

Born, Fort Polk, Louisiana, January 6, 1963.
Bats Both. Throws Left. Height 6 feet, 3 inches. Weight, 205 pounds.

Year Club	Lea	G	IP	W	L	Pct	SO	BB	H	ERA	SAVES
1984 West Palm Beach	Fla. St.	8	39⅓	1	4	.200	27	22	51	4.58	0
1985 West Palm Beach a ...	Fla. St.	24	128	7	10	.412	71	79	135	4.57	0
1986 Vermont	Eastern	22	136⅔	10	6	.625	96	74	109	2.83	0
1987 Nashville b	A.A.	18	98⅓	2	8	.200	74	44	97	4.30	0
1988 Nashville	A.A.	27	182	11	10	.524	*161	56	149	3.02	0
1988 Cincinnati	N.L.	10	61⅓	4	5	.444	39	20	60	3.96	0
1989 Cincinnati	N.L.	69	95⅓	8	3	.727	98	40	67	2.93	0
1990 Cincinnati	N.L.	56	154⅓	12	9	.571	117	70	131	2.74	2
1991 Cincinnati c-d-e	N.L.	39	108⅓	3	5	.375	77	34	92	2.91	1
1992 Cincinnati f	N.L.	64	81⅓	4	2	.667	90	26	79	2.99	26
1993 Seattle g-h-i	A.L.	34	34⅔	1	3	.250	48	17	22	2.34	18
1994 Philadelphia j-k	N.L.					INJURED—Did Not Play					
1995 Philadelphia	N.L.	25	22	2	5	.286	12	15	23	7.36	0
1995 Seattle l-m	A.L.	30	47⅔	2	1	.667	58	16	23	1.51	14
1996 Seattle	A.L.	70	75⅔	4	7	.364	73	38	68	4.04	20
1997 Seattle n-o	A.L.	71	69⅓	3	8	.273	55	47	89	7.27	14
Major League Totals ....9 Yrs.		468	750	43	48	.473	667	323	654	3.50	95
Division Series											
1995 Seattle	A.L.	4	7⅓	1	0	1.000	9	3	4	2.45	1
1997 Seattle	A.L.	2	2⅓	0	0	.000	1	0	2	0.00	0
Divisional Series Totals 6			9⅔	1	0	1.000	10	3	6	1.86	1
Championship Series											
1990 Cincinnati	N.L.	4	5	1	1	.500	3	3	4	1.80	0
1995 Seattle	A.L.	3	6	1	0	1.000	5	1	1	0.00	1
Championship Series Totals 7			11	2	1	.667	8	4	5	0.82	1

Year	Club	Lea	G	IP	W	L	Pct	SO	BB	H	ERA	SAVES
	World Series Record											
1990 Cincinnati		N.L.	1	1	0	0	.000	0	0	1	0.00	0

a Traded by Montreal Expos to Cincinnati Reds organization with infielder Tim Barker for infielder Wayne Krenchicki, March 31, 1986.
b On disabled list from April 6 to June 26, 1987.
c On disabled list from May 26 to June 11 and June 17 to July 19, 1991.
d Suspended seven games by National League for September 9 admittedly hitting batter with pitch, October 3 to October 6, 1991 and first four games of 1992 season.
e Appeared in two additional games as pinch runner.
f Traded to Seattle Mariners for outfielder Kevin Mitchell, November 17, 1992.
g Suspended four games by American League for June 6 fight from July 9 to July 15, 1993.
h On disabled list from July 21 to August 5 and August 8 to end of 1993 season.
i Released, November 18, 1993; signed with Philadelphia Phillies organization, February 2, 1994.
j On disabled list from March 31 to end of 1994 season.
k Filed for free agency, October 17; re-signed with Philadelphia Phillies organization, December 6, 1994.
l Released by Philadelphia Phillies, July 9, 1995.
m Signed with Seattle Mariners, July 14, 1995.
n Filed for free agency, November 7, 1997.
o Signed as free agent with Baltimore Orioles organization, December 15, 1997.

CHECO, ROBINSON
Born, Santo Domingo, Dominican Republic, September 9, 1971.
Bats Right. Throws Right. Height, 6 feet, 1 inch. Weight, 185 pounds.

Year	Club	Lea	G	IP	W	L	Pct	SO	BB	H	ERA	SAVES
1997 Sarasota		Fla. St.	11	56	1	4	.200	63	27	54	5.30	0
1997 Trenton		Eastern	1	7⅔	1	0	1.000	9	1	6	2.35	0
1997 Pawtucket		Int.	9	55⅓	4	2	.667	56	16	41	3.42	0
1997 Boston a		A.L.	5	13⅓	1	1	.500	14	3	12	3.38	0

a On disabled list from April 1 to May 13, 1997.

CHRISTIANSEN, JASON SAMUEL
Born, Omaha, Nebraska, September 21, 1969.
Bats Right. Throws Left. Height, 6 feet, 5 inches. Weight, 230 pounds.

Year	Club	Lea	G	IP	W	L	Pct	SO	BB	H	ERA	SAVES
1991 Pirates		Gulf Coast	6	8	1	0	1.000	8	1	4	0.00	1
1991 Welland		N.Y.-Penn.	8	21⅓	0	1	.000	17	12	15	2.53	0
1992 Augusta		So. Atl.	10	20	1	0	1.000	21	8	12	1.80	2
1992 Salem		Carolina	38	50	3	1	.750	59	22	47	3.24	2
1993 Salem		Carolina	57	71⅓	1	1	.500	70	24	48	3.15	4
1993 Carolina		Southern	2	2⅔	0	0	.000	2	1	3	0.00	0
1994 Carolina		Southern	28	38⅔	2	1	.667	43	14	30	2.09	2
1994 Buffalo		A.A.	33	33⅔	3	1	.750	39	16	19	2.41	0
1995 Pittsburgh		N.L.	63	56⅓	1	3	.250	53	34	49	4.15	0
1996 Calgary		P.C.	2	11	1	0	1.000	10	1	9	3.27	0
1996 Pittsburgh		N.L.	33	44⅓	3	3	.500	38	19	56	6.70	0
1997 Carolina		Southern	8	15	0	1	.000	25	5	17	4.20	1
1997 Pittsburgh a		N.L.	39	33⅔	3	0	1.000	37	17	37	2.94	0
Major League Totals		3 Yrs.	135	134⅓	7	6	.538	128	70	142	4.69	0

a On disabled list from April 1 to June 28, 1997.

CLARK, MARK WILLARD
Born, Bath, Illinois, May 12, 1968.
Bats Right. Throws Right. Height, 6 feet, 5 inches. Weight, 225 pounds.

Year	Club	Lea	G	IP	W	L	Pct	SO	BB	H	ERA	SAVES
1988 Hamilton		N.Y.-Penn.	15	94⅓	6	7	.462	60	32	88	3.05	0
1989 Savannah		So. Atl.	27	173⅔	*14	9	.609	132	52	143	2.44	0
1990 St. Petersburg		Fla. St.	10	62	3	2	.600	58	14	63	3.05	0
1990 Arkansas		Texas	19	115⅓	5	11	.313	87	37	111	3.82	0
1991 Arkansas a		Texas	15	92⅓	5	5	.500	76	30	99	4.00	0
1991 Louisville		A.A.	7	45⅓	3	2	.600	29	15	43	2.98	0
1991 St. Louis		N.L.	7	22⅓	1	1	.500	13	11	17	4.03	0
1992 Louisville		A.A.	9	61	4	4	.500	38	15	56	2.80	0
1992 St. Louis b		N.L.	20	113⅓	3	10	.231	44	36	117	4.45	0
1993 Charlotte		Int.	2	13	1	0	1.000	12	2	9	2.08	0
1993 Cleveland c		A.L.	26	109⅓	7	5	.583	57	25	119	4.28	0
1994 Cleveland d		A.L.	20	127⅓	11	3	.786	60	40	133	3.82	0

Year Club	Lea	G	IP	W	L	Pct	SO	BB	H	ERA	SAVES
1995 Buffalo e .............A.A.		5	35⅓	4	0	1.000	17	10	39	3.57	0
1995 Cleveland ............A.L.		22	124⅔	9	7	.563	68	42	143	5.27	0
1996 New York f .............N.L.		32	212⅓	14	11	.560	142	48	217	3.43	0
1997 New York-Chicago g ....N.L.		32	205	14	8	.636	123	59	213	3.82	0
Major League Totals ....7 Yrs.		159	914⅓	59	45	.567	507	261	959	4.07	0

a On disabled list from April 9 to May 7, 1991.
b Traded to Cleveland Indians with shortstop Juan Andujar for outfielder Mark Whiten, March 31, 1993.
c On disabled list from July 17 to September 8, 1993.
d On disabled list from July 21 to end of 1994 season.
e Re-signed with Cleveland Indians, December 20, 1995.
f Traded to New York Mets for outfielder Ryan Thompson and pitcher Reid Cornelius, March 31, 1996.
g Traded to Chicago Cubs with outfielder Lance Johnson and player-to-be-named for pitcher Mel Rojas, pitcher Turk Wendell and outfielder Brian McRae, August 8, 1997. Chicago Cubs received infielder Manny Alexander to complete trade, August 14, 1997.

CLEMENS, WILLIAM ROGER
Born, Dayton, Ohio, August 4, 1962.
Bats Right. Throws Right. Height, 6 feet, 4 inches. Weight, 220 pounds.

Year Club	Lea	G	IP	W	L	Pct	SO	BB	H	ERA	SAVES
1983 Winter Haven ....Fla. St.		4	29	3	1	.750	36	0	22	1.24	0
1983 New Britain ....Eastern		7	52	4	1	.800	59	12	31	1.38	0
1984 Pawtucket ....Eastern		7	46⅔	2	3	.400	50	14	39	1.93	0
1984 Boston ..............A.L.		21	133⅓	9	4	.692	126	29	146	4.32	0
1985 Boston a ............A.L.		15	98⅓	7	5	.583	74	37	83	3.29	0
1986 Boston b ............A.L.		33	254	*24	4	*.857	238	67	179	*2.48	0
1987 Boston c ............A.L.		36	281⅔	*20	9	.690	256	83	248	2.97	0
1988 Boston ..............A.L.		35	264	18	12	.600	*291	62	217	2.93	0
1989 Boston ..............A.L.		35	253⅓	17	11	.607	230	93	215	3.13	0
1990 Boston d ............A.L.		31	228⅓	21	6	.778	209	54	193	*1.93	0
1991 Boston e ............A.L.		35	*271⅓	18	10	.643	*241	65	219	*2.62	0
1992 Boston ..............A.L.		32	246⅔	18	11	.621	208	62	203	*2.41	0
1993 Pawtucket ....Int.		1	3⅔	0	0	.000	8	4	1	0.00	0
1993 Boston f ............A.L.		29	191⅔	11	14	.440	160	67	175	4.46	0
1994 Boston ..............A.L.		24	170⅔	9	7	.563	168	71	124	2.85	0
1995 Sarasota ....Fla. St.		1	4	0	0	.000	7	2	0	0.00	0
1995 Pawtucket ....Int.		1	5	0	0	.000	5	3	1	0.00	0
1995 Boston g ............A.L.		23	140	10	5	.667	132	60	141	4.18	0
1996 Boston h-i ..........A.L.		34	242⅔	10	13	.435	257	106	216	3.63	0
1997 Toronto j ...........A.L.		34	264	21	7	.750	292	68	204	2.05	0
Major League Totals ....14 Yrs.		417	3040	213	118	.644	2882	924	2563	2.97	0
Division Series											
1995 Boston ..............A.L.		1	7	0	0	.000	5	1	5	3.86	0
Championship Series											
1986 Boston ..............A.L.		3	22⅔	1	1	.500	17	7	22	4.37	0
1988 Boston ..............A.L.		1	7	0	0	.000	8	0	6	3.86	0
1990 Boston ..............A.L.		2	7⅔	0	1	.000	4	5	7	3.52	0
Championship Series Totals 6			37⅓	1	2	.333	29	12	35	4.10	0
World Series Record											
1986 Boston ..............A.L.		2	11⅓	0	0	.000	11	6	9	3.18	0

a On disabled list from July 8 to August 3 and August 21 to end of 1985 season.
b Selected Most Valuable Player and Cy Young Award winner in American League for 1986.
c Selected Cy Young Award winner in American League for 1987.
d Suspended five games by American League for bumping and threatening umpire and refusing to leave dugout after ejection during Game Four, 1990 American League Championship Series, from April 26 to May 1, 1991.
e Selected Cy Young Award winner in American League for 1991.
f On disabled list from June 19 to July 16, 1993.
g On disabled list from April 16 to June 2, 1995.
h Filed for free agency, November 5, 1996.
i Signed with Toronto Blue Jays, December 13, 1996.
j Selected Cy Young Award Winner in American League for 1997.

CLEMONS, CHRISTOPHER HALE
Born, Baytown, Texas, October 31, 1972.
Bats Right. Throws Right. Height, 6 feet, 4 inches. Weight, 220 pounds.

Year Club	Lea	G	IP	W	L	Pct	SO	BB	H	ERA	SAVES
1994 White Sox ....Gulf Coast		2	7	0	1	.000	5	1	5	3.86	0
1994 Hickory ....So. Atl.		12	69⅓	4	2	.667	42	18	74	4.41	0
1995 Pr William ....Carolina		27	137	7	12	.368	92	64	136	4.73	0

Year	Club		Lea	G	IP	W	L	Pct	SO	BB	H	ERA	SAVES
1996 Pr William	. . . . .Carolina			6	36	1	4	.200	26	8	36	2.25	0
1996 Birmingham	. . . . . . .Southern			13	94⅓	5	2	.714	69	40	91	3.15	0
1997 Chicago a	. . . . .A.L.			5	12⅔	0	2	.000	8	11	19	8.53	0
1997 Nashville	. . . . .A.A.			22	124⅓	5	5	.500	70	65	115	4.55	0

a Selected in expansion draft by Arizona Diamondbacks, November 18, 1997.

CLONTZ, JOHN BRADLEY (BRAD)
Born, Stuart, Virginia, April 25, 1971.
Bats Right. Throws Right. Height, 6 feet, 1 inch. Weight, 180 pounds.

Year	Club	Lea	G	IP	W	L	Pct	SO	BB	H	ERA	SAVES
1992 Pulaski	. . . . .Appal.		4	5⅔	0	0	.000	7	2	3	1.59	1
1992 Macon	. . . . .So. Atl.		17	23	2	1	.667	18	10	19	3.91	2
1993 Durham	. . . . .Carolina		51	75⅓	1	7	.125	79	26	69	2.75	10
1994 Greenville	. . . . .Southern		39	45	1	2	.333	49	10	32	1.20	27
1994 Richmond	. . . . .Int.		24	25⅔	0	0	.000	21	9	19	2.10	11
1995 Atlanta	. . . . .N.L.		59	69	8	1	.889	55	22	71	3.65	4
1996 Atlanta	. . . . .N.L.		81	80⅔	6	3	.667	49	33	78	5.69	1
1997 Richmond	. . . . .Int.		16	22	0	0	.000	24	2	10	0.00	6
1997 Atlanta	. . . . .N.L.		51	48	5	1	.833	42	18	52	3.75	1
Major League Totals	. . . . .3 Yrs.		191	197⅔	19	5	.792	146	73	201	4.51	6
Division Series												
1995 Atlanta	. . . . .N.L.		1	1⅓	0	0	.000	2	0	0	0.00	0
Championship Series												
1995 Atlanta	. . . . .N.L.		1	0⅓	0	0	.000	0	0	1	0.00	0
1996 Atlanta	. . . . .N.L.		1	0⅔	0	0	.000	0	0	0	0.00	0
Championship Series Totals	2		1	0	0	.000	0	0	1	0.00	0
World Series Record												
1995 Atlanta	. . . . .N.L.		2	3⅓	0	0	.000	2	0	2	2.70	0
1996 Atlanta	. . . . .N.L.		3	1⅔	0	0	.000	2	1	1	0.00	0
World Series Totals	5		5	0	0	.000	4	1	3	1.80	0

CLOUDE, KENNETH BRIAN
Born, Baltimore, Maryland, January 9, 1975.
Bats Right. Throws Right. Height, 6 feet, 1 inch. Weight, 200 pounds.

Year	Club	Lea	G	IP	W	L	Pct	SO	BB	H	ERA	SAVES
1994 Mariners	. . . . .Arizona		12	52⅓	3	4	.429	61	19	36	2.06	0
1995 Wisconsin	. . . . .Midwest		25	161	9	8	.529	140	63	137	3.24	0
1996 Lancaster	. . . . .California		28	168⅓	15	4	.789	161	60	167	4.22	0
1997 Memphis	. . . . .Southern		22	132⅔	11	7	.611	124	48	131	3.87	0
1997 Seattle	. . . . .A.L.		10	51	4	2	.667	46	26	41	5.12	0

COLON, BARTOLO
Born, Altamira, Dominican Republic, May 24, 1975.
Bats Right. Throws Right. Height, 6 feet. Weight, 185 pounds.

Year	Club	Lea	G	IP	W	L	Pct	SO	BB	H	ERA	SAVES
1994 Burlington	. . . . .Appal.		12	66	7	4	.636	84	44	46	3.14	0
1995 Kinston	. . . . .Carolina		21	128⅔	13	3	.813	152	39	91	1.96	0
1996 Canton-Akrn	. . . . . . .Eastern		13	62	2	2	.500	56	25	44	1.74	0
1996 Buffalo	. . . . .A.A.		8	15	0	0	.000	19	8	16	6.00	0
1997 Buffalo	. . . . .A.A.		10	56⅔	7	1	.875	54	23	45	2.22	0
1997 Cleveland	. . . . .A.L.		19	94	4	7	.364	66	45	107	5.65	0

CONE, DAVID BRIAN
Born, Kansas City, Missouri, January 2, 1963.
Bats Left. Throws Right. Height, 6 feet, 1 inch. Weight, 190 pounds.

Year	Club	Lea	G	IP	W	L	Pct	SO	BB	H	ERA	SAVES
1981 Sarasota Royals	. . .Gulf Coast		14	67	6	4	.600	45	33	52	2.55	0
1982 Charleston	. . . . .So. Atl.		16	104⅔	9	2	.818	87	47	84	2.06	0
1982 Fort Myers	. . . . .Fla. St.		10	72⅓	7	1	.875	57	25	56	2.12	0
1983 Jacksonville a	. . . . . .Southern			INJURED—Did Not Play								
1984 Memphis	. . . . .Southern		29	178⅔	8	12	.400	110	114	162	4.28	0

Year	Club	Lea	G	IP	W	L	Pct	SO	BB	H	ERA	SAVES
1985 Omaha	A.A.	28	158⅔	9	15	.375	115	*93	157	4.65	0
1986 Omaha	A.A.	39	71	8	4	.667	63	25	60	2.79	14
1986 Kansas City b	A.L.	11	22⅔	0	0	.000	21	13	29	5.56	0
1987 Tidewater	Int.	3	11	0	1	.000	10	6	10	5.73	0
1987 New York c	N.L.	21	99⅓	5	6	.454	68	44	87	3.71	1
1988 New York	N.L.	35	231⅓	20	3	*.870	213	80	178	2.22	0
1989 New York	N.L.	34	219⅔	14	8	.636	190	74	183	3.52	0
1990 New York d	N.L.	31	211⅔	14	10	.583	*233	65	177	3.23	0
1991 New York	N.L.	34	232⅔	14	14	.500	*241	73	204	3.29	0
1992 New York e	N.L.	27	196⅔	13	7	.650	214	*82	162	2.88	0
1992 Toronto f	A.L.	8	53	4	3	.571	47	29	39	2.55	0
1993 Kansas City	A.L.	34	254	11	14	.440	191	114	205	3.33	0
1994 Kansas City g	A.L.	23	171⅔	16	5	.762	132	54	130	2.94	0
1995 Toronto-New York h-i-j	A.L.	30	229⅓	18	8	.692	191	88	195	3.57	0
1996 Norwich	Eastern	2	10	0	0	.000	13	1	9	0.90	0
1996 New York k	A.L.	11	72	7	2	.778	71	34	50	2.88	0
1997 New York l	A.L.	29	195	12	6	.667	222	86	155	2.82	0
Major League Totals . . . . . . 12 Yrs.		328	2189	148	86	.632	2034	836	1794	3.13	1
Division Series											
1995 New York	A.L.	2	15⅔	1	0	1.000	14	9	15	4.60	0
1996 New York	A.L.	1	6	0	1	.000	8	2	8	9.00	0
1997 New York	A.L.	1	3⅓	0	0	.000	2	2	7	16.20	0
Divisional Series Totals 4		25	1	1	.500	24	13	30	7.20	0
Championship Series											
1988 New York	N.L.	3	12	1	1	.500	9	5	10	4.50	0
1992 Toronto	A.L.	2	12	1	1	.500	9	5	11	3.00	0
1996 New York	A.L.	1	6	0	0	.000	5	5	5	3.00	0
Championship Series Totals 6		30	2	2	.500	23	15	26	3.60	0
World Series Record											
1992 Toronto	A.L.	2	10⅓	0	0	.000	8	8	9	3.48	0
1996 New York	A.L.	1	6	1	0	1.000	3	4	4	1.50	0
World Series Totals 3		16⅓	1	0	1.000	11	12	13	2.76	0

a On disabled list from April 8 to end of 1983 season.
b Traded to New York Mets with catcher Chris Jelic for pitchers Rick Anderson and Mauro Gozzo and catcher Ed Hearn, March 27, 1987.
c On disabled list from May 29 to August 13, 1987.
d Appeared in one additional game as pinch hitter.
e Traded to Toronto Blue Jays for infielder Jeff Kent and player to be named, August 27; New York Mets acquired outfielder Ryan Thompson to complete trade, September 1, 1992.
f Filed for free agency, October 30; signed with Kansas City Royals, December 8, 1992.
g Selected Cy Young Award winner in American League for 1994.
h Traded to Toronto Blue Jays for infielder Chris Stynes, infielder Anthony Medrano and pitcher David Sinnes, April 6, 1995.
i Traded to New York Yankees for pitcher Marty Janzen, pitcher Jason Jarvis and pitcher Mike Gordon, July 28, 1995.
j Filed for free agency, November 12, 1995. Resigned with New York Yankees, December 21, 1995.
k On disabled list from May 3 to September 2, 1996.
l On disabled list from August 18 to September 20, 1997.

COOK, DENNIS BRYAN
Born, Dickinson, Texas, October 4, 1962.
Bats Left. Throws Left. Height, 6 feet, 3 inches. Weight, 185 pounds.

Year	Club	Lea	G	IP	W	L	Pct	SO	BB	H	ERA	SAVES
1985 Clinton	Midwest	13	83	5	4	.556	40	27	73	3.36	0
1986 Fresno	California	27	170	12	7	.632	*173	100	141	3.97	1
1987 Shreveport	Texas	16	105⅔	9	2	.818	98	20	94	2.13	0
1987 Phoenix	P.C.	12	62	2	5	.286	24	26	72	5.23	0
1988 Phoenix	P.C.	26	141⅓	11	9	.550	110	51	138	3.88	0
1988 San Francisco	N.L.	4	22	2	1	.667	13	11	9	2.86	0
1989 Phoenix a	P.C.	12	78	7	4	.636	85	19	73	3.12	0
1989 S. F.-Philadelphia	N.L.	23	121	7	8	.467	67	38	110	3.72	0
1990 Phil.-Los Angeles b-c	N.L.	47	156	9	4	.692	64	56	155	3.92	1
1991 San Antonio	Texas	7	50⅔	1	3	.250	45	10	43	2.49	0
1991 Albuquerque	P.C.	14	91⅓	7	3	.700	84	32	73	3.63	0
1991 Los Angeles d	N.L.	20	17⅔	1	0	1.000	8	7	12	0.51	0
1992 Cleveland	A.L.	32	158	5	7	.417	96	50	156	3.82	0
1993 Cleveland	A.L.	25	54	5	5	.500	34	16	62	5.67	0
1993 Charlotte e	Int.	12	42⅔	3	2	.600	40	6	46	5.06	0
1994 Chicago f	A.L.	38	33	3	1	.750	26	14	29	3.55	0

Year	Club	Lea	G	IP	W	L	Pct	SO	BB	H	ERA	SAVES
1995 Cleveland-Texas g	A.L.	46	57⅔	0	2	.000	53	26	63	4.52	2
1996 Texas h-i	A.L.	60	70⅓	5	2	.714	64	35	53	4.09	0
1997 Florida j	N.L.	59	62⅓	1	2	.333	63	28	64	3.90	0
Major League Totals ....10 Yrs.		354	752	38	32	.543	488	281	713	3.93	3
Division Series											
1996 Texas	A.L.	2	1⅓	0	0	.000	0	1	0	0.00	0
1997 Florida	N.L.	2	3	1	0	1.000	3	1	0	0.00	0
Divisional Series Totals 4		4⅓		1	0	1.000	3	2	0	0.00	0
Championship Series											
1997 Florida	N.L.	2	2⅓	0*	0	.000	2	0	0	0.00	0
World Series Record											
1997 Florida	N.L.	3	3⅔	1	0	1.000	5	1	1	0.00	0

a Traded by San Francisco Giants to Philadelphia Phillies with pitcher Terry Mulholland and third baseman/outfielder Charlie Hayes for pitcher Steve Bedrosian and player to be named, June 18; San Francisco acquired infielder Rich Parker to complete trade, August 6, 1989.
b Appeared in one additional game as pinch runner and five additional games as pinch hitter.
c Traded to Los Angeles Dodgers for catcher Darrin Fletcher, September 13, 1990.
d Traded to Cleveland Indians with pitcher Mike Christopher for pitcher Rudy Seanez, December 11, 1991.
e Refused assignment to minor leagues and became free agent, October 5, 1993; signed with Chicago White Sox organization, January 5, 1994.
f Claimed on waivers by Cleveland Indians, October 17, 1994.
g Traded to Texas Rangers for infielder Guillermo Mercedes, June 22, 1995.
h Filed for free agency, October 29, 1996.
i Signed with Florida Marlins, December 10, 1996.
j Traded to New York Mets for outfielder Fletcher Baines and pitcher Scott Comer, December 18, 1997.

COOKE, STEVEN MONTAGUE

Born, Kaual, Hawaii, January 14, 1970.
Bats Right. Throws Left. Height, 6 feet, 6 inches. Weight, 230 pounds.

Year	Club	Lea	G	IP	W	L	Pct	SO	BB	H	ERA	SAVES
1990 Welland	N.Y.-Penn.	11	46	2	3	.400	43	17	36	2.35	0
1991 Augusta	So. Atl.	11	60⅔	5	4	.556	52	35	50	2.82	0
1991 Salem	Carolina	2	13	1	0	1.000	5	2	14	4.85	0
1991 Carolina	Southern	9	55⅔	3	3	.500	46	19	39	2.26	0
1992 Carolina	Southern	6	36	2	2	.500	38	12	31	3.00	0
1992 Buffalo	A.A.	13	74⅓	6	3	.667	52	36	71	3.75	0
1992 Pittsburgh	N.L.	11	23	2	0	1.000	10	4	22	3.52	1
1993 Pittsburgh	N.L.	32	210⅓	10	10	.500	132	59	207	3.89	0
1994 Pittsburgh	N.L.	25	134⅓	4	11	.267	74	46	157	5.02	0
1995 Augusta a	So. Atl.	1	5	1	0	1.000	6	1	2	0.00	0
1995 Carolina	Southern	1	5	0	0	.000	4	5	5	7.20	0
1996 Pittsburgh	N.L.	3	8⅓	0	0	.000	7	5	11	7.56	0
1996 Carolina	Southern	12	53⅔	1	5	.167	45	26	56	4.53	0
1997 Pittsburgh b-c	N.L.	32	167⅓	9	15	.375	109	77	184	4.30	0
Major League Totals ....5 Yrs.		103	543⅔	25	36	.410	332	191	581	4.34	1

a On disabled list entire 1995 season through June 19, 1996.
b Released by Pittsburgh Pirates, December 15, 1997.
c Signed as free agent with Cincinnati Reds, December 22, 1997.

CORDOVA, FRANCISCO

Born, Veracruz, Mexico, April 26, 1972.
Bats Right. Throws Right. Height, 5 feet, 11 inches. Weight, 163 pounds.

Year	Club	Lea	G	IP	W	L	Pct	SO	BB	H	ERA	SAVES
1992 Mex. City Reds	Mex.	16	28	3	0	1.000	14	14	28	5.79	0
1993 Mex. City Reds	Mex.	43	106	9	2	.818	71	47	96	3.23	4
1994 Mex. City Reds	Mex.	41	150⅓	15	4	.789	104	43	122	2.33	8
1995 Mex. City Reds	Mex.	27	125	13	0	1.000	88	42	131	3.10	4
1996 Pittsburgh a	N.L.	59	99	4	7	.364	95	20	103	4.09	12
1997 Pittsburgh b-c	N.L.	29	178⅔	11	8	.579	121	49	175	3.63	0
Major League Totals ....2 Yrs.		88	277⅔	15	15	.500	216	69	278	3.79	12

a Signed by Pittsburgh Pirates as non-drafted free agent, January 18, 1996.
b Pitched first 9 innings of combined no-hitter (with Ricardo Rincon) against Houston Astros, winning 3-0 in 10 innings, July 12, 1997.
c On disabled list from August 22 to September 6, 1997.

CORMIER, RHEAL PAUL

Born, Moncton, New Brunswick, Canada, April 23, 1967.
Bats Left. Throws Left. Height, 5 feet, 10 inches. Weight, 185 pounds.

Year Club	Lea	G	IP	W	L	Pct	SO	BB	H	ERA	SAVES
1989 St. Petersburg	Fla. St.	26	169⅔	12	7	.632	122	33	141	2.23	0
1990 Arkansas	Texas	22	121⅓	5	12	.294	102	30	133	5.04	0
1990 Louisville	A.A.	4	24	1	1	.500	9	3	18	2.25	0
1991 Louisville	A.A.	21	127⅔	7	9	.438	74	31	140	4.23	0
1991 St. Louis	N.L.	11	67⅔	4	5	.444	38	8	74	4.12	0
1992 Louisville	A.A.	1	4	0	1	.000	1	0	8	6.75	0
1992 St. Louis	N.L.	31	186	10	10	.500	117	33	194	3.68	0
1993 St. Louis a	N.L.	38	145⅓	7	6	.538	75	27	163	4.33	0
1994 Arkansas	Texas	2	9⅓	1	0	1.000	11	0	9	1.93	0
1994 Louisville	A.A.	3	22	1	2	.333	13	8	21	4.50	0
1994 St. Louis b	N.L.	7	39⅔	3	2	.600	26	7	40	5.45	0
1995 Boston c-d	A.L.	48	115	7	5	.583	69	31	131	4.07	0
1996 Montreal e	N.L.	33	159⅔	7	10	.412	100	41	165	4.17	0
1997 Montreal f-g-h	N.L.	1	1⅓	0	1	.000	0	1	4	33.75	0
Major League Totals 7 Yrs.		169	714⅔	38	39	.494	425	148	771	4.18	0
Division Series											
1995 Boston	A.L.	2	0⅔	0	0	.000	2	1	2	13.50	0

a On disabled list from August 18 to September 7, 1993.
b On disabled list from April 28 to May 12 and May 21 to July 31, 1994.
c Traded to Boston Red Sox with outfielder Mark Whiten for infielder Scott Cooper, pitcher Cory Bailey and player to be named later, April 8, 1995.
d Traded to Montreal Expos with first baseman Ryan McGuire and pitcher Shayne Bennett for infielder/outfielder Wil Cordero and pitcher Bryan Eversgerd, January 10, 1966.
e On disabled list from August 23 to September 10, 1996.
f On disabled list from April 6 to September 29, 1997.
g Filed for free agency, October 30, 1997.
h Signed with Cleveland Indians organization, December 18, 1997.

CORSI, JAMES BERNARD (JIM)

Born, Newton, Massachusetts, September 9, 1961.
Bats Right. Throws Right. Height, 6 feet, 1 inch. Weight, 220 pounds.

Year Club	Lea	G	IP	W	L	Pct	SO	BB	H	ERA	SAVES
1982 Oneonta	N.Y.-Penn.	1	3	0	0	.000	6	2	5	0.00	0
1982 Paintsville	Appal.	8	31	0	2	.000	20	13	32	2.90	0
1983 Greensboro	So. Atl.	12	50	2	2	.500	37	33	59	4.14	1
1983 Oneonta a	N.Y.-Penn.	11	59	3	6	.333	47	21	76	4.27	0
1984 b					Out of Organized Baseball						
1985 Greensboro	So. Atl.	41	78⅔	5	8	.385	84	23	94	4.23	9
1986 New Britain	Eastern	29	51⅓	2	3	.400	38	20	52	2.28	3
1987 Modesto c	California	19	30	3	1	.750	45	10	23	3.60	6
1987 Huntsville	Southern	28	48	8	1	.889	33	15	30	2.81	4
1988 Tacoma	P.C.	50	59	2	5	.286	48	23	60	2.75	16
1988 Oakland	A.L.	11	21⅓	0	1	.000	10	6	20	3.80	0
1989 Tacoma	P.C.	23	28⅓	2	3	.400	23	9	40	4.13	8
1989 Oakland	A.L.	22	38⅓	1	2	.333	21	10	26	1.88	0
1990 Tacoma d-e	P.C.	5	6	0	0	.000	3	1	9	1.50	0
1991 Tucson	P.C.	2	3	0	0	.000	4	0	2	0.00	0
1991 Houston f	N.L.	47	77⅔	0	5	.000	53	23	76	3.71	0
1992 Tacoma	P.C.	26	29⅓	0	0	.000	21	10	22	1.23	12
1992 Oakland g	A.L.	32	44	4	2	.667	19	18	44	1.43	0
1993 High Desert	California	3	9	0	1	.000	6	2	11	3.00	0
1993 Florida h-i	N.L.	15	20⅓	0	2	.000	7	10	28	6.64	0
1994 Brevard City	Fla. St.	6	11	0	1	.000	11	0	8	1.64	0
1994 Edmonton	P.C.	15	22	0	1	.000	15	10	29	4.50	0
1995 Edmonton	P.C.	3	3	0	0	.000	3	1	0	0.00	3
1995 Oakland j	A.L.	38	45	2	4	.333	26	26	31	2.20	2
1996 Modesto	California	1	1	0	0	.000	2	0	0	0.00	0
1996 Oakland k-l	A.L.	56	73⅔	6	0	1.000	43	34	71	4.03	3
1997 Pawtucket	Int.	2	2⅓	0	0	.000	3	1	2	0.00	1
1997 Red Sox	Gulf Coast	3	4	1	0	1.000	6	0	2	0.00	0
1997 Boston m-n-o	A.L.	52	57⅔	5	3	.625	40	21	56	3.43	2
Major League Totals 8 Yrs.		273	378	18	19	.486	219	148	352	3.26	7

a On disabled list from April 11 to May 11, 1983.
b Released by New York Yankees, April 10, 1984; signed with Boston Red Sox organization, April 1, 1985.
c Released by Boston Red Sox, April 2; signed with Oakland Athletics organization, April 12, 1987.
d On disabled list from March 29 to end of 1990 season.
e Not offered 1991 contract, December 20, 1990; signed with Houston Astros, January 31, 1991.

f Released, November 19, 1991; signed with Oakland Athletics organization, March 16, 1992.
g Selected by Florida Marlins in expansion draft, November 17, 1992.
h On disabled list from April 1 to April 30 and July 6 to end of the 1993 season.
i Became free agent, October 15, 1993; re-signed with Florida Marlins, January 24, 1994.
j On disabled list from June 22 to August 8, 1995.
k On disabled list from April 28 to May 19, 1996.
l Filed for free agency, November 4, 1996.
m On disabled list from June 2 to July 1, 1997.
n Filed for free agency, November 3, 1997.
o Re-signed with Boston Red Sox, December 4, 1997.

CRABTREE, TIMOTHY LYLE (TIM)
Born, Jackson, Michigan, October 13, 1969.
Bats Right. Throws Right. Height, 6 feet, 4 inches. Weight, 205 pounds.

Year	Club	Lea	G	IP	W	L	Pct	SO	BB	H	ERA	SAVES
1992	St. Catharines	N.Y.-Penn.	12	69	6	3	.667	47	22	45	1.57	0
1992	Knoxville	Southern	3	19	0	2	.000	13	4	14	0.95	0
1993	Knoxville	Southern	27	158²/₃	9	14	.391	67	59	178	4.08	0
1994	Syracuse	Int.	51	108	2	6	.250	58	49	125	4.17	2
1995	Syracuse	Int.	26	31¹/₃	0	2	.000	22	12	38	5.40	5
1995	Toronto	A.L.	31	32	0	2	.000	21	13	30	3.09	0
1996	Toronto a	A.L.	53	67¹/₃	5	3	.625	57	22	59	2.54	1
1997	St. Cathrnes	N.Y.-Penn.	2	3	0	0	.000	3	0	3	3.00	0
1997	Syracuse	Int.	3	3²/₃	0	0	.000	3	1	7	9.82	1
1997	Toronto b	A.L.	37	40²/₃	3	3	.500	26	17	65	7.08	2
Major League Totals	3 Yrs.		121	140	8	8	.500	104	52	154	3.99	3

a On disabled list from August 16 to September 6, 1996.
b On disabled list from June 4 to August 4, 1997.

CREEK, PAUL DOUGLAS (DOUG)
Born, Winchester, Virginia, March 1, 1969.
Bats Left. Throws Left. Height, 5 feet, 10 inches. Weight, 205 pounds.

Year	Club	Lea	G	IP	W	L	Pct	SO	BB	H	ERA	SAVES
1991	Hamilton	N.Y.-Penn.	9	38²/₃	3	2	.600	45	18	39	5.12	1
1991	Savannah	So.Atl.	5	28¹/₃	2	1	.667	32	17	24	4.45	0
1992	Springfield	Midwest	6	38¹/₃	4	1	.800	43	13	32	2.58	0
1992	St.Petersburg	Fla.St.	13	73¹/₃	5	4	.556	63	37	57	2.82	0
1993	Arkansas	Texas	25	147²/₃	11	10	.524	128	48	142	4.02	0
1993	Louisville	A.A.	2	14	0	0	.000	9	9	10	3.21	0
1994	Louisville	A.A.	7	26¹/₃	1	4	.200	16	23	37	8.54	0
1994	Arkansas	Texas	17	92	3	10	.231	65	36	96	4.40	0
1995	Arkansas	Texas	26	34¹/₃	4	2	.667	50	16	24	2.88	1
1995	Louisville	A.A.	26	30²/₃	3	2	.600	29	21	20	3.23	0
1995	St. Louis	N.L.	6	6²/₃	0	0	.000	10	3	2	0.00	0
1996	San Francisco	N.L.	63	48¹/₃	0	2	.000	38	32	45	6.52	0
1997	San Francisco	N.L.	3	13¹/₃	1	2	.333	14	14	12	6.75	0
1997	Phoenix a	P.C.	25	129²/₃	8	6	.571	137	66	140	4.93	0
Major League Totals	3 Yrs.		72	68¹/₃	1	4	.200	62	49	59	5.93	0

a Sold to Chicago White Sox, November 7, 1997.

CROWELL, JAMES E.
Born, Minneapolis, Minnesota, May 14, 1974.
Bats Left. Throws Left. Height, 6 feet, 4 inches. Weight, 225 pounds.

Year	Club	Lea	G	IP	W	L	Pct	SO	BB	H	ERA	SAVES
1995	Watertown	N.Y.-Penn.	12	56²/₃	5	2	.714	48	27	50	2.86	0
1996	Columbus	So. Atl.	28	165¹/₃	7	10	.412	104	69	163	4.14	0
1997	Kinston	Carolina	17	114	9	4	.692	94	26	96	2.37	0
1997	Akron a	Eastern	3	18	1	0	1.000	7	11	13	4.50	0
1997	Chattanooga	Southern	3	19	2	1	.667	14	5	19	2.84	0
1997	Indianapls	A.A.	3	19²/₃	1	1	.500	6	8	19	2.75	0
1997	Cincinnati	N.L.	2	6¹/₃	0	1	.000	3	5	12	9.95	0

a Traded by Cleveland Indians to Cincinnati Reds with pitcher Danny Graves, pitcher Scott Winchester and infielder Damian Jackson for pitcher John Smiley and infielder Jeff Branson, July 31, 1997.

CUNNANE, WILLIAM JOSEPH (WILL)
Born, Suffern, New York, April 24, 1974.
Bats Right. Throws Right. Height, 6 feet, 2 inches. Weight, 175 pounds.

Year	Club	Lea	G	IP	W	L	Pct	SO	BB	H	ERA	SAVES
1993 Marlins	....	Gulf Coast	16	66⅔	3	3	.500	64	8	75	2.70	2
1994 Kane County	....	Midwest	32	138⅔	11	3	.786	106	23	110	1.43	1
1995 Portland	....	Eastern	21	117⅔	9	2	.818	83	34	120	3.67	0
1996 Portland a	....	Eastern	25	151⅔	10	12	.455	101	30	156	3.74	0
1997 San Diego	....	N.L.	54	91⅓	6	3	.667	79	49	114	5.81	0

a Drafted by San Diego Padres from Florida Marlins organization in Rule V draft, December 9, 1996.

DAAL (CORDERO), OMAR JESUS
Born, Maracaibo, Venezuela, March 1, 1972.
Bats Left. Throws Left. Height, 6 feet, 3 inches. Weight 175 pounds.

Year	Club	Lea	G	IP	W	L	Pct	SO	BB	H	ERA	SAVES
1990-91	....			Played in Dominican Summer League								
1992 Albuquerque	....	P.C.	12	10⅓	0	2	.000	9	11	14	7.84	0
1992 San Antonio	....	Texas	35	57⅓	2	6	.250	52	33	60	5.02	5
1993 Albuquerque	....	P.C.	6	5⅓	1	1	.500	2	3	5	3.38	2
1993 Los Angeles	....	N.L.	47	35⅓	2	3	.400	19	21	36	5.09	0
1994 Albuquerque	....	P.C.	11	34⅔	4	2	.667	28	16	38	5.19	1
1994 Los Angeles	....	N.L.	24	13⅔	0	0	.000	9	5	12	3.29	0
1995 Albuquerque	....	P.C.	17	53⅓	2	3	.400	46	26	56	4.05	1
1995 Los Angeles a	....	N.L.	28	20	4	0	1.000	11	15	29	7.20	0
1996 Montreal	....	N.L.	64	87⅓	4	5	.444	82	37	74	4.02	0
1997 Ottawa	....	Int.	2	8	0	1	.000	9	1	10	5.63	0
1997 Syracuse	....	Int.	5	33⅔	3	0	1.000	29	10	18	0.53	0
1997 Montreal	....	N.L.	33	30⅓	1	2	.333	16	15	48	9.79	1
1997 Toronto b-c	....	A.L.	9	27	1	1	.500	28	6	34	4.00	0

| Major League Totals | .... | 5 Yrs. | 205 | 213⅔ | 12 | 11 | .522 | 165 | 99 | 233 | 5.27 | 1 |

a Traded to Montreal Expos for pitcher Rick Clelland, December 15, 1995.
b Claimed on waivers by Toronto Blue Jays, July 24, 1997.
c Selected in expansion draft by Arizona Diamondbacks, November 18, 1997.

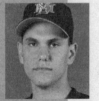

D'AMICO, JEFFREY CHARLES (JEFF)
Born, St. Petersburg, Florida, December 27, 1975.
Bats Right. Throws Right. Height, 6 feet, 7 inches. Weight, 250 pounds.

Year	Club	Lea	G	IP	W	L	Pct	SO	BB	H	ERA	SAVES
1995 Beloit	....	Midwest	21	132	13	3	.813	119	31	102	2.39	0
1996 El Paso	....	Texas	13	96	5	4	.556	76	13	89	3.19	0
1996 Milwaukee	....	A.L.	17	86	6	6	.500	53	31	88	5.44	0
1997 Beloit	....	Midwest	1	3	0	0	.000	7	1	0	0.00	0
1997 Milwaukee a	....	A.L.	23	135⅔	9	7	.563	94	43	139	4.71	0

| Major League Totals | .... | 2 Yrs. | 40 | 221⅔ | 15 | 13 | .536 | 147 | 74 | 227 | 4.99 | 0 |

a On disabled list from July 19 to September 2, 1997.

DARWIN, DANNY WAYNE
Born, Bonham, Texas, October 25, 1955.
Bats Right. Throws Right. Height, 6 feet, 3 inches. Weight, 195 pounds.

Year	Club	Lea	G	IP	W	L	Pct	SO	BB	H	ERA	SAVES
1976 Asheville	....	W. Carolinas	16	102	6	3	.667	76	48	96	3.62	0
1977 Tulsa a	....	Texas	23	154	13	4	.765	129	72	130	2.51	0
1978 Tucson	....	P.C.	23	125	8	9	.471	126	83	147	6.26	0
1978 Texas	....	A.L.	3	9	1	0	1.000	8	1	11	4.00	0
1979 Tucson	....	P.C.	13	95	6	6	.500	65	42	89	3.60	0
1979 Texas	....	A.L.	20	78	4	4	.500	58	30	50	4.04	0
1980 Texas b	....	A.L.	53	110	13	4	.765	104	50	98	2.62	8
1981 Texas	....	A.L.	22	146	9	9	.500	98	57	115	3.64	0
1982 Texas	....	A.L.	56	89	10	8	.556	61	37	95	3.44	7
1983 Texas c	....	A.L.	28	183	8	13	.381	92	62	175	3.49	0
1984 Texas d	....	A.L.	35	223⅔	8	12	.400	123	54	249	3.94	1
1985 Milwaukee e	....	A.L.	39	217⅔	8	18	.308	125	65	212	3.80	2
1986 Milwaukee f	....	A.L.	27	130⅓	6	8	.429	80	35	120	3.52	0
1986 Houston	....	N.L.	12	54⅓	5	2	.714	40	9	50	2.32	0
1987 Houston g	....	N.L.	33	195⅔	9	10	.474	134	69	184	3.59	0

Year Club	Lea	G	IP	W	L	Pct	SO	BB	H	ERA	SAVES
1988 Houston . . . . .N.L.		44	192	8	13	.381	129	48	189	3.84	3
1989 Houston . . . . .N.L.		68	122	11	4	.733	104	33	92	2.36	7
1990 Houston h-i . . . . .N.L.		48	162⅔	11	4	.733	109	31	136	*2.21	2
1991 Boston j . . . . .A.L.		12	68	3	6	.333	42	15	71	5.16	0
1992 Boston . . . . .A.L.		51	161⅓	9	9	.500	124	53	159	3.96	3
1993 Boston . . . . .A.L.		34	229⅓	15	11	.577	130	49	196	3.26	0
1994 Boston k-l . . . . .A.L.		13	75⅔	7	5	.583	54	24	101	6.30	0
1995 Oklahoma City . . . . .A.A.		1	3	0	0	.000	4	0	1	0.00	0
1995 Toronto-Texas m-n-o-p .A.L.		20	99	3	10	.231	58	31	131	7.46	0
1996 Pittsburgh-Houston q-r-s .N.L.		34	164⅔	10	11	.476	96	27	160	3.77	0
1997 Chicago t . . . . .A.L.		21	113⅓	4	8	.333	62	31	130	4.13	0
1997 San Francisco u-v . . . . . .N.L.		10	44	1	3	.250	30	14	51	4.91	0
Major League Totals . . . . . . .20 Yrs.		683	2868	163	172	.487	1861	825	2775	3.75	32

a On disabled list from April 25 to May 4 and May 22 to June 11, 1977.
b On disabled list from June 5 to June 26, 1980.
c On disabled list from March 25 to April 10 and August 9 to September 1, 1983.
d Traded to Milwaukee Brewers as part of four team deal sending catcher Don Slaught from Kansas City Royals to Texas Rangers, catcher Jim Sundberg from Milwaukee to Kansas City, pitcher Tim Leary from the New York Mets to Kansas City and then to Milwaukee, pitcher Fred Wills from Kansas City to New York, January 18, 1985, and catcher Bill Hance from Texas to Milwaukee to complete deal, January 30, 1985.
e Filed for free agency, November 12; re-signed with Milwaukee Brewers, December 22, 1985.
f Traded to Houston Astros for pitchers Don August and Mark Knudson, August 15, 1985.
g Filed for free agency, October 27, 1987; re-signed with Houston Astros, January 8, 1988.
h Appeared in four additional games as pinch runner.
i Granted special free agency by arbitrator, December 7; signed with Boston Red Sox, December 19, 1990.
j On disabled list from April 23 to May 22 and July 5 to end of 1991 season.
k On disabled list from June 16 to end of 1994 season.
l Filed for free agency, October 17, 1994.
m Signed with Toronto Blue Jays, April 10, 1995.
n Released by Toronto Blue Jays, July 18, 1995.
o Signed with Texas Rangers organization, July 31, 1995.
p Not offered 1996 contract, November 2, 1995.
q Signed with Pittsburgh Pirates organization, January 31, 1996.
r Traded to Houston Astros for pitcher Rich Loiselle, July 23, 1996.
s Signed with Chicago White Sox organization, February 6, 1997.
t Traded to San Francisco Giants with pitcher Wilson Alvarez and pitcher Roberto Hernandez for infielder Mike Caruso, outfielder Brian Manning, pitcher Lorenzo Barcelo, pitcher Keith Foulke, pitcher Bob Howry and pitcher Ken Vining, July 31, 1997.
u Filed for free agency, October 30, 1997.
v Re-signed with San Francisco Giants, December 5, 1997.

DAVIS, TIMOTHY HOWARD
Born, Marianna, Florida, July 14, 1970.
Bats Left. Throws Left. Height, 5 feet, 11 inches. Weight, 165 pounds.

Year Club	Lea	G	IP	W	L	Pct	SO	BB	H	ERA	SAVES
1993 Appleton . . . . .Midwest		16	77⅔	10	2	.833	89	33	54	1.85	2
1993 Riverside . . . . .California		18	30⅔	3	0	1.000	56	9	14	1.76	7
1994 Calgary . . . . .P.C.		6	39⅓	3	1	.750	43	8	35	1.82	0
1994 Seattle . . . . .A.L.		42	49⅓	2	2	.500	28	25	57	4.01	2
1995 Tacoma . . . . .P.C.		2	13⅓	0	1	.000	13	4	15	5.40	0
1995 Seattle a . . . . .A.L.		5	24	2	1	.667	19	18	30	6.38	0
1996 Everett . . . . .Northwest		1	2	0	0	.000	5	1	0	0.00	0
1996 Tacoma . . . . .P.C.		8	17	0	1	.000	19	10	19	5.29	0
1996 Seattle b . . . . .A.L.		40	42⅔	2	2	.500	34	17	43	4.01	0
1997 Tacoma . . . . .P.C.		1	5	1	0	1.000	5	3	4	3.60	0
1997 Seattle c . . . . .A.L.		2	6⅔	0	0	.000	10	4	6	6.75	0
Major League Totals . . . . .4 Yrs.		89	122⅔	6	5	.545	91	64	136	4.62	2

a On disabled list from September 8 to October 3, 1995.
b On disabled list from May 27 to July 11, 1996.
c On disabled list from April 24 to September 29, 1997.

DEHART, RICK ALLEN
Born, Topeka, Kansas, March 21, 1970.
Bats Left. Throws Left. Height, 6 feet, 1 inch. Weight, 180 pounds.

Year Club	Lea	G	IP	W	L	Pct	SO	BB	H	ERA	SAVES
1992 Albany . . . . .So. Atl.		38	117	9	6	.600	133	40	91	2.46	3
1993 San Berndno . . . . . .California		9	53⅓	4	3	.571	44	25	56	3.04	0
1993 Harrisburg . . . . .Eastern		12	34	2	4	.333	18	19	45	7.68	0
1993 Wst Plm Bch . . . . .Fla. St.		7	42	1	3	.250	33	17	42	3.00	0

Year	Club	Lea	G	IP	W	L	Pct	SO	BB	H	ERA	SAVES
1994 Wst Plm Bch	Fla. St.	30	136⅓	9	7	.563	88	34	132	3.37	0
1995 Harrisburg	Eastern	35	93	6	7	.462	64	39	94	4.84	0
1996 Harrisburg	Eastern	30	43⅔	1	2	.333	30	19	46	2.68	1
1997 Ottawa	Int.	43	63	0	4	.000	57	22	60	4.00	2
1997 Montreal	N.L.	23	29⅓	2	1	.667	29	14	33	5.52	0

DEJEAN, MICHEL DWAIN
Born, Baton Rouge, Louisiana, September 28, 1970.
Bats Right. Throws Right. Height, 6 feet, 2 inches. Weight, 205 pounds.

Year	Club	Lea	G	IP	W	L	Pct	SO	BB	H	ERA	SAVES
1992 Oneonta	N.Y.-Penn.	20	20⅔	0	0	.000	20	3	12	0.44	16
1993 Greensboro	So. Atl.	20	18	2	3	.400	16	8	22	5.00	9
1994 Tampa	Fla. St.	34	34	0	2	.000	22	13	39	2.38	16
1994 Albany	Eastern	16	24⅔	0	2	.000	13	15	22	4.38	4
1995 Norwich	Eastern	59	78⅓	5	5	.500	57	34	58	2.99	20
1996 New Haven a	Eastern	16	22⅓	0	0	.000	12	8	20	3.22	11
1996 Colo Sprngs	P.C.	30	40⅓	0	2	.000	31	21	52	5.13	1
1997 Colo Sprngs	P.C.	10	10	0	1	.000	9	7	17	5.40	4
1997 New Haven	Eastern	2	3	0	1	.000	2	2	3	6.00	0
1997 Colorado b	N.L.	55	67⅔	5	0	1.000	38	24	74	3.99	2

a Traded by New York Yankees to Colorado Rockies with pitcher Steve Shoemaker for catcher Joe Girardi, November 20, 1995.
b On disabled list from July 18 to August 8, 1997.

DELA MAZA, ROLAND ROBERT
Born, Granada Hills, California, November 11, 1971.
Bats Right. Throws Right. Height, 6 feet, 2 inches. Weight, 195 pounds.

Year	Club	Lea	G	IP	W	L	Pct	SO	BB	H	ERA	SAVES
1993 Watertown	N.Y.-Penn.	15	100	10	3	.769	81	14	90	2.52	0
1994 Columbus	So. Atl.	21	112⅔	13	2	.867	97	25	102	2.96	0
1995 Canton-Akrn	Eastern	7	37⅓	2	1	.667	27	18	35	4.10	0
1995 Kinston	Carolina	26	110⅓	6	0	1.000	100	28	99	2.37	1
1996 Canton-Akrn	Eastern	40	139⅔	9	7	.563	132	49	122	4.38	1
1997 Buffalo a	A.A.	34	115	9	4	.692	73	43	104	2.90	2
1997 Kansas City	A.L.	1	2	0	0	.000	1	1	1	4.50	0

a Traded by Cleveland Indians organization to Kansas City Royals for outfielder Bip Roberts, August 31, 1997.

DELUCIA, RICHARD ANTHONY
Born, Reading, Pennsylvania, October 7, 1964.
Bats Right. Throws Right. Height, 6 feet. Weight, 185 pounds.

Year	Club	Lea	G	IP	W	L	Pct	SO	BB	H	ERA	SAVES
1986 Bellingham	Northwest	13	74	8	2	.800	69	24	44	*1.70	0
1987 Salinas a	California	1	1	0	0	.000	1	0	2	9.00	0
1988 San Bernardino	California	22	127⅔	7	8	.467	118	58	110	3.10	0
1989 Williamsport b	Eastern	10	54⅔	3	4	.429	41	13	59	3.79	0
1990 San Bernardino	California	5	30⅔	4	1	.800	35	3	19	2.05	0
1990 Williamsport	Eastern	18	115	6	6	.500	76	30	92	2.11	0
1990 Calgary	P.C.	5	32⅓	2	2	.500	23	12	30	3.62	0
1990 Seattle	A.L.	5	36	1	2	.333	20	9	30	2.00	0
1991 Seattle	A.L.	32	182	12	13	.480	98	78	176	5.09	0
1992 Seattle c	A.L.	30	83⅔	3	6	.333	66	35	100	5.49	1
1992 Calgary	P.C.	8	40⅓	4	2	.667	38	14	32	2.45	1
1993 Seattle d	A.L.	30	42⅔	3	6	.333	48	23	46	4.64	0
1993 Calgary e	P.C.	8	44	1	5	.167	38	20	45	5.73	1
1994 Indianapolis f-g	A.A.	36	43	5	1	.833	52	24	22	2.30	19
1994 Cincinnati	N.L.	8	10⅔	0	0	.000	15	5	9	4.22	0
1995 St. Louis h	N.L.	56	82⅓	8	7	.533	76	36	63	3.39	0
1996 San Jose	California	5	7⅓	0	0	.000	11	3	5	2.45	0
1996 San Francisco i	N.L.	56	61⅔	3	6	.333	55	31	62	5.84	0
1997 San Francisco j	N.L.	3	1⅔	0	0	.000	2	0	6	10.80	0
1997 Anaheim k-l-m	A.L.	33	42⅓	6	4	.600	42	27	29	3.61	3
Major League Totals	8 Yrs.	253	543	36	44	.450	422	244	521	4.62	4

a On disabled list from April 10 to end of 1987 season.
b On disabled list from May 31 to July 2 and July 7 to end of 1989 season.

232

c On disabled list from August 5 to September 1, 1992.
d On disabled list from June 28 to July 22, 1993.
e Released by Seattle Mariners, March 29; signed with Cincinnati Reds organization, April 3, 1994.
f Became free agent, October 15; signed with Baltimore Orioles organization, November 17, 1994.
g Drafted by St. Louis Cardinals from Baltimore Orioles organization, December 5, 1994.
h Traded by St. Louis Cardinals to San Francisco Giants with pitchers Allen Watson and Doug Creek for infielder Royce Clayton, December 14, 1995.
i On disabled list from April 1 to May 2 and July 27 to August 23, 1996.
j Traded to Anaheim Angels for player to be named later, April 14, 1997. San Francisco Giants received pitcher Travis Thurmond to complete trade, May 22, 1997.
k On disabled list from July 15 to September 2, 1997.
l Filed for free agency, November 3, 1997.
m Re-signed with Anaheim Angels, December 7, 1997.

DESSENS, ELMER

Born, Hermosillo, Mexico, January 13, 1972.
Bats Right. Throws Right. Height, 6 feet. Weight, 190 pounds.

Year	Club	Lea	G	IP	W	L	Pct	SO	BB	H	ERA	SAVES
1994 Mexico	Mexican		37	127²/₃	11	4	.733	51	32	121	2.04	3
1995 Carolina	Southern		27	152	15	8	.652	68	21	170	2.49	0
1996 Calgary	P.C.		6	34¹/₃	2	2	.500	15	15	40	3.15	0
1996 Carolina	Southern		5	11²/₃	0	1	.000	7	4	15	5.40	0
1996 Pittsburgh a	N.L.		15	25	0	2	.000	13	4	40	8.28	0
1997 Pittsburgh	N.L.		3	3¹/₃	0	0	.000	2	0	2	0.00	0
Major League Totals	2 Yrs.		18	28¹/₃	0	2	.000	15	4	42	7.31	0

a On disabled list from July 31 to September 10, 1996.

DICKSON, JASON ROYCE

Born, London, Ontario, Canada, March 30, 1973.
Bats Left. Throws Right. Height, 6 feet. Weight, 190 pounds.

Year	Club	Lea	G	IP	W	L	Pct	SO	BB	H	ERA	SAVES
1994 Boise	Northwest		9	44¹/₃	3	1	.750	37	18	40	3.86	1
1995 Cedar Rapids	Midwest		25	173	14	6	.700	134	45	151	2.86	0
1996 Midland	Texas		8	55¹/₃	5	2	.714	40	10	55	3.58	0
1996 Vancouver	P.C.		18	130¹/₃	7	11	.389	70	40	134	3.80	0
1996 California	A.L.		7	43¹/₃	1	4	.200	20	18	52	4.57	0
1997 Anaheim	A.L.		33	203²/₃	13	9	.591	115	56	236	4.29	0
Major League Totals	2 Yrs.		40	247	14	13	.519	135	74	288	4.34	0

DIPOTO, GERARD PETER (JERRY)

Born, Jersey City, New Jersey, May 24, 1968.
Bats Right. Throws Right. Height, 6 feet, 2 inches. Weight, 200 pounds.

Year	Club	Lea	G	IP	W	L	Pct	SO	BB	H	ERA	SAVES
1989 Watertown	N.Y.-Penn.		14	87¹/₃	6	5	.545	98	39	75	3.61	0
1990 Kinston	Carolina		24	145¹/₃	11	4	.733	143	77	129	3.78	0
1990 Canton	Eastern		3	14	1	0	1.000	12	4	11	2.57	0
1991 Canton	Eastern		28	156	6	11	.353	97	74	143	3.81	0
1992 Colorado Springs	P.C.		50	122	9	9	.500	62	66	148	4.94	2
1993 Charlotte	Int.		34	46²/₃	6	3	.667	44	13	34	1.93	12
1993 Cleveland	A.L.		46	56¹/₃	4	4	.500	41	30	57	2.40	11
1994 Charlotte	Int.		25	34¹/₃	3	2	.600	26	12	37	3.15	9
1994 Cleveland a-b	A.L.		7	15²/₃	0	0	.000	9	10	26	8.04	0
1995 New York	N.L.		58	78²/₃	4	6	.400	49	29	77	3.78	2
1996 New York c	N.L.		57	77¹/₃	7	2	.778	52	45	91	4.19	0
1997 Colorado d	N.L.		74	95²/₃	5	3	.625	74	33	108	4.70	16
Major League Totals	5 Yrs.		242	323²/₃	20	15	.571	225	147	359	4.12	29

a On disabled list from March 25 to June 12, 1994.
b Traded to New York Mets with pitchers Dave Mlicki and Paul Byrd and player to be named for outfielder Jeromy Burnitz and pitcher Joe Roa, November 18; New York acquired second baseman Jesus Azuaje to complete trade, December 6, 1994.
c Traded to Colorado Rockies for pitcher Armando Reynoso, November 27, 1996.
c Outrighted by Detroit Tigers, October 23, 1997.
d Signed contract extension with Colorado Rockies, January 17, 1998.

DISHMAN, GLENELG EDWARD (GLENN)

Born, Baltimore, Maryland, November 5, 1970.
Bats Right. Throws Left. Height, 6 feet, 1 inch. Weight, 195 pounds.

Year	Club	Lea	G	IP	W	L	Pct	SO	BB	H	ERA	SAVES
1993	Spokane	Northwest	12	77²/₃	6	3	.667	79	13	59	2.20	0
1993	Rancho Cuca	California	2	11¹/₃	0	1	.000	6	5	14	7.15	0
1994	Wichita	Texas	27	169¹/₃	11	8	.579	165	42	156	2.82	0
1994	Las Vegas	P.C.	2	13	1	1	.500	12	1	15	3.46	0
1995	Las Vegas	P.C.	14	106	6	3	.667	64	20	91	2.55	0
1995	San Diego	N.L.	19	97	4	8	.333	43	34	104	5.01	0
1996	Las Vegas	P.C.	26	155	6	8	.429	115	43	177	5.57	0
1996	San Diego-Philadelphia a-b	N.L.	7	9¹/₃	0	0	.000	3	3	12	7.71	0
1997	Toledo	Int.	21	114	7	6	.538	77	32	112	3.87	1
1997	Detroit c-d	A.L.	7	29	1	2	.333	20	8	30	5.28	0
Major League Totals	3 Yrs.		33	135¹/₃	5	10	.333	66	45	146	5.25	0

a Claimed on waivers by Philadelphia Phillies, September 12, 1996.
b Claimed on waivers by Detroit Tigers, October 3, 1996.
c Outrighted by Detroit Tigers, October 23, 1997.
d Filed for free agency, November 19, 1997.

DRABEK, DOUGLAS DEAN

Born, Victoria, Texas, July 25, 1962.
Bats Right. Throws Right. Height, 6 feet, 1 inch. Weight, 185 pounds.

Year	Club	Lea	G	IP	W	L	Pct	SO	BB	H	ERA	SAVES
1983	Niagara Falls	N.Y.-Penn.	16	103²/₃	6	7	.462	103	48	99	3.65	0
1984	Appleton	Midwest	1	5	1	0	1.000	6	3	3	1.80	0
1984	Glens Falls a	Eastern	19	124²/₃	12	5	.706	75	44	90	2.24	0
1984	Nashville	Southern	4	31	1	2	.333	22	10	30	2.52	0
1985	Albany	Eastern	26	*192²/₃	13	7	.650	*153	55	153	2.99	0
1986	Columbus	Int.	8	42	1	4	.200	23	25	50	7.29	0
1986	New York b	A.L.	27	131²/₃	7	8	.467	76	50	126	4.10	0
1987	Pittsburgh c	N.L.	29	176¹/₃	11	12	.478	120	46	165	3.88	0
1988	Pittsburgh	N.L.	33	219¹/₃	15	7	.682	127	50	194	3.08	0
1989	Pittsburgh	N.L.	35	244¹/₃	14	12	.538	123	69	215	2.80	0
1990	Pittsburgh d	N.L.	33	231²/₃	*22	6	*.786	131	56	190	2.76	0
1991	Pittsburgh e	N.L.	35	234²/₃	15	14	.517	142	62	245	3.07	0
1992	Pittsburgh f-g	N.L.	34	256²/₃	15	11	.577	177	54	218	2.77	0
1993	Houston	N.L.	34	237²/₃	9	*18	.333	157	60	242	3.79	0
1994	Houston h	N.L.	23	164²/₃	12	6	.667	121	45	132	2.84	0
1995	Houston	N.L.	31	185	10	9	.526	143	54	205	4.77	0
1996	Houston i-j-k	N.L.	30	175¹/₃	7	9	.438	137	60	208	4.57	0
1997	Chicago l-m	A.L.	31	169¹/₃	12	11	.522	85	69	170	5.74	0
Major League Totals	12 Yrs.		375	2426¹/₃	149	123	.548	1539	675	2310	3.58	0

Championship Series

Year	Club	Lea	G	IP	W	L	Pct	SO	BB	H	ERA	SAVES
1990	Pittsburgh	N.L.	2	16¹/₃	1	1	.500	13	3	12	1.65	0
1991	Pittsburgh	N.L.	2	15	1	1	.500	10	5	10	0.60	0
1992	Pittsburgh	N.L.	3	17	0	3	.000	10	7	18	3.71	0
Championship Series Totals	7			48¹/₃	2	5	.286	33	15	40	2.05	0

a Traded by Chicago White Sox to New York Yankees organization with pitcher Kevin Hickey to complete July 18 trade in which Chicago acquired infielder Roy Smalley for two players to be named, August 13, 1984.
b Traded to Pittsburgh Pirates with pitchers Brian Fisher and Logan Easley for pitchers Rick Rhoden, Pat Clements and Cecilio Guante, November 26, 1986.
c On disabled list from April 26 to May 18, 1987.
d Selected Cy Young Award winner in National League for 1990.
e Appeared in one additional game as pinch runner.
f Appeared in one additional game as pinch hitter.
g Filed for free agency, October 26; signed with Houston Astros, December 1, 1992.
h Appeared in one additional game as pinch runner.
i On disabled list from August 23 to September 8, 1996.
j Filed for free agency, November 18, 1996.
k Signed with Chicago White Sox, January 14, 1997.
l Filed for free agency, October 30, 1997.
m Signed as free agent with Baltimore Orioles, December 11, 1997.

DREIFORT, DARREN JAMES

Born, Wichita, Kansas, May 18, 1972.

Bats Right. Throws Right. Height, 6 feet, 2 inches. Weight, 205 pounds.

Year Club	Lea	G	IP	W	L	Pct	SO	BB	H	ERA	SAVES
1994 San Antonio	Texas	8	35⅓	3	1	.750	32	13	36	2.80	0
1994 Albuquerque	P.C.	1	6⅓	1	0	1.000	3	3	8	5.68	0
1994 Los Angeles a	N.L.	27	29	0	5	.000	22	15	45	6.21	6
1995 Los Angeles b	N.L.			INJURED—Did Not Play							
1996 Albuquerque	P.C.	18	86⅓	5	6	.455	75	52	88	4.17	0
1996 Los Angeles c	N.L.	19	23⅔	1	4	.200	24	12	23	4.94	0
1997 Albuquerque	P.C.	2	5⅔	0	0	.000	3	1	2	1.59	0
1997 Los Angeles d	N.L.	48	63	5	2	.714	63	34	45	2.86	4
Major League Totals	3 Yrs.	94	115⅔	6	11	.353	109	61	113	4.12	10
Division Series											
1996 Los Angeles	N.L.	1	0⅔	0	0	.000	0	0	0	0.00	0

a Appeared in one additional game as pinch hitter.
b On disabled list entire 1995 season.
c On disabled list from April 1 to May 16, 1996.
d On disabled list from May 12 to June 17, 1997.

ECKERSLEY, DENNIS LEE

Born, Oakland, California, October 3, 1954.

Bats Right. Throws Right. Height, 6 feet, 2 inches. Weight, 195 pounds.

Year Club	Lea	G	IP	W	L	Pct	SO	BB	H	ERA	SAVES
1972 Reno	California	12	75	5	5	.500	56	33	87	4.80	0
1973 Reno	California	31	202	12	8	.600	218	91	182	3.65	0
1974 San Antonio	Texas	23	167	*14	3	*.824	*163	60	141	3.40	0
1975 Cleveland	A.L.	34	187	13	7	.650	152	90	147	2.60	2
1976 Cleveland	A.L.	36	199	13	12	.520	200	78	155	3.44	1
1977 Cleveland a-b	A.L.	33	247	14	13	.519	191	54	214	3.53	0
1978 Boston	A.L.	35	268	20	8	.714	162	71	258	2.99	0
1979 Boston	A.L.	33	247	17	10	.630	150	59	234	2.99	0
1980 Boston	A.L.	30	198	12	14	.462	121	44	188	4.27	0
1981 Boston	A.L.	23	154	9	8	.529	79	35	160	4.27	0
1982 Boston	A.L.	33	224⅓	13	13	.500	127	43	228	3.73	0
1983 Boston	A.L.	28	176⅓	9	13	.409	77	39	223	5.61	0
1984 Boston c	A.L.	9	64⅔	4	4	.500	33	13	71	5.01	0
1984 Chicago d	N.L.	24	160⅓	10	8	.556	81	36	152	3.03	0
1985 Chicago e	N.L.	25	169⅓	11	7	.611	117	19	145	3.08	0
1986 Chicago f	N.L.	33	201	6	11	.353	137	43	226	4.57	0
1987 Oakland	A.L.	54	115⅔	6	8	.429	113	17	99	3.03	16
1988 Oakland	A.L.	60	72⅔	4	2	.667	70	11	52	2.35	*45
1989 Oakland g	A.L.	51	57⅔	4	0	1.000	55	3	32	1.56	33
1990 Oakland	A.L.	63	73⅓	4	2	.667	73	4	41	0.61	48
1991 Oakland	A.L.	67	76	5	4	.556	87	9	60	2.96	43
1992 Oakland h	A.L.	69	80	7	1	.875	93	11	62	1.91	51
1993 Oakland	A.L.	64	67	2	4	.333	80	13	67	4.16	36
1994 Oakland i	A.L.	45	44⅓	5	4	.556	47	13	49	4.26	19
1995 Oakland j	A.L.	52	50⅓	4	6	.400	40	11	53	4.83	29
1996 St. Louis k	N.L.	63	60	0	6	.000	49	6	65	3.30	30
1997 St. Louis l-m	N.L.	57	53	1	5	.167	45	8	49	3.91	36
Major League Totals	23 Yrs.	1021	3246	193	170	.532	2379	730	3030	3.49	389
Division Series											
1996 St. Louis	N.L.	3	3⅔	0	0	.000	2	0	3	0.00	3
Championship Series											
1984 Chicago	N.L.	1	5⅓	0	1	.000	0	0	9	8.44	0
1988 Oakland	A.L.	4	6	0	0	.000	5	2	1	0.00	4
1989 Oakland	A.L.	4	5⅔	0	0	.000	2	0	4	1.59	3
1990 Oakland	A.L.	3	3⅓	0	0	.000	3	0	2	0.00	2
1992 Oakland	A.L.	3	3	0	0	.000	2	0	8	6.00	1
1996 St. Louis	N.L.	3	3⅓	1	0	1.000	4	0	2	0.00	1
Championship Series Totals		18	26⅔	1	1	.500	16	2	26	2.70	11
World Series Record											
1988 Oakland	A.L.	2	1⅔	0	1	.000	2	1	2	10.80	0
1989 Oakland	A.L.	2	1⅔	0	0	.000	0	0	0	0.00	1
1990 Oakland	A.L.	2	1⅓	0	1	.000	1	0	3	6.75	0
World Series Totals		6	4⅔	0	2	.000	3	1	5	5.79	1

a Pitched no-hit, no-run game against California Angels, winning 1-0, May 30, 1977.
b Traded to Boston Red Sox with catcher Fred Kendall for catcher Bo Diaz, infielder Ted Cox and pitchers Mike Paxton and Rick Wise, March 30, 1978.
c Traded to Chicago Cubs with infielder Mike Brumley for first baseman Bill Buckner, May 25, 1984.
d Opted for free agency in Re-Entry Draft, November 8; re-signed with Chicago Cubs, November 28, 1984.
e On disabled list from August 11 to end of 1985 season.
f Traded to Oakland Athletics for outfielder Dave Wilder, April 3, 1987.
g On disabled list from May 29 to July 13, 1989.
h Selected Most Valuable Player and Cy Young Award winner in American League for 1992.
i Filed for free agency, October 22, 1994.
j Re-signed with Oakland Athletics, April 3, 1995.
k On disabled list from May 19 to June 13, 1996.
l Filed for free agency, October 29, 1997.
m Signed as free agent with Boston Red Sox, December 9, 1997.

EISCHEN, JOSEPH RAYMOND

Born, West Covina, California, May 25, 1970.
Bats Left. Throws Left. Height, 6 feet, 1 inch. Weight, 190 pounds.

Year	Club	Lea	G	IP	W	L	Pct	SO	BB	H	ERA	SAVES
1989 Butte	Pioneer	12	52⅔	3	7	.300	57	38	50	5.30	0
1990 Gastonia	So. Atl.	17	73⅓	3	7	.300	69	40	51	2.70	0
1991 Charlotte-W.Palm B. a	Fla. St.	26	142⅔	8	12	.400	106	79	134	3.87	0
1992 West Palm Beach	Fla. St.	27	169⅔	9	8	.529	167	*83	128	3.08	0
1993 Harrisburg	Eastern	20	119⅓	14	4	.778	110	60	122	3.62	0
1993 Ottawa	Int.	6	40⅔	2	2	.500	29	15	34	3.54	0
1994 Ottawa	Int.	48	62	2	6	.250	57	40	54	4.94	2
1994 Montreal	N.L.	1	⅔	0	0	.000	1	0	4	54.00	0
1995 Ottawa	Int.	11	15⅔	2	1	.667	13	8	9	1.72	0
1995 Albuquerque	P.C.	13	16⅓	3	0	1.000	14	3	8	0.00	2
1995 Los Angeles b	N.L.	17	20⅓	0	0	.000	15	11	19	3.10	0
1996 Los Angeles	N.L.	28	43⅓	0	1	.000	36	20	48	4.78	0
1996 Detroit c	A.L.	24	25	1	1	.500	15	14	27	3.24	0
1997 Cincinnati d-e-f	N.L.	1	1⅓	0	0	.000	2	1	2	6.75	0
1997 Indianapolis	A.A.	26	42⅔	1	0	1.000	26	13	41	1.27	2
Major League Totals	4 Yrs.	71	90⅔	1	2	.333	69	46	100	4.37	0

a Traded by Texas Rangers to Montreal Expos organization with pitchers Travis Buckley and Jonathan Hurst for pitcher Dennis (Oil Can) Boyd, July 21, 1989.
b Traded to Los Angeles Dodgers with outfielder Roberto Kelly for outfielder Henry Rodriquez and infielder Jeff Treadway, May 24, 1995.
c Traded to Detroit Tigers with pitcher John Cummings for outfielder Chad Curtis, July 31, 1996.
d Traded to Cincinnati Reds for player to be named later, March 16, 1997. San Diego Padres received infielder Ray Brown to complete trade, March 19, 1997.
e On disabled list from April 1 to April 26 and April 29 to September 29, 1997.
f Released by Cincinnati Reds, December 19, 1997.

ELDRED, CALVIN JOHN

Born, Cedar Rapids, Iowa, November 24, 1967.
Bats Right. Throws Right. Height, 6 feet, 4 inches. Weight, 235 pounds.

Year	Club	Lea	G	IP	W	L	Pct	SO	BB	H	ERA	SAVES
1989 Beloit	Midwest	5	31⅓	2	1	.667	32	11	23	2.30	0
1990 Stockton	California	7	50	4	2	.667	75	19	31	1.62	0
1990 El Paso	Texas	19	110⅓	5	4	.556	93	47	126	4.49	0
1991 Denver	A.A.	29	*185	13	9	.591	*168	84	161	3.75	0
1991 Milwaukee	A.L.	3	16	2	0	1.000	10	6	20	4.50	0
1992 Denver	A.A.	19	141	10	6	.625	99	42	122	3.00	0
1992 Milwaukee	A.L.	14	100⅓	11	2	.846	62	23	76	1.79	0
1993 Milwaukee	A.L.	36	*258	16	16	.500	180	91	232	4.01	0
1994 Milwaukee	A.L.	25	179	11	11	.500	98	84	158	4.68	0
1995 Milwaukee a	A.L.	4	23⅔	1	1	.500	18	10	24	3.42	0
1996 New Orleans	A.A.	6	32⅓	2	2	.500	30	17	24	3.34	0
1996 Milwaukee b	A.L.	15	84⅔	4	4	.500	50	38	82	4.46	0
1997 Milwaukee	A.L.	34	202	13	15	.464	122	89	207	4.99	0
Major League Totals	7 Yrs.	131	863⅔	58	49	.542	540	341	799	4.16	0

a On disabled list from May 15 to October 2, 1995.
b On disabled list from April 1 to July 14, 1996.

EMBREE, ALAN DUANE

Born, Vancouver, Washington, January 23, 1970.
Bats Left. Throws Left. Height, 6 feet, 2 inches. Weight, 185 pounds.

Year	Club	Lea	G	IP	W	L	Pct	SO	BB	H	ERA	SAVES
1990 Burlington	Appal.	15	81²/₃	4	4	.500	58	30	87	2.64	0
1991 Columbus	So. Atl.	27	155¹/₃	10	8	.556	137	77	126	3.59	0
1992 Kinston	Carolina	15	101	10	5	.667	115	32	89	3.30	0
1992 Canton-Akron	Eastern	12	79	7	2	.778	56	28	61	2.28	0
1992 Cleveland	A.L.	4	18	0	2	.000	12	8	19	7.00	0
1993 Canton-Akron	Eastern	1	5¹/₃	0	0	.000	4	3	3	3.38	0
1994 Canton-Akron	Eastern	30	157	9	16	.360	81	64	183	5.50	0
1995 Buffalo	A.A.	30	40²/₃	3	4	.429	56	19	31	0.89	5
1995 Cleveland	A.L.	23	24²/₃	3	2	.600	23	16	23	5.11	1
1996 Buffalo	A.A.	20	34¹/₃	4	1	.800	46	14	26	3.93	5
1996 Cleveland a	A.L.	24	31	1	1	.500	33	21	30	6.39	0
1997 Atlanta b	N.L.	66	46	3	1	.750	45	20	36	2.54	0
Major League Totals	4 Yrs.	117	119²/₃	7	6	.538	113	65	108	4.74	1
Division Series											
1996 Cleveland	A.L.	3	1	0	0	.000	1	0	0	9.00	0
Championship Series											
1995 Cleveland	A.L.	1	0¹/₃	0	0	.000	1	0	0	0.00	0
1997 Atlanta	N.L.	1	1	0	0	.000	1	1	0	0.00	0
Championship Series Totals	2	1¹/₃	0	0	.000	2	1	0	0.00	0
World Series Record											
1995 Cleveland	A.L.	4	3¹/₃	0	0	.000	2	2	2	2.70	0

a On disabled list from August 1 to September 7, 1996.
b Traded to Atlanta Braves with outfielder Kenny Lofton for outfielder Marquis Grissom and outfielder David Justice, March 25, 1997.

ERDOS, TODD MICHAEL

Born, Washington, Pennsylvania, November 21, 1973.
Bats Right. Throws Right. Height, 6 feet, 1 inch. Weight, 205 pounds.

Year	Club	Lea	G	IP	W	L	Pct	SO	BB	H	ERA	SAVES
1992 Padres	Arizona	12	57²/₃	3	4	.429	61	18	36	2.65	0
1992 Spokane	Northwest	2	13	1	0	1.000	11	5	9	0.69	0
1993 Waterloo	Midwest	11	47²/₃	1	9	.100	27	31	64	8.31	0
1993 Spokane	Northwest	16	90¹/₃	5	6	.455	64	53	73	3.19	0
1995 Rancho Cuca	California	1	2²/₃	0	0	.000	4	0	5	13.50	0
1995 Clinton	Midwest	5	5	0	0	.000	1	8	4	5.40	0
1995 Idaho Falls	Pioneer	32	41¹/₃	5	3	.625	48	30	34	3.48	1
1996 Rancho Cuca	California	55	67¹/₃	3	3	.500	82	37	63	3.74	17
1997 Mobile	Southern	55	59	1	4	.200	49	22	45	3.36	27
1997 San Diego a	N.L.	11	13²/₃	2	0	1.000	13	4	17	5.27	0

a Selected in expansion draft by Arizona Diamondbacks, November 18, 1997.

ERICKS, JOHN EDWARD

Born, Tinley Park, Illinois, June 16, 1967.
Bats Right. Throws Right. Height, 6 feet, 7 inches. Weight, 220 pounds.

Year	Club	Lea	G	IP	W	L	Pct	SO	BB	H	ERA	SAVES
1988 Johnson City	Appal.	9	41	3	2	.600	41	27	27	3.73	0
1989 Savannah	So. Atl.	28	167¹/₃	11	10	.524	211	101	90	2.04	0
1990 St. Petersburg	Fla. St.	4	23	2	1	.667	25	6	16	1.57	0
1990 Arkansas	Texas	4	15¹/₃	1	2	.333	19	19	17	9.39	0
1991 Arkansas	Texas	25	139²/₃	5	14	.263	103	84	138	4.77	0
1992 Arkansas	Texas	13	75	2	6	.250	71	29	69	4.08	0
1994 Salem	Carolina	17	52¹/₃	4	2	.667	71	20	42	3.10	1
1994 Carolina	Southern	11	57	2	4	.333	64	19	42	2.68	0
1995 Calgary	P.C.	5	29	2	1	.667	25	13	20	2.48	0
1995 Pittsburgh	N.L.	19	106	3	9	.250	80	50	108	4.58	0
1996 Calgary	P.C.	14	30	1	2	.333	40	15	31	4.20	1
1996 Pittsburgh	N.L.	28	46²/₃	4	5	.444	46	19	56	5.79	8
1997 Pittsburgh a	N.L.	10	9¹/₃	1	0	1.000	6	4	7	1.93	6
1997 Pirates	Gulf Coast	9	13	0	0	.000	18	5	5	3.46	0
1997 Calgary	P.C.	6	7	0	0	.000	10	1	14	12.86	0
Major League Totals	3 Yrs.	57	162	8	14	.364	132	73	171	4.78	14

a On disabled list from April 29 to September 29, 1997.

ERICKSON, SCOTT GAVIN

Born, Long Beach, California, February 2, 1968.
Bats Right. Throws Right. Height, 6 feet, 4 inches. Weight, 222 pounds.

Year Club	Lea	G	IP	W	L	Pct	SO	BB	H	ERA	SAVES
1989 Visalia ....California		12	78⅔	3	4	.429	59	22	79	2.97	0
1990 Orlando ....Southern		15	101	8	3	.727	69	24	75	3.03	0
1990 Minnesota ...........A.L.		19	113	8	4	.667	53	51	108	2.87	0
1991 Minnesota a ...........A.L.		32	204	*20	8	.714	108	71	189	3.18	0
1992 Minnesota ............A.L.		32	212	13	12	.520	101	83	197	3.40	0
1993 Minnesota b ...........A.L.		34	218⅔	8	*19	.296	116	71	*266	5.19	0
1994 Minnesota c-d-e .......A.L.		23	144	8	11	.421	104	59	173	5.44	0
1995 Minnesota-Baltimore f-g-h A.L.		32	196⅓	13	10	.565	106	67	213	4.81	0
1996 Baltimore ............A.L.		34	222⅓	13	12	.520	100	66	262	5.02	0
1997 Baltimore ............A.L.		34	221⅔	16	7	.696	131	61	218	3.69	0
Major League Totals ....8 Yrs.		240	1532	99	83	.544	819	529	1626	4.24	0
Division Series											
1996 Baltimore ............A.L.		1	6⅔	0	0	.000	6	2	6	4.05	0
1997 Baltimore ............A.L.		1	6⅔	1	0	1.000	6	2	7	4.05	0
Divisional Series Totals 2		2	13⅓	1	0	1.000	12	4	13	4.05	0
Championship Series											
1991 Minnesota ............A.L.		1	4	0	0	.000	2	5	3	4.50	0
1996 Baltimore ............A.L.		2	11⅓	0	1	.000	8	4	14	2.38	0
1997 Baltimore ............A.L.		2	12⅔	1	0	1.000	6	1	15	4.26	0
Championship Series Totals 5		5	28	1	1	.500	16	10	32	3.54	0
World Series Record											
1991 Minnesota ............A.L.		2	10⅔	0	0	.000	5	4	10	5.06	0

a On disabled list from June 30 to July 15, 1991.
b On disabled list from April 2 to April 17, 1993.
c Pitched no-hit, no-run game against Milwaukee Brewers, winning 6-0, April 27, 1994.
d On disabled list from May 15 to May 31, 1994.
e Declared restricted free agent under Major League Baseball implemented labor proposal, December 23, 1994.
f Re-signed with Minnesota Twins, April 29, 1995.
g Traded to Baltimore Orioles for pitcher Scott Klingenbeck and player to be named later, July 7, 1995.
h Minnesota Twins received outfielder Kimera Bartee to complete trade, September 19, 1995.

ESCOBAR, KELVIM JOSE

Born, LaGuaira, Venezuela, April 11, 1976.
Bats Right. Throws Right. Height, 6 feet, 1 inch. Weight, 205 pounds.

Year Club	Lea	G	IP	W	L	Pct	SO	BB	H	ERA	SAVES
1994 Blue Jays ....Gulf Coast		11	65	4	4	.500	64	18	56	2.35	0
1995 Medcine Hat ....Pioneer		14	69⅓	3	3	.500	75	33	66	5.71	0
1996 Dunedin ....Fla. St.		18	110⅓	9	5	.643	113	33	101	2.69	0
1996 Knoxville ....Southern		10	54	3	4	.429	44	24	61	5.33	0
1997 Dunedin ....Fla. St.		3	12	0	1	.000	16	3	16	3.75	0
1997 Knoxville ....Southern		5	24⅓	2	1	.667	31	16	20	3.70	0
1997 Toronto .............A.L.		27	31	3	2	.600	36	19	28	2.90	14

ESHELMAN, VAUGHN MICHAEL

Born, Philadelphia, Pennsylvania, May 22, 1969.
Bats Left. Throws Left. Height, 6 feet, 3 inches. Weight, 205 pounds.

Year Club	Lea	G	IP	W	L	Pct	SO	BB	H	ERA	SAVES
1991 Bluefield ....Appal.		3	14	1	0	1.000	15	9	10	0.64	0
1991 Kane County ......Midwest		11	77⅔	5	3	.625	90	35	57	2.32	0
1993 Frederick ....Carolina		24	143⅓	7	10	.412	122	59	128	3.89	0
1994 Bowie ....Eastern		27	166⅓	11	9	.550	133	60	175	4.00	0
1995 Trenton ....Eastern		2	7	0	1	.000	7	0	3	0.00	0
1995 Boston a ............A.L.		23	81⅔	6	3	.667	41	36	86	4.85	0
1996 Pawtucket ....Int.		7	43⅔	1	2	.333	28	19	40	4.33	0
1996 Boston b .............A.L.		39	87⅔	6	3	.667	59	58	112	7.08	0
1997 Boston c-d ..........A.L.		21	42⅔	3	3	.500	18	17	58	6.33	0
1997 Pawtucket ....Int.		14	66⅔	3	4	.429	57	22	63	4.86	1
Major League Totals ....3 Yrs.		83	212	15	9	.625	118	111	256	6.07	0

a On disabled list from May 25 to June 13 and July 6 to July 24 and August 25 to September 9, 1995.
b On disabled list from April 1 to April 25, 1996.
c Claimed on waivers by Oakland Athletics, October 15, 1997.
d Selected in expansion draft by Tampa Bay Devil Rays, November 18, 1997.

ESTES, AARON SHAWN (SHAWN)

Born, San Bernardino, California, February 18, 1973.
Bats Both. Throws Left. Height, 6 feet, 2 inches. Weight, 185 pounds.

Year	Club	Lea	G	IP	W	L	Pct	SO	BB	H	ERA	SAVES
1991 Bellingham	......	Northwest	9	34	1	3	.250	35	55	27	6.88	0
1992 Bellingham	......	Northwest	15	77	3	3	.500	77	45	84	4.32	0
1993 Appleton	....	Midwest	19	83⅓	5	9	.357	65	52	108	7.24	0
1994 Mariners	....	Arizona	5	20	0	3	.000	31	6	16	3.15	0
1994 Appleton	....	Midwest	5	19⅔	0	2	.000	28	17	19	4.58	0
1995 Wisconsin	....	Midwest	2	10	0	0	.000	11	5	5	0.90	0
1995 Burlington	....	Midwest	4	15⅓	0	0	.000	22	12	13	4.11	0
1995 San Jose	......	California	9	49⅔	5	2	.714	61	17	32	2.17	0
1995 Shreveport	....	Texas	4	22⅓	2	0	1.000	18	10	14	2.01	0
1995 San Francisco a	....	N.L.	3	17⅓	0	3	.000	14	5	16	6.75	0
1996 Phoenix	....	P.C.	18	110⅓	9	3	.750	95	38	92	3.43	0
1996 San Francisco	....	N.L.	11	70	3	5	.375	60	39	63	3.60	0
1997 San Francisco b	....	N.L.	32	201	19	5	.792	181	100	162	3.18	0
Major League Totals	3 Yrs.		46	288⅓	22	13	.629	255	144	241	3.50	0
Divisional Series												
1997 San Francisco	....	N.L.	1	3	0	0	.000	3	4	5	15.00	0

a Traded to San Francisco Giants with infielder Wilson Delgado for pitcher Salomon Torres, May 20, 1995.
b On disabled list from April 1 to April 7, 1997.

EYRE, SCOTT ALAN

Born, Inglewood, California, May 30, 1972.
Bats Left. Throws Left. Height, 6 feet, 1 inch. Weight, 160 pounds.

Year	Club	Lea	G	IP	W	L	Pct	SO	BB	H	ERA	SAVES
1992 Butte	....	Pioneer	15	80⅔	7	3	.700	94	39	71	2.90	0
1993 Chston-Sc	....	So. Atl.	26	143⅔	11	7	.611	154	59	115	3.45	0
1994 South Bend	....	Midwest	19	111⅓	8	4	.667	111	37	108	3.47	0
1995 White Sox	....	Gulf Coast	9	27⅓	0	2	.000	40	12	16	2.30	0
1996 Birmingham	......	Southern	27	158⅓	12	7	.632	137	79	170	4.38	0
1997 Birmingham	......	Southern	22	126⅔	13	5	.722	127	55	110	3.84	0
1997 Chicago	....	A.L.	11	60⅔	4	4	.500	36	31	62	5.04	0

FASSERO, JEFFREY JOSEPH

Born, Springfield, Illinois, January 5, 1963.
Bats Left. Throws Left. Height, 6 feet, 1 inch. Weight, 195 pounds.

Year	Club	Lea	G	IP	W	L	Pct	SO	BB	H	ERA	SAVES
1984 Johnson City	......	Appal.	13	66⅔	4	7	.364	59	39	65	4.59	1
1985 Springfield	....	Midwest	29	119	4	8	.333	65	45	126	4.01	1
1986 St. Petersburg	......	Fla. St.	26	*176	13	7	.650	112	56	156	2.45	0
1987 Arkansas	....	Texas	28	151⅓	10	7	.588	118	67	168	4.10	0
1988 Arkansas	....	Texas	70	78	5	5	.500	72	41	97	3.58	17
1989 Louisville	....	A.A.	22	112	3	10	.231	73	47	136	5.22	0
1989 Arkansas a-b	....	Texas	6	44	4	1	.800	38	12	32	1.64	0
1990 Canton c	....	Eastern	61	64⅓	5	4	.556	61	24	66	2.80	6
1991 Indianapolis	....	A.A.	18	18⅓	3	0	1.000	12	7	11	1.47	4
1991 Montreal	....	N.L.	51	55⅓	2	5	.286	42	17	39	2.44	8
1992 Montreal	....	N.L.	70	85⅔	8	7	.533	63	34	81	2.84	1
1993 Montreal	....	N.L.	56	149⅔	12	5	.706	140	54	119	2.29	1
1994 Montreal d	....	N.L.	21	138⅔	8	6	.571	119	40	119	2.99	0
1995 Montreal	....	N.L.	30	189	13	14	.481	164	74	207	4.33	0
1996 Montreal e	....	N.L.	34	231⅔	15	11	.577	222	55	217	3.30	0
1997 Seattle	....	A.L.	35	234⅓	16	9	.640	189	84	226	3.61	0
Major League Totals	7 Yrs.		297	1084⅓	74	57	.565	939	358	1008	3.29	10
Division Series												
1997 Seattle	....	A.L.	1	8	1	0	1.000	3	4	3	1.13	0

a Drafted by Chicago White Sox from St. Louis Cardinals organization in minor league draft, December 5, 1989.
b Released by Chicago White Sox, March 28; signed with Cleveland Indians organization, April 7, 1990.
c Became free agent, October 15, 1990; signed with Montreal Expos organization, January 3, 1991.
d On disabled list from July 24 to August 10, 1994.
e Traded to Seattle Mariners with pitcher Alex Pachecho for catcher Chris Widger, pitcher Matt Wagner and pitcher Trey Moore, October 29, 1996.

FERNANDEZ, ALEXANDER (ALEX)

Born, Miami Beach, Florida, August 13, 1969.
Bats Right. Throws Right. Height, 6 feet, 1 inch. Weight, 215 pounds.

Year	Club	Lea	G	IP	W	L	Pct	SO	BB	H	ERA	SAVES
1990 Sarasota White Sox	...	Gulf C.	2	10	1	0	1.000	10	1	11	3.60	0
1990 Sarasota	....	Fla. St.	2	14⅔	1	1	.500	23	3	8	1.84	0
1990 Birmingham	....	Southern	4	25	4	0	1.000	27	6	20	1.08	0
1990 Chicago	....	A.L.	13	87⅔	5	5	.500	61	34	89	3.80	0
1991 Chicago	....	A.L.	34	191⅓	9	13	.409	145	88	186	4.51	0
1992 Chicago	....	A.L.	29	187⅔	8	11	.421	95	50	199	4.27	0
1992 Vancouver	....	P.C.	4	28⅔	2	1	.667	27	6	15	0.94	0
1993 Chicago	....	A.L.	34	247⅓	18	9	.667	169	67	221	3.13	0
1994 Chicago a	....	A.L.	24	170⅓	11	7	.611	122	50	163	3.86	0
1995 Chicago b	....	A.L.	30	203⅔	12	8	.600	159	65	200	3.80	0
1996 Chicago c	....	A.L.	35	258	16	10	.615	200	72	248	3.45	0
1997 Florida	....	N.L.	32	220⅔	17	12	.586	183	69	193	3.59	0
Major League Totals	....	8 Yrs.	231	1567	96	75	.561	1134	495	1499	3.76	0
Division Series												
1997 Florida	....	N.L.	1	7	1	0	1.000	5	0	7	2.57	0
Championship Series												
1993 Chicago	....	A.L.	2	15	0	2	.000	10	6	15	1.80	0
1997 Florida	....	N.L.	1	2⅔	0	1	.000	3	1	6	16.88	0
Championship Series Totals	....	3		17⅔	0	3	.000	13	7	21	4.08	0

a Declared restricted free agent under Major League Baseball implemented labor proposal, December 23, 1994.
b Re-signed with Chicago White Sox, April 5, 1995.
c Signed with Florida Marlins, December 9, 1996.

FERNANDEZ, OSVALDO

Born, Holguin, Cuba, November 4, 1968.
Bats Right. Throws Right. Height, 6 feet, 2 inches. Weight, 190 pounds.

Year	Club	Lea	G	IP	W	L	Pct	SO	BB	H	ERA	SAVES
1996 San Francisco a	....	N.L.	30	171⅔	7	13	.350	106	57	193	4.61	0
1997 Phoenix	....	P.C.	2	12	0	0	.000	4	3	10	3.00	0
1997 San Francisco b	....	N.L.	11	56⅓	3	4	.429	31	15	74	4.95	0
Major League Totals	....	2 Yrs.	41	228	10	17	.370	137	72	267	4.70	0

a Signed with San Francisco Giants, January 16, 1996.
b On disabled list from May 20 to June 20 and June 26 to September 29, 1997.

FETTERS, MICHAEL LEE

Born, Van Nuys, California, December 19, 1964.
Bats Right. Throws Right. Height, 6 feet, 4 inches. Weight, 215 pounds.

Year	Club	Lea	G	IP	W	L	Pct	SO	BB	H	ERA	SAVES
1986 Salem	....	Northwest	12	72	4	2	.667	72	51	60	3.38	0
1987 Palm Springs	......	California	19	116	9	7	.563	105	73	106	3.57	0
1988 Midland	....	Texas	20	114	8	8	.500	101	67	116	5.92	0
1988 Edmonton	....	P.C.	2	14	2	0	1.000	11	10	8	1.93	0
1989 Edmonton	....	P.C.	26	168	12	8	.600	144	72	160	3.80	0
1989 California	....	A.L.	1	3⅓	0	0	.000	4	1	5	8.10	0
1990 Edmonton	....	P.C.	5	27⅓	1	1	.500	26	13	22	0.99	0
1990 California	....	A.L.	26	67⅔	1	1	.500	35	20	77	4.12	1
1991 Edmonton	....	P.C.	11	61	2	7	.222	43	26	65	4.87	0
1991 California a	....	A.L.	19	44⅔	2	5	.286	24	28	53	4.84	0
1992 Milwaukee b	....	A.L.	50	62⅔	5	1	.833	43	24	38	1.87	2
1993 Milwaukee	....	A.L.	45	59⅓	3	3	.500	23	22	59	3.34	0
1994 Milwaukee c	....	A.L.	42	46	1	4	.200	31	27	41	2.54	17
1995 Milwaukee d-e	....	A.L.	40	34⅔	0	3	.000	33	20	40	3.38	22
1996 Milwaukee	....	A.L.	61	61⅓	3	3	.500	53	26	65	3.38	32
1997 Tucson	....	P.C.	2	1⅔	0	0	.000	0	1	1	10.80	0
1997 Milwaukee f-g	....	A.L.	51	70⅓	5	1	.167	62	33	62	3.45	6
Major League Totals	.....	9 Yrs.	335	450	16	25	.390	308	201	440	3.38	80

a Traded to Milwaukee Brewers with pitcher Glenn Carter for pitcher Chuck Crim, December 10, 1991.
b On disabled list from May 3 to May 19, 1992.
c Declared restricted free agent under Major League Baseball implemented labor proposal, December 23, 1994.
d Re-signed with Milwaukee Brewers, April 13, 1995.
e On disabled list from May 25 to June 9, 1995.
f On disabled list from April 4 to May 5, 1997.
g Traded to Cleveland Indians with pitcher Ben McDonald and pitcher Ron Villone for outfielder Marquis Grissom and pitcher Jeff Juden, December 8, 1997. Traded to Oakland Athletics for pitcher Steve Karsay, December 8, 1997.

FINLEY, CHARLES EDWARD
Born, Monroe, Louisiana, November 26, 1962.
Bats Left. Throws Left. Height, 6 feet, 6 inches. Weight, 214 pounds.

Year Club	Lea	G	IP	W	L	Pct	SO	BB	H	ERA	SAVES
1985 Salem	Northwest	18	29	3	1	.750	32	10	34	4.66	5
1986 Quad City	Midwest	10	12	1	0	1.000	16	3	4	0.00	6
1986 California	A.L.	25	46⅓	3	1	.750	37	23	40	3.30	0
1987 California	A.L.	35	90⅔	2	7	.222	63	43	102	4.67	0
1988 California	A.L.	31	194⅓	9	15	.375	111	82	191	4.17	0
1989 California a	A.L.	29	199⅔	16	9	.640	156	82	171	2.57	0
1990 California	A.L.	32	236	18	9	.667	177	81	210	2.40	0
1991 California	A.L.	34	227⅓	18	9	.667	171	101	205	3.80	0
1992 California b	A.L.	31	204⅓	7	12	.368	124	98	212	3.96	0
1993 California	A.L.	35	251⅓	16	14	.533	187	82	243	3.15	0
1994 California	A.L.	25	*183⅓	10	10	.500	148	71	178	4.32	0
1995 California c	A.L.	32	203	15	12	.556	195	93	192	4.21	0
1996 California	A.L.	35	238	15	16	.484	215	94	241	4.16	0
1997 Lk Elsinore	California	2	9	0	0	.000	12	4	5	2.00	0
1997 Anaheim d	A.L.	25	164	13	6	.684	155	65	152	4.23	0
Major League Totals	12 Yrs.	369	2238⅓	142	120	.542	1739	915	2137	3.69	0
Championship Series											
1986 California	A.L.	3	2	0	0	.000	1	0	1	0.00	0

a On disabled list from August 22 to September 15, 1989.
b On disabled list from April 7 to April 22, 1992.
c Filed for free agency, November 12, 1995. Re-signed, January 4, 1996.
d On disabled list from April 1 to April 15 and August 20 to September 29, 1997.

FLORIE, BRYCE BETTENCOURT
Born, Charleston, South Carolina, May 21, 1970.
Bats Right. Throws Right. Height, 6 feet. Weight, 185 pounds.

Year Club	Lea	G	IP	W	L	Pct	SO	BB	H	ERA	SAVES
1988 Scottsdale Padres	Arizona	11	38⅓	4	5	.444	29	22	52	7.98	0
1989 Charleston, SC	So. Atl.	12	44	1	7	.125	22	42	54	6.95	0
1989 Spokane	Northwest	14	61	4	5	.444	50	40	79	7.08	0
1990 Waterloo	Midwest	14	65⅔	4	5	.444	38	37	60	4.39	0
1991 Waterloo	Midwest	23	133	7	6	.538	90	79	119	3.92	0
1992 High Desert	California	26	137⅔	9	7	.563	106	114	99	4.12	0
1992 Charleston, SC	So. Atl.	1	5	0	1	.000	5	0	5	1.80	0
1993 Wichita	Texas	27	154⅔	11	8	.579	133	100	128	3.96	0
1994 Las Vegas	P.C.	50	71⅔	2	5	.286	67	47	76	5.15	1
1994 San Diego	N.L.	9	9⅓	0	0	.000	8	3	8	0.96	0
1995 San Diego	N.L.	47	68⅔	2	2	.500	68	38	49	3.01	1
1996 San Diego a-b	N.L.	39	49⅓	2	2	.500	51	27	45	4.01	0
1996 Milwaukee	A.L.	15	19	0	1	.000	12	13	20	6.63	0
1997 Milwaukee c-d	A.L.	32	75	4	4	.500	53	42	74	4.32	0
Major League Totals	4 Yrs.	142	221⅓	8	9	.471	192	123	196	3.90	1

a Traded to Milwaukee Brewers with pitcher Ron Villone and outfielder Marc Newfield for outfielder Greg Vaughan and player to be named later, July 31, 1996.
b San Diego Padres received outfielder Gerald Parent to complete trade, September 16, 1996.
c On disabled list from August 21 to September 8, 1997.
d Traded to Detroit Tigers with player to be named later for pitcher Mike Myers, pitcher Rick Greene and infielder Santiago Perez, November 21, 1997.

FOSSAS, EMILIO ANTONIO (TONY)
Born, Havana, Cuba, September 23, 1957.
Bats Left. Throws Left. Height, 6 feet. Weight, 187 pounds.

Year Club	Lea	G	IP	W	L	Pct	SO	BB	H	ERA	SAVES
1979 Sarasota Rangers	Gulf C.	10	60	6	3	.667	49	26	54	3.00	0
1980 Asheville	So. Atl.	30	*197	12	8	.600	140	69	187	3.15	2
1981 Tulsa	Texas	38	106	5	6	.455	57	44	113	4.16	2
1982 Burlington	Midwest	25	146	8	9	.471	115	33	121	3.08	0
1983 Tulsa	Texas	24	132⅔	8	7	.533	103	46	123	4.21	0
1983 Oklahoma City	A.A.	10	35	1	2	.333	23	12	55	7.97	0
1984 Tulsa	Texas	4	10	0	1	.000	7	3	12	4.50	2
1984 Oklahoma City	A.A.	29	121	5	9	.357	74	34	143	4.31	0
1985 Oklahoma City a	A.A.	30	109⅔	7	6	.538	49	36	121	4.76	2
1986 Edmonton	P.C.	7	43⅓	3	3	.500	15	12	53	4.57	0

Year	Club	Lea	G	IP	W	L	Pct	SO	BB	H	ERA	SAVES
1987 Edmonton b	.....P.C.		40	117⅓	6	8	.429	54	29	151	4.99	0
1988 Oklahoma City	.......A.A.		52	66⅔	3	0	1.000	42	16	64	2.84	4
1988 Texas c	.......A.L.		5	5⅔	0	0	.000	0	2	11	4.76	0
1989 Denver	.......A.A.		24	35⅓	5	1	.833	35	11	27	2.04	6
1989 Milwaukee	.......A.L.		51	61	2	2	.500	42	22	57	3.54	1
1990 Denver	.......A.A.		25	35⅔	5	2	.714	45	10	29	1.51	4
1990 Milwaukee d	.......A.L.		32	29⅓	2	3	.400	24	10	44	6.44	0
1991 Boston	.......A.L.		64	57	3	2	.600	29	28	49	3.47	1
1992 Boston e	.......A.L.		60	29⅔	1	2	.333	19	14	31	2.43	2
1993 Boston f	.......A.L.		71	40	1	1	.500	39	15	38	5.17	0
1994 Pawtucket	.......Int.		11	9⅔	2	0	1.000	8	3	4	0.00	0
1994 Boston g	.......A.L.		44	34	2	0	1.000	31	15	35	4.76	1
1995 St. Louis h	.......N.L.		58	36⅔	3	0	1.000	40	10	28	1.47	0
1996 St. Louis	.......N.L.		65	47	0	4	.000	36	21	43	2.68	2
1997 St. Louis i-j	.......N.L.		71	51⅔	2	7	.222	41	26	62	3.83	0
Major League Totals ....10 Yrs.			521	392	16	21	.432	301	163	398	3.70	7
Championship Series												
1996 St. Louis	.......N.L.		5	4⅓	0	0	.000	1	3	1	2.08	0

a Became free agent, October 15; signed with California Angels organization, December 31, 1985.
b Became free agent, October 15; signed with Texas Rangers organization, December 12, 1987.
c Became free agent, October 15, 1988; signed with Milwaukee Brewers organization, January 21, 1989.
d Released, December 3, 1990; signed with Boston Red Sox, January 23, 1991.
e Released, December 11, 1992, re-signed with Boston Red Sox organization, January 18, 1993.
f Not offered 1994 contract, December 20, 1993; re-signed with Boston Red Sox, January 20, 1994.
g Not offered 1995 contract, December 23, 1994.
h Signed with St. Louis Cardinals organization, April 10, 1995.
i Filed for free agency, October 27, 1997.
j Signed as free agent with Seattle Mariners, December 16, 1997.

FOSTER, KEVIN CHRISTOPHER
Born, Evanston, Illinois, January 13, 1969.
Bats Right. Throws Right. Height, 6 feet, 1 inch. Weight, 160 pounds.

Year	Club	Lea	G	IP	W	L	Pct	SO	BB	H	ERA	SAVES
1990 Bradenton Expos	.....Gulf C.		4	10⅔	2	0	1.000	11	6	9	5.06	0
1990 Gate City	.........Pioneer		10	55	1	7	.125	52	34	43	4.58	0
1991 Sumter	.....So. Atl.		34	102	10	4	.714	111	68	62	2.74	1
1992 West Palm Beach a	...Fla. St.		16	69⅓	7	2	.778	66	31	45	1.95	0
1993 Jacksonville b	.....Southern		12	65⅔	4	4	.500	72	29	53	3.97	0
1993 Scranton	.......Int.		17	71	1	1	.500	59	29	63	3.93	0
1993 Philadelphia	.......N.L.		2	6⅔	0	1	.000	6	7	13	14.85	0
1994 Reading c	.........Eastern		1	6	0	1	.000	3	1	7	6.00	0
1994 Orlando	.........Southern		3	19	1	0	1.000	21	2	8	0.95	0
1994 Iowa	.......A.A.		6	33⅔	3	1	.750	35	14	28	4.28	0
1994 Chicago	.......N.L.		13	81	3	4	.429	75	35	70	2.89	0
1995 Chicago	.......N.L.		30	167⅔	12	11	.522	146	65	149	4.51	0
1996 Iowa	.......A.A.		18	115	7	6	.538	87	46	106	4.30	0
1996 Chicago	.......N.L.		17	87	7	6	.538	53	35	98	6.21	0
1997 Chicago d	.......N.L.		26	146⅓	10	7	.588	118	66	141	4.61	0
Major League Totals ....5 Yrs.			88	488⅔	32	29	.525	398	208	471	4.71	0

a Traded by Montreal Expos to Seattle Mariners organization for player to be named, November 20; Montreal
   acquired catcher Miah Bradbury to complete trade, December 8, 1992.
b Traded by Seattle Mariners organization to Philadelphia Phillies organization for pitcher Bob Ayrault, June 13, 1993.
c Traded by Philadelphia Phillies to Chicago Cubs organization for pitcher Shawn Boskie, April 12, 1994.
d On disabled list from August 17 to September 1, 1997.

FOULKE, KEITH CHARLES
Born, San Diego, California, October 19, 1972.
Bats Right. Throws Right. Height, 6 feet. Weight, 195 pounds.

Year	Club	Lea	G	IP	W	L	Pct	SO	BB	H	ERA	SAVES
1994 Everett	.........Northwest		4	19⅓	2	0	1.000	22	3	17	0.93	0
1995 San Jose	........California		28	177⅓	13	6	.684	168	32	166	3.50	0
1996 Shreveport	.........Texas		27	182⅔	12	7	.632	129	35	149	2.76	0
1997 Phoenix	.......P.C.		12	76	5	4	.556	54	15	79	4.50	0
1997 Nashville	.......A.A.		1	4⅔	0	0	.000	4	0	8	5.79	0
1997 San Francisco a	........N.L.		11	44⅔	1	5	.167	33	18	60	8.26	0
1997 Chicago	.......N.L.		16	28⅔	3	0	1.000	21	5	28	3.45	3
Major League Totals ....1 Yrs.			27	73⅓	4	5	.444	54	23	88	6.38	3

a Traded to Chicago White Sox with infielder Mike Caruso, outfielder Brian Manning, pitcher Lorenzo Barcelo, pitcher Bob Howry and pitcher Ken Vining for pitcher Wilson Alvarez, pitcher Danny Darwin and pitcher Roberto Hernandez, July 31, 1997.

FOX, CHAD DOUGLAS

Born, Coronado, California, September 3, 1970.
Bats Right. Throws Right. Height, 6 feet, 3 inches. Weight 175 pounds.

Year	Club	Lea	G	IP	W	L	Pct	SO	BB	H	ERA	SAVES
1992	Princeton	Appal.	15	49⅓	4	2	.667	37	34	55	4.74	0
1993	Chston-Wv	So. Atl.	27	135⅔	9	12	.429	81	97	138	5.37	0
1994	Winston-Sal	Carolina	25	156⅓	12	5	.706	137	94	121	3.86	0
1995	Chattanooga	Southern	20	80	4	5	.444	56	52	76	5.06	0
1996	Richmond a	Int.	18	93⅓	3	10	.231	87	49	91	4.72	0
1997	Richmond	Int.	13	24⅓	1	0	1.000	25	14	24	3.70	0
1997	Atlanta b	N.L.	30	27⅓	0	1	.000	28	16	24	3.29	0

a Traded by Cincinnati Reds with player-to-be-name to Atlanta Braves for outfielder Mike Kelly, January 9, 1996; Atlanta received pitcher Ray King to complete deal, April 26, 1996.
b Traded to Milwaukee Brewers for outfielder Gerald Williams, December 11, 1997.

FRANCO, JOHN ANTHONY

Born, Brooklyn, New York, September 17, 1960.
Bats Left. Throws Left. Height, 5 feet, 10 inches. Weight, 185 pounds.

Year	Club	Lea	G	IP	W	L	Pct	SO	BB	H	ERA	SAVES
1981	Vero Beach	Fla. St.	13	79	7	4	.636	60	41	78	3.53	0
1982	San Antonio	Texas	17	105⅓	10	5	.667	76	58	137	4.96	0
1982	Albuquerque	P.C.	5	27⅓	1	2	.333	24	15	41	7.24	0
1983	Albuquerque a	P.C.	11	15	0	0	.000	8	11	10	5.40	0
1983	Indianapolis	A.A.	23	115	6	10	.375	54	42	148	4.85	2
1984	Cincinnati	N.L.	54	79⅓	6	2	.750	55	36	74	2.61	4
1984	Wichita	A.A.	6	9⅓	1	0	1.000	11	4	8	5.79	0
1985	Cincinnati	N.L.	67	99	12	3	.800	61	40	83	2.18	12
1986	Cincinnati	N.L.	74	101	6	6	.500	84	44	90	2.94	29
1987	Cincinnati	N.L.	68	82	8	5	.615	61	27	76	2.52	32
1988	Cincinnati	N.L.	70	86	6	6	.500	46	27	60	1.57	*39
1989	Cincinnati b	N.L.	60	80⅔	4	8	.333	60	36	77	3.12	32
1990	New York	N.L.	55	67⅔	5	3	.625	56	21	66	2.53	*33
1991	New York	N.L.	52	55⅓	5	9	.357	45	18	61	2.93	30
1992	New York c	N.L.	31	33	6	2	.750	20	11	24	1.64	15
1993	New York d	N.L.	35	36⅓	4	3	.571	29	19	46	5.20	10
1994	New York e	N.L.	47	50	1	4	.200	42	19	47	2.70	*30
1995	New York f	N.L.	48	51⅔	5	3	.625	41	17	48	2.44	29
1996	New York	N.L.	51	54	4	3	.571	48	21	54	1.83	28
1997	New York	N.L.	59	60	5	3	.625	53	20	49	2.55	36
Major League Totals		14 Yrs.	771	936	77	60	.562	701	356	855	2.57	359

a Traded by Los Angeles Dodgers to Cincinnati Reds organization with pitcher Brett Wise for infielder Rafael Landestoy, May 9, 1983.
b Traded to New York Mets with outfielder Don Brown for pitchers Randy Myers and Kip Gross, December 7, 1989.
c On disabled list from June 29 to August 1 and August 26 to end of 1992 season.
d On disabled list from April 17 to May 7 and August 3 to August 27, 1993.
e Filed for free agency, October 17, 1994.
f Re-signed with New York Mets, April 5, 1995.

FRASCATORE, JOHN VINCENT

Born, New York, N.Y., February 4, 1970.
Bats Right. Throws Right. Height, 6 feet, 1 inch. Weight, 210 pounds.

Year	Club	Lea	G	IP	W	L	Pct	SO	BB	H	ERA	SAVES
1991	Hamilton	N.Y.-Penn.	30	30⅓	2	7	.222	18	22	44	9.20	1
1992	Savannah	So. Atl.	50	58⅔	5	7	.417	56	29	49	3.84	23
1993	Springfield	Midwest	27	157⅓	7	12	.368	126	33	157	3.78	0
1994	Arkansas	Texas	12	78⅓	7	3	.700	63	15	76	3.10	0
1994	St. Louis	N.L.	1	3⅓	0	1	.000	2	2	7	16.20	0
1994	Louisville	A.A.	13	85	8	3	.727	58	33	82	3.39	0
1995	Louisville	A.A.	28	82	2	8	.200	55	34	89	3.95	5
1995	St. Louis	N.L.	14	32⅔	1	1	.500	21	16	39	4.41	0

Year	Club	Lea	G	IP	W	L	Pct	SO	BB	H	ERA	SAVES
1996 Louisville	...........A.A.	36	156⅓	6	13	.316	95	42	180	5.18	0
1997 St. Louis	............N.L.	59	80	5	2	.714	58	33	74	2.48	0
Major League Totals	......3 Yrs.	74	116	6	4	.600	81	51	120	3.41	0

GARCIA, RAMON ANTONIO

Born, Guanare, Venezuela, December 9, 1969.
Bats Right. Throws Right. Height, 6 feet, 2 inches. Weight, 205 pounds.

Year	Club	Lea	G	IP	W	L	Pct	SO	BB	H	ERA	SAVES
1989 White Sox	.......Gulf Coast	14	53	6	4	.600	52	17	34	3.06	0
1990 Sarasota	..........Fla. St.	26	157⅓	9	14	.391	130	45	155	3.95	0
1990 Vancouver	...........P.C.	1	1	0	0	.000	1	0	2	0.00	0
1991 Birmingham	......Southern	6	38⅔	4	0	1.000	38	11	27	0.93	0
1991 Vancouver	............P.C.	4	26⅔	2	2	.500	17	7	24	4.05	0
1991 Chicago	..............A.L.	16	78⅓	4	4	.500	40	31	79	5.40	0
1992 Vancouver	...........P.C.	28	170	9	11	.450	79	56	165	3.71	0
1993 Nashville a	............A.A.	7	42⅔	4	1	.800	25	11	45	4.01	0
1994 Chicago b	.............A.L.			INJURED—Did Not Play							
1995	....			INJURED—Did Not Play							
1996 New Orleans c	........A.A.	11	38⅓	2	1	.667	32	12	31	1.88	0
1996 Milwaukee d	........A.L.	37	75⅔	4	4	.500	40	21	84	6.66	4
1997 Houston	............N.L.	42	158⅔	9	8	.529	120	52	155	3.69	1
Major League Totals	........3 Yrs.	95	312⅔	17	16	.515	200	104	318	4.84	5
Division Series												
1997 Houston	.................N.L.	2	1	0	0	.000	1	1	1	0.00	0

a On disabled list for balance of 1993 season.
b Released by Chicago White Sox, March 9, 1994.
c Signed as free agent by Milwaukee Brewers organization, April 3, 1996.
d Drafted by Houston Astros in Rule V draft, December 9, 1996.

GARDNER, MARK ALLAN

Born, Los Angeles, California, March 1, 1962.
Bats Right. Throws Right. Height, 6 feet, 1 inch. Weight, 200 pounds.

Year	Club	Lea	G	IP	W	L	Pct	SO	BB	H	ERA	SAVES
1985 Jamestown	......N.Y.-Penn.	3	13	0	0	.000	16	4	9	2.77	0
1985 West Palm Beach	.....Fla. St.	10	60⅔	5	4	.556	44	18	54	2.37	0
1986 Jacksonville	......Southern	29	168⅔	10	11	.476	140	90	144	3.84	0
1987 Indianapolis	...........A.A.	9	46	3	3	.500	41	28	48	5.67	0
1987 Jacksonville	......Southern	17	101	4	6	.400	78	42	101	4.19	0
1988 Indianapolis	...........A.A.	13	84⅓	4	2	.667	71	32	65	2.77	0
1988 Jacksonville	......Southern	15	112⅓	6	3	.667	130	36	72	1.60	0
1989 Indianapolis	...........A.A.	24	163⅓	12	4	.750	*175	59	122	2.37	0
1989 Montreal	.............N.L.	7	26⅓	0	3	.000	21	11	26	5.13	0
1990 Montreal	.............N.L.	27	152⅓	7	9	.438	135	61	129	3.42	0
1991 Indianapolis	...........A.A.	6	31	2	0	1.000	38	16	26	3.48	0
1991 Montreal a-b	..........N.L.	27	168⅓	9	11	.450	107	75	139	3.85	0
1992 Montreal c	............N.L.	33	179⅔	12	10	.545	132	60	179	4.36	0
1993 Omaha	................A.A.	8	48⅓	4	2	.667	41	19	34	2.79	0
1993 Kansas City d-e	.......A.L.	17	91⅔	4	6	.400	54	36	92	6.19	0
1994 Edmonton	..............P.C.	1	6	1	0	1.000	11	1	4	0.00	0
1994 Brevard City	........Fla. St.	1	5	1	0	1.000	3	1	1	0.00	0
1994 Florida f-g	.............N.L.	20	92⅓	4	4	.500	57	30	97	4.87	0
1995 Florida h-i	............N.L.	39	102⅓	5	5	.500	87	43	109	4.49	1
1996 San Jose j	.......California	1	5⅔	0	0	.000	7	0	4	3.18	0
1996 San Francisco k	........N.L.	30	179⅓	12	7	.632	145	57	200	4.42	0
1997 San Francisco	........N.L.	30	180⅓	12	9	.571	136	57	188	4.29	0
Major League Totals	........9 Yrs.	230	1173	65	64	.504	874	430	1159	4.37	1

a On disabled list from April 2 to May 14, 1991.
b Pitched nine no-hit, no-run innings against Los Angeles Dodgers, losing 1-0 in tenth inning, July 26, 1991.
c Traded to Kansas City Royals with pitcher Doug Platt for catcher Tim Spehr and pitcher Jeff Shaw, December 9, 1992.
d On disabled list from July 7 to August 27, 1993.
e Released, December 8, 1993; signed with Florida Marlins organization, January 3, 1994.
f On disabled list from June 8 to June 25, 1994.
g Declared restricted free agent under Major League Baseball implemented labor proposal, December 23, 1994.
h Re-signed with Florida Marlins, April 4, 1995.

i Filed for free agency, October 4, 1995; signed with Florida Marlins organization, December 8, 1995.
j Signed with San Francisco Giants, March 29, 1996.
k On disabled list from July 3 to July 21, 1996.

GLAVINE, THOMAS MICHAEL
Born, Concord, Massachusetts, March 25, 1966.
Bats Left. Throws Left. Height, 6 feet, 1 inch. Weight, 190 pounds.

Year	Club	Lea	G	IP	W	L	Pct	SO	BB	H	ERA	SAVES
1984 Bradenton Braves	....Gulf C.		8	32⅓	2	3	.400	34	13	29	3.34	0
1985 Sumter	...........So. Atl.		26	168⅔	9	6	.600	174	73	114	*2.35	0
1986 Greenville	........Southern		22	145⅓	11	6	.647	114	70	129	3.41	0
1986 Richmond	............Int.		7	40	1	5	.167	12	27	40	5.63	0
1987 Richmond	............Int.		22	150⅓	6	12	.333	91	56	142	3.35	0
1987 Atlanta	...............N.L.		9	50⅓	2	4	.333	20	33	55	5.54	0
1988 Atlanta	...............N.L.		34	195⅓	7	*17	.292	84	63	201	4.56	0
1989 Atlanta	...............N.L.		29	186	14	8	.636	90	40	172	3.68	0
1990 Atlanta a	..........N.L.		33	214⅓	10	12	.455	129	78	232	4.28	0
1991 Atlanta b-c	........N.L.		34	246⅔	*20	11	.645	192	69	201	2.55	0
1992 Atlanta d	...........N.L.		33	225	*20	8	.714	129	70	197	2.76	0
1993 Atlanta	...............N.L.		36	239⅓	*22	6	.786	120	90	236	3.20	0
1994 Atlanta e	..........N.L.		25	165⅓	13	9	.591	140	70	173	3.97	0
1995 Atlanta	...............N.L.		29	198⅔	16	7	.696	127	66	182	3.08	0
1996 Atlanta	...............N.L.		36	235⅓	15	10	.600	181	85	222	2.98	0
1997 Atlanta	...............N.L.		33	240	14	7	.667	152	79	197	2.96	0
Major League Totals	.......11 Yrs.		331	2196⅓	153	99	.607	1364	743	2068	3.40	0
Division Series												
1995 Atlanta	...............N.L.		1	7	0	0	.000	3	1	5	2.57	0
1996 Atlanta	...............N.L.		1	6⅔	1	0	1.000	7	3	5	1.35	0
1997 Atlanta	...............N.L.		1	6	1	0	1.000	4	5	5	4.50	0
Divisional Series Totals	3			19⅔	2	0	1.000	14	9	15	2.75	0
Championship Series												
1991 Atlanta	...............N.L.		2	14	0	2	.000	11	6	12	3.21	0
1992 Atlanta	...............N.L.		2	7⅓	0	2	.000	2	3	13	12.27	0
1993 Atlanta	...............N.L.		1	7	1	0	1.000	5	0	6	2.57	0
1995 Atlanta	...............N.L.		1	7	0	0	.000	5	2	7	1.29	0
1996 Atlanta	...............N.L.		2	13	1	1	.500	9	0	10	2.08	0
1997 Atlanta	...............N.L.		2	13⅓	1	1	.500	9	11	13	5.40	0
Championship Series Totals	10			61⅔	3	6	.333	41	22	61	4.23	0
World Series Record												
1991 Atlanta	...............N.L.		2	13⅓	1	1	.500	8	7	8	2.70	0
1992 Atlanta	...............N.L.		2	17	1	1	.500	8	4	10	1.59	0
1995 Atlanta	...............N.L.		2	14	2	0	1.000	11	6	4	1.29	0
1996 Atlanta	...............N.L.		1	7	0	1	.000	8	3	4	1.29	0
World Series Totals	7			51⅓	4	3	.571	35	20	26	1.75	0

a Appeared in one additional game as pinch runner.
b Appeared in one additional game as pinch hitter and one additional game as pinch runner.
c Selected Cy Young Award winner in National League for 1991.
d Appeared in two additional games as pinch hitter.
e Appeared in one additional game as pinch hitter.

GOMES, WAYNE MAURICE
Born, Hampton, Virginia, January 15, 1973.
Bats Right. Throws Right. Height, 6 feet. Weight, 215 pounds.

Year	Club	Lea	G	IP	W	L	Pct	SO	BB	H	ERA	SAVES
1993 Batavia	..........N.Y.-Penn.		5	7⅓	1	0	1.000	11	8	1	1.23	0
1993 Clearwater	..........Fla. St.		9	7⅔	0	0	.000	13	9	4	1.17	4
1994 Clearwater	..........Fla. St.		23	104⅓	6	8	.429	102	82	85	4.74	0
1995 Reading	...........Eastern		22	104⅔	7	4	.636	102	70	89	3.96	0
1996 Reading	...........Eastern		67	64⅓	0	4	.000	79	48	53	4.48	24
1997 Scranton-WB	...........Int.		26	38	3	1	.750	36	24	31	2.37	7
1997 Philadelphia	...........N.L.		37	42⅔	5	1	.833	24	24	45	5.27	0

245

GONZALEZ, GEREMIS SEGUNDO (JEREMI)
Born, Maracaibo, Venezuela, January 8, 1975.
Bats Right. Throws Right. Height, 6 feet, 2 inches. Weight, 200 pounds.

Year Club	Lea	G	IP	W	L	Pct	SO	BB	H	ERA	SAVES
1992 Rockies/Cub	Arizona	14	45	0	5	.000	39	22	65	7.80	0
1993 Huntington	Appal.	12	67²/₃	3	9	.250	42	38	82	6.25	0
1994 Peoria	Midwest	13	71¹/₃	1	7	.125	39	32	86	5.55	0
1994 Williamsprt	N.Y.-Penn.	16	80²/₃	4	6	.400	64	29	83	4.24	1
1995 Rockford a	Midwest	12	65¹/₃	4	4	.500	36	28	63	5.10	0
1995 Daytona	Fla. St.	19	44¹/₃	5	1	.833	30	13	34	1.22	4
1996 Orlando b	Southern	17	97	6	3	.667	85	28	95	3.34	0
1997 Iowa	A.A.	10	62	2	2	.500	58	21	47	3.48	0
1997 Chicago	N.L.	23	144	11	9	.550	93	69	126	4.25	0

a On suspended list from June 1 to June 3, 1995.
b On disabled list from July 6 to August 10, 1996.

GOODEN, DWIGHT EUGENE
Born, Tampa, Florida, November 16, 1964.
Bats Right. Throws Right. Height, 6 feet, 3 inches. Weight, 210 pounds.

Year Club	Lea	G	IP	W	L	Pct	SO	BB	H	ERA	SAVES
1982 Kingsport	Appalachian	9	65²/₃	5	4	.556	66	25	53	2.47	0
1982 Little Falls	N.Y.-Penn.	2	13	0	1	.000	18	3	11	4.15	0
1983 Lynchburg	Carolina	27	191	*19	4	.826	*300	*112	121	*2.50	0
1984 New York a	N.L.	31	218	17	9	.654	*276	73	161	2.60	0
1985 New York b	N.L.	35	*276²/₃	*24	4	.857	*268	69	198	*1.53	0
1986 New York	N.L.	33	250	17	6	.739	200	80	197	2.84	0
1987 Lynchburg	Carolina	1	4	0	0	.000	3	2	2	0.00	0
1987 Tidewater	Int.	4	22	3	0	1.000	24	9	20	2.05	0
1987 New York c	N.L.	25	179²/₃	15	7	.682	148	53	162	3.21	0
1988 New York	N.L.	34	248¹/₃	18	9	.667	175	57	242	3.19	0
1989 New York d	N.L.	19	118¹/₃	9	4	.692	101	47	93	2.89	1
1990 New York e	N.L.	34	232²/₃	19	7	.731	223	70	229	3.83	0
1991 New York f	N.L.	27	190	13	7	.650	150	56	185	3.60	0
1992 New York g-h	N.L.	31	206	10	13	.435	145	70	197	3.67	0
1993 New York i	N.L.	29	208³/₄	12	15	.444	149	61	188	3.45	0
1994 Norfolk	Int.	1	3	0	0	.000	4	1	0	0.00	0
1994 Binghamton	Eastern	1	5	1	0	1.000	4	1	2	0.00	0
1994 New York j-k-l	N.L.	7	41¹/₃	3	4	.429	40	15	46	6.31	0
1995 m		SUSPENDED—Did Not Play									
1996 New York n	A.L.	29	170²/₃	11	7	.611	126	88	169	5.01	0
1997 Norwich	Eastern	3	18	3	0	1.000	14	5	13	3.00	0
1997 New York o-p-q	A.L.	20	106¹/₃	9	5	.643	66	53	116	4.91	0
Major League Totals .... 13 Yrs.		354	2446²/₃	177	97	.646	2067	792	2183	3.31	1

Divisional Series

1997 New York	A.L.	1	5²/₃	0	0	.000	5	3	5	1.59	0

Championship Series

1986 New York	N.L.	2	17	0	1	.000	9	5	16	1.06	0
1988 New York	N.L.	3	18¹/₃	0	0	.000	20	8	10	2.95	0
Championship Series Totals 5			35¹/₃	0	1	.000	29	13	26	2.04	0

World Series Record

1986 New York	N.L.	2	9	0	2	.000	9	4	17	8.00	0

a Selected Rookie of the Year in National League for 1984.
b Selected Cy Young Award winner in National League for 1985.
c On disabled list from April 1 to June 5, 1987.
d On disabled list from July 2 to September 1, 1989.
e Appeared in one additional game as pinch runner.
f On disabled list from August 24 to end of 1991 season.
g On disabled list from July 18 to August 8, 1992.
h Appeared in two additional games as pinch hitter.
i Appeared in one additional game as pinch hitter.
j On disabled list from April 22 to June 9, 1994.
k Suspended 60 days by Commissioner's Office for violating drug aftercare program from July 28 to end of 1994 season and first 16 days of 1995 season; suspension extended to entire 1995 season for repeated violations of drug aftercare program, November 4, 1994.
l Filed for free agency, October 17, 1994.
m Signed with New York Yankees, October 16, 1995.
n Pitched no-hit, no-run game against Seattle Mariners, winning 2-0, May 14, 1996.
o On disabled list from April 6 to June 15, 1997.
p Filed for free agency, November 3, 1997.
q Signed as free agent with Cleveland Indians, December 8, 1997.

GORDON, THOMAS (TOM)
Born, Sebring, Florida, November 18, 1967.
Bats Right. Throws Right. Height, 5 feet, 9 inches. Weight, 180 pounds.

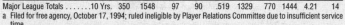

Year	Club	Lea	G	IP	W	L	Pct	SO	BB	H	ERA	SAVES
1986 Sarasota Royals	Gulf C.	9	44	3	1	.750	47	23	31	1.02	0
1986 Omaha	A.A.	1	1⅓	0	0	.000	3	2	6	47.25	0
1987 Eugene	Northwest	15	72⅓	*9	0	*1.000	91	47	48	2.86	1
1987 Fort Myers	Fla. St.	3	13⅔	1	0	1.000	11	17	5	2.63	0
1988 Appleton	Midwest	17	118	7	5	.583	*172	43	69	2.06	0
1988 Memphis	Southern	6	47⅓	6	0	1.000	62	17	16	0.38	0
1988 Omaha	A.A.	3	20⅓	3	0	1.000	29	15	11	1.33	0
1988 Kansas City	A.L.	5	15⅔	0	2	.000	18	7	16	5.17	0
1989 Kansas City	A.L.	49	163	17	9	.654	153	86	122	3.64	1
1990 Kansas City	A.L.	32	195⅓	12	11	.522	175	99	192	3.73	0
1991 Kansas City	A.L.	45	158	9	14	.391	167	87	129	3.87	1
1992 Kansas City	A.L.	40	117⅔	6	10	.375	98	55	116	4.59	0
1993 Kansas City	A.L.	48	155⅔	12	6	.667	143	77	125	3.58	1
1994 Kansas City a-b	A.L.	24	155⅓	11	7	.611	126	87	136	4.35	0
1995 Kansas City c-d-e-f	A.L.	31	189	12	12	.500	119	89	204	4.43	0
1996 Boston	A.L.	34	215⅔	12	9	.571	171	105	249	5.59	0
1997 Boston	A.L.	42	182⅔	6	10	.375	159	78	155	3.74	11
Major League Totals	10 Yrs.	350	1548	97	90	.519	1329	770	1444	4.21	14

a Filed for free agency, October 17, 1994; ruled ineligible by Player Relations Committee due to insufficient service time.
b Declared restricted free agent under Major League Baseball implemented labor proposal, December 23, 1994.
c Re-signed with Kansas City Royals, April 28, 1995.
d On disabled list from May 8 to May 24, 1995.
e Filed for free agency, November 12, 1995.
f Signed with Boston Red Sox, December 21, 1995.

GORECKI, RICHARD JOHN
Born, Evergreen Park, Illinois, August 27, 1973.
Bats Right. Throws Right. Height, 6 feet, 3 inches. Weight, 167 pounds.

Year	Club	Lea	G	IP	W	L	Pct	SO	BB	H	ERA	SAVES
1991 Great Falls	Pioneer	13	51	0	3	.000	56	27	44	4.41	0
1992 Bakersfield	California	25	129	11	7	.611	115	90	122	4.05	0
1993 San Antonio	Texas	26	156	6	9	.400	118	62	136	3.35	0
1994 Albuquerque	P.C.	22	103	8	6	.571	73	60	119	5.07	0
1995 Vero Beach	Fla. St.	6	27	1	2	.333	24	9	19	0.67	0
1997 San Berndno	California	14	51	2	3	.400	58	32	38	3.88	0
1997 San Antonio	Texas	7	45⅓	4	2	.667	33	15	26	1.39	0
1997 Los Angeles a	N.L.	4	6	1	0	1.000	6	6	9	15.00	0

a Selected in expansion draft by Tampa Bay Devil Rays, November 18, 1997.

GRACE, MICHAEL JAMES (MIKE)
Born, Joliet, Illinois, June 20, 1970.
Bats Right. Throws Right. Height, 6 feet, 4 inches. Weight, 220 pounds.

Year	Club	Lea	G	IP	W	L	Pct	SO	BB	H	ERA	SAVES
1991 Batavia	N.Y.-Penn.	6	32⅓	1	2	.333	36	14	20	1.39	0
1991 Spartanburg	So.Atl.	6	33⅓	3	1	.750	23	9	24	1.89	0
1992 Spartanburg	So.Atl.	6	27⅓	0	1	.000	21	8	25	4.94	0
1994 Spartanburg	So.Atl.	15	80⅓	5	5	.500	45	20	84	4.82	0
1995 Reading	Eastern	24	147⅓	13	6	.684	118	35	137	3.54	0
1995 Scranton-WB	Int.	2	17	2	0	1.000	13	2	17	1.59	0
1995 Philadelphia	N.L.	2	11⅓	1	1	.500	7	4	10	3.18	0
1996 Philadelphia a	N.L.	12	80	7	2	.778	49	16	72	3.49	0
1997 Reading	Eastern	4	20⅓	1	3	.250	10	6	28	5.75	0
1997 Scranton-WB	Int.	12	75	5	6	.455	55	27	84	4.56	0
1997 Philadelphia b	N.L.	6	39	3	2	.600	26	10	32	3.46	0
Major League Totals	3 Yrs.	20	130⅓	11	5	.688	82	30	114	3.45	0

a On disabled list from June 3 to September 30, 1996.
b On disabled list from April 1 to June 25, 1997.

GRANGER, JEFFREY ADAM

Born, San Pedro, California, December 16, 1971.
Bats Right. Throws Left. Height, 6 feet, 4 inches. Weight, 200 pounds.

Year	Club	Lea	G	IP	W	L	Pct	SO	BB	H	ERA	SAVES
1993	Eugene	Northwest	8	36	3	3	.500	56	10	28	3.00	0
1993	Kansas City	A.L.	1	1	0	0	.000	1	2	3	27.00	0
1994	Kansas City	A.L.	2	9⅓	0	1	.000	3	6	13	6.75	0
1994	Memphis	Southern	25	139⅔	7	7	.500	112	61	155	3.87	0
1995	Wichita	Texas	18	95⅔	4	7	.364	81	40	122	5.93	0
1996	Omaha	A.A.	45	77	5	3	.625	68	29	65	2.34	4
1996	Kansas City a	A.L.	15	16⅓	0	0	.000	11	10	21	6.61	0
1997	Pittsburgh	N.L.	9	5	0	0	.000	4	8	10	18.00	0
1997	Calgary	P.C.	30	82⅔	1	7	.125	68	33	111	5.55	1
Major League Totals	4 Yrs.		27	31⅔	0	1	.000	19	26	47	9.09	0

a Traded to Pittsburgh Pirates with infielder Joe Randa and pitchers Jeff Martin and Jeff Wallace for infielders Jay Bell and Jeff King, December 13, 1996.

GREEN, TYLER SCOTT

Born, Springfield, Ohio, February 18, 1970.
Bats Right. Throws Right. Height, 6 feet, 5 inches. Weight, 210 pounds.

Year	Club	Lea	G	IP	W	L	Pct	SO	BB	H	ERA	SAVES
1991	Batavia	N.Y.-Penn.	3	15	1	0	1.000	19	6	7	1.20	0
1991	Clearwater	Fla. St.	2	13	2	0	1.000	20	8	3	1.38	0
1992	Reading	Eastern	12	62⅓	6	3	.667	67	20	46	1.88	0
1992	Scranton-WB	Int.	2	10⅓	0	1	.000	15	12	7	6.10	0
1993	Philadelphia	N.L.	3	7⅓	0	0	.000	7	5	16	7.36	0
1993	Scranton-WB	Int.	28	118⅓	6	10	.375	87	43	102	3.95	0
1994	Scranton-WB	Int.	27	162	7	16	.304	95	77	179	5.56	0
1995	Philadelphia	N.L.	26	140⅔	8	9	.471	85	66	157	5.31	0
1996	Philadelphia a	N.L.			INJURED—Did Not Play							
1997	Scranton-WB	Int.	12	72⅓	4	8	.333	40	29	80	6.10	0
1997	Philadelphia b	N.L.	14	76⅔	4	4	.500	58	45	72	4.93	0
Major League Totals	3 Yrs.		43	224⅔	12	13	.480	150	116	245	5.25	0

a On disabled list from March 30 to end of 1996 season.
b On disabled list from April 1 to June 2, 1997.

GROOM, WEDSEL GARY JR. (BUDDY)

Born, Dallas, Texas, July 10, 1965.
Bats Left. Throws Left. Height, 6 feet, 2 inches. Weight, 200 pounds.

Year	Club	Lea	G	IP	W	L	Pct	SO	BB	H	ERA	SAVES
1987	Sarasota White Sox	Gulf C.	4	12	1	0	1.000	8	2	12	0.75	1
1987	Daytona Beach	Fla. St.	11	68	7	2	.778	29	33	60	3.59	0
1988	Tampa	Fla. St.	27	*195	13	10	.565	118	51	181	2.54	0
1989	Birmingham	Southern	26	167	13	8	.619	94	78	172	4.52	0
1990	Birmingham a	Southern	20	115	6	8	.429	66	48	135	5.07	0
1991	London	Eastern	11	51⅔	7	1	.875	39	12	51	3.48	0
1991	Toledo	Int.	24	75	2	5	.286	49	25	75	4.32	1
1992	Toledo	Int.	16	109⅓	7	7	.500	71	23	102	2.80	0
1992	Detroit	A.L.	12	38⅔	0	5	.000	15	22	48	5.82	1
1993	Toledo	Int.	16	102	9	3	.750	78	30	98	2.74	0
1993	Detroit	A.L.	19	36⅔	0	2	.000	15	13	48	6.14	0
1994	Toledo	Int.	5	4	0	0	.000	6	0	2	2.25	0
1994	Detroit	A.L.	40	32	0	1	.000	27	13	31	3.94	1
1995	Toledo	Int.	6	33	2	3	.400	24	4	31	1.91	0
1995	Detroit b-c	A.L.	23	40⅔	1	3	.250	23	26	55	7.52	1
1995	Florida d-e	N.L.	14	15	1	2	.333	12	6	26	7.20	0
1996	Oakland	A.L.	72	77⅓	5	0	1.000	57	34	85	3.84	2
1997	Oakland	A.L.	78	64⅔	2	2	.500	45	24	75	5.15	3
Major League Totals	6 Yrs.		258	305	9	15	.375	194	138	368	5.31	8

a Drafted by Detroit Tigers organization from Chicago White Sox organization in minor league draft, December 5, 1990.
b Traded to Florida Marlins for player to be named later, August 7, 1995.
c Detroit Tigers received pitcher Mike Myers to complete trade, August 9, 1995.
d Waived by Florida Marlins, October 4, 1995.
e Signed with Oakland Athletics organization, December 2, 1995.

GUARDADO, EDWARD ADRIAN

Born, Stockton, California, October 2, 1970.
Bats Right. Throws Left. Height, 6 feet. Weight, 193 pounds.

Year	Club	Lea	G	IP	W	L	Pct	SO	BB	H	ERA	SAVES
1991 Elizabethon	Appal.	14	92	8	4	.667	106	31	67	1.86	0
1992 Kenosha	Midwest	18	101	5	10	.333	103	30	106	4.37	0
1992 Visalia	California	7	49⅓	7	0	1.000	39	10	47	1.64	0
1993 Nashville	Southern	10	65⅓	4	0	1.000	57	10	53	1.24	0
1993 Minnesota	A.L.	19	94⅔	3	8	.273	46	36	123	6.18	0
1994 Salt Lake City	P.C.	24	151	12	7	.632	87	51	171	4.83	0
1994 Minnesota	A.L.	4	17	0	2	.000	8	4	26	8.47	0
1995 Minnesota	A.L.	51	91⅓	4	9	.308	71	45	99	5.12	2
1996 Minnesota	A.L.	83	73⅔	6	5	.545	74	33	61	5.25	4
1997 Minnesota	A.L.	69	46	0	4	.000	54	11	45	3.91	1
Major League Totals	5 Yrs.	226	322⅔	13	28	.317	253	135	354	5.47	7

GUBICZA, MARK STEVEN

Born, Philadelphia, Pennsylvania, August 14, 1962.
Bats Right. Throws Right. Height, 6 feet, 5 inches. Weight, 225 pounds.

Year	Club	Lea	G	IP	W	L	Pct	SO	BB	H	ERA	SAVES
1981 Sarasota Royals	Gulf Coast	11	56	*8	1	*.889	40	23	39	2.25	0
1982 Ft. Myers a	Fla. St.	11	48	2	5	.286	36	25	49	4.13	0
1983 Jacksonville	Southern	28	196	14	12	.538	*146	93	146	3.08	0
1984 Kansas City	A.L.	29	189	10	14	.417	111	75	172	4.05	0
1985 Kansas City	A.L.	29	177⅓	14	10	.583	99	77	160	4.06	0
1986 Kansas City b	A.L.	35	180⅔	12	6	.667	118	84	155	3.64	0
1987 Kansas City	A.L.	35	241⅔	13	18	.419	166	120	231	3.98	0
1988 Kansas City	A.L.	35	269⅔	20	8	.714	183	83	237	2.70	0
1989 Kansas City	A.L.	36	255	15	11	.577	173	63	252	3.04	0
1990 Kansas City c	A.L.	16	94	4	7	.364	71	38	101	4.50	0
1991 Omaha	A.A.	3	16⅓	2	1	.667	12	4	20	3.31	0
1991 Kansas City d	A.L.	26	133	9	12	.429	89	42	168	5.68	0
1992 Kansas City e-f	A.L.	18	111⅓	7	6	.538	81	36	110	3.72	0
1993 Kansas City g	A.L.	49	104⅓	5	8	.385	80	43	128	4.66	2
1994 Kansas City h	A.L.	22	130	7	9	.438	59	26	158	4.50	0
1995 Kansas City i	A.L.	33	213⅓	12	14	.462	81	62	222	3.75	0
1996 Kansas City j-k	A.L.	19	119⅓	4	12	.250	55	34	132	5.13	0
1997 Anaheim l-m-n	A.L.	2	4⅔	0	1	.000	5	3	13	25.07	0
1997 Lk Elsinore	California	2	4	0	1	.000	1	1	12	15.75	0
Major League Totals	14 Yrs.	384	2223⅓	132	136	.493	1371	786	2239	3.96	2
Championship Series											
1985 Kansas City	A.L.	2	8⅓	1	0	1.000	4	4	4	3.24	0

a On disabled list from June 29 to end of 1982 season.
b On disabled list from June 6 to June 21, 1986.
c On disabled list from June 30 to end of 1990 season.
d On disabled list from March 30 to May 13, 1991.
e On disabled list July 11 to end of 1992 season.
f Filed for free agency, October 30; re-signed with Kansas City Royals, November 25, 1992.
g Filed for free agency, November 3; re-signed with Kansas City Royals, December 8, 1993.
h Filed for free agency, October 27; re-signed with Kansas City Royals, December 12, 1994.
i Filed for free agency, November 12, 1995; re-signed with Kansas City Royals, December 7, 1995.
j On disabled list from July 6 to September 30, 1996.
k Traded to California Angels with pitcher Mike Bovee for designated hitter Chili Davis, October 28, 1996.
l On disabled list from April 12 to September 29, 1997.
m Filed for free agency, October 30, 1997.
n Signed with Anaheim Angels organization, December 8, 1997.

GUNDERSON, ERIC ANDREW

Born, Portland, Oregon, March 29, 1966
Bats Left. Throws Left. Height, 6 feet. Weight, 195 pounds.

Year	Club	Lea	G	IP	W	L	Pct	SO	BB	H	ERA	SAVES
1987 Everett	Northwest	15	98⅔	8	4	.667	99	34	80	2.46	0
1988 San Jose	California	20	149⅓	12	5	.706	151	52	131	2.65	0
1988 Shreveport	Texas	7	36⅔	1	2	.333	28	13	45	5.15	0
1989 Shreveport	Texas	11	72⅔	8	2	.800	61	23	68	2.72	0
1989 Phoenix	P.C.	14	85⅔	2	4	.333	56	36	93	5.04	0
1990 Phoenix	P.C.	16	82	5	7	.417	41	46	137	8.23	0
1990 Shreveport	Texas	8	52⅔	2	2	.500	44	17	51	3.25	0

Year	Club	Lea	G	IP	W	L	Pct	SO	BB	H	ERA	SAVES
1990 San Francisco	....	N.L.	7	19⅔	1	2	.333	14	11	24	5.49	0
1991 San Francisco a	....	N.L.	2	3⅓	0	0	.000	2	1	6	5.40	1
1991 Phoenix	....	P.C.	40	107	7	6	.538	53	44	153	6.14	3
1992 Jacksnville b	.....	Southern	15	23⅓	2	0	1.000	23	7	18	2.31	2
1992 Calgary	....	P.C.	27	52⅓	0	2	.000	50	31	57	6.02	5
1992 Seattle	....	A.L.	9	9⅓	2	1	.667	2	5	12	8.68	0
1993 Calgary c	....	P.C.	5	6⅔	0	1	.000	3	8	14	18.90	0
1993 Binghamton	....	Eastern	20	22⅓	2	1	.667	26	14	20	5.24	1
1993 Norfolk d-e	......	Int.	6	34	3	2	.600	26	9	41	3.71	0
1994 St. Lucie	....	Fla. St.	3	4⅔	1	0	1.000	6	0	4	0.00	1
1994 Norfolk	....	Int.	19	36⅔	3	1	.750	31	17	25	3.68	1
1994 New York	....	N.L.	14	9	0	0	.000	4	4	5	0.00	0
1995 New York f-g	....	N.L.	30	24⅓	1	1	.500	19	8	25	3.70	0
1995 Boston h-i	....	A.L.	19	12⅓	2	1	.667	9	9	13	5.11	0
1996 Pawtucket	....	Int.	26	33⅔	2	1	.667	34	9	38	3.48	2
1996 Boston j	....	A.L.	28	17⅓	0	1	.000	7	8	21	8.31	0
1997 Texas k-l	....	A.L.	60	49⅔	2	1	.667	31	15	45	3.26	1
Major League Totals	....	7 Yrs.	169	145	8	7	.533	88	61	151	4.59	2

a Released, March 31; signed with Seattle Mariners organization, April 9, 1992.
b On disabled list from April 10 to April 17, 1992.
c Released by Seattle Mariners, May 29; signed with New York Mets organization, June 10, 1993.
d Became free agent, October 15; signed with San Diego Padres, December 23, 1993.
e Released by San Diego Padres, March 14; signed with New York Mets organization, May 5, 1994.
f Released, August 2, 1995.
g Claimed on waivers by Seattle Mariners, August 4, 1995.
h Designated for assignment by Seattle Mariners, August 7, 1995.
i Claimed on waivers by Boston Red Sox, August 10, 1995.
j Opted for free agency, October 7, 1996.
k Signed as free agent with Texas Rangers organization, January 24, 1997.
l On disabled list from August 19 to September 8, 1997.

GUTHRIE, MARK ANDREW
Born, Buffalo, New York, September 22, 1965.
Bats Both. Throws Left. Height, 6 feet, 4 inches. Weight, 206 pounds.

Year	Club	Lea	G	IP	W	L	Pct	SO	BB	H	ERA	SAVES
1987 Visalia	....	California	4	12	2	1	.667	9	5	10	4.50	0
1988 Visalia	....	California	25	171⅓	12	9	.571	182	86	169	3.31	0
1989 Orlando	....	Southern	14	96	8	3	.727	103	38	75	1.97	0
1989 Portland	....	P.C.	7	44⅓	3	4	.429	35	16	45	3.65	0
1989 Minnesota	....	A.L.	13	57⅓	2	4	.333	38	21	66	4.55	0
1990 Portland	....	P.C.	9	42⅓	1	3	.250	39	12	47	2.98	0
1990 Minnesota	....	A.L.	24	144⅔	7	9	.438	101	39	154	3.79	0
1991 Minnesota a	....	A.L.	41	98	7	5	.583	72	41	116	4.32	2
1992 Minnesota	....	A.L.	54	75	2	3	.400	76	23	59	2.88	5
1993 Minnesota b	....	A.L.	22	21	2	1	.667	15	16	20	4.71	0
1994 Minnesota	....	A.L.	50	51⅓	4	2	.667	38	18	65	6.14	1
1995 Minnesota	....	A.L.	36	42⅓	5	3	.625	48	16	47	4.46	0
1995 Los Angeles c	....	N.L.	24	19⅔	0	2	.000	19	9	19	3.66	0
1996 Los Angeles d-e	....	N.L.	66	73	2	3	.400	56	22	65	2.22	1
1997 Los Angeles	....	N.L.	62	69⅓	1	4	.200	42	30	71	5.32	1
Major League Totals	....	9 Yrs.	392	651⅓	32	36	.471	505	235	682	4.07	10
Division Series												
1995 Los Angeles	....	N.L.	3	1⅓	0	0	.000	1	1	2	6.75	0
1996 Los Angeles	....	N.L.	1	0⅓	0	0	.000	1	1	0	0.00	0
Division Series Totals	....	4		1⅔	0	0	.000	2	2	2	5.40	0
Championship Series												
1991 Minnesota	....	A.L.	2	2⅔	1	0	1.000	0	0	0	0.00	0
World Series Record												
1991 Minnesota	....	A.L.	4	4	0	1	.000	3	4	3	2.25	0

a Appeared in one additional game as pinch runner.
b On disabled list from May 29 to end of 1993 season.
c Traded to Los Angeles Dodgers with pitcher Kevin Tapani for pitcher Jose Parra, pitcher Greg Hansell and infielder Ron Coomer, July 31, 1995. Minnesota Twins received outfielder Chris Latham to complete trade, October 30, 1995.
d Filed for free agency, October 29, 1996.
e Re-signed with Los Angeles Dodgers, November 6, 1996.

GUZMAN (CORREA), JUAN ANDRES

Born, Santo Domingo, Dominican Republic, October 28, 1966.
Bats Right. Throws Right. Height, 5 feet, 11 inches. Weight, 195 pounds.

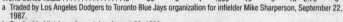

Year	Club	Lea	G	IP	W	L	Pct	SO	BB	H	ERA	SAVES
1985	Bradenton Dodgers ...Gulf C.		21	42	5	1	.833	43	25	39	3.86	4
1986	Vero Beach ....Fla. St.		26	131⅓	10	9	.526	96	90	114	3.49	0
1987	Bakersfield a .....California		22	110	5	6	.455	113	84	106	4.75	0
1988	Knoxville ....Southern		46	84	4	5	.444	90	61	52	2.36	6
1989	Syracuse ....Int.		14	20⅓	1	1	.500	28	30	13	3.98	0
1989	Knoxville ....Southern		22	47⅔	1	4	.200	50	60	34	6.23	0
1990	Knoxville ....Southern		37	157	11	9	.550	138	80	145	4.24	1
1991	Syracuse ....Int.		12	67	4	5	.444	67	42	46	4.03	0
1991	Toronto .............A.L.		23	138⅔	10	3	.769	123	66	98	2.99	0
1992	Toronto b ...........A.L.		28	180⅔	16	5	.762	165	72	135	2.64	0
1992	Syracuse ....Int.		1	3	0	0	.000	3	1	6	6.00	0
1993	Toronto .............A.L.		33	221	14	3	*.824	194	110	211	3.99	0
1994	Toronto .............A.L.		25	147⅓	12	11	.522	124	76	165	5.68	0
1995	Syracuse ....Int.		1	5	0	0	.000	5	3	1	0.00	0
1995	Toronto c ...........A.L.		24	135⅓	4	14	.222	94	73	151	6.32	0
1996	Toronto d ...........A.L.		27	187⅔	11	8	.579	165	53	158	2.93	0
1997	Toronto e ...........A.L.		13	60	3	6	.333	52	31	48	4.95	0
1997	Dunedin ....Fla. St.		2	4	0	0	.000	3	1	3	0.00	0
Major League Totals ....7 Yrs.			173	1070⅔	70	50	.583	917	481	966	4.03	0
Championship Series												
1991	Toronto .............A.L.		1	5⅔	1	0	1.000	2	4	4	3.18	0
1992	Toronto .............A.L.		2	13	2	0	1.000	11	5	12	2.08	0
1993	Toronto .............A.L.		2	13	2	0	1.000	9	9	8	2.08	0
Championship Series Totals 5				31⅔	5	0	1.000	22	18	24	2.27	0
World Series Record												
1992	Toronto .............A.L.		1	8	0	0	.000	7	1	8	1.13	0
1993	Toronto .............A.L.		2	12	0	1	.000	12	8	10	3.75	0
World Series Totals 3				20	0	1	.000	19	9	18	2.70	0

a Traded by Los Angeles Dodgers to Toronto Blue Jays organization for infielder Mike Sharperson, September 22, 1987.
b On disabled list from August 4 to August 29, 1992.
c On disabled list from May 16 to June 5 and August 10 to August 29, 1995.
d On disabled list from May 23 to June 7, 1996.
e On disabled list from May 29 to June 27 and July 16 to September 29, 1997.

HALL, MICHAEL DARREN

Born, Marysville, Ohio, July 14, 1964.
Bats Right. Throws Right. Height, 6 feet, 3 inches. Weight, 205 pounds.

Year	Club	Lea	G	IP	W	L	Pct	SO	BB	H	ERA	SAVES
1986	Medicne Hat ....Pioneer		17	89⅓	5	7	.417	60	47	91	3.83	0
1987	Myrtle Bch ....So. Atl.		41	66⅔	5	5	.500	68	28	57	3.51	6
1988	Dunedin ....Fla. St.		4	9⅓	1	1	.500	15	5	6	1.93	1
1988	Knoxville ....Southern		37	40⅓	3	2	.600	33	17	28	2.23	17
1989	Dunedin ....Fla. St.		16	51	1	4	.200	42	21	46	3.53	0
1989	Knoxville ....Southern		13	19⅔	0	2	.000	10	10	21	3.66	1
1990	Knoxville ....Southern		28	33⅓	3	5	.375	28	33	29	4.86	1
1991	Knoxville ....Southern		42	69⅓	5	3	.625	78	27	56	2.60	2
1992	Syracuse ....Int.		55	69	4	6	.400	49	35	62	4.30	5
1993	Syracuse ....Int.		60	79⅓	6	7	.462	68	31	75	5.33	13
1994	Syracuse ....Int.		6	5⅔	1	0	1.000	7	2	5	1.59	3
1994	Toronto .............A.L.		30	31⅔	2	3	.400	28	14	26	3.41	17
1995	Toronto a-b .........A.L.		17	16⅓	0	2	.000	11	9	21	4.41	3
1996	Los Angeles c ........N.L.		9	12	0	2	.000	12	5	13	6.00	0
1996	Yakima ....Northwest		2	3	0	1	.000	4	0	5	3.00	0
1997	Los Angeles .........N.L.		63	54⅔	3	2	.600	39	26	58	2.30	2
Major League Totals ....4 Yrs.			119	114⅔	5	9	.357	90	54	118	3.30	22

a On disabled list June 19 to July 4 and July 30 to end of 1996 season.
b Released by Toronto Blue Jays, October 10, 1996.
c Signed as free agent with Los Angeles Dodgers, November 1, 1996.

HAMILTON, JOHNS JOSEPH (JOEY)
Born, Statesboro, Georgia, September 9, 1970.
Bats Right. Throws Right. Height, 6 feet, 4 inches. Weight, 220 pounds.

Year Club	Lea	G	IP	W	L	Pct	SO	BB	H	ERA	SAVES
1992 Charleston, SC	So. Atl.	7	34⅔	2	2	.500	35	4	37	3.38	0
1992 High Desert	California	9	49⅓	4	3	.571	43	18	46	2.74	0
1992 Wichita	Texas	6	34⅔	3	0	1.000	26	11	33	2.86	0
1993 Rancho Cucamonga	Calif.	2	11	1	0	1.000	6	2	11	4.09	0
1993 Wichita	Texas	15	90⅔	4	9	.308	50	36	101	3.97	0
1993 Las Vegas	P.C.	8	47	3	2	.600	33	22	49	4.40	0
1994 Las Vegas	P.C.	9	59⅓	3	5	.375	32	22	69	2.73	0
1994 San Diego	N.L.	16	108⅔	9	6	.600	61	29	98	2.98	0
1995 San Diego	N.L.	31	204⅓	6	9	.400	123	56	189	3.08	0
1996 San Diego	N.L.	34	211⅔	15	9	.625	184	85	206	4.17	0
1997 San Diego a	N.L.	31	192⅔	12	7	.632	124	69	199	4.25	0
Major League Totals 4 Yrs.		112	717⅓	42	31	.575	492	237	692	3.70	
Division Series											
1996 San Diego	N.L.	1	6	0	1	.000	6	0	5	4.50	0

a On disabled list from April 24 to May 17, 1997.

HAMMOND, CHRISTOPHER ANDREW
Born, Atlanta, Georgia, January 21, 1966.
Bats Left. Throws Left. Height, 6 feet, 1 inch. Weight, 195 pounds.

Year Club	Lea	G	IP	W	L	Pct	SO	BB	H	ERA	SAVES
1986 Sarasota Reds	Gulf C.	7	41⅔	3	2	.600	53	17	27	2.81	0
1986 Tampa	Fla. St.	5	21⅔	0	2	.000	5	13	25	3.32	0
1987 Tampa	Fla. St.	25	170	11	11	.500	126	60	174	3.55	0
1988 Chattanooga	Southern	26	182⅔	*16	5	.762	127	77	127	*1.72	0
1989 Nashville	A.A.	24	157⅓	11	7	.611	142	96	144	3.38	0
1990 Nashville	A.A.	24	149	*15	1	*.938	*149	63	118	*2.17	0
1990 Cincinnati	N.L.	3	11⅓	0	2	.000	4	12	13	6.35	0
1991 Cincinnati a	N.L.	20	99⅔	7	7	.500	50	48	92	4.06	0
1992 Cincinnati b-c	N.L.	28	147⅓	7	10	.412	79	55	149	4.21	0
1993 Florida d	N.L.	32	191	11	12	.478	108	66	207	4.66	0
1994 Portland	Eastern	1	2	0	0	.000	2	0	0	0.00	0
1994 Brevard City	Fla. St.	2	7⅓	0	0	.000	5	3	4	1.23	0
1994 Florida e	N.L.	13	73⅓	4	4	.500	40	23	79	3.07	0
1995 Brevard City	Fla. St.	1	4	0	0	.000	4	0	3	0.00	0
1995 Charlotte	Int.	1	4	0	0	.000	3	2	3	0.00	0
1995 Florida f	N.L.	25	161	9	6	.600	126	47	157	3.80	0
1996 Brevard Cty	Fla. St.	1	4	0	0	.000	8	0	3	0.00	0
1996 Charlotte	Int.	1	5	1	0	1.000	3	0	5	7.20	0
1996 Florida g-h-i	N.L.	38	81	5	8	.385	50	27	104	6.56	0
1997 Boston j-k	A.L.	29	65⅓	3	4	.429	48	27	81	5.92	1
Major League Totals 8 Yrs.		188	830	46	53	.465	505	305	882	4.51	1

a On disabled list from July 27 to September 1, 1991.
b Appeared in two additional games as pinch runner.
c Traded to Florida Marlins for third baseman Gary Scott and player to be named, March 27; Cincinnati Reds acquired pitcher Hector Carrasco to complete trade, September 10, 1993.
d Appeared in one additional game as pinch hitter.
e On disabled list from June 11 to August 2, 1994.
f On disabled list from April 25 to May 13 and August 3 to August 19, 1995.
g On disabled list from June 9 to July 14, 1996.
h Waived by Florida Marlins, October 3, 1996.
i Filed for free agency, October 4, 1996.
j On disabled list from June 28 to September 29, 1997.
k Filed for free agency, October 30, 1997.

HAMPTON, MICHAEL WILLIAM
Born, Brooksville, Florida, September 9, 1972.
Bats Right. Throws Left. Height, 5 feet, 10 inches. Weight, 190 pounds.

Year Club	Lea	G	IP	W	L	Pct	SO	BB	H	ERA	SAVES
1990 Tempe Mariners	Arizona	14	64⅓	*7	2	.778	59	40	52	2.66	0
1991 San Bernardino	California	18	73⅔	1	7	.125	57	47	71	5.25	0
1991 Bellingham	Northwest	9	57	5	2	.714	65	26	32	1.58	0
1992 San Bernardino	California	25	170	13	8	.619	132	66	163	3.12	0
1992 Jacksonville	Southern	2	10⅓	0	1	.000	6	1	13	4.35	0

Year Club	Lea	G	IP	W	L	Pct	SO	BB	H	ERA	SAVES
1993 Seattle ...........A.L.		13	17	1	3	.250	8	17	28	9.53	1
1993 Jacksonville a ......Southern		15	87⅓	6	4	.600	84	33	71	3.71	0
1994 Houston .............N.L.		44	41⅓	2	1	.667	24	16	46	3.70	0
1995 Houston b ...........N.L.		24	150⅔	9	8	.529	115	49	141	3.35	0
1996 Houston .............N.L.		27	160⅓	10	10	.500	101	49	175	3.59	0
1997 Houston .............N.L.		34	223	15	10	.600	139	77	217	3.83	0
Major League Totals ....5 Yrs.		142	592⅓	37	32	.536	387	208	607	3.80	1
Division Series											
1997 Houston .............N.L.		1	4⅔	0	1	.000	2	8	2	11.57	0

a Traded by Seattle Mariners to Houston Astros with outfielder Mike Felder for outfielder Eric Anthony, December 10, 1993.
b On disabled list from May 15 to June 13, 1995.

HANEY, CHRISTOPHER DEANE

Born, Baltimore, Maryland, November 16, 1968.
Bats Left. Throws Left. Height, 6 feet, 3 inches. Weight, 195 pounds.

Year Club	Lea	G	IP	W	L	Pct	SO	BB	H	ERA	SAVES
1990 Jamestown ......N.Y.-Penn.		6	28	3	0	1.000	26	10	17	0.96	1
1990 Rockford ....Midwest		8	53	2	4	.333	45	6	40	2.21	0
1990 Jacksonville ....Southern		1	6	1	0	1.000	6	3	6	0.00	0
1991 Harrisburg ....Eastern		12	83⅓	5	3	.625	68	31	65	2.16	0
1991 Indianapolis ........A.A.		2	10⅓	1	1	.500	8	6	14	4.35	0
1991 Montreal ...........N.L.		16	84⅔	3	7	.300	51	43	94	4.04	0
1992 Montreal a-b .........N.L.		9	38	2	3	.400	27	10	40	5.45	0
1992 Indianapolis c ........A.A.		15	84	5	2	.714	61	42	88	5.14	0
1992 Kansas City ...........A.L.		7	42	2	3	.400	27	16	35	3.86	0
1993 Omaha ..............A.A.		8	47⅔	6	1	.857	32	14	43	2.27	0
1993 Kansas City ...........A.L.		23	124	9	9	.500	65	53	141	6.02	0
1994 Omaha ..............A.A.		18	104⅔	8	7	.533	78	37	125	5.25	0
1994 Kansas City ...........A.L.		6	28⅓	2	2	.500	18	11	36	7.31	0
1995 Kansas City d ........A.L.		16	81⅓	3	4	.429	31	33	78	3.65	0
1996 Kansas City ...........A.L.		35	228	10	14	.417	115	51	267	4.70	0
1997 Omaha ..............A.A.		4	19	1	0	1.000	7	6	16	3.79	0
1997 Wichita ....Texas		2	6⅔	0	1	.000	2	0	5	2.70	0
1997 Kansas City e .........A.L.		8	24⅔	1	2	.333	16	5	29	4.38	0
Major League Totals ....7 Yrs.		120	651	32	44	.421	350	222	720	4.82	0

a On disabled list from April 12 to July 16, 1992.
b Appeared in one additional game as pinch runner.
c Traded by Montreal Expos to Kansas City Royals with pitcher Bill Sampen for third baseman Sean Berry and pitcher Archie Corbin, August 29, 1992.
d On disabled list from July 13 to October 2, 1995.
e On disabled list from April 15 to June 17 and June 27 to September 3, 1997.

HANSELL, GREGORY MICHAEL (GREG)

Born, Bellflower, California, March 12, 1971.
Bats Right. Throws Right. Height, 6 feet, 5 inches. Weight, 215 pounds.

Year Club	Lea	G	IP	W	L	Pct	SO	BB	H	ERA	SAVES
1989 Red Sox ....Gulf Coast		10	57	3	2	.600	44	23	51	2.53	2
1990 Winter Havn ....Fla.St.		21	115⅓	7	10	.412	79	64	95	3.59	0
1990 St. Lucie ....Fla.St.		6	38	2	4	.333	16	15	34	2.84	0
1991 Bakersfield ......California		25	150⅔	14	5	.737	132	42	142	2.87	0
1992 Albuquerque ..........P.C.		13	68⅔	1	5	.167	38	35	84	5.24	0
1992 San Antonio ....Texas		14	92⅓	6	4	.600	64	33	80	2.83	0
1993 Albuquerque ..........P.C.		26	101⅓	5	10	.333	60	60	131	6.93	0
1994 Albuquerque ..........P.C.		47	123⅓	10	2	.833	101	31	109	2.99	8
1995 Los Angeles .........N.L.		20	19⅓	0	1	.000	13	6	29	7.45	0
1995 Albuquerque ..........P.C.		8	16	1	1	.500	15	6	25	8.44	1
1995 Salt Lake .............P.C.		7	32⅓	3	1	.750	17	4	39	5.01	0
1996 Minnesota ...........A.L.		50	74⅓	3	0	1.000	46	31	83	5.69	3
1997 Milwaukee a-b ........A.L.		3	4⅔	0	0	.000	5	1	5	9.64	0
1997 Tucson ...............P.C.		40	87⅓	2	3	.400	76	27	99	4.64	2
Major League Totals ....3 Yrs.		73	98⅓	3	1	.750	64	38	117	6.22	3

a Outrighted by Milwaukee Brewers, August 7, 1997.
b Signed with Arizona Diamondbacks organization, December 18, 1997.

HANSON, ERIK BRIAN

Born, Kinnelon, New Jersey, May 18, 1965.
Bats Right. Throws Right. Height, 6 feet, 6 inches. Weight, 210 pounds.

Year	Club	Lea	G	IP	W	L	Pct	SO	BB	H	ERA	SAVES
1986 Chattanooga	Southern	3	9⅓	0	0	.000	11	4	10	3.86	0
1987 Chattanooga	Southern	21	131⅓	8	10	.444	131	43	102	2.60	0
1987 Calgary	P.C.	8	47⅓	1	3	.250	43	21	38	3.61	0
1988 Calgary	P.C.	27	161⅔	12	7	.632	*154	57	92	4.23	0
1988 Seattle	A.L.	6	41⅔	2	3	.400	36	12	35	3.24	0
1989 Calgary	P.C.	8	38	4	2	.667	37	11	51	6.87	0
1989 Seattle a	A.L.	17	113⅓	9	5	.643	75	32	103	3.18	0
1990 Seattle	A.L.	33	236	18	9	.667	211	68	205	3.24	0
1991 Seattle b	A.L.	27	174⅔	8	8	.500	143	56	182	3.81	0
1991 Calgary	P.C.	1	6	0	0	.000	5	2	1	1.50	0
1992 Seattle c	A.L.	31	186⅔	8	*17	.320	112	57	209	4.82	0
1993 Seattle d-e	A.L.	31	215	11	12	.478	163	60	215	3.47	0
1994 Cincinnati f-g	N.L.	22	122⅔	5	5	.500	101	23	137	4.11	0
1995 Boston h-i-j	A.L.	29	186⅔	15	5	.750	139	59	187	4.24	0
1996 Toronto	A.L.	35	214⅓	13	17	.433	156	102	243	5.41	0
1997 Dunedin	Fla. St.	2	7	0	0	.000	5	1	7	1.29	0
1997 Toronto k	A.L.	3	15	0	0	.000	18	6	15	7.80	0
Major League Totals 10 Yrs.		234	1506⅓	89	81	.524	1154	475	1531	4.08	0
Division Series											
1995 Boston	A.L.	1	8	0	1	.000	5	4	4	4.50	0

a On disabled list from May 25 to August 3, 1989.
b On disabled list from May 12 to May 27 and May 29 to June 21, 1991.
c On disabled list from August 22 to September 12, 1992.
d Appeared in two additional games as pinch runner.
e Traded to Cincinnati Reds with second baseman Bret Boone for pitcher Bobby Ayala and catcher Dan Wilson, November 2, 1993.
f On disabled list from August 9 to end of 1994 season.
g Filed for free agency, October 22, 1994; ruled ineligible for free agency by Player Relations Committee due to insufficient service time.
h Signed with Boston Red Sox, April 11, 1995.
i Filed for free agency, November 12, 1995.
j Signed with Toronto Blue Jays, December 22, 1995.
k On disabled list from April 1 to April 17 and April 23 to September 14, 1997.

HARNISCH, PETER THOMAS (PETE)

Born, Commack, New York, September 23, 1966.
Bats Right. Throws Right. Height, 6 feet. Weight, 207 pounds.

Year	Club	Lea	G	IP	W	L	Pct	SO	BB	H	ERA	SAVES
1987 Bluefield	Appal.	9	52⅔	3	1	.750	64	26	38	2.56	0
1987 Hagerstown	Carolina	4	20	1	2	.333	18	14	17	2.25	0
1988 Charlotte	Southern	20	132⅓	7	6	.538	141	52	113	2.58	0
1988 Rochester	Int.	7	58⅓	4	1	.800	43	14	44	2.16	0
1988 Baltimore	A.L.	2	13	0	2	.000	10	9	13	5.54	0
1989 Rochester	Int.	12	87⅓	5	5	.500	59	35	60	2.58	0
1989 Baltimore	A.L.	18	103⅓	5	9	.357	70	64	97	4.62	0
1990 Baltimore a	A.L.	31	188⅔	11	11	.500	122	86	189	4.34	0
1991 Houston	N.L.	33	216⅔	12	9	.571	172	83	169	2.70	0
1992 Houston b	N.L.	34	206⅔	9	10	.474	164	64	182	3.70	0
1993 Houston	N.L.	33	217⅔	16	9	.640	185	79	171	2.98	0
1994 Tucson	P.C.	1	5	0	0	.000	1	1	2	0.00	0
1994 Houston c-d-e-f	N.L.	17	95	8	5	.615	62	39	100	5.40	0
1995 New York g-h	N.L.	18	110	2	8	.200	82	24	111	3.68	0
1996 St. Lucie	Fla.St.	2	13	1	0	1.000	12	0	11	2.77	0
1996 New York i	N.L.	31	194⅔	8	12	.400	114	61	195	4.21	0
1997 Mets	Gulf Coast	1	3	0	0	.000	5	0	7	12.00	0
1997 St. Lucie	Fla. St.	2	12	1	0	1.000	7	4	5	3.00	0
1997 Norfolk	Int.	3	16⅔	1	1	.500	16	10	16	5.40	0
1997 New York j-k	N.L.	6	25⅔	0	1	.000	12	11	35	8.06	0
1997 Milwaukee l-m	A.L.	4	14	1	1	.500	10	12	13	5.14	0
Major League Totals 10 Yrs.		227	1385⅓	72	77	.483	1003	532	1275	3.88	0

a Traded to Houston Astros with pitcher Curt Schilling and outfielder Steve Finley for first baseman Glenn Davis, January 10, 1991.
b Suspended three games by National League for June 24 blatantly throwing behind batter, July 7 to July 10, 1992.
c Appeared in one additional game as pinch runner.
d On disabled list from May 23 to June 30, 1994.
e Traded to New York Mets for one or two players to be named, November 28; Houston Astros acquired pitcher Andy Beckerman to complete trade, December 6, 1994.

f Not offered 1995 contract and became free agent, December 23, 1994.
g Re-signed with New York Mets, April 6, 1995.
h On disabled list from August 2 to October 2, 1995.

i On disabled list from April 1 to April 14, 1996.
j On disabled list from April 2 to August 5, 1997.
k Traded to Milwaukee Brewers for outfielder Donnie Moore, August 31, 1997.
l Filed for free agency, October 27, 1997.
m Signed as free agent with Milwaukee Brewers, January 22, 1998.

HARRIS, HERNANDO PETROCELLI (PEP)

Born, Lancaster, South Carolina, September 23, 1972.
Bats Right. Throws Right. Height, 6 feet, 2 inches. Weight, 185 pounds.

Year	Club	Lea	G	IP	W	L	Pct	SO	BB	H	ERA	SAVES
1991	Burlington	Appal.	13	65²/₃	4	3	.571	47	31	67	3.29	0
1992	Columbus	So.Atl.	18	90²/₃	7	4	.636	57	51	88	3.67	0
1993	Columbus	So.Atl.	26	119	7	8	.467	82	44	113	4.24	0
1994	Kinston	Carolina	27	32²/₃	4	1	.800	37	16	21	1.93	8
1994	Canton-Akrn	Eastern	24	20¹/₃	2	0	1.000	15	13	9	2.21	12
1995	Buffalo	A.A.	14	32²/₃	2	1	.667	18	15	32	2.48	0
1995	Canton-Akrn	Eastern	32	83	6	3	.667	40	23	78	2.39	10
1996	Midland	Texas	6	39	2	2	.500	28	9	47	5.31	0
1996	Vancouver	P.C.	18	118¹/₃	9	3	.750	61	46	135	4.56	0
1996	California a	A.L.	11	32¹/₃	2	0	1.000	20	17	31	3.90	0
1997	Anaheim	A.L.	61	79²/₃	5	4	.556	56	38	82	3.62	0
Major League Totals	2 Yrs.		72	112	7	4	.636	76	55	113	3.70	0

a Traded to California Angels with pitcher Jason Grimsley for pitcher Brian Anderson, February 15, 1996.

HASEGAWA, SHIGETOSHI

Born, Kobe, Japan, August 1, 1968.
Bats Right. Throws Right. Height, 5 feet, 11 inches. Weight, 160 pounds.

Year	Club	Lea	G	IP	W	L	Pct	SO	BB	H	ERA	SAVES
1991	Orix a	Japan Pac.	28	185	12	9	.571	111	50	...	3.55	1
1992	Orix	Japan Pac.	24	143¹/₃	6	8	.428	86	51	...	3.27	1
1993	Orix	Japan Pac.	23	159²/₃	12	6	.667	86	48	...	2.71	0
1994	Orix	Japan Pac.	25	156¹/₃	11	9	.550	86	46	...	3.11	1
1995	Orix	Japan Pac.	24	171	12	7	.632	91	51	...	2.89	0
1996	Orix	Japan Pac.	18	87²/₃	4	6	.400	55	40	...	5.34	1
1997	Anaheim b	A.L.	50	116²/₃	3	7	.300	83	46	118	3.93	0

a Selected Pacific League Rookie of the Year for 1991.
b Signed as free agent by Anaheim Angels, January 9, 1997.

HAWKINS, LA TROY

Born, Gary, Indiana, December 21, 1972.
Bats Right. Throws Right. Height, 6 feet, 5 inches. Weight, 195 pounds.

Year	Club	Lea	G	IP	W	L	Pct	SO	BB	H	ERA	SAVES
1991	Twins	Gulf Coast	11	55	4	3	.571	47	26	62	4.75	0
1992	Twins	Gulf Coast	6	36¹/₃	3	2	.600	35	10	36	3.22	0
1992	Elizabethtown	Appal.	5	26²/₃	0	1	.000	36	11	21	3.38	0
1993	Ft. Wayne	Midwest	26	157¹/₃	15	5	.750	179	41	110	2.06	0
1994	Ft. Myers	Fla. St.	6	38²/₃	4	0	1.000	36	6	32	2.33	0
1994	Nashville	Southern	11	73¹/₃	9	2	.818	53	28	50	2.33	0
1994	Salt Lake	P.C.	12	81²/₃	5	4	.556	37	33	92	4.08	0
1995	Salt Lake	P.C.	22	144¹/₃	9	7	.563	74	40	150	3.55	0
1995	Minnesota	A.L.	6	27	2	3	.400	9	12	39	8.67	0
1996	Minnesota	A.L.	7	26¹/₃	1	1	.500	24	9	42	8.20	0
1996	Salt Lake	P.C.	20	137²/₃	9	8	.529	99	31	138	3.92	0
1997	Salt Lake	P.C.	14	76	9	4	.692	53	16	100	5.45	0
1997	Minnesota	A.L.	20	103¹/₃	6	12	.333	58	47	134	5.84	0
Major League Totals	3 Yrs.		33	156²/₃	9	16	.360	91	68	215	6.72	0

HAYNES, JIMMY WAYNE
Born, LaGrange, Georgia, September 5, 1972.
Bats Right. Throws Right. Height, 6 feet, 4 inches. Weight, 175 pounds.

Year	Club	Lea	G	IP	W	L	Pct	SO	BB	H	ERA	SAVES
1991	Orioles	Gulf Coast	14	62	3	2	.600	67	21	44	1.60	2
1992	Kane County	Midwest	24	144	7	11	.389	141	45	131	2.56	0
1993	Frederick	Carolina	27	172⅓	12	8	.600	174	61	139	3.03	0
1994	Rochester	Int.	3	13⅓	1	0	1.000	14	6	20	6.75	0
1994	Bowie	Eastern	25	173⅔	13	8	.619	177	46	154	2.90	0
1995	Rochester	Int.	26	167	12	8	.600	140	49	162	3.29	0
1995	Baltimore	A.L.	4	24	2	1	.667	22	12	11	2.25	0
1996	Rochester	Int.	5	28⅔	1	1	.500	24	18	31	5.65	0
1996	Baltimore	A.L.	26	89	3	6	.333	65	58	122	8.29	1
1997	Rochester	Int.	16	102	5	4	.556	113	55	89	3.44	0
1997	Edmonton	P.C.	5	29⅔	0	2	.000	24	11	36	4.85	0
1997	Oakland a	A.L.	13	73⅓	3	6	.333	65	40	74	4.42	0
Major League Totals		3 Yrs.	43	186⅓	8	13	.381	152	110	207	5.99	1

a Traded to Oakland Athletics with player to be named later for outfielder Geronimo Berroa, June 27, 1997. Oakland Athletics received pitcher Mark Seaver to complete trade, September 2, 1997.

HELLING, RICKY ALLEN (RICK)
Born, Devil's Lake, North Dakota, December 15, 1970.
Bats Right. Throws Right. Height, 6 feet, 3 inches. Weight, 220 pounds.

Year	Club	Lea	G	IP	W	L	Pct	SO	BB	H	ERA	SAVES
1992	Charlotte	Fla. St.	3	19⅔	1	1	.500	20	4	13	2.29	0
1993	Tulsa	Texas	26	177⅓	12	8	.600	188	46	150	3.60	0
1993	Okla City	A.A.	2	11	1	1	.500	17	3	5	1.64	0
1994	Texas	A.L.	9	52	3	2	.600	25	18	62	5.88	0
1994	Okla City	A.A.	20	132⅓	4	12	.250	85	43	153	5.78	0
1995	Texas	A.L.	3	12⅓	0	2	.000	5	8	17	6.57	0
1995	Okla City	A.A.	20	109⅔	4	8	.333	80	41	132	5.33	0
1996	Okla City	A.A.	23	140	12	4	.750	157	38	124	2.96	0
1996	Texas a	A.L.	6	20⅓	1	2	.333	16	9	23	7.52	0
1996	Florida	N.L.	5	27⅔	2	1	.667	26	7	14	1.95	0
1997	Florida b	N.L.	31	76	2	6	.250	53	48	61	4.38	0
1997	Texas	A.L.	10	55	3	3	.500	46	21	47	4.58	0
Major League Totals		4 Yrs.	64	243⅓	11	16	.407	171	111	224	4.85	0

a Acquired by Florida Marlins, September 3, 1996, as player-to-be-named-later in trade which sent pitcher John Burkette to Texas Rangers for pitcher Ryan Dempster, August 8, 1996.

b Traded to Texas Rangers for pitcher Ed Vosberg, August 12, 1997.

HENRIQUEZ, OSCAR EDUARDO
Born, LaGuaira, Venezuela, January 28, 1974.
Bats Right. Throws Right. Height, 6 feet, 6 inches. Weight, 220 pounds.

Year	Club	Lea	G	IP	W	L	Pct	SO	BB	H	ERA	SAVES
1993	Asheville	So. Atl.	27	150	9	10	.474	117	70	154	4.44	0
1995	Kissimmee	Fla. St.	20	44⅔	3	4	.429	36	30	40	5.04	1
1996	Kissimmee	Fla. St.	37	34	0	4	.000	40	29	28	3.97	15
1997	New Orleans	A.A.	60	74	4	5	.444	80	27	65	2.80	12
1997	Houston a	N.L.	4	4	0	1	.000	3	3	2	4.50	0

a Traded to Florida Marlins with pitcher Manuel Barrios and player to be named later for outfielder Moises Alou, November 11, 1997.

HENRY, FLOYD BLUFORD III (BUTCH)
Born, El Paso, Texas, October 7, 1968.
Bats Left. Throws Left. Height, 6 feet, 1 inch. Weight, 205 pounds.

Year	Club	Lea	G	IP	W	L	Pct	SO	BB	H	ERA	SAVES
1987	Billings	Pioneer	9	35	4	0	1.000	38	12	37	4.63	1
1988	Cedar Rapds	Midwest	27	187	16	2	.889	163	56	144	2.26	0
1989	Chattanooga	Southern	7	26⅓	1	3	.250	19	12	22	3.42	0
1990	Chattanooga a	Southern	24	143⅓	8	8	.500	95	58	151	4.21	0
1991	Tucson	P.C.	27	153⅔	10	11	.476	97	42	192	4.80	0
1992	Houston b	N.L.	28	165⅔	6	9	.400	96	41	185	4.02	0
1993	Colorado c	N.L.	30	84⅔	2	8	.200	39	24	117	6.59	0

Year Club	Lea	G	IP	W	L	Pct	SO	BB	H	ERA	SAVES
1993 Ottawa	Int.	5	31⅓	3	1	.750	25	1	34	3.73	0
1993 Montreal	N.L.	10	18⅓	1	1	.500	8	4	18	3.93	0
1994 Ottawa	Int.	2	14	2	0	1.000	11	2	11	0.00	0
1994 Montreal	N.L.	24	107⅓	8	3	.727	70	20	97	2.43	1
1995 Montreal d	N.L.	21	126⅔	7	9	.438	60	28	133	2.84	0
1996 Boston e	A.L.			INJURED—Did Not Play							
1997 Sarasota	Fla. St.	2	8⅓	0	1	.000	7	0	8	5.40	0
1997 Boston f	A.L.	36	84⅓	7	3	.700	51	19	89	3.52	6
Major League Totals ....5 Yrs.		139	587	31	33	.484	324	136	639	3.77	7

a Traded by Cincinnati Reds organization to Houston Astros with catcher Terry McGriff and pitcher Keith Kaiser for second baseman Bill Doran, August 31, 1990.
b Selected by Colorado Rockies in expansion draft, November 17, 1992.
c Traded to Montreal Expos for pitcher Kent Bottenfield, July 16, 1993.
d Claimed on waivers by Boston Red Sox, October 13, 1995.
e On disabled list from March 22 through end of 1996 season.
f On disabled list from May 5 to June 23, 1997.

HENRY, RICHARD DOUGLAS (DOUG)
Born, Sacramento, California, December 10, 1963.
Bats Right. Throws Right. Height, 6 feet, 4 inches. Weight, 205 pounds.

Year Club	Lea	G	IP	W	L	Pct	SO	BB	H	ERA	SAVES
1986 Beloit	Midwest	27	143⅓	7	8	.467	115	56	153	4.65	1
1987 Beloit	Midwest	31	132⅔	8	9	.471	106	51	145	4.88	2
1988 Stockton	California	23	70⅔	7	1	.875	71	31	46	1.78	7
1988 El Paso	Texas	14	45⅔	4	0	1.000	50	19	33	3.15	0
1989 El Paso a	Texas	1	2	0	0	.000	2	3	3	13.50	0
1989 Stockton	California	4	11	0	1	.000	9	3	9	0.00	0
1990 Stockton	California	4	8	1	0	1.000	13	3	4	1.13	1
1990 El Paso	Texas	15	30⅔	1	0	1.000	25	11	31	2.93	9
1990 Denver	A.A.	27	50⅔	2	3	.400	54	27	46	4.44	8
1991 Denver	A.A.	32	57⅔	3	2	.600	47	20	47	2.18	14
1991 Milwaukee	A.L.	32	36	2	1	.667	28	14	16	1.00	15
1992 Milwaukee	A.L.	68	65	1	4	.200	52	24	64	4.02	29
1993 Milwaukee	A.L.	54	55	4	4	.500	38	25	67	5.56	17
1994 El Paso	Texas	6	8⅓	1	0	1.000	10	2	7	5.40	3
1994 New Orleans	A.A.	10	14⅔	1	0	1.000	10	10	5	1.84	3
1994 Milwaukee b-c	A.L.	25	31⅓	2	3	.400	20	23	32	4.60	0
1995 New York	N.L.	51	67	3	6	.333	62	25	48	2.96	4
1996 New York	N.L.	58	75	2	8	.200	58	36	82	4.68	9
1997 San Francisco d-e ..	N.L.	75	70⅔	4	5	.444	69	41	70	4.71	3
Major League Totals ....7 Yrs.		363	400	18	31	.367	327	188	379	4.07	77
Divisional Series											
1997 San Francisco	N.L.	1	2	0	0	.000	2	3	1	0.00	0

a On disabled list from July 7 to August 10, 1989.
b On disabled list from March 29 to April 27, 1994.
c Traded to New York Mets for two players to be named, November 30; Milwaukee Brewers acquired catcher Javier Gonzalez as partial completion of trade, December 6, 1994.
d Filed for free agency, October 27, 1997.
e Signed with Houston Astros, November 26, 1997.

HENTGEN, PATRICK GEORGE
Born, Detroit, Michigan, November 13, 1968.
Bats Right. Throws Right. Height, 6 feet, 2 inches. Weight, 200 pounds.

Year Club	Lea	G	IP	W	L	Pct	SO	BB	H	ERA	SAVES
1986 St. Catharines	N.Y.-Penn.	13	40	0	4	.000	30	30	38	4.50	1
1987 Myrtle Beach	So. Atl.	32	*188	11	5	.688	131	60	145	2.35	0
1988 Dunedin	Fla. St.	31	151⅓	3	12	.200	125	65	139	3.45	0
1989 Dunedin	Fla. St.	29	151⅓	9	8	.529	148	71	123	2.68	0
1990 Knoxville	Southern	28	153⅓	9	5	.643	142	68	121	3.05	0
1991 Syracuse	Int.	31	171	8	9	.471	*155	*90	146	4.47	0
1991 Toronto	A.L.	3	7⅓	0	0	.000	3	3	5	2.45	0
1992 Syracuse	Int.	4	20⅓	1	2	.333	17	8	15	2.66	0
1991 Toronto a	A.L.	28	50⅓	5	2	.714	39	32	49	5.36	0
1993 Toronto	A.L.	34	216⅓	19	9	.679	122	74	215	3.87	0
1994 Toronto	A.L.	24	174⅔	13	8	.619	147	59	158	3.40	0
1995 Toronto	A.L.	30	200⅔	10	14	.417	135	90	236	5.11	0

Year	Club	Lea	G	IP	W	L	Pct	SO	BB	H	ERA	SAVES
1996 Toronto b .............A.L.			35	265²/₃	20	10	.667	177	94	238	3.22	0
1997 Toronto .............A.L.			35	264	15	10	.600	160	71	253	3.68	0
Major League Totals ....7 Yrs.			189	1179	82	53	.607	783	423	1154	3.88	0
Championship Series												
1993 Toronto .............A.L.			1	3	0	1	.000	3	2	9	18.00	0
World Series Record												
1993 Toronto .............A.L.			1	6	1	0	1.000	6	3	5	1.50	0

a On disabled list from August 13 to September 29, 1992.
b Selected Cy Young Award Winner in American League for 1996.

HEREDIA, FELIX
Born, Barahona, Dominican Republic, June 18, 1976.
Bats Left. Throws Left. Height, 6 feet. Weight, 160 pounds.

Year	Club	Lea	G	IP	W	L	Pct	SO	BB	H	ERA	SAVES
1993 Marlins ....Gulf Coast			12	62	5	1	.833	53	11	50	2.47	0
1994 Kane County ....Midwest			24	68	4	5	.444	65	14	86	5.69	3
1995 Brevard Cty ....Fla. St.			34	95²/₃	6	4	.600	76	36	101	3.57	1
1996 Portland ....Eastern			55	60	8	1	.889	42	15	48	1.50	5
1996 Florida ...............N.L.			21	16²/₃	1	1	.500	10	10	21	4.32	0
1997 Florida ...............N.L.			56	56²/₃	5	3	.625	54	30	53	4.29	0
Major League Totals ....2 Yrs.			77	73¹/₃	6	4	.600	64	40	74	4.30	0
Championship Series												
1997 Florida ...............N.L.			2	3¹/₃	0	0	.000	4	2	3	5.40	0
World Series Record												
1997 Florida ...............N.L.			4	5¹/₃	0	0	.000	5	1	2	0.00	0

HERMANSON, DUSTIN MICHAEL
Born, Springfield, Ohio, December 21, 1972.
Bats Right. Throws Right. Height, 6 feet, 3 inches. Weight, 195 pounds.

Year	Club	Lea	G	IP	W	L	Pct	SO	BB	H	ERA	SAVES
1994 Wichita ....Texas			16	21	1	0	1.000	30	6	13	0.43	8
1994 Las Vegas .............P.C.			7	7¹/₃	0	0	.000	6	5	6	6.14	3
1995 Las Vegas .............P.C.			31	36	0	1	.000	42	29	35	3.50	11
1995 San Diego ...........N.L.			26	31²/₃	3	1	.750	19	22	35	6.82	0
1996 Las Vegas .............P.C.			42	46	1	4	.200	54	27	41	3.13	21
1996 San Diego a ...........N.L.			8	13²/₃	1	0	1.000	11	4	18	8.56	0
1997 Montreal b ...........N.L.			32	158¹/₃	8	8	.500	136	66	134	3.69	0
Major League Totals ....3 Yrs.			66	203³/₃	12	9	.571	166	92	187	4.51	0

a Traded to Florida Marlins for infielder Quilvio Veras, November 21, 1996.
b Traded to Montreal Expos with outfielder Joe Orsulak for infielder Cliff Floyd, March 26, 1997.

HERNANDEZ, EISLER LIVAN
Born, Villa Clara, Cuba, February 20, 1975.
Bats Right. Throws Right. Height, 6 feet, 2 inches. Weight, 220 pounds.

Year	Club	Lea	G	IP	W	L	Pct	SO	BB	H	ERA	SAVES
1996 Charlotte ....Int.			10	49	2	4	.333	45	34	61	5.14	0
1996 Portland ....Eastern			15	93¹/₃	9	2	.818	95	34	81	4.34	0
1996 Florida ...............N.L.			1	3	0	0	.000	2	2	3	0.00	0
1997 Portland ....Eastern			1	4	0	0	.000	2	7	2	2.25	0
1997 Charlotte ....Int.			14	81¹/₃	5	3	.625	58	38	76	3.98	0
1997 Florida ...............N.L.			17	96¹/₃	9	3	.750	72	38	81	3.18	0
Major League Totals ....2 Yrs.			18	99¹/₃	9	3	.750	74	40	84	3.08	0
Division Series												
1997 Florida ...............N.L.			1	4	0	0	.000	3	0	3	2.25	0
Championship Series												
1997 Florida ...............N.L.			2	10²/₃	2	0	1.000	16	2	5	0.84	0
World Series Record												
1997 Florida ...............N.L.			2	13²/₃	2	0	1.000	7	10	15	5.27	0

HERNANDEZ, ROBERTO MANUEL

Born, Santurce, Puerto Rico, November 11, 1964.
Bats Right. Throws Right. Height, 6 feet, 4 inches. Weight, 235 pounds.

Year	Club	Lea	G	IP	W	L	Pct	SO	BB	H	ERA	SAVES
1986 Salem	Northwest		10	55	2	2	.500	38	42	57	4.58	0
1987 Quad City a	Midwest		7	21	2	3	.400	21	12	24	6.86	1
1988 Quad City	Midwest		24	164²/₃	9	10	.474	114	48	157	3.17	0
1988 Midland	Texas		3	12¹/₃	0	2	.000	7	8	16	6.57	0
1989 Palm Springs	California		7	42²/₃	1	4	.200	33	16	49	4.64	0
1989 Midland b	Texas		12	64	2	7	.222	42	30	94	6.89	0
1989 South Bend	Midwest		4	24¹/₃	1	1	.500	17	17	19	3.33	0
1990 Birmingham	Southern		17	108	8	5	.615	62	43	102	3.67	0
1990 Vancouver	P.C.		11	79¹/₃	3	5	.375	49	26	73	2.84	0
1991 Vancouver	P.C.		7	44²/₃	4	1	.800	40	23	41	3.22	0
1991 Sarasota White Sox	Gulf C.		1	6	0	0	.000	7	0	2	0.00	0
1991 Birmingham	Southern		4	22²/₃	2	1	.667	25	6	11	1.99	0
1991 Chicago	A.L.		9	15	1	0	1.000	6	7	18	7.80	0
1992 Vancouver	P.C.		9	20²/₃	3	3	.500	23	11	13	2.61	2
1992 Chicago	A.L.		43	71	7	3	.700	68	20	45	1.65	12
1993 Chicago	A.L.		70	78²/₃	3	4	.429	71	20	66	2.29	38
1994 Chicago	A.L.		45	47²/₃	4	4	.500	50	19	44	4.91	14
1995 Chicago c	A.L.		60	59²/₃	3	7	.300	84	28	63	3.92	32
1996 Chicago	A.L.		72	84²/₃	6	5	.545	85	38	65	1.91	38
1997 Chicago d	A.L.		46	48	5	1	.833	47	24	38	2.44	27
1997 San Francisco e-f	N.L.		28	32²/₃	5	2	.714	35	14	29	2.48	4
Major League Totals	7 Yrs.		373	437¹/₃	34	26	.567	446	170	368	2.84	165
Divisional Series												
1997 San Francisco	N.L.		3	1¹/₃	0	1	.000	1	3	5	20.25	0
Championship Series												
1993 Chicago	A.L.		4	4	0	0	.000	1	0	4	0.00	1

a On disabled list from May 6 to May 21 and June 14 to August 14, 1987.
b Traded by California Angels to Chicago White Sox for outfielder Mark Davis, August 2, 1989.
c Signed with Chicago White Sox, April 28, 1995.
d Traded to San Francisco Giants with pitcher Wilson Alvarez and pitcher Danny Darwin for infielder Mike Caruso, outfielder Brian Manning, pitcher Lorenzo Barcelo, pitcher Keith Foulke, pitcher Bob Howry and pitcher Ken Vining, July 31, 1997.
e Filed for free agency, October 30, 1997.
f Signed with Tampa Bay Devil Rays, November 18, 1997.

HERSHISER, OREL LEONARD IV

Born, Buffalo, New York, September 16, 1958.
Bats Right, Throws Right. Height, 6 feet, 3 inches. Weight, 198 pounds.

Year	Club	Lea	G	IP	W	L	Pct	SO	BB	H	ERA	SAVES
1979 Clinton	Midwest		15	43	4	0	1.000	33	17	33	2.09	0
1980 San Antonio	Texas		49	109	5	9	.357	75	59	120	3.55	0
1981 San Antonio	Texas		42	102	7	6	.538	95	50	94	4.68	0
1982 Albuquerque	P.C.		47	123²/₃	9	6	.600	93	63	121	3.71	0
1983 Albuquerque	P.C.		49	134¹/₃	10	8	.556	95	57	132	4.09	16
1983 Los Angeles	N.L.		8	8	0	0	.000	5	6	7	3.38	1
1984 Los Angeles	N.L.		45	189²/₃	11	8	.579	150	50	160	2.66	2
1985 Los Angeles	N.L.		36	239²/₃	19	3	*.864	157	68	179	2.03	0
1986 Los Angeles	N.L.		35	231¹/₃	14	14	.500	153	86	213	3.85	0
1987 Los Angeles	N.L.		37	*264²/₃	16	16	.500	190	74	247	3.06	1
1988 Los Angeles a	N.L.		35	*267	*23	8	.742	178	73	208	2.26	1
1989 Los Angeles	N.L.		35	*256²/₃	15	*15	.500	178	77	226	2.31	0
1990 Los Angeles b	N.L.		4	25¹/₃	1	1	.500	16	4	26	4.26	0
1991 Bakersfield	California		2	11	2	0	1.000	6	1	5	0.82	0
1991 San Antonio	Texas		1	7	0	1	.000	5	1	11	2.57	0
1991 Albuquerque	P.C.		1	5	0	0	.000	5	0	5	0.00	0
1991 Los Angeles c-d	N.L.		21	112	7	2	.778	73	32	112	3.46	0
1992 Los Angeles e	N.L.		33	210²/₃	10	15	.400	130	69	209	3.67	0
1993 Los Angeles	N.L.		33	215²/₃	12	14	.462	141	72	201	3.59	0
1994 Los Angeles f	N.L.		21	135¹/₃	6	6	.500	72	42	146	3.79	0
1995 Cleveland g-h-i-j	A.L.		26	167¹/₃	16	6	.727	111	51	151	3.87	0
1996 Cleveland	A.L.		33	206	15	9	.625	125	58	238	4.24	0
1997 Cleveland k-l-m	A.L.		32	195¹/₃	14	6	.700	107	69	199	4.47	0
Major League Totals	15 Yrs.		434	2724²/₃	179	123	.593	1786	831	2522	3.25	5
Division Series												
1995 Cleveland	A.L.		1	7¹/₃	1	0	1.000	7	2	3	0.00	0
1996 Cleveland	A.L.		1	5	0	0	.000	3	3	7	5.40	0
1997 Cleveland	A.L.		2	11¹/₃	0	0	.000	4	2	14	3.97	0
Divisional Series Totals			4	23²/₃	1	0	1.000	14	7	24	3.04	0

259

Year	Club	Lea	G	IP	W	L	Pct	SO	BB	H	ERA	SAVES
Championship Series												
1985 Los Angeles ..........N.L.			2	15⅓	1	0	1.000	5	6	17	3.52	0
1988 Los Angeles ..........N.L.			4	24⅔	1	0	1.000	15	7	18	1.10	1
1995 Cleveland ............A.L.			2	14	2	0	1.000	15	3	9	1.29	0
1997 Cleveland ............A.L.			1	7	0	0	.000	7	1	4	0.00	0
Championship Series Totals 9				61	4	0	1.000	42	17	48	1.62	1
World Series Record												
1988 Los Angeles ..........N.L.			2	18	2	0	1.000	17	6	7	1.00	0
1995 Cleveland ............A.L.			2	14	1	1	.500	13	4	8	2.57	0
1997 Cleveland ............A.L.			2	10	0	2	.000	5	6	15	11.70	0
World Series Totals 6				42	3	3	.500	35	16	30	4.07	0

a Selected Cy Young Award winner in National League for 1988.
b On disabled list from April 27 to end of 1990 season.
c On disabled list from March 15 to May 29, 1991.
d Filed for free agency, November 1; re-signed with Los Angeles Dodgers, December 3, 1991.
e Appeared in two additional games as pinch hitter.
f Filed for free agency, October 21, 1994.
g Signed with Cleveland Indians, April 8, 1995.
h On disabled list from June 22 to July 7, 1995.
i Filed for free agency, November 12, 1995.
j Re-signed with Cleveland Indians, November 15, 1995.
k On disabled list from July 29 to August 13, 1997.
l Filed for free agency, October 29, 1997.
m Signed with San Francisco Giants, December 9, 1997.

HILL, KENNETH WADE

Born, Lynn, Massachusetts, December 14, 1965.
Bats Right. Throws Right. Height, 6 feet, 2 inches. Weight, 200 pounds.

Year	Club	Lea	G	IP	W	L	Pct	SO	BB	H	ERA	SAVES
1985 Gastonia ....So. Atl.			15	69	3	6	.333	48	57	60	4.96	0
1986 Gastonia ....So. Atl.			22	122⅓	9	5	.643	86	80	95	2.79	0
1986 Glens Falls a ......Eastern			1	7	0	1	.000	4	6	4	5.14	0
1986 Arkansas ....Texas			3	18	1	2	.333	9	7	18	4.50	0
1987 Arkansas ....Texas			18	53⅔	3	5	.375	48	30	60	5.20	2
1987 St. Petersburg .....Fla. St.			18	41	1	3	.250	32	17	38	4.17	2
1988 Arkansas ....Texas			22	115⅓	9	9	.500	107	50	129	4.92	0
1988 St. Louis b ..........N.L.			4	14	0	1	.000	6	6	16	5.14	0
1989 Louisville ...........A.A.			3	18	0	2	.000	18	10	13	3.50	0
1989 St. Louis ...........N.L.			33	196⅔	7	*15	.318	112	*99	186	3.80	0
1990 Louisville ...........A.A.			12	85⅓	6	1	.857	104	27	47	1.79	0
1990 St. Louis ...........N.L.			17	78⅔	5	6	.455	58	33	79	5.49	0
1991 Louisville ...........A.A.			1	1	0	0	.000	2	0	0	0.00	0
1991 St. Louis c-d .........N.L.			30	181⅓	11	10	.524	121	67	147	3.57	0
1992 Montreal ............N.L.			33	218	16	9	.640	150	75	187	2.68	0
1993 Ottawa ....Int.			1	4	0	0	.000	0	1	1	0.00	0
1993 Montreal e-f .........N.L.			28	183⅔	9	7	.563	90	74	163	3.23	0
1994 Montreal g-h .........N.L.			23	154⅓	*16	5	.762	85	44	145	3.32	0
1995 St. Louis ...........N.L.			18	110⅓	6	7	.462	50	45	125	5.06	0
1995 Cleveland i-j-k-l ......A.L.			12	74⅓	4	1	.800	48	32	77	3.98	0
1996 Texas .............A.L.			35	250⅔	16	10	.615	170	95	250	3.63	0
1997 Tulsa m ....Texas			1	5	0	0	.000	3	1	2	0.00	0
1997 Texas-Anaheim n-o-p ....A.L.			31	190	9	12	.429	106	95	194	4.55	0
Major League Totals ....10 Yrs.			264	1652⅔	99	83	.544	996	665	1569	3.76	0
Division Series												
1995 Cleveland ............A.L.			1	1⅓	1	0	1.000	2	0	1	0.00	0
1996 Texas ..............A.L.			1	6	0	0	.000	1	3	5	4.50	0
Division Series Totals 2				7⅓	1	0	1.000	3	3	6	3.68	0
Championship Series												
1995 Cleveland ............A.L.			1	7	1	0	1.000	6	3	5	0.00	0
World Series Record												
1995 Cleveland ............A.L.			2	7⅓	0	1	.000	1	4	7	4.26	0

a Traded by Detroit Tigers to St. Louis Cardinals organization with first baseman Mike Laga for catcher Mike Heath, August 10, 1986.
b On disabled list from March 26 to May 9, 1988.
c On disabled list from August 11 to September 1, 1991.
d Traded to Montreal Expos for first baseman Andres Galarraga, November 25, 1991.
e Appeared in one additional game as pinch hitter.
f On disabled list from June 26 to July 17, 1993.
g Appeared in one additional game as pinch hitter.

h Declared restricted free agent under Major League Baseball implemented labor proposal, December 23, 1994.
i Traded to St. Louis Cardinals for pitcher Bryan Eversgerd, pitcher Kirk Bollinger and outfielder Darond Stovall, April 5, 1995.
j Traded to Cleveland Indians for infielder David Bell, pitcher Rick Heiserman and catcher Pepe McNeal, July 27, 1995.
k Filed for free agency, November 12, 1995.
l Signed with Texas Rangers, December 23, 1995.
m On disabled list from May 1 to May 24, 1997.
n Traded to Anaheim Angels for catcher Jim Leyritz and player to be named later, July 29, 1997. Texas Rangers received infielder Rob Sasser to complete trade, October 31, 1997.
o Filed for free agency, November 7, 1997.
p Re-signed with Anaheim Angels, November 16, 1997.

HITCHCOCK, STERLING ALEX

Born, Fayetteville, North Carolina, April 29, 1971.
Bats Left. Throws Left. Height, 6 feet, 1 inch. Weight, 192 pounds.

Year	Club	Lea	G	IP	W	L	Pct	SO	BB	H	ERA	SAVES
1989	Sarasota Yankees	Gulf C.	13	76⅔	*9	1	.900	*98	27	48	1.64	0
1990	Greensboro	So. Atl.	27	173⅓	12	12	.500	*171	60	122	2.91	0
1991	Prince William	Carolina	19	119⅓	7	7	.500	101	26	111	2.64	0
1992	Albany	Eastern	24	146⅔	6	9	.400	*155	42	116	2.58	0
1992	New York	A.L.	3	13	0	2	.000	6	6	23	8.31	0
1993	Oneonta	N.Y.-Penn.	1	1	0	0	.000	0	0	0	0.00	0
1993	Columbus a	Int.	16	76⅔	3	5	.375	85	28	80	4.81	0
1993	New York	A.L.	6	31	1	2	.333	26	14	32	4.65	0
1994	Albany	Eastern	1	5	1	0	1.000	7	0	4	1.80	0
1994	Columbus	Int.	10	50	3	4	.429	47	18	53	4.32	0
1994	New York	A.L.	23	49⅓	4	1	.800	37	29	48	4.20	2
1995	New York b	A.L.	27	168⅓	11	10	.524	121	68	155	4.70	0
1996	Seattle c	A.L.	35	196⅔	13	9	.591	132	73	245	5.35	0
1997	San Diego d	N.L.	32	161	10	11	.476	106	55	172	5.20	0
1997	San Diego	N.L.	70	81⅓	6	4	.600	111	24	59	2.66	37
Major League Totals	5 Yrs.		309	368⅔	30	23	.566	421	128	276	3.03	135
Division Series												
1995	New York	A.L.	2	1⅔	0	0	.000	1	2	2	5.40	0

a On disabled list from May 23 to July 21, 1993.
b Traded by New York Yankees to Seattle Mariners with infielder Russ Davis for pitchers Jeff Nelson and Jim Mecir and infielder Tino Martinez, December 7, 1995.
c Traded to San Diego Padres for pitcher Scott Sanders, December 6, 1996.
d On disabled list from June 6 to July 3, 1997.

HOFFMAN, TREVOR WILLIAM

Born, Bellflower, California, October 13, 1967.
Bats Right. Throws Right. Height, 6 feet, 1 inch. Weight, 205 pounds.

Year	Club	Lea	G	IP	W	L	Pct	SO	BB	H	ERA	SAVES
1991	Cedar Rapids	Midwest	27	33⅔	1	1	.500	52	13	22	1.87	12
1991	Chattanooga	Southern	14	14	1	0	1.000	23	7	10	1.93	8
1992	Chattanooga	Southern	6	29⅔	3	0	1.000	31	11	22	1.52	0
1992	Nashville a	A.A.	42	65⅓	4	6	.400	63	32	57	4.27	6
1993	Florida-San Diego b	N.L.	67	90	4	6	.400	79	39	80	3.90	5
1994	San Diego	N.L.	47	56	4	4	.500	68	20	39	2.57	20
1995	San Diego	N.L.	55	53⅓	7	4	.636	52	14	48	3.88	31
1996	San Diego	N.L.	70	88	9	5	.643	111	31	50	2.25	42
1997	San Diego	N.L.	70	81⅓	6	4	.600	111	24	59	2.66	37
Major League Totals	5 Yrs.		309	368⅔	30	23	.566	421	128	276	3.03	135
Division Series												
1996	San Diego	N.L.	2	1⅔	0	1	.000	2	1	3	10.80	0

Record as Position Player

Year	Club	Lea	Pos	G	AB	R	H	2B	3B	HR	RBI	SB	Avg
1989	Bellingham	Pioneer	SS	61	201	22	50	5	0	1	20	1	.249
1990	Charleston	So. Atl.	SS-3B	103	278	41	59	10	1	2	23	3	.212

a Selected by Florida Marlins from Cincinnati Reds organization in expansion draft, November 17, 1992.
b Traded to San Diego Padres with pitchers Andres Berumen and Jose Martinez for infielder Greg Sheffield and pitcher Rich Rodriguez, June 25, 1993.

HOLMES, DARREN LEE

Born, Asheville, North Carolina, April 25, 1966.
Bats Right. Throws Right. Height, 6 feet. Weight, 200 pounds.

Year	Club	Lea	G	IP	W	L	Pct	SO	BB	H	ERA	SAVES
1984	Great Falls	Pioneer	18	44⅔	2	5	.286	29	30	53	6.65	0
1985	Vero Beach	Fla. St.	33	63⅔	4	3	.571	46	35	57	3.11	2
1986	Vero Beach	Fla. St.	11	64⅔	3	6	.333	59	39	55	2.92	0
1987	Vero Beach a-b	Fla. St.	19	99⅔	6	4	.600	46	53	111	4.52	0
1988	San Luis Potosi	Mexican	23	139⅔	9	9	.500	110	92	151	4.64	0
1988	Albuquerque	P.C.	1	5⅓	0	1	.000	1	1	6	5.06	0
1989	San Antonio c	Texas	17	110⅓	5	8	.385	81	44	102	3.83	1
1989	Albuquerque	P.C.	9	38⅔	1	4	.200	31	18	50	7.45	0
1990	Albuquerque	P.C.	56	92⅔	12	2	.857	99	39	78	3.11	13
1990	Los Angeles d	N.L.	14	17⅓	0	1	.000	19	11	15	5.19	0
1991	Beloit	Midwest	2	2	0	0	.000	3	0	0	0.00	0
1991	Denver	A.A.	1	1	0	0	.000	2	2	1	9.00	0
1991	Milwaukee e	A.L.	40	76⅓	1	4	.200	59	27	90	4.72	3
1992	Denver	A.A.	12	13	0	0	.000	12	1	7	1.38	7
1992	Milwaukee f	A.L.	41	42⅓	4	4	.500	31	11	35	2.55	6
1993	Colorado Springs	P.C.	3	8⅔	1	0	1.000	9	1	1	0.00	0
1993	Colorado	N.L.	62	66⅔	3	3	.500	60	20	56	4.05	25
1994	Asheville	So. Atl.	2	3	0	0	.000	7	0	1	0.00	0
1994	Colorado Springs	P.C.	4	7⅔	0	1	.000	12	3	11	8.22	0
1994	Colorado g	N.L.	29	28⅓	0	3	.000	33	24	35	6.35	3
1995	Colorado	N.L.	68	66⅔	6	1	.857	61	28	59	3.24	14
1996	Colorado	N.L.	62	77	5	4	.556	73	28	78	3.97	1
1997	Colorado h-i-j	N.L.	42	89⅓	9	2	.818	70	36	113	5.34	3
Major League Totals		8 Yrs.	358	464	28	22	.560	406	185	481	4.33	55
	Division Series											
1995	Colorado	N.L.	3	1⅔	1	0	1.000	2	0	6	0.00	0

a On disabled list from April 9 to May 4, 1987.
b Loaned by Los Angeles Dodgers organization to San Luis Potosi of Mexican League, March 28; returned to Los Angeles organization, August 31, 1988.
c On disabled list from June 2 to June 10, 1989.
d Traded to Milwaukee Brewers for catcher Bert Heffernan, December 20, 1990.
e On disabled list from July 3 to July 18, 1991.
f Selected by Colorado Rockies in expansion draft, November 17, 1992.
g On disabled list from June 5 to June 24 and July 21 to August 11, 1994.
h On disabled list from April 30 to May 15, 1997.
i Filed for free agency, October 27, 1997.
j Signed as free agent with New York Yankees, December 22, 1997.

HOLT, CHRISTOPHER MICHAEL (CHRIS)

Born, Dallas, Texas, September 18, 1971.
Bats Right. Throws Right. Height, 6 feet, 4 inches. Weight, 205 pounds.

Year	Club	Lea	G	IP	W	L	Pct	SO	BB	H	ERA	SAVES
1992	Auburn	N.Y.-Penn.	14	83	2	5	.286	81	24	75	4.45	0
1993	Quad City	Midwest	26	186⅓	11	10	.524	176	54	162	2.27	0
1994	Jackson	Texas	26	167	10	9	.526	111	22	169	3.45	0
1995	Jackson	Texas	5	32⅓	2	2	.500	24	5	27	1.67	0
1995	Tucson	P.C.	20	118⅔	5	8	.385	69	32	155	4.10	0
1996	Tucson	P.C.	28	186⅓	9	6	.600	137	38	209	3.72	0
1996	Houston	N.L.	4	4⅔	0	1	.000	0	3	5	5.79	0
1997	Houston	N.L.	33	209⅔	8	12	.400	95	61	211	3.52	0
Major League Totals		2 Yrs.	37	214⅓	8	13	.381	95	64	216	3.57	0

HOLTZ, MICHAEL JAMES (MIKE)

Born, Arlington, Virginia, October 10, 1972.
Bats Left. Throws Left. Height, 5 feet, 9 inches. Weight, 172 pounds.

Year	Club	Lea	G	IP	W	L	Pct	SO	BB	H	ERA	SAVES
1994	Boise	Northwest	22	35	0	0	.000	59	11	22	0.51	11
1995	Lk Elsinore	California	56	82⅔	4	4	.500	101	23	70	2.29	3
1996	Midland	Texas	33	41	1	2	.333	41	9	52	4.17	2
1996	California	A.L.	30	29⅓	3	3	.500	31	19	21	2.45	0
1997	Anaheim	A.L.	66	43⅓	3	4	.429	40	15	38	3.32	2
Major League Totals		2 Yrs.	96	72⅔	6	7	.462	71	34	59	2.97	2

HUDEK, JOHN RAYMOND

Born, Tampa, Florida, August 8, 1966.
Bats Both. Throws Right. Height, 6 feet, 1 inch. Weight, 200 pounds.

Year	Club	Lea	G	IP	W	L	Pct	SO	BB	H	ERA	SAVES
1988 South Bend		Midwest	26	54⅔	7	2	.778	35	21	45	1.98	8
1989 Sarasota		Fla. St.	27	43	1	3	.250	39	13	22	1.67	15
1989 Birmingham		Southern	18	17	1	1	.500	10	9	14	4.24	11
1990 Birmingham		Southern	42	92⅓	6	6	.500	67	52	84	4.58	4
1991 Birmingham		Southern	51	65⅔	5	10	.333	49	28	58	3.84	13
1992 Birmingham		Southern	5	11⅔	0	1	.000	9	11	9	2.31	1
1992 Vancouver a		P.C.	39	85⅓	8	1	.889	61	45	69	3.16	2
1993 Toledo b		Int.	16	38⅔	1	3	.250	32	22	44	5.82	0
1993 Tucson		P.C.	13	19	3	1	.750	18	11	17	3.79	0
1994 Tucson		P.C.	6	7⅓	0	0	.000	14	3	3	4.91	2
1994 Houston		N.L.	42	39⅓	0	2	.000	39	18	24	2.97	16
1995 Houston c		N.L.	19	20	2	2	.500	24	5	19	5.40	7
1996 Kissimmee		Fla. St.	2	3	0	0	.000	3	2	2	0.00	0
1996 Tucson		P.C.	17	20⅓	1	0	1.000	26	8	17	3.10	4
1996 Houston d		N.L.	15	16	2	0	1.000	14	5	12	2.81	2
1997 New Orleans		A.A.	19	20⅔	0	0	.000	26	3	3	0.44	7
1997 Houston e		N.L.	40	40⅔	1	3	.250	36	33	38	5.98	4
Major League Totals		4 Yrs.	116	116	5	7	.417	118	61	93	4.42	29

a Drafted by Detroit Tigers from Chicago White Sox organization, December 7, 1992.
b Claimed on waivers by Houston Astros from Detroit Tigers organization, July 29, 1993.
c On disabled list from June 23 to October 2, 1995.
d On disabled list from April 1 to July 15, 1996.
e Traded to New York Mets for outfielder Carl Everett, December 22, 1997.

HUDSON, JOSEPH PAUL (JOE)

Born, Philadelphia, Pennsylvania, September 29, 1970.
Bats Both. Throws Right. Height, 6 feet, 1 inch. Weight, 175 pounds.

Year	Club	Lea	G	IP	W	L	Pct	SO	BB	H	ERA	SAVES
1992 Elmira		N.Y.-Penn.	19	72	3	3	.500	38	33	76	4.38	0
1993 Lynchburg		Carolina	49	84⅓	8	6	.571	62	38	97	4.06	6
1994 Sarasota		Fla. St.	30	48⅓	3	1	.750	33	27	42	2.23	7
1994 New Britain		Eastern	23	39	5	3	.625	24	18	49	3.92	0
1995 Trenton		Eastern	22	31⅔	0	1	.000	24	17	20	1.71	8
1995 Boston		A.L.	39	46	0	1	.000	29	23	53	4.11	1
1996 Pawtucket		Int.	25	33⅓	1	1	.500	18	21	29	3.51	5
1996 Boston		A.L.	36	45	3	5	.375	19	32	57	5.40	1
1997 Pawtucket		Int.	29	32	2	1	.667	14	23	25	2.25	7
1997 Boston		A.L.	26	35⅔	3	1	.750	14	14	39	3.53	0
Major League Totals		3 Yrs.	101	126⅔	6	7	.462	62	69	149	4.41	2
Division Series												
1995 Boston		A.L.	1	1	0	0	.000	0	1	2	0.00	0

HURTADO, EDWIN AMILGAR

Born, Barquismeto, Venezuela, February 1, 1970.
Bats Right. Throws Right. Height, 6 feet, 3 inches. Weight, 215 pounds.

Year	Club	Lea	G	IP	W	L	Pct	SO	BB	H	ERA	SAVES
1993 St. Catharines		N.Y.-Penn.	15	101	10	2	.833	87	34	69	2.50	0
1994 Hagerstown		So. Atl.	33	134⅓	11	2	.846	121	46	118	2.95	2
1995 Knoxville		Southern	11	54⅔	2	4	.333	38	25	54	4.45	0
1995 Toronto a		A.L.	14	77⅔	5	2	.714	33	40	81	5.45	0
1996 Seattle b		A.L.	16	47⅔	2	5	.286	36	30	61	7.74	0
1996 Tacoma		P.C.	5	31⅓	1	2	.333	26	12	23	3.73	0
1997 Seattle		A.L.	13	19	1	2	.333	10	15	25	9.00	0
1997 Tacoma		P.C.	20	132⅓	10	6	.625	100	37	139	3.88	0
Major League Totals		3 Yrs.	43	144⅓	8	9	.471	79	85	167	6.67	2

a Traded to Seattle Mariners with pitcher Paul Menhart for pitcher Bill Risley and infielder Miguel Cairo, December 18, 1995.
b On disabled list from September 1 to September 30, 1996.

HUTTON, MARK STEVEN
Born, Adelaide, Australia, February 6, 1970.
Bats Right. Throws Right. Height, 6 feet, 6 inches. Weight, 225 pounds.

Year	Club	Lea	G	IP	W	L	Pct	SO	BB	H	ERA	SAVES
1989	Oneonta	N.Y.-Penn.	12	66⅓	6	2	.750	62	24	70	4.07	0
1990	Greensboro	So. Atl.	21	81⅓	1	10	.091	72	62	77	6.31	0
1991	Fort Lauderdale ...	Fla. St.	24	147	5	8	.385	117	65	98	2.45	0
1991	Columbus	Int.	1	6	1	0	1.000	5	5	3	1.50	0
1992	Albany	Eastern	25	165⅓	13	7	.650	128	66	146	3.59	0
1992	Columbus	Int.	1	5	0	1	.000	4	2	7	5.40	0
1993	Columbus	Int.	21	133	10	4	.714	112	53	98	3.18	0
1993	New York	A.L.	7	22	1	1	.500	12	17	24	5.73	0
1994	Columbus	Int.	22	34⅔	2	5	.286	27	12	31	3.63	3
1994	New York	A.L.	2	3⅔	0	0	.000	1	0	4	4.91	0
1995	Columbus	Int.	11	52⅓	2	6	.250	23	24	64	8.43	0
1996	Tampa	Fla. St.	3	5	0	0	.000	6	1	2	1.80	0
1996	Columbus	Int.	2	2	0	0	.000	3	2	0	0.00	0
1996	New York	A.L.	12	30⅓	0	2	.000	25	18	32	5.04	0
1996	Florida a-b	N.L.	13	56⅓	5	1	.833	31	18	47	3.67	0
1997	Florida-Colorado c-d ...	N.L.	40	60⅓	3	2	.600	39	26	72	4.48	0
Major League Totals .....4 Yrs.			74	172⅔	9	6	.600	108	79	179	4.48	0

a On disabled list from April 15 to May 29, 1996.
b Traded to Florida Marlins for pitcher David Weathers, July 31, 1996.
c Traded to Colorado Rockies for infielder Craig Counsell, July 27, 1997.
d Traded to Cincinnati Reds for outfielder Curtis Goodwin, December 10, 1997.

IRABU, HIDEKI
Born, Hyogo, Japan, May 5, 1969.
Bats Right. Throws Right. Height, 6 feet, 4 inches. Weight, 240 pounds.

Year	Club	Lea	G	IP	W	L	Pct	SO	BB	H	ERA	SAVES
1988	Lotte	Japan Pac.	14	39⅓	2	5	.286	21	15	30	3.69	1
1989	Lotte	Japan Pac.	33	51	0	2	.000	50	27	37	3.53	9
1990	Lotte	Japan Pac.	24	125⅔	8	5	.615	102	72	110	3.78	0
1991	Lotte	Japan Pac.	24	100⅔	3	8	.273	79	70	110	6.88	0
1992	Chiba Lotte	Japan Pac.	28	77	0	5	.000	55	37	78	3.88	0
1993	Chiba Lotte	Japan Pac.	32	142⅓	8	7	.533	160	56	125	3.10	1
1994	Chiba Lotte	Japan Pac.	27	207⅓	*15	10	.600	*239	94	170	3.04	0
1995	Chiba Lotte	Japan Pac.	28	203	11	11	.500	*239	72	158	*2.53	0
1996	Chiba Lotte	Japan Pac.	23	157⅓	.12	6	.667	167	59	108	*2.40	0
1997	Tampa a-b	Fla. St.	2	9	1	0	1.000	12	0	4	0.00	0
1997	Norwich	Eastern	2	10	1	1	.500	9	0	13	4.50	0
1997	Columbus	Int.	4	27	2	0	1.000	28	5	19	1.67	0
1997	New York	A.L.	13	53⅓	5	4	.556	56	20	69	7.09	0

a Rights acquired by San Diego Padres from Chiba Lotte Orions.
b Traded to New York Yankees by San Diego Padres with infielder Homer Bush, outfielder Gordon Amerson and player to be named later for outfielder Ruben Rivera, pitcher Rafael Medina and cash (reported to be $3 million), May 30, 1997. New York Yankees received outfielder Vernon Maxwell to complete trade, June 9, 1997.

ISRINGHAUSEN, JASON DERIK
Born, Brighton, Illinois, September 7, 1972.
Bats Right. Throws Right. Height, 6 feet, 3 inches. Weight, 195 pounds.

Year	Club	Lea	G	IP	W	L	Pct	SO	BB	H	ERA	SAVES
1992	Mets	Gulf Coast	6	29	2	4	.333	25	17	26	4.34	0
1992	Kingsport	Appal.	7	36	4	1	.800	24	12	32	3.25	0
1993	Pittsfield	N.Y.-Penn.	15	90⅓	7	4	.636	104	28	68	3.29	0
1994	St. Lucie	Fla. St.	14	101	6	4	.600	59	27	76	2.23	0
1994	Binghamton	Eastern	14	92⅓	5	4	.556	69	23	78	3.02	0
1995	Binghamton	Eastern	6	41	2	1	.667	59	12	26	2.85	0
1995	Norfolk	Int.	12	87	9	1	.900	75	24	64	1.55	0
1995	New York	N.L.	14	93	9	2	.818	55	31	88	2.81	0
1996	New York a	N.L.	27	171⅔	6	14	.300	114	73	190	4.77	0
1997	Mets	Gulf Coast	1	4⅔	1	0	1.000	7	1	2	1.93	0
1997	St. Lucie	Fla. St.	2	12	1	0	1.000	15	5	8	0.00	0
1997	Norfolk	Int.	3	20	0	2	.000	17	8	20	4.05	0
1997	New York b	N.L.	6	29⅔	2	2	.500	25	22	40	7.58	0
Major League Totals .... 3 Yrs.			47	294⅓	17	18	.486	194	126	318	4.43	0

a On disabled list from August 13 to September 1, 1996.
b On disabled list from April 1 to August 27, 1997.

JACKSON, MICHAEL RAY (MIKE)

Born, Houston, Texas, December 22, 1964.
Bats Right. Throws Right. Height, 6 feet. Weight, 223 pounds.

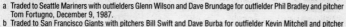

Year Club	Lea	G	IP	W	L	Pct	SO	BB	H	ERA	SAVES
1984 Spartanburg	So. Atl.	14	80⅔	7	2	.778	77	50	53	2.68	0
1985 Peninsula	Carolina	31	125⅓	7	9	.438	96	53	127	4.60	1
1986 Reading	Eastern	30	43⅓	2	3	.400	42	22	25	1.66	6
1986 Portland	P.C.	17	22⅔	3	1	.750	23	13	18	3.18	3
1986 Philadelphia	N.L.	9	13⅓	0	0	.000	3	4	12	3.38	0
1987 Maine	Int.	2	11	1	0	1.000	13	5	9	0.82	2
1987 Philadelphia a	N.L.	55	109⅓	3	10	.231	93	56	88	4.20	1
1988 Seattle	A.L.	62	99⅓	6	5	.545	76	43	74	2.63	4
1989 Seattle	A.L.	65	99⅓	4	6	.400	94	54	81	3.17	7
1990 Seattle	A.L.	63	77⅓	5	7	.417	69	44	64	4.54	3
1991 Seattle b	A.L.	72	88⅔	7	7	.500	74	34	64	3.25	14
1992 San Francisco	N.L.	67	82	6	6	.500	80	33	76	3.73	2
1993 San Francisco c	N.L.	*81	77⅓	6	6	.500	70	24	58	3.03	1
1994 San Francisco d-e	N.L.	36	42⅓	3	2	.600	51	11	23	1.49	4
1995 Chattanooga	Southern	3	3	0	0	.000	2	0	2	0.00	0
1995 Indianapolis	A.A.	2	2	0	0	.000	1	0	0	0.00	0
1995 Cincinnati f-g-h	N.L.	40	49	6	1	.857	41	19	38	2.39	2
1996 Seattle i-j	A.L.	73	72	1	1	.500	70	24	61	3.62	6
1997 Cleveland	A.L.	71	75	2	5	.286	74	29	59	3.24	15
Major League Totals ....12 Yrs.		694	885	49	56	.467	795	375	698	3.33	59
Division Series											
1995 Cincinnati	N.L.	3	3⅔	0	0	.000	1	0	4	0.00	0
1997 Cleveland	A.L.	4	4⅓	1	0	1.000	5	1	3	0.00	0
Division Series Totals 7		8	1	0	1.000	6	1	7	0.00	0
Championship Series											
1995 Cincinnati	N.L.	3	2⅓	0	1	.000	1	4	5	23.14	0
1997 Cleveland	A.L.	5	4⅓	0	0	.000	7	1	1	0.00	0
Championship Series Totals 8		6⅔	0	1	.000	8	5	6	8.10	0
World Series Record											
1997 Cleveland	A.L.	4	4⅔	0	0	.000	4	3	5	1.93	0

a Traded to Seattle Mariners with outfielders Glenn Wilson and Dave Brundage for outfielder Phil Bradley and pitcher Tom Fortugno, December 9, 1987.
b Traded to San Francisco Giants with pitchers Bill Swift and Dave Burba for outfielder Kevin Mitchell and pitcher Mike Remlinger, December 11, 1991.
c On disabled list from July 24 to August 9, 1993.
d On disabled list from June 17 to July 2 and July 7 to end of 1994 season.
e Filed for free agency, October 18, 1994.
f Signed with Cincinnati Reds, April 8, 1995.
g On disabled list from April 25 to June 5, 1995.
h Filed for free agency, November 12, 1995.
i Signed with Seattle Mariners, February 2, 1996.
j Filed for free agency, October 30, 1996.

JACOME, JASON JAMES

Born, Tulsa, Oklahoma, November 24, 1970.
Bats Left. Throws Left. Height, 6 feet, 1 inch. Weight, 175 pounds.

Year Club	Lea	G	IP	W	L	Pct	SO	BB	H	ERA	SAVES
1991 Kingsport	Appal.	12	55⅓	5	4	.556	48	13	35	1.63	2
1992 Columbia	So. Atl.	8	52⅔	4	1	.800	49	15	40	1.03	0
1992 St. Lucie	Fla. St.	17	114⅓	6	7	.462	66	30	98	2.83	0
1993 St. Lucie	Fla. St.	14	99⅓	6	3	.667	66	23	106	3.08	0
1993 Binghamton	Eastern	14	87	8	4	.667	56	38	85	3.21	0
1994 Norfolk	Int.	19	126⅔	8	6	.571	80	42	138	2.84	0
1994 New York	N.L.	8	54	4	3	.571	30	17	54	2.67	0
1995 Norfolk	Int.	8	43⅔	2	4	.333	31	13	40	3.92	0
1995 New York	N.L.	5	21	0	4	.000	11	15	33	10.29	0
1995 Kansas City a	A.L.	15	84	4	6	.400	39	21	101	5.36	0
1996 Kansas City	A.L.	49	47⅔	0	4	.000	32	22	67	4.72	1
1997 Buffalo b	A.A.	7	37	3	1	.750	23	10	41	3.16	0
1997 Kansas City-Cleveland	A.L.	28	49⅓	2	0	1.000	27	20	58	5.83	0
Major League Totals ....4 Yrs.		105	256	10	17	.370	139	95	313	5.17	1

a Traded to Kansas City Royals with pitcher Allen McDill for pitcher Geno Morones and pitcher Derek Wallace, July 21, 1995.
b Claimed on waivers by Cleveland Indians, May 8, 1997.

JAMES, MICHAEL ELMO (MIKE)
Born, Ft. Walton Beach, Florida, August 15, 1967.
Bats Right. Throws Right. Height, 6 feet, 4 inches. Weight, 215 pounds.

Year	Club	Lea	G	IP	W	L	Pct	SO	BB	H	ERA	SAVES
1988 Great Falls	.........Pioneer		14	67	7	1	.875	59	41	61	3.76	0
1989 Bakersfield	.......California		27	159²/₃	11	8	.579	127	78	144	3.78	0
1990 San Antonio	.........Texas		26	157	11	4	.733	97	78	144	3.32	0
1991 San Antonio	.........Texas		15	89¹/₃	9	5	.643	74	51	88	4.53	0
1991 Albuquerque	..........P.C.		13	45	1	3	.250	39	30	51	6.60	0
1992 San Antonio	.........Texas		8	54	2	1	.667	52	20	39	2.67	0
1992 Albuquerque	..........P.C.		18	46²/₃	2	1	.667	33	22	55	5.59	1
1993 Albuquerque	..........P.C.		16	31¹/₃	1	0	1.000	32	19	38	7.47	2
1993 Vero Beach	.........Fla. St.		30	60¹/₃	2	3	.400	60	33	54	4.92	5
1994 Vancouver	..........P.C.		37	91¹/₃	5	3	.625	66	34	101	5.22	8
1995 Lake Elsinore	......California		5	5²/₃	0	0	.000	8	3	9	9.53	0
1995 California a	............A.L.		46	55²/₃	3	0	1.000	36	26	49	3.88	1
1996 California	............A.L.		69	81	5	5	.500	65	42	62	2.67	1
1997 Anaheim b	...........A.L.		58	62²/₃	5	5	.500	57	28	69	4.31	7
Major League Totals	........3 Yrs.		173	199¹/₃	13	10	.565	158	96	180	3.52	9

a On disabled list from May 11 to June 1, 1995.
b On disabled list from July 3 to July 27, 1997.

JANZEN, MARTIN THOMAS (MARTY)
Born, Homestead, Florida, May 31, 1973.
Bats Right. Throws Right. Height, 6 feet, 3 inches. Weight, 197 pounds.

Year	Club	Lea	G	IP	W	L	Pct	SO	BB	H	ERA	SAVES
1992 Yankees	........Gulf Coast		12	68²/₃	7	2	.778	73	15	55	2.36	0
1992 Greensboro	.........So. Atl.		2	5	0	0	.000	5	1	5	3.60	1
1993 Yankees	........Gulf Coast		5	22¹/₃	0	1	.000	19	3	20	1.21	0
1994 Greensboro	.........So. Atl.		17	104	3	7	.300	92	25	98	3.89	0
1995 Tampa	.............Fla. St.		18	113²/₃	10	3	.769	104	30	102	2.61	0
1995 Norwich	...........Eastern		3	20	1	2	.333	16	7	17	4.95	0
1995 Knoxville	.........Southern		7	48	5	1	.833	44	14	35	2.63	0
1996 Syracuse	.............Int.		10	55²/₃	3	4	.429	34	24	74	7.76	0
1996 Toronto	.............A.L.		15	73²/₃	4	6	.400	47	38	95	7.33	0
1997 Syracuse	.............Int.		22	65	0	5	.000	56	36	76	7.20	1
1997 Toronto a	.............A.L.		12	25	2	1	.667	17	13	23	3.60	0
Major League Totals	........2 Yrs.		27	98²/₃	6	7	.462	64	51	118	6.39	0

a Selected in expansion draft by Arizona Diamondbacks, November 18, 1997.

JARVIS, KEVIN THOMAS
Born, Lexington, Kentucky, August 1, 1969.
Bats Left. Throws Right. Height, 6 feet, 2 inches. Weight, 200 pounds.

Year	Club	Lea	G	IP	W	L	Pct	SO	BB	H	ERA	SAVES
1991 Princeton	...........Appal.		13	85²/₃	5	6	.455	79	29	73	2.42	0
1992 Cedar Rapids	.......Midwest		1	1	0	0	.000	0	0	1	0.00	0
1992 Charleston, WV	.....So. Atl.		28	133	6	8	.429	131	37	123	3.11	0
1993 Winston-Salem	......Carolina		21	145	8	7	.533	101	48	133	3.41	0
1993 Chattanooga	......Southern		7	37¹/₃	3	1	.750	18	11	26	1.69	0
1994 Indianapolis	...........A.A.		21	132¹/₃	10	2	.833	90	34	136	3.54	0
1994 Cincinnati	.............N.L.		6	17²/₃	1	1	.500	10	5	22	7.13	0
1995 Indianapolis	...........A.A.		10	60²/₃	4	2	.667	37	18	62	4.45	0
1995 Cincinnati	.............N.L.		19	79	3	4	.429	33	32	91	5.70	0
1996 Indianapolis	...........A.A.		8	42²/₃	4	3	.571	32	12	45	5.06	0
1996 Cincinnati	.............N.L.		24	120¹/₃	8	9	.471	63	43	152	5.98	0
1997 Toledo a	.............Int.		2	8	0	1	.000	5	4	7	6.75	0
1997 Cincinnati b-c	.............N.L.		9	13¹/₃	0	1	.000	12	7	21	10.13	1
1997 Minnesota-Detroit d-e	...A.L.		23	54²/₃	0	3	.000	36	22	78	7.08	0
Major League Totals	........4 Yrs.		81	285	12	18	.400	154	109	364	6.38	1

a Claimed on waivers by Detroit Tigers, May 2, 1997.
b Claimed on waivers by Minnesota Twins, May 9, 1997.
c Claimed on waivers by Detroit Tigers, June 17, 1997.
d On disabled list from June 25 to July 14, 1997.
e Released by Detroit Tigers, December 12, 1997.

JOHNSON, DANE EDWARD

Born, Coral Gables, Florida, February 10, 1963.
Bats Right. Throws Right. Height, 6 feet, 5 inches. Weight, 205 pounds.

Year	Club	Lea	G	IP	W	L	Pct	SO	BB	H	ERA	SAVES
1984 Medicne Hat	....	Pioneer	10	41⅔	1	5	.167	15	59	43	8.42	0
1985 Florence	....	So. Atl.	10	34⅓	0	4	.000	25	37	27	6.29	1
1986 Florence	....	So. Atl.	31	123⅔	8	12	.400	68	114	136	6.99	0
1987 Dunedin	....	Fla. St.	18	59	2	5	.286	25	49	68	5.80	0
1988 Dunedin	....	Fla. St.	32	104⅔	11	6	.647	73	89	91	4.73	0
1989 Myrtle Bch. a	....	So. Atl.	4	5⅔	0	0	.000	5	4	5	1.59	0
1990–91	....				Played in Chinese Professional League, Taiwan							
1992	....				Out of Organized Baseball							
1993 El Paso b	....	Texas	15	25⅓	2	2	.500	26	10	23	3.91	1
1993 New Orleans c	....	A.A.	13	15	0	0	.000	10	4	11	2.40	6
1994 Chicago d	....	A.L.	15	12⅓	2	1	.667	7	11	16	6.57	0
1994 Nashville	....	A.A.	39	44	1	5	.167	40	18	40	2.25	24
1995 Nashville e	....	A.A.	46	56	4	4	.500	51	28	48	2.41	15
1996 Syracuse f	....	Int.	43	51⅓	3	2	.600	51	17	37	2.45	22
1996 Toronto g	....	A.L.	10	9	0	0	.000	7	5	5	3.00	0
1997 Edmonton	....	P.C.	14	16	1	1	.500	13	8	17	5.63	6
1997 Oakland h	....	A.L.	38	45⅔	4	1	.800	43	31	49	4.53	2
Major League Totals	....	3 Yrs.	63	67	6	2	.750	57	47	70	4.70	2

a Released by Toronto Blue Jays organization, July 12, 1989.
b Signed as free agent by Milwaukee Brewers organization, June 5, 1993.
c Opted for free agency, October 15, 1993.
d Signed as free agent by Chicago White Sox, January 28, 1994.
e Opted for free agency, October 16, 1995.
f Signed as free agent with Toronto Blue Jays organization, February 10, 1996.
g Claimed on waivers by Oakland Athletics, October 2, 1996.
h Released and signed with Toronto Blue Jays organization, October 29, 1997.

JOHNSON, JASON MICHAEL

Born, Santa Barbara, California, October 27, 1973.
Bats Right. Throws Right. Height, 6 feet, 6 inches. Weight, 220 pounds.

Year	Club	Lea	G	IP	W	L	Pct	SO	BB	H	ERA	SAVES
1992 Pirates	....	Gulf Coast	5	7⅓	2	0	1.000	3	6	6	3.68	0
1993 Pirates	....	Gulf Coast	9	54	1	4	.200	39	14	48	2.33	0
1993 Welland	....	N.Y.-Penn.	6	35	1	5	.167	19	9	33	4.63	0
1994 Augusta	....	So. Atl.	20	102⅔	2	12	.143	69	32	119	4.03	0
1995 Augusta	....	So. Atl.	11	53⅔	3	5	.375	42	17	57	4.36	0
1995 Lynchburg	....	Carolina	10	55	1	4	.200	41	20	58	4.91	0
1996 Lynchburg	....	Carolina	15	44⅓	1	4	.200	27	12	56	6.50	0
1996 Augusta	....	So. Atl.	14	84	4	4	.500	83	25	82	3.11	0
1997 Lynchburg	....	Carolina	17	99⅓	8	4	.667	92	30	98	3.71	0
1997 Carolina	....	Southern	9	57⅓	3	3	.500	63	16	56	4.08	0
1997 Pittsburgh a	....	N.L.	3	6	0	0	.000	3	1	10	6.00	0

a Selected in expansion draft by Tampa Bay Devil Rays, November 18, 1997.

JOHNSON, MICHAEL KEITH

Born, Edmonton, Alberta, Canada, October 3, 1975.
Bats Left. Throws Right. Height, 6 feet, 2 inches. Weight, 175 pounds.

Year	Club	Lea	G	IP	W	L	Pct	SO	BB	H	ERA	SAVES
1993 Blue Jays	....	Gulf Coast	16	44⅓	0	2	.000	31	22	51	4.87	1
1994 Medicne Hat	....	Pioneer	9	36⅓	1	3	.250	8	22	48	4.46	0
1995 Blue Jays	....	Gulf Coast	3	15	0	2	.000	13	8	20	7.20	0
1995 Medicne Hat	....	Pioneer	19	49	4	1	.800	32	25	46	3.86	3
1996 Hagerstown	....	So. Atl.	29	162⅔	11	8	.579	155	39	157	3.15	0
1997 Baltimore a	....	A.L.	14	39⅔	0	1	.000	29	16	52	7.94	2
1997 Montreal	....	N.L.	11	50	2	5	.286	28	21	54	5.94	0
Major League Totals	....	1 Yrs.	25	89⅔	2	6	.250	57	37	106	6.83	2

a Traded to Montreal Expos for player to be named later, July 31, 1997. Baltimore Orioles received pitcher Everett Stull to complete trade, October 31, 1997.

JOHNSON, RANDALL DAVID (RANDY)

Born, Walnut Creek, California, September 10, 1964.
Bats Right. Throws Left. Height, 6 feet, 10 inches. Weight, 225 pounds.

Year	Club	Lea	G	IP	W	L	Pct	SO	BB	H	ERA	SAVES
1985	Jamestown	N.Y.-Penn.	8	27⅓	0	3	.000	21	24	29	5.93	0
1986	West Palm Beach	Fla. St.	26	119⅔	8	7	.533	133	94	89	3.16	0
1987	Jacksonville	Southern	25	140	11	8	.579	*163	128	100	3.73	0
1988	Indianapolis	A.A.	20	113⅓	8	7	.533	111	72	85	3.26	0
1988	Montreal	N.L.	4	26	3	0	1.000	25	7	23	2.42	0
1989	Montreal	N.L.	7	29⅔	0	4	.000	26	26	29	6.67	0
1989	Indianapolis a	A.A.	3	18	1	1	.500	17	9	13	2.00	0
1989	Seattle	A.L.	22	131	7	9	.438	104	70	118	4.40	0
1990	Seattle b-c	A.L.	33	219⅔	14	11	.560	194	*120	174	3.65	0
1991	Seattle	A.L.	33	201⅓	13	10	.565	228	*152	151	3.98	0
1992	Seattle d	A.L.	31	210⅓	12	14	.462	*241	*144	154	3.77	0
1993	Seattle	A.L.	35	255⅓	19	8	.704	*308	99	185	3.24	1
1994	Seattle	A.L.	23	172	13	6	.684	*204	72	132	3.19	0
1995	Seattle e	A.L.	30	214⅓	18	2	.900	*294	65	159	2.48	0
1996	Everett	Northwest	1	2	0	0	.000	5	0	0	0.00	0
1996	Seattle f	A.L.	14	61⅓	5	0	1.000	85	25	48	3.67	1
1997	Seattle	A.L.	30	213	20	4	.833	291	77	147	2.28	0
Major League Totals		10 Yrs.	262	1734	124	68	.646	2000	857	1320	3.37	2
Division Series												
1995	Seattle	A.L.	2	10	2	0	1.000	16	6	5	2.70	0
1997	Seattle	A.L.	2	13	0	2	.000	16	6	14	5.54	0
Division Series Totals		4	23	2	2	.500	32	12	19	4.30	0	
Championship Series												
1995	Seattle	A.L.	2	15⅓	0	1	.000	13	2	12	2.35	0

a Traded by Montreal Expos to Seattle Mariners with pitchers Brian Holman and Gene Harris for pitcher Mark Langston and player to be named, May 25; Montreal acquired pitcher Mike Campbell to complete trade, July 31, 1989.
b Pitched no-hit, no-run game against Detroit Tigers, winning 2-0, June 2, 1990.
c Suspended three games by American League for June 30 fight from July 11 to July 13, 1990.
d On disabled list from June 11 to June 27, 1992.
e Selected Cy Young Award Winner in American League for 1995.
f On disabled list from May 13 to August 6 and August 27 to September 30, 1996.

JONES, DOUGLAS REID (DOUG)

Born, Covina, California, June 24, 1957.
Bats Right. Throws Right. Height, 6 feet, 2 inches. Weight, 195 pounds.

Year	Club	Lea	G	IP	W	L	Pct	SO	BB	H	ERA	SAVES
1978	Newark a	N.Y.-Penn.	15	38	2	4	.333	27	15	49	5.21	2
1979	Burlington	Midwest	28	*190	10	10	.500	115	73	144	*1.75	0
1980	Stockton	California	11	76	6	2	.750	54	31	63	2.84	0
1980	Vancouver	P.C.	8	53	3	2	.600	28	15	52	3.23	0
1980	Holyoke	Eastern	8	62	5	3	.625	39	26	57	2.90	0
1981	El Paso	Texas	15	90	5	7	.417	62	28	121	5.80	0
1981	Vancouver	P.C.	11	80	5	3	.625	38	22	79	3.04	0
1982	Milwaukee	A.L.	4	2⅔	0	0	.000	1	1	5	10.13	0
1982	Vancouver	P.C.	23	106	5	8	.385	60	31	109	2.97	2
1983	Vancouver b	P.C.	3	7	0	1	.000	4	5	10	10.29	0
1984	Vancouver c	P.C.	3	8	1	0	1.000	2	3	0	10.13	0
1984	El Paso d	Texas	16	109⅓	6	8	.429	62	35	120	4.28	7
1985	Waterbury	Eastern	39	116	9	4	.692	113	36	123	3.65	0
1986	Maine	Int.	43	116⅓	5	6	.455	98	27	105	*2.09	9
1986	Cleveland	A.L.	11	18	1	0	1.000	12	6	18	2.50	1
1987	Buffalo	A.A.	23	61⅔	5	2	.714	61	12	49	2.04	7
1987	Cleveland	A.L.	49	91⅓	6	5	.545	87	24	101	3.15	8
1988	Cleveland	A.L.	51	83⅓	3	4	.429	72	16	69	2.27	37
1989	Cleveland	A.L.	59	80⅔	7	10	.412	65	13	76	2.34	32
1990	Cleveland	A.L.	66	84⅓	5	5	.500	55	22	66	2.56	43
1991	Cleveland	A.L.	36	63⅓	4	8	.333	48	17	87	5.54	7
1991	Colorado Springs e	P.C.	17	35⅔	2	2	.500	29	5	30	3.28	7
1992	Houston	N.L.	80	111⅔	11	8	.579	93	17	96	1.85	36
1993	Houston f	N.L.	71	85⅓	4	10	.286	66	21	102	4.54	26
1994	Philadelphia g	N.L.	47	54	2	4	.333	38	6	55	2.17	27
1995	Baltimore h-i-j	A.L.	52	46⅔	0	4	.000	42	16	55	5.01	22
1996	Chicago k-l	N.L.	28	32⅓	2	2	.500	26	7	41	5.01	2
1996	New Orleans	A.A.	13	24	0	3	.000	17	6	28	3.75	6

Year Club	Lea	G	IP	W	L	Pct	SO	BB	H	ERA	SAVES
1996 Milwaukee m .........A.L.		24	31⅔	5	0	1.000	34	13	31	3.41	1
1997 Milwaukee n-o-p ......A.L.		75	80⅓	6	6	.500	82	9	62	2.02	36
Major League Totals ....13 Yrs.		653	865⅔	56	66	.459	721	188	864	3.10	278

a On disabled list from June 20 to July 12, 1978.
b On disabled list from April 11 to September 1, 1983.
c On disabled list from April 25 to May 30, 1984.
d Became free agent, October 15, 1984; signed with Cleveland Indians organization, April 3, 1985.
e Not offered 1992 contract, December 20, 1991; signed with Houston Astros organization, January 24, 1992.
f Traded to Philadelphia Phillies with pitcher Jeff Juden for pitcher Mitch Williams, December 2, 1993.
g Filed for free agency, October 20, 1994.
h Signed with Baltimore Orioles, April 8, 1995.
i Not offered 1996 contract, November 1, 1995.
j Signed with Chicago Cubs, December 28, 1995.
k Released by Chicago Cubs, May 16, 1996.
l Filed for free agency, November 6, 1996.
m Signed with Milwaukee Brewers organization, December 7, 1996.
n On disabled list from July 16 to August 2, 1997.
o Filed for free agency, October 27, 1997.
p Re-signed with Milwaukee Brewers, November 18, 1997.

JONES, ROBERT JOSEPH (BOBBY)
Born, Fresno, California, February 10, 1970.
Bats Right. Throws Right. height, 6 feet, 4 inches. Weight, 210 pounds.

Year Club	Lea	G	IP	W	L	Pct	SO	BB	H	ERA	SAVES
1991 Columbia ....So. Atl.		5	24⅓	3	1	.750	35	3	20	1.85	0
1992 Binghamton ....Eastern		24	158	12	4	.750	143	43	118	1.88	0
1993 Norfolk ....Int.		24	166	12	10	.545	126	32	149	3.63	0
1993 New York .............N.L.		9	61⅔	2	4	.333	35	22	61	3.65	0
1994 New York .............N.L.		24	160	12	7	.632	80	56	157	3.15	0
1995 New York .............N.L.		30	195⅔	10	10	.500	127	53	209	4.19	0
1996 New York .............N.L.		31	195⅔	12	8	.600	116	46	219	4.42	0
1997 New York .............N.L.		30	193⅓	15	9	.625	125	63	177	3.63	0
Major League Totals ....5 Yrs.		124	806⅓	51	38	.573	483	240	823	3.86	0

JONES, TODD BARTON (GIVIN)
Born, Marietta, Georgia, April 24, 1968.
Bats Left. Throws Right. Height, 6 feet, 3 inches. Weight, 200 pounds.

Year Club	Lea	G	IP	W	L	Pct	SO	BB	H	ERA	SAVES
1989 Auburn ..........N.Y.-Penn.		11	49⅔	2	3	.400	71	42	47	5.44	0
1990 Osceola ....Fla. St.		27	151⅓	12	10	.545	106	109	124	3.51	0
1991 Osceola ....Fla. St.		14	72⅓	4	4	.500	51	35	69	4.35	0
1991 Jackson ....Texas		10	55⅓	4	3	.571	37	39	51	4.88	0
1992 Jackson ....Texas		61	66	3	7	.300	60	44	52	3.14	25
1992 Tucson ................P.C.		3	4	0	1	.000	4	10	1	4.50	0
1993 Tucson ................P.C.		41	48⅔	4	2	.667	45	31	49	4.44	12
1993 Houston .............N.L.		27	37⅓	1	2	.333	25	15	28	3.13	2
1994 Houston .............N.L.		48	72⅔	5	2	.714	63	26	52	2.72	5
1995 Houston .............N.L.		68	99⅔	6	5	.545	96	52	89	3.07	15
1996 Tucson ................P.C.		1	2	0	0	.000	0	2	1	0.00	0
1996 Houston a-b ........N.L.		51	57⅓	6	3	.667	44	32	61	4.40	17
1997 Detroit ...............A.L.		68	70	5	4	.556	70	35	60	3.09	31
Major League Totals ....5 Yrs.		262	337	23	16	.590	298	160	290	3.23	70

a On disabled list from July 19 to August 12 and August 18 to September 12, 1996.
b Traded to Detroit Tigers with outfielder Brian Hunter, infielder Orlando Miller and pitcher Doug Brocail for catcher Brad Ausmus, pitcher C.J. Nitkowski, pitcher Jose Lima, pitcher Trever Miller and infielder Daryle Ward, December 10, 1996.

JORDAN, RICARDO
Born, Boynton Beach, Florida, June 27, 1970.
Bats Left. Throws Left. Height, 5 feet, 11 inches. Weight, 165 pounds.

Year Club	Lea	G	IP	W	L	Pct	SO	BB	H	ERA	SAVES
1990 Dunedin ....Fla. St.		13	22⅔	0	2	.000	16	19	15	2.38	0
1991 Myrtle Beach ....So. Atl.		29	144⅔	9	8	.529	152	79	101	2.74	1
1992 Dunedin ....Fla. St.		45	47	0	5	.000	49	28	44	3.83	15

Year	Club	Lea	G	IP	W	L	Pct	SO	BB	H	ERA	SAVES
1993 Dunedin	Fla. St.	15	24⅔	2	0	1.000	24	15	20	4.38	1
1993 Knoxville	Southern	25	36⅔	1	4	.200	35	18	33	2.45	2
1994 Knoxville	Southern	53	64⅓	4	3	.571	70	23	54	2.66	17
1995 Syracuse	Int.	13	12⅓	0	0	.000	17	7	15	6.57	0
1995 Toronto a	A.L.	15	15	1	0	1.000	10	13	18	6.60	1
1996 Scranton-W.B.	Int.	32	39⅓	3	3	.500	40	22	40	5.26	1
1996 Philadelphia b	N.L.	26	25	2	2	.500	17	12	18	1.80	0
1997 Norfolk	Int.	34	29	0	1	.000	34	24	20	2.79	1
1997 New York c	N.L.	22	27	1	2	.333	19	15	31	5.33	0
Major League Totals	3 Yrs.	63	67	4	4	.500	46	40	67	4.30	1

a Traded with outfielder Howard Battle to Philadelphia Phillies for pitcher Paul Quantril, December 6, 1995.
b Traded to New York Mets along with pitcher Toby Borland, in exchange for first baseman Rico Brogna, November 27, 1996.
c Outrighted by New York Mets, October 15, 1997.

JUDEN, JEFFREY DANIEL

Born, Salem, Massachusetts, January 19, 1971.
Bats Right. Throws Right. Height, 6 feet, 7 inches. Weight, 245 pounds.

Year	Club	Lea	G	IP	W	L	Pct	SO	BB	H	ERA	SAVES
1989 G. C. Astros	Gulf Coast	9	39⅔	1	4	.200	49	17	33	3.40	0
1990 Osceola	Fla. St.	15	91	10	1	*.909	85	42	72	2.27	0
1990 Columbus	Southern	11	52	1	3	.250	40	42	55	5.37	0
1991 Jackson	Texas	16	95⅔	6	3	.667	75	44	84	3.10	0
1991 Tucson	P.C.	10	56⅔	3	2	.600	51	25	56	3.18	0
1991 Houston	N.L.	4	18	0	2	.000	11	7	19	6.00	0
1992 Tucson	P.C.	26	147	9	10	.474	120	71	149	4.04	0
1993 Tucson	P.C.	27	169	11	6	.647	156	*76	174	4.63	0
1993 Houston a	N.L.	2	5	0	1	.000	7	4	4	5.40	0
1994 Philadelphia	N.L.	6	27⅔	1	4	.200	22	12	29	6.18	0
1994 Scranton b	Int.	6	25⅓	2	2	.500	28	19	30	8.53	0
1995 Scranton-Wilkes Barre	Int.	14	83⅓	6	4	.600	65	33	73	4.10	0
1995 Philadelphia c	N.L.	13	62⅔	2	4	.333	47	31	53	4.02	0
1996 San Francisco-Montreal	N.L.	58	74⅓	5	0	1.000	61	34	61	3.27	0
1997 Montreal d	N.L.	22	130	11	5	.688	107	57	125	4.22	0
1997 Cleveland	A.L.	8	31⅓	0	1	.000	29	15	32	5.46	0
Major League Totals	6 Yrs.	113	349	19	17	.528	284	160	323	4.36	0
Championship Series											
1997 Cleveland	A.L.	3	1	0	0	.000	2	2	2	0.00	0
World Series Record											
1997 Cleveland	A.L.	2	2	0	0	.000	0	2	2	4.50	0

a Traded to Philadelphia Phillies with pitcher Doug Jones for pitcher Mitch Williams, December 2, 1993.
b On disabled list from June 24 to July 24 and July 25 to end of 1994 season.
c Traded to San Francisco Giants for infielder Mike Benjamin, August 17, 1995.
d Traded to Cleveland Indians for pitcher Steve Kline and player to be named later, July 31, 1997.

KAMIENIECKI, SCOTT ANDREW

Born, Mount Clemens, Michigan, April 19, 1964.
Bats Right. Throws Right. Height, 6 feet. Weight, 195 pounds.

Year	Club	Lea	G	IP	W	L	Pct	SO	BB	H	ERA	SAVES
1987 Albany	Eastern	10	37	1	3	.250	19	33	41	5.35	0
1987 Prince William	Carolina	19	112⅓	9	5	.643	84	78	91	4.17	0
1988 Prince William	Carolina	15	100⅓	6	7	.462	72	50	115	4.40	0
1988 Fort Lauderdale	Fla. St.	12	77	3	6	.333	51	40	71	3.62	0
1989 Albany	Eastern	24	151	10	9	.526	*140	57	142	3.70	1
1990 Albany	Eastern	22	132	10	9	.526	99	61	113	3.20	0
1991 Columbus	Int.	11	76⅓	6	3	.667	58	20	61	2.36	0
1991 New York a	A.L.	9	55⅓	4	4	.500	34	22	54	3.90	0
1992 Fort Lauderdale	Fla. St.	1	7	1	0	1.000	3	0	8	1.29	0
1992 Columbus	Int.	2	13	1	0	1.000	12	4	6	0.69	0
1992 New York b	A.L.	28	188	6	14	.300	88	74	193	4.36	0
1993 Columbus	Int.	1	6	1	0	1.000	4	0	5	1.50	0
1993 New York	A.L.	30	154⅓	10	7	.588	72	59	163	4.08	1
1994 New York	A.L.	22	117⅓	8	6	.571	71	59	115	3.76	0
1995 Tampa	Fla. St.	1	5	1	0	1.000	2	1	6	1.80	0
1995 Columbus	Int.	1	6⅔	1	0	1.000	10	1	2	0.00	0
1995 New York c	A.L.	17	89⅔	7	6	.538	43	49	83	4.01	0

270

Year Club	Lea	G	IP	W	L	Pct	SO	BB	H	ERA	SAVES
1996 Tampa	Fla. St.	3	23	2	1	.667	17	4	20	1.17	0
1996 New York d-e	A.L.	7	22⅔	1	2	.333	15	19	36	11.12	0
1996 Columbus f	Int.	5	30⅓	2	1	.667	27	8	33	5.64	0
1997 Baltimore g-h	A.L.	30	179⅓	10	6	.625	109	67	179	4.01	0
Major League Totals	7 Yrs.	143	806⅔	46	45	.505	432	349	823	4.26	1
Championship Series											
1997 Baltimore	A.L.	2	8	1	0	1.000	5	2	4	0.00	0
Division Series											
1995 New York	A.L.	1	5	0	0	.000	4	4	9	7.20	0

a On disabled list from August 3 to end of 1991 season.
b On disabled list from April 2 to April 29, 1992.
c On disabled list from May 6 to July 15, 1995.
d On disabled list from April 1 to April 24 and July 31 to September 30, 1996.
e Not offered contract by New York Yankees, December 21, 1996.
f Signed with Baltimore Orioles organization, January 22, 1997.
g Filed for free agency, October 30, 1997.
h Re-signed with Baltimore Orioles, December 5, 1997.

KARCHNER, MATTHEW DEAN (MATT)

Born, Berwick, Pennsylvania, June 28, 1967.
Bats Right. Throws Right. Height, 6 feet, 4 inches. Weight, 245 pounds.

Year Club	Lea	G	IP	W	L	Pct	SO	BB	H	ERA	SAVES
1989 Eugene	Northwest	8	30	1	1	.500	25	8	30	3.90	0
1990 Appleton	Midwest	27	71	2	7	.222	58	31	70	4.82	0
1991 Baseball City	Fla. St.	38	73	6	3	.667	65	25	49	1.97	5
1992 Memphis	Southern	33	141	8	8	.500	88	35	161	4.47	1
1993 Memphis	Southern	6	30	3	2	.600	14	4	34	4.20	0
1994 Birmingham	Southern	39	43	5	2	.714	29	14	36	1.26	6
1994 Nashville	A.A.	17	26⅓	4	2	.667	19	7	18	1.37	2
1995 Nashville	A.A.	28	37⅓	3	3	.500	29	10	39	1.45	9
1995 Chicago	A.L.	31	32	4	2	.667	24	12	33	1.69	0
1996 Chicago a	A.L.	50	59⅓	7	4	.636	46	41	61	5.76	1
1996 Nashville	A.A.	1	0⅔	0	0	.000	0	0	0	0.00	0
1997 Nashville	A.A.	13	18⅔	2	1	.667	11	6	12	1.93	3
1997 Chicago	A.L.	52	52⅔	3	1	.750	30	26	50	2.91	15
Major League Totals	3 Yrs.	133	144	14	7	.667	100	79	144	3.81	16

a On disabled list from August 11 to September 30, 1996.

KARL, RANDALL SCOTT (SCOTT)

Born, Fontana, California, August 9, 1971.
Bats Left. Throws Left. Height, 6 feet, 2 inches. Weight, 195 pounds.

Year Club	Lea	G	IP	W	L	Pct	SO	BB	H	ERA	SAVES
1992 Helena	Pioneer	9	61⅔	7	0	1.000	57	16	54	1.46	0
1993 El Paso	Texas	27	180	13	8	.619	95	35	172	2.45	0
1994 El Paso	Texas	8	54⅔	5	1	.833	51	15	44	2.96	0
1994 New Orleans	A.A.	15	89	5	5	.500	54	33	92	3.84	0
1995 New Orleans	A.A.	8	46⅓	3	4	.429	29	12	47	3.30	0
1995 Milwaukee	A.L.	25	124	6	7	.462	59	50	141	4.14	0
1996 Milwaukee	A.L.	32	207⅓	13	9	.591	121	72	220	4.86	0
1997 Milwaukee	A.L.	32	193⅓	10	13	.435	119	67	212	4.47	0
Major League Totals	3 Yrs.	89	524⅔	29	29	.500	299	189	573	4.55	0

KARP, RYAN JASON

Born, Los Angeles, California, April 5, 1970.
Bats Left. Throws Left. Height, 6 feet, 4 inches. Weight, 220 pounds.

Year Club	Lea	G	IP	W	L	Pct	SO	BB	H	ERA	SAVES
1992 Oneonta	N.Y.-Penn.	14	70⅓	6	4	.600	58	30	66	4.09	0
1993 Greensboro	So. Atl.	17	109⅓	13	1	.929	132	40	73	1.81	0
1993 Pr William	Carolina	8	49	3	2	.600	34	12	35	2.20	0
1993 Albany	Eastern	3	13	0	0	.000	10	9	13	4.15	0
1994 Reading	Eastern	21	121⅓	4	11	.267	96	54	123	4.45	0
1995 Reading	Eastern	7	47	1	2	.333	37	15	44	3.06	0
1995 Philadelphia	N.L.	1	2	0	0	.000	2	3	1	4.50	0

Year	Club	Lea	G	IP	W	L	Pct	SO	BB	H	ERA	SAVES
1995 Scranton-WB	Int.	13	81⅓	7	1	.875	73	31	81	4.20	0
1996 Scranton-WB	Int.	7	41	1	1	.500	30	14	35	3.07	0
1997 Scranton-WB	Int.	32	73	4	3	.571	55	42	72	4.19	1
1997 Philadelphia a	N.L.	15	15	1	1	.500	18	9	12	5.40	0
Major League Totals ....2 Yrs.		16	17	1	1	.500	20	12	13	5.29	0

a Selected in expansion draft by Tampa Bay Devil Rays, November 18, 1997.

KARSAY, STEFAN ANDREW (STEVE)
Born, Flushing, New York, March 24, 1972.
Bats Right. Throws Right. Height, 6 feet, 3 inches. Weight, 210 pounds

Year	Club	Lea	G	IP	W	L	Pct	SO	BB	H	ERA	SAVES
1990 St. Cathrnes	N.Y.-Penn.	5	22⅔	1	1	.500	25	12	11	0.79	0
1991 Myrtle Bch	So. Atl.	20	110⅔	4	9	.308	100	48	96	3.58	0
1992 Dunedin	Fla. St.	16	85⅔	6	3	.667	87	29	56	2.73	0
1993 Knoxville	Southern	19	104	8	4	.667	100	32	98	3.38	0
1993 Huntsville a-b	Southern	2	14	0	0	.000	22	3	13	5.14	0
1993 Oakland	A.L.	8	49	3	3	.500	33	16	49	4.04	0
1994 Oakland c	A.L.	4	28	1	1	.500	15	8	26	2.57	0
1995 Oakland	A.L.			INJURED—Did Not Play							
1996 Modesto	California	14	34	0	1	.000	31	1	35	2.65	0
1997 Oakland d-e	A.L.	24	132⅔	3	12	.200	92	47	166	5.77	0
Major League Totals ....3 Yrs.		36	209⅔	7	16	.304	140	71	241	4.94	0

a On disabled list from July 3 to July 16, 1993.
b Traded by Toronto Blue Jays to Oakland Athletics organization with player to be named for outfielder Rickey Henderson July 31; Oakland acquired outfielder Jose Herrera to complete trade, August 7, 1993.
c On disabled list from April 26 to end of 1994 season.
d On disabled list from August 6 to September 29, 1997.
e Traded to Cleveland Indians for pitcher Mike Fetters, December 8, 1997.

KEAGLE, GREGORY CHARLES (GREG)
Born, Corning, New York, June 28, 1971.
Bats Right. Throws Right. Height, 6 feet, 1 inch. Weight 185 pounds.

Year	Club	Lea	G	IP	W	L	Pct	SO	BB	H	ERA	SAVES
1993 Spokane	Northwest	15	83	3	3	.500	77	40	80	3.25	0
1994 Rancho Cuca	California	14	92	11	1	.917	91	41	62	2.05	0
1994 Wichita	Texas	13	70⅓	3	9	.250	57	32	84	6.27	0
1995 Memphis	Southern	15	81	4	9	.308	82	41	82	5.11	0
1995 Rancho Cuca	California	2	14	0	0	.000	11	2	14	4.50	0
1995 Las Vegas	P.C.	14	75⅔	7	6	.538	49	42	76	4.28	0
1996 Toledo	Int.	6	27	2	3	.400	24	11	42	10.00	0
1996 Detroit a	A.L.	26	87⅔	3	6	.333	70	68	104	7.39	0
1997 Toledo	Int.	23	151⅓	11	7	.611	140	61	136	3.81	0
1997 Detroit	A.L.	11	45⅓	3	5	.375	33	18	58	6.55	0
Major League Totals ....2 Yrs.		37	133	6	11	.353	103	86	162	7.11	0

a On disabled list from July 7 to August 21, 1996.
a Traded by San Diego Padres to Seattle Mariners with pitcher Andy Benes for outfielders Marc Newfield and ron Villone, July 31, 1995.
b Drafted by Detroit in Rule V draft, December 4, 1995.

KEY, JAMES EDWARDS (JIMMY)
Born, Huntsville, Alabama, April 22, 1961.
Bats Right, Throws Left. Height, 6 feet, 1 inch. Weight, 185 pounds.

Year	Club	Lea	G	IP	W	L	Pct	SO	BB	H	ERA	SAVES
1982 Medicine Hat	Pioneer	5	31⅓	2	1	.667	25	10	27	2.30	0
1982 Florence	S. Atlantic	9	58	5	2	.714	49	18	59	3.72	0
1983 Knoxville	Southern	14	101	6	5	.545	57	40	86	2.85	0
1983 Syracuse	Int.	16	89⅓	4	8	.333	71	33	87	4.13	0

272

Year	Club	Lea	G	IP	W	L	Pct	SO	BB	H	ERA	SAVES
1984 Toronto	A.L.	63	62	4	5	.444	44	32	70	4.65	10
1985 Toronto	A.L.	35	212⅔	14	6	.700	85	50	188	3.00	0
1986 Toronto	A.L.	36	232	14	11	.560	141	74	222	3.57	0
1987 Toronto	A.L.	36	261	17	8	.680	161	66	210	*2.76	0
1988 Dunedin	Fla. St.	4	21⅓	2	0	1.000	11	1	15	0.00	0
1988 Toronto a	A.L.	21	131⅓	12	5	.706	65	30	127	3.29	0
1989 Toronto b	A.L.	33	216	13	14	.481	118	27	226	3.88	0
1990 Dunedin	Fla. St.	3	18	2	0	1.000	14	3	21	2.50	0
1990 Toronto c	A.L.	27	154⅓	13	7	.650	88	22	169	4.25	0
1991 Toronto	A.L.	33	209⅓	16	12	.571	125	44	207	3.05	0
1992 Toronto d	A.L.	33	216⅔	13	13	.500	117	59	2.05	3.53	0
1993 New York	A.L.	34	236⅔	18	6	.750	173	43	219	3.00	0
1994 New York	A.L.	25	168	*17	4	.810	97	52	177	3.27	0
1995 New York e	A.L.	5	30⅓	1	2	.333	14	6	40	5.64	0
1996 Tampa	Fla. St.	2	13	0	0	.000	11	1	10	2.77	0
1996 Yankees	Gulf Coast	1	5	1	0	1.000	10	0	3	0.00	0
1996 New York f-g	A.L.	30	169⅓	12	11	.522	116	58	171	4.68	0
1997 Baltimore	A.L.	34	212⅓	16	10	.615	141	82	210	3.43	0
Major League Totals ....14 Yrs.		445	2512⅓	180	114	.612	1485	645	2441	3.49	10
Division Series											
1996 New York	A.L.	1	5	0	0	.000	3	1	5	3.60	0
1997 Baltimore	A.L.	1	4⅔	0	1	.000	4	0	8	3.86	0
Division Series Totals 2			9⅔	0	1	.000	7	1	13	3.72	0
Championship Series											
1985 Toronto	A.L.	2	8⅔	0	1	.000	5	2	15	5.19	0
1989 Toronto	A.L.	1	6	1	0	1.000	2	2	7	4.50	0
1991 Toronto	A.L.	1	6	0	0	.000	1	1	5	3.00	0
1992 Toronto	A.L.	1	3	0	0	.000	1	2	2	0.00	0
1996 New York	A.L.	1	8	1	0	1.000	5	1	3	2.25	0
1997 Baltimore	A.L.	2	7	0	0	.000	7	3	5	2.57	0
Championship Series Totals 8			38⅔	2	1	.667	21	11	37	3.26	0
World Series Record											
1992 Toronto	A.L.	2	9	2	0	1.000	6	0	6	1.00	0
1996 New York	A.L.	2	11⅓	1	1	.500	1	5	15	3.97	0
World Series Totals 4			20⅓	3	1	.750	7	5	21	2.66	0

a On disabled list from April 15 to June 29, 1988.
b On disabled list from August 3 to August 19, 1989.
c On disabled list from May 23 to June 22, 1990.
d Filed for free agency, October 27; signed with New York Yankees, December 10, 1992.
e On disabled list from May 17 to October 2, 1995.
f On disabled list from May 16 to May 31 and June 11 to June 26, 1996.
g Signed with Baltimore Orioles, December 6, 1996.

KILE, DARRYL ANDREW

Born, Garden Grove, California, December 2, 1968.
Bats Right. Throws Right. Height, 6 feet, 5 inches. Weight, 185 pounds.

Year	Club	Lea	G	IP	W	L	Pct	SO	BB	H	ERA	SAVES
1988 Gulf Coast Astros	Gulf C.	12	59⅔	5	3	.625	54	33	48	3.17	0
1989 Columbus	Southern	20	125⅔	11	6	.647	108	68	74	2.58	0
1989 Tucson	P.C.	6	25⅔	2	1	.667	18	13	33	5.96	0
1990 Tucson a	P.C.	26	123⅓	5	10	.333	77	68	147	6.64	0
1991 Houston	N.L.	37	153⅔	7	11	.389	100	84	144	3.69	0
1992 Tucson	P.C.	9	56⅓	4	1	.800	43	32	50	3.99	0
1992 Houston	N.L.	22	125⅓	5	10	.333	90	63	124	3.95	0
1993 Houston b	N.L.	32	171⅔	15	8	.652	141	69	152	3.51	0
1994 Houston	N.L.	24	147⅔	9	6	.600	105	*82	153	4.57	0
1995 Tucson	P.C.	4	24⅓	2	1	.667	15	12	29	8.51	0
1995 Houston	N.L.	25	127	4	12	.250	113	73	114	4.96	0
1996 Houston	N.L.	35	219	12	11	.522	219	97	233	4.19	0
1997 Houston c-d	N.L.	34	255⅔	19	7	.731	205	94	208	2.57	0
Major League Totals ....7 Yrs.		209	1200	71	65	.522	973	562	1128	3.79	0
Division Series											
1997 Houston	N.L.	1	7	0	1	.000	4	2	2	2.57	0

a On disabled list from April 10 to April 20, 1990.
b Pitched no-hit game against New York Mets, winning 7-1, September 8, 1993.
c Filed for free agency, October 28, 1997.
d Signed with Colorado Rockies, December 5, 1997.

KING, CURTIS ALBERT

Born, Norristown, Pennsylvania, October 25, 1970.
Bats Right. Throws Right. Height, 6 feet, 5 inches. Weight, 205 pounds.

Year Club	Lea	G	IP	W	L	Pct	SO	BB	H	ERA	SAVES
1994 New Jersey	N.Y.-Penn.	5	20⅔	1	0	1.000	14	11	19	2.61	0
1994 Savannah	So. Atl.	8	53	4	1	.800	40	9	37	1.87	0
1995 St. Pete	Fla. St.	28	136	7	8	.467	65	49	117	2.58	0
1996 Arkansas	Texas	5	5	0	1	.000	5	6	15	19.80	1
1996 St. Pete	Fla. St.	48	55⅔	3	3	.500	27	24	41	2.75	30
1997 Arkansas	Texas	32	36⅓	2	3	.400	29	10	38	4.46	16
1997 Louisville	A.A.	16	22	2	1	.667	9	6	19	2.05	3
1997 St. Louis	N.L.	30	29⅓	4	2	.667	13	11	38	2.76	0

KLINE, STEVEN JAMES

Born, Sunbury, Pennsylvania, August 22, 1972.
Bats Both. Throws Left. Height, 6 feet, 2 inches. Weight, 200 pounds.

Year Club	Lea	G	IP	W	L	Pct	SO	BB	H	ERA	SAVES
1993 Burlington	Appal.	2	7⅓	1	1	.500	4	2	11	4.91	0
1993 Watertown	N.Y.-Penn.	13	79	5	4	.556	45	12	77	3.19	0
1994 Columbus	So. Atl.	28	185⅔	18	5	.783	174	36	175	3.01	0
1995 Canton-Akrn	Eastern	14	89⅓	2	3	.400	45	30	86	2.42	0
1996 Canton-Akrn	Eastern	25	146⅔	8	12	.400	107	55	168	5.46	0
1997 Buffalo	A.A.	20	51⅓	3	3	.500	41	13	53	4.03	1
1997 Cleveland a	A.L.	20	26⅓	3	1	.750	17	13	42	5.81	0
1997 Montreal	N.L.	26	26⅓	1	3	.250	20	10	31	6.15	0
Major League Totals	1 Yrs.	46	52⅔	4	4	.500	37	23	73	5.98	0

a Traded to Montreal Expos with player to be named later for pitcher Jeff Juden, July 31, 1997.

KRIVDA, RICK MICHAEL

Born, McKeesport, Pennsylvania, January 19, 1970.
Bats Right. Throws Right. Height, 6 feet, 1 inch. Weight, 180 pounds.

Year Club	Lea	G	IP	W	L	Pct	SO	BB	H	ERA	SAVES
1991 Bluefield	Appal.	15	67	7	1	.875	79	24	48	1.88	1
1992 Kane Country	Midwest	18	121⅔	12	5	.706	124	41	108	3.03	0
1992 Frederick	Carolina	9	57⅓	5	1	.833	64	15	51	2.98	0
1993 Bowie	Eastern	22	125⅔	7	5	.583	108	50	114	3.08	0
1993 Rochester	Int.	5	33⅓	3	0	1.000	23	16	20	1.89	0
1994 Rochester	Int.	28	163	9	10	.474	122	73	149	3.53	0
1995 Rochester	Int.	16	101⅔	6	5	.545	74	32	96	3.19	0
1995 Baltimore	A.L.	13	75⅓	2	7	.222	53	25	76	4.54	0
1996 Rochester	Int.	8	44	3	1	.750	34	15	51	4.30	0
1996 Baltimore	A.L.	22	81⅔	3	5	.375	54	39	89	4.96	0
1997 Rochester	Int.	22	146	14	2	.875	128	34	122	3.39	0
1997 Baltimore	A.L.	10	50	4	2	.667	29	18	67	6.30	0
Major League Totals	3 Yrs.	45	207	9	14	.391	136	82	232	5.13	0

LANGSTON, MARK EDWARD

Born, San Diego, California, August 20, 1960.
Bats Right. Throws Left. Height, 6 feet, 2 inches. Weight, 184 pounds.

Year Club	Lea	G	IP	W	L	Pct	SO	BB	H	ERA	SAVES
1981 Bellingham	Northwest	13	85	7	3	.700	97	46	81	3.39	0
1981 Bakersfield	California	26	177⅓	12	7	.632	161	102	143	2.54	0
1983 Chattanooga	Southern	28	198	14	9	.609	142	102	187	3.59	1
1984 Seattle	A.L.	35	225	17	10	.630	*204	*118	188	3.40	0
1985 Seattle a	A.L.	24	126⅔	7	14	.333	72	91	122	5.47	0
1986 Seattle	A.L.	37	239⅓	12	14	.462	*245	123	234	4.85	0
1987 Seattle	A.L.	35	272	19	13	.594	*262	114	242	3.84	0
1988 Seattle	A.L.	35	261⅓	15	11	.577	235	110	222	3.34	0
1989 Seattle b	A.L.	10	73⅓	4	5	.444	60	19	60	3.56	0
1989 Montreal c	N.L.	24	176⅔	12	9	.571	175	93	138	2.39	0
1990 California d	A.L.	33	223	10	17	.370	195	104	215	4.40	0
1991 California	A.L.	34	246⅓	19	8	.704	183	96	190	3.00	0
1992 California e	A.L.	32	229	13	14	.481	174	74	206	3.66	0

Year Club	Lea	G	IP	W	L	Pct	SO	BB	H	ERA	SAVES
1993 California .............A.L.	A.L.	35	256⅓	16	11	.593	196	85	220	3.20	0
1994 California f ...........A.L.	A.L.	18	119⅓	7	8	.467	109	54	121	4.68	0
1995 California ............A.L.	A.L.	31	200⅓	15	7	.682	142	64	212	4.63	0
1996 Lk Elsinore ....California	California	1	4	0	0	.000	5	0	3	0.00	0
1996 California g ..........A.L.	A.L.	18	123⅓	6	5	.545	83	45	116	4.82	0
1997 Lk Elsinore ....California	California	3	14	0	2	.000	10	2	11	3.21	0
1997 Anaheim h-i-j ........A.L.	A.L.	9	47⅔	2	4	.333	30	29	61	5.85	0
Major League Totals ....14 Yrs.		410	2819⅔	174	150	.537	2365	1219	2547	3.88	0

a On disabled list from June 7 through July 22, 1985.
b Traded to Montreal Expos with player to be named for pitchers Gene Harris, Brian Holman and Randy Johnson, May 25; Montreal acquired pitcher Mike Campbell to complete trade, July 31, 1989.
c Filed for free agency, October 30; signed with California Angels, December 1, 1989.
d Pitched first seven innings of no-hit, no-run game, completed by Mike Witt, against Seattle Mariners, winning 1-0, April 12, 1990.
e Appeared in one additional game as pinch runner.
f On disabled list from April 6 to May 11, 1994.
g On disabled list from May 6 to June 1 and July 12 to July 28 and August 10 to September 30, 1996.
h On disabled list from May 23 to August 20 and August 21 to September 29, 1997.
i Filed for free agency, October 28, 1997.
j Signed with San Diego Padres organization, January 7, 1998.

LEITER, ALOIS TERRY (AL)
Born, Toms River, New Jersey, October 23, 1965.
Bats Left. Throws Left. Height, 6 feet, 3 inches. Weight, 215 pounds.

Year Club	Lea	G	IP	W	L	Pct	SO	BB	H	ERA	SAVES
1984 Oneonta ........N.Y.-Penn.	N.Y.-Penn.	10	57	3	2	.600	48	26	52	3.63	0
1985 Oneonta ........N.Y.-Penn.	N.Y.-Penn.	6	38	3	2	.600	34	25	27	2.37	0
1985 Fort Lauderdale .....Fla. St.	Fla. St.	17	82	1	6	.143	44	57	87	6.48	0
1986 Fort Lauderdale .....Fla. St.	Fla. St.	22	117⅔	4	8	.333	101	90	96	4.05	0
1987 Albany a ....Eastern	Eastern	15	78	3	3	.500	71	37	64	3.35	0
1987 Columbus ....Int.	Int.	5	23⅓	1	4	.200	23	15	21	6.17	0
1987 New York .............A.L.	A.L.	4	22⅔	2	2	.500	28	15	24	6.35	0
1988 Columbus ....Int.	Int.	4	13	0	2	.000	12	14	5	3.46	0
1988 New York b ...........A.L.	A.L.	14	57⅓	4	4	.500	60	33	49	3.92	0
1989 New York-Toronto-c-d ..A.L.	A.L.	5	33⅓	1	2	.333	26	23	32	5.67	0
1989 Dunedin ....Fla. St.	Fla. St.	3	8	0	2	.000	4	5	11	5.63	0
1990 Dunedin ....Fla. St.	Fla. St.	6	24	0	0	.000	14	12	18	2.63	0
1990 Syracuse e ....Int.	Int.	15	78	3	8	.273	69	68	59	4.62	0
1990 Toronto .............A.L.	A.L.	4	6⅓	0	0	.000	5	2	1	0.00	0
1991 Dunedin ....Fla. St.	Fla. St.	4	9⅔	0	0	.000	5	7	5	1.86	0
1991 Toronto f .............A.L.	A.L.	3	1⅔	0	0	.000	1	5	3	27.00	0
1992 Syracuse ....Int.	Int.	27	163⅓	8	9	.471	108	64	159	3.86	0
1992 Toronto .............A.L.	A.L.	1	1	0	0	.000	0	2	1	9.00	0
1993 Toronto g ............A.L.	A.L.	34	105	9	6	.600	66	56	93	4.11	2
1994 Toronto h-i ..........A.L.	A.L.	20	111⅔	6	7	.462	100	65	125	5.08	0
1995 Toronto j-k ..........A.L.	A.L.	28	183	11	11	.500	153	108	162	3.64	0
1996 Florida l .............N.L.	N.L.	33	215⅓	16	12	.571	200	119	153	2.93	0
1997 Florida m-n ..........N.L.	N.L.	27	151⅓	11	9	.550	132	91	133	4.34	0
Major League Totals ....11 Yrs.		173	888⅔	60	53	.531	771	519	776	4.01	2
Division Series											
1997 Florida ...............N.L.	N.L.	1	4	0	0	.000	3	3	7	9.00	0
Championship Series											
1993 Toronto ...........A.L.	A.L.	2	2⅔	0	0	.000	2	2	4	3.38	0
1997 Florida ...............N.L.	N.L.	2	8⅓	0	1	.000	6	2	13	4.32	0
Championship Series Totals 4			11	0	1	.000	8	4	17	4.09	0
World Series Record											
1993 Toronto .............A.L.	A.L.	3	7	1	0	1.000	5	2	12	7.71	0
1997 Florida ...............N.L.	N.L.	2	10⅔	0	0	.000	10	10	10	5.06	0
World Series Totals 5			17⅔	1	0	1.000	15	12	22	6.11	0

a On disabled list from May 1 to May 23, 1987.
b On disabled list from June 22 to July 26, 1988.
c Traded to Toronto Blue Jays for outfielder Jesse Barfield, April 30, 1989.
d On disabled list from May 11 to end of 1989 season.
e On disabled list from May 20 to June 13, 1990.
f On disabled list from April 22 to end of 1991 season.
g On disabled list from April 24 to May 9, 1993.
h On disabled list from June 9 to June 24, 1994.
i Declared restricted free agent under Major League Baseball implemented labor proposal, December 23, 1994.
j Signed with Toronto Blue Jays, April 28, 1995.

k Filed for free agency, November 12, 1995; signed with Florida Marlins, December 14, 1995.
l Pitched no-hit, no-run game against Colorado Rockies, May 11, 1996.
m On disabled list from May 1 to May 20 and August 13 to August 29, 1997.
n Traded to New York Mets with infielder Ralph Milliard for pitcher Jesus Sanchez, pitcher A. J. Burnett and outfielder Robert Stratton, February 6, 1998.

LEITER, MARK EDWARD
Born, Joliet, Illinois, April 13, 1963.
Bats Right. Throws Right. Height, 6 feet, 3 inches. Weight, 210 pounds.

Year Club	Lea	G	IP	W	L	Pct	SO	BB	H	ERA	SAVES
1983 Bluefield	Appal.	6	36²/₃	2	1	.667	35	13	33	2.70	0
1983 Hagerstown	Carolina	8	36	1	5	.167	18	28	42	7.25	0
1984 Hagerstown	Carolina	27	139¹/₃	8	*13	.381	105	108	132	5.62	0
1985 Hagerstown	Carolina	34	83¹/₃	2	8	.200	82	29	77	3.46	8
1985 Charlotte	Southern	5	6¹/₃	0	1	.000	8	2	3	1.42	1
1986 Charlotte a	Southern			INJURED—Did Not Play							
1987 Charlotte b	Southern			INJURED—Did Not Play							
1988 Charlotte c-d	Southern			INJURED—Did Not Play							
1989 Ft. Lauderdale	Fla. St.	6	35¹/₃	2	2	.500	22	5	27	1.53	1
1989 Columbus	Int.	22	90	9	6	.600	70	34	102	5.00	0
1990 Columbus	Int.	30	122²/₃	9	4	.692	115	27	114	3.60	1
1990 New York e	A.L.	8	26¹/₃	1	1	.500	21	9	33	6.84	0
1991 Toledo f	Int.	5	6²/₃	1	0	1.000	7	3	6	0.00	1
1991 Detroit f	A.L.	38	134²/₃	9	7	.563	103	50	125	4.21	1
1992 Detroit g	A.L.	35	112	8	5	.615	75	43	116	4.18	0
1993 Detroit h-i	A.L.	27	106²/₃	6	6	.500	70	44	111	4.72	0
1994 California	A.L.	40	95¹/₃	4	7	.364	71	35	99	4.72	2
1995 San Francisco k	N.L.	30	195²/₃	10	12	.455	129	55	185	3.82	0
1996 San Francisco l-n	N.L.	35	205	8	12	.400	164	69	219	4.92	0
1997 Philadelphia o	N.L.	31	182¹/₃	10	17	.370	148	64	216	5.67	0
Major League Totals	8 Yrs.	244	1058¹/₃	56	67	.455	781	369	1104	4.69	3

a On disabled list from March 30 to end of 1986 season.
b On disabled list from March 26 to end of 1987 season.
c On disabled list from April 1 to June 13, 1988.
d Released by Baltimore Orioles, June 13; signed with New York Yankees organization, September 29, 1988.
e Traded to Detroit Tigers for infielder Torey Lovullo, March 19, 1991.
f On disabled list from June 5 to June 25, 1991.
g On disabled list from August 3 to August 24, 1992.
h On disabled list from August 8 to end of 1993 season.
i Released, March 15; signed with California Angels, March 20, 1994.
j Not offered 1995 contract, December 23, 1994.
k Signed with San Francisco Giants organization, April 8, 1995.
l Traded to Montreal Expos for pitcher Tim Scott and pitcher Kirk Reuter, July 30, 1996.
m Filed for free agency, November 5, 1996.
n Signed with Philadelphia Phillies, December 11, 1996.
o On disabled list from June 12 to July 6, 1997.

LESKANIC, CURTIS JOHN
Born, Homestead, Pennsylvania, April 2, 1968.
Bats Right. Throws Right. Height, 6 feet. Weight, 180 pounds.

Year Club	Lea	G	IP	W	L	Pct	SO	BB	H	ERA	SAVES
1990 Kinston	Carolina	14	73¹/₃	6	5	.545	71	30	61	3.68	0
1991 Kinston a	Carolina	28	174¹/₃	*15	8	.652	*163	91	143	2.79	0
1992 Orlando	Southern	26	152²/₃	9	11	.450	126	64	158	4.30	0
1992 Portland b	P.C.	5	15¹/₃	1	2	.333	14	8	16	9.98	0
1993 Wichita c	Texas	7	44¹/₃	2	.600		42	17	37	3.45	0	
1993 Colorado Springs	P.C.	9	44¹/₃	4	3	.571	38	26	39	4.47	0
1993 Colorado	N.L.	18	57	1	5	.167	30	27	59	5.37	0
1994 Colorado Springs	P.C.	21	130¹/₃	5	7	.417	98	54	129	3.31	0
1994 Colorado	N.L.	8	22¹/₃	1	1	.500	17	10	27	5.64	0
1995 Colorado	N.L.	76	98	6	3	.667	107	33	83	3.40	10
1996 Colo Sprngs	P.C.	3	3	0	0	.000	2	1	5	3.00	0
1996 Colorado d	N.L.	70	73²/₃	7	5	.583	76	38	82	6.23	6
1997 Salem	Carolina	2	2¹/₃	0	0	.000	3	1	5	3.86	0
1997 Colo Sprngs	P.C.	10	19	0	0	.000	20	18	11	3.79	2
1997 Colorado e	N.L.	55	58¹/₃	4	0	1.000	53	24	59	5.55	2
Major League Totals	5 Yrs.	227	309¹/₃	19	14	.576	283	132	310	5.00	18
Division Series											
1995 Colorado	N.L.	3	3	0	1	.000	4	0	3	6.00	0

a Traded by Cleveland Indians to Minnesota Twins organization with pitcher Oscar Munoz, March 28, 1992.
b Selected by Colorado Rockies from Minnesota Twins organization in expansion draft, November 17, 1993.
c Loaned by Colorado Rockies to San Diego Padres organization from April 4 to May 20, 1993.
d On disabled list from May 30 to June 20, 1996.
e On disabled list from April 1 to April 12, 1997.

LEVINE, ALAN BRIAN

Born, Park Ridge, Illinois, May 22, 1968.
Bats Left. Throws Right. Height, 6 feet, 3 inches. Weight, 180 pounds.

Year Club	Lea	G	IP	W	L	Pct	SO	BB	H	ERA	SAVES
1991 Utica ...........N.Y.-Penn.		16	85	6	4	.600	83	26	75	3.18	1
1992 South Bend ....Midwest		23	156⅔	9	5	.643	131	36	151	2.81	0
1992 Sarasota ....Fla. St.		3	15⅔	0	2	.000	11	5	17	4.02	0
1993 Sarasota ....Fla. St.		27	161⅓	11	8	.579	129	50	169	3.68	0
1994 Birmingham .....Southern		18	114⅓	5	9	.357	94	44	117	3.31	0
1994 Nashville ............A.A.		8	24	0	2	.000	24	11	34	7.87	0
1995 Nashville ............A.A.		3	14	0	2	.000	14	7	20	5.14	0
1995 Birmingham .....Southern		43	73	4	3	.571	68	25	61	2.34	7
1996 Nashville ............A.A.		43	61⅔	4	5	.444	45	24	58	3.65	12
1996 Chicago ..............A.L.		16	18⅓	0	1	.000	12	7	22	5.40	0
1997 Nashville ............A.A.		26	35⅓	1	1	.500	29	11	58	7.13	2
1997 Chicago a ...........A.L.		25	27⅓	2	2	.500	22	16	35	6.91	0
Major League Totals ....2 Yrs.		41	45⅔	2	3	.400	34	23	57	6.31	0

a Traded to Texas Rangers with pitcher Larry Thomas for infielder Benji Gil, December 19, 1997.

LIDLE, CORY FULTON

Born, Hollywood, California, March 22, 1972.
Bats Right. Throws Right. Height, 5 feet, 11 inches. Weight, 175 pounds.

Year Club	Lea	G	IP	W	L	Pct	SO	BB	H	ERA	SAVES
1991 Twins ....Gulf Coast		4	4⅔	1	1	.500	5	0	5	5.79	0
1992 Elizabethtn ....Appal.		19	43⅔	2	1	.667	32	21	40	3.71	6
1993 Pocatello a-b-c ......Pioneer		17	106⅔	8	4	.667	91	54	104	4.13	1
1994 Stockton ....California		25	42⅔	1	2	.333	38	13	60	4.43	4
1994 Beloit.............Midwest		13	69	3	4	.429	62	11	65	2.61	0
1995 El Paso ....Texas		45	109⅔	5	4	.556	78	36	126	3.36	2
1996 Binghamton d ....Eastern		27	190⅓	14	10	.583	141	49	186	3.31	0
1997 Norfolk ....Int.		7	42	4	2	.667	34	10	46	3.64	0
1997 New York e .........N.L.		54	81⅔	7	2	.778	54	20	86	3.53	2

a Released by Minnesota Twins organization, April 1, 1993.
b Signed by Pocatello, May 28, 1993.
c Sold to Milwaukee Brewers, September 17, 1993.
d Traded to New York Mets for catcher Kelly Stinnett, January 17, 1996.
e Selected in expansion draft by Arizona Diamondbacks, November 18, 1997.

LIEBER, JONATHAN RAY

Born, Council Bluffs, Iowa, April 2, 1970.
Bats Left. Throws Right. Height, 6 feet, 3 inches. Weight, 220 pounds.

Year Club	Lea	G	IP	W	L	Pct	SO	BB	H	ERA	SAVES
1992 Eugene ....Northwest		5	31	3	0	1.000	23	2	26	1.16	0
1992 Baseball City ....Fla. St.		7	31	3	3	.500	19	8	45	4.65	0
1993 Wilmington ....Carolina		17	114⅔	9	3	.750	89	9	125	2.67	0
1993 Memphis-Carol. a ..Southern		10	55	6	3	.667	45	16	71	5.07	0
1994 Carolina ....Southern		3	21	2	0	1.000	21	2	13	1.29	0
1994 Buffalo ...............A.A.		3	21⅓	1	1	.500	21	1	16	1.69	0
1994 Pittsburgh ...........N.L.		17	108⅔	6	7	.462	71	25	116	3.73	0
1995 Calgary ...............P.C.		14	77	1	5	.167	34	19	122	7.01	0
1995 Pittsburgh ...........N.L.		21	72⅔	4	7	.364	45	14	103	6.32	0
1996 Pittsburgh ...........N.L.		51	142	9	5	.643	94	28	156	3.99	1
1997 Pittsburgh ...........N.L.		33	188⅓	11	14	.440	160	51	193	4.49	0
Major League Totals ....4 Yrs.		122	511⅔	30	33	.476	370	118	568	4.45	1

a Traded by Kansas City Royals to Pittsburgh Pirates organization with pitcher Dan Miceli for pitcher Stan Belinda, July 31, 1993.

LIGTENBERG, KERRY DALE

Born, Rapid City, South Dakota, May 11, 1971.
Bats Right. Throws Right. Height, 6 feet, 2 inches. Weight, 185 pounds.

Year	Club	Lea	G	IP	W	L	Pct	SO	BB	H	ERA	SAVES
1994 Minneapolis		NCL	19	114⅓	5	5	.500	94	44	103	3.31	0
1995 Minneapolis		PRA	17	108⅔	11	2	.846	100	26	101	2.73	0
1996 Durham		Carolina	49	59⅔	7	4	.636	76	16	58	2.41	20
1997 Greenville		Southern	31	35⅓	3	1	.750	43	14	20	2.04	16
1997 Richmond		Int.	14	25	0	3	.000	35	2	21	4.32	1
1997 Atlanta		N.L.	15	15	1	0	1.000	19	4	12	3.00	1
Championship Series												
1997 Atlanta		N.L.	2	3	0	0	.000	4	0	1	0.00	0

LIMA (RODRIGUEZ), JOSE DESIDERIO

Born, Santiago, Dominican Republic, September 30, 1972.
Bats Right. Throws Right. Height, 6 feet, 2 inches. Weight, 170 pounds.

Year	Club	Lea	G	IP	W	L	Pct	SO	BB	H	ERA	SAVES
1990 Bristol		Appal.	14	75⅓	3	8	.273	64	22	89	5.02	1
1991 Lakeland		Fla. St.	4	8⅔	0	1	.000	5	2	16	10.38	0
1991 Fayetteville		So. Atl.	18	58	1	3	.250	60	25	53	4.97	0
1992 Lakeland		Fla. St.	25	151	5	11	.313	137	21	132	3.16	0
1993 London		Eastern	27	177	8	*13	.381	138	59	160	4.07	0
1994 Toledo		Int.	23	142⅓	7	9	.438	117	48	124	3.60	0
1994 Detroit		A.L.	3	6⅔	0	1	.000	7	3	11	13.50	0
1995 Lakeland		Fla. St.	4	21	3	1	.750	20	0	23	2.57	0
1995 Toledo		Int.	11	74⅔	5	3	.625	40	14	69	3.01	0
1995 Detroit		A.L.	15	73⅔	3	9	.250	37	18	85	6.11	0
1996 Toledo		Int.	12	69	5	4	.556	57	12	93	6.78	0
1996 Detroit a		A.L.	39	72⅔	5	6	.455	59	22	87	5.70	3
1997 Houston		N.L.	52	75	1	6	.143	63	16	79	5.28	2
Major League Totals	4 Yrs.		109	228	9	22	.290	166	59	262	5.92	5
Division Series												
1997 Houston		N.L.	1	1	0	0	.000	1	1	0	0.00	0

a Traded to Houston Astros with catcher Brad Ausmus, pitcher C.J. Nitkowski, pitcher Trever Miller and infielder Daryle Ward for outfielder Brian Hunter, infielder Orlando Miller, pitcher Todd Jones and pitcher Doug Brocail, December 10, 1996.

LIRA, ANTONIO FELIPE (FELIPE)

Born, Santa Teresa, Venezuela, April 26, 1972.
Bats Right. Throws Right. Height, 6 feet. Weight, 170 pounds.

Year	Club	Lea	G	IP	W	L	Pct	SO	BB	H	ERA	SAVES
1990 Bristol		Appal.	13	78⅓	5	5	.500	71	16	70	2.41	1
1990 Lakeland		Fla. St.	1	1⅔	0	0	.000	4	3	3	5.40	0
1991 Fayetteville		So. Atl.	15	73⅓	5	5	.500	56	19	79	4.66	1
1992 Lakeland		Fla. St.	32	109	11	5	.688	84	16	95	2.39	1
1993 London		Eastern	22	152	10	4	.714	122	39	157	3.38	0
1993 Toledo		Int.	5	31⅓	1	2	.333	23	11	32	4.60	0
1994 Toledo		Int.	26	151⅓	7	12	.368	110	45	171	4.70	0
1995 Detroit		A.L.	37	146⅓	9	13	.409	89	56	151	4.31	1
1996 Detroit		A.L.	32	194⅔	6	14	.300	113	66	204	5.22	0
1997 Everett		Northwest	1	5	1	0	1.000	9	2	6	3.60	0
1997 Tacoma		P.C.	3	21	2	0	1.000	17	5	21	3.43	0
1997 Detroit-Seattle a		A.L.	28	110⅔	5	11	.313	73	55	132	6.34	0
Major League Totals	3 Yrs.		97	451⅔	20	38	.345	275	177	487	5.20	1

a Traded to Seattle Mariners with pitcher Omar Olivares for pitcher Scott Sanders and pitcher Dean Crow, July 18, 1997.

LLOYD, GRAEME JOHN

Born, Victoria, Australia, April 9, 1967.
Bats Left. Throws Left. Height, 6 feet, 7 inches. Weight, 230 pounds.

Year	Club	Lea	G	IP	W	L	Pct	SO	BB	H	ERA	SAVES
1988 Myrtle Beach		So. Atl.	41	59⅔	3	2	.600	43	30	71	3.62	2
1989 Dunedin		Fla. St.	2	2⅔	0	0	.000	0	1	6	10.13	0
1989 Myrtle Beach a		So. Atl.	1	5	0	0	.000	3	0	5	5.40	0

Year	Club	Lea	G	IP	W	L	Pct	SO	BB	H	ERA	SAVES
1990 Myrtle Beach	So. Atl.	19	49²/₃	5	2	.714	42	16	51	2.72	6
1991 Dunedin	Fla. St.	50	60¹/₃	2	5	.286	39	25	54	2.24	24
1991 Knoxville	Southern	2	1²/₃	0	0	.000	2	1	1	0.00	0
1992 Knoxville b-c	Southern	49	92	4	8	.333	65	25	79	1.96	14
1993 Milwaukee d-e	A.L.	55	63²/₃	3	4	.429	31	13	64	2.83	0
1994 Milwaukee	A.L.	43	47	2	3	.400	31	15	49	5.17	3
1995 Milwaukee f	A.L.	33	32	0	5	.000	13	8	28	4.50	4
1996 Milwaukee-New York g	A.L.	65	56²/₃	2	6	.250	30	22	61	4.28	0
1997 New York	A.L.	46	49	1	1	.500	26	20	55	3.31	0
Major League Totals ....5 Yrs.		242	248¹/₃	8	19	.296	131	78	257	3.91	8
Division Series											
1996 New York	A.L.	2	1	0	0	.000	0	0	1	0.00	0
1997 New York	A.L.	2	1¹/₃	0	0	.000	1	0	0	0.00	0
Divisional Series Totals 4			2¹/₃	0	0	.000	1	0	1	0.00	0
Championship Series											
1996 New York	A.L.	2	1²/₃	0	0	.000	1	0	0	0.00	0
World Series Record											
1996 New York	A.L.	4	2²/₃	1	0	1.000	4	0	0	0.00	0

a On disabled list from June 29 to September 1, 1989.
b Drafted by Philadelphia Phillies from Toronto Blue Jays organization, December 7, 1992.
c Traded by Philadelphia Phillies to Milwaukee Brewers for pitcher John Trisler, December 8, 1992.
d On disabled list from August 20 to September 4, 1993.
e Suspended three games by American League for participating in August 24 brawl while on disabled list from September 5 to September 7, 1993.
f On disabled list from July 25 to September 10, 1995.
g Traded to New York Yankees with infielder Pat Listach for outfielder Gerald Williams and pitcher Bob Wickman. Yankees received pitcher Ricky Bones as a player-to-be-named-later, August 23, 1996. Listach was injured before trade and his deal was nullified when Yankees received infielder Gabby Martinez to complete transaction, November 5, 1996.

LOAIZA, ESTEBAN ANTONIO VEYNA
Born, Tijuana, Mexico, December 31, 1971.
Bats Right. Throws Right. Height, 6 feet, 4 inches. Weight, 190 pounds.

Year	Club	Lea	G	IP	W	L	Pct	SO	BB	H	ERA	SAVES
1991 Pirates	Gulf Coast	11	51²/₃	5	1	.833	41	14	48	2.26	0
1992 Augusta	So. Atl.	26	143¹/₃	10	8	.556	123	60	134	3.89	0
1993 Salem	Carolina	17	109	6	7	.462	61	30	113	3.39	0
1993 Carolina	Southern	7	43	2	1	.667	40	12	39	3.77	0
1994 Carolina	Southern	24	154¹/₃	10	5	.667	115	30	169	3.79	0
1995 Pittsburgh	N.L.	32	172²/₃	8	9	.471	85	55	205	5.16	0
1996 Calgary	P.C.	12	69¹/₃	3	4	.429	38	25	61	4.02	0
1996 Pittsburgh	N.L.	10	52²/₃	2	3	.400	32	19	65	4.96	0
1997 Pittsburgh	N.L.	33	196¹/₃	11	11	.500	122	56	214	4.13	0
Major League Totals ....3 Yrs.		75	421²/₃	21	23	.477	239	130	484	4.65	0

LOISELLE, RICHARD FRANK (RICH)
Born, Neenah, Wisconsin, January 12, 1972.
Bats Right. Throws Right. Height, 6 feet, 5 inches. Weight, 225 pounds.

Year	Club	Lea	G	IP	W	L	Pct	SO	BB	H	ERA	SAVES
1991 Padres	Arizona	12	61¹/₃	2	3	.400	47	26	72	3.52	0
1992 Chston-Sc	So. Atl.	19	97	4	8	.333	64	42	93	3.71	0
1993 Waterloo	Midwest	10	59¹/₃	1	5	.167	47	29	55	3.94	0
1993 Rancho Cuca	California	14	82²/₃	5	8	.385	53	34	109	5.77	0
1994 Rancho Cuca	California	27	156²/₃	9	10	.474	120	76	160	3.96	0
1995 Memphis	Southern	13	78²/₃	6	3	.667	48	33	82	3.55	0
1995 Las Vegas	P.C.	8	27¹/₃	2	2	.500	16	9	36	7.24	0
1995 Tucson	P.C.	2	10¹/₃	0	0	.000	4	4	8	2.61	0
1996 Jackson	Texas	16	98²/₃	7	4	.636	65	27	107	3.47	0
1996 Tucson	P.C.	5	33¹/₃	2	2	.500	31	11	28	2.43	0
1996 Calgary	P.C.	8	50²/₃	2	2	.500	41	16	64	4.09	0
1996 Pittsburgh a	N.L.	5	20²/₃	1	0	1.000	9	8	22	3.05	0
1997 Pittsburgh	N.L.	72	72²/₃	1	5	.167	66	24	76	3.10	29
Major League Totals ....2 Yrs.		77	93¹/₃	2	5	.286	75	32	98	3.09	29

a Traded to Pittsburgh Pirates by Houston Astros organization for pitcher Danny Darwin, July 23, 1996.

LOPEZ, ALBERT ANTHONY

Born, Mesa, Arizona, August 18, 1971.
Bats Right. Throws Right. Height, 6 feet, 1 inch. Weight, 205 pounds.

Year	Club	Lea	G	IP	W	L	Pct	SO	BB	H	ERA	SAVES
1991	Burlington	Appal.	13	73⅓	4	5	.444	81	23	61	3.44	0
1992	Columbus	So. Atl.	16	97	7	2	.778	117	33	80	2.88	0
1992	Kinston	Carolina	10	64	5	2	.714	44	26	56	3.52	0
1993	Canton	Eastern	16	110	9	4	.692	80	47	79	3.11	0
1993	Cleveland	A.L.	9	49⅔	3	1	.750	25	32	49	5.98	0
1993	Charlotte	Int.	3	12	1	0	1.000	7	2	8	2.25	0
1994	Charlotte	Int.	22	144	13	3	.813	105	42	136	3.94	0
1994	Cleveland	A.L.	4	17	1	2	.333	18	6	20	4.24	0
1995	Buffalo	A.A.	18	101⅓	5	10	.333	82	51	101	4.44	0
1995	Cleveland	A.L.	6	23	0	0	.000	22	7	17	3.13	0
1996	Buffalo	A.A.	17	104⅔	10	2	.833	89	40	90	3.87	0
1996	Cleveland	A.L.	13	62	5	4	.556	45	22	80	6.39	0
1997	Akron	Eastern	1	1	0	0	.000	2	0	2	0.00	0
1997	Buffalo	A.A.	7	11⅓	1	0	1.000	13	2	6	0.00	1
1997	Cleveland a-b	A.L.	37	76⅔	3	7	.300	63	40	101	6.93	0
Major League Totals		5 Yrs.	69	228⅓	12	14	.462	173	107	267	5.99	0

a On disabled list from July 2 to July 29 and August 14 to September 1, 1997.
b Selected in expansion draft by Tampa Bay Devil Rays, November 18, 1997.

LORRAINE, ANDREW JASON

Born, Los Angeles, California, August 11, 1972.
Bats Left. Throws Left. Height, 6 feet, 3 inches. Weight, 195 pounds.

Year	Club	Lea	G	IP	W	L	Pct	SO	BB	H	ERA	SAVES
1993	Boise	Northwest	6	42	4	1	.800	39	6	33	1.29	0
1994	California	A.L.	4	18⅔	0	2	.000	10	11	30	10.61	0
1994	Vancouver	P.C.	22	142	12	4	.750	90	34	156	3.42	0
1995	Vancouver a	P.C.	18	97⅔	6	6	.500	51	30	105	3.96	0
1995	Nashville	A.A.	7	39	4	1	.800	26	12	51	6.00	0
1995	Chicago	A.L.	5	8	0	0	.000	5	2	3	3.38	0
1996	Edmonton b	P.C.	30	141	8	10	.444	73	46	181	5.68	0
1997	Edmonton	P.C.	23	117⅔	8	6	.571	75	34	143	4.74	0
1997	Oakland	A.L.	12	29⅔	3	1	.750	18	15	45	6.37	0
Major League Totals		3 Yrs.	21	56⅓	3	3	.500	33	28	78	7.35	0

a Traded to Chicago White Sox with outfielder McKay Christensen, and pitchers Bill Simas and John Snyder for pitchers Jim Abbott and Tim Fortugno.
b Traded to Oakland Athletics with pitcher Charlie Poe for outfielder Danny Tartabull, January 22, 1996.

LOWE, DEREK CHRISTOPHER

Born, Dearborn, Michigan, June 1, 1973.
Bats Right. Throws Right. Height, 6 feet, 6 inches. Weight, 170 pounds.

Year	Club	Lea	G	IP	W	L	Pct	SO	BB	H	ERA	SAVES
1991	Mariners	Arizona	12	71	5	3	.625	60	21	58	2.41	0
1992	Bellingham	Northwest	14	85⅔	7	3	.700	66	22	69	2.42	0
1993	Riverside	California	27	154	12	9	.571	80	60	189	5.26	0
1994	Jacksnville	Southern	26	151⅓	7	10	.412	75	50	177	4.94	0
1995	Mariners	Arizona	2	9⅔	1	0	1.000	11	2	5	0.93	0
1995	Port City	Southern	10	53⅓	1	6	.143	30	22	70	6.07	0
1996	Port City	Southern	10	65	5	3	.625	33	17	56	3.05	0
1996	Tacoma	P.C.	17	105	6	9	.400	54	37	118	4.54	0
1997	Tacoma	P.C.	10	57⅓	3	4	.429	49	20	53	3.45	0
1997	Pawtucket	Int.	6	30⅓	4	0	1.000	21	11	23	2.37	0
1997	Seattle-Boston a	A.L.	20	69	2	6	.250	52	23	74	6.13	0
Major League Totals		1 Yrs.	20	69	2	6	.250	52	23	74	6.13	0

a Traded to Boston Red Sox with catcher Jason Varitek for pitcher Heathcliff Slocumb, July 31, 1997.

LUDWICK, ERIC DAVID

Born, Whiteman Afb, Missouri, December 14, 1971.
Bats Right. Throws Right. Height, 6 feet, 5 inches. Weight, 210 pounds.

Year	Club	Lea	G	IP	W	L	Pct	SO	BB	H	ERA	SAVES
1993	Pittsfield	N.Y.-Penn.	10	51	4	4	.500	40	18	51	3.18	0
1994	St. Lucie	Fla. St.	27	150⅓	7	13	.350	77	77	162	4.55	0
1995	Binghamton	Eastern	23	143⅓	12	5	.706	131	68	108	2.95	0

Year	Club	Lea	G	IP	W	L	Pct	SO	BB	H	ERA	SAVES
1995 Norfolk	....	Int.	4	20	1	1	.500	9	7	22	5.85	0
1996 Louisville	....	A.A.	11	60⅓	3	4	.429	73	24	55	2.83	0
1996 St. Louis a	....	N.L.	6	10	0	1	.000	12	3	11	9.00	0
1997 Louisville	....	A.A.	24	80	6	8	.429	85	26	67	2.93	4
1997 Edmonton	....	P.C.	6	19	1	1	.500	20	4	22	3.32	0
1997 St. Louis b	....	N.L.	5	6⅔	0	1	.000	7	6	12	9.45	0
1997 Oakland c	....	A.L.	6	24	1	4	.200	14	16	32	8.25	0
Major League Totals .... 2 Yrs.			17	40⅔	1	6	.143	33	25	55	8.63	0

a Traded to St. Louis Cardinals by New York Mets organization with pitcher Erik Hiljus and outfielder Yudith Ozorio for outfielder Bernard Gilkey, January 22, 1996.
b Traded to Oakland Athletics with pitcher T.J. Mathews and pitcher Blake Stein for infielder Mark McGwire, July 31, 1997.
c Traded to Florida Marlins for infielder Kurt Abbott, December 19, 1997.

MADDUX, GREGORY ALAN

Born, San Angelo, Texas, April 14, 1966.
Bats Right. Throws Right. Height, 6 feet. Weight, 175 pounds.

Year	Club	Lea	G	IP	W	L	Pct	SO	BB	H	ERA	SAVES
1984 Pikeville	....	Appalachian	14	85⅔	6	2	.750	62	41	63	2.63	0
1985 Peoria	....	Midland	27	186	13	9	.591	125	52	176	3.19	0
1986 Pittsfield	....	Eastern	8	62⅔	4	3	.571	35	15	49	2.69	0
1986 Iowa	....	A.A.	18	128⅓	10	1	*.909	65	30	127	3.02	0
1986 Chicago	....	N.L.	6	31	2	4	.333	20	11	44	5.52	0
1987 Iowa	....	A.A.	4	27⅔	3	0	1.000	22	12	17	0.98	0
1987 Chicago a	....	N.L.	30	155⅔	6	14	.300	101	74	181	5.61	0
1988 Chicago	....	N.L.	34	249	18	8	.692	140	81	230	3.18	0
1989 Chicago	....	N.L.	35	238⅓	19	12	.613	135	82	222	2.95	0
1990 Chicago	....	N.L.	35	237	15	15	.500	144	71	*242	3.46	0
1991 Chicago	....	N.L.	39	*263	15	11	.577	198	66	232	3.35	0
1992 Chicago b-c	....	N.L.	35	*268	*20	11	.645	199	70	201	2.18	0
1993 Atlanta d	....	N.L.	36	*267	20	10	.667	197	52	228	*2.36	0
1994 Atlanta e	....	N.L.	25	*202	*16	6	.727	156	31	150	*1.56	0
1995 Atlanta f	....	N.L.	28	209⅔	19	2	.905	181	23	147	1.63	0
1996 Atlanta	....	N.L.	35	245	15	11	.577	172	28	225	2.72	0
1997 Atlanta	....	N.L.	33	232⅔	19	4	.826	177	20	200	2.20	0
Major League Totals .... 12 Yrs.			369	2598⅓	184	108	.630	1820	609	2302	2.81	0
Division Series												
1995 Atlanta	....	N.L.	2	14	1	0	1.000	7	2	19	4.50	0
1996 Atlanta	....	N.L.	1	7	1	0	1.000	7	0	3	0.00	0
1997 Atlanta	....	N.L.	1	9	1	0	1.000	6	1	7	1.00	0
Divisional Series Totals 4				30	3	0	1.000	20	3	29	2.40	0
Championship Series												
1989 Chicago	....	N.L.	2	7⅓	0	1	.000	5	4	13	13.50	0
1993 Atlanta	....	N.L.	2	12⅔	1	1	.500	11	7	11	4.97	0
1995 Atlanta	....	N.L.	1	8	1	0	1.000	4	2	7	1.13	0
1996 Atlanta	....	N.L.	2	14⅓	1	1	.500	10	2	15	2.51	0
1997 Atlanta	....	N.L.	2	13	0	2	.000	16	4	9	1.38	0
Championship Series Totals 9				55⅓	3	5	.375	46	19	55	4.07	0
World Series Record												
1995 Atlanta	....	N.L.	2	16	1	1	.500	8	3	9	2.25	0
1996 Atlanta	....	N.L.	2	15⅔	1	1	.500	5	1	14	1.72	0
World Series Totals 4				31⅔	2	2	.500	13	4	23	1.99	0

a Appeared in two games as pinch hitter.
b Selected Cy Young Award winner in National League for 1992.
c Filed for free agency, October 26; signed with Atlanta Braves, December 9, 1992.
d Selected Cy Young Award winner in National League for 1993.
e Selected Cy Young Award winner in National League for 1994.
f Selected Cy Young Award Winner in National League for 1995.

MADDUX, MICHAEL AUSLEY

Born, Dayton, Ohio, August 27, 1961.
Bats Right. Throws Right. Height, 6 feet, 2 inches. Weight, 188 pounds.

Year	Club	Lea	G	IP	W	L	Pct	SO	BB	H	ERA	SAVES
1982 Bend	....	Northwest	11	65⅓	3	6	.333	59	26	68	3.99	0
1983 Spartanburg	....	W. Carolinas	13	84⅓	4	6	.400	85	47	98	5.44	0
1983 Peninsula	....	Carolina	14	99⅓	8	4	.667	76	35	92	3.62	0

Year Club	Lea	G	IP	W	L	Pct	SO	BB	H	ERA	SAVES
1983 Reading	Eastern	1	3	0	0	.000	2	1	4	6.00	0
1984 Reading	Eastern	20	116	3	*12	.200	77	49	143	5.04	0
1984 Portland	P.C.	8	45	2	4	.333	22	17	58	5.80	0
1985 Portland	P.C.	27	166	9	12	.429	96	15	195	5.31	0
1986 Portland	P.C.	12	84	5	2	.714	65	22	70	2.36	0
1986 Philadelphia	N.L.	16	78	3	7	.300	44	34	88	5.42	0
1987 Maine	Int.	18	103	6	6	.500	71	26	116	4.35	0
1987 Philadelphia	N.L.	7	17	2	0	1.000	15	5	17	2.65	0
1988 Maine	Int.	5	23⅔	0	2	.000	18	10	25	4.18	0
1988 Philadelphia a	N.L.	25	88⅔	4	3	.571	59	34	91	3.76	0
1989 Scranton	Int.	19	123	7	7	.500	100	26	119	3.66	0
1989 Philadelphia b	N.L.	16	43⅔	1	3	.250	26	14	52	5.15	1
1990 Albuquerque	P.C.	20	108	8	5	.615	85	32	122	4.25	0
1990 Los Angeles c	N.L.	11	20⅔	0	1	.000	11	4	24	6.53	0
1991 San Diego	N.L.	64	98⅔	7	2	.778	57	27	78	2.46	5
1992 San Diego d-e	N.L.	50	79⅔	2	2	.500	60	24	71	2.37	5
1993 New York	N.L.	58	75	3	8	.273	57	27	67	3.60	5
1994 New York f-g	N.L.	27	44	2	1	.667	32	13	45	5.11	2
1995 Pittsburgh	N.L.	8	9	1	0	1.000	4	3	14	9.00	0
1995 Boston h-i-j-k	A.L.	36	89⅔	4	1	.800	65	15	86	3.61	1
1996 Pawtucket	Int.	3	14	2	0	1.000	9	2	13	3.21	0
1996 Boston l-m-n	A.L.	23	64⅓	3	2	.600	32	27	76	4.48	0
1997 Tacoma	P.C.	1	5	0	0	.000	5	2	1	0.00	0
1997 Seattle o-p-q-r	A.L.	6	10⅔	1	0	1.000	7	8	20	10.13	0
1997 Las Vegas s	P.C.	3	16	0	2	.000	13	9	23	5.63	0
Major League Totals	12 Yrs.	347	719	33	30	.524	469	235	729	4.02	19
Division Series											
1995 Boston	A.L.	2	3	0	0	.000	1	1	2	0.00	0

a On disabled list from April 22 to June 1, 1988.
b Released, November 20; signed with Los Angeles Dodgers organization, December 21, 1989.
c Became free agent, October 15, 1990; signed with San Diego Padres, April 7, 1991.
d On disabled list from April 5 to April 26, 1992.
e Traded to New York Mets for pitchers Roger Mason and Mike Freitas, December 17, 1992.
f On disabled list from April 29 to May 13, 1994.
g Filed for free agency, October 20, 1994.
h Signed with Pittsburgh Pirates organization, April 10, 1995.
i Released, May 17, 1995.
j Signed with Boston Red Sox, May 30, 1995.
k Filed for free agency, November 12, 1995.
l On disabled list from May 6 to August 2, 1996.
m Filed for free agency, November 1, 1996.
n Re-signed with Boston Red Sox, December 7, 1996.
o Released by Boston Red Sox, March 26, 1997.
p Signed with Seattle Mariners organization, April 7, 1997.
q On disabled list from June 22 to July 13, 1997.
r Released by Seattle Mariners, July 23, 1997.
s Signed with San Diego Padres organization, August 16, 1997.

MADURO, CALVIN GREGORY
Born, Santa Cruz, Aruba, September 5, 1974.
Bats Right. Throws Right. Height, 6 feet. Weight, 175 pounds.

Year Club	Lea	G	IP	W	L	Pct	SO	BB	H	ERA	SAVES
1992 Orioles	Gulf Coast	13	71⅓	1	4	.200	66	26	56	2.27	0
1993 Bluefield	Appal.	14	91	9	4	.692	83	17	90	3.96	0
1994 Frederick	Carolina	27	152⅓	9	8	.529	137	59	132	4.25	0
1995 Frederick	Carolina	20	122⅓	8	5	.615	120	34	109	2.94	0
1995 Bowie	Eastern	7	35⅓	0	6	.000	26	27	39	5.09	0
1996 Bowie	Eastern	19	124⅓	9	7	.563	87	36	116	3.26	0
1996 Rochester	Int.	8	43⅔	3	5	.375	40	18	49	4.74	0
1996 Philadelphia	N.L.	4	15⅓	0	1	.000	11	3	13	3.52	0
1997 Philadelphia	N.L.	15	71	3	7	.300	31	41	83	7.23	0
1997 Scranton-WB	Int.	13	79⅓	6	4	.600	53	57	71	4.99	0
Major League Totals	2 Yrs.	19	86⅓	3	8	.273	42	44	96	6.57	0

MAGNANTE, MICHAEL ANTHONY
Born, Glendale, California, June 17, 1965.
Bats Left. Throws Left. Height, 6 feet, 1 inch. Weight, 190 pounds.

Year Club	Lea	G	IP	W	L	Pct	SO	BB	H	ERA	SAVES
1988 Eugene	Northwest	3	16	1	1	.500	26	2	10	0.56	0
1988 Appleton	Midwest	9	47⅔	3	2	.600	40	15	48	3.21	0
1988 Baseball City	Fla. St.	4	24	1	1	.500	19	8	19	4.13	0

Year Club	Lea	G	IP	W	L	Pct	SO	BB	H	ERA	SAVES
1989 Memphis ....Southern		26	157⅓	8	9	.471	118	53	137	3.66	0
1990 Omaha a ...........A.A.		13	76⅔	2	5	.286	56	25	72	4.11	0
1991 Omaha ..............A.A.		10	65⅔	6	1	.857	50	23	53	3.02	0
1991 Kansas City ........A.L.		38	55	0	1	.000	42	23	55	2.45	0
1992 Kansas City b .......A.L.		44	89⅓	4	9	.308	31	35	115	4.94	0
1993 Omaha ..............A.A.		33	105⅓	2	6	.250	74	29	97	3.67	2
1993 Kansas City .........A.L.		7	35⅓	1	2	.333	16	11	37	4.08	0
1994 Kansas City c .......A.L.		36	47	2	3	.400	21	16	55	4.60	0
1995 Omaha ..............A.A.		15	57	5	1	.833	38	13	55	2.84	0
1995 Kansas City ........A.L.		28	44⅔	1	1	.500	28	16	45	4.23	0
1996 Omaha ..............A.A.		1	3	1	0	1.000	6	0	3	0.00	0
1996 Kansas City d-e .......A.L.		38	54	2	2	.500	32	24	58	5.67	0
1997 New Orleans ..........A.A.		17	24	2	3	.400	23	5	31	4.50	1
1997 Houston ..............N.L.		40	47⅔	3	1	.750	43	11	39	2.27	1
Major League Totals ....7 Yrs.		231	373	13	19	.406	213	136	404	4.13	1
Division Series											
1997 Houston ...........N.L.		2	2	0	0	.000	2	0	4	4.50	0

a On disabled list from June 17 to end of 1990 season.
b On disabled list from July 2 to July 20, 1992.
c On disabled list from July 16 to July 31, 1994.
d On disabled list from May 19 to June 13, 1996.
e Waived by Kansas City Royals, October 3, 1996.

MAHAY, RONALD MATTHEW
Born, Crestwood, Illinois, June 28, 1971.
Bats Left. Throws Left. Height, 6 feet, 2 inches. Weight, 185 pounds.

Year Club	Lea	G	IP	W	L	Pct	SO	BB	H	ERA	SAVES
1995 Boston ..............A.L.		5	20	3	4	2	0	1	3	0	.200
1996 Sarasota ....Fla. St.		31	70⅔	2	2	.500	68	35	61	3.82	2
1996 Trenton ....Eastern		1	3⅔	0	1	.000	0	6	12	29.45	0
1997 Trenton ....Eastern		17	40⅔	3	3	.500	47	13	29	3.10	5
1997 Pawtucket ....Int.		2	4⅔	1	0	1.000	6	1	3	0.00	0
1997 Boston ..............A.L.		28	25	3	0	1.000	22	11	19	2.52	0
Major League Totals ....2 Yrs.		33	25	3	0	1.000	28	12	23	2.52	0

MARTIN, THOMAS EDGAR
Born, Charleston, South Carolina, May 21, 1970.
Bats Left. Throws Left. Height, 6 feet, 1 inch. Weight, 185 pounds.

Year Club	Lea	G	IP	W	L	Pct	SO	BB	H	ERA	SAVES
1989 Bluefield ....Appal.		8	39	3	3	.500	31	25	36	4.62	0
1989 Erie ............N.Y.-Penn.		7	40⅔	0	5	.000	44	25	42	6.64	0
1990 Wausau ....Midwest		9	40	2	3	.400	45	27	31	2.48	0
1991 Kane County ......Midwest		38	99	4	10	.286	106	56	92	3.64	6
1992 High Desert ....California		11	16⅓	0	2	.000	10	16	23	9.37	0
1992 Waterloo ....Midwest		39	55	2	6	.250	57	22	62	4.25	3
1993 Rancho Cuca .....California		47	59⅓	1	4	.200	53	39	72	5.61	0
1994 Greenville ....Southern		36	74	5	6	.455	51	24	82	4.62	0
1995 Tigres ....Mexican		1	1⅓	0	1	.000	0	1	5	27.00	0
1995 Richmond ....Int.		7	9	0	0	.000	3	10	10	9.00	0
1996 Tucson ..............P.C.		5	6	0	0	.000	1	2	6	0.00	0
1996 Jackson ....Texas		57	75	6	2	.750	58	42	71	3.24	3
1997 Houston a-b-c .........N.L.		55	56	5	3	.625	36	23	52	2.09	2
Division Series											
1997 Houston ..............N.L.		2	0⅔	0	0	.000	0	1	1	0.00	0

a On disabled list from May 30 to June 15, 1997.
b Selected on expansion draft by Arizona Diamondbacks, November 18, 1997.
c Traded to Cleveland Indians with infielder Travis Fryman for infielder Matt Williams, December 1, 1997.

MARTINEZ (AQUINO), PEDRO
Born, Villa Mella, Dominican Republic, November 29, 1968.
Bats Left. Throws Left. Height, 6 feet, 2 inches. Weight, 185 pounds.

Year Club	Lea	G	IP	W	L	Pct	SO	BB	H	ERA	SAVES
1987 Spokane ....Northwest		18	51⅔	4	1	.800	42	36	57	3.83	0
1988 Spokane ....Northwest		15	99⅔	8	3	.727	89	32	108	4.24	0
1989 Charleston ....So. Atl.		27	187	14	8	.636	158	64	147	1.97	0

Year	Club	Lea	G	IP	W	L	Pct	SO	BB	H	ERA	SAVES
1990	Wichita	Texas	24	129⅓	6	10	.375	88	70	139	4.80	0
1991	Wichita	Texas	26	156⅔	11	10	.524	95	57	169	5.23	0
1992	Wichita	Texas	26	168⅓	11	7	.611	142	52	153	2.99	0
1993	Las Vegas	P.C.	15	87⅔	3	5	.375	65	40	94	4.72	0
1993	San Diego	N.L.	32	37	3	1	.750	32	13	23	2.43	0
1994	San Diego a	N.L.	48	68⅓	3	2	.600	52	49	52	2.90	3
1995	Tucson	P.C.	20	34	1	1	.500	21	13	44	6.62	2
1995	Houston b-c	N.L.	25	20⅔	6	3	.000	17	16	29	7.40	0
1996	Norfolk	Int.	34	56⅔	4	4	.500	37	20	45	3.02	2
1996	New York-Cincinnati d-e-f	N.L.	9	10	0	0	.000	9	8	13	6.30	0
1997	Indianapols	A.A.	28	80⅓	4	3	.571	36	35	70	3.47	0
1997	Cincinnati g	N.L.	8	6⅔	1	1	.500	4	7	8	9.45	0
Major League Totals		5 Yrs.	122	142⅔	7	4	.636	114	93	125	3.97	3

a Traded to Houston Astros with outfielders Derek Bell and Phil Plantier, pitcher Doug Brocail, shortstop Ricky Gutierrez and infielder Craig Shipley for third baseman Ken Caminiti, shortstop Andujar Cedeño, outfielder Steve Finley, pitcher Brian Williams, first baseman Roberto Petagine and player to be named, December 28, 1994.
b Traded to San Diego Padres for infielder Ray Holbert, October 10, 1995.
c Traded to New York Mets for outfielder Jeff Barry, December 15, 1995.
d Traded to Cincinnati Reds for outfielder Andre King, September 11, 1996.
e Outrighted by Cincinnati Reds, November 4, 1996.
f On disabled list from June 29 to July 24 and July 31 to August 27, 1996.
g Filed for free agency, November 18, 1997.

MARTINEZ, PEDRO JAMIE

Born, Manoguyabo, Dominican Republic, July 25, 1971.
Bats Right. Throws Right. Height, 5 feet, 11 inches. Weight, 170 pounds.

Year	Club	Lea	G	IP	W	L	Pct	SO	BB	H	ERA	SAVES
1988	Santo Domingo	Domin. Sum.	8	49⅓	5	1	.833	28	16	45	3.12	0
1989	Santo Domingo	Domin. Sum.	13	85⅔	7	2	.778	63	25	59	2.75	1
1990	Great Falls	Pioneer	14	77	8	3	.727	82	40	74	3.62	0
1991	Bakersfield	California	10	61⅓	8	0	1.000	83	19	41	2.05	0
1991	San Antonio	Texas	12	76⅔	7	5	.583	74	31	57	1.76	0
1991	Albuquerque	P.C.	6	39⅓	3	3	.500	35	16	28	3.66	0
1992	Albuquerque	P.C.	20	125⅓	7	6	.538	124	57	104	3.81	0
1992	Los Angeles	N.L.	2	8	0	1	.000	8	1	6	2.25	0
1993	Albuquerque	P.C.	1	3	0	0	.000	4	1	1	3.00	0
1993	Los Angeles a	N.L.	65	107	10	5	.667	119	57	76	2.61	2
1994	Montreal	N.L.	24	144⅔	11	5	.688	142	45	115	3.42	1
1995	Montreal	N.L.	30	194⅔	14	10	.583	174	66	158	3.51	0
1996	Montreal	N.L.	33	216⅔	13	10	.565	222	70	189	3.70	0
1997	Montreal b-c	N.L.	31	241⅓	17	8	.680	305	67	158	1.90	0
Major League Totals		6 Yrs.	185	912⅓	65	39	.625	970	306	702	3.00	3

a Traded to Montreal Expos for second baseman Delino DeShields, November 19, 1993.
b Traded to Boston Red Sox for pitcher Carl Pavano and player to be named later, November 18, 1997.
c Selected Cy Young Award Winner in National League for 1997.

MARTINEZ, RAMON JAIME

Born, Santo Domingo, Dominican Republic, March 22, 1968.
Bats Right. Throws Right. Height, 6 feet, 4 inches. Weight, 176 pounds.

Year	Club	Lea	G	IP	W	L	Pct	SO	BB	H	ERA	SAVES
1985	Bradenton Dodgers	Gulf C.	23	59	4	1	.800	42	23	57	2.59	1
1986	Bakersfield	California	20	106	4	8	.333	78	63	119	4.75	0
1987	Vero Beach	Fla. St.	25	170⅓	16	5	.762	148	78	128	2.17	0
1988	San Antonio	Texas	14	95	8	4	.667	89	34	79	2.46	0
1988	Albuquerque	P.C.	10	58⅔	5	2	.714	49	32	43	2.76	0
1988	Los Angeles	N.L.	9	35⅔	1	3	.250	23	22	27	3.79	0
1989	Albuquerque	P.C.	18	113	10	2	.833	127	50	92	2.79	0
1989	Los Angeles	N.L.	15	98⅔	6	4	.600	89	41	79	3.19	0
1990	Los Angeles	N.L.	33	234⅓	20	6	.769	223	67	191	2.92	0
1991	Los Angeles	N.L.	33	220⅓	17	13	.567	150	69	190	3.27	0
1992	Los Angeles a	N.L.	25	150⅔	8	11	.421	101	69	141	4.00	0
1993	Los Angeles b	N.L.	32	211⅔	10	12	.455	127	*104	202	3.44	0
1994	Los Angeles c	N.L.	24	170	12	7	.632	119	56	160	3.97	0
1995	Los Angeles d-e-f	N.L.	30	206⅓	17	7	.708	138	81	176	3.66	0
1996	San Antonio	Texas	1	2⅔	0	0	.000	1	3	0	0.00	0
1996	Vero Beach	Fla. St.	1	7	1	0	1.000	10	0	5	0.00	0
1996	Los Angeles g	N.L.	28	168⅔	15	6	.714	133	86	153	3.42	0
1997	Los Angeles h	N.L.	22	133⅔	10	5	.667	120	68	123	3.64	0
Major League Totals		10 Yrs.	251	1630	116	74	.611	1223	663	1442	3.48	0

Year	Club	Lea	G	IP	W	L	Pct	SO	BB	H	ERA	SAVES
	Division Series											
1995 Los Angeles ..........N.L.			1	4⅓	0	1	.000	3	2	10	14.45	0
1996 Los Angeles ..........N.L.			1	8	0	0	.000	6	3	3	1.13	0
Division Series Totals 2				12⅓	0	1	.000	9	5	13	5.84	0

a Appeared in one additional game as pinch runner.
b Suspended five games for June 15 intentionally hitting batter with pitch from July 8 to July 12, 1993.
c Declared restricted free agent under Major League Baseball implemented labor proposal, December 23, 1994.
d Pitched no-hit, no-run game against Florida Marlins, July 14, 1995.
e Filed for free agency, November 12, 1995.
f Re-signed with Los Angeles Dodgers, November 20, 1995.
g On disabled list from April 7 to May 14, 1996.
h On disabled list from June 15 to August 20, 1997.

MASATO, YOSHII
Born, Osaka, Japan, April 20, 1965.
Bats Right. Throws Right. Height, 6 feet, 2 inches. Weight, 210 pounds.

Year	Club	Lea	G	IP	W	L	Pct	SO	BB	H	ERA	SAVES
1985 Kintetsu ....Japan Pac.			2	3	0	1	.000	1	3	6	21.00	0
1986 Kintetsu ....Japan Pac.			2	2⅓	0	0	.000	2	2	10	23.14	0
1987 Kintetsu ....Japan Pac.			13	36	2	1	.667	23	12	45	4.75	24
1988 Kintetsu ....Japan Pac.			50	80⅓	10	2	.833	44	27	76	2.69	20
1989 Kintetsu ....Japan Pac.			47	84⅓	5	5	.500	44	37	77	2.99	15
1990 Kintetsu ....Japan Pac.			45	74⅓	8	9	.471	55	30	80	3.39	2
1991 Kintetsu ....Japan Pac.			21	26⅓	2	1	.667	13	6	30	3.42	0
1992 Kintetsu ....Japan Pac.			9	11⅔	1	0	1.000	4	2	10	2.31	0
1993 Kintetsu ....Japan Pac.			22	104⅔	5	5	.500	66	25	100	2.67	0
1994 Kintetsu a ......Japan Pac.			21	97	7	7	.500	42	37	118	5.47	0
1995 Yakult ....Japan Cent.			25	147⅓	10	7	.588	91	39	127	3.12	0
1996 Yakult ....Japan Cent.			25	180⅓	10	7	.588	145	47	177	3.24	0
1997 Yakult b ....Japan Cent.			28	174⅓	13	6	.684	104	48	149	2.99	0

a Traded to Yakult Swallows, October, 1994.
b Signed as a free agent with New York Mets, January 13, 1998.

MATHEWS, TERRY ALAN
Born, Alexandria, Louisiana, October 5, 1964.
Bats Left. Throws Right. Height, 6 feet, 2 inches. Weight, 225 pounds.

Year	Club	Lea	G	IP	W	L	Pct	SO	BB	H	ERA	SAVES
1987 Gastonia ....So. Atl.			34	48⅓	3	3	.500	46	32	53	5.59	0
1988 Charlotte ....Fla. St.			27	163⅓	13	6	.684	94	49	138	2.80	0
1989 Tulsa ....Texas			10	45⅓	2	5	.286	32	24	53	6.15	0
1989 Charlotte ....Fla. St.			10	59⅓	4	2	.667	30	17	55	3.64	0
1990 Tulsa ....Texas			14	86⅓	5	7	.417	48	36	88	4.27	0
1990 Oklahoma City .......A.A.			12	70⅔	2	7	.222	36	15	81	3.69	0
1991 Oklahoma City .......A.A.			18	95⅓	5	6	.455	63	34	98	3.49	1
1991 Texas ...............A.L.			34	57⅓	4	0	1.000	51	16	54	3.61	1
1992 Texas a .............A.L.			40	42⅓	2	4	.333	26	31	48	5.95	0
1992 Oklahoma City b .......A.A.			9	16⅔	1	1	.500	13	7	17	4.32	1
1993 Jackson ....Texas			17	103	6	5	.545	74	29	116	3.67	0
1993 Tucson c .............P.C.			16	33	5	0	1.000	34	11	40	3.55	2
1994 Edmonton ............P.C.			13	84	4	4	.500	46	22	88	4.29	0
1994 Florida ..............N.L.			24	43	2	1	.667	21	9	45	3.35	0
1995 Charlotte ....Int.			2	3⅔	0	0	.000	5	0	5	4.91	0
1995 Florida d ............N.L.			57	82⅔	4	4	.500	72	27	70	3.38	3
1996 Florida ..............N.L.			57	55	2	4	.333	49	27	59	4.91	4
1996 Baltimore e-f .........A.L.			14	18⅔	2	2	.500	13	7	20	3.38	0
1997 Baltimore ............A.L.			57	63⅓	4	4	.500	39	36	63	4.41	1
Major League Totals ....6 Yrs.			283	362⅓	20	19	.513	271	155	359	4.12	9
	Division Series											
1996 Baltimore ............A.L.			3	2⅔	0	0	.000	2	1	3	0.00	0
1997 Baltimore ............A.L.			1	1	0	0	.000	1	0	2	18.00	0
Division Series Totals 4				3⅔	0	0	.000	3	1	5	4.91	0
	Championship Series											
1996 Baltimore ............A.L.			3	2⅓	0	0	.000	3	2	0	0.00	0

a On disabled list from July 29 to September 12, 1992.
b Sold by Texas Rangers to Houston Astros organization, April 4, 1993.
c Became free agent, October 15; signed with Florida Marlins organization, November 10, 1993.

d On disabled list from August 19 to September 3, 1995.
e On disabled list from April 2 to April 17, 1996.
f Traded to Baltimore Orioles for player to be named later, August 21, 1996. Florida Marlins received catcher Greg Zaun to complete trade, August 23, 1996.

MATHEWS, TIMOTHY JAY (T.J.)

Born, Belleville, Illinois, January 9, 1970.
Bats Right. Throws Right. Height, 6 feet, 2 inches. Weight, 200 pounds.

Year	Club	Lea	G	IP	W	L	Pct	SO	BB	H	ERA	SAVES
1992	Hamilton	N.Y.-Penn.	14	86⅔	10	1	.909	89	30	70	2.18	0
1993	Springfield	Midwest	25	159⅓	12	9	.571	144	29	121	2.71	0
1994	St. Petersburg	Fla. St.	11	66⅓	5	5	.500	62	23	52	2.44	0
1994	Arkansas	Texas	16	97	5	5	.500	93	24	83	3.15	0
1995	Louisville	A.A.	32	66⅔	9	4	.692	50	27	60	2.70	1
1995	St. Louis	N.L.	23	29⅔	1	1	.500	28	11	21	1.52	2
1996	St. Louis	N.L.	67	83⅔	2	6	.250	80	32	62	3.01	6
1997	St. Louis a	N.L.	40	46	4	4	.500	46	18	41	2.15	0
1997	Oakland	A.L.	24	28⅔	6	2	.750	24	12	34	4.40	3
Major League Totals		3 Yrs.	154	188	13	13	.500	178	73	158	2.78	11
	Division Series											
1996	St. Louis	N.L.	1	1	1	0	1.000	2	0	1	0.00	0
	Championship Series											
1996	St. Louis	N.L.	2	0⅔	0	0	.000	2	1	2	0.00	0

a Traded to Oakland Athletics with pitcher Eric Ludwick and pitcher Blake Stein for first baseman Mark McGwire, July 31, 1997.

MAY, DARRELL KEVIN

Born, San Bernadino, California, June 13, 1972.
Bats Left. Throws Left. Height, 6 feet, 2 inches. Weight, 170 pounds.

Year	Club	Lea	G	IP	W	L	Pct	SO	BB	H	ERA	SAVES
1992	Braves	Gulf Coast	12	53	4	3	.571	61	13	34	1.36	1
1993	Macon	So. Atl.	17	104⅓	10	4	.714	111	22	81	2.24	0
1993	Durham	Carolina	9	51⅔	5	2	.714	47	16	44	2.09	0
1994	Durham	Carolina	12	74⅔	8	2	.800	73	17	74	3.01	0
1994	Greenville	Southern	11	63⅔	5	3	.625	42	17	61	3.11	0
1995	Greenville	Southern	15	91⅓	2	8	.200	79	20	81	3.55	0
1995	Richmond	Int.	9	51	4	2	.667	42	16	53	3.71	0
1995	Atlanta	N.L.	2	4	0	0	.000	1	0	10	11.25	0
1996	Pittsburgh a	N.L.	5	8⅔	0	1	.000	5	4	15	9.35	0
1996	Calgary b-c	P.C.	23	131⅔	7	6	.538	75	36	146	4.10	0
1996	California d	A.L.	5	2⅔	0	0	.000	1	2	3	10.13	0
1997	Vancouver	P.C.	13	80	7	5	.583	62	31	65	3.26	0
1997	Anaheim	A.L.	29	51⅔	2	1	.667	42	25	56	5.23	0
Major League Totals		3 Yrs.	41	67	2	2	.500	49	31	84	6.31	0

a Waived by Atlanta Braves, March 30, 1996.
b Claimed by Pittsburgh Pirates, April 4, 1996.
c Released by Pittsburgh Pirates organization, September 4, 1996.
d Claimed by California Angels, September 6, 1996.

MCCARTHY, GREGORY O'NEIL (GREG)

Born, Norwalk, Connecticut, October 30, 1968.
Bats Left. Throws Left. Height, 6 feet, 2 inches. Weight, 195 pounds.

Year	Club	Lea	G	IP	W	L	Pct	SO	BB	H	ERA	SAVES
1987	Utica	N.Y.-Penn.	20	29⅔	4	1	.800	40	23	14	0.91	3
1988	Spartanburg	So. Atl.	34	64⅔	4	2	.667	65	52	52	4.04	2
1989	Spartanburg	So. Atl.	24	112	5	8	.385	115	80	90	4.18	0
1990	Clearwater a	Fla. St.	42	59⅔	1	3	.250	67	38	47	3.47	5
1991	Montreal b	N.L.	(INJURED—Did Not Play)									
1992	Kinston	Carolina	23	27⅓	3	0	1.000	37	9	14	0.00	12
1993	Kinston	Carolina	9	10⅔	0	0	.000	14	13	8	1.69	2
1993	Canton-Akrn	Eastern	33	34⅓	2	3	.400	39	37	28	4.72	6
1994	Canton-Akrn	Eastern	22	32	2	3	.400	39	23	19	2.25	9
1994	Charlotte c	Int.	18	23⅓	1	0	1.000	21	28	17	6.94	0

Year	Club	Lea	G	IP	W	L	Pct	SO	BB	H	ERA	SAVES
1995 Birmingham d	Southern	38	44⅔	3	3	.500	48	29	37	5.04	3
1996 Tacoma	P.C.	39	68⅓	4	2	.667	90	53	58	3.29	4
1996 Seattle	A.L.	10	9⅔	0	0	.000	7	4	8	1.86	0
1997 Tacoma	P.C.	22	22	2	1	.667	34	16	21	3.27	3
1997 Seattle	A.L.	37	29⅔	1	1	.500	34	16	26	5.46	0
Major League Totals .... 2 Yrs.		47	39⅓	1	1	.500	41	20	34	4.58	0

a Drafted by Montreal Expos from Philadelphia Phillies organization in Rule V draft, December 3, 1990.
b Drafted by Cleveland Indians in Rule V draft, December 2, 1991.
c Signed as minor league free agent by Chicago White Sox, November 14, 1994.
d Signed as minor league free agent by Seattle Mariners, December 14, 1995.

McDONALD, LARRY BENARD

Born, Baton Rouge, Louisiana, November 24, 1967.
Bats Right. Throws Right. Height, 6 feet, 7 inches. Weight, 214 pounds.

Year	Club	Lea	G	IP	W	L	Pct	SO	BB	H	ERA	SAVES
1989 Frederick	Carolina	2	9	0	0	.000	9	0	10	2.00	0
1989 Baltimore	A.L.	6	7⅓	1	0	1.000	3	4	8	8.59	0
1990 Hagerstown	Eastern	3	11	0	1	.000	15	3	11	6.55	0
1990 Rochester	Int.	7	44	3	3	.500	37	21	33	2.86	0
1990 Baltimore a	A.L.	21	118⅔	8	5	.615	65	35	88	2.43	0
1991 Rochester	Int.	2	7	0	1	.000	7	5	10	7.71	0
1991 Baltimore b	A.L.	21	126⅓	6	8	.429	85	43	126	4.84	0
1992 Baltimore	A.L.	35	227	13	13	.500	158	74	213	4.24	0
1993 Baltimore	A.L.	34	220⅓	13	14	.481	171	86	185	3.39	0
1994 Baltimore c	A.L.	24	157⅓	14	7	.667	94	54	151	4.06	0
1995 Rochester	Int.	1	3⅔	0	0	.000	1	4	1	2.45	0
1995 Baltimore d	A.L.	14	80	3	6	.333	62	38	67	4.16	0
1996 Milwaukee e	A.L.	35	221⅔	12	10	.545	146	67	228	3.90	0
1997 Milwaukee f	A.L.	21	133	8	7	.533	110	36	120	4.06	0
Major League Totals .... 9 Yrs.		211	1291⅓	78	70	.527	894	437	1186	3.91	0

a On disabled list from April 6 to May 22, 1990.
b On disabled list from March 29 to April 19 and May 24 to June 30, 1991.
c Declared restricted free agent under Major League Baseball implemented labor proposal, December 23, 1994.
d On disabled list from June 17 to July 14 and July 20 to September 11, 1995.
e Signed with Milwaukee Brewers, January 20, 1996.
f On disabled list from July 17 to September 29, 1997.

McELROY, CHARLES DWAYNE (CHUCK)

Born, Galveston, Texas, October 1, 1967.
Bats Left. Throws Left. Height, 6 feet. Weight, 195 pounds.

Year	Club	Lea	G	IP	W	L	Pct	SO	BB	H	ERA	SAVES
1986 Utica	N.Y.-Penn.	14	94⅔	4	6	.400	91	28	85	2.95	0
1987 Spantanburg	So. Atl.	24	130⅓	14	4	.778	115	48	117	3.11	0
1987 Clearwater	Fla. St.	2	7⅓	1	0	1.000	7	4	1	0.00	0
1988 Reading	Eastern	28	160	9	12	.429	93	70	172	4.50	0
1989 Reading	Eastern	32	47	3	1	.750	39	14	39	2.68	12
1989 Scranton	Int.	14	15⅓	1	2	.333	12	11	13	2.93	3
1989 Philadelphia	N.L.	11	10⅓	0	0	.000	8	4	12	1.74	0
1990 Scranton	Int.	57	76	6	8	.429	78	34	62	2.72	7
1990 Philadelphia a	N.L.	16	14	0	1	.000	16	10	24	7.71	0
1991 Chicago b	N.L.	71	101⅓	6	2	.750	92	57	73	1.95	3
1992 Chicago	N.L.	72	83⅔	4	7	.364	83	51	73	3.55	6
1993 Iowa	A.A.	9	15⅔	0	1	.000	13	9	19	4.60	2
1993 Chicago c	N.L.	49	47⅓	2	2	.500	31	25	51	4.56	0
1994 Cincinnati	N.L.	52	57⅔	1	2	.333	38	15	52	2.34	5
1995 Cincinnati d	N.L.	44	40⅓	3	4	.429	27	15	46	6.02	0
1996 Indianapolis	A.A.	5	13⅓	1	1	.500	10	4	11	2.70	0
1996 Cincinnati	N.L.	12	12⅓	2	0	1.000	13	10	13	6.57	0
1996 California e-f	A.L.	40	36⅔	5	1	.833	32	13	32	2.95	0
1997 Anaheim-Chicago g-h-i	A.L.	61	75	1	3	.250	62	22	73	3.84	1
Major League Totals .... 9 Yrs.		428	478⅔	24	22	.522	402	222	449	3.53	15

a Traded to Chicago Cubs with pitcher Bob Scanlan for pitcher Mitch Williams, April 7, 1991.
b Appeared in one game as pinch runner.
c Traded to Cincinnati Reds for pitchers Larry Luebbers and Mike Anderson and catcher Darron Cox, December 10, 1993.
d On disabled list from June 7 to June 23, 1995.

e On disabled list from August 11 to August 28 and April 1 to April 28, 1996.
f Traded to California Angels for pitcher Lee Smith, May 27, 1996.
g Traded to Chicago White Sox with catcher Jorge Fabregas for outfielder Tony Phillips and catcher Chad Kreuter, May 18, 1997.
h Selected on expansion draft by Arizona Diamondbacks, November 18, 1997.
i Traded to Colorado Rockies for outfielder Harvey Pulliam, November 19, 1997.

McMICHAEL, GREGORY WINSTON (GREG)

Born, Knoxville, Tennessee, December 1, 1966.
Bats Right. Throws Right. Height, 6 feet, 3 inches. Weight, 215 pounds.

Year	Club	Lea	G	IP	W	L	Pct	SO	BB	H	ERA	SAVES
1988	Burlington	Appal.	3	21	2	0	1.000	20	4	17	2.57	0
1988	Kinston	Carolina	11	77⅓	4	2	.667	35	18	57	2.68	0
1989	Canton	Eastern	26	170	11	11	.500	101	64	164	3.49	0
1990	Canton	Eastern	13	40⅓	2	3	.400	19	17	39	3.35	0
1990	Colorado Springs a	P.C.	12	59	2	3	.400	34	30	72	5.80	0
1991	Durham	Carolina	36	79⅔	5	6	.455	82	29	83	3.62	2
1992	Greenville	Southern	15	46⅓	4	2	.667	53	13	37	1.36	1
1992	Richmond	Int.	19	90⅓	6	5	.545	86	34	89	4.38	2
1993	Atlanta	N.L.	74	91⅔	2	3	.400	89	29	68	2.06	19
1994	Atlanta	N.L.	51	58⅔	4	6	.400	47	19	66	3.84	21
1995	Atlanta	N.L.	67	80⅔	7	2	.778	74	32	64	2.79	2
1996	Atlanta b	N.L.	73	86⅔	5	3	.625	78	27	84	3.22	2
1997	New York	N.L.	73	87⅔	7	10	.412	81	27	73	2.98	7
Major League Totals	5 Yrs.		338	405⅓	25	24	.510	369	134	355	2.91	51
Division Series												
1995	Atlanta	N.L.	3	1⅓	0	0	.000	1	2	1	6.75	0
1996	Atlanta	N.L.	2	1⅓	0	0	.000	3	1	1	6.75	0
Division Series Totals	4			2⅔	0	0	.000	4	3	2	6.75	0
Championship Series												
1993	Atlanta	N.L.	4	4	0	1	.000	1	2	7	6.75	0
1995	Atlanta	N.L.	3	2⅔	1	0	1.000	2	1	0	0.00	1
1996	Atlanta	N.L.	3	2	0	1	.000	3	1	4	9.00	0
Championship Series Totals	10			8⅔	1	2	.333	6	4	11	5.19	1
World Series Record												
1995	Atlanta	N.L.	3	3⅓	0	0	.000	2	2	3	2.70	0
1996	Atlanta	N.L.	2	1	0	0	.000	1	0	5	27.00	0
World Series Totals	5			4⅓	0	0	.000	3	2	8	8.31	0

a Released by Cleveland Indians, April 2; signed with Atlanta Braves organization, April 16, 1991.
b Traded to New York Mets for pitcher Paul Byrd and player to be named later, November 25, 1996.

MECIR, JAMES JASON (JIM)

Born, Queens, New York, May 16, 1970.
Bats Both. Throws Right. Height, 6 feet, 1 inch. Weight, 195 pounds.

Year	Club	Lea	G	IP	W	L	Pct	SO	BB	H	ERA	SAVES
1991	San Bernardino	California	14	70⅓	3	5	.375	48	37	72	4.22	1
1992	San Bernardino	California	14	61⅔	4	5	.444	53	26	72	4.67	0
1993	Riverside	California	26	145⅓	9	11	.450	85	58	160	4.33	0
1994	Jacksonville	Southern	46	80⅓	6	5	.545	53	35	73	2.69	13
1995	Tacoma	P.C.	40	69⅔	1	4	.200	46	28	63	3.10	8
1995	Seattle a	A.L.	2	4⅔	0	0	.000	3	2	5	0.00	0
1996	New York	A.L.	26	40⅓	1	1	.500	38	23	42	5.13	0
1996	Columbus	Int.	33	47⅔	3	3	.500	52	15	37	2.27	7
1997	New York b-c	A.L.	25	33⅔	0	4	.000	25	10	36	5.88	0
1997	Columbus	Int.	24	27	1	1	.500	34	6	14	1.00	11
Major League Totals	3 Yrs.		53	78⅔	1	5	.167	66	35	83	5.15	0

a Traded by Seattle Mariners to New York Yankees with pitcher Jeff Nelson and infielder Tino Martinez for pitcher Sterling Hitchcock and infielder Russ Davis, December 7, 1995.
b Sent to Boston Red Sox as player to be named later for designated hitter Mike Stanley and infielder Randy Brown, September 29, 1997.
c Selected in expansion draft by Tampa Bay Devil Rays, November 18, 1997.

MENDOZA, RAMIRO
Born, Los Santos, Panama, June 15, 1972.
Bats Right. Throws Right. Height, 6 feet, 2 inches. Weight, 154 pounds.

Year	Club	Lea	G	IP	W	L	Pct	SO	BB	H	ERA	SAVES
1993	Yankees ....Gulf Coast		15	67⅔	4	5	.444	61	7	59	2.79	1
1993	Greensboro ....So. Atl.		2	3⅓	0	1	.000	3	5	3	2.45	0
1994	Tampa ....Fla. St.		22	134⅓	12	6	.667	110	35	133	3.01	0
1995	Norwich ....Eastern		19	89⅔	5	6	.455	68	33	87	3.21	0
1995	Columbus ....Int.		2	14	1	0	1.000	13	2	10	2.57	0
1996	Columbus ....Int.		15	97	6	2	.750	61	19	96	2.51	0
1996	New York .............A.L.		12	53	4	5	.444	34	10	80	6.79	0
1997	Columbus ....Int.		1	6⅓	0	0	.000	4	1	7	5.68	0
1997	New York .............A.L.		39	133⅔	8	6	.571	82	28	157	4.24	2
Major League Totals ....2 Yrs.			51	186⅔	12	11	.522	116	38	237	4.97	2
Division Series												
1997	New York .............A.L.		2	3⅔	1	1	.500	2	0	3	2.45	0

MENHART, PAUL GERARD
Born, St. Louis, Missouri, March 25, 1969.
Bats Right. Throws Right. Height, 6 feet, 2 inches. Weight, 190 pounds.

Year	Club	Lea	G	IP	W	L	Pct	SO	BB	H	ERA	SAVES
1990	St. Catharines ....N.Y.-Penn.		8	40	0	5	.000	38	19	34	4.05	0
1990	Myrtle Beach ....So. Atl.		5	30⅔	3	0	1.000	18	5	18	0.59	0
1991	Dunedin ....Fla. St.		20	128⅓	10	6	.625	114	34	114	2.66	0
1992	Knoxville ....Southern		28	177⅔	10	11	.476	104	38	181	3.85	0
1993	Syracuse ....Int.		25	151	9	10	.474	108	67	143	3.64	0
1995	Syracuse ....Int.		10	51⅓	2	4	.333	30	25	62	6.31	0
1995	Toronto a .............A.L.		21	78⅔	1	4	.200	50	47	72	4.92	0
1996	Seattle b .............A.L.		11	42	2	2	.500	18	25	55	7.29	0
1996	Tacoma ...............P.C.		6	26	0	3	.000	12	16	53	11.08	0
1997	Tacoma ...............P.C.		15	61⅓	4	7	.364	51	34	76	6.16	1
1997	Las Vegas ............P.C.		11	66⅓	0	7	.000	44	21	78	5.97	0
1997	San Diego ............N.L.		9	44	2	3	.400	22	13	42	4.70	0
Major League Totals ....3 Yrs.			41	164⅔	5	9	.357	90	85	169	5.47	0

a Traded to Seattle Mariners with pitcher Edwin Hurtado for pitcher Bill Risley and infielder Miguel Cairo, December 18, 1995.
b On disabled list from August 14 to September 30, 1996.

MERCEDES, JOSE MIGUEL
Born, El Seibo, Dominican Republic, March 5, 1971.
Bats Right. Throws Right. Height, 6 feet, 1 inch. Weight, 199 pounds.

Year	Club	Lea	G	IP	W	L	Pct	SO	BB	H	ERA	SAVES
1992	Orioles ....Gulf Coast		8	35⅓	2	3	.400	21	13	31	1.78	0
1992	Kane County ....Midwest		8	47⅓	3	2	.600	45	15	40	2.66	0
1993	Bowie ....Eastern		26	147	6	8	.429	75	65	170	4.78	0
1994	El Paso a ....Texas		3	9⅔	2	0	1.000	8	4	13	4.66	0
1994	New Orleans ...........A.A.		3	18⅓	0	0	.000	7	8	19	4.91	0
1994	Milwaukee .............A.L.		19	31	2	0	1.000	11	16	22	2.32	0
1995	Milwaukee b ..........A.L.		5	7⅓	0	1	.000	6	8	12	9.82	0
1996	Milwaukee .............A.L.		11	16⅔	0	2	.000	6	5	20	9.18	0
1996	New Orleans ...........A.A.		25	101	3	7	.300	47	28	109	3.56	1
1997	Milwaukee .............A.L.		29	159	7	10	.412	80	53	146	3.79	0
Major League Totals ....4 Yrs.			64	214	9	13	.409	103	82	200	4.21	0

a Drafted from Baltimore Orioles organization by Milwaukee Brewers in Rule V draft, December 13, 1993.
b On disabled list from May 14 through end of 1995 season.

MERCKER, KENT FRANKLIN
Born, Dublin, Ohio, February 1, 1968.
Bats Left. Throws Left. Height, 6 feet, 2 inches. Weight, 195 pounds.

Year	Club	Lea	G	IP	W	L	Pct	SO	BB	H	ERA	SAVES
1986	Bradenton Braves ....Gulf C.		9	47⅓	4	3	.571	42	16	37	2.47	0
1987	Durham a ....Carolina		3	11⅔	0	1	.000	14	6	11	5.40	0
1988	Durham ....Carolina		19	127⅔	11	4	.733	159	47	102	2.75	0
1988	Greenville ....Southern		9	48⅓	3	1	.750	60	26	36	3.35	0

Year	Club	Lea	G	IP	W	L	Pct	SO	BB	H	ERA	SAVES
1989 Richmond	Int.	27	168⅔	9	12	.429	*144	*95	107	3.20	0
1989 Atlanta	N.L.	2	4⅓	0	0	.000	4	6	8	12.46	0
1990 Richmond b	Int.	12	58⅓	5	4	.556	69	27	60	3.55	1
1990 Atlanta	N.L.	36	48⅓	4	7	.364	39	24	43	3.17	7
1991 Atlanta c-d	N.L.	50	73⅓	5	3	.625	62	35	56	2.58	6
1992 Atlanta	N.L.	53	68⅓	3	2	.600	49	35	51	3.42	6
1993 Atlanta	N.L.	43	66	3	1	.750	59	36	52	2.86	0
1994 Atlanta e-f	N.L.	20	112⅓	9	4	.692	111	45	90	3.45	0
1995 Atlanta g-h	N.L.	29	143	7	8	.467	102	61	140	4.15	0
1996 Buffalo	A.A.	3	16	0	2	.000	11	9	11	3.94	0
1996 Baltimore-Cleveland i-j-k	A.L.	24	69⅔	4	6	.400	29	38	83	6.98	0
1997 Cincinnati l-m-n	N.L.	28	144⅔	8	11	.421	75	62	135	3.92	0
Major League Totals	9 Yrs.	285	730	43	42	.506	530	342	658	3.91	19
Division Series											
1995 Atlanta	N.L.	1	0⅓	0	0	.000	0	0	0	0.00	0
Championship Series											
1991 Atlanta	N.L.	1	0⅔	0	1	.000	0	2	0	13.50	0
1992 Atlanta	N.L.	2	3	0	0	.000	1	1	1	0.00	0
Championship Series Totals	3	3⅔	0	1	.000	1	3	1	2.45	0
World Series Record											
1991 Atlanta	N.L.	2	1	0	0	.000	1	0	0	0.00	0
1995 Atlanta	N.L.	1	2	0	0	.000	2	2	1	4.50	0
World Series Totals	3	3	0	0	.000	3	2	1	3.00	0

a On disabled list from April 2 to August 1, 1987.
b On disabled list from March 30 to May 6, 1990.
c On disabled list from August 9 to August 24, 1991.
d Pitched first six innings of no-hit, no-run game completed by Mark Wohlers (7th and 8th innings) and Alejandro Pena (9th inning) against San Diego Padres, winning 1-0, September 11, 1991.
e Pitched no-hit, no-run game against Los Angeles Dodgers, winning 6-0, April 8, 1994.
f Declared restricted free agent under Major League Baseball implemented labor proposal, December 23, 1994.
g Re-signed with Atlanta Braves, April 27, 1995.
h Traded to Baltimore Orioles for pitcher Joe Borowski and Rachaad Stewart, December 17, 1995.
i Traded to Cleveland Indians for desigated hitter Eddie Murray, July 21, 1996.
j Filed for free agency, November 4, 1996.
k Signed with Cincinnati Reds, December 10, 1996.
l On disabled list from August 17 to September 1, 1997.
m Filed for free agency, October 27, 1997.
n Signed as free agent with St. Louis Cardinals, December 16, 1997.

MESA, JOSE RAMON
Born, Azua, Dominican Republic, May 22, 1966.
Bats Right. Throws Right. Height, 6 feet, 3 inches. Weight, 225 pounds.

Year	Club	Lea	G	IP	W	L	Pct	SO	BB	H	ERA	SAVES
1982 Bradenton Blue Jays	G.C.	13	83⅓	6	4	.600	40	20	58	2.70	1
1983 Florence	So. Atl.	28	141⅓	6	12	.333	91	93	153	5.48	0
1984 Florence	So. Atl.	7	38⅓	4	3	.571	35	25	38	3.76	0
1984 Kinston a	Carolina	10	50⅔	5	2	.714	24	28	51	3.91	0
1985 Kinston	Carolina	30	106⅓	5	10	.333	71	79	110	6.16	1
1986 Ventura	California	24	142⅓	10	6	.625	113	58	141	3.86	0
1986 Knoxville	Southern	9	41⅓	2	2	.500	30	23	40	4.35	0
1987 Knoxville b	Southern	35	*193⅓	10	*13	.435	115	104	*206	5.21	0
1987 Baltimore	A.L.	6	31⅓	1	3	.250	17	15	38	6.03	0
1988 Rochester c	Int.	11	15⅔	0	3	.000	15	14	21	8.62	0
1989 Hagerstown d	Eastern	3	13	0	0	.000	12	4	9	1.38	0
1989 Rochester	Int.	7	10	0	2	.000	3	6	10	5.40	0
1990 Hagerstown e	Eastern	15	79	5	5	.500	72	30	77	3.42	0
1990 Rochester	Int.	4	26	1	2	.333	23	12	21	2.42	0
1990 Baltimore	A.L.	7	46⅔	3	2	.600	24	27	37	3.86	0
1991 Rochester	Int.	8	51⅓	3	3	.500	48	30	37	3.86	0
1991 Baltimore f-g	A.L.	23	123⅔	6	11	.353	64	62	151	5.97	0
1992 Balt.-Cleveland h	A.L.	28	160⅔	7	12	.368	62	70	169	4.59	0
1993 Cleveland i	A.L.	34	208⅔	10	12	.455	118	62	232	4.92	0
1994 Cleveland	A.L.	51	73	7	5	.583	63	26	71	3.82	2
1995 Cleveland	A.L.	62	64	3	0	1.000	58	17	49	1.13	46
1996 Cleveland	A.L.	69	72⅓	2	7	.222	64	28	69	3.73	39
1997 Cleveland	A.L.	66	82⅓	4	4	.500	69	28	83	2.40	16
Major League Totals	9 Yrs.	346	862⅔	43	56	.434	539	335	899	4.28	103

Year	Club	Lea	G	IP	W	L	Pct	SO	BB	H	ERA	SAVES
	Division Series											
1995 Cleveland		.A.L.	2	2	0	0	.000	0	2	0	0.00	1
1996 Cleveland		.A.L.	2	4⅔	0	1	.000	7	0	8	3.86	0
1997 Cleveland		.A.L.	2	3⅓	0	0	.000	2	1	5	2.70	1
Division Series Totals		.6		10	0	1	.000	9	3	13	2.70	1
	Championship Series											
1995 Cleveland		.A.L.	4	4	0	0	.000	1	1	3	2.25	1
1997 Cleveland		.A.L.	4	5⅓	1	0	1.000	5	3	5	3.38	2
Championship Series Totals		.8		9⅓	1	0	1.000	6	4	8	2.89	3
	World Series Record											
1995 Cleveland		.A.L.	2	4	1	0	1.000	4	1	5	4.50	1
1997 Cleveland		.A.L.	5	5	0	0	.000	5	1	10	5.40	1
World Series Totals		.7		9	1	0	1.000	9	2	15	5.00	2

a On disabled list from August 27 to end of 1984 season.
b Traded by Toronto Blue Jays to Baltimore Orioles with pitcher Oswald Peraza for pitcher Mike Flanagan, August 31, 1987.
c On disabled list from June 29 to end of 1988 season.
d On disabled list from May 27 to end of 1989 season.
e On disabled list from April 6 to April 25, 1990.
f On disabled list from August 21 to September 6, 1991.
g Appeared in one additional game as pinch runner.
h Traded to Cleveland Indians for outfielder Kyle Washington, July 14, 1992.
i Suspended three games by American League for March 30 fight from April 5 to April 8, 1993.

MICELI, DANIEL
Born, Newark, New Jersey, September 9, 1970.
Bats Right. Throws Right. Height, 6 feet, 1 inch. Weight, 185 pounds.

Year	Club	Lea	G	IP	W	L	Pct	SO	BB	H	ERA	SAVES
1990 Baseball City Royals	. .Gulf C.	*27	53	3	4	.429	48	29	45	3.91	4
1991 Eugene	. . . . .Northwest	25	33⅔	0	1	.000	43	18	18	2.14	10
1992 Appleton	. . . . .Midwest	23	23⅓	1	1	.500	44	4	12	1.93	9
1992 Memphis	. . . . .Southern	32	37⅔	3	0	1.000	46	13	20	1.91	4
1993 Mem.-Carolina a	. . .Southern	53	71	6	6	.500	87	43	65	4.69	17
1993 Pittsburgh	. . . . .N.L.	9	5⅓	0	0	.000	4	3	6	5.06	0
1994 Buffalo	. . . . .A.A.	19	24	1	1	.500	31	6	15	1.88	2
1994 Pittsburgh	. . . . .N.L.	28	27⅓	2	1	.667	27	11	28	5.93	2
1995 Pittsburgh	. . . . .N.L.	58	58	4	4	.500	56	28	61	4.66	21
1996 Carolina	. . . . .Southern	3	9	1	0	1.000	17	1	4	1.00	1
1996 Pittsburgh b	. . . . .N.L.	44	85⅔	2	10	.167	66	45	99	5.78	1
1997 Detroit c	. . . . .N.L.	71	82⅔	3	2	.600	79	38	77	5.01	3
Major League Totals	. . . . . . .5 Yrs.	210	259	11	17	.393	232	125	271	5.28	27

a Traded by Kansas City Royals to Pittsburgh Pirates organization with pitcher Jon Lieber for pitcher Stan Belinda, July 31, 1993.
b Traded to Detroit Tigers for pitcher Clint Sodowsky, November 1, 1996.
c Traded to San Diego Padres with designated hitter Donne Wall and infielder Ryan Balfe for pitcher Tim Worrell and outfielder Trey Beamon, November 19, 1997.

MILLER, KURT EVERETT
Born, Tucson, Arizona, August 24, 1972.
Bats Right. Throws Right. Height, 6 feet, 5 inches. Weight, 205 pounds.

Year	Club	Lea	G	IP	W	L	Pct	SO	BB	H	ERA	SAVES
1990 Welland	. . . . .N.Y.-Penn.	14	65⅔	3	2	.600	62	37	59	3.29	0
1991 Augusta a-b	. . . . .So. Atl.	21	115⅓	6	7	.462	103	57	89	2.50	0
1992 Charlotte	. . . . .Fla. St.	12	75⅓	5	4	.556	58	29	51	2.39	0
1992 Tulsa	. . . . .Texas	16	88	7	5	.583	73	35	82	3.68	0
1993 Tulsa c	. . . . .Texas	18	96	6	8	.429	68	45	102	5.06	0
1993 Edmonton	. . . . .P.C.	9	48	3	3	.500	19	34	42	4.50	0
1994 Edmonton	. . . . .P.C.	23	125⅔	7	*13	.350	58	64	164	6.88	0
1994 Florida	. . . . .N.L.	4	20	1	3	.250	11	7	26	8.10	0
1996 Charlotte	. . . . .Int.	12	65⅔	3	5	.375	38	26	77	4.66	0
1996 Florida	. . . . .N.L.	26	46⅓	1	3	.250	30	33	57	6.80	0
1997 Brevard Cty	. . . . .Fla. St.	2	5	0	0	.000	7	2	6	1.80	0
1997 Charlotte	. . . . .Int.	21	27⅔	2	1	.667	31	22	25	3.58	0
1997 Florida d-e	. . . . .N.L.	7	7⅓	0	1	.000	7	7	12	9.82	0
Major League Totals	. . . . .3 Yrs.	37	73⅔	2	7	.222	48	47	95	7.45	0

a On disabled list from July 10 to August 3, 1991.
b Traded by Pittsburgh Pirates to Texas Rangers organization with player to be named for third baseman Steve Buechele, August 30; Texas organization acquired pitcher Hector Fajardo to complete trade, September 6, 1991.
c Traded by Texas Rangers to Florida Marlins with pitcher Robb Nen for pitcher Cris Carpenter, July 17, 1993.
d On disabled list from April 1 to September 1, 1997.
e Traded to Chicago Cubs for player to be named later, November 18, 1997.

MILLER, TRAVIS EUGENE
Born, Dayton, Ohio, November 2, 1972.
Bats Right. Throws Left. Height, 6 feet, 3 inches. Weight, 205 pounds.

Year	Club	Lea	G	IP	W	L	Pct	SO	BB	H	ERA	SAVES
1994	Fort Wayne	Midwest	11	55⅓	4	1	.800	50	12	52	2.60	0
1994	Nashville	Southern	1	6⅓	0	0	.000	4	2	3	2.84	0
1995	New Britain	Eastern	28	162⅔	7	9	.438	151	65	172	4.37	0
1996	Salt Lake	P.C.	27	160⅓	8	10	.444	143	57	187	4.83	0
1996	Minnesota	A.L.	7	26⅓	1	2	.333	15	9	45	9.23	0
1997	Salt Lake	P.C.	21	125⅔	10	6	.625	86	57	140	4.73	0
1997	Minnesota	A.L.	13	48⅓	1	5	.167	26	23	64	7.63	0
Major League Totals	2 Yrs.		20	74⅔	2	7	.222	41	32	109	8.20	0

MILLS, ALAN BERNARD
Born, Lakeland, Florida, October 18, 1966.
Bats Right. Throws Right. Height, 6 feet, 1 inch. Weight, 192 pounds.

Year	Club	Lea	G	IP	W	L	Pct	SO	BB	H	ERA	SAVES
1986	Salem a	Northwest	14	83⅔	6	6	.500	50	60	77	4.63	0
1987	Prince William	Carolina	35	85⅔	2	11	.154	53	54	102	6.09	1
1988	Prince William	Carolina	42	93⅔	3	8	.273	59	43	93	4.13	4
1989	Ft. Lauderdale	Fla. St.	22	31	1	4	.200	25	9	40	3.77	6
1989	Prince William	Carolina	26	39⅔	6	1	.857	44	13	22	0.91	7
1990	Columbus	Int.	17	29⅓	3	3	.500	30	14	22	3.38	6
1990	New York	A.L.	36	41⅓	1	5	.167	24	33	48	4.10	0
1991	Columbus	Int.	38	113⅔	7	5	.583	77	75	109	4.43	8
1991	New York b	A.L.	6	16⅓	1	1	.500	11	8	16	4.41	0
1992	Rochester	Int.	3	5	0	1	.000	8	2	6	5.40	1
1992	Baltimore	A.L.	35	103⅓	10	4	.714	60	54	78	2.61	2
1993	Baltimore c	A.L.	45	100⅓	5	4	.556	68	51	80	3.23	4
1994	Baltimore	A.L.	47	45⅓	3	3	.500	44	24	43	5.16	2
1995	Rochester	Int.	1	2⅔	0	1	.000	2	5	2	0.00	0
1995	Orioles	Gulf Coast	1	2	0	0	.000	1	2	3	0.00	0
1995	Baltimore	A.L.	21	23	3	0	1.000	16	18	30	7.43	0
1996	Baltimore d	A.L.	49	54⅔	3	2	.600	50	35	40	4.28	3
1997	Baltimore e	A.L.	39	38⅔	2	3	.400	32	33	41	4.89	0
Major League Totals	8 Yrs.		278	423⅓	28	22	.560	305	256	376	3.93	11
Division Series												
1997	Baltimore	A.L.	1	1	0	0	.000	1	0	1	0.00	0
Championship Series												
1996	Baltimore	A.L.	3	2⅓	0	0	.000	3	1	3	3.86	0
1997	Baltimore	A.L.	3	3⅓	0	1	.000	3	2	1	2.70	0
Championship Series Totals	6			5⅔	0	1	.000	6	3	4	3.18	0

a Traded by California Angels to New York Yankees organization to complete December 19, 1986 trade in which New York acquired pitcher Ron Romanick and player to be named for catcher Butch Wynegar, June 22, 1987.
b Traded to Baltimore Orioles for two players to be named, February 29; New York Yankees acquired pitchers Francisco de la Rosa, March 5, and Mark Carper to complete trade, June 8, 1992.
c Suspended four games by American League for June 6 fight from June 26 to June 29, 1993.
d On disabled list from April 1 to May 11, 1996.
e On disabled list from April 10 to June 15, 1997.

MILLWOOD, KEVIN AUSTIN
Born, Gastonia, North Carolina, December 24, 1974.
Bats Right. Throws Right. Height, 6 feet, 4 inches. Weight, 205 pounds.

Year	Club	Lea	G	IP	W	L	Pct	SO	BB	H	ERA	SAVES
1993	Braves	Gulf Coast	12	50	3	3	.500	49	28	36	3.06	0
1994	Macon	So. Atl.	12	32⅔	0	5	.000	24	32	31	5.79	1
1994	Danville	Appal.	13	46	3	3	.500	56	34	42	3.72	1

Year	Club	Lea	G	IP	W	L	Pct	SO	BB	H	ERA	SAVES
1995 Macon ....So. Atl.			29	103	5	6	.455	89	57	86	4.63	0
1996 Durham ....Carolina			33	149⅓	6	9	.400	139	58	138	4.28	1
1997 Greenville ....Southern			11	61⅓	3	5	.375	61	24	59	4.11	0
1997 Richmond ....Int.			9	60⅔	7	0	1.000	46	16	38	1.93	0
1997 Atlanta ...............N.L.			12	51⅓	5	3	.625	42	21	55	4.03	0

MIMBS, MICHAEL RANDALL (MIKE)
Born, Macon, Georgia, February 13, 1969.
Bats Left. Throws Left. Height, 6 feet, 2 inches. Weight, 180 pounds.

Year	Club	Lea	G	IP	W	L	Pct	SO	BB	H	ERA	SAVES
1990 Great Falls ....Pioneer			3	6⅔	0	0	.000	7	5	4	4.05	0
1990 Yakima ....Northwest			12	67⅓	4	3	.571	72	39	59	3.88	0
1991 Vero Beach ....Fla. St.			24	141⅔	12	4	.750	132	70	124	2.67	0
1992 San Antonio ....Texas			24	129⅔	10	8	.556	87	73	132	4.23	1
1993 St. Paul ....Northern			20	98⅓	8	2	.800	97	45	94	3.20	0
1994 Harrisburg ....Eastern			32	153⅔	11	4	.733	145	61	130	3.46	0
1995 Philadelphia .........N.L.			35	136⅔	9	7	.563	93	75	127	4.15	1
1996 Scranton-WB ....Int.			7	29	2	1	.667	20	5	27	2.48	0
1996 Philadelphia a ...........N.L.			21	99⅓	3	9	.250	56	41	116	5.53	0
1997 Philadelphia ...........N.L.			17	28⅔	0	3	.000	29	27	31	7.53	0
1997 Scranton-WB ....Int.			11	43⅔	4	2	.667	41	20	52	5.98	0
Major League Totals ....3 Yrs.			73	264⅔	12	19	.387	178	143	274	5.03	1

a On disabled list from August 7 to September 2, 1996.

MINOR, BLAS
Born, Merced, California, March 20, 1966.
Bats Right. Throws Right. Height, 6 feet, 3 inches. Weight, 203 pounds.

Year	Club	Lea	G	IP	W	L	Pct	SO	BB	H	ERA	SAVES
1988 Princeton ....Appal.			15	16⅓	0	1	.000	23	5	18	4.41	7
1989 Salem ....Carolina			39	86⅔	3	5	.375	62	31	91	3.63	0
1990 Harrisburg ....Eastern			38	94	6	4	.600	98	29	81	3.06	5
1990 Buffalo ...............A.A.			1	2⅔	0	1	.000	2	2	2	3.38	0
1991 Buffalo a ...............A.A.			17	36	2	2	.500	25	15	46	5.75	0
1991 Carolina ....Southern			3	12⅔	0	0	.000	18	7	9	2.84	0
1992 Buffalo ...............A.A.			45	96⅓	5	4	.556	60	26	72	2.43	18
1992 Pittsburgh ...........N.L.			1	2	0	0	.000	0	0	3	4.50	0
1993 Pittsburgh ...........N.L.			65	94⅓	8	6	.571	84	26	94	4.10	2
1994 Buffalo ...............A.A.			33	51⅓	1	2	.333	61	12	47	2.98	11
1994 Pittsburgh b ...........N.L.			17	19	0	1	.000	17	9	27	8.05	1
1995 New York c ...........N.L.			35	46⅔	4	2	.667	43	13	44	3.66	1
1996 New York ...........N.L.			17	25⅔	0	0	.000	20	6	23	3.51	0
1996 Seattle d ...........A.L.			11	25⅓	0	1	.000	14	11	27	4.97	0
1996 Tacoma ...............P.C.			7	9⅔	1	2	.333	8	3	15	8.38	1
1997 New Orleans ...........A.A.			23	31⅔	3	3	.500	27	9	20	2.27	6
1997 Houston e ...........N.L.			11	12	1	0	1.000	6	5	13	4.50	1
1997 Tucson ...............P.C.			12	29	2	2	.500	21	15	36	4.03	1
Major League Totals ....6 Yrs.			157	225	13	10	.565	184	70	231	4.40	5

a On disabled list from June 8 to June 24 and June 28 to August 12, 1991.
b Claimed on waivers by New York Mets from Pittsburgh Pirates, November 4, 1994.
c On disabled list from July 24 to August 24, 1995.
d Traded to Seattle Mariners for infielder Randy Vickers, June 9, 1996.
e Signed with Houston Astros, July 17, 1997.

MLICKI, DAVID JOHN
Born, Cleveland, Ohio, June 8, 1968.
Bats Right. Throws Right. Height, 6 feet, 4 inches. Weight, 190 pounds.

Year	Club	Lea	G	IP	W	L	Pct	SO	BB	H	ERA	SAVES
1990 Burlington ....Appal.			8	18	3	1	.750	17	6	16	3.50	0
1990 Watertown .......N.Y.-Penn.			7	32	3	0	1.000	28	11	33	3.38	0
1991 Columbus ....So. Atl.			22	115⅔	8	6	.571	136	70	101	4.20	0
1992 Canton ....Eastern			27	172⅔	11	9	.550	146	80	143	3.60	0
1992 Cleveland ..............A.L.			4	21⅔	0	2	.000	16	16	23	4.98	0
1993 Canton a ....Eastern			6	23	2	1	.667	21	8	15	0.39	0

Year Club	Lea	G	IP	W	L	Pct	SO	BB	H	ERA	SAVES
1993 Cleveland	A.L.	3	13⅓	0	0	.000	7	6	11	3.38	0
1994 Charlotte b	Int.	28	165⅓	6	10	.375	152	64	179	4.25	0
1995 New York	N.L.	29	160⅔	9	7	.563	123	54	160	4.26	0
1996 New York	N.L.	51	90	6	7	.462	83	33	95	3.30	1
1997 New York	N.L.	32	193⅔	8	12	.400	157	76	194	4.00	0
Major League Totals	5 Yrs.	119	479⅓	23	28	.451	386	185	483	3.98	1

a On disabled list from April 4 to August 4, 1993.
b Traded by Cleveland Indians to New York Mets with pitchers Jerry DiPoto and Paul Byrd and player to be named for outfielder Jeremy Burnitz and pitcher Joe Roa, November 18; New York organization acquired second baseman Jesus Azuaje to complete trade, December 6, 1994.

MOEHLER, BRIAN MERRITT

Born, Rockingham, North Carolina, December 31, 1971.
Bats Right. Throws Right. Height, 6 feet, 3 inches. Weight, 225 pounds.

Year Club	Lea	G	IP	W	L	Pct	SO	BB	H	ERA	SAVES
1993 Niagara Fls	N.Y.-Penn.	12	58⅔	6	5	.545	38	27	51	3.22	0
1994 Lakeland	Fla. St.	26	164⅔	12	12	.500	92	65	153	3.01	0
1995 Jacksnville	Southern	28	162⅓	8	10	.444	89	52	176	4.82	0
1996 Jacksnville	Southern	28	173⅓	15	6	.714	120	50	186	3.48	0
1996 Detroit	A.L.	2	10⅓	0	1	.000	2	8	11	4.35	0
1997 Detroit a	A.L.	31	175⅓	11	12	.478	97	61	198	4.67	0
Major League Totals	2 Yrs.	33	185⅔	11	13	.458	99	69	209	4.65	0

a On disabled list from August 7 to August 22, 1997.

MOHLER, MICHAEL ROSS

Born, Dayton, Ohio, July 26, 1968.
Bats Right. Throws Left. Height, 6 feet, 2 inches. Weight, 195 pounds.

Year Club	Lea	G	IP	W	L	Pct	SO	BB	H	ERA	SAVES
1990 Madison	Midwest	42	63⅓	1	1	.500	72	32	56	3.41	1
1991 Modesto	California	21	122⅔	9	4	.692	98	45	106	2.86	0
1991 Huntsville	Southern	8	53	4	2	.667	27	20	55	3.57	0
1992 Huntsville	Southern	44	80⅓	3	8	.273	56	39	72	3.59	3
1993 Oakland	A.L.	42	64⅓	1	6	.143	42	44	57	5.60	0
1994 Modesto	California	7	29⅓	1	1	.500	29	6	21	2.76	1
1994 Tacoma	P.C.	17	63⅔	1	3	.250	50	21	66	3.53	0
1994 Oakland	A.L.	1	2⅓	0	1	.000	4	2	2	7.71	0
1995 Edmonton	P.C.	29	45	2	1	.667	28	20	40	2.60	5
1995 Oakland	A.L.	28	23⅔	1	1	.500	15	18	16	3.04	1
1996 Oakland	A.L.	72	81	6	3	.667	64	41	79	3.67	7
1997 Oakland	A.L.	62	101⅔	1	10	.091	66	54	116	5.13	1
Major League Totals	5 Yrs.	205	273	9	21	.300	191	159	270	4.65	9

MONTGOMERY, JEFFREY THOMAS (JEFF)

Born, Wellston, Ohio, January 7, 1962.
Bats Right. Throws Right. Height, 5 feet, 11 inches. Weight, 180 pounds.

Year Club	Lea	G	IP	W	L	Pct	SO	BB	H	ERA	SAVES
1983 Billings	Pioneer	20	44⅔	6	2	.750	90	13	31	2.42	5
1984 Tampa	Fla. St.	31	44⅓	5	3	.625	56	30	29	2.44	*14
1984 Vermont	Eastern	22	25⅓	2	0	1.000	20	24	14	2.13	4
1985 Vermont	Eastern	*53	101	5	3	.625	89	48	63	2.05	9
1986 Denver	A.A.	30	151⅔	11	7	.611	78	57	162	4.39	1
1987 Nashville	A.A.	24	139	8	5	.615	121	51	132	4.14	0
1987 Cincinnati a	N.L.	14	19⅓	2	2	.500	13	9	25	6.52	0
1988 Omaha	A.A.	20	28⅓	1	2	.333	36	11	15	1.91	13
1988 Kansas City	A.L.	45	62⅔	7	2	.778	47	30	54	3.45	1
1989 Kansas City	A.L.	63	92	7	3	.700	94	25	66	1.37	18
1990 Kansas City	A.L.	73	94⅓	6	5	.545	94	34	81	2.39	24
1991 Kansas City	A.L.	67	90	4	4	.500	77	28	83	2.90	33
1992 Kansas City	A.L.	65	82⅔	1	6	.143	69	27	61	2.18	39
1993 Kansas City	A.L.	69	87⅓	7	5	.583	66	23	65	2.27	*45
1994 Kansas City	A.L.	42	44⅔	2	3	.400	50	15	48	4.03	27
1995 Kansas City b-c	A.L.	54	65⅔	2	3	.400	49	25	60	3.43	31
1996 Kansas City	A.L.	48	63⅓	4	6	.400	45	19	59	4.26	24

Year Club	Lea	G	IP	W	L	Pct	SO	BB	H	ERA	SAVES
1997 Omaha	A.A.	2	2	0	0	.000	2	1	1	0.00	0
1997 Kansas City d	A.L.	55	59⅓	1	4	.200	48	18	53	3.49	14
Major League Totals ....11 Yrs.		595	761⅓	43	43	.500	652	253	655	2.91	256

a Traded to Kansas City Royals for outfielder Van Snider, February 13, 1988.
b Filed for free agency, November 12, 1995.
c Re-signed with Kansas City Royals, December 15, 1995.
d On disabled list from April 18 to May 3, 1997.

MOREL, RAMON RAFAEL
Born, Villa Gonzalez, Dominican Republic, August 15, 1974.
Bats Right. Throws Right. Height, 6 feet, 2 inches. Weight, 175 pounds.

Year Club	Lea	G	IP	W	L	Pct	SO	BB	H	ERA	SAVES
1992 Pirates	Gulf Coast	14	45⅔	2	2	.500	29	11	49	4.34	0
1993 Welland	N.Y.-Penn.	16	77	7	8	.467	51	21	90	4.21	0
1994 Augusta	So. Atl.	28	168⅔	10	7	.588	152	24	157	2.83	0
1995 Lynchburg	Carolina	12	72⅔	3	7	.300	44	13	80	3.47	0
1995 Carolina	Southern	10	69	3	3	.500	34	10	71	3.52	0
1995 Pittsburgh	N.L.	5	6⅓	0	1	.000	3	2	6	2.84	0
1996 Carolina	Southern	11	63⅔	2	5	.286	44	16	75	5.09	0
1996 Pittsburgh	N.L.	29	42	2	1	.667	22	19	57	5.36	0
1997 Calgary	P.C.	27	101⅔	6	7	.462	72	42	131	5.75	0
1997 Pittsburgh-Chicago a	N.L.	8	11⅓	0	0	.000	7	7	14	4.77	0
Major League Totals ....3 Yrs.		42	59⅔	2	2	.500	32	28	77	4.98	0

a Claimed on waivers by Chicago Cubs, September 11, 1997.

MORGAN, MICHAEL THOMAS (MIKE)
Born, Tulare, California, October 8, 1959.
Bats Right. Throws Right. Height, 6 feet, 2 inches. Weight, 220 pounds.

Year Club	Lea	G	IP	W	L	Pct	SO	BB	H	ERA	SAVES
1978 Oakland	A.L.	3	12	0	3	.000	0	8	19	7.50	0
1978 Vancouver	P.C.	14	92	5	6	.455	31	54	109	5.58	0
1979 Ogden	P.C.	13	101	5	5	.500	42	49	93	3.48	0
1979 Oakland	A.L.	13	77	2	10	.167	17	50	102	5.96	0
1980 Ogden a-b	P.C.	20	115	6	9	.400	46	77	135	5.40	0
1981 Nashville c	Southern	26	169	8	7	.533	100	83	164	4.42	0
1982 New York d	A.L.	30	150⅓	7	11	.389	71	67	167	4.37	0
1983 Toronto e	A.L.	16	45⅓	0	3	.000	22	21	48	5.16	0
1983 Syracuse	Int.	5	19	0	3	.000	17	13	20	5.59	1
1984 Syracuse f	Int.	34	*185⅔	13	11	.542	105	*100	167	4.07	1
1985 Seattle g	A.L.	2	6	1	1	.500	2	5	11	12.00	0
1985 Calgary	P.C.	1	2	0	0	.000	0	0	3	4.50	0
1986 Seattle	A.L.	37	216⅓	11	*17	.393	116	86	243	4.53	1
1987 Seattle h	A.L.	34	207	12	17	.414	85	53	245	4.65	0
1988 Rochester	Int.	3	17	0	2	.000	7	6	19	4.76	0
1988 Baltimore i-j	A.L.	22	71⅓	1	6	.143	29	23	70	5.43	1
1989 Los Angeles	N.L.	40	152⅔	8	11	.421	72	33	130	2.53	0
1990 Los Angeles	N.L.	33	211	11	15	.423	106	60	216	3.75	0
1991 Los Angeles k	N.L.	34	236⅓	14	10	.583	140	61	197	2.78	1
1992 Chicago	N.L.	34	240	16	8	.667	123	79	203	2.55	0
1993 Chicago l	N.L.	32	207⅔	10	15	.400	111	74	206	4.03	0
1994 Chicago m	N.L.	15	80⅔	2	10	.167	57	35	111	6.69	0
1995 Orlando	Southern	2	10⅔	0	2	.000	5	7	13	7.59	0
1995 Chicago-St. Louis n-o-p	N.L.	21	131⅓	7	7	.500	61	34	133	3.56	0
1996 St. Petersburg	Fla. St.	1	5⅔	1	0	1.000	4	1	4	0.00	0
1996 Louisville	A.A.	4	23	1	3	.250	10	11	29	7.04	0
1996 St. Louis-Cincinnati q-r-s	N.L.	23	130⅓	6	11	.353	74	47	146	4.62	0
1997 Cincinnati t-u-v	N.L.	31	162	9	12	.429	103	49	165	4.78	0
Major League Totals ....17 Yrs.		420	2338	117	167	.412	1189	785	2412	4.07	3

a On disabled list from May 14 to June 27, 1980.
b Traded by Oakland Athletics to New York Yankees organization for infielder Fred Stanley and Brian Doyle, November 3, 1980.
c On disabled list from April 9 to April 22, 1981.
d Traded to Toronto Blue Jays with infielder Fred McGriff and outfielder Dave Collins for pitcher Dale Murray and outfielder Tom Dodd, December 9, 1982.
e On disabled list from July 2 to August 23, 1983.
f Drafted by the Seattle Mariners from Toronto Blue Jays organization, December 3, 1984.

g On disabled list from April 17 to end of 1985 season.
h Traded to Baltimore Orioles for pitcher Ken Dixon, December 9, 1987.
i On disabled list from June 9 to July 19 and from August 12 to end of 1988 season.
j Traded to Los Angeles Dodgers for outfielder Mike Devereaux, March 13, 1989.
k Filed for free agency, October 28; signed with Chicago Cubs, December 3, 1991.
l On disabled list from June 14 to June 29, 1993.
m On disabled list from May 9 to May 25, June 5 to June 22, and July 28 to end of 1994 season.
n On disabled list from April 25 to May 25 and July 4 to July 24, 1995.
o Traded to St. Louis Cardinals with infielder Paul Torres and catcher Francisco Morales for infielder Todd Zeile, June 16, 1995.
p Filed for free agency, November 12, 1995; re-signed with St. Louis Cardinals, December 7, 1995.
q On disabled list from April 1 to May 18, 1996.
r Released by St. Louis Cardinals, August 28, 1996.
s Signed with Cincinnati Reds, September 3, 1996.
  On disabled list from June 8 to June 24, 1997.
u Filed for free agency, October 28, 1997.
v Signed as free agent by Minnesota Twins, December 15, 1997.

MORMAN, ALVIN
Born, Rockingham, North Carolina, January 6, 1969.
Bats Left. Throws Left. Height, 6 feet, 3 inches. Weight, 210 pounds.

Year	Club	Lea	G	IP	W	L	Pct	SO	BB	H	ERA	SAVES
1991 Astros	.........Gulf Coast		11	16⅔	1	0	1.000	24	5	15	2.16	1
1991 Osceola	...........Fla. St.		3	6	0	0	.000	3	2	5	1.50	0
1992 Asheville	..........So. Atl.		57	75⅓	8	0	1.000	70	26	60	1.55	15
1993 Jackson	.............Texas		19	97⅓	8	2	.800	101	28	77	2.96	0
1994 Tucson	...............P.C.		58	74	3	7	.300	49	26	84	5.11	5
1995 Tucson	...............P.C.		45	48⅓	5	1	.833	36	20	50	3.91	3
1996 Houston	...............N.L.		53	42	4	1	.800	31	24	43	4.93	0
1997 New Orleans a	........A.A.		8	10	0	1	.000	14	2	11	4.50	0
1997 Buffalo	...............A.A.		3	3⅓	0	0	.000.	3	0	2	0.00	0
1997 Cleveland b	...........A.L.		34	18⅓	0	0	.000	13	14	19	5.89	2
Major League Totals	........2 Yrs.		87	60⅓	4	1	.800	44	38	62	5.22	2
Division Series												
1997 Cleveland	.............A.L.		1	0	0	0	.000	0	1	0	INF	0
Championship Series												
1997 Cleveland	.............A.L.		2	1⅓	0	0	.000	1	0	0	0.00	0
World Series Record												
1997 Cleveland	.............A.L.		2	0⅓	0	0	.000	1	2	0	0.00	0

a Traded to Cleveland Indians for pitcher Jose Cabrera, May 9, 1997.
b On disabled list from July 29 to September 1, 1997.

MORRIS, MATTHEW CHRISTIAN
Born, Middletown, New York, August 9, 1994.
Bats Right. Throws Right. Height, 6 feet, 5 inches. Weight, 210 pounds.

Year	Club	Lea	G	IP	W	L	Pct	SO	BB	H	ERA	SAVES
1995 New Jersey	......N.Y.-Penn.		2	11	2	0	1.000	13	3	12	1.64	0
1995 St. Petersburg	.......Fla. St.		6	34	3	2	.600	31	11	22	2.38	0
1996 Arkansas	............Texas		27	167	12	12	.500	120	48	178	3.88	0
1996 Louisville	...............A.A.		1	8	0	1	.00	9	1	8	3.38	0
1997 St. Louis	.............N.L.		33	217	12	9	.571	149	69	208	3.19	0

MOYER, JAMIE
Born, Sellersville, Pennsylvania, November 18, 1962.
Bats Left. Throws Left. Height, 6 feet. Weight, 170 pounds.

Year	Club	Lea	G	IP	W	L	Pct	SO	BB	H	ERA	SAVES
1984 Geneva	..........N.Y.-Penn.		14	*104⅔	*9	3	.750	*120	31	59	1.89	0
1985 Winston-Salem	.....Carolina		12	94	8	2	.800	94	22	82	2.30	0
1985 Pittsfield	...........Eastern		15	96⅔	7	6	.538	51	32	99	3.72	0
1986 Pittsfield	...........Eastern		6	41	3	1	.750	42	16	27	0.88	0
1986 Iowa	.................A.A.		6	42⅓	3	2	.600	25	11	25	2.55	0
1986 Chicago	..............N.L.		16	87⅓	7	4	.636	45	42	107	5.05	0
1987 Chicago	..............N.L.		35	201	12	15	.444	147	97	210	5.10	0
1988 Chicago a	............N.L.		34	202	9	15	.375	121	55	212	3.48	0
1989 Charlotte Rangers	....Gulf C.		3	11	1	0	1.000	18	1	8	1.64	0
1989 Tulsa	................Texas		2	12⅓	1	1	.500	9	3	16	5.11	0

Year	Club	Lea	G	IP	W	L	Pct	SO	BB	H	ERA	SAVES
1989 Texas b	A.L.	15	76	4	9	.308	44	33	84	4.86	0
1990 Texas c	A.L.	33	102⅓	2	6	.250	58	39	115	4.66	0
1991 Louisville	A.A.	20	125⅔	5	10	.333	69	43	125	3.80	0
1991 St. Louis d-e	N.L.	8	31⅓	0	5	.000	20	16	38	5.74	0
1992 Toledo f	Int.	21	138⅔	10	8	.556	80	37	128	2.86	0
1993 Rochester	Int.	8	54	6	0	1.000	41	13	42	1.67	0
1993 Baltimore	A.L.	25	152	12	9	.571	90	38	154	3.43	0
1994 Baltimore	A.L.	23	149	5	7	.417	87	38	158	4.77	0
1995 Baltimore g-h	A.L.	27	115⅔	8	6	.571	65	30	117	5.21	0
1996 Boston-Seattle i-j-k	A.L.	34	160⅓	13	8	.813	79	46	177	3.98	0
1997 Tacoma	P.C.	1	5	1	0	1.000	6	0	1	0.00	0
1997 Seattle l	A.L.	30	188⅔	17	5	.773	113	43	187	3.86	0
Major League Totals	11 Yrs.	280	1466	89	84	.514	869	477	1559	4.36	0
Divisional Series											
1997 Seattle	A.L.	1	4⅔	0	1	.000	2	1	5	5.79	0

a Traded to Texas Rangers with outfielder Rafael Palmeiro and pitcher Drew Hall for infielders Curtis Wilkerson and Luis Benetiz, pitchers Mitch Williams, Paul Kilgus and Steve Wilson, and outfielder Pablo Delgado, December 5, 1988.
b On disabled list from May 31 to September 1, 1989.
c Released, November 13, 1990; signed with St. Louis Cardinals organization, January 10, 1991.
d Became free agent, October 15, 1991; signed with Chicago Cubs organization, January 8, 1992.
e Released by Chicago Cubs, March 30; signed with Detroit Tigers organization, May 24, 1992.
f Became free agent, October 15; signed with Baltimore Orioles organization, December 19, 1992.
g Filed for free agency, November 12, 1995.
h Re-signed with Baltimore Orioles, December 23, 1995.
i Traded to Seattle Mariners for outfielder Darren Bragg, July 30, 1996.
j Filed for free agency, October 29, 1996.
k Re-signed with Seattle Mariners, November 20, 1996.
l On disabled list from April 1 to April 29, 1997.

MULHOLLAND, TERENCE JOHN (TERRY)

Born, Uniontown, Pennsylvania, March 9, 1963.
Bats Right. Throws Left. Height, 6 feet, 3 inches. Weight, 215 pounds.

Year	Club	Lea	G	IP	W	L	Pct	SO	BB	H	ERA	SAVES
1984 Everett	Northwest	3	19	1	0	1.000	15	4	10	0.00	0
1984 Fresno	California	9	42⅔	5	2	.714	39	36	32	2.95	0
1985 Shreveport	Texas	26	176⅔	9	8	.529	122	87	166	2.90	0
1986 Phoenix	P.C.	17	111	8	5	.615	77	56	112	4.46	0
1986 San Francisco	N.L.	15	54⅔	1	7	.125	27	35	51	4.94	0
1987 Phoenix	P.C.	37	171⅓	7	12	.368	94	90	200	5.07	1
1988 Phoenix	P.C.	19	100⅔	7	3	.700	57	44	116	3.58	0
1988 San Francisco a	N.L.	9	46	2	1	.667	18	7	50	3.72	0
1989 Phoenix	P.C.	13	78⅓	4	5	.444	61	26	67	2.99	0
1989 S.F.-Philadelphia b	N.L.	25	115⅓	4	7	.364	66	36	137	4.92	0
1990 Scranton	Int.	1	6	0	1	.000	2	2	9	3.00	0
1990 Philadelphia c-d	N.L.	33	180⅔	9	10	.474	75	42	172	3.34	0
1991 Philadelphia e	N.L.	34	232	16	13	.552	142	49	231	3.61	0
1992 Philadelphia	N.L.	32	229	13	11	.542	125	46	227	3.81	0
1993 Philadelphia f	N.L.	29	191	12	9	.571	116	40	177	3.25	0
1994 New York f-g	A.L.	24	120⅔	6	7	.462	72	37	150	6.49	0
1995 Phoenix	P.C.	1	4	0	0	.000	4	1	4	2.25	0
1995 San Francisco h-i-j	N.L.	29	149	5	13	.278	65	38	190	5.80	0
1996 Philadelphia	N.L.	21	133⅓	8	7	.533	52	21	157	4.66	0
1996 Seattle k-m	A.L.	12	69⅓	5	4	.556	34	28	75	4.67	0
1997 Chicago-San Francisco n-o	N.L.	40	186⅔	6	13	.316	99	51	190	4.24	0
Major League Totals	11 Yrs.	303	1707⅔	87	102	.460	891	430	1807	4.29	0
Championship Series											
1993 Philadelphia	N.L.	1	5	0	1	.000	2	1	9	7.20	0
World Series Record											
1993 Philadelphia	N.L.	2	10⅔	1	0	1.000	5	3	14	6.75	0

a On disabled list from August 1 to end of 1988 season.
b Traded to Philadelphia Phillies with pitcher Dennis Cook and infielder Charlie Hayes for pitcher Steve Bedrosian and player to be named, June 18; San Francisco Giants acquired infielder Rich Parker to complete trade, August 6, 1989.
c On disabled list from June 9 to June 28, 1990.
d Pitched no-hit, no-run game against San Francisco Giants, winning 6-0, August 15, 1990.
e Appeared in one additional game as pinch runner.
f Traded to New York Yankees with player to be named for pitchers Bobby Munoz and Ryan Karp and infielder Kevin Jordan, February 9; New York acquired pitcher Jeff Patterson to complete trade, November 8, 1994.
g Filed for free agency, October 27, 1994.

h Signed with San Francisco Giants, April 8, 1995.
i On disabled list from June 6 to July 4, 1995.
j Filed for free agency, November 12, 1995.
k Traded to Seattle Mariners for infielder Desi Relaford, July 31, 1996.
l Filed for free agency, October 28, 1996.
m Signed with Chicago Cubs, December 9, 1996.
n Claimed on waivers by San Francisco Giants, August 8, 1997.
o Filed for free agency, October 27, 1997.

MUNOZ, MICHAEL ANTHONY

Born, Baldwin Park, California, July 12, 1965.
Bats Left. Throws Left. Height, 6 feet, 3 inches. Weight, 200 pounds.

Year	Club	Lea	G	IP	W	L	Pct	SO	BB	H	ERA	SAVES
1986	Great Falls	Pioneer	14	18⅓	4	4	.500	49	38	85	3.21	0
1987	Bakersfield	California	52	118	8	7	.533	80	43	125	3.74	9
1988	San Antonio	Texas	56	71⅔	7	2	.778	71	24	63	1.00	14
1989	Albuquerque	P.C.	60	79	6	4	.600	81	40	72	3.08	6
1989	Los Angeles	N.L.	3	2⅔	0	0	.000	3	2	5	16.88	0
1990	Albuquerque	P.C.	49	59⅓	4	1	.800	40	19	65	4.25	6
1990	Los Angeles a	N.L.	8	5⅔	0	1	.000	2	3	6	3.18	0
1991	Toledo	Int.	38	54	2	3	.400	38	35	44	3.83	8
1991	Detroit	A.L.	6	9⅓	0	0	.000	3	5	14	9.64	0
1992	Detroit	A.L.	65	48	1	2	.333	23	25	44	3.00	2
1993	Detroit b	A.L.	8	3	0	1	.000	1	6	4	6.00	0
1993	Colorado Springs	P.C.	40	37⅔	1	2	.333	30	9	46	1.67	3
1993	Colorado	N.L.	21	18	2	1	.667	16	9	21	4.50	0
1994	Colorado	N.L.	57	45⅔	4	2	.667	32	31	37	3.74	1
1995	Colorado	N.L.	64	43⅔	2	4	.333	37	27	54	7.42	2
1996	Colo Sprngs	P.C.	10	13⅓	1	1	.500	13	6	8	2.03	3
1996	Colorado c	N.L.	54	44⅔	2	2	.500	45	16	55	6.65	0
1997	Colorado d-e	N.L.	64	45⅔	3	3	.500	26	13	52	4.53	2
Major League Totals	9 Yrs.		350	266⅓	14	16	.467	188	137	292	5.24	7
Division Series												
1995	Colorado	N.L.	4	1⅓	0	1	.000	1	1	4	13.50	0

a Traded to Detroit Tigers for pitcher Mike Wilkins, October 1, 1990.
b Refused assignment to minor leagues and became free agent, May 11; signed with Colorado Rockies organization, May 14, 1993.
c On disabled list from July 27 to August 15, 1996.
d Filed for free agency, October 27, 1997.
e Re-signed with Colorado Rockies, December 20, 1997.

MUNOZ, ROBERTO (BOBBY)

Born, Rio Piedras, Puerto Rico, March 3, 1968.
Bats Right. Throws Right. Height, 6 feet, 7 inches. Weight, 237 pounds.

Year	Club	Lea	G	IP	W	L	Pct	SO	BB	H	ERA	SAVES
1989	Sarasota Yankees	Gulf C.	2	10⅓	1	1	.500	13	4	5	3.48	0
1989	Fort Lauderdale	Fla. St.	3	13⅓	1	2	.333	2	7	16	4.72	0
1990	Greensboro	So. Atl.	25	132⅔	5	12	.294	100	58	133	3.73	0
1991	Fort Lauderdale	Fla. St.	19	108	5	8	.385	53	40	91	2.33	0
1991	Columbus	Int.	1	3	0	1	.000	2	3	8	24.00	0
1992	Albany	Eastern	22	112⅓	7	5	.583	66	70	96	3.28	0
1993	Columbus	Int.	22	31⅓	3	1	.750	16	8	24	1.44	10
1993	New York a	A.L.	38	45⅔	3	3	.500	33	26	48	5.32	0
1994	Scranton	Int.	6	34	2	3	.400	24	14	27	2.12	0
1994	Philadelphia	N.L.	21	104⅓	7	5	.583	59	35	101	2.67	1
1995	Reading	Eastern	4	15	0	4	.000	8	3	28	10.80	0
1995	Scranton-Wilkes Barre	Int.	2	16	1	0	1.000	10	3	8	0.56	0
1995	Philadelphia b	N.L.	3	15⅔	0	2	.000	6	9	15	5.74	0
1996	Clearwater	Fla. St.	2	14	1	1	.500	7	2	15	1.93	0
1996	Scranton-WB	Int.	8	50⅔	4	2	.667	34	7	50	3.91	0
1996	Reading	Eastern	4	27⅔	0	1	.000	29	8	24	2.93	0
1996	Philadelphia c	N.L.	8	25⅓	0	3	.000	8	7	42	7.82	0
1997	Philadelphia d	N.L.	8	33⅓	1	5	.167	20	15	47	8.91	0
1997	Las Vegas e	P.C.	17	22⅔	0	2	.000	13	11	30	9.93	0
1997	Albuquerque	P.C.	18	31	0	3	.000	20	15	43	4.35	0
Major League Totals	5 Yrs.		76	224⅓	11	18	.379	126	92	253	4.93	1

a Traded to Philadelphia Phillies with pitcher Ryan Karp and infielder Kevin Jordan for pitcher Terry Mulholland and player to be named, February 9; New York Yankees acquired pitcher Jeff Patterson to complete trade, November 8, 1994.
b On disabled list from April 25 to July 22 and August 3 to October 2, 1995.
c On disabled list from April 1 to June 11 and June 17 to July 22 and August 8 to September 30, 1996.
d Released by Philadelphia Phillies, May 19, 1997.
e Signed with San Diego Padres organization, May 19, 1997.

MURRAY, HEATH ROBERTSON

Born, Troy, Ohio, April 19, 1973.
Bats Left. Throws Left. Height, 6 feet, 4 inches. Weight, 205 pounds.

Year	Club	Lea	G	IP	W	L	Pct	SO	BB	H	ERA	SAVES
1994 Spokane		Northwest	15	99⅓	5	6	.455	78	18	101	2.90	0
1995 Rancho Cuca		California	14	92⅓	9	4	.692	81	38	80	3.12	0
1995 Memphis		Southern	14	77⅓	5	4	.556	71	42	83	3.38	0
1996 Memphis		Southern	27	174	13	9	.591	156	60	154	3.21	0
1997 Las Vegas		P.C.	19	109	6	8	.429	99	41	142	5.45	0
1997 San Diego a		N.L.	17	33⅓	1	2	.333	16	21	50	6.75	0

a On disabled list from June 20 to July 10, 1997.

MUSSINA, MICHAEL COLE

Born, Williamsport, Pennsylvania, December 8, 1968.
Bats Right. Throws Right. Height, 6 feet, 2 inches. Weight, 185 pounds.

Year	Club	Lea	G	IP	W	L	Pct	SO	BB	H	ERA	SAVES
1990 Hagerstown		Eastern	7	42⅓	3	0	1.000	40	7	34	1.49	0
1990 Rochester		Int.	2	13⅓	0	0	.000	15	4	8	1.35	0
1991 Rochester a		Int.	19	122⅓	10	4	.714	107	31	108	2.87	0
1991 Baltimore		A.L.	12	87⅔	4	5	.444	52	21	77	2.87	0
1992 Baltimore		A.L.	32	241	18	5	*.783	130	48	212	2.54	0
1993 Bowie		Eastern	2	8	1	0	1.000	10	1	5	2.25	0
1993 Baltimore b		A.L.	25	167⅔	14	6	.700	117	44	163	4.46	0
1994 Baltimore		A.L.	24	176⅓	16	5	.762	99	42	163	3.06	0
1995 Baltimore		A.L.	32	221⅔	19	9	.679	158	50	187	3.29	0
1996 Baltimore		A.L.	36	243⅓	19	11	.633	204	69	264	4.81	0
1997 Baltimore		A.L.	33	224⅔	15	8	.652	218	54	197	3.20	0
Major League Totals		7 Yrs.	194	1362⅓	105	49	.682	978	328	1263	3.50	0
Division Series												
1996 Baltimore		A.L.	1	6	0	0	.000	6	2	7	4.50	0
1997 Baltimore		A.L.	2	14	2	0	1.000	16	3	7	1.93	0
Division Series Totals		3	20	2	0	1.000	22	5	14	2.70	0
Championship Series												
1996 Baltimore		A.L.	1	7⅔	0	1	.000	6	2	8	5.87	0
1997 Baltimore		A.L.	2	15	0	0	.000	25	4	4	0.60	0
Championship Series Totals		3	22⅔	0	1	.000	31	6	12	2.38	0

a On disabled list from May 5 to May 12, 1991.
b On disabled list from July 22 to August 20, 1993.

MYERS, MICHAEL STANLEY (MIKE)

Born, Cook County, Illinois, June 26, 1969.
Bats Left. Throws Left. Height, 6 feet, 3 inches. Weight, 200 pounds.

Year	Club	Lea	G	IP	W	L	Pct	SO	BB	H	ERA	SAVES
1990 Everett		Northwest	15	85⅓	4	5	.444	73	30	91	3.90	0
1991 Clinton		Midwest	11	65⅓	5	3	.625	59	18	61	2.62	0
1991 Giants		Arizona	1	3	0	1	.000	2	2	5	12.00	0
1992 Clinton		Midwest	7	37⅔	1	2	.333	32	8	28	1.19	0
1992 San Jose		California	8	54⅔	5	1	.833	40	17	43	2.30	0
1993 Edmonton		P.C.	27	161⅔	7	14	.333	112	52	195	5.18	0
1994 Brevard City		Fla. St.	3	11⅓	0	0	.000	15	4	7	0.79	0
1994 Edmonton		P.C.	12	60	1	5	.167	55	21	78	5.55	0
1995 Charlotte		Int.	37	36⅔	0	5	.000	24	15	41	5.65	0
1995 Toledo		Int.	6	8⅓	0	0	.000	8	3	6	4.32	0
1995 Florida		N.L.	2	2	0	0	.000	0	3	1	0.00	0
1995 Detroit a-b		A.L.	11	6⅓	1	0	1.000	4	4	10	9.95	0

Year Club	Lea	G	IP	W	L	Pct	SO	BB	H	ERA	SAVES
1996 Detroit ..............A.L.		83	64⅔	1	5	.167	69	34	70	5.01	6
1997 Detroit c ..............A.L.		88	53⅔	0	4	.000	50	25	58	5.70	2
Major League Totals ....3 Yrs.		184	126⅔	2	9	.182	123	66	139	5.47	8

a Buddy Grrom was traded to Florida Marlins for player to be named later, August 7, 1995.
b Detroit Tigers received pitcher Mike Myers to complete trade, August 9, 1995.
c Traded to Milwaukee Brewers with pitcher Rick Greene and infielder Santiago Perez for pitcher Bryce Florie and player to be named later, November 21, 1997.

MYERS, RANDALL KIRK
Born, Vancouver, Washington, September 19, 1962.
Bats Left. Throws Left. Height, 6 feet, 1 inch. Weight, 230 pounds.

Year Club	Lea	G	IP	W	L	Pct	SO	BB	H	ERA	SAVES
1982 Kingsport ....Appal.		13	74⅓	6	3	.667	*86	69	68	4.12	0
1983 Columbia ....Southern		28	173⅓	14	10	.583	164	108	146	3.63	0
1984 Lynchburg ....Carolina		23	157	13	5	.722	171	61	123	*2.06	0
1984 Jackson ....Texas		5	35	2	1	.667	35	16	29	2.06	0
1985 Jackson ....Texas		19	120⅓	4	8	.333	116	69	99	3.96	0
1985 Tidewater ....Int.		8	44	1	1	.500	25	20	40	1.84	0
1985 New York ............N.L.		1	2	0	0	.000	2	1	0	0.00	0
1986 Tidewater ....Int.		45	65	6	7	.462	79	44	44	2.35	12
1986 New York ............N.L.		10	10⅔	0	0	.000	13	9	11	4.22	0
1987 Tidewater ....Int.		5	7⅓	0	0	.000	13	4	6	4.91	3
1987 New York ............N.L.		54	75	3	6	.333	92	30	61	3.96	6
1988 New York ............N.L.		55	68	7	3	.700	69	17	45	1.72	26
1989 New York a ..........N.L.		65	84⅓	7	4	.636	88	40	62	2.35	24
1990 Cincinnati ............N.L.		66	86⅔	4	6	.400	98	38	59	2.08	31
1991 Cincinnati b ..........N.L.		58	132	6	13	.316	108	80	116	3.55	6
1992 San Diego c-d ........N.L.		66	79⅔	3	6	.333	66	34	84	4.29	38
1993 Chicago e ............N.L.		73	75⅓	2	4	.333	86	26	65	3.11	*53
1994 Chicago ..............N.L.		38	40⅓	1	5	.167	32	16	40	3.79	21
1995 Chicago f-g ..........N.L.		57	55⅓	1	2	.333	59	28	49	3.88	38
1996 Baltimore ............A.L.		62	58⅔	4	4	.500	74	29	60	3.53	31
1997 Baltimore h-i ..........A.L.		61	59⅔	2	3	.400	56	22	47	1.51	45
Major League Totals ....13 Yrs.		666	828	40	56	.417	843	370	699	3.08	319
Division Series											
1996 Baltimore ............A.L.		3	3	0	0	.000	3	0	0	0.00	2
1997 Baltimore ............A.L.		2	2	0	0	.000	5	0	0	0.00	1
Division Series Totals 5		5	0	0	.000	8	0	0	0.00	3	
Championship Series											
1988 New York ............N.L.		3	4⅔	2	0	1.000	0	2	1	0.00	0
1990 Cincinnati ............N.L.		4	5⅔	0	0	.000	7	3	2	0.00	3
1996 Baltimore ............A.L.		3	4	0	1	.000	2	3	4	2.25	0
1997 Baltimore ............A.L.		4	5⅓	0	1	.000	7	3	6	5.06	1
Championship Series Totals 14		19⅔	2	2	.500	16	11	13	1.83	4	
World Series Record											
1990 Cincinnati ..............N.L.		3	3	0	0	.000	3	0	2	0.00	1

a Traded to Cincinnati Reds with pitcher Kip Gross for pitcher John Franco and outfielder Don Brown, December 7, 1989.
b Traded to San Diego Padres for outfielder/infielder Bip Roberts and player to be named, December 8; Cincinnati Reds acquired outfielder Craig Pueschner to complete trade, December 9, 1991.
c Entered one game as pinch hitter and remained in game as pitcher.
d Filed for free agency, October 26; signed with Chicago Cubs, December 9, 1992.
e Appeared in one additional game as pinch hitter.
f Filed for free agency, November 12, 1995.
g Signed with Baltimore Orioles, December 14, 1995.
h Filed for free agency, October 27, 1997.
i Signed with Toronto Blue Jays, November 26, 1997.

MYERS, RODNEY LUTHER
Born, Rockford, Illinois, June 26, 1969.
Bats Right. Throws Right. Height, 6 feet, 1 inch. Weight, 200 pounds.

Year Club	Lea	G	IP	W	L	Pct	SO	BB	H	ERA	SAVES
1990 Eugene ....Northwest		6	22⅔	0	2	.000	17	13	19	1.19	0
1991 Appleton ....Midwest		9	27⅓	1	1	.500	29	26	22	2.60	0
1992 Lethbridge ....Pioneer		15	103⅓	5	8	.385	76	61	93	4.01	0
1993 Rockford ....Midwest		12	85⅓	7	3	.700	65	18	65	1.79	0

Year Club	Lea	G	IP	W	L	Pct	SO	BB	H	ERA	SAVES
1993 Memphis ....Southern		12	65⅔	3	6	.333	42	32	73	5.62	0
1994 Wilmington ....Carolina		4	9⅓	1	1	.500	9	1	9	4.82	1
1994 Memphis ....Southern		42	69⅔	5	1	.833	53	29	45	1.03	9
1995 Omaha ...............A.A.		38	48⅓	4	5	.444	38	19	52	4.10	2
1996 Chicago ...............N.L.		45	67⅓	2	1	.667	50	38	61	4.68	0
1997 Iowa ................A.A.		24	140⅔	7	8	.467	79	38	140	4.09	0
1997 Chicago ..............N.L.		5	9	0	0	.000	6	7	12	6.00	0
Major League Totals ....2 Yrs.		50	76⅓	2	1	.667	56	45	73	4.83	0

NAGY, CHARLES HARRISON

Born, Bridgeport, Connecticut, May 5, 1967.
Bats Left. Throws Right. Height, 6 feet, 3 inches. Weight, 200 pounds.

Year Club	Lea	G	IP	W	L	Pct	SO	BB	H	ERA	SAVES
1989 Kinston ....Carolina		13	95⅓	8	4	.667	99	24	69	1.51	0
1989 Canton ....Eastern		15	94	4	5	.444	65	32	102	3.35	0
1990 Canton ....Eastern		23	175	13	8	.619	99	39	132	2.52	0
1990 Cleveland ............A.L.		9	45⅔	2	4	.333	26	21	58	5.40	0
1991 Cleveland ............A.L.		33	211⅓	10	15	.400	109	66	228	4.13	0
1992 Cleveland ............A.L.		33	252	17	10	.630	169	57	245	2.96	0
1993 Canton ....Eastern		2	8	0	0	.000	4	2	8	1.13	0
1993 Cleveland a ............A.L.		9	48⅔	2	6	.250	30	13	66	6.29	0
1994 Cleveland ............A.L.		23	169⅓	10	8	.556	108	48	175	3.45	0
1995 Cleveland ............A.L.		29	178	16	6	.727	139	61	194	4.55	0
1996 Cleveland ............A.L.		32	222	17	5	.773	167	61	217	3.41	0
1997 Cleveland ............A.L.		34	227	15	11	.577	149	77	253	4.28	0
Major League Totals ....8 Yrs.		202	1354	89	65	.578	897	404	1436	3.93	0
Division Series											
1995 Cleveland ............A.L.		1	7	1	0	1.000	6	5	4	1.29	0
1996 Cleveland ............A.L.		2	11⅓	0	1	.000	13	5	15	7.15	0
1997 Cleveland ............A.L.		1	3⅔	0	1	.000	1	6	2	9.82	0
Division Series Totals 4			22	1	2	.333	20	16	21	5.73	0
Championship Series											
1995 Cleveland ............A.L.		1	8	0	0	.000	6	0	5	1.13	0
1997 Cleveland ............A.L.		2	13	0	0	.000	5	5	17	2.77	0
Championship Series Totals 3			21	0	0	.000	11	5	22	2.14	0
World Series Record											
1995 Cleveland ............A.L.		1	7	0	0	.000	4	1	8	6.43	0
1997 Cleveland ............A.L.		2	7	0	1	.000	5	5	8	6.43	0
World Series Totals 3			14	0	1	.000	9	6	16	6.43	0

a On disabled list from May 17 to October 1, 1993.

NAULTY, DANIEL DONOVAN (DAN)

Born, Los Angeles, California, January 6, 1970.
Bats Right. Throws Right. Height, 6 feet, 6 inches. Weight, 210 pounds.

Year Club	Lea	G	IP	W	L	Pct	SO	BB	H	ERA	SAVES
1992 Kenosha ....Midwest		6	18	0	1	.000	14	7	22	5.50	0
1993 Ft. Myers ....Fla. St.		7	30	0	3	.000	20	14	41	5.70	0
1993 Ft. Wayne ....Midwest		18	116	6	8	.429	96	48	101	3.26	0
1994 Ft. Myers ....Fla. St.		16	88⅓	8	4	.667	83	32	78	2.95	0
1994 Nashville ....Southern		9	47⅓	0	7	.000	29	22	48	5.89	0
1995 Salt Lake ...............P.C.		42	90⅓	2	6	.250	76	47	92	5.18	4
1996 Minnesota a ............A.L.		49	57	3	2	.600	56	35	43	3.79	4
1997 Twins ....Gulf Coast		2	4	0	0	.000	3	3	2	2.25	0
1997 Salt Lake ...............P.C.		6	6⅓	0	1	.000	5	2	11	11.37	0
1997 Minnesota b ...........A.L.		29	30⅔	1	1	.500	23	10	29	5.87	1
Major League Totals ....2 Yrs.		78	87⅔	4	3	.571	79	45	72	4.52	5

a On disabled list from August 5 to September 30, 1996.
b On disabled list from May 26 to September 1, 1997.

NAVARRO (CINTRON), JAIME
Born, Bayamon, Puerto Rico, March 27, 1967.
Bats Right. Throws Right. Height, 6 feet, 4 inches. Weight, 225 pounds.

Year	Club	Lea	G	IP	W	L	Pct	SO	BB	H	ERA	SAVES
1987 Helena	....	Pioneer	13	85²/₃	4	3	.571	95	18	87	3.57	0
1988 Stockton	....	California	26	174²/₃	15	5	.750	151	74	148	3.09	0
1989 El Paso	....	Texas	11	76²/₃	5	2	.714	78	35	61	2.47	0
1989 Denver	....	A.A.	3	20	1	1	.500	17	7	24	3.60	0
1989 Milwaukee	....	A.L.	19	109²/₃	7	8	.467	56	32	119	3.12	0
1990 Denver	....	A.A.	6	40²/₃	2	3	.400	28	14	41	4.20	0
1990 Milwaukee	....	A.L.	32	149¹/₃	8	7	.533	75	41	176	4.46	1
1991 Milwaukee	....	A.L.	34	234	15	12	.556	114	73	237	3.92	0
1992 Milwaukee	....	A.L.	34	246	17	11	.607	100	64	224	3.33	0
1993 Milwaukee	....	A.L.	35	214¹/₃	11	12	.478	114	73	254	5.33	0
1994 Milwaukee	....	A.L.	29	89²/₃	4	9	.308	65	35	115	6.62	0
1995 Chicago a-b-c	....	N.L.	29	200¹/₃	14	6	.700	128	56	194	3.28	0
1996 Chicago	....	N.L.	35	236²/₃	15	12	.556	158	72	244	3.92	0
1997 Chicago	....	A.L.	33	209²/₃	9	14	.391	142	73	267	5.79	0
Major League Totals	9 Yrs.		280	1689²/₃	100	91	.524	952	519	1830	4.31	1

a Not offered 1996 contract, April 7, 1995.
b Signed with Chicago Cubs, April 9, 1995.
c Filed for free agency, November 12, 1995; re-signed with Chicago Cubs, December 8, 1995.

NEAGLE, DENNIS EDWARD JR. (DENNY)
Born, Prince Georges County, Maryland, September 13, 1968.
Bats Left. Throws Left. Height 6 feet, 4 inches. Weight, 217 pounds.

Year	Club	Lea	G	IP	W	L	Pct	SO	BB	H	ERA	SAVES
1989 Elizabethton	....	Appal.	6	22	1	2	.333	32	8	20	4.50	1
1989 Kenosha	....	Midwest	6	43²/₃	2	1	.667	40	16	25	1.65	0
1990 Visalia	....	California	10	63	8	0	1.000	92	16	39	1.43	0
1991 Orlando	....	Southern	17	121¹/₃	12	3	.800	94	31	94	2.45	0
1991 Portland	....	P.C.	19	104²/₃	9	4	.692	94	32	101	3.27	0
1991 Minnesota a-b	....	A.L.	7	20	0	1	.000	14	7	28	4.05	0
1992 Pittsburgh c	....	N.L.	55	86¹/₃	4	6	.400	77	43	81	4.48	2
1993 Buffalo	....	A.A.	3	3¹/₃	0	0	.000	6	2	3	0.00	0
1993 Pittsburgh	....	N.L.	50	81¹/₃	3	5	.375	73	37	82	5.31	1
1994 Pittsburgh	....	N.L.	24	137	9	10	.474	122	49	135	5.12	0
1995 Pittsburgh	....	N.L.	31	209²/₃	13	8	.619	150	45	221	3.43	0
1996 Pittsburgh-Atlanta d	....	N.L.	33	221¹/₃	16	9	.640	149	48	226	3.49	0
1997 Atlanta	....	N.L.	34	233¹/₃	20	5	.800	172	49	204	2.97	0
Major League Totals	7 Yrs.		234	989	65	44	.596	757	278	977	3.83	3
Championship Series												
1992 Pittsburgh	....	N.L.	2	1²/₃	0	0	.000	0	3	4	27.00	0
1996 Atlanta	....	N.L.	2	7²/₃	0	0	.000	8	3	2	2.35	0
1997 Atlanta	....	N.L.	2	12	1	0	1.000	9	1	5	0.00	0
Championship Series Totals	6			21¹/₃	1	0	1.000	17	7	11	2.95	0
World Series Record												
1996 Atlanta	....	N.L.	2	6	0	0	.000	3	4	5	3.00	0

a On disabled list from July 28 to August 12, 1991.
b Traded to Pittsburgh Pirates with outfielder Midre Cummings for pitcher John Smiley, March 17, 1992.
c Appeared in one additional game as pinch runner.
d Traded to Atlanta Braves for infielder Ron Wright, outfielder Corey Pointer and pitcher Jason Schmidt, August 29, 1996.

NELSON, JEFFREY ALLAN
Born, Baltimore, Maryland, November 17, 1996.
Bats Right. Throws Right. Height, 6 feet, 8 inches. Weight, 235 pounds.

Year	Club	Lea	G	IP	W	L	Pct	SO	BB	H	ERA	SAVES
1984 Great Falls	....	Pioneer	1	0²/₃	0	0	.000	1	3	3	54.00	0
1984 Bradenton Dodgers	.....	G.C.	9	13¹/₃	0	0	.000	7	6	6	1.35	0
1985 Bradenton Dodgers	.....	G.C.	14	47¹/₃	0	5	.000	31	32	72	5.51	0
1986 Bakersfield a	.....	California	24	71¹/₃	0	7	.000	37	84	80	5.74	0
1986 Great Falls	....	Pioneer	3	2	0	0	.000	1	3	5	13.50	0
1987 Salinas	....	California	17	80	3	7	.300	43	71	80	5.74	0
1988 San Bernardino	.....	California	27	149¹/₃	8	9	.471	94	91	163	5.54	0
1989 Williamsport b	.....	Eastern	15	92¹/₃	7	5	.583	61	53	72	3.31	0

Year	Club	Lea	G	IP	W	L	Pct	SO	BB	H	ERA	SAVES
1990 Williamsport	Eastern		10	43⅓	1	4	.200	14	18	65	6.44	0
1990 Peninsula	Carolina		18	60	2	2	.500	49	25	47	3.15	6
1991 Jacksonville	Southern		21	28⅓	4	0	1.000	34	9	23	1.27	12
1991 Calgary	P.C.		28	32⅓	3	4	.429	26	15	39	3.90	7
1992 Seattle	A.L.		66	81	1	7	.125	46	44	71	3.44	6
1992 Calgary	P.C.		2	3⅔	1	0	1.000	0	1	0	0.00	0
1993 Calgary	P.C.		5	7⅔	1	0	1.000	6	2	6	1.17	1
1993 Seattle	A.L.		71	60	5	3	.625	61	34	57	4.35	1
1994 Calgary	P.C.		18	25⅓	1	4	.200	30	7	21	2.84	8
1994 Seattle	A.L.		28	42⅓	0	0	.000	44	20	35	2.76	0
1995 Seattle c	A.L.		62	78⅔	7	3	.700	96	27	58	2.17	2
1996 New York	A.L.		73	74⅓	4	4	.500	91	36	75	4.36	2
1997 New York	A.L.		77	78⅔	3	7	.300	81	37	53	2.86	2
Major League Totals	6 Yrs.		377	415	20	24	.455	419	198	349	3.32	13
Division Series												
1995 Seattle	A.L.		3	5⅔	0	1	.000	7	3	7	3.18	0
1996 New York	A.L.		2	3⅔	1	0	1.000	5	2	2	0.00	0\
1997 New York	A.L.		4	4	0	0	.000	0	2	4	0.00	0
Division Series Totals			9	13⅓	1	1	.500	12	7	13	1.35	0
Championship Series												
1995 Seattle	A.L.		3	3	0	0	.000	3	5	3	0.00	0
1996 New York	A.L.		2	2⅓	0	1	.000	2	0	5	11.57	0
Championship Series Totals			5	5⅓	0	1	.000	5	5	8	5.06	0
World Series Record												
1996 New York	A.L.		3	4⅓	0	0	.000	5	1	1	0.00	0

a Drafted by Seattle Mariners from Los Angeles Dodgers organization in minor league draft, December 9, 1986.
b On disabled list from July 16 to end of 1989 season.
c Traded by Seattle Mariners to New York Yankees with infielder Tino Martinez and pitcher Jim Mecir for infielder Russ Davis and pitcher Sterling Hitchcock, December 7, 1995.

NEN, ROBERT ALLEN

Born, San Pedro, California, November 28, 1969.
Bats Right. Throws Right. Height, 6 feet, 4 inches. Weight, 200 pounds.

Year	Club	Lea	G	IP	W	L	Pct	SO	BB	H	ERA	SAVES
1987 Sarasota Rangers	Gulf C.		2	2⅓	0	0	.000	4	3	4	7.71	0
1988 Gastonia	So. Atl.		14	48⅓	0	5	.000	36	45	69	7.45	0
1988 Butte	Pioneer		14	48⅓	4	5	.444	30	45	65	8.75	0
1989 Gastonia	So. Atl.		24	138⅓	7	4	.636	146	76	96	2.41	0
1990 Charlotte a	Fla. St.		11	53⅔	1	4	.200	38	36	44	3.69	0
1990 Tulsa	Texas		7	26⅔	0	5	.000	21	21	23	5.06	0
1991 Tulsa b	Texas		6	28	0	2	.000	23	20	24	5.79	0
1992 Tulsa c	Texas		4	25	1	1	.500	20	2	21	2.16	0
1993 Oklahoma City	A.A.		6	28⅓	0	2	.000	12	18	45	6.67	0
1993 Texas d-e	A.L.		9	22⅔	1	1	.500	12	26	28	6.35	0
1993 Florida	N.L.		15	33⅓	1	0	1.000	27	20	35	7.02	0
1994 Florida	N.L.		44	58	5	5	.500	60	17	46	2.95	15
1995 Florida	N.L.		62	65⅔	0	7	.000	68	23	62	3.29	23
1996 Florida	N.L.		75	83	5	1	.833	92	21	67	1.95	35
1997 Florida f	N.L.		73	74	9	3	.750	81	40	72	3.89	35
Major League Totals	5 Yrs.		278	336⅔	21	17	.553	340	147	310	3.61	108
Division Series												
1997 Florida	N.L.		2	2	1	0	1.000	2	2	1	0.00	0
Championship Series												
1997 Florida	N.L.		2	2	0	0	.000	1	0	0	0.00	2
World Series Record												
1997 Florida	N.L.		4	4⅔	0	0	.000	7	2	8	7.71	2

a On disabled list from March 28 to April 26 and May 6 to May 24, 1990.
b On disabled list from April 18 to June 10, June 29 to July 8 and July 9 to end of 1991 season.
c On disabled list from April 29 to end of 1992 season.
d On disabled list from June 13 to July 17, 1993.
e Traded to Florida Marlins with pitcher Kurt Miller for pitcher Cris Carpenter, July 17, 1993.
f Traded to San Francisco Giants for pitcher Joe Fontenot, pitcher Mike Villano and pitcher Mick Pageler, November 18, 1997.

NOMO, HIDEO

Born, Osaka, Japan, August 31, 1968.
Bats Right. Throws Right. Height, 6 feet, 2 inches. Weight, 210 pounds.

Year	Club	Lea	G	IP	W	L	Pct	SO	BB	H	ERA	SAVES
1990 Kintetsu	....	Japan Pac.	29	235	18	8	.692	287	109	...	2.91	0
1991 Kintetsu	....	Japan Pac.	31	242⅓	17	11	.607	287	128	...	3.05	1
1992 Kintetsu	....	Japan Pac.	30	216⅔	18	8	.692	228	117	150	2.66	0
1993 Kintetsu	....	Japan Pac.	32	243⅓	17	12	.586	276	148	201	3.70	0
1994 Kintetsu	....	Japan Pac.	17	114	8	7	.533	126	86	103	3.63	0
1995 Bakersfield	....	California	1	5⅓	0	1	.000	6	1	6	3.38	0
1995 Los Angeles a-b	....	N.L.	28	191⅓	13	6	.684	236	78	124	2.54	0
1996 Los Angeles c	....	N.L.	33	228⅓	16	11	.593	234	85	180	3.19	0
1997 Los Angeles	....	N.L.	33	207⅓	14	12	.538	233	92	193	4.25	0
Major League Totals	....	3 Yrs.	94	627	43	29	.597	703	255	497	3.34	0
Division Series												
1995 Los Angeles	....	N.L.	1	5	0	1	.000	6	2	7	9.00	0
1996 Los Angeles	....	N.L.	1	3⅔	0	1	.000	3	5	5	12.27	0
Division Series Totals	....	2		8⅔	0	2	.000	9	7	12	10.38	0

a Signed with Los Angeles Dodgers organization, February 13, 1995.
b Selected Rookie of the Year in National League for 1995.
c Pitched no-hit, no-run game against Colorado Rockies, winning 9-0, September 17, 1996.

OGEA, CHAD WAYNE

Born, Lake Charles, Louisiana, November 9, 1970.
Bats Right. Throws Right. Height, 6 feet, 2 inches. Weight, 200 pounds.

Year	Club	Lea	G	IP	W	L	Pct	SO	BB	H	ERA	SAVES
1992 Kinston	....	Carolina	21	139⅓	13	3	.813	123	29	135	3.49	0
1992 Canton	....	Eastern	7	49	6	1	.857	40	12	38	2.20	0
1993 Charlotte	....	Int.	29	181⅔	13	8	.619	135	54	169	3.81	0
1994 Charlotte	....	Int.	24	163⅔	9	10	.474	113	34	146	3.85	1
1994 Cleveland	....	A.L.	4	16⅓	0	1	.000	11	10	21	6.06	0
1995 Buffalo	....	A.A.	4	17⅔	0	1	.000	11	8	16	4.58	0
1995 Cleveland	....	A.L.	20	106⅓	8	3	.727	57	29	95	3.05	0
1996 Buffalo	....	A.A.	5	25⅔	0	1	.000	20	6	27	5.26	0
1996 Cleveland a	....	A.L.	29	146⅔	10	6	.625	101	42	151	4.79	0
1997 Buffalo	....	A.A.	1	21	1	1	.500	11	6	24	4.29	0
1997 Cleveland b	....	A.L.	21	126⅓	8	9	.471	80	47	139	4.99	0
Major League Totals	....	4 Yrs.	74	395⅔	26	19	.578	249	128	406	4.44	0
Division Series												
1996 Cleveland	....	A.L.	1	0⅓	0	0	.000	0	1	0	0.00	0
1997 Cleveland	....	A.L.	1	5⅓	0	0	.000	1	0	2	1.69	0
Division Series Totals	....	2		5⅔	0	0	.000	1	1	2	1.59	0
Championship Series												
1995 Cleveland	....	A.L.	1	0⅔	0	0	.000	2	0	1	0.00	0
1997 Cleveland	....	A.L.	2	14	0	2	.000	7	5	12	3.21	0
Championship Series Totals	....	3		14⅔	0	2	.000	9	5	13	3.07	0
World Series Record												
1997 Cleveland	....	A.L.	2	11⅔	2	0	1.000	5	3	11	1.54	0

a On disabled list from April 28 to May 28, 1996.
b On disabled list from June 24 to September 1, 1997.

OJALA, KIRT STANLEY

Born, Kalamazoo, Michigan, December 24, 1968.
Bats Left. Throws Left. Height, 6 feet, 2 inches. Weight, 200 pounds.

Year	Club	Lea	G	IP	W	L	Pct	SO	BB	H	ERA	SAVES
1990 Oneonta	....	N.Y.-Penn.	14	79	7	2	.778	87	43	75	2.16	0
1991 Pr William	....	Carolina	25	156⅔	8	7	.533	112	61	120	2.53	0
1992 Albany	....	Eastern	24	151⅔	12	8	.600	116	80	130	3.62	0
1993 Albany	....	Eastern	1	6⅓	1	0	1.000	6	2	5	0.00	0
1993 Columbus	....	Int.	31	126	8	9	.471	83	71	145	5.50	0
1994 Columbus	....	Int.	25	148	11	7	.611	81	46	157	3.83	0
1995 Columbus	....	Int.	32	145⅔	8	7	.533	107	54	138	3.95	1
1996 Indianapols	....	A.A.	22	133⅔	7	7	.500	92	31	143	3.77	0
1997 Charlotte	....	Int.	25	149	8	7	.533	119	55	148	3.50	0
1997 Florida a	....	N.L.	7	28⅔	1	2	.333	19	18	28	3.14	0

a Signed with Arizona Diamondbacks, November 25, 1997.

OLIVARES (PALQU), OMAR

Born, Mayaguez, Puerto Rico, July 6, 1967.
Bats Right. Throws Right. Height, 6 feet, 1 inch. Weight, 193 pounds.

Year	Club	Lea	G	IP	W	L	Pct	SO	BB	H	ERA	SAVES
1987	Charleston, SC	So. Atl.	31	170⅓	4	14	.222	86	57	182	4.60	0
1988	Charleston, SC	So. Atl.	24	185⅓	13	6	.684	94	43	166	2.23	0
1988	Riverside	California	4	23⅓	3	0	1.000	16	9	18	1.16	0
1989	Wichita a	Texas	26	*185⅔	12	11	.522	79	61	175	3.39	0
1990	Louisville	A.A.	23	159⅓	10	11	.476	88	59	127	2.82	0
1990	St. Louis	N.L.	9	49⅓	1	1	.500	20	17	45	2.92	0
1991	Louisville	A.A.	6	36⅓	1	2	.333	27	16	39	3.47	0
1991	St. Louis	N.L.	28	167⅓	11	7	.611	91	61	148	3.71	1
1992	St. Louis b-c	N.L.	32	197	9	9	.500	124	63	189	3.84	0
1993	St. Louis d-e	N.L.	58	118⅔	5	3	.625	63	54	134	4.17	1
1994	Louisville	A.A.	9	47⅓	2	1	.667	38	16	47	4.37	0
1994	St. Louis f	N.L.	14	73⅔	3	4	.429	26	37	84	5.74	1
1995	Colorado Springs	P.C.	3	11⅔	0	1	.000	6	2	14	5.40	0
1995	Scranton-Wilkes Barre	Int.	7	44⅓	0	3	.000	28	20	49	4.87	0
1995	Colo.-Philadelphia g-h-i	N.L.	16	41⅔	1	4	.200	22	23	55	6.91	0
1996	Toledo	Int.	1	5⅓	1	0	1.000	5	3	4	8.44	0
1996	Detroit j	A.L.	25	160	7	11	.389	81	75	169	4.89	0
1997	Detroit-Seattle k-l	A.L.	32	177⅓	6	10	.375	103	81	191	4.98	0
Major League Totals	8 Yrs.		214	985	43	49	.467	530	411	1015	4.46	3

a Traded by San Diego Padres to St. Louis Cardinals organization for outfielder Alex Cole and pitcher Steve Peters, February 27, 1990.
b On disabled list from May 25 to June 13, 1992.
c Appeared in on additional games as pinch runner and three additional games as pinch hitter.
d On disabled list from June 4 to June 19, 1993.
e Appeared in one additional game as pinch hitter and one game as pinch runner.
f Appeared in one additional game as pinch hitter.
g Signed with Colorado Rockies, April 9, 1995.
h Claimed on waivers by Philadelphia Phillies, July 11, 1995.
i Designated for assignment by Philadelphia Phillies, July 27, 1995.
j On disabled list from April 16 to May 30, 1996.
k Traded to Seattle Mariners with pitcher Felipe Lira for pitcher Scott Sanders and pitcher Dean Crow, July 18, 1997.
l Filed for free agency, October 30, 1997.
m Signed as free agent with Anaheim Angels, December 11, 1997.

OLIVER, DARREN CHRISTOPHER

Born, Rio Linda, California, October 6, 1970.
Bats Right. Throws Left. Height, 6 feet. Weight, 200 pounds.

Year	Club	Lea	G	IP	W	L	Pct	SO	BB	H	ERA	SAVES
1988	G.C. Rangers	Gulf C.	12	54⅓	5	1	.833	59	18	39	2.15	0
1989	Gastonia	So. Atl.	24	122⅓	8	7	.533	108	82	86	3.16	0
1990	G.C. Rangers a	Gulf C.	3	6	0	0	.000	7	1	1	0.00	0
1990	Gastonia	So. Atl.	1	2	0	0	.000	2	4	1	13.50	0
1991	Charlotte b	Fla. St.	2	8	0	1	.000	12	3	6	4.50	0
1992	Charlotte	Fla. St.	8	25	1	0	1.000	33	10	11	0.72	2
1992	Tulsa c	Texas	3	14⅓	0	1	.000	14	4	15	3.14	0
1993	Tulsa	Texas	46	73⅓	7	5	.583	77	41	51	1.96	6
1993	Texas	A.L.	2	3⅓	0	0	.000	4	1	2	2.70	0
1994	Oklahoma City	A.A.	6	7⅓	0	0	.000	6	3	1	0.00	1
1994	Texas	A.L.	43	50	4	0	1.000	50	35	40	3.42	2
1995	Texas d	A.L.	17	49	4	2	.667	39	32	47	4.22	0
1996	Charlotte	Fla. St.	2	12	0	1	.000	9	3	8	3.00	0
1996	Texas	A.L.	30	173⅔	14	6	.700	112	76	190	4.66	0
1997	Texas	A.L.	32	201⅓	13	12	.520	104	82	213	4.20	0
Major League Totals	5 Yrs.		124	477⅓	35	20	.636	309	226	492	4.28	2
Division Series												
1996	Texas	A.L.	1	8	0	1	.000	3	2	6	3.38	0

a On disabled list from April 6 to August 9, 1990.
b On disabled list from May 1 to end of 1991 season.
c On disabled list from July 1 to end of 1992 season.
d On disabled list from June 27 to October 2, 1995.

OLSON, GREGG WILLIAM

Born, Omaha, Nebraska, October 11, 1966.
Bats Right. Throws Right. Height, 6 feet, 4 inches. Weight, 212 pounds.

Year	Club	Lea	G	IP	W	L	Pct	SO	BB	H	ERA	SAVES
1988	Hagerstown	Carolina	8	9	1	0	1.000	9	2	5	2.00	4
1988	Charlotte	Southern	8	15⅓	0	1	.000	22	6	24	5.87	1
1988	Baltimore	A.L.	10	11	1	1	.500	9	10	10	3.27	0
1989	Baltimore a	A.L.	64	85	5	2	.714	90	46	57	1.69	27
1990	Baltimore	A.L.	64	74⅓	6	5	.545	74	31	57	2.42	37
1991	Baltimore b	A.L.	72	73⅔	4	6	.400	72	29	74	3.18	31
1992	Baltimore	A.L.	60	61⅓	1	5	.167	58	24	46	2.05	36
1993	Baltimore c-d	A.L.	50	45	0	2	.000	44	18	37	1.60	29
1994	Richmond	Int.	8	11⅓	0	0	.000	13	8	8	1.59	2
1994	Atlanta e-f-g	N.L.	16	14⅔	0	2	.000	10	13	19	9.20	1
1995	Buffalo	A.A.	18	21⅔	1	0	1.000	25	9	16	2.49	13
1995	Omaha	A.A.	1	1	0	0	.000	1	1	0	0.00	0
1995	Cleve.-Kansas City h-i-j	A.L.	23	33	3	3	.500	21	19	28	4.09	3
1996	Indianapolis	A.A.	7	6⅓	0	0	.000	4	6	6	4.26	4
1996	Detroit k-l	A.L.	43	43	3	0	1.000	29	28	43	5.02	8
1996	Houston m-n	N.L.	9	9⅓	1	0	1.000	8	7	12	4.82	0
1997	Omaha o-p-q	A.A.	9	35⅓	3	1	.750	20	10	30	3.31	0
1997	Minnesota-Kansas City	A.L.	45	50	4	3	.571	34	28	58	5.58	1
Major League Totals		10 Yrs.	456	500⅓	28	29	.491	449	253	441	3.20	173

a Selected Rookie of the Year in American League for 1989.
b Pitched ninth inning of combined no-hit, no-run game started by Bob Milacki (six innings) followed by Mike Flanagan (7th inning) and Mark Williamson (8th) against Oakland Athletics, saving 2-0 victory, July 13, 1991.
c On disabled list from August 9 to September 20, 1993.
d Not offered 1994 contract, December 20, 1993; signed with Atlanta Braves, February 8, 1994.
e On disabled list from March 26 to May 29, 1994.
f Filed for free agency, October 18, 1994; ruled ineligible by Player Relations Committee due to insufficient service time.
g Not offered 1995 contract, December 23, 1994.
h Signed with Cleveland Indians organization, March 14, 1995.
i Sold to Kansas City Royals, July 24, 1995.
j Filed for free agency, November 12, 1995. Signed with St. Louis Cardinals organization, January 23, 1996.
k Signed with St. Louis Cardinals organization, January 23, 1996.
l Traded to Detroit Tigers for infielder Yuri Sanchez, April 26, 1996.
m Traded to Houston Astros for player to be named later and player to be named later, August 27, 1996.
n Filed for free agency, October 28, 1996.
o Released by Minnesota Twins, May 16, 1997.
p Signed with Kansas City Royals organization, May 24, 1997.
q Filed for free agency, October 28, 1997.

OQUIST, MICHAEL LEE

Born, La Junta, Colorado, May 30, 1968.
Bats Right. Throws Right. Height, 6 feet, 2 inches. Weight, 175 pounds.

Year	Club	Lea	G	IP	W	L	Pct	SO	BB	H	ERA	SAVES
1989	Erie	N.Y.-Penn.	15	97⅔	7	4	.636	109	25	86	3.59	0
1990	Frederick	Carolina	25	166⅓	9	8	.529	170	48	134	2.81	0
1991	Hagerstown	Eastern	27	166⅓	10	9	.526	136	62	168	4.06	0
1992	Rochester	Int.	26	153⅓	10	12	.455	111	45	164	4.11	0
1993	Rochester	Int.	28	149⅓	9	8	.529	128	41	144	3.50	0
1993	Baltimore	A.L.	5	11⅔	0	0	.000	8	4	12	3.86	0
1994	Baltimore	A.L.	15	58⅓	3	3	.500	39	30	75	6.17	0
1994	Rochester	Int.	13	50⅔	3	2	.600	36	15	54	3.73	3
1995	Baltimore a-b	A.L.	27	54	2	1	.667	27	41	51	4.17	0
1995	Rochester	Int.	7	12	0	0	.000	11	5	17	5.25	2
1996	Las Vegas	P.C.	27	140⅓	9	4	.692	110	44	136	2.89	1
1996	San Diego c-d	N.L.	8	7⅔	0	0	.000	4	4	6	2.35	0
1997	Edmonton	P.C.	9	52⅔	6	1	.857	37	16	57	3.25	0
1997	Modesto	California	2	3⅔	0	0	.000	5	1	5	4.91	0
1997	Oakland e	A.L.	19	107⅔	4	6	.400	72	43	111	5.02	0
Major League Totals		5 Yrs.	74	239⅓	9	10	.474	150	122	255	4.96	0

a Opted for free agency, October 16, 1995.
b Signed as free agent with San Diego Padres organization, December 21, 1995.
c Opted for free agency, October 16, 1996.
d Signed as free agent with Oakland Athletics organization, November 19, 1996.
e On disabled list from July 14 to August 20, 1997.

OROSCO, JESSE RUSSELL

Born, Santa Barbara, California, April 21, 1957.

Bats Right. Throws Left. Height, 6 feet, 2 inches. Weight, 205 pounds.

Year Club	Lea	G	IP	W	L	Pct	SO	BB	H	ERA	SAVES
1978 Elizabethton a	Appal.	20	40	4	4	.500	48	20	29	1.13	6
1979 New York	N.L.	18	35	1	2	.333	22	22	33	4.89	0
1979 Tidewater	Int.	16	81	4	4	.500	55	43	82	3.89	0
1980 Jackson	Texas	37	71	4	4	.500	85	62	52	3.68	3
1981 Tidewater	Int.	46	87	9	5	.643	81	32	80	3.31	8
1981 New York	N.L.	8	17⅓	0	1	.000	18	6	13	1.59	1
1982 New York	N.L.	54	109⅓	4	10	.286	89	40	92	2.72	4
1983 New York	N.L.	62	110	13	7	.650	84	38	76	1.47	17
1984 New York	N.L.	60	87	10	6	.625	85	34	58	2.59	31
1985 New York	N.L.	54	79	8	6	.571	68	34	66	2.73	17
1986 New York	N.L.	58	81	8	6	.571	62	35	64	2.33	21
1987 New York b	N.L.	58	77	3	9	.250	78	31	78	4.44	16
1988 Los Angeles c	N.L.	55	53	3	2	.600	43	30	41	2.72	9
1989 Cleveland	A.L.	69	78	3	4	.429	79	26	54	2.08	3
1990 Cleveland	A.L.	55	64⅔	5	4	.556	55	38	58	3.90	2
1991 Cleveland d	A.L.	47	45⅔	2	0	1.000	36	15	52	3.74	0
1992 Milwaukee e	A.L.	59	39	3	1	.750	40	13	33	3.23	1
1993 Milwaukee	A.L.	57	56⅔	3	5	.375	67	17	47	3.18	8
1994 Milwaukee f	A.L.	40	39	3	1	.750	36	26	32	5.08	0
1995 Baltimore g	A.L.	65	49⅔	2	4	.333	58	27	28	3.26	3
1996 Baltimore h-i	A.L.	66	55⅓	3	1	.750	52	28	42	3.40	0
1997 Baltimore	A.L.	71	50⅓	6	3	.667	46	30	29	2.32	0
Major League Totals ... 18 Yrs.		956	1127⅓	80	72	.526	1018	490	896	2.95	133
Division Series											
1996 Baltimore	A.L.	4	1	0	1	.000	2	3	2	36.00	0
1997 Baltimore	A.L.	2	1⅓	0	0	.000	1	0	1	0.00	0
Division Series Totals ... 6			2⅓	0	1	.000	3	3	3	15.43	0
Championship Series											
1986 New York	N.L.	4	8	3	0	1.000	10	2	5	3.38	0
1988 Los Angeles	N.L.	4	2⅓	0	0	.000	0	3	4	7.71	0
1996 Baltimore	A.L.	4	2	0	0	.000	2	1	2	4.50	0
1997 Baltimore	A.L.	2	1⅓	0	0	.000	1	1	0	0.00	0
Championship Series Totals ... 14			13⅔	3	0	1.000	13	7	11	3.95	0
World Series Record											
1986 New York	N.L.	4	5⅔	0	0	.000	6	0	2	0.00	2

a Traded by Minnesota Twins to New York Mets to complete December 8, 1978 trade in which Minnesota acquired pitcher Jerry Koosman for pitcher Greg Field and player to be named, February 7, 1979.

b Traded to Los Angeles Dodgers as part of three team deal in which New York acquired pitchers Wally Whitehurst and Kevin Tapani from Oakland and Jack Savage from Los Angeles; Oakland A's acquired pitchers Bob Welch and Matt Young from Los Angeles and sent pitcher Jay Howell and shortstop Alfredo Griffin to Los Angeles, December 11, 1987.

c Filed for free agency, November 3; signed with Cleveland Indians, December 3, 1988.

d Traded to Milwaukee Brewers for player to be named, December 6, 1991.

e Filed for free agency, November 5; re-signed with Milwaukee Brewers, December 3, 1992.

f Filed for free agency, October 27, 1994.

g Signed with Baltimore Orioles, April 8, 1995.

h Filed for free agency, October 28, 1996.

i Re-signed with Baltimore Orioles, November 20, 1996.

OSBORNE, DONOVAN ALAN

Born, Roseville, California, June 21, 1969.

Bats Both. Throws Left. Height, 6 feet, 2 inches. Weight, 195 pounds.

Year Club	Lea	G	IP	W	L	Pct	SO	BB	H	ERA	SAVES
1990 Hamilton	N.Y.-Penn.	4	20	0	2	.000	14	5	21	3.60	0
1990 Savannah	So. Atl.	6	41⅓	2	2	.500	28	7	40	2.61	0
1991 Arkansas	Texas	26	166	8	12	.400	130	43	177	3.63	0
1992 St. Louis	N.L.	34	179	11	9	.550	104	38	179	3.77	0
1993 St. Louis	N.L.	26	155⅔	10	7	.588	83	47	153	3.76	0
1994 St. Louis b	N.L.	INJURED—Did Not Play									
1995 Arkansas	Texas	2	11	0	1	.000	6	2	12	2.45	0
1995 Louisville	A.A.	1	7	0	1	.000	3	0	8	3.86	0
1995 St. Louis c	N.L.	19	113⅓	4	6	.400	82	34	112	3.81	0
1996 St. Pete	Fla. St.	1	6	1	0	1.000	2	0	2	0.00	0
1996 Louisville	A.A.	1	7	1	0	1.000	3	2	6	2.57	0
1996 St. Louis d	N.L.	30	198⅔	13	9	.591	134	57	191	3.53	0

Year	Club	Lea	G	IP	W	L	Pct	SO	BB	H	ERA	SAVES
1997 Louisville	....	A.A.	3	13⅓	0	1	.000	13	5	13	4.72	0
1997 St. Louis e	....	N.L.	14	80⅓	3	7	.300	51	23	84	4.93	0
Major League Totals	5 Yrs.		123	727	41	38	.519	454	199	733	3.84	0
Division Series												
1996 St. Louis	....	N.L.	1	4	0	0	.000	5	0	7	9:00	0
Championship Series												
1996 St. Louis	....	N.L.	2	7⅔	1	1	.500	6	4	12	9.39	0

a Appeared in three additional games as pinch runner.
b On disabled list from March 30 to end of 1994 season.
c On disabled list from May 15 to July 14, 1995.
d On disabled list from April 1 to April 17, 1996.
e On disabled list from May 3 to July 29, 1997.

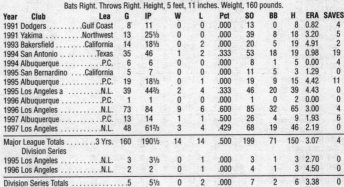

OSUNA, ANTONIO PEDRO
Born, Sinaloa, Mexico, April 12, 1973.
Bats Right. Throws Right. Height, 5 feet, 11 inches. Weight, 160 pounds.

Year	Club	Lea	G	IP	W	L	Pct	SO	BB	H	ERA	SAVES
1991 Dodgers	....	Gulf Coast	8	11	0	0	.000	13	0	8	0.82	4
1991 Yakima	....	Northwest	13	25⅓	0	0	.000	39	8	18	3.20	5
1993 Bakersfield	....	California	14	18⅓	0	2	.000	20	5	19	4.91	2
1994 San Antonio	....	Texas	35	46	1	2	.333	53	18	19	0.98	19
1994 Albuquerque	....	P.C.	6	6	0	0	.000	8	1	5	0.00	4
1995 San Bernardino	....	California	5	7	0	0	.000	11	5	3	1.29	0
1995 Albuquerque	....	P.C.	19	18⅓	0	1	.000	19	9	15	4.42	11
1995 Los Angeles a	....	N.L.	39	44⅔	2	4	.333	46	20	39	4.43	0
1996 Albuquerque	....	P.C.	1	1	0	0	.000	1	0	2	0.00	0
1996 Los Angeles	....	N.L.	73	84	9	6	.600	85	32	65	3.00	4
1997 Albuquerque	....	P.C.	13	14	1	1	.500	26	4	9	1.93	6
1997 Los Angeles	....	N.L.	48	61⅔	3	4	.429	68	19	46	2.19	0
Major League Totals	3 Yrs.		160	190⅓	14	14	.500	199	71	150	3.07	4
Division Series												
1995 Los Angeles	....	N.L.	3	3⅓	0	1	.000	3	1	3	2.70	0
1996 Los Angeles	....	N.L.	2	2	0	1	.000	4	1	3	4.50	0
Division Series Totals	....	.5		5⅓	0	2	.000	7	2	6	3.38	0

a On disabled list from May 19 to June 16, 1995.

PANIAGUA, JOSE LUIS
Born, San Jose De Ocoa, Dominican Republic, August 20, 1973.
Bats Right. Throws Right. Height, 6 feet, 2 inches. Weight, 185 pounds.

Year	Club	Lea	G	IP	W	L	Pct	SO	BB	H	ERA	SAVES
1993 Expos	....	Gulf Coast	4	27	3	0	1.000	25	5	13	0.67	0
1994 Wst Plm Bch	....	Fla. St.	26	141	9	9	.500	110	54	131	3.64	0
1995 Harrisburg	....	Eastern	25	126⅓	7	12	.368	89	62	140	5.34	0
1996 Harrisburg a	....	Eastern	3	18	3	0	1.000	16	2	12	0.00	0
1996 Ottawa	....	Int.	15	85	9	5	.643	61	23	72	3.18	0
1996 Montreal	....	N.L.	13	51	2	4	.333	27	23	55	3.53	0
1997 Wst Plm Bch	....	Fla. St.	2	10	1	0	1.000	11	2	5	0.00	0
1997 Ottawa	....	Int.	22	137⅔	8	10	.444	87	44	164	4.64	0
1997 Montreal	....	N.L.	9	18	1	2	.333	8	16	29	12.00	0
Major League Totals	2 Yrs.		22	69	3	6	.333	35	39	84	5.74	0

a On disabled list from May 21 to June 11, 1996.
b Selected in expansion draft by Tampa Bay Devil Rays, November 18, 1997.

PARK, CHAN HO
Born, Kong Ju City, South Korea, June 30, 1973.
Bats Right. Throws Right. Height, 6 feet, 2 inches. Weight, 185 pounds.

Year	Club	Lea	G	IP	W	L	Pct	SO	BB	H	ERA	SAVES
1994 Los Angeles	....	N.L.	2	4	0	0	.000	6	5	5	11.25	0
1994 San Antonio	....	Texas	20	101⅓	5	7	.417	100	57	91	3.64	0
1995 Albuquerque	....	P.C.	23	110	6	7	.462	101	76	93	4.91	0
1995 Los Angeles	....	N.L.	2	4	0	0	.000	7	2	2	4.50	0
1996 Los Angeles	....	N.L.	48	108⅔	5	5	.500	119	71	82	3.64	0
1997 Los Angeles	....	N.L.	32	192	14	8	.636	166	70	149	3.38	0
Major League Totals	4 Yrs.		84	308⅔	19	13	.594	298	148	238	3.59	

PATTERSON, DANNY SHANE

Born, San Gabriel, California, February 17, 1971.
Bats Right. Throws Right. Height, 6 feet. Weight, 170 pounds.

Year	Club	Lea	G	IP	W	L	Pct	SO	BB	H	ERA	SAVES
1990 Butte	....	Pioneer	13	28⅓	0	3	.000	18	14	36	6.35	1
1991 Rangers	....	Gulf Coast	11	50	5	3	.625	46	12	43	3.24	0
1992 Gastonia	....	So. Atl.	23	105⅓	4	6	.400	84	33	106	3.59	0
1993 Charlotte	....	Fla. St.	47	68	5	6	.455	41	28	55	2.51	7
1994 Charlotte	....	Fla. St.	7	13⅔	1	0	1.000	9	5	13	4.61	0
1994 Tulsa	....	Texas	30	44	1	4	.200	33	17	35	1.64	6
1995 Tulsa	....	Texas	26	36⅓	2	2	.500	24	13	45	6.19	5
1995 Okla City	....	A.A.	14	27⅓	1	0	1.000	9	9	23	1.65	2
1996 Okla City	....	A.A.	44	80⅓	6	2	.750	53	15	79	1.68	10
1996 Texas	....	A.L.	7	8⅔	0	0	.000	5	3	10	0.00	0
1997 Tulsa	....	Texas	2	2	0	0	.000	0	0	5	4.50	0
1997 Texas a	....	A.L.	54	71	10	6	.625	69	23	70	3.42	1
Major League Totals	....	2 Yrs.	61	79⅔	10	6	.625	74	26	80	3.05	1

Division Series

Year	Club	Lea	G	IP	W	L	Pct	SO	BB	H	ERA	SAVES
1996 Texas	....	A.L.	1	0⅓	0	0	.000	0	0	1	0.00	0

a On disabled list from May 17 to June 14, 1997.

PATTERSON, ROBERT CHANDLER (BOB)

Born, Jacksonville, Florida, May 16, 1959.
Bats Right. Throws Left. Height, 6 feet, 2 inches. Weight, 192 pounds.

Year	Club	Lea	G	IP	W	L	Pct	SO	BB	H	ERA	SAVES
1982 Sarasota Padres	...	Gulf Coast	8	52	4	3	.571	65	7	60	2.94	0
1982 Reno	....	California	4	25⅓	1	0	1.000	10	5	28	3.55	0
1983 Beaumont	....	Texas	43	116⅔	8	4	.667	97	36	107	4.01	11
1984 Las Vegas	....	P.C.	*60	143⅓	8	9	.471	97	37	129	3.27	13
1985 Las Vegas	....	P.C.	42	186⅓	10	11	.476	146	52	187	3.14	6
1985 San Diego a	....	N.L.	3	4	0	0	.000	1	3	13	24.75	0
1986 Hawaii	....	P.C.	25	156	9	6	.600	*137	44	146	3.40	1
1986 Pittsburgh	....	N.L.	11	36⅓	2	3	.400	20	5	49	4.95	0
1987 Vancouver	....	P.C.	14	89	5	2	.714	92	30	62	2.12	0
1987 Pittsburgh	....	N.L.	15	43	1	4	.200	27	22	49	6.70	0
1988 Buffalo b	....	A.A.	4	31	2	0	1.000	20	4	26	2.32	0
1989 Buffalo	....	A.A.	31	177⅓	12	6	.667	103	35	177	3.35	1
1989 Pittsburgh	....	N.L.	12	26⅔	4	3	.571	20	8	23	4.05	1
1990 Pittsburgh	....	N.L.	55	94⅔	8	5	.615	70	21	88	2.95	5
1991 Pittsburgh	....	N.L.	54	65⅔	4	3	.571	57	15	67	4.11	2
1992 Pittsburgh c	....	N.L.	60	64⅔	6	3	.667	43	23	59	2.92	9
1993 Texas d	....	A.L.	52	52⅔	2	4	.333	46	11	59	4.78	1
1994 California e-f	....	A.L.	47	42	2	3	.400	30	15	35	4.07	1
1995 California g-h	....	A.L.	62	53⅓	5	2	.714	41	13	48	3.04	0
1996 Chicago i	....	N.L.	79	54⅔	3	3	.500	53	22	46	3.13	8
1997 Chicago	....	N.L.	76	59⅓	1	6	.143	58	10	47	3.34	0
Major League Totals	....	12 Yrs.	526	597	38	39	.494	466	168	583	3.96	27

Championship Series

Year	Club	Lea	G	IP	W	L	Pct	SO	BB	H	ERA	SAVES
1990 Pittsburgh	....	N.L.	2	1	0	0	.000	0	2	1	0.00	1
1991 Pittsburgh	....	N.L.	1	2	0	0	.000	3	0	1	0.00	0
1992 Pittsburgh	....	N.L.	2	1⅔	0	0	.000	1	1	3	5.40	0
Championship Series Totals	....	5		4⅔	0	0	.000	4	3	5	1.93	1

a Traded to Pittsburgh Pirates organization for outfielder Marvell Wynne, April 3, 1986.
b On disabled list from April 28 to end of 1988 season.
c Released, November 20; signed with Texas Rangers organization, December 8, 1992.
d Refused assignment to minor leagues and became free agent, October 4, 1993; signed with California Angels organization, January 18, 1994.
e Filed for free agency, October 21, 1994; ruled ineligible by Player Relations Committee due to insufficient service time.
f Not offered 1995 contract, December 23, 1994.
g Signed with California Angels organization, April 8, 1995.
h Filed for free agency, November 12, 1995.
i Signed with Chicago Cubs, January 16, 1996.

PAVLIK, ROGER ALLEN

Born, Houston, Texas, October 4, 1967.
Bats Right. Throws Right. Height, 6 feet, 3 inches. Weight, 220 pounds.

Year Club	Lea	G	IP	W	L	Pct	SO	BB	H	ERA	SAVES
1986 Sara. Rangers a	Gulf C.	INJURED—Did Not Play									
1987 Gastonia b	So. Atl.	15	67⅓	2	7	.222	55	42	66	4.95	0
1988 Gastonia	So. Atl.	18	84	2	12	.143	89	59	94	4.61	0
1988 Butte	Pioneer	8	49	3	0	1.000	56	34	46	4.59	0
1989 Charlotte	Fla. St.	26	118⅔	3	8	.273	98	72	92	3.41	1
1990 Charlotte	Fla. St.	11	66⅓	5	3	.625	76	40	50	2.44	0
1990 Tulsa	Texas	16	100⅓	6	5	.545	91	71	66	2.33	0
1991 Oklahoma City c	A.A.	8	26	0	5	.000	43	26	19	5.19	0
1992 Oklahoma City	A.A.	18	117⅔	7	5	.583	104	51	90	2.98	0
1992 Texas	A.L.	13	62	4	4	.500	45	34	66	4.21	0
1993 Oklahoma City	A.A.	6	37	3	2	.600	32	14	26	1.70	0
1993 Texas	A.L.	26	166⅓	12	6	.667	131	80	151	3.41	0
1994 Charlotte	Fla. St.	3	16⅔	2	1	.667	15	2	13	1.08	0
1994 Oklahoma City	A.A.	5	29	2	2	.500	38	7	26	3.10	0
1994 Texas d	A.L.	11	50⅓	2	5	.286	31	30	61	7.69	0
1995 Texas	A.L.	31	191⅔	10	10	.500	149	90	174	4.37	0
1996 Texas	A.L.	34	201	15	8	.652	127	81	216	5.19	0
1997 Rangers	Gulf Coast	2	7	0	0	.000	5	0	8	1.29	0
1997 Tulsa	Texas	1	5	0	0	.000	4	2	3	3.60	0
1997 Okla City	A.A.	1	6	0	0	.000	4	0	2	0.00	0
1997 Texas e-f-g	A.L.	11	57⅔	3	5	.375	35	31	59	4.37	0
Major League Totals ....6 Yrs.		126	729	46	38	.548	518	346	727	4.59	0
Division Series											
1996 Texas	A.L.	1	2⅔	0	1	.000	1	0	4	6.75	0

a On disabled list from June 5 to end of 1986 season.
b On disabled list from June 4 to August 6, 1987.
c On disabled list from April 25 to July 28, 1991.
d On disabled list from March 25 to May 14, June 12 to July 2, and July 3 to July 24, 1994.
e On disabled list from May 7 to September 2, 1997.
f Not offered 1996 contract, December 20, 1997.
g Re-signed with Texas Rangers, December 23, 1997.

PERCIVAL, TROY EUGENE

Born, Fontana, California, August 9, 1969.
Bats Right. Throws Right. Height, 6 feet, 3 inches. Weight, 200 pounds.

Year Club	Lea	G	IP	W	L	Pct	SO	BB	H	ERA	SAVES
1991 Boise	Northwest	28	38⅓	2	0	1.000	63	18	23	1.41	12
1992 Palm Springs	California	11	10⅔	1	1	.500	16	8	6	5.06	2
1992 Midland	Texas	20	19	3	0	1.000	21	11	18	2.37	5
1993 Vancouver	P.C.	18	18⅔	0	1	.000	19	13	24	6.27	4
1994 Vancouver	P.C.	49	61	2	6	.250	73	29	63	4.13	15
1995 California	A.L.	62	74	3	2	.600	94	26	37	1.95	3
1996 California	A.L.	62	74	0	2	.000	100	31	38	2.31	36
1997 Lk Elsinore	California	2	2	0	0	.000	3	0	1	0.00	0
1997 Anaheim a	A.L.	55	52	5	5	.500	72	22	40	3.46	27
Major League Totals ....3 Yrs.		179	200	8	9	.471	266	79	115	2.48	66

a On disabled list from April 7 to May 16, 1997.

PEREZ, CARLOS GROSS

Born, Nigua, Dominican Republic, April 14, 1971.
Bats Left. Throws Left. Height, 6 feet, 3 inches. Weight, 195 pounds.

Year Club	Lea	G	IP	W	L	Pct	SO	BB	H	ERA	SAVES
1990 Expos	Gulf Coast	13	35⅔	3	1	.750	38	15	24	2.52	2
1991 Sumter	So. Atl.	16	73⅔	2	2	.500	69	32	57	2.44	0
1992 Rockford	Midwest	7	9⅓	0	1	.000	8	5	12	5.79	1
1993 Burlington	Midwest	12	16⅔	1	0	1.000	21	9	13	3.24	0
1993 San Berndno	California	20	131	8	7	.533	98	44	120	3.44	0
1994 Harrisburg	Eastern	12	79	7	2	.778	69	18	55	1.94	1
1994 Ottawa	Int.	17	119	7	5	.583	82	41	130	3.33	0
1995 Montreal	N.L.	28	141⅓	10	8	.556	106	28	142	3.69	0
1997 Montreal	N.L.	33	206⅔	12	13	.480	110	48	206	3.88	0
Major League Totals ....2 Yrs.		61	348	22	21	.512	216	76	348	3.80	0

PERISHO, MATTHEW ALAN
Born, Burlington, Iowa, June 8, 1975.
Bats Left. Throws Left. Height, 6 feet. Weight, 175 pounds.

Year	Club	Lea	G	IP	W	L	Pct	SO	BB	H	ERA	SAVES
1993 Angels		Arizona	11	64	7	3	.700	65	23	58	3.66	0
1994 Cedar Rapds		Midwest	27	147⅔	12	9	.571	107	88	165	4.33	0
1995 Lake Elsinore		California	24	115⅓	8	9	.471	68	60	137	6.32	0
1996 Lake Elsinore		California	21	128⅔	7	5	.583	97	58	131	4.20	0
1996 Midland		Texas	8	53⅓	3	2	.600	50	20	48	3.21	0
1997 Midland		Texas	10	73	5	2	.714	62	26	60	2.96	0
1997 Vancouver		P.C.	9	52⅓	4	4	.500	47	29	68	5.33	0
1997 Anaheim a		A.L.	11	45	0	2	.000	35	28	59	6.00	0

a Traded to Texas Rangers for infielder Mike Bell, October 31, 1997.

PERSON, ROBERT ALAN
Born, Lowell, Massachusetts, October 6, 1969.
Bats Right. Throws Right. Height, 5 feet, 11 inches. Weight, 180 pounds.

Year	Club	Lea	G	IP	W	L	Pct	SO	BB	H	ERA	SAVES
1989 Burlington		Appal.	10	34	0	1	.000	19	17	23	3.18	1
1990 Kinston		Carolina	4	16⅔	1	0	1.000	7	9	17	2.70	0
1990 Indians		Gulf Coast	5	7⅓	0	2	.000	8	4	10	7.36	2
1990 Watertown		N.Y.-Penn.	5	16⅓	1	0	1.000	19	7	8	1.10	0
1991 Kinston		Carolina	11	52	3	5	.375	45	42	56	4.67	0
1991 Bend		Northwest	2	10	1	1	.500	6	5	6	3.60	0
1991 South Bend		Midwest	13	76⅓	4	3	.571	66	56	50	3.30	0
1992 Sarasota		Fla. St.	19	105⅓	5	7	.417	85	62	90	3.59	0
1993 High Desert		California	28	169	12	10	.545	107	48	184	4.69	0
1994 Binghamton		Eastern	31	159	9	6	.600	130	68	124	3.45	0
1995 Binghamton		Eastern	26	66⅔	5	4	.556	65	25	46	3.11	7
1995 Norfolk		Int.	5	32	2	1	.667	33	13	30	4.50	0
1995 New York		N.L.	3	12	1	0	1.000	10	2	5	0.75	0
1996 Norfolk		Int.	8	43	5	0	1.000	32	21	33	3.35	0
1996 New York a		N.L.	27	89⅔	4	5	.444	76	35	86	4.52	0
1997 Syracuse		Int.	1	7	1	0	1.000	5	2	4	0.00	0
1997 Toronto b		A.L.	23	128⅓	5	10	.333	99	60	125	5.61	0
Major League Totals	3 Yrs.		53	230	10	15	.400	185	97	216	4.93	0

a Traded to Toronto Blue Jays for first baseman John Olerud, December 21, 1996.
b On disabled list from May 8 to May 27 and September 9 to September 29, 1997.

PETERS, CHRISTOPHER MICHAEL (CHRIS)
Born, Fort Thomas, Kentucky, January 28, 1972.
Bats Left. Throws Left. Height, 6 feet, 1 inch. Weight, 170 pounds.

Year	Club	Lea	G	IP	W	L	Pct	SO	BB	H	ERA	SAVES
1993 Welland		N.Y.-Penn.	16	27⅔	1	0	1.000	25	20	33	4.55	0
1994 Salem		Carolina	3	3⅓	1	0	1.000	2	1	5	13.50	0
1994 Augusta		So. Atl.	54	60⅔	4	5	.444	83	33	51	4.30	4
1995 Lynchburg		Carolina	24	144⅔	11	5	.688	132	35	126	2.43	0
1995 Carolina		Southern	2	14	2	0	1.000	7	2	9	1.29	0
1996 Carolina		Southern	14	92	7	3	.700	69	34	73	2.64	0
1996 Calgary		P.C.	4	27⅔	1	1	.500	16	8	18	0.98	0
1996 Pittsburgh		N.L.	16	64	2	4	.333	28	25	72	5.63	0
1997 Calgary		P.C.	14	51⅓	2	4	.333	55	30	52	4.38	1
1997 Pittsburgh		N.L.	31	37⅓	2	2	.500	17	21	38	4.58	0
Major League Totals	2 Yrs.		47	101⅓	4	6	.400	45	46	110	5.24	0

PETKOVSEK, MARK JOSEPH
Born, Beaumont, Texas, November 18, 1965.
Bats Right. Throws Right. Height, 6 feet, 1 inch. Weight, 185 pounds.

Year	Club	Lea	G	IP	W	L	Pct	SO	BB	H	ERA	SAVES
1987 Rangers		Gulf Coast	3	5⅔	0	0	.000	7	2	4	3.18	0
1987 Charlotte		Fla. St.	11	56	3	4	.429	23	17	67	4.02	0
1988 Charlotte		Fla. St.	28	175⅔	10	11	.476	95	42	156	2.97	0
1989 Oklahoma City		A.A.	6	30⅔	0	4	.000	8	18	39	7.34	0

311

Year Club	Lea	G	IP	W	L	Pct	SO	BB	H	ERA	SAVES
1989 Tulsa	Texas	21	140	8	5	.615	66	35	144	3.47	0
1990 Oklahoma City	A.A.	28	151	7	14	.333	81	42	187	5.25	0
1991 Texas	A.L.	4	9⅓	0	1	.000	6	4	21	14.46	0
1991 Oklahoma City	A.A.	25	149⅔	9	8	.529	67	38	162	4.93	0
1992 Buffalo	A.A.	32	150⅓	8	8	.500	49	44	150	3.53	1
1993 Buffalo	A.A.	14	70⅔	3	4	.429	27	16	74	4.33	0
1993 Pittsburgh	N.L.	26	32⅓	3	0	1.000	14	9	43	6.96	0
1994 Tucson	P.C.	25	138⅓	10	7	.588	69	40	176	4.62	0
1995 Louisville	A.A.	8	54⅓	4	1	.800	30	8	38	2.32	0
1995 St. Louis	N.L.	26	137⅓	6	6	.500	71	35	136	4.00	0
1996 St. Petersburg	Fla. St.	3	6	0	0	.000	5	0	6	4.50	0
1996 Louisville	A.A.	2	3	0	1	.000	4	1	5	9.00	0
1996 St. Louis a	N.L.	48	88⅔	11	2	.846	45	35	83	3.55	0
1997 St. Louis	N.L.	55	96	4	7	.364	51	31	109	5.06	2
Major League Totals	5 Yrs.	159	363⅔	24	16	.600	187	114	392	4.70	2
Division Series											
1996 St. Louis	N.L.	1	2	0	0	.000	1	0	0	0.00	0
Championship Series											
1996 St. Louis	N.L.	6	7⅓	0	1	.000	7	3	11	7.36	0

a On disabled list from April 1 to April 19, 1996.

PETTITTE, ANDREW EUGENE (ANDY)

Born, Baton Rouge, Louisiana, June 15, 1972.
Bats Left. Throws Left. Height, 6 feet, 5 inches. Weight, 235 pounds.

Year Club	Lea	G	IP	W	L	Pct	SO	BB	H	ERA	SAVES
1991 Yankees	Gulf Coast	6	36⅔	4	1	.800	51	8	16	0.98	0
1991 Oneonta	N.Y.-Penn.	6	33	2	2	.500	32	16	33	2.18	0
1992 Greensboro	So. Atl.	27	168	10	4	.714	130	55	141	2.20	0
1993 Prince William	Carolina	26	159⅔	11	9	.550	129	47	146	3.04	0
1993 Albany	Eastern	1	5	1	0	1.000	6	2	5	3.60	0
1994 Albany	Eastern	11	73	7	2	.778	50	18	60	2.71	0
1994 Columbus	Int.	16	96⅔	7	2	.778	61	21	101	2.98	0
1995 Columbus	Int.	2	11⅔	0	0	.000	8	0	7	0.00	0
1995 New York	A.L.	31	175	12	9	.571	114	63	183	4.17	0
1996 New York	A.L.	35	221	21	8	.724	162	72	229	3.87	0
1997 New York	A.L.	35	240⅓	18	7	.720	166	65	233	2.88	0
Major League Totals	3 Yrs.	101	636⅓	51	24	.680	442	200	645	3.58	0
Division Series											
1995 New York	A.L.	1	7	0	0	.000	0	3	9	5.14	0
1996 New York	A.L.	1	6⅓	0	0	.000	3	6	4	5.68	0
1997 New York	A.L.	2	11⅔	0	2	.000	5	1	15	8.49	0
Division Series Totals		4	25	0	2	.000	8	10	28	6.84	0
Championship Series											
1996 New York	A.L.	2	15	1	0	1.000	7	5	10	3.60	0
World Series Record											
1996 New York	A.L.	2	10⅔	1	1	.500	5	4	11	5.91	0

PICHARDO, HIPOLITO ANTONIO

Born, Jicome Esperanza, Dominican Republic, August 22, 1969.
Bats Right. Throws Right. Height, 6 feet, 1 inch. Weight, 185 pounds.

Year Club	Lea	G	IP	W	L	Pct	SO	BB	H	ERA	SAVES
1988 Boardwalk Royals	Gulf C.	1	1⅓	0	0	.000	3	1	3	13.50	0
1989 Appleton	Midwest	12	75⅔	5	4	.556	50	18	58	2.97	0
1990 Baseball City a	Fla. St.	11	45	1	6	.143	40	25	47	3.80	0
1991 Memphis	Southern	34	99	3	11	.214	75	38	116	4.27	0
1992 Memphis	Southern	2	14	0	0	.000	10	1	13	0.64	0
1992 Kansas City	A.L.	31	143⅔	9	6	.600	59	49	148	3.95	0
1993 Kansas City b	A.L.	30	165	7	8	.467	70	53	183	4.04	0
1994 Kansas City	A.L.	45	67⅔	5	3	.625	36	24	82	4.92	3
1995 Kansas City c	A.L.	44	64	8	4	.667	43	30	66	4.36	1
1996 Kansas City	A.L.	57	68	3	5	.375	43	26	74	5.43	3
1997 Omaha	A.A.	5	4⅔	0	0	.000	3	3	5	5.79	1
1997 Kansas City d-e	A.L.	47	49	3	5	.375	34	24	51	4.22	11
Major League Totals	6 Yrs.	254	557⅓	35	31	.530	285	206	604	4.34	18

a On disabled list from April 23 to May 2 and June 8 to August 3, 1990.
b On disabled list from August 14 to September 1, 1993.
c On disabled list from August 15 to September 1, 1995.
d On disabled list from July 5 to August 26, 1997.
e Filed for free agency, October 31, 1997.

PISCIOTTA, MARC GEORGE

Born, Edison, New Jersey, August 7, 1970.
Bats Right. Throws Right. Height, 6 feet, 5 inches. Weight, 240 pounds.

Year	Club	Lea	G	IP	W	L	Pct	SO	BB	H	ERA	SAVES
1991	Welland	N.Y.-Penn.	24	34	1	1	.500	47	20	16	0.26	8
1992	Augusta	So. Atl.	20	79⅓	4	5	.444	54	43	91	4.54	1
1993	Augusta	So. Atl.	34	43⅔	5	2	.714	49	17	31	2.68	12
1993	Salem a	Carolina	20	18⅓	0	0	.000	13	13	23	2.95	12
1994	Carolina b	Southern	26	25⅔	3	4	.429	21	15	32	5.61	5
1994	Salem	Carolina	31	29⅓	1	4	.200	23	13	24	1.53	19
1995	Carolina	Southern	56	69⅓	6	4	.600	57	45	60	4.15	9
1996	Calgary c	P.C.	57	65⅔	2	7	.222	46	46	71	4.11	1
1997	Iowa	A.A.	42	45⅔	6	2	.750	48	23	29	2.36	22
1997	Chicago	N.L.	24	28⅓	3	1	.750	21	16	20	3.18	0

a Drafted from Pittsburgh Pirates organization by Colorado Rockies in Rule V draft, December 13, 1993.
b Returned to Pittsburgh Pirates by Colorado Rockies, March 28, 1994.
c Claimed on waivers by Chicago Cubs, November 20, 1996.

PITTSLEY, JAMES MICHAEL

Born, DuBois, Pennsylvania, April 3, 1974.
Bats Right. Throws Right. Height, 6 feet, 7 inches. Weight, 220 pounds.

Year	Club	Lea	G	IP	W	L	Pct	SO	BB	H	ERA	SAVES
1992	Royals	Gulf Coast	9	43⅓	4	1	.800	47	15	27	3.32	0
1992	Baseball Cy	Fla. St.	1	3	0	0	.000	4	1	2	0.00	0
1993	Rockford	Midwest	15	80⅓	5	5	.500	87	32	76	4.26	0
1994	Wilmington	Carolina	27	161⅔	11	5	.688	171	42	154	3.17	0
1995	Kansas City	A.L.	1	3⅓	0	0	.000	0	1	7	13.50	0
1995	Omaha	A.A.	8	47⅔	4	1	.800	39	16	38	3.21	0
1996	Wilmington	Carolina	2	9	0	1	.000	10	5	13	11.00	0
1996	Wichita	Texas	3	22	3	0	1.000	7	5	9	0.41	0
1996	Omaha	A.A.	13	70⅓	7	1	.875	53	39	74	3.97	0
1997	Omaha	A.A.	7	38⅔	1	2	.333	30	20	36	4.42	0
1997	Kansas City	A.L.	21	112	5	8	.385	52	54	120	5.46	0
Major League Totals		2 Yrs.	22	115⅓	5	8	.385	52	55	127	5.70	0

PLESAC, DANIEL THOMAS

Born, Gary, Indiana, February 4, 1962.
Bats Left. Throws Left. Height, 6 feet, 5 inches. Weight, 215 pounds.

Year	Club	Lea	G	IP	W	L	Pct	SO	BB	H	ERA	SAVES
1983	Paintsville	Appal.	14	82⅓	*9	1	*.900	*85	57	76	3.50	0
1984	Stockton	California	16	108⅓	6	6	.500	101	50	106	3.32	0
1984	El Paso	Texas	7	39	2	2	.500	24	16	43	3.46	0
1985	El Paso	Texas	25	150⅓	12	5	.706	128	68	171	3.97	0
1986	Milwaukee	A.L.	51	91	10	7	.588	75	29	81	2.97	14
1987	Milwaukee	A.L.	57	79⅓	5	6	.455	89	23	63	2.61	23
1988	Milwaukee	A.L.	50	52⅓	1	2	.333	52	12	46	2.41	30
1989	Milwaukee	A.L.	52	61⅓	3	4	.429	52	17	47	2.35	33
1990	Milwaukee	A.L.	66	69	3	7	.300	65	31	67	4.43	24
1991	Milwaukee a	A.L.	45	92⅓	2	7	.222	61	39	92	4.29	8
1992	Milwaukee b	A.L.	44	79	5	4	.556	54	35	64	2.96	1
1993	Chicago	N.L.	57	62⅔	2	1	.667	47	21	74	4.74	0
1994	Chicago c	N.L.	54	54⅔	2	3	.400	53	13	61	4.61	1
1995	Pittsburgh	N.L.	58	60⅓	4	4	.500	57	27	53	3.58	3
1996	Pittsburgh d-e	N.L.	73	70⅓	6	5	.545	76	24	67	4.09	11
1997	Toronto	A.L.	73	50⅓	2	4	.333	61	19	47	3.58	1
Major League Totals		12 Yrs.	680	822⅔	45	54	.455	742	290	762	3.54	149

a On disabled list from April 22 to May 12, 1991.
b Filed for free agency, October 27; signed with Chicago Cubs, December 8, 1992.

c Filed for free agency, October 14; signed with Pittsburgh Pirates, November 8, 1994.
d Traded to Toronto Blue Jays with outfielder Orlando Merced and infielder Carlos Garcia for pitcher Jose Silva, pitcher Jose Pett, infielder Brandon Cromer and players to be named later, November 14, 1996.
e Pittsburgh Pirates received pitcher Mike Halperin, infielder Abraham Nunez and catcher Craig Wilson to complete trade, December 11, 1996.

PLUNK, ERIC VAUGHN

Born, Wilmington, California, September 3, 1963.
Bats Right. Throws Right. Height, 6 feet, 5 inches. Weight, 220 pounds.

Year	Club	Lea	G	IP	W	L	Pct	SO	BB	H	ERA	SAVES
1981	Bradenton Yankees	Gulf C.	11	54	3	4	.429	47	20	56	3.84	0
1982	Paintsville	Appal.	12	64	6	3	.667	59	30	64	4.64	0
1983	Ft. Lauderdale a	Fla. St.	20	125	8	10	.444	109	63	115	2.74	0
1984	Ft. Lauderdale b	Fla. St.	28	176⅓	12	12	.500	*152	*123	153	2.86	0
1985	Huntsville	Southern	13	79⅓	8	2	.800	68	56	61	3.40	0
1985	Tacoma	P.C.	11	53	0	5	.000	43	50	51	5.77	1
1986	Tacoma	P.C.	6	32⅔	2	3	.400	31	33	25	4.68	0
1986	Oakland	A.L.	26	120⅓	4	7	.364	98	102	91	5.31	0
1987	Tacoma	P.C.	24	34⅔	1	1	.500	56	17	21	1.56	9
1987	Oakland	A.L.	32	95	4	6	.400	90	62	91	4.74	2
1988	Oakland c	A.L.	49	78	7	2	.778	79	39	62	3.00	5
1989	Oakland-New York d	A.L.	50	104⅓	8	6	.571	85	64	82	3.28	1
1990	New York	A.L.	47	72⅔	6	3	.667	67	43	58	2.72	0
1991	New York e-f	A.L.	43	111⅔	2	5	.286	103	62	128	4.76	0
1992	Canton	Eastern	9	15⅓	1	2	.333	19	5	11	1.72	0
1992	Cleveland g	A.L.	58	71⅓	9	6	.600	50	38	61	3.64	4
1993	Cleveland	A.L.	70	71	4	5	.444	77	30	61	2.79	15
1994	Cleveland	A.L.	41	71	7	2	.778	73	37	61	2.54	3
1995	Cleveland	A.L.	56	64	6	2	.750	71	27	48	2.67	2
1996	Cleveland h	A.L.	56	77⅔	3	2	.600	85	34	56	2.43	2
1997	Cleveland	A.L.	55	65⅓	4	5	.444	66	36	62	4.66	0
Major League Totals	12 Yrs.		583	1003	64	51	.557	944	574	861	3.69	34
Division Series												
1995	Cleveland	A.L.	1	1⅓	0	0	.000	1	1	1	0.00	0
1996	Cleveland	A.L.	3	4	0	1	.000	6	2	1	6.75	0
1997	Cleveland	A.L.	1	1⅓	0	1	.000	1	0	4	27.00	0
Division Series Totals		5	6⅔	0	2		.000	8	3	6	9.45	0
Championship Series												
1988	Oakland	A.L.	1	0⅓	0	0	.000	1	0	1	0.00	0
1995	Cleveland	A.L.	3	2	0	0	.000	2	3	1	9.00	0
1997	Cleveland	A.L.	1	0⅔	1	0	1.000	0	0	1	0.00	0
Championship Series Totals		5	3	1	0		1.000	3	3	3	6.00	0
World Series Record												
1988	Oakland	A.L.	2	1⅔	0	0	.000	3	0	0	0.00	0
1997	Cleveland	A.L.	3	3	0	1	.000	3	4	3	9.00	0
World Series Totals		5	4⅔	0	1		.000	6	4	3	5.79	0

a On disabled list from August 11 to August 26, 1983.
b Traded by New York Yankees to Oakland Athletics organization with outfielder Stan Javier and pitchers Jay Howell, Jose Rijo and Tim Birtsas for pitcher Bert Bradley and outfielder Rickey Henderson, December 5, 1984.
c On disabled list from July 2 to July 17, 1988.
d Traded to New York Yankees with pitcher Greg Cadaret and outfielder Luis Polonia for outfielder Rickey Henderson, June 21, 1989.
e Released, November 21; signed with Toronto Blue Jays organization, December 12, 1991.
f Released by Toronto Blue Jays, March 27; signed with Cleveland Indians organization, April 9, 1992.
g Filed for free agency, October 27; re-signed with Cleveland Indians, November 11, 1992.
h Re-signed with Cleveland Indians, December 10, 1996.

POOLE, JAMES RICHARD

Born, Rochester, New York, April 28, 1966.
Bats Left. Throws Left. Height, 6 feet, 2 inches. Weight, 203 pounds.

Year	Club	Lea	G	IP	W	L	Pct	SO	BB	H	ERA	SAVES
1988	Vero Beach	Fla. St.	10	14⅓	1	1	.500	12	9	13	3.77	0
1989	Vero Beach	Fla. St.	*60	78⅓	11	4	.733	93	24	58	1.61	19
1989	Bakersfield	California	1	1⅔	0	0	.000	1	0	2	0.00	0
1990	San Antonio	Texas	54	63⅔	6	7	.462	77	27	55	2.40	16
1990	Los Angeles a	N.L.	16	10⅔	0	0	.000	6	8	7	4.22	0
1991	Oklahoma City	A.A.	10	12⅓	0	0	.000	14	1	4	0.00	3

Year	Club	Lea	G	IP	W	L	Pct	SO	BB	H	ERA	SAVES
1991	Texas-Baltimore b	A.L.	29	42	3	2	.600	38	12	29	2.36	1
1991	Rochester	Int.	27	29	3	2	.600	25	9	29	2.79	9
1992	Hagerstown	Eastern	7	13	0	1	.000	4	1	14	2.77	0
1992	Rochester c	Int.	32	42⅓	1	6	.143	30	18	40	5.31	10
1992	Baltimore	A.L.	6	3⅓	0	0	.000	3	1	3	0.00	0
1993	Baltimore	A.L.	55	50⅓	2	1	.667	29	21	30	2.15	2
1994	Baltimore d	A.L.	38	20⅓	1	0	1.000	18	11	32	6.64	0
1995	Buffalo	A.A.	1	2⅔	0	0	.000	0	2	7	27.00	0
1995	Cleveland e	A.L.	42	50⅓	3	3	.500	41	17	40	3.75	0
1996	Cleveland	A.L.	32	26⅔	4	0	1.000	19	14	29	3.04	0
1996	San Francisco f	N.L.	35	23⅔	2	1	.667	19	13	15	2.66	0
1997	San Francisco	N.L.	63	49⅓	3	1	.750	26	25	73	7.11	0
Major League Totals	8 Yrs.		316	276⅔	18	8	.692	199	122	258	3.87	3

Division Series

Year	Club	Lea	G	IP	W	L	Pct	SO	BB	H	ERA	SAVES
1995	Cleveland	A.L.	1	1⅔	0	0	.000	2	1	2	5.40	0

Championship Series

Year	Club	Lea	G	IP	W	L	Pct	SO	BB	H	ERA	SAVES
1995	Cleveland	A.L.	1	1	0	0	.000	2	0	0	0.00	0

World Series Record

Year	Club	Lea	G	IP	W	L	Pct	SO	BB	H	ERA	SAVES
1995	Cleveland	A.L.	2	2⅓	0	1	.000	1	0	1	3.86	0

a Traded to Texas Rangers with cash for pitchers Steve Allen and David Lynch, December 29, 1990.
b Claimed on waivers by Baltimore Orioles, May 31, 1991.
c On disabled list from April 3 to June 23, 1992.
d Not offered 1995 contract, December 23, 1994.
e Signed with Cleveland Indians organization, March 14, 1995.
f Traded to San Francisco Giants for infielder Mark Carreon, July 9, 1996.

PORTUGAL, MARK STEVEN

Born, Los Angeles, California, October 30, 1962.
Bats Right. Throws Right. Height, 6 feet. Weight, 190 pounds.

Year	Club	Lea	G	IP	W	L	Pct	SO	BB	H	ERA	SAVES
1981	Elizabethton	Appal.	14	85	7	1	.875	65	39	65	3.71	1
1982	Wisconsin Rapids	Midwest	36	119	9	8	.529	95	62	110	4.01	2
1983	Visalia	California	24	131⅓	10	5	.667	132	84	142	4.18	0
1984	Orlando	Southern	27	196	14	7	.667	110	113	171	2.98	0
1985	Toledo a	Int.	19	128⅔	8	5	.615	89	60	129	3.78	0
1985	Minnesota	A.L.	6	24⅓	1	3	.250	12	14	24	5.55	0
1986	Toledo	Int.	6	45	5	1	.833	30	23	34	2.60	0
1986	Minnesota	A.L.	27	112⅔	6	10	.375	67	50	112	4.31	1
1987	Portland	P.C.	17	102	1	10	.091	69	50	108	6.00	0
1987	Minnesota	A.L.	13	44	1	3	.250	28	24	58	7.77	0
1988	Portland	P.C.	3	19⅔	2	0	1.000	9	8	15	1.37	0
1988	Minnesota b-c	A.L.	26	57⅔	3	3	.500	31	17	60	4.53	3
1989	Tucson	P.C.	17	116⅔	7	5	.583	90	32	107	3.78	0
1989	Houston	N.L.	20	108	7	1	.875	86	37	91	2.75	0
1990	Houston	N.L.	32	196⅔	11	10	.524	136	67	187	3.62	0
1991	Houston d-e	N.L.	32	168⅓	10	12	.455	120	59	163	4.49	1
1992	Houston f-g	N.L.	18	101⅓	6	3	.667	62	41	76	2.66	0
1993	Houston h	N.L.	33	208	18	4	*.818	131	77	194	2.77	0
1994	San Francisco i	N.L.	21	137⅓	10	8	.556	87	45	135	3.93	0
1995	San Francisco-Cinc. j	N.L.	31	181⅔	11	10	.524	96	56	185	4.01	0
1996	Cincinnati k-l-m	N.L.	27	156	8	9	.471	93	42	146	3.98	0
1997	Philadelphia n	N.L.	3	13⅔	0	2	.000	2	5	17	4.61	0
Major League Totals	13 Yrs.		289	1509⅔	92	78	.541	951	534	1448	3.83	5

Championship Series

Year	Club	Lea	G	IP	W	L	Pct	SO	BB	H	ERA	SAVES
1995	Cincinnati	N.L.	1	1	0	1	.000	0	1	3	36.00	0

a On disabled list from July 22 to August 2, 1985.
b On disabled list from August 7 to August 28, 1988.
c Traded to Houston Astros for pitcher Todd McClure, December 4, 1988.
d On disabled list from July 18 to August 12, 1991.
e Appeared in one additional game as pinch runner.
f On disabled list from June 15 to July 4 and July 10 to September 24, 1992.
g Suspended one game by Houston Astros for leaving ballpark before end of game, July 10, 1992.
h Filed for free agency, October 25; signed with San Francisco Giants, November 21, 1993.
i On disabled list from June 19 to July 3 and August 3 to end of 1994 season.
j Traded to Cincinnati Reds with pitcher Dave Burba and outfielder Darren Lewis for outfielder Deion Sanders, pitcher
   John Roper, pitcher Ricky Pickett, pitcher Scott Service and infielder David McCarty, July 21, 1995.
k On disabled list from August 27 to September 15, 1996.
l Filed for free agency, November 18, 1996.
m Signed with Philadelphia Phillies, December 11, 1996.
n On disabled list from April 1 to April 20 and May 4 to September 29, 1997.

POWELL, JAMES WILLARD (JAY)
Born, Meridian, Mississippi, January 9, 1972.
Bats Right. Throws Right. Height, 6 feet, 4 inches. Weight, 220 pounds.

Year	Club	Lea	G	IP	W	L	Pct	SO	BB	H	ERA	SAVES
1993 Albany	.So. Atl.		6	27²/₃	0	2	.000	29	13	29	4.55	0
1994 Frederick	.Carolina		26	123¹/₃	7	7	.500	87	54	132	4.96	1
1995 Portland	.Eastern		50	53	5	4	.556	53	15	42	1.87	24
1995 Florida	.N.L.		9	8¹/₃	0	0	.000	4	6	7	1.08	0
1996 Brevard Cty	.Fla. St.		1	2	0	0	.000	4	0	0	0.00	0
1996 Florida a	.N.L.		67	71¹/₃	4	3	.571	52	36	71	4.54	2
1997 Florida	.N.L.		74	79²/₃	7	2	.778	65	30	71	3.28	2
Major League Totals	.3 Yrs.		150	159¹/₃	11	5	.688	121	72	149	3.73	4
Championship Series												
1997 Florida	.N.L.		1	0²/₃	0	0	.000	0	0	0	0.00	0
World Series Record												
1997 Florida	.N.L.		4	3²/₃	1	0	1.000	2	4	5	7.36	0

a On disabled list from April 20 to May 10, 1996.

PRIETO, ARIEL
Born, Havana, Cuba, October 22, 1969.
Bats Right. Throws Right. Height, 6 feet, 3 inches. Weight, 225 pounds.

Year	Club	Lea	G	IP	W	L	Pct	SO	BB	H	ERA	SAVES
1995 Oakland a	.A.L.		14	58	2	6	.250	37	32	57	4.97	0
1996 Modesto	.California		2	9	0	0	.000	8	2	9	3.00	1
1996 Edmonton	.P.C.		3	15²/₃	3	0	1.000	18	6	11	0.57	0
1996 Oakland b	.A.L.		21	125²/₃	6	7	.462	75	54	130	4.15	0
1997 Edmonton	.P.C.		2	6	0	0	.000	7	1	4	1.50	0
1997 Oakland c	.A.L.		22	125	6	8	.429	90	70	155	5.04	0
Major League Totals	.3 Yrs.		57	308²/₃	14	21	.400	202	156	342	4.67	0

a On disabled list from August 19 to September 3, 1995.
b On disabled list from May 19 to July 28, 1996.
c On disabled list from July 13 to August 17 and August 23 to September 29, 1997.

PULSIPHER, WILLIAM THOMAS (BILL)
Born, Fort Benning, Georgia, October 9, 1973.
Bats Left. Throws Left. Height, 6 feet, 3 inches. Weight, 210 pounds.

Year	Club	Lea	G	IP	W	L	Pct	SO	BB	H	ERA	SAVES
1992 Pittsfield	.N.Y.-Penn.		14	95	6	3	.667	83	56	88	2.84	0
1993 Capital City	.So. Atl.		6	43¹/₃	2	3	.400	29	12	34	2.08	0
1993 St. Lucie	.Fla. St.		13	96¹/₃	7	3	.700	102	39	63	2.24	0
1994 Binghamton	.Eastern		28	201	14	9	.609	171	89	179	3.22	0
1995 Norfolk	.Int.		13	91²/₃	6	4	.600	63	33	84	3.14	0
1995 New York a	.N.L.		17	126²/₃	5	7	.417	81	45	122	3.98	0
1996 New York a	.N.L.				(INJURED—Did Not Play)							
1997 G.C. Mets	.Gulf C.		2	5	0	0	.000	4	1	3	1.80	0
1997 St. Lucie b	.Fla. St.		12	36²/₃	1	4	.200	35	35	29	5.89	0
1997 Binghamton	.Eastern		10	12²/₃	0	0	.000	12	7	11	1.42	0
1997 Norfolk	.Int.		8	24²/₃	0	5	.000	18	38	23	7.87	0

a On disabled list entire season.
b On disabled list March 31 to May 3 and August 15 to 25, 1997.

QUANTRILL, PAUL JOHN
Born, London, Ontario, Canada, November 3, 1966.
Bats Left. Throws Right. Height, 6 feet, 1 inch. Weight, 185 pounds.

Year	Club	Lea	G	IP	W	L	Pct	SO	BB	H	ERA	SAVES
1989 Sarasota Red Sox	...Gulf C.		2	5	0	0	.000	5	0	2	0.00	2
1989 Elmira	.N.Y.-Penn.		20	76	5	4	.556	57	12	90	3.43	2
1990 Winter Haven	.Fla. St.		7	45²/₃	2	5	.286	14	6	46	4.14	0
1990 New Britain	.Eastern		22	132²/₃	7	11	.389	53	23	149	3.53	0
1991 New Britain	.Eastern		5	35	2	1	.667	18	8	32	2.06	0
1991 Pawtucket	.Int.		25	155²/₃	10	7	.588	74	29	165	4.45	0
1992 Pawtucket	.Int.		19	119	6	8	.429	56	20	143	4.46	0
1992 Boston	.A.L.		27	49¹/₃	2	3	.400	24	15	55	2.19	1

Year	Club	Lea	G	IP	W	L	Pct	SO	BB	H	ERA	SAVES
1993 Boston	....	A.L.	49	138	6	12	.333	66	44	151	3.91	1
1994 Boston a	....	A.L.	17	23	1	1	.500	15	5	25	3.52	0
1994 Scranton	....	Int.	8	57	3	3	.500	36	6	55	3.47	0
1994 Philadelphia	......	N.L.	18	30	2	2	.500	13	10	39	6.00	1
1995 Philadelphia b	...	N.L.	33	179⅓	11	12	.478	103	44	212	4.67	0
1996 Toronto	....	A.L.	38	134⅓	5	14	.263	86	51	172	5.43	0
1997 Toronto	....	A.L.	77	88	6	7	.462	56	17	103	1.94	5
Major League Totals	6 Yrs.		259	642	33	51	.393	363	186	757	4.12	8

a Traded to Philadelphia Phillies with outfielder Billy Hatcher for outfielder Wes Chamberlain and pitcher Mike Sullivan, May 31, 1994.
b Traded by Philadelphia Phillies to Toronto Blue Jays for infielder Howard Battle and pitcher Ricardo Jordan, December 6, 1995.

RADINSKY, SCOTT DAVID
Born, Glendale, California, March 3, 1968.
Bats Left. Throws Left. Height, 6 feet, 3 inches. Weight, 204 pounds.

Year	Club	Lea	G	IP	W	L	Pct	SO	BB	H	ERA	SAVES
1986 Sara. White Sox	...	Gulf Coast	7	26⅔	1	0	1.000	18	17	24	3.38	0
1987 Peninsula		Carolina	12	39	1	7	.125	37	32	43	5.77	0
1987 Sara. White Sox	.....	Gulf C.	11	58⅓	3	3	.500	41	39	43	2.31	0
1988 Sara. White Sox a	....	Gulf C.	5	3⅓	0	0	.000	7	4	2	5.40	0
1989 South Bend	....	Midwest	53	61⅔	7	5	.583	83	19	39	1.75	31
1990 Chicago	....	A.L.	62	52⅓	6	1	.857	46	36	47	4.82	4
1991 Chicago	....	A.L.	67	71⅓	5	5	.500	49	23	53	2.02	8
1992 Chicago	....	A.L.	68	59⅓	3	7	.300	48	34	54	2.73	15
1993 Chicago	....	A.L.	73	54⅔	8	2	.800	44	19	61	4.28	4
1994 Chicago b	....	A.L.	INJURED—Did Not Play									
1995 South Bend	....	Midwest	6	9⅔	0	0	.000	11	0	5	0.00	2
1995 Chicago c	....	A.L.	46	38	2	1	.667	14	17	46	5.45	1
1996 San Berndno	.....	California	3	4⅓	0	0	.000	4	2	2	2.08	0
1996 Los Angeles d	....	N.L.	58	52⅓	5	1	.833	48	17	52	2.41	1
1997 Los Angeles	....	N.L.	75	62⅓	5	1	.833	44	21	54	2.89	3
Major League Totals	7 Yrs.		449	390⅓	34	18	.654	293	167	367	3.34	36
Division Series												
1996 Los Angeles	....	N.L.	2	1⅓	0	0	.000	2	1	0	0.00	0
Championship Series												
1993 Chicago	....	A.L.	4	1⅔	0	0	.000	1	1	3	10.80	0

a On disabled list from April 8 to end of 1988 season.
b On disabled list from March 1 to end of 1994 season.
c On disabled list from July 17 to August 15, 1995.
d On disabled list from April 1 to April 12, 1996.

RADKE, BRAD WILLIAM
Born, Eau Claire, Wisconsin, October 27, 1972.
Bats Right. Throws Right. Height, 6 feet, 2 inches. Weight, 180 pounds.

Year	Club	Lea	G	IP	W	L	Pct	SO	BB	H	ERA	SAVES
1991 Twins	....	Gulf Coast	10	49⅔	3	4	.429	46	14	41	3.08	1
1992 Kenosha	....	Midwest	26	165⅔	10	10	.500	127	47	149	2.93	0
1993 Ft. Myers	....	Fla. St.	14	92	3	5	.375	69	21	85	3.82	0
1993 Nashville	....	Southern	13	76	2	6	.250	76	16	81	4.62	0
1994 Nashville	....	Southern	29	186⅓	12	9	.571	123	34	167	2.66	0
1995 Minnesota	....	A.L.	29	181	11	14	.440	75	47	195	5.32	0
1996 Minnesota	....	A.L.	35	232	11	16	.407	148	57	231	4.46	0
1997 Minnesota	....	A.L.	35	239⅔	20	10	.667	174	48	238	3.87	0
Major League Totals	3 Yrs.		99	652⅔	42	40	.512	397	152	664	4.48	0

RAGGIO, BRADY JOHN
Born, Los Angeles, California, September 17, 1972.
Bats Right. Throws Right. Height, 6 feet, 4 inches. Weight, 210 pounds.

Year	Club	Lea	G	IP	W	L	Pct	SO	BB	H	ERA	SAVES
1992 Cardinals	....	Arizona	14	48⅓	4	3	.571	48	7	51	3.54	1
1994 New Jersey	......	N.Y.-Penn.	4	27	3	0	1.000	20	4	28	1.67	0
1994 Madison	....	Midwest	11	67⅓	4	3	.571	66	14	63	3.21	0

Year	Club	Lea	G	IP	W	L	Pct	SO	BB	H	ERA	SAVES
1995 Peoria	Midwest	8	48⅔	3	0	1.000	34	2	42	1.85	0
1995 St. Pete	Fla. St.	20	47⅓	2	3	.400	35	13	43	3.80	0
1996 Arkansas	Texas	26	162⅓	9	10	.474	123	40	160	3.22	0
1997 Louisville	A.A.	22	138	8	11	.421	91	32	145	4.17	0
1997 St. Louis	N.L.	15	31⅓	1	2	.333	21	16	44	6.89	0

RAPP, PATRICK LELAND

Born, Jennings, Louisiana, July 13, 1967.
Bats Right. Throws Right. Height, 6 feet, 3 inches. Weight, 205 pounds.

Year	Club	Lea	G	IP	W	L	Pct	SO	BB	H	ERA	SAVES
1989 Pocatello	Pioneer	16	73	4	6	.400	40	29	90	5.30	0
1990 Clinton	Midwest	27	167⅓	14	10	.583	132	79	132	2.64	0
1991 San Jose	California	16	90	7	5	.583	73	37	88	2.50	0
1991 Shreveport	Texas	10	60⅓	6	2	.750	46	22	52	2.69	0
1992 Phoenix	P.C.	39	121	7	8	.467	79	40	115	3.05	3
1992 San Francisco a	N.L.	3	10	0	2	.000	3	6	8	7.20	0
1993 Edmonton	P.C.	17	107⅔	8	3	.727	93	34	89	3.43	0
1993 Florida	N.L.	16	94	4	6	.400	57	39	101	4.02	0
1994 Florida b	N.L.	24	133⅓	7	8	.467	75	69	132	3.85	0
1995 Charlotte	Int.	1	6	0	1	.000	5	1	6	6.00	0
1995 Florida	N.L.	28	167⅓	14	7	.667	102	76	158	3.44	0
1996 Charlotte	Int.	2	11	1	1	.500	9	4	18	8.18	0
1996 Florida	N.L.	30	162⅓	8	16	.333	86	91	184	5.10	0
1997 Phoenix c-d	P.C.	3	15	2	0	1.000	6	9	16	3.60	0
1997 Florida-San Francisco	N.L.	27	141⅔	5	8	.385	92	72	158	4.83	0
Major League Totals	6 Yrs.	128	708⅔	38	47	.447	415	353	741	4.31	0

a Selected by Florida Marlins in expansion draft, November 17, 1992.
b Appeared in one additional game as pinch runner.
c Traded to San Francisco Giants for pitcher Brandon Leese and pitcher Bobby Rector, July 18, 1997. On disabled list from July 20 to August 6, 1997.
d Released by San Francisco Giants, December 19, 1997.

REED, RICHARD ALLEN (RICK)

Born, Huntington, West Virginia, August 16, 1965.
Bats Right. Throws Right. Height, 6 feet, 1 inch. Weight, 195 pounds.

Year	Club	Lea	G	IP	W	L	Pct	SO	BB	H	ERA	SAVES
1986 Pirates	Gulf Coast	8	24	0	2	.000	15	6	20	3.75	0
1986 Macon	So. Atl.	1	6⅓	0	0	.000	1	2	5	2.84	0
1987 Macon	So. Atl.	46	93⅔	8	4	.667	92	29	80	2.50	7
1988 Salem	Carolina	15	72⅓	6	2	.750	73	17	56	2.74	0
1988 Harrisburg	Eastern	2	16	1	0	1.000	17	2	11	1.13	0
1988 Pittsburgh	N.L.	2	12	1	0	1.000	6	2	10	3.00	0
1988 Buffalo	A.A.	10	77	5	2	.714	50	12	62	1.64	0
1989 Buffalo	A.A.	20	125⅔	9	8	.529	75	28	130	3.72	0
1989 Pittsburgh	N.L.	15	54⅔	1	4	.200	34	11	62	5.60	0
1990 Pittsburgh	N.L.	13	53⅔	2	3	.400	27	12	62	4.36	1
1990 Buffalo	A.A.	15	91	7	4	.636	63	21	82	3.46	0
1991 Pittsburgh	N.L.	1	4⅓	0	0	.000	2	1	8	10.38	0
1991 Buffalo	A.A.	25	167⅔	14	4	.778	102	26	151	2.15	0
1992 Macon a-b	A.A.	11	62	5	4	.556	35	12	67	4.35	1
1992 Kansas City	A.L.	19	100⅓	3	7	.300	49	20	105	3.68	0
1993 Omaha	A.A.	19	128⅓	11	4	.733	58	14	116	3.09	0
1993 Okla City	A.A.	5	34⅓	1	3	.250	21	2	43	4.19	0
1993 Kansas City-Texas c-d	A.L.	3	7⅔	1	0	1.000	5	2	12	5.87	0
1994 Okla City	A.A.	2	11⅔	1	1	.500	8	0	10	3.86	0
1994 Texas e-f	A.L.	4	16⅔	1	1	.500	12	7	17	5.94	0
1994 Indianaplis	A.A.	21	140⅓	9	5	.643	79	19	162	4.68	0
1995 Cincinnati	N.L.	4	17	0	0	.000	10	3	18	5.82	0
1995 Indianapolis	A.A.	22	135	11	4	.733	92	26	127	3.33	0
1996 Norfolk g	Int.	28	182	8	10	.444	128	33	164	3.16	0
1997 New York	N.L.	33	208⅓	13	9	.591	113	31	186	2.89	0
Major League Totals	9 Yrs.	94	474⅔	22	24	.478	258	89	480	3.87	1

a Released by Pittsburgh Pirates organization, April 3, 1992.
b Signed as free agent with Kansas City Royals organization, April 4, 1992.
c Released by Kansas City Royals, August 5, 1993.
d Signed as free agent by Texas Rangers, August 11, 1993.

e Released by Texas Rangers, May 13, 1994.
f Signed as free agent with Cincinnati Reds organization, May 13, 1994.
g Signed by New York Mets as a minor league free agent, November 20, 1995.

REED, STEVEN VINCENT
Born, Los Angeles, California, March 11, 1966.
Bats Right. Throws Right. Height, 6 feet, 2 inches. Weight, 205 pounds.

Year	Club	Lea	G	IP	W	L	Pct	SO	BB	H	ERA	SAVES
1988 Pocatello	.........Pioneer		31	46	4	1	.800	49	8	42	2.54	*13
1989 Clinton	..........Midwest		60	94⅔	5	3	.625	104	38	54	1.05	26
1989 San Jose	........California		2	2	0	0	.000	3	1	0	0.00	0
1990 Shreveport	...........Texas		45	60⅓	3	1	.750	59	20	53	1.64	8
1991 Shreveport	...........Texas		15	21⅔	2	0	1.000	26	3	17	0.83	7
1991 Phoenix	.............P.C.		41	56⅓	2	3	.400	46	12	62	4.31	6
1992 Shreveport	...........Texas		27	29	1	0	1.000	33	0	18	0.62	23
1992 Phoenix	.............P.C.		29	31	0	1	.000	30	10	27	3.48	20
1992 San Francisco a	.......N.L.		18	15⅔	1	0	1.000	11	3	13	2.30	0
1993 Colorado Springs	.....P.C.		11	12⅓	0	0	.000	10	3	8	0.00	7
1993 Colorado	............N.L.		64	84⅓	9	5	.643	51	30	80	4.48	3
1994 Colorado	............N.L.		*61	64	3	2	.600	51	26	79	3.94	3
1995 Colorado	............N.L.		71	84	5	2	.714	79	21	61	2.14	3
1996 Colorado	............N.L.		70	75	4	3	.571	51	19	66	3.96	0
1997 Colorado b-c	.......N.L.		63	62⅓	4	6	.400	43	27	49	4.04	6
Major League Totals	........6 Yrs.		347	385⅓	26	18	.591	286	126	348	3.62	15
Division Series												
1995 Colorado	............N.L.		3	2⅔	0	0	.000	3	1	2	0.00	0

a Selected by Colorado Rockies in expansion draft, November 17, 1992.
b Released by Colorado Rockies, December 22, 1997.
c Signed as free agent with San Francisco Giants, December 24, 1997.

REKAR, BRYAN ROBERT
Born, Oaklawn, Illinois, June 3, 1972.
Bats Right. Throws Right. Height, 6 feet, 3 inches. Weight, 205 pounds.

Year	Club	Lea	G	IP	W	L	Pct	SO	BB	H	ERA	SAVES
1993 Bend	...........Northwest		13	75	3	5	.375	59	18	81	4.08	0
1994 Central Valley	.....California		22	111⅓	6	6	.500	91	31	120	3.48	0
1995 New Haven	........Eastern		12	80⅓	6	3	.667	80	16	65	2.13	0
1995 Colorado Springs	.......P.C.		7	48⅓	4	2	.667	39	13	29	1.49	0
1995 Colorado	............N.L.		15	85	4	6	.400	60	24	95	4.98	0
1996 Colo Sprngs	...........P.C.		19	123	8	8	.500	75	36	138	4.46	0
1996 Colorado	............N.L.		14	58⅓	2	4	.333	25	26	87	8.95	0
1997 Colorado a	............N.L.		2	9⅓	1	0	1.000	4	6	11	5.79	0
1997 Colo Sprngs	...........P.C.		28	145	10	9	.526	116	39	169	5.46	0
Major League Totals	........3 Yrs.		31	152⅔	7	10	.412	89	56	193	6.54	0

a Selected in expansion draft by Tampa Bay Devil Rays, November 18, 1997.

REMLINGER, MICHAEL JOHN
Born, Middletown, New York, March 26, 1966.
Bats Left. Throws Left. height, 6 feet. Weight, 195 pounds.

Year	Club	Lea	G	IP	W	L	Pct	SO	BB	H	ERA	SAVES
1987 Everett	.........Northwest		2	5	0	0	.000	11	5	1	3.60	0
1987 Clinton	..........Midwest		6	30	2	1	.667	43	14	21	3.30	0
1987 Shreveport	..........Texas		6	34⅓	4	2	.667	51	22	14	2.36	0
1988 Shreveport a	.........Texas		3	13	1	0	1.000	18	4	7	0.69	0
1989 Shreveport	..........Texas		16	90⅔	4	6	.400	92	73	68	2.98	0
1989 Phoenix	.............P.C.		11	43	1	6	.143	28	52	51	9.21	0
1990 Shreveport	...........Texas		25	147⅔	9	11	.450	75	72	149	3.90	0
1991 Phoenix	.............P.C.		19	108⅔	5	5	.500	68	59	134	6.38	0
1991 San Francisco b	.......N.L.		8	35	2	1	.667	19	20	36	4.37	0
1992 Calgary	..............P.C.		21	70⅓	1	7	.125	24	48	97	6.65	0
1992 Jacksonville	......Southern		5	26	1	1	.500	21	11	25	3.46	0
1993 Calgary	..............P.C.		19	84⅔	4	3	.571	51	52	100	5.53	0
1993 Jacksonville c	......Southern		7	39⅔	1	3	.250	23	19	40	6.58	0
1994 Norfolk	..............Int.		12	63	2	4	.333	45	25	57	3.14	0

319

Year Club	Lea	G	IP	W	L	Pct	SO	BB	H	ERA	SAVES
1994 New York	N.L.	10	54⅔	1	5	.167	33	35	55	4.61	0
1995 Indianapolis	A.A.	41	46⅔	5	3	.625	58	32	40	4.05	0
1995 New York-Cincinnati d-e	N.L.	7	6⅔	0	1	.000	7	5	9	6.75	0
1996 Indianapolis	A.A.	28	89⅓	4	3	.571	97	44	64	2.52	0
1996 Cincinnati	N.L.	19	27⅓	0	1	.000	19	19	24	5.60	0
1997 Cincinnati	N.L.	69	124	8	8	.500	145	60	100	4.14	2
Major League Totals ....5 Yrs.		113	247⅔	11	16	.407	223	139	224	4.51	2

a On disabled list from April 30 to end of 1988 season.
b Traded to Seattle Mariners with outfielder Kevin Mitchell for pitchers Bill Swift, Mike Jackson and Dave Burba, December 11, 1991.
c Became free agent, October 15; signed with New York Mets organization, November 22, 1993.
d Traded to Cincinnati Reds for outfielder Cobi Cradle, May 11, 1995.
e Traded to Kansas City Royals as part of three team deal with St. Louis Cardinals, December 4, 1995.

REYES, CARLOS ALBERTO
Born, Miami, Florida, April 4, 1969.
Bats Both. Throws Right. Height, 6 feet 1 inch. Weight, 190 pounds.

Year Club	Lea	G	IP	W	L	Pct	SO	BB	H	ERA	SAVES
1991 Bradenton Braves	Gulf C.	20	45⅔	3	2	.600	37	9	44	1.77	5
1992 Macon	So. Atl.	23	60	2	3	.400	57	11	57	2.10	2
1992 Durham	Carolina	21	40⅔	2	1	.667	33	10	31	2.43	5
1993 Greenville	Southern	33	70	8	1	.889	57	24	64	2.06	2
1993 Richmond a	Int.	18	28⅔	1	0	1.000	30	11	30	3.77	1
1994 Modesto	California	3	5	0	0	.000	3	0	2	0.00	0
1994 Oakland b	A.L.	27	78	0	3	.000	57	44	71	4.15	1
1995 Oakland c	A.L.	40	69	4	6	.400	48	28	71	5.09	0
1996 Oakland	A.L.	46	122⅓	7	10	.412	78	61	134	4.78	0
1997 Columbus	Int.	1	2	0	0	.000	2	0	5	18.00	0
1997 Edmonton	P.C.	5	31	2	0	1.000	23	3	30	3.48	0
1997 Oakland d	A.L.	37	77⅓	3	4	.429	43	25	101	5.82	0
Major League Totals ....4 Yrs.		150	346⅔	14	23	.378	226	158	377	4.93	1

a Drafted by Oakland Athletics from Atlanta Braves organization, December 13, 1993.
b On disabled list from July 18 to August 4, 1994.
c On disabled list from July 19 to October 2, 1995.
d On disabled list from August 21 to September 12, 1997.

REYES, DENNIS
Born, Higuera De Zaragoza, Mexico, April 19, 1977.
Bats Left. Throws Left. Height, 6 feet, 3 inches. Weight, 246 pounds.

Year Club	Lea	G	IP	W	L	Pct	SO	BB	H	ERA	SAVES
1994 Vero Beach	Fla. St.	9	41⅔	2	4	.333	25	18	58	6.70	0
1994 Great Falls	Pioneer	14	66⅔	7	1	.875	70	25	71	3.78	0
1995 Mexico	Mexican	17	58⅔	5	5	.500	44	41	76	6.60	0
1995 Vero Beach	Fla. St.	3	10	1	0	1.000	9	6	8	1.80	0
1996 San Berndno	California	29	166	11	12	.478	176	77	166	4.17	0
1997 San Antonio	Texas	12	80⅓	8	1	.889	66	28	79	3.02	0
1997 Albuquerque	P.C.	10	57⅓	6	3	.667	45	33	70	5.65	0
1997 Los Angeles	N.L.	14	47	2	3	.400	36	18	51	3.83	0

REYES, RAFAEL ALBERTO
Born, San Cristobal, Dominican Republic, April 10, 1971.
Bats Right. Throws Right. Height, 6 feet, 1 inch. Weight, 195 pounds.

Year Club	Lea	G	IP	W	L	Pct	SO	BB	H	ERA	SAVES
1990 West Palm Beach	Fla. St.	16	57	5	4	.556	47	32	58	4.74	1
1991 Rockford	Midwest	3	11⅓	0	1	.000	10	2	14	5.56	0
1992 Albany	So. Atl.	27	27⅓	0	2	.000	29	13	24	3.95	4
1993 Burlington	Midwest	53	74	7	6	.538	80	26	52	2.68	11
1994 Harrisburg	Eastern	60	69⅓	2	2	.500	60	13	68	3.25	35
1995 Milwaukee	A.L.	27	33⅓	1	1	.500	29	18	19	2.43	1
1996 Beloit	Midwest	13	19⅔	1	0	1.000	22	6	17	1.83	0
1996 Milwaukee	A.L.	5	5⅔	1	0	1.000	2	2	8	7.94	0

Year	Club	Lea	G	IP	W	L	Pct	SO	BB	H	ERA	SAVES
1997	Tucson ..............P.C.		38	57⅓	2	4	.333	70	34	52	5.02	7
1997	Milwaukee ...........A.L.		19	29⅔	1	2	.333	28	9	32	5.46	1
Major League Totals ....3 Yrs.			51	68⅔	3	3	.500	59	29	59	4.19	2

REYNOLDS, RICHARD SHANE

Born, Bastrop, Louisiana, March 26, 1968.
Bats Right. Throws Right. Height, 6 feet, 3 inches. Weight, 210 pounds.

Year	Club	Lea	G	IP	W	L	Pct	SO	BB	H	ERA	SAVES
1989	Auburn ..........N.Y.-Penn.		6	35	3	2	.600	23	14	36	2.31	0
1989	Asheville ....So. Atl.		8	51⅓	8	5	.625	33	21	53	3.68	0
1990	Columbus ....Southern		29	155⅓	9	10	.474	92	70	181	4.81	0
1991	Jackson ....Texas		27	151	8	9	.471	116	62	165	4.47	0
1992	Tucson ...............P.C.		25	142	9	8	.529	106	34	156	3.68	1
1992	Houston ..............N.L.		8	25⅓	1	3	.250	10	6	42	7.11	0
1993	Tucson ...............P.C.		25	139⅓	10	6	.625	106	21	147	3.62	1
1993	Houston ..............N.L.		5	11	0	0	.000	10	6	11	0.82	0
1994	Houston ..............N.L.		33	124	8	5	.615	110	21	128	3.05	0
1995	Houston ..............N.L.		30	189⅓	10	11	.476	175	37	196	3.47	0
1996	Houston ..............N.L.		35	239	16	10	.615	204	44	227	3.65	0
1997	New Orleans .........A.A.		1	5	1	0	1.000	6	1	3	0.00	0
1997	Houston a .............N.L.		30	181	9	10	.474	152	47	189	4.23	0
Major League Totals ....6 Yrs.			141	769⅔	44	39	.530	661	161	793	3.72	0
Divisional Series												
1997	Houston ..............N.L.		1	6	0	1	.000	5	1	5	3.00	0

a On disabled list from June 10 to July 14, 1997.

REYNOSO (GUTIERREZ), MARTIN ARMANDO

Born, San Luis Potosi, Mexico, May 1, 1996.
Bats Right. Throws Right. Height, 6 feet. Weight, 196 pounds.

Year	Club	Lea	G	IP	W	L	Pct	SO	BB	H	ERA	SAVES
1988	Saltillo ....Mexican		32	180	11	11	.500	92	85	176	4.30	2
1989	Saltillo ....Mexican		27	160⅓	13	9	.591	107	64	155	3.48	0
1990	Saltillo a ....Mexican		27	200⅔	*20	3	*.870	*170	73	174	2.60	0
1990	Richmond ....Int.		4	24	3	1	.750	15	7	26	2.25	0
1991	Richmond ....Int.		22	131	10	6	.625	97	39	117	*2.61	0
1991	Atlanta ...............N.L.		6	23⅓	2	1	.667	10	10	26	6.17	0
1992	Richmond ....Int.		28	169⅓	12	9	.571	108	52	156	2.66	0
1992	Atlanta b .............N.L.		3	7⅔	1	0	1.000	2	2	11	4.70	1
1993	Colorado Springs .......P.C.		4	22⅓	2	1	.667	22	8	19	3.22	0
1993	Colorado c ............N.L.		30	189	12	11	.522	117	63	206	4.00	0
1994	Colorado d ............N.L.		9	52⅓	3	4	.429	25	22	54	4.82	0
1995	Colorado Springs .......P.C.		5	23	2	1	.667	17	6	14	1.57	0
1995	Colorado e ............N.L.		20	93	7	7	.500	40	36	116	5.32	0
1996	Colorado f ............N.L.		30	168⅔	8	9	.471	88	49	195	4.96	0
1997	St. Lucie ....Fla. St.		2	10	1	1	.500	6	1	9	2.70	0
1997	New York g ............N.L.		16	91⅓	6	3	.667	47	29	95	4.53	0
Major League Totals ....7 Yrs.			114	625⅓	39	35	.527	329	211	703	4.69	1
Division Series												
1995	Colorado ..............N.L.		1	1	0	0	.000	0	0	2	0.00	0

a Purchased by Atlanta Braves organization from Saltillo Sarape Makers of Mexican League, August 15, 1990.
b Selected by Colorado Rockies in expansion draft, November 17, 1992.
c Appeared in one additional game as pinch runner.
d On disabled list from May 21 to end of 1994 season.
e On disabled list from April 25 to June 18, 1995.
f Traded to New York Mets for pitcher Jerry DiPoto, November 27, 1996.
g On disabled list from April 1 to April 15 and July 17 to September 29, 1997.

RHODES, ARTHUR LEE
Born, Waco, Texas, October 24, 1969.
Bats Left. Throws Left. Height, 6 feet, 2 inches. Weight, 206 pounds.

Year Club	Lea	G	IP	W	L	Pct	SO	BB	H	ERA	SAVES
1988 Bluefield	Appal.	11	35⅓	3	4	.429	44	15	29	3.31	0
1989 Erie	N.Y.-Penn.	5	31	2	0	1.000	45	10	13	1.16	0
1989 Frederick	Carolina	7	24⅓	2	2	.500	28	19	19	5.18	0
1990 Frederick	Carolina	13	80⅔	4	6	.400	103	21	62	2.12	0
1990 Hagerstown	Eastern	12	72⅓	3	4	.429	60	39	62	3.73	0
1991 Hagerstown a	Eastern	19	106⅔	7	4	.636	115	47	73	2.70	0
1991 Baltimore	A.L.	8	36	0	3	.000	23	23	47	8.00	0
1992 Rochester	Int.	17	101⅔	6	6	.500	115	46	84	3.72	0
1992 Baltimore	A.L.	15	94⅓	7	5	.583	77	38	87	3.63	0
1993 Rochester	Int.	6	26⅔	1	1	.500	33	15	26	4.05	0
1993 Baltimore b	A.L.	17	85⅔	5	6	.455	49	49	91	6.51	0
1994 Frederick	Carolina	1	5	0	0	.000	7	0	3	0.00	0
1994 Rochester	Int.	15	90⅓	7	5	.583	86	34	70	2.79	0
1994 Baltimore c	A.L.	10	52⅔	3	5	.375	47	30	51	5.81	0
1995 Baltimore	A.L.	19	75⅓	2	5	.286	77	48	68	6.21	0
1996 Baltimore	A.L.	28	53	9	1	.900	62	23	48	4.08	1
1997 Baltimore	A.L.	53	95⅓	10	3	.769	102	26	75	3.02	1
Major League Totals ....7 Yrs.		150	492⅓	36	28	.563	437	237	467	5.01	2
Division Series											
1996 Baltimore	A.L.	2	1	0	0	.000	1	1	1	9.00	0
1997 Baltimore	A.L.	1	2⅓	0	0	.000	4	0	0	0.00	0
Division Series Totals 3			3⅓	0	0	.000	5	1	1	2.70	0
Championship Series											
1996 Baltimore	A.L.	3	2	0	0	.000	2	0	2	0.00	0
1997 Baltimore	A.L.	2	2⅓	0	0	.000	2	3	2	0.00	0
Championship Series Totals 5			4⅓	0	0	.000	4	3	4	0.00	0

a On disabled list from May 13 to June 5, 1991.
b On disabled list from May 10 to July 31, 1993.
c On disabled list from May 2 to May 21, 1994.

RIGBY, BRADLEY KENNETH
Born, Milwaukee, Wisconsin, May 14, 1973.
Bats Right. Throws Right. Height, 6 feet, 6 inches. Weight, 203 pounds.

Year Club	Lea	G	IP	W	L	Pct	SO	BB	H	ERA	SAVES
1994 Modesto	California	11	23⅔	2	1	.667	28	10	20	3.80	2
1995 Modesto	California	31	154⅔	11	4	.733	145	48	135	3.84	2
1996 Huntsville	Southern	26	159⅓	9	12	.429	127	59	161	3.95	0
1997 Edmonton	P.C.	15	82⅓	8	4	.667	49	26	95	4.37	0
1997 Oakland a	A.L.	14	77⅔	1	7	.125	34	22	92	4.87	0

a On disabled list from August 8 to August 23, 1997.

RINCON, RICARDO (ESPINOZA)
Born, Veracruz, Mexico, April 13, 1970.
Bats Left. Throws Left. Height, 6 feet. Weight, 190 pounds.

Year Club	Lea	G	IP	W	L	Pct	SO	BB	H	ERA	SAVES
1990 Torreon	Mexican	19	47⅔	3	0	1.000	29	32	53	3.78	0
1991 Torreon	Mexican	32	74⅓	2	8	.200	66	48	99	6.54	1
1992 Torreon	Mexican	49	89⅔	6	5	.545	91	46	87	3.91	4
1993 Torreon	Mexican	57	82⅓	7	3	.700	81	36	80	3.17	8
1994 Mex. City Reds	Mexican	20	53⅓	2	4	.333	38	20	57	3.21	1
1995 Mex. City Reds	Mexican	27	75	6	6	.500	41	41	86	5.16	3
1996 Mex. City Reds	Mexican	50	78⅔	5	3	.625	60	27	58	2.97	10
1997 Pittsburgh a	N.L.	62	60	4	8	.333	71	24	51	3.45	4

a On disabled list from June 20 to July 5, 1997.

RISLEY, WILLIAM CHARLES

Born, Chicago, Illinois, May 29, 1967.
Bats Right. Throws Right. Height, 6 feet, 2 inches. Weight, 215 pounds.

Year	Club	Lea	G	IP	W	L	Pct	SO	BB	H	ERA	SAVES
1987	Sarasota Reds	Gulf C.	11	52⅓	1	4	.200	50	26	38	1.89	0
1988	Greensboro	So. Atl.	23	120⅓	8	4	.667	135	84	82	4.11	0
1989	Cedar Rapids	Midwest	27	140⅔	9	10	.474	128	81	87	3.90	0
1990	Cedar Rapids	Midwest	22	137⅔	8	9	.471	123	68	99	2.81	0
1991	Chattanooga	Southern	19	108⅓	5	7	.417	77	60	81	3.16	0
1991	Nashville a	A.A.	8	44	3	5	.375	32	26	45	4.91	0
1992	Montreal	N.L.	1	5	1	0	1.000	2	1	4	1.80	0
1992	Indianapolis	A.A.	25	95⅔	5	8	.385	64	47	105	6.40	0
1993	Ottawa	Int.	41	63⅔	2	4	.333	74	34	51	2.54	1
1993	Montreal b	N.L.	2	3	0	0	.000	2	2	2	6.00	0
1994	Calgary	P.C.	6	12	0	0	.000	15	4	13	3.00	1
1994	Seattle	A.L.	37	52⅓	9	6	.600	61	19	31	3.44	0
1995	Tacoma	P.C.	1	1	0	0	.000	2	1	0	0.00	0
1995	Seattle c-d	A.L.	45	60⅓	2	1	.667	65	18	55	3.13	1
1996	Syracuse	Int.	2	1	0	0	.000	0	1	0	0.00	0
1996	St. Cathrnes	N.Y.-Penn.	3	7	0	0	.000	10	2	3	1.29	0
1996	Toronto e	A.L.	25	41⅔	0	1	.000	29	25	33	3.89	0
1997	Dunedin	Fla. St.	8	12	0	2	.000	11	3	9	4.50	0
1997	Syracuse	Int.	11	15⅓	1	2	.333	20	10	19	8.22	0
1997	Toronto f	A.L.	3	4⅓	0	1	.000	2	2	3	8.31	0
Major League Totals		6 Yrs.	113	166⅔	12	9	.571	161	67	128	3.56	1

Division Series

1995	Seattle	A.L.	4	3	0	0	.000	1	0	2	6.00	1

Championship Series

1995	Seattle	A.L.	3	2⅔	0	0	.000	2	1	2	0.00	0

a Traded by Cincinnati Reds to Montreal Expos with pitcher John Wetteland for outfielder Dave Martinez, pitcher Scott Ruskin and infielder Willie Greene, December 11, 1991.
b Claimed on waivers by Seattle Mariners, March 17, 1994.
c On disabled list from May 29 to June 13, 1995.
d Traded to Toronto Blue Jays with infielder Miguel Cairo for pitchers Edwin Hutado and Paul Menhart, December 18, 1995.
e On disabled list from May 10 to June 11 and June 26 to July 31, 1996.
f On disabled list from April 1 to September 12, 1997.

RITCHIE, TODD EVERETT

Born, Portsmouth, Virginia, November 7, 1971.
Bats Right. Throws Right. Height, 6 feet, 3 inches. Weight, 205 pounds.

Year	Club	Lea	G	IP	W	L	Pct	SO	BB	H	ERA	SAVES
1990	Elizabethtn	Appal.	11	65	5	2	.714	49	24	45	1.94	0
1991	Kenosha	Midwest	21	116⅔	7	6	.538	101	50	113	3.55	0
1992	Visalia	California	28	172⅔	11	9	.550	129	65	193	5.06	0
1993	Nashville	Southern	12	46⅔	3	2	.600	41	15	46	3.66	0
1994	Nashville	Southern	4	17	0	2	.000	9	7	24	4.24	0
1995	New Britain	Eastern	24	113	4	9	.308	60	54	135	5.73	0
1996	New Britain	Eastern	29	82⅔	3	7	.300	53	30	101	5.44	4
1996	Salt Lake	P.C.	16	24⅔	0	4	.000	19	11	27	5.47	0
1997	Minnesota	A.L.	42	74⅔	2	3	.400	44	28	87	4.58	0

RITZ, KEVIN D.

Born, Eatonstown, New Jersey, June 8, 1965.
Bats Right. Throws Right. Height, 6 feet, 4 inches. Weight, 220 pounds.

Year	Club	Lea	G	IP	W	L	Pct	SO	BB	H	ERA	SAVES
1986	Gastonia	So. Atl.	7	36	1	2	.333	34	21	29	4.21	0
1986	Lakeland	Fla. St.	18	86	3	9	.250	39	45	114	5.57	1
1987	Glens Falls	Eastern	25	152⅓	8	8	.500	78	71	174	4.90	0
1988	Glens Falls	Eastern	26	136⅔	8	10	.444	75	70	115	3.82	0
1989	Toledo	Int.	16	102⅔	7	8	.467	74	60	95	3.16	0
1989	Detroit	A.L.	12	74	4	6	.400	56	44	75	4.38	0
1990	Toledo	Int.	20	89⅔	3	6	.333	57	59	93	5.22	0
1990	Detroit	A.L.	4	7⅓	0	4	.000	3	14	14	11.05	0
1991	Toledo	Int.	20	126⅓	8	7	.533	105	60	116	3.28	0
1991	Detroit	A.L.	11	15⅓	0	3	.000	9	22	17	11.74	0
1992	Detroit a-b	A.L.	23	80⅓	2	5	.286	57	44	88	5.60	0

Year Club	Lea	G	IP	W	L	Pct	SO	BB	H	ERA	SAVES
1993 Colorado c-d-e .... .A.L.		INJURED—Did Not Play									
1994 Colorado Springs .... .P.C.		9	35	5	0	1.000	27	6	26	1.29	0
1994 Colorado .... .N.L.		15	73⅔	5	6	.455	53	35	88	5.62	0
1995 Colorado .... .N.L.		31	173⅓	11	11	.500	120	65	171	4.21	2
1996 Colorado .... .N.L.		35	213	17	11	.607	105	105	236	5.28	0
1997 Colorado f .... .N.L.		18	107⅓	6	8	.429	56	46	142	5.87	0
Major League Totals .... .8 Yrs.		149	744⅓	45	54	.455	459	375	831	5.28	2
Division Series											
1995 Colorado .... .N.L.		2	7	0	0	.000	5	3	12	7.71	0

a On disabled list from August 4 to end of 1992 season.
b Selected by Colorado Rockies in expansion draft, November 17, 1992.
c Refused assignment to minor leagues and became free agent, April 3; assignment rescinded due to injury and placed on disabled list, April 4, 1993.
d On disabled list from April 4 to the end of 1993 season.
e Released, October 12; re-signed by Colorado Rockies, December 21, 1993.
f On disabled list from July 11 to September 29, 1997.

RIVERA, MARIANO
Born, Panama City, Panama, November 29, 1969.
Bats Right. Throws Right. Height, 6 feet, 4 inches. Weight, 170 pounds.

Year Club	Lea	G	IP	W	L	Pct	SO	BB	H	ERA	SAVES
1990 Yankees .... .Gulf Coast		22	52	5	1	.833	58	7	17	0.17	1
1991 Greensboro .... .So. Atl.		29	114⅔	4	9	.308	123	36	103	2.75	0
1992 Ft. Lauderdale ...... .Fla. St.		10	59⅓	5	3	.625	42	5	40	2.28	0
1993 Yankees .... .Gulf Coast		2	4	0	1	.000	6	1	2	2.25	0
1993 Greensboro .... .So. Atl.		10	39⅓	1	0	1.000	32	15	31	2.06	0
1994 Tampa .... .Fla. St.		7	36⅔	3	0	1.000	27	12	34	2.21	0
1994 Albany .... .Eastern		9	63⅓	3	0	1.000	39	8	58	2.27	0
1994 Columbus .... .Int.		6	31	4	2	.667	23	10	34	5.81	0
1995 Columbus .... .Int.		7	30	2	2	.500	30	3	25	2.10	0
1995 New York .... .A.L.		19	67	5	3	.625	51	30	71	5.51	0
1996 New York .... .A.L.		61	107⅔	8	3	.727	130	34	73	2.09	5
1997 New York .... .A.L.		66	71⅔	6	4	.600	68	20	65	1.88	43
Major League Totals .... .3 Yrs.		146	246⅓	19	10	.655	249	84	209	2.96	48
Division Series											
1995 New York .... .A.L.		3	5⅓	1	0	1.000	8	1	3	0.00	0
1996 New York .... .A.L.		2	4⅔	0	0	.000	1	1	0	0.00	0
1997 New York .... .A.L.		2	2	0	0	.000	1	0	2	4.50	1
Divisional Series Totals 7			12	1	0	1.000	10	2	5	0.75	1
Championship Series											
1996 New York .... .A.L.		2	4	1	0	1.000	5	1	6	0.00	0
World Series Record											
1996 New York .... .A.L.		4	5⅔	0	0	.000	4	3	4	1.59	0

ROA, JOSEPH RODGER
Born, Southfield, Michigan, October 11, 1971.
Bats Right. Throws Right. Height, 6 feet, 1 inch. Weight, 194 pounds.

Year Club	Lea	G	IP	W	L	Pct	SO	BB	H	ERA	SAVES
1989 Braves .... .Gulf Coast		13	37⅓	2	2	.500	21	10	40	2.89	0
1990 Pulaski .... .Appal.		14	75⅔	4	2	.667	49	26	55	2.97	0
1991 Macon a .... .So. Atl.		30	141	13	3	.813	96	33	106	2.17	1
1992 St. Lucie .... .Fla. St.		26	156⅓	9	7	.563	61	15	176	3.63	0
1993 Binghamton .... .Eastern		32	167⅓	12	7	.632	73	24	190	3.87	0
1994 Binghamton .... .Eastern		3	20	2	1	.667	11	1	18	1.80	0
1994 Norfolk b .... .Int.		25	167⅔	8	8	.500	74	34	184	3.49	0
1995 Buffalo .... .A.A.		25	164⅔	17	3	.850	93	28	168	3.50	0
1995 Cleveland .... .A.L.		1	6	0	1	.000	0	2	9	6.00	0
1996 Cleveland .... .A.L.		1	1⅔	0	0	.000	0	3	4	10.80	0
1996 Buffalo c .... .A.A.		26	165⅓	11	8	.579	82	36	161	3.27	0
1997 San Francisco .... .N.L.		28	65⅔	2	5	.286	34	20	86	5.21	0
1997 Phoenix .... .P.C.		6	36	3	1	.750	16	11	43	4.75	0
Major League Totals .... .3 Yrs.		30	73⅓	2	6	.250	34	25	99	5.40	0

a Traded by Atlanta Braves to New York Mets for pitcher Alejandro Pena, August 29, 1991.
b Traded to Cleveland Indians with outfielder Jeromy Burnitz for pitchers Dave Mlicki, Paul Byrd and Jerry DiPoto, November 18, 1994.

c Traded to San Francisco Giants as player to be named later in November 13 trade which sent third baseman Matt Williams to Cleveland Indians for pitcher Julian Tavorez, infielders Jeff Kent and Jose Vizcaino, December 16, 1996. Outfielder Trenidad Hubbard was sent to Cleveland on the same day to complete the transaction.

ROBERTSON, RICHARD WAYNE

Born, Nacogdoches, Texas, September 15, 1968.
Bats Left. Throws Left. Height, 6 feet, 4 inches. Weight, 175 pounds.

Year	Club	Lea	G	IP	W	L	Pct	SO	BB	H	ERA	SAVES
1990	Welland	N.Y.-Penn.	16	64⅓	3	4	.429	80	55	51	3.08	0
1991	Salem	Carolina	12	45⅔	2	4	.333	32	42	34	4.93	0
1991	Augusta	So. Atl.	13	74	4	7	.364	62	51	73	4.99	0
1992	Salem	Carolina	6	37	3	0	1.000	27	10	29	3.41	0
1992	Carolina	Southern	20	124⅔	6	7	.462	107	41	127	3.03	0
1993	Buffalo	A.A.	23	132⅓	9	8	.529	71	52	141	4.28	0
1993	Pittsburgh	N.L.	9	9	0	1	.000	5	4	15	6.00	0
1994	Buffalo	A.A.	18	118⅔	5	10	.333	71	36	112	3.11	0
1994	Pittsburgh a	N.L.	8	15⅔	0	0	.000	8	10	20	6.89	0
1995	Salt Lake	P.C.	7	44⅓	5	0	1.000	40	12	31	2.44	0
1995	Minnesota	A.L.	25	51⅔	2	0	1.000	38	31	48	3.83	0
1996	Minnesota	A.L.	36	186⅓	7	17	.292	114	116	197	5.12	0
1997	Minnesota b	A.L.	31	147	8	12	.400	69	70	169	5.69	0
Major League Totals		5 Yrs.	109	409⅔	17	30	.362	234	231	449	5.25	0

a Claimed on waivers by Minnesota Twins from Pittsburgh Pirates, November 4, 1994.
b Released by Minnesota Twins, December 15, 1997.

RODRIGUEZ, FELIX ANTONIO

Born, Montecristi, Dominican Republic, December 5, 1972.
Bats Right. Throws Right. Height, 6 feet, 1 inch. Weight, 180 pounds.

Year	Club	Lea	G	IP	W	L	Pct	SO	BB	H	ERA	SAVES
1993	Vero Beach	Fla. St.	32	132	8	8	.500	80	71	109	3.75	0
1994	San Antonio	Texas	26	136⅓	6	8	.429	126	88	106	4.03	0
1995	Los Angeles	N.L.	11	10⅔	1	1	.500	5	5	11	2.53	0
1995	Albuquerque	P.C.	14	51	3	2	.600	46	26	52	4.24	0
1996	Albuquerque a	P.C.	27	107⅓	3	9	.250	65	60	111	5.53	0
1997	Indianapolis	A.A.	23	26⅔	3	3	.500	26	16	22	1.01	1
1997	Cincinnati b	N.L.	26	46	0	0	.000	34	28	48	4.30	0
Major League Totals		2 Yrs.	37	56⅔	1	1	.500	39	33	59	3.97	0

a Released by Los Angeles Dodgers organization and signed as free agent by Cincinnati Reds organization, December 23, 1996.
b Traded to Arizona Diamondbacks for player to be named later, November 11, 1997. Cincinnati Reds received pitcher Scott Winchester to complete trade, November 18, 1997.

RODRIGUEZ, FRANCISCO (FRANK)

Born, Brooklyn, New York, December 11, 1972.
Bats Right. Throws Right. Height, 6 feet. Weight, 175 pounds.

Year	Club	Lea	G	IP	W	L	Pct	SO	BB	H	ERA	SAVES
1992	Lynchburg	Carolina	25	148⅔	12	7	.632	129	65	125	3.09	0
1993	New Britain	Eastern	28	170⅔	7	11	.389	151	78	147	3.74	0
1994	Pawtucket	Int.	28	186	8	13	.381	*160	60	182	3.92	0
1995	Pawtucket	Int.	13	27	1	1	.500	18	8	19	4.00	2
1995	Boston-Minnesota a-b	A.L.	25	105⅔	5	8	.385	59	57	114	6.13	0
1996	Minnesota	A.L.	38	206⅔	13	14	.481	110	78	218	5.05	21997
1997	Minnesota	A.L.	43	142⅓	3	6	.333	65	60	147	4.62	0
Major League Totals		3 Yrs.	106	454⅔	21	28	.429	234	195	479	5.17	2

Record as Position Player

Year	Club	Lea	Pos	G	AB	R	H	2B	3B	HR	RBI	SB	Avg
1991	Winter Haven Red Sox	Gulf C.	SS	3	14	3	7	0	1	0	3	0	.500
1991	Elmira	N.Y.-Penn.	SS	67	255	36	69	5	3	6	31	3	.271

a Traded to Minnesota Twins with player to be named later for pitcher Rick Aquilera, July 6, 1995.
b Minnesota Twins received outfielder Jermane Johnson to complete trade, October 11, 1995.

325

RODRIGUEZ, NERIO

Born, San Pedro De Macoris, Dominican Republic, March 22, 1973.
Bats Right. Throws Right. Height, 6 feet, 1 inch. Weight, 195 pounds.

Year	Club	Lea	G	IP	W	L	Pct	SO	BB	H	ERA	SAVES
1995 High Desert	....	California	7	10	0	0	.000	10	7	8	1.80	0
1996 Frederick	....	Carolina	24	111⅓	8	7	.533	114	40	83	2.26	2
1996 Rochester	....	Int.	2	15	1	0	1.000	6	2	10	1.80	0
1996 Baltimore	....	A.L.	8	16⅔	0	1	.000	12	7	18	4.32	0
1997 Rochester	....	Int.	27	168⅓	11	10	.524	160	62	124	3.90	0
1997 Baltimore	....	A.L.	6	22	2	1	.667	11	8	21	4.91	0
Major League Totals	....	2 Yrs.	14	38⅔	2	2	.500	23	15	39	4.66	0

RODRIGUEZ, RICHARD ANTHONY (RICH)

Born, Downey, California, March 1, 1963.
Bats Left. Throws Left. Height, 6 feet. Weight, 205 pounds.

Year	Club	Lea	G	IP	W	L	Pct	SO	BB	H	ERA	SAVES
1984 Little Fls	....	N.Y.-Penn.	25	35⅓	2	1	.667	27	36	28	2.80	0
1985 Columbia	....	So. Atl.	49	80⅓	6	3	.667	71	36	89	4.03	6
1986 Jackson	....	Texas	13	33	3	4	.429	15	15	51	9.00	0
1986 Lynchburg	....	Carolina	36	45⅓	2	1	.667	38	19	37	3.57	3
1987 Lynchburg	....	Carolina	69	68	3	1	.750	59	26	69	2.78	5
1988 Jackson a	....	Texas	47	78⅓	2	7	.222	68	42	66	2.87	6
1989 Wichita	....	Texas	54	74⅓	8	3	.727	40	37	74	3.63	8
1990 Las Vegas	....	P.C.	27	59	3	4	.429	46	22	50	3.51	8
1990 San Diego	....	N.L.	32	47⅔	1	1	.500	22	16	52	2.83	1
1991 San Diego b	....	N.L.	64	80	3	1	.750	40	44	66	3.26	0
1992 San Diego c	....	N.L.	61	91	6	3	.667	64	29	77	2.37	0
1993 San Diego-Florida d-e	...	N.L.	70	76	2	4	.333	43	33	73	3.79	3
1994 St. Louis f	....	N.L.	56	60⅓	3	5	.375	43	26	62	4.03	0
1995 St. Louis g-i	....	N.L.	1	1⅔	0	0	.000	0	0	0	0.00	0
1996 Omaha j-k-l	....	A.A.	47	70	2	3	.400	68	20	75	3.99	3
1997 San Francisco m-n-o	....	N.L.	71	65⅓	4	3	.571	32	21	65	3.17	1
Major League Totals	....	7 Yrs.	355	422	19	17	.528	244	169	395	3.20	5
Division Series												
1997 San Francisco	....	N.L.	2	1	0	0	.000	0	0	1	0.00	0

a Traded by New York Mets to San Diego Padres organization for infielders Brad Pounders and Bill Stevenson, January 13, 1989.
b Appeared in one additional game as pinch runner.
c Entered one game as pinch hitter and remained in game as pitcher.
d Traded to Florida Marlins with infielder Gary Sheffield for pitchers Trevor Hoffman, Andres Berumen and Jose Martinez, June 25, 1993.
e Released, March 29; signed with St. Louis Cardinals, April 3, 1994.
f Declared restricted free agent under Major League Baseball implemented labor proposal, December 23, 1994.
g Re-signed with St. Louis Cardinals, April 5, 1995.
h On disabled list from April 27 to October 2, 1995.
i Released by St. Louis Cardinals, November 21, 1995.
j Signed as free agent by Cincinnati Reds, January 2, 1996.
k Released by Cincinnati Reds, March 23, 1996.
l Signed by Kansas City Royals, April 9, 1996.
m Signed as free agent by San Francisco Giants, November 14, 1996.
n Filed for free agency, October 30, 1997.
o Re-signed with San Francisco Giants, December 7, 1997.

ROGERS, KENNETH SCOTT

Born, Savannah, Georgia, November 10, 1964.
Bats Left. Throws Left. Height, 6 feet, 1 inch. Weight, 205 pounds.

Year	Club	Lea	G	IP	W	L	Pct	SO	BB	H	ERA	SAVES
1982 Sarasota Rangers	....	Gulf C.	2	3	0	0	.000	4	0	0	0.00	0
1983 Sarasota Rangers	....	Gulf C.	15	53⅓	4	1	.800	36	20	40	2.36	1
1984 Burlington	....	Midwest	39	92⅔	4	7	.364	93	33	87	3.98	3
1985 Daytona Beach	....	Fla. St.	6	10	0	1	.000	9	11	12	7.20	0
1985 Burlington	....	Midwest	33	95	2	5	.286	96	61	67	2.84	4
1986 Tulsa a	....	Texas	10	26⅓	0	3	.000	23	18	39	9.91	0
1986 Salem	....	Carolina	12	66	2	7	.222	46	26	75	6.27	0
1987 Charlotte b	....	Fla. St.	5	17	0	3	.000	14	8	17	4.76	0
1987 Tulsa	....	Texas	28	69	1	5	.167	59	35	80	5.35	2
1988 Charlotte c	....	Fla. St.	8	35⅓	2	0	1.000	26	11	22	1.27	1

Year	Club	Lea	G	IP	W	L	Pct	SO	BB	H	ERA	SAVES
1988 Tulsa	Texas	13	83⅓	4	6	.400	76	34	73	4.00	0
1989 Texas	A.L.	73	73⅔	3	4	.429	63	42	60	2.93	2
1990 Texas	A.L.	69	97⅔	10	6	.625	74	42	93	3.13	15
1991 Texas	A.L.	63	109⅔	10	10	.500	73	61	121	5.42	5
1992 Texas	A.L.	*81	78⅔	3	6	.333	70	26	80	3.09	6
1993 Texas	A.L.	35	208⅓	16	10	.615	140	71	210	4.10	0
1994 Texas d-e-f	A.L.	24	167⅓	11	8	.579	120	52	169	4.46	0
1995 Texas g-h	A.L.	31	208	17	7	.708	140	76	192	3.38	0
1996 New York	A.L.	30	179	12	8	.600	92	83	179	4.68	0
1997 New York i	A.L.	31	145	6	7	.462	78	62	161	5.65	0
Major League Totals ....9 Yrs.		437	1267⅓	88	66	.571	850	515	1265	4.20	28
Division Series											
1996 New York	A.L.	2	2	0	0	.000	1	2	5	9.00	0
Championship Series											
1996 New York	A.L.	1	3	0	0	.000	3	2	5	12.00	0
World Series Record											
1996 New York	A.L.	1	2	0	0	.000	0	2	5	22.50	0

a On disabled list from April 12 to April 30, 1986.
b On disabled list from March 28 to April 30, 1987.
c On disabled list from March 20 to May 15, 1988.
d Pitched perfect no-hit, no-run game against California Angels, winning 4-0, July 28, 1994.
e Filed for free agency, October 19, 1994; ruled ineligible by Player Relations Committee due to insufficient service time.
f Declared restricted free agent under Major League Baseball implemented labor proposal, December 23, 1994.
g Re-signed with Texas Rangers, April 7, 1995.
h Filed for free agency, November 12, 1995. Signed with New York Yankees, December 30, 1995.
i Traded to Oakland Athletics for player to be named later, November 7, 1997. New York Yankees received infielder Scott Brosius to complete trade, November 18, 1997.

ROJAS (MEDRANO), MELQUIADES (MEL)

Born, Haina, Dominican Republic, December 10, 1966.
Bats Right. Throws Right. Height, 5 feet, 11 inches. Weight, 195 pounds.

Year	Club	Lea	G	IP	W	L	Pct	SO	BB	H	ERA	SAVES
1986 Bradenton Expos	Gulf C.	13	55⅓	4	5	.444	34	27	63	4.88	0
1987 Burlington	Midwest	25	158⅔	8	9	.471	100	67	146	3.80	0
1988 Rockford a	Midwest	12	73⅓	6	4	.600	72	29	52	2.45	0
1988 West Palm Beach b ...	Fla. St.	2	5	1	0	1.000	4	1	4	3.60	0
1989 Jacksonville	Southern	34	112	10	7	.588	104	57	62	2.49	5
1990 Indianapolis	A.A.	17	97⅔	2	4	.333	64	47	84	3.13	0
1990 Montreal	N.L.	23	40	3	1	.750	26	24	34	3.60	1
1991 Indianapolis	A.A.	14	52⅔	4	2	.667	55	14	50	4.10	1
1991 Montreal	N.L.	37	48	3	3	.500	37	13	42	3.75	6
1992 Indianapolis	A.A.	4	8⅓	2	1	.667	7	3	10	5.40	0
1992 Montreal	N.L.	68	100⅔	7	1	.875	70	34	71	1.43	10
1993 Montreal c	N.L.	66	88⅓	5	8	.385	48	30	80	2.95	10
1994 Montreal	N.L.	58	84	3	2	.600	84	21	71	3.32	16
1995 Montreal	N.L.	59	67⅔	1	4	.200	61	29	69	4.12	30
1996 Montreal d	N.L.	74	81	7	4	.636	92	28	56	3.22	36
1997 Chicago-New York e	N.L.	77	85⅓	0	6	.000	93	36	78	4.64	15
Major League Totals ....8 Yrs.		462	595	29	29	.500	511	215	501	3.27	124

a On disabled list from May 7 to June 14, 1988.
b On disabled list from August 8 to end of 1988 season.
c On disabled list from July 4 to July 19, 1993.
d Signed with Chicago Cubs, December 10, 1996.
e Traded to New York Mets with pitcher Turk Wendell and outfielder Brian McRae for outfielder Lance Johnson, pitcher Mark Clark and player to be named later, August 8, 1997. Chicago Cubs received infielder Manny Alexander to complete trade, August 14, 1997.

ROSADO, JOSE ANTONIO

Born, Jersey City, New Jersey, November 9, 1974.
Bats Left. Throws Left. Height, 6 feet. Weight, 175 pounds.

Year	Club	Lea	G	IP	W	L	Pct	SO	BB	H	ERA	SAVES
1994 Royals	Gulf Coast	14	64⅔	6	2	.750	56	7	45	1.25	0
1995 Wilmington	Carolina	25	138	10	7	.588	117	30	128	3.13	0
1996 Wichita	Texas	2	13	2	0	1.000	12	1	10	0.00	0
1996 Omaha	A.A.	15	96⅔	8	3	.727	82	38	80	3.17	0

Year	Club	Lea	G	IP	W	L	Pct	SO	BB	H	ERA	SAVES
1996	Kansas City	A.L.	16	106⅔	8	6	.571	64	26	101	3.21	0
1997	Kansas City	A.L.	33	203⅓	9	12	.429	129	73	208	4.69	0
Major League Totals		2 Yrs.	49	310	17	18	.486	193	99	309	4.18	0

RUEBEL, MATTHEW ALEXANDER (MATT)

Born, Cincinnati, Ohio, October 16, 1969.
Bats Left. Throws Left. Height, 6 feet, 2 inches. Weight, 180 pounds.

Year	Club	Lea	G	IP	W	L	Pct	SO	BB	H	ERA	SAVES
1991	Welland	N.Y.-Penn.	6	27⅔	1	1	.500	27	11	16	1.95	0
1991	Augusta	So. Atl.	8	47	3	4	.429	35	25	43	3.83	0
1992	Augusta	So. Atl.	12	64⅔	5	2	.714	65	19	53	2.78	0
1992	Salem	Carolina	13	78⅓	1	6	.143	46	43	77	4.71	0
1993	Salem	Carolina	19	33⅓	1	4	.200	29	32	34	5.94	0
1993	Augusta	So. Atl.	23	63⅓	5	5	.500	50	34	51	2.42	0
1994	Carolina	Southern	6	16⅓	1	1	.500	14	3	28	6.61	0
1994	Salem	Carolina	21	86⅓	6	6	.500	72	27	87	3.44	0
1995	Carolina	Southern	27	169⅓	13	5	.722	136	45	150	2.76	0
1996	Calgary	P.C.	13	76⅓	5	3	.625	48	28	89	4.60	0
1996	Pittsburgh	N.L.	26	58⅔	1	1	.500	22	25	64	4.60	1
1997	Pittsburgh a	N.L.	44	62⅔	3	2	.600	50	27	77	6.32	0
Major League Totals		2 Yrs.	70	121⅓	4	3	.571	72	52	141	5.49	1

a On disabled list from May 5 to May 21, 1997.

RUETER, KIRK WESLEY

Born, Hoyleton, Illinois, December 1, 1970.
Bats Left. Throws Left. Height, 6 feet, 3 inches. Weight, 195 pounds.

Year	Club	Lea	G	IP	W	L	Pct	SO	BB	H	ERA	SAVES
1991	Bradenton Expos	Gulf C.	5	19	1	1	.500	19	4	16	0.95	0
1991	Sumter	So. Atl.	8	40⅔	3	1	.750	27	10	32	1.33	0
1992	Rockford	Midwest	26	174⅓	11	9	.550	153	36	150	2.58	0
1993	Harrisburg	Eastern	9	59⅔	5	0	1.000	36	7	47	1.36	0
1993	Ottawa	Int.	7	43⅓	4	2	.667	27	3	46	2.70	0
1993	Montreal	N.L.	14	85⅔	8	0	1.000	31	18	85	2.73	0
1994	Ottawa	Int.	1	2	0	0	.000	1	0	1	4.50	0
1994	Montreal	N.L.	20	92⅓	7	3	.700	50	23	106	5.17	0
1995	Ottawa	Int.	20	120⅔	9	7	.563	67	25	120	3.06	0
1995	Montreal	N.L.	9	47⅓	5	3	.625	28	9	38	3.23	0
1996	Ottawa	Int.	3	15	1	2	.333	3	3	21	4.20	0
1996	Phoenix	P.C.	5	25⅔	1	2	.333	15	12	25	3.51	0
1996	Montreal-San Francisco a	N.L.	20	102	6	8	.429	46	27	109	3.97	0
1997	San Francisco	N.L.	32	190⅔	13	6	.684	115	51	194	3.45	0
Major League Totals		5 Yrs.	95	518	39	20	.661	270	128	532	3.72	0
	Division Series											
1997	San Francisco	N.L.	1	7	0	0	.000	5	3	4	1.29	0

a On disabled list from May 10 to May 26, 1996.

RUFFCORN, SCOTT PATRICK

Born, Austin, Texas, December 12, 1969.
Bats Right. Throws Right. Height, 6 feet, 4 inches. Weight, 210 pounds.

Year	Club	Lea	G	IP	W	L	Pct	SO	BB	H	ERA	SAVES
1991	Sarasota White Sox ...	Gulf C	4	11⅓	0	0	.000	15	5	8	3.18	0
1991	South Bend	Midwest	9	43⅔	1	3	.250	45	25	35	3.92	0
1992	Sarasota	Fla. St.	25	160⅓	14	5	.737	140	39	122	2.19	0
1993	Birmingham	Southern	20	135	9	4	.692	*141	52	108	2.73	0
1993	Nashville	A.A.	7	45	2	2	.500	44	8	30	2.80	0
1993	Chicago	A.L.	3	10	0	2	.000	2	10	9	8.10	0
1994	Nashville	A.A.	24	165⅔	*15	3	.833	144	40	139	2.72	0
1994	Chicago	A.L.	2	6⅓	0	2	.000	3	5	15	12.79	0
1995	Nashville	A.A.	2	0⅓	0	0	.000	0	3	3	108.00	0
1995	Sarasota White Sox ...	Gulf C	3	10	0	0	.000	7	5	7	0.90	0
1995	Birmingham	Southern	3	16	0	2	.000	13	10	17	5.63	0
1995	Chicago	A.L.	4	8	0	0	.000	5	13	10	7.87	0

Year Club	Lea	G	IP	W	L	Pct	SO	BB	H	ERA	SAVES
1996 Nashville	A.A.	24	149	13	4	.765	129	61	142	3.87	0
1996 Chicago	A.L.	3	6⅓	0	1	.000	3	6	10	11.37	0
1997 Scranton-WB	Int.	5	31	2	0	1.000	20	10	22	1.16	0
1997 Philadelphia b-c	N.L.	18	39⅔	0	3	.000	33	36	42	7.71	0
Major League Totals	5 Yrs.	30	70⅓	0	8	.000	46	70	86	8.57	0

a Sold to Philadelphia Phillies, January 10, 1997.
b On disabled list from August 18 to September 29, 1997.
c Filed for free agency, October 7, 1997.

RUFFIN, BRUCE WAYNE

Born, Lubbock, Texas, October 4, 1963.
Bats Right. Throws Left. Height, 6 feet, 2 inches. Weight, 213 pounds.

Year Club	Lea	G	IP	W	L	Pct	SO	BB	H	ERA	SAVES
1985 Clearwater	Fla. St.	14	97	5	5	.500	74	34	87	2.88	0
1986 Reading	Eastern	16	90⅓	8	4	.667	68	26	89	3.29	0
1986 Philadelphia	N.L.	21	146⅓	9	4	.692	70	44	138	2.46	0
1987 Philadelphia	N.L.	35	204⅔	11	14	.440	93	73	236	4.35	0
1988 Philadelphia	N.L.	55	144⅓	6	10	.375	82	80	151	4.43	3
1989 Scranton	Int.	9	50	5	1	.833	44	39	44	4.68	0
1989 Philadelphia	N.L.	24	125⅔	6	10	.375	70	62	152	4.44	0
1990 Philadelphia	N.L.	32	149	6	13	.316	79	62	178	5.38	0
1991 Philadelphia a	N.L.	31	119	4	7	.364	85	38	125	3.78	0
1992 Milwaukee	A.L.	25	58	1	6	.143	45	41	66	6.67	0
1992 Denver b	A.A.	4	28⅔	3	0	1.000	17	8	28	0.94	0
1993 Colorado	N.L.	59	139⅔	6	5	.545	126	69	145	3.87	2
1994 Colorado	N.L.	56	55⅔	4	5	.444	65	30	55	4.04	16
1995 New Haven	Eastern	2	2	0	0	.000	2	0	1	0.00	0
1995 Colorado c	N.L.	37	34	0	1	.000	23	19	26	2.12	11
1996 Colorado	N.L.	71	69⅔	7	5	.583	74	29	55	4.00	24
1997 Colo. Springs	P.C.	2	2⅔	0	0	.000	2	0	1	3.38	0
1997 Colorado d-e-f	N.L.	23	22	0	2	.000	31	18	18	5.32	7
Major League Totals	12 Yrs.	469	1268	60	82	.423	843	565	1345	4.19	63
Division Series											
1995 Colorado	N.L.	4	3⅓	0	0	.000	2	2	3	2.70	0

a Traded to Milwaukee Brewers for infielder Dale Sveum, December 11, 1991.
b Filed for free agency, November 5; signed with Colorado Rockies organization, December 7, 1992.
c On disabled list from May 29 to June 17 and June 26 to August 22, 1995.
d On disabled list from May 19 to June 17 and June 27 to September 29, 1997.
e Filed for free agency, October 31, 1997.
f Signed as free agent with Colorado Rockies organization, January 2, 1998.

RUSCH, GLENDON JAMES

Born, Seattle, Washington, November 7, 1974.
Bats Left. Throws Left. Height, 6 feet, 2 inches. Weight, 170 pounds.

Year Club	Lea	G	IP	W	L	Pct	SO	BB	H	ERA	SAVES
1993 Royals	Gulf Coast	11	62	4	2	.667	48	11	43	1.60	0
1993 Rockford	Midwest	2	8	0	1	.000	8	7	10	3.38	0
1994 Rockford	Midwest	28	114	8	5	.615	122	34	111	4.66	1
1995 Wilmington	Carolina	26	165⅔	14	6	.700	147	34	110	1.74	0
1996 Omaha	A.A.	28	169⅔	11	9	.550	117	40	177	3.98	0
1997 Omaha	A.A.	1	6	0	1	.000	2	1	7	4.50	0
1997 Kansas City a	A.L.	30	170⅓	6	9	.400	116	52	206	5.50	0

a On disabled list from June 16 to July 1, 1997.

SABERHAGEN, BRET WILLIAM

Born, Chicago Heights, Illinois, April 11, 1964.
Bats Right. Throws Right. Height, 6 feet, 1 inch. Weight, 200 pounds.

Year Club	Lea	G	IP	W	L	Pct	SO	BB	H	ERA	SAVES
1984 Kansas City	A.L.	38	157⅔	10	11	.476	73	36	138	3.48	1
1985 Kansas City a	A.L.	32	235⅓	20	6	.769	158	38	211	2.87	0
1986 Kansas City b	A.L.	30	156	7	12	.368	112	29	165	4.15	0
1987 Kansas City	A.L.	33	257	18	10	.643	163	53	246	3.36	0

Year	Club	Lea	G	IP	W	L	Pct	SO	BB	H	ERA	SAVES
1988	Kansas City	A.L.	35	260⅔	14	16	.467	171	59	271	3.80	0
1989	Kansas City c	A.L.	36	262⅓	23	6	.793	193	43	209	2.16	0
1990	Kansas City d	A.L.	20	135	5	9	.357	87	28	146	3.27	0
1991	Kansas City e-f-g	A.L.	28	196⅓	13	8	.619	136	45	165	3.07	0
1992	New York h	N.L.	17	97⅔	3	5	.375	81	27	84	3.50	0
1993	New York i-j	N.L.	19	139⅓	7	7	.500	93	17	131	3.29	0
1994	New York	N.L.	24	177⅓	14	4	.778	143	13	169	2.74	0
1995	New York-Colorado k	N.L.	25	153	7	6	.538	100	33	165	4.17	0
1996	Colorado l	N.L.	INJURED—Did Not Play									
1996	Colorado	N.L.	INJURED—Did Not Play									
1997	Lowell	N.Y.-Penn.	1	3	0	0	.000	2	0	1	0.00	0
1997	Trenton m	Eastern	2	8	0	0	.000	9	1	2	0.00	0
1997	Pawtucket	Int.	2	11	0	1	.000	9	1	11	3.27	0
1997	Boston n-o	A.L.	6	26	0	1	.000	14	10	30	6.58	0
Major League Totals	13 Yrs.		343	2253⅔	141	101	.583	1524	431	2130	3.30	1

a Selected Cy Young Award winner in American League for 1985.
b On disabled list from August 11 to September 1, 1986.
c Selected Cy Young Award winner in American League for 1989.
d On disabled list from July 16 to September 10, 1990.
e On disabled list from June 14 to July 12, 1991.
f Pitched no-hit, no-run game against Chicago White Sox, winning 7-0, August 26, 1991.
g Traded to New York Mets with infielder Bill Pecota for outfielder Kevin McReynolds and infielders Gregg Jefferies and Keith Miller, December 11, 1991.
h On disabled list from May 16 to July 18 and August 2 to September 7, 1992.
i On disabled list from August 3 to end of 1993 season.
j Suspended five days by team for July 27, 1993 spraying bleach in clubhouse from April 3 to April 8, 1994.
k Traded to Colorado Rockies with player to be named later for pitcher Juan Acevado and pitcher Arnold Gooch, July 21, 1995.
l Released by Colorado Rockies and signed as free agent with Boston Red Sox organization, December 9, 1996.
m On disabled list from April 1 to August 22, 1997.
n Filed for free agency, October 31, 1997.
o Re-signed with Boston Red Sox, November 17, 1997.

SAGER, ANTHONY JOSEPH (A.J.)

Born, Columbus, Ohio, March 3, 1965.
Bats Right. Throws Right. Height, 6 feet, 4 inches. Weight, 220 pounds.

Year	Club	Lea	G	IP	W	L	Pct	SO	BB	H	ERA	SAVES
1988	Spokane	Northwest	15	98⅔	8	3	.727	74	27	123	5.11	0
1989	Charleston, SC	So. Atl.	26	167⅔	14	9	.609	105	40	166	3.38	0
1990	Wichita	Texas	26	154⅓	11	12	.478	79	29	200	5.48	0
1991	Wichita	Texas	10	65⅓	4	3	.571	31	16	69	4.13	0
1991	Las Vegas	P.C.	18	109	7	5	.583	61	20	127	4.71	0
1992	Las Vegas	P.C.	30	60	1	7	.125	40	17	89	7.95	1
1993	Wichita	Texas	11	73⅓	5	3	.625	49	16	69	3.19	0
1993	Las Vegas	P.C.	21	90	6	5	.545	58	18	91	3.70	1
1994	Las Vegas	P.C.	23	40⅔	1	4	.200	23	8	57	4.43	5
1994	San Diego a	N.L.	22	46⅔	1	4	.200	26	16	62	5.98	0
1995	Colorado Springs	P.C.	23	133⅔	8	5	.615	80	23	153	3.50	0
1995	Colorado b	N.L.	10	14⅔	0	0	.000	10	7	19	7.36	0
1996	Toledo	Int.	18	37⅔	1	0	1.000	24	3	38	2.63	0
1996	Detroit	A.L.	22	79	4	5	.444	52	29	91	5.01	0
1997	Detroit	A.L.	38	84	3	4	.429	53	24	81	4.18	3
Major League Totals	4 Yrs.		92	224⅓	8	13	.381	141	76	253	5.05	3

a Became free agent, October 15, 1994.
b Signed with Colorado Rockies, December 1, 1995.

SALKELD, ROGER WILLIAM

Born, Burbank, California, March 6, 1971.
Bats Right. Throws Right. Height, 6 feet, 5 inches. Weight, 215 pounds.

Year	Club	Lea	G	IP	W	L	Pct	SO	BB	H	ERA	SAVES
1989	Bellingham	Northwest	8	42	2	2	.500	55	10	27	1.29	0
1990	San Berndno	California	25	153⅓	11	5	.688	167	83	140	3.40	0
1991	Jacksnville	Southern	23	153⅓	8	8	.500	159	55	131	3.05	0
1991	Calgary	P.C.	4	19⅓	2	1	.667	21	13	18	5.12	0
1993	Jacksnville	Southern	14	77	4	3	.571	56	29	71	3.27	0
1993	Seattle	A.L.	3	14⅓	0	0	.000	13	4	13	2.51	0
1994	Seattle	A.L.	13	59	2	5	.286	46	45	76	7.17	0
1994	Calgary	P.C.	13	67⅓	3	7	.300	54	39	74	6.15	0

Year	Club	Lea	G	IP	W	L	Pct	SO	BB	H	ERA	SAVES
1995 Tacoma ..............P.C.			4	15	1	0	1.000	11	7	8	1.80	1
1995 Indianapols ...........A.A.			20	119⅓	12	2	.857	86	57	96	4.22	0
1996 Cincinnati .............N.L.			29	116	8	5	.615	82	54	114	5.20	0
1996 Indianapolis b .........A.A.			36	88	4	8	.333	88	54	91	6.75	1
Major League Totals ....3 Yrs.			45	189⅓	10	10	.500	141	103	203	5.61	0

a Traded to Cincinnati Reds for pitcher Tim Belcher, May 15, 1995.
b Signed as free agent with Houston Astros organization, December 29, 1997.

SANDERS, SCOTT GERALD
Born, Hannibal, Missouri, March 25, 1969.
Bats Right. Throws Right. Height, 6 feet, 4 inches. Weight, 215 pounds.

Year	Club	Lea	G	IP	W	L	Pct	SO	BB	H	ERA	SAVES
1990 Spokane ....Northwest			3	19	2	1	.667	21	5	12	0.95	0
1990 Waterloo ....Midwest			7	37	2	2	.500	29	21	43	4.86	0
1991 Waterloo ....Midwest			4	26⅓	3	0	1.000	18	6	17	0.68	0
1991 High Desert ....California			21	132⅔	9	6	.600	93	72	114	3.66	0
1992 Wichita ....Texas			14	87⅔	7	5	.583	95	37	85	3.49	0
1992 Las Vegas .............P.C.			14	72	3	6	.333	51	31	97	5.50	0
1993 Las Vegas .............P.C.			24	152⅓	5	10	.333	*161	62	170	4.96	0
1993 San Diego ...........N.L.			9	52⅓	3	3	.500	37	23	54	4.13	0
1994 San Diego a ...........N.L.			23	111	4	8	.333	109	48	103	4.78	1
1995 Las Vegas .............P.C.			1	3	0	0	.000	2	1	3	0.00	0
1995 San Diego b ...........N.L.			17	90	5	5	.500	88	31	79	4.30	0
1996 San Diego c ...........N.L.			46	144	9	5	.643	157	48	117	3.38	0
1997 Seattle-Detroit d .......A.L.			47	139⅔	6	14	.300	120	62	152	5.86	2
Major League Totals ....5 Yrs.			142	537	27	35	.435	511	212	505	4.54	3
Division Series												
1996 San Diego ...........N.L.			1	4⅓	0	0	.000	4	4	3	8.31	0

a On disabled list from May 2 to May 17, 1984.
b On disabled list from July 18 to September 8 and September 8 to October 2, 1995.
c Traded to Seattle Mariners for pitcher Sterling Hitchcock, December 6, 1996.
d Traded to Detroit Tigers with pitcher Dean Crow for pitcher Omar Olivares and pitcher Felipe Lira, July 18, 1997.

SANTANA, JULIO FRANKLIN
Born, San Pedro De Macoris, Dominican Republic, January 20, 1973.
Bats Right. Throws Right. Height, 6 feet. Weight, 175 pounds.

Year	Club	Lea	G	IP	W	L	Pct	SO	BB	H	ERA	SAVES
1993 Rangers ....Gulf Coast			26	39	4	1	.800	50	7	31	1.38	7
1994 Charlstn-Sc ....So. Atl.			16	91⅓	6	7	.462	103	44	65	2.46	0
1994 Tulsa ....Texas			11	71⅓	7	2	.778	45	41	50	2.90	0
1995 Okla City ............A.A.			2	3	0	2	.000	6	7	9	39.00	0
1995 Charlotte ....Fla. St.			5	31⅓	0	3	.000	27	16	32	3.73	0
1995 Tulsa ....Texas			15	103	6	4	.600	71	52	91	3.15	0
1996 Okla City ............A.A.			29	185⅔	11	12	.478	113	66	171	4.02	0
1997 Okla City .............A.A.			1	3	0	0	.000	1	2	9	15.00	0
1997 Texas a .............A.L.			30	104	4	6	.400	64	49	141	6.75	0

a On disabled list from July 15 to August 10, 1997.

SANTIAGO, JOSE RAFAEL
Born, Fajardo, Puerto Rico, November 5, 1974.
Bats Right. Throws Right. Height, 6 feet, 3 inches. Weight, 200 pounds.

Year	Club	Lea	G	IP	W	L	Pct	SO	BB	H	ERA	SAVES
1994 Royals ....Gulf Coast			10	19	1	0	1.000	10	7	17	2.37	2
1995 Spokane ....Northwest			22	48⅔	2	4	.333	32	20	60	3.14	1
1996 Lansing ....Midwest			54	77	7	6	.538	55	21	78	2.57	19
1997 Wilmington ....Carolina			4	3⅔	1	1	.500	1	1	3	4.91	2
1997 Lansing ....Midwest			9	13	1	0	1.000	8	6	10	2.08	1
1997 Kansas City ...........A.L.			4	4⅔	0	0	.000	1	2	7	1.93	0
1997 Wichita a ....Texas			22	27	2	1	.667	12	8	32	4.00	3

a On disabled list from June 18 to July 9, 1997.

SAUNDERS, ANTHONY SCOTT
Born, Baltimore, Maryland, April 29, 1974.
Bats Left. Throws Left. Height, 6 feet, 2 inches. Weight, 205 pounds.

Year	Club	Lea	G	IP	W	L	Pct	SO	BB	H	ERA	SAVES
1992 Marlins	.........Gulf Coast		24	45⅔	4	1	.800	37	13	29	1.18	7
1993 Kane County	.......Midwest		23	83⅓	6	1	.857	87	32	72	2.27	1
1994 Brevard Cty	.........Fla. St.		10	60	5	5	.500	46	9	54	3.15	0
1995 Brevard Cty		Fla. St.	13	71	6	5	.545	54	15	60	3.04	0
1996 Portland	..........Eastern		26	167⅔	13	4	.765	156	62	121	2.63	0
1997 Charlotte	..............Int.		3	13	1	0	1.000	9	6	9	2.77	0
1997 Florida a-b	.............N.L.		22	111⅓	4	6	.400	102	64	99	4.61	0
Championship Series												
1997 Florida	...............N.L.		1	5⅓	0	0	.000	3	3	4	3.38	0
World Series Record												
1997 Florida	...............N.L.		1	2	0	1	.000	2	3	7	27.00	0

a On disabled list from May 19 to July 10, 1997.
b Selected in expansion draft by Tampa Bay Devil Rays, November 18, 1997.

SCHILLING, CURTIS MONTAGUE (CURT)
Born, Anchorage, Alaska, November 14, 1966.
Bats Right. Throws Right. Height, 6 feet, 4 inches. Weight, 225 pounds.

Year	Club	Lea	G	IP	W	L	Pct	SO	BB	H	ERA	SAVES
1986 Elmira	.........N.Y.-Penn.		16	93⅔	7	3	.700	75	31	92	2.59	0
1987 Greensboro	.........So. Atl.		29	184	8	*15	.348	*189	65	179	3.82	0
1988 New Britain a	......Eastern		21	106	8	5	.615	62	40	91	2.97	1
1988 Charlotte	.........Southern		7	45⅓	5	2	.714	32	23	36	3.18	0
1988 Baltimore	...............A.L.		4	14⅔	0	3	.000	4	10	22	9.82	0
1989 Rochester	...............Int.		27	*185⅓	*13	11	.542	109	59	176	3.21	0
1989 Baltimore	...............A.L.		5	8⅔	0	1	.000	6	3	10	6.23	0
1990 Rochester	...............Int.		15	87⅓	4	4	.500	83	25	95	3.92	0
1990 Baltimore b	...........A.L.		35	46	1	2	.333	32	19	38	2.54	3
1991 Tucson	..............P.C.		13	23⅔	0	1	.000	21	12	16	3.42	3
1991 Houston c	...............N.L.		56	75⅔	3	5	.375	71	39	79	3.81	8
1992 Philadelphia	...........N.L.		42	226⅓	14	11	.560	147	59	165	2.35	2
1993 Philadelphia	...........N.L.		34	235⅓	16	7	.696	186	57	234	4.02	0
1994 Reading	..........Eastern		1	4	0	0	.000	4	1	6	0.00	0
1994 Scranton	...............Int.		2	10	0	0	.000	6	5	6	1.80	0
1994 Philadelphia d	........N.L.		13	82⅓	2	8	.200	58	28	87	4.48	0
1995 Philadelphia e	........N.L.		17	116	7	5	.583	114	26	96	3.57	0
1996 Clearwater	.........Fla. St.		2	14	2	0	1.000	17	1	9	1.29	0
1996 Scranton-W.B.	......Int.		2	13	1	0	1.000	10	5	9	1.38	0
1996 Philadelphia f	........N.L.		26	183⅓	9	10	.474	182	50	149	3.19	0
1997 Philadelphia	...........N.L.		35	254⅓	17	11	.607	319	58	208	2.97	0
Major League Totals	........10 Yrs.		267	1242⅔	69	63	.523	1119	349	1088	3.38	13
Championship Series												
1993 Philadelphia	...........N.L.		2	16	0	0	.000	19	5	11	1.69	0
World Series Record												
1993 Philadelphia	...........N.L.		2	15⅓	1	1	.500	9	5	13	3.52	0

a Traded by Boston Red Sox to Baltimore Orioles organization with outfielder Brady Anderson for pitcher Mike
  Boddicker, July 29, 1988.
b Traded to Houston Astros with pitcher Pete Harnisch and outfielder Steve Finley for first baseman Glenn Davis,
  January 10, 1991.
c Traded to Philadelphia Phillies for pitcher Jason Grimsley, April 2, 1992.
d On disabled list from May 17 to July 25, 1994.
e On disabled list from July 19 to October 2, 1995.
f On disabled list from April 1 to May 14, 1996.

SCHMIDT, JASON DAVID
Born, Kelso, Washington, January 29, 1973.
Bats Right. Throws Right. Height, 6 feet, 5 inches. Weight, 185 pounds.

Year	Club	Lea	G	IP	W	L	Pct	SO	BB	H	ERA	SAVES
1991 Braves	..........Gulf Coast		11	45⅓	3	4	.429	44	23	32	2.38	0
1992 Macon	.........So. Atl.		7	24⅔	0	3	.000	33	19	31	4.01	0
1992 Pulaski	.............Appal.		11	58⅓	3	4	.429	56	31	55	4.01	0
1993 Durham	..........Carolina		22	116⅔	7	11	.389	110	47	128	4.94	0
1994 Greenville	.........Southern		24	140⅔	8	7	.533	131	54	135	3.65	0
1995 Richmond	..............Int.		19	116	8	6	.571	95	48	97	2.25	0

Year Club	Lea	G	IP	W	L	Pct	SO	BB	H	ERA	SAVES
1995 Atlanta ............N.L.		9	25	2	2	.500	19	18	27	5.76	0
1996 Greenville ....Southern		1	2	0	0	.000	2	0	4	9.00	0
1996 Richmond ....Int.		7	45⅔	3	0	1.000	41	19	36	2.56	0
1996 Atlanta-Pittsburgh a-b ...N.L.		19	96⅓	5	6	.455	74	53	108	5.70	0
1997 Pittsburgh ...........N.L.		32	187⅔	10	9	.526	136	76	193	4.60	0
Major League Totals ....3 Yrs.		60	309	17	17	.500	229	147	328	5.04	0

a Traded to Pittsburgh Pirates with infielder Ron Wright and outfielder Corey Pointer for pitcher Denny Neagle, August 29, 1996.
b On disabled list from July 15 to August 28, 1996.

SCHOUREK, PETER ALAN
Born, Austin, Texas, May 10, 1969.
Bats Left. Throws Left. Height, 6 feet, 5 inches. Weight, 205 pounds.

Year Club	Lea	G	IP	W	L	Pct	SO	BB	H	ERA	SAVES
1987 Little Falls .......N.Y.-Penn.		12	78⅓	4	5	.444	57	34	70	3.68	0
1988 Little Falls a ....N.Y.-Penn.		INJURED—Did Not Play									
1989 Columbia ....So. Atl.		27	136	5	9	.357	131	66	120	2.85	1
1989 St. Lucie ....Fla. St.		2	4	0	0	.000	4	2	3	2.25	0
1990 St. Lucie ....Fla. St.		5	37	4	1	.800	28	8	29	0.97	0
1990 Tidewater ....Int.		2	14	1	0	1.000	14	5	9	2.57	0
1990 Jackson ....Texas		19	124⅓	11	4	.733	94	39	109	3.04	0
1991 New York ...........N.L.		35	86⅓	5	4	.556	67	43	82	4.27	2
1991 Tidewater ....Int.		4	25	1	1	.500	17	10	18	2.52	0
1992 Tidewater ....Int.		8	52⅔	2	5	.286	42	23	46	2.73	0
1992 New York b ..........N.L.		22	136	6	8	.429	60	44	137	3.64	0
1993 New York c ..........N.L.		41	128⅓	5	12	.294	72	45	168	5.96	0
1994 Cincinnati ...........N.L.		22	81⅓	7	2	.778	69	29	90	4.09	0
1995 Cincinnati ...........N.L.		29	190⅓	18	7	.720	160	45	158	3.22	0
1996 Cincinnati d .........N.L.		12	67⅓	4	5	.444	54	24	79	6.01	0
1997 Cincinnati e-f-g ......N.L.		18	84⅔	5	8	.385	59	38	78	5.42	0
Major League Totals ....7 Yrs.		179	774⅓	50	46	.521	541	268	792	4.44	2
Division Series											
1995 Cincinnati ...........N.L.		1	7	1	0	1.000	5	3	5	2.57	0
Championship-Series											
1995 Cincinnati ...........N.L.		2	14⅓	0	1	.000	13	3	14	1.26	0

a On disabled list from March 29 to end of 1988 season.
b Appeared in one additional game as pinch runner.
c Claimed on waivers by Cincinnati Reds, April 7, 1994.
d On disabled list from June 1 to August 22 and July 2 to September 30, 1996.
e On disabled list from June 14 to July 18 and July 31 to September 2, 1997.
f Released by Cincinnati Reds, October 10, 1997.
g Signed with Houston Astros organization, January 9, 1998.

SCOTT, TIMOTHY DALE
Born, Hanford, California, November 16, 1966.
Bats Right. Throws Right. Height, 6 feet, 2 inches. Weight, 205 pounds.

Year Club	Lea	G	IP	W	L	Pct	SO	BB	H	ERA	SAVES
1984 Great Falls ....Pioneer		13	78	5	4	.556	44	38	90	4.38	0
1985 Bakersfield a ......California		12	63⅔	3	4	.429	31	28	84	5.80	0
1986 Vero Beach b ....Fla. St.		20	95⅓	5	4	.556	37	34	113	3.40	0
1987 Bakersfield ....California		7	32⅓	2	3	.400	29	10	33	4.45	0
1987 San Antonio c ....Texas		2	5⅓	0	1	.000	6	2	14	16.88	0
1988 Bakersfield d ......California		36	64⅓	4	8	.333	59	26	52	3.64	7
1989 San Antonio ....Texas		48	68	4	2	.667	64	36	71	3.71	4
1990 San Antonio ....Texas		30	47	3	3	.500	52	14	35	2.85	7
1990 Albuquerque e .........P.C.		17	15	2	1	.667	15	14	14	4.20	3
1991 Las Vegas ............P.C.		41	111	8	8	.500	74	39	133	5.19	0
1991 San Diego ...........N.L.		2	1	0	0	.000	1	0	2	9.00	0
1992 Las Vegas ............P.C.		24	28	1	2	.333	28	3	20	2.25	15
1992 San Diego ...........N.L.		34	37⅔	4	1	.800	30	21	39	5.26	0
1993 San Diego-Montreal f ....N.L.		56	71⅔	7	2	.778	65	34	69	3.01	1
1994 Montreal g ...........N.L.		40	53⅓	5	2	.714	37	18	51	2.70	1
1995 Montreal ............N.L.		62	63⅓	2	0	1.000	57	23	52	3.98	2
1996 Montreal-San Francisco h-i .N.L.		65	66	5	7	.417	47	30	65	4.64	1
1997 Colo Sprngs j-k-l-m-n-o ..P.C.		12	14⅔	0	0	.000	18	3	7	1.23	3
1997 San Diego-Colorado .....N.L.		17	21	1	1	.500	16	7	30	8.14	0
Major League Totals ....7 Yrs.		276	314	24	13	.649	253	133	308	4.13	5

333

a On disabled list from July 23 to end of 1985 season.
b On disabled list from April 9 to May 15, 1986.
c On disabled list from May 18 to end of 1987 season.
d On disabled list from May 6 to May 27, 1988.
e Became free agent, October 15; signed with San Diego Padres organization, November 1, 1990.
f Traded to Montreal Expos for infielder Archi Cianfrocco, June 23, 1993
g On disabled list from June 6 to June 21, 1994.
h Traded to San Francisco Giants with pitcher Kirk Reuter for pitcher Mark Leiter, July 30, 1996.
i Claimed on waivers by Cincinnati Reds, October 13, 1996.
j Signed with San Diego Padres organization, January 30, 1997.
k Released by San Diego Padres, May 18, 1997.
l Signed with Colorado Rockies organization, May 27, 1997.
m Claimed on waivers by Seattle Mariners, July 10, 1997.
n On disabled list from July 4 to September 29, 1997.
o Signed with Los Angeles Dodgers organization, December 17, 1997.

SELE, AARON HELMER
Born, Golden Valley, Minnesota, June 25, 1970.
Bats Right. Throws Right. Height, 6 feet, 5 inches. Weight, 205 pounds.

Year Club	Lea	G	IP	W	L	Pct	SO	BB	H	ERA	SAVES
1991 Winter Haven . . . . .Fla. St.		13	69	3	6	.333	51	32	65	4.96	1
1992 Lynchburg . . . . .Carolina		20	127	13	5	.722	112	46	104	2.91	0
1992 New Britain . . . . .Eastern		7	33	2	1	.667	29	15	43	6.27	0
1993 Pawtucket . . . . .Int.		14	94⅓	8	2	.800	87	23	74	2.19	0
1993 Boston . . . . .A.L.		18	111⅔	7	2	.778	93	48	100	2.74	0
1994 Boston . . . . .A.L.		22	143⅓	8	7	.533	105	60	140	3.83	0
1995 Sarasota . . . . .Fla. St.		2	7	0	0	.000	8	1	6	0.00	0
1995 Trenton . . . . .Eastern		2	8	0	1	.000	9	2	8	3.38	0
1995 Pawtucket . . . . .Int.		2	5	0	0	.000	1	2	9	9.00	0
1995 Boston a . . . . .A.L.		6	32⅓	3	1	.750	21	14	32	3.06	0
1996 Pawtucket . . . . .Int.		1	3	0	0	.000	4	1	3	6.00	0
1996 Boston b . . . . .A.L.		29	157⅓	7	11	.389	137	67	192	5.32	0
1997 Boston c . . . . .A.L.		33	177⅓	13	12	.520	122	80	196	5.38	0
Major League Totals . . . . .5 Yrs.		108	622	38	33	.535	478	269	660	4.41	0

a On disabled list from May 24 to October 2, 1995.
b On disabled list from August 14 to September 1, 1996.
c Traded to Texas Rangers with pitcher Mark Brandenburg for catcher Jim Leyritz and outfielder Damon Buford, November 6, 1997.

SERAFINI, DANIEL JOSEPH
Born, San Francisco, California, January 25, 1974.
Bats Both. Throws Left. Height, 6 feet, 1 inch. Weight, 185 pounds.

Year Club	Lea	G	IP	W	L	Pct	SO	BB	H	ERA	SAVES
1992 Twins . . . . .Gulf Coast		8	29⅔	1	0	1.000	33	15	27	3.64	0
1993 Ft. Wayne . . . . .Midwest		27	140⅔	10	8	.556	147	83	117	3.65	0
1994 Ft. Myers . . . . .Fla. St.		23	136⅔	9	9	.500	130	57	149	4.61	0
1995 New Britain . . . . .Eastern		27	162⅔	12	9	.571	123	72	155	3.38	0
1995 Salt Lake . . . . .P.C.		1	4	0	0	.000	4	1	4	6.75	1
1996 Minnesota . . . . .A.L.		1	4⅓	0	1	.000	1	2	7	10.38	0
1996 Salt Lake . . . . .P.C.		25	130⅔	7	7	.500	109	58	164	5.58	0
1997 Salt Lake . . . . .P.C.		28	152	9	7	.563	118	55	166	4.97	0
1997 Minnesota . . . . .A.L.		6	26⅓	2	1	.667	15	11	27	3.42	0
Major League Totals . . . . . . .2 Yrs.		7	30⅔	2	2	.500	16	13	34	4.40	0

SERVICE, SCOTT DAVID
Born, Cincinnati, Ohio, February 26, 1967.
Bats Right. Throws Right. Height, 6 feet, 6 inches. Weight, 226 pounds.

Year Club	Lea	G	IP	W	L	Pct	SO	BB	H	ERA	SAVES
1986 Spartanburg . . . . .So. Atl.		14	58⅔	1	6	.143	49	34	68	5.83	0
1986 Utica . . . . .N.Y.-Penn.		10	70⅔	5	4	.556	43	18	65	2.67	0
1986 Clearwater . . . . .Fla. St.		4	25⅓	1	2	.333	19	15	20	3.20	0

Year	Club	Lea	G	IP	W	L	Pct	SO	BB	H	ERA	SAVES
1987 Reading	Eastern	5	19²/₃	0	3	.000	12	16	22	7.78	0
1987 Clearwater	Fla. St.	21	137²/₃	13	4	.765	73	32	127	2.48	0
1988 Reading	Eastern	10	56²/₃	3	4	.429	39	22	52	2.86	0
1988 Maine	Int.	19	110¹/₃	8	8	.500	87	31	109	3.67	0
1988 Philadelphia	N.L.	5	5¹/₃	0	0	.000	6	1	7	1.69	0
1989 Reading	Eastern	23	85²/₃	6	6	.500	82	23	71	3.26	1
1989 Scranton	Int.	23	33¹/₃	3	1	.750	24	23	27	2.16	6
1990 Scranton a	Int.	45	96	5	4	.556	94	44	95	4.76	2
1991 Indianapolis	A.A.	18	121¹/₃	6	7	.462	91	39	83	2.97	0
1992 Montreal	N.L.	5	7	0	0	.000	11	5	15	14.14	0
1992 Indianapolis-Nash. b	A.A.	52	95	8	2	.800	112	44	66	1.89	6
1993 Indianapolis c	A.A.	21	30¹/₃	4	2	.667	28	17	25	4.45	2
1993 Colorado-Cincin. d-e	N.L.	29	46	2	2	.500	50	32	91	4.30	2
1994 Indianapolis	A.A.	40	58¹/₃	5	5	.500	67	27	35	2.31	13
1994 Cincinnati	N.L.	6	7¹/₃	1	2	.333	5	3	8	7.36	0
1995 Indianapolis	A.A.	36	41¹/₃	4	1	.800	48	15	33	2.18	18
1995 San Francisco f	N.L.	28	31	3	1	.750	30	20	18	3.19	0
1996 Indianapolis	A.A.	35	48	1	4	.200	58	10	34	3.00	15
1996 Cincinnati g	N.L.	34	48	1	0	1.000	46	18	51	3.94	0
1997 Indianapols	A.A.	33	34	3	2	.600	53	12	30	3.71	15
1997 Omaha	A.A.	16	14²/₃	0	0	.000	16	4	9	0.00	9
1997 Cincinnati h-i-j	N.L.	4	5¹/₃	0	0	.000	3	1	11	11.81	0
1997 Kansas City	A.L.	12	17	0	3	.000	19	5	17	4.76	0
Major League Totals .... 7 Yrs.		123	167	7	8	.467	163	69	171	4.74	2

a Became free agent, October 15; signed with Montreal Expos organization, November 13, 1990.
b Refused assignment to minor leagues and became free agent, June 9; signed with Cincinnati Reds organization, June 12, 1992.
c Claimed on waivers by Colorado Rockies from Cincinnati Reds organization, June 27, 1993.
d Claimed on waivers by Cincinnati Reds, July 7, 1993.
e Appeared in one additional game as pinch hitter.
f Traded to San Francisco Giants with outfielder Deion Sanders, pitcher John Roper, pitcher Ricky Pickett and infielder David McCarty for pitcher Dave Burba, pitcher Mark Portugal and outfielder Darren Lewis, July 21, 1995.
g Waived by San Francisco Giants, March 26, 1996. Signed with Cincinnati Reds.
h Claimed on waivers by Oakland Athletics, March 27, 1997.
i Claimed on waivers by Cincinnati Reds, April 4, 1997.
j Traded to Kansas City Royals with pitcher Hector Carrasco for outfielder Jon Nunnally and outfielder Chris Stynes, July 15, 1997.

SHAW, JEFFREY LEE

Born, Washington Court House, Ohio, July 7, 1966.
Bats Right. Throws Right. Height, 6 feet, 2 inches. Weight, 200 pounds.

Year	Club	Lea	G	IP	W	L	Pct	SO	BB	H	ERA	SAVES
1986 Batavia	N.Y.-Penn.	14	88²/₃	8	4	.667	71	35	79	2.54	0
1987 Waterloo	Midwest	28	184¹/₃	11	11	.500	117	56	192	3.52	0
1988 Williamsport	Eastern	27	163²/₃	5	*19	.208	61	75	*173	3.63	0
1989 Canton	Eastern	30	154¹/₃	7	10	.412	95	67	134	3.62	0
1990 Colorado Springs	P.C.	17	98²/₃	10	3	.769	55	52	98	4.29	0
1990 Cleveland	A.L.	12	48²/₃	3	4	.429	25	20	73	6.66	0
1991 Colorado Springs	P.C.	12	75²/₃	6	3	.667	55	25	77	4.64	0
1991 Cleveland	A.L.	29	72¹/₃	0	5	.000	31	27	72	3.36	1
1992 Colorado Springs	P.C.	25	155	10	5	.667	84	45	174	4.76	0
1992 Cleveland a-b	A.L.	2	7²/₃	0	1	.000	3	4	7	8.22	0
1993 Ottawa	Int.	2	4	0	0	.000	1	2	5	0.00	0
1993 Montreal	N.L.	55	95²/₃	2	7	.222	50	32	91	4.14	0
1994 Montreal	N.L.	46	67¹/₃	5	2	.714	47	15	67	3.88	1
1995 Montreal	N.L.	50	62¹/₃	1	6	.143	45	26	58	4.62	3
1995 Chicago c	A.L.	9	9²/₃	0	0	.000	6	1	12	6.52	0
1996 Cincinnati d	N.L.	78	104²/₃	8	6	.571	69	29	99	2.49	4
1997 Cincinnati	N.L.	78	94²/₃	4	2	.667	74	12	79	2.38	42
Major League Totals .... 8 Yrs.		359	563	23	33	.411	350	166	558	3.77	51

a Refused assignment to minor leagues and became free agent, October 8; signed with Kansas City Royals organization, November 9, 1992.
b Traded by Kansas City Royals with catcher Tim Spehr for pitchers Mark Gardner and Doug Piatt, December 9, 1992.
c Traded to Chicago White Sox for pitcher Jose DeLeon, August 27, 1995.
d Signed with Cincinnati Reds organization, January 2, 1996.

SHUEY, PAUL KENNETH

Born, Lima, Ohio, September 16, 1970.
Bats Right. Throws Right. Height, 6 feet, 3 inches. Weight, 215 pounds.

Year	Club	Lea	G	IP	W	L	Pct	SO	BB	H	ERA	SAVES
1992 Columbus	....	So. Atl.	14	78	5	5	.500	73	47	62	3.35	0
1993 Canton	....	Eastern	27	61²/₃	4	8	.333	41	36	76	7.30	0
1993 Kinston	....	Carolina	15	22¹/₃	1	0	1.000	27	8	29	4.84	0
1994 Kinston	....	Carolina	13	12	1	0	1.000	16	3	10	3.75	8
1994 Charlotte	....	.Int.	20	23¹/₃	2	1	.667	25	10	15	1.93	10
1994 Cleveland a	....	.A.L.	14	11²/₃	0	1	.000	16	12	14	8.49	5
1995 Buffalo	....	A.A.	25	27¹/₃	1	2	.333	27	7	21	2.63	11
1995 Cleveland b	....	.A.L.	7	6¹/₃	0	2	.000	5	5	5	4.26	0
1996 Buffalo	....	A.A.	19	33¹/₃	3	2	.600	57	9	14	0.81	4
1996 Cleveland	....	.A.L.	42	53²/₃	5	2	.714	44	26	45	2.85	4
997 Buffalo	....	A.A.	2	5	0	0	.000	6	4	4	3.60	0
1997 Akron	....	Eastern	3	8	0	0	.000	9	0	10	3.38	0
1997 Cleveland c	....	.A.L.	40	45	4	2	.667	46	28	52	6.20	2
Major League Totals	....	4 Yrs.	103	116²/₃	9	7	.563	111	71	116	4.78	11

Division Series

Year	Club	Lea	G	IP	W	L	Pct	SO	BB	H	ERA	SAVES
1996 Cleveland	....	.A.L.	3	2	0	0	.000	2	2	5	9.00	0

a On disabled list from June 27 to July 21, 1994.
b On disabled list from May 4 to May 22, 1995.
c On disabled list from April 25 to May 18 and June 19 to July 4 and July 11 to August 1, 1997.

SILVA, JOSE LEONEL

Born, Tijuana, Mexico, December 19, 1973.
Bats Right. Throws Right. Height, 6 feet, 5 inches. Weight, 210 pounds.

Year	Club	Lea	G	IP	W	L	Pct	SO	BB	H	ERA	SAVES
1992 Blue Jays	....	Gulf Coast	12	59¹/₃	6	4	.600	78	18	42	2.28	0
1993 Hagerstown	....	So. Atl.	24	142²/₃	12	5	.706	161	62	103	2.52	0
1994 Dunedin	....	.Fla. St.	8	43	0	2	.000	41	24	41	3.77	0
1994 Knoxville	....	Southern	16	91¹/₃	4	8	.333	71	31	89	4.14	0
1995 Knoxville	....	Southern	3	2	0	0	.000	2	6	3	9.00	0
1996 Knoxville	....	Southern	22	44	2	3	.400	26	22	45	4.91	0
1996 Toronto a	....	.A.L.	2	2	0	0	.000	0	0	5	13.50	0
1997 Calgary	....	.P.C.	17	66	5	1	.833	54	22	74	3.41	0
1997 Pittsburgh	....	.N.L.	11	36¹/₃	2	1	.667	30	16	52	5.94	0
Major League Totals	....	2 Yrs.	13	38¹/₃	2	1	.667	30	16	57	6.34	0

a Traded to Pittsburgh Pirates with pitcher Jose Pett, infielder Brandon Cromer, and players to be named later for outfielder Orlando Merced, infielder Carlos Garcia and pitcher Dan Plesac, November 14, 1996. Pittsburgh received pitcher Mike Halperin, infielder Abraham Nunez and catcher Craig Wilson to complete trade, December 11, 1996.

SIMAS, WILLIAM ANTHONY (BILL)

Born, Hanford, California, November 28, 1971.
Bats Left. Throws Right. Height, 6 feet, 3 inches. Weight, 220 pounds.

Year	Club	Lea	G	IP	W	L	Pct	SO	BB	H	ERA	SAVES
1992 Boise	....	Northwest	14	70²/₃	6	5	.545	39	29	82	3.95	1
1993 Cedar Rapids	....	Midwest	35	80	5	8	.385	62	36	93	4.95	6
1994 Midland	....	Texas	13	15¹/₃	2	0	1.000	12	2	5	0.59	6
1994 Lake Elsinor	....	California	37	47	5	2	.714	34	10	44	2.11	13
1995 Vancouver	....	.P.C.	30	38	6	3	.667	44	14	44	3.55	6
1995 Nashville	....	.A.A.	7	11²/₃	1	1	.500	12	3	12	3.86	0
1995 Chicago a	....	.A.L.	14	14	1	1	.500	16	10	15	2.57	0
1996 Chicago	....	.A.L.	64	72²/₃	2	8	.200	65	39	75	4.58	2
1997 Chicago b	....	.A.L.	40	41¹/₃	3	1	.750	38	24	46	4.14	1
Major League Totals	....	3 Yrs.	118	128	6	10	.375	119	73	136	4.22	3

a Traded to Chicago White Sox with outfielder McKay Christensen, pitcher Andrew Lorraine and pitcher John Snyder for pitcher Jim Abbott and pitcher Tim Fortugno, July 27, 1995.
b On disabled list from July 20 to August 5 and August 15 to September 29, 1997.

SIROTKA, MICHAEL ROBERT (MIKE)
Born, Houston, Texas, May 13, 1971.
Bats Left. Throws Left. Height, 6 feet, 1 inch. Weight, 190 pounds.

Year Club	Lea	G	IP	W	L	Pct	SO	BB	H	ERA	SAVES
1993 White Sox	Gulf Coast	3	5	0	0	.000	8	2	4	0.00	0
1993 South Bend	Midwest	7	10⅓	0	1	.000	12	6	12	6.10	0
1994 South Bend	Midwest	27	196⅔	12	9	.571	173	58	183	3.07	0
1995 Birmingham	Southern	16	101⅓	7	6	.538	79	22	95	3.20	0
1995 Nashville	A.A.	8	54	1	5	.167	34	13	51	2.83	0
1995 Chicago	A.L.	6	34⅓	1	2	.333	19	17	39	4.19	0
1996 Nashville	A.A.	15	90	7	5	.583	58	24	90	3.60	0
1996 Chicago	A.L.	15	26⅓	1	2	.333	11	12	34	7.18	0
1997 Nashville	A.A.	19	112⅓	7	5	.583	92	22	115	3.28	0
1997 Chicago	A.L.	7	32	3	0	1.000	24	5	36	2.25	0
Major League Totals ....3 Yrs.		28	92⅔	5	4	.556	54	34	109	4.37	0

SLOCUMB, HEATHCLIFF
Born, Jamaica, New York, June 7, 1966.
Bats Right. Throws Right. Height, 6 feet, 3 inches. Weight, 220 pounds.

Year Club	Lea	G	IP	W	L	Pct	SO	BB	H	ERA	SAVES
1984 Kingsport	Appal.	1	0⅓	0	0	.000	0	1	0	0.00	0
1984 Little Falls	N.Y.-Penn.	4	9	0	0	.000	10	16	8	11.00	0
1985 Kingsport	Appal.	11	52⅓	3	2	.600	29	31	47	3.78	0
1986 Little Falls a	N.Y.-Penn.	25	43⅔	3	1	.750	41	36	24	1.65	1
1987 Winston-Salem	Carolina	9	27⅓	1	2	.333	27	26	26	6.26	0
1987 Peoria	Midwest	16	104	10	4	.714	81	42	97	2.60	0
1988 Winston-Salem	Carolina	25	119⅔	6	6	.500	78	90	122	4.96	1
1989 Peoria	Midwest	49	55⅔	5	3	.625	52	33	31	1.78	22
1990 Charlotte	Southern	43	50⅓	3	1	.750	37	32	50	2.15	12
1990 Iowa	A.A.	20	27	3	2	.600	21	18	16	2.00	1
1991 Iowa	A.A.	12	13⅓	1	0	1.000	9	6	10	4.05	1
1991 Chicago	N.L.	52	62⅔	2	1	.667	34	30	53	3.45	1
1992 Iowa	A.A.	25	41⅔	1	3	.250	47	16	36	2.59	7
1992 Chicago	N.L.	30	36	0	3	.000	27	21	52	6.50	1
1993 Iowa	A.A.	10	12	1	0	1.000	10	8	7	1.50	7
1993 Chicago b	N.L.	10	10⅔	1	0	1.000	4	4	7	3.38	0
1993 Charlotte	Int.	23	30⅓	3	2	.600	25	11	25	3.56	1
1993 Cleveland c	A.L.	20	27⅓	3	1	.750	18	16	28	4.28	0
1994 Philadelphia	N.L.	52	72⅓	5	1	.833	58	28	75	2.86	0
1995 Philadelphia d	N.L.	61	65⅓	5	6	4.55	63	35	64	2.89	32
1996 Boston	A.L.	75	83⅓	5	5	.500	88	55	68	3.02	31
1997 Boston-Seattle e	A.L.	76	75	0	9	.000	64	49	84	5.16	27
Major League Totals ....7 Yrs.		376	432⅔	21	26	.447	356	238	431	3.79	92
Division Series											
1997 Seattle	A.L.	2	2	0	0	.000	3	3	3	4.50	0

a Drafted by Chicago Cubs from New York Mets organization in minor league draft, December 9, 1988.
b Traded to Cleveland Indians for shortstop Jose Hernandez, June 1, 1993.
c Traded to Philadelphia Phillies for outfielder Ruben Amaro, November 2, 1993.
d Traded to Boston Red Sox with pitcher Larry Wimberly and outfielder Rick Holyfield for outfielder Lee Tinsley, outfielder Glenn Murray and pitcher Ken Ryan, January 29, 1996.
e Traded to Seattle Mariners for catcher Jason Varitek and pitcher Derek Lowe, July 31, 1997.

SMALL, AARON JAMES
Born, Oxnard, California, November 23, 1971.
Bats Right. Throws Right. Height, 6 feet, 5 inches. Weight, 200 pounds.

Year Club	Lea	G	IP	W	L	Pct	SO	BB	H	ERA	SAVES
1989 Medicine Hat	Pioneer	15	70⅔	1	7	.125	40	31	80	5.86	0
1990 Myrtle Beach	So. Atl.	27	147⅔	9	9	.500	96	56	150	2.80	0
1991 Dunedin	Fla. St.	24	148⅓	8	7	.533	92	42	129	2.73	0
1992 Knoxville	Southern	27	135	5	12	.294	79	61	152	5.27	0
1993 Knoxville	Southern	48	93	4	4	.500	44	40	99	3.39	16
1994 Syracuse	Int.	13	24⅓	3	2	.600	15	9	19	2.22	0
1994 Knoxville	Southern	29	96⅓	5	5	.500	75	38	92	2.99	5
1994 Toronto	A.L.	1	2	0	0	.000	0	2	5	9.00	0
1995 Syracuse	Int.	1	1⅔	0	0	.000	2	1	3	5.40	0
1995 Charlotte	Int.	33	40⅔	2	1	.667	31	10	36	2.88	10

Year	Club	Lea	G	IP	W	L	Pct	SO	BB	H	ERA	SAVES
1995 Florida a		N.L.	7	6⅓	1	0	1.000	5	6	7	1.42	0
1996 Edmonton		P.C.	25	119⅔	8	6	.571	83	28	111	4.29	1
1996 Oakland b-c		A.L.	12	28⅔	1	3	.250	17	22	37	8.16	0
1997 Edmonton		P.C.	1	5	1	0	1.000	4	0	1	0.00	0
1997 Oakland		A.L.	71	96⅔	9	5	.643	57	40	109	4.28	4
Major League Totals	4 Yrs.		91	133⅔	11	8	.579	79	70	158	5.05	4

a Signed with Florida Marlins, April 26, 1995.
b Claimed on waivers by Seattle Mariners, January 23, 1996.
c Claimed on waivers by Oakland Athletics, January 29, 1996.

SMILEY, JOHN PATRICK

Born, Phoenixville, Pennsylvania, March 17, 1965.
Bats Left. Throws Left. Height, 6 feet, 4 inches. Weight, 212 pounds.

Year	Club	Lea	G	IP	W	L	Pct	SO	BB	H	ERA	SAVES
1983 Bradenton Pirates		Gulf C.	12	65⅓	3	4	.429	42	27	69	5.92	0
1984 Macon a		So. Atl.	21	130	5	11	.313	73	41	119	3.95	0
1985 Prince William		Carolina	10	56	2	2	.500	45	27	64	5.14	0
1985 Macon		So. Atl.	16	88⅔	3	8	.273	70	37	84	4.67	0
1986 Prince William		Carolina	48	90	2	4	.333	93	40	64	3.10	0
1986 Pittsburgh		N.L.	12	11⅔	1	0	1.000	9	4	4	3.86	0
1987 Pittsburgh		N.L.	63	75	5	5	.500	58	50	69	5.76	4
1988 Pittsburgh		N.L.	34	205	13	11	.542	129	46	185	3.25	0
1989 Pittsburgh		N.L.	28	205⅓	12	8	.600	123	49	174	2.81	0
1990 Pittsburgh b		N.L.	26	149⅓	9	10	.474	86	36	161	4.64	0
1991 Pittsburgh c		N.L.	33	207⅔	*20	8	*.714	129	44	194	3.08	0
1992 Minnesota d		A.L.	34	241	16	9	.640	163	65	205	3.21	0
1993 Cincinnati e		N.L.	18	105⅔	3	9	.250	60	31	117	5.62	0
1994 Cincinnati		N.L.	24	158⅔	11	10	.524	112	37	169	3.86	0
1995 Cincinnati f		N.L.	28	176⅔	12	5	.706	124	39	173	3.46	0
1996 Cincinnati		N.L.	35	217⅓	13	14	.481	171	54	207	3.64	0
1997 Cincinnati g-h		N.L.	20	117	9	10	.474	94	31	139	5.23	0
1997 Cleveland		A.L.	6	37⅓	2	4	.333	26	10	45	5.54	0
Major League Totals	12 Yrs.		361	1907⅔	126	103	.550	1284	496	1842	3.80	4
Division Series												
1995 Cincinnati		N.L.	1	6	0	0	.000	1	0	9	3.00	0
Championship Series												
1990 Pittsburgh		N.L.	1	2	0	0	.000	0	0	2	0.00	0
1991 Pittsburgh		N.L.	2	2⅔	0	2	.000	3	1	8	23.63	0
1995 Cincinnati		N.L.	1	5	0	0	.000	1	0	5	3.60	0
Championship Series Totals	4			9⅔	0	2	.000	4	1	15	8.38	0

a On disabled list from April 27 to May 27, 1984.
b On disabled list from May 19 to July 1, 1990.
c Traded to Minnesota Twins for pitcher Denny Neagle and outfielder Midre Cummings, March 17, 1992.
d Filed for free agency, October 26; signed with Cincinnati Reds, November 30, 1992.
e On disabled list from July 3 to end of 1993 season.
f On disabled list from August 22 to September 6, 1995.
g On disabled list from June 2 to June 17, 1997.
h Traded to Cleveland Indians with infielder Jeff Branson for pitcher Danny Graves, pitcher Jim Crowell, pitcher Scott Winchester and infielder Damian Jackson, July 31, 1997.

SMITH, PETER JOHN (PETE)

Born, Weymouth, Mass., February 27, 1966.
Bats Right. Throws Right. Height, 6 feet, 2 inches. Weight, 200 pounds.

Year	Club	Lea	G	IP	W	L	Pct	SO	BB	H	ERA	SAVES
1984 Phillies		Gulf Coast	8	37	1	2	.333	35	16	28	1.46	0
1985 Clearwater a		Fla. St.	26	153	12	10	.545	86	80	135	3.29	0
1986 Greenville		Southern	24	104⅔	1	8	.111	64	78	117	5.85	0
1987 Greenville		Southern	29	177⅓	9	9	.500	119	67	162	3.35	1
1987 Atlanta		N.L.	6	31⅔	1	2	.333	11	14	39	4.83	0
1988 Atlanta		N.L.	32	195⅓	7	15	.318	124	88	183	3.69	0
1989 Atlanta		N.L.	28	142	5	14	.263	115	57	144	4.75	0
1990 Atlanta		N.L.	13	77	5	6	.455	56	24	77	4.79	0
1990 Greenville		Southern	2	3⅓	0	0	.000	2	0	1	0.00	0
1991 Macon		So. Atl.	3	9⅔	0	0	.000	14	2	15	8.38	0
1991 Richmond		Int.	10	51	3	3	.500	41	24	66	7.24	0
1991 Atlanta		N.L.	14	48	1	3	.250	29	22	48	5.06	0

Year	Club	Lea	G	IP	W	L	Pct	SO	BB	H	ERA	SAVES
1992	Richmond	Int.	15	109⅓	7	4	.636	93	24	75	2.14	0
1992	Atlanta	N.L.	12	79	7	0	1.000	43	28	63	2.05	0
1993	Atlanta b	N.L.	20	90⅔	4	8	.333	53	36	92	4.37	0
1994	New York c	N.L.	21	131⅓	4	10	.286	62	42	145	5.55	0
1995	Cincinnati	N.L.	11	24⅓	1	2	.333	14	7	30	6.66	0
1995	Charlotte	Int.	10	49	2	1	.667	20	17	51	3.86	0
1996	Las Vegas d-e	P.C.	26	169	11	9	.550	95	42	192	4.95	0
1997	Las Vegas	P.C.	6	33⅔	3	2	.600	24	6	38	4.28	0
1997	San Diego f-g	N.L.	37	118	7	6	.538	68	52	120	4.81	1
Major League Totals 10 Yrs.			194	937⅓	42	66	.389	575	370	941	4.46	1

a Traded by Philadelphia Phillies to Atlanta Braves with catcher Ozzie Virgil for pitcher Steve Bedrosian and outfielder Milt Thompson, December 10, 1985.
b Traded to New York Mets for outfielder Dave Gallagher, November 24, 1993.
c Released by New York Mets and signed as free agent by Cincinnati Reds, December 1, 1994.
d Released by Cincinnati Reds and signed as free agent with Florida Marlins, November 15, 1995.
e Signed as minor league free agent by San Diego Padres, December 12, 1995.
f Filed for free agency, October 30, 1997.
g Re-signed with San Diego Padres, December 16, 1997.

SMOLTZ, JOHN ANDREW

Born, Detroit, Michigan, May 15, 1967.
Bats Right. Throws Right. Height, 6 feet, 3 inches. Weight, 185 pounds.

Year	Club	Lea	G	IP	W	L	Pct	SO	BB	H	ERA	SAVES
1986	Lakeland	Fla. St.	17	96	7	8	.467	47	31	86	3.56	0
1987	Glens Falls a	Eastern	21	130	4	10	.286	86	81	131	5.68	0
1987	Richmond	Int.	3	16	0	1	.000	5	11	17	6.19	0
1988	Richmond	Int.	20	135⅓	10	5	.667	115	37	118	2.79	0
1988	Atlanta	N.L.	12	64	2	7	.222	37	33	74	5.48	0
1989	Atlanta	N.L.	29	208	12	11	.522	168	72	160	2.94	0
1990	Atlanta b	N.L.	34	231⅓	14	11	.560	170	*90	206	3.85	0
1991	Atlanta c	N.L.	36	229⅔	14	13	.519	148	77	206	3.80	0
1992	Atlanta d	N.L.	35	246⅔	15	12	.556	*215	80	206	2.85	0
1993	Atlanta	N.L.	35	243⅔	15	11	.577	208	100	208	3.62	0
1994	Atlanta e	N.L.	21	134⅔	6	10	.375	113	48	120	4.14	0
1995	Atlanta f	N.L.	29	192⅔	12	7	.632	193	72	166	3.18	0
1996	Atlanta g-h	N.L.	35	253⅔	24	8	.750	276	55	199	2.94	0
1997	Atlanta	N.L.	35	256	15	12	.556	241	63	234	3.02	0
Major League Totals 10 Yrs.			301	2060⅓	129	102	.558	1769	690	1779	3.40	0
Division Series												
1995	Atlanta	N.L.	1	5⅔	0	0	.000	6	1	5	7.94	0
1996	Atlanta	N.L.	1	9	1	0	1.000	7	2	4	1.00	0
1997	Atlanta	N.L.	1	9	1	0	1.000	11	1	3	1.00	0
Division Series Totals 3				23⅔	2	0	1.000	24	4	12	2.66	0
Championship Series												
1991	Atlanta	N.L.	2	15⅓	2	0	1.000	15	3	14	1.76	0
1992	Atlanta	N.L.	3	20⅓	2	0	1.000	19	10	14	2.66	0
1993	Atlanta	N.L.	1	6⅓	0	1	.000	10	5	8	0.00	0
1995	Atlanta	N.L.	1	7	0	0	.000	2	2	7	2.57	0
1996	Atlanta	N.L.	2	15	2	0	1.000	12	3	12	1.20	0
1997	Atlanta	N.L.	1	6	0	1	.000	9	5	5	7.50	0
Championship Series Totals 10				70	6	2	.750	67	28	60	2.31	0
World Series Record												
1991	Atlanta	N.L.	2	14⅓	0	0	.000	11	1	13	1.26	0
1992	Atlanta	N.L.	2	13⅓	1	0	1.000	12	7	13	2.70	0
1995	Atlanta	N.L.	1	2⅓	0	0	.000	4	2	6	15.43	0
1996	Atlanta	N.L.	2	14	1	1	.500	14	8	6	0.64	0
World Series Totals 7				44	2	1	.667	41	18	38	2.25	0

a Traded by Detroit Tigers to Atlanta Braves organization for pitcher Doyle Alexander, August 12, 1987.
b Appeared in four additional games as pinch runner.
c Appeared in two additional games as pinch runner.
d Appeared in one additional game as pinch hitter.
e Suspended eight games by National League for May 14 hitting batter with pitch, June 20 to June 28, 1994.
f Selected Cy Young Award Winner in National League for 1996.
g Filed for free agency, October 31, 1996.
h Re-signed with Atlanta Braves, November 20, 1996.

SODOWSKY, CLINT REA
Born, Ponca City, Oklahoma, July 13, 1972.
Bats Left. Throws Right. Height, 6 feet, 3 inches. Weight, 180 pounds.

Year	Club	Lea	G	IP	W	L	Pct	SO	BB	H	ERA	SAVES
1991	Bristol	Appal.	14	55	0	5	.000	44	34	49	3.76	0
1992	Bristol	Appal.	15	56	2	2	.500	48	29	46	3.54	0
1993	Fayetteville	So. Atl.	27	155⅔	14	10	.583	80	51	177	5.09	0
1994	Lakeland	Fla. St.	19	110⅓	6	3	.667	73	34	111	3.83	0
1995	Jacksonville	Southern	19	123⅔	5	5	.500	77	50	102	2.55	0
1995	Toledo	Int.	9	60	5	1	.833	32	30	47	2.85	0
1995	Detroit	A.L.	6	23⅓	2	2	.500	14	18	24	5.01	0
1996	Detroit a	A.L.	7	24⅓	1	3	.250	9	20	40	11.84	0
1996	Toledo	Int.	19	118⅔	6	8	.429	59	51	128	3.94	0
1997	Calgary	P.C.	8	13⅔	0	1	.000	9	6	19	6.59	1
1997	Pittsburgh b-c	N.L.	45	52	2	2	.500	51	34	49	3.63	0
Major League Totals		3 Yrs.	58	99⅔	5	7	.417	74	72	113	5.96	0

a Traded to Pittsburgh Pirates for pitcher Dan Miceli, November 1, 1996.
b On disabled list from August 26 to September 10, 1997.
c Selected in expansion draft by Arizona Diamondbacks, November 18, 1997.

SPOLJARIC, PAUL NIKOLA
Born, Kelowna, British Columbia, Canada, September 24, 1970.
Bats Right. Throws Left. Height, 6 feet, 3 inches. Weight, 205 pounds.

Year	Club	Lea	G	IP	W	L	Pct	SO	BB	H	ERA	SAVES
1990	Medicine Hat	Pioneer	15	66⅓	3	7	.300	62	35	57	4.34	1
1991	St. Catharines	N.Y.-Penn.	4	18⅔	0	2	.000	21	9	21	4.82	0
1992	Myrtle Beach	So. Atl.	26	162⅔	10	8	.556	161	58	111	2.82	0
1993	Dunedin	Fla. St.	4	26	3	0	1.000	29	12	16	1.38	0
1993	Knoxville	Southern	7	43⅓	4	1	.800	51	22	30	2.28	0
1993	Syracuse	Int.	18	95⅓	8	7	.533	88	52	97	5.29	0
1994	Syracuse	Int.	8	47⅓	1	5	.167	38	28	47	5.70	0
1994	Knoxville	Southern	17	102	6	5	.545	79	48	88	3.62	0
1994	Toronto	A.L.	2	2⅓	0	1	.000	2	9	5	38.57	0
1995	Syracuse	Int.	43	87⅔	2	10	.167	108	54	69	4.93	10
1996	Syracuse	Int.	17	22	3	0	1.000	24	6	20	3.27	4
1996	St. Cathrnes	N.Y.-Penn.	2	5	0	0	.000	7	0	3	0.00	0
1996	Toronto a	A.L.	28	38	2	2	.500	38	19	30	3.08	1
1997	Dunedin	Fla. St.	4	10⅔	0	0	.000	10	2	10	1.69	0
1997	Toronto-Seattle b-c	A.L.	57	70⅔	0	3	.000	70	36	61	3.69	3
Major League Totals		3 Yrs.	87	111	2	6	.250	110	64	96	4.22	4
Division Series												
1997	Seattle	A.L.	2	1⅔	0	0	.000	1	0	4	0.00	0

a On disabled list from July 25 to August 18, 1996.
b On disabled list from April 1 to April 18, 1997.
c Traded to Seattle Mariners with pitcher Mike Timlin for outfielder Jose Cruz, July 31, 1997.

SPRADLIN, JERRY CARL
Born, Fullerton, California, June 14, 1967.
Bats Both. Throws Right. Height, 6 feet, 7 inches. Weight, 240 pounds.

Year	Club	Lea	G	IP	W	L	Pct	SO	BB	H	ERA	SAVES
1988	Billings	Pioneer	17	47⅔	4	1	.800	23	14	45	3.21	0
1989	Greensboro	So. Atl.	42	94⅔	7	2	.778	56	23	88	2.76	2
1990	Cedar Rapids	Midwest	5	12	0	1	.000	6	5	13	3.00	0
1990	Chston-Wv	So. Atl.	43	74⅓	3	4	.429	39	17	74	2.54	17
1991	Chattanooga	Southern	48	96	7	3	.700	73	32	95	3.09	4
1992	Cedar Rapids	Midwest	1	2⅓	1	0	1.000	4	0	5	7.71	0
1992	Chattanooga	Southern	59	65⅓	3	3	.500	35	13	52	1.38	34
1993	Indianapolis	A.A.	34	56⅔	3	2	.600	46	12	58	3.49	1
1993	Cincinnati	N.L.	37	49	2	1	.667	24	9	44	3.49	2
1994	Cincinnati	N.L.	6	8	0	0	.000	4	2	12	10.13	0
1994	Indianapolis a	A.A.	28	73⅓	3	3	.500	49	16	87	3.68	3
1994	Edmonton	P.C.	6	10⅔	1	0	1.000	3	4	12	2.53	1
1995	Charlotte	Int.	41	59⅓	3	3	.500	38	15	59	3.03	1
1996	Indianapolis b	A.A.	49	100	6	8	.429	79	23	94	3.33	15
1996	Cincinnati c	N.L.	1	0⅓	0	0	.000	0	0	0	0.00	0
1997	Philadelphia	N.L.	76	81⅔	4	8	.333	67	27	86	4.74	1
Major League Totals		4 Yrs.	120	139	6	9	.400	95	38	142	4.60	3

a Claimed on waivers by Florida Marlins organization, August 4, 1994.
b Released by Florida Marlins and signed by Cincinnati Reds as free agent, February 11, 1996.
c Signed as minor league free agent by Philadelphia Phillies, December 5, 1996.

SPRINGER, DENNIS LEROY

Born, Fresno, California, February 12, 1965.
Bats Right. Throws Right. Height, 5 feet, 10 inches. Weight, 185 pounds.

Year	Club	Lea	G	IP	W	L	Pct	SO	BB	H	ERA	SAVES
1987	Great Falls	Pioneer	23	65 2/3	4	3	.571	54	16	70	2.88	6
1988	Bakersfield	California	32	154	13	7	.650	108	62	135	3.27	2
1988	Vero Beach	Fla. St.	1	5 2/3	0	0	.000	4	2	6	4.76	0
1989	San Antonio	Texas	19	140	6	8	.429	89	46	128	3.15	0
1989	Albuquerque	P.C.	8	41	4	1	.800	18	14	58	4.83	0
1990	Albuquerque	P.C.	2	6 1/3	0	0	.000	2	7	10	5.68	0
1990	San Antonio	Texas	24	163 1/3	8	6	.571	77	n	147	3.31	0
1991	San Antonio	Texas	30	164 2/3	10	10	.500	138	91	153	4.43	0
1992	San Antonio	Texas	18	122	6	7	.462	73	49	114	4.35	0
1992	Albuquerque	P.C.	11	62	2	7	.222	36	22	70	5.66	0
1993	Albuquerque	P.C.	35	130 2/3	3	8	.273	69	39	173	5.99	0
1994	Reading	Eastern	24	135	5	8	.385	118	44	125	3.40	2
1995	Scranton-WB	Int.	30	171	10	11	.476	115	47	163	4.68	0
1995	Philadelphia	N.L.	4	22 1/3	0	3	.000	15	9	21	4.84	0
1996	Vancouver	P.C.	16	109 1/3	10	3	.769	78	36	89	2.72	0
1996	California a	A.L.	20	94 2/3	5	6	.455	64	43	91	5.51	0
1997	Vancouver	P.C.	2	15	1	1	.500	7	6	12	3.00	0
1997	Anaheim b	A.L.	32	194 2/3	9	9	.500	75	73	199	5.18	0
Major League Totals		3 Yrs.	56	311 2/3	14	18	.438	154	125	311	5.26	0

a Signed with California Angels organization, January 5, 1996.
b Selected in expansion draft by Tampa Bay Devil Rays, November 18, 1997.

SPRINGER, RUSSELL PAUL

Born, Alexandria, Louisiana, November 7, 1968.
Bats Right. Throws Right. Height, 6 feet, 4 inches. Weight, 195 pounds.

Year	Club	Lea	G	IP	W	L	Pct	SO	BB	H	ERA	SAVES
1990	Tampa Yankees	Gulf Coast	4	15	0	2	.000	17	4	10	1.20	0
1990	Greensboro	So. Atl.	10	56 1/3	2	3	.400	51	31	51	3.67	0
1991	Fort Lauderdale	Fla. St.	25	152 1/3	5	9	.357	138	62	118	3.49	0
1991	Albany	Eastern	2	15	1	0	1.000	16	6	9	1.80	0
1992	Columbus	Int.	20	123 2/3	8	5	.615	95	54	89	2.69	0
1992	New York a	A.L.	14	16	0	0	.000	12	10	18	6.19	0
1993	Vancouver	P.C.	11	59	5	4	.556	40	33	58	4.27	0
1993	California b	A.L.	14	60	1	6	.143	31	32	73	7.20	0
1994	Vancouver	P.C.	12	83	7	4	.636	58	19	77	3.04	0
1994	California	A.L.	18	45 2/3	2	2	.500	28	14	53	5.52	2
1995	Vancouver	P.C.	6	34	2	0	1.000	23	23	24	3.44	0
1995	California	A.L.	19	51 2/3	1	2	.333	38	25	60	6.10	1
1995	Philadelphia c-d	N.L.	14	26 2/3	0	0	.000	32	10	22	3.71	0
1996	Philadelphia	N.L.	51	96 2/3	3	10	.231	94	38	106	4.66	0
1997	Jackson	Texas	1	1	0	0	.000	2	0	2	9.00	0
1997	Houston e-f	N.L.	54	55 1/3	3	3	.500	74	27	48	4.23	3
Major League Totals		6 Yrs.	184	352	10	23	.303	309	156	380	5.34	6
Divisional Series												
1997	Houston	N.L.	2	1 2/3	0	0	.000	3	1	2	5.40	0

a Traded to California Angels with first baseman J. T. Snow and pitcher Jerry Nielsen for pitcher Jim Abbott, December 6, 1992.
b On disabled list from August 2 to end of 1993 season.
c Kevin Flora was traded to Philadelphia Phillies with player to be named later for outfielder Dave Gallagher, August 9, 1995.
d Philadelphia Phillies received pitcher Russ Springer to complete trade, August 15, 1995.
e On disabled list from June 17 to July 10, 1997.
f Selected in expansion draft by Arizona Diamondbacks, November 18, 1997.

STANIFER, ROBERT WAYNE

Born, Easley, South Carolina, March 10, 1972.
Bats Right. Throws Right. Height, 6 feet, 3 inches. Weight 205 pounds.

Year	Club	Lea	G	IP	W	L	Pct	SO	BB	H	ERA	SAVES
1994 Elmira	.........N.Y.-Penn.		9	49	2	1	.667	38	12	54	2.57	0
1994 Brevard Cty	.........Fla. St.		5	24⅓	1	2	.333	12	10	32	6.29	0
1995 Brevard Cty	.........Fla. St.		18	82⅔	3	6	.333	45	15	97	4.14	0
1996 Brevard Cty	.........Fla. St.		22	49	4	2	.667	32	9	54	2.39	0
1996 Portland	...........Eastern		18	34⅓	3	1	.750	33	9	27	1.57	2
1997 Charlotte	.............Int.		22	27⅔	4	0	1.000	25	7	34	4.88	5
1997 Florida	.............N.L.		36	45	1	2	.333	28	16	43	4.60	1

STANTON, WILLIAM MICHAEL

Born, Galena Park, Texas, June 2, 1967.
Bats Left. Throws Left. Height, 6 feet, 1 inch. Weight, 190 pounds.

Year	Club	Lea	G	IP	W	L	Pct	SO	BB	H	ERA	SAVES
1987 Pulaski	...........Appal.		15	83⅓	4	8	.333	82	42	64	3.24	0
1988 Burlington	.........Midwest		30	154	11	5	.688	160	69	154	3.62	0
1988 Durham	..........Carolina		2	12⅓	1	0	1.000	14	5	14	1.46	0
1989 Greenville	........Southern		47	51⅓	4	1	.800	54	31	32	1.58	19
1989 Richmond	.............Int.		13	20	2	0	1.000	20	13	6	0.00	8
1989 Atlanta	...............N.L.		20	24	0	1	.000	27	8	17	1.50	7
1990 Atlanta a	.............N.L.		7	7	0	3	.000	7	4	16	18.00	2
1990 Greenville	........Southern		4	5⅔	0	1	.000	5	3	7	1.59	0
1991 Atlanta	...............N.L.		74	78	5	5	.500	54	21	62	2.88	7
1992 Atlanta	...............N.L.		65	63⅔	5	4	.556	44	20	59	4.10	8
1993 Atlanta	...............N.L.		63	52	4	6	.400	43	29	51	4.67	27
1994 Atlanta b	.............N.L.		49	45⅔	3	1	.750	35	26	41	3.55	3
1995 Atlanta	...............N.L.		26	19⅓	1	1	.500	13	6	31	5.59	1
1995 Boston c-d-e	.............A.L.		22	21	1	0	1.000	10	8	17	3.00	0
1996 Boston-Texas f-g	.......A.L.		81	78⅔	4	4	.500	60	27	78	3.66	1
1997 New York	.............A.L.		64	66⅔	6	1	.857	70	34	50	2.57	3
Major League Totals	........9 Yrs.		471	456	29	26	.527	363	183	422	3.69	59
Division Series												
1995 Boston	...............A.L.		1	2⅓	0	0	.000	4	0	1	0.00	0
1996 Texas	...............A.L.		3	3⅓	0	1	.000	3	3	2	2.70	0
1997 New York	...............A.L.		3	1	0	0	.000	3	1	1	0.00	0
Division Series Totals	7			6⅔	0	1	.000	10	4	4	1.35	0
Championship Series												
1991 Atlanta	...............N.L.		3	3⅔	0	0	.000	3	3	4	2.45	0
1992 Atlanta	...............N.L.		5	4⅓	0	0	.000	5	2	2	0.00	0
1993 Atlanta	...............N.L.		1	1	0	0	.000	0	1	1	0.00	0
Championship Series Totals	9			9	0	0	.000	8	6	7	1.00	0
World Series Record												
1991 Atlanta	...............N.L.		5	7⅓	1	0	1.000	7	2	5	0.00	0
1992 Atlanta	...............N.L.		4	5	0	0	.000	1	2	3	0.00	1
World Series Totals	9			12⅓	1	0	1.000	8	4	8	0.00	1

a On disabled list from April 27 to end of 1990 season.
b Not offered 1995 contract, December 23, 1994.
c Re-signed with Atlanta Braves, April 12, 1995.
d Traded to Boston Red Sox for player to be named later and outfielder Marc Lewis, July 31, 1995.
e Atlanta Braves received pitcher Michael Jacobs and outfielder Marc Lewis to complete trade, August 31, 1995.
f Traded to Texas Rangers with player to be named later for pitcher Mark Brandenberg and pitcher Kerry Lacy, July 31, 1996.
g Filed for free agency, October 27, 1996. Signed with New York Yankees, December 11, 1996.

STEPHENSON, GARRETT CHARLES

Born, Takoma Park, Maryland, January 2, 1972.
Bats Right. Throws Right. Height, 6 feet, 5 inches. Weight, 203 pounds.

Year	Club	Lea	G	IP	W	L	Pct	SO	BB	H	ERA	SAVES
1992 Bluefield	...........Appal.		12	32⅓	3	1	.750	30	7	35	4.73	0
1993 Albany	.............So. Atl.		30	171⅓	16	7	.696	147	44	142	2.84	1
1994 Frederick	..........Carolina		18	107⅓	7	5	.583	133	36	91	4.02	0
1994 Bowie	.............Eastern		7	36⅔	3	2	.600	32	11	47	5.15	0
1995 Bowie	............Eastern		29	175⅓	7	10	.412	139	47	154	3.64	0

Year	Club	Lea	G	IP	W	L	Pct	SO	BB	H	ERA	SAVES
1996 Baltimore	A.L.	3	6⅓	0	1	.000	3	3	13	12.79	0
1996 Rochester c	Int.	23	121⅔	7	6	.538	86	44	123	4.81	0
1997 Scranton-WB	Int.	7	29	3	1	.750	27	12	27	5.90	0
1997 Philadelphia b	N.L.	20	117	8	6	.571	81	38	104	3.15	0
Major League Totals .... 2 Yrs.		23	123⅓	8	7	.533	84	41	117	3.65	0

a Claimed on waivers by Philadelphia Phillies from Baltimore Orioles, September 4, 1996, completing trade of August 29, 1996, in which third baseman Todd Zeile and outfielder Pete Incaviglia went from Philadelphia to Baltimore in exchange for pitcher Calvin Maduro.
b On disabled list from June 5 to June 22 and August 18 to September 2, 1997.

STOTTLEMYRE, TODD VERNON
Born, Yakima, Washington, May 20, 1965.
Bats Left. Throws Right. Height, 6 feet, 3 inches. Weight, 200 pounds.

Year	Club	Lea	G	IP	W	L	Pct	SO	BB	H	ERA	SAVES
1986 Ventura	California	17	103⅔	9	4	.692	104	36	76	2.43	0
1986 Knoxville	Southern	18	99	8	7	.533	81	49	93	4.18	0
1987 Syracuse	Int.	34	186⅔	11	*13	.458	143	*87	189	4.44	0
1988 Syracuse	Int.	7	48⅓	5	0	1.000	51	8	36	2.05	0
1988 Toronto	A.L.	28	98	4	8	.333	67	46	109	5.69	0
1989 Syracuse	Int.	10	55⅔	3	2	.600	45	15	46	3.23	0
1989 Toronto	A.L.	27	127⅔	7	7	.500	63	44	137	3.88	0
1990 Toronto	A.L.	33	203	13	17	.433	115	69	214	4.34	0
1991 Toronto	A.L.	34	219	15	8	.652	116	75	194	3.78	0
1992 Toronto a-b	A.L.	28	174	12	11	.522	98	63	175	4.50	0
1993 Toronto c	A.L.	30	176⅔	11	12	.478	98	69	204	4.84	0
1994 Toronto d	A.L.	26	140⅔	7	7	.500	105	48	149	4.22	1
1995 Oakland e-f	A.L.	31	209⅔	14	7	.667	205	80	228	4.55	0
1996 St. Louis	N.L.	34	223⅓	14	11	.560	194	93	191	3.87	0
1997 St. Louis	N.L.	28	181	12	9	.571	160	65	155	3.88	0
Major League Totals .... 10 Yrs.		299	1753	109	97	.529	1221	652	1756	4.29	1
Division Series											
1996 St. Louis	N.L.	1	6⅔	1	0	1.000	7	2	5	1.35	0
Championship Series											
1989 Toronto	A.L.	1	5	0	1	.000	3	2	7	7.20	0
1991 Toronto	A.L.	1	3⅔	0	1	.000	3	1	7	9.82	0
1992 Toronto	A.L.	1	3⅔	0	0	.000	1	0	3	2.45	0
1993 Toronto	A.L.	1	6	0	1	.000	4	4	6	7.50	0
1996 St. Louis	N.L.	3	8	1	1	.500	11	3	15	12.38	0
Championship Series Totals 7		26⅓	1	4	.200	22	10	38	8.54	0
World Series Record											
1992 Toronto	A.L.	4	3⅔	0	0	.000	4	0	4	0.00	0
1993 Toronto	A.L.	1	2	0	0	.000	1	4	3	27.00	0
World Series Totals 5		5⅔	0	0	.000	5	4	7	9.53	0

a On disabled list from June 20 to July 16, 1992.
b Suspended by American League for August 5 umpire bumping from September 23 to September 27, 1992.
c On disabled list from May 25 to June 12, 1993.
d Filed for free agency, October 17, 1994.
e Signed with Oakland Athletics, April 11, 1995.
f Traded to St. Louis for pitcher Bret Wagner, pitcher Jay Witasick, pitcher Carl Dale and outfielder Allen Battle, January 9, 1996.

SULLIVAN, WILLIAM SCOTT
Born, Tuscaloosa, Alabama, March 13, 1971.
Bats Right. Throws Right. Height, 6 feet, 4 inches. Weight, 210 pounds.

Year	Club	Lea	G	IP	W	L	Pct	SO	BB	H	ERA	SAVES
1993 Billings	Pioneer	18	54	5	0	1.000	79	25	33	1.67	3
1994 Chattanooga	Southern	34	121⅓	11	7	.611	111	40	101	3.41	7
1995 Cincinnati	N.L.	3	3⅔	0	0	.000	2	4	4	4.91	0
1995 Indianapolis	A.A.	44	58⅔	4	3	.571	54	24	51	3.53	1
1996 Indianapolis	A.A.	53	108⅔	5	2	.714	77	37	95	2.73	1
1996 Cincinnati	N.L.	7	8	0	0	.000	3	5	7	2.25	0
1997 Indianapols	A.A.	19	27⅔	3	1	.750	23	4	16	1.30	2
1997 Cincinnati	N.L.	59	97⅓	5	3	.625	96	30	79	3.24	1
Major League Totals .... 3 Yrs.		69	109	5	3	.625	101	37	90	3.22	1

SUPPAN, JEFFREY SCOT (JEFF)

Born, Oklahoma City, Oklahoma, January 2, 1975.
Bats Right. Throws Right. Height, 6 feet, 1 inch. Weight, 200 pounds.

Year	Club	Lea	G	IP	W	L	Pct	SO	BB	H	ERA	SAVES
1993 Red Sox	........Gulf Coast		10	57²/₃	4	3	.571	64	16	52	2.18	0
1994 Sarasota	...........Fla. St.		27	174	13	7	.650	173	50	153	3.26	0
1995 Trenton	...........Eastern		15	99	6	2	.750	88	26	86	2.36	0
1995 Pawtucket	.............Int.		7	45²/₃	2	3	.400	32	9	50	5.32	0
1995 Boston	..............A.L.		8	22²/₃	1	2	.333	19	5	29	5.96	0
1996 Pawtucket	.............Int.		22	145¹/₃	10	6	.625	142	25	130	3.22	0
1996 Boston a	..............A.L.		1	22²/₃	1	1	.500	13	13	29	7.54	0
1997 Pawtucket	.............Int.		9	60²/₃	5	1	.833	40	15	51	3.71	0
1997 Boston	..............A.L.		23	112¹/₃	7	3	.700	67	36	140	5.69	0
Major League Totals	........3 Yrs.		39	157²/₃	9	6	.600	99	54	198	5.99	0

a On disabled list from August 25 to September 30, 1996.\
b Selected in expansion draft by Arizona Diamondbacks, November 18, 1997.

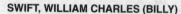

SWIFT, WILLIAM CHARLES (BILLY)

Born, South Portland, Maine, October 27, 1961.
Bats Right. Throws Right. Height, 6 feet. Weight, 191 pounds.

Year	Club	Lea	G	IP	W	L	Pct	SO	BB	H	ERA	SAVES
1985 Chattanooga a	.....Southern		7	39	2	1	.667	21	21	34	3.69	0
1985 Seattle	..............A.L.		23	120²/₃	6	10	.375	55	48	131	4.77	0
1986 Calgary	...............P.C.		10	57	4	4	.500	29	22	57	3.95	1
1986 Seattle	..............A.L.		29	115¹/₃	2	9	.192	55	55	148	5.46	0
1987 Calgary b	...............P.C.		5	18	0	0	.000	5	13	32	8.84	0
1988 Seattle	..............A.L.		38	174²/₃	8	12	.400	47	65	199	4.59	0
1989 San Bernardino	....California		2	10	1	0	1.000	4	2	8	0.00	0
1989 Seattle c	..............A.L.		37	130	7	3	.700	45	38	140	4.43	1
1990 Seattle	..............A.L.		55	128	6	4	.600	42	21	135	2.39	6
1991 Seattle d-e	..............A.L.		71	90¹/₃	1	2	.333	48	26	74	1.99	17
1992 San Francisco f-g	......N.L.		30	164²/₃	10	4	.714	77	43	*2.08	1
1993 San Francisco	..............N.L.		34	232²/₃	21	8	.724	157	55	195	2.82	0
1994 San Francisco h-i-j	......N.L.		17	109¹/₃	8	7	.533	62	31	109	3.38	0
1995 Colorado k-l	...........N.L.		19	105²/₃	9	3	.750	68	43	122	4.94	0
1996 Salem	...........Carolina		2	6	0	0	.000	4	1	9	4.50	0
1996 Colorado m	...........N.L.		7	18¹/₃	1	1	.500	5	5	23	5.40	2
1997 Salem	...........Carolina		1	4	0	1	.000	1	0	4	6.75	0
1997 Colo Sprngs	...............P.C.		1	3	0	1	.000	4	3	4	12.00	0
1997 Rochester	.............Int.		2	3²/₃	0	1	.000	2	3	2	4.91	0
1997 Colorado n-o-p	........N.L.		14	65¹/₃	4	6	.400	29	26	85	6.34	0
Major League Totals	........12 Yrs.		374	1455	83	69	.546	690	456	1505	3.76	27
Division Series												
1995 Colorado	.............N.L.		1	6	0	0	.000	3	2	7	6.00	0

a On disabled list from Jay 6 to May 21, 1985.
b On disabled list from June 4 to end of 1987 season.
c On disabled list from March 28 to April 27, 1989.
d On disabled list from April 11 to April 26, 1991.
e Traded to San Francisco Giants with pitchers Mike Jackson and Dave Burba for outfielder Kevin Mitchell and pitcher Mike Remlinger, December 11, 1991.
f Appeared in four additional games as pinch runner, and entered one game as pinch runner and remained in game as pitcher.
g On disabled list from May 23 to June 21 and August 25 to September 7, 1992.
h Appeared in one additional game as pinch runner.
i On disabled list from May 18 to June 6 and June 24 to July 22, 1994.
j Filed for free agency, October 14, 1994.
k Signed with Colorado Rockies, April 8, 1995.
l On disabled list from May 28 to June 16 and July 26 to September 1, 1995.
m On disabled list from April 1 to June 3 and June 4 to August 27, 1996.
n On disabled list from May 13 to July 11, 1997.
o Released by Colorado Rockies, August 20, 1997.
p Signed with Baltimore Orioles organization, August 26, 1997.

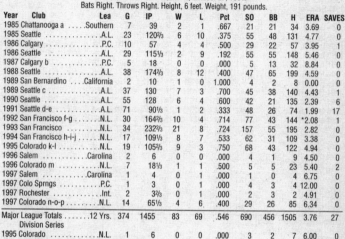

SWINDELL, FOREST GREGORY (GREG)

Born, Houston, Texas, January 2, 1965.
Bats Right. Throws Left. Height, 6 feet, 3 inches. Weight, 225 pounds.

Year	Club	Lea	G	IP	W	L	Pct	SO	BB	H	ERA	SAVES
1986 Waterloo	..........Midwest		3	18	2	1	.667	25	3	12	1.00	0
1986 Cleveland	.............A.L.		9	61²/₃	5	2	.714	46	15	57	4.23	0
1987 Cleveland a	............A.L.		16	102¹/₃	3	8	.273	97	37	112	5.10	0
1988 Cleveland	.............A.L.		33	242	18	14	.563	180	45	234	3.20	0

Year	Club	Lea	G	IP	W	L	Pct	SO	BB	H	ERA	SAVES
1989 Cleveland b	A.L.	28	184⅓	13	6	.684	129	51	170	3.37	0
1990 Cleveland	A.L.	34	214⅔	12	9	.571	135	47	245	4.40	0
1991 Cleveland c	A.L.	33	238	9	16	.360	169	31	241	3.48	0
1992 Cincinnati d-e	N.L.	31	213⅔	12	8	.600	138	41	210	2.70	0
1993 Houston f	N.L.	31	190⅓	12	13	.480	124	40	215	4.16	0
1994 Houston	N.L.	24	148⅓	8	9	.471	74	26	175	4.37	0
1995 Houston	N.L.	33	153	10	9	.526	96	39	180	4.47	0
1996 Houston g	N.L.	8	23	0	3	.000	15	11	35	7.83	0
1996 Cleveland h-i-j-k	A.L.	13	28⅔	1	1	.500	21	8	31	6.59	0
1997 Minnesota	A.L.	65	115⅔	7	4	.636	75	25	102	3.58	1
Major League Totals 12 Yrs.		358	1915⅔	110	102	.519	1299	416	2007	3.88	1

a On disabled list from July 2 to end of 1987 season.
b On disabled list from July 26 to August 30, 1989.
c Traded to Cincinnati Reds for pitchers Jack Armstrong, Scott Scudder and Joe Turek, November 15, 1991.
d On disabled list from August 23 to September 7, 1992.
e Filed for free agency, October 26; signed with Houston Astros, December 4, 1992.
f On disabled list from July 6 to July 25, 1993.
g Waived by Houston Astros, June 3, 1996.
h Signed with Cleveland Indians, June 15, 1996.
i On disabled list from July 4 to July 21 and April 20 to May 22, 1996.
j Designated for assignment by Cleveland Indians, August 28, 1996.
k Filed for free agency, October 3, 1996.

TAPANI, KEVIN RAY

Born, Des Moines, Iowa, February 18, 1964.
Bats Right. Throws Right. Height, 6 feet. Weight, 188 pounds.

Year	Club	Lea	G	IP	W	L	Pct	SO	BB	H	ERA	SAVES
1986 Medford	Northwest	2	8⅓	1	0	1.000	9	3	6	0.00	0
1986 Modesto	California	11	69	6	1	.857	44	22	74	2.48	0
1986 Huntsville	Southern	1	6	1	0	1.000	2	1	8	6.00	0
1986 Tacoma	P.C.	1	2	0	1	.000	1	1	5	15.43	0
1987 Modesto a	California	24	148	10	7	.588	121	60	122	3.76	0
1988 St. Lucie b	Fla. St.	3	19	1	0	1.000	11	4	17	1.42	0
1988 Jackson	Texas	24	62⅓	5	1	.833	35	19	45	2.74	3
1989 Tidewater	Int.	17	109	7	5	.583	63	25	113	3.47	0
1989 New York c	N.L.	3	7⅓	0	0	.000	2	4	5	3.68	0
1989 Portland	P.C.	6	41	4	2	.667	30	12	38	2.20	0
1989 Minnesota	A.L.	5	32⅔	2	2	.500	21	8	34	3.86	0
1990 Minnesota d	A.L.	28	159⅓	12	8	.600	101	29	164	4.07	0
1991 Minnesota	A.L.	34	244	16	9	.640	135	40	225	2.99	0
1992 Minnesota a	A.L.	34	220	16	11	.593	138	48	226	3.97	0
1993 Minnesota	A.L.	36	225⅔	12	15	.444	150	57	243	4.43	0
1994 Minnesota e	A.L.	24	156	11	7	.611	91	39	181	4.62	0
1995 Minnesota	A.L.	20	133⅔	6	11	.353	88	34	155	4.92	0
1995 Los Angeles f-g	N.L.	13	57	4	2	.667	43	14	72	5.05	0
1996 Chicago h-i-j	A.L.	34	225⅓	13	10	.565	150	76	236	4.59	0
1997 Orlando	Southern	1	4	0	0	.000	2	2	3	4.50	0
1997 Daytona	Fla. St.	1	4⅔	0	0	.000	4	2	5	3.86	0
1997 Rockford	Midwest	2	11	1	0	1.000	7	0	5	0.82	0
1997 Iowa	A.A.	1	9	0	1	.000	4	1	5	4.00	0
1997 Chicago k	N.L.	13	85	9	3	.750	55	23	77	3.39	0
Major League Totals 9 Yrs.		244	1546	101	78	.564	974	372	1618	4.13	0

Division Series
| 1995 Los Angeles | N.L. | 2 | 0⅓ | 0 | 0 | .000 | 1 | 4 | 0 | 81.00 | 0 |

Championship Series
| 1991 Minnesota | A.L. | 2 | 10⅓ | 0 | 1 | .000 | 9 | 3 | 16 | 7.84 | 0 |

World Series Record
| 1991 Minnesota | A.L. | 2 | 12 | 1 | 1 | .500 | 7 | 2 | 13 | 4.50 | 0 |

a Traded by Oakland Athletics to New York Mets organization as part of a three-team trade in which New York also acquired pitchers Wally Whitehurst from Oakland and Jack Savage from Los Angeles Dodgers, Oakland acquired pitchers Bob Welch and Matt Young from Los Angeles and Los Angeles acquired pitcher Jay Howell and short stop Alfredo Griffin from Oakland and pitcher Jesse Orosco from New York, December 11, 1987.
b On disabled list from March 28 to May 7 and June 3 to June 24, 1988.
c Traded to Minnesota Twins organization with pitchers Tim Drummond, Rick Aguilera and David West and player to be named for pitcher Frank Viola, July 31; Minnesota acquired pitcher Jack Savage to complete trade, October 16, 1989.
d On disabled list from August 17 to September 11, 1990.
e Declared restricted free agent under Major League Baseball implemented labor proposal, December 23, 1994.
f Re-signed with Minnesota Twins, April 5, 1995.

Traded to Los Angeles Dodgers with pitcher Mark Guthrie for pitcher Jose Parra, pitcher Greg Hansell and infielder Ron Coomer, July 31, 1995. Minnesota Twins received outfielder Chris Latham to complete trade, October 30, 1995.
h Signed with Chicago White Sox, February 3, 1996.
i Filed for free agency, October 29, 1996.
j Signed with Chicago Cubs, December 13, 1996.
k On disabled list from April 1 to July 22, 1997.

TATIS, RAMON FRANCISCO

Born, Guayubin, Dominican Republic, January 5, 1973.
Bats Left. Throws Left. Height, 6 feet, 2 inches. Weight, 185 pounds.

Year Club	Lea	G	IP	W	L	Pct	SO	BB	H	ERA	SAVES
1992 Mets	Gulf Coast	11	36	1	3	.250	25	15	56	8.50	0
1993 Kingsport	Appal.	13	42⅔	0	2	.000	25	23	51	6.12	1
1994 Kingsport	Appal.	13	40⅔	1	3	.250	36	31	35	3.32	0
1995 Pittsfield	N.Y.-Penn.	13	79⅓	4	5	.444	69	27	88	3.63	0
1995 Columbia	So. Atl.	18	32	2	3	.400	27	14	34	5.63	0
1996 St. Lucie	Fla. St.	46	74⅓	4	2	.667	46	38	71	3.39	6
1997 Chicago a	N.L.	56	55⅔	1	1	.500	33	29	66	5.34	0

a Selected on expansion draft by Tampa Bay Devil Rays, November 18, 1997.

TAVAREZ, JULIAN

Born, Santiago, Dominican Republic, May 22, 1973.
Bats Right. Throws Right. Height, 6 feet, 2 inches. Weight, 165 pounds.

Year Club	Lea	G	IP	W	L	Pct	SO	BB	H	ERA	SAVES
1990–91			Played in Dominican Summer League								
1992 Burlington	Appal.	14	87⅓	6	3	.667	69	12	86	2.68	0
1993 Kinston	Carolina	18	119	11	5	.688	107	28	102	2.42	0
1993 Canton	Eastern	3	19	2	1	.667	11	1	14	0.95	0
1993 Cleveland	A.L.	8	37	2	2	.500	19	13	53	6.57	0
1994 Charlotte	Int.	26	176	15	6	.714	102	43	167	3.48	0
1994 Cleveland	A.L.	1	1⅔	0	1	.000	0	1	6	21.60	0
1995 Cleveland	A.L.	57	85	10	2	.833	68	21	76	2.44	0
1996 Buffalo	A.A.	2	14	1	0	1.000	10	3	10	1.29	0
1996 Cleveland	A.L.	51	80⅔	4	7	.364	46	22	101	5.36	0
1997 San Francisco	N.L.	89	88⅓	6	4	.600	38	34	91	3.87	0
Major League Totals	5 Yrs.	206	292⅔	22	16	.579	171	91	327	4.31	0
Division Series											
1995 Cleveland	A.L.	3	2⅔	0	0	.000	3	0	5	6.75	0
1996 Cleveland	A.L.	2	1⅓	0	0	.000	1	2	1	0.00	0
Division Series Totals	5	4	0	0	.000	4	2	6	4.50	0
Championship Series											
1995 Cleveland	A.L.	4	3⅓	0	1	.000	2	1	3	2.70	0
World Series											
1995 Cleveland	A.L.	5	4⅓	0	0	.000	1	2	3	0.00	0

a Traded to San Francisco Giants, with infielder Jeff Kent, infielder Jose Vizcano and a player to be named later for infielder Matt Williams and a player to be named later, November 13, 1996.

1997 San Francisco	N.L.	3	4	0	1	.000	0	2	4	4.50	0
Division Series Totals	8	8	0	1	.000	4	4	10	4.50	0

TAYLOR, WILLIAM HOWELL

Born, Monticello, Florida, October 16, 1961.
Bats Right. Throws Right. Height, 6 feet, 8 inches. Weight, 230 pounds.

Year Club	Lea	G	IP	W	L	Pct	SO	BB	H	ERA	SAVES
1980 Asheville	So. Atl.	6	14	0	2	.000	12	9	24	10.93	0
1980 Sarasota Rangers	Gulf C.	14	35	0	0	.000	22	16	36	2.31	0
1981 Sarasota Rangers	Gulf C.	12	53	4	2	.667	35	29	42	2.72	0
1981 Asheville	So. Atl.	14	64	1	7	.125	44	35	76	4.64	0
1982 Wausau-Burlington a	Mid.	37	112	7	9	.438	95	63	100	4.18	4
1983 Salem	Carolina	7	41⅔	1	1	.500	42	42	30	6.26	0
1983 Tulsa	Texas	21	76	5	8	.385	75	51	86	6.87	0
1984 Tulsa	Texas	42	80	5	3	.625	80	51	65	3.83	7
1985 Tulsa	Texas	20	103⅔	3	9	.250	87	48	84	3.47	0

Year	Club	Lea	G	IP	W	L	Pct	SO	BB	H	ERA	SAVES
1986 Tulsa ....Texas			11	68⅓	3	7	.300	64	37	65	3.95	0
1986 Oklahoma City .........A.A.			16	101⅔	5	5	.500	68	57	94	4.60	0
1987 Oklahoma City .........A.A.			28	168⅓	*12	9	.571	100	91	198	5.61	0
1988 Oklahoma City b-c ......A.A.			20	82	4	8	.333	42	35	98	5.49	1
1989 Las Vegas d-e .........P.C.			47	79	7	4	.636	71	27	93	5.13	1
1990 Durham ....Carolina			5	8⅓	0	0	.000	10	1	8	3.24	0
1990 Richmond ....Int.			2	3	0	0	.000	0	0	4	0.00	0
1991 Greenville ....Southern			59	77⅔	6	2	.750	65	15	49	1.51	22
1992 Richmond f ....Int.			47	79	2	3	.400	82	27	72	2.28	12
1993 Richmond g ....Int.			59	68⅓	2	4	.333	81	26	56	1.98	*26
1994 Oakland h ...........A.L.			41	46⅓	1	3	.250	48	18	38	3.50	1
1996 Edmonton .............P.C.			7	11⅓	0	0	.000	13	3	10	0.79	4
1996 Oakland i ...........A.L.			55	60⅓	6	3	.667	67	25	52	4.33	17
1997 Oakland ...............A.L.			72	73	3	4	.429	66	36	70	3.82	23
Major League Totals ....3 Yrs.			168	179⅔	10	10	.500	181	79	160	3.91	41

a Loaned by Texas Rangers to Seattle Mariners organization, April 15; returned to Texas Rangers organization, June 23, 1982.
b On disabled list from June 7 to August 7, 1988.
c Became free agent October 15, 1988; signed with San Diego Padres organization, March 30, 1989.
d On disabled list from May 22 to June 30, 1989.
e Became free agent, October 15, 1989; signed with Atlanta Braves organization, August 16, 1990.
f Drafted by Toronto Blue Jays from Atlanta Braves organization, December 7, 1992; returned to Atlanta Braves organization, April 1, 1993.
g Became free agent, October 15; signed with Oakland Athletics organization, December 17, 1993.
h On disabled list from July 27 to end of 1994 season.
i On disabled list from August 16 to September 13, 1996.

TELEMACO, AMAURY
Born, Higuey, Dominican Republic, January 19, 1974.
Bats Right. Throws Right. Height, 6 feet, 4 inches. Weight 220 pounds.

Year	Club	Lea	G	IP	W	L	Pct	SO	BB	H	ERA	SAVES
1992 Huntington ....Appal.			12	76⅓	3	5	.375	93	17	71	4.01	0
1992 Peoria ....Midwest			2	5⅔	0	1	.000	5	5	9	7.94	0
1993 Peoria ....Midwest			23	143⅔	8	11	.421	133	54	129	3.45	0
1994 Daytona ....Fla. St.			11	76⅔	7	3	.700	59	23	62	3.40	0
1994 Orlando ....Southern			12	62⅔	3	5	.375	49	20	56	3.45	0
1995 Orlando ....Southern			22	147⅔	8	8	.500	151	42	112	3.29	0
1996 Iowa .................A.A.			8	50	3	1	.750	42	18	38	3.06	0
1996 Chicago a ...........N.L.			25	97⅓	5	7	.417	64	31	108	5.46	0
1997 Orlando ....Southern			1	8	1	0	1.000	6	2	9	2.25	0
1997 Chicago .............N.L.			10	38	0	3	.000	29	11	47	6.16	0
1997 Iowa .................A.A.			18	113⅔	5	9	.357	75	38	121	4.51	0
Major League Totals ....2 Yrs.			35	135⅓	5	10	.333	93	42	155	5.65	0

a On disabled list from August 20 to September 4, 1996.

TELFORD, ANTHONY CHARLES
Born, San Jose, California, March 6, 1966.
Bats Right. Throws Right. Height, 6 feet, 1 inch. Weight, 180 pounds.

Year	Club	Lea	G	IP	W	L	Pct	SO	BB	H	ERA	SAVES
1987 Newark .........N.Y.-Penn.			6	17⅔	1	0	1.000	27	3	16	1.02	0
1987 Hagerstown ....Carolina			2	11⅓	1	0	1.000	10	5	9	1.59	0
1987 Rochester ....Int.			1	2	0	0	.000	3	3	0	0.00	0
1988 Hagerstown ....Carolina			1	7	1	0	1.000	10	0	3	0.00	0
1989 Frederick ....Carolina			9	25⅔	2	1	.667	19	12	25	4.21	1
1990 Frederick ....Carolina			8	53⅔	4	2	.667	49	11	35	1.68	0
1990 Hagerstown ....Eastern			14	96	10	2	.833	73	25	80	1.97	0
1990 Baltimore ...........A.L.			8	36⅓	3	3	.500	20	19	43	4.95	0
1991 Rochester ....Int.			27	157⅓	12	9	.571	115	48	166	3.95	0
1991 Baltimore ...........A.L.			9	26⅔	0	0	.000	24	6	27	4.05	0
1992 Rochester ....Int.			27	181	12	7	.632	129	64	183	4.18	0
1993 Baltimore ...........A.L.			3	7⅓	0	0	.000	6	1	11	9.82	0
1993 Rochester a ....Int.			38	90⅔	7	7	.500	66	33	98	4.27	2
1994 Richmond ....Int.			38	142⅔	10	6	.625	111	41	148	4.23	0
1995 Edmonton b-c .........P.C.			8	36⅓	3	2	.600	17	16	47	7.18	0
1995 Canton-Akrn. ....Eastern			2	11	2	0	1.000	4	4	6	0.82	0
1995 Buffalo d .............A.A.			16	39	4	1	.800	24	10	35	3.46	0

Year	Club	Lea	G	IP	W	L	Pct	SO	BB	H	ERA	SAVES
1996 Ottawa e	....	Int.	30	118⅓	7	2	.778	69	34	128	4.11	0
1997 Montreal	....	N.L.	65	89	4	6	.400	61	33	77	3.24	1
Major League Totals	....	4 Yrs.	85	159⅓	7	9	.438	111	59	158	4.07	1

a Released by Baltimore Orioles and signed as free agent with Atlanta Braves organization, November 23, 1993.
b Signed by Oakland Athletics organization, November 17, 1994.
c Signed by Cleveland Indians organization, June 15, 1994.
d Released by Cleveland Indians organization, October 15, 1995.
e Signed as free agent with Montreal Expos organization, February 22, 1996.

TELGHEDER, DAVID WILLIAM
Born, Middletown, New York, November 11, 1966.
Bats Right. Throws Right. Height, 6 feet, 3 inches. Weight, 212 pounds.

Year	Club	Lea	G	IP	W	L	Pct	SO	BB	H	ERA	SAVES
1989 Pittsfield	....	N.Y.-Penn.	13	58⅔	5	3	.625	65	9	43	2.45	2
1990 Columbia	....	So. Atl.	14	99⅓	9	3	.750	81	10	79	1.54	0
1990 St. Lucie	....	Fla. St.	14	96	9	4	.692	77	14	84	3.00	0
1991 Williamsport	....	Eastern	28	167⅓	13	11	.542	90	33	185	3.60	0
1992 Tidewater	....	Int.	28	169	6	14	.300	118	36	173	4.21	0
1993 Norfolk	....	Int.	13	76⅓	7	3	.700	52	19	81	2.95	1
1993 New York	....	N.L.	24	75⅔	6	2	.750	35	21	82	4.76	0
1994 New York	....	N.L.	6	10	0	1	.000	4	8	11	7.20	0
1994 Norfolk	....	Int.	23	158⅔	8	10	.444	83	26	156	3.40	0
1995 Norfolk	....	Int.	29	92½	5	4	.556	75	8	77	2.24	3
1995 New York a-b	....	N.L.	7	25⅔	1	2	.333	16	7	34	5.61	0
1996 Edmonton	....	P.C.	17	101⅓	8	6	.571	59	23	102	4.17	0
1996 Modesto	....	California	1	6	1	0	1.000	3	1	4	1.50	0
1996 Oakland	....	A.L.	16	79⅓	4	7	.364	43	26	92	4.65	0
1997 Modesto	....	California	2	5⅓	0	0	.000	4	2	3	3.38	0
1997 Oakland c-d-e	....	A.L.	20	101	4	6	.400	55	35	134	6.06	0
Major League Totals	......	5 Yrs.	73	291⅔	15	18	.455	153	97	353	5.34	0

a Outrighted by New York Mets, October 16, 1995.
b Signed with Oakland Athletics organization, December 2, 1995.
c On disabled list from June 24 to September 8, 1997.
d Outrighted by Oakland Athletics, September 13, 1997.
e Signed with Oakland Athletics organization, December 5, 1997.

TEWKSBURY, ROBERT ALAN (BOB)
Born, Concord, New Hampshire, November 30, 1960.
Bats Right. Throws Right. Height, 6 feet, 4 inches. Weight, 208 pounds.

Year	Club	Lea	G	IP	W	L	Pct	SO	BB	H	ERA	SAVES
1981 Oneonta	....	N.Y.-Penn.	14	90	7	3	.700	62	37	85	3.40	0
1982 Ft. Lauderdale	......	Fla. St.	24	182⅓	*15	4	.789	92	47	146	*1.88	1
1983 Nashville a	....	Southern	7	51	5	1	.833	15	10	49	2.82	0
1983 Ft. Lauderdale	....	Fla. St.	2	16	2	0	1.000	5	1	6	0.00	0
1984 Nashville b	....	Southern	26	172	11	9	.550	78	42	185	2.83	0
1985 Albany	....	Eastern	17	106⅔	6	5	.545	63	19	101	3.59	0
1985 Columbus c	....	Int.	6	44	3	0	1.000	21	5	27	1.02	0
1986 Columbus	....	Int.	2	10	1	0	1.000	4	2	6	2.70	0
1986 New York	....	A.L.	23	130⅓	9	5	.643	49	31	144	3.31	0
1987 Columbus	....	Int.	11	74⅔	6	1	.857	32	11	68	2.53	0
1987 New York d	....	A.L.	8	33⅓	1	4	.200	12	7	47	6.75	0
1987 Chicago e	....	N.L.	7	18	0	4	.000	10	13	32	6.50	0
1988 Iowa	....	A.A.	10	67	4	2	.667	43	10	73	3.76	0
1988 Chicago f-g	....	N.L.	1	3⅓	0	0	.000	1	2	6	8.10	0
1989 Louisville	....	A.A.	28	*189	*13	5	.722	72	34	170	2.43	1
1989 St. Louis	....	N.L.	7	30	1	0	1.000	17	10	25	3.30	0
1990 Louisville	....	A.A.	6	40⅔	3	2	.600	22	3	41	2.43	0
1990 St. Louis	....	N.L.	28	145⅓	10	9	.526	50	15	151	3.47	1
1991 St. Louis	....	N.L.	30	191	11	12	.478	75	38	206	3.25	0
1992 St. Louis	....	N.L.	33	233	16	5	*762	91	20	217	2.16	0
1993 St. Louis	....	N.L.	32	213⅔	17	10	.630	97	20	*258	3.83	0
1994 St. Louis h	....	N.L.	24	155⅔	12	10	.545	79	22	*190	5.32	0
1995 Charlotte	....	Fla. St.	1	6	1	0	1.000	4	0	3	0.00	0
1995 Texas i-j-k-l	....	A.L.	21	129⅔	8	7	.533	53	20	169	4.58	0

Year	Club	Lea	G	IP	W	L	Pct	SO	BB	H	ERA	SAVES
1996	San Diego m	N.L.	36	206⅔	10	10	.500	126	43	224	4.31	0
1997	Minnesota n	A.L.	26	168⅔	8	13	.381	92	31	200	4.22	0
Major League Totals		12 Yrs.	276	1658⅔	103	89	.536	752	272	1869	3.84	1

a On disabled list from April 8 to June 7, 1983.
b On disabled list from April 9 to April 27, 1984.
c On disabled list from June 10 to July 25, 1985.
d Traded to Chicago Cubs with pitchers Rich Scheid and Dean Wilkins for pitcher Steve Trout, July 11, 1987.
e On disabled list from August 13 to end of 1987 season.
f On disabled list from May 22 to June 12, 1988.
g Became free agent, October 15; signed with St. Louis Cardinals organization, December 19, 1988.
h Filed for free agency, October 21, 1994.
i Signed with Texas Rangers, April 8, 1995.
j On disabled list from July 23 to August 26, 1995.
k Not offered 1996 contract, November 2, 1995.
l Signed by San Diego Padres, December 18, 1995.
m Filed for free agency, October 31, 1996.
n On disabled list from May 5 to May 25 and July 18 to August 17, 1997.

THOMAS, LARRY WAYNE

Born, Miami, Florida, October 25, 1969.
Bats Right. Throws Left. Height, 6 feet, 1 inch. Weight, 190 pounds.

Year	Club	Lea	G	IP	W	L	Pct	SO	BB	H	ERA	SAVES
1991	Utica	N.Y.-Penn.	11	73⅓	1	3	.250	61	25	55	1.47	0
1991	Birmingham	Southern	2	6	0	0	.000	2	4	6	3.00	0
1992	Sarasota	Fla. St.	8	55⅔	5	0	1.000	50	7	44	1.62	0
1992	Birmingham	Southern	17	120⅔	8	6	.571	72	30	102	1.94	0
1993	Nashville	A.A.	18	100⅔	4	6	.400	67	32	114	5.99	0
1993	Sarasota	Fla. St.	8	61⅔	4	2	.667	27	15	52	2.48	0
1993	Birmingham	Southern	1	7	0	1	.000	5	1	9	5.14	0
1994	Birmingham	Southern	24	144	5	10	.333	77	53	159	4.63	0
1995	Birmingham	Southern	35	40⅓	4	1	.800	47	15	24	1.34	2
1995	Chicago	A.L.	17	13⅔	0	0	.000	12	6	8	1.32	0
1996	Chicago a	A.L.	57	30⅔	2	3	.400	20	14	32	3.23	0
1997	Chicago b	A.L.	5	3⅓	0	0	.000	0	2	3	8.10	0
1997	Nashville	A.A.	44	48	3	2	.600	53	18	47	3.94	2
Major League Totals		3 Yrs.	79	47⅔	2	3	.400	32	22	43	3.02	0

a On disabled list from August 17 to September 6, 1996
b Traded to Texas Rangers with pitcher Alan Levine for infielder Benji Gil, December 19, 1997.

THOMPSON, JUSTIN WILLARD

Born, San Antonio, Texas, March 8, 1973.
Bats Left. Throws Left. Height, 6 feet, 4 inches. Weight, 215 pounds.

Year	Club	Lea	G	IP	W	L	Pct	SO	BB	H	ERA	SAVES
1991	Bristol	Appal.	10	50	2	5	.286	60	24	45	3.60	0
1992	Fayettevlle	So. Atl.	20	95	4	4	.500	88	40	79	2.18	0
1993	Lakeland	Fla. St.	11	55⅔	4	4	.500	46	16	65	3.56	0
1993	London	Eastern	14	83⅔	3	6	.333	72	37	96	4.09	0
1995	Lakeland	Fla. St.	6	24	2	1	.667	20	8	30	4.88	0
1995	Jacksnville	Southern	18	123	6	7	.462	98	38	110	3.73	0
1996	Fayettevlle	So. Atl.	1	3	0	0	.000	5	0	1	3.00	0
1996	Visalia	California	1	3	0	0	.000	7	2	2	0.00	0
1996	Toledo	Int.	13	84⅓	6	3	.667	69	26	74	3.42	0
1996	Detroit a	A.L.	11	59	1	6	.143	44	31	62	4.58	0
1997	Detroit b	A.L.	32	223⅓	15	11	.577	151	66	188	3.02	0
Major League Totals		2 Yrs.	43	282⅓	16	17	.485	195	97	250	3.35	0

a On disabled list from June 3 to August 17, 1996.
b On disabled list from July 6 to July 21, 1997.

THOMPSON, MARK RADFORD

Born, Russellville, Kentucky, April 7, 1971.
Bats Right. Throws Right. Height, 6 feet, 2 inches. Weight, 205 pounds.

Year	Club	Lea	G	IP	W	L	Pct	SO	BB	H	ERA	SAVES
1992	Bend	Northwest	16	*106⅓	8	4	.667	*102	31	81	1.95	0
1993	Central Valley	California	11	69⅔	3	2	.600	72	18	46	2.20	0

Year Club	Lea	G	IP	W	L	Pct	SO	BB	H	ERA	SAVES
1993 Colorado Springs a .......P.C.		4	33⅓	3	0	1.000	22	11	31	2.70	0
1994 Colorado Springs .......P.C.		23	140⅓	8	9	.471	82	57	169	4.49	0
1994 Colorado .............N.L.		2	9	1	1	.500	5	8	16	9.00	0
1995 Colorado Springs .......P.C.		11	62	5	3	.625	38	25	73	6.10	0
1995 Colorado .............N.L.		21	51	2	3	.400	30	22	73	6.53	0
1996 Colorado .............N.L.		34	169⅔	9	11	.450	99	74	189	5.30	0
1997 Colorado b ...........N.L.		6	29⅔	3	3	.500	9	13	40	7.89	0
1997 Asheville ....So. Atl.		4	13⅓	0	2	.000	9	5	11	2.70	0
1997 Colo Sprngs. .........P.C.		1	3	0	0	.000	1	1	6	12.00	0
Major League Totals ....4 Yrs.		63	259⅓	15	18	.455	143	117	318	5.97	0
Division Series											
1995 Colorado .............N.L.		1	1	0	0	.000	0	0	0	0.00	1

a On disabled list from July 26 to end of 1993 season.
b On disabled list from May 8 to September 29, 1997.

THOMSON, JOHN CARL
Born, Vicksburg, Mississippi, October 1, 1973.
Bats Right. Throws Right. Height, 6 feet, 3 inches. Weight, 175 pounds.

Year Club	Lea	G	IP	W	L	Pct	SO	BB	H	ERA	SAVES
1993 Rockies ....Arizona		11	50⅔	3	5	.375	36	31	43	4.62	0
1994 Asheville ....So. Atl.		19	88⅓	6	6	.500	79	33	70	2.85	0
1994 Central Val ....California		9	49⅓	3	1	.750	41	18	43	3.28	0
1995 New Haven ....Eastern		26	131⅓	7	8	.467	82	56	132	4.18	0
1996 New Haven ....Eastern		16	97⅔	9	4	.692	86	27	82	2.86	0
1996 Colo Sprngs ...........P.C.		11	69⅔	4	7	.364	62	26	76	5.04	0
1997 Colo Sprngs ...........P.C.		7	42	4	2	.667	49	14	36	3.43	0
1997 Colorado .............N.L.		27	166⅓	7	9	.438	106	51	193	4.71	0

THURMAN, MICHAEL RICHARD
Born, Corvallis, Oregon, July 22, 1973.
Bats Right. Throws Right. Height, 6 feet, 4 inches. Weight, 190 pounds.

Year Club	Lea	G	IP	W	L	Pct	SO	BB	H	ERA	SAVES
1994 Vermont .........N.Y.-Penn.		2	6⅔	0	1	.000	3	2	6	5.40	0
1995 Albany ....So. Atl.		22	110⅓	3	8	.273	77	32	133	5.47	0
1996 Wst Plm Bch ....Fla. St.		19	113⅔	6	8	.429	68	23	122	3.40	0
1996 Harrisburg ....Eastern		4	24⅔	3	1	.750	14	5	25	5.11	0
1997 Harrisburg ....Eastern		20	115⅔	9	6	.600	85	30	102	3.81	0
1997 Ottawa ....Int.		4	19⅔	1	3	.250	15	9	17	5.49	0
1997 Montreal .............N.L.		5	11⅔	1	0	1.000	8	4	8	5.40	0

TIMLIN, MICHAEL AUGUST
Born, Midland, Texas, March 10, 1966.
Bats Right. Throws Right. Height, 6 feet, 4 inches. Weight, 210 pounds.

Year Club	Lea	G	IP	W	L	Pct	SO	BB	H	ERA	SAVES
1987 Medicine Hat ....Pioneer		13	75⅓	4	8	.333	66	26	79	5.14	0
1988 Myrtle Beach ....So. Atl.		35	151	10	6	.625	106	77	119	2.86	0
1989 Dunedin ....Fla. St.		33	88⅔	5	8	.385	64	36	90	3.25	7
1990 Dunedin ....Fla. St.		42	50⅓	7	2	.778	46	16	36	1.43	22
1990 Knoxville ....Southern		17	26	1	2	.333	21	7	20	1.73	8
1991 Toronto a ...........A.L.		63	108⅓	11	6	.647	85	50	94	3.16	3
1992 Dunedin ....Fla. St.		6	10	0	0	.000	7	2	9	0.90	1
1992 Syracuse ....Int.		7	11⅓	0	1	.000	7	5	15	8.74	3
1992 Toronto b ...........A.L.		26	43⅔	0	2	.000	35	20	45	4.12	1
1993 Dunedin ....Fla. St.		4	9	0	0	.000	8	0	4	1.00	1
1993 Toronto .............A.L.		54	55⅔	4	2	.667	49	27	63	4.69	1
1994 Toronto c ...........A.L.		34	40	0	1	.000	38	20	41	5.17	2
1995 Syracuse ....Int.		8	17⅓	1	1	.500	13	4	13	1.04	0
1995 Toronto d ...........A.L.		31	42	4	3	.571	36	17	38	2.14	5
1996 Toronto .............A.L.		59	56⅔	1	6	.143	52	18	47	3.65	31
1997 Toronto-Seattle e .......A.L.		64	72⅔	6	4	.600	45	20	69	3.22	10
Major League Totals ....7 Yrs.		331	419	26	24	.520	340	172	397	3.63	53

Year	Club	Lea	G	IP	W	L	Pct	SO	BB	H	ERA	SAVES
	Division Series											
1997	Seattle	A.L.	1	0⅔	0	0	.000	1	1	3	54.00	0
	Championship Series											
1991	Toronto	A.L.	4	5⅔	0	1	.000	5	2	5	3.18	0
1992	Toronto	A.L.	2	1⅓	0	0	.000	1	0	4	6.75	0
1993	Toronto	A.L.	1	2⅓	0	0	.000	2	0	3	3.86	0
Championship Series Totals			7	9⅓	0	1	.000	8	2	12	3.86	0
	World Series Record											
1992	Toronto	A.L.	2	1⅓	0	0	.000	0	0	0	0.00	1
1993	Toronto	A.L.	2	2⅓	0	0	.000	4	0	2	0.00	0
World Series Totals			4	3⅔	0	0	.000	4	0	2	0.00	1

a On disabled list from August 1 to August 15, 1991.
b On disabled list from March 27 to June 12, 1992.
c On disabled list from May 25 to June 9, 1994.
d On disabled list from June 22 to August 18, 1995.
e Traded to Seattle Mariners with pitcher Paul Spoljaric for outfielder Jose Cruz, July 31, 1997.

TOMKO, BRETT DANIEL

Born, Cleveland, Ohio, April 7, 1973.
Bats Right. Throws Right. Height, 6 feet, 4 inches. Weight, 215 pounds.

Year	Club	Lea	G	IP	W	L	Pct	SO	BB	H	ERA	SAVES
1995	Chston-Wv	So. Atl.	9	49	4	2	.667	46	9	41	1.84	0
1996	Chattanooga	Southern	27	157⅔	11	7	.611	164	54	131	3.88	0
1997	Indianapolis	A.A.	10	61	6	3	.667	60	9	53	2.95	0
1997	Cincinnati	N.L.	22	126	11	7	.611	95	47	106	3.43	0

TRACHSEL, STEPHEN CHRISTOPHER

Born, Oxnard, California, October 31, 1970.
Bats Right. Throws Right. Height, 6 feet, 3 inches. Weight, 185 pounds.

Year	Club	Lea	G	IP	W	L	Pct	SO	BB	H	ERA	SAVES
1991	Geneva	N.Y.-Penn.	2	14⅓	1	0	1.000	7	6	10	1.26	0
1991	Winston-Salem	Carolina	12	73⅔	4	4	.500	69	19	70	3.67	0
1992	Charlotte	Southern	29	191	13	8	.619	135	35	180	3.06	0
1993	Iowa	A.A.	27	170⅔	13	6	.684	135	45	170	3.96	0
1993	Chicago	N.L.	3	19⅔	0	2	.000	14	3	16	4.58	0
1994	Iowa	A.A.	2	9	0	2	.000	8	7	11	10.00	0
1994	Chicago a	N.L.	22	146	9	7	.563	108	54	133	3.21	0
1995	Chicago	N.L.	30	160⅔	7	13	.350	117	76	174	5.15	0
1996	Orlando	Southern	2	13	0	1	.000	12	0	11	2.77	0
1996	Chicago	N.L.	31	205	13	9	.591	132	62	181	3.03	0
1997	Chicago	N.L.	34	201⅓	8	12	.400	160	69	225	4.51	0
Major League Totals		5 Yrs.	120	732⅔	37	43	.463	531	264	729	3.98	0

a On disabled list from July 20 to August 4, 1994.

TRLICEK, RICHARD ALAN

Born, Houston, Texas, August 26, 1969.
Bats Right. Throws Right. Height, 6 feet, 3 inches. Weight, 200 pounds.

Year	Club	Lea	G	IP	W	L	Pct	SO	BB	H	ERA	SAVES
1987	Utica	N.Y.-Penn.	10	37⅓	2	5	.286	22	31	43	4.10	0
1988	Batavia	N.Y.-Penn.	8	31⅔	2	3	.400	26	31	27	7.39	0
1989	Sumter a-b	So. Atl.	15	93⅔	6	5	.545	72	40	73	2.59	0
1989	Durham c	Carolina	1	8	0	0	.000	4	1	3	1.13	0
1990	Dunedin	Fla. St.	26	154⅓	5	8	.385	125	72	128	3.73	0
1991	Knoxville	Southern	41	51⅓	2	5	.286	55	22	36	2.45	16
1992	Toronto	A.L.	2	1⅔	0	0	.000	1	2	2	10.80	0
1992	Syracuse	Int.	35	43⅓	1	1	.500	35	31	37	4.36	10
1993	Los Angeles d	N.L.	41	64	1	2	.333	41	21	59	4.08	1
1994	New Britain e	Eastern	6	24⅔	0	1	.000	13	6	12	0.73	0
1994	Pawtucket	Int.	11	27⅓	2	1	.667	19	13	19	2.63	0
1994	Boston f-g	A.L.	12	22⅓	1	1	.500	7	16	32	8.06	0
1995	Phoenix h-i	P.C.	38	63	5	4	.556	43	21	72	5.29	0
1995	Canton-Akrn	Eastern	24	38⅓	5	3	.625	27	16	33	3.05	3

Year Club	Lea	G	IP	W	L	Pct	SO	BB	H	ERA	SAVES
1996 Norfolk j-k-l . . . . .Int.		62	77	4	5	.444	54	16	52	1.87	10
1996 New York m . . . . .N.L.		5	5⅓	0	1	.000	3	3	3	3.38	0
1997 Boston n-o . . . . .A.L.		18	23⅓	3	4	.429	10	18	26	4.63	0
1997 New York p-q-r . . . . . . .N.L.		9	9	0	0	.000	4	5	10	8.00	0
Major League Totals . . . . .5 Yrs.		87	125⅔	5	8	.385	66	65	132	5.23	1

a Released by Philadelphia Phillies organization, March 23, 1989.
b Signed as free agent by Atlanta Braves organization, April 2, 1989.
c Traded to Toronto Blue Jays for catcher Ernie Whitt and outfielder Kevin Batiste, December 17, 1989.
d Claimed off waivers by Los Angeles Dodgers, March 16, 1993.
e Claimed off waivers by Boston Red Sox, April 1, 1994.
f Released by Boston Red Sox, December 5, 1994.
g Signed as free agent by San Francisco Giants, January 27, 1995.
h Released by San Francisco Giants, July 18, 1995.
i Signed as free agent by Cleveland Indians, July 28, 1995.
j Signed by Detroit Tigers as a free agent, November 30, 1995.
k Released by Detroit Tigers, March 27, 1996.
l Signed as free agent by New York Mets, March 28, 1996.
m Claimed on waivers by Boston Red Sox, October 14, 1996.
n Traded to New York Mets for pitcher Toby Borland, May 12, 1997.
o Signed with New York Mets organization, December 19, 1997.
p On disabled list from June 12 to September 29, 1997.
q Outrighted by New York Mets, October 8, 1997.
r Signed by New York Mets, December 19, 1997.

TROMBLEY, MICHAEL SCOTT
Born, Springfield, Massachusetts, April 14, 1967.
Bats Right. Throws Right. Height, 6 feet, 2 inches. Weight, 208 pounds.

Year Club	Lea	G	IP	W	L	Pct	SO	BB	H	ERA	SAVES
1989 Kenosha . . . . .Midwest		12	49	5	1	.833	41	13	45	3.12	2
1989 Visalia . . . . .California		6	42	2	2	.500	31	11	31	2.14	0
1990 Visalia . . . . .California		27	176	14	6	.700	164	50	163	3.43	0
1991 Orlando . . . . .Southern		27	*191	12	7	.632	*175	57	153	2.54	0
1992 Portland . . . . .P.C.		25	165	10	8	.556	138	58	149	3.65	0
1992 Minnesota . . . . .A.L.		10	46⅓	3	2	.600	38	17	43	3.30	0
1993 Minnesota . . . . .A.L.		44	114⅓	6	6	.500	85	41	131	4.88	2
1994 Salt Lake City . . . . .P.C.		11	60⅔	4	4	.500	63	20	75	5.04	0
1994 Minnesota . . . . .A.L.		24	48⅓	2	0	1.000	32	18	56	6.33	0
1995 Salt Lake . . . . .P.C.		12	69⅔	5	3	.625	59	26	71	3.62	0
1995 Minnesota a . . . . .A.L.		20	97⅔	4	8	.333	68	42	107	5.62	0
1996 Salt Lake . . . . .P.C.		24	36⅔	2	2	.500	38	10	24	2.45	10
1996 Minnesota . . . . .A.L.		43	68⅔	5	1	.833	57	25	61	3.01	6
1997 Minnesota . . . . .A.L.		67	82⅓	2	3	.400	74	31	77	4.37	1
Major League Totals . . . . .6 Yrs.		208	457⅔	22	20	.524	354	174	475	4.66	9

a Outrighted by Minnesota Twins, November 28, 1995.

URBINA, UGUETH URTAIN
Born, Caracas, Venezuela, February 15, 1974.
Bats Right. Throws Right. Height, 6 feet, 2 inches. Weight, 185 pounds.

Year Club	Lea	G	IP	W	L	Pct	SO	BB	H	ERA	SAVES
1991 Expos . . . . .Gulf Coast		10	63	3	3	.500	51	10	58	2.29	0
1992 Albany . . . . .So. Atl.		24	142⅓	7	13	.350	100	54	111	3.22	0
1993 Burlington . . . . .Midwest		16	108⅓	10	1	.909	107	36	78	1.99	0
1993 Harrisburg . . . . .Eastern		11	70	4	5	.444	45	32	66	3.99	0
1994 Harrisburg . . . . .Eastern		21	120⅔	9	3	.750	86	43	96	3.28	0
1995 West Palm Beach . . . . .Fla. St.		2	9	1	0	1.000	11	1	4	0.00	0
1995 Ottawa . . . . .Int.		13	68	6	2	.750	55	26	46	3.04	0
1995 Montreal . . . . .N.L.		7	23⅓	2	2	.500	15	14	26	6.17	0
1996 Wst Plm Bch . . . . .Fla. St.		3	14	1	1	.500	21	3	13	1.29	0
1996 Ottawa . . . . .Int.		5	23⅔	2	0	1.000	28	6	17	2.66	0
1996 Montreal . . . . .N.L.		33	114	10	5	.667	108	44	102	3.71	0
1997 Montreal . . . . .N.L.		63	64⅓	5	8	.385	84	29	52	3.78	27
Major League Totals . . . . .3 Yrs.		103	201⅔	17	15	.531	207	87	180	4.02	27

VALDES, ISMAEL

Born, Victoria, Tamaulipas, Mexico, August 21, 1973.
Bats Right. Throws Right. Height, 6 feet, 3 inches. Weight, 185 pounds.

Year	Club	Lea	G	IP	W	L	Pct	SO	BB	H	ERA	SAVES
1991 Kissimmee Dodgers	Gulf C.	10	50⅓	2	2	.500	44	13	44	2.32	0
1992				Played in Dominican Summer League								
1993 San Antonio	Texas	3	13	1	0	1.000	11	0	12	1.38	0
1994 San Antonio	Texas	8	55⅓	2	3	.400	55	9	54	3.38	0
1994 Albuquerque	P.C.	8	45	4	1	.800	39	13	44	3.40	0
1994 Los Angeles	N.L.	21	28⅓	3	1	.750	28	10	21	3.18	0
1995 Los Angeles	N.L.	33	197⅔	13	11	.542	150	51	168	3.05	1
1996 Los Angeles	N.L.	33	225	15	7	.682	173	54	219	3.32	0
1997 Los Angeles a	N.L.	30	196⅔	10	11	.476	140	47	171	2.65	0
Major League Totals	4 Yrs.	117	647⅔	41	30	.577	491	162	579	3.03	1
Division Series											
1995 Los Angeles	N.L.	1	7	0	0	.000	6	1	3	0.00	0
1996 Los Angeles	N.L.	1	6⅓	0	1	.000	5	0	5	4.26	0
Division Series Totals	2	13⅓	0	1	.000	11	1	8	2.03	0

a On disabled list from July 6 to July 28, 1997.

VALDES, MARK CHRISTOPHER

Born, Dayton, Ohio, December 20, 1971.
Bats Right. Throws Right. Height, 6 feet. Weight, 170 pounds.

Year	Club	Lea	G	IP	W	L	Pct	SO	BB	H	ERA	SAVES
1993 Elmira	N.Y.-Penn.	3	9⅔	0	2	.000	15	7	8	5.59	0
1994 Kane County	Midwest	11	76⅓	7	4	.636	68	21	62	2.95	0
1994 Portland	Eastern	15	99	8	4	.667	70	39	77	2.55	0
1995 Charlotte	Int.	27	170⅓	9	13	.409	104	59	189	4.86	0
1995 Florida	N.L.	3	7	0	0	.000	2	9	17	14.14	0
1996 Portland	Eastern	10	64⅓	6	2	.750	49	12	60	2.66	0
1996 Charlotte	Int.	8	51	2	4	.333	24	15	66	5.12	0
1996 Florida	N.L.	11	48⅔	1	3	.250	13	23	63	4.81	0
1997 Montreal	N.L.	48	95	4	4	.500	54	39	84	3.13	2
Major League Totals	3 Yrs.	62	150⅔	5	7	.417	69	71	164	4.18	2

VAN LANDINGHAM, WILLIAM JOSEPH

Born, Columbia, Tennessee, July 16, 1970.
Bats Right. Throws Right. Height, 6 feet, 2 inches. Weight, 210 pounds.

Year	Club	Lea	G	IP	W	L	Pct	SO	BB	H	ERA	SAVES
1991 Everett	Northwest	15	77	8	4	.667	86	79	58	4.09	0
1992 San Jose	California	6	21	1	3	.250	18	13	22	5.57	0
1992 Clinton	Midwest	10	54	0	4	.000	59	29	49	5.67	0
1993 San Jose	California	27	163⅓	*14	8	.636	*171	87	167	5.12	0
1993 Phoenix	P.C.	1	7	0	1	.000	2	0	8	6.43	0
1994 Shreveport	Texas	8	51⅓	4	3	.571	45	11	41	2.81	0
1994 Phoenix	P.C.	5	29	1	1	.500	29	14	21	2.48	0
1994 San Francisco	N.L.	16	84	8	2	.800	56	43	70	3.54	0
1995 San Jose	California	1	6⅔	1	0	1.000	5	2	4	0.00	0
1995 San Francisco a	N.L.	18	122⅔	6	3	.667	95	40	124	3.67	0
1996 San Francisco	N.L.	32	181⅔	9	14	.391	97	78	196	5.40	0
1997 San Francisco b	N.L.	18	89	4	7	.364	52	59	80	4.96	0
1997 Phoenix c-d	P.C.	4	17	1	1	.500	7	21	20	9.00	0
Major League Totals	4 Yrs.	84	477⅓	27	26	.509	300	220	470	4.54	0

a On disabled list from April 25 to June 6, 1995.
b Outrighted by San Francisco Giants, August 6, 1997.
c Released by San Francisco Giants organization, December 19, 1997.
d Signed with Anaheim Angels, January 10, 1998.

VERAS, DARIO ANTONIO
Born, Santiago, Dominican Republic, March 13, 1973.
Bats Right. Throws Right. Height, 6 feet, 2 inches. Weight, 165 pounds.

Year	Club	Lea	G	IP	W	L	Pct	SO	BB	H	ERA	SAVES
1993	Bakersfield	California	7	13⅓	1	0	1.000	11	8	13	7.43	0
1993	Vero Beach	Fla. St.	24	54⅔	2	2	.500	31	14	59	2.80	2
1994	Rancho Cuca	California	59	79	9	2	.818	56	25	66	2.05	3
1995	Memphis	Southern	58	82⅔	7	3	.700	70	27	81	3.81	1
1996	Memphis	Southern	29	42⅔	3	1	.750	47	9	38	2.32	1
1996	Las Vegas	P.C.	19	40⅓	6	2	.750	30	6	41	2.90	1
1996	San Diego	N.L.	23	29	3	1	.750	23	10	24	2.79	0
1997	Mobile	Southern	5	5	0	0	.000	5	3	8	9.00	0
1997	Rancho Cuca	California	2	3	0	0	.000	3	1	3	6.00	1
1997	Las Vegas	P.C.	12	14⅓	0	2	.000	13	6	14	5.02	2
1997	San Diego a	N.L.	23	24⅔	2	1	.667	21	12	28	5.11	0
Major League Totals		2 Yrs.	46	53⅔	5	2	.714	44	22	52	3.86	0
Division Series												
1996	San Diego	N.L.	2	1	0	0	.000	1	0	1	0.00	0

a On disabled list from April 23 to May 9 and May 14 to July 28, 1997.

VERES, DAVID SCOTT
Born, Montgomery, Alabama, October 19, 1966.
Bats Right. Throws Right. Height, 6 feet, 2 inches. Weight, 195 pounds.

Year	Club	Lea	G	IP	W	L	Pct	SO	BB	H	ERA	SAVES
1986	Medford	Northwest	15	77⅓	5	2	.714	60	57	58	3.26	0
1987	Modesto	California	26	148⅓	8	9	.471	124	108	124	4.79	0
1988	Modesto	California	19	125	4	11	.267	91	78	100	3.31	0
1988	Huntsville	Southern	8	39	3	4	.429	17	15	50	4.15	0
1989	Huntsville	Southern	29	159⅓	8	11	.421	105	83	160	4.86	0
1990	Tacoma a	P.C.	32	151⅔	11	8	.579	88	88	136	4.69	1
1991	Albuquerque b	P.C.	57	100⅔	7	6	.538	81	52	89	4.47	5
1992	Tucson	P.C.	29	52⅔	2	3	.400	46	17	60	5.30	0
1993	Tucson	P.C.	43	130⅓	6	10	.375	122	32	156	4.90	5
1994	Tucson	P.C.	16	24	1	1	.500	19	10	17	1.88	1
1994	Houston	N.L.	32	41	3	3	.500	28	7	39	2.41	1
1995	Houston c	N.L.	72	103⅓	5	1	.833	94	30	89	2.26	1
1996	Montreal	N.L.	68	77⅔	6	3	.667	81	32	85	4.17	4
1997	Montreal d-e	N.L.	53	62	2	3	.400	47	27	68	3.48	1
Major League Totals		4 Yrs.	225	284	16	10	.615	250	96	281	3.07	7

a Traded by Oakland Athletics to Los Angeles Dodgers organization for pitcher Kevin Campbell, January 15, 1991.
b Became free agent, October 15; signed Houston Astros organization, May 28, 1992.
c Traded to Montreal Expos with catcher Raul Chavez for infielder Sean Berry, December 20, 1995.
d On disabled list from August 18 to September 17, 1997.
e Traded to Montreal Expos with player to be named later for outfielder Terry Jones and player to be named later, December 10, 1997.

VERES, RANDOLF RUHLAND (RANDY)
Born, Sacramento, California, November 25, 1965.
Bats Right. Throws Right. Height, 6 feet, 3 inches. Weight, 189 pounds.

Year	Club	Lea	G	IP	W	L	Pct	SO	BB	H	ERA	SAVES
1985	Helena	Pioneer	13	77⅓	7	4	.636	67	36	66	3.84	0
1986	Beloit a	Midwest	23	113⅓	4	12	.250	87	52	132	3.89	0
1987	Beloit	Midwest	21	127	10	6	.625	98	52	132	3.12	0
1988	Stockton	California	20	110	8	4	.667	96	77	94	3.35	0
1988	El Paso	Texas	6	39⅓	3	2	.600	31	12	35	3.66	0
1989	El Paso	Texas	8	43⅓	2	3	.400	41	25	43	4.78	0
1989	Denver	A.A.	17	107	6	7	.462	80	38	108	3.95	0
1989	Milwaukee	A.L.	3	8⅓	0	1	.000	8	4	9	4.32	0
1990	Denver	A.A.	16	50⅓	1	6	.143	36	27	60	5.19	2
1990	Milwaukee b	A.L.	26	41⅔	0	3	.000	16	16	38	3.67	1
1991	Richmond c	Int.	9	25	0	2	.000	12	10	32	5.04	0
1991	Phoenix	P.C.	19	43	3	0	1.000	41	14	42	3.56	1
1992	Phoenix d-e	P.C.	12	13⅓	0	2	.000	13	13	14	8.10	1
1993	Canton f-g	Eastern	13	57	1	5	.167	49	19	59	4.89	0
1994	Iowa	A.A.	33	55⅓	5	6	.455	42	11	43	2.93	5
1994	Chicago h	N.L.	10	9⅔	1	1	.500	5	2	12	5.59	0
1995	Charlotte	Int.	6	6⅔	1	0	1.000	5	5	3	2.70	1

Year	Club	Lea	G	IP	W	L	Pct	SO	BB	H	ERA	SAVES
1995 Florida i		N.L.	47	48²⁄₃	4	4	.500	31	22	46	3.88	1
1996 Detroit j		A.L.	25	30¹⁄₃	0	4	.000	28	23	38	8.31	0
1997 Kansas City k-l		A.L.	24	35¹⁄₃	4	0	1.000	28	7	36	3.31	1
1997 Omaha		A.A.	11	15	1	1	.500	19	5	15	6.60	0
Major League Totals	.6 Yrs.		135	174	9	13	.409	116	74	179	4.60	3

a On disabled list from August 17 to end of 1986 season.
b Released, April 5; signed with Atlanta Braves organization, May 3, 1991.
c Released by Atlanta Braves, June 12; signed with San Francisco Giants organization, June 19, 1991.
d On disabled list from May 16 to end of 1992 season.
e Became free agent, October 16, 1992; signed with Cleveland Indians organization, June 15, 1993.
f On disabled list from July 9 to July 16, 1993.
g Became free agent, October 15; signed with Chicago Cubs organization, December 3, 1993.
h Released, November 16, 1994.
i Traded to Detroit Tigers for pitcher Matt Brunson, March 11, 1996.
j Designated for assignment by Detroit Tigers, May 29, 1996.
k Released by Kansas City Royals, August 26, 1997.
l On disabled list from June 24 to September 29, 1997.

VILLONE, RONALD THOMAS (RON)
Born, Englewood, New Jersey, January 16, 1970.
Bats Left. Throws Left. Height, 6 feet, 3 inches. Weight, 230 pounds.

Year	Club	Lea	G	IP	W	L	Pct	SO	BB	H	ERA	SAVES
1993 Riverside	California	16	83¹⁄₃	7	4	.636	82	62	74	4.21	0
1993 Jacksonville	Southern	11	63²⁄₃	3	4	.429	66	41	49	4.38	0
1994 Jacksonville	Southern	41	79¹⁄₃	6	7	.462	94	68	56	3.86	8
1995 Tacoma	P.C.	22	29²⁄₃	1	0	1.000	43	19	9	0.61	13
1995 Seattle	A.L.	19	19¹⁄₃	0	2	.000	26	23	20	7.91	0
1995 San Diego a-b	N.L.	19	25²⁄₃	2	1	.667	37	11	24	4.21	1
1996 Las Vegas	P.C.	23	22	2	1	.667	29	9	13	1.64	3
1996 San Diego c	N.L.	21	18¹⁄₃	1	1	.500	19	7	17	2.95	0
1996 Milwaukee	A.L.	23	24²⁄₃	0	0	.000	19	18	14	3.28	2
1996 Milwaukee d	A.L.	50	52²⁄₃	1	0	1.000	40	36	54	3.42	0
Major League Totals	.3 Yrs.	132	140²⁄₃	4	4	.500	141	95	129	4.09	3

a Traded to San Diego Padres with outfielder Marc Newfield for pitcher Andy Benes and player to be named later, July 31, 1995.
b Seattle Mariners received pitcher Greg Keagle to complete trade, September 16, 1995.
c Traded to Milwaukee Brewers with pitcher Bryce Florie and outfielder Marc Newfield for outfielder Greg Vaughan and player to be named later, July 31, 1996. San Diego Padres received outfielder Gerald Parent to complete trade, September 16, 1996.
d Traded to Cleveland Indians with pitcher Ben McDonald and pitcher Mike Fetters for outfielder Marquis Grissom and pitcher Jeff Juden, December 8, 1997.

VOSBERG, EDWARD JOHN
Born, Tucson, Arizona, September 28, 1961.
Bats Left. Throws Left. Height, 6 feet, 1 inch. Weight, 190 pounds.

Year	Club	Lea	G	IP	W	L	Pct	SO	BB	H	ERA	SAVES
1983 Reno	California	15	97	6	6	.500	70	39	111	3.90	0
1983 Beaumont	Texas	1	7	1	0	1.000	1	2	2	0.00	0
1984 Beaumont	Texas	27	183²⁄₃	13	11	.542	100	74	196	3.43	0
1985 Beaumont	Texas	27	175	9	11	.450	124	69	178	3.91	0
1986 Las Vegas	P.C.	25	129²⁄₃	7	8	.467	93	64	136	4.72	0
1986 San Diego	N.L.	5	13²⁄₃	0	1	.000	8	9	17	6.59	0
1987 Las Vegas	P.C.	34	167²⁄₃	9	8	.529	75	97	154	3.92	0
1988 Las Vegas a	P.C.	45	128	11	7	.611	75	56	137	4.15	2
1989 Tucson-Albuq. b-c	P.C.	35	107²⁄₃	6	8	.429	86	54	139	6.02	3
1990 San Francisco	N.L.	18	24¹⁄₃	1	1	.500	12	12	21	5.55	0
1990 Phoenix d	P.C.	24	34	1	3	.250	28	16	36	2.65	3
1991 Edmonton-Calg. e-f	P.C.	28	38	0	3	.000	29	17	57	6.87	2
1992						Played in Italian Professional League					
1993 Iowa g	A.A.	52	63	5	1	.833	64	22	67	3.57	3
1994 Tacoma	P.C.	26	53²⁄₃	4	2	.667	54	19	39	3.35	0
1994 Oakland h	A.L.	16	13²⁄₃	0	2	.000	12	5	16	3.95	0
1995 Oklahoma City	A.A.	1	1²⁄₃	1	0	1.000	2	1	1	0.00	0
1995 Texas i	A.L.	44	36	5	5	.500	36	16	32	3.00	4
1996 Texas	A.L.	52	44	1	1	.500	32	21	51	3.27	8
1997 Texas j	A.L.	42	41	1	2	.333	29	15	44	4.61	0
1997 Florida k	N.L.	17	12	1	1	.500	8	6	15	3.75	1
Major League Totals	.6 Yrs.	194	184²⁄₃	9	13	.409	137	84	196	4.14	13

Year	Club	Lea	G	IP	W	L	Pct	SO	BB	H	ERA	SAVES
	Division Series											
1996 Texas	A.L.	1	0	0	0	.000	0	0	1	INF	0	
	Championship Series											
1997 Florida	N.L.	2	2⅔	0	0	.000	3	1	2	0.00	0	
	World Series Record											
1997 Florida	N.L.	2	3	0	0	.000	2	3	3	6.00	0	

a Traded by San Diego Padres to Houston Astros organization for catcher Dan Walters, December 13, 1988.
b Traded by Houston Astros to Los Angeles Dodgers organization to complete July 22 trade in which Houston acquired outfielder Javier Ortiz for player to be named, August 1, 1989.
c Became free agent October 15, 1989; signed with San Francisco Giants organization, March 13, 1990.
d Became free agent, October 15; signed with California Angels organization, December 4, 1990.
e Released by California Angels, May 11; signed with Seattle Mariners organization, May 20, 1991.
f Released by Seattle Mariners, July 10, 1991; signed with Chicago Cubs organization, March 17, 1993.
g Became free agent, October 15; signed with Oakland Athletics organization, December 3, 1993.
h Drafted by Los Angeles Dodgers from Oakland Athletics organization, December 5, 1994.
i Signed with Texas Rangers organization, April 25, 1995.
j Traded to Florida Marlins for pitcher Rick Helling, August 12, 1997.
k Traded to San Diego Padres for pitcher Chris Clark, November 21, 1997.

WADE, HAWATHA TERRELL (TERRELL)

Born, Rembert, South Carolina, January 25, 1973.
Bats Left. Throws Left. Height, 6 feet, 3 inches. Weight, 205 pounds.

Year	Club	Lea	G	IP	W	L	Pct	SO	BB	H	ERA	SAVES
1991 Braves	Gulf Coast	10	23	2	0	1.000	22	15	29	6.26	0	
1992 Idaho Falls	Pioneer	13	50⅓	1	4	.200	54	42	59	6.44	0	
1993 Macon	So. Atl.	14	83⅓	8	2	.800	121	36	57	1.73	0	
1993 Durham	Carolina	5	33	2	1	.667	47	18	26	3.27	0	
1993 Greenville	Southern	8	42	2	1	.667	40	29	32	3.21	0	
1994 Greenville	Southern	21	105⅔	9	3	.750	105	58	87	3.83	0	
1994 Richmond	Int.	4	24	2	2	.500	26	15	23	2.63	0	
1995 Richmond	Int.	24	142	10	9	.526	124	63	137	4.56	0	
1995 Atlanta	N.L.	3	4	0	1	.000	3	4	3	4.50	0	
1996 Atlanta	N.L.	44	69⅔	5	0	1.000	79	47	57	2.97	1	
1997 Atlanta a-b	N.L.	12	42	2	3	.400	35	16	60	5.36	0	
1997 Greenville	Southern	8	12⅔	0	2	.000	14	8	15	4.97	0	
Major League Totals	3 Yrs.	59	115⅔	7	4	.636	117	67	120	3.89	1	
	Championship Series											
1996 Atlanta	N.L.	1	0⅓	0	0	.000	1	0	0	0.00	0	
	World Series Record											
1996 Atlanta	N.L.	2	0⅔	0	0	.000	0	1	0	0.00	0	

a On disabled list from June 7 to September 29, 1997.
b Selected in expansion draft by Tampa Bay Devil Rays, November 18, 1997.

WAGNER, PAUL ALAN

Born, Milwaukee, Wisconsin, November 14, 1967.
Bats Right. Throws Right. Height, 6 feet, 1 inch. Weight, 202 pounds.

Year	Club	Lea	G	IP	W	L	Pct	SO	BB	H	ERA	SAVES
1989 Welland	N.Y.-Penn.	13	50⅓	4	5	.444	36	15	54	4.47	0	
1990 Augusta	So. Atl.	35	72	7	7	.500	71	30	71	2.75	4	
1990 Salem	Carolina	11	36	0	1	.000	28	17	39	5.00	2	
1991 Salem	Carolina	25	158⅓	11	6	.647	113	60	124	3.12	0	
1992 Carolina	Southern	19	121⅔	6	6	.500	101	47	104	3.03	0	
1992 Buffalo	A.A.	8	39⅓	3	3	.500	19	14	51	5.49	0	
1992 Pittsburgh	N.L.	6	13	2	0	1.000	5	5	9	0.69	0	
1993 Pittsburgh a	N.L.	44	141⅓	8	8	.500	114	42	143	4.27	2	
1994 Pittsburgh	N.L.	29	119⅔	7	8	.467	86	50	136	4.59	0	
1995 Pittsburgh b	N.L.	33	165	5	16	.238	120	72	174	4.80	1	
1996 Pirates	Gulf Coast	1	3	0	0	.000	4	0	2	0.00	0	
1996 Pittsburgh c	N.L.	16	81⅔	4	8	.333	81	39	86	5.40	0	
1997 Carolina	Southern	12	16	0	1	.000	20	16	25	10.13	0	
1997 Pittsburgh d-e	N.L.	14	16	0	0	.000	9	13	17	3.94	0	
1997 Milwaukee f	A.L.	2	2	1	0	1.000	0	0	3	9.00	0	
Major League Totals	6 Yrs.	144	538⅔	27	40	.403	415	221	568	4.59	3	

a On disabled list from August 3 to August 18, 1993.
b On disabled list from July 3 to July 21, 1995.
c On disabled list from June 7 to July 2 and July 20 to September 30, 1996.

d On disabled list from April 1 to July 18, 1997.
e Released by Pittsburgh Pirates, August 26, 1997.
f Signed with Milwaukee Brewers, September 1, 1997.

WAGNER, WILLIAM EDWARD (BILLY)

Born, Tannersville, Virginia, July 25, 1971.
Bats Left. Throws Left. Height, 5 feet, 10 inches. Weight, 180 pounds.

Year Club	Lea	G	IP	W	L	Pct	SO	BB	H	ERA	SAVES
1993 Auburn	N.Y.-Penn.	7	28⅔	1	3	.250	31	25	25	4.08	0
1994 Quad City	Midwest	26	153	8	9	.471	204	91	99	3.29	0
1995 Jackson	Texas	12	70	2	2	.500	77	36	49	2.57	0
1995 Tucson	P.C.	13	76⅓	5	3	.625	80	32	70	3.18	0
1995 Houston	N.L.	1	0⅓	0	0	.000	0	0	0	0.00	0
1996 Tucson	P.C.	12	74	6	2	.750	86	33	62	3.28	0
1996 Houston a	N.L.	37	51⅔	2	2	.500	67	30	28	2.44	9
1997 Houston	N.L.	62	66⅓	7	8	.467	106	30	49	2.85	23
Major League Totals	3 Yrs.	100	118⅓	9	10	.474	173	60	77	2.66	32
Division Series											
1997 Houston	N.L.	1	1	0	0	.000	2	0	3	18.00	0

a On disabled list from August 23 to September 7, 1996.

WAKEFIELD, TIMOTHY STEPHEN (TIM)

Born, Melborne, Florida, August 2, 1966.
Bats Right. Throws Right. Height, 6 feet, 2 inches. Weight, 204 pounds.

Year Club	Lea	G	IP	W	L	Pct	SO	BB	H	ERA	SAVES
1989 Welland	N.Y.-Penn.	18	39⅔	1	1	.500	42	21	30	3.40	2
1990 Salem	Carolina	28	190⅓	10	14	.417	127	85	187	4.73	0
1991 Buffalo	A.A.	1	4⅔	0	1	.000	4	1	8	11.57	0
1991 Carolina	Southern	26	183	15	8	.652	123	51	155	2.90	0
1992 Buffalo	A.A.	20	135⅓	10	3	.769	71	51	122	3.06	0
1992 Pittsburgh	N.L.	13	92	8	1	.889	51	35	76	2.15	0
1993 Carolina	Southern	9	56⅔	3	5	.375	36	22	68	6.99	0
1993 Pittsburgh	N.L.	24	128⅓	6	11	.353	59	75	145	5.61	0
1994 Buffalo	A.A.	30	175⅔	5	15	.250	83	98	197	5.84	0
1995 Pawtucket	Int.	4	25	2	1	.667	14	9	23	2.52	0
1995 Boston a-b	A.L.	27	195⅓	16	8	.667	119	68	163	2.95	0
1996 Boston	A.L.	32	211⅔	14	13	.519	140	90	238	5.14	0
1997 Boston c	A.L.	35	201⅓	12	15	.444	151	87	193	4.25	0
Major League Totals	5 Yrs.	131	828⅔	56	48	.538	520	355	815	4.15	0
Division Series											
1995 Boston	A.L.	1	5⅓	0	1	.000	4	5	5	11.81	0

a Released by Pittsburgh Pirates, April 20, 1995.
b Signed by Boston Red Sox, April 27, 1995.
c On disabled list from April 15 to May 6, 1997.

WALKER, JAMES ROSS (JAIME)

Born, McMinnville, Tennessee, July 1, 1971.
Bats Left. Throws Left. Height, 6 feet, 2 inches. Weight, 190 pounds.

Year Club	Lea	G	IP	W	L	Pct	SO	BB	H	ERA	SAVES
1992 Auburn	N.Y.-Penn.	15	83⅓	4	6	.400	67	21	75	3.13	0
1993 Quad City	Midwest	25	131⅔	3	11	.214	121	48	140	5.13	0
1994 Quad City	Midwest	32	125	8	10	.444	104	42	133	4.18	1
1995 Jackson	Texas	50	58	4	2	.667	38	24	59	4.50	2
1996 Jackson	Texas	45	101	5	1	.833	79	35	94	2.50	2
1997 Wichita	Texas	5	6⅔	0	1	.000	6	5	6	9.45	0
1997 Kansas City a-b	A.L.	50	43	3	3	.500	24	20	46	5.44	0

a Traded to Kansas City Royals with outfielder Jermaine Dye for infielder Keith Lockhart and outfielder Michael Tucker, March 27, 1997.
b On disabled list from June 5 to June 24, 1997.

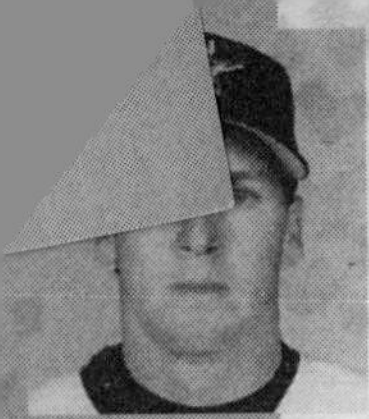

WALL, DONNELL LEE (DONNE)

Born, Potosi, Missouri, July 11, 1967.
Bats Right. Throws Right. Height, 6 feet, 1 inch. Weight, 180 pounds.

Year	Club	Lea	G	IP	W	L	Pct	SO	BB	H	ERA	SAVES
1989	Auburn	N.Y.-Penn.	12	65⅓	7	0	1.000	69	12	45	1.79	1
1990	Asheville	So. Atl.	28	132	6	8	.429	111	47	149	5.18	1
1991	Burlington	Midwest	16	106⅔	7	5	.583	102	21	73	2.03	0
1991	Osceloa	Fla. St.	12	77⅓	6	3	.667	62	11	55	2.09	0
1992	Osceloa	Fla. St.	7	41	3	1	.750	30	8	37	2.63	0
1992	Jackson	Texas	18	114⅓	9	6	.600	99	26	114	3.54	0
1992	Tucson	P.C.	2	8	0	0	.000	2	1	11	1.13	0
1993	Tucson	P.C.	25	131⅔	6	4	.600	89	35	147	3.83	0
1994	Tucson	P.C.	26	148⅓	11	8	.579	84	35	171	4.43	0
1995	Tucson	P.C.	28	177⅓	17	6	.739	119	32	190	3.30	0
1995	Houston	N.L.	6	24⅓	3	1	.750	16	5	33	5.55	0
1996	Tucson	P.C.	8	52⅓	3	3	.500	36	6	67	4.13	0
1996	Houston	N.L.	26	150	9	8	.529	99	34	170	4.56	0
1997	Houston a-b	N.L.	8	41⅔	2	5	.286	25	16	53	6.26	0
1997	New Orleans	A.A.	17	110	8	7	.533	84	24	109	3.85	0
Major League Totals		3 Yrs.	40	216	14	14	.500	140	55	256	5.00	0

a Claimed on waivers by Cincinnati Reds, October 7, 1997.
b Traded to Detroit Tigers with catcher Paul Bako for outfielder Melvin Nieves, November 11, 1997.

WASDIN, JOHN TRUMAN

Born, Fort Belvoir, Virginia, August 5, 1972.
Bats Right. Throws Right. Height, 6 feet, 2 inches. Weight, 190 pounds.

Year	Club	Lea	G	IP	W	L	Pct	SO	BB	H	ERA	SAVES
1993	Athletics	Arizona	1	3	0	0	.000	1	0	3	3.00	0
1993	Madison	Midwest	9	48⅓	2	3	.400	40	9	32	1.86	0
1993	Modesto	California	3	16⅓	0	3	.000	11	4	17	3.86	0
1994	Modesto	California	6	26⅔	3	1	.750	30	5	17	1.69	0
1994	Huntsville	Southern	21	141⅔	12	3	.800	108	29	126	3.43	0
1995	Edmonton	P.C.	29	174⅓	12	8	.600	111	38	193	5.52	0
1995	Oakland	A.L.	5	17⅓	1	1	.500	6	3	14	4.67	0
1996	Edmonton	P.C.	9	50	2	1	.667	30	17	52	4.14	0
1996	Oakland	A.L.	25	131⅓	8	7	.533	75	50	145	5.96	0
1997	Boston	A.L.	53	124⅔	4	6	.400	84	38	121	4.40	0
Major League Totals		3 Yrs.	83	273⅓	13	14	.481	165	91	280	5.17	0

WATSON, ALLEN KENNETH

Born, Jamaica, New York, November 18, 1970.
Bats Left. Throws Left. Height, 6 feet, 3 inches. Weight, 190 pounds.

Year	Club	Lea	G	IP	W	L	Pct	SO	BB	H	ERA	SAVES
1991	Hamilton	N.Y.-Penn.	8	39⅓	1	1	.500	46	17	22	2.52	0
1991	Savannah	So. Atl.	3	13⅔	1	1	.500	12	8	16	3.95	0
1992	St. Petersburg	Fla. St.	14	89⅔	5	4	.556	80	18	81	1.91	0
1992	Arkansas	Texas	14	96⅓	8	5	.615	93	23	77	2.15	0
1992	Louisville	A.A.	2	12⅔	1	0	1.000	9	5	8	1.46	0
1993	Louisville	A.A.	17	120⅔	5	4	.556	86	31	101	2.91	0
1993	St. Louis	N.L.	16	86	6	7	.462	49	28	90	4.60	0
1994	St. Louis	N.L.	22	115⅔	6	5	.545	74	53	130	5.52	0
1995	Arkansas	Texas	1	5	1	0	1.000	7	0	4	0.00	0
1995	Louisville	A.A.	4	24	2	2	.500	19	6	20	2.63	0
1995	St. Louis a-b	N.L.	21	114⅓	7	9	.438	49	41	126	4.96	0
1996	San Jose	California	2	6⅓	0	0	.000	12	0	7	1.42	0
1996	San Francisco c-d	N.L.	29	185⅔	8	12	.400	128	69	189	4.61	0
1997	Anaheim	A.L.	35	199	12	12	.500	141	73	220	4.93	0
Major League Totals		5 Yrs.	123	700⅔	39	45	.464	441	264	755	4.91	0

a On disabled list from June 7 to July 8, 1995.
b Traded by St. Louis Cardinals to San Francisco Giants with pitchers Rich Delucia and Doug Creek for infielder Royce Clayton, December 14, 1995.
c On disabled list from July 2 to July 25, 1996.
d Traded to California Angels with pitcher Fausto Macey for infielder J.T. Snow, November 27, 1996.

WEATHERS, JOHN DAVID

Born, Lawrenceburg, Tennessee, September 25, 1969.
Bats Right. Throws Right. Height, 6 feet, 3 inches. Weight, 205 pounds.

Year	Club	Lea	G	IP	W	L	Pct	SO	BB	H	ERA	SAVES
1988	St. Catharines	N.Y.-Penn.	15	62²/₃	4	4	.500	36	26	58	3.02	0
1989	Myrtle Beach	So. Atl.	31	172²/₃	11	*13	.458	111	86	163	3.86	0
1990	Dunedin	Fla. St.	27	158	10	7	.588	96	59	158	3.70	0
1991	Knoxville	Southern	24	139¹/₃	10	7	.588	114	49	121	2.45	0
1991	Toronto	A.L.	15	14²/₃	1	0	1.000	13	17	15	4.91	0
1992	Syracuse a	Int.	12	48¹/₃	1	4	.200	30	21	48	4.66	0
1992	Toronto b	A.L.	2	3¹/₃	0	0	.000	3	2	5	8.10	0
1993	Edmonton	P.C.	22	141	11	4	.733	117	47	150	3.83	0
1993	Florida	N.L.	14	45²/₃	2	3	.400	34	13	57	5.12	0
1994	Florida c	N.L.	24	135	8	12	.400	72	59	166	5.27	0
1995	Brevard City	Fla. St.	1	4	0	0	.000	3	1	4	0.00	0
1995	Charlotte	Int.	1	5	0	1	.000	0	5	10	9.00	0
1995	Florida d	N.L.	28	90¹/₃	4	5	.444	60	52	104	5.98	0
1996	Charlotte	Int.	1	2¹/₃	0	0	.000	0	3	5	7.71	0
1996	Florida e	N.L.	31	71¹/₃	2	2	.500	40	28	85	4.54	0
1996	Columbus	Int.	3	16²/₃	0	2	.000	7	5	20	5.40	0
1996	New York	A.L.	11	17¹/₃	0	2	.000	13	14	23	9.35	0
1997	Columbus	Int.	5	36²/₃	2	2	.500	35	7	35	3.19	0
1997	Buffalo f-g	A.A.	11	68²/₃	4	3	.571	51	17	71	3.15	0
1997	New York-Cleveland h	A.L.	19	25²/₃	1	3	.250	18	15	38	8.42	0
Major League Totals	7 Yrs.		144	403¹/₃	18	27	.400	253	200	493	5.67	0

Division Series

1996	New York	A.L.	2	5	1	0	1.000	5	0	1	0.00	0

Championship Series

1996	New York	A.L.	2	3	1	0	1.000	0	0	3	0.00	0

World Series Record

1996	New York	A.L.	3	3	0	0	.000	3	3	2	3.00	0

a On disabled list from May 11 to July 31, 1992.
b Selected by Florida Marlins in expansion draft, November 17, 1992.
c Appeared in two additional games as pinch runner.
d On disabled list from June 26 to July 13, 1995.
e Traded to New York Yankees for pitcher Mark Hutton, July 31, 1996.
f Traded to Cleveland Indians for outfielder Chad Curtis, June 9, 1997.
g Outrighted by Cleveland Indians, August 8, 1997.
h Signed as free agent with Cincinnati Reds, December 19, 1997.

WELLS, DAVID LEE

Born, Torrance, California, May 20, 1963.
Bats Left. Throws Left. Height, 6 feet, 4 inches. Weight, 225 pounds.

Year	Club	Lea	G	IP	W	L	Pct	SO	BB	H	ERA	SAVES
1982	Medicine Flat	Pioneer	12	64¹/₃	4	3	.571	53	32	71	5.18	0
1983	Kinston	Carolina	25	157	6	5	.545	115	71	141	3.73	0
1984	Kinston	Carolina	7	42	1	6	.143	44	19	51	4.71	0
1984	Knoxville a	Southern	8	59	3	2	.600	34	17	58	2.59	0
1985	Knoxville b	Southern		INJURED—Did Not Play	0	0						
1986	Florence	So. Atl.	4	12²/₃	0	0	.000	14	9	7	3.55	0
1986	Ventura	California	5	19	2	1	.667	26	4	13	1.89	0
1986	Knoxville c	Southern	10	40	1	3	.250	32	18	42	4.05	0
1986	Syracuse	Int.	3	3²/₃	0	1	.000	2	1	6	9.82	0
1987	Syracuse	Int.	43	109¹/₃	4	6	.400	106	32	102	3.87	6
1987	Toronto	A.L.	18	29¹/₃	4	3	.571	32	12	37	3.99	1
1988	Syracuse	Int.	6	5²/₃	0	0	.000	8	2	7	0.00	3
1988	Toronto	A.L.	41	64¹/₃	3	5	.375	56	31	65	4.62	4
1989	Toronto	A.L.	54	86¹/₃	7	4	.636	78	28	66	2.40	2
1990	Toronto	A.L.	43	189	11	6	.647	115	45	165	3.14	3
1991	Toronto	A.L.	40	198¹/₃	15	10	.600	106	49	188	3.72	1
1992	Toronto d	A.L.	41	120	7	9	.438	62	36	138	5.40	2
1993	Detroit e-f	A.L.	32	187	11	9	.550	139	42	183	4.19	0
1994	Lakeland	Fla. St.	2	6	0	0	.000	3	0	5	0.00	0
1994	Detroit g	A.L.	16	111¹/₃	5	7	.417	71	24	113	3.96	0
1995	Detroit	A.L.	18	130¹/₃	10	3	.769	83	37	120	3.04	0
1995	Cincinnati h-i	N.L.	11	72²/₃	6	5	.545	50	16	74	3.59	0
1996	Baltimore j-k	A.L.	34	224¹/₃	11	14	.440	130	51	247	5.14	0
1997	New York	A.L.	32	218	16	10	.615	156	45	239	4.21	0
Major League Totals	11 Yrs.		380	1631	106	85	.555	1078	416	1635	4.02	13

Year	Club	Lea	G	IP	W	L	Pct	SO	BB	H	ERA	SAVES
	Division Series											
1995 Cincinnati	....	.N.L.	1	6⅓	1	0	1.000	8	1	6	0.00	0
1996 Baltimore	....	.A.L.	2	13⅔	1	0	1.000	6	4	15	4.61	0
1997 New York	....	.A.L.	1	9	1	0	1.000	1	0	5	1.00	0
Divisional Series Totals	....	.4		29	3	0	1.000	15	5	26	2.48	0
	Championship Series											
1989 Toronto	....	.A.L.	1	1	0	0	.000	1	2	0	0.00	0
1991 Toronto	....	.A.L.	4	7⅔	0	0	.000	9	2	6	2.35	0
1995 Cincinnati	....	.N.L.	1	6	0	1	.000	3	2	8	4.50	0
1996 Baltimore	....	.A.L.	6	6⅔	1	0	1.000	6	3	8	4.05	0
Championship Series Totals	....	.7		21⅓	1	1	.500	19	9	22	3.38	0
	World Series Record											
1992 Toronto	....	.A.L.	4	4⅓	0	0	.000	3	2	1	0.00	0

a On disabled list from June 24 to end of 1984 season.
b On disabled list from April 10 to end of 1985 season.
c On disabled list from July 7 to August 20, 1986.
d Released, March 30; signed with Detroit Tigers, April 3, 1993.
e On disabled list from August 1 to August 20, 1993.
f Filed for free agency, October 28; re-signed with Detroit Tigers, December 14, 1993.
g On disabled list from April 16 to June 4, 1994.
h Traded to Cincinnati Reds for pitcher C.J. Nitkowski, pitcher Dave Tuttle and player to be named later, July 31, 1995. Detroit Tigers received infielder Mark Lewis to complete trade, November 16, 1995.
i Signed with Seattle Mariners organization, December 8, 1995.
j Filed for free agency, October 29, 1996.
k Signed with New York Yankees, December 17, 1996.

WELLS, ROBERT LEE
Born, Yakima, Washington, November 1, 1966.
Bats Right. Throws Right. Height, 6 feet. Weight, 180 pounds.

Year	Club	Lea	G	IP	W	L	Pct	SO	BB	H	ERA	SAVES
1989 Martinsville	....	.Appal.	4	6	0	0	.000	3	2	8	4.50	0
1990 Spartanburg	....	.So. Atl.	20	113	5	8	.385	73	40	94	2.87	0
1990 Clearwater	....	.Fla. St.	6	14⅓	0	2	.000	11	6	17	4.91	1
1991 Clearwater	....	.Fla. St.	24	75⅓	7	2	.778	66	19	63	3.11	0
1991 Reading	....	.Eastern	1	5	1	0	1.000	3	1	4	3.60	0
1992 Clearwater	....	.Fla. St.	9	9⅓	1	0	1.000	9	3	10	3.86	5
1992 Reading	....	.Eastern	3	15⅓	0	1	.000	11	5	12	1.17	0
1993 Clearwater	....	.Fla. St.	12	27⅔	1	0	1.000	24	6	23	0.98	2
1993 Scranton	....	.Int.	11	19⅓	1	1	.500	8	5	19	2.79	0
1994 Reading	....	.Eastern	14	19⅓	1	3	.250	19	3	18	2.79	4
1994 Scranton	....	.Int.	11	14⅔	0	2	.000	13	6	18	2.45	0
1994 Philadelphia a	....	.N.L.	5	5	1	0	1.000	3	3	4	1.80	0
1994 Calgary	....	.P.C.	6	31⅔	3	2	.600	17	9	43	6.54	0
1994 Seattle	....	.A.L.	1	4	1	0	1.000	3	1	4	2.25	0
1995 Seattle b	....	.A.L.	30	76⅔	4	3	.571	38	39	88	5.75	0
1996 Seattle	....	.A.L.	36	130⅔	12	7	.632	94	46	141	5.30	0
1997 Seattle	....	.A.L.	46	67⅓	2	0	1.000	51	18	88	5.75	2
Major League Totals	....	.4 Yrs.	119	283⅔	20	10	.667	189	107	325	5.43	2
	Division Series											
1995 Seattle	....	.A.L.	1	1	0	0	.000	0	1	2	9.00	0
1997 Seattle	....	.A.L.	1	1⅓	0	0	.000	1	0	1	0.00	0
Divisional Series Totals	....	.2		2⅓	0	0	.000	1	1	3	3.86	0
	Championship Series											
1995 Seattle	....	.A.L.	1	3	0	0	.000	2	2	2	3.00	0

a Claimed on waivers by Seattle Mariners, June 30, 1994.
b Designated for assignment by Seattle Mariners, November 29, 1995.

WENDELL, STEVEN JOHN (TURK)
Born, Pittsfield, Massachusetts, May 19, 1967.
Bats Both. Throws Right. Height, 6 feet, 2 inches. Weight, 190 pounds.

Year	Club	Lea	G	IP	W	L	Pct	SO	BB	H	ERA	SAVES
1988 Pulaski	....	.Appal.	14	*101	3	8	.273	87	30	85	3.83	0
1989 Burlington	....	.Midwest	22	159	9	11	.450	153	41	127	2.21	0
1989 Greenville	....	.Southern	1	3⅔	0	0	.000	3	1	7	9.82	0
1989 Durham	....	.Carolina	3	24	2	0	1.000	27	6	13	1.13	0

Year	Club	Lea	G	IP	W	L	Pct	SO	BB	H	ERA	SAVES
1990	Greenville	Southern	36	91	4	9	.308	85	48	105	5.74	2
1990	Durham	Carolina	6	38⅔	1	3	.250	26	15	24	1.86	0
1991	Greenville	Southern	25	147⅔	11	3	.786	122	51	130	2.56	0
1991	Richmond a	Int.	3	21	0	2	.000	18	16	20	3.43	0
1992	Iowa b	A.A.	4	25	2	0	1.000	12	15	17	1.44	0
1993	Iowa	A.A.	25	148⅔	10	8	.556	110	47	148	4.60	0
1993	Chicago	N.L.	7	22⅔	1	2	.333	15	8	24	4.37	0
1994	Iowa	A.A.	23	168	11	6	.647	118	28	141	2.95	0
1994	Chicago	N.L.	6	14⅓	1	0	1.000	9	10	22	11.93	0
1995	Daytona	Fla. St.	4	7⅔	0	0	.000	8	1	5	1.17	0
1995	Orlando	Southern	5	7	1	0	1.000	7	4	6	3.86	1
1995	Chicago c	N.L.	43	60⅓	3	1	.750	50	24	71	4.92	0
1996	Chicago	N.L.	70	79⅓	4	5	.444	75	44	58	2.84	18
1997	Chicago-New York d	N.L.	65	76⅓	3	5	.375	64	53	68	4.36	5
Major League Totals	5 Yrs.		191	253	11	14	.440	213	139	243	4.45	23

a Traded by Atlanta Braves to Chicago Cubs organization with pitcher Yorkis Perez for catcher Damon Berryhill and pitcher Mike Bielecki, September 29, 1991.
b On disabled list from May 4 to end of 1992 season.
c On disabled list from April 25 to May 27, 1995.
d Traded to New York Mets with pitcher Mel Rojas and outfielder Brian McRae for outfielder Lance Johnson, pitcher Mark Clark and player to be named later, August 8, 1997. Chicago Cubs received infielder Manny Alexander to complete trade, August 14, 1997.

WENGERT, DONALD PAUL (DON)
Born, Sioux City, Iowa, November 6, 1969.
Bats Right. Throws Right. Height, 6 feet, 2 inches. Weight, 205 pounds.

Year	Club	Lea	G	IP	W	L	Pct	SO	BB	H	ERA	SAVES
1992	Sou Oregon	Northwest	6	37	2	0	1.000	29	7	32	1.46	0
1992	Madison	Midwest	7	40	3	4	.429	29	17	42	3.38	0
1993	Madison	Midwest	13	78⅔	6	5	.545	46	18	79	3.32	0
1993	Modesto	California	12	70⅓	3	6	.333	43	29	75	4.73	0
1994	Modesto	California	10	42⅔	4	1	.800	52	11	40	2.95	2
1994	Huntsville	Southern	17	99⅓	6	4	.600	92	33	86	3.26	0
1995	Edmonton	P.C.	16	39	1	1	.500	20	16	55	7.38	1
1995	Oakland	A.L.	19	29⅔	1	1	.500	16	12	30	3.34	0
1996	Oakland a	A.L.	36	161⅓	7	11	.389	75	60	200	5.58	0
1997	Oakland b	A.L.	49	134	5	11	.313	68	41	177	6.04	2
Major League Totals	3 Yrs.		104	325	13	23	.361	159	113	407	5.57	2

a On disabled list from July 24 to August 8, 1996.
b Traded to San Diego Padres with infielder David Newhan for pitcher Doug Bochtler and infielder Jorge Velandia, November 26, 1997.

WETTELAND, JOHN KARL
Born, San Mateo, California, August 21, 1966.
Bats Right. Throws Right. Height, 6 feet, 2 inches. Weight, 215 pounds.

Year	Club	Lea	G	IP	W	L	Pct	SO	BB	H	ERA	SAVES
1985	Great Falls	Pioneer	11	20⅔	1	1	.500	23	15	17	3.92	0
1986	Bakersfield	California	15	67	0	7	.000	38	46	71	5.78	0
1986	Great Falls	Pioneer	12	69⅓	4	3	.571	59	40	70	5.45	0
1987	Vero Beach	Fla. St.	27	175⅔	12	7	.632	144	92	150	3.13	0
1988	San Antonio	Texas	25	162⅓	10	8	.556	140	*77	141	3.88	0
1989	Albuquerque	P.C.	10	69	5	3	.625	73	20	61	3.65	0
1989	Los Angeles	N.L.	31	102⅔	5	8	.385	96	34	81	3.77	1
1990	Albuquerque	P.C.	8	29	2	2	.500	26	13	27	5.59	0
1990	Los Angeles	N.L.	22	43	2	4	.333	36	17	44	4.81	0
1991	Albuquerque	P.C.	41	61⅓	4	3	.571	55	26	48	2.79	*20
1991	Los Angeles c-d	N.L.	6	9	1	0	1.000	9	3	5	0.00	0
1992	Montreal	N.L.	67	83⅓	4	4	.500	99	36	64	2.92	37
1993	West Palm Beach	Fla. St.	2	3	0	0	.000	6	0	0	0.00	0
1993	Montreal e	N.L.	70	85⅓	9	3	.750	113	28	58	1.37	43
1994	Montreal f-g	N.L.	52	63⅔	4	6	.400	68	21	46	2.83	25
1995	New York h-i	A.L.	60	61⅓	1	5	.167	66	14	40	2.93	31
1996	New York j-k-l-m	A.L.	62	63⅔	2	3	.400	69	21	54	2.83	43
1997	Texas	A.L.	61	65	7	2	.778	63	21	43	1.94	31
Major League Totals	9 Yrs.		431	577	35	35	.500	619	195	435	2.81	211

Year	Club	Lea	G	IP	W	L	Pct	SO	BB	H	ERA	SAVES
	Division Series											
1995 New York		A.L.	3	4⅓	0	1	.000	5	2	8	14.54	0
1996 New York		A.L.	3	4	0	0	.000	4	4	2	0.00	2
Division Series Totals			6	8⅓	0	1	.000	9	6	10	7.56	2
	Championship Series											
1996 New York		A.L.	4	4	0	0	.000	5	1	2	4.50	1
	World Series Record											
1996 New York		A.L.	5	4⅓	0	0	.000	6	1	4	2.08	4

a Drafted by Detroit Tigers from Los Angeles Dodgers organization, December 5, 1987; returned to Los Angeles organization, March 29, 1988.
b On disabled list from May 1 to May 8 and June 3 to June 29, 1991.
c Traded to Cincinnati Reds with pitcher Tim Belcher for outfielder Eric Davis and pitcher Kip Gross, November 27, 1991.
d Traded by Cincinnati Reds to Montreal Expos with pitcher Bill Risley for outfielder Dave Martinez, infielder Willie Greene and pitcher Scott Ruskin, December 11, 1991.
e On disabled list from April 4 to April 23, 1993.
f On disabled list from April 18 to May 3, 1994.
g Declared restricted free agent under Major League Baseball implemented labor proposal, December 23, 1994.
h Traded to New York Yankees for outfielder Fernando Seguignol and player to be named later, April 5, 1995.
i Re-signed with New York Yankees, June 7, 1995.
j Re-signed with New York Yankees, February 13, 1996.
k On disabled list from August 13 to September 6, 1996.
l Filed for free agency, November 4, 1996.
m Signed with Texas Rangers, December 16, 1996.

WHISENANT, MATTHEW MICHAEL
Born, Los Angeles, California, June 8, 1971.
Bats Both. Throws Left. Height, 6 feet, 3 inches. Weight, 215 pounds.

Year	Club	Lea	G	IP	W	L	Pct	SO	BB	H	ERA	SAVES
1997 Brevard Cty		Fla. St.	2	3⅓	0	0	.000	4	3	3	8.10	0
1997 Charlotte		Int.	16	15	2	1	.667	19	12	16	7.20	0
1997 Florida a-b		N.L.	4	2⅔	0	0	.000	4	6	4	16.88	0
1997 Kansas City		A.L.	24	19	1	0	1.000	16	12	15	2.84	0
Major League Totals	1 Yrs.		28	21⅔	1	0	1.000	20	18	19	4.57	0

a On disabled list from April 1 to July 4, 1997.
b Traded to Kansas City Royals for catcher Matt Treanor, July 29, 1997.

WHITE, GABRIEL ALLEN
Born, Sebring, Florida, November 20, 1971.
Bats Left. Throws Left. Height, 6 feet, 2 inches. Weight, 200 pounds.

Year	Club	Lea	G	IP	W	L	Pct	SO	BB	H	ERA	SAVES
1990 Expos		Gulf Coast	11	57⅓	4	2	.667	41	12	50	3.14	0
1991 Sumter		So. Atl.	24	149	6	9	.400	140	53	127	3.26	0
1992 Rockford		Midwest	27	187	14	8	.636	176	61	148	2.84	0
1993 Harrisburg		Eastern	16	100	7	2	.778	80	28	80	2.16	0
1993 Ottawa		Int.	6	40⅓	2	1	.667	28	6	38	3.12	0
1994 Wst Plm Bch		Fla. St.	1	6	1	0	1.000	4	1	2	1.50	0
1994 Montreal		N.L.	7	23⅔	1	1	.500	17	11	24	6.08	1
1994 Ottawa		Int.	14	73	8	3	.727	48	28	77	5.05	0
1995 Ottawa		Int.	12	62⅓	2	3	.400	37	17	58	3.90	0
1995 Montreal a		N.L.	19	25⅔	1	2	.333	25	9	26	7.01	0
1996 Indianapols		A.A.	11	68⅓	6	3	.667	51	9	69	2.77	0
1997 Indianapols		A.A.	20	118	7	4	.636	62	18	119	2.82	0
1997 Cincinnati		N.L.	12	41	2	2	.500	25	8	39	4.39	1
Major League Totals	3 Yrs.		38	90⅓	4	5	.444	67	28	89	5.58	2

a Traded to Cincinnati Reds for outfielder Jhonny Carvajal December 15, 1995.

WHITESIDE, MATTHEW CHRISTOPHER
Born, Sikeston, Missouri, August 8, 1967.
Bats Right. Throws Right. Height, 6 feet. Weight, 195 pounds.

Year	Club	Lea	G	IP	W	L	Pct	SO	BB	H	ERA	SAVES
1990 Butte		Pioneer	18	57⅓	4	4	.500	45	25	57	3.45	2
1991 Gastonia		So. Atl.	48	62⅔	3	1	.750	71	21	43	2.15	29
1992 Tulsa		Texas	33	33⅔	0	1	.000	30	3	31	2.41	21

Year	Club	Lea	G	IP	W	L	Pct	SO	BB	H	ERA	SAVES
1992 Oklahoma City	A.A.	12	11⅓	1	0	1.000	13	3	7	0.79	8
1992 Texas	A.L.	20	28	1	1	.500	13	11	26	1.93	4
1993 Oklahoma City	A.A.	8	11⅓	2	1	.667	10	8	17	5.56	1
1993 Texas	A.L.	60	73	2	1	.667	39	23	78	4.32	1
1994 Texas	A.L.	47	61	2	2	.500	37	28	68	5.02	1
1995 Texas a-b	A.L.	40	53	5	4	.556	46	19	48	4.08	3
1996 Okla City	A.A.	36	94	9	6	.600	52	24	95	3.45	0
1996 Okla c	A.L.	14	32⅓	0	1	.000	15	11	43	6.68	0
1997 Okla City	A.A.	10	28	1	1	.500	11	13	30	3.54	1
1997 Texas	A.L.	42	72⅔	4	1	.800	44	26	85	5.08	0
Major League Totals ...... 6 Yrs.		223	320	14	10	.583	194	118	348	4.61	9

a On disabled list from May 9 to May 25, 1995.
b Signed with Texas Rangers organization, November 29, 1995.
c Not offered 1996 contract, October 31, 1996.

WICKMAN, ROBERT JOE (BOB)
Born, Green Bay, Wisconsin, February 6, 1969.
Bats Right. Throws Right. Height, 6 feet, 1 inch. Weight, 212 pounds.

Year	Club	Lea	G	IP	W	L	Pct	SO	BB	H	ERA	SAVES
1990 Sara. White Sox	Gulf C.	2	11	2	0	1.000	15	1	7	2.45	0
1990 Sarasota	Fla. St.	2	13⅔	0	1	.000	8	4	17	1.98	0
1990 South Bend	Midwest	9	65⅓	7	2	.778	50	16	50	1.38	0
1991 Sarasota	Fla. St.	7	44	5	1	.833	32	11	43	2.05	0
1991 Birmingham a	Southern	20	131⅓	6	10	.375	81	50	127	3.56	0
1992 Columbus	Int.	23	157	12	5	.706	108	55	131	2.92	0
1992 New York	A.L.	8	50⅓	6	1	.857	21	20	51	4.11	0
1993 New York	A.L.	41	140	14	4	.778	70	69	156	4.63	4
1994 New York	A.L.	*53	70	5	4	.556	56	27	54	3.09	6
1995 New York	A.L.	63	80	2	4	.333	51	33	77	4.05	1
1996 New York-Milwaukee b	A.L.	70	95⅔	7	1	.875	75	44	106	4.42	0
1997 Milwaukee	A.L.	74	95⅔	7	6	.538	78	41	89	2.73	1
Major League Totals ...... 6 Yrs.		309	531⅔	41	20	.672	351	234	533	3.91	12
Division Series												
1995 New York	A.L.	3	3	0	0	.000	3	0	5	0.00	0

a Traded by Chicago White Sox to New York Yankees organization with pitchers Melido Perez and Domingo Jean for second baseman Steve Sax and cash, January 10, 1992.
b Traded to Milwaukee Brewers with outfielder Gerald Williams for pitcher Graeme Lloyd, pitcher Ricky Bones and infielder Pat Listach, August 23, 1996. Listach trade voided due to prior injury and New York Yankees received infielder Gabby Martinez to complete trade, November 5, 1996.

WILKINS, MARC ALLEN
Born, Mansfield, Ohio, October 21, 1970.
Bats Right. Throws Right. Height, 5 feet, 11 inches. Weight, 200 pounds.

Year	Club	Lea	G	IP	W	L	Pct	SO	BB	H	ERA	SAVES
1992 Welland	N.Y.-Penn.	28	42	4	2	.667	42	24	49	7.29	1
1993 Augusta	So. Atl.	48	77	5	6	.455	73	31	83	4.21	1
1994 Salem	Carolina	28	151	8	5	.615	90	45	155	3.70	0
1995 Carolina	Southern	37	99⅓	5	3	.625	80	44	91	3.99	0
1996 Carolina	Southern	11	24⅔	2	3	.400	19	11	19	4.01	0
1996 Pittsburgh	N.L.	47	75	4	3	.571	62	36	75	3.84	1
1997 Pittsburgh	N.L.	70	75⅔	9	5	.643	47	33	65	3.69	2
Major League Totals ...... 2 Yrs.		117	150⅔	13	8	.619	109	69	140	3.76	3

WILLIAMS, GREGORY SCOTT (WOODY)
Born, Houston, Texas, August 19, 1966.
Bats Right. Throws Right. Height, 6 feet. Weight, 190 pounds.

Year	Club	Lea	G	IP	W	L	Pct	SO	BB	H	ERA	SAVES
1988 St. Catharines	N.Y.-Penn.	12	76	8	2	.800	58	21	48	1.54	0
1988 Knoxville	Southern	6	28⅓	2	2	.500	25	12	27	3.81	0
1989 Dunedin	Fla. St.	20	81⅓	3	5	.375	60	27	63	2.32	3
1989 Knoxville	Southern	14	71	3	5	.375	51	33	61	3.55	1
1990 Syracuse	Int.	3	9	0	1	.000	8	4	15	10.00	0

Year	Club	Lea	G	IP	W	L	Pct	SO	BB	H	ERA	SAVES
1990 Knoxville	Southern	42	126	7	9	.438	74	39	111	3.14	5
1991 Knoxville	Southern	18	42⅔	3	2	.600	37	14	42	3.59	3
1991 Syracuse	Int.	31	54⅔	3	4	.429	37	27	52	4.12	6
1992 Syracuse	Int.	25	120⅔	6	8	.429	81	41	115	3.13	1
1993 Syracuse	Int.	12	16⅓	1	1	.500	16	5	15	2.20	3
1993 Dunedin	Fla. St.	2	4	0	0	.000	2	2	0	0.00	0
1993 Toronto	A.L.	30	37	3	1	.750	24	22	40	4.38	0
1994 Syracuse	Int.	1	1⅔	0	0	.000	1	0	0	0.00	1
1994 Toronto	A.L.	38	59⅓	1	3	.250	56	33	44	3.64	0
1995 Toronto	A.L.	23	53⅔	1	2	.333	41	28	44	3.69	0
1995 Syracuse	Int.	5	7⅔	0	0	.000	13	5	5	3.52	1
1996 Dunedin	Fla. St.	2	7⅔	0	2	.000	11	2	9	8.22	0
1996 St. Cathrnes	N.Y.-Penn.	2	7⅓	0	0	.000	12	4	7	3.68	0
1996 Syracuse	Int.	7	32	3	1	.750	33	7	22	1.41	0
1996 Toronto a	A.L.	12	59	4	5	.444	43	21	64	4.73	0
1997 Toronto	A.L.	31	194⅔	9	14	.391	124	66	201	4.35	0
Major League Totals	5 Yrs.	134	403⅔	18	25	.419	288	170	393	4.21	0

a On disabled list from April 1 to May 31 and June 7 to July 26, 1996.

WILLIAMS, MICHAEL DARREN

Born, Radford, Virginia, July 29, 1969.
Bats Right. Throws Right. Height 6 feet, 2 inches. Weight, 199 pounds.

Year	Club	Lea	G	IP	W	L	Pct	SO	BB	H	ERA	SAVES
1990 Batavia	N.Y.-Penn.	27	47	2	3	.400	42	13	39	2.30	11
1991 Clearwater	Fla. St.	14	93⅓	7	3	.700	76	14	65	1.74	0
1991 Reading	Eastern	15	100	7	5	.583	50	34	92	3.69	0
1992 Reading	Eastern	3	15⅔	1	2	.333	12	7	17	5.17	0
1992 Philadelphia	N.L.	5	28⅔	1	1	.500	5	7	29	5.34	0
1992 Scranton	Int.	16	92⅔	9	1	.900	59	30	84	2.43	0
1993 Scranton	Int.	14	97⅓	9	2	.818	53	16	93	2.87	0
1993 Philadelphia	N.L.	17	51	1	3	.250	33	22	50	5.29	0
1994 Scranton	Int.	14	84	2	7	.222	53	36	91	5.79	0
1994 Philadelphia	N.L.	12	50⅓	2	4	.333	29	20	61	5.01	0
1995 Scranton-WB	Int.	3	9⅔	0	1	.000	8	2	8	4.66	0
1995 Philadelphia	N.L.	33	87⅔	3	3	.500	57	29	78	3.29	0
1996 Philadelphia	N.L.	32	167	6	14	.300	103	67	188	5.44	0
1997 Omaha	A.A.	20	79	3	6	.333	68	38	71	4.22	5
1997 Kansas City a-b-c	A.L.	10	14	0	2	.000	10	8	20	6.43	1
Major League Totals	6 Yrs.	109	398⅔	13	27	.325	237	153	426	4.92	1

a Signed with Boston Red Sox organization, February 15, 1997.
b Outrighted by Kansas City Royals, July 3, 1997.
c Signed with Pittsburgh Pirates organization, December 18, 1997.

WINCHESTER, SCOTT J.

Born, Midland, Michigan, April 20, 1973.
Bats Right. Throws Right. Height, 6 feet, 2 inches. Weight, 210 pounds.

Year	Club	Lea	G	IP	W	L	Pct	SO	BB	H	ERA	SAVES
1995 Watertown	N.Y.-Penn.	23	28⅔	3	1	.750	27	6	24	2.83	11
1996 Columbus	So. Atl.	52	61⅓	7	3	.700	60	16	50	3.23	26
1997 Kinston a	Carolina	34	36⅔	2	1	.667	45	11	21	1.47	29
1997 Akron	Eastern	6	7	0	0	.000	8	2	8	3.86	1
1997 Chattanooga	Southern	9	10⅔	2	1	.667	3	3	9	1.69	3
1997 Indianapols	A.A.	4	5⅔	0	0	.000	2	2	2	0.00	0
1997 Cincinnati b-c	N.L.	5	6	0	0	.000	3	2	9	6.00	0

a Traded to Cincinnati Reds with pitcher Danny Graves, pitcher Jim Crowell and infielder Damian Jackson for pitcher John Smiley and infielder Jeff Branson, July 31, 1997.
b Selected on expansion draft by Arizona Diamondbacks, November 18, 1997.
c Sent to Cincinnati Reds as player to be named later for pitcher Felix Rodriguez, November 18, 1997.

WITT, ROBERT ANDREW (BOBBY)

Born, Arlington, Virginia, May 11, 1964.
Bats Right. Throws Right. Height, 6 feet, 2 inches. Weight, 205 pounds.

Year	Club	Lea	G	IP	W	L	Pct	SO	BB	H	ERA	SAVES
1985	Tulsa	Texas	11	35	0	6	.000	39	44	26	6.43	0
1986	Texas	A.L.	31	157⅔	11	9	.550	174	*143	130	5.48	0
1987	Tulsa	Texas	1	5	0	1	.000	2	6	5	5.40	0
1987	Oklahoma City	A.A.	1	5	1	0	1.000	2	3	5	9.00	0
1987	Texas a	A.L.	26	143	8	10	.444	160	*140	114	4.91	0
1988	Oklahoma City	A.A.	11	76⅔	4	6	.400	70	47	69	4.34	0
1988	Texas	A.L.	22	174⅓	8	10	.444	148	101	134	3.92	0
1989	Texas	A.L.	31	194⅓	12	13	.480	166	*114	182	5.14	0
1990	Texas b	A.L.	35	222	17	10	.630	221	110	197	3.36	0
1991	Oklahoma City	A.A.	2	8	1	1	.500	12	8	3	1.13	0
1991	Texas c	A.L.	17	88⅔	3	7	.300	82	74	84	6.09	0
1992	Texas-Oakland d	A.L.	31	193	10	14	.417	125	114	183	4.29	0
1993	Oakland	A.L.	35	220	14	13	.519	131	91	226	4.21	0
1994	Oakland e-f	A.L.	24	135⅔	8	10	.444	111	70	151	5.04	0
1995	Florida g-h-i	N.L.	19	110⅔	2	7	.222	95	47	104	3.90	0
1995	Texas j	A.L.	10	61⅓	3	4	.429	46	21	81	4.55	0
1996	Texas	A.L.	33	199⅔	16	12	.571	157	96	235	5.41	0
1997	Texas k-l	A.L.	34	209	12	12	.500	121	74	245	4.82	0
Major League Totals	12 Yrs.		346	2109⅓	124	131	.486	1737	1195	2066	4.63	0
Division Series												
1996	Texas	A.L.	1	3⅓	0	0	.000	3	2	4	8.10	0
Championship Series												
1992	Oakland	A.L.	1	1	0	0	.000	1	1	2	18.00	0

a On disabled list from May 21 to June 20, 1987.
b Appeared in two games as pinch runner.
c On disabled list from May 27 to August 1, 1991.
d Traded to Oakland Athletics with outfielder Ruben Sierra, pitcher Jeff Russell and cash for outfielder Jose Canseco, August 31, 1992.
e Appeared in one additional game as pinch runner.
f Filed for free agency, October 17, 1994.
g Signed with Florida Marlins, April 8, 1995.
h Traded to Texas Rangers for two players to be named later, August 8, 1995.
i Florida Marlins received pitcher Wilson Heredia on August 11, 1995 and outfielder Scott Posednik on October 10, 1995 to complete trade.
j Not offered 1996 contract, November 2, 1995.
k Filed for free agency, October 27, 1997.
l Re-signed with Texas Rangers, December 19, 1997.

WOHLERS, MARK EDWARD

Born, Holyoke, Massachusetts, January 23, 1970.
Bats Right. Throws Right. Height, 6 feet, 4 inches. Weight, 207 pounds.

Year	Club	Lea	G	IP	W	L	Pct	SO	BB	H	ERA	SAVES
1988	Pulaski	Appal.	13	59⅔	5	3	.625	49	50	47	3.32	0
1989	Sumter	So. Atl.	14	68	2	7	.222	51	59	74	6.49	0
1989	Pulaski	Appal.	14	46	1	1	.500	50	28	48	5.48	0
1990	Sumter	So. Atl.	37	52⅓	5	4	.556	85	20	27	1.88	5
1990	Greenville	Southern	14	15⅔	0	1	.000	20	14	14	4.02	6
1991	Greenville	Southern	28	31⅓	0	0	.000	44	13	9	0.57	21
1991	Richmond	Int.	23	26⅓	1	0	1.000	22	12	23	1.03	11
1991	Atlanta a	N.L.	17	19⅔	3	1	.750	13	13	17	3.20	2
1992	Richmond	Int.	27	34⅓	0	2	.000	33	17	32	3.93	9
1992	Atlanta	N.L.	32	35⅓	1	2	.333	17	14	28	2.55	4
1993	Richmond	Int.	25	29⅓	1	3	.250	39	11	21	1.84	4
1993	Atlanta	N.L.	46	48	6	2	.750	45	22	37	4.50	0
1994	Atlanta	N.L.	51	51	7	2	.778	58	33	51	4.59	1
1995	Atlanta	N.L.	65	64⅔	7	3	.700	90	24	51	2.09	25
1996	Atlanta	N.L.	77	77⅓	2	4	.333	100	21	71	3.03	39
1997	Atlanta	N.L.	71	69⅓	5	7	.417	92	38	57	3.50	33
Major League Totals	7 Yrs.		359	365⅓	31	21	.596	415	165	312	3.33	104
Division Series												
1995	Atlanta	N.L.	3	2⅔	0	1	.000	4	2	6	6.75	2
1996	Atlanta	N.L.	3	3⅓	0	0	.000	4	0	1	0.00	2
1997	Atlanta	N.L.	1	1	0	0	.000	1	0	1	0.00	1
Division Series Totals			7	7	0	1	.000	9	2	8	2.57	5
Championship Series												
1991	Atlanta	N.L.	3	1⅔	0	0	.000	1	1	3	0.00	0
1992	Atlanta	N.L.	3	3	0	0	.000	2	1	2	0.00	0

Year Club	Lea	G	IP	W	L	Pct	SO	BB	H	ERA	SAVES
1993 Atlanta	N.L.	4	5⅓	0	1	.000	10	3	2	3.38	0
1995 Atlanta	N.L.	4	5	1	0	1.000	8	0	2	1.80	0
1996 Atlanta	N.L.	3	3	0	0	.000	4	0	0	0.00	2
1997 Atlanta	N.L.	1	1	0	0	.000	1	1	0	0.00	0
Championship Series Totals		18	19	1	1	.500	26	6	9	1.42	2
World Series Record											
1991 Atlanta	N.L.	3	1⅔	0	0	.000	1	2	2	0.00	0
1992 Atlanta	N.L.	2	0⅔	0	0	.000	0	1	0	0.00	0
1995 Atlanta	N.L.	4	5	0	0	.000	3	3	4	1.80	2
1996 Atlanta	N.L.	4	4⅓	0	0	.000	4	2	7	6.23	0
World Series Totals		13	11⅔	0	0	.000	8	8	13	3.09	2

a Pitched seventh and eighth innings of combined no-hit, no-run game started by Kent Mercker (six innings) and completed by Alejandro Pena (9th inning) against San Diego Padres, won 1-0, September 11, 1991.

WOLCOTT, ROBERT WILLIAM (BOB)

Born, Huntington Beach, California, September 8, 1973.
Bats Right. Throws Right. Height, 6 feet. Weight, 190 pounds.

Year Club	Lea	G	IP	W	L	Pct	SO	BB	H	ERA	SAVES
1992 Bellingham	Northwest	9	22⅓	0	1	.000	17	19	25	6.85	0
1993 Bellingham	Northwest	15	95⅓	8	4	.667	79	26	70	2.64	0
1994 Calgary	P.C.	1	6	0	1	.000	5	3	6	3.00	0
1994 Riverside	California	26	180⅔	14	8	.636	142	50	173	2.84	0
1995 Port City	Southern	12	86	7	3	.700	53	13	60	2.20	0
1995 Tacoma	P.C.	13	79⅓	6	3	.667	43	16	94	4.08	0
1995 Seattle	A.L.	7	36⅔	3	2	.600	19	14	43	4.42	0
1996 Lancaster	California	1	6	0	1	.000	6	0	9	10.50	0
1996 Tacoma	P.C.	3	12⅓	0	2	.000	16	3	17	7.30	0
1996 Seattle	A.L.	30	149⅓	7	10	.412	78	54	179	5.73	0
1997 Tacoma	P.C.	7	37	1	3	.250	29	7	40	5.11	0
1997 Seattle a	A.L.	19	100	5	6	.455	58	29	129	6.03	0
Major League Totals	3 Yrs.	56	286	15	18	.455	155	97	351	5.66	0
Championship Series											
1995 Seattle	A.L.	1	7	1	0	1.000	2	5	8	2.57	0

a Selected in expansion draft by Arizona Diamondbacks, November 18, 1997.

WOODARD, STEVEN LARRY

Born, Hartselle, Alabama, May 15, 1975.
Bats Left. Throws Right. Height, 6 feet, 4 inches. Weight, 225 pounds.

Year Club	Lea	G	IP	W	L	Pct	SO	BB	H	ERA	SAVES
1994 Brewers	Arizona	15	82⅔	8	0	1.000	85	13	68	2.40	0
1995 Beloit	Midwest	21	115	7	4	.636	94	31	113	4.54	0
1996 Stockton	California	28	181⅓	12	9	.571	142	33	201	4.02	0
1997 El Paso	Texas	19	136⅓	14	3	.824	97	25	136	3.17	0
1997 Tucson	P.C.	1	7	1	0	1.000	6	1	3	0.00	0
1997 Milwaukee a	A.L.	7	36⅔	3	3	.500	32	6	39	5.15	0

a On disabled list from August 28 to September 29, 1997.

WORRELL, TIMOTHY HOWARD

Born, Pasadena, California, July 5, 1967.
Bats Right. Throws Right. Height, 6 feet, 4 inches. Weight, 200 pounds.

Year Club	Lea	G	IP	W	L	Pct	SO	BB	H	ERA	SAVES
1990 Charleston SC	So. Atl.	20	110⅔	5	8	.385	68	28	120	4.64	0
1991 Waterloo	Midwest	14	86⅓	8	4	.667	83	33	70	3.34	0
1991 High Desert	California	11	63⅔	5	2	.714	70	33	65	4.24	0
1992 Wichita	Texas	19	125⅔	8	6	.571	109	32	115	2.86	0
1992 Las Vegas	P.C.	10	63⅓	4	2	.667	32	19	61	4.26	0
1993 Las Vegas	P.C.	15	87	5	6	.455	89	26	102	5.48	0
1993 San Diego	N.L.	21	100⅔	2	7	.222	52	43	104	4.92	0
1994 San Diego a	N.L.	3	14⅔	0	1	.000	14	5	9	3.68	0
1995 Rancho Cuca	California	9	22⅔	0	2	.000	17	6	25	5.16	1
1995 Las Vegas	P.C.	10	24	0	2	.000	18	17	27	6.00	0

Year Club	Lea	G	IP	W	L	Pct	SO	BB	H	ERA	SAVES
1995 San Diego b	N.L.	9	13⅓	1	0	1.000	13	6	16	4.72	0
1996 San Diego	N.L.	50	121	9	7	.563	99	39	109	3.05	1
1997 San Diego c	N.L.	60	106⅓	4	8	.333	81	50	116	5.16	3
Major League Totals	5 Yrs.	143	356	16	23	.410	259	143	354	4.30	4
Division Series											
1996 San Diego	N.L.	2	3⅔	0	0	.000	2	1	4	2.45	0

a On disabled list from April 19 to end of 1994 season.
b On disabled list from April 25 to October 2, 1995.
a Selected in expansion draft by Arizona Diamondbacks, November 18, 1997.
c Traded to Detroit Tigers with outfielder Trey Beamon for pitcher Dan Miceli, designated hitter Donne Wall and infielder Ryan Balfe, November 19, 1997.

WORRELL, TODD ROLAND

Born, Arcadia, California, September 28, 1959.
Bats Right. Throws Right. Height, 6 feet, 5 inches. Weight, 222 pounds.

Year Club	Lea	G	IP	W	L	Pct	SO	BB	H	ERA	SAVES
1982 Erie	N.Y.-Penn.	9	51⅔	4	1	.800	57	15	52	3.31	0
1983 Louisville	A.A.	15	79⅔	4	2	.667	46	42	76	4.74	0
1983 Arkansas	Texas	10	70⅓	5	2	.714	74	37	57	3.07	0
1984 Arkansas	Texas	18	100⅓	3	10	.231	68	67	109	4.49	0
1984 St. Petersburg	Fla. St.	8	47⅓	3	2	.600	33	24	41	2.09	0
1985 Louisville	A.A.	34	127⅔	8	6	.571	126	47	114	3.60	11
1985 St. Louis	N.L.	17	21⅔	3	0	1.000	17	7	17	2.91	5
1986 St. Louis a	N.L.	74	103⅔	9	10	.474	73	41	86	2.08	*36
1987 St. Louis	N.L.	75	94⅔	8	6	.571	92	34	86	2.66	33
1988 St. Louis	N.L.	68	90	5	9	.357	78	34	69	3.00	32
1989 St. Louis b	N.L.	47	51⅔	3	5	.375	41	26	42	2.96	20
1989 Louisville	A.A.	1	1	0	0	.000	1	0	0	0.00	0
1990 St. Louis c	N.L.		INJURED—Did Not Play								
1991 Louisville	A.A.	3	3	0	0	.000	4	3	4	18.00	0
1991 St. Louis d	N.L.		INJURED—Did Not Play								
1992 St. Louis e	N.L.	67	64	5	3	.625	64	25	45	2.11	3
1993 Bakersfield	California	2	2	0	0	.000	5	0	1	0.00	0
1993 Albuquerque	P.C.	7	8⅔	1	0	1.000	13	2	7	1.04	0
1993 Los Angeles f	N.L.	35	38⅔	1	1	.500	31	11	46	6.05	5
1994 Los Angeles g	N.L.	38	42	6	5	.545	44	12	37	4.29	11
1995 Los Angeles	N.L.	59	62⅓	4	1	.800	61	19	50	2.02	32
1996 Los Angeles	N.L.	72	65⅓	4	6	.400	66	15	70	3.03	44
1997 Los Angeles h	N.L.	65	59⅔	2	6	.250	61	23	60	5.28	35
Major League Totals	11 Yrs.	617	693⅔	50	52	.490	628	247	608	3.09	256
Division Series											
1996 Los Angeles	N.L.	1	1	0	0	.000	1	1	0	0.00	0
Championship Series											
1985 St. Louis	N.L.	4	6⅓	1	0	1.000	3	2	4	1.42	0
1987 St. Louis	N.L.	3	4⅓	0	0	.000	6	1	4	2.08	1
Championship Series Totals		7	10⅔	1	0	1.000	9	3	8	1.69	1
World Series Record											
1985 St. Louis	N.L.	3	4⅔	0	1	.000	6	2	4	3.86	1
1987 St. Louis	N.L.	4	7	0	0	.000	3	4	6	1.29	2
World Series Totals		7	11⅔	0	1	.000	9	6	10	2.31	3

a Selected Rookie of the Year in National League for 1986.
b On disabled list from May 14 to June 7, 1989.
c On disabled list from March 30 to end of 1990 season.
d On disabled list from April 4 to end of 1991 season.
e Filed for free agency, October 26; signed with Los Angeles Dodgers, December 9, 1992.
f On disabled list from April 8 to May 26 and June 11 to July 15, 1993.
g On disabled list from May 5 to May 23, 1994.
h Filed for free agency, October 28, 1997.

WRIGHT, JAMEY ALAN

Born, Oklahoma City, Oklahoma, December 24, 1974.
Bats Right. Throws Right. Height, 6 feet, 6 inches. Weight, 205 pounds.

Year Club	Lea	G	IP	W	L	PCT	SO	BB	H	ERA	SAVES
1993 Rockies	Arizona	8	36	1	3	.250	26	9	35	4.00	0
1994 Asheville	So. Atl.	28	143⅓	7	14	.333	103	59	188	5.97	0

Year	Club	Lea	G	IP	W	L	Pct	SO	BB	H	ERA	SAVES
1995 Salem	Carolina	26	171	10	8	.556	95	72	160	2.47	0
1995 New Haven	Eastern	1	3	0	1	.000	0	3	6	9.00	0
1996 New Haven	Eastern	7	44²/3	5	1	.833	54	12	27	0.81	0
1996 Colo Sprngs	P.C.	9	59²/3	4	2	.667	40	22	53	2.72	0
1996 Colorado	N.L.	16	91¹/3	4	4	.500	45	41	105	4.93	0
1997 Salem	Carolina	1	1	0	1	.000	1	1	1	9.00	0
1997 Colo Sprngs	P.C.	2	11	1	0	1.000	11	5	9	1.64	0
1997 Colorado a	N.L.	26	149²/3	8	12	.400	59	71	198	6.25	0
Major League Totals ....2 Yrs.		42	241	12	16	.429	104	112	303	5.75	0

a On disabled list from May 15 to June 8, 1997.

WRIGHT, JARET SAMUEL

Born, Anaheim, California, December 29, 1975.
Bats Right. Throws Right. Height, 6 feet, 2 inches. Weight, 220 pounds.

Year	Club	Lea	G	IP	W	L	Pct	SO	BB	H	ERA	SAVES
1994 Burlington	Appal.	4	13¹/3	0	1	.000	16	9	13	5.40	0
1995 Columbus	So. Atl.	24	129	5	6	.455	113	79	93	3.00	0
1996 Kinston	Carolina	19	101	7	4	.636	109	55	65	2.50	0
1997 Akron	Eastern	8	54	3	3	.500	59	23	43	3.67	0
1997 Buffalo	A.A.	7	45	4	1	.800	47	19	30	1.80	0
1997 Cleveland	A.L.	16	90¹/3	8	3	.727	63	35	81	4.38	0
Division Series											
1997 Cleveland	A.L.	2	11¹/3	2	0	1.000	10	7	11	3.97	0
Championship Series											
1997 Cleveland	A.L.	1	3	0	0	.000	3	2	6	15.00	0
World Series Record											
1997 Cleveland	A.L.	2	12¹/3	1	0	1.000	12	10	7	2.92	0

YAN, ESTEBAN LUIS

Born, Campina Del Seibo, Dominican Republic, June 22, 1974.
Bats Right. Throws Right. Height, 6 feet, 4 inches. Weight, 230 pounds.

Year	Club	Lea	G	IP	W	L	Pct	SO	BB	H	ERA	SAVES
1993 Danville	Appal.	14	71¹/3	4	7	.364	50	24	73	3.03	0
1994 Macon	So. Atl.	28	170²/3	11	12	.478	121	34	155	3.27	0
1995 Wst Plm Bch	Fla. St.	24	137²/3	6	8	.429	89	33	139	3.07	1
1996 Bowie	Eastern	9	16	0	2	.000	16	8	18	5.63	0
1996 Baltimore	A.L.	4	9¹/3	0	0	.000	7	3	13	5.79	0
1996 Rochester	Int.	22	71²/3	5	4	.556	61	18	75	4.27	1
1997 Rochester	Int.	34	119	11	5	.688	131	37	107	3.10	2
1997 Baltimore a	A.L.	3	9²/3	0	1	.000	4	7	20	15.83	0
Major League Totals ....2 Yrs.		7	19	0	1	.000	11	10	33	10.89	0

a Selected in expansion draft by Tampa Bay Devil Rays, November 18, 1997.